THE NEW MILLENNIUM Atlas of the United States, Canada, & the World

Maps created by

MapQuest.com, Inc.

MAPQUEST.COM™

Gareth Stevens Publishing
MILWAUKEE

PRIMEDIA Reference Inc. Staff

Director of Editorial Production
Andrea J. Pitluk

Director–Purchasing and Production
Edward A. Thomas

Deputy Editor
William A. McGeveran, Jr.

Senior Editor
Lori Wiesenfeld

Associate Editors
Beth R. Ellis
Mark S. O'Malley

Vice President & Editorial Director
Robert Famighetti

MapQuest.com, Inc. Staff

Project Manager Keith Winters

Project Coordinator
(Encyclopedia map set) Nancy Hamme
Associate Project Coordinator
(Encyclopedia map set) Andrew DeWitt

Project Coordinator
(Atlas) Andrew Green
Associate Project Coordinator
(Atlas) Matt Tharp

Layout & Design
Jeannine Schonta, Andy Skinner

Research & Compilation
Marley Amstutz, Laura Hartwig, Bill Truninger

Research Librarian Luis Freile

GIS
John Fix, Mark Leitzell, Brad Sauder, Dave Folk, Larry Meyers

Cartographers
Zach Davis, Brian Goudreau, Kendall Marten, Todd Martin, Jeff Martz, Tara Petrilli, Justin Morrill, Tracey Morrill, Linda Peters, Hylon Plumb, Robert Rizzutti

Editors
Robert Harding, Dana Wolf

Production Support
Shawna Roberts

Imagesetting/Proofing
Chris Gruber, Fred Hofferth

For a free color catalog describing Gareth Stevens Publishing's list of high-quality books and multimedia programs, call 1-800-542-2595 (USA) or 1-800-461-9120 (Canada). Gareth Stevens Publishing's Fax: (414) 225-0377.

Library of Congress Cataloging-in-Publication Data available upon request from publisher. Fax: (414) 225-0377 for the attention of the Publishing Records Department.

ISBN 0-8368-2491-1

This edition first published in 2000 by
Gareth Stevens Publishing
1555 North RiverCenter Drive, Suite 201
Milwaukee, Wisconsin 53212 USA

Printed in the United States of America

1 2 3 4 5 6 7 8 9 04 03 02 01 00

TABLE OF CONTENTS

The WORLD in the 21st CENTURY

4 WORLD

6 ASIA and OCEANIA

8 Japan
9 North Korea, South Korea, Taiwan
10 China
11 Vietnam, Laos, Cambodia, Mongolia
12 Thailand, Burma (Myanmar), Philippines
13 Indonesia, Brunei, Singapore, Malaysia
14 Australia
15 Papua New Guinea, New Zealand, Federated States of Micronesia
16 Marshall Is., Nauru, Solomon Is., Tuvalu
17 Kiribati, Fiji, Palau, Tonga
18 Vanuatu, New Caledonia & Dependencies, Samoa, American Samoa
19 Nepal, Maldives, Bhutan, Sri Lanka
20 India
21 Bangladesh, Pakistan
22 Afghanistan, Iran, Turkmenistan
23 Kazakhstan, Uzbekistan, Kyrgyzstan, Tajikistan
24 Iraq, Kuwait, Saudi Arabia
25 Bahrain, Qatar, United Arab Emirates, Yemen, Oman
26 Lebanon, Israel, Jordan
27 Turkey, Cyprus, Syria

28 EUROPE

30 Great Britain & Northern Ireland
31 Republic of Ireland
32 Denmark, Netherlands
33 Belgium, Liechtenstein, Luxembourg
34 France
35 Monaco, Switzerland
36 Portugal, Malta, Gibraltar, Andorra
37 Spain
38 Italy
39 Austria, Vatican City, San Marino
40 Germany
41 Poland
42 Czech Republic, Slovakia
43 Hungary, Romania
44 Russia
45 Armenia, Georgia, Azerbaijan
46 Estonia, Latvia, Lithuania
47 Belarus, Ukraine
48 Slovenia, Croatia, Bosnia & Hercegovina, F.Y.R. Macedonia
49 Albania, Yugoslavia
50 Moldova, Bulgaria
51 Greece
52 Iceland, Norway
53 Sweden, Finland

54 AFRICA

56 Egypt, Libya
57 Algeria, Tunisia, Morocco
58 Western Sahara, Cape Verde, Mali, Mauritania
59 Chad, Niger, Sudan
60 Eritrea, Djibouti, Ethiopia, Somalia
61 Kenya, Uganda, Rwanda, Burundi
62 Senegal, The Gambia, Guinea, Guinea-Bissau
63 Sierra Leone, Côte d'Ivoire, São Tomé & Príncipe, Liberia
64 Ghana, Burkina Faso, Benin, Togo
65 Nigeria, Cameroon
66 Equatorial Guinea, Republic of the Congo, Gabon, Central African Republic
67 Comoros, Democratic Republic of the Congo, Zambia
68 Tanzania, Malawi, Mozambique
69 Mauritius, Zimbabwe, Botswana, Madagascar
70 Angola, Namibia, Seychelles
71 South Africa, Swaziland, Lesotho

72 SOUTH AMERICA

74 Argentina
75 Paraguay, Uruguay
76 Chile
77 Peru, Bolivia
78 Colombia
79 Ecuador, Venezuela
80 Guyana, Suriname, French Guiana
81 Brazil

82 NORTH AMERICA

84 Mexico
85 Belize, Guatemala
86 Honduras, El Salvador, Costa Rica
87 Nicaragua, Panama
88 Cuba, Jamaica
89 Dominican Republic, Haiti, Bahamas, Turks & Caicos Is.
90 Puerto Rico, Antigua & Barbuda, St. Kitts & Nevis, Dominica
91 St. Lucia, Barbados, St. Vincent & the Grenadines, Grenada, Trinidad & Tobago
92 Canada
93 Canadian Provincial & Territorial Flags
94 Alberta
95 British Columbia
96 Manitoba
97 New Brunswick
98 Newfoundland
99 Northwest Territories, Nunavut
100 Nova Scotia, Prince Edward Island
101 Ontario, Québec
102 Southern Ontario
103 Southern Québec
104 Saskatchewan
105 Yukon Territory

LEGEND

POLAR REGIONS

106 Arctic Regions, Greenland
107 Antarctica

108 WORLD INDEX

UNITED STATES

126 U.S. Political
127 U.S. Physical
128 Alabama
129 Alaska
130 Arizona
131 Arkansas
132 California
133 Colorado
134 Connecticut
135 Delaware
136 Florida
137 Georgia
138 Hawaii
139 Idaho
140 Illinois
141 Indiana
142 Iowa
143 Kansas
144 Kentucky
145 Louisiana
146 Maine
147 Maryland
148 Massachusetts
149 Michigan
150 Minnesota
151 Mississippi
152 Missouri
153 Montana
154 Nebraska
155 Nevada
156 New Hampshire
157 New Jersey
158 New Mexico
159 New York
160 North Carolina
161 North Dakota
162 Ohio
163 Oklahoma
164 Oregon
165 Pennsylvania
166 Rhode Island
167 South Carolina
168 South Dakota
169 Tennessee
170 Texas
171 Utah
172 Vermont
173 Virginia
174 Washington
175 West Virginia
176 Wisconsin
177 Wyoming

178 STATE INDEXES

General

- National Capital
- Territorial Capital
- Other City
- International Boundary (subject area)
- International Boundary (non-subject)
- Internal Boundary (state, province, etc.)
- Disputed Boundary
- Perennial River
- Intermittent River
- Canal
- Dam

U.S. States, Canadian Provinces & Territories

(additions and changes to general legend)

- State Capital
- County Seat
- Built Up Area
- State Boundary
- County Boundary
- National Park
- Other Park, Forest, Grassland
- Indian, Other Reservation
- Point of Interest
- Mountain Peak
- Continental Divide
- Time Zone Boundary
- Limited Access Highway
- Other Major Road
- 90 Highway Shield

PROJECTION

The only true representation of the earth, free of distortion, is a globe. Maps are flat, and the process by which the geographic locations (latitude and longitude) are transformed from a three-dimensional sphere to a two-dimensional flat map is called a Projection.

For a detailed explanation of Projections, see ***MapScope*** in Volume 2 of ***Funk & Wagnalls New Encyclopedia.***

This example is used on pages 20, 21 for India, Bangladesh, and Pakistan.

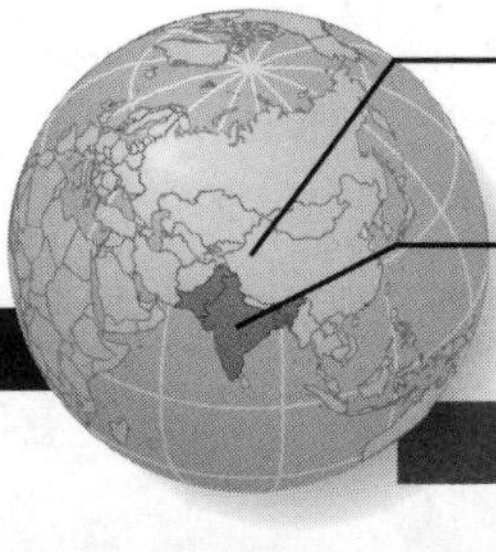

The Globe is centered on the continent of Asia, as shown on pages 6, 7.

The subject countries are shown in a stronger red/brown color.

LOCATOR

TYPES OF SCALE

Visual Scale

Every map has a bar scale, or a Visual Scale, that can be used for measuring. It shows graphically the relationship between map distance and ground distance.

Miles

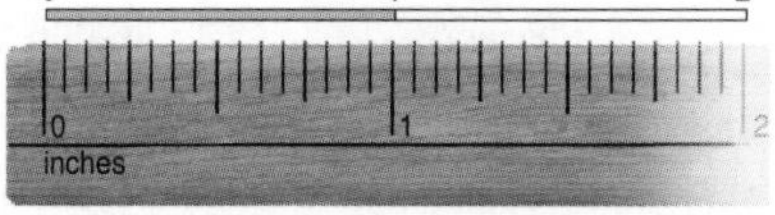

One inch represents 1 mile

Kilometers

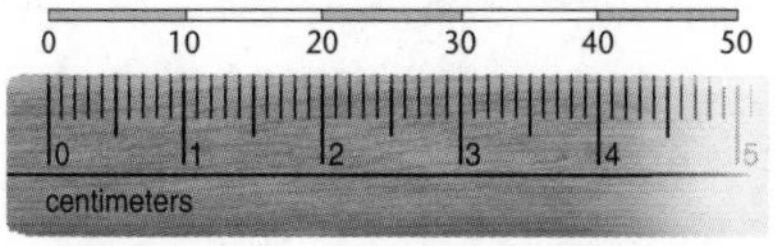

One centimeter represents 10 kilometers

Representative Fraction

The scale of a map, expressed as a numerical ratio of map distance to ground distance, is called a Representative Fraction (or RF). It is usually written as 1/50,000 or 1:50,000, meaning that one unit of measurement on the map represents 50,000 of the same units on the ground.

THE WORLD IN THE 21ST CENTURY

The following eight-page section looks at the growing world population and the impact of environmental change as we move into a new century and millennium. Topics covered are:

World Population Trends ....pages S-1,2
Life & Health S-3,4
Climate & Global Warming S-5,6
Deforestation S-7,8

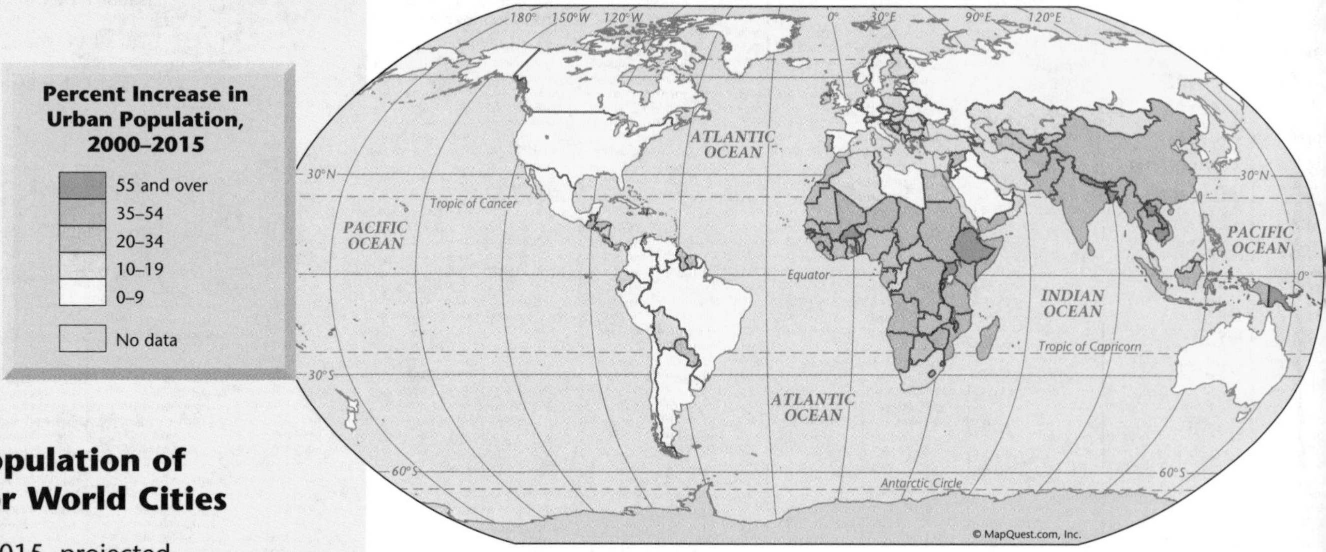

Source: *UN World Resources*, pp. 274–275.

Urban Population Growth, 2000–2015

The world population will become increasingly urbanized in the early 21st century. It is predicted that the largest increases in urban population will occur in Africa and southern and eastern Asia.

Population of Major World Cities

2015, projected

1 Tokyo 28,887,000
2 Mumbai............26,218,000
3 Lagos................24,640,000
4 São Paulo 20,320,000
5 Mexico City......19,180,000
6 Shanghai 17,969,000
7 New York..........17,602,000
8 Calcutta............17,305,000
9 Delhi 16,860,000
10 Beijing.............15,572,000
11 Los Angeles 14,217,000
12 Buenos Aires 13,856,000
13 Seoul 12,980,000
14 Rio de Janeiro ..11,860,000
15 Osaka 10,609,000

These figures are for "urban agglomerations," which are densely populated urban areas, larger than the cities by themselves.

Source: UN, Dept. for Economic and Social Information and Policy Analysis

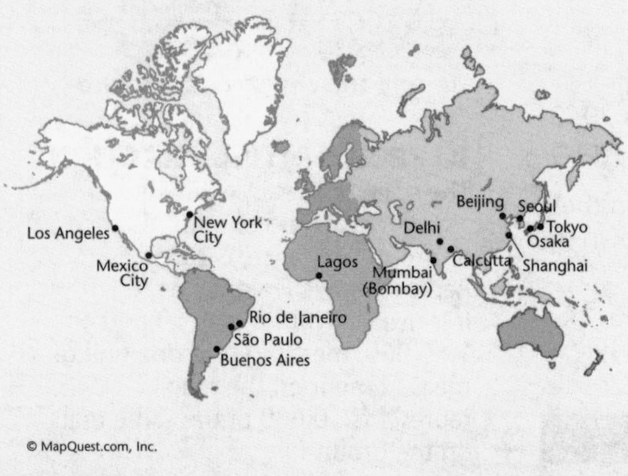

Population Growth: Urban vs. Rural Areas, 1950–2015

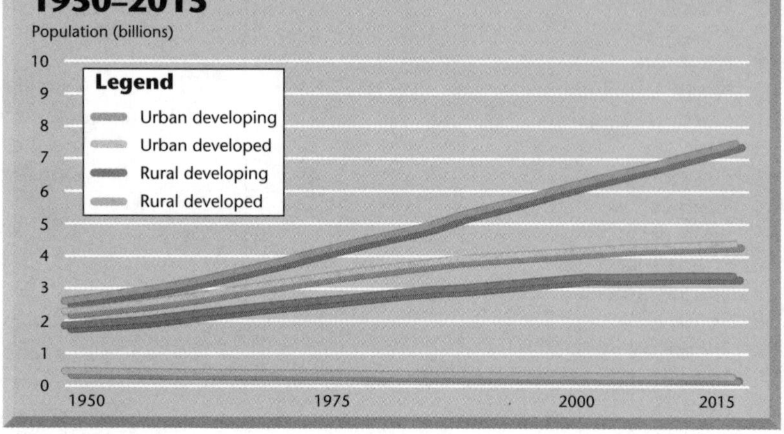

Source: *UN World Resources*, p. 146.

Population growth in rural areas will taper off where it has not already. But urban growth will increase, especially in the developing nations.

Developed regions include United States, Canada, Japan, Europe, and Australia and New Zealand.

Developing regions include Africa, Asia (excluding Japan), South America and Central America, Mexico, and Oceania (excluding Australia and New Zealand). The European successor states of the former Soviet Union are classified as developed regions, while the Asian successor states are classified as developing regions.

Population Density, 2000

Population

Persons per sq. mi.	Persons per sq. km.
and over	200 and over
60–519	100–199
30–259	50–99
25–129	10–49
1–24	1–9
under 1	under 1

© MapQuest.com, Inc.

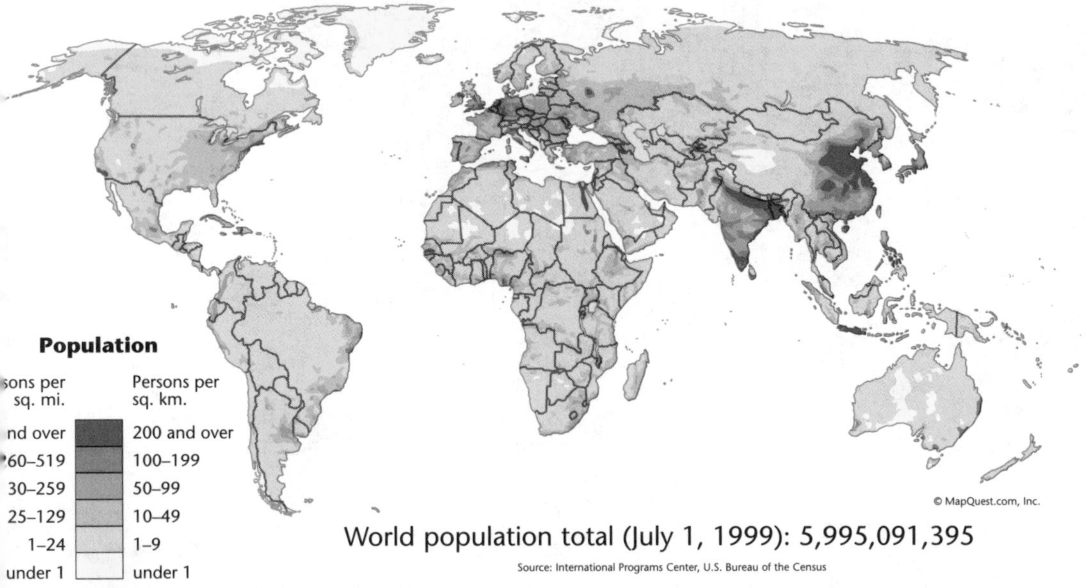

World population total (July 1, 1999): 5,995,091,395

Source: International Programs Center, U.S. Bureau of the Census

Population Density, Largest Countries

2000

People per square mile

China	330
India	800
United States	70
Indonesia	290
Brazil	50
Russia	20

2050

People per square mile

China	360
India	1,400
United States	100
Indonesia	450
Brazil	70
Russia	20

The world will become more crowded in the 21st century. In mid-1999, China already had the highest population in the world, with an estimated 1.2 billion inhabitants, one-fifth of the total population. India had reached 1 billion, while the United States had the world's third-largest population, with about 273 million, followed by Indonesia, Brazil, and Russia.

Source: Bureau of the Census, U.S. Dept. of Commerce

Anticipated World Population Growth

Population (billions)

Fertility rates
- High
- Medium
- Low

Developing regions

Developed regions

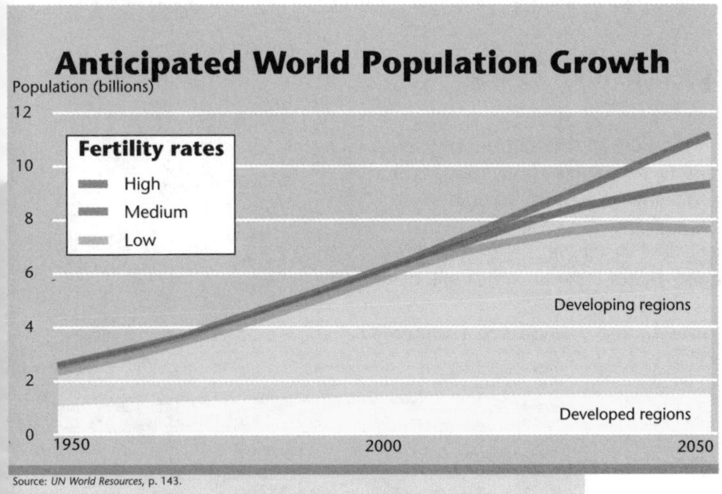

Source: *UN World Resources*, p. 143.

The world population has grown from about 2 billion in 1950 to 6 billion today, and could almost double by 2050. Most of the growth will continue to occur in developing regions, where fertility rates (number of children born per woman of childbearing age) are relatively high.

Where the fertility rate is around 2 children per woman of childbearing age, the population will tend to stabilize. This figure indicates roughly that couples, over a lifetime, are replacing themselves without adding to the population.

Population experts at the United Nations actually give three different projections for future population growth. Under a **high** fertility-rate projection, which assumes rates would stabilize at an average of 2.6 in high-fertility regions and 2.1 in low-fertility regions, the global population would reach 11.2 billion by 2050. Under a **medium** projection, which assumes rates would ultimately stabilize at around replacement levels, the population would rise to 9.4 billion by 2050. Under a **low** fertility-rate projection, which assumes rates would eventually stabilize at lower-than-replacement levels, the world population would still reach about 7.7 billion by 2050.

Population Projections by Continent

NORTH AMERICA
475,815
617,249
728,136

EUROPE*
588,240
696,838
727,289

ASIA
3,641,354
4,774,053
5,406,328

AFRICA
778,434
1,317,493
2,012,567

SOUTH AMERICA
343,294
451,641
519,878

AUSTRALIA & PACIFIC IS.
30,029
38,512
42,829

Population (in thousands)

YEAR
1999 2025 2050

Population projections based on medium fertility rate

*Including Russia

© MapQuest.com, Inc.

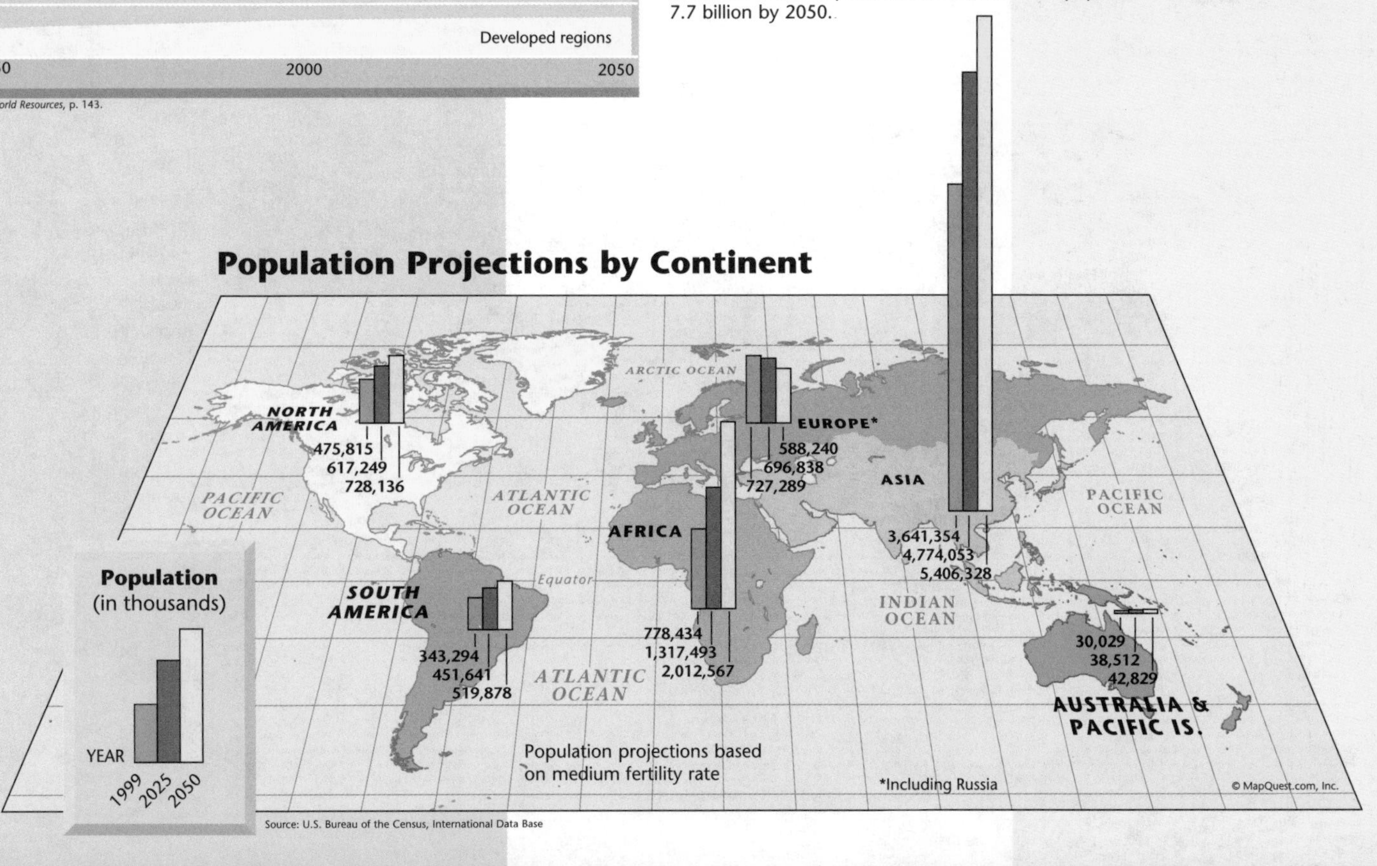

Source: U.S. Bureau of the Census, International Data Base

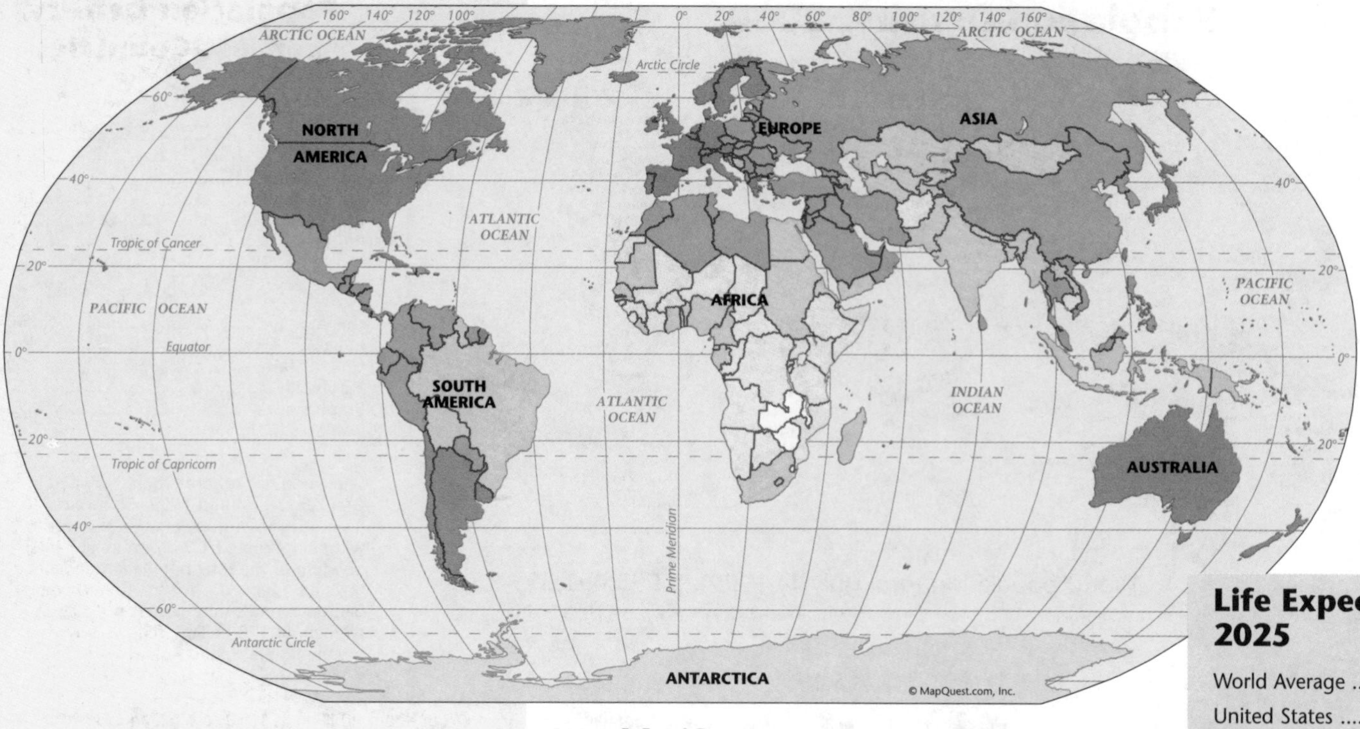

World Life Expectancy, 1999

Life Expectancy
(in years)

- 75–84
- 65–74
- 50–64
- 40–49
- Less than 40
- No data

Life expectancy at birth is a common measure of the number of years a person may expect to live. There are many factors, such as nutrition, sanitation, health and medical services, that contribute to helping people live longer.

As some of the above factors improve in the developing countries, life expectancy there should increase. But most of Sub-Saharan Africa will have less than average life expectancies.

Although it is not indicated here, females almost always have a longer life expectancy than males.

World Life Expectancy, 2025

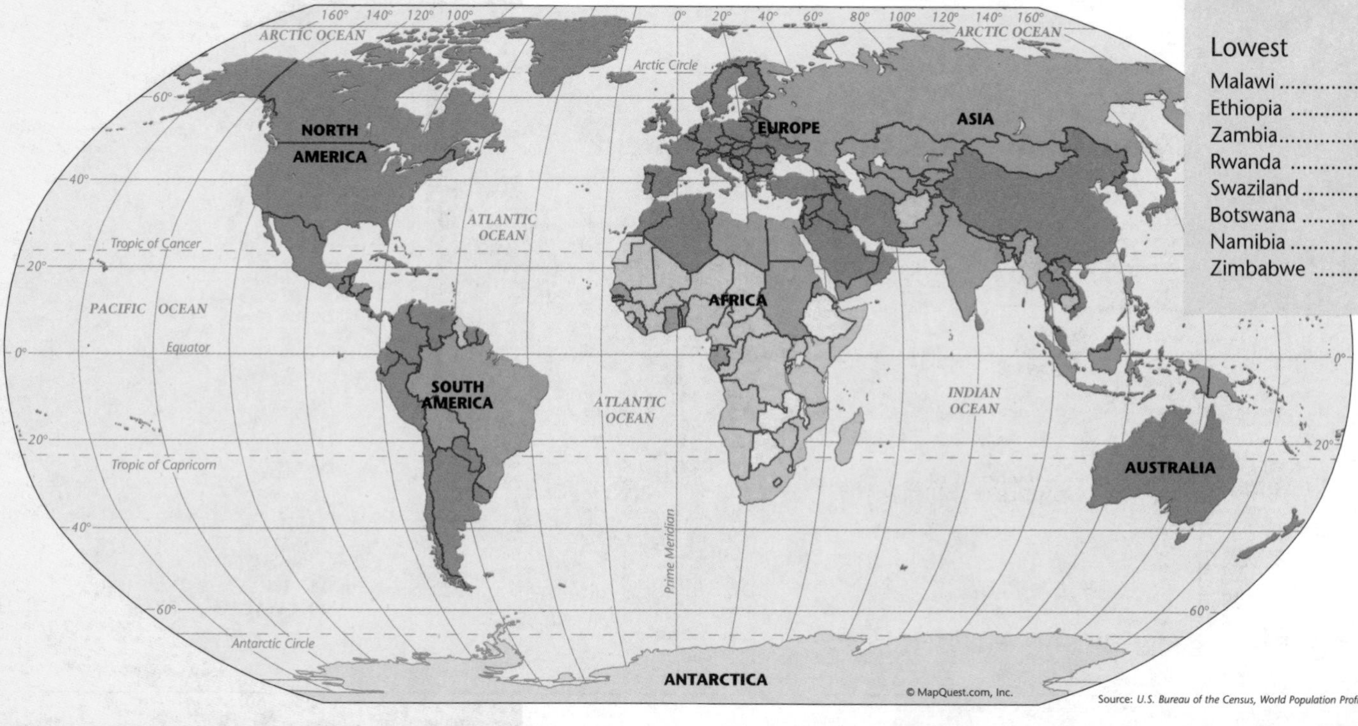

Source: *U.S. Bureau of the Census, World Population Profile:* 1998

Life Expectancy, 2025

World Average 7
United States 7

Highest

Andorra 8
Austria 8
Australia 8
Canada..............................8
Cyprus 8
Dominica 8
Israel 8
Japan 8
Kuwait 8
Monaco 8
San Marino.........................8
Singapore...........................8
Taiwan 8

Lowest

Malawi 4
Ethiopia 4
Zambia...............................4
Rwanda 4
Swaziland...........................4
Botswana 4
Namibia 5
Zimbabwe 5

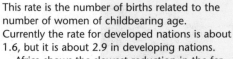

Infant Mortality Averages, 2015–2020

by continent with highest and lowest country

World Average 35

Africa 55	Europe 8
Sierra Leone 114	Albania 20
Mauritius 8	Austria
	& 14 others...........5
Asia 32	
Afghanistan 118	North America 22
Japan 4	Haiti 82
	Canada...................5
Australia & Oceania ..15	U.S. 5
Papua	
New Guinea 37	South America 23
Australia 5	Guyana..................37
	Chile......................9

1995–2000

© MapQuest.com, Inc.

Infant Mortality

Infant mortality means the number of deaths before the age of one per 1,000 live births. It is a fairly common way of judging how healthy a country is. Presently there are about 14 countries with infant mortality rates lower than that of the United States.

With improvements in sanitation and health care, it is expected that infant mortality will decline substantially in the 21st century. However, it will continue to be a serious problem especially in Sub-Saharan Africa and other developing regions

Infant Mortality Rate
(per 1,000 live births)

- 85–169
- 50–85
- 25–49
- 10–24
- Less than 10
- No data

2015–2020

© MapQuest.com, Inc.

Source: UN Population Division and UN Children's Fund

Food & Nutrition

There has been a general trend towards better nutrition, but Sub-Saharan Africa remains a problem area: increasing numbers of people will be suffering from undernutrition.

On a worldwide basis, the food supply seems adequate. Unfortunately the availability of food and the distribution of people don't always match up.

Undernutrition in Developing Countries, 1969-2010

million persons suffering from undernutrition

500 400 300 200 100 0

1969-71   1979-81   1990-92   2010

Legend
- Latin America and the Caribbean
- Near East and North Africa
- Sub-Saharan Africa
- East and Southeast Asia
- South Asia

Fertility

This rate is the number of births related to the number of women of childbearing age. Currently the rate for developed nations is about 1.6, but it is about 2.9 in developing nations.

Africa shows the slowest reduction in the fertility rate. With improvements in infant mortality and the implementation of family planning programs, the rate should stabilize.

Average Daily per Capita Calorie Supply, 1992–1994

by continent with highest and lowest country

BOSNIA AND HERZEGOVINA 1,734

BELGIUM 3,700

AFGHANISTAN 2,121

CHINA 3,082

UNITED STATES 3,609

HAITI 1,721

PERU 2,121

LIBYA 3,288

SOMALIA 1,533

SOLOMON ISLANDS 2,046

ARGENTINA 3,076

NEW ZEALAND 3,314

Source: UN Food and Agriculture Organization, UN Population Division, U.S. Department of Agriculture

© MapQuest.com, Inc.

Trends in Fertility Rates

Legend
- Africa
- Asia
- South and Central America
- Developed
- Developing

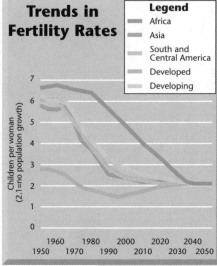

Children per woman (2.1=no population growth)

7 6 5 4 3 2 1 0

1950 1960 1970 1980 1990 2000 2010 2020 2030 2040 2050

Source: UN Population Division

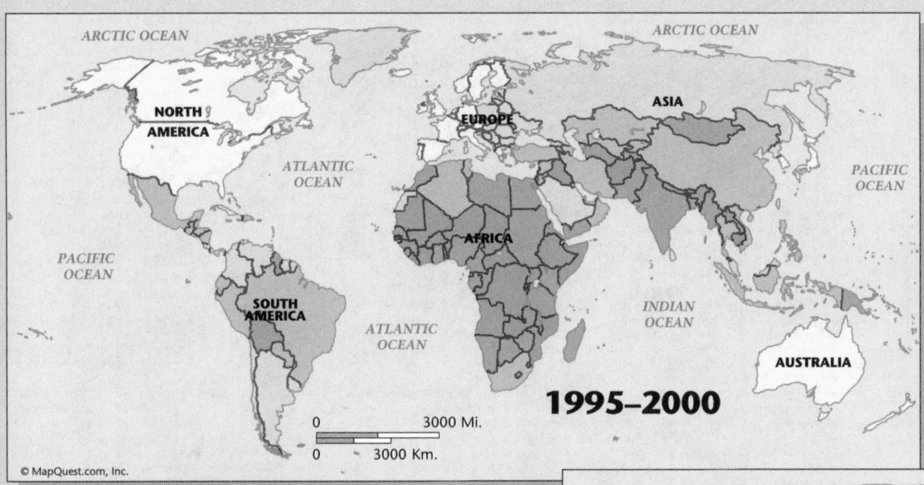

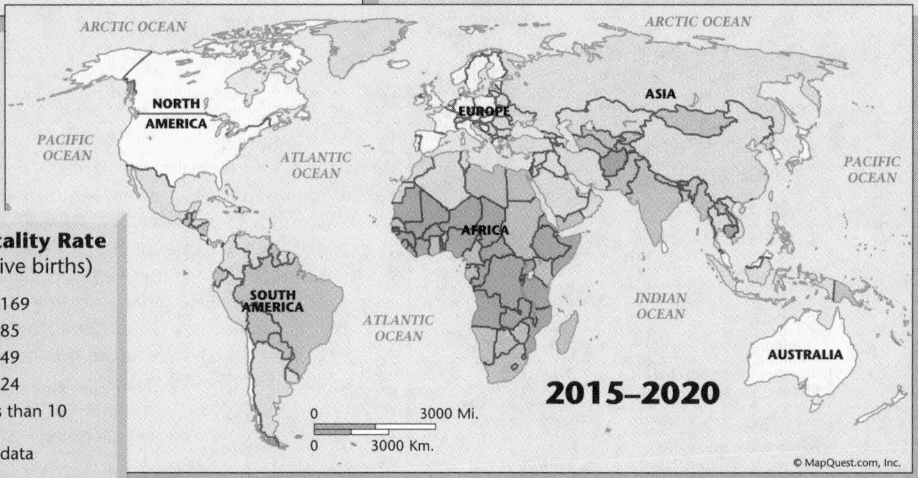

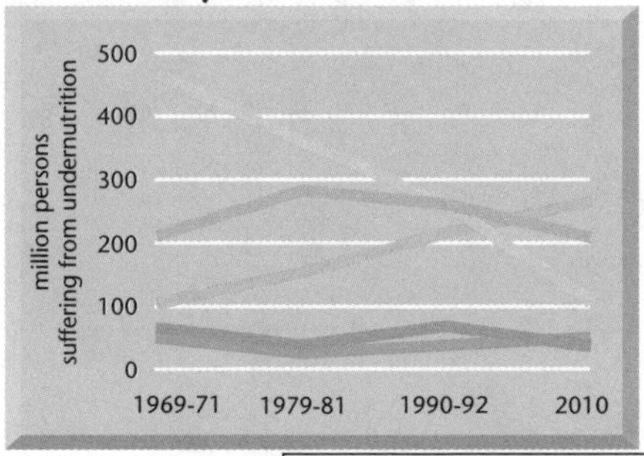

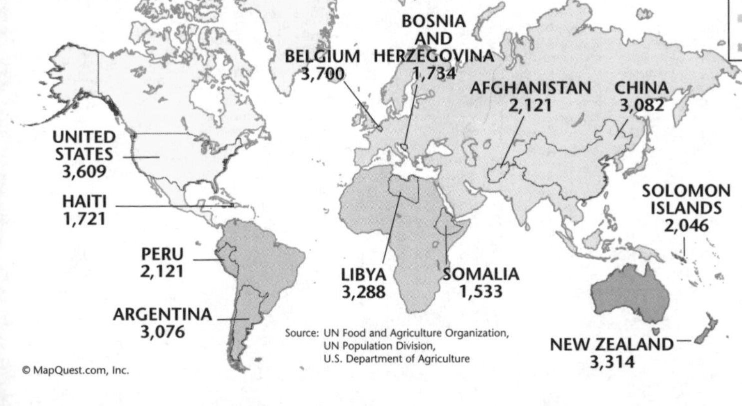

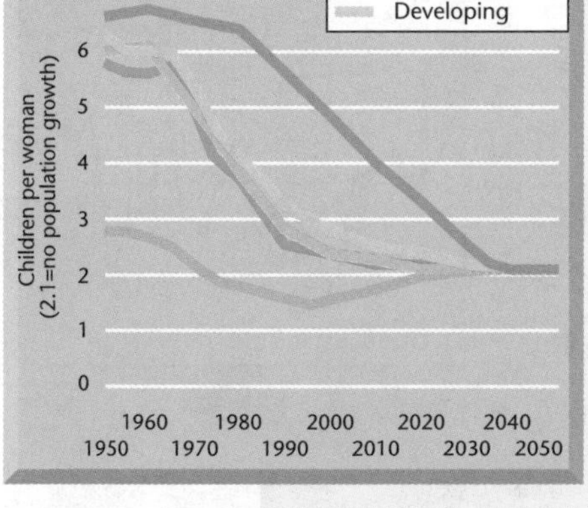

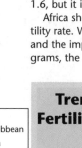

Global Warming

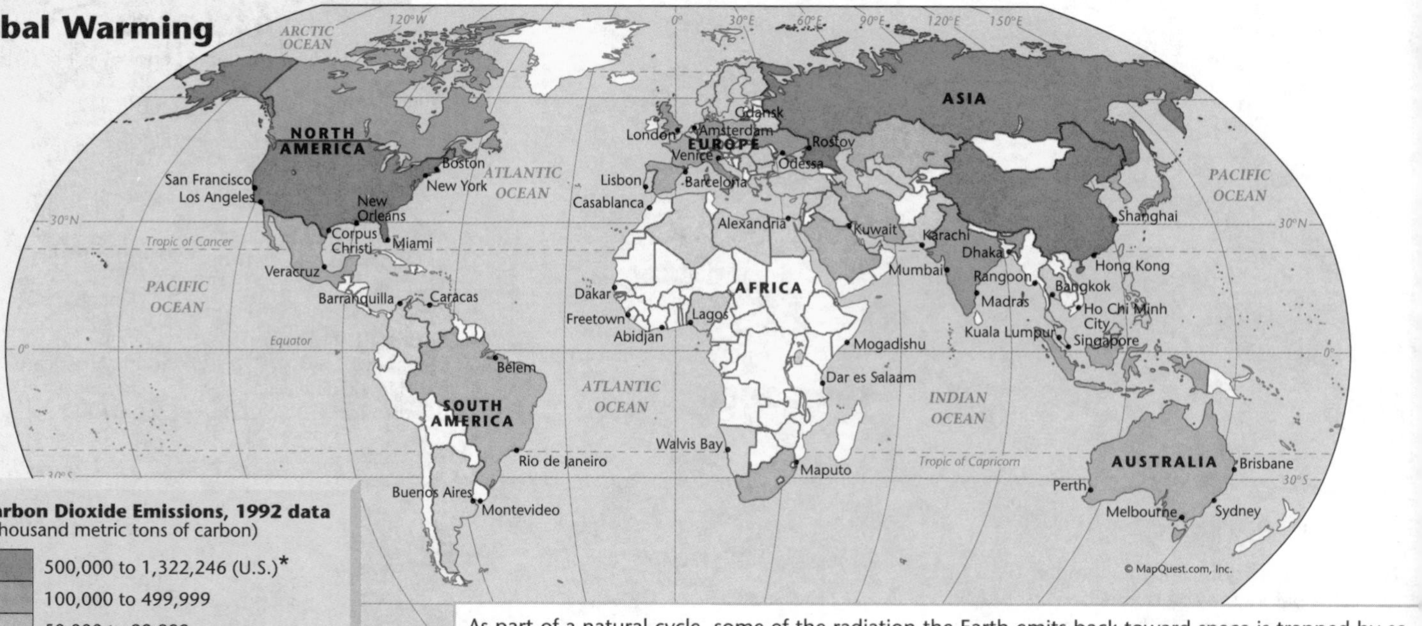

Carbon Dioxide Emissions, 1992 data
(thousand metric tons of carbon)

- 500,000 to 1,322,246 (U.S.)*
- 100,000 to 499,999
- 50,000 to 99,999
- 10,000 to 49,999
- 5,000 to 9,999
- 0 to 4,999
- No current data availible

* The highest CO_2 levels are found in the United States

• Major cities that would be affected by a rise in sea level

Source: *Estimates or Global, Regional, and National Annual CO2 Emissions from Fossil-Fuel Burning Hydraulic Cement Production, and Gas Flaring: 1950–1992*, Oak Ridge National Laboratory, 1995

As part of a natural cycle, some of the radiation the Earth emits back toward space is trapped by so-called greenhouse gases in the atmosphere. Over the past two centuries, however, concentrations of these greenhouse gases have increased. Carbon dioxide (CO2), for example, has been building up because of such activities as the burning of fossil fuels like coal, oil, and natural gas, as well as deforestation (forests absorb huge amounts of carbon dioxide, therby helping to regulate climate). The increase in greenhouse gases may help explain why the average temperature at the Earth's surface has risen approximately 0.7 degrees (over 1°Fahrenheit) over the past century. Some experts project the average surface temperature will increase by roughly 1-3°C (2 to 6° F) in the 21st century. If global warming does continue, large portions of the polar ice caps may melt, inundating coastal low lands. As a result, crop production and natural habitats could undergo major changes. Increased temperatures could also have serious health effects.

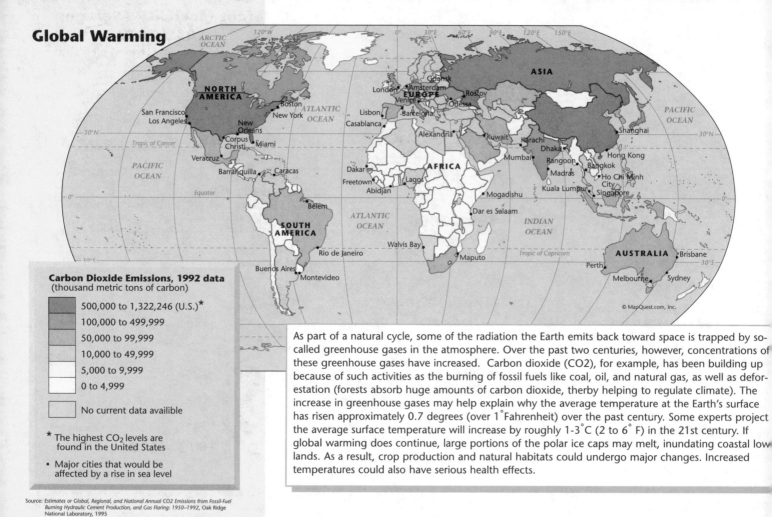

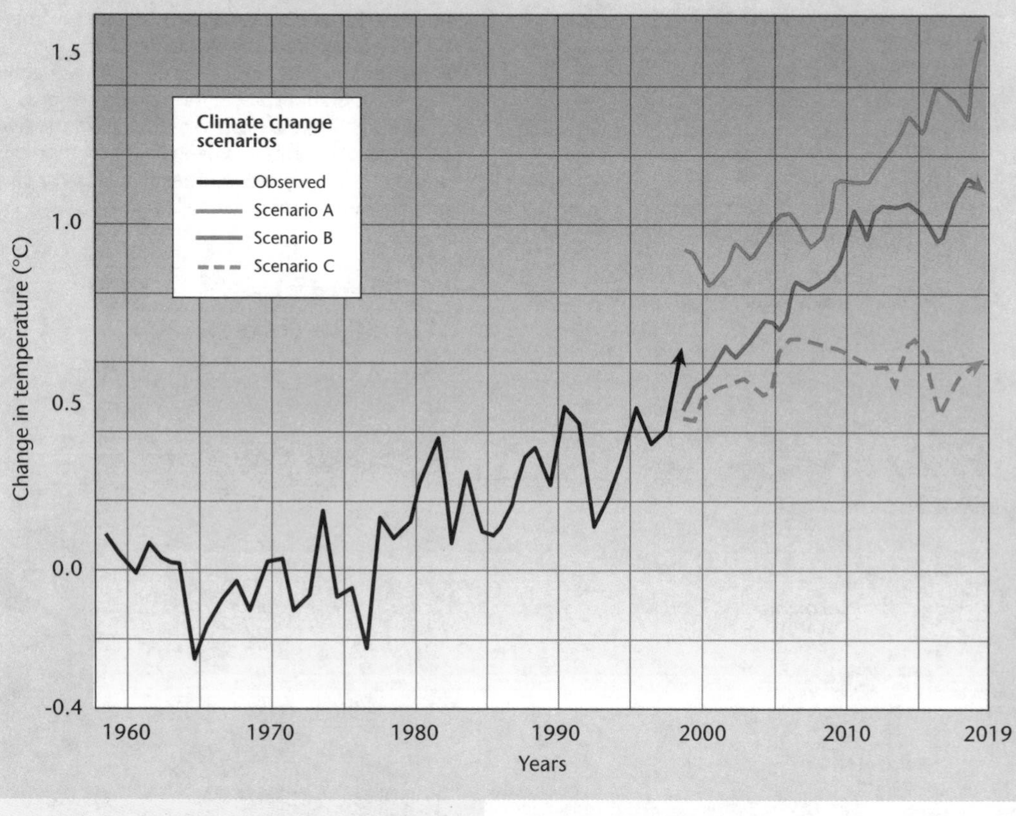

Projections of Rising Global Temperature

Scientists differ over the magnitude of the climate changes an increase in greenhouse gases may cause. The graph at left shows how average global surface temperatures would be affected under three different scenarios up to the year 2019. Scenario B, which a group of NASA scientists believes to be the most likely, assumes a moderate increase in greenhouse gases. In Scenario A, they grow at a fast rate, while Scenario C assumes no increase in greenhouse gases. (A temperature change of 1°C is equivalent to a change of 1.8°F.)

Sources: NASA Goddard Institute for Space Studies.

Changing Surface Temperatures, 1960–1998

Surface temperature changes, 1960–1998 (°C)

	2.2
	1.8
	1.4
	1.0
	0.6
	0.2
	-0.2
	-0.6
	-1.0
	-1.4
	No data

The changes in land surface temperatures shown on the map at left are derived from several thousand meteorological stations and satellite measurements. (A change of 1°C is equivalent to 1.8°F.)

Source: NASA Goddard Institute for Space Studies. Data collected from NOAA National Climate Data Center in Ashville, North Carolina.

© MapQuest.com, Inc.

Rising Weather-Related Deaths

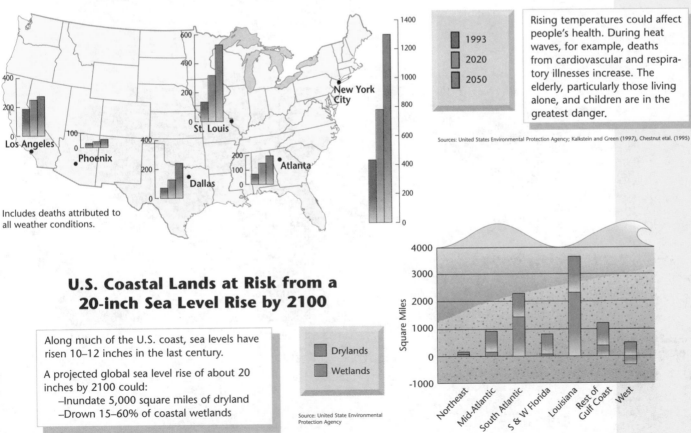

	1993
	2020
	2050

Rising temperatures could affect people's health. During heat waves, for example, deaths from cardiovascular and respiratory illnesses increase. The elderly, particularly those living alone, and children are in the greatest danger.

Sources: United States Environmental Protection Agency; Kalkstein and Green (1997), Chestnut etal. (1995)

Includes deaths attributed to all weather conditions.

U.S. Coastal Lands at Risk from a 20-inch Sea Level Rise by 2100

Along much of the U.S. coast, sea levels have risen 10–12 inches in the last century.

A projected global sea level rise of about 20 inches by 2100 could:
–Inundate 5,000 square miles of dryland
–Drown 15–60% of coastal wetlands

	Drylands
	Wetlands

Source: United State Environmental Protection Agency

Square Miles

Northeast, Mid-Atlantic, South Atlantic, S & W Florida, Louisiana, Rest of Gulf Coast, West

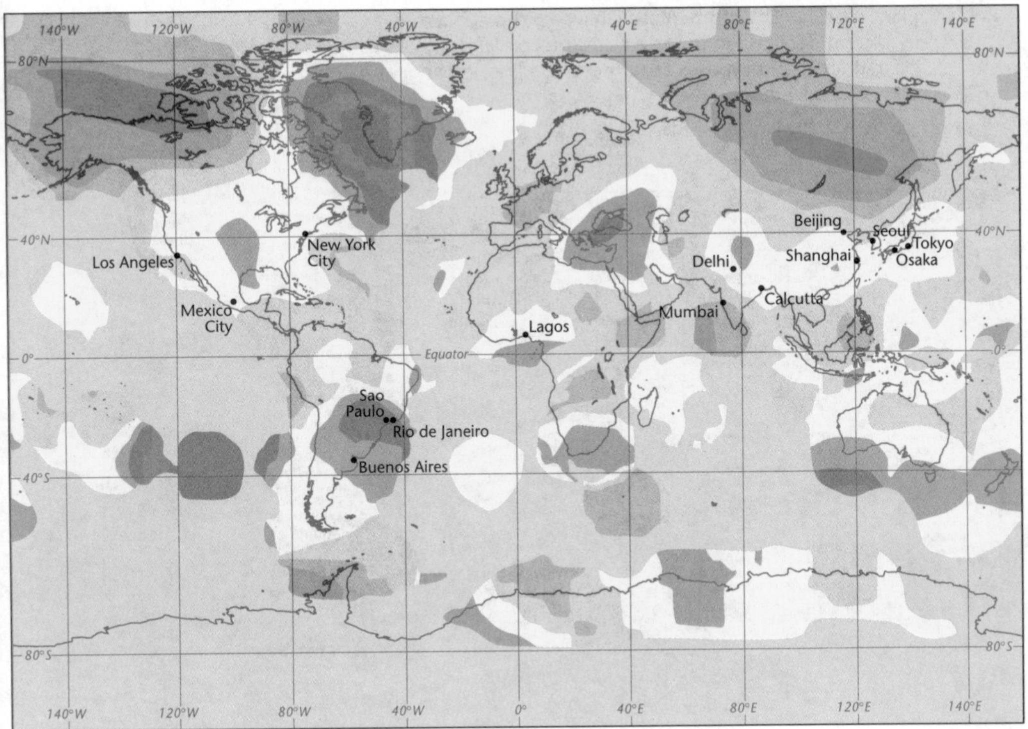

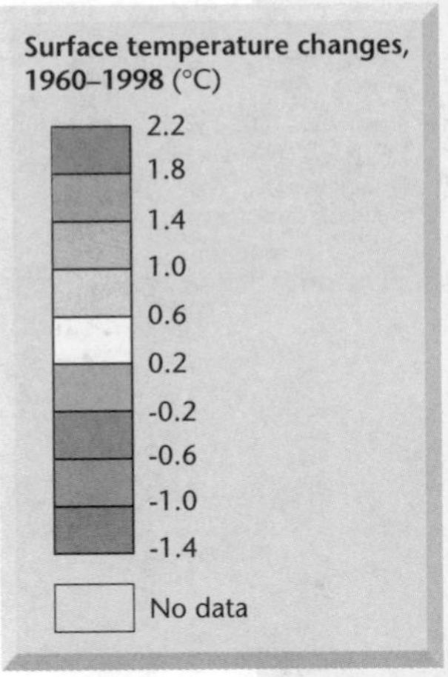

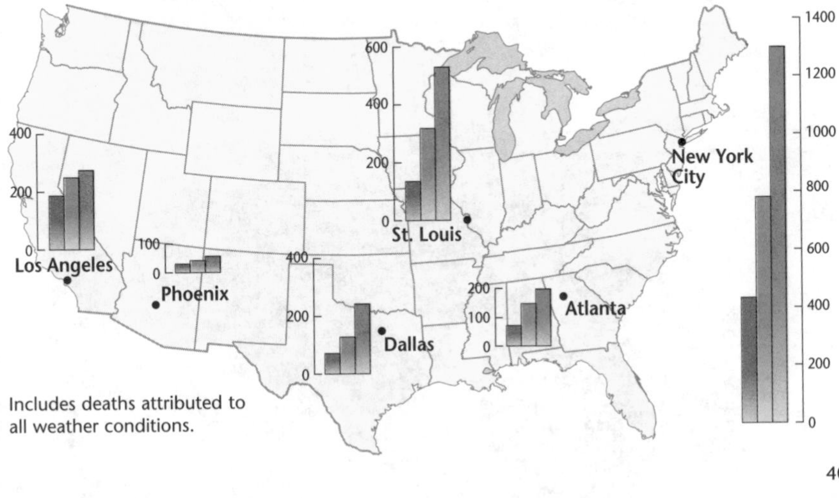

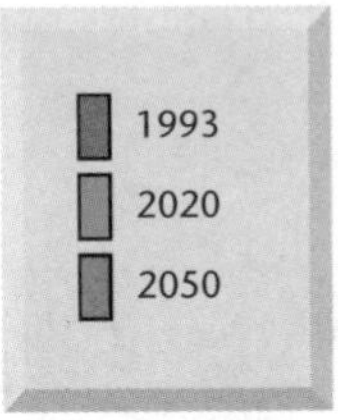

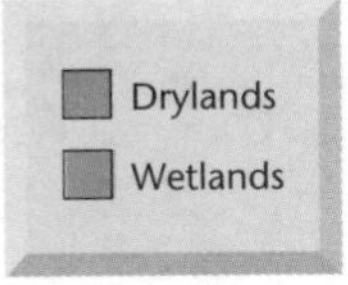

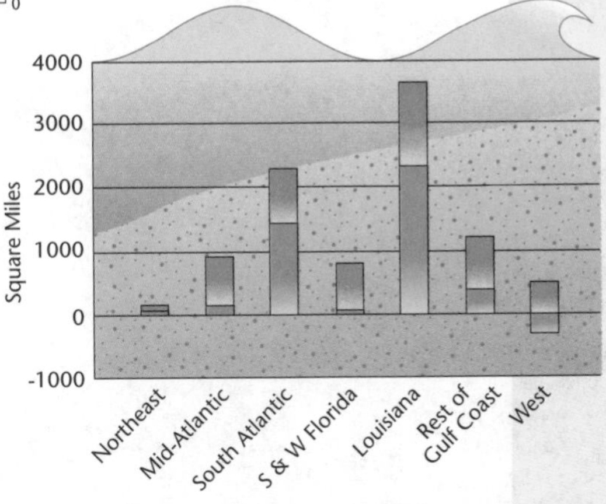

World Forest Cover

Forests help regulate climate by storing huge amounts of carbon dioxide, while providing habitats for countless animal and plant species. Environmentalists have voiced concern over a long-term decrease in forest cover, as forest lands have been cleared for such purposes as farming, logging, mining, and urban expansion.

Forest Cover

- Forest cover 8,000 years ago that has been lost
- Remaining forest cover (much of it fragmented)

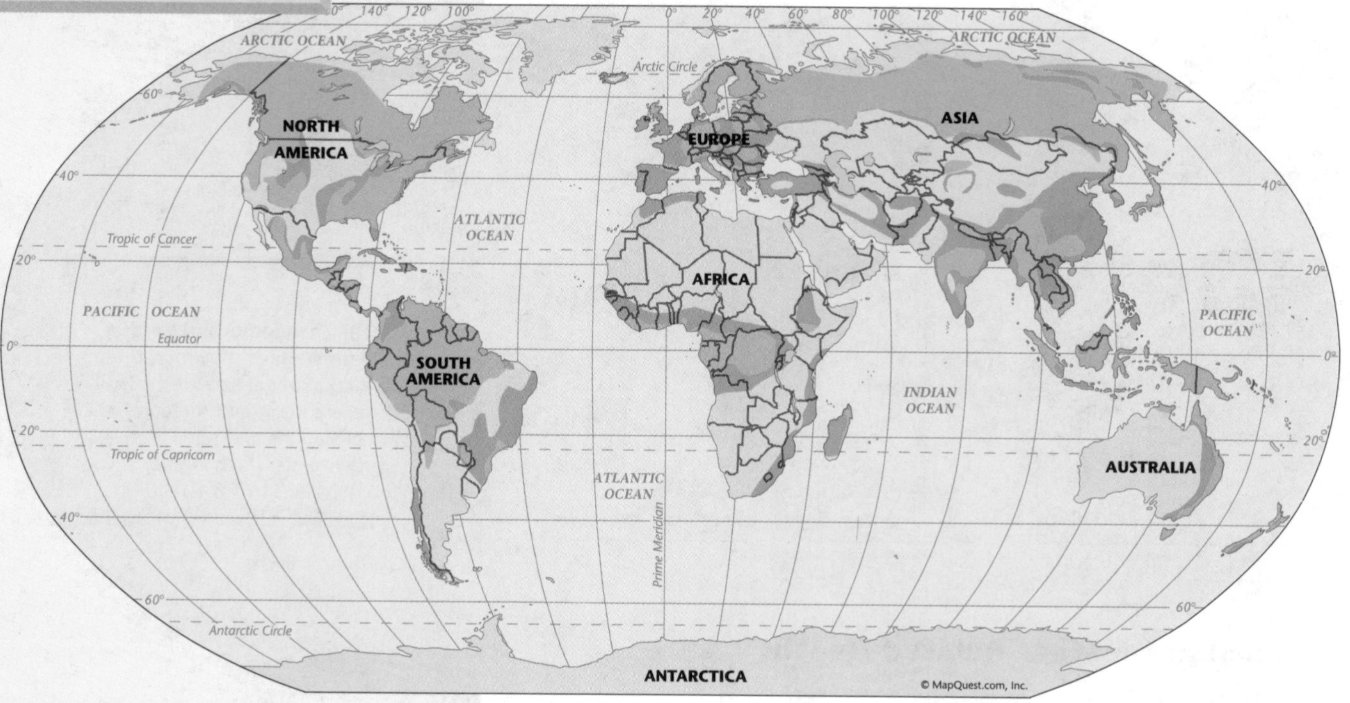

Source: *Forest Frontiers Initiative*, World Resource Institute, 1998

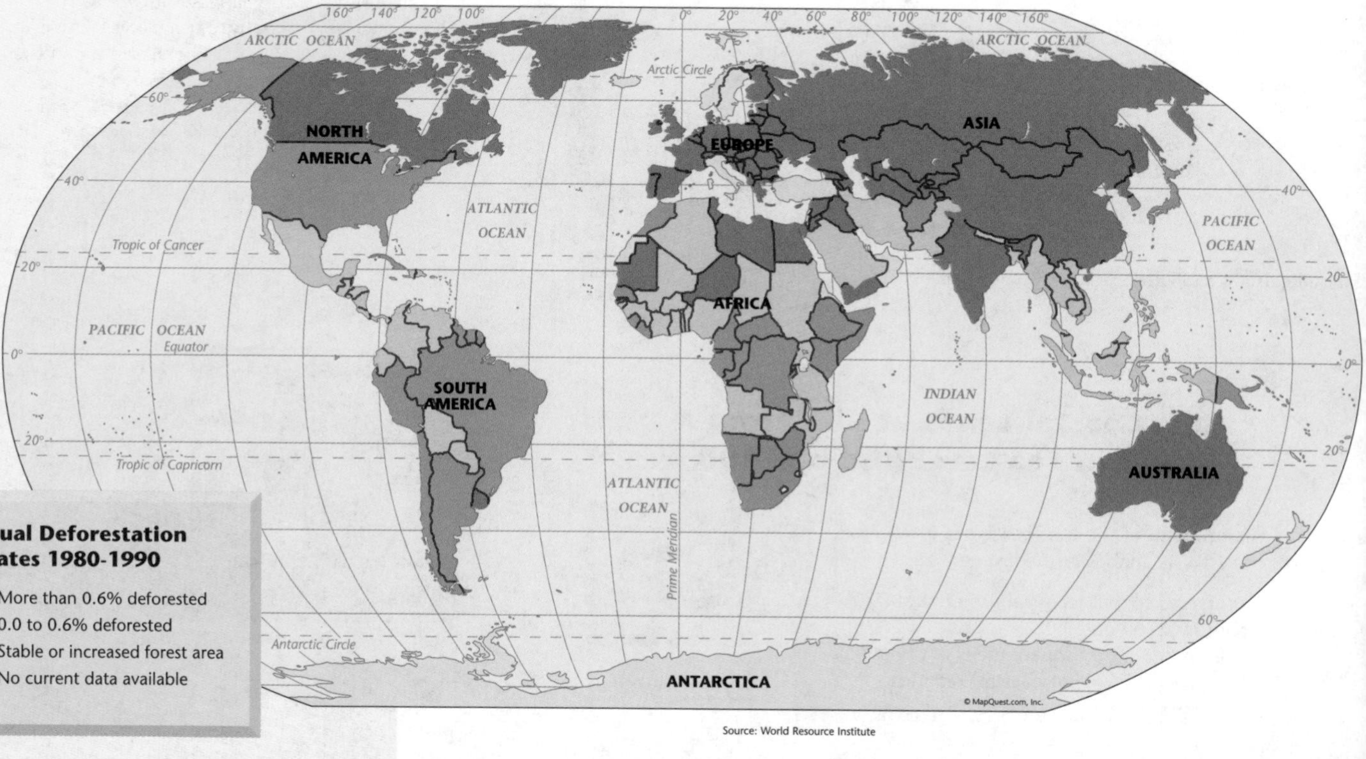

Annual Deforestation Rates 1980-1990

- More than 0.6% deforested
- 0.0 to 0.6% deforested
- Stable or increased forest area
- No current data available

Source: World Resource Institute

Tropical Rain Forests

...pical rain forests, found around the Earth with-...0 degrees of the equator, contain more than... of the world's plant and animal species, ...des being home to many indigenous peoples. ...y are vital to the balance of nature. In the past ...years alone, about one-fifth of the acreage has ...n cleared for logging and other purposes. ...se rain forests, including the major forests pin-...nted, remain under serious threat.

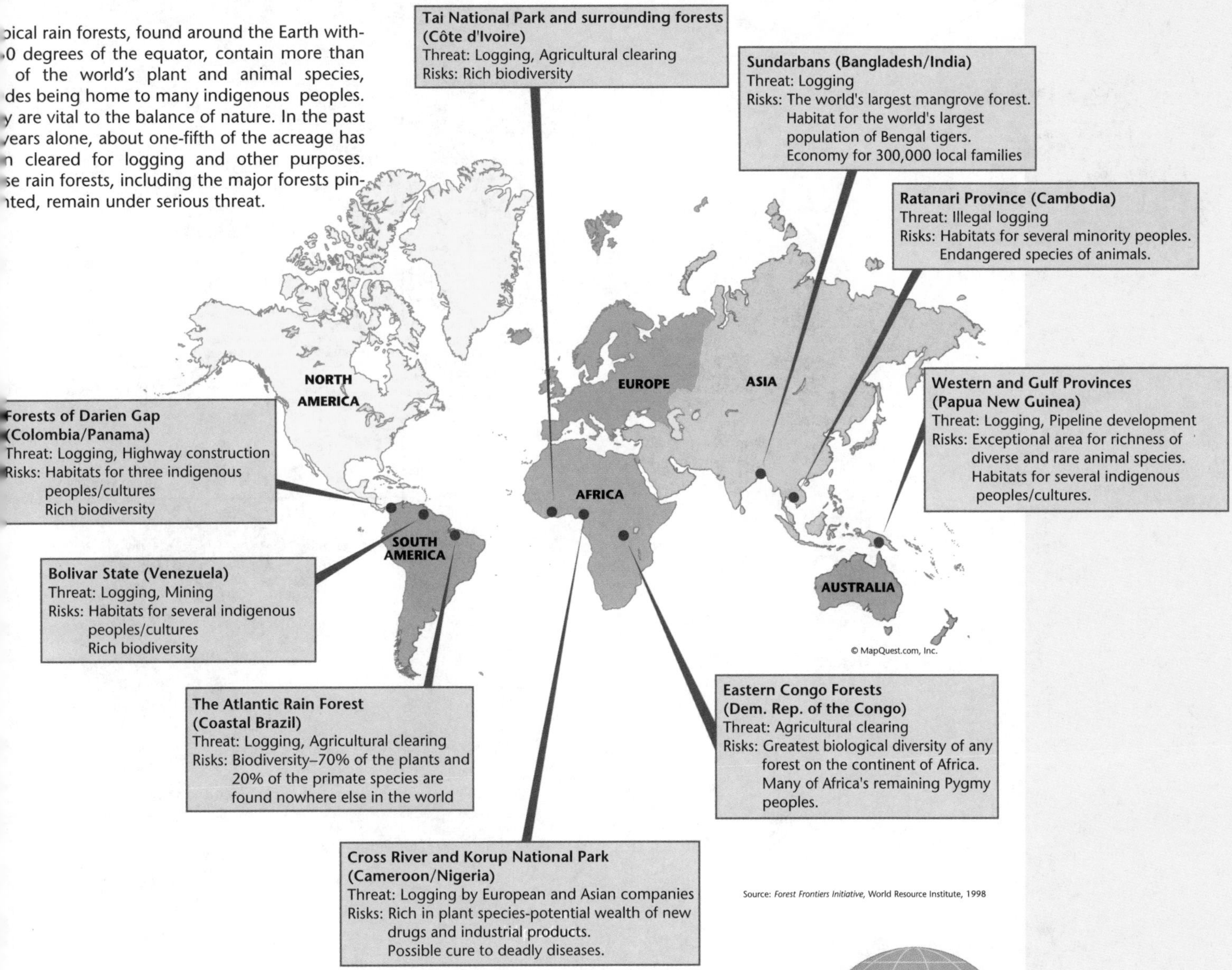

Tai National Park and surrounding forests (Côte d'Ivoire)
Threat: Logging, Agricultural clearing
Risks: Rich biodiversity

Sundarbans (Bangladesh/India)
Threat: Logging
Risks: The world's largest mangrove forest. Habitat for the world's largest population of Bengal tigers. Economy for 300,000 local families

Ratanari Province (Cambodia)
Threat: Illegal logging
Risks: Habitats for several minority peoples. Endangered species of animals.

Forests of Darien Gap (Colombia/Panama)
Threat: Logging, Highway construction
Risks: Habitats for three indigenous peoples/cultures Rich biodiversity

Western and Gulf Provinces (Papua New Guinea)
Threat: Logging, Pipeline development
Risks: Exceptional area for richness of diverse and rare animal species. Habitats for several indigenous peoples/cultures.

Bolivar State (Venezuela)
Threat: Logging, Mining
Risks: Habitats for several indigenous peoples/cultures Rich biodiversity

The Atlantic Rain Forest (Coastal Brazil)
Threat: Logging, Agricultural clearing
Risks: Biodiversity–70% of the plants and 20% of the primate species are found nowhere else in the world

Eastern Congo Forests (Dem. Rep. of the Congo)
Threat: Agricultural clearing
Risks: Greatest biological diversity of any forest on the continent of Africa. Many of Africa's remaining Pygmy peoples.

Cross River and Korup National Park (Cameroon/Nigeria)
Threat: Logging by European and Asian companies
Risks: Rich in plant species-potential wealth of new drugs and industrial products. Possible cure to deadly diseases.

NORTH AMERICA · EUROPE · ASIA · AFRICA · SOUTH AMERICA · AUSTRALIA

© MapQuest.com, Inc.

Source: *Forest Frontiers Initiative*, World Resource Institute, 1998

Percentage of Frontier Forest
Under Moderate or High Threat of Destruction (through 2030)

Source: *Forest Frontiers Initiative*, World Resource Institute, 1998

WORLD 39%

AFRICA 77%
NORTH AMERICA 26%
CENTRAL AMERICA 87%
SOUTH AMERICA 54%
EUROPE 100%
ASIA 60%
RUSSIA 19%
OCEANIA 76%

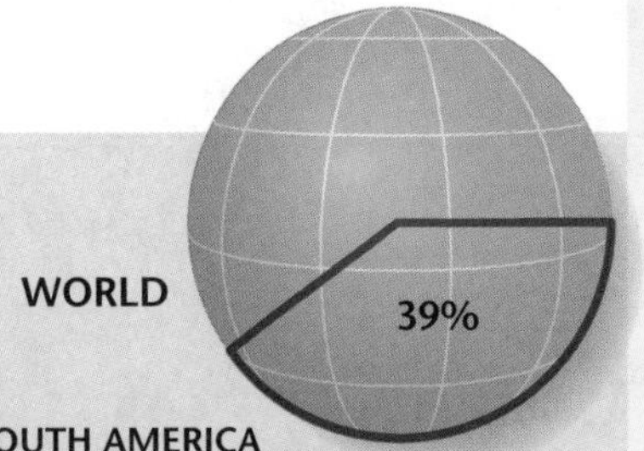

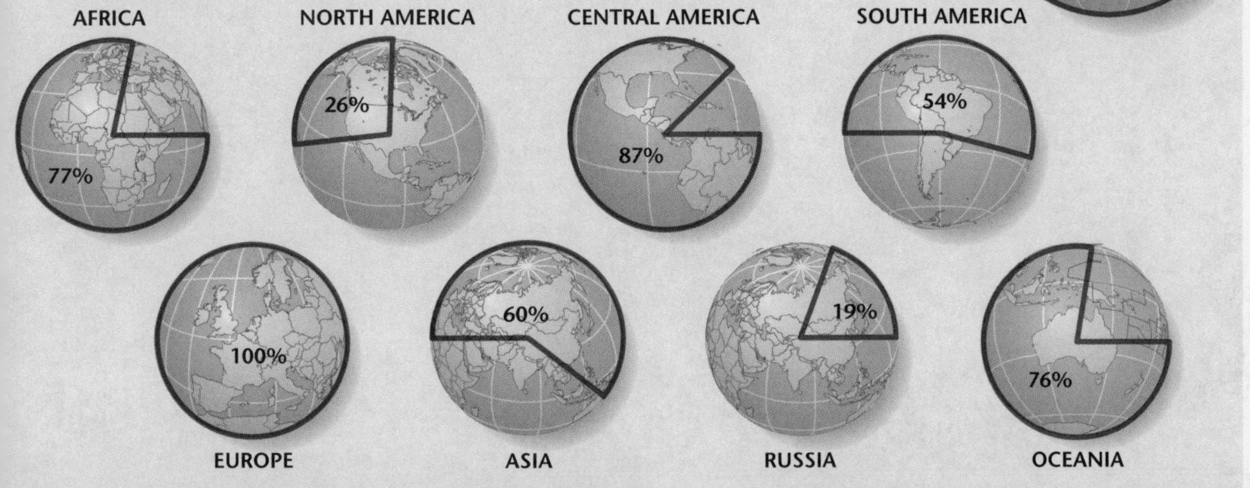

Frontier Forests

According to the World Resources Institute, only about one-fifth of Earth's forest cover of 8,000 years ago survives unfragmented, in the large unspoiled tracts it calls frontier forests. These forests are big enough to provide stable habitats for a rich diversity of plant and animal species. Most surviving forests are in the far north or the tropics, and are under threat.

The World

Scale at the equator
1:116,400,000

0   1000   2000   3000 mi

0   1000   2000   3000   4000 km

Robinson Projection

ARCTIC OCEAN

180° 160° 140° 120° 100° 80° 60°

80°

ALASKA (U.S.)

60°

NORTH AMERICA

CANADA

International Date Line (Sunday)

40°

ROCKY MOUNTAINS

UNITED STATES

ATLANTIC OCEAN

Tropic of Cancer

20°

MEXICO

See inset below

HAWAII (U.S.)

PACIFIC OCEAN

VENEZUELA   GUYANA
                        SURINAME
COLOMBIA   FRENCH GUIANA
                        (France)

0°   Equator

Galápagos Is.
(Ecuador)   ECUADOR

KIRIBATI

PERU

SOUTH AMERICA

BRAZIL

SAMOA

ANDES MOUNTAINS

BOLIVIA

TONGA

PARAGUAY

20°   Tropic of Capricorn

URUGUAY

40°

CHILE ARGENTINA

Falkland Is.
(Br.)

South
Georgia
(Br.)

60°

Antarctic Circle

© MapQuest.com, Inc.

90°   80°   FLORIDA   70°
                           (U.S.)

Gulf Of
Mexico   BAHAMAS

Tropic of Cancer   Tropic of Cancer   60°

CUBA   ATLANTIC OCEAN
                    Turks and
                    Caicos Is. (Br.)

20°

MEXICO   HAITI DOMINICAN   Virgin Islands
                               REPUBLIC   (U.S. and Br.)   ANTIGUA AND
     BELIZE   BARBUDA
                    JAMAICA   Puerto Rico ST. KITTS
GUATEMALA   (U.S.)   AND NEVIS   Guadeloupe
                                                          (France)
  HONDURAS   Caribbean Sea   DOMINICA
EL SALVADOR   Martinique
                                             (France)   ST. LUCIA
    NICARAGUA   Netherlands ST. VINCENT AND BARBADOS
                    Aruba   Antilles   THE GRENADINES
PACIFIC   (Netherlands)   (Netherlands)   GRENADA
OCEAN   TRINIDAD AND
                                                TOBAGO
10°
    COSTA
    RICA

PANAMA   VENEZUELA

COLOMBIA   GUYANA
90°   80°

N

1:30,000,000

0   250   500   750 mi

0   250   500   750   1000 km

Bipolar Oblique Conic Conformal Projection

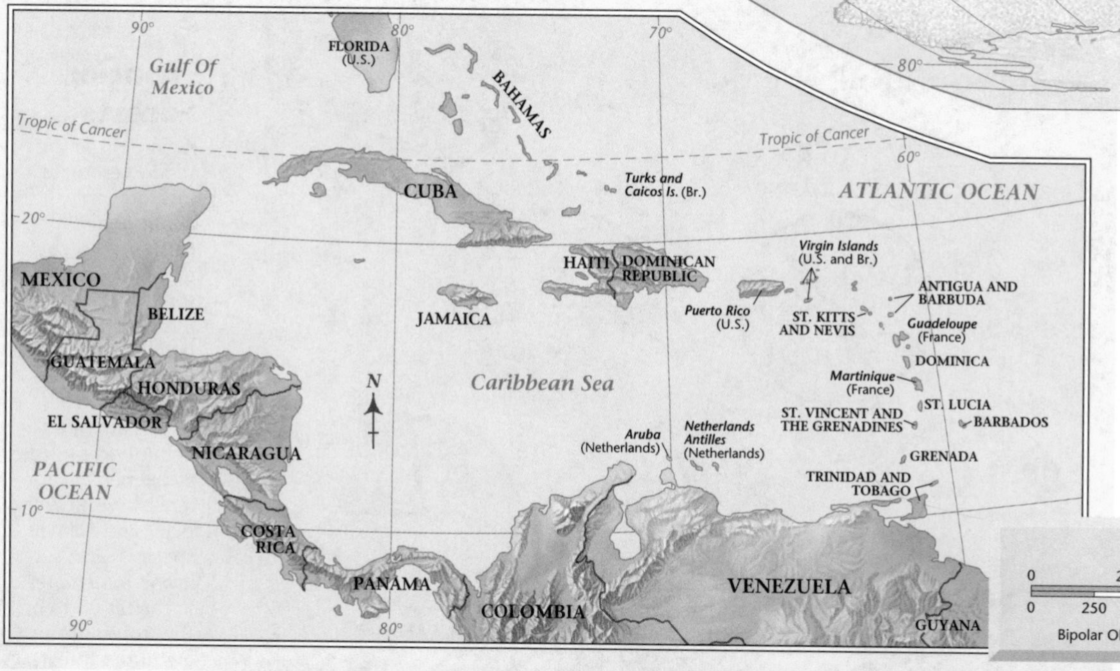

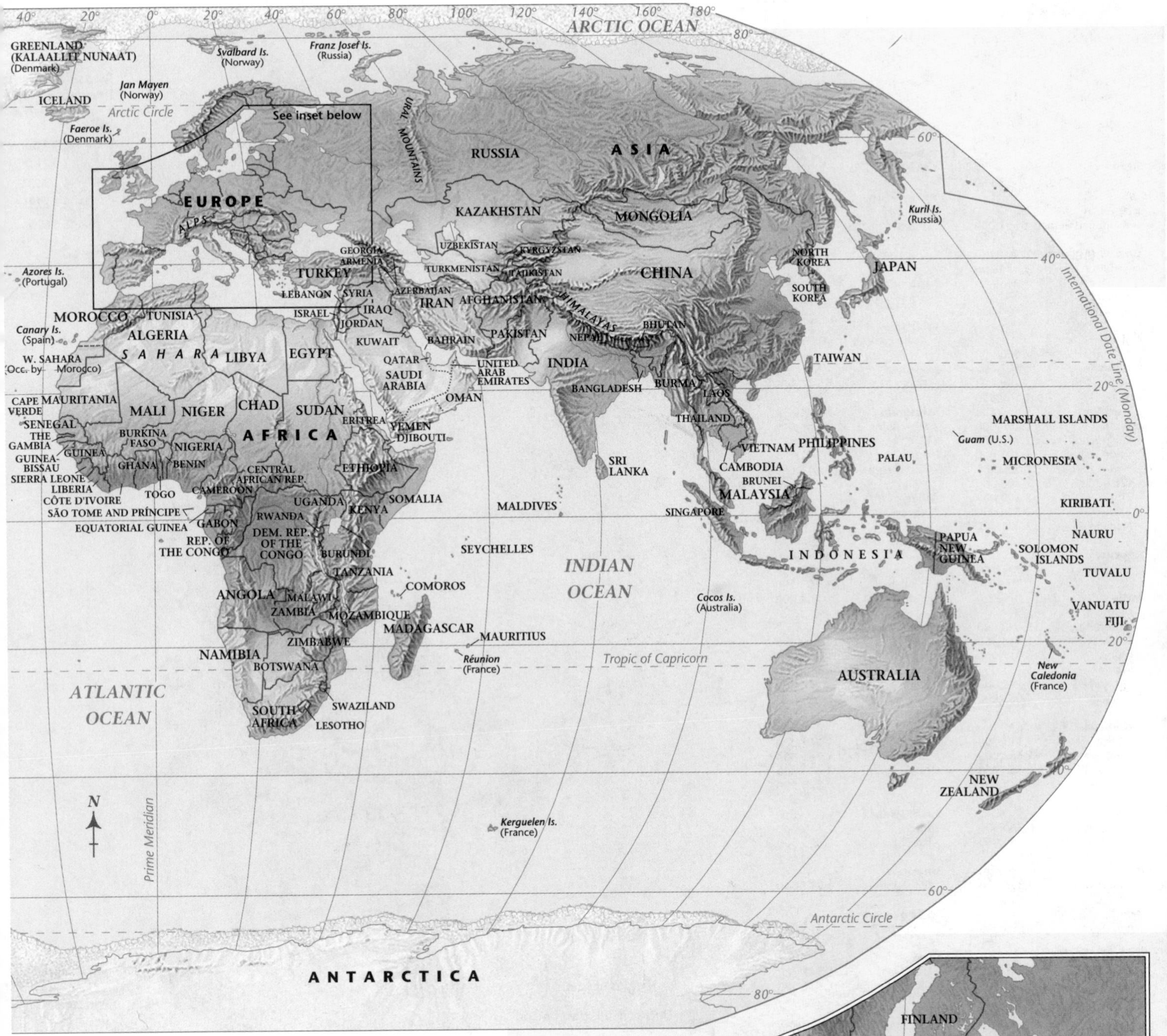
ARCTIC OCEAN
GREENLAND (KALAALLIT NUNAAT) (Denmark)
Svalbard Is. (Norway)
Franz Josef Is. (Russia)
Jan Mayen (Norway)
ICELAND
Arctic Circle
See inset below
Faeroe Is. (Denmark)
URAL MOUNTAINS
RUSSIA
ASIA
EUROPE
ALPS
KAZAKHSTAN
MONGOLIA
Kuril Is. (Russia)
GEORGIA
ARMENIA
UZBEKISTAN
KYRGYZSTAN
TURKMENISTAN
TAJIKISTAN
AZERBAIJAN
NORTH KOREA
SOUTH KOREA
JAPAN
CHINA
Azores Is. (Portugal)
TURKEY
LEBANON
SYRIA
ISRAEL
IRAQ
JORDAN
IRAN
AFGHANISTAN
HIMALAYAS
PAKISTAN
BHUTAN
NEPAL
International Date Line (Monday)
MOROCCO
TUNISIA
Canary Is. (Spain)
ALGERIA
SAHARA
LIBYA
EGYPT
KUWAIT
BAHRAIN
QATAR
SAUDI ARABIA
UNITED ARAB EMIRATES
OMAN
INDIA
TAIWAN
W. SAHARA (Occ. by Morocco)
BANGLADESH
BURMA
LAOS
THAILAND
CAPE VERDE
MAURITANIA
MALI
NIGER
CHAD
SUDAN
ERITREA
YEMEN
DJIBOUTI
SENEGAL
THE GAMBIA
BURKINA FASO
GUINEA
GUINEA-BISSAU
SIERRA LEONE
LIBERIA
CÔTE D'IVOIRE
TOGO
GHANA
BENIN
NIGERIA
AFRICA
CENTRAL AFRICAN REP.
ETHIOPIA
CAMEROON
SOMALIA
SRI LANKA
VIETNAM
CAMBODIA
PHILIPPINES
BRUNEI
MALAYSIA
SINGAPORE
PALAU
Guam (U.S.)
MARSHALL ISLANDS
MICRONESIA
KIRIBATI
NAURU
SÃO TOME AND PRÍNCIPE
EQUATORIAL GUINEA
GABON
RWANDA
UGANDA
KENYA
MALDIVES
REP. OF THE CONGO
DEM. REP. OF THE CONGO
BURUNDI
TANZANIA
SEYCHELLES
INDIAN OCEAN
INDONESIA
PAPUA NEW GUINEA
SOLOMON ISLANDS
TUVALU
ANGOLA
MALAWI
ZAMBIA
COMOROS
MOZAMBIQUE
MADAGASCAR
MAURITIUS
Cocos Is. (Australia)
VANUATU
FIJI
NAMIBIA
ZIMBABWE
BOTSWANA
Réunion (France)
Tropic of Capricorn
AUSTRALIA
New Caledonia (France)
ATLANTIC OCEAN
SOUTH AFRICA
SWAZILAND
LESOTHO
NEW ZEALAND
N
Prime Meridian
Kerguelen Is. (France)
Antarctic Circle
ANTARCTICA

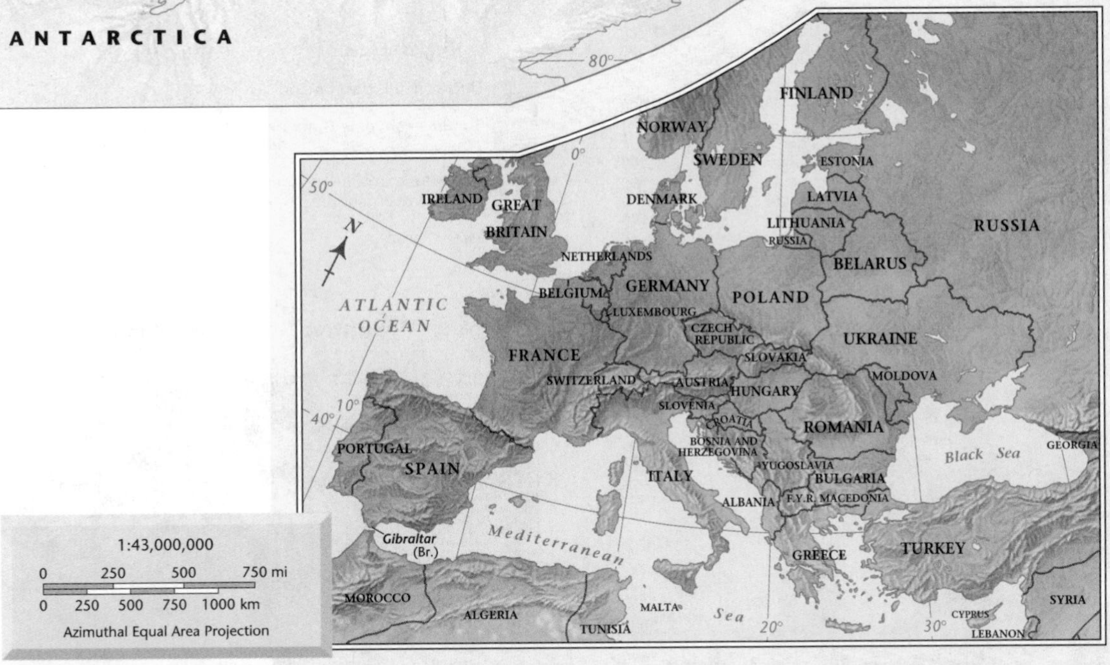
FINLAND
NORWAY
SWEDEN
ESTONIA
IRELAND
GREAT BRITAIN
DENMARK
LATVIA
LITHUANIA
RUSSIA
NETHERLANDS
BELARUS
BELGIUM
GERMANY
POLAND
LUXEMBOURG
ATLANTIC OCEAN
CZECH REPUBLIC
UKRAINE
FRANCE
SLOVAKIA
SWITZERLAND
AUSTRIA
MOLDOVA
HUNGARY
SLOVENIA
CROATIA
ROMANIA
PORTUGAL
SPAIN
BOSNIA AND HERZEGOVINA
YUGOSLAVIA
BULGARIA
Black Sea
GEORGIA
ITALY
ALBANIA
F.Y.R. MACEDONIA
Gibraltar (Br.)
Mediterranean Sea
GREECE
TURKEY
MOROCCO
ALGERIA
TUNISIA
MALTA
CYPRUS
LEBANON
SYRIA
1:43,000,000
0 250 500 750 mi
0 250 500 750 1000 km
Azimuthal Equal Area Projection

MAJOR CITIES

Afghanistan	(metro)
Kabul	2,029,000
Bahrain	
Manama	151,000
Bangladesh	(metro)
Dhaka	8,545,000
Bhutan	
Thimphu	8,900
Brunei	
Band. Seri Begawan	51,000
Burma (Myanmar)	(metro)
Rangoon	3,873,000
Cambodia	
Phnom Penh	800,000
China	
Shanghai	7,500,000
Hong Kong	6,502,000
Beijing	5,700,000
Tianjin	4,500,000
Shenyang	3,600,000
Wuhan	3,200,000
Guangzhou	2,900,000
Chongqing	2,700,000
Harbin	2,500,000
Chengdu	2,500,000
Zibo	2,200,000
Xi'an	2,200,000
Nanjing	2,091,000
Cyprus	
Nicosia	193,000
India	(metro)
Mumbai	
(Bombay)	12,572,000
Calcutta	10,916,000
Delhi	8,375,000
Madras	5,361,000
Hyderabad	4,280,000
Bangalore	4,087,000
Indonesia	
Jakarta	9,113,000
Surabaya	2,664,000
Bandung	2,356,000
Medan	1,844,000
Iran	
Tehran	6,750,000
Mashhad	1,964,000
Iraq	(metro)
Baghdad	4,336,000
Israel	
Jerusalem	585,000
Japan	
Tokyo	7,968,000
Yokohama	3,320,000
Osaka	2,600,000
Nagoya	2,151,000
Sapporo	1,774,000
Kyoto	1,464,000
Kobe	1,420,000
Fukuoka	1,296,000
Kawasaki	1,209,000
Hiroshima	1,115,000
Jordan	(metro)
Amman	1,183,000
Kazakhstan	
Almaty	1,064,000

North Korea	
P'yŏngyang	2,741,000
South Korea	
Seoul	10,231,000
Pusan	3,814,000
Taegu	2,449,000
Kuwait	
Kuwait	29,000
Kyrgyzstan	
Bishkek	589,000
Laos	
Vientiane	377,000
Lebanon	(metro)
Beirut	1,826,000
Malaysia	(metro)
Kuala Lumpur	1,236,000
Maldives	
Male	55,000
Mongolia	
Ulan Bator	536,000
Nepal	
Kathmandu	419,000
Oman	
Masqat	85,000
Pakistan	(metro)
Karachi	5,181,000
Lahore	2,953,000
Faisalabad	1,104,000
Islamabad	204,000
Philippines	
Manila	1,655,000
Qatar	
Doha	236,000
Russia (Asian)	
Novosibirsk	1,368,000
Yekaterinburg	1,277,000
Omsk	1,161,000
Chelyabinsk	1,084,000
Krasnoyarsk	870,000
Saudi Arabia	(metro)
Riyadh	2,619,000
Jiddah	1,492,000
Singapore	
Singapore	3,737,000
Sri Lanka	
Colombo	615,000
Syria	
Damascus	1,549,000
Halab (Aleppo)	1,542,000
Taiwan	
Taipei	1,770,000
Tajikistan	
Dushanbe	529,000
Thailand	(metro)
Bangkok	6,547,000
Turkey (Asian)	
Ankara	2,938,000
İzmir	2,130,000
Turkmenistan	
Ashgabat	407,000
United Arab Emirates	
Abu Dhabi (metro)	799,000
Uzbekistan	(metro)
Tashkent	2,282,000
Vietnam	(metro)
Ho Chi Minh City	3,521,000
Hanoi	1,236,000
Yemen	(metro)
Sana	927,000

International comparability of city population
data is limited by various data inconsistencies.

Gross National Product (GNP) per capita

- $36,410
- $21,500
- $8625
- $2785
- $695
- $0
- No data

Vegetation

- Unclassified Highlands and Ice Cap
- Tundra and Alpine Tundra
- Coniferous Forest
- Midlatitude Deciduous Forest
- Subtropical Broadleaf Evergreen Forest
- Mixed Forest
- Midlatitude Scrub
- Midlatitude Grassland
- Desert
- Tropical Seasonal and Scrub
- Tropical Rain Forest
- Tropical Savanna

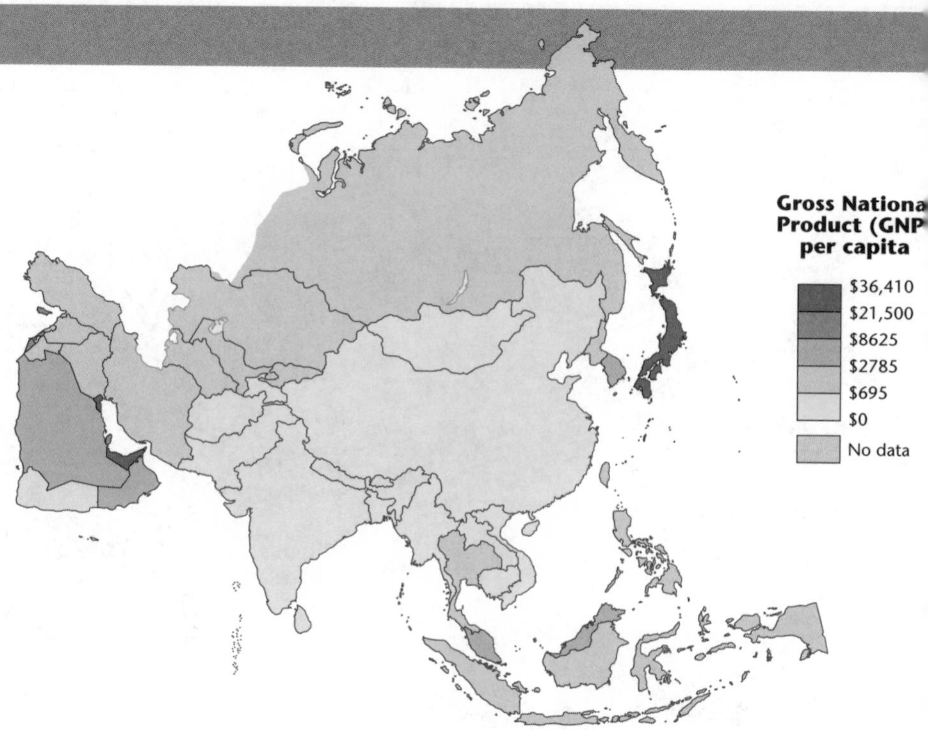

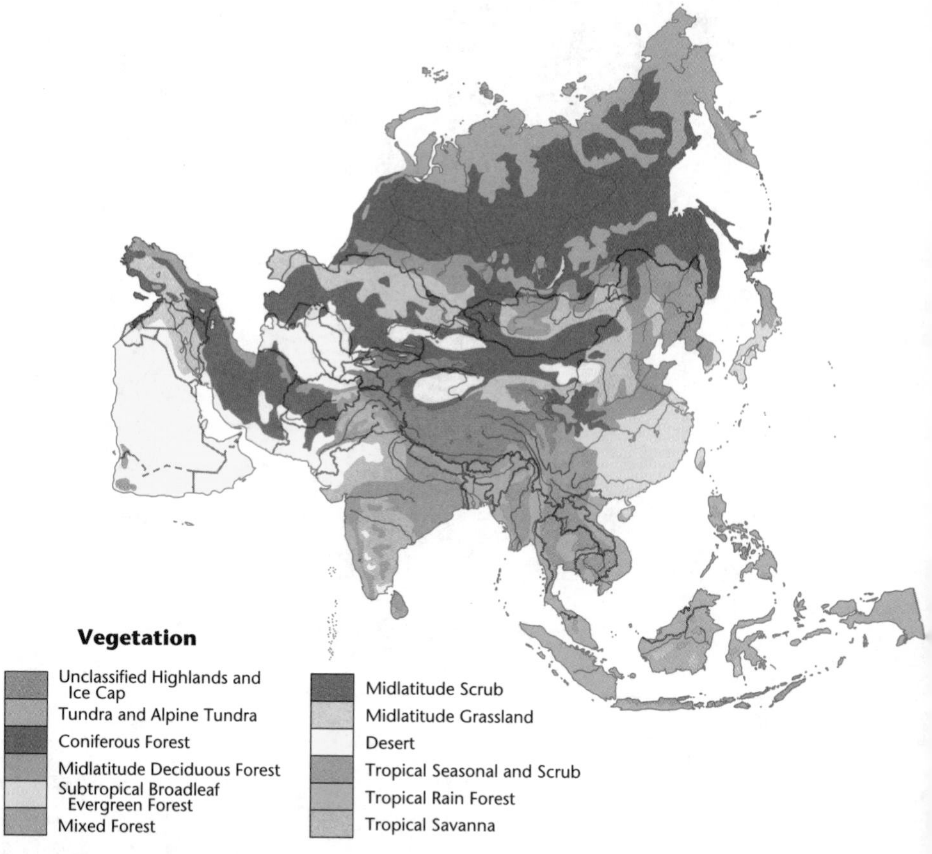

Asia: Population, by nation (in millions)*

CHINA	INDIA	INDON.	PAKIS.	BANGL.	JAPAN	PHILIP.	All other Asian countries
1254.2	1000.8	216.1	138.1	127.1	126.2	79.4	699.5*

*Excluding Russia

© MapQuest.com, Inc.

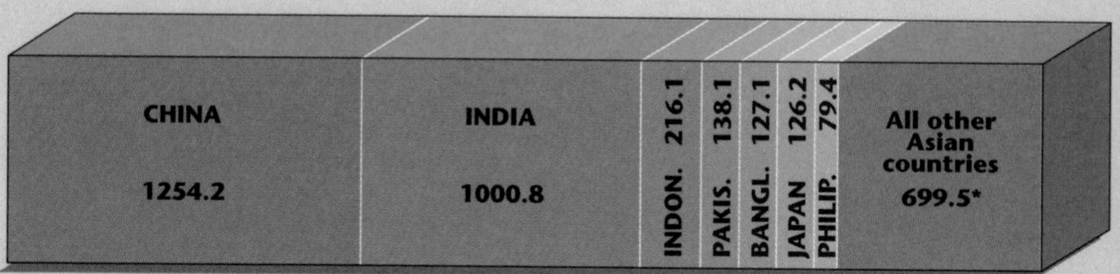

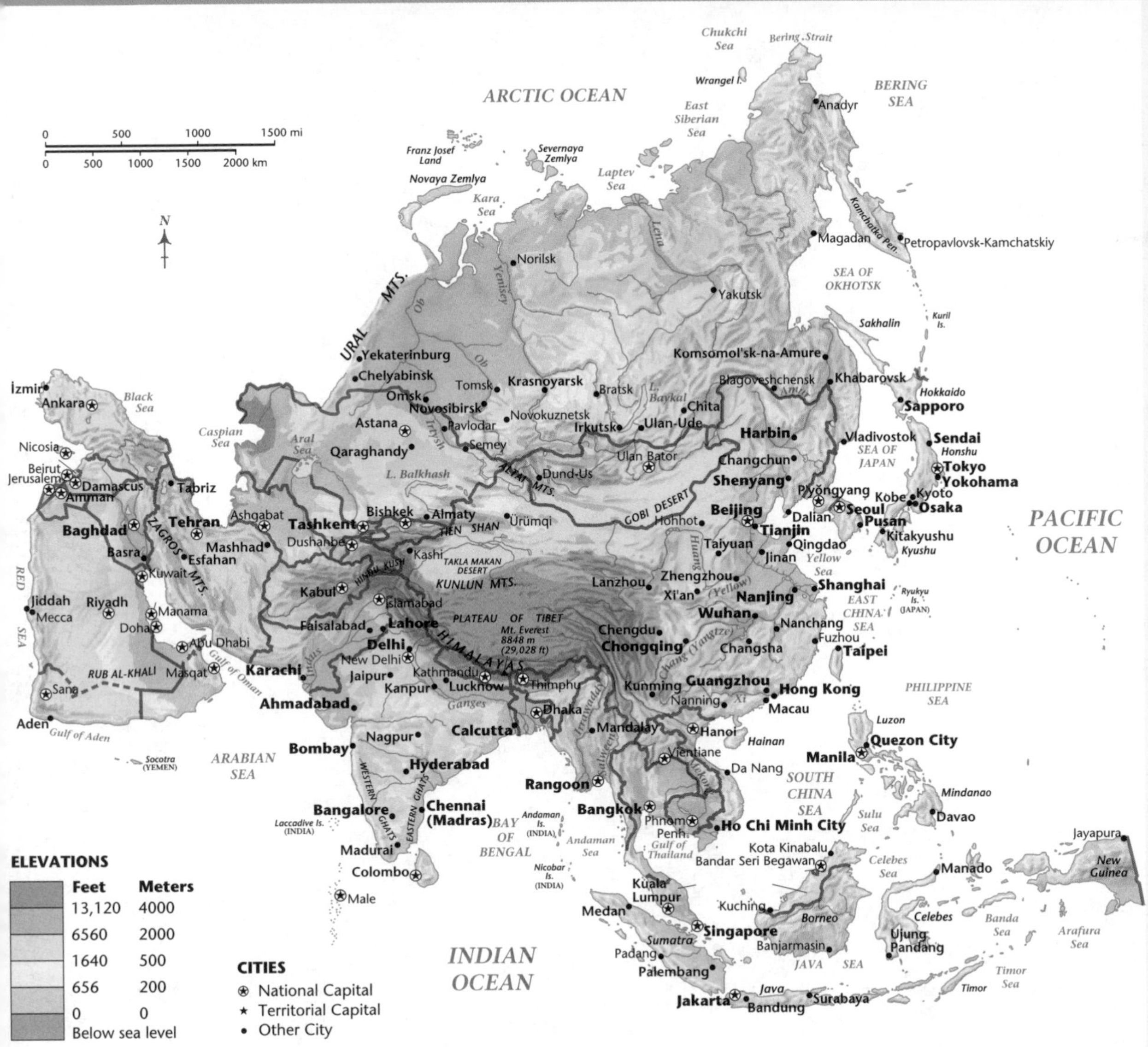
ARCTIC OCEAN
PACIFIC OCEAN
INDIAN OCEAN
0 500 1000 1500 mi
0 500 1000 1500 2000 km
N
Chukchi Sea
Bering Strait
BERING SEA
Wrangel I.
East Siberian Sea
Franz Josef Land
Severnaya Zemlya
Novaya Zemlya
Laptev Sea
Kara Sea
Anadyr
Kamchatka Pen.
Petropavlovsk-Kamchatskiy
Magadan
SEA OF OKHOTSK
Norilsk
Yakutsk
Sakhalin
Kuril Is.
URAL MTS.
Yekaterinburg
Chelyabinsk
Komsomol'sk-na-Amure
Khabarovsk
Hokkaido
Sapporo
İzmir
Ankara
Black Sea
Omsk
Tomsk
Krasnoyarsk
Bratsk
Blagoveshchensk
Novosibirsk
Novokuznetsk
Chita
Astana
Pavlodar
Irkutsk
Ulan-Ude
Harbin
Vladivostok
Sendai
Honshu
Caspian Sea
Aral Sea
Qaraghandy
Semey
ALTAI MTS.
Ulan Bator
Changchun
SEA OF JAPAN
Tokyo
Yokohama
Nicosia
Beirut
Jerusalem
Damascus
Amman
Tabriz
L. Balkhash
Dund-Us
Shenyang
P'yongyang
Kobe
Kyoto
Osaka
Bishkek
Almaty
Ashgabat
Tashkent
Dushanbe
TIEN SHAN
Ürümqi
GOBI DESERT
Hohhot
Beijing
Tianjin
Dalian
Seoul
Pusan
Kitakyushu
Kyushu
Baghdad
Tehran
ZAGROS MTS.
Mashhad
Esfahan
Basra
Kashi
TAKLA MAKAN DESERT
Taiyuan
Jinan
Qingdao
Yellow Sea
Kuwait
HINDU KUSH
KUNLUN MTS.
Lanzhou
Zhengzhou
Xi'an
Shanghai
Ryukyu Is. (JAPAN)
Kabul
Islamabad
PLATEAU OF TIBET
Nanjing
EAST CHINA SEA
RED SEA
Jiddah
Mecca
Riyadh
Manama
Doha
Faisalabad
Lahore
Mt. Everest 8848 m (29,028 ft)
Wuhan
Nanchang
Delhi
New Delhi
HIMALAYAS
Chengdu
Chongqing
Changsha
Fuzhou
Taipei
Abu Dhabi
Gulf of Oman
Karachi
Jaipur
Kathmandu
Thimphu
RUB AL-KHALI
Masqat
Kanpur
Lucknow
Kunming
Guangzhou
Hong Kong
PHILIPPINE SEA
Sana
Ganges
Nanning
Macau
Ahmadabad
Dhaka
Aden
Gulf of Aden
Calcutta
Mandalay
Hanoi
Luzon
Bombay
Nagpur
Hainan
Quezon City
Manila
Socotra (YEMEN)
ARABIAN SEA
Hyderabad
Vientiane
Da Nang
Rangoon
SOUTH CHINA SEA
Mindanao
Bangalore
Chennai (Madras)
Andaman Is. (INDIA)
Bangkok
Phnom Penh
Ho Chi Minh City
Davao
Laccadive Is. (INDIA)
BAY OF BENGAL
Andaman Sea
Gulf of Thailand
Sulu Sea
Jayapura
Madurai
Kota Kinabalu
Bandar Seri Begawan
Celebes Sea
Manado
New Guinea
Colombo
Nicobar Is. (INDIA)
Kuala Lumpur
Kuching
Borneo
Male
Medan
Singapore
Celebes
Banda Sea
Arafura Sea
Sumatra
Banjarmasin
Ujung Pandang
Padang
JAVA SEA
Palembang
Timor Sea
Timor
Jakarta
Java
Bandung
Surabaya
ELEVATIONS
Feet Meters
13,120 4000
6560 2000
1640 500
656 200
0 0
Below sea level
CITIES
National Capital
Territorial Capital
Other City

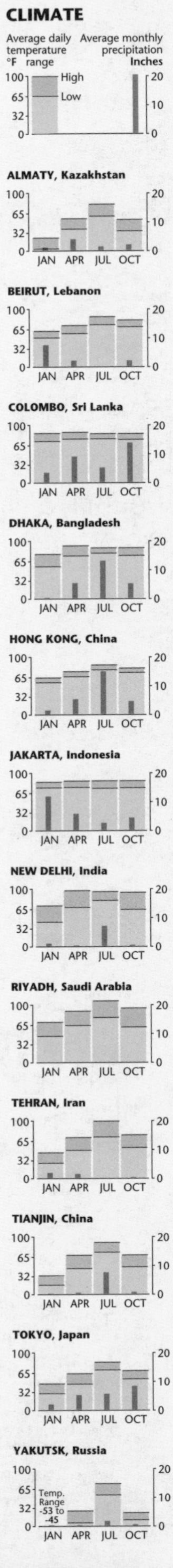
CLIMATE
Average daily temperature °F range
Average monthly precipitation Inches
High
Low
ALMATY, Kazakhstan
BEIRUT, Lebanon
COLOMBO, Sri Lanka
DHAKA, Bangladesh
HONG KONG, China
JAKARTA, Indonesia
NEW DELHI, India
RIYADH, Saudi Arabia
TEHRAN, Iran
TIANJIN, China
TOKYO, Japan
YAKUTSK, Russia
Temp. Range -53 to -45
JAN APR JUL OCT

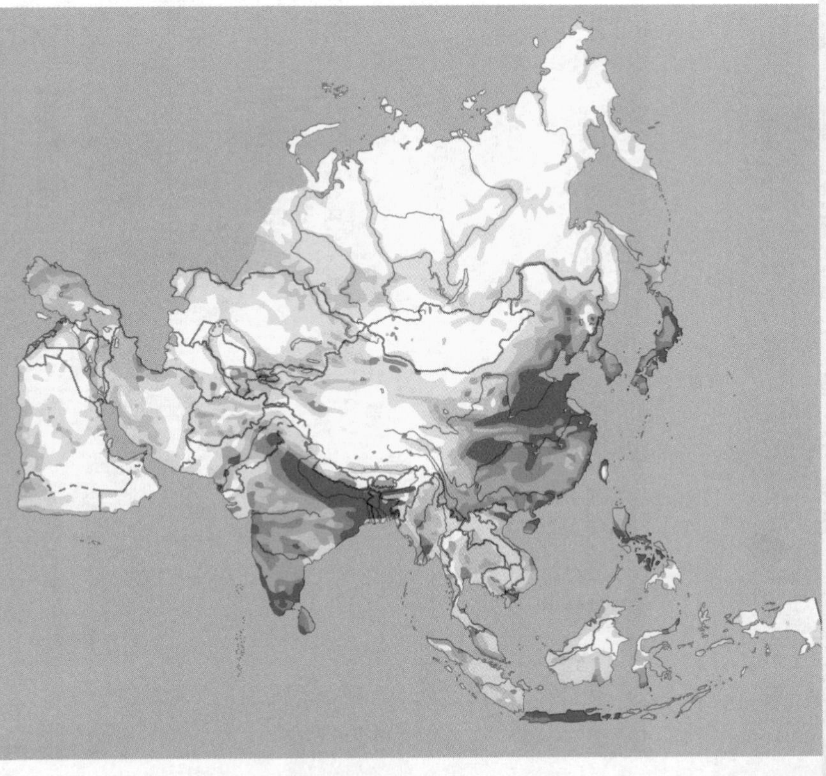
Population
Persons per sq mi
Persons per sq km
Over 520 Over 200
260–519 100–199
130–259 50–99
25–129 10–49
1–24 1–9
0 0

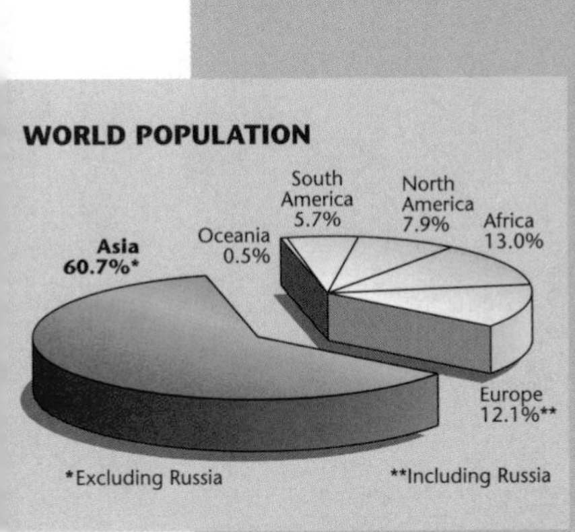
WORLD POPULATION
Asia 60.7%*
Oceania 0.5%
South America 5.7%
North America 7.9%
Africa 13.0%
Europe 12.1%**
*Excluding Russia
**Including Russia

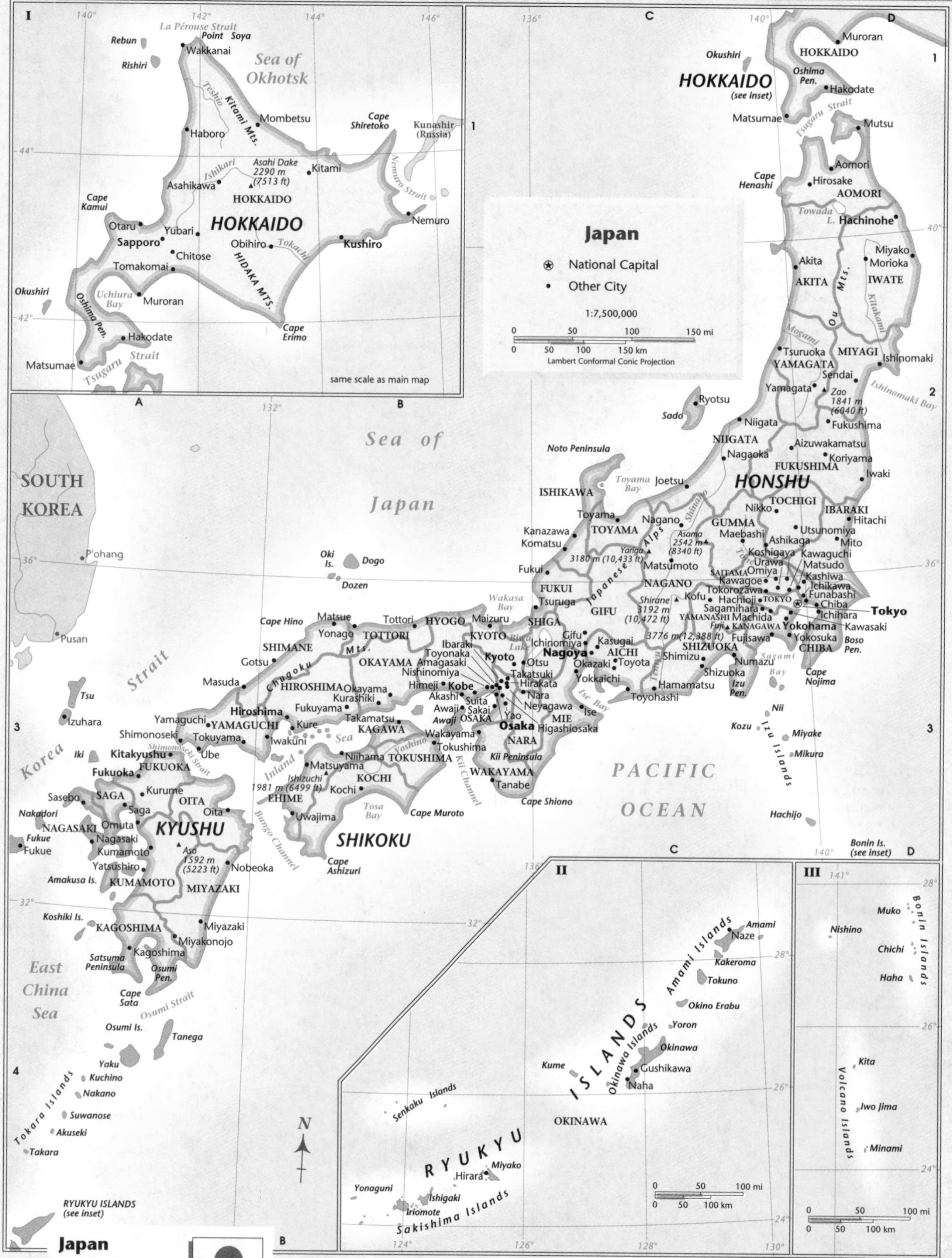

Japan

Capital: Tokyo
Area: 145,850 sq. mi.
377,850 sq. km.
Population: 126,182,000
Largest City: Tokyo
Language: Japanese
Monetary Unit: Yen

Japan: Map Index

Prefectures

Aichi	C3
Akita	D2
Aomori	D1
Chiba	D3
Ehime	B3
Fukui	C3
Fukuoka	A3
Fukushima	C2
Gifu	C3
Gumma	C2
Hiroshima	B3
Hokkaido	D1, Inset I
Hyogo	B3
Ibaraki	D2
Ishikawa	C2
Iwate	D2
Kagawa	B3
Kagoshima	A4
Kanagawa	C3
Kochi	B3
Kumamoto	A3
Kyoto	B3
Mie	C3
Miyagi	D2
Miyazaki	A3
Nagano	C3
Nagasaki	A3
Nara	B3
Niigata	C2
Oita	A3
Okayama	B3
Okinawa	Inset II
Osaka	B3
Saga	A3
Saitama	C2
Shiga	C3
Shimane	B3
Shizuoka	C3
Tochigi	C2
Tokushima	B3
Tokyo	C3
Tottori	B3
Toyama	C2
Wakayama	B3
Yamagata	C2
Yamaguchi	A3
Yamanashi	C3

Cities and Towns

Aizuwakamatsu	C2
Akashi	B3
Akita	D2
Amagasaki	B3
Aomori	D1
Asahikawa	Inset I
Ashikaga	C2
Awaji	B3
Chiba	D3
Chitose	Inset I
Fujisawa	C3
Fukue	A3
Fukui	C2
Fukuoka	A3
Fukushima	D2
Fukuyama	B3
Funabashi	D3
Gifu	C3
Gotsu	B3
Gushikawa	Inset II
Haboro	Inset I
Hachinohe	D1
Hachioji	C3
Hakodate	D1, Inset I
Hamamatsu	C3
Higashiosaka	B3
Himeji	B3
Hirakata	B3
Hirara	Inset II
Hirosake	D1
Hiroshima	B3
Hitachi	D2
Ibaraki	B3
Ichihara	D3
Ichikawa	D3
Ichinomiya	C3
Ise	C3
Ishinomaki	D2
Iwaki	D2
Iwakuni	B3
Izuhara	A3
Joetsu	C2
Kagoshima	A4
Kanazawa	C2
Kashiwa	D3
Kasugai	C3
Kawagoe	C3
Kawaguchi	C3
Kawasaki	C3
Kitakyushu	A3
Kitami	Inset I
Kobe	B3
Kochi	B3
Kofu	C3
Komatsu	C2
Koriyama	D2
Koshigaya	C3
Kumamoto	A3
Kurashiki	B3
Kure	B3
Kurume	A3
Kushiro	Inset I
Kyoto	B3
Machida	C3
Maebashi	C2
Maizuru	B3
Masuda	A3
Matsudo	C3
Matsue	B3
Matsumae	D1, Inset I
Matsumoto	C2
Matsuyama	B3
Mito	D2
Miyako	D2
Miyakonojo	A4
Miyazaki	A4
Mombetsu	Inset I
Morioka	D2
Muroran	D1, Inset I
Mutsu	D1
Nagano	C2
Nagaoka	C2
Nagasaki	A3
Nagoya	C3
Naha	Inset II
Nara	B3
Naze	Inset II
Nemuro	Inset I
Neyagawa	B3
Niigata	C2
Niihama	B3
Nikko	C2
Nishinomiya	B3
Nobeoka	A3
Numazu	C3
Obihiro	Inset I
Oita	A3
Okayama	B3
Okazaki	C3
Omiya	C3
Omuta	A3
Osaka	B3
Otaru	Inset I
Otsu	B3
Ryotsu	C2
Saga	A3
Sagamihara	C3
Sakai	B3
Sapporo	Inset I
Sasebo	A3
Sendai	D2
Shimizu	C3
Shimonoseki	A3
Shizuoka	C3
Suita	B3
Takamatsu	B3
Takatsuki	B3
Tanabe	B3
Tokorozawa	C3
Tokushima	B3
Tokuyama	A3
Tokyo, *capital*	C3
Tomakomai	Inset I
Tottori	B3
Toyama	C2
Toyohashi	C3
Toyonaka	B3
Toyota	C3
Tsuruga	C3
Tsuruoka	C2
Ube	A3
Urawa	C3
Utsunomiya	C2
Uwajima	B3
Wakayama	B3
Wakkanai	Inset I
Yamagata	D2
Yamaguchi	A3
Yao	B3
Yatsushiro	A3

Japan: Map Index
Yokkaichi C3
Yokohama C3
Yokosuka C3
Yonago B3
Yubari .... Inset I

Other Features
Akuseki, *island* A4
Amakusa, *islands* A3
Amami, *island* .... Inset II
Amami, *islands* .... Inset II
Asahi Dake, *mt.* .... Inset I
Asama, *mt.* C2
Ashizuri, *cape* B3
Aso, *mt.* A3
Awaji, *island* B3
Biwa, *lake* B3
Bonin, *islands* .... Inset III
Boso, *peninsula* D3
Bungo, *channel* B3
Chichi, *island* .... Inset III
Chugoku, *mts.* B3
Dogo, *island* B2
Dozen, *island* B2
East China, *sea* A4
Erimo, *cape* .... Inset I
Fuji, *mt.* C3
Fukue, *island* A3
Hachijo, *island* C3
Haha, *island* .... Inset III
Henashi, *cape* C1
Hidaka, *mts.* .... Inset I
Hino, *cape* B3
Hokkaido, *island* .... D1, Inset I
Honshu, *island* C2
Iki, *island* A3
Inland, *sea* B3
Iriomote, *island* .... Inset II
Ise, *bay* C3
Ishigaki, *island* .... Inset II
Ishikari, *river* .... Inset I
Ishinomaki, *bay* D2
Ishizuchi, *mt.* B3
Iwo Jima, *island* .... Inset III
Izu, *islands* C3
Izu, *peninsula* C3
Japan, *sea* B2
Japanese Alps, *mts.* C3
Kakeroma, *island* .... Inset II
Kamui, *cape* .... Inset I
Kii, *channel* B3
Kii, *peninsula* B3
Kita, *island* .... Inset III
Kitakami, *river* D2
Kitami, *mts.* .... Inset I
Korea, *strait* A3
Koshiki, *islands* A4
Kozu, *island* C3
Kuchino, *island* A4
Kume, *island* .... Inset II
Kyushu, *island* A3
La Pérouse, *strait* .... Inset I
Mikura, *island* C3
Minami, *island* .... Inset III
Miyake, *island* C3
Miyako, *island* .... Inset II
Mogami, *river* D2
Muko, *island* .... Inset III
Muroto, *cape* B3
Nakadori, *island* A3
Nakano, *island* A4
Nemuro, *strait* .... Inset I
Nii, *island* C3
Nishino, *island* .... Inset III
Nojima, *cape* D3
Noto, *peninsula* C2
Okhotsk, *sea* .... Inset I
Oki, *islands* B2
Okinawa, *island* .... Inset II
Okinawa, *islands* .... Inset II
Okino Erabu, *island* .... Inset II
Okushiri, *island* .... C1, Inset I
Oshima, *peninsula* .... D1, Inset I
Osumi, *islands* A4
Osumi, *peninsula* A4
Osumi, *strait* A4
Ou, *mts.* D2
Rebun, *island* .... Inset I
Rishiri, *island* .... Inset I
Ryukyu, *islands* .... A4, Inset II
Sado, *island* C2
Sagami, *bay* C3
Sakishima, *islands* .... Inset II
Sata, *cape* A4
Satsuma, *peninsula* A4
Senkaku, *islands* .... Inset II
Shikoku, *island* B3
Shimonoseki, *strait* A3
Shinano, *river* C2
Shiono, *cape* B3
Shirane, *mt.* C3
Shiretoko, *cape* .... Inset I
Soya, *point* .... Inset I
Suwanose, *island* A4
Takara, *island* A4
Tanega, *island* A4
Tenryu, *river* C3
Teshio, *river* .... Inset I
Tokachi, *river* .... Inset I
Tokara, *islands* A4
Tokuno, *island* .... Inset II
Tone, *river* C2
Tosa, *bay* B3
Towada, *lake* D1
Toyama, *bay* C2
Tsu, *island* A3
Tsugaru, *strait* .... D1, Inset I
Uchiura, *bay* .... Inset I
Volcano, *islands* .... Inset III
Wakasa, *bay* B3
Yaku, *island* A4
Yariga, *mt.* C2
Yonaguni, *island* .... Inset II
Yoron, *island* .... Inset II
Yoshino, *river* B3
Zao, *mt.* D2

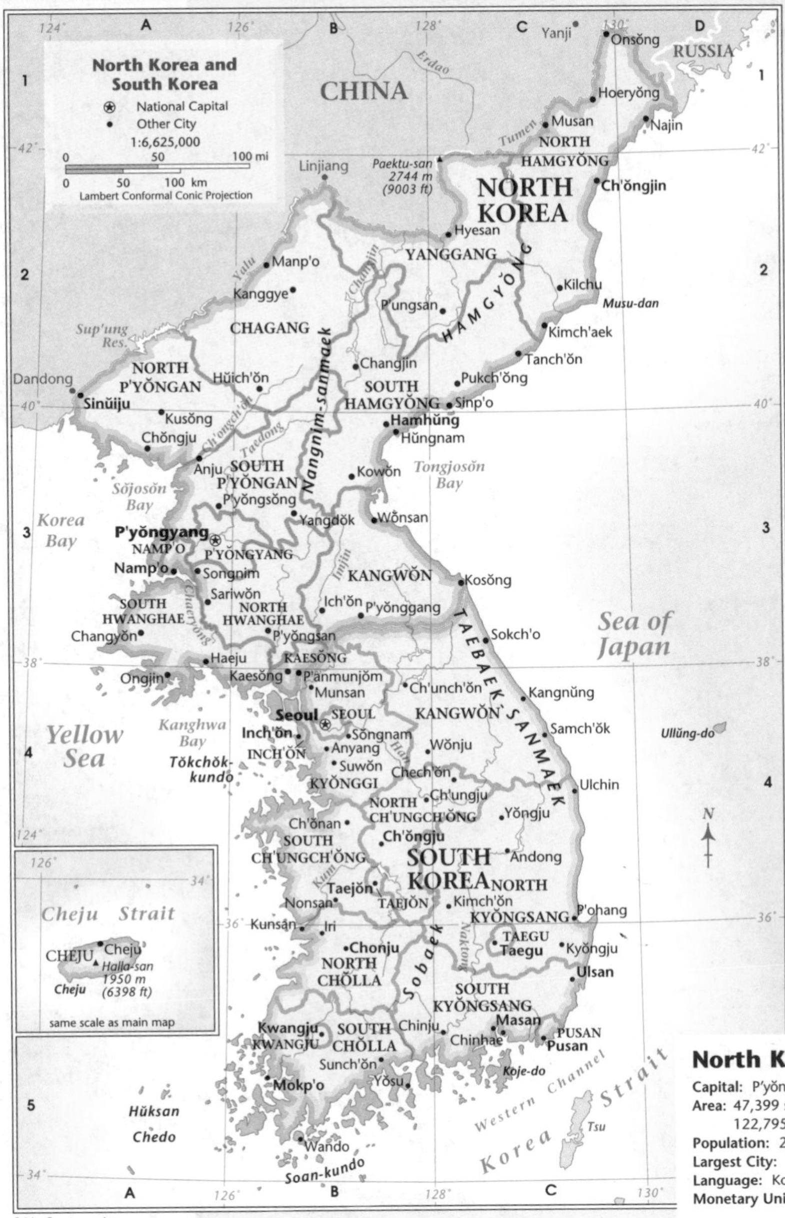

© MapQuest.com, Inc.

North Korea

Capital: P'yŏngyang
Area: 47,399 sq. mi.
122,795 sq. km.
Population: 21,386,000
Largest City: P'yŏngyang
Language: Korean
Monetary Unit: Won

South Korea

Capital: Seoul
Area: 38,330 sq. mi.
99,301 sq. km.
Population: 46,885,000
Largest City: Seoul
Language: Korean
Monetary Unit: Won

North Korea: Map Index

Provinces
Chagang B2
Kaesŏng B3
Kangwŏn B3
Namp'o A3
North Hamgyŏng C1
North Hwanghae B3
North P'yŏngan A2
P'yŏngyang A3
South Hamgyŏng B2
South Hwanghae A3
South P'yŏngan B3
Yanggang B2

Cities and Towns
Anju A3
Changjin B2
Changyŏn A3
Ch'ŏngjin C2
Chŏngju A3
Haeju A3
Hamhŭng B3
Hoeryŏng C1
Hŭich'ŏn B2
Hŭngnam B3
Hyesan C2
Ich'ŏn B3
Kaesŏng B4
Kanggye B2
Kilchu C2
Kimch'aek C2
Kosŏng C3
Kowŏn B3
Kusŏng A3
Manp'o B2
Musan C1
Najin D1
Namp'o A3
Ongjin A4
Onsŏng C1
P'anmunjŏm B4
Pukch'ŏng C2
P'ungsan C2
P'yŏnggang B3
P'yŏngsan B3
P'yŏngsŏng A3
P'yŏngyang, *capital* A3
Sariwŏn A3
Sinp'o C2
Sinŭiju A2
Songnim A3
Tanch'ŏn C2
Wŏnsan B3
Yangdŏk B3

Other Features
Chaeryŏng, *river* A3
Changjin, *river* B2
Ch'ongch'ŏn, *river* A3
Hamgyŏng, *mts.* C2
Imjin, *river* B3
Kanghwa, *bay* A4
Korea, *bay* A3
Musu-dan, *point* C2
Nangnim-sanmaek, *mts.* B3
Paektu-san, *mt.* C2
Sŏjosŏn, *bay* A3
Sup'ung, *reservoir* A2
Taedong, *river* B3
Tongjosŏn, *bay* B3
Tumen, *river* C1
Yalu, *river* B2

South Korea: Map Index

Provinces
Cheju .... Inset
Inch'ŏn B4
Kangwŏn B4
Kwangju B5
Kyŏnggi B4
North Chŏlla B5
North Ch'ungch'ŏng B4
North Kyŏngsang C4
Pusan C5
Seoul B4
South Chŏlla B5
South Ch'ungch'ŏng B4
South Kyŏngsang C5
Taegu C5
Taejŏn B4

Cities and Towns
Andong C4
Anyang B4
Chech'ŏn C4
Cheju .... Inset
Chinhae C5
Chinju C5
Chonju B5
Ch'ŏnan B4
Ch'ŏngju B4
Ch'unch'ŏn B4
Ch'ungju B4
Inch'ŏn B4
Iri B5
Kangnŭng C4
Kimch'ŏn C4
Kunsan B5
Kwangju B5
Kyŏngju C5
Masan C5
Mokp'o B5
Munsan B4
Nonsan B4
P'ohang C4
Pusan C5
Samch'ŏk C4
Seoul, *capital* B4
Sokch'o C3
Sŏngnam B4
Sunch'ŏn B5
Suwŏn B4
Taegu C5
Taejŏn B4
Ulchin C4
Ulsan C5
Wŏnju B4
Wando B5
Yŏngju C4
Yŏsu B5

Other Features
Cheju, *island* .... Inset
Cheju, *strait* .... Inset
Halla-san, *mt.* .... Inset
Han, *river* B4
Hŭksan Chedo, *islands* A5
Kanghwa, *bay* A4
Koje-do, *island* C5
Korea, *strait* C5
Kum, *river* B4
Naktong, *river* C5
Soan-kundo, *islands* B5
Sobaek, *mts.* B5
Taebaek-Sanmaek, *mts.* C3
Tŏkchŏk-kundo, *islands* A4
Ullŭng-do, *island* D4
Western, *channel* C5

© MapQuest.com, Inc.

Taiwan

Capital: Taipei
Area: 13,969 sq. mi.
36,189 sq. km.
Population: 22,113,000
Largest City: Taipei
Language: Mandarin Chinese
Monetary Unit: New Taiwan dollar

Taiwan: Map Index

Cities and Towns
Changhua B1
Chiai B2
Chilung B1
Chunan B1
Chungho B1
Chungli B1
Fangliao B2
Fengshan B2
Fengyüan B1
Hengch'un B2
Hsinchu B1
Hsinchuang B1
Hsintien B1
Hsinying B2
Hualien B2
Ilan B1
Kangshan B2
Kaohsiung B2
Makung A2
Miaoli B1
Nant'ou B1
Panch'iao B1
P'ingtung B2
Shanchung B1
T'aichung B1
T'ainan B2
Taipei, *capital* B1
T'aitung B2
Tanshui B1
T'aoyüan B1
Touliu B2
Yungho B1

Other Features
Choshui, *river* B2
Chungyang, *range* B2
East China, *sea* B1
Kaop'ing, *river* B2
Lan, *island* B2
Lü, *island* B2
Luzon, *strait* B3
P'enghu (Pescadores), *islands* A2
Pescadores, *channel* A2
Philippine, *sea* B2
South China, *sea* A2
Taiwan, *strait* A1
Tanshui, *river* B1
Tsengwen, *river* B2
Yü Shan, *mt.* B2

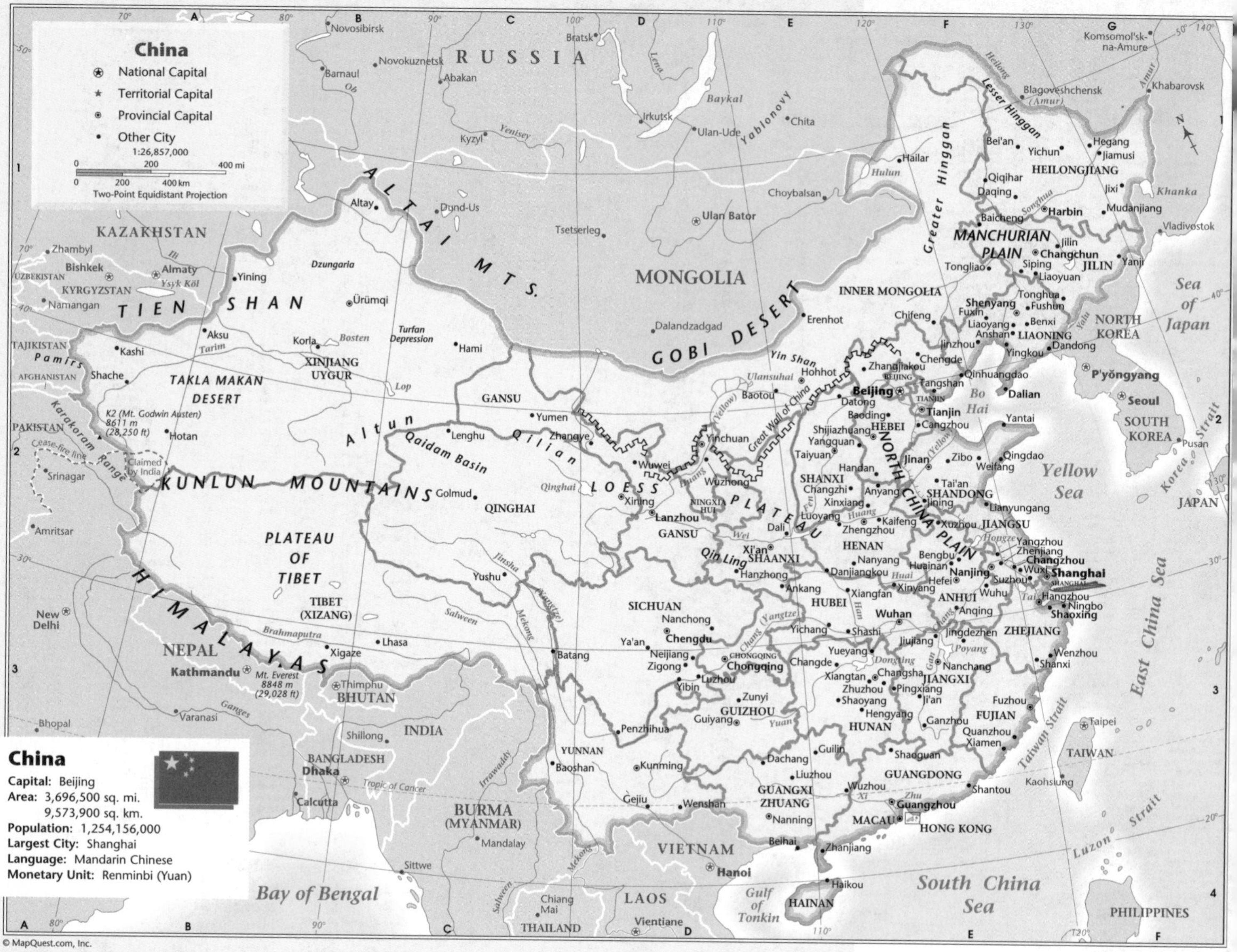

China

Capital: Beijing
Area: 3,696,500 sq. mi.
9,573,900 sq. km.
Population: 1,254,156,000
Largest City: Shanghai
Language: Mandarin Chinese
Monetary Unit: Renminbi (Yuan)

China: Map Index

Internal Divisions
Provinces
Anhui E2
Fujian E3
Gansu C1, D2
Guangdong E3
Guizhou D3
Hainan D4
Hebei E2
Heilongjiang F1
Henan E2
Hubei E2
Hunan E3
Jiangsu E2
Jiangxi E3
Jilin F1
Liaoning F1
Qinghai C2
Shaanxi D2
Shandong E2
Shanxi E2
Sichuan D2
Yunnan C3
Zhejiang E3

Autonomous Regions
Guangxi Zhuang D3
Inner Mongolia E1
Ningxia Hui D2
Tibet (Xizang) B2
Xinjiang Uygur B1

Independent Municipalities
Beijing E1
Chongqing D3
Shanghai F2
Tianjin E2

Special Administrative Regions (S.A.R.)
Hong Kong ..... E3, Inset
Macau E3

Cities and Towns
Aberdeen ..... Inset
Aksu B1
Altay B1
Ankang D2
Anqing E2
Anshan F1
Anyang E2
Baicheng F1
Baoding E2
Baoshan C3
Baotou E1
Batang C3
Bei'an F1
Beihai D3
Beijing, *capital* E2
Bengbu E2
Benxi F1
Cangzhou E2
Changchun F1
Changde E3
Changsha E3
Changzhi E2
Changzhou F2
Chek Keng ..... Inset
Chengde E1
Chengdu D2
Chifeng E1
Chongqing D3
Chung Hau ..... Inset
Dachang D3
Dali D2
Dalian F2
Dandong F1
Danjiangkou E2
Daqing F1
Datong E1
Erenhot E1
Fushun F1
Fuxin F1
Fuzhou E3
Ganzhou E3
Gejiu D3
Golmud C2
Guangzhou E3
Guilin E3
Guiyang D3
Haikou E4
Hailar E1
Hami C1
Handan E2
Hangzhou F2
Hanzhong D2
Harbin F1
Hefei E2
Hegang G1
Hengyang E3
Hohhot E1
Hotan A2
Huainan E2
Jiamusi G1
Ji'an E3
Jilin F1
Jinan E2
Jingdezhen E3
Jining E2
Jinzhou F1
Jiujiang E3
Jixi G1
Kaifeng E2
Kashi A2
Korla B1
Kowloon ..... Inset
Kunming D3
Lanzhou D2
Lenghu C2
Lhasa C3
Lianyungang E2
Liaoyang F1
Liaoyuan F1
Liuzhou D3
Lo Wu ..... Inset
Luoyang E2
Luzhou D3
Mudanjiang F1
Nanchang E3
Nanchong D2
Nanjing E2
Nanning D3
Nanyang E2
Neijiang D3
New Kowloon ..... Inset
Ningbo F3
Penzhihua D3
Pingxiang E3
Qingdao F2
Qinhuangdao E2
Qiqihar F1
Quanzhou E3
Sai Kung ..... Inset
Shache A2
Shanghai F2
Shantou E3
Shanxi F3
Shaoguan E3
Shaoxing F3
Shaoyang E3
Shashi E2
Sha Tin ..... Inset
Shek Pik ..... Inset
Shenyang F1
Shijiazhuang E2
Siping F1
Suzhou F2
Tai'an E2
Taiyuan E2
Tangshan E2
Tianjin E2
Tonghua F1
Tongliao F1
Tsuen Wan ..... Inset
Tuen Mun ..... Inset
Ürümqi B1
Weifang E2
Wenshan D3
Wenzhou F3
Wuhan E2
Wuhu E2
Wuwei D2
Wuxi F2
Wuzhong D2
Wuzhou E3
Xiamen E3
Xi'an D2
Xiangfan E2
Xiangtan E3
Xigaze B3
Xining D2
Xinxiang E2
Xinyang E2
Xuzhou E2
Ya'an D2
Yangquan E2
Yangzhou E2
Yanji F1
Yantai F2
Yibin D3
Yichang E2
Yichun F1
Yinchuan D2
Yingkou F1
Yining B1
Yuen Long ..... Inset
Yueyang E3
Yumen C2
Yushu C2
Zhangjiakou E1
Zhangye D2
Zhanjiang E3
Zhengzhou E2
Zhenjiang E2
Zhuzhou E3
Zibo E2
Zigong D3
Zunyi D3

Other Features
Altai, *mts.* B1
Altun, *range* B2
Bayan Har, *range* C2
Bo Hai, *gulf* E2
Bosten, *lake* B1
Brahmaputra, *river* B3
Chang (Yangtze), *river* D2, E2
Deep, *bay* ..... Inset
Dongting, *lake* E3
Dzungaria, *desert basin* B1
East China, *sea* F3
Fen, *river* E2
Gan, *river* E3
Gobi, *desert* D1
Greater Hinggan, *range* F1
Great Wall of China D2
Han, *river* E2
Heilong (Amur), *river* F1
Himalayas, *mts.* B3
Hong Kong, *island* ..... Inset
Hongze, *lake* E2
Huai, *river* E2
Huang (Yellow), *river* D2, E2
Hulun, *lake* E1
Indus, *river* A2
Jinsha (Yangtze), *river* C2
Khanka, *lake* G1
Kunlun, *mts.* B2
K2 (Godwin Austen), *mt.* A2
Lantau, *island* ..... Inset
Lesser Hinggan, *range* F1
Liao, *river* F1
Loess, *plateau* D2
Lop, *lake* C1
Manchurian, *plain* F1
Mekong, *river* C2
Nan Ling, *mts.* E3
New Territories, *island* ..... Inset
North China, *plain* E2
Pamirs, *region* A2
Poyang, *lake* E3
Qaidam, *basin* C2
Qilian, *range* C2
Qinghai, *lake* C2
Qin Ling, *mts.* D2
Salween, *river* C2
Songhua, *river* F1
South China, *sea* ..... E4, Inset
Stonecutters (S.I.), *island* ..... Inset
Tai, *lake* F2
Taiwan, *strait* E3
Takla Makan, *desert* B2
Tanggula, *range* C2
Tarim, *river* B1
Tibet, *plateau* B2
Tien Shan, *range* A1
Tonkin, *gulf* D4
Turfan, *depression* C1
Ulansuhai, *lake* D1
Wei, *river* D2
Xi, *river* E3
Yalu, *river* F1
Yangtze, *river* C2, D2
Yellow, *sea* F2
Yin Shan, *mts.* E1
Yuan, *river* D3
Zhu, *river* E3

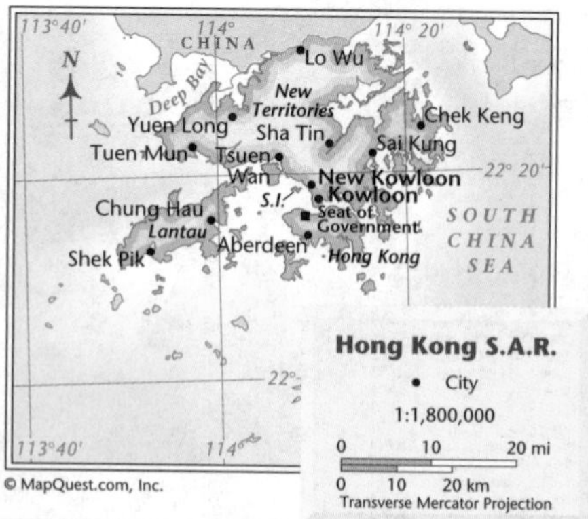

Vietnam: Map Index

Cities and Towns
Bac Lieu A5
Bien Hoa B4
Buon Me Thuot B4
Ca Mau A5
Cam Ranh B4
Can Tho A4
Cao Bang B1
Chau Doc A4
Da Lat B4
Da Nang B3
Dien Bien Phu A2
Dong Hoi B3
Ha Giang A1
Haiphong B2
Hanoi, *capital* A2
Hoa Binh A2
Ho Chi Minh City B4
Hon Gai B2
Hue B3
Khe Sanh B3
Kontum B3
Lang Son B2
Lao Cai A1
Long Xuyen A4
My Tho B4
Nam Dinh B2
Nha Trang B4
Phan Rang B4
Phan Thiet B4
Pleiku B4
Quang Ngai B3
Quang Tri B3
Qui Nhon B4
Rach Gia A4
Soc Trang A5
Son La A2
Tay Ninh B4
Thai Nguyen A2
Thanh Hoa A2
Tuy Hoa B4
Viet Tri A2
Vinh A2
Vung Tau- Con Dao B4
Yen Bai A2

Other Features
Annam, *mts.* A2
Ba, *river* B3
Black (Da), *river* A2
Ca, *river* A2
Central, *highlands* B4
Con Son, *islands* B5
Cu Lao Thu, *island* B4
Dao Phu Quoc, *island* A4
Dong Nai, *river* B4
Fan Si Pan, *mt.* A1
Gam, *river* A1
Lo, *river* A1
Ma, *river* A2
Mekong, *delta* B5
Mekong, *river* A4
Mui Bai Bung, *point* A5
Ngoc Linh, *mt.* B3
Red (Hong), *river* A2
Tonkin, *gulf* B2

Vietnam

Capital: Hanoi
Area: 127,246 sq. mi.
329,653 sq. km.
Population: 77,311,000
Largest City: Ho Chi Minh City
Language: Vietnamese
Monetary Unit: Dong

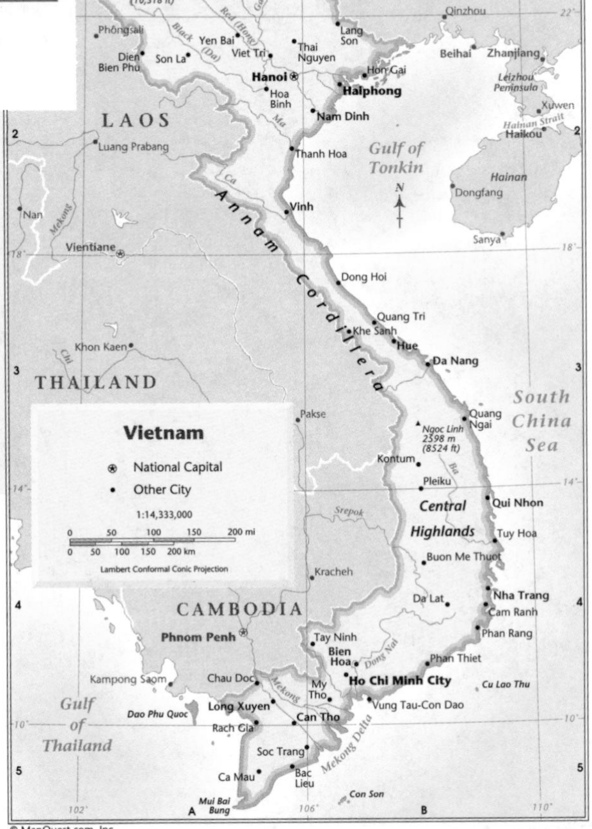

Laos: Map Index

Cities and Towns
Attapu D4
Ban Houayxay A1
Champasak C4
Louang Namtha A1
Luang Prabang B2
Muang Khammouan C3
Muang Không C4
Muang Khôngxédôn C4
Muang Paklay A2
Muang Pakxan B2
Muang Vangviang B2
Muang Xaignabouri A2
Muang Xay A1
Muang Xépôn D3
Muang Xon B1
Pakse C4
Phôngsali B1
Saravan D4
Savannakhet C3
Vientiane, *capital* B3
Xam Nua C1
Xiangkhoang B2

Other Features
Annam, *range* C3
Banghiang, *river* C3
Bolovens, *plateau* D4
Kong, *river* D4
Luang Prabang, *range* A3
Mekong, *river* A1, C3
Nam Ngum, *reservoir* B2
Ou, *river* B1
Phou Bia, *mt.* B2
Xiangkhoang, *plateau* B2

Laos

Capital: Vientiane
Area: 91,429 sq. mi.
236,085 sq. km.
Population: 5,407,000
Largest City: Vientiane
Language: Lao
Monetary Unit: New kip

Mongolia

Capital: Ulan Bator
Area: 604,800 sq. mi.
1,566,839 sq. km.
Population: 2,617,000
Largest City: Ulan Bator
Language: Mongolian
Monetary Unit: Tughrik

Mongolia: Map Index

Cities and Towns
Altay B2
Arvayheer C2
Baruun-Urt D2
Bayanhongor C2
Bulgan C2
Buyant-Uhaa D3
Choybalsan D2
Dalandzadgad C3
Darhan C2
Dund-Us B2
Erdenet C2
Mandalgovĭ C2
Mörön C2
Ölgiy A2
Öndörhaan D2
Sühbaatar C2
Tamsagbulag D2
Tsetserleg C2
Ulaangom B2
Ulaan-Uul C2
Ulan Bator, *capital* C2
Uliastay B2

Other Features
Altai, *mts.* B2
Bööntsagaan, *lake* B2
Dörgön, *lake* B2
Dzavhan, *river* B2
Gobi, *desert* C3
Hangayn, *mts.* B2
Har Us, *lake* B2
Hovd, *river* B2
Hövsgöl, *lake* C1
Hyargas, *lake* B2
Ih Bogd Uul, *mt.* C3
Kerulen, *river* D2
Mongolian, *plateau* C2
Onon, *river* D2
Orhon, *river* C2
Selenge Mörön, *river* C2
Tavan Bogd Uul, *mt.* A2
Tesiyn, *river* B2
Tuul, *river* C2
Uvs, *lake* B1

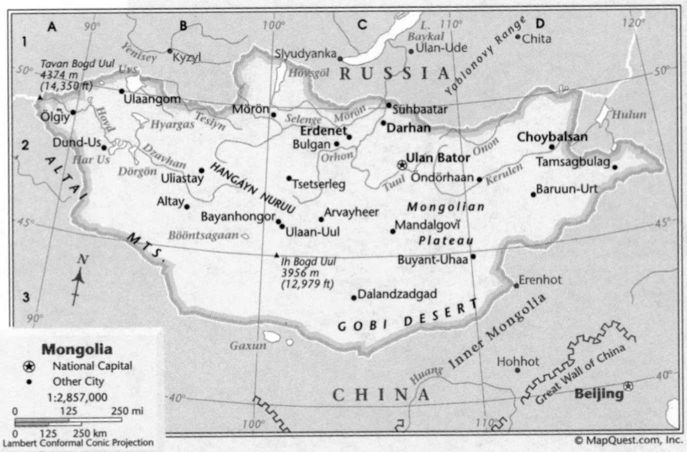

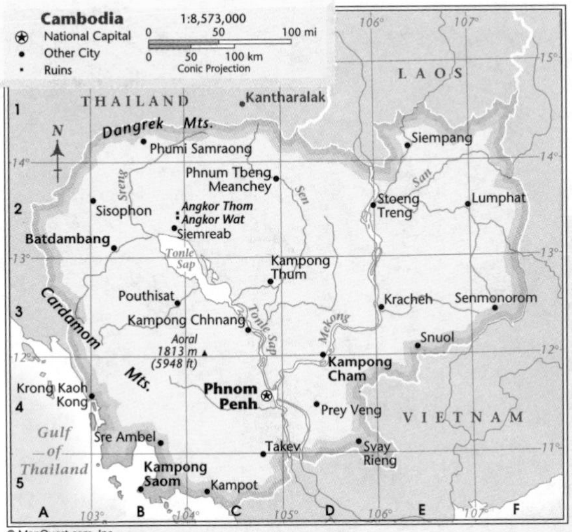

Cambodia

Capital: Phnom Penh
Area: 70,238 sq. mi.
181,964 sq. km.
Population: 11,627,000
Largest City: Phnom Penh
Language: Khmer
Monetary Unit: New riel

Cambodia: Map Index

Cities and Towns
Batdambang B2
Kampong Cham D4
Kampong Chhnang C3
Kampong Saom B5
Kampong Thum C3
Kampot C5
Kracheh E3
Krong Kaoh Kong A4
Lumphat F2
Phnom Penh, *capital* C4
Phnum Tbeng Meanchey C2
Phumi Samraong B1
Pouthisat B3
Prey Veng D4
Senmonorom F3
Siempang E1
Siemreab B2
Sisophon B2
Snuol E3
Sre Ambel B4
Stoeng Treng D2
Svay Rieng D4
Takev C5

Other Features
Angkor Thom, *ruins* B2
Angkor Wat, *ruins* B2
Aoral, *mt.* C3
Cardamom, *mts.* A3
Dangrek, *mts.* B1
Mekong, *river* D3
San, *river* E2
Sen, *river* D2
Sreng, *river* B2
Thailand, *gulf* A4
Tonle Sap, *lake* B2, C3
Tonle Sap, *river* B2

Thailand

Capital: Bangkok
Area: 198,115 sq. mi.
513,251 sq. km.
Population: 60,609,000
Largest City: Bangkok
Language: Thai
Monetary Unit: Baht

Thailand: Map Index

Cities and Towns

Aranyaprathet	C3
Bangkok, *capital*	B3
Ban Phai	C2
Buriram	C3
Chaiyaphum	C3
Chiang Mai	B2
Chiang Rai	B2
Chon Buri	B3
Chumphon	B4
Hat Yai	B5
Hua Hin	B3
Khon Kaen	C2
Lampang	B2
Lamphun	B2
Loei	C2
Lop Buri	B3
Nakhon Phanom	C2
Nakhon Ratchasima	C3
Nakhon Sawan	B2
Nakhon Si Thammarat	B4
Nam Tok	B3
Narathiwat	B5
Nong Khai	C2
Nonthaburi	B3
Pattani	B5
Phatthalung	B5
Phayao	B2
Phetchabun	C2
Phetchaburi	B3
Phichit	B2
Phitsanulok	B2
Phrae	B2
Phra Nakhon Si Ayutthaya	B3
Phuket	B5
Prachuap Khiri Khan	B4
Ranong	B4
Ratchaburi	B3
Rayong	B3
Roi Et	C2
Sakon Nakhon	C2
Sara Buri	B3
Sattahip	B3
Sisaket	C3
Songkhla	B5
Sukhothai	B2
Surat Thani	B4
Surin	C3
Tak	B2
Takua Pa	B4
Trang	B5
Trat	C3
Ubon Ratchathani	C3
Udon Thani	C2
Uttaradit	B2
Yala	B5

Other Features

Bilauktaung, *range*	B3
Chao Phraya, *river*	B3
Chi, *river*	C2
Dangrek, *mts.*	C3
Dawna, *range*	B2
Inthanon, *mt.*	B2
Khorat, *plateau*	C3
Ko Chang, *island*	C3
Ko Kut, *island*	C3
Ko Phangan, *island*	B4
Ko Samui, *island*	B4
Ko Tarutao, *island*	B5
Kra, *isthmus*	B4
Laem, *mt.*	B3
Lam Pao, *reservoir*	C2
Luang, *mt.*	B4
Mae Klong, *river*	B3
Malacca, *strait*	B5
Malay, *peninsula*	B4
Mekong, *river*	C3
Mun, *river*	C3
Nan, *river*	B2
Pa Sak, *river*	B3
Phetchabun, *range*	B3
Ping, *river*	B2
Salween, *river*	A2
Sirinthorn, *reservoir*	C3
Srinagarind, *reservoir*	B3
Tanen, *range*	B2
Thailand, *gulf*	B4
Thale Luang, *lagoon*	B5
Yom, *river*	B2

Thailand

⊛ National Capital
● Other City

1:14,667,000

0 ___ 100 ___ 200 mi
0 ___ 100 ___ 200 km
Lambert Conformal Conic Projection

© MapQuest.com, Inc.

Burma: Map Index

States and Divisions

Chin, *state*	B2
Irrawaddy, *division*	B3
Kachin, *state*	C1
Karen, *state*	C2
Kayah, *state*	C2
Magwe, *division*	B2
Mandalay, *division*	B2
Mon, *state*	C3
Pegu, *division*	B3
Rakhine, *state*	B2
Rangoon, *division*	B3
Sagaing, *division*	B2
Shan, *state*	C2
Tenasserim, *division*	C4

Cities and Towns

Bassein	B3
Bhamo	C1
Haka	B2
Henzada	B3
Kawthaung	C4
Keng Tung	C2
Kyaukpyu	B2
Lashio	C2
Loi-kaw	C2
Mandalay	C2
Maymyo	C2
Meiktila	B2
Mergui	B3
Monywa	B2
Moulmein	C3
Myingyan	B2
Myitkyina	C1
Pa-an	C3
Pegu	C3
Prome	B2
Putao	C1
Rangoon, *capital*	C3
Sagaing	B2
Shwebo	B2
Sittwe	B2
Tamu	B1
Taunggyi	C2
Tavoy	C3
Toungoo	C2
Ye	C3

Other Features

Andaman, *sea*	B3
Arakan Yoma, *mts.*	B2
Bengal, *bay*	B3
Bilauktaung, *range*	C3
Cheduba, *island*	B2
Chin, *hills*	B2
Chindwin, *river*	B1
Coco, *islands*	B3
Hkakabo Razi, *mt.*	C1
Irrawaddy, *river*	B2
Martaban, *gulf*	C3
Mekong, *river*	C2
Mergui, *archipelago*	C4
Mouths of the Irrawaddy, *delta*	B3
Preparis, *island*	B3
Ramree, *island*	B2
Salween, *river*	C2
Shan, *plateau*	C2
Sittang, *river*	C2
Tavoy, *point*	C3
Thailand, *gulf*	C4

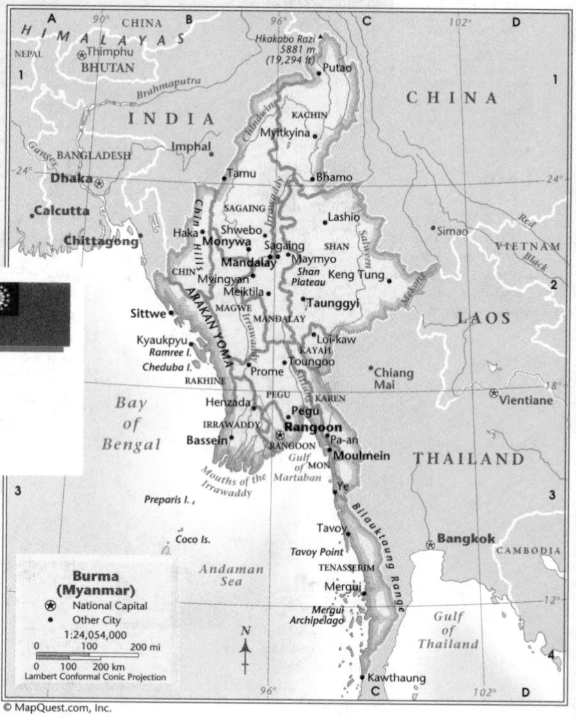

Burma (Myanmar)

Capital: Rangoon
Area: 261,228 sq. mi.
676,756 sq. km.
Population: 48,081,000
Largest City: Rangoon
Language: Burmese
Monetary Unit: Kyat

Burma (Myanmar)

⊛ National Capital
● Other City

1:24,054,000

0 ___ 100 ___ 200 mi
0 ___ 100 ___ 200 km
Lambert Conformal Conic Projection

© MapQuest.com, Inc.

Philippines

⊛ National Capital
● Other City

1:16,000,000

0 ___ 100 ___ 200 mi
0 ___ 100 ___ 200 km
Lambert Conformal Conic Projection

Philippines

Capital: Manila
Area: 115,860 sq. mi.
300,155 sq. km.
Population: 79,346,000
Largest City: Manila
Languages: Pilipino, English
Monetary Unit: Philippine peso

Philippines: Map Index

Regions

Bicol	B3
Cagayan Valley	B2
Central Luzon	A3
Central Mindanao	C5
Central Visayas	B4
*Cordillera Autonomous Region	B2
Eastern Visayas	C4
Ilocos	B2
*Moslem Mindanao Autonomous Region	B5
National Capital Region	B3
Northern Mindanao	C4
Southern Mindanao	C5
Southern Tagalog	B3
Western Mindanao	B5
Western Visayas	B4

Cities and Towns

Angeles	B3
Bacolod	B4
Baguio	B2
Basilan	B5
Batangas	B3
Bislig	C4
Butuan	C4
Cabanatuan	B3
Cadiz	B4
Cagayan de Oro	C4
Calapan	B3
Calbayog	C3
Cebu	B4
Cotabato	C5
Dagupan	B2
Davao	C5
Dipolog	B4
Dumaguete	B4
General Santos	C5
Iligan	C4
Iloilo	B4
Jolo	B5
Laoag	B2
Legazpi	B3
Lipa	B3
Lucena	B3
Mamburao	B3
Mandaue	B4
Manila, *capital*	B3
Masbate	B3
Naga	B3
Olongapo	B3
Ormoc	C4
Pagadian	B5
Puerto Princesa	A4
Quezon City	B3
Roxas	B4
San Carlos	B4
San Fernando	B2
San Pablo	B3
Silay	B4
Surigao	C4
Tacloban	C4
Tuguegarao	B2
Vigan	B2
Zamboanga	B5

Other Features

Agusan, *river*	C4
Apo, *volcano*	C5
Babuyan, *channel*	B2
Babuyan, *islands*	B2
Balabac, *island*	A5
Balabac, *strait*	A5
Bashi, *channel*	B1
Basilan, *island*	B5
Bataan, *peninsula*	B3
Batan, *islands*	B1
Bohol, *island*	C4
Bohol, *sea*	C4
Cagayan, *islands*	B4
Cagayan, *river*	B2
Cagayan Sulu, *island*	A5
Calamian, *islands*	A3
Caramoan, *peninsula*	C3
Catanduanes, *island*	C3
Celebes, *sea*	B5
Cordillera Central, *mts.*	B2
Corregidor, *island*	B3
Cuyo, *islands*	B4
Davao, *gulf*	C5
Dinagat, *island*	C4
Diuata, *mts.*	C4
Jolo, *island*	B5
Laguna de Bay, *lake*	B3
Lamon, *bay*	B3
Leyte, *island*	C4
Lingayen, *gulf*	B2
Luzon, *island*	B3
Luzon, *strait*	B1
Manila, *bay*	B3
Marinduque, *island*	B3
Masbate, *island*	B3
Mayon, *volcano*	B3
Mindanao, *island*	C5
Mindoro, *island*	B3
Mindoro, *strait*	B3
Moro, *gulf*	C5
Negros, *island*	B4
Palawan, *island*	A4
Panay, *gulf*	B4
Panay, *island*	B4
Philippine, *sea*	C3
Pulangi, *river*	C5
Samar, *island*	C4
Samar, *sea*	C4
Siargao, *island*	C4
Sibuyan, *island*	B3
Sibuyan, *sea*	B3
Sierra Madre, *mts.*	B3
South China, *sea*	A3
Sulu, *archipelago*	B5
Sulu, *sea*	A4
Tablas, *island*	B4
Tawi Tawi, *island*	A5
Visayan, *islands*	B4
Visayan, *sea*	B4
Zambales, *mts.*	B3
Zamboanga, *peninsula*	B5

*Not on map

© MapQuest.com, Inc.

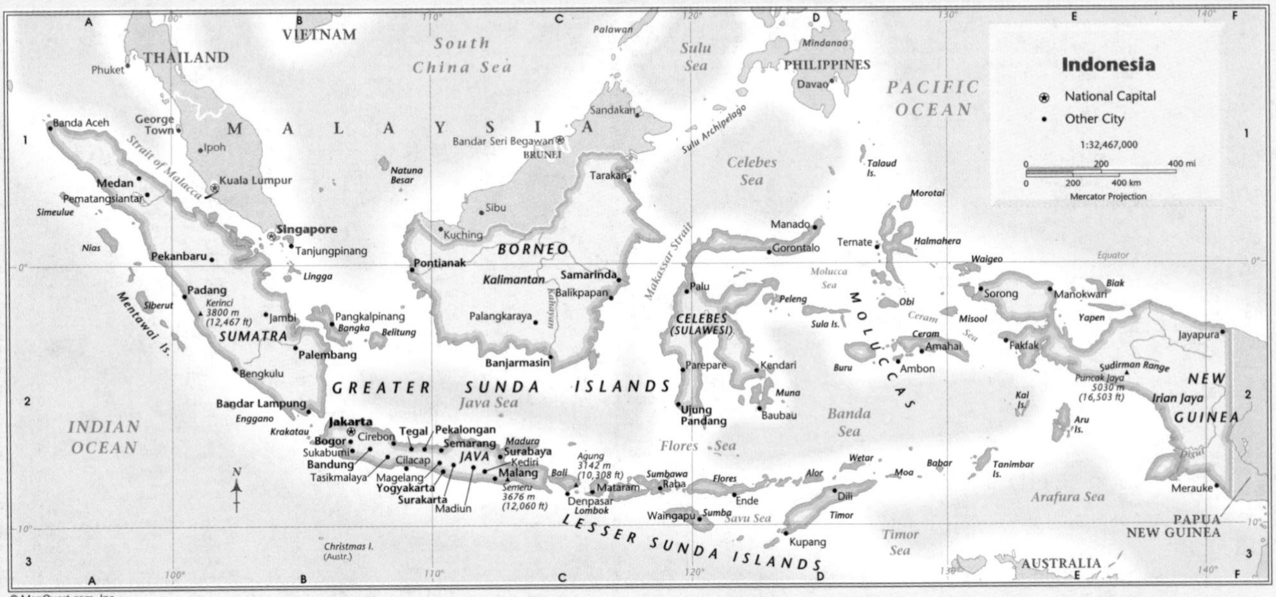

Indonesia:
Map Index

Cities and Towns

Amahai D2
Ambon D2
Balikpapan C2
Banda Aceh A1
Bandar Lampung B2
Bandung B2
Banjarmasin C2
Baubau D2
Bengkulu B2
Bogor B2
Cilacap B2
Cirebon B2
Denpasar C2
Dili D2
Ende D2
Fakfak E2
Gorontalo D1
Jakarta, *capital* B2
Jambi B2
Jayapura F2
Kediri C2
Kendari D2
Kupang D3
Madiun C2
Magelang C2
Malang C2
Manado D1
Manokwari E2
Mataram C2
Medan A1
Merauke F2
Padang B2
Palangkaraya C2
Palembang B2
Palu C2
Pangkalpinang B2
Parepare C2
Pekalongan B2
Pekanbaru B1
Pematangsiantar A1
Pontianak B2
Raba C2
Samarinda C2
Semarang C2
Sorong E2
Sukabumi B2
Surabaya C2
Surakarta C2
Tanjungpinang B1
Tarakan C1
Tasikmalaya B2
Tegal B2
Ternate D1
Ujung Pandang C2
Waingapu D2
Yogyakarta C2

Other Features

Agung, *mt.* C2
Alor, *island* D2
Arafura, *sea* E2
Aru, *islands* E2
Babar, *island* D2
Bali, *island* C2
Banda, *sea* D2
Bangka, *island* B2
Belitung, *island* B2
Biak, *island* E2
Borneo, *island* C1
Buru, *island* D2
Celebes (Sulawesi), *island* D2
Celebes, *sea* D1
Ceram, *island* D2
Ceram, *sea* D2
Digul, *river* E2
Enggano, *island* B2
Flores, *island* D2
Flores, *sea* C2
Greater Sunda, *islands* B2
Halmahera, *island* D1
Irian Jaya, *region* E2
Java, *island* C2
Java, *sea* C2
Jaya, *mt.* E2
Kahayan, *river* C2
Kai, *islands* E2
Kalimantan, *region* C2
Kerinci, *mt.* B2
Krakatau, *island* B2
Lesser Sunda, *islands* C2
Lingga, *island* B2
Lombok, *island* C2
Madura, *island* C2
Makassar, *strait* C2
Malacca, *strait* A1
Mentawai, *islands* A2
Misool, *island* E2
Moa, *island* D2
Molucca, *sea* D2
Moluccas, *islands* D2
Morotai, *island* D1
Muna, *island* D2
Natuna Besar, *island* B1
New Guinea, *island* E2
Nias, *island* A1
Obi, *island* D2
Peleng, *island* D2
Savu, *sea* D2
Semeru, *mt.* C2
Siberut, *island* A2
Simeulue, *island* A1
South China, *sea* C1
Sudirman, *range* E2
Sula, *islands* D2
Sulu, *sea* D1
Sumatra, *island* B2
Sumba, *island* D2
Sumbawa, *island* C2
Talaud, *islands* D1
Tanimbar, *islands* E2
Timor, *island* D2
Timor, *sea* D3
Waigeo, *island* E2
Wetar, *island* D2
Yapen, *island* E2

Indonesia

Capital: Jakarta
Area: 741,052 sq. mi.
1,919,824 sq. km.
Population: 216,108,000
Largest City: Jakarta
Language: Bahasa Indonesian
Monetary Unit: New rupiah

Brunei

Capital: Bandar Seri Begawan
Area: 2,226 sq. mi.
5,767 sq. km.
Population: 323,000
Largest City: Bandar Seri Begawan
Language: Malay
Monetary Unit: Brunei dollar

Brunei: Map Index

Cities and Towns

Badas A2
Bandar Seri Begawan, *capital* B2
Bangar C2
Batang Duri C2
Jerudong B2
Kerangan Nyatan B3
Kuala Abang B2
Kuala Belait A2
Labi A3
Labu C2
Lumut A2
Medit B2
Muara C1
Seria A2
Sukang B3
Tutong B2

Other Features

Belait, *river* B3
Brunei, *bay* C1
Brunei, *river* B2
Bukit Pagon, *mt.* C3
Pandaruan, *river* C2
South China, *sea* A2
Temburong, *river* C2
Tutong, *river* B2

Singapore:
Map Index

Cities and Towns

Bedok B1
Bukit Panjang B1
Bukit Timah B1
Changi B1
Choa Chu Kang A1
Jurong A1
Kranji B1
Nee Soon B1
Punggol B1
Queenstown B1
Sembawang B1
Serangoon B1
Singapore, *capital* B1
Tampines B1
Thong Hoe A1
Toa Payoh B1
Tuas A1
Woodlands B1

Other Features

Ayer Chawan, *island* A1
Bukum, *island* B2
Johor, *strait* B1
Keppel, *harbor* B2
Pandan, *strait* A2
Semakau, *island* B2
Senang, *island* A2
Sentosa, *island* B2
Singapore, *island* B1
Singapore, *strait* B2
Tekong, *island* C1
Timah, *hill* B1
Ubin, *island* B1

Singapore

Capital: Singapore
Area: 247 sq. mi.
640 sq. km.
Population: 3,532,000
Largest City: Singapore
Languages: Mandarin Chinese, English, Malay, Tamil
Monetary Unit: Singapore dollar

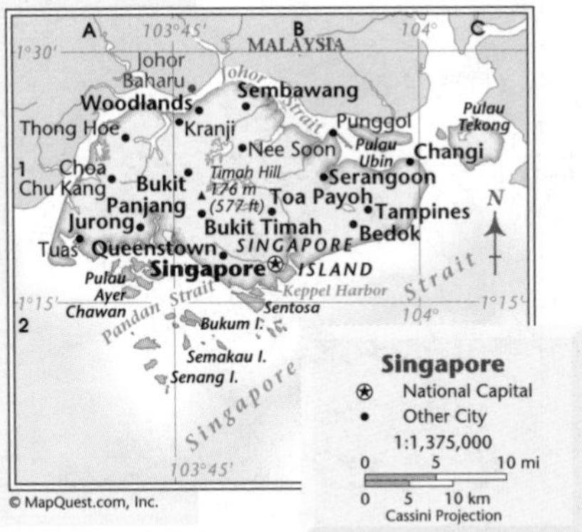

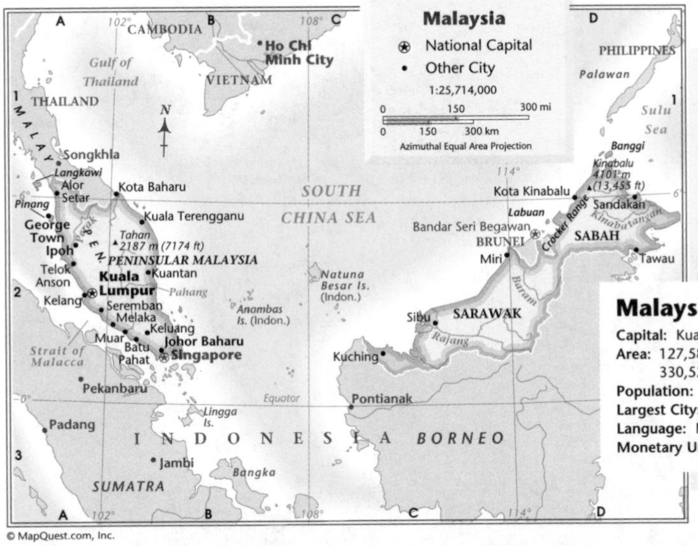

Malaysia:
Map Index

Cities and Towns

Alor Setar A1
Batu Pahat B2
George Town A2
Ipoh A2
Johor Baharu B2
Kelang A2
Keluang B2
Kota Baharu B1
Kota Kinabalu D2
Kuala Lumpur, *capital* A2
Kuala Terengganu B2
Kuantan B2
Kuching C2
Melaka B2
Miri D2
Muar B2
Sandakan D2
Seremban A2
Sibu C2
Tawau D2
Telok Anson A2

Other Features

Banggi, *island* D1
Baram, *river* D2
Crocker, *range* D2
Kinabalu, *mt.* D1
Kinabatangan, *river* D2
Labuan, *island* D2
Langkawi, *island* A1
Malacca, *strait* A2
Malay, *peninsula* A1
Pahang, *river* B2
Peninsular Malaysia, *region* B2
Perak, *river* A2
Pinang, *island* A2
Rajang, *river* C2
Sabah, *state* D2
Sarawak, *state* C2
Tahan, *mt.* B2

Malaysia

Capital: Kuala Lumpur
Area: 127,584 sq. mi.
330,529 sq. km.
Population: 21,376,000
Largest City: Kuala Lumpur
Language: Malay
Monetary Unit: Ringgit

AUSTRALIA

Australia: Map Index

States and Territories
- Australian Capital Territory.......D3
- New South Wales D3
- Northern Territory....................C2
- Queensland. D2
- South Australia.........................C2
- Tasmania. D4
- Victoria D3
- Western Australia.....................B2

Aboriginal Lands
- Alawa-Ngandji C1
- Balwina B2
- Central Australia B2
- Central Desert...........................C2
- Daly River.................................B1
- Haasts Bluff C2
- Lake Mackay.............................B2
- Nganyatjara B2
- Petermann B2
- Pitjantjatjara.............................C2
- Waani/Garawa C1
- Yandeyarra A2
- Unnamed B2
- Unnamed..................................C1
- Unnamed..................................D1

Cities and Towns
- Adelaide, S.A., *capital* ..C3, Inset II
- Albany, W.A..............................A3
- Albury, N.S.W. D3
- Alice Springs, N.T.....................C2
- Altona, Vic. ....Inset V
- Armadale, W.A. ....Inset I
- Armidale, N.S.W. E3
- Asquith, N.S.W. ....Inset IV
- Auburn, N.S.W. ....Inset IV
- Balcatta, W.A. ....Inset I
- Bald Hills, Qld. ....Inset III
- Ballarat, Vic..............................D3
- Bankstown, N.S.W............Inset IV
- Bayswater, W.A. ....Inset I
- Beenleigh, Qld. ....Inset III
- Belmont, W.A......................Inset I
- Bendigo, Vic. D3
- Berwick, Vic. ....Inset V
- Blacktown, N.S.W. ....Inset IV
- Botany, N.S.W..................Inset IV
- Bourke, N.S.W. D3
- Bowen, Qld. D2
- Box Hill, Vic. ....Inset V
- Brighton, S.A. ....Inset II
- Brighton, Qld. ....Inset III
- Brighton, Vic.......................Inset V
- Brisbane, Qld., *capital* ....E2, Inset III
- Broadmeadows, Vic. ....Inset V
- Broken Hill, N.S.W. D3
- Broome, W.A............................B1
- Brown Plains, Qld.............Inset III
- Bunbury, W.A. A3
- Bundaberg, Qld........................E2
- Burnside, S.A. ....Inset II
- Byford, W.A. ....Inset I
- Cairns, Qld. D1
- Campbelltown, S.A. ....Inset II
- Campbelltown, N.S.W. ....Inset IV
- Canberra, A.C.T., *national capital* D3
- Cannington, W.A. ....Inset I
- Canterbury, N.S.W. ....Inset IV
- Carnarvon, W.A. A2
- Castle Hill, N.S.W. ....Inset IV
- Caulfield, Vic. ....Inset V
- Ceduna, S.A. C3
- Charleville, Qld. D2
- Charters Towers, Qld. D2
- Chelsea, Vic. ....Inset V
- Chermside, Qld. ....Inset III
- City Beach, W.A. ....Inset I
- Cleveland, Qld. ....Inset III
- Cloncurry, Qld. D2
- Coburg, Vic. ....Inset V
- Coober Pedy, S.A. C2
- Coopers Plains, Qld. ....Inset III
- Cranbourne, Vic. ....Inset V
- Cronulla, N.S.W. ....Inset IV
- Dampier, W.A. A2
- Dandenong, Vic. ....Inset V
- Darwin, N.T., *capital* C1
- Dee Why, N.S.W. ....Inset IV
- Devonport, Tas. D4
- Doncaster, Vic. ....Inset V
- Dubbo, N.S.W. D3
- Elizabeth, S.A. ....Inset II
- Eltham, Vic. ....Inset V
- Emerald, Qld. D2
- Enfield, S.A. ....Inset II
- Epping, N.S.W. ....Inset IV
- Esperance, W.A........................B3
- Essendon, Vic. ....Inset V
- Fairfield, N.S.W. ....Inset IV
- Ferntree Gully, Vic. ....Inset V
- Ferny Grove, Qld. .... Inset III
- Frankston, Vic. .... Inset V
- Fremantle, W.A. ....A3, Inset I
- Geelong, Vic. D3
- Geraldton, W.A. A2
- Gladstone, Qld. E2
- Glenelg, S.A. .... Inset II
- Glen Forrest, W.A. .... Inset I
- Gold Coast, Qld. E2
- Goodna, Qld. .... Inset III
- Gosford, N.S.W.........................E3
- Gosnells, W.A. .... Inset I
- Grafton, N.S.W. E2
- Grange, S.A. .... Inset II
- Greenslopes, Qld. .... Inset III
- Griffith, N.S.W. D3
- Gympie, Qld.............................E2
- Heidelberg, Vic. .... Inset V
- Hobart, Tas., *capital* D4
- Holland Park, Qld. .... Inset III
- Holroyd, N.S.W. ....Inset IV
- Hornsby, N.S.W. .... Inset IV
- Hurstville, N.S.W. .... Inset IV
- Inala, Qld. .... Inset III
- Ipswich, Qld. .... Inset III
- Kalamunda, W.A. .... Inset I
- Kalgoorlie, W.A........................B3
- Katherine, N.T..........................C1
- Keilor, Vic. .... Inset V
- Kelmscott, W.A. .... Inset I
- Kersbrook, S.A. .... Inset II
- Kwinana, W.A. .... Inset I
- Kwinana Beach, W.A. .... Inset I
- La Perouse, N.S.W. .... Inset IV
- Launceston, Tas. D4
- Leichhardt, N.S.W. .... Inset IV
- Lilydale, Vic. .... Inset V
- Lismore, N.S.W.........................E2
- Liverpool, N.S.W. .... Inset IV
- Lobethal, S.A. .... Inset II
- Logan, Qld. .... Inset III
- Longreach, Qld.........................D2
- Mackay, Qld. D2
- Mandurah, W.A........................A3
- Manly, Qld. .... Inset III
- Manly, N.S.W. .... Inset IV
- Marion, S.A. .... Inset II
- Maryborough, Qld. E2
- Melbourne, Vic., *capital*....................D3, Inset V
- Melville, W.A. .... Inset I
- Merredin, W.A. A3
- Midland, W.A. .... Inset I
- Mildura, Vic. D3
- Mitcham, S.A. .... Inset II
- Mona Vale, N.S.W............ Inset IV
- Moorabbin, Vic. .... Inset V
- Mordialloc, Vic. .... Inset V
- Moree, N.S.W. D2
- Morningside, Qld. .... Inset III
- Mosman Park, W.A. .... Inset I
- Mount Barker, S.A. .... Inset II
- Mount Gambier, S.A. D3
- Mount Gravatt, Qld. .... Inset III
- Mount Isa, Qld.........................C2
- Mount Nebo, Qld. ....Inset III
- Mullaloo, W.A. .... Inset I
- Narrogin, W.A. A3
- Nedlands, W.A. .... Inset I
- Newcastle, N.S.W. E3
- Newman, W.A..........................A2
- Newmarket, Qld. .... Inset III
- Noarlunga, S.A. .... Inset II
- North Adelaide, S.A. .... Inset II
- Northcote, Vic. .... Inset V
- North Sydney, N.S.W. ..... Inset IV
- Nunawading, Vic. .... Inset V
- Oakleigh, Vic. .... Inset V
- Orange, N.S.W. D3
- Parramatta, N.S.W. .... Inset IV
- Perth, W.A., *capital* ....A3, Inset I
- Petrie, Qld. .... Inset III
- Pickering Brook, W.A. .... Inset I
- Port Adelaide, S.A. .... Inset II
- Port Augusta, S.A. C3
- Port Hedland, W.A....................A2
- Port Lincoln, S.A. C3
- Port Macquarie, N.S.W. E3
- Port Pirie, S.A. C3
- Prahran, Vic. .... Inset V
- Preston, Vic. .... Inset V
- Queenstown, Tas. D4
- Randwick, N.S.W. .... Inset IV
- Redcliffe, Qld. .... Inset III
- Redland Bay, Qld. .... Inset III
- Reynella, S.A. .... Inset II
- Ringwood, Vic. .... Inset V
- Rockdale, N.S.W. .... Inset IV
- Rockhampton, Qld. E2
- Roma, Qld. D2
- Ryde, N.S.W. .... Inset IV
- St. Ives, N.S.W. .... Inset IV
- St. Kilda, S.A. .... Inset II
- St. Kilda, Vic. .... Inset V
- Salisbury, S.A. .... Inset II
- Samford, Qld. .... Inset III
- Sandgate, Qld. .... Inset III
- Scarborough, W.A. .... Inset I
- Spearwood, W.A. .... Inset I
- Springvale, Vic. .... Inset V
- Stirling, W.A. .... Inset I
- Stirling, S.A. .... Inset II
- Sunshine, Vic. .... Inset V
- Sutherland, N.S.W. .... Inset IV
- Sydney, N.S.W., *capital,* ....E3, Inset IV
- Tamworth, N.S.W. E3
- Taree, N.S.W.............................E3
- Tea Tree Gully, S.A. .... Inset II
- Tennant Creek, N.T. C1
- Tom Price, W.A.........................A2
- Toowoomba, Qld. E2
- Townsville, Qld. D1
- Unley, S.A. .... Inset II
- Victoria Park, W.A. .... Inset I
- Victoria Point, Qld. .... Inset III
- Wagga Wagga, N.S.W.............D3
- Wanneroo, W.A. .... Inset I
- Warrnambool, Vic. D3
- Waverley, Vic. .... Inset V
- Weipa, Qld. D1
- Whyalla, S.A.............................C3
- Willoughby, N.S.W. .... Inset IV
- Wollongong, N.S.W. E3
- Woodside, S.A. .... Inset II
- Woodville, S.A. .... Inset II
- Woomera, S.A..........................C3
- Wyndham, W.A. B1
- Wynnum, Qld. .... Inset III

Other Features
- Arafura, *sea*.............................C1
- Arnhem, *cape*...........................C1
- Arnhem Land, *region* C1
- Ashburton, *river*.......................A2
- Ashmore and Cartier, *islands* B1
- Australian Alps, *mts*..................D3
- Barkly, *tableland* C1
- Bass, *strait*...............................D3
- Bate, *bay*..........................Inset IV
- Blue, *mts.* E3
- Botany, *bay*......................Inset IV
- Brisbane, *river*..................Inset III
- Burdekin, *river*.........................D1
- Canning, *river* .... Inset I
- Cape York, *peninsula*...............D1
- Carpentaria, *gulf* C1
- Coral, *sea* E1
- Daly, *river*...............................C1
- Darling, *range* A3
- Darling, *river*...........................D3
- Drysdale River Natl. Park B1
- Eyre, *lake* C2
- Eyre, *peninsula* C3
- Fitzroy, *river*............................B1
- Flinders, *range*.........................C3
- Flinders, *river* D1
- Frome, *lake*.............................D2
- Gairdner, *lake*..........................C3
- Garden, *island*.................... Inset I
- Gascoyne *river*.........................A2
- Gibson, *desert*..........................B2
- Gilbert, *river*............................D1
- Great Artesian, *basin*................D2
- Great Australian, *bight*.............B3
- Great Barrier, *reef*....................D1
- Great Dividing, *range*........D1, D3
- Great Sandy, *desert*..................B2
- Great Victoria, *desert* B2
- Gregory Natl. Park C1
- Grey, *range* D2
- Groote Eylandt, *island* C1
- Hamersley, *range*.....................A2
- Hobsons, *bay*.................... Inset V
- Jackson, *port* ....Inset IV
- Kakadu Natl. Park C1
- Kangaroo, *island* C3
- Kimberley, *plateau* B1
- King Leopold, *range* B1
- Kosciusko, *mt*...........................D3
- Lakefield Natl. Park D1
- Leeuwin, *cape* A3
- Leichhardt, *river* D1
- Leveque, *cape*...........................B1
- Logan, *river* ....Inset III
- Macdonnell, *ranges*..................C2
- Melville, *island* C1
- Mitchell, *river*...........................D1
- Moreton, *bay* ....Inset III
- Murchison, *river* A2
- Murray, *river* D3
- Murrumbidgee, *river*................D3
- Musgrave, *ranges*.....................C2
- New England, *range* E3
- North West, *cape* A2
- Nullarbor, *plain* B3
- Port Phillip, *bay*................ Inset V
- Roper, *river*..............................C1
- Rudall River Natl. Park B2
- St. Vincent, *gulf*.................Inset II
- Samsonvale, *lake* ....Inset III
- Simpson, *desert*........................C2
- Simpson Desert Natl. Park........C2
- Spencer, *gulf* C3
- Swan, *river* .... Inset I
- Tasman, *sea*..............................E3
- Timor, *sea* B1
- Torrens, *lake*............................C2
- Torrens, *river* ....Inset II
- Torres, *strait*............................D1
- Uluru (Ayers Rock) C2
- Victoria, *river*...........................C1
- Witjira Natl. Park......................C2
- Yampi, *sound*...........................B1
- York, *cape* D1

Australia

Capital: Canberra
Area: 2,966,200 sq. mi.
7,684,456 sq. km.
Population: 18,784,000
Largest City: Sydney
Language: English
Monetary Unit: Australian dollar

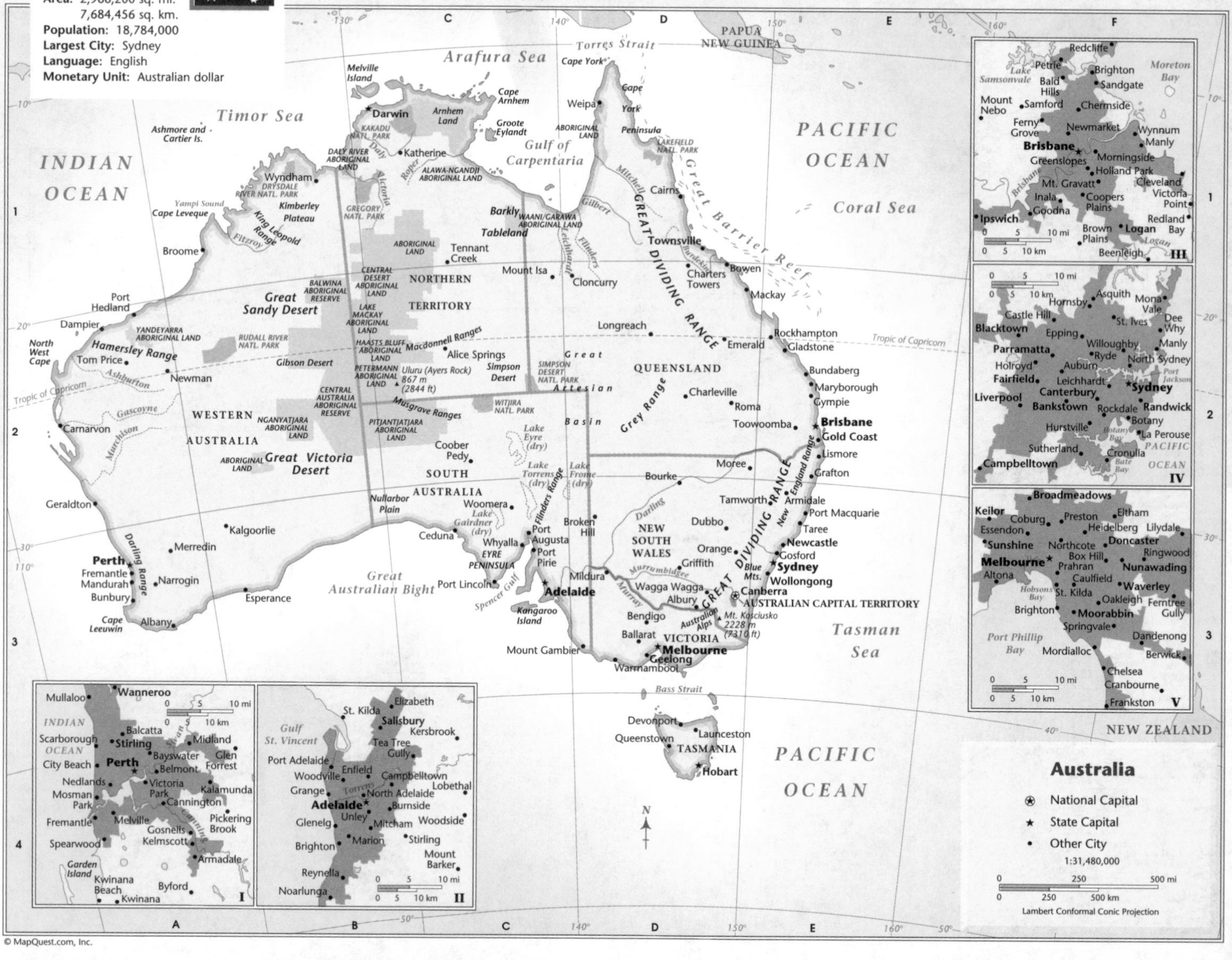

New Zealand

Capital: Wellington
Area: 104,454 sq. mi.
270,606 sq. km.
Population: 3,662,000
Largest City: Auckland
Language: English
Monetary Unit: New Zealand dollar

New Zealand: Map Index

Cities and Towns
Alexandra....A4
Ashburton....B3
Auckland....B2
Blenheim....B3
Christchurch....B3
Collingwood....B3
Dunedin....B4
East Coast Bays....B2
Gisborne....C2
Greymouth....B3
Hamilton....C2
Hastings....C2
Hicks Bay....C2
Invercargill....A4
Kaeo....B2
Kaikoura....B3
Kaitaia....B2
Kawhia....B2
Lower Hutt....B3
Manukau....B2
Milford Sound....A3
Napier....C2
Nelson....B3
New Plymouth....B2
Oamaru....B4
Palmerston North....C3
Queenstown....A3
Rotorua....C2
Taumaruni....C2
Taupo....C2
Tauranga....C2
Timaru....B3
Waimamaku....B2
Wanganui....C2
Wellington, *capital*....B3
Westport....B3
Whakatane....C2
Whangarei....B2

Other Features
Aspiring, *mt.*....A3
Banks, *peninsula*....B3
Canterbury, *bight*....B3
Canterbury, *plains*....B3
Clutha, *river*....A4
Cook, *mt.*....B3
Cook, *strait*....B3
Coromandel, *peninsula*....C2
East, *cape*....C2
Egmont, *cape*....B2
Egmont, *mt.*....B2
Farewell, *cape*....B3
Foveaux, *strait*....A4
Great Barrier, *island*....C2
Hawea, *lake*....A3
Hawke, *bay*....C2
Ngauruhoe, *mt.*....C2
North, *cape*....B1
North, *island*....B2
North Taranaki, *bight*....B2
Palliser, *cape*....C3
Pegasus, *bay*....B3
Plenty, *bay*....C2
Puysegur, *point*....A4
Rangitikei, *river*....C2
Raukumara, *range*....C2
Ruahine, *range*....C2
Ruapehu, *mt.*....C2
South, *island*....A3
Southern Alps, *mts.*....A3
Southland, *plains*....A4
South Taranaki, *bight*....B2
South West, *cape*....A4
Stewart, *island*....A4
Tararua, *range*....C3
Tasman, *bay*....B3
Tasman, *sea*....A2
Taupo, *lake*....C2
Te Anau, *lake*....A4
Tekapo, *lake*....B3
Three Kings, *islands*....B1
Tongariro, *mt.*....C2
Waikato, *river*....C2
Wairau, *river*....B3
Waitaki, *river*....B3
Wanaka, *lake*....A3

Papua New Guinea: Map Index

Cities and Towns
Alotau....B3
Arawa....B2
Daru....A2
Goroka....A2
Kavieng....B2
Kerema....A2
Kimbe....B2
Lae....A2
Lorengau....A2
Madang....A2
Morehead....A2
Mount Hagen....A2
Popondetta....A2
Port Moresby, *capital*....A2
Rabaul....B2
Vanimo....A2
Wabag....A2
Wau....A2
Wewak....A1

Other Features
Admiralty, *islands*....A2
Bismarck, *archipelago*....A2
Bismarck, *range*....A2
Bismarck, *sea*....A2
Bougainville, *island*....B2
Buka, *island*....B2
Central, *range*....A2
Coral, *sea*....A3
D'Entrecasteaux, *islands*....B2
Feni, *islands*....B2
Fly, *river*....A2
Gazelle, *peninsula*....B2
Green, *islands*....B2
Huon, *peninsula*....A2
Karkar, *island*....A2
Lihir, *group*....B2
Louisiade, *archipelago*....B3
Manus, *island*....A2
Markham, *river*....A2
Milne, *bay*....B3
Murray, *lake*....A2
Mussau, *island*....A2
New Britain, *island*....B2
New Guinea, *island*....A2
New Hanover, *island*....B2
New Ireland, *island*....B2
Ninigo, *group*....A2
Nuguria, *islands*....B2
Owen Stanley, *range*....A2
Papua, *gulf*....A2
Purari, *river*....A2
Ramu, *river*....A2
Rossel, *island*....B3
St. George's, *channel*....B2
Sepik, *river*....A2
Solomon, *sea*....B2
Tabar, *islands*....B2
Tagula, *island*....B3
Tanga, *islands*....B2
Tauu, *islands*....B3
Torres, *strait*....A2
Trobriand, *islands*....B2
Umboi, *island*....A2
Whiteman, *range*....A2
Wilhelm, *mt.*....A2
Witu, *island*....A2
Woodlark (Muyua), *island*....B2

Papua New Guinea

Capital: Port Moresby
Area: 178,704 sq. mi.
462,964 sq. km.
Population: 4,705,000
Largest City: Port Moresby
Language: English
Monetary Unit: Kina

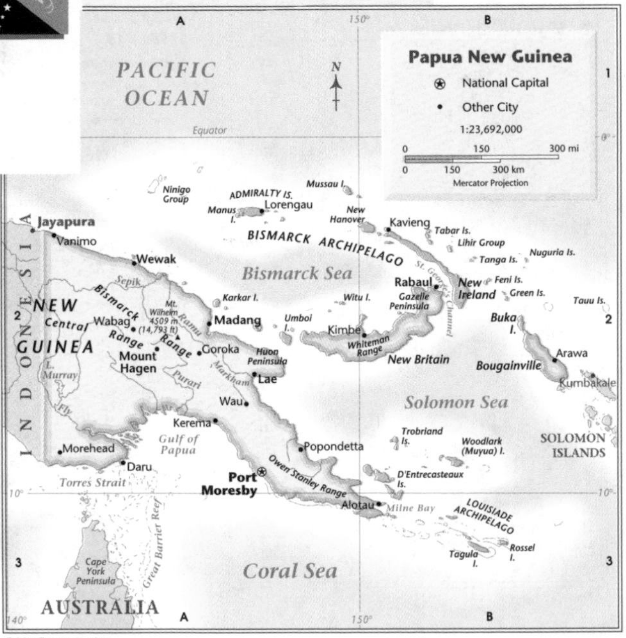

© MapQuest.com, Inc.

MAJOR CITIES

Australia		Papua New Guinea	(metro)
Sydney	3,935,000	Morobe	439,725
Melbourne	3,322,000	Western Highlands	398,376
Brisbane	1,548,000	Southern Highlands	390,240
Perth	1,319,000	Eastern Highlands	316,802
Adelaide	1,083,000	Madang	288,317
New Zealand		Port Moresby	271,813
Auckland	998,000		
Wellington	335,000		
Christchurch	331,000		
Hamilton	159,000		
Dunedin	112,000		

© MapQuest.com, Inc.

Micronesia: Map Index

Cities and Towns
Colonia....A2
Kosrae....D2
Palikir, *capital*....C2
Weno....C2

Other Features
Caroline, *islands*....B2
Chuuk, *islands*....C2
Eauripik, *atoll*....B2
Faraulep, *atoll*....B2
Kapingamarangi, *atoll*....C2
Kosrae, *island*....D2
Mortlock, *islands*....C2
Murilo, *atoll*....C2
Namoluk, *atoll*....C2
Namonuito, *atoll*....C2
Ngulu, *atoll*....A2
Nukuoro, *atoll*....C2
Oroluk, *atoll*....C2
Pohnpei, *island*....D2
Pulusuk, *island*....B2
Ulithi, *atoll*....B2
Weno, *island*....C2
Yap, *islands*....A2

Micronesia

Capital: Palikir
Area: 271 sq. mi.
702 sq. km.
Population: 132,000
Largest City: Palikir
Language: English
Monetary Unit: U.S. dollar

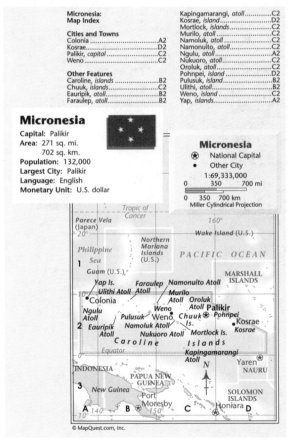

© MapQuest.com, Inc.

Marshall Islands

⊛ National Capital
● Other City
1:25,750,000

0   150   300 mi
0   150   300 km
Mercator Projection

Marshall Islands

Capital: Majuro
Area: 70 sq. mi.
181 sq. km.
Population: 66,000
Largest City: Majuro
Language: English
Monetary Unit: U.S. dollar

Marshall Islands: Map Index

City
Majuro, capital.....................C2

Other Features
Ailinglapalap, island............B2
Ailuk, island.........................B1
Arno, island..........................C2
Aur, island............................C2
Bikar, island..........................C1
Bikini, island.........................B1
Ebon, island..........................B3
Enewetak, island...................A1
Jaluit, island..........................B2
Kwajalein, island...................B2
Lae, island.............................B2
Likiep, island.........................B1
Majuro, island.......................C2
Maloelap, island....................C2
Mili, island.............................C2
Namu, island.........................B2
Ralik, island chain.................A1
Ratak, island chain................B1
Roi, island..............................B2
Rongelap, island....................B1
Rongerik, island.....................B1
Taka, island............................B1
Taongi, island.........................B1
Ujae, island............................B2
Ujelang, island.......................A2
Wotho, island.........................B1
Wotje, island..........................B2

Nauru

⊛ National Capital
● Other City
1:135,000

0   1   2 mi
0   1   2 km
Lambert Conformal Conic Projection

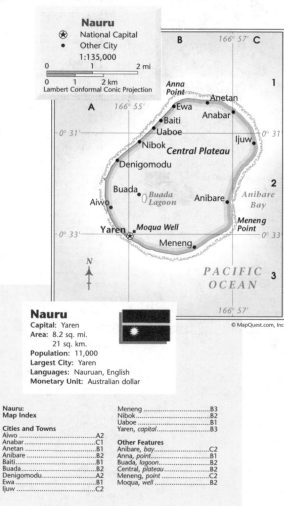

Nauru

Capital: Yaren
Area: 8.2 sq. mi.
21 sq. km.
Population: 11,000
Largest City: Yaren
Languages: Nauruan, English
Monetary Unit: Australian dollar

Nauru: Map Index

Cities and Towns
Aiwo......................................A2
Anabar...................................C1
Anetan...................................B1
Anibare..................................B2
Baiti.......................................B1
Buada....................................B2
Denigomodu..........................A2
Ewa.......................................B1
Ijuw.......................................C2

Meneng..................................B3
Nibok.....................................B2
Uaboe....................................B2
Yaren, capital........................B3

Other Features
Anibare, bay..........................C2
Anna, point............................B1
Buada, lagoon........................B2
Central, plateau......................B2
Meneng, point........................C2
Moqua, well...........................B2

Solomon Islands

⊛ National Capital
● Other City
1:24,100,000

0   150   300 mi
0   150   300 km
Mercator Projection

Solomon Islands: Map Index

Cities and Towns
Auki.......................................B1
Buala.....................................A1
Gizo.......................................A1
Honiara, capital.....................A1
Kirakira.................................B2
Sasamungga..........................A1

Other Features
Bellona, island.......................A2
Choiseul, island.....................A1
Guadalcanal, island...............A1
Indispensable, reefs..............B2
Malaita, island.......................B1
Maramasike, island...............B1
Nendo, island.........................C2
New Georgia Group,
islands..............................A1
Ontong Java, island...............A1
Popomanaseu, mt..................B1
Rennell, island.......................A2
San Cristobal, island.............B2
Santa Cruz, islands...............C2
Santa Isabel, island...............A1
Solomon, sea.........................A2
Utupua, island........................C2
Vanikolo, islands....................C2
Vella Lavella, island..............A1

Solomon Islands

Capital: Honiara
Area: 10,954 sq. mi.
28,378 sq. km.
Population: 455,000
Largest City: Honiara
Language: English
Monetary Unit: Dollar

Tuvalu

Capital: Funafuti
Area: 9.4 sq. mi.
24.4 sq. km.
Population: 11,000
Largest City: Funafuti
Languages: Tuvaluan, English
Monetary Unit: Tuvalu dollar,
Australian dollar

Tuvalu: Map Index

City
Funafuti, capital.....................C3

Other Features
Funafuti, island......................C3
Nanumanga, island...............B2
Nanumea, island....................B1
Niulakita, island.....................C4
Niutao, island.........................B2
Nui, island.............................B2
Nukufetau, island...................C2
Nukulaelae, island.................C2
Vaitupu, island.......................C2

Tuvalu

⊛ National Capital
● Other City
1:12,500,000

0   75   150 mi
0   75   150 km
Mercator Projection

© MapQuest.com, Inc.

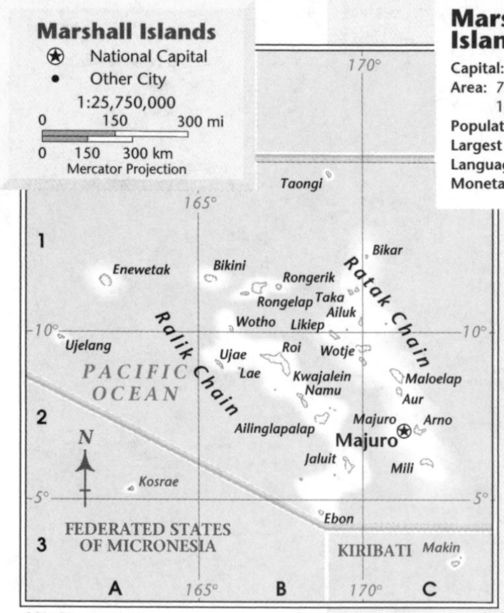

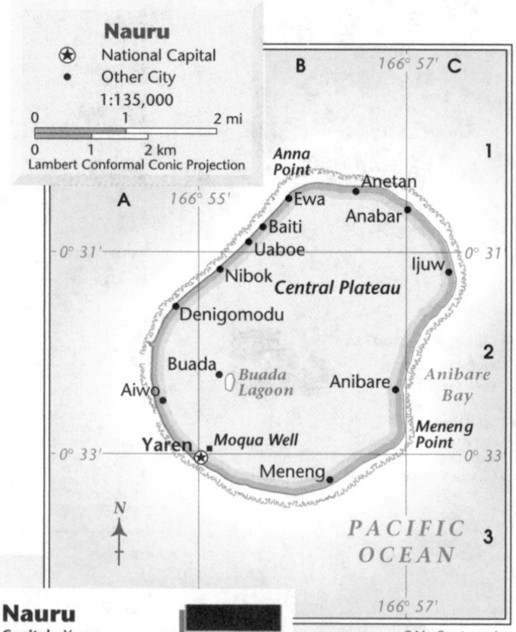

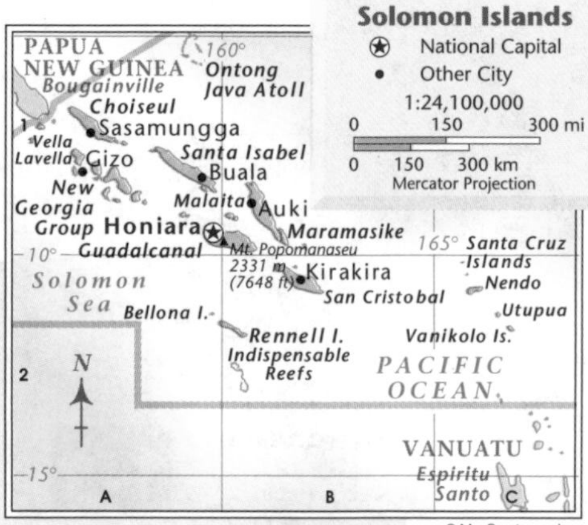

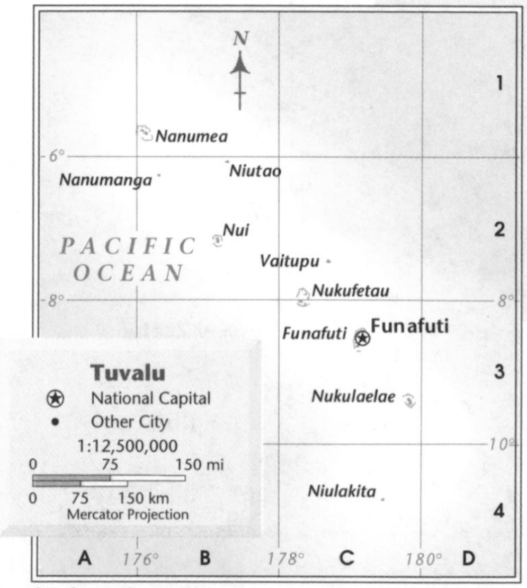

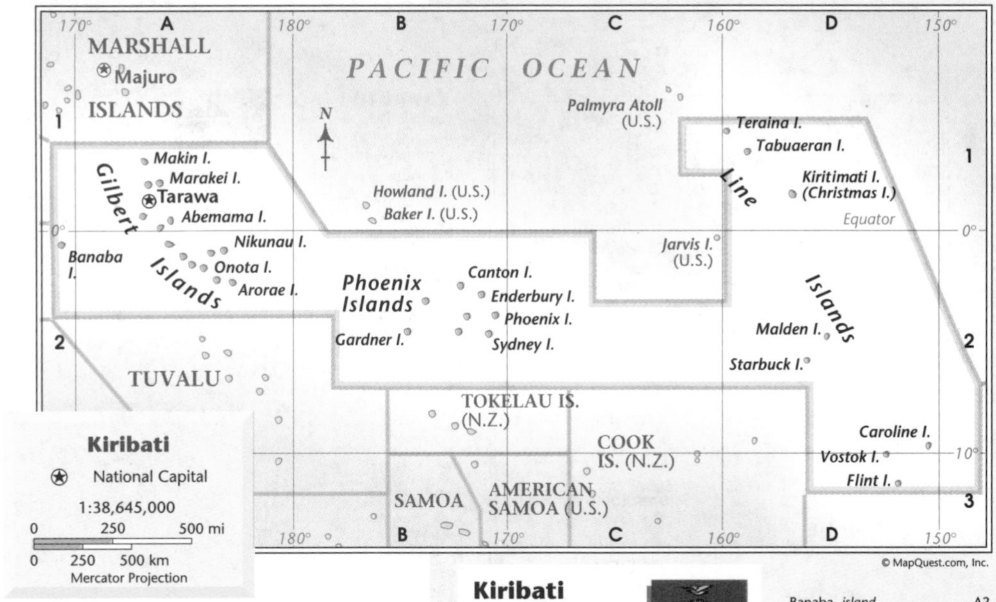

© MapQuest.com, Inc.

Kiribati

Capital: Tarawa
Area: 313 sq. mi.
811 sq. km.
Population: 86,000
Largest City: Tarawa
Languages: I-Kiribati (Gilbertese), English
Monetary Unit: Australian dollar

Kiribati: Map Index

City

Tarawa, *capital*	A1

Other Features

Abemama, *island*	A1
Arorae, *island*	A2
Banaba, *island*	A2
Canton, *island*	B2
Caroline, *island*	D2
Enderbury, *island*	B2
Flint, *island*	D3
Gardner, *island*	B2
Gilbert, *islands*	A1
Kiritimati (Christmas), *island*	D1
Line, *islands*	D1
Makin, *island*	A1
Malden, *island*	D2
Marakei, *island*	A1
Nikunau, *island*	A2
Onota, *island*	A2
Phoenix, *island*	B2
Phoenix, *islands*	B2
Starbuck, *island*	D2
Sydney, *island*	B2
Tabuaeran, *island*	D1
Teraina, *island*	D1
Vostok, *island*	D3

Fiji: Map Index

Cities and Towns

Galoa	B3
Labasa	B2
Lami	B3
Lautoka	A2
Lomawai	A3
Nabouwalu	B2
Nadi	A2
Naduri	B2
Nakodu	B2
Navua	B3
Suva, *capital*	B3
Vunisea	B3

Other Features

Beqa, *island*	B3
Bligh Water, *sound*	B2
Cicia, *island*	C2
Cikobia, *island*	C1
Gau, *island*	B3
Great Sea, *reef*	B1
Kadavu, *island*	B3
Kadavu, *passage*	A3
Kioa, *island*	C2
Koro, *island*	B2
Koro, *sea*	B2
Lakeba, *island*	C3
Lakeba, *passage*	C3
Lau, *island group*	C2
Laucala, *island*	C2
Moala, *island group*	B3
Nadi, *bay*	A2
Navua, *river*	A3
Ono, *island*	B3
Ovalau, *island*	B2
Qamea, *island*	C2
Qelelevu, *island*	C2
Rabi, *island*	C2
Soso, *bay*	B3
Taveuni, *island*	C2
Tomanivi, *mt.*	B2
Udu, *point*	C2
Vanua Balavu, *island*	C2
Vanua Levu, *island*	B2
Vatu Lele, *island*	A3
Vetauua, *island*	C1
Viti Levu, *island*	A2
Vunaniu, *bay*	A3
Washington, *cape*	A3
Yasawa, *island group*	A2

Fiji

Capital: Suva
Area: 7,056 sq. mi.
18,280 sq. km.
Population: 813,000
Largest City: Suva
Languages: Fijian, Hindi, English
Monetary Unit: Fiji dollar

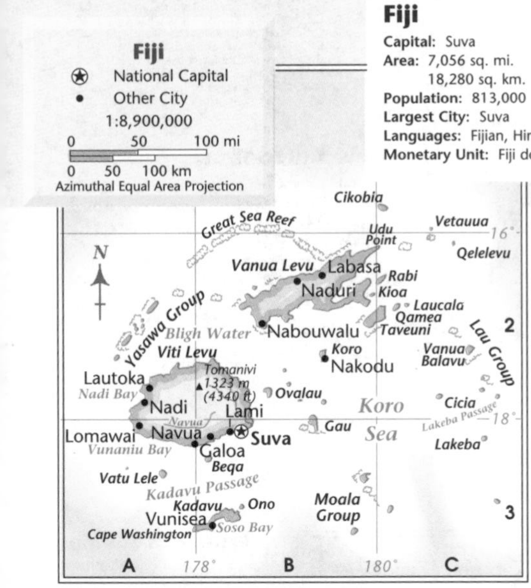

© MapQuest.com, Inc.

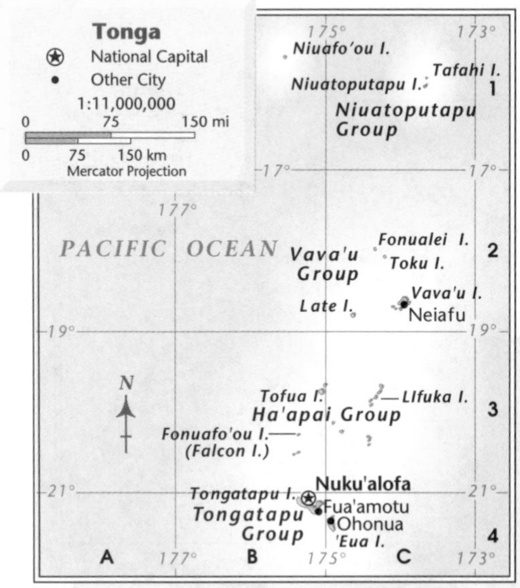

© MapQuest.com, Inc.

Tonga

Capital: Nuku'alofa
Area: 301 sq. mi.
780 sq. km.
Population: 109,000
Largest City: Nuku'alofa
Languages: Tongan, English
Monetary Unit: Pa'anga

Tonga: Map Index

Cities and Towns

Fua'amotu	B4
Neiafu	C2
Nuku'alofa, *capital*	B4
Ohonua	C4

Other Features

'Eua, *island*	C4
Fonuafo'ou (Falcon), *island*	B3
Fonualei, *island*	C2
Ha'apai, *island group*	B3
Late, *island*	C2
Lifuka, *island*	C3
Niuafo'ou, *island*	B1
Niuatoputapu, *island*	C1
Niuatoputapu, *island group*	C1
Tafahi, *island*	C1
Tofua, *island*	B3
Toku, *island*	C2
Tongatapu, *island*	B4
Tongatapu, *island group*	B4
Vava'u, *island*	C2
Vava'u, *island group*	C2

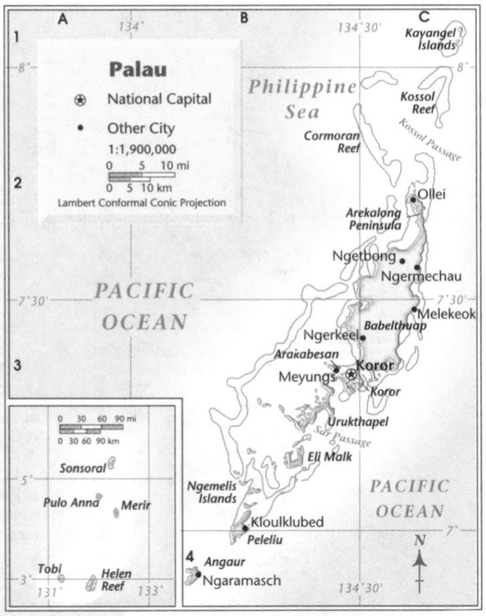

© MapQuest.com, Inc.

Palau: Map Index

Cities and Towns

Kloulklubed	B3
Koror, *capital*	B3
Melekeok	C3
Meyungs	B3
Ngaramasch	B4
Ngerkeel	B3
Ngermechau	C2
Ngetbong	C2
Ollei	C2

Other Features

Angaur, *island*	B4
Arakabesan, *island*	B3
Arekalong, *peninsula*	C2
Babelthuap, *island*	C3
Cormoran, *reef*	B2
Eli Malk, *island*	B3
Helen, *reef*	Inset
Kayangel, *islands*	C1
Koror, *island*	C3
Kossol, *passage*	C2
Kossol, *reef*	C2
Merir, *island*	Inset
Ngemelis, *islands*	B3
Peleliu, *island*	B4
Philippine, *sea*	B2
Pulo Anna, *island*	Inset
Sar, *passage*	B3
Sonsoral, *island*	Inset
Tobi, *island*	Inset
Urukthapel, *island*	B3

Palau

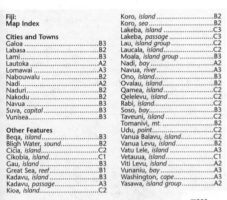

Capital: Koror
Area: 177 sq. mi.
458 sq. km.
Population: 18,000
Largest City: Koror
Languages: English, Sonsorolese, Angaur, Japanese, Tobi, Palauan
Monetary Unit: U.S. dollar

Vanuatu

Capital: Vila
Area: 4,707 sq. mi.
12,194 sq. km.
Population: 189,000
Largest City: Vila
Languages: French, English, Bislama
Monetary Unit: Vatu

Vanuatu:
Map Index

Cities and Towns
Anelghowhat C5
Isangel C4
Lakatoro B3
Lamap B3
Luganville C2
Marino C2
Potnarvin C4
Sola B1
Vila, *capital* C3

Other Features
Ambrym, *island* C3
Anatom, *island* C5
Aoba, *island* B2
Banks, *islands* B1
Coral, *sea* C3
Éfaté, *island* C3
Épi, *island* C3
Erromango, *island* C4
Espiritu Santo, *island* B2
Futuna, *island* C4
Homo, *bay* B2
Maéwo, *island* C2
Malakula, *island* B3
Pentecost, *island* C2
Santa Maria, *island* B2
Tabwemasana, *mt.* B2
Tanna, *island* C4
Torres, *islands* B1
Vanua Lava, *island* B1

Vanuatu

⊛ National Capital
• Other City
1:12,400,000
0   75   150 mi
0   75   150 km
Lambert Conformal Conic Projection

New Caledonia

★ Territorial Capital
• Other City
1:19,650,000
0   125   250 mi
0   125   250 km
Lambert Conformal Conic Projection

New
Caledonia:
Map Index

Cities and Towns
Bourail C2
Koné C2
Koumac C2
Nouméa, *capital* C2
Thio C2

Other Features
Astrolabe, *reefs* C2

Avon, *islands* A2
Bélep, *islands* C2
Chesterfield, *islands* A2
Coral, *sea* B2
D'Entrecasteaux, *reefs* C1
Huon, *islands* B1
Lifou, *island* D2
Loyalty, *islands* C2
Maré, *island* D2
New Caledonia, *island* C2
Ouvéa, *island* C2
Pines, *island* D2
Sandy, *island* B2

New Caledonia

Capital: Nouméa
Area: 8,548 sq. mi.
21,912 sq. km.
Population: 197,000
Largest City: Nouméa
Language: French
Monetary Unit: CFA Franc

Samoa

⊛ National Capital
• Other City
1:3,000,000
0   20   40 mi
0   20   40 km
Mercator Projection

Samoa

Capital: Apia
Area: 1,093 sq. mi.
2,832 sq. km.
Population: 230,000
Largest City: Apia
Languages: Samoan, English
Monetary Unit: Tala

Samoa:
Map Index

Cities and Towns
Apia, *capital* C2
Asau A2
Fagamalo B1
Falelatai B2
Falelima A2
Matautu C2
Poutasi C3
Pu'apu'a B2
Safotu B1
Sala'ilua A2
Salelologa B2

Solosolo C2
Taga A2
Ti'avea D2
Tuasivi B2

Other Features
Apolima, *island* B2
Apolima, *strait* B2
Manono, *island* B2
Nu'ulua, *island* D3
Nu'utele, *island* C3
Safata, *bay* C3
Savai'i, *island* A2
Silisili, *mt.* B2
Upolu, *island* C2

American Samoa

★ Territorial Capital
• Other City
1:1,429,000
0   10   20 mi
0   10   20 km
Conformal Conic Projection

American Samoa:
Map Index

Cities and Towns
Aoa C1
Aua C1
Fagasa B1
Fagatogo B1
Faleniu B1
Leone B1
Nuuuli B1
Pago Pago, *capital* B1
Pavaiai B2

Other Features
Aunuu, *island* C1
Ofu, *island* A1
Olosega, *island* A1
Pola, *island* C1
Rose, *island* B1
Swains, *island* A1
Tau, *island* A1
Tutuila, *island* A1, C2

American Samoa

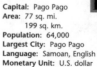

Capital: Pago Pago
Area: 77 sq. mi.
199 sq. km.
Population: 64,000
Largest City: Pago Pago
Language: Samoan, English
Monetary Unit: U.S. dollar

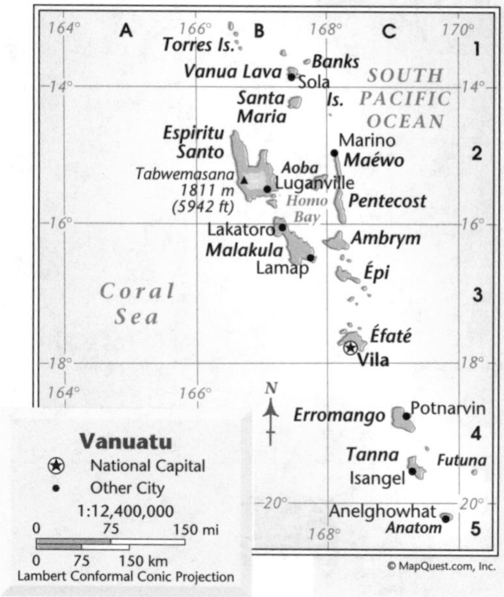

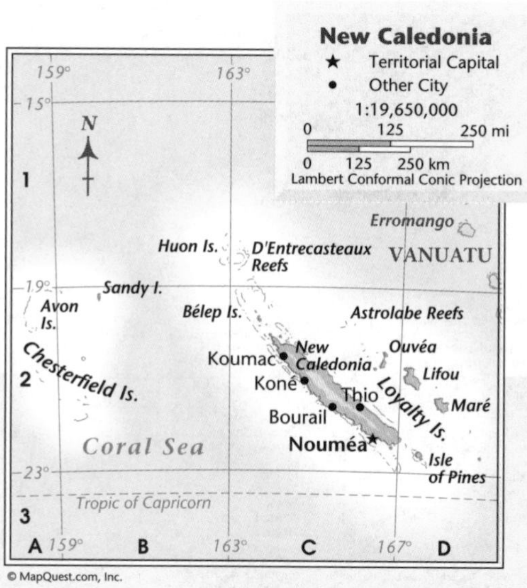

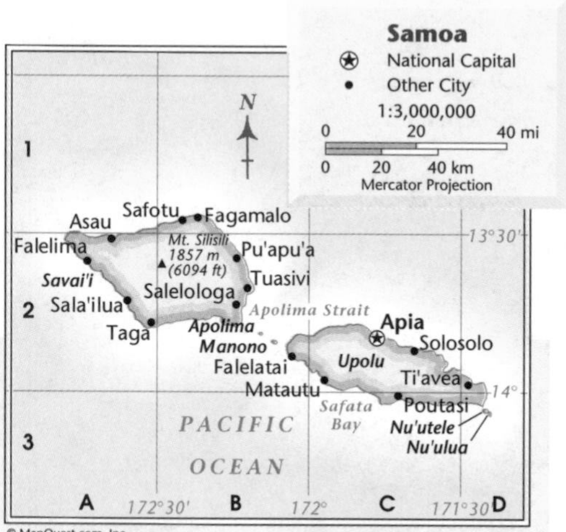

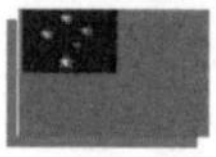

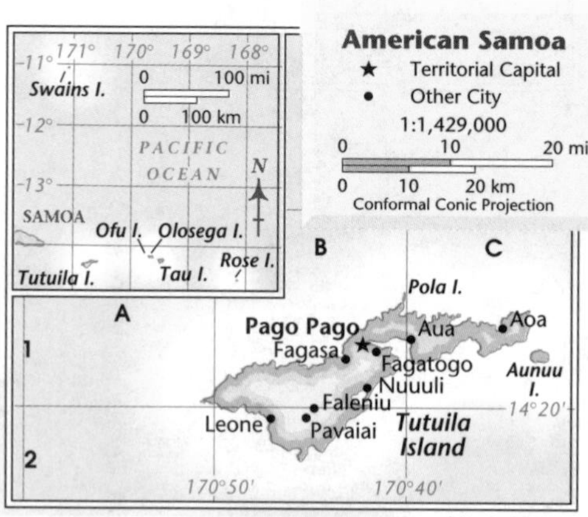

Nepal

★	National Capital
•	Other City

1:7,778,000

0   50   100 mi
0   50   100 km

Lambert Conformal Conic Projection

© MapQuest.com, Inc.

Maldives

Capital: Male
Area: 115 sq. mi.
  298 sq. km.
Population: 300,000
Largest City: Male
Language: Divehi
Monetary Unit: Rufiyaa

Nepal

Capital: Kathmandu
Area: 56,827 sq. mi.
  147,220 sq. km.
Population: 24,303,000
Largest City: Kathmandu
Language: Nepali
Monetary Unit: Rupee

Nepal: Map Index

Cities and Towns

Baglung	B2
Bhairahawa	B2
Bhaktapur	C2
Biratnagar	D3
Birendranagar	B2
Birganj	C2
Butwal	B2
Dandeldhura	A2
Dhangarhi	A2
Dhankuta	D2
Dharan	D3
Hetauda	C2
Ilam	D3
Janakpur	C3
Jumla	B2
Kathmandu, capital	C2
Lalitpur	C2
Mustang	B2
Nepalganj	B2
Pokhara	B2
Rajbiraj	C3
Silgarhi	B2
Simikot	B1
Sindhuli Garhi	C2
Tulsipur	B2

Other Features

Annapurna, mt.	B2
Api, mt.	A2
Arun, river	D2
Bagmati, river	C2
Bheri, river	B2
Churia, mts.	B2
Dhaulagiri, mt.	B2
Everest, mt.	C2
Himalayas, mts.	B2
Kali, river	B2
Kanchenjunga, mt.	D2
Karnali, river	B2
Kathmandu, valley	C2
Mahabharat, range	B2
Narayani, river	B2
Rapti, river	B2
Sarda, river	A2
Seti, river	A2
Sun Kosi, river	C2
Terai, region	A2, C3

Maldives: Map Index

City

Male, capital	A2

Other Features

Addu, atoll	A5
Ari, atoll	A3
Equatorial, channel	A5
Fadiffolu, atoll	A2
Felidu, atoll	A3
Haddummati, atoll	A4
Horsburgh, atoll	A2
Ihavandiffulu, atoll	A1
Kardiva, channel	A2
Kolumadulu, atoll	A3
Malcolm, atoll	A1
Male, atoll	A2
Miladummadulu, atoll	A1
Mulaku, atoll	A3
Nilandu, atoll	A3
North Malosmadulu, atoll	A2
One and Half Degree, channel	A4
South Male, atoll	A3
South Malosmadulu, atoll	A2
Suvadiva, atoll	A4
Tiladummati, atoll	A1
Veimandu, channel	A3

Maldives

★	National Capital

1:11,579,000

0   75   150 mi
0   75   150 km

Lambert Conformal Conic Projection

© MapQuest.com, Inc.

Sri Lanka: Map Index

Provinces

Central	B4
Eastern	C4
North Central	B3
Northern	B2
North Western	B4
Sabaragamuwa	B5
Southern	B5
Uva	C5
Western	A4

Cities and Towns

Amparai	C4
Anuradhapura	B3
Batticaloa	C4
Colombo, capital	A5
Dehiwala-Mt. Lavinia	A5
Galle	B5
Hambantota	C5
Jaffna	B2
Kalutara	A5
Kandy	B4
Kilinochchi	B2
Kotte	A5
Kurunegala	B4
Mankulam	B2
Mannar	A3
Matale	B4
Matara	B6
Moratuwa	A5
Mullaittivu	B2
Negombo	A4
Nuwara Eliya	B5
Point Pedro	B2
Polonnaruwa	C4
Pottuvil	C5
Puttalam	A3
Ratnapura	B5
Trincomalee	C3
Vavuniya	B3

Other Features

Adam's, peak	B4
Adam's Bridge, shoal	A3
Aruvi, river	B3
Bengal, bay	C3
Delft, island	A2
Dondra Head, cape	B6
Jaffna, lagoon	B2
Kalu, river	B5
Kelani, river	B4
Mahaweli Ganga, river	C4
Mannar, gulf	A3
Mannar, island	A2
Palk, strait	A2
Pidurutalagala, mt.	B4
Trincomalee, harbor	C3
Yan, river	B3

Sri Lanka

Capital: Colombo
Area: 25,332 sq. mi.
  65,627 sq. km.
Population: 19,145,000
Largest City: Colombo
Language: Sinhalese
Monetary Unit: Rupee

Sri Lanka

★	National Capital
•	Other City

1:6,400,000

0   40   80 km

Mercator Projection

© MapQuest.com, Inc.

Bhutan

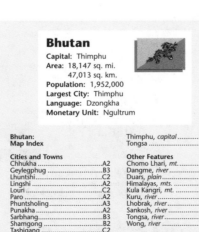

Capital: Thimphu
Area: 18,147 sq. mi.
  47,013 sq. km.
Population: 1,952,000
Largest City: Thimphu
Language: Dzongkha
Monetary Unit: Ngultrum

Bhutan: Map Index

Cities and Towns

Chhukha	A2
Geylegphug	B3
Lhuntshi	C2
Lingshi	A1
Louri	C2
Paro	A2
Phuntsholing	A3
Punakha	B2
Sarbhang	B3
Shamgong	B2
Tashigang	C2
Thimphu, capital	A2
Tongsa	B2

Other Features

Chomo Lhari, mt.	A1
Dangme, river	C2
Duars, plain	A3
Himalayas, mts.	B1
Kula Kangri, mt.	B1
Kuru, river	C2
Lhobrak, river	B2
Sankosh, river	B2
Tongsa, river	B2
Wong, river	A2

Bhutan

★	National Capital
•	Other City

1:6,053,000

0   25   50   75 mi
0   25   50   75 km

Lambert Conformal Conic Projection

© MapQuest.com, Inc.

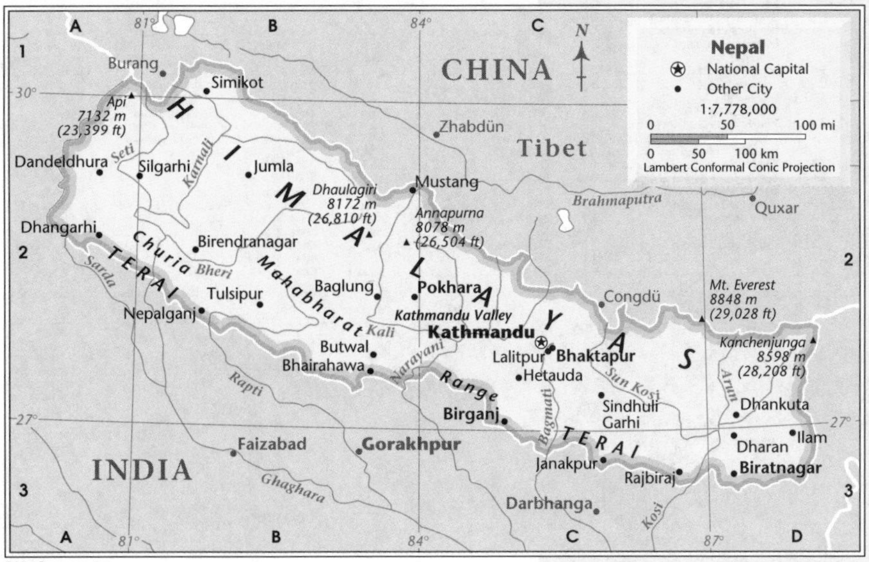

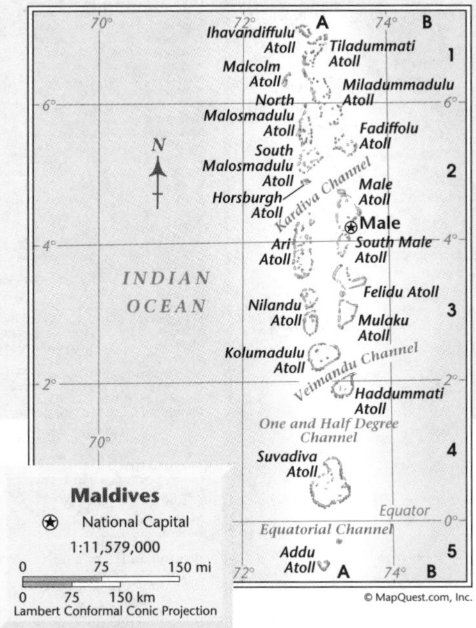

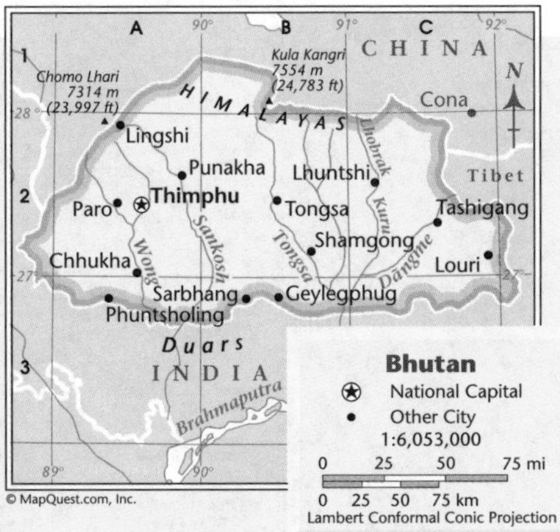

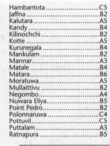

India:
Map Index

Internal Divisions

Andaman and Nicobar Islands (territory) F6
Andhra Pradesh (state) C5
Arunachal Pradesh (state) F3
Assam (state) F3
Bihar (state) E4
Chandigarh (territory) C2
Dadra and Nagar Haveli (territory) B4
Daman and Diu (territory) B4
Delhi (territory) C3
Goa (state) B5
Gujarat (state) B4
Haryana (state) C3
Himachal Pradesh (state) C2
Jammu and Kashmir (state) C2
Karnataka (state) C6
Kerala (state) C6
Lakshadweep (territory) B6
Madhya Pradesh (state) C4
Maharashtra (state) B5
Manipur (state) F4
Meghalaya (state) F3
Mizoram (state) F4
Nagaland (state) F3
Orissa (state) D4
Pondicherry (territory) C6
Punjab (state) C2
Rajasthan (state) B3
Sikkim (state) E3
Tamil Nadu (state) C6
Tripura (state) F4
Uttar Pradesh (state) C3
West Bengal (state) E4

Cities and Towns

Agartala F4
Agra C3
Ahmadabad B4
Aizawl F4
Ajmer B3
Akola C4
Alampur Inset II
Aligarh C3
Allahabad D3
Alleppey (Alappuzha) C7
Amdanga Inset II
Amravati C4
Amritsar B2
Andheri Inset I
Ara D3
Asansol E4
Aurangabad C5
Babu Bheri Inset II
Baidyabati Inset II
Bally Inset II
Bamangachi Inset II
Banana F7
Bandra Inset I
Bangalore C6
Bansbaria Inset II
Barakpur Inset II
Baranagar Inset II
Barasat Inset II
Bareilly C3
Bargachia Inset II
Bauria Inset II
Behala Inset II
Belapurpada Inset I
Belgaum B5
Bellary C5
Bhadrakh E4
Bhadreswar Inset II
Bhagalpur E3
Bhamapur D5
Bhandup Inset I
Bharatpur C3
Bhatapara D4
Bhatpara Inset II
Bhavnagar B4
Bhayandar Inset I
Bhimpur Inset II
Bhiwandi Inset I
Bhopal C4
Bhubaneswar E4
Bhuj A4
Bihar E3
Bijapur C5
Bikaner B3
Bilaspur D4
Bishnupur Inset II
Borivli Inset I
Buj-Buj Inset II
Burdwan E4
Burhanpur C4
Calcutta E4, Inset II
Chandannagar Inset II
Chandigarh C2
Chandrapur C5
Chembur Inset I
Chene Inset I
Chennai (Madras) D6
Cherrapunji F3
Chirner Inset I
Cochin (Kochi) C7
Coimbatore C6
Cuddalore C6
Cuttack E4
Daman B4
Darbhanga E3
Darjiling E3
Dehra Dun C2
Delhi C3
Dhulagarh Inset II
Dibrugarh F3
Dispur F3
Diu B4
Dum-Dum Inset II
Dumjor Inset II
Faizabad D3
Gandhinagar B4
Ganganagar B3
Gangtok E3
Garden Reach Inset II
Garulia Inset II
Gauhati F3
Gaya E4
Ghatkopar Inset I
Gorakhpur D3
Gulbarga C5
Guntur C5
Gwalior C3
Halisahar Inset II
Haora E4, Inset II
Hisabpur Inset II
Hubli-Dharwar C5
Hugli-Chunchura Inset II
Hyderabad C5
Imphal F4
Indore C4
Itanagar F3
Jabalpur C4
Jadabpur Inset II
Jagdalpur D5
Jaipur C3
Jammu B2
Jamnagar B4
Jampur Inset II
Jamshedpur E4
Janai Inset II
Jejur Inset II
Jhansi C3
Jodhpur B3
Joka Inset II
Jullundur C2
Junagadh B4
Kakinada D5
Kalwa Inset I
Kaman Inset I
Kamarhati Inset II
Kanchipuram C6
Kanchrapara Inset II
Kanpur D3
Kansaripara Inset II
Kasinathpur Inset II
Kathgodam C3
Kharagpur E4
Kohima F3
Kolhapur B5
Kolshet Inset I
Konnagar Inset II
Kota C3
Kozhikode C6
Kurla Inset I
Kurnool C5
Lakhpat A4
Lucknow D3
Ludhiana C2
Madurai C7
Malad Inset I
Malegaon B4
Mangalore B6
Mathura C3
Meerut C3
Moradabad C3
Mulund Inset I
Mumbai (Bombay) B5, Inset I
Mumbra Inset I
Mysore C6
Nagpur C4
Naihati Inset II
Nalikul Inset II
Nanded C5
Nangi Inset II
Nanole Inset I
Nasik B4
Nellore C6
New Delhi, *capital* C3
Nizamabad C5
Ongole C5
Panaji B5
Panihati Inset II
Patiala C2
Patna E3
Paye Inset I
Polba Inset II
Pondicherry C6
Port Blair F6
Pune B5
Raipur D4
Rajkot B4
Rajpur Inset II
Ramanbati Inset II
Ranchi E4
Raurkela D4
Rishra Inset II
Saharanpur Panipat C3
Salem C6
Sambalpur D4
Sankrail Inset II
Sasaram D4
Sheva Inset I
Shillong F3
Sholapur C5
Shrirampur Inset II
Silvassi B4
Simla C2
Singur Inset II
Sonarpur Inset II
South Dum-Dum Inset II
Srinagar B2
Sugandha Inset II
Surat B4
Thane Inset I
Thanjavur C6
Tiruchchirappalli C6
Titagarh Inset II
Trivandrum (Thiruvananthapuram) C7
Trombay Inset I
Tuticorin C7
Udaipur B4

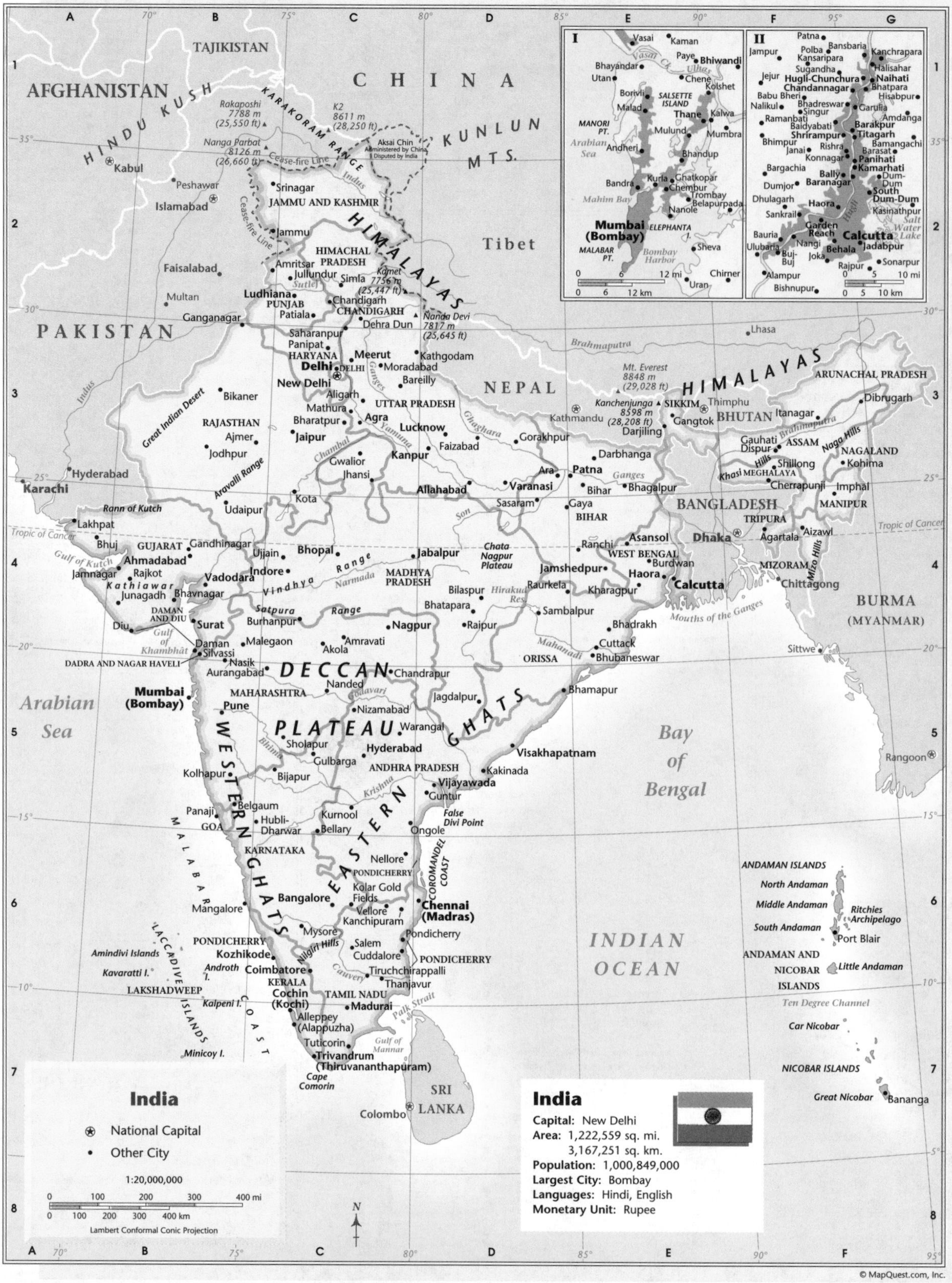

Bangladesh

* ⊛ National Capital
* • Other City

1:7,491,000

0   50   100 mi
0   50   100 km
Azimuthal Equal Area Projection

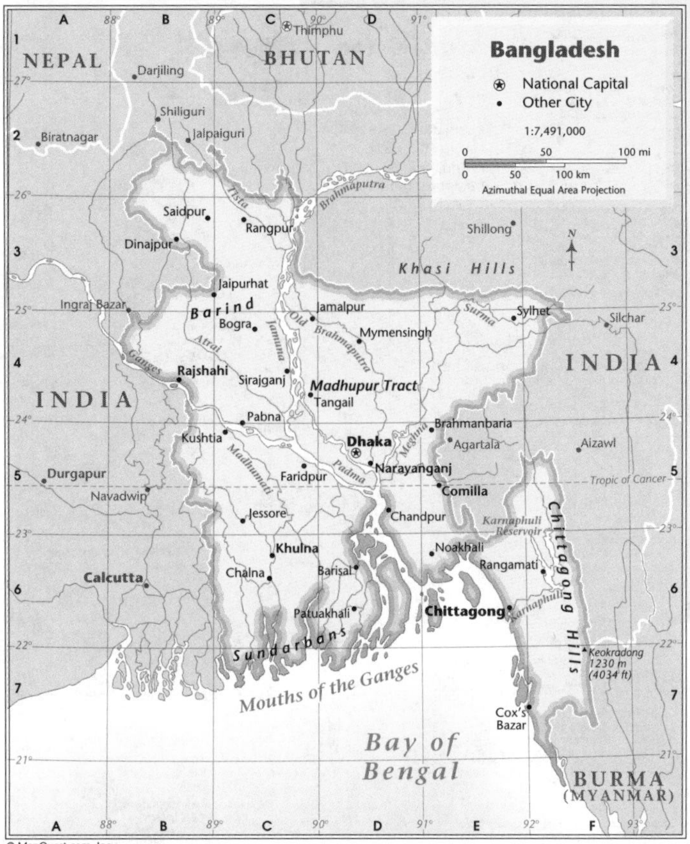

© MapQuest.com, Inc.

Bangladesh

Capital: Dhaka
Area: 57,295 sq. mi.
148,433 sq. km.
Population: 127,118,000
Largest City: Dhaka
Language: Bengali
Monetary Unit: Taka

Bangladesh: Map Index

Cities and Towns

Barisal	D6
Bogra	C4
Brahmanbaria	E5
Chalna	C6
Chandpur	D5
Chittagong	E6
Comilla	E5
Cox's Bazar	E7
Dhaka, *capital*	D5
Dinajpur	B3
Faridpur	C5
Jaipurhat	B3
Jamalpur	C4
Jessore	C5
Khulna	C6
Kushtia	C5
Mymensingh	D4
Narayanganj	D5
Noakhali	E6
Pabna	C4
Patuakhali	D6
Rajshahi	B4
Rangamati	F6
Rangpur	C3
Saidpur	B3
Sirajganj	C4
Sylhet	E4
Tangail	C4

Other Features

Atrai, *river*	B4
Barind, *region*	B4
Bengal, *bay*	D7
Brahmaputra, *river*	D3
Chittagong Hills, *region*	F5
Ganges, *river*	B4
Jamuna, *river*	C4
Karnaphuli, *reservoir*	F6
Karnaphuli, *river*	E6
Keokradong, *mt.*	F7
Madhumati, *river*	C5
Madhupur Tract, *region*	D4
Meghna, *river*	D5
Mouths of the Ganges, *delta*	C7
Old Brahmaputra, *river*	C4
Padma, *river*	D5
Sundarbans, *region*	C7
Surma, *river*	E3
Tista, *river*	C2

India: Map Index

Ujjain	C4
Ulubaria	Inset II
Uran	Inset I
Utan	Inset I
Vadodara	B4
Varanasi	D3
Vasai	Inset I
Vellore	C6
Vijayawada	D5
Visakhapatnam	D5
Warangal	C5

Other Features

Amindivi, *islands*	B6
Andaman, *islands*	F6
Androth, *island*	B6
Arabian, *sea*	A5, Inset I
Aravalli, *range*	B3
Bengal, *bay*	E5
Bhima, *river*	C5
Brahmaputra, *river*	F3
Car Nicobar, *island*	F7
Cauvery, *river*	C6
Chambal, *river*	C4
Chata Nagpur, *plateau*	D4
Comorin, *cape*	C7
Coromandel, *coast*	D6
Deccan, *plateau*	C5
Eastern Ghats, *mts.*	C6
Elephanta, *island*	Inset I
False Divi, *point*	D5
Ganges, *river*	E3
Ghaghara, *river*	D3
Godavari, *river*	C5
Great Indian, *desert*	B3
Great Nicobar, *island*	F7
Himalayas, *mts.*	C2, E3
Hirakud, *reservoir*	D4
Hugli, *river*	Inset II
Indus, *river*	C2
Kalpeni, *island*	B7
Kamet, *mt.*	C2
Kanchenjunga, *mt.*	E3
Karakoram, *range*	C1
Kathiawar, *peninsula*	B4
Kavaratti, *island*	B6
Khambhat, *gulf*	B4
Khasi, *hills*	F3
Kolar, *gold fields*	C6
Krishna, *river*	C5
Kutch, *gulf*	A4
Laccadive, *islands*	B6
Little Andaman, *island*	F6
Mahanadi, *river*	D4
Mahim, *bay*	Inset I
Malabar, *coast*	B6
Malabar, *point*	Inset I
Mannar, *gulf*	C7
Manori, *point*	Inset I
Middle Andaman, *island*	F6
Minicoy, *island*	B7
Mizo, *hills*	F4
Mouths of the Ganges, *delta*	E4
Mumbai, *harbor*	Inset I
Naga, *hills*	F3
Nanda Devi, *mt.*	C2
Narmada, *river*	C4
Nicobar, *islands*	F7
Nilgiri, *hills*	C6
North Andaman, *island*	F6
Palk, *strait*	C7
Rann of Kutch, *mud flat*	B4
Ritchies, *archipelago*	F6
Salsette, *island*	Inset I
Salt Water, *lake*	Inset II
Satpura, *range*	C4
Son, *river*	D4
South Andaman, *island*	F6
Sutlej, *river*	C2
Ten Degree, *channel*	F7
Ulhas, *river*	Inset I
Vasai, *creek*	Inset I
Vindhya, *range*	C4
Western Ghats, *mts.*	B5
Yamuna, *river*	C3

Pakistan

Capital: Islamabad
Area: 339,697 sq. mi.
880,044 sq. km.
Population: 138,123,000
Largest City: Karachi
Languages: Urdu, English
Monetary Unit: Pakistani rupee

Pakistan: Map Index

Internal Divisions

Azad Kashmir Province	D2
Baluchistan Province	B4
Federally Administrated Tribal Areas	C3
Islamabad Capital Territory	D3
Northern Areas	D2
North-West Frontier Province	D2
Punjab Province	D3
Sind Province	C5

Cities and Towns

Bahawalpur	D4
Bela	C4
Chiniot	D3
Chitral	D2
Dadu	C4
Dera Ghazi Khan	D3
Dera Ismail Khan	D3
Faisalabad	D3
Gilgit	E2
Gujranwala	E3
Gujrat	E3
Gwadar	B5
Hyderabad	C5
Islamabad, *capital*	D3
Jhang Sadar	D3
Jhelum	D3
Karachi	C5
Kasur	E3
Khuzdar	C4
Lahore	E3
Larkana	C4
Mardan	D2
Mianwali	D3
Mirpur Khas	C5
Multan	D3
Muzaffarabad	D2
Nawabshah	C4
Nok Kundi	B4

Okara	D3
Panjgur	B4
Peshawar	D3
Quetta	C3
Rahimyar Khan	D4
Rawalpindi	D3
Sahiwal	D3
Sargodha	D3
Shikarpur	C4
Sialkot	E3
Sukkur	C4
Surab	C4

Other Features

Arabian, *sea*	B6
Central Makran, *range*	B4
Chagai, *hills*	B4
Chenab, *river*	D3
Hindu Kush, *mts.*	D2
Indus, *river*	C4, E2
Jhelum, *river*	D3
Karakoram, *range*	E2
Khojak, *pass*	C3
Khyber, *pass*	D2
Kirthar, *range*	C4
Konar, *river*	D2
K2 (Godwin Austen), *mt.*	E2
Makran Coast, *range*	B5
Mouths of the Indus, *delta*	C5
Nal, *river*	C4
Nanga Parbat, *mt.*	E2
Nara, *canal*	C4
Nowshak, *mt.*	D2
Rakaposhi, *mt.*	E2
Ravi, *river*	D3
Safed Koh, *range*	D3
Siahan, *range*	B4
Sulaiman, *range*	D3
Sutlej, *river*	D4
Thar, *desert*	D4
Tirich Mir, *mt.*	D2
Toba Kakar, *range*	C3
Zhob, *river*	C3

Pakistan

* ⊛ National Capital
* • Other City

1:19,538,000

0   150   300 mi
0   150   300 km
Lambert Conformal Conic Projection

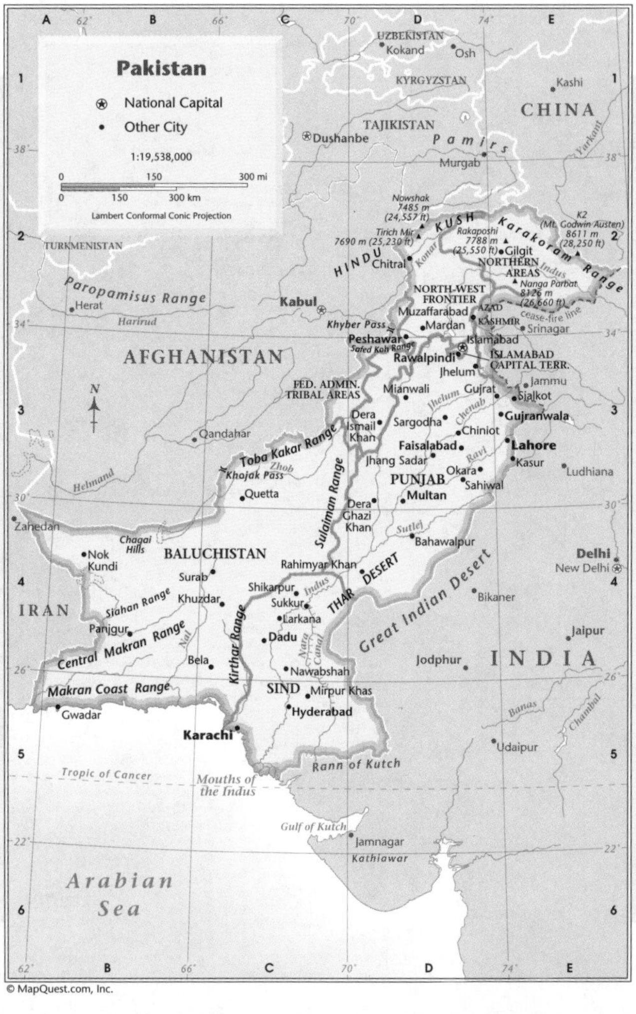

© MapQuest.com, Inc.

Afghanistan: Map Index

Cities and Towns

Asadabad	C2
Baghlan	B1
Balkh	B1
Bamian	B2
Baraki Barak	B2
Chaghcharan	B2
Charikar	B1
Farah	A2
Feyzabad	C1
Gardez	B2
Ghazni	B2
Herat	A2
Jalalabad	B2
Kabul, capital.	B2
Khowst	B2
Konduz	B1

Kowt-e Ashrow	B2
Lashkar Gah	A2
Mazar-e Sharif	B1
Meymaneh	B1
Qalat	A2
Qaleh-ye Now	A2
Qandahar	A2
Samangan	B1
Sar-e Pol	B1
Sheberghan	B1
Shindand	A2
Taloqan	B1
Tarin Kowt	B2
Zaranj	A2
Zareh Sharan	B2

Other Features

Amu Darya, river	B1
Arghandab, river	B2
Farah, river	A2
Fuladi, mt.	B2
Gowd-e Zereh, lake	A3
Hamun-e Saberi, lake	A2
Harirud, river	A2
Helmand, river	A2
Hindu Kush, range	B1
Kabul, river	B2
Khojak, pass	B2
Khyber, pass	C2
Konar, river	C1
Konduz, river	B1
Morghab, river	A1
Nowshak, mt.	C1
Panj, river	C1
Paropamisus, range	A2
Registan, region	A2
Shibar, pass	B2
Vakhan, region	C1

Afghanistan

Capital: Kabul
Area: 251,825 sq. mi.
  652,396 sq. km.
Population: 25,825,000
Largest City: Kabul
Languages: Pashto, Dari Persian
Monetary Unit: Afghani

Afghanistan
⊛ National Capital
• Other City
1:10,870,000
0 50 100 150 mi
0 50 100 150 km
Lambert Conformal Conic Projection

Iran

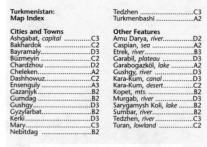

Capital: Tehran
Area: 632,457 sq. mi.
  1,638,490 sq. km.
Population: 65,180,000
Largest City: Tehran
Languages: Persian, Turkic, Luri, Kurdish
Monetary Unit: Rial

Iran: Map Index

Cities and Towns

Abadan	B3
Ahvaz	B3
Arak	B3
Ardabil	B2
Bakhtaran	B3
Bam	D4
Bandar Beheshti	E4
Bandar-e Abbas	D4
Bandar-e Anzali	B2
Bandar-e Bushehr	C4
Bandar-e Khomeyni	B3
Bandar-e Torkeman	C2
Birjand	D3
Dezful	B3

Esfahan	C3
Hamadan	B3
Ilam	B3
Iranshahr	E4
Jask	D4
Karaj	C2
Kashan	C3
Kerman	D3
Khorramabad	B3
Khorramshahr	B3
Khvoy	A2
Mashhad	D2
Neyshabur	D2
Orumiyeh (Urmia)	A2
Qazvin	B2
Qom	C3
Rasht	B2
Sabzevar	D2
Sanandaj	B2
Sari	C2
Shahr-e Kord	C3
Shiraz	C4
Sirjan	D4
Tabriz	B2
Tehran, capital	C2
Yasuj	C3
Yazd	C3
Zabol	E3
Zahedan	E4
Zanjan	B2

Other Features

Aras, river	B2

Atrak, river	D2
Azerbaijan, region	B2
Bakhtiari, region	B3
Baluchistan, region	E4
Caspian, sea	C2
Damavand, mt.	C2
Dasht-e Kavir, desert	D3
Dasht-e Lut, desert	D3
Elburz, mts.	C2
Halil, river	D4
Hamun-e Jaz Murian, lake	D4
Hashtadan, region	E3
Hormuz, strait	D4
Karun, river	B3
Kavir-e Namak, desert	D3
Kerman, region	D4
Kharg, island	C4
Khorasan, region	D2
Khuzestan, region	B3
Kopet, mts.	D2
Kul, river	D4
Larestan, region	D4
Mand, river	C4
Mazandaran, region	C2
Oman, gulf	D5
Persian, gulf	C4
Qareh, river	B3
Qeshm, island	D4
Shatt al-Arab, river	B3
Urmia, lake	B2
Yazd, region	C3
Zagros, mts.	B3

Iran
⊛ National Capital
• Other City
1:20,571,000
0 150 300 mi
0 150 300 km
Lambert Conformal Conic Projection

Turkmenistan: Map Index

Cities and Towns

Ashgabat, capital	C3
Bakhardok	C2
Bayramaly	D3
Büzmeyin	C2
Chardzhou	D2
Cheleken	A2
Dashhowuz	C1
Ensenguly	A3
Gazanjyk	B2
Gumdag	B2
Gushgy	D3
Gyzylarbat	B2
Kerki	D3
Mary	C3
Nebitdag	B2

Tedzhen	C3
Turkmenbashi	A2

Other Features

Amu Darya, river	D2
Caspian, sea	B3
Etrek, river	B3
Garabil, plateau	D3
Garabogazköl, lake	A2
Gushgy, river	D3
Kara-Kum, canal	D3
Kara-Kum, desert	C2
Kopet, mts.	B2
Murgab, river	D3
Sarygamysh Koli, lake	B2
Sumbar, river	B2
Tedzhen, river	C3
Turan, lowland	C2

Turkmenistan

Capital: Ashgabat
Area: 188,417 sq. mi.
  488,127 sq. km.
Population: 4,366,000
Largest City: Ashgabat
Languages: Turkmen, Russian, Uzbek
Monetary Unit: Manat

Turkmenistan
⊛ National Capital
• Other City
1:16,929,000
0 100 200 mi
0 100 200 km
Lambert Conformal Conic Projection

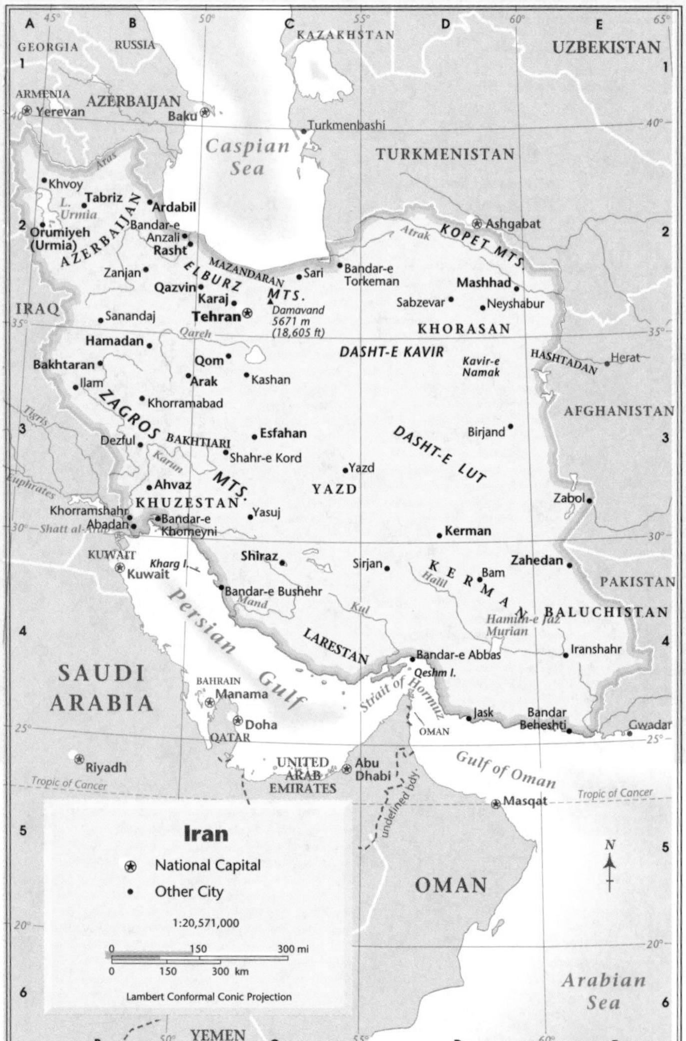

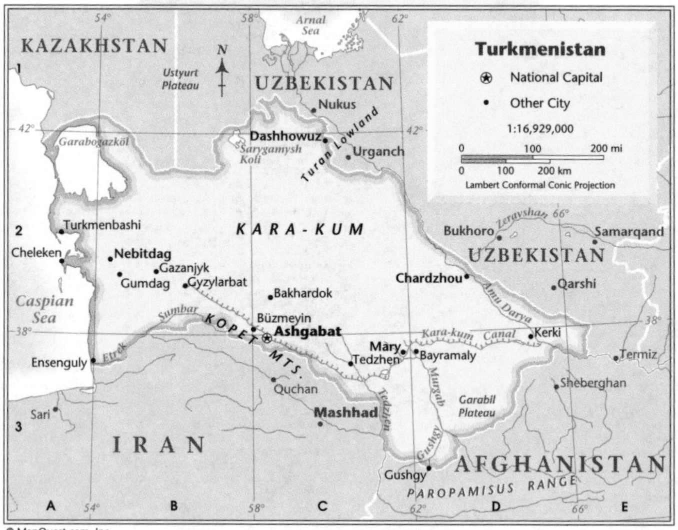

Kazakhstan Map Index

Beyneu B2
Ekibastuz D1
Embi B2
Esil C1
Kokshetau C1
Leneinsk C2
Lepsi D2
Oral B1
Öskemen
  (Ust-Kamenogorsk) E1
Pavlodar D1
Petropavl C1
Qaraghandy (Karaganda) ..D2
Qostanay C1
Qyzylorda C2
Rudnyy C1
Saryshaghan D2
Semey (Semipalatinsk) ...E1
Shalqar B2
Shymkent (Chimkent) C2
Taldyqorghan D2
Temirtau D1
Zaysan E2
Zhambyl (Dzhambul) ...D2
Zhezqazgham C2

Other Features
Alakol, lake E2
Aral, sea B2
Balkhash, lake D2
Betpak Dala, plain C2
Caspian, depression ...B2
Caspian, sea A2
Ili, river D2
Irtysh, river D1
Ishim, river C1
Kazakh Upland region ...C1
Khan-Tengri, mt. E2
Muyun Kum, desert ...D2
Syrdarya, river C2
Tengiz, lake C2
Tobol, river C1
Torghay, plateau C1
Ural, river B2
Ustyurt, plateau B2
Zaysan, lake E2

Kazakhstan
Capital: Astana
Area: 1,049,200 sq. mi.
  2,718,135 sq. km.
Population: 16,825,000
Largest City: Almaty
Language: Kazakh
Monetary Unit: Tenge

Kazakhstan: Map Index

Cities and Towns
Astana (Aqmola), capital D1
Almaty (Alma-Ata) D2
Aqtau B2
Aqtobe B1
Aral C2
Arqalyq.....................C1
Atbasar C1
Atyrau B2
Ayagöz E2
Balkhash D2

© MapQuest.com, Inc.

Kazakhstan
⊛ National Capital
• Other City
1:26,667,000
0 — 125 — 250 mi
0 — 125 — 250 km
Lambert Conformal Conic Projection

Uzbekistan
⊛ National Capital
• Other City
1:14,725,000
0 — 40 — 80 mi
0 — 40 — 80 km
Lambert Conformal Conic Projection

© MapQuest.com, Inc.

Uzbekistan
Capital: Tashkent
Area: 172,700 sq. mi.
  447,409 sq. km.
Population: 24,102,000
Largest City: Tashkent
Languages: Uzbek, Russian
Monetary Unit: Ruble

Uzbekistan: Map Index

Cities and Towns
Andizhan D2
Bukhara B3
Farghona D2
Gulistan C2
Jizzakh C2
Khujayli A2
Muynoq A2
Namangan D2
Nawoiy C2
Nukus A2
Olmaliq C2
Qarshi C3
Qunghirot A2
Quqon D2
Samarqand C3
Tashkent, capital C2
Termiz C3
Uchquduq B2
Urganch B2
Zarafshon B2

Other Features
Amu Darya, river B2
Aral, sea A2
Chirchiq, river C2
Fergana, valley D2
Kyzylkum, desert B2
Syrdarya, river C2
Turan, lowland A2
Ustyurt, plateau A2
Zeravshan, river B2

Kyrgyzstan Map Index

Cities and Towns
At-Bashy D2
Balykchy E1
Bishkek, capital D1
Cholpon-Ata E1
Jalal-Abad D2
Jangy-Bazar B2
Karakol F1
Kara-Say F2
Kyzyl-Kyya D2
Naryn E2
Osh C2
Özgön C2
Sary Tash C3
Songköl D2
Sülüktü A3
Talas C1
Tash Kömür C2

Tokmok D1
Toktogul C2

Other Features
Alay, mts. C3
Chatkal, river B2
Chu, river D1
Jengish Chokusu, mt. G1
Kyzyl-Suu, river C3
Naryn, river E2
Tien Shan, mts. E2
Toxkan, river E2
Ysyk-Köl, lake E1

Kyrgyzstan
Capital: Bishkek
Area: 76,642 sq. mi.
  198,554 sq. km.
Population: 4,546,000
Largest City: Bishkek
Language: Kirghiz
Monetary Unit: Som

© MapQuest.com, Inc.

Kyrgyzstan
⊛ National Capital
• Other City
1:14,286,000
0 — 75 — 150 mi
0 — 75 — 150 km
Lambert Conformal Conic Projection

Tajikistan
Capital: Dushanbe
Area: 55,300 sq. mi.
  143,264 sq. km.
Population: 6,103,000
Largest City: Dushanbe
Language: Tajik
Monetary Unit: Ruble

Tajikistan: Map Index

Cities and Towns
Dangara A1
Dushanbe, capital A1
Jirgatol B1
Kalai Khum B1
Kansay B2
Khorugh B2
Khudzhand A1
Konibodom A2
Kulob A2
Morghob B1
Navabad A2
Norak A2
Panj A2
Panjakent A2
Qurghonteppa A2
Tursunzoda A1
Uroteppa A1
Zarafobod A1

Other Features
Alay, mts. B1
Bartang, river B1

Communisim, mt. B1
Darya, river A2
Kofarnihon, river A2
Morghob, river B1
Oqsu, river C2

Pamirs, mts. B2
Panj, river B2
Pyandzh, river A2
Qarokul, lake B1
Surkhob, river B1

Syrdarya, river A1, B1
Turkeston, mts. A1
Vahsh, river A1
Zeravshan, mts. A1
Zeravshan, river A1

Tajikistan
⊛ National Capital
• Other City
1:7,622,000
0 — 40 — 80 mi
0 — 40 — 80 km
Lambert Conformal Conic Projection

© MapQuest.com, Inc.

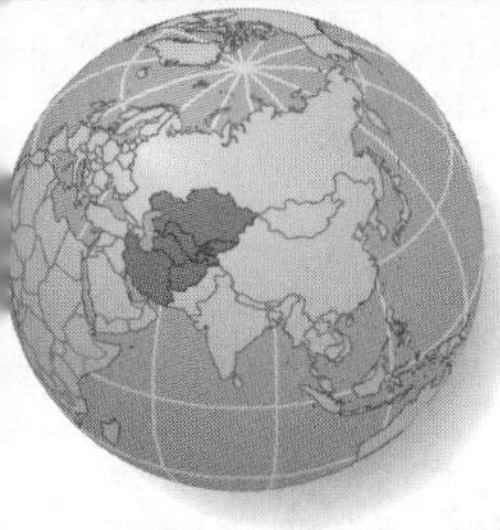

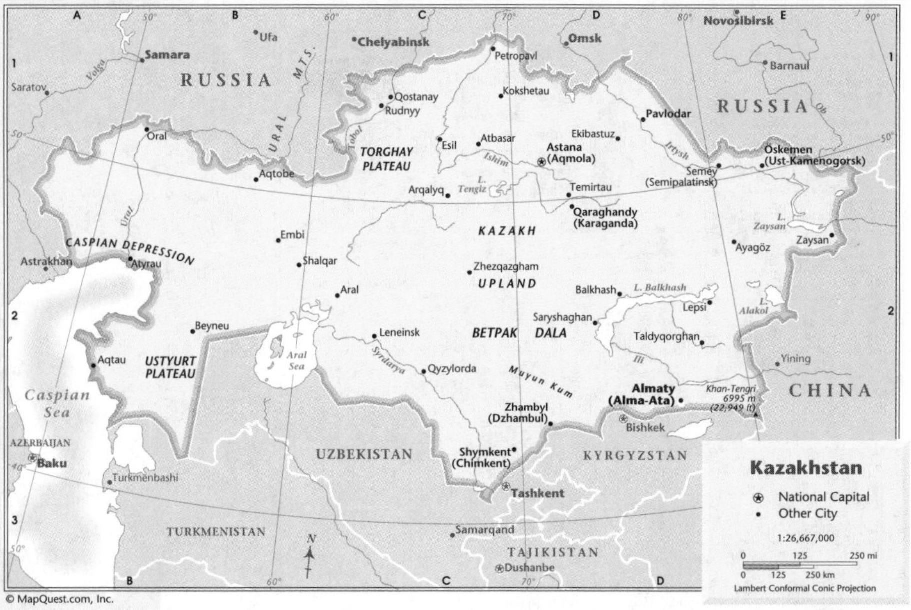

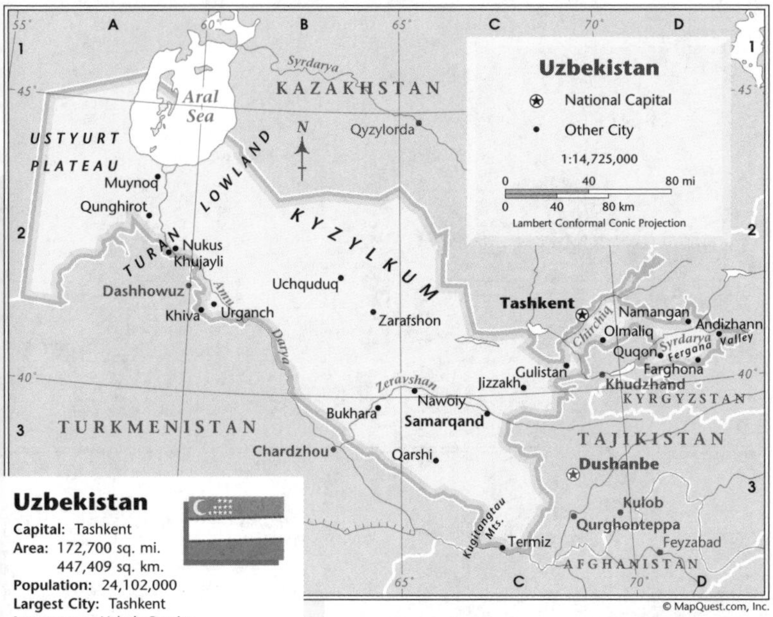

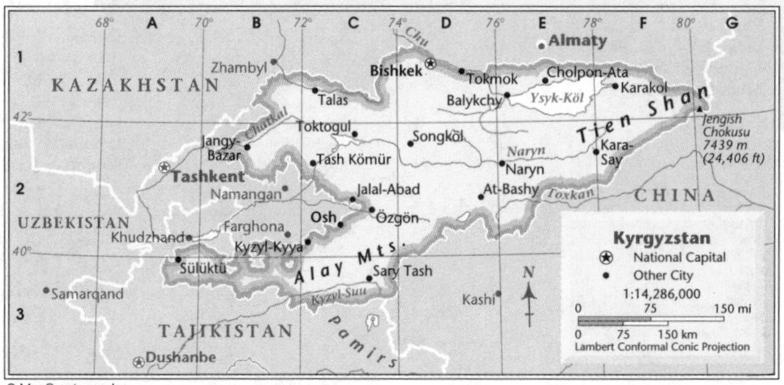

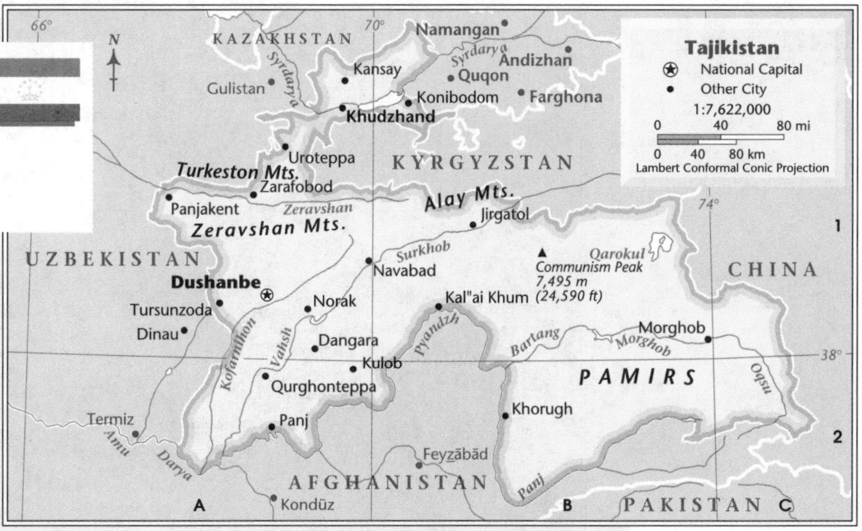

Iraq:
Map Index

Cities and Towns
Amarah, al-........................C2
Baghdad, *capital*...............B2
Baqubah B2
Basra C2
Dahuk...............................B1
Diwaniyah, ad- C2
Fallujah, al- B2
Hadithah, al- B2
Hillah, al- B2
Irbil B1
Karbala B2
Khanaqin C2
Kirkuk B1
Kut, al- C2
Mosul B1
Najaf, an- B2
Nasiriyah, an- C2
Qayyarah, al- B1
Ramadi, ar- B2
Rutbah, ar- B2
Samarra B2
Samawah, as- C2
Sulaymaniyah, as-..............C1
Tall Afar.............................B1
Tikrit B2
Umm Qasr C2

Other Features
Babylon, *ruins* B2
Diyala, *river*.......................C2
Euphrates, *river*..................C2
Great Zab, *river*..................B1
Haji Ibrahim, *mt.*.................B1
Little Zab, *river* B1
Mesopotamia, *region*..........B2
Milh, *lake* B2
Persian, *gulf* C3
Shatt al-Arab, *river* C2
Syrian, *desert*.....................B2
Tigris, *river* B1

Iraq

Capital: Baghdad
Area: 167,975 sq. mi.
435,169 sq. km.
Population: 22,427,000
Largest City: Baghdad
Language: Arabic
Monetary Unit: Dinar

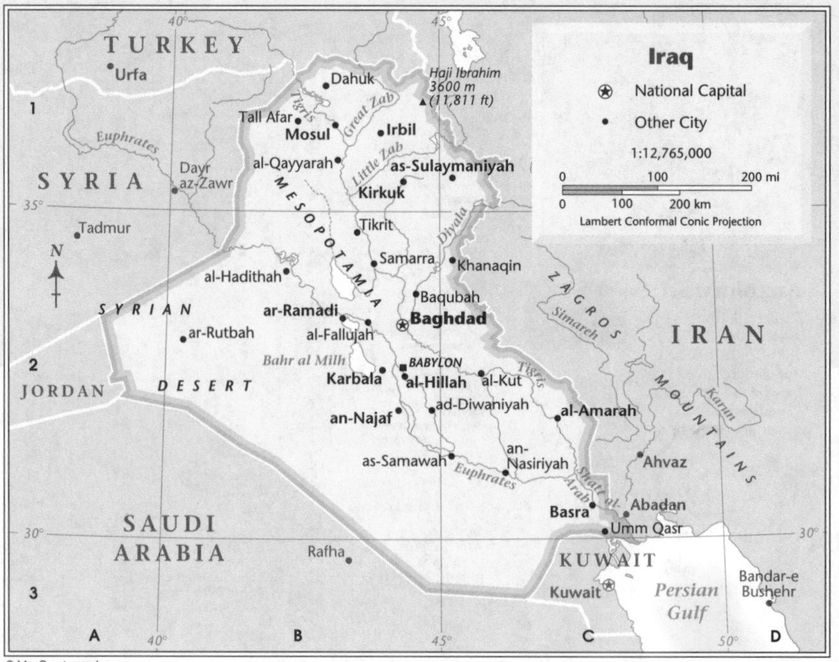

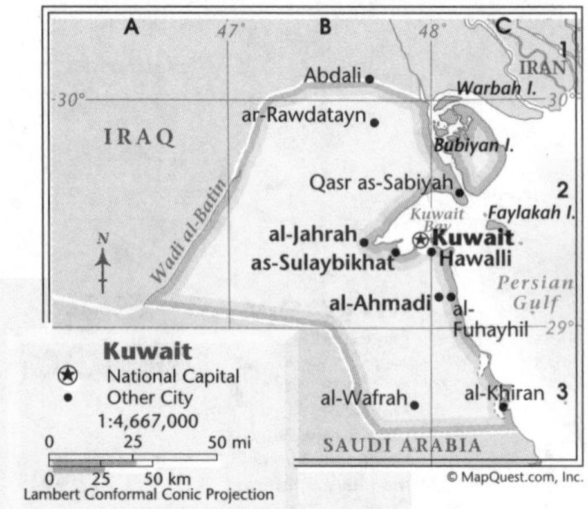

Kuwait

Capital: Kuwait
Area: 6,880 sq. mi.
17,924 sq. km.
Population: 1,991,000
Largest City: Kuwait
Language: Arabic
Monetary Unit: Dinar

Kuwait:
Map Index

Cities and Towns
Abdali B1
Ahmadi, al-........................C2
Fuhayhil, al- C2
Hawalli C2
Jahrah, al- B2
Khiran, al-..........................C3
Kuwait, *capital* B2
Qasr as-Sabiyah C2
Rawdatayn, ar- B2
Sulaybikhat, as-.................B2
Wafrah, al- B3

Other Features
Bubiyan, *island* C2
Faylakah, *island*.................C2
Kuwait, *bay*.......................B2
Persian, *gulf* C2
Wadi al-Batin, *river* A2
Warbah, *island* C1

Saudi Arabia

Capital: Riyadh
Area: 865,000 sq. mi.
2,240,933 sq. km.
Population: 21,505,000
Largest City: Riyadh
Language: Arabic
Monetary Unit: Riyal

Saudi Arabia:
Map Index

Cities and Towns
Abha B2
Badanah B1
Buqayq C1
Buraydah B1
Dammam, ad- C1
Dhahran C1
Hail B1
Harad C1
Hillah, al- B2
Hufuf, al- C1
Jawf, al-.............................A1
Jiddah A2
Jizan B2
Jubayl, al- C1
Khamis Mushayt B2
Kharj, al- B1
Mecca A2
Medina A1
Najran B2
Qalat Bishah B2
Qunfudhah, al- B2
Rafha.................................B1
Ras al-Khafji.......................C1
Ras Tanura.........................C1
Riyadh, *capital*..................B1
Sulayyil, as- B2
Tabuk A1
Taif, at- B2
Turayf A1
Unayzah B1
Wajh, al- A1
Yanbu al-Bahr.....................A1

Other Features
Asir, *region* B2
Dahna, ad-, *desert*..............B1
Farasan, *islands* B2
Hasa, al-, *region* C1
Hijaz, al-, *region* A1
Jabal Tuwayq, *mts.*.............B2
Nafud, an-, *desert*...............B1
Najd, *region* B1
Persian, *gulf* C1
Red, *sea* A1
Rub al-Khali
(Empty Quarter), *desert* ...C2
Sabkhat Matti, *salt flat*........C2
Sawda, *mt.* B2
Syrian, *desert*......................A1
Umm as-Samim, *salt flat* C2
Wadi al-Hamd, *river*............A1

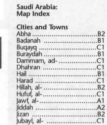

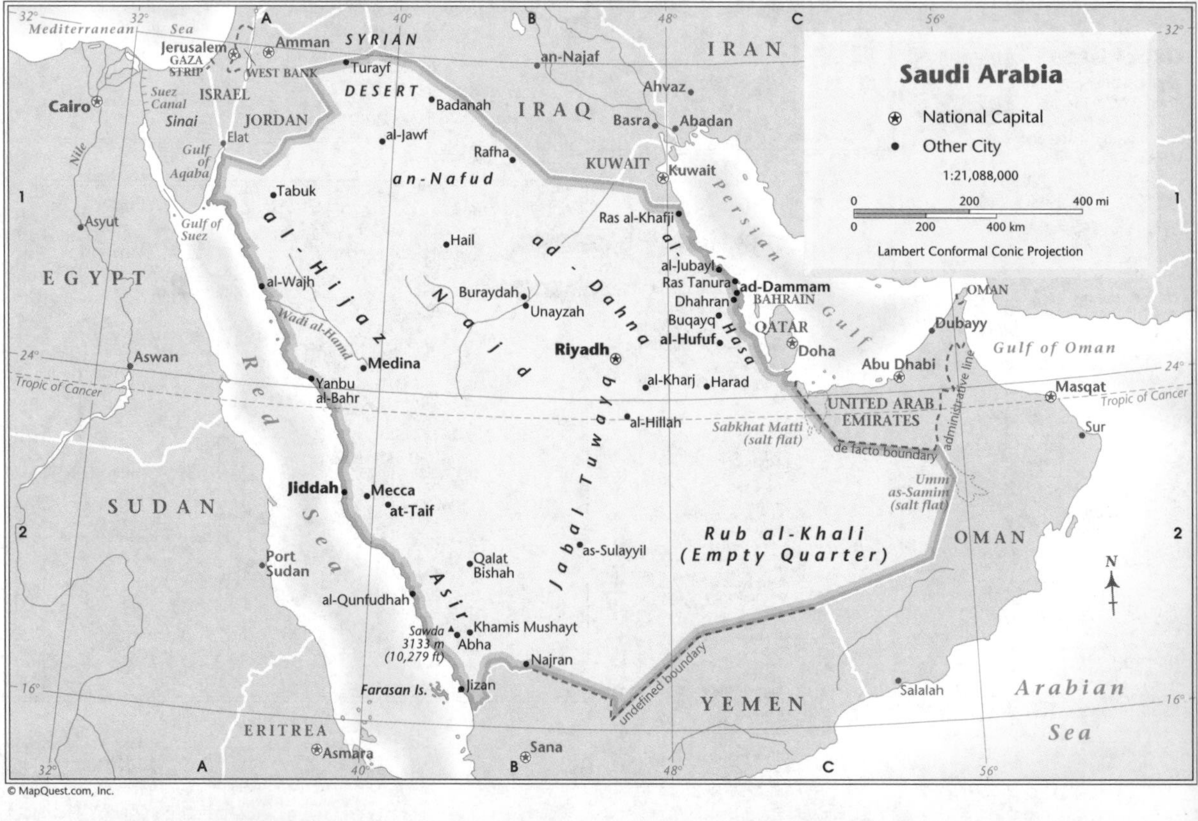

Bahrain and Qatar
National Capital
Other City
1:2,842,000
0 10 20 mi
0 10 20 km
Transverse Mercator Projection

Bahrain and Qatar: Map Index

Bahrain Cities and Towns

Askar	B1
Mamtalah, al-	B2
Manama, *capital*	B1
Mina Salman	B1

Other Features

Bahrain, *gulf*	A2
Hawar, *islands*	B2
Jiddah, *island*	A1
Muharraq, al-, *island*	B1
Ras al-Barr, *cape*	B2
Sitrah, *island*	B1
Umm an-Nasan, *island*	A1

Qatar Cities and Towns

Doha, *capital*	D3
Dukhan	B3
Jumayliyah, al-	C2
Khawr, al-	D2
Ruways, ar-	C1
Umm Bab	B3
Umm Said (Musayid)	D4
Wakrah, al-	D3

Other Features

Dawhat as-Salwa, *bay*	B3
Ras Laffan, *cape*	D2
Ras Rakan, *cape*	C1
Tuwayyir al-Hamir, *hill*	C4

Bahrain

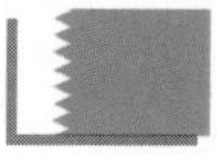

Capital: Manama
Area: 268 sq. mi.
694 sq. km.
Population: 629,000
Largest City: Manama
Language: Arabic
Monetary Unit: Dinar

Qatar

Capital: Doha
Area: 4,412 sq. mi.
11,430 sq. km.
Population: 724,000
Largest City: Doha
Language: Arabic
Monetary Unit: Riyal

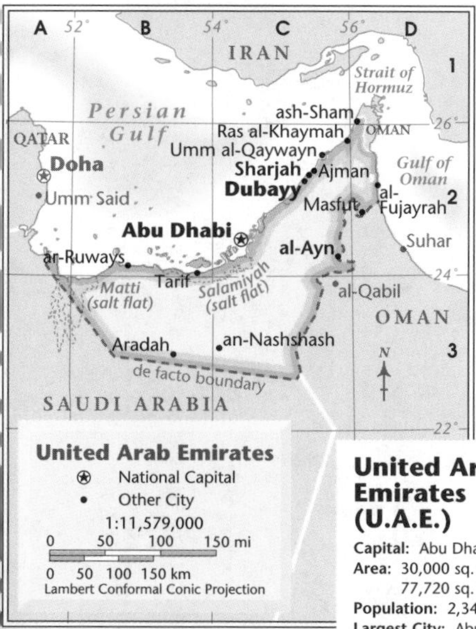

United Arab Emirates
National Capital
Other City
1:11,579,000
0 50 100 150 mi
0 50 100 150 km
Lambert Conformal Conic Projection

United Arab Emirates (U.A.E.)

Capital: Abu Dhabi
Area: 30,000 sq. mi.
77,720 sq. km.
Population: 2,344,000
Largest City: Abu Dhabi
Language: Arabic
Monetary Unit: Dirham

United Arab Emirates: Map Index

Cities and Towns

Abu Dhabi, *capital*	C2
Ajman	C2
Aradah	B3
Ayn, al-	C2
Dubayy	C2
Fujayrah, al-	D2
Masfut	D2
Nashshash, an-	C3
Ras al-Khaymah	C2
Ruways, ar-	B2
Sham, ash-	D1
Sharjah	C2
Tarif	B2
Umm al-Qaywayn	C2

Other Features

Hormuz, *strait*	D1
Matti, *salt flat*	B3
Oman, *gulf*	D2
Persian, *gulf*	B1
Salamiyah, *salt flat*	C3

Yemen: Map Index

Cities and Towns

Aden	B2
Ahwar	B2
Amran	A1
Ataq	B2
Balhaf	B2
Bayda, al-	B2
Dhamar	A2
Ghaydah, al-	C1
Habarut	C1
Hadiboh	C2
Hajjah	A1
Hawf	C1
Hazm, al-	A1
Hudaydah, al-	A2
Ibb	A2
Lahij	A2
Madinat ash-Shab	A2
Marib	B1
Maydi	A1
Mocha (Mukha, al-)	A2
Mukalla, al-	B2
Qalansiyah	C2
Qishn	C1
Rida	A2
Sadah	A1
Sana, *capital*	A1
Sanaw	C1
Sayhut	C1
Saywun	B1
Shabwah	B1
Taizz	A2
Zabid	A2

Other Features

Abd al-Kuri, *island*	C2
Aden, *gulf*	B2
Arabian, *sea*	C2
Bab al-Mandab, *strait*	A2
Hadhramaut, *district*	B1
Jabal an-Nabi Shuayb, *mt.*	A1
Jabal Zuqar, *island*	A2
Kamaran, *island*	A1
Perim, *island*	A2
Ras al-Kalb, *cape*	B2
Ras Fartak, *cape*	C1
Red, *sea*	A2
Socotra, *island*	C2
The Brothers, *islands*	C2
Wadi al-Masilah, *river*	B1

Yemen

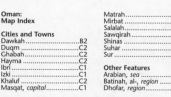

Capital: Sana
Area: 205,356 sq. mi.
532,010 sq. km.
Population: 16,942,000
Largest City: Sana
Language: Arabic
Monetary Unit: Riyal

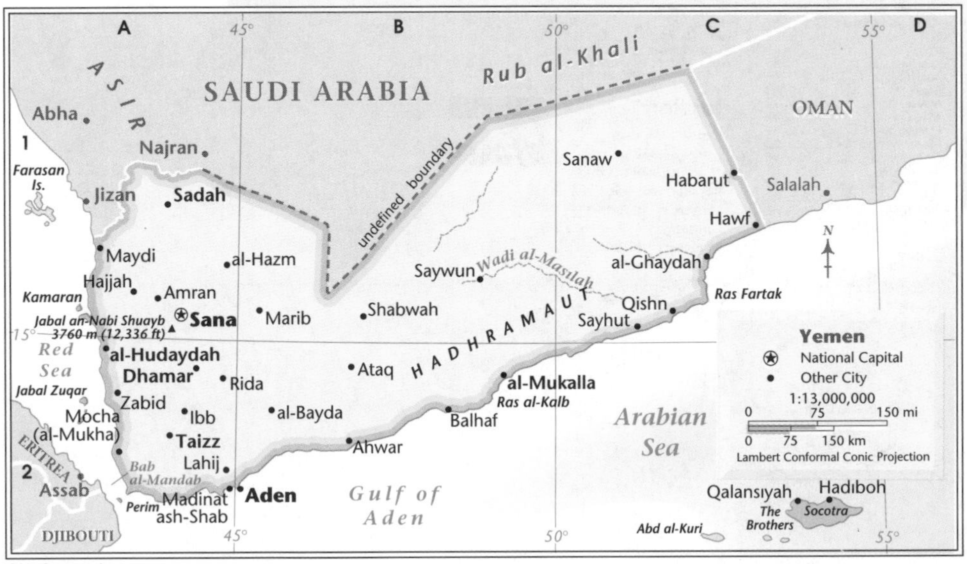

Yemen
National Capital
Other City
1:13,000,000
0 75 150 mi
0 75 150 km
Lambert Conformal Conic Projection

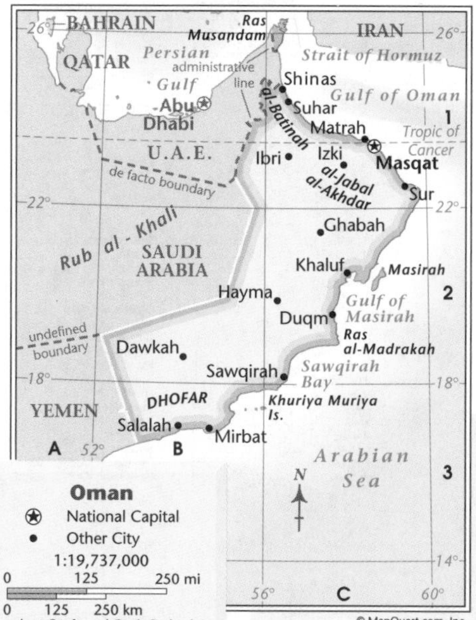

Oman
National Capital
Other City
1:19,737,000
0 125 250 mi
0 125 250 km
Lambert Conformal Conic Projection

Oman: Map Index

Cities and Towns

Dawkah	B2
Duqm	C2
Ghabah	C2
Hayma	C2
Ibri	C1
Izki	C1
Khaluf	C2
Masqat, *capital*	C1
Matrah	C1
Mirbat	B3
Salalah	B3
Sawqirah	C2
Shinas	C1
Suhar	C1
Sur	C1

Other Features

Arabian, *sea*	C3
Batinah, al-, *region*	C1
Dhofar, *region*	B3
Hormuz, *strait*	C1
Jabal al-Akhdar, al-, *mts.*	C1
Khuriya Muriya, *islands*	C3
Masirah, *gulf*	C2
Masirah, *island*	C2
Oman, *gulf*	C1
Persian, *gulf*	B1
Ras al-Madrakah, *cape*	C2
Ras Musandam, *cape*	C1
Sawqirah, *bay*	C2

Oman

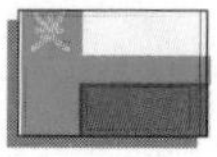

Capital: Masqat
Area: 118,150 sq. mi.
305,829 sq. km.
Population: 2,447,000
Largest City: Masqat
Language: Arabic
Monetary Unit: Rial Omani

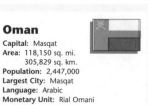

Lebanon

Capital: Beirut
Area: 3,950 sq. mi.
10,233 sq. km.
Population: 3,563,000
Largest City: Beirut
Languages: Arabic, French
Monetary Unit: Pound

Lebanon: Map Index

Cities and Towns

Amyun A1
Baalbek B1
Babda A2
Batrun, al- A1
Beirut, *capital* A2
Bint Jubayl B1
Bsharri B1
Damur, ad- A1
Duma A2
Halba B1
Hirmil, al- B1
Jazzin A2
Jubayl A1
Juniyah A2
Marj Uyun A2
Nabatiyah at-Tahta, an- ...A2
Qubayyat, al- B1
Rashayya A2
Riyaq B2
Sidon (Sayda) A2
Sur (Tyre) A2
Tripoli (Tarabulus) A1
Zahlah A2

Other Features

Anti-Lebanon, *mts.* B1
Awwali, *river* A2
Bekaa, *valley* A2
Byblos, *ruins* A1
Hermon, *mt.* A2
Ibrahim, *river* A1
Kebir, *river* A1
Lebanon, *mts.* B1
Litani, *river* A2
Orontes, *river* B1
Qurnat as-Sawda, *mt.* .B1

Israel

⊛ National Capital
• Other City
⊢⊣ Canal

1:2,838,000

0   20   40 mi
0 20 40 km

Cassini-Soldner Transverse
Cylindrical Projection

Jordan: Map Index

Cities and Towns

Amman, *capital* A2
Aqabah, al- A3
Azraq ash-Shishan B2
Bair B2
Irbid A1
Jafr, al- B2
Jarash A1
Karak, al- A2
Maan A2
Madaba A2
Mafraq, al- B1
Mudawwarah, al- B3
Qatranah, al- B2
Ramtha, ar- B1
Ras an-Naqb A2
Salt, as- A1
Tafilah, at- A2
Zarqa, az- B1

Other Features

Aqaba, *gulf* A3
Arabah, al-, *river* A2
Dead Sea, *lake* A2
Jabal Ramm, *mt.* A3
Jordan, *river* A2
Petra, *ruins* A2
Syrian, *desert* B1
Tiberias, *lake* A1
Wadi as-Sirhan, *depression* ..B2

Jordan

Capital: Amman
Area: 34,342 sq. mi.
88,969 sq. km.
Population: 4,561,000
Largest City: Amman
Language: Arabic
Monetary Unit: Dinar

Jordan

⊛ National Capital
• Other City

1:3,250,000

0   50   100 mi
0 50 100 km

Lambert Conformal Conic Projection

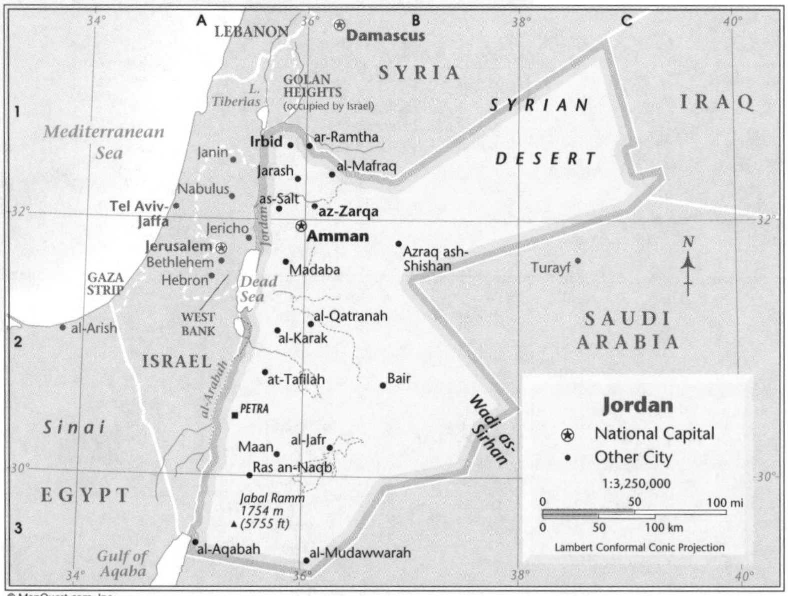

Israel

Capital: Jerusalem
Area: 7,992 sq. mi.
20,705 sq. km.
Population: 5,750,000
Largest City: Jerusalem
Languages: Hebrew, Arabic
Monetary Unit: New Shekel

Israel: Map Index

Districts

Central B1
Haifa B1
Jerusalem B2
Northern B1
Southern B2
Tel Aviv B1

Cities and Towns

Acre (Akko) B1
Ashdod B2
Ashqelon B2
Beersheba B2
Dimona B2
Elat B3
Hadera B1
Haifa B1
Herzliyya B1
Holon B1
Jerusalem, *capital* .....B
Lod (Lydda) ....B
Mizpe Ramon ....B
Nahariyya ....B
Nazareth ....B
Netanya ....B
Petah Tiqwa ....B
Qiryat Gat ....B
Qiryat Shemona ....B
Ramat Gan ....B
Ramla ....B
Rehovot ....B
Tel Aviv-Jaffa ....B
Tiberias ....B
Yotvata ....B
Zefat ....B

Other Features

Aqaba, *gulf* ....B
Arabah, al-, *river* .....B
Besor, *river* ....B
Dead, *sea* ....B
Galilee, *region* ....B
Haifa, *bay* ....B
Jezreel (Esdraelon), *plain* ..B
Jordan, *river* ....B
Judea, *plain* ....B
Masada, *ruins* ....B
Meron, *mt.* ....B
Negev, *region* ....B
Ramon, *mt.* ....B
Samarian, *hills* ....B
Sharon, *plain* ....B
Tiberias (Galilee), *lake* .B
Zevulun, *plain* ....B

© MapQuest.com, Inc.

Turkey

Capital: Ankara
Area: 300,948 sq. mi.
779,658 sq. km.
Population: 65,599,000
Largest City: İstanbul
Language: Turkish
Monetary Unit: Lira

Turkey
⊛ National Capital
• Other City
1:11,125,000
0   75   150 mi
0   75   150 km
Lambert Conformal Conic Projection

© MapQuest.com, Inc.

Turkey: Map Index

Cities and Towns

Adana C3
Adapazarı B2
Afyon B2
Ağrı E2
Aksaray C3
Alanya C3
Amasya C2
Ankara, *capital* C2
Antalya B3
Antioch (Antakya) D3
Artvin E2
Aydın A3
Balıkesir A2
Batman E3
Bolu B2
Bursa B2
Çanakkale A2
Çankırı C2
Çorum C2
Denizli B3
Divriği D2
Diyarbakır E3
Edirne A2
Elâziğ D2
Erzincan D2
Erzurum E2
Eskişehir B2
Eyüp B2
Fethiye B3
Gaziantep D3
Gelibolu (Gallipoli) A2
Giresun D2
İskenderun D3
Isparta B3
İstanbul B2
İzmir A2
İzmit B2
Kadıköy A2
Karaman C3
Kars E2
Kastamonu C2
Kayseri C2
Kırıkkale C2
Kırşehir C2
Konya C3
Kütahya B2
Malatya D2

Manisa A2
Maraş D3
Mardin E3
Mersin C3
Muğla B3
Muş E2
Niğde C3
Ordu D2
Samsun D2
Siirt E3

Silifke C3
Sinope C2
Sivas D2
Tarsus C3
Tekirdağ A2
Thrace A2
Tokat D2
Trabzon D2
Urfa D3
Usak B2

Üsküdar B2
Van E2
Zonguldak B2

Other Features
Aegean, *sea* A3
Anatolia, *region* B2
Antalya, *gulf* B3
Ararat (Ağri Daği), *mt.* .E2
Aras, *river* E2

Atatürk, *reservoir* D3
Beyşehir, *lake* B3
Black, *sea* C1
Bosporus, *strait* B2
Burdur, *lake* B3
Büyük Menderes, *rivers* ..A3
Ceyhan, *river* D3
Cilician Gates, *pass* ...C3
Çoruh, *river* E2
Çukorova, *region* C3

Eğridir, *lake* B2
Erciyas Daği, *mt.* C2
Euphrates, *river* D2
Great Zab, *river* E3
İskenderun, *gulf* D3
Keban, *reservoir* D2
Kızıl Irmak, *river* C2
Kura, *river* E2
Marmara, *sea* B2
Mediterranean, *sea* B4

Murat, *river* E2
Pontic, *mts.* C2
Sakarya, *river* B2
Seyhan, *river* C3
Taurus, *mts.* B3
Tigris, *river* E2
Tuz, *lake* C2
Ulu Dağ (Mt. Olympus), *mt.* ..B2
Van, *lake* E2
Yesilirmak, *river* D2

Cyprus
⊛ National Capital
• Other City
1:5,091,000
0   25   50 mi
0   25   50 km
Lambert Conformal Conic Projection

© MapQuest.com, Inc.

Cyprus:
Map Index

Cities and Towns
Episkopi A2
Famagusta B1
Kokkina A1
Kyrenia B1
Lapithos B1
Larnaca B2
Lefka A2
Lefkoniko B1
Limassol A2
Morphou A1
Nicosia, *capital* A2
Paphos A2
Peyia A2
Polis A1

Yialousa C1

Other Features
Akrotiri, *bay* B2
Andreas, *cape* C1
Arnauti, *cape* A1
British Sovereign
  Base Area A2, B2
Famagusta, *bay* C1
Gata, *cape* B2
Greco, *cape* C2
Karpas, *peninsula* C1
Kormakiti, *cape* A1
Kyrenia, *range* B1
Mesaoria, *plain* B1
Morphou, *bay* A1
Olympus, *mt.* A2
Troödos, *mts.* A2

Cyprus

Capital: Nicosia
Area: 3,572 sq. mi.
9,254 sq. km.
Population: 754,000
Largest City: Nicosia
Languages: Greek, Turkish
Monetary Unit: Pound

Syria
⊛ National Capital
• Other City
1:9,250,000
0   60   120 mi
0   60   120 km
Azimuthal Equal Area Projection

© MapQuest.com, Inc.

Syria:
Map Index

Cities and Towns
Abu Kamal B2
Azaz A1
Baniyas A2
Damascus, *capital* A3
Dara A3
Dayr az-Zawr B2
Halab (Aleppo) A1
Hamah A2
Hasakah, al- B1
Homs A2
Idlib A2
Ladhiqiyah, al- (Latakia) ..A2
Madinat ath-Thawrah ...B2
Manbij A1
Nabk, an- A2
Qamishli, al- B1

Qunaytirah, al- A3
Raqqah, ar- B2
Sab Abar A3
Salahiyah A2
Sukhnah, as- B2
Suwar, as- B2
Suwayda, as- A3
Tadmur B2
Tartus A2

Other Features
Anti-Lebanon, *mts.* A3
Buhayrat al-Asad, *lake* .B2
Euphrates (al-Furat), *river* ..B2
Golan Heights, *occupied*
  territory A3
Hermon, *mt.* A3
Jabal an-Nusayriyah, *mts.* ..A2
Jazirah, al-, *region* B1
Khabur, *river* B1

Mediterranean, *sea* A2
Orontes, *river* A2
Palmyra, *ruins* B2
Syrian, *desert* B3
Tigris, *river* C1

Syria

Capital: Damascus
Area: 71,498 sq. mi.
185,228 sq. km.
Population: 17,214,000
Largest City: Damascus
Language: Arabic
Monetary Unit: Pound

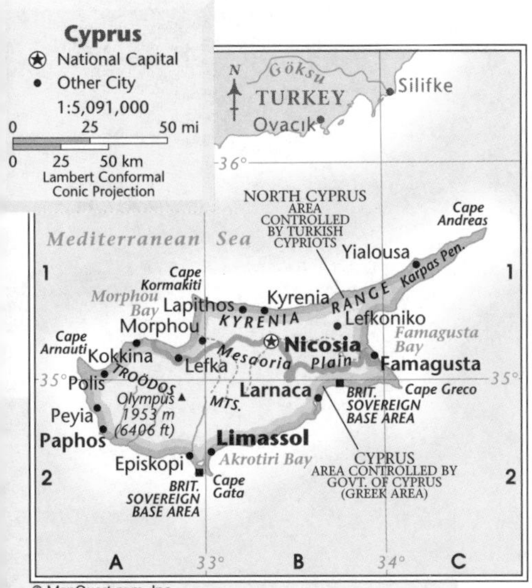

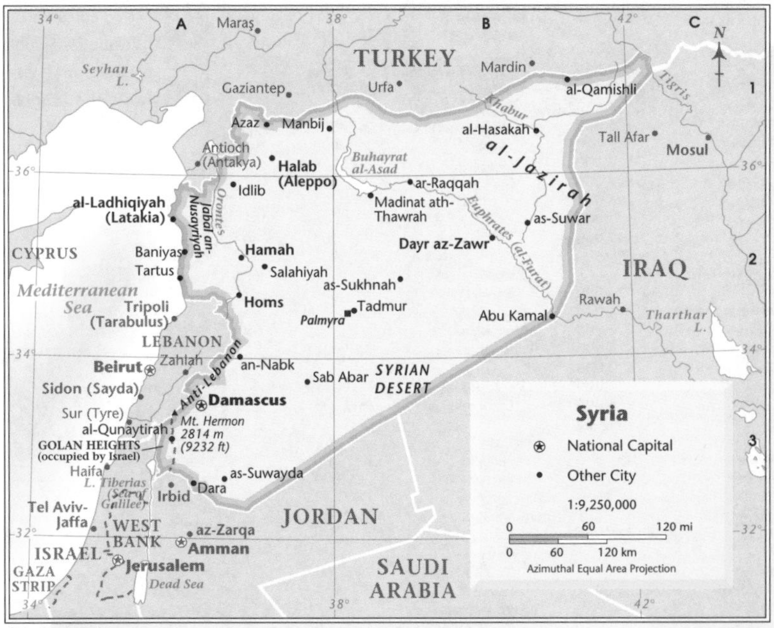

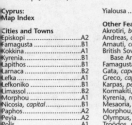

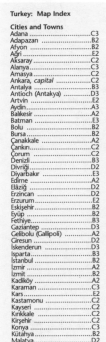

MAJOR CITIES

Albania
Tiranë   244,000

Andorra
Andorra la Vella   16,000

Armenia   (metro)
Yerevan   1,278,000

Austria
Vienna   1,540,000

Azerbaijan   (metro)
Baku   1,848,000

Belarus   (metro)
Minsk   1,708,000

Belgium   (metro)
Brussels   948,000
Antwerp   456,000

Bosnia and Hercegovina
Sarajevo   416,000

Bulgaria
Sofia   1,117,000

Croatia   (metro)
Zagreb   981,000

Czech Republic
Prague   1,200,000

Denmark
Copenhagen   632,000

Estonia
Tallinn   424,000

Finland
Helsinki   532,000

France
Paris   2,152,000
Lyon   1,260,000
Marseille   1,200,000

Georgia   (metro)
Tbilisi   1,342,000

Germany
Berlin   3,458,000
Hamburg   1,708,000
Munich   1,226,000
Cologne   964,000
Frankfurt   647,000
Essen   612,000
Dortmund   597,000
Stuttgart   586,000
Düsseldorf   571,000
Leipzig   549,000

Great Britain
London   7,074,000
Birmingham   1,021,000
Leeds   727,000
Glasgow   616,000
Sheffield   530,000
Bradford   483,000
Liverpool   468,000
Edinburgh   449,000

Greece   (metro)
Athens   3,073,000

Hungary
Budapest   1,897,000

Iceland
Reykjavík   105,000

Ireland
Dublin   482,000

Italy
Rome   2,645,000
Milan   1,304,000
Naples   1,046,000
Turin   920,000
Palermo   688,000
Genoa   654,000

Latvia
Riga   821,000

Liechtenstein
Vaduz   5,000

Lithuania
Vilnius   580,000

Luxembourg
Luxembourg   77,000

F.Y.R. Macedonia
Skopje   430,000

Malta
Valletta   7,000

Moldova
Chişinău   656,000

Monaco
Monaco   27,000

Netherlands
Amsterdam   717,000
Rotterdam   591,000

Norway
Oslo   492,000

Poland
Warsaw   1,633,000
Łódź   820,000
Kraków   745,000
Wrocław   642,000

Portugal
Lisbon   582,000

Romania
Bucharest   2,037,000

Russia (European)
Moscow   8,368,000
St. Petersburg   4,232,000
Nizh. Novgorod   1,376,000
Samara   1,184,000
Ufa   1,093,000
Kazan   1,076,000
Perm   1,031,000
Rostov-na-Donu   1,014,000
Volgograd   999,000

San Marino
San Marino   3,000

Slovakia
Bratislava   452,000

Slovenia
Ljubljana   273,000

Spain
Madrid   2,867,000
Barcelona   1,509,000
Valencia   747,000
Seville   697,000

Sweden
Stockholm   718,000

Switzerland
Zürich   342,000
Bern   129,000

Turkey (European)
İstanbul   6,620,000

Ukraine
Kiev   2,630,000
Kharkiv   1,555,000
Dnipropetrovsk   1,147,000
Donetsk   1,088,000
Odesa   1,046,000

Yugoslavia   (metro)
Belgrade   1,204,000

International comparability of city population
data is limited by various data inconsistencies.

© MapQuest.com, Inc.

Gross National Product (GNP) per capita

- $36,410
- $21,500
- $8625
- $2785
- $695
- $0
- No data

Vegetation

- Tundra
- Coniferous Forest
- Deciduous Forest
- Mixed Forest
- Midlatitude Scrubland
- Midlatitude Grassland
- Unclassified Highlands or Ice Cap

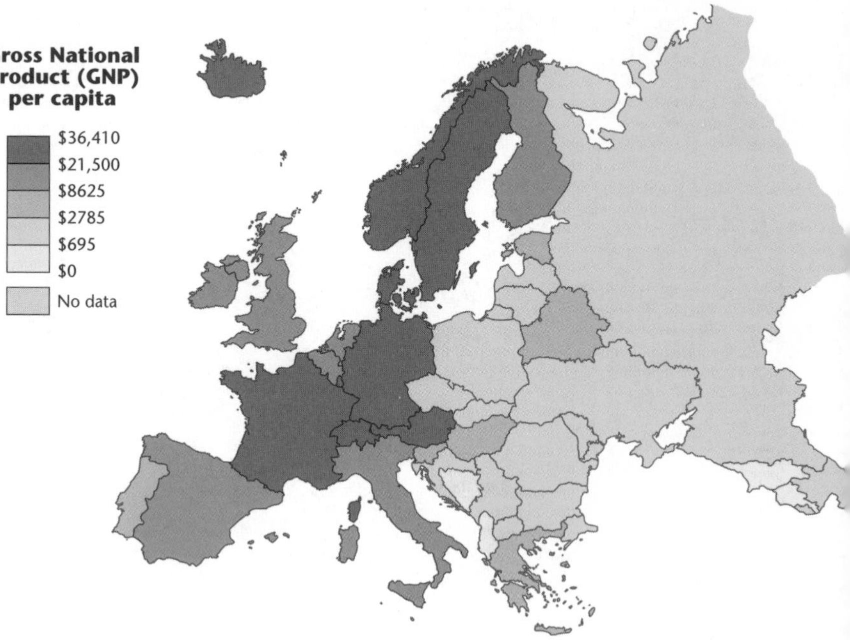

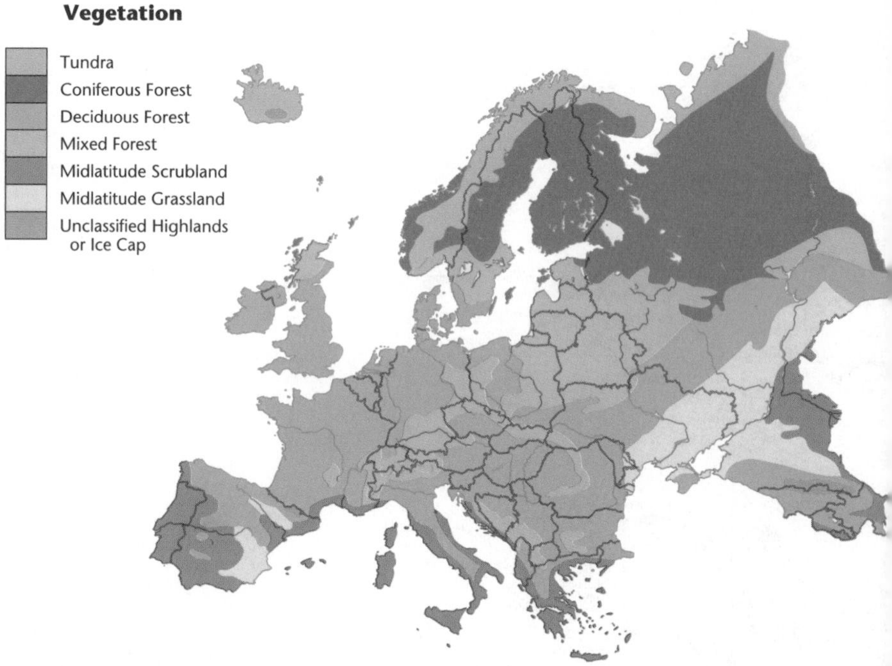

Europe: Population, by nation (in millions)*

| RUSSIA 146.4* | GER. 82.1 | GR. BRIT. 59.1 | FRANCE 59.0 | ITALY 56.7 | UKRAINE 49.8 | SPAIN 39.1 | POLAND 38.6 | ROM. 22.3 | NETH. 15.8 | All other European countries 158.3 |

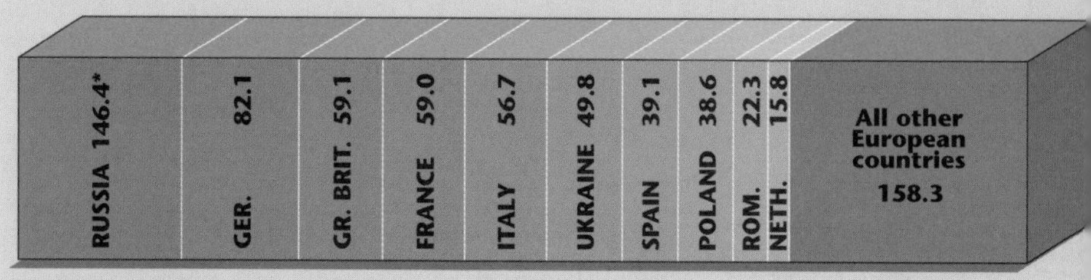

*Including Asian Russia as well as the more populous European portion of the country.

CITIES
National Capital
Territorial Capital
Other City
ELEVATIONS
Feet Meters
13,120 4000
6560 2000
1640 500
656 200
0 0
Below sea level
ATLANTIC OCEAN
Norwegian Sea
North Sea
Barents Sea
White Sea
Baltic Sea
Bay of Biscay
MEDITERRANEAN SEA
Tyrrhenian Sea
Ionian Sea
Adriatic Sea
Aegean Sea
Black Sea
Caspian Sea
Sea of Azov
ICELAND
Reykjavík
Akureyri
NORWAY
SWEDEN
FINLAND
RUSSIA
ESTONIA
LATVIA
LITHUANIA
BELARUS
UKRAINE
POLAND
GERMANY
DENMARK
NETHERLANDS
BELGIUM
LUXEMBOURG
FRANCE
SWITZERLAND
AUSTRIA
CZECH REP.
SLOVAKIA
HUNGARY
ROMANIA
MOLDOVA
BULGARIA
YUGOSLAVIA
BOSNIA AND HERZEGOVINA
CROATIA
SLOVENIA
ALBANIA
GREECE
TURKEY
ITALY
SPAIN
PORTUGAL
IRELAND
GREAT BRITAIN
GEORGIA
ARMENIA
AZERBAIJAN
LAPLAND
URAL MTS.
CAUCASUS
ALPS
PYRENEES
CARPATHIAN MTS.
APENNINES
NORTHERN EUROPEAN PLAIN
IBERIAN PENINSULA
Moscow
St. Petersburg
Helsinki
Stockholm
Oslo
Copenhagen
Tallinn
Riga
Vilnius
Minsk
Kiev
Warsaw
Berlin
Prague
Vienna
Budapest
Bratislava
Bucharest
Chişinău
Sofia
Belgrade
Sarajevo
Zagreb
Ljubljana
Skopje
Tiranë
Athens
Rome
Bern
Paris
London
Dublin
Brussels
Amsterdam
Luxembourg
Madrid
Lisbon
Tbilisi
Yerevan
Baku
Valletta
Mt. Elbrus 5642 m (18,510 ft)
Mont Blanc 4807 m (15,771 ft)
Pico de Aneto 3404 m (11,169 ft)
Mt. Etna 3369 m (11,053 ft)
N
0 250 500 750 mi
0 250 500 750 1000 km

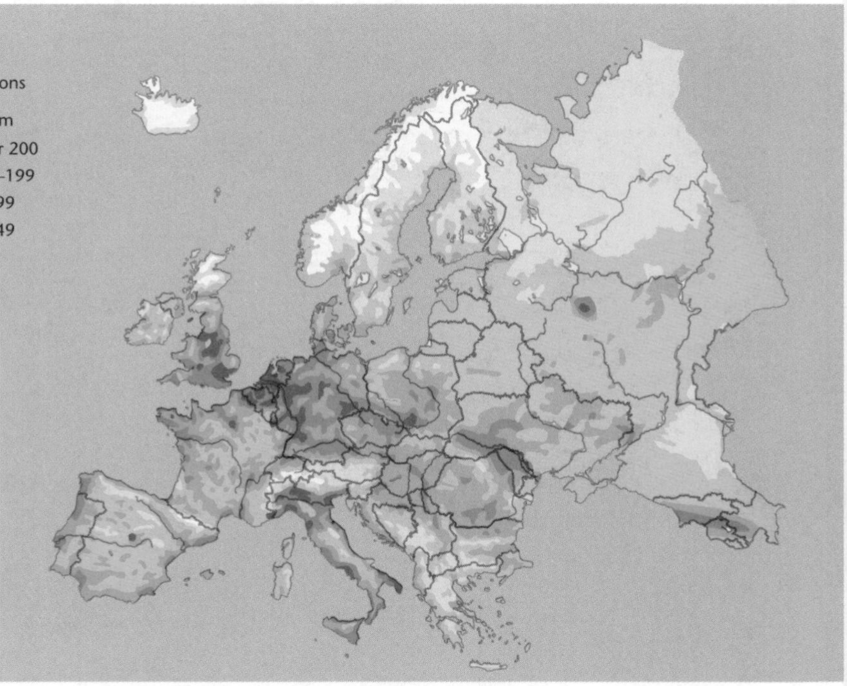
Population
Persons per sq mi
Persons per sq km
Over 520 Over 200
260–519 100–199
130–259 50–99
25–129 10–49
1–24 1–9
0 0

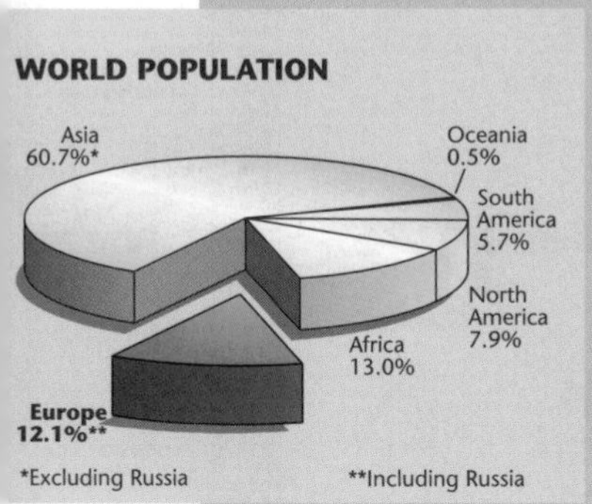
WORLD POPULATION
Asia 60.7%*
Oceania 0.5%
South America 5.7%
North America 7.9%
Africa 13.0%
Europe 12.1%**
*Excluding Russia
**Including Russia

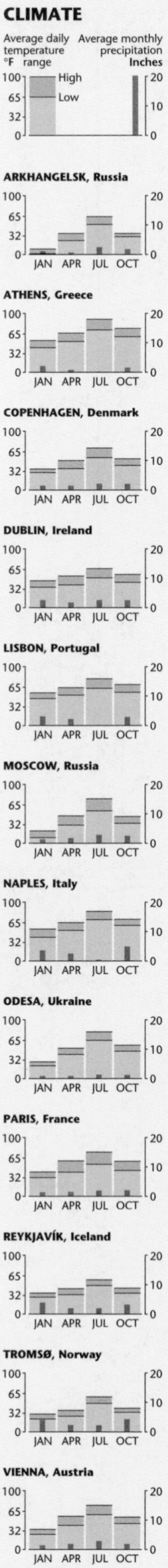
CLIMATE
Average daily temperature °F range
Average monthly precipitation Inches
High
Low
ARKHANGELSK, Russia
ATHENS, Greece
COPENHAGEN, Denmark
DUBLIN, Ireland
LISBON, Portugal
MOSCOW, Russia
NAPLES, Italy
ODESA, Ukraine
PARIS, France
REYKJAVÍK, Iceland
TROMSØ, Norway
VIENNA, Austria
JAN APR JUL OCT

Great Britain

Capital: London
Area: 94,251 sq. mi.
244,174 sq. km.
Population: 59,133,000
Largest City: London
Language: English
Monetary Unit: Pound

Great Britain: Map Index

CHANNEL ISLANDS
Features

Alderney, *island*...........Inset II
Guernsey, *island* ....Inset II
Jersey, *island* ....Inset II
St. Malo, *gulf* ....Inset II
Sark, *island* ....Inset II

ENGLAND
Cities and Towns

Aylesbury ....Inset III
Banbury C3
Barnsley C3
Barnstaple B3
Barrow-in-Furness B2
Basildon ....Inset III
Bath C3
Bedford C3
Berwick-upon-Tweed C2
Birkenhead B3
Birmingham C3
Blackburn C3
Blackpool C3
Bolton C3
Boston C3
Bournemouth C4
Bradford C3
Braintree ....Inset III
Brentwood ....Inset III
Brighton C4
Bristol C3
Burnley C3
Bury C3
Bury St. Edmunds D3
Buxton C3
Camberley ....Inset III
Cambridge D3
Canterbury D3
Carlisle C2
Chatham ....Inset III
Chelmsford ....D3, Inset III
Cheltenham C3
Chester C3
Chesterfield C3
Chichester C4
Colchester D3
Coventry C3
Cowes C4
Crawley ....Inset III
Crewe C3
Darlington C2
Derby C3
Doncaster C3
Dorchester C4
Dorking ....Inset III
Dover D3
Dudley C3
Dunstable ....Inset III
Durham C2
Eastbourne D4
Ely D3
Epsom ....Inset III
Ewell ....Inset III
Exeter B4
Farnham ....Inset III
Felixstowe D3
Fleetwood C3
Folkestone D3
Gateshead C2
Gillingham D3
Glastonbury C3
Gloucester C3
Gosport C4
Grantham C3
Gravesend ....Inset III
Great Yarmouth D3
Grimsby C3
Guildford C3
Halifax C3
Harlow ....Inset III
Harrogate C2
Haslemere ....Inset III
Hastings D4
Hereford C3
Hertford ....Inset III
High Wycombe ....Inset III
Hove C4
Huddersfield C3
Ipswich D3
Kendal C2
Kenilworth C3
Kidderminster C3
King's Lynn D3
Kingston upon Hull C3
Kingston upon ThamesInset III
Lancaster C2
Launceston B4
Leeds C3
Leicester C3
Lewes D4
Lichfield C3
Lincoln C3
Liverpool C3
London, *capital* ....C3, Inset III
Lowestoft D3
Luton C3
Maidstone D3
Manchester C3
Margate D3
Matlock C3
Middlesbrough C2
Newcastle-under-Lyme C3
Newcastle upon Tyne C2
Newmarket D3
Newquay B4
Northallerton C2
Northampton C3
North Shields C2
Norwich D3
Nottingham C3
Oldham C3
Oxford C3
Penrith C2
Penzance B4
Peterborough C3
Plymouth B4
Poole C4
Portsmouth C4
Preston C3
Reading C3
Reigate ....Inset III
Rochdale C3
Rotherham C3
St. Albans ....C3, Inset III

Republic of Ireland

Capital: Dublin
Area: 27,137 sq. mi.
70,303 sq. km.
Population: 3,632,000
Largest City: Dublin
Languages: English, Irish
Monetary Unit: Punt, Euro

Republic of Ireland: Map Index

Counties
Carlow C2
Cavan C2
Clare B2
Cork B3
Donegal B1
Dublin C2
Galway B2
Kerry B2
Kildare C2
Kilkenny C2
Laois C2
Leitrim B1
Limerick B2
Longford C2
Louth C2
Mayo B2
Meath C2
Monaghan C1
Offaly C2
Roscommon B2
Sligo B1
Tipperary North Riding B2
Tipperary South Riding B2
Waterford C2
Westmeath C2
Wexford C2
Wicklow C2

Cities and Towns
Ardara B1
Arklow C2
Athlone C2
Ballina B1
Bantry B3
Blarney B3
Carlingford C1
Carlow C2
Carrick-on-Shannon B2
Cashel C2
Castlebar B2
Cavan C2
Clara C2
Clifden A2
Clonmel C2
Cóbh B3
Cork B3
Dingle A2
Donegal B1
Drogheda C2
Dublin, *capital* C2
Dundalk C2
Dungarvan C2
Dún Laoghaire C2
Ennis B2
Ennistymon B2
Galway B2
Kildare C2
Kilkee B2
Kilkenny C2
Killarney B2
Letterkenny C1
Lifford C1
Limerick B2
Longford C2
Mallow B2
Maynooth C2
Monaghan C1
Mullingar C2
Naas C2
Nenagh B2
Port Laoise C2
Roscommon B2
Roscrea C2
Rosslare C2
Shannon B2
Sligo B1
Swords C2
Tipperary B2
Tralee B2
Trim C2
Tuam B2
Tullamore C2
Waterford C2
Westport B2
Wexford C2
Wicklow C2
Youghal C3

Other Features
Achill, *island* A2
Allen, *lake* B1
Aran, *islands* B2
Bantry, *bay* B3
Barrow, *river* C2
Benwee Head, *cape* B1
Blackwater, *river* B2
Blackwater, *river* C1
Boggeragh, *mts.* B2
Boyne, *river* C2
Caha, *mts.* B3
Carlingford, *lake* C1
Carnsore, *point* C2
Carrantuohill, *mt.* B3
Celtic, *sea* B3
Clear, *cape* B3
Conn, *lake* B1
Connaught, *province* B2
Connemara, *region* B2
Corrib, *lake* B2
Derg, *lake* B2
Dingle, *bay* A2
Donegal, *bay* B1
Erne, *river* B1
Errigal, *mt.* B1
Finn, *river* C1
Foyle, *inlet* C1
Galway, *bay* B2
Grand, *canal* C2
Irish, *sea* D2
Killala, *bay* B1
Knockboy, *mt.* B3
Lee, *river* B3
Leinster, *province* C2
Loop Head, *cape* B2
Malin Head, *cape* C1
Mask, *lake* B2
Maumturk, *mts.* B2
Mizen Head, *cape* B3
Moher, *cliffs* B2
Munster, *province* B2
Ree, *lake* B2
Royal, *canal* C2
Saint George's, *channel* C3
Shannon, *river* B2
Suir, *river* C2
Twelve Pins, *mt.* B2
Ulster, *province* C1
Wicklow, *mts.* C2
Wicklow Head, *cape* D2

© MapQuest.com, Inc.

Great Britain: Map Index
St. Austell B4
St. Helens C3
Salford C3
Salisbury C3
Scarborough C2
Scunthorpe C3
Sheffield C3
Shrewsbury C3
Slough Inset III
Solihull C3
Southampton C4
Southend-on-Sea D3
Southport C3
South Shields C2
Stafford C3
Stevenage Inset III
Stoke-on-Trent C3
Stratford-upon-Avon C3
Sunderland C2
Swindon C3
Taunton C3
Telford C3
Tewkesbury C3
Thetford D3
Tiverton B4
Tonbridge Inset III
Torbay B4
Trowbridge C3
Truro B4
Tunbridge Wells D3
Wakefield C3
Walsall C3
Warrington C3
Warwick C3
Watford Inset III
Westminster Inset III
Whitehaven B2
Wigan C3
Winchester C3
Windsor Inset III
Wolverhampton C3
Worcester C3
Yeovil C4
York C3

Other Features
Avon, *river* C3
Black Country, *region* C3
Bristol, *channel* B3
Cheviot, *hills* C2
Cotswold, *hills* C3
Cumbrian, *mts.* B2
Dartmoor, *plateau* B4
Dee, *river* B3
Dover, *strait* D4
English, *channel* C4
Exmoor, *plateau* B3
Fens, *region* D3
Flodden Field, *plain* C2
Humber, *river* D3
Irish, *sea* B3
Lake, *district* B2
Land's End, *promontory* B4
Liverpool, *bay* B3
Lyme, *bay* C4
Mersey, *river* C3
Midlands, *region* C3
North, *sea* D2
North Downs, *hills* C3
North Foreland, *promontory* D3
Ouse, *river* C2, D3
Pennines, *mts.* C2
Scafell Pike, *mt.* B2
Scilly, *islands* A4
Severn, *river* C3
South Downs, *hills* C3
Spithead, *channel* C4
Start, *point* B4
Tees, *river* C2
Thames, *river* C3, Inset III
Trent, *river* C3
Tweed, *river* C2
Tyne, *river* C2
Wash, *bay* D3
Wight, *island* C4
Wye, *river* C3
Yare, *river* D3

ISLE OF MAN
City
Douglas B2

NORTHERN IRELAND
Cities and Towns
Armagh A2
Ballymena A2
Bangor B2
Belfast B2
Coleraine A2
Holywood B2
Larne B2
Londonderry A2
Newry A2
Omagh A2
Portadown A2
Strangford B2

Other Features
Antrim, *mts.* A2
Bann, *river* A2
Erne, *river* A2
Foyle, *lake* A2
Foyle, *river* A2
Giant's Causeway, *headland* A2
Irish, *sea* B3
Lough Erne, *lake* A2
Mourne, *mts.* A2
Neagh, *lake* A2
North, *channel* A2
Rathlin, *island* A2
Slieve Donard, *mt.* B2
Sperrin, *mts.* A2
Upper Lough Erne, *lake* A2

SCOTLAND
Cities and Towns
Aberdeen C1
Aviemore B1
Ayr B2
Campbeltown B2
Clydebank B2
Cupar C2
Dornoch B1
Dumfries B2
Dundee C2
Dunfermline B2
Edinburgh B2
Elgin B1
Fort William B2
Fraserburgh C1
Glasgow B2
Greenock B2
Hamilton B2
Hawick C2
Inverness B1
Kilmarnock B2
Kirkcaldy B2
Kirkwall Inset I
Kyle of Lochalsh B1
Lairg B1
Lerwick Inset I
Mallaig B1
Montrose C2
Motherwell B2
Newtown St. Boswells C2
Oban B2
Paisley B2
Perth B2
Peterhead C1
Pitlochry B2
Portree A1
St. Andrews C2
Scone B2
Sconser A1
Stirling B2
Stornoway A1
Stranraer B2
Thurso B1
Ullapool B1
Wick B1

Other Features
Arran, *island* B2
Barra, *island* A2
Bass Rock, *islet* C2
Bell Rock (Inchcape), *reef* C2
Ben Nevis, *mt.* B2
Bute, *island* B2
Cheviot, *hills* C2
Clyde, *estuary* B2
Clyde, *river* B2
Coll, *island* A2
Colonsay, *island* A2
Dee, *river* C1
Dornoch, *estuary* B1
Duncansby, *cape* B1
Dunsinane, *mt.* B2
Eigg, *island* A2
Fair, *island* Inset I
Forth, *estuary* C2
Forth, *river* B2
Grampian, *mts.* B2
Hebrides, *sea* A1
Hoy, *island* Inset I
Inner Hebrides, *islands* A2
Islay, *island* A2
Jura, *island* B2
Katrine, *lake* B2
Kinnairds, *cape* C1
Lammermuir, *hills* C2
Lewis, *island* A1
Linnhe, *lake* B2
Lomond, *lake* B2
Lorne, *estuary* A2
Mainland, *island* Inset I
Merrick, *mt.* B2
Minch, *strait* B1
Moray, *estuary* B1
Mull, *island* A2
Ness, *lake* B1
North Uist, *island* A1
Ochil, *hills* B2
Orkney, *islands* Inset I
Outer Hebrides, *islands* A1
Rhum, *island* A1
Sanday, *island* Inset I
Shetland, *islands* Inset I
Sidlaw, *hills* B2
Skye, *island* A1
Solway, *estuary* B2
Southern Uplands, *mts.* B2
South Ronaldsay, *island* Inset I
South Uist, *island* A1
Spey, *river* B1
Stronsay, *island* Inset I
Tay, *estuary* C2
Tay, *lake* B2
Tay, *river* B2
Tiree, *island* A2
Tweed, *river* C2
Unst, *island* Inset I
Westray, *island* Inset I
Wrath, *cape* B1
Yell, *island* Inset I

WALES
Cities and Towns
Aberystwyth B3
Bangor B3
Caerleon C3
Caernarfon B3
Cardiff B3
Carmarthen B3
Conwy B3
Fishguard B3
Holyhead B3
Lampeter B3
Llandrindod Wells B3
Merthyr Tydfil B3
Milford Haven B3
Mold B3
Newport C3
Pembroke B3
Port Talbot B3
Rhondda B3
St. David's B3
Swansea B3
Welshpool B3

Other Features
Anglesey, *island* B3
Bala, *lake* B3
Brecon Beacons, *mts.* B3
Bristol, *channel* B3
Cambrian, *mts.* B3
Cardigan, *bay* B3
Dee, *river* B3
Lleyn, *peninsula* B3
Menai, *strait* B3
Snowdon, *mt.* B3
Teifi, *river* B3
Tywi, *river* B3
Usk, *river* C3
Wye, *river* C3

Denmark

Capital: Copenhagen
Area: 16,639 sq. mi.
43,080 sq. km.
Population: 5,357,000
Largest City: Copenhagen
Language: Danish
Monetary Unit: Krone

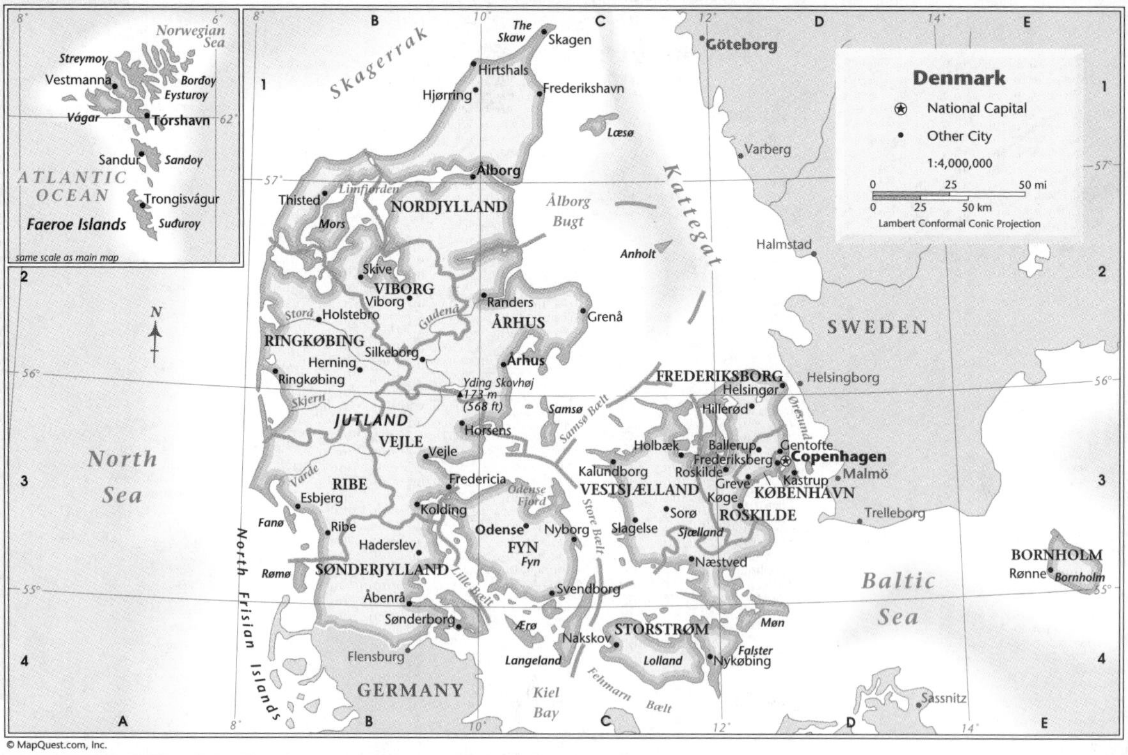

Denmark: Map Index

Counties
Århus C2
Bornholm E3
Frederiksborg D2
Fyn C3
København D3
Nordjylland B2
Ribe B3
Ringkøbing B2
Roskilde D3
Sønderjylland B3
Storstrøm C4
Vejle B3
Vestsjælland C3
Viborg B2

Cities and Towns
Åbenrå B3
Ålborg B1
Århus C2
Ballerup D3
Copenhagen, *capital* D3
Esbjerg B3
Fredericia B3
Frederiksberg D3
Frederikshavn C1
Gentofte D3
Grenå C2
Greve D3
Haderslev B3
Helsingør D2
Herning B2
Hillerød D3
Hirtshals B1
Hjørring B1
Holbæk C3
Holstebro B2
Horsens B3
Kalundborg C3
Kastrup D3
Køge D3
Kolding B3
Næstved C3
Nakskov C4
Nyborg C3
Nykøbing C4
Odense C3
Randers C2
Ribe B3
Ringkøbing B2
Rønne E3
Roskilde D3
Sandur ....Inset
Silkeborg B2
Skagen C1
Skive B2
Slagelse C3
Sønderborg B4
Sorø C3
Svendborg C3
Thisted B2
Tórshavn ....Inset
Trongisvágur ....Inset
Vejle B3
Vestmanna ....Inset
Viborg B2

Other Features
Ærø, *island* C4
Ålborg, *bay* C2
Anholt, *island* C2
Baltic, *sea* D3
Borðoy, *island* ....Inset
Bornholm, *island* E3
Eysturoy, *island* ....Inset
Faeroe, *islands* ....Inset
Falster, *island* D4
Fanø, *island* B3
Fehmarn, *strait* C4
Fyn, *island* C3
Gudenå, *river* B2
Jutland, *peninsula* B3
Kattegat, *strait* C2
Læsø, *island* C1
Langeland, *island* C4
Lille, *strait* B3
Limfjorden, *channel* B2
Lolland, *island* C4
Møn, *island* D4
Mors, *island* B2
North, *sea* A3
North Frisian, *islands* B4
Norwegian, *sea* ....Inset
Odense, *fjord* C3
Øresund, *sound* D3
Rømø, *island* B3
Samsø, *island* C3
Samsø, *strait* C3
Sandoy, *island* ....Inset
Sjælland, *island* C3
Skagerrak, *strait* B1
Skaw, *cape* C1
Skjern, *river* B3
Storå, *river* B2
Store, *strait* C3
Streymoy, *island* ....Inset
Suðuroy, *island* ....Inset
Vágar, *island* ....Inset
Varde, *river* B3
Yding Skovhøj, *hill* B2

Netherlands: Map Index

Provinces
Drenthe D2
Flevoland C2
Friesland C1
Gelderland D2
Groningen D1
Limburg C3
North Brabant C3
North Holland B2
Overijssel D2
South Holland B2
Utrecht C2
Zeeland A3

Cities and Towns
Alkmaar B2
Almelo D2
Amersfoort C2
Amsterdam, *capital* B2
Apeldoorn C2
Arnhem C3
Assen D2
Bergen op Zoom B3
Breda B3
Delft B2
Delfzijl D1
Den Helder B2
Deventer D2
Doetinchem D3
Dordrecht B3
Edam C2
Ede C2
Eindhoven C3
Emmeloord C2
Emmen D2
Enschede D2
Gouda B2
Groningen D1
Haarlem B2
Heerenveen C2
Heerlen C4
Hengelo D2
Hilversum C2
Hoogeveen D2
Hoorn C2
Leeuwarden C1
Leiden B2
Lelystad C2
Maastricht C4
Meppel D2
Middelburg A3
Nijmegen C3
Oss C3
Otterlo C2
Roermond D3
Rotterdam B3
Scheveningen B2
Schiedam B3
's Hertogenbosch C3
Sittard C4
Sneek C1
The Hague B2
Tilburg C3
Utrecht C2
Venlo D3
Vlaardingen B3
Vlissingen A3
Weert C3
Zaanstad B2
Zwolle D2

Other Features
Ameland, *island* C1
Eems, *river* D1
Flevoland, *polder* C2
IJssel, *river* D2
IJsselmeer, *sea* C2
Maas, *river* C3, D3
Neder Rijn, *river* C3
New Waterway, *channel* B3
Northeast, *polder* C2
North Holland, *canal* B2
North Sea, *canal* B2
Oosterschelde, *channel* A3
Overflakkee, *island* B3
Princess Margriet, *canal* C1
Schiermonnikoog, *island* D1
Schouwen, *island* A3
Terschelling, *island* C1
Texel, *island* B1
Tholen, *island* B3
Vaalserberg, *mt.* D4
Vlieland, *island* B1
Waal, *river* C3
Waddenzee, *sound* C1
Walcheren, *island* A3
Westerschelde, *channel* A3
West Frisian, *islands* B1
Wilhelmina, *canal* B3
Zuid-Willemsvaart, *canal* C3

Netherlands

Capital: Amsterdam
Area: 16,033 sq. mi.
41,536 sq. km.
Population: 15,808,000
Largest City: Amsterdam
Language: Dutch
Monetary Unit: Guilder, Euro

Belgium

- ⊛ National Capital
- • Other City
- ⊥⊥⊥⊥ Canal

1:2,381,000

0 — 20 — 40 mi
0 — 20 — 40 km
Lambert Conformal Conic Projection

© MapQuest.com, Inc.

Belgium:
Map Index

Internal Divisions

Antwerp (province)	C1
Brussels Cap. Region	C2
East Flanders (province)	B2
Flanders (region)	C1
Flemish Brabant (province)	C2
Hainaut (province)	B2
Liège (province)	D2
Limburg (province)	D1
Luxembourg (province)	D3
Namur (province)	C2
Walloon Brabant (province)	C2
Wallonia (region)	C2
West Flanders (province)	B1

Cities and Towns

Aalst	C2
Anderlecht	C2
Antwerp	C1
Arlon	D3
Ath	B2
Bastogne	D2
Binche	C2
Brugge	B1
Brussels, capital	C2
Charleroi	C2
Chimay	C2
Dinant	C2
Gembloux	C2
Genk	D2
Ghent	B1
Halle	C2
Hasselt	D2
Ixelles	C2
Knokke	B1
Kortrijk	B2
La Louvière	C2
Leuven	C2
Liège	D2
Limbourg	D2
Malmédy	E2
Mechelen	C1
Mons	B2
Mouscron	B2
Namur	C2
Neufchâteau	D3
Oostende	A1
Poperinge	A2
Roeselare	B2
Schaerbeek	C2
Sint-Niklaas	C1
Sint-Truiden	D2
Spa	D2
Tournai	B2
Turnhout	C1
Uccle	C2
Verviers	D2
Wavre	C2
Ypres	A2
Zeebrugge	B1

Other Features

Albert, canal	C1
Ardennes, plateau	D2
Botrange, mt.	E2
Brugge-Ghent, canal	B1
Dender, river	B2
Kempenland, region	D1
Leie, river	B2
Maas, river	D2
Meuse, river	D2
Oostende-Brugge, canal	B1
Ourthe, river	D2
Rupel, river	C1
Sambre, river	C2
Schelde, river	B2
Semois, river	D3
Senne, river	C2

Belgium

Capital: Brussels
Area: 11,787 sq. mi.
30,536 sq. km.
Population: 10,182,000
Largest City: Brussels
Languages: Flemish, French, German
Monetary Unit: Belgian franc, Euro

Luxembourg

- ⊛ National Capital
- • Other City

1:1,700,000

0 — 10 — 20 mi
0 — 10 — 20 km
Azimuthal Equal Area Projection

© MapQuest.com, Inc.

Luxembourg:
Map Index

Cities and Towns

Clervaux	B1
Diekirch	B2
Differdange	A2
Dudelange	B2
Echternach	B2
Esch-sur-Alzette	A2
Ettelbruck	B2
Grevenmacher	B2
Larochette	B2
Luxembourg, capital	B2
Mersch	B2
Redange	A2
Remich	B2
Troisvierges	B1
Vianden	B2
Wiltz	A2

Other Features

Alzette, river	B2
Ardennes, plateau	A1
Bon Pays, region	B2
Buurgplaatz, mt.	B1
Clerve, river	B1
Mosel, river	B2
Our, river	B1
Sûre, river	A2, B2

Liechtenstein

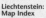

Capital: Vaduz
Area: 62 sq. mi.
161 sq. km.
Population: 32,000
Largest City: Vaduz
Language: German
Monetary Unit: Swiss franc

Liechtenstein:
Map Index

Cities and Towns

Balzers	B2
Eschen	B1
Gamprin	B1
Malbun	B2
Mauren	B1
Planken	B1
Ruggell	B1
Schaan	B1
Schellenberg	B1
Triesen	B2
Triesenberg	B2
Vaduz, capital	B2

Other Features

Alps, range	A2
Grauspitz, mt.	A2
Rhine, canal	B1, B2
Rhine, river	A1, A2
Samina, river	B2

Liechtenstein

- ⊛ National Capital
- • Other City

1:500,000

0 — 2.5 — 5 mi
0 — 2.5 — 5 km
Oblique Mercator Projection

© MapQuest.com, Inc.

Luxembourg

Capital: Luxembourg
Area: 999 sq. mi.
2,588 sq. km.
Population: 429,000
Largest City: Luxembourg
Languages: French, German
Monetary Unit: Luxembourg franc, Euro

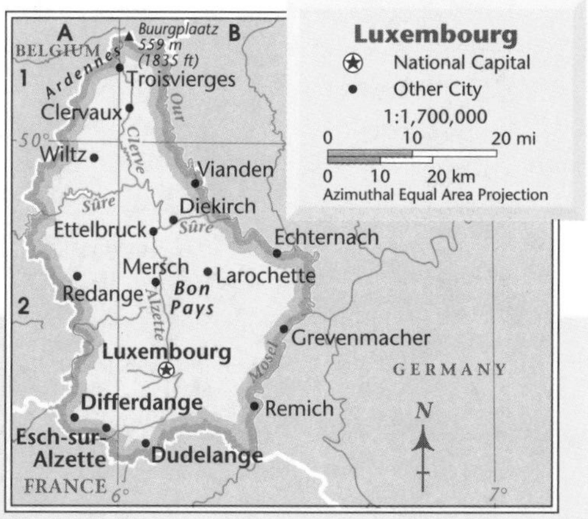

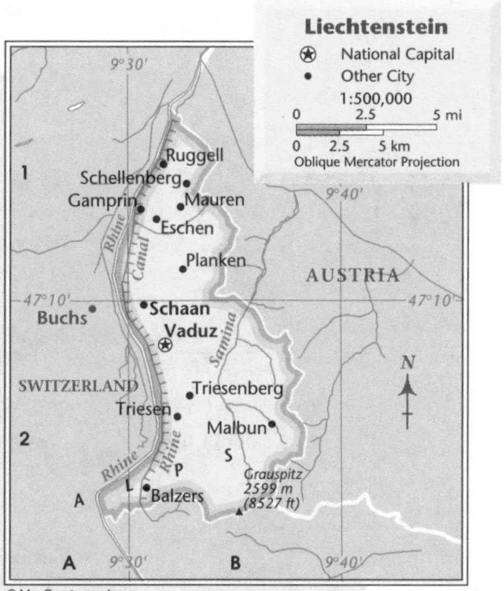

France
National Capital
Other City
1:5,625,000
0 50 100 mi
0 50 100 km
Lambert Conformal Conic Projection
GREAT BRITAIN
ENGLAND
London
Bristol
Exeter
Plymouth
Brighton
Portsmouth
Dover
Bristol Channel
English Channel
Strait of Dover
Thames
Channel Islands (Br.)
Guernsey
Sark
Jersey
Golfe de Saint-Malo
Cap de la Hague
Utah Beach
Omaha Beach
Cotentin
NETHERLANDS
Eindhoven
BELGIUM
Brussels
Brugge
Ghent
Antwerp
Liège
Namur
Meuse
Ardennes
LUXEMBOURG
Luxembourg
GERMANY
Essen
Düsseldorf
Cologne
Bonn
Koblenz
Rhine
Wiesbaden
Trier
Saar
Mannheim
Saarbrücken
Karlsruhe
Freiburg
SWITZERLAND
Bern
Basel
Aare
Lausanne
L. Geneva
Geneva
ITALY
Turin
Cuneo
Po
MONACO
ANDORRA
SPAIN
Santander
Burgos
Pamplona
Soria
Saragossa
Lérida
Tarragona
Gerona
Castellón de la Plana
Duero
Ebro
Bay of Biscay
Mediterranean Sea
Golfe du Lion
NORD-PAS-DE-CALAIS
Dunkirk (Dunkerque)
Calais
Boulogne-sur-Mer
Lille
Roubaix
Tourcoing
Lens
Douai
Arras
Valenciennes
Cambrai
Abbeville
PICARDIE
Amiens
Somme
Beauvais
Compiègne
Soissons
Laon
Aisne
Oise
HAUTE-NORMANDIE
Dieppe
Le Havre
Rouen
Trouville
Deauville
Seine
Évreux
BASSE-NORMANDIE
Cherbourg
Bayeux
Caen
Saint-Lô
Orne
Mont-Saint-Michel
Alençon
ÎLE-DE-FRANCE
Paris
Chantilly
Versailles
Dreux
Chartres
Fontainebleau
CHAMPAGNE-ARDENNE
Charleville Mézières
Sedan
Reims
Argonne
Marne
Châlons-sur-Marne
Saint-Dizier
Troyes
Chaumont
Aube
LORRAINE
Verdun
Metz
Bar-le-Duc
Nancy
Moselle
Épinal
VOSGES
ALSACE
Strasbourg
Colmar
Mulhouse
BRETAGNE
Brest
Morlaix
Saint-Brieuc
Saint-Malo
Rance
Quimper
Pointe du Raz
Rennes
Vilaine
Lorient
Vannes
Carnac
Belle-Île
PAYS DE LA LOIRE
Laval
Le Mans
Angers
Loire
Saint-Nazaire
Nantes
Saumur
Cholet
Île d'Yeu
La Roche-sur-Yon
CENTRE
Orléans
Montargis
Yonne
Blois
Tours
Vienne
Vierzon
Bourges
Châteauroux
BOURGOGNE
Auxerre
Dijon
Nevers
Le Creusot
Cluny
Mâcon
FRANCHE-COMTÉ
Belfort Gap
Belfort
Vesoul
Besançon
Dôle
JURA
POITOU-CHARENTES
Châtellerault
Poitiers
Niort
Île de Ré
La Rochelle
Rochefort
Île d'Oléron
Charente
Saintes
Cognac
Angoulême
LIMOUSIN
Limoges
Guéret
AUVERGNE
Montluçon
Vichy
Allier
Clermont-Ferrand
MASSIF CENTRAL
Aurillac
Le Puy
RHÔNE-ALPES
Roanne
Saône
Bourg-en-Bresse
Lyon
Saint-Étienne
Annecy
Aix-les-Bains
Chambéry
Grenoble
Isère
Valence
Privas
Mont Blanc 4807 m (15,771 ft)
Chamonix-Mont-Blanc
Great St. Bernard Pass
Little St. Bernard Pass
ALPS
Rhône
AQUITAINE
Gironde
Bordeaux
Arcachon
Bergerac
Dordogne
Périgueux
Brive-la-Gallarde
Garonne
Agen
LANDES
Adour
Biarritz
Bayonne
Pau
Lourdes
Tarbes
MIDI-PYRÉNÉES
Lot
Cahors
Rodez
Montauban
Albi
Auch
Toulouse
Carcassonne
Foix
Pic de Vignemale 3298 m (10,820 ft)
PYRENEES
LANGUEDOC-ROUSSILLON
Mende
CÉVENNES
Alès
Nîmes
Montpellier
Béziers
Narbonne
Perpignan
PROVENCE-ALPES-CÔTE-D'AZUR
Montélimar
Gap
Briançon
Digne
Maritime Alps
Avignon
Arles
Durance
Draguignan
Aix-en-Provence
Marseille
Toulon
Nice
Cannes
Fréjus
St.-Tropez
Same scale as main map
Mediterranean Sea
CORSICA
CORSE
Calvi
Bastia
Ajaccio
Porto-Vecchio
I
II
L'Isle-Adam
Luzarches
Louvres
Dammartin-en-Goële
Pontoise
Meulan
Taverny
Domont
Conflans-Sainte-Honorine
Sarcelles
Maisons-Laffitte
Argenteuil
Saint-Denis
Sevran
Poissy
Levallois-Perret
Clichy
Bondy
Chelles
Saint-Germain-en-Laye
Nanterre
Paris
Montreuil
Saint-Cloud
Boulogne-Billancourt
Vincennes
Sèvres
Pontchartrain
Versailles
Gentilly
Maurepas
Choisy-le Roi
Créteil
Ozoir-la-Ferrière
Massy
Villeneuve-Saint-Georges
Chevreuse
Palaiseau
Coubert
Les Ulis
Savigny-sur-Orge
Limours
Évry
Arpajon
Corbeil-Essonnes
Mennecy
Etrechy
Ballancourt-sur-Essonne
Melun
0 5 10 mi
0 5 10 km

Switzerland

Capital: Bern
Area: 15,943 sq. mi.
41,303 sq. km.
Population: 7,275,000
Largest City: Zürich
Languages: German, French, Italian
Monetary Unit: Swiss franc

Switzerland
National Capital
Other City
1:3,090,000
Lambert Conformal Conic Projection

© MapQuest.com, Inc.

Monaco
National Capital
1:74,470
Lambert Conformal Conic Projection

© MapQuest.com, Inc.

Monaco: Map Index

Districts
Fontvieille A2
La Condamine B1
Monaco, *capital* B1
Monte Carlo B1

Other Features
Casino B1
Fontvieille, *port* B2
Monaco, *port* B1
Palace B2
Sporting Club C1

Monaco

Capital: Monaco
Area: 0.75 sq. mi.
1.94 sq. km.
Population: 32,000
Language: French
Monetary Unit: French franc or Monégasque franc

Switzerland: Map Index

Cantons
Aargau C1
Appenzell Ausser-Rhoden D1
Appenzell Inner-Rhoden D1
Basel-Land B1
Basel-Stadt B1
Bern B2
Fribourg B2
Geneva A2
Glarus D2
Graubünden D2
Jura B1
Lucerne C1
Neuchâtel A2
Nidwalden C2
Obwalden C2
Sankt Gallen D1
Schaffhausen C1
Schwyz C1
Solothurn B1
Thurgau C1
Ticino C2
Uri C2
Valais B2
Vaud A2
Zug C1
Zürich C1

Cities and Towns
Aarau C1
Altdorf C2
Baden C1
Basel B1
Bellinzona D2
Bern, *capital* B2
Biel B1
Bolligen B2
Bulle B2
Chur D2
Davos D2
Einsiedeln C1
Fribourg B2
Frutigen B2
Geneva A2
Horgèn C1
Interlaken B2
La Chaux-de-Fonds A1
Lausanne A2
Locarno C2
Lucerne C1
Lugano C3
Montreux A2
Morges A2
Neuchâtel A2
St. Moritz D2
Sankt Gallen D1
Schaffhausen C1
Schwyz C1
Sempach C1
Sion B2
Thun B2
Uster C1
Winterthur C1
Yverdon A2
Zermatt B2
Zug C1
Zürich C1

Other Features
Aare, *river* B1, B2
Alps, *mts.* B2
Bernese Alps, *mts.* B2
Biel, *lake* B1
Brienzersee, *lake* B2
Constance (Bodensee), *lake* D1
Doubs, *river* A1
Dufourspitze, *mt.* B3
Engadine, *valley* D2
Geneva, *lake* A2
Inn, *river* D2
Jungfrau, *mt.* B2
Jura, *mts.* A2
Lepontine Alps, *mts.* C2
Lucerne, *lake* C2
Lugano, *lake* C3
Maggiore, *lake* C2
Matterhorn, *mt.* B3
Neuchâtel, *lake* A2
Pennine Alps, *mts.* B2
Reuss, *river* C2
Rhaetian Alps, *mts.* D2
Rhine, *river* C1, D2
Rhône, *river* B2
St. Gotthard, *pass* C2
St. Gotthard, *tunnel* C2
Splügen, *pass* D2
Staubbach, *falls* B2
Thunersee, *lake* B2
Ticino, *river* C2
Walensee, *lake* D1
Zürichsee, *lake* C1

France

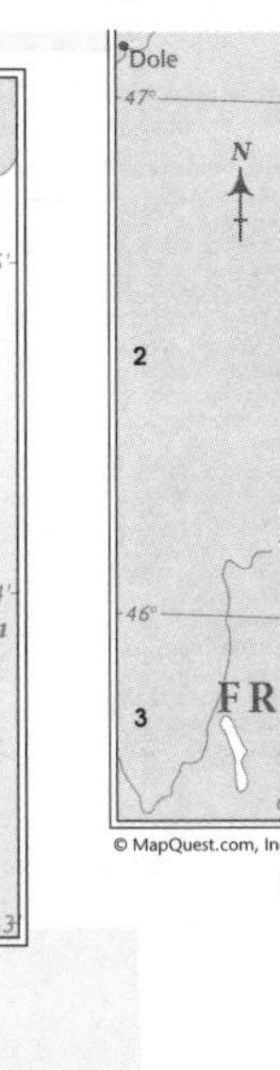

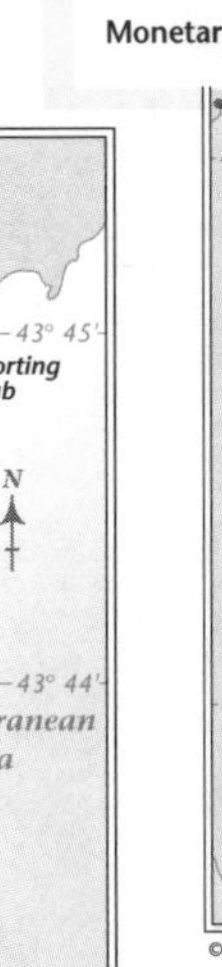

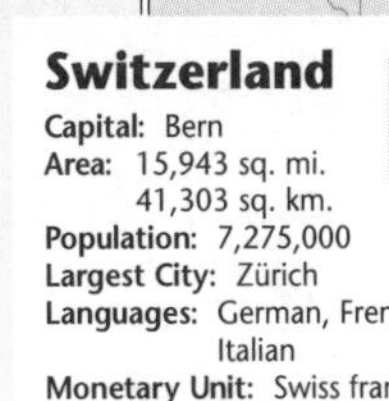

Capital: Paris
Area: 210,026 sq. mi.
544,109 sq. km.
Population: 58,978,000
Largest City: Paris
Language: French
Monetary Unit: Franc, Euro

France: Map Index

Regions
Alsace D2
Aquitaine B4
Auvergne C4
Basse-Normandie B2
Bourgogne C3
Bretagne B2
Centre C3
Champagne-Ardenne D2
Corse .... Inset I
Franche-Comté D3
Haute-Normandie C2
Île-de-France C2
Languedoc-Roussillon C5
Limousin C4
Lorraine D2
Midi-Pyrénées C5
Nord-Pas-de-Calais C1
Pays De La Loire B3
Picardie C2
Poitou-Charentes C3
Provence-Alpes-Côte-d'Azur D4
Rhône-Alpes D4

Cities and Towns
Abbeville C1
Agen C4
Aix-en-Provence D5
Aix-les-Bains D4
Ajaccio .... Inset I
Albi C5
Alençon C2
Alès D4
Amiens C2
Angers B3
Angoulême C4
Annecy D4
Arachon B4
Argenteuil .... Inset II
Arles D5
Arpajon .... Inset II
Arras C1
Auch C5
Aurillac C4
Auxerre C3
Avignon D5
Ballancourt-sur-Essonne .... Inset II
Bar-le-Duc D2
Bastia .... Inset I
Bayeux B2
Bayonne B5
Beauvais C2
Belfort D3
Bergerac C4
Besançon D3
Béziers C5
Biarritz B5
Blois C3
Bondy .... Inset II
Bordeaux B4
Boulogne-Billancourt .... Inset II
Boulogne-sur-Mer C1
Bourg-en-Bresse D3
Bourges C3
Brest A2
Briançon D4
Brive-la-Gallarde C4
Caen B2
Cahors C4
Calais C1
Calvi .... Inset I
Cambrai C1
Cannes D5
Carcassonne C5
Carnac B3
Châlons-sur-Marne D2
Chambéry D4
Chamonix-Mont-Blanc D4
Chantilly C2
Charleville Mézières D2
Chartres C2
Châteauroux C3
Châtellerault C3
Chaumont D2
Chelles .... Inset II
Cherbourg B2
Chevreuse .... Inset II
Choisy-le Roi .... Inset II
Cholet B3
Clermont-Ferrand C4
Clichy .... Inset II
Cluny D3
Cognac B4
Colmar D2
Compiègne C2
Conflans-Sainte-Honorine .... Inset II
Corbeil-Essonnes .... Inset II
Coubert .... Inset II
Créteil .... Inset II
Dammartin-en-Goële .... Inset II
Deauville C2
Dieppe C2
Digne D4
Dijon D3
Dôle D3
Domont .... Inset II
Douai C1
Draguignan D5
Dreux C2
Dunkirk (Dunkerque) C1
Épinal D2
Etrechy .... Inset II
Évreux C2
Évry .... Inset II
Foix C5
Fontainebleau C2
Fréjus D5
Gap D4
Gentilly .... Inset II
Grenoble D4
Guéret C3
Laon C2
La Rochelle B3
La-Roche-sur-Yon B3
Laval B2
Le Creusot D3
Le Havre C2
Le Mans C2
Lens C1
Le Puy C4
Les Ulis .... Inset II
Levallois-Perret .... Inset II
Lille C1
Limoges C4
Limours .... Inset II
L'Isle-Adam .... Inset II
Lorient B3
Lourdes B5
Louvres .... Inset II
Luzarches .... Inset II
Lyon D4
Mâcon D3
Maisons-Laffitte .... Inset II
Marseille D5
Massy .... Inset II
Maurepas .... Inset II
Melun .... Inset II
Mende C4
Mennecy .... Inset II
Metz D2
Meulan .... Inset II
Montargis C2
Montauban C4
Montélimar D4
Montluçon C3
Montpellier C5
Montreuil .... Inset II
Mont-Saint-Michel B2
Morlaix B2
Mulhouse D3
Nancy D2
Nanterre .... Inset II
Nantes B3
Narbonne C5
Nevers C3
Nice D5
Nîmes D5
Niort B3
Orléans C3
Ozoir-la-Ferrière .... Inset II
Palaiseau .... Inset II
Paris, *capital* .... C2, Inset II
Pau B5
Périgueux C4
Perpignan C5
Poissy .... Inset II
Poitiers C3
Pontchartrain .... Inset II
Pontoise .... Inset II
Porto-Vecchio .... Inset I
Privas D4
Quimper A2
Reims D2
Rennes B2
Roanne D3
Rochefort B4
Rodez C4
Roubaix C1
Rouen C2
Saint-Brieuc B2
Saint-Cloud .... Inset II
Saint-Denis .... Inset II
Saint-Dizier D2
Saintes B4
Saint-Étienne D4
Saint-Germain-en-Laye .... Inset II
Saint-Lô B2
Saint-Malo B2
Saint-Nazaire B3
Saint-Tropez D5
Sarcelles .... Inset II
Saumur B3
Savigny-sur-Orge .... Inset II
Sedan D2
Sevran .... Inset II
Sèvres .... Inset II
Soissons C2
Strasbourg D2
Tarbes C5
Taverny .... Inset II
Toulon D5
Toulouse C5
Tourcoing C1
Tours C3
Trouville C2
Troyes D2
Valence D4
Valenciennes C1
Vannes B3
Verdun D2
Versailles .... C2, Inset II
Vesoul D3
Vichy C3
Vierzon C3
Villeneuve-Saint-Georges .... Inset II
Vincennes .... Inset II

Other Features
Adour, *river* B5
Aisne, *river* D2
Allier, *river* C3
Alps, *range* D4
Ardennes, *region* D1
Argonne, *forest* D2
Aube, *river* D3
Belfort, *gap* D3
Belle, *island* B3
Biscay, *bay* B4
Blanc, *mt.* D4
Cévennes, *mts.* C4
Charente, *river* B4
Corsica, *island* .... Inset I
Cotentin, *peninsula* B2
Dordogne, *river* C4
Dover, *strait* C1
Durance, *river* D5
English, *channel* B2
Garonne, *river* C4
Geneva, *lake* D3
Gironde, *river* B4
Hague, *cape* B2
Isère, *river* D4
Jura, *mts.* D3
Landes, *region* B5
Lion, *gulf* D5
Little St. Bernard, *pass* D4
Loire, *river* C3
Lot, *river* C4
Maritime Alps, *range* D4
Marne, *river* .... C2, Inset II
Massif Central, *plateau* C4
Meuse, *river* D2
Moselle, *river* D2
Oise, *river* .... C2, Inset II
Oléron, *island* B4
Omaha, *beach* B2
Orne, *river* B2
Pyrenees, *range* C5
Rance, *river* B2
Raz, *point* A3
Ré, *island* B3
Rhine, *river* D2
Rhône, *river* D4
Saint-Malo, *gulf* B2
Sambre, *river* C1
Saône, *river* D3
Seine, *river* .... C2, Inset II
Somme, *river* C2
Utah, *beach* B2
Vienne, *river* C3
Vignemale, *mt.* B5
Vilaine, *river* B3
Vosges, *mts.* D2
Yeu, *island* B3
Yonne, *river* C2

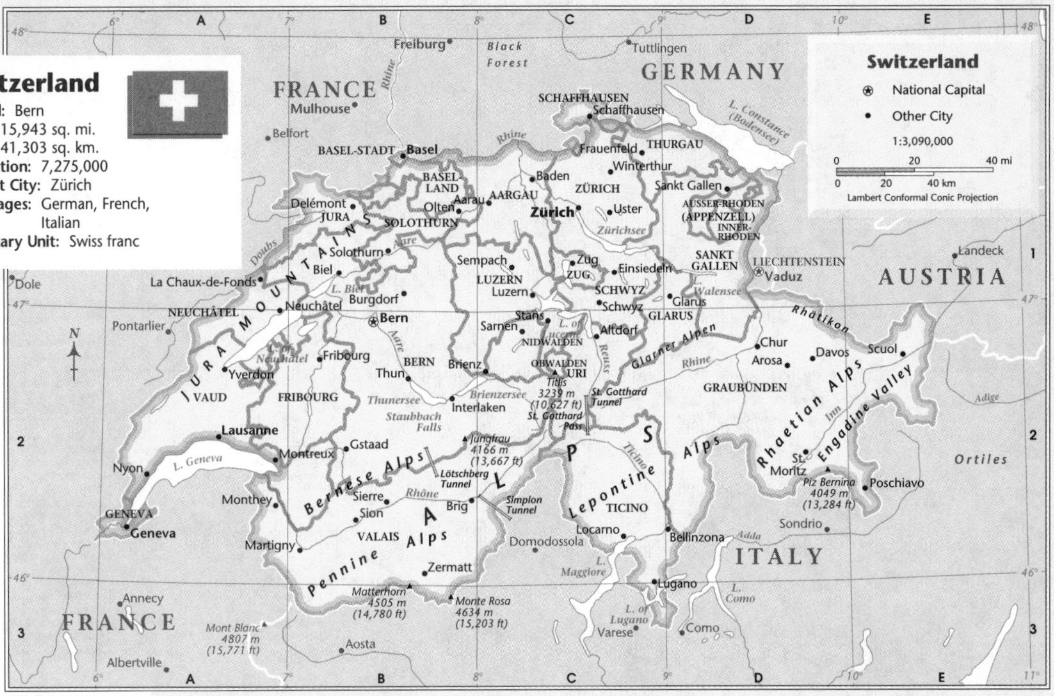

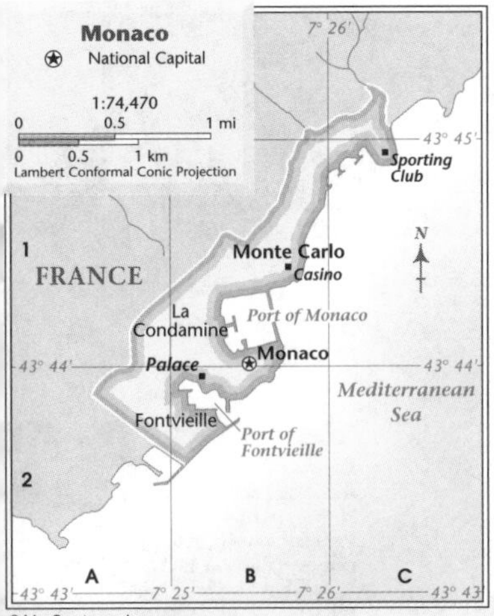

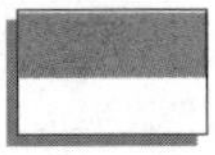

© MapQuest.com, Inc.

Portugal: Map Index

Districts

Aveiro	A2
Beja	A4
Braga	A2
Bragança	B2
Castelo Branco	B2
Coimbra	A2
Évora	B3
Faro	A4
Guarda	B2
Leiria	A3
Lisbon	A3
Oporto (Porto)	A2
Portalegre	B3
Santarém	A3
Setúbal	A3
Viana do Castelo	A2
Vila Real	B2
Viseu	B2

Cities and Towns

Abrantes	A3
Almada	A3
Amadora	A3
Aveiro	A2
Barreiro	A3
Beja	B3
Braga	A2
Bragança	B2
Caidasm da Rainha	A3
Castelo Branco	B3
Chaves	B2
Coimbra	A2
Covilhã	B2
Elvas	B3
Estoril	A3
Évora	B3
Faro	B4
Figueira da Foz	A2
Grândola	A3
Guarda	B2
Guimarães	A2
Lagos	A4
Leiria	A3
Leixões	A2
Lisbon, *capital*	A3
Mafra	A3
Moura	B3
Odemira	A4
Oeiras	A3
Oporto (Porto)	A2
Peniche	A3
Portalegre	B3
Portimão	A4
Queluz	A3
Santarém	A3
Setúbal	A3
Sines	A4
Valença	A1
Viana do Castelo	A2
Vila do Conde	A2
Vila Nova de Gaia	A2
Vila Real	B2
Vila Real de Santo Antonio	B4
Viseu	B2

Other Features

Algarve, *region*	A4
Cádiz, *gulf*	B4
Carvoeiro, *cape*	A3
Chança, *river*	B4
Douro, *river*	B2
Espichel, *cape*	A3
Estrela, *mt.*	B2
Estrela, *mts.*	B2
Guadiana, *river*	B3
Lima, *river*	A2
Minho, *river*	A1
Mondego, *cape*	A2
Mondego, *river*	B2
Roca, *cape*	A3
Sado, *river*	A3
São Vicente, *cape*	A4
Seda, *river*	B3
Setúbal, *bay*	A3
Sor, *river*	B3
Sorraia, *river*	A3
Tagus, *river*	A3
Tâmega, *river*	B2
Zêzere, *river*	A3

Portugal

Capital: Lisbon
Area: 35,672 sq. mi.
92,415 sq. km.
Population: 9,918,000
Largest City: Lisbon
Language: Portuguese
Monetary Unit: Escudo, Euro

Malta

Capital: Valletta
Area: 122 sq. mi.
316 sq. km.
Population: 382,000
Largest City: Valletta
Languages: Maltese, English
Monetary Unit: Maltese lira

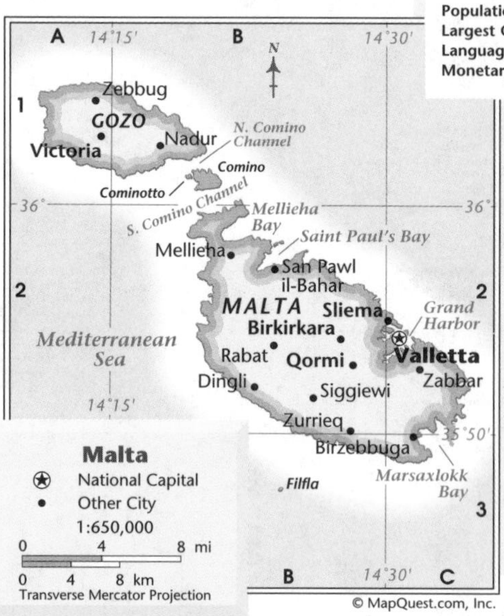

© MapQuest.com, Inc.

Malta: Map Index

Cities and Towns

Birkirkara	B
Birzebbuga	C
Dingli	B
Mellieha	B
Nadur	B
Qormi	B
Rabat	B
San Pawl il-Bahar	B
Siggiewi	B
Sliema	C
Valletta, *capital*	C
Victoria	A
Zabbar	C
Zebbug	A
Zurrieq	B

Other Features

Comino, *island*	B
Cominotto, *island*	B
Filfla, *island*	B
Gozo, *island*	A
Grand, *harbor*	C
Malta, *island*	B
Marsaxlokk, *bay*	C
Mellieha, *bay*	B
North Comino, *channel*	B
Saint Paul's, *bay*	B
South Comino, *channel*	B

Gibraltar

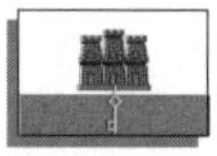

Area: 2.25 sq. mi.
5.83 sq. km.
Population: 29,000
Language: English
Monetary Unit: British Pound

Gibraltar: Map Index

Features

Catalan, *bay*	A2
Detached, *mole*	A2
Eastern, *beach*	A2
Fortress Headquarters	A3
Gibraltar, *bay*	A2
Gibraltar, *harbor*	A2
Gibraltar, *strait*	A4
Governor's Residence	A2
Great Europa, *point*	A4
Highest point	A3
Little, *bay*	A4
Mediterranean, *sea*	A3
North, *mole*	A2
North Front, *airfield*	A1
Rosia, *bay*	A3
Saint Michael's, *cave*	A3
Sandy, *bay*	A3
Signal, *hill*	A2
South, *mole*	A3
The Rock, *prom.*	A2

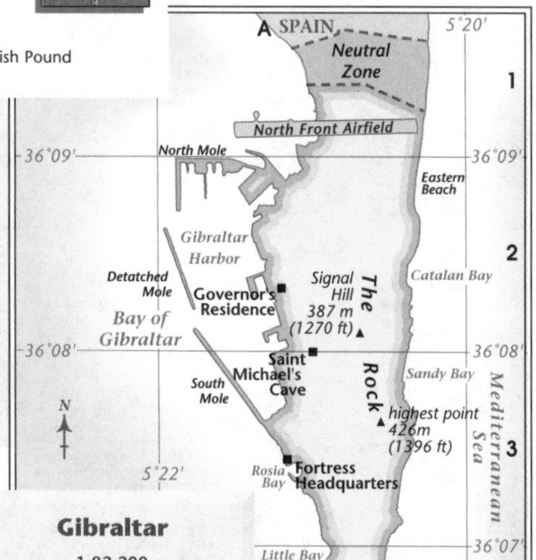

© MapQuest.com, Inc.

Andorra

Capital: Andorra la Vella
Area: 181 sq. mi.
469 sq. km.
Population: 66,000
Largest City: Andorra la Vella
Language: Catalan
Monetary Unit: French franc

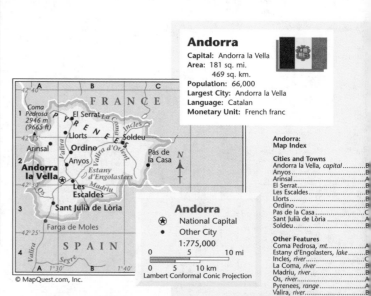

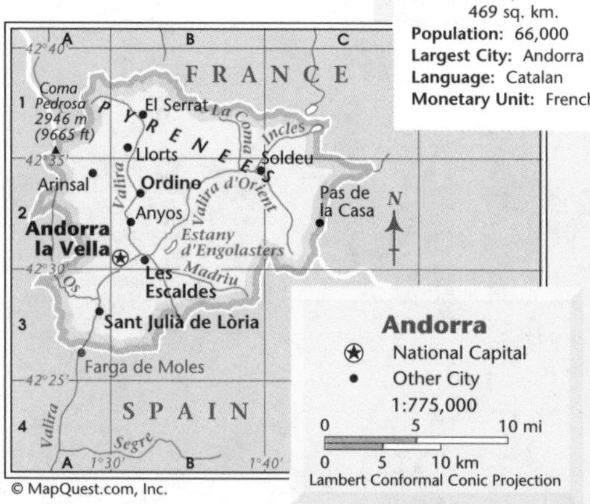

© MapQuest.com, Inc.

Andorra: Map Index

Cities and Towns

Andorra la Vella, *capital*	B
Anyos	B
Arinsal	A
El Serrat	B
Les Escaldes	B
Llorts	B
Ordino	B
Pas de la Casa	C
Sant Julià de Lòria	A
Soldeu	B

Other Features

Coma Pedrosa, *mt.*	A
Estany d'Engolasters, *lake*	B
Incles, *river*	C
La Coma, *river*	B
Madriu, *river*	B
Os, *river*	A
Pyrenees, *range*	A
Valira, *river*	B
Valira d'Orient, *river*	B

Spain: Map Index

Regions

Andalusia D4
Aragón F2
Asturias C1
Balearic Islands G3
Basque Country E1
Canary Islands Inset I
Cantabria D1
Castile-La Mancha E3
Castile-León D1, E1
Catalonia G2
Estremadura C3
Galicia C1
La Rioja E1
Madrid E2
Murcia F4
Navarra F1
Valencia F2, F3

Cities and Towns

Águilas F4
Albacete F3
Alcalá de Henares Inset II
Alcañiz F2
Alcázar de San Juan E3
Alcira F3
Alcobendas Inset II
Alcorcón E2, Inset II
Alcoy F3
Algeciras D4
Alicante F3
Almadén D3
Almansa F3
Almendralejo C3
Almería E4
Antequera D4
Aranda de Duero E2
Aranjuez E2
Astorga C1
Ávila D2
Avilés D1
Badajoz C3
Badalona H2
Baracaldo E1
Barcelona H2
Baza E4
Béjar D2
Benavente D1
Benidorm F3
Bilbao E1
Burgos E1
Cáceres C3
Cádiz C4
Calatayud F2
Cartagena F4
Castellón de la Plana F3
Ceuta D5
Cieza F3
Ciudadela H2
Ciudad Real E3
Ciudad Rodrigo C2
Córdoba D4
Cornellá de Llogregat G2
Coslada Inset II
Cuenca E2
Don Benito D3
Dos Hermanas D4
Écija D4
Elche F3
El Ferrol B1
Figueras H1
Fuenlabrada Inset II
Gerona H2
Getafe E2, Inset II
Gijón D1
Granada E4
Guadalajara E2
Guecho E1
Guernica y Luno E1
Hellín F3
Hospitalet H2
Huelva C4
Huesca F1
Ibiza G3
Jaén E4
Jerez de la Frontera C4
La Coruña B1
La Laguna Inset I
La Roda E3
Las Palmas Inset I
Leganés Inset II
León D1
Lérida G2
Linares E3
Logroño E1
Loja D4
Lorca F4
Lucena D4
Lugo C1
Madrid, *capital* E2, Inset II
Mahón J3
Málaga D4
Marbella D4
Mataró H2
Medina del Campo D2
Mérida C3
Mieres D1
Miranda de Ebro E1
Monforte C1
Morón de la Frontera D4
Móstoles Inset II
Murcia F4
Orense C1
Oviedo D1
Palencia D1
Palma H3
Pamplona F1
Plasencia C2
Ponferrada C1
Pontevedra B1
Puertollano D3
Reinosa D1
Reus G2
Sabadell H2
Sagunto F3
Salamanca D2
San Baudilio de Llobregat G2
San Fernando C4
San Sebastián F1
Santa Coloma de Gramanet H2
Santa Cruz de Tenerife Inset I
Santander E1
Santiago de Compostela B1
Segovia D2
Seville D4
Soria E2
Talavera de la Reina D3
Tarragona G2
Tarrasa H2
Telde Inset I
Teruel F2
Toledo D3
Tomelloso E3
Torrejón de Ardoz Inset II
Torrelavega D1
Torrente F3
Tortosa G2
Úbeda E3
Valdepeñas E3
Valencia F3
Valladolid D2
Vich H2
Vigo B1
Villarreal de los Infantes F3
Vitoria E1
Yecla F3
Zafra C3
Zamora D2
Zaragoza F2

Other Features

Alarcón, *reservoir* E3
Alboran, *sea* E4
Alcántara, *reservoir* C3
Almendra, *reservoir* C2
Aneto, *mt.* G1
Balearic, *islands* G3
Balearic, *sea* G2
Béticos, *mts.* D4
Biscay, *bay* D1
Brava, *coast* H2
Buendía, *reservoir* E2
Cabrera, *island* H3
Cádiz, *gulf* C4
Canaray, *islands* Inset I
Cantábrica, *mts.* C1
Cijara, *reservoir* D3
Duero, *river* D2
Ebro, *river* F1
Esla, *river* D2
Finisterre, *cape* B1
Formentera, *island* G3
Fuerteventura, *island* Inset I
Gata, *cape* E4
Gibraltar, *strait* D5
Gomera, *island* Inset I
Gran Canaria, *island* Inset I
Gredos, *mts.* D2
Guadalquivir, *river* D4
Guadarrama, *mts.* D2
Guadiana, *river* C3
Hierro, *island* Inset I
Ibérico, *mts.* E1
Ibiza, *island* G3
Jarama, *river* Inset II
Júcar, *river* F3
Lanzarote, *island* Inset I
La Palma, *island* Inset I
Majorca, *island* H3
Mediterranean, *sea* E4
Mequinenza, *reservoir* F2
Meseta, *plateau* D3
Miño, *river* B1
Minorca, *island* H2
Morena, *mts.* D3
Mulhacén, *mt.* E4
Nao, *cape* G3
Nevada, *mts.* E4
Orellana, *reservoir* D3
Ortegal, *cape* C1
Palos, *cape* F4
Pyrenees, *mts.* F1
Ricobayo, *reservoir* D2
Segura, *river* E3
Sol, *coast* D4
Tagus, *river* D3
Tenerife, *island* Inset I
Toledo, *mts.* D3
Tormes, *river* D2
Tortosa, *cape* G2
Valdecañas, *reservoir* D3
Valencia, *gulf* G3
Zújar, *reservoir* D3

Spain

Capital: Madrid
Area: 194,898 sq. mi.
504,917 sq. km.
Population: 39,168,000
Largest City: Madrid
Language: Spanish
Monetary Unit: Peseta, Euro

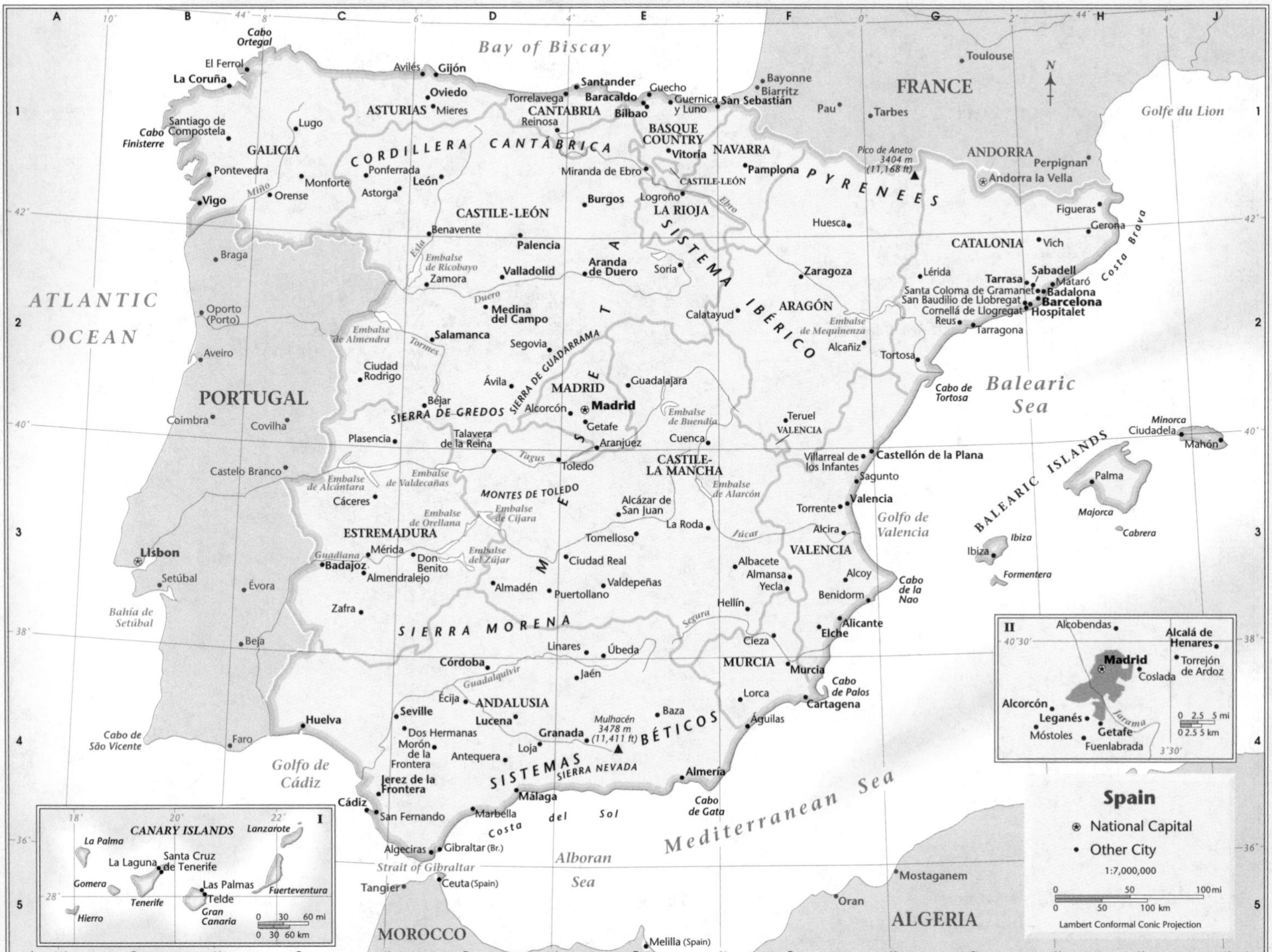

GERMANY
AUSTRIA
SWITZERLAND
LIECHTENSTEIN
HUNGARY
SLOVENIA
CROATIA
BOSNIA AND HERZEGOVINA
FRANCE
MONACO
SAN MARINO
VATICAN CITY
MALTA
TUNISIA
J U R A
A L P S
A L P S
Maritime Alps
A P E N N I N E S
Dinaric Alps
Dolomites
Basel
Zürich
Bern
Lausanne
L. Geneva
Geneva
Rhône
Rhine
L. Constance
Bregenz
Lech
Inn
Innsbruck
Salzburg
Enns
Mur
Rába
Graz
Klagenfurt
Brenner Pass
Merano
Bolzano
Cortina d'Ampezzo
TRENTINO-ALTO ADIGE
FRIULI-VENEZIA GIULIA
Udine
Gorizia
Aquileia
Trieste
Ljubljana
Zagreb
Pécs
Drava
Danube
Osijek
Sava
Una
Rijeka
Istria
Krk
Cres
Pag
Pula
Banja Luka
Zadar
Dugi Otok
Split
Brač
Hvar
Vis
Korčula
Lastovo
Mljet
Dubrovnik
Mostar
Neretva
Sarajevo
Sondrio
L. Lugano
L. Como
L. Maggiore
Oglio
Adige
Plave
Trento
Belluno
VENETO
Mt. Blanc 4807 m (15,771 ft)
VALLE D'AOSTA
Aosta
Monte Rosa 4634 m (15,203 ft)
Como
Bergamo
Monza
Milan
Novara
Vercelli
Brescia
L. Garda
Verona
Vicenza
Treviso
Venice
Gulf of Venice
Padua (Padova)
Mantua (Mantova)
Chioggia
Rovigo
LOMBARDY
Plain of Lombardy
Pavia
Turin
Asti
Piacenza
Cremona
Po
Alessandria
Parma
EMILIA-ROMAGNA
Ferrara
PIEDMONT
Reggio nell'Emilia
Modena
Canossa
Bologna
Ravenna
Cuneo
Genoa
LIGURIA
Savona
Monte Cimone 2165 m (7103 ft)
Faenza
Forlì
Gulf of Genoa
La Spezia
Rimini
Ventimiglia
San Remo
Nice
Cannes
Pesaro
Pistoia
Lucca
Prato
Pisa
Arno
Florence
Livorno
TUSCANY
Ancona
Ligurian Sea
San Gimignano
Arezzo
MARCHE
Siena
Cortona
Macerata
L. Trasimeno
Perugia
Montepulciano
Cap Corse
Elba
Grosseto
UMBRIA
Ascoli Piceno
Bastia
Pianosa
Maremma
Spoleto
Teramo
L. Bolsena
Terni
Tiber
CORSICA (Fr.)
Giglio
Montecristo
Viterbo
Rieti
Monte Corno 2914 m (9560 ft)
Pescara
Chieti
Adriatic Sea
L'Aquila
LATIUM
Sangro
Ajaccio
Civitavecchia
L. Bracciano
Campagna di Roma
Rome
ABRUZZI
Termoli
Testa del Gargano
Castel Gandolfo
Frosinone
MOLISE
San Severo
Manfredonia
Isernia
Campobasso
Foggia
Pontine Marshes
Latina
APULIA (PUGLIA)
Barletta
Punta Caprara
Asinara
Gaeta
Bari
Capua
Vesuvius 1277 m (4190 ft)
Benevento
Monopoli
Olbia
Pontine Is.
Caserta
Naples
Avellino
Sassari
Alghero
SARDINIA
Torre del Greco
Ischia
Bay of Naples
CAMPANIA
Salerno
Potenza
Matera
Brindisi
Capri
Sorrento
BASILICATA
Taranto
Lecce
Nuoro
Tirso
Monte Cervati 1898 m (6225 ft)
Gulf of Salerno
Tyrrhenian Sea
Otranto
Oristano
Monti del Gennargentu
Gulf of Taranto
SARDINIA
Cape Santa Maria di Leuca
CALABRIA
Botte Donato 1929 m (6329 ft)
Cosenza
San Pietro
Cagliari
Carbonia
Sant' Antioco
Gulf of Cagliari
Cape Carbonara
Crotone
Cape Teulada
Catanzaro
Ustica
Stromboli
Ionian Sea
Lipari Is.
Montalto 1957 m (6422 ft)
Cape San Vito
Messina
Egadi Is.
Palermo
Cefalù
Mt. Etna 3369 m (11,053 ft)
Reggio di Calabria
Trapani
Strait of Messina
Cape Spartivento
Marsala
Strait of Sicily
Caltanissetta
Enna
Catania
Agrigento
SICILY
Gela
Syracuse (Siracusa)
Cape Bon
SICILY
Ragusa
Pantelleria
Cape Passero
Mediterranean Sea
Gozo
Malta
Valletta
N
A
B
C
D
1
2
3
8°
12°
16°
44°
40°
36°
Italy
National Capital
Other City
1:5,614,000
0 50 100 150 mi
0 50 100 150 km
Lambert Conformal Conic Projection
Italy
Capital: Rome
Area: 116,333 sq. mi. 301,381 sq. km.
Population: 56,735,000
Largest City: Rome
Language: Italian
Monetary Unit: Lira, Euro

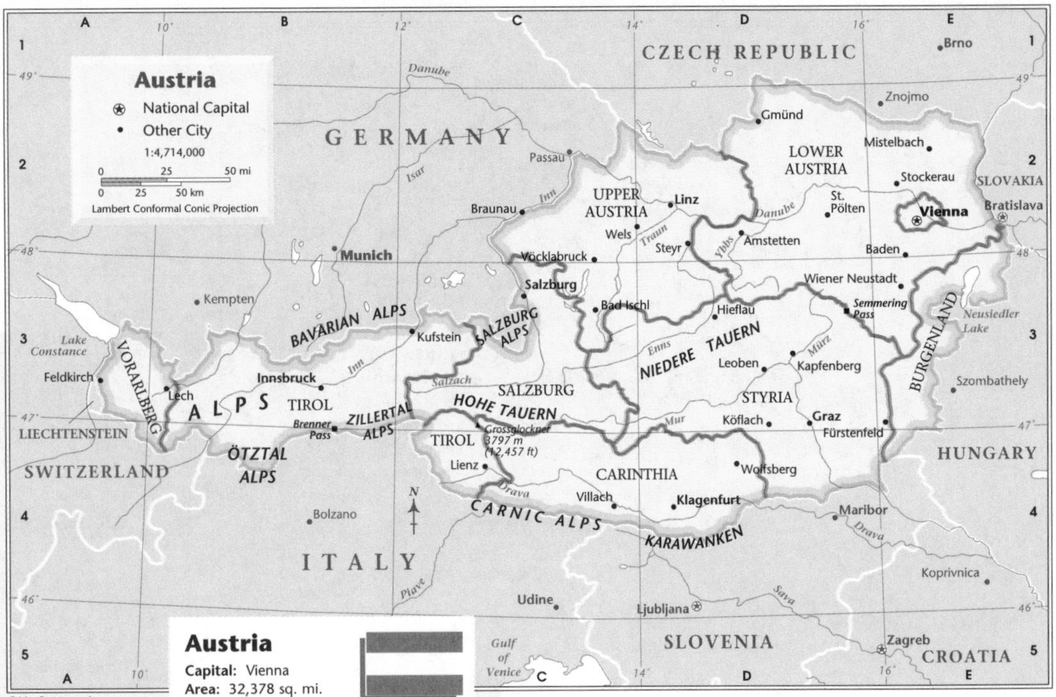

Austria

Capital: Vienna
Area: 32,378 sq. mi.
83,881 sq. km.
Population: 8,139,000
Largest City: Vienna
Language: German
Monetary Unit: Schilling, Euro

Austria: Map Index

Provinces
- Burgenland E3
- Carinthia C4
- Lower Austria D2
- Salzburg C3
- Styria D3
- Tirol B3, C4
- Upper Austria C2
- Vienna E2
- Vorarlberg A3

Cities and Towns
- Amstetten D2
- Baden E2
- Bad Ischl C3
- Braunau C2
- Feldkirch A3
- Fürstenfeld E3
- Gmünd D2
- Graz D3
- Hieflau D3
- Innsbruck B3
- Kapfenberg D3
- Klagenfurt D4
- Köflach D3
- Kufstein C3
- Lech B3
- Leoben D3
- Lienz C4
- Linz D2
- Mistelbach E2
- Salzburg C3
- Sankt Pölten D2
- Steyr D2
- Stockerau E2
- Vienna, *capital* E2
- Villach C4
- Vöcklabruck C2
- Wels C2
- Wiener Neustadt E3
- Wolfsberg D4

Other Features
- Alps, *range* B3
- Bavarian Alps, *range* B3
- Brenner, *pass* B3
- Carnic Alps, *range* C4
- Constance, *lake* A3
- Danube, *river* D2
- Drava, *river* C4
- Enns, *river* D3
- Grossglockner, *mt.* C3
- Hohe Tauern, *mts.* C3
- Inn, *river* B3, C2
- Karawanken, *range* D4
- Mur, *river* D3
- Mürz, *river* D3
- Neusiedler, *lake* E3
- Niedere Tauern, *range* D3
- Ötztal Alps, *range* B4
- Salzach, *river* C3
- Salzburg Alps, *range* C3
- Semmering, *pass* D3
- Traun, *river* C2
- Ybbs, *river* D2
- Zillertal Alps, *range* B3

Vatican City

Area: 108.7 acres
Population: 811
Languages: Italian, Latin
Monetary Unit: Lira

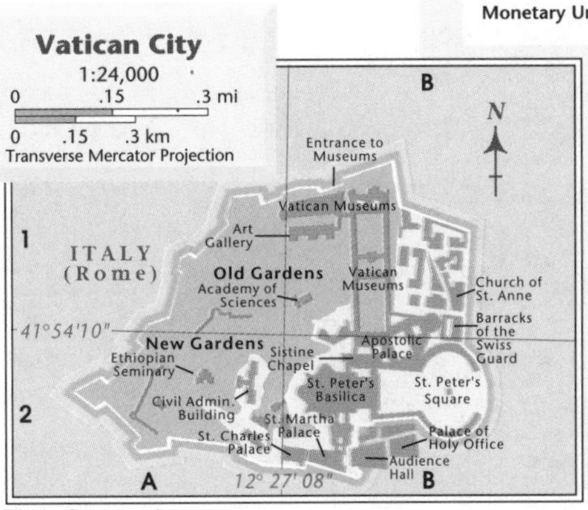

© MapQuest.com, Inc.

Vatican City: Map Index

Features
- Academy of Sciences B1
- Apostolic Palace B2
- Art Gallery B1
- Audience Hall B2
- Barracks of the Swiss Guard B1
- Church of St. Anne B1
- Civil Administration Building A2
- Entrance to Museums B1
- Ethiopian Seminary A2
- New Gardens A2
- Old Gardens A1
- Palace of Holy Office B2
- St. Charles Palace B2
- St. Martha Palace B2
- St. Peter's Basilica B2
- St. Peter's Square B2
- Sistine Chapel B2
- Vatican Museums B1

Italy: Map Index

Regions
- Abruzzi C2
- Apulia C2
- Basilicata C2
- Calabria D3
- Campania C2
- Emilia-Romagna B1
- Friuli-Venezia Giulia C1
- Latium C2
- Liguria B1
- Lombardy B1
- Marche C2
- Molise C2
- Piedmont A1
- Puglia C2
- Sardinia B3
- Sicily C3
- Trentino-Alto Adige B1
- Tuscany B2
- Umbria C2
- Valle d'Aosta A1
- Veneto B1

Cities and Towns
- Agrigento C3
- Alessandria B1
- Alghero B2
- Ancona C2
- Aosta A1
- Aquileia C1
- Arezzo B2
- Ascoli Piceno C2
- Asti B1
- Avellino C2
- Bari D2
- Barletta D2
- Belluno C1
- Benevento C2
- Bergamo B1
- Bologna B1
- Bolzano B1
- Brescia B1
- Brindisi D2
- Cagliari B3
- Caltanissetta C3
- Campobasso C2
- Canossa B1
- Capua C2
- Carbonia B3
- Caserta C2
- Castel Gandolfo C2
- Catania C3
- Catanzaro D3
- Cefalù C3
- Chieti C2
- Chioggia C1
- Civitavecchia B2
- Como B1
- Cortina d'Ampezzo C1
- Cortona B2
- Cosenza D3
- Cremona B1
- Crotone D3
- Cuneo A1
- Enna C3
- Faenza B1
- Ferrara B1
- Florence B2
- Foggia C2
- Forlì C1
- Frosinone C2
- Gaeta C2
- Gela C3
- Genoa B1
- Gorizia C1
- Grosseto B2
- Isernia C2
- L'Aquila C2
- La Spezia B1
- Latina C2
- Lecce D2
- Livorno B2
- Lucca B2
- Macerata C2
- Manfredonia C2
- Mantova B1
- Mantua (Mantova) B1
- Marsala C3
- Matera D2
- Merano B1
- Messina C3
- Milan B1
- Modena B1
- Monopoli D2
- Montepulciano B2
- Monza B1
- Naples C2
- Novara B1
- Nuoro B2
- Olbia B2
- Oristano B3
- Otranto D2
- Padova B1
- Padua (Padova) B1
- Palermo C3
- Parma B1
- Pavia B1
- Perugia C2
- Pesaro C2
- Pescara C2
- Pisa B2
- Pistoia B2
- Placenza B1
- Potenza C2
- Prato B2
- Ragusa C3
- Ravenna C1
- Reggio di Calabria C3
- Reggio nell'Emilia B1
- Rieti C2
- Rimini C1
- Rome, *capital* C2
- Rovigo B1
- Salerno C2
- San Gimignano B2
- San Remo A2
- San Severo C2
- Sassari B2
- Savona B1
- Siena B2
- Siracusa C3
- Sondrio B1
- Sorrento C2
- Spoleto C2
- Syracuse (Siracusa) C3
- Taranto D2
- Teramo C2
- Termoli C2
- Terni C2
- Torre del Greco C2
- Trapani C3
- Trento B1
- Treviso C1
- Trieste C1
- Turin A1
- Udine C1
- Venice C1
- Ventimiglia A2
- Vercelli B1
- Verona B1
- Vicenza B1
- Viterbo C2

Other Features
- Adige, *river* B1
- Adriatic, *sea* C2
- Alps, *mts.* A1, B1
- Apennines, *range* B1
- Arno, *river* B2
- Asinara, *island* B2
- Blanc, *mt.* A1
- Bolsena, *lake* B2
- Botte Donato, *mt.* D3
- Bracciano, *lake* C2
- Brenner, *pass* B1
- Cagliari, *gulf* B3
- Campagna di Roma, *region* C2
- Caprara, *point* B2
- Capri, *island* C2
- Carbonara, *cape* B3
- Cervati, *mt.* C2
- Cimone, *mt.* B1
- Como, *lake* B1
- Corno, *mt.* C2
- Dolomites, *range* B1
- Egadi, *islands* C3
- Elba, *island* B2
- Etna, *mt.* C3
- Garda, *lake* B1
- Gennargentu, *mts.* B2
- Genoa, *gulf* B1
- Giglio, *island* B2
- Ionian, *sea* D3
- Ischia, *island* C2
- Ligurian, *sea* B2
- Lipari, *islands* C3
- Lombardy, *plain* B1
- Lugano, *lake* B1
- Maggiore, *lake* B1
- Maremma, *region* B2
- Mediterranean, *sea* C3
- Messina, *strait* C3
- Montalto, *mt.* C3
- Montecristo, *island* B2
- Naples, *bay* C2
- Oglio, *river* B1
- Pantelleria, *island* C3
- Passero, *cape* C3
- Pianosa, *island* B2
- Piave, *river* C1
- Po, *river* A1, B1
- Pontine, *islands* C2
- Pontine, *marshes* C2
- Rosa, *mt.* A1
- Salerno, *gulf* C2
- Sangro, *river* C2
- San Pietro, *island* B3
- Santa Maria di Leuca, *cape* D3
- Sant'Antioco, *island* B3
- San Vito, *cape* C3
- Sardinia, *island* B2
- Sicily, *island* C3
- Sicily, *strait* B3
- Spartivento, *cape* D3
- Stromboli, *island* C3
- Taranto, *gulf* D2
- Testa del Gargano, *point* D2
- Teulada, *cape* B3
- Tiber, *river* C2
- Tirso, *river* B2
- Trasimeno, *lake* C2
- Tyrrhenian, *sea* B2
- Ustica, *island* C3
- Venice, *gulf* C1
- Vesuvius, *volcano* C2

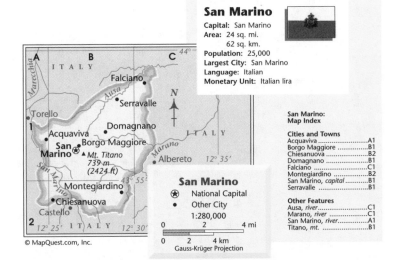

San Marino

Capital: San Marino
Area: 24 sq. mi.
62 sq. km.
Population: 25,000
Largest City: San Marino
Language: Italian
Monetary Unit: Italian lira

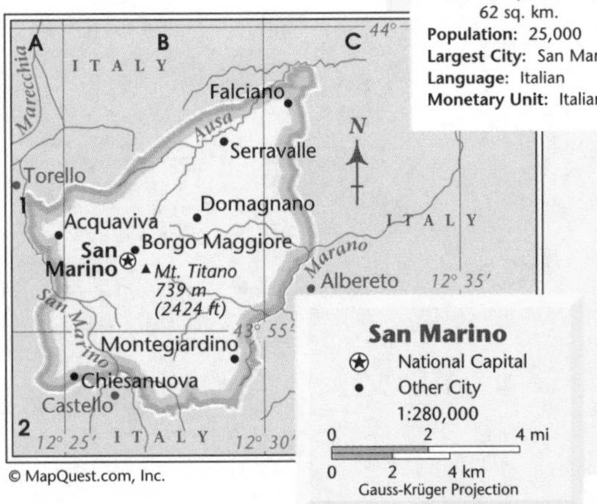

© MapQuest.com, Inc.

San Marino: Map Index

Cities and Towns
- Acquaviva A1
- Borgo Maggiore B1
- Chiesanuova B2
- Domagnano B1
- Falciano C1
- Montegiardino B2
- San Marino, *capital* B1
- Serravalle B1

Other Features
- Ausa, *river* C1
- Marano, *river* C1
- San Marino, *river* A1
- Titano, *mt.* B1

DENMARK
Sønderborg
Baltic Sea
Bornholm (Den.)
Flensburg
Kiel Bay
Rødby Havn
Rügen
Sassnitz
North Frisian Is.
Schleswig
North Sea
Puttgarden
Fehmarn
Stralsund
Pomeranian Bay
Mecklenburg Bay
Kiel
Nord-Ostsee Canal
Helgoland
Neumünster
Rostock
Greifswald
SCHLESWIG-HOLSTEIN
Lübeck
Wismar
Güstrow
Świnoujście
East Frisian Is.
Cuxhaven
Schwerin
MECKLENBURG-WESTERN POMERANIA
Oderhaff
Wilhelmshaven
Bremerhaven
HAMBURG
Hamburg
Schweriner See
Neubrandenburg
Emden
Nordenham
Szczecin
BREMEN
Lüneburger Heide
Müritz
Neustrelitz
Groningen
Lüneburg
Bremen
Oldenburg
NORTHERN EUROPEAN PLAIN
Elbe
Havel
Schwedt
POLAND
Uelzen
Wittenberge
Ems
LOWER SAXONY
BRANDENBURG
Eberswalde
Gorzów Wielkopolski
Oder
Nienburg
Stendal
Warta
Nordhorn
BERLIN
Spandau
Berlin
Frankfurt an der Oder
Mittelland Canal
Brandenburg
Potsdam
NETHERLANDS
Hannover
Wolfsburg
Osnabrück
Brunswick
Weser
Hildesheim
Eisenhüttenstadt
Odra
Arnhem
Bielefeld
Hameln
Salzgitter
Magdeburg
Luckenwalde
Münster
Detmold
Guben
Zielona Góra
Bocholt
NORTH RHINE-WESTPHALIA
Goslar
Halberstadt
Wittenberg
Neisse
Kleve
Harz
Bernburg
Dessau
Spree
Gelsenkirchen
Recklinghausen
Paderborn
Marl
Hamm
SAXONY-ANHALT
Cottbus
Bottrop
Herne
Lippstadt
Oberhausen
Lünen
Northeim
Duisburg
Dortmund
Saale
Moers
Bochum
Büren
Göttingen
Eisleben
Halle
Mulde
Mülheim an der Ruhr
Essen
Witten
Arnsberg
Nordhausen
Krefeld
Ratingen
Hagen
Kassel
Leipzig
Riesa
Düsseldorf
Wuppertal
Ruhr
Mönchengladbach
Neuss
Remscheid
Werra
Mühlhausen
Meissen
Bautzen
Görlitz
Solingen
Fulda
Dresden
Maas
Leverkusen
Naumburg
SAXONY
Maastricht
Cologne
Bergisch Gladbach
HESSE
Eisenach
Weimar
Freiberg
Zittau
Aachen
Siegen
Gotha
Erfurt
Jena
Gera
Chemnitz
Liberec
Liège
Bonn
Marburg
THURINGIA
Zwickau
Thuringian Forest
Suhl
ERZGEBIRGE
Remagen
Giessen
Lahn
Wetzlar
Fulda
Plauen
BELGIUM
Rhine
Fichtelberg 1214 m (3983 ft)
Koblenz
Bad Ems
Frankenwald
Frankfurt am Main
Taunus
Coburg
Hof
Eifel
Hanau
Kulmbach
Karlovy Vary
Labe
Wiesbaden
Offenbach
Spessart
Schweinfurt
Prague
Bingen
Mainz
Bayreuth
Fichtelgebirge
Mosel
Bad Kreuznach
Darmstadt
Main
Bamberg
CZECH REPUBLIC
LUXEMBOURG
Hunsrück
Odenwald
Oberpfälzer Wald
Trier
RHINELAND-PALATINATE
Worms
Würzburg
Jura
Weiden
Plzeň
Luxembourg
SAARLAND
Ludwigshafen am Rhein
Mannheim
Erlangen
Main-Danube Canal
Fürth
Saar
Kaiserslautern
Heidelberg
Nuremberg
Amberg
Vltava
Neunkirchen
Bohemian Forest
Saarbrücken
Speyer
Ansbach
Pirmasens
Franconian Jura
Moselle
Metz
Heilbronn
Bayerischer Wald
Karlsruhe
Regensburg
Ludwigsburg
Pforzheim
Straubing
Schwäbisch Gmünd
Nancy
Baden-Baden
Stuttgart
Esslingen
Ingolstadt
Strasbourg
Göppingen
Heidenheim
Vosges
Black Forest
BAVARIA
Isar
FRANCE
Tübingen
Landshut
Passau
Meuse
Reutlingen
Swabian Jura
Ulm
Augsburg
Neckar
Danube
Lech
Dachau
Inn
BADEN-WÜRTTEMBERG
Munich
Salzach
Ammersee
Freiburg
Memmingen
Mulhouse
Kaufbeuren
Starnberg See
Rosenheim
Chiem See
Salzburg
Singen
Ravensburg
Kempten
AUSTRIA
Saône
Bad Reichenhall
Basel
Constance
Friedrichshafen
BAVARIAN ALPS
Lindau
Aare
L. Constance
Oberammergau
Hindelang
Garmisch-Partenkirchen
Zürich
Zugspitze 2962 m (9718 ft)
Vaduz
Innsbruck
LIECHTENSTEIN
Lucerne
SWITZERLAND
Chur
ITALY
ALPS
Bolzano
Germany
Capital: Berlin
Area: 137,735 sq. mi. 356,826 sq. km.
Population: 82,087,000
Largest City: Berlin
Language: German
Monetary Unit: Mark, Euro
Germany
National Capital
Other City
1:4,066,000
0 25 50 75 mi
0 25 50 75 km
Lambert Conformal Conic Projection
N

Poland

Capital: Warsaw
Area: 120,727 sq. mi.
312,764 sq. km.
Population: 38,609,000
Largest City: Warsaw
Language: Polish
Monetary Unit: Zloty

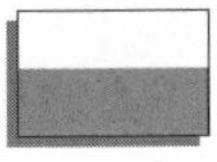

Poland: Map Index

Cities and Towns

Biała Podlaska	F2
Białystok	F2
Bielsko-Biała	D4
Bydgoszcz	C2
Bytom	D3
Chełm	F3
Chojnice	C2
Chorzów	D3
Ciechanów	E2
Częstochowa	D3
Darłowo	C1
Elbląg	D1
Ełk	F2
Gdańsk	D1
Gdynia	D1
Gliwice	D3
Głogów	C3
Gorzów Wielkopolski	B2
Grudziądz	D2
Hel	D1
Jelenia Góra	B3
Katowice	D3
Kielce	E3
Kołobrzeg	B1
Konin	D2
Koszalin	C1
Kraków	D1
Krosnow	E4
Kutno	D2
Legnica	C3
Leszno	C3
Łódź	D3
Łomża	F2
Lublin	F3
Nowy Sącz	E4
Nysa	C3
Olsztyn	E2
Opole	C3
Ostrołęka	E2
Piła	C2
Piotrków Trybunalski	D3
Płock	D2
Poznań	F4
Przemyśl	E3
Puck	D1
Puławy	E3
Radom	E3
Ruda Śląska	D3
Rybnik	D3
Rzeszów	F3
Sczcecinek	C2
Siedlce	F2
Sieradz	D3
Skierniewice	E3
Słupsk	C1
Sosnowiec	D3
Suwałki	F1
Świnoujście	B2
Szczecin	B2
Tarnobrzeg	E3
Tarnów	E3
Toruń	D2
Tychy	D3
Ustka	C1
Wałbrzych	C3
Warsaw, capital	E2
Władysławowo	D1
Włocławek	D2
Wodzisław Śląski	D3
Wrocław	C3
Zabrze	D3
Zakopane	D4
Zamość	F3
Zielona Góra	B3

Other Features

Baltic, sea	B1
Beskid, mts.	D4
Bug, river	E2, F3
Carpathian, mts.	E4
Frisches Haff, bay	D1
Gdańsk, gulf	D1
High Tatra, mts.	D4
Mamry, lake	E1
Narew, river	E2
Neisse, river	B3
Noteć, river	C2, D2
Oder, river	B2, C3
Pilica, river	E3
Pomeranian, bay	B1
Rysy, mt.	E4
San, river	F3
Silesia, region	C3
Śniardwy, lake	E2
Sudeten, mts.	B3
Vistula, river	D2, E3
Warta, river	B2, C2
Wieprz, river	F3

Map labels (Poland map):

BALTIC SEA · Rügen · Pomeranian Bay · Ustka · Władysławowo · Puck · Hel · Gulf of Gdańsk · Vistula Lagoon · RUSSIA · Kaliningrad · Kaunas · LITHUANIA · Vilnius · Darłowo · Słupsk · Gdynia · Gdańsk · Koszalin · Kołobrzeg · Świnoujście · Elbląg · L. Mamry · Suwałki · Sczcecinek · Chojnice · Olsztyn · L. Śniardwy · Ełk · Hrodna · GERMANY · Szczecin · Grudziądz · Narew · Łomża · Białystok · Baranavichy · BELARUS · Piła · Noteć · Bydgoszcz · Toruń · Vistula · Ciechanów · Ostrołęka · Gorzów Wielkopolski · Berlin · Oder · Warta · Poznań · Włocławek · Płock · Bug · Warsaw · Siedlce · Brest · Konin · Kutno · Pripyats · Zielona Góra · Leszno · Skierniewice · Biała Podlaska · Lutsk · Leipzig · Głogów · Sieradz · Łódź · Pilica · Radom · Puławy · Lublin · Chełm · Elbe · Dresden · Legnica · Jelenia Góra · Wrocław · Silesia · Piotrków Trybunalski · Kielce · Zamość · Neisse · Wałbrzych · Częstochowa · Opole · Nysa · Ruda Śląska · Bytom · Chorzów · Sosnowiec · Katowice · Rybnik · Gliwice · Zabrze · Wodzisław Śląski · Tychy · Kraków · Tarnobrzeg · San · Rzeszów · Przemyśl · Lviv · UKRAINE · Hradec Králové · Sudeten · Wieprz · Bug · Ostrava · Bielsko-Biała · Olomouc · Beskid Mts. · Zakopane · Nowy Sącz · CARPATHIAN MOUNTAINS · Tarnów · Krosnow · Dnestr · CZECH REPUBLIC · High Tatra · Rysy · 2499 m (8199 ft) · SLOVAKIA · © MapQuest.com, Inc.

Poland

- ⊛ National Capital
- • Other City
- ⊥⊥⊥ Canal

1:6,687,500

0 — 50 — 100 mi
0 — 50 — 100 km

Lambert Conformal Conic Projection

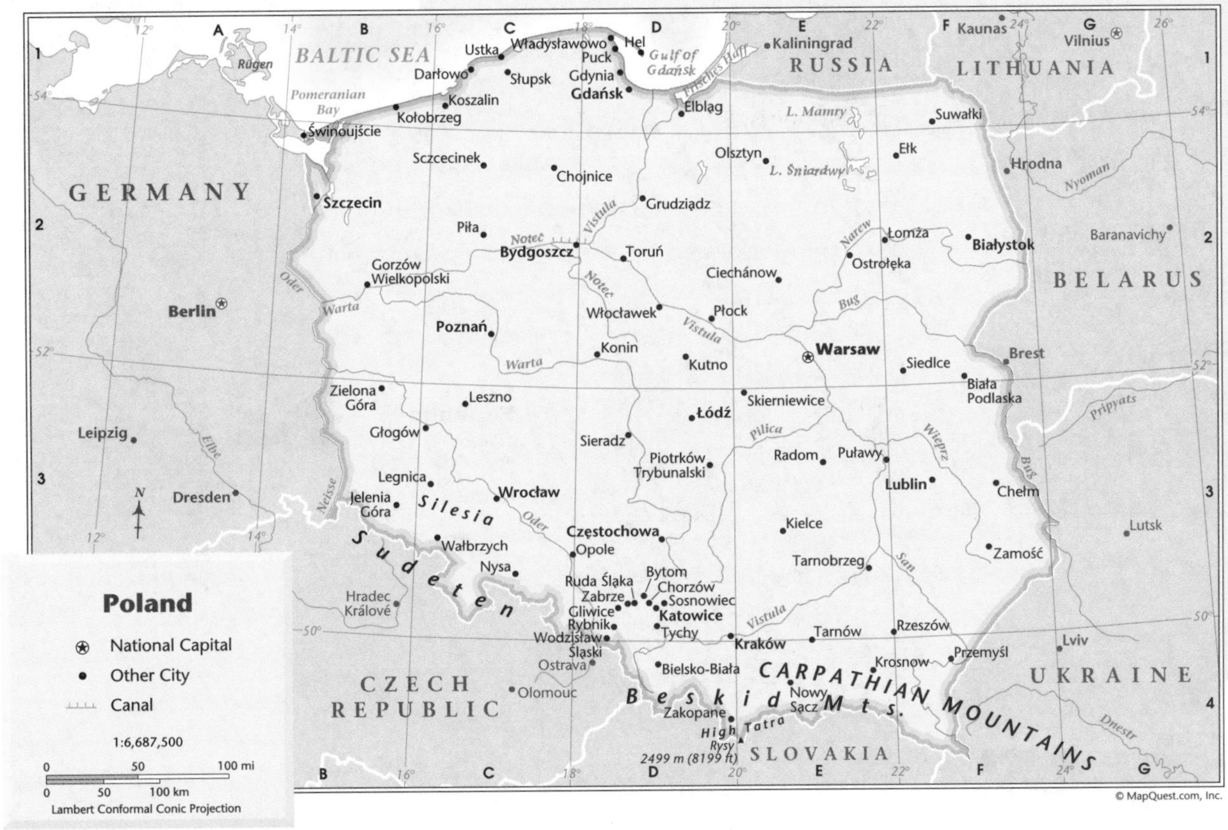

Germany: Map Index

States

Baden-Württemberg	B4
Bavaria	B4
Berlin	C2
Brandenburg	C2
Bremen	B2
Hamburg	B2
Hesse	B3
Lower Saxony	B2
Mecklenburg-Western Pomerania	C2
North Rhine-Westphalia	A3
Rhineland-Palatinate	A4
Saarland	A4
Saxony	C3
Saxony-Anhalt	B3
Schleswig-Holstein	B2
Thuringia	B3

Cities and Towns

Aachen	A3
Amberg	B4
Ansbach	B4
Arnsberg	B3
Augsburg	B4
Bad Ems	A3
Baden-Baden	B4
Bad Kreuznach	A4
Bad Reichenhall	C5
Bamberg	B4
Bautzen	C3
Bayreuth	B4
Bergisch Gladbach	A3
Berlin, capital	C2
Bernburg	B3
Bielefeld	B2
Bingen	A3
Bocholt	A3
Bochum	A3
Bonn	A3
Bottrop	A3
Brandenburg	B2
Bremen	B2
Bremerhaven	B2
Brunswick	B2
Büren	B3
Chemnitz	C3
Coburg	B3
Cologne	A3
Constance	B5
Cottbus	C3
Cuxhaven	B2
Dachau	B4
Darmstadt	B4
Dessau	B3
Detmold	B3
Dortmund	A3
Dresden	C3
Duisburg	A3
Düsseldorf	A3
Eberswalde	C2
Eisenach	B3
Eisenhüttenstadt	C2
Eisleben	B3
Emden	A2
Erfurt	B3
Erlangen	B4
Essen	A3
Esslingen	B4
Flensburg	B1
Frankfurt am Main	B3
Frankfurt an der Oder	C2
Freiberg	C3
Freiburg	A5
Friedrichshafen	B5
Fulda	B3
Fürth	B4
Garmisch-Partenkirchen	B5
Gelsenkirchen	A3
Gera	B3
Giessen	B3
Göppingen	B4
Görlitz	C3
Goslar	B3
Gotha	B3
Göttingen	B3
Greifswald	C1
Guben	C3
Güstrow	C2
Hagen	A3
Halberstadt	B3
Halle	B3
Hamburg	B2
Hameln	B2
Hamm	A3
Hanau	B3
Hannover	B2
Heidelberg	B4
Heidenheim	B4
Heilbronn	B4
Herne	A3
Hildesheim	B2
Hindelang	B5
Hof	B3
Ingolstadt	B4
Jena	B3
Kaiserslautern	A4
Karlsruhe	B4
Kassel	B3
Kaufbeuren	B5
Kempten	B5
Kiel	B1
Kleve	A3
Koblenz	A3
Krefeld	A3
Kulmbach	B3
Landshut	C4
Leipzig	B3
Leverkusen	A3
Lindau	B5
Lippstadt	B3
Lübeck	B2
Luckenwalde	C2
Ludwigsburg	B4
Ludwigshafen am Rhein	B4
Lüneburg	B2
Lünen	A3
Magdeburg	B2
Mainz	B4
Mannheim	B4
Marburg	B3
Marl	A3
Meissen	C3
Memmingen	B5
Moers	A3
Mönchengladbach	A3
Mühlhausen	B3
Mülheim an der Ruhr	A3
Munich	B4
Münster	A3
Naumburg	B3
Neubrandenburg	C2
Neumünster	B1
Neunkirchen	A4
Neuss	A3
Neustrelitz	C2
Nienburg	B2
Nordenham	B2
Nordhausen	B3
Nordhorn	A2
Northeim	B3
Nuremberg	B4
Oberammergau	B5
Oberhausen	A3
Offenbach	B3
Offenburg	A4
Oldenburg	B2
Osnabrück	B2
Paderborn	B3
Passau	C4
Pforzheim	B4
Pirmasens	A4
Plauen	C3
Potsdam	C2
Puttgarden	B1
Ratingen	A3
Ravensburg	B5
Recklinghausen	A3
Regensburg	C4
Remagen	A3
Remscheid	A3
Reutlingen	B4
Riesa	C3
Rosenheim	C5
Rostock	C1
Saarbrücken	A4
Salzgitter	B2
Sassnitz	C1
Schleswig	B1
Schwäbisch Gmünd	B4
Schwedt	C2
Schweinfurt	B3
Schwerin	B2
Siegen	B3
Singen	B5
Solingen	A3
Spandau	C2
Speyer	B4
Stendal	B2
Stralsund	C1
Straubing	C4
Stuttgart	B4
Suhl	B3
Trier	A4
Tübingen	B4
Uelzen	B2
Ulm	B4
Weiden	C4
Weimar	B3
Wetzlar	B3
Wiesbaden	B3
Wilhelmshaven	B2
Wismar	B2
Witten	A3
Wittenberg	C3
Wittenberge	B2
Wolfsburg	B2
Worms	B4
Wuppertal	A3
Würzburg	B4
Zittau	C3
Zwickau	C3

Other Features

Ammersee, lake	B4
Baltic, sea	C1
Bavarian Alps, mts.	B5
Bayerischer Wald, mts.	C4
Black, forest	B4
Bohemian, forest	C4
Chiem, lake	C5
Constance, lake	B5
Danube, river	B4
East Frisian, islands	A2
Eifel, plateau	A3
Elbe, river	B2, C3
Ems, river	A3
Erzgebirge, mts.	C3
Fehmarn, island	B1
Fichtelberg, mt.	C3
Fichtelgebirge, mts.	C3
Franconian Jura, mts	B4
Frankenwald, mts.	B3
Fulda, river	B3
Harz, mts.	B3
Havel, river	C2
Helgoland, island	A1
Hünsruck, mts.	A4
Inn, river	C4
Isar, river	C4
Kiel, bay	B1
Lahn, river	B3
Lech, river	B4
Lüneburger Heide, region	B2
Main, river	B4
Main-Danube, canal	B4
Mecklenburg, bay	B1
Mittelland, canal	B2
Mosel, river	A4
Mulde, river	C3
Müritz, lake	C2
Neckar, river	B4
Neisse, river	C3
Nord-Ostsee, canal	B1
North, sea	A1
Northern European, plain	B2
North Frisian, islands	B1
Oberpfälzer Wald, mts.	C4
Odenwald, forest	B4
Oder, river	C2
Oderhaff, lake	C2
Pomeranian, bay	C1
Rhine, river	A3, A4
Rügen, island	C1
Ruhr, river	B3
Saale, river	B3
Saar, river	A4
Salzach, river	C4
Schweriner, lake	B2
Spessart, mts.	B4
Spree, river	C3
Starnberg, lake	B5
Swabian Jura, mts.	B4
Taunus, mts.	B3
Thuringian, forest	B3
Werra, river	B3
Weser, river	B3
Zugspitze, mt.	B5

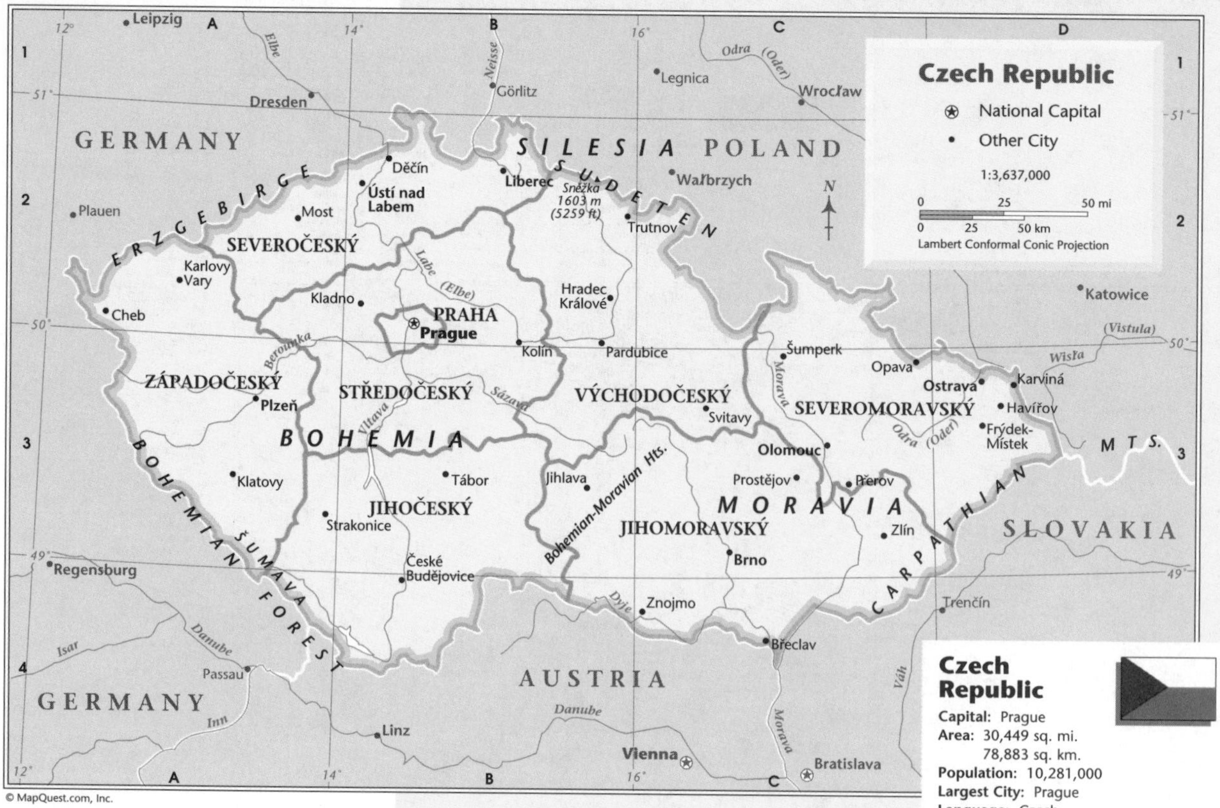

Czech Republic

Capital: Prague
Area: 30,449 sq. mi.
78,883 sq. km.
Population: 10,281,000
Largest City: Prague
Language: Czech
Monetary Unit: Koruna

Czech Republic: Map Index

Administrative Regions

Jihočeský....B3
Jihomoravský....C3
Praha....B2
Severočeský....A2
Severomoravský....C3
Středočeský....B3
Východočeský....B3
Západočeský....A3

Cities and Towns

Břeclav....C4
Brno....C3
České Budějovice....B4
Cheb....A2
Děčín....B2
Frýdek-Místek....D3
Havířov....D3
Hradec Králové....B2
Jihlava....B3
Karlovy Vary....A2
Karviná....D3
Kladno....B2
Klatovy....A3
Kolín....B2
Liberec....B2
Most....A2
Olomouc....C3
Opava....C3
Ostrava....D3
Pardubice....B2
Plzeň....A3
Prague, *capital*....B2
Přerov....C3
Prostějov....C3
Strakonice....A3
Šumperk....C3
Svitavy....C3
Tábor....B3
Trutnov....B2
Ústí nad Labem....B2
Zlín....C3
Znojmo....C4

Other Features

Berounka, *river*....A3
Bohemia, *region*....A3
Bohemian, *forest*....A3
Bohemian-Moravian, *heights*....B3
Carpathian, *mts.*....C4
Dyje, *river*....B4
Erzgebirge, *mts.*....A2
Labe, *Elbe, river*....B2
Morava, *river*....C3
Moravia, *region*....C3
Odra, *Oder, river*....C3
Sázava, *river*....B3
Silesia, *region*....B2
Sněžka, *mt.*....B2
Sudeten, *mts.*....B2
Šumava, *mts.*....A3
Vltava, *river*....B3

Slovakia

Capital: Bratislava
Area: 18,933 sq. mi.
49,049 sq. km.
Population: 5,396,000
Largest City: Bratislava
Language: Slovak
Monetary Unit: New Koruna

Slovakia: Map Index

Regions

Banskobystrický....C2
Bratislavský....A2
Košický....C2
Nitriansky....B2
Prešovský....C2
Trenčiansky....A2
Trnavský....A2
Žilinský....B2

Cities and Towns

Banská Bystrica....B2
Bardejov....C2
Bratislava, *capital*....A2
Humenné....C2
Komárno....B3
Košice....C2
Levice....B2
Liptovský Mikuláš....B2
Lučenec....B2
Martin....B2
Michalovce....C2
Nitra....B2
Nové Zamky....B3
Piešťany....A2
Poprad....C2
Považská Bystrica....B2
Prešov....C2
Prievidza....B2
Ružomberok....B2
Spišská Nová Ves....C2
Trenčín....B2
Trnava....A2
Žilina....B2
Zvolen....B2

Other Features

Biele Karpaty, *mts.*....A2
Carpathian, *mts.*....A2
Danube, *river*....A3
Gerlachovka, *mt.*....C2
Hornád, *river*....C2
Hron, *river*....B2
Ipeľ, *river*....B2
Laborec, *river*....C2
Male Karpaty, *mts.*....A2
Morava, *river*....A2
Ondava, *river*....C2
Slaná, *river*....C2
Slovenskérudohorie, *mts.*....B2
Tatra, *range*....B2
Váh, *river*....A2

Romania: Map Index

Cities and Towns

Alba Iulia....B2
Alexandria....C4
Arad....A2
Bacău....D2
Baia Mare....B2
Bîrlad....D2
Bistrița....C2
Botoșani....D2
Brăila....D3
Brașov....C3
Bucharest, *capital*....D3
Buzău....D3
Călărași....D3
Cernavodă....E3
Cluj-Napoca....B2
Constanța....E3
Craiova....B3
Dej....B2
Deva....B3
Dorohoi....D2
Drobeta-Turnu Severin....B3
Făgăras....C3
Fetești....D3
Focșani....D3
Galați....E3
Giurgiu....C4
Hunedoara....B3
Iași....D2
Lugoj....A3
Lupeni....B3
Medgidia....E3
Mediaș....C2
Miercurea Ciuc....C2
Oltenița....D3
Onești....D2
Oradea....A2
Petrila....B3
Petroșani....B3
Piatra Neamț....D2
Pitești....C3
Ploiești....D3
Rădăuți....C2
Reghin....C2
Reșița....A3
Rîmnicu Vîlcea....C3
Roman....D2
Salonța....A2
Satu Mare....B2
Sfîntu Gheorghe....C3
Sibiu....C3
Sighetul Marmației....B2

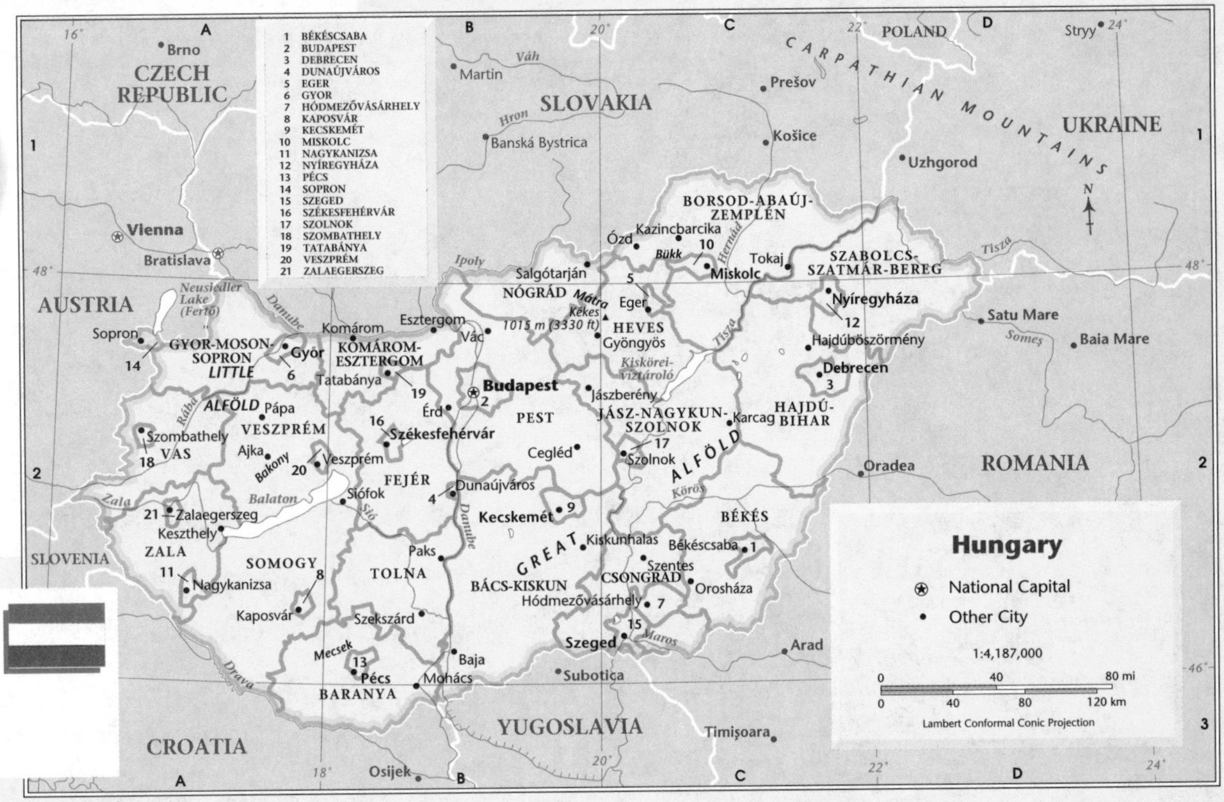

Hungary

Capital: Budapest
Area: 35,919 sq. mi.
93,054 sq. km.
Population: 10,186,000
Largest City: Budapest
Language: Hungarian
Monetary Unit: Forint

Hungary: Map Index

Counties
Bács-Kiskun B2
Baranya B3
Békés C2
Békéscsaba C2
Borsod-Abaúj-Zemplén C1
Budapest (city) B2
Csongrád C2
Debrecen C2
Dunaújváros B2
Eger C2
Fejér B2
Győr A2
Győr-Moson- Sopron A2
Hajdú-Bihar C2
Heves C2
Hódmezővásárhely C2
Jász-Nagykun-Szolnok C2
Kaposvár A2
Kecskemét B2
Komárom-Esztergom B2
Miskolc C1
Nagykanizsa A2
Nógrád B2
Nyíregyháza C2
Pécs B2
Pest B2
Somogy A2
Sopron A2
Szabolcs- Szatmár-Bereg C1
Szeged C2
Székesfehérvár B2
Szolnok C2
Szombathely A2
Tatabánya B2
Tolna B2
Vas A2
Veszprém A2
Zala .... A
Zalaegerszeg A2

Cities and Towns
Ajka A2
Baja B2
Békéscsaba C2
Budapest, *capital* B2
Cegléd B2
Debrecen C2
Dunaújváros B2
Eger C2
Érd B2
Esztergom B2
Gyöngyös B2
Győr A2
Hajdúböszörmény C2
Hódmezővásárhely C2
Jászberény B2
Kaposvár A2
Karcag C2
Kazincbarcika C1
Kecskemét B2
Keszthely A2
Kiskunhalas B2
Komárom B2
Miskolc C1
Mohács B2
Nagykanizsa A2
Nyíregyháza C2
Orosháza C2
Ózd C1
Paks B2
Pápa A2
Pécs B2
Salgótarján B1
Siófok B2
Sopron A2
Szeged C2
Székesfehérvár B2
Szekszárd B2
Szentes C2
Szolnok C2
Szombathely A2
Tatabánya B2
Tokaj C1
Vác B2
Veszprém A2
Zalaegerszeg A2

Other Features
Bakony, *mts.* A2
Balaton, *lake* A2
Bükk, *mts.* C1
Danube, *river* A2, B2
Drava, *river* A2
Great Alföld, *plain* B2
Hernád, *river* C1
Ipoly, *river* B1
Kékes, *mt.* C2
Kiskörei-víztároló, *lake* C2
Körös, *river* C2
Little Alföld, *plain* A2
Maros, *river* C2
Mátra, *mts.* B2
Mecsek, *mts.* B2
Neusiedler (Fertő), *lake* A2
Rába, *river* A2
Sió, *river* B2
Tisza, *river* C2
Zala, *river* A2

Romania

Capital: Bucharest
Area: 91,699 sq. mi.
267,174 sq. km.
Population: 22,334,000
Largest City: Bucharest
Language: Romanian
Monetary Unit: Leu

Sighişoara C2
Siret D2
Slatina C3
Slobozia D3
Suceava D2
Tecuci D3
Timişoara A3
Tîrgovişte C3
Tîrgu Jiu B3
Tîrgu-Mureş C2
Tîrgu Neamţ D2
Tîrgu Ocna D2
Tulcea E3
Turda B2
Turnu Măgurele C4
Vaslui D2
Zalău B2

Other Features
Apuseni, *mts.* B2
Argeş, *river* C3
Banat, *region* A3
Bicaz, *reservoir* D2
Bihor, *mts.* B2
Bistriţa, *river* C2
Carpathian, *mts.* B1
Danube, *river* B3, D3, E3
Dobruja, *region* E4
Ialomiţa, *river* D3
Iron Gate, *reservoir* B3
Jiu, *river* B3
Moldavia, *region* D2
Moldoveanu, *mt.* C3
Mouths of the Danube, *delta* E3
Mureş, *river* B2
Olt, *river* C3
Prut, *river* E2
Razelm, *lake* E3
Siret, *river* D2
Someş, *river* B2
Transylvanian Alps, *mts.* B3
Walachia, *region* B3

Part of Russia extends onto the continent of Asia.

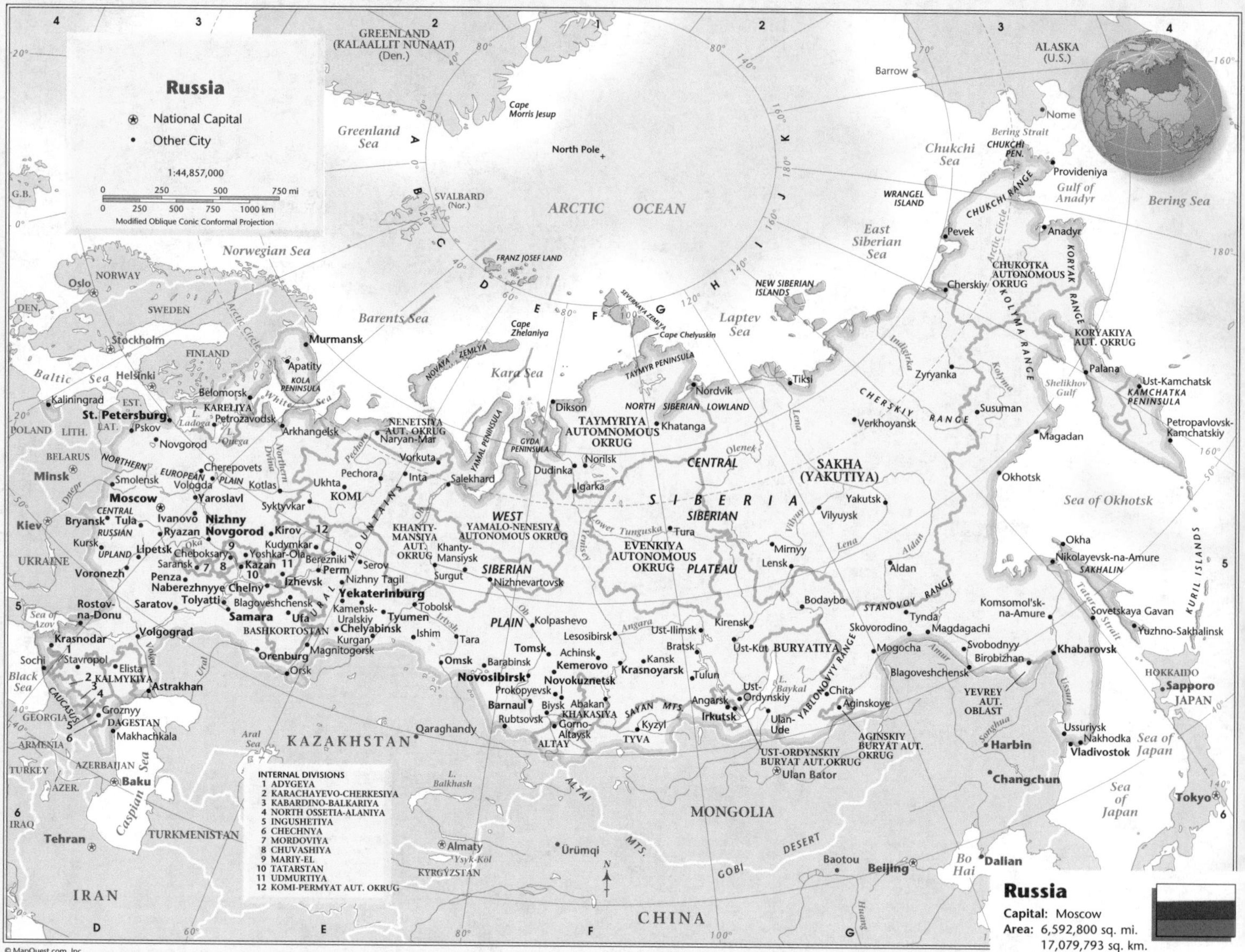

Russia

Capital: Moscow
Area: 6,592,800 sq. mi.
17,079,793 sq. km.
Population: 146,394,000
Largest City: Moscow
Language: Russian
Monetary Unit: Ruble

Russia: Map Index

Internal Divisions
Adygeya (republic) D5
Aginskiy Buryat (autonomous okrug) G4
Altay (republic) F4
Bashkortostan (republic) D4
Buryatiya (republic) G4
Chechnya (republic) D5
Chukotka (autonomous okrug) J3
Chuvashiya (republic) D4
Dagestan (republic) D5
Evenkiya (autonomous okrug) F3
Ingushetiya (republic) D5
Kabardino-Balkariya (republic) D5
Kalmykiya (republic) D5
Karachayevo-Cherkesiya (republic) D5
Kareliya (republic) C3
Khakasiya (republic) F4
Khanty-Mansiya (autonomous okrug) E3
Komi (republic) D3
Komi-Permyat (autonomous okrug) D3
Koryakiya (autonomous okrug) J3
Mariy-El (republic) D4
Mordoviya (republic) D4
Nenetsiya (autonomous okrug) D3
North Ossetia Alaniya (republic) D5
Tatarstan (republic) D4
Taymyriya (autonomous okrug) F2
Tyva (republic) F4
Udmurtiya (republic) D4
Ust-Ordynskiy Buryat (autonomous okrug) G5
Sakha (Yakutiya) (republic) H3
Yamalo-Nenesiya (autonomous okrug) E3
Yevrey (autonomous oblast) H5

Cities and Towns
Abakan F4
Achinsk F4
Aginskoye G4
Aldan H4
Anadyr J3
Angarsk G4
Apatity C3
Arkhangelsk D3
Astrakhan D5
Barabinsk E4
Barnaul F4
Belomorsk C3
Berezniki D4
Birobizhan H5
Biysk F4
Blagoveshchensk D4
Blagoveshchensk H4
Bodaybo G4
Bratsk G4
Bryansk C4
Cheboksary D4
Chelyabinsk E4
Cherepovets C4
Cherskiy J3
Chita G4
Dikson F2
Dudinka F3
Elista D5
Gorno-Altaysk F4
Groznyy D5
Igarka F3
Inta E3
Irkutsk G4
Ishim E4
Ivanovo D4
Izhevsk D4
Kaliningrad C4
Kamensk-Uralskiy D4
Kansk F4
Kazan D4
Kemerovo F4
Khabarovsk H5
Khanty-Mansiysk E3
Khatanga G2
Kirensk G4
Kolpashevo F4
Komsomol'sk-na-Amure H4
Kotlas D3
Krasnodar C5
Krasnoyarsk F4
Kudymkar D4
Kurgan E4
Kursk C4
Kyzyl F4
Lensk G3
Lesosibirsk F4
Lipetsk C4
Magadan I4
Magdagachi H4
Magnitogorsk D4
Makhachkala D5
Mirnyy G3
Mogocha G4
Moscow, *capital* C4
Murmansk C3
Naberezhnyye Chelny D4
Nakhodka H5
Naryan-Mar D3
Nikolayevsk-na-Amure I4
Nizhnevartovsk E3
Nizhny Novgorod D4
Nizhny Tagil D4
Nordvik G2
Norilsk F3
Novgorod C4
Novokuznetsk F4
Novosibirsk F4
Okha I4
Okhotsk I4
Omsk E4
Orenburg D4
Orsk D4
Palana J4
Penza D4
Pechora D3
Perm D4
Petropavlovsk-Kamchatskiy I4
Petrozavodsk C3
Pevek J3
Prokopyevsk F4
Provideniya K3
Pskov C4
Rostov-na-Donu C5
Rubtsovsk F4
Ryazan C4
St. Petersburg C4
Salekhard E3
Samara D4
Saransk D4
Saratov D4
Serov E4
Skovorodino H4
Smolensk C4
Sochi C5
Sovetskaya Gavan I5
Stavropol D5
Surgut E3
Susuman I3
Svobodnyy H4
Syktyvkar D3
Tara E4
Tiksi H2
Tobolsk E4
Tolyatti D4
Tomsk F4
Tula C4
Tulun G4
Tura G3
Tynda H4
Tyumen E4
Ufa D4
Ukhta D3
Ulan-Ude G4
Ussuriysk H5
Ust-Ilimsk G4
Ust-Kamchatsk J4
Ust-Kut G4
Ust-Ordynskiy G4
Verkhoyansk H3
Vilyuysk H3
Vladivostok H5
Volgograd D5
Vologda C4
Vorkuta E3
Voronezh C4
Vyatka D4
Yakutsk H3
Yaroslavl C4
Yekaterinburg E4
Yoshkar-Ola D4
Yuzhno-Sakhalinsk I5
Zyryanka I3

Other Features
Aldan, *river* H4
Amur, *river* H4
Anadyr, *gulf* K3
Angara, *river* F4
Azov, *sea* C5
Baltic, *sea* B4
Barents, *sea* C2
Baykal, *lake* G4
Bering, *sea* K4
Bering, *strait* K3
Black, *sea* C5
Caspian, *sea* D6
Caucasus, *mts.* D5
Central Russian, *upland* C4
Central Siberian, *plateau* G3
Central, *range* I4
Chelyuskin, *cape* G2
Cherskiy, *range* H3
Chukchi, *peninsula* K3
Chukchi, *range* J3
Chukchi, *sea* K2
Dnepr, *river* C4
Dzhugdzhur, *range* H4
East Siberian, *sea* J2
Franz Josef Land, *islands* D1
Gyda, *peninsula* E2
Indigirka, *river* I3
Irtysh, *river* E4
Kamchatka, *peninsula* J4
Kara, *sea* E2
Kola, *peninsula* C3
Kolyma, *range* J3
Kolyma, *river* I3
Koryak, *range* J3
Kuril, *islands* I5
Ladoga, *lake* C3
Laptev, *sea* H2
Lena, *river* H3
Lower Tunguska, *river* F3
New Siberian, *islands* I2
North Siberian, *lowland* G2
Northern Divina, *river* D3
Northern European, *plain* C4
Novaya Zemlya, *islands* D2
Ob, *river* E3
Oka, *river* D4
Okhotsk, *sea* I4
Olenek, *river* G3
Onega, *lake* C3
Pechora, *river* D3
Sakhalin, *island* I4
Sayan, *mts.* F4
Severnaya Zemlya, *islands* F1
Shelikhov, *gulf* I3
Siberia, *region* G3
Sikhote Alin, *range* H5
Stanovoy, *range* H4
Tatar, *strait* I4
Taymyr, *peninsula* G2
Ural, *mts.* D4
Ural, *river* D5
Ussuri, *river* H5
Verkhoyansk, *range* H3
Vilyuy, *river* G3
Volga, *river* D5
West Siberian, *plain* E3
White, *sea* C3
Wrangel, *island* J2
Yablonovyy, *range* G4
Yamal, *peninsula* E3
Yenisey, *river* F3
Zhelaniya, *cape* E2

Armenia

Capital: Yerevan
Area: 11,500 sq. mi.
29,793 sq. km.
Population: 3,409,000
Largest City: Yerevan
Language: Armenian
Monetary Unit: Dram

Armenia:
Map Index

Cities and Towns

Alaverdi	B1
Ararat	B3
Artashat	B3
Artik	A2
Artsvashen	C2
Dilijan	B2
Ejmiatsin	B2
Gavarr	C2
Goris	D3

Gyumri	A2
Hoktemberyan	B2
Hrazdan	B2
Ijevan	C2
Kafan	D3
Kirovakan	B2
Martuni	C2
Meghri	D4
Sisian	D3
Sotk	C2
Stepanavan	B2
Tashir	B1
Vardenis	C2

Vayk	C3
Yerevan, *capital*	B2
Other Features	
Akhuryan, *river*	A2
Aragats, *mt.*	B2
Aras, *river*	B2
Arpa, *river*	C3
Debed, *river*	B2
Hrazdan, *river*	B2
Lesser Caucasus, *mts.*	B1
Sevan, *lake*	C2
Vorotan, *river*	C3

Armenia

⊛ National Capital
• Other City

1:3,000,000

0   25   50 mi
0   25   50 km
Azimuthal Equal Area Projection

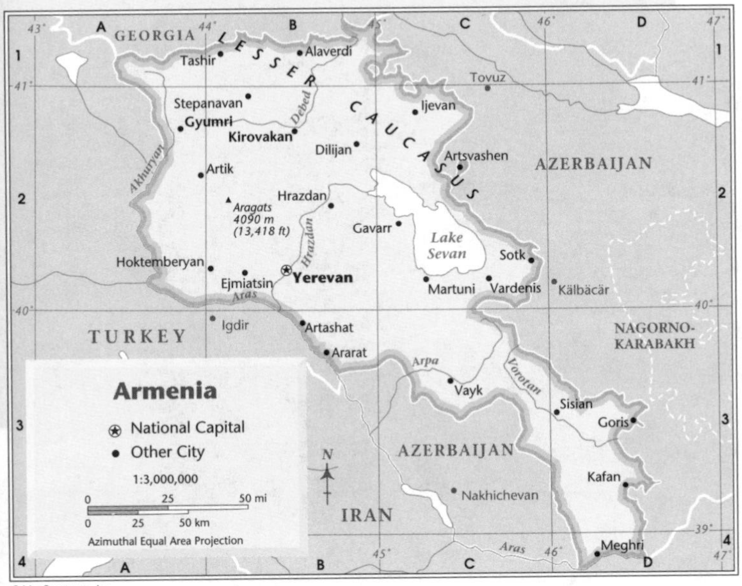

Georgia:
Map Index

Cities and Towns

Akhalkalaki	B4
Akhaltsikhe	B4
Akhmeta	C3
Batumi	A4
Bolnisi	C4
Borjomi	B4
Chiatura	B3
Gagra	A2
Gori	C4
Gudauta	A2
Jvari	B3
Khashuri	B4
Kobuleti	A3
Kutaisi	B3
Lagodekhi	D4
Marneuli	C4
Mtskheta	C4
Ochamchire	A3
Ozurgeti	A3
Poti	A3
Rustavi	C4
Samtredia	B3
Senaki	B3
Sukhumi	A3
Tbilisi, *capital*	C4
Telavi	C4
Tqvarcheli	A3
Tsiteli-Tsqaro	D4
Tskhinvali	B3

Tsnori	C4
Zestaponi	B3
Zugdidi	A3
Other Features	
Abkhazia, *autonomous*	
republic	A3
Ajaria, *autonomous republic*	A4
Alazani, *river*	C4
Caucasus, *mts.*	A2
Enguri, *river*	A3
Iori, *river*	C4
Lesser Caucasus, *mts.*	B4
Mqinvartsveri, *mt.*	C3
Mtkvari, *river*	C4
Rioni, *river*	B3
Shkhara, *mt.*	B3
South Ossetia, *region*	B3

Georgia

Capital: Tbilisi
Area: 26,900 sq. mi.
69,689 sq. km.
Population: 5,067,000
Largest City: Tbilisi
Language: Georgian
Monetary Unit: Lari

Azerbaijan:
Map Index

Cities and Towns

Ağcabädi	B2
Ağdam	B3
Ağstafa	A2
Älät	C3
Äli Bayramli	C3
Astara	C3
Baku, *capital*	C2
Balakän	B2
Bärdä	B2
Biläsuvar	C3
Gäncä	B2
Göyçay	B2
Kälbäcär	B2
Länkäran	C3
Mingäçevir	B2
Nakhichevan	A3
Quba	C2
Şahbuz	A3
Şaki	B2

Salyan	C3
Sumqayit	C2
Tovuz	A2
Xaçmaz	C2
Xankändi	B3
Yevlax	B2
Zaqatala	B2
Other Features	
Abşeron, *peninsula*	C2
Aras, *river*	B3
Bazardüzü Daği, *mt.*	B2
Caucasus, *range*	A1
Karabakh, *canal*	B2
Kür, *river*	A2, C2
Kür-Aras, *lowland*	B2
Lesser Caucasus, *range*	A2
Mingäçevir, *reservoir*	B2
Nagorno-Karabakh,	
autonomous region	B2
Samur, *river*	B2
Talish, *mts.*	C3

Azerbaijan

Capital: Baku
Area: 33,400 sq. mi.
86,528 sq. km.
Population: 7,908,000
Largest City: Baku
Language: Azerbaijani
Monetary Unit: Manat

Azerbaijan

⊛ National Capital
• Other City

1:5,673,000

0   25   50 mi
0   25   50 km
Azimuthal Equal Area Projection

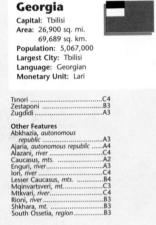

Estonia:
Map Index

Cities and Towns

Haapsalu	B2
Kärdla	B1
Keila	C1
Kohtla-Järve	D1
Kunda	D1
Kuressaare	B2
Mustvee	D2
Narva	E1
Paldiski	C1
Pärnu	C2
Rapla	C1
Tallinn, *capital*	C1
Tapa	C1
Tartu	D2
Tõrva	C2
Türi	C2
Valga	D3
Viljandi	C2
Virtsu	B2
Võru	D3

Other Features

Baltic, *sea*	A1
Finland, *gulf*	C1
Hiiumaa, *island*	B2
Irbe, *strait*	A3
Munamägi, *mt.*	D3
Narva, *river*	D1
Pärnu, *river*	C2
Pedja, *river*	D2
Peipus, *lake*	D2
Pskov, *lake*	D3
Riga, *gulf*	B3
Saaremaa, *island*	B2
Võrts Järv, *lake*	D2

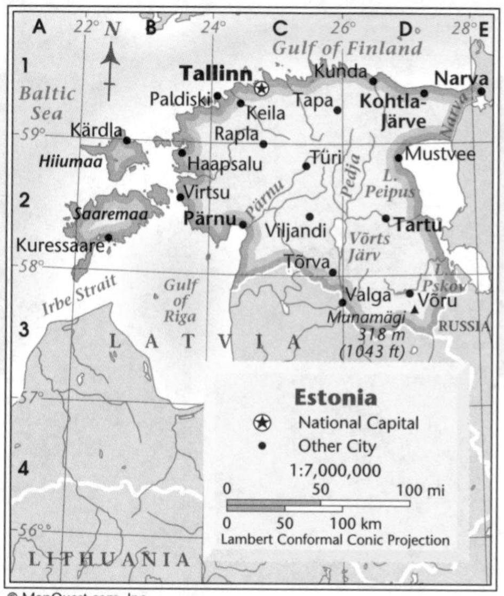

Estonia

Capital: Tallinn
Area: 17,413 sq. mi.
45,111 sq. km.
Population: 1,409,000
Largest City: Tallinn
Language: Estonian
Monetary Unit: Kroon

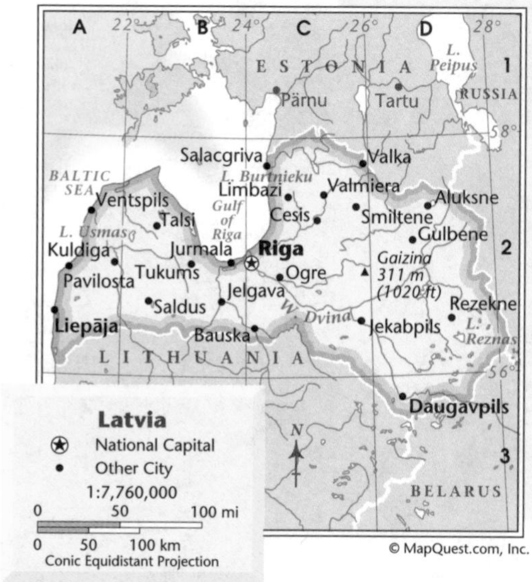

Latvia

Capital: Riga
Area: 24,900 sq. mi.
64,508 sq. km.
Population: 2,354,000
Largest City: Riga
Language: Latvian
Monetary Unit: Lat

Latvia:
Map Index

Cities and Towns

Aluksne	D2
Bauska	C2
Cesis	C2
Daugavpils	D3
Gulbene	D2
Jekabpils	C2
Jelgava	B2
Jurmala	B2
Kuldiga	A2
Liepāja	A2
Limbazi	C2
Ogre	C2
Pavilosta	A2
Rezekne	D2
Riga, *capital*	C2
Salacgriva	C2
Saldus	B2
Smiltene	C2
Talsi	B2
Tukums	B2
Valka	C2
Valmiera	C2
Ventspils	A2

Other Features

Baltic, *sea*	A2
Burtnieku, *lake*	C2
Gaizina, *mt.*	C2
Reznas, *lake*	D2
Riga, *gulf*	B2
Usmas, *lake*	B2
Western Dvina, *river*	C2

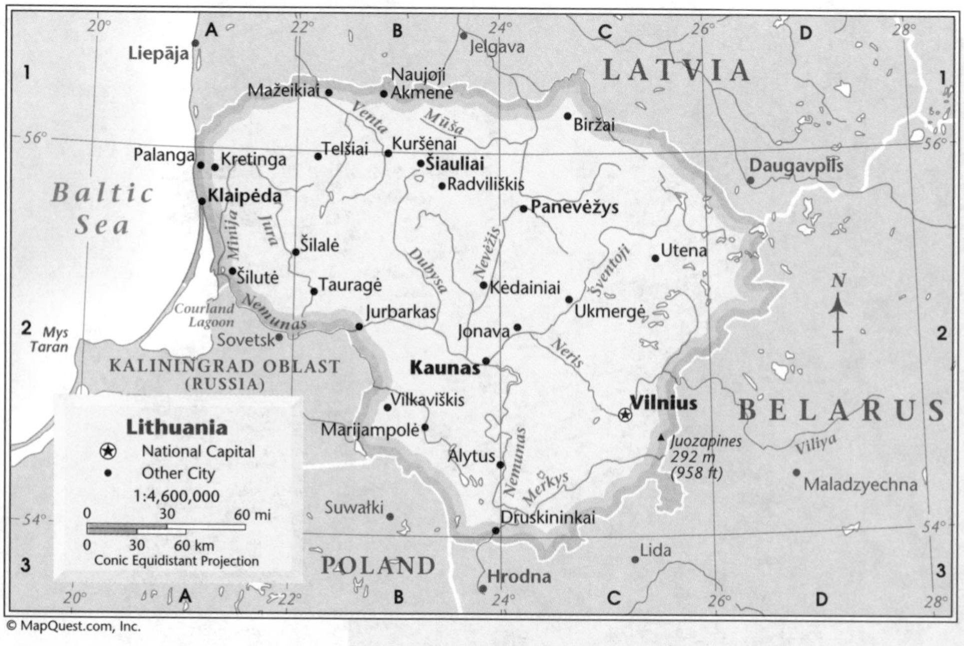

Lithuania

Capital: Vilnius
Area: 25,213 sq. mi.
65,319 sq. km.
Population: 3,585,000
Largest City: Vilnius
Language: Lithuanian
Monetary Unit: Litas

Lithuania:
Map Index

Cities and Towns

Alytus	C2
Biržai	C1
Druskininkai	B2
Jonava	C2
Jurbarkas	B2
Kaunas	B2
Kėdainiai	B2
Klaipėda	A2
Kretinga	A2
Kuršėnai	B1
Marijampolė	B2
Mažeikiai	B1
Naujoji Akmenė	B1
Palanga	A2
Panevėžys	C2
Radviliškis	B2
Šiauliai	B2
Šilalė	B2
Šilutė	A2
Tauragė	B2
Telšiai	B2
Ukmergė	C2
Utena	C2
Vilkaviškis	B2
Vilnius, *capital*	C2

Other Features

Baltic, *sea*	A2
Courland, *lagoon*	A2
Dubysa, *river*	B2
Juozapines, *mt.*	C2
Jura, *river*	A2
Merkys, *river*	C2
Minija, *river*	A2
Mūša, *river*	B1
Nemunas, *river*	A2, C2
Neris, *river*	C2
Nevėžis, *river*	B2
Šventoji, *river*	C2
Venta, *river*	B1

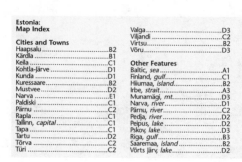

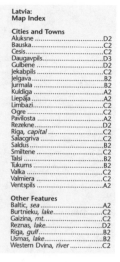

© MapQuest.com, Inc.

Belarus

Capital: Minsk
Area: 80,134 sq. mi.
207,601 sq. km.
Population: 10,402,000
Largest City: Minsk
Languages: Belarussian, Russian
Monetary Unit: Belarus ruble

Belarus: Map Index

Cities and Towns
Asipovichy D3
Babruysk D3
Baranavichy C3
Brest A3
Homyel E3
Hrodna A3
Krychaw E3
Lida B3
Mahilyow E3
Maladzyechna C2
Mazyr D3
Minsk, *capital* C3
Orsha E2
Pastavy C2
Pinsk C3
Polotsk D2
Rechytsa E3
Salihorsk C3
Smilovichi D3
Smolevichi D2
Vawkavysk B3
Vitsyebsk E2
Zhlobin D3

Other Features
Bug, *river* A3
Byarezina, *river* D3
Byelaruskaya Hrada, *range* C3
Dnepr, *river* E3
Dnepr-Bug, *canal* B3
Dzyarzhynskaya Hara, *mt.* C3
Nyoman, *river* B3
Pripyats, *marshes* C4
Pripyats, *river* C3
Ptsich, *river* D3
Sozh, *river* E3
Western Dvina, *river* D2

Ukraine: Map Index

Cities and Towns
Balaklava C4
Belaya Tserkov C2
Berdyansk D3
Cherkassy C2
Chernigov C1
Chernivtsi B2
Chornobyl' C1
Dneprodzerzhinsk C2
Dnipropetrovsk D2
Donetsk D2
Feodosiya D3
Gorlovka D2
Ivano-Frankovsk A2
Izmail B3
Kachovka C3
Kerch D3
Kharkiv D1
Kherson C3
Khmelnytskyy B2
Khust A2
Kiev, *capital* C1
Kirovograd C2
Konotop C1
Korosten B1
Kotovsk B2
Kovel A1
Kramatorsk D2
Kremenchug C2
Kryvyi Rih C2
Lisichansk D2
Luhansk D2
Lutsk B1
Lviv A2
Makeyevka D2
Mariupol D3
Melitopol D3
Mogilev Podolskiy B2
Mykolaiv C3
Nikopol C2
Odesa C3
Pervomaysk C2
Poltava C2
Priluki C1
Rovno B1
Sevastopol C4
Shostka C1
Simferopol C4
Sumy C1
Ternopol B2
Uman C2
Uzhgorod A2
Vinnitsa B2
Yalta C4
Yevpatoriya C3
Zaporizhzhia D2
Zhitomir B1

Other Features
Azov, *sea* D3
Black, *sea* C3
Bug, *river* A1
Carpathian, *mts.* A2
Crimean, *mts.* C4
Crimean, *peninsula* C3
Desna, *river* C1
Dneprodzerzhinsk, *reservoir* C2
Dnieper, *river* C1,C3
Dniester, *river* B2
Donets, *basin* D2
Donets, *river* D2
Hoverla, *mt.* A2
Kakhovka, *reservoir* C3
Karkinit, *bay* C3
Kerch, *strait* D3
Kiev, *reservoir* C1
Kremenchug, *reservoir* C2
Pripyat, *river* A1
Prut, *river* B2
Psel, *river* C1
Sluch, *river* B1
Southern Bug, *river* B2
Taganrog, *gulf* D3
Tisza, *river* A2
Volyno-Podol'skaya Vozvyshennost, *uplands* B2
Vorskla, *river* C1

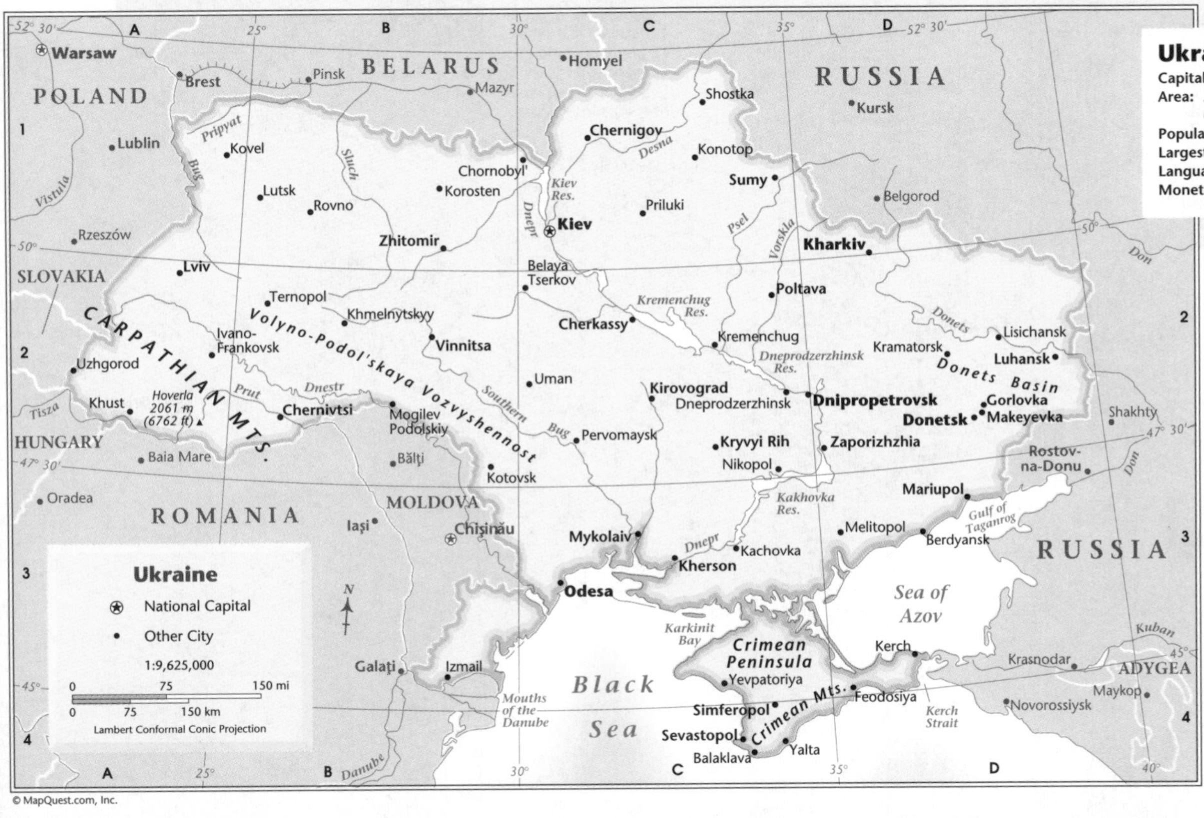

© MapQuest.com, Inc.

Ukraine

Capital: Kiev
Area: 233,100 sq. mi.
603,886 sq. km.
Population: 49,811,000
Largest City: Kiev
Languages: Ukrainian, Russian
Monetary Unit: Hryvnya

Slovenia

Capital: Ljubljana
Area: 7,821 sq. mi.
　　　20,262 sq. km.
Population: 1,971,000
Largest City: Ljubljana
Languages: Slovenian, Serbo-Croatian
Monetary Unit: Tolar

Slovenia:
Map Index

Cities and Towns
Celje C2
Idrija B2
Jesenice B2
Kočevje B3
Koper A3
Kranj B2
Krško C3
Ljubljana, *capital* B2
Maribor C2
Murska Sobota D2
Nova Gorica A3
Novo Mesto C3
Postojna B3
Ptuj C2

Other Features
Adriatic, *sea* A3
Drava, *river* C2
Julian Alps, *mts.* A2
Krka, *river* B3
Kupa, *river* B3
Mura, *river* C2
Sava, *river* B2
Savinja, *river* B2
Trieste, *gulf* A3
Triglav, *mt.* A2

© MapQuest.com, Inc.

Croatia

National Capital
Other City
1:9,700,000

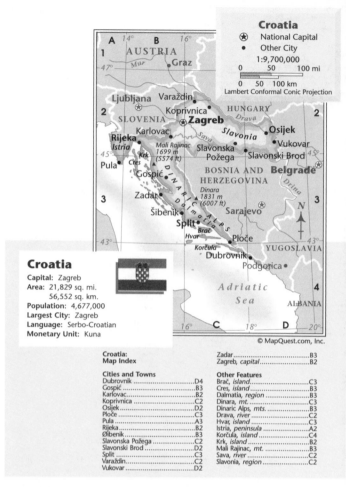

© MapQuest.com, Inc.

Croatia

Capital: Zagreb
Area: 21,829 sq. mi.
　　　56,552 sq. km.
Population: 4,677,000
Largest City: Zagreb
Language: Serbo-Croatian
Monetary Unit: Kuna

Croatia:
Map Index

Cities and Towns
Dubrovnik D4
Gospić B3
Karlovac B2
Koprivnica C2
Osijek D2
Ploče C3
Pula A3
Rijeka B2
Øibenik B3
Slavonska Požega C2
Slavonski Brod D2
Split C3
Varaždin C2
Vukovar D2

Zadar B3
Zagreb, *capital* B2

Other Features
Brač, *island* C3
Cres, *island* B3
Dalmatia, *region* B3
Dinara, *mt.* C3
Dinaric Alps, *mts.* B3
Drava, *river* C2
Hvar, *island* C3
Istria, *peninsula* A2
Korčula, *island* C4
Krk, *island* B2
Mali Rajinac, *mt.* B3
Sava, *river* C2
Slavonia, *region* C2

Bosnia and Hercegovina:
Map Index

Cities and Towns
Banja Luka B1
Bihać A1
Bijeljina C1
Bosanska Gradiška B1
Bosanska Krupa A1
Brčko B1
Bugojno B1
Derventa B1
Doboj B1
Foča B2
Gacko B2
Goražde B2
Gračanica B1
Jajce B1
Livno B2
Mostar B2
Pale B2
Prijedor A1
Sanski Most A1
Sarajevo, *capital* B2
Srebrenica B1
Teslić B1
Trebinje B1
Tuzla B1
Zavidovići B1
Zenica B1
Zvornik C1

Other Features
Bosna, *river* B1
Dinara, *mt.* A2
Dinaric Alps, *mts.* A2
Drina, *river* C1
Neretva, *river* B2
Sava, *river* B1
Una, *river* A1
Vrbas, *river* B1

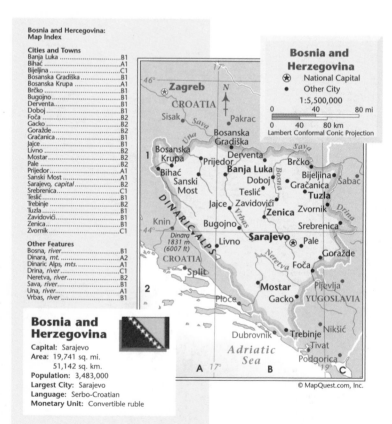

© MapQuest.com, Inc.

Bosnia and Herzegovina

Capital: Sarajevo
Area: 19,741 sq. mi.
　　　51,142 sq. km.
Population: 3,483,000
Largest City: Sarajevo
Language: Serbo-Croatian
Monetary Unit: Convertible ruble

F.Y.R. Macedonia

Capital: Skopje
Area: 9,928 sq. mi.
　　　25,720 sq. km.
Population: 2,023,000
Largest City: Skopje
Languages: Macedonian, Albanian, Serbo-Croatian, Turkish
Monetary Unit: Denar

F.Y.R. Macedonia:
Map Index

Cities and Towns
Bitola B2
Blatec C2
Debar A2
Gevgelija C2
Kavadarci C2
Kičevo A2
Kočani C2
Kruševo B2
Kumanovo B1
Ohrid A2
Prilep B2
Skopje, *capital* B2
Štip C2
Struga A2
Strumica C2
Tetovo A1
Titov Veles B2

Other Features
Belasica, *mts.* C2
Bregalnica, *river* C2
Crna, *river* B1
Crna Gora, *mts.* B1
Doiran, *lake* C2
Jakupica, *mts.* B2
Korab, *mt.* A2
Kožuf, *mts.* C2
Nidže, *mts.* B3
Ogražden, *mts.* C2
Ohrid, *lake* A3
Prespa, *lake* B3
Treska, *river* C2
Vardar, *river* C2

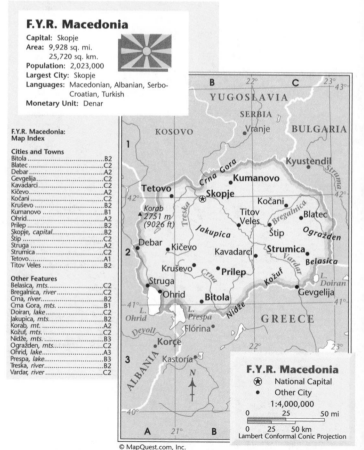

© MapQuest.com, Inc.

F.Y.R. Macedonia

National Capital
Other City
1:4,000,000

0　　25　　50 mi
0　　25　　50 km
Lambert Conformal Conic Projection

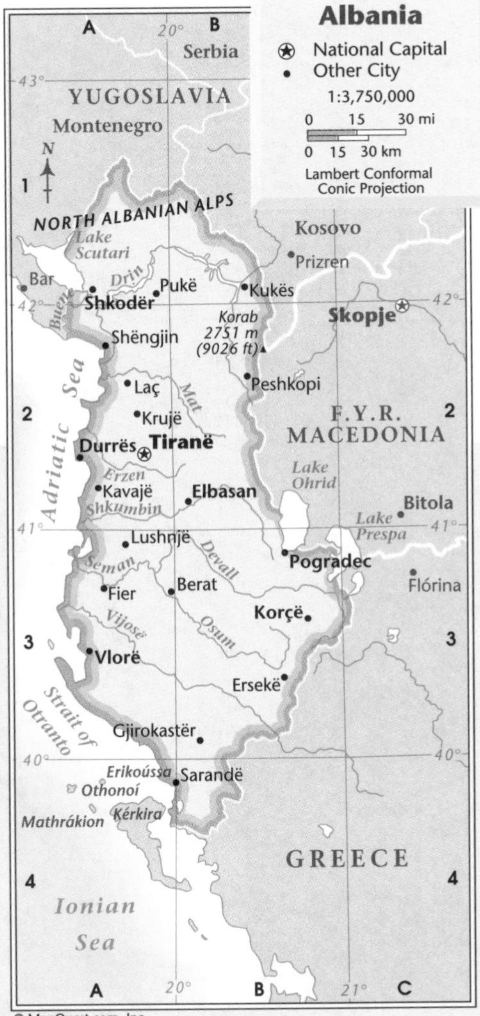

© MapQuest.com, Inc.

© MapQuest.com, Inc.

Albania:
Map Index

Cities and Towns
- Berat A3
- Durrës A2
- Elbasan B2
- Ersekë B3
- Fier A3
- Gjirokastër B3
- Kavajë A2
- Korçë B3
- Krujë A2
- Kukës B1
- Laç A2
- Lushnjë A3
- Peshkopi B2
- Pogradec B3
- Pukë A1
- Sarandë A4
- Shëngjin A2
- Shkodër A1
- Tiranë, *capital* A2
- Vlorë A3

Other Features
- Adriatic, *sea* A2
- Buene, *river* A2
- Devoll, *river* B3
- Drin, *river* A1
- Erzen, *river* A2
- Ionian, *sea* A4
- Korab, *mt.* B2
- Mat, *river* B2
- North Albanian Alps, *range* A1
- Ohrid, *lake* B2
- Osum, *river* B3
- Otranto, *strait* A3
- Prespa, *lake* C3
- Scutari, *lake* A1
- Seman, *river* A3
- Shkumbin, *river* A2
- Vijosë, *river* A3

Albania

Capital: Tiranë
Area: 11,100 sq. mi.
28,756 sq. km.
Population: 3,365,000
Largest City: Tiranë
Languages: Albanian, Greek
Monetary Unit: Lek

Yugoslavia:
Map Index

Internal Divisions
- Kosovo (province) B3
- Montenegro (republic) A3
- Serbia (republic) B2
- Vojvodina (province) A2

Cities and Towns
- Bačka Palanka A2
- Bar A3
- Bečej B2
- Belgrade, *capital* B2
- Bor C2
- Čačak B3
- Cetinje A3
- Đakovica B3
- Kikinda B2
- Kosovska Mitrovica B3
- Kragujevac B2
- Kraljevo B3
- Kruševac B3
- Leskovac B3
- Nikšić A3
- Niš B3
- Novi Pazar B3
- Novi Sad A2
- Pančevo B2
- Peć B3
- Pirot C3
- Pljevlja A3
- Podgorica A3
- Požarevac B2
- Priboj A3
- Priština B3
- Prizren B3
- Prokuplje B3
- Šabac A2
- Senta B2
- Smederevo B2
- Sombor A2
- Sremska Mitrovica A2
- Subotica A1
- Svetozarevo B3
- Uroševac B3
- Užice A3
- Valjevo A2
- Vranje B3
- Vrbas A2
- Vršac B2
- Zaječar C3
- Zrenjanin B2

Other Features
- Adriatic, *sea* A4
- Balkan, *mts.* C3
- Beli Drim, *river* B3
- Crna Gora, *mts.* B3
- Danube, *river* A2, B2
- Đaravica, *mt.* B3
- Dinaric Alps, *mts.* A3
- Drina, *river* A2
- Durmitor, *mts.* A3
- Fruška Gora, *mts.* A2
- Ibar, *river* B3
- Jastrebac, *mts.* B3
- Južna, *river* B3
- Kopaonik, *mts.* B3
- Kotor, *gulf* A3
- Morava, *river* B3
- Nisăva, *river* C3
- North Albanian Alps, *mts.* B3
- Šar Planina, *mts.* B3
- Sava, *river* A2
- Scutari, *lake* A3
- Tara, *river* A3
- Tisa, *river* B2
- Velika Morava, *river* B2
- Veliki, *canal* A2
- Zapandna Morava, *river* B3
- Zeta, *river* A3
- Zlatibor, *mts.* A3

Yugoslavia

Capital: Belgrade
Area: 39,449 sq. mi.
102,199 sq. km.
Population: 11,207,000
Largest City: Belgrade
Language: Serbo-Croatian
Monetary Unit: New Yugoslav dinar

Moldova

National Capital
Other City
1:4,800,000

Capital: Chişinău
Area: 13,012 sq. mi.
33,710 sq. km.
Population: 4,461,000
Largest City: Chişinău
Languages: Moldovan, Russian
Monetary Unit: Moldovan leu

Moldova:
Map Index

Cities and Towns
Bălţi	A2
Basarabeasca	B2
Bender (Tighina)	B2
Briceni	A1
Cahul	B3
Căuşeni	B2
Chişinău, *capital*	B2
Comrat	B2
Dubăsari	B2
Făleşti	A2
Floreşti	B2
Leova	B2
Orhei	B2
Rîbniţa	B2
Rîşcani	A2
Soroca	B1
Tiraspol	B2
Ungheni	A2

Other Features
Botna, *river*	B2
Bugeac, *region*	B3
Codri, *region*	A3
Cogalnic, *river*	B2
Dnestr, *river*	B2
Ialpug, *river*	B2
Prut, *river*	A1, B3
Raut, *river*	B2

Bulgaria:
Map Index

Administrative Regions
Burgas	E3
Khaskovo	D4
Lovech	C2
Montana	B2
Plovdiv	C3
Ruse	E2
Sofia City	B3
Sofiya	B3
Varna	F2
Stara Zagora	D3
Svilengrad	E4
Svishtov	D2
Tŭrgovishte	E2
Varna	F2
Veliko Tŭrnovo	D2
Vidin	A2
Vratsa	B2
Yambol	E3

Other Features
Arda, *river*	C4
Balkan, *mts.*	B2
Danube, *river*	B2
Golyama Kamchiya, *river*	E2
Iskŭr, *river*	C2
Kamchiya, *river*	F2
Luda Kamchiya, *river*	E3
Ludogorie, *region*	E2
Maritsa, *river*	D3
Mesta, *river*	B4
Musala, *mt.*	B3
Ogosta, *river*	B2
Osŭm, *river*	C3
Rhodope, *mts.*	C4
Rila, *mts.*	B3
Sredna Gora, *mts.*	C3
Struma, *river*	A3
Stryama, *river*	C3
Thrace, *region*	D4
Thracian, *plain*	C3
Tundzha, *river*	E3
Yantra, *river*	D2

Cities and Towns
Asenovgrad	C3
Aytos	F3
Blagoevgrad	B4
Burgas	F3
Dimitrovgrad	D3
Dobrich	F2
Elkhovo	E3
Gabrovo	D3
Kazanlŭk	D3
Khaskovo	D4
Kozloduy	B2
Kŭrdzhali	D4
Kyustendil	A3
Lom	B2
Lovech	C2
Madan	C4
Montana	B2
Oryakhovo	B2
Panagyurishte	C3
Pazardzhik	C3
Pernik	B3
Petrich	B4
Pleven	C2
Plovdiv	C3
Primorsko	F3
Razgrad	E2
Ruse	D2
Samokov	B3
Shumen	E2
Silistra	F1
Sliven	E3
Smolyan	C4
Sofia, *capital*	B3

Bulgaria

Capital: Sofia
Area: 42,855 sq. mi.
111,023 sq. km.
Population: 8,195,000
Largest City: Sofia
Language: Bulgarian
Monetary Unit: Lev

Bulgaria

National Capital
Other City

1:3,210,000

Lambert Conformal Conic Projection

Greece

⊛ National Capital

• Other City

1:6,500,000

0   75   150 mi

0   75   150 km

Lambert Conformal Conic Projection

© MapQuest.com, Inc.

Greece:
Map Index

Regions

Attica	B2
Central Greece	B2
Central Macedonia	B1
Crete	C4
Eastern Macedonia and Thrace	C1
Epirus	B2
Ionian Islands	B2
Northern Aegean	C2
Peloponnesus	B3
Southern Aegean	C3
Thessaly	B2
Western Greece	B3
Western Macedonia	B1

Cities and Towns

Agrínion	B2
Akharnaí	Inset
Alexandroúpolis	C1
Árgos	B3
Asprópirgos	Inset
Athens, capital	B3, Inset
Áyios Dhimítrios	Inset
Corinth	Inset
Dháfni	Inset
Elevsís	Inset
Ellinikón	Inset
Glifádha	Inset
Ioánnina	B2
Iráklion	C4
Kalámai	B3

Kalamáki	Inset
Kallithéa	Inset
Kastoría	B1
Kateríni	B1
Kavála	C1
Keratsínion	Inset
Kérkira	A2
Khalándrion	Inset
Khalkís	B2
Khaniá	B4
Kifisiá	Inset
Komotiní	C1
Kozáni	B1
Lamía	B2
Lárisa	B2
Mándra	Inset
Mesolóngion	B2
Mitilíni	C2
Néa Liósia	Inset
Neápolis	B3
Níkaia	Inset
Paianía	Inset
Pátrai	B2
Peristéri	Inset
Pílos	B3
Piraiévs	B3, Inset
Préveza	B2
Rhodes	D3
Selínia	Inset
Sérrai	B1
Sparta	B3
Thásos	C1
Thessaloníki	B1
Trikala	B2
Véroia	B1

Vólos	B2
Xánthi	C1

Other Features

Aegean, sea	C2
Aigáleo, mts.	Inset
Aíyina, island	B3
Akhelóös, river	B2
Alfios, river	B3
Aliákmon, river	B1
Ándros, island	C3
Astipálaia, island	C3
Áthos, mt.	C1
Corinth, gulf	B2
Corinth, isthmus	B3
Crete, island	C4
Crete, sea	C4
Cyclades, islands	C3
Delos, island	C3
Dodecanese, islands	C3
Elevsís, bay	Inset
Euboea, island	B2
Idhra, island	B3
Ikaría, island	C3
Ionian, islands	B2
Ionian, sea	A2
Itháki, island	B2
Kárpathos, island	C4
Kefallinía, island	B2
Kérkira, island	A1
Khalkidhikí, peninsula	B1
Khíos, island	C2
Kifissós, river	B2
Kíthira, island	B3
Kos, island	C3

Lésvos, island	C2
Límnos, island	C2
Míkonos, island	C3
Milos, island	C3
Náxos, island	C3
Northern Sporades, islands	B2
Olympus, mt.	B1
Páros, island	C3
Pindus, mts.	B2
Piniós, river	B2
Prespa, lake	B1
Rhodes, island	D3
Salamís, island	Inset
Sámos, island	C3
Samothráki, island	C1
Saronic, gulf	Inset
Skíros, island	C2
Struma, river	B1
Thásos, island	C1
Thíra, island	C3
Zákinthos, island	B3

Greece

Capital: Athens
Area: 50,949 sq. mi.
      131,992 sq. km.
Population: 10,707,000
Largest City: Athens
Language: Greek
Monetary Unit: Drachma

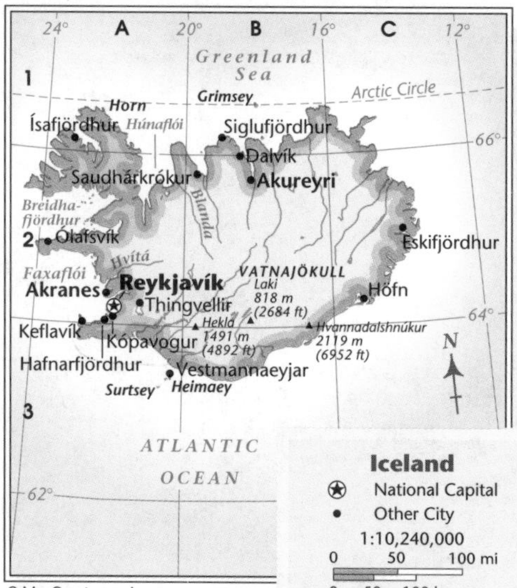

Iceland

⊛ National Capital

• Other City

1:10,240,000

0 50 100 mi

0 50 100 km

Lambert Conformal Conic Projection

Iceland

Capital: Reykjavík
Area: 36,699 sq. mi.
95,075 sq. km.
Population: 273,000
Largest City: Reykjavík
Language: Icelandic
Monetary Unit: New Icelandic króna

Iceland: Map Index

Cities and Towns

Akranes A2
Akureyri B2
Dalvík B2
Eskifjördhur C2
Hafnarfjördhur A3
Höfn C2
Ísafjördhur A1
Keflavík A3
Kópavogur A2
Ólafsvík A2
Reykjavík, *capital* A2
Saudhárkrókur B2
Siglufjördhur B1
Thingvellir A2
Vestmannaeyjar A3

Other Features

Blanda, *river* B2
Breidhafjördhur, *fjord* A2
Faxaflói, *bay* A2
Greenland, *sea* B1
Grimsey, *island* B1
Heimaey, *island* A3
Hekla, *volcano* B3
Horn, *cape* A1
Húnaflói, *bay* A2
Hvannadalshnúkur, *mt.* B3
Hvítá, *river* A2
Laki, *volcano* B2
Surtsey, *island* A3
Vatnajökull, *ice cap* B2

Norway

Capital: Oslo
Area: 125,050 sq. mi.
323,964 sq. km.
Population: 4,439,000
Largest City: Oslo
Language: Norwegian
Monetary Unit: Norwegian krone

Norway: Map Index

Cities and Towns

Ålesund B3
Alta E1
Arendal B4
Bergen B3
Bodø C2
Drammen C4
Dumbås B3
Egersund B4
Florø A3
Fredrikstad C4
Gjøvik C3
Hamar C3
Hammerfest E1
Harstad D2
Haugesund B4
Kinsarvik B3
Kirkenes F2
Kristiansand B4
Kristiansund B3
Lakselv F1
Leikanger B3
Lillehammer C3
Mo C2
Molde B3
Mosjøen C2
Moss C4
Namsos C3
Narvik D2
Oslo, *capital* C3
Skien B4
Stavanger B4
Steinkjer C3
Tromsø D2
Trondheim C3
Vadsø F1

Other Features

Barents, *sea* E1
Boknafjord, *fjord* B4
Dovrefjell, *mts.* B3
Finnmark, *plateau* E2
Glåma, *river* C3
Glittertinden, *mt.* B3
Hallingdal, *valley* B3
Hardangerfjord, *fjord* B4
Hardangervidda, *plateau* B3
Jotunheimen, *mts.* B3
Lofoten, *islands* C2
Mjøsa, *lake* C3
North, *cape* F1
North, *sea* A3
Norwegian, *sea* A2
Oslofjord, *fjord* C4
Skagerrak, *strait* B4
Sognafjord, *fjord* B3
Tana, *river* F1
Trondheimsfjord, *fjord* B3
Vesterålen, *islands* C2

Finland: Map Index

Internal Divisions

Eastern Finland (province)	C2
Lapland (province)	C1
Oulu (province)	C1
Southern Finland (province)	C2
Western Finland (province)	B2
Central Finland (region)	C2
Central Ostrobothnia (region)	B2
Etelä-Savo (region)	C2
Häme (region)	B2
Itä-Uusimaa (region)	C2
Kainuu (region)	C2
Kymenlaakso (region)	C2
North Karelia (region)	C2
Northern Ostrobothnia (region)	C1
Ostrobothnia (region)	B2
Päijät Häme (region)	C2
Pirkanmaa (region)	B2
Satakunta (region)	B2
Savo (region)	B2
South Karelia (region)	C2
South Ostrobothnia (region)	B2
South-West Finland (region)	B2
Uusimaa (region)	B2

Cities and Towns

Espoo	B2
Hämeenlinna	B2
Hangö	B3
Helsinki, *capital*	B2
Hyvinkää	B2
Iisalmi	C2
Imatra	C2
Ivalo	C1
Jakobstad	B2
Jämsä	C2
Joensuu	C2
Jyväskylä	C2
Kajaani	C2
Kemi	B1
Kemijärvi	C1
Kokkola	B2
Kolari	B1
Kotka	C2
Kouvola	C2
Kuopio	C2
Lahti	C2
Lappeenranta	C2
Lieksa	D2
Mariehamn (Maarianhamina)	A2
Mikkeli	C2
Muonio	B1
Oulu	C1
Pori	B2
Raahe	B2
Rauma	B2
Rovaniemi	C1
Salo	B2
Savonlinna	C2
Seinäjoki	B2
Tampere	B2
Tornio	B1
Turku	B2
Vaasa	B2
Vantaa	B2
Varkaus	C2
Ylivieska	B2

Other Features

Åland, *islands*	B2
Baltic, *sea*	B3
Bothnia, *gulf*	B2
Finland, *gulf*	C3
Haltiatunturi, *mt.*	B1
Iijoki, *river*	C1
Inari, *lake*	C1
Kemijoki, *river*	C1
Kivi, *lake*	C2
Lapland, *region*	B1
Lokka, *reservoir*	C1
Muoniojoki, *river*	B1
Näsi, *lake*	B2
Oulu, *lake*	C2
Oulujoki, *river*	C2
Ounasjoki, *river*	B1
Päijänne, *lake*	C2
Pielinen, *lake*	C2
Saimaa, *lake*	C2
Tenojoki, *river*	C1
Torniojoki, *river*	B1
Ylikitka, *lake*	C1

Finland

- ★ National Capital
- • Other City

1:10,000,000

0   50   100   150 mi
0   50   100   150   200 km

Lambert Conformal Conic Projection

Finland

Capital: Helsinki
Area: 130,559 sq. mi.
338,236 sq. km.
Population: 5,158,000
Largest City: Helsinki
Languages: Finnish, Swedish
Monetary Unit: Markka, Euro

Sweden

- ★ National Capital
- • Other City

1:11,333,000

0   50   100   150 mi
0   50   100   150 km

Lambert Conformal Conic Projection

Sweden

Capital: Stockholm
Area: 173,732 sq. mi.
450,083 sq. km.
Population: 8,911,000
Largest City: Stockholm
Language: Swedish
Monetary Unit: Krona

Sweden: Map Index

Counties

Älvsborg	B3
Blekinge	C3
Gävleborg	B2
Göteborg och Bohus	B3
Gotland	C3
Halland	B3
Jämtland	B2
Jönköping	B3
Kalmar	C3
Kopparberg	B2
Kristianstad	B3
Kronoberg	B3
Malmöhus	B3
Norrbotten	C1
Örebro	B3
Östergötland	B3
Skaraborg	B3
Södermanland	C3
Stockholm	C3
Uppsala	C3
Värmland	B3
Västerbotten	C2
Västernorrland	C2
Västmanland	C3

Cities and Towns

Borås	B3
Eskilstuna	C3
Falun	B2
Gällivare	D1
Gävle	C2
Göteborg	B3
Halmstad	B3
Haparanda	D1
Härnösand	C2
Helsingborg	B3
Hudiksvall	C2
Jönköping	B3
Kalmar	C3
Karlskrona	C3
Karlstad	B3
Kiruna	D1
Kristianstad	B3
Kristinehamn	B3
Linköping	C3
Luleå	D1
Lund	B3
Malmberget	D1
Malmö	B3
Norrköping	C3
Örebro	B3
Örnsköldsvik	C2
Orrefors	C3
Östersund	B2
Sarjektjakko	C1
Skellefteå	D2
Söderhamn	C2
Södertälje	C3
Sundsvall	C2
Trollhättan	B3
Uddevalla	B3
Umeå	D2
Uppsala	C3
Västerås	C3
Växjö	B3
Visby	C3

Other Features

Ångermanälven, *river*	C2
Baltic, *sea*	C3
Bothnia, *gulf*	D2
Dalälven, *river*	C2
Faxälven, *river*	C2
Göta, *canal*	B3
Gotland, *island*	C3
Hornavan, *lake*	C1
Indalsälven, *river*	B2
Kalixälven, *river*	D1
Kattegat, *strait*	B3
Kebnekaise, *mt.*	C1
Kjølen, *mts.*	B2
Klarälven, *river*	B2
Ljusnanälven, *river*	B2
Luleälven, *river*	D1
Mälaren, *lake*	C3
Muonioälven, *river*	D1
Norra Storfjället, *mt.*	C1
Öland, *island*	C3
Øresund, *sound*	B3
Osterdalälven, *river*	B2
Skagerrak, *strait*	A3
Skåne, *region*	B3
Skellefteälven, *river*	B3
Småland, *region*	B3
Storavan, *lake*	C1
Storsjön, *lake*	B2
Torneälven, *river*	D1
Uddjaur, *lake*	C1
Umeälven, *river*	C2
Vänern, *lake*	B3
Vättern, *lake*	B3
Vindelälven, *river*	C2

© MapQuest.com, Inc.

© MapQuest.com, Inc.

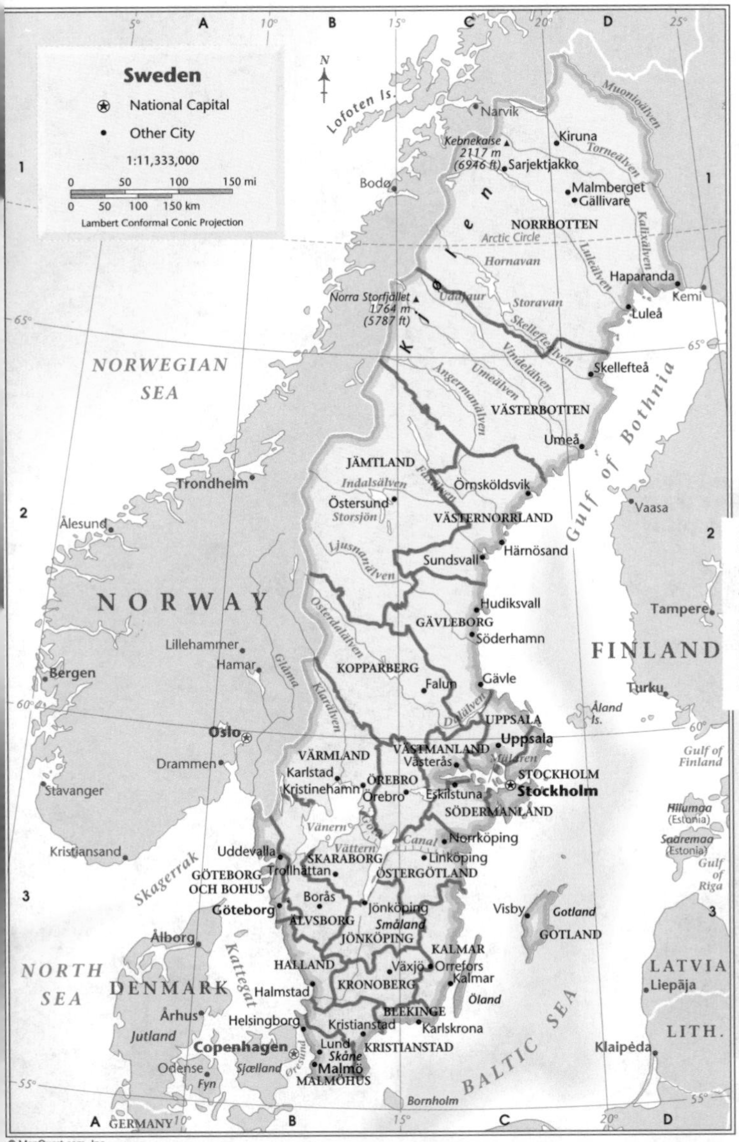

MAJOR CITIES

Algeria
Algiers — 1,483,000
Oran — 590,000
Constantine — 483,000

Angola — (metro)
Luanda — 2,081,000

Benin
Cotonou — 402,000
Porto-Novo — 144,000

Botswana
Gaborone — 183,000

Burkina Faso
Ouagadougou — 824,000

Burundi
Bujumbura — 235,440

Cameroon — (metro)
Douala — 1,320,000
Yaoundé — 1,119,000

Cape Verde
Praia — 61,000

Central African Republic
Bangui — 474,000

Chad — (metro)
N'Djamena — 826,000

Comoros — (metro)
Moroni — 30,000

Congo, Democratic Republic of the
Kinshasa — 3,800,000
Lubumbashi — 739,000

Congo, Republic of the
Brazzaville (metro) — 1,004,000

Côte d'Ivoire
Abidjan — 2,793,000
Yamoussoukro — 107,000

Djibouti — (metro)
Djibouti — 450,000

Egypt
Cairo — 6,789,000
Alexandria — 3,328,000
Port Said — 470,000
Suez — 418,000

Equatorial Guinea
Malabo — 38,000

Eritrea
Asmara — 358,000

Ethiopia
Addis Ababa — 2,085,000

Gabon
Libreville — 275,000

The Gambia
Banjul — 40,000

Ghana — (metro)
Accra — 1,673,000

Guinea — (metro)
Conakry — 1,558,000

Guinea-Bissau
Bissau — 138,000

Kenya
Nairobi — 959,000
Mombasa — 401,000

Lesotho
Maseru — 109,000

Liberia — (metro)
Monrovia — 962,000

Libya — (metro)
Tripoli — 1,682,000

Madagascar — (metro)
Antananarivo — 876,000

Malawi
Blantyre — 332,000
Lilongwe — 234,000

Mali
Bamako — 810,000

Mauritania
Nouakchott — 550,000

Mauritius
Port Louis — 146,000

Morocco
Casablanca — 2,943,000
Fez — 564,000
Rabat — 1,220,000

Mozambique — (metro)
Maputo — 2,212,000

Namibia
Windhoek — 114,000

Niger
Niamey — 392,000

Nigeria
Lagos — 1,300,000
Ibadan — 1,300,000
Abuja — 250,000

Rwanda
Kigali — 237,000

São Tomé & Príncipe
São Tomé — 43,000

Senegal
Dakar — 1,641,000

Seychelles — (metro)
Victoria — 24,000

Sierra Leone
Freetown — 470,000

Somalia
Mogadishu — 997,000

South Africa
Cape Town — 2,350,000
Johannesburg — 1,916,000
Durban — 1,137,000
Pretoria — 1,080,000
Port Elizabeth — 853,000
Bloemfontein — 300,000

Sudan
Omdurman — 1,271,000
Khartoum — 947,000

Swaziland
Mbabane — 38,000

Tanzania — (metro)
Dar es-Salaam — 1,747,000

Togo
Lomé — 600,000

Tunisia
Tunis — 674,000

Uganda — (metro)
Kampala — 954,000

Western Sahara
el-Aaiún — 90,000

Zambia — (metro)
Lusaka — 1,317,000

Zimbabwe — (metro)
Harare — 1,410,000

International comparability of city population data is limited by various data inconsistencies.

Vegetation
- Coniferous Forest
- Mixed Forest
- Midlatitude Scrubland
- Midlatitude Grassland
- Desert
- Tropical Seasonal and Scrub
- Tropical Rain Forest
- Tropical Savanna

Gross National Product (GNP) per capita
- $36,410
- $21,500
- $8625
- $2785
- $695
- $0
- No data

© MapQuest.com, Inc.

Africa: Population, by nation (in millions)

NIGERIA 113.8 | EGYPT 67.3 | ETHIOPIA 59.7 | CONGO, DEM.REP. 50.5 | S. AFR. 43.4 | SUDAN 34.5 | TANZ. 31.3 | ALGERIA 31.1 | MOROC. 29.7 | KENYA 28.8 | All other African countries 288.3

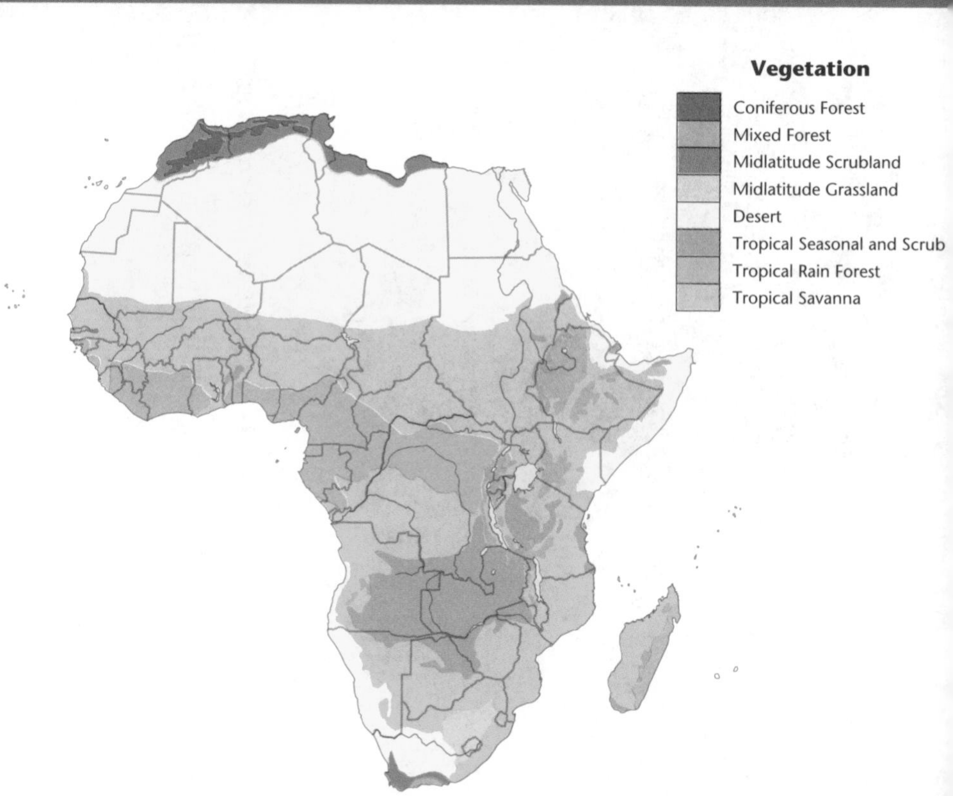

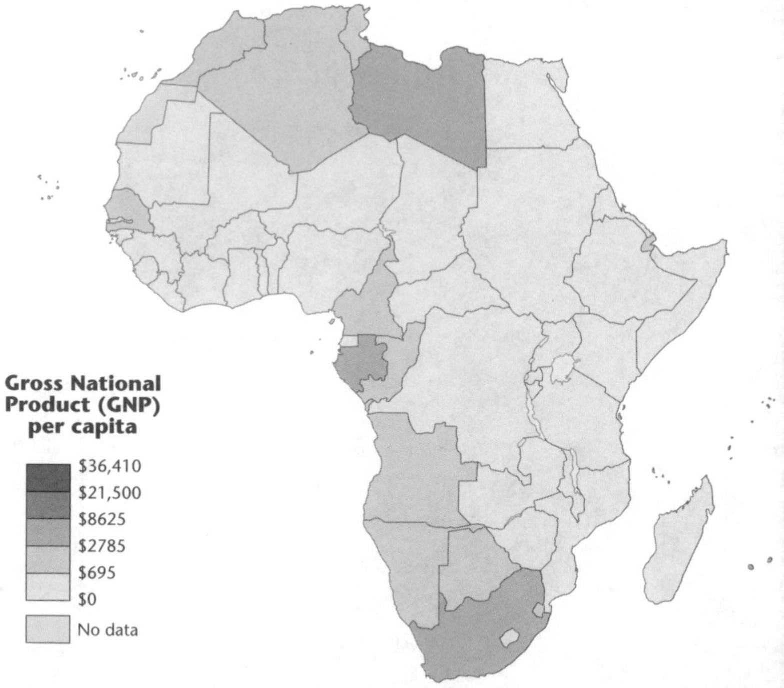

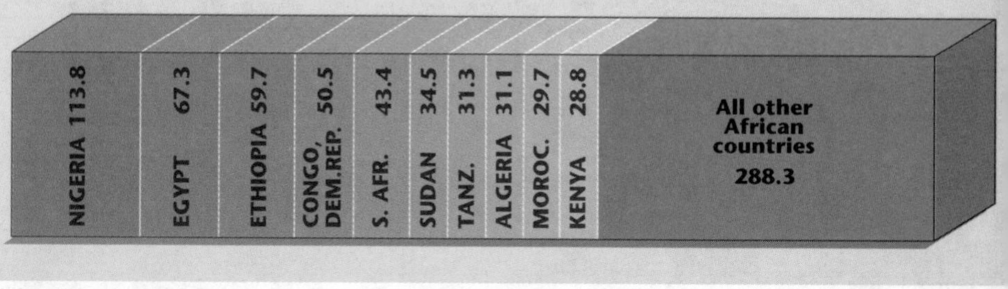

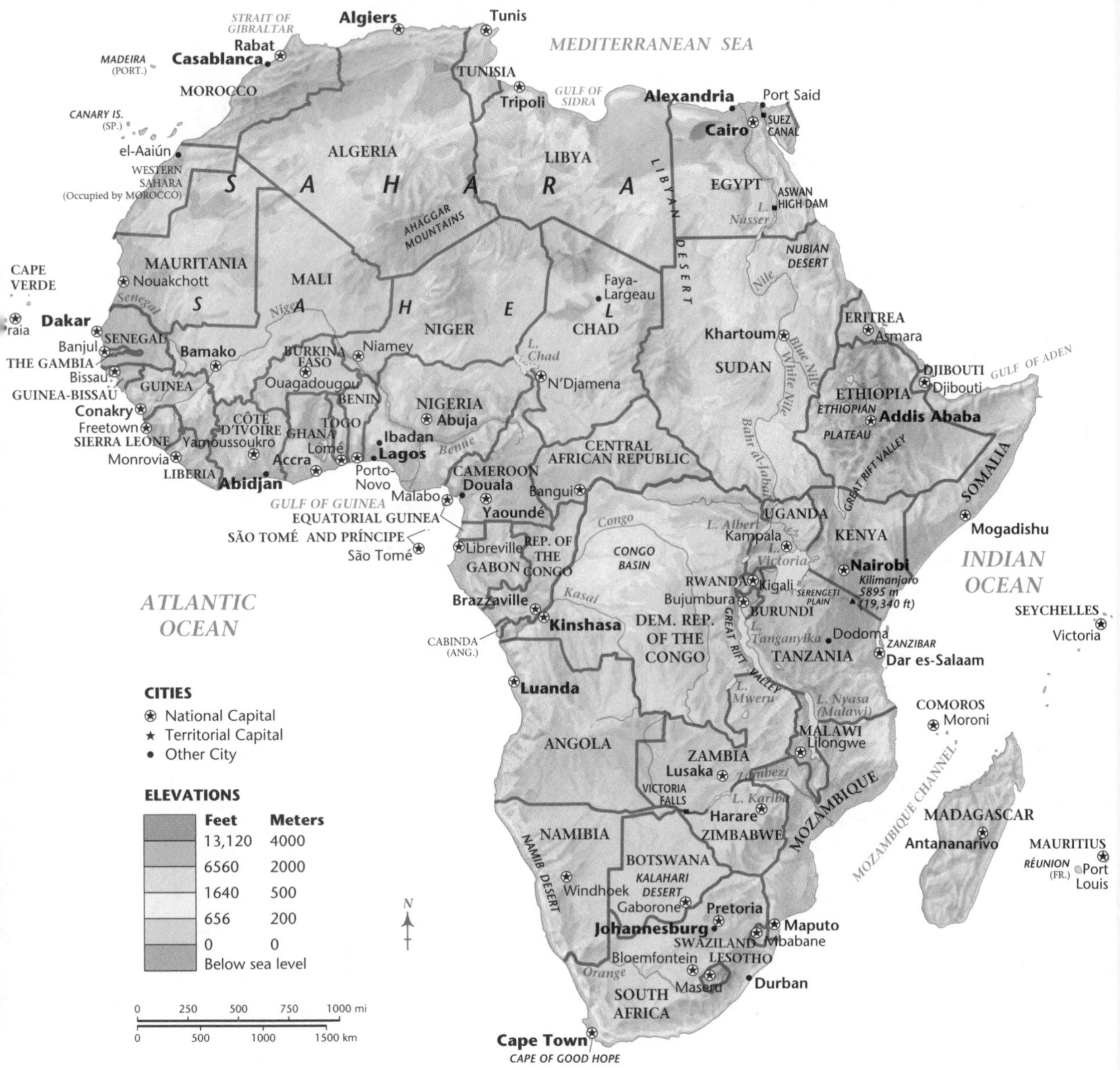

STRAIT OF GIBRALTAR
Algiers
Tunis
Rabat
MADEIRA (PORT.)
Casablanca
MEDITERRANEAN SEA
TUNISIA
MOROCCO
Tripoli
GULF OF SIDRA
Alexandria
Port Said
CANARY IS. (SP.)
Cairo
SUEZ CANAL
el-Aaiún
ALGERIA
LIBYA
WESTERN SAHARA (Occupied by MOROCCO)
S A H A R A
LIBYAN DESERT
EGYPT
ASWAN HIGH DAM
L. Nasser
AHAGGAR MOUNTAINS
NUBIAN DESERT
CAPE VERDE
MAURITANIA
Nouakchott
MALI
Faya-Largeau
Nile
Senegal
S A H E L
Niger
NIGER
CHAD
ERITREA
Asmara
Dakar
Praia
SENEGAL
Banjul
THE GAMBIA
Bissau
GUINEA-BISSAU
Bamako
BURKINA FASO
Niamey
Khartoum
L. Chad
SUDAN
Blue Nile
White Nile
DJIBOUTI
Djibouti
GULF OF ADEN
GUINEA
Ouagadougou
N'Djamena
Conakry
BENIN
NIGERIA
Abuja
ETHIOPIA
ETHIOPIAN PLATEAU
Addis Ababa
Freetown
SIERRA LEONE
CÔTE D'IVOIRE
Yamoussoukro
GHANA
TOGO
Lomé
Ibadan
Lagos
Benue
CENTRAL AFRICAN REPUBLIC
Bahr al-Jabal
GREAT RIFT VALLEY
SOMALIA
Monrovia
LIBERIA
Abidjan
Accra
Porto-Novo
CAMEROON
Douala
Malabo
Bangui
GULF OF GUINEA
EQUATORIAL GUINEA
Yaoundé
UGANDA
L. Albert
Kampala
KENYA
Mogadishu
SÃO TOMÉ AND PRÍNCIPE
São Tomé
Congo
Libreville
REP. OF THE CONGO
GABON
CONGO BASIN
L. Victoria
Nairobi
INDIAN OCEAN
RWANDA
Kigali
SERENGETI PLAIN
Kilimanjaro 5895 m (19,340 ft)
Bujumbura
BURUNDI
Kasai
Brazzaville
Kinshasa
ATLANTIC OCEAN
DEM. REP. OF THE CONGO
GREAT RIFT VALLEY
L. Tanganyika
Dodoma
ZANZIBAR
TANZANIA
Dar es-Salaam
SEYCHELLES
Victoria
CABINDA (ANG.)
Luanda
L. Mweru
L. Nyasa (Malawi)
COMOROS
Moroni
CITIES
National Capital
Territorial Capital
Other City
MALAWI
Lilongwe
ANGOLA
ZAMBIA
Lusaka
Zambezi
MOZAMBIQUE CHANNEL
ELEVATIONS
Feet Meters
13,120 4000
6560 2000
1640 500
656 200
0 0
Below sea level
VICTORIA FALLS
L. Kariba
Harare
ZIMBABWE
MOZAMBIQUE
MADAGASCAR
Antananarivo
NAMIBIA
MAURITIUS
RÉUNION (FR.)
Port Louis
NAMIB DESERT
BOTSWANA
KALAHARI DESERT
Windhoek
Gaborone
Pretoria
N
Johannesburg
Maputo
SWAZILAND
Mbabane
Bloemfontein
LESOTHO
Orange
Maseru
Durban
SOUTH AFRICA
0 250 500 750 1000 mi
0 500 1000 1500 km
Cape Town
CAPE OF GOOD HOPE

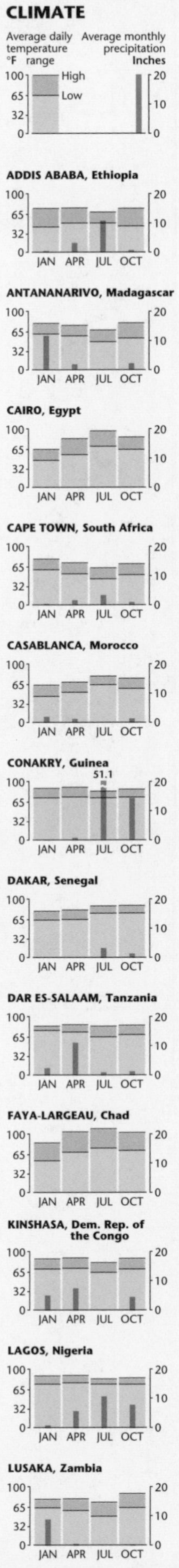

CLIMATE
Average daily temperature °F range
Average monthly precipitation Inches
High
Low
100 65 32 0
20 10 0
ADDIS ABABA, Ethiopia
ANTANANARIVO, Madagascar
CAIRO, Egypt
CAPE TOWN, South Africa
CASABLANCA, Morocco
CONAKRY, Guinea
51.1
DAKAR, Senegal
DAR ES-SALAAM, Tanzania
FAYA-LARGEAU, Chad
KINSHASA, Dem. Rep. of the Congo
LAGOS, Nigeria
LUSAKA, Zambia
JAN APR JUL OCT

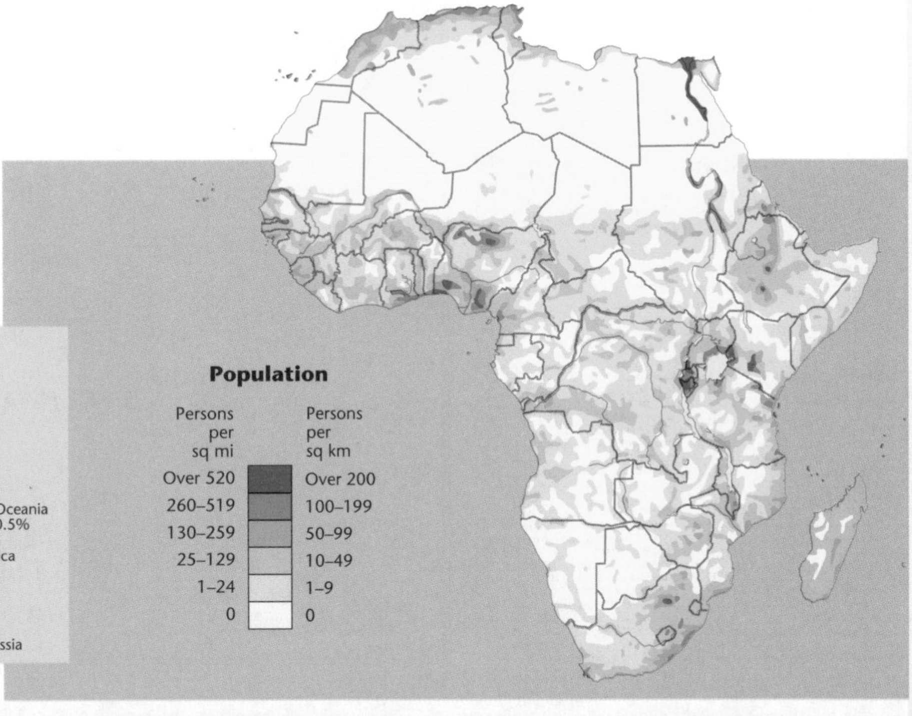

Population
Persons per sq mi
Persons per sq km
Over 520 Over 200
260–519 100–199
130–259 50–99
25–129 10–49
1–24 1–9
0 0

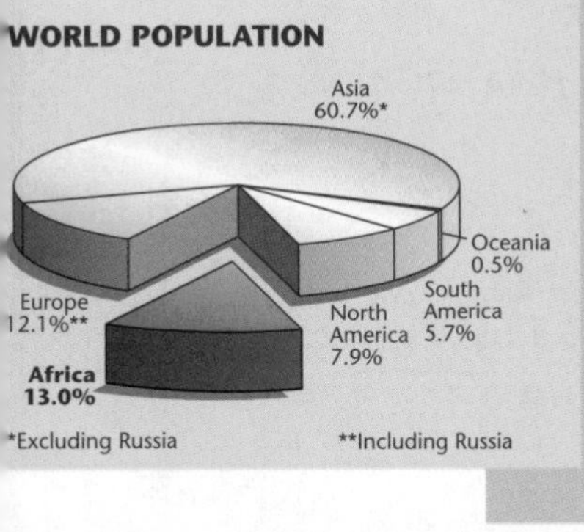

WORLD POPULATION
Asia 60.7%*
Oceania 0.5%
South America 5.7%
North America 7.9%
Europe 12.1%**
Africa 13.0%
*Excluding Russia
**Including Russia

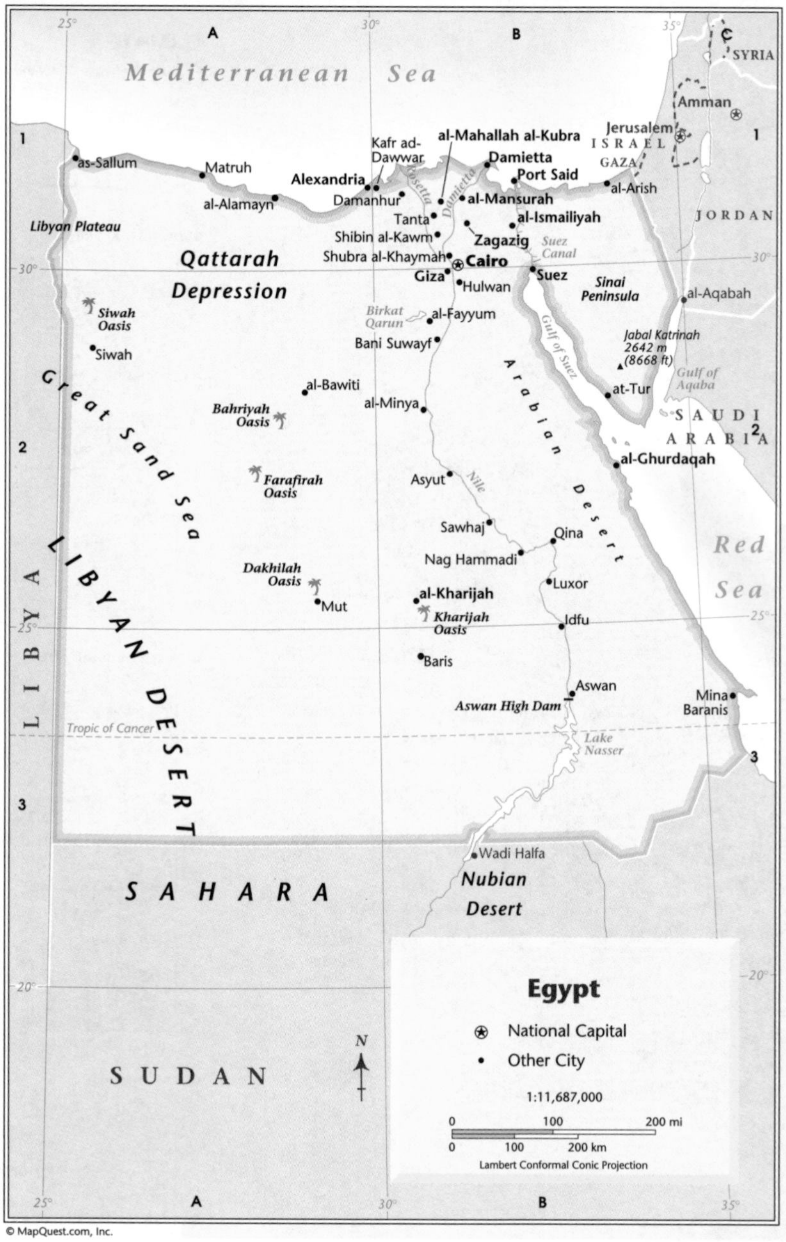

Egypt

Capital: Cairo
Area: 385,229 sq. mi.
998,003 sq. km.
Population: 67,273,906
Largest City: Cairo
Language: Arabic
Monetary Unit: Pound

Egypt: Map Index

Cities and Towns
Alamayn, al- A1
Alexandria A1
Arish, al- B1
Aswan B3
Asyut B2
Bani Suwayf B2
Baris B3
Bawiti, al- A2
Cairo, *capital* B1
Damanhur B1
Damietta B1
Fayyum, al- B2
Ghurdaqah, al- B2
Giza B2
Hulwan B2
Idfu B3
Ismailiyah, al- B1
Kafr ad-Dawwar B1
Kharijah, al- B2
Luxor B2
Mahallah al-Kubra, al- B1
Mansurah, al- B1
Matruh A1
Mina Baranis C3
Minya, al- B2
Mut A2
Nag Hammadi B2
Port Said B1
Qina B2
Sallum, as- A1
Sawhaj B2
Shibin al-Kawm B1
Shubra al-Khaymah B1
Siwah A2
Suez B2
Tanta B1
Tur, at- B2
Zagazig B1

Other Features
Aqaba, *gulf* B2
Arabian, *desert* B2
Aswan High, *dam* B3
Bahriyah, *oasis* A2
Birkat Qarun, *lake* B2
Dakhilah, *oasis* A2
Damietta, *river* B1
Farafirah, *oasis* A2
Great Sand Sea, *desert* A2
Jabal Katrinah, *mt.* B2
Kharijah, *oasis* B2
Libyan, *desert* A2
Libyan, *plateau* A1
Nasser, *lake* B3
Nile, *river* B2
Qattarah, *depression* A2
Red, *sea* C2
Rosetta, *river* B1
Sahara, *desert* A3
Sinai, *peninsula* B2
Siwah, *oasis* A2
Suez, *canal* B1
Suez, *gulf* B2

Libya

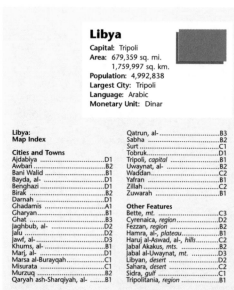

Capital: Tripoli
Area: 679,359 sq. mi.
1,759,997 sq. km.
Population: 4,992,838
Largest City: Tripoli
Language: Arabic
Monetary Unit: Dinar

Libya: Map Index

Cities and Towns
Ajdabiya D1
Awbari B2
Bani Walid B1
Bayda, al- D1
Benghazi D1
Birak B2
Darnah D1
Ghadamis A1
Gharyan B1
Ghat B3
Jaghbub, al- D2
Jalu D2
Jawf, al- D3
Khums, al- B1
Marj, al- D1
Marsa al-Burayqah C1
Misurata C1
Murzuq B2
Qaryah ash-Sharqiyah, al- B1
Qatrun, al- B3
Sabha B2
Surt C1
Tobruk D1
Tripoli, *capital* B1
Uwaynat, al- B2
Waddan C2
Yafran B1
Zillah C2
Zuwarah B1

Other Features
Bette, *mt.* C3
Cyrenaica, *region* D2
Fezzan, *region* B2
Hamra, al-, *plateau* B1
Haruj al-Aswad, al-, *hills* C2
Jabal Akakus, *mts.* B2
Jabal al-Uwaynat, *mt.* D3
Libyan, *desert* D2
Sahara, *desert* C2
Sidra, *gulf* C1
Tripolitania, *region* B1

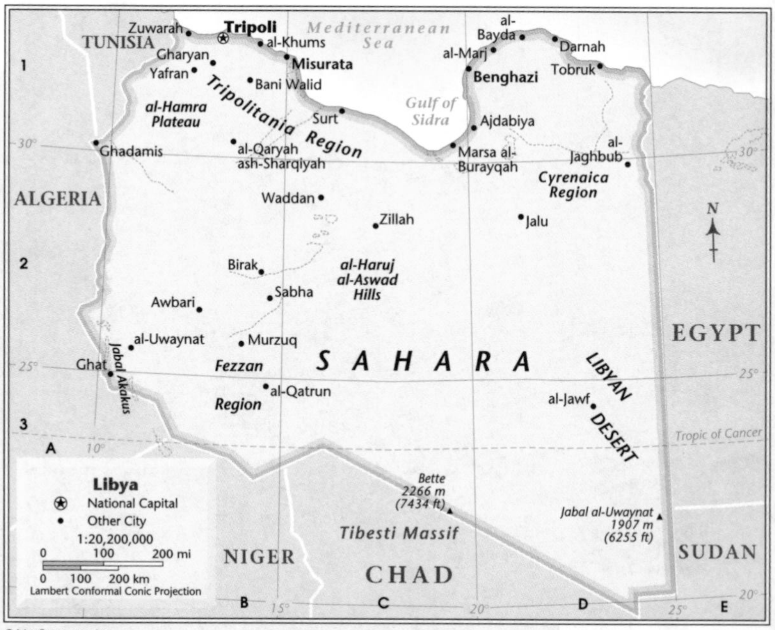

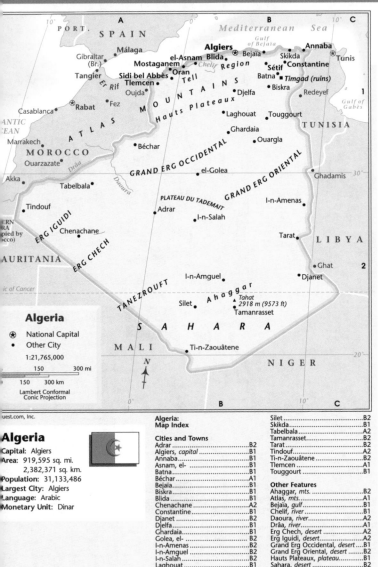

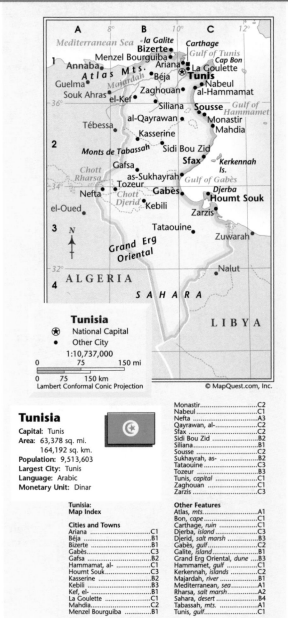

Algeria

* National Capital
* Other City

1:21,765,000

0   150   300 mi
0 150 300 km

Lambert Conformal Conic Projection

Algeria

Capital: Algiers
Area: 919,595 sq. mi.
2,382,371 sq. km.
Population: 31,133,486
Largest City: Algiers
Language: Arabic
Monetary Unit: Dinar

Algeria: Map Index

Cities and Towns

Adrar	B2
Algiers, *capital*	B1
Annaba	B1
Asnam, el-	B1
Batna	B1
Béchar	A1
Bejaïa	B1
Biskra	B1
Blida	B1
Chenachane	A2
Constantine	B1
Djanet	B2
Djelfa	B1
Ghardaïa	B1
Golea, el-	B2
I-n-Amenas	B2
I-n-Amguel	B2
I-n-Salah	B2
Laghouat	B1
Mostaganem	B1
Oran	A1
Ouargla	B1
Sétif	B1
Sidi bel Abbès	A1
Silet	B2
Skikda	B1
Tabelbala	A2
Tamanrasset	B2
Tarat	B2
Tindouf	A2
Ti-n-Zaouâtene	B2
Tlemcen	A1
Touggourt	B1

Other Features

Ahaggar, *mts.*	B2
Atlas, *mts.*	A1
Bejaïa, *gulf*	B1
Chelif, *river*	B1
Daoura, *river*	A2
Drâa, *river*	A1
Erg Chech, *desert*	A2
Erg Iguidi, *desert*	A2
Grand Erg Occidental, *desert*	B1
Grand Erg Oriental, *desert*	B2
Hauts Plateaux, *plateau*	B1
Sahara, *desert*	B2
Tademait, *plateau*	B2
Tahat, *mt.*	B2
Tanezrouft, *mts.*	A2
Tell Region	B1
Timgad, *ruins*	B1

Tunisia

* National Capital
* Other City

1:10,737,000

0   75   150 mi
0 75 150 km

Lambert Conformal Conic Projection

© MapQuest.com, Inc.

Tunisia

Capital: Tunis
Area: 63,378 sq. mi.
164,192 sq. km.
Population: 9,513,603
Largest City: Tunis
Language: Arabic
Monetary Unit: Dinar

Tunisia: Map Index

Cities and Towns

Ariana	C1
Béja	B1
Bizerte	B1
Gabès	C3
Gafsa	B2
Hammamat, al-	C1
Houmt Souk	C3
Kasserine	B2
Kebili	B3
Kef, el-	B1
La Goulette	C1
Mahdia	C2
Menzel Bourguiba	B1
Monastir	C2
Nabeul	C1
Nefta	A3
Qayrawan, al-	C2
Sfax	C2
Sidi Bou Zid	B2
Siliana	B1
Sousse	C2
Sukhayrah, as-	B2
Tataouine	C3
Tozeur	B3
Tunis, *capital*	C1
Zaghouan	C1
Zarzis	C3

Other Features

Atlas, *mts.*	A1
Bon, *cape*	C1
Carthage, *ruin*	C1
Djerba, *island*	C3
Djerid, *salt marsh*	B3
Gabès, *gulf*	C2
Galite, *island*	B1
Grand Erg Oriental, *dune*	B3
Hammamet, *gulf*	C1
Kerkennah, *islands*	C2
Majardah, *river*	B1
Mediterranean, *sea*	A1
Rharsa, *salt marsh*	A2
Sahara, *desert*	B4
Tabassah, *mts.*	A1
Tunis, *gulf*	C1

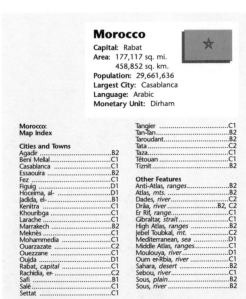

Morocco

Capital: Rabat
Area: 177,117 sq. mi.
458,852 sq. km.
Population: 29,661,636
Largest City: Casablanca
Language: Arabic
Monetary Unit: Dirham

Morocco: Map Index

Cities and Towns

Agadir	B2
Beni Mellal	C1
Casablanca	C1
Essaouira	B2
Fez	C1
Figuig	D1
Hoceima, al-	D1
Jadida, el-	B1
Kenitra	C1
Khouribga	C1
Larache	C1
Marrakech	B2
Meknès	C1
Mohammedia	C1
Ouarzazate	C2
Ouezzane	C1
Oujda	D1
Rabat, *capital*	C1
Rachidia, er-	C2
Safi	B1
Salé	C1
Settat	C1
Tangier	C1
Tan-Tan	B2
Taroudant	B2
Tata	C2
Taza	C1
Tétouan	C1
Tiznit	B2

Other Features

Anti-Atlas, *ranges*	B2
Atlas, *mts.*	B2
Dades, *river*	C2
Drâa, *river*	B2, C2
Er Rif, *range*	C1
Gibraltar, *strait*	C1
High Atlas, *ranges*	C2
Jebel Toubkal, *mt.*	B2
Mediterranean, *sea*	D1
Middle Atlas, *ranges*	C1
Moulouya, *river*	D1
Oum er-Rbia, *river*	C1
Sahara, *desert*	B2
Sebou, *river*	C1
Sous, *plain*	B2
Sous, *river*	B2

Morocco

* National Capital
* Other City

1:13,222,000

0   75   150 mi
0 75 150 km

Azimuthal Equal Area Projection

© MapQuest.com, Inc.

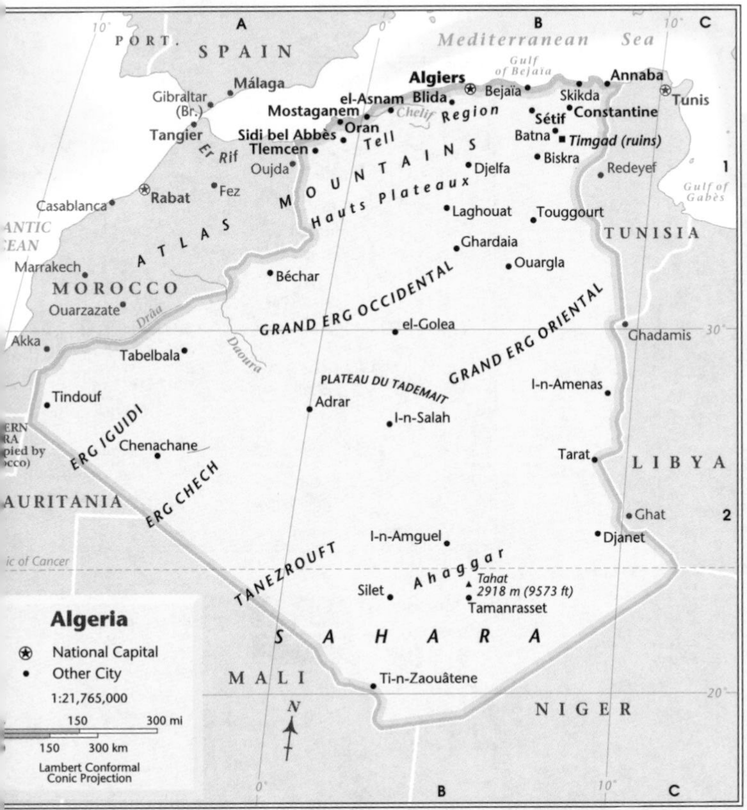

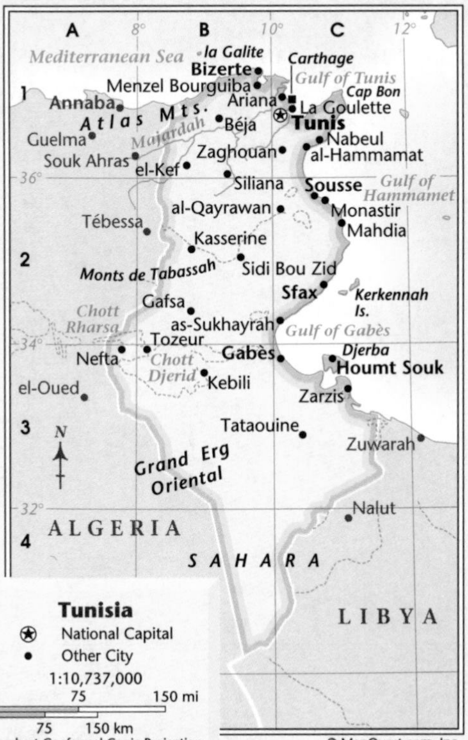

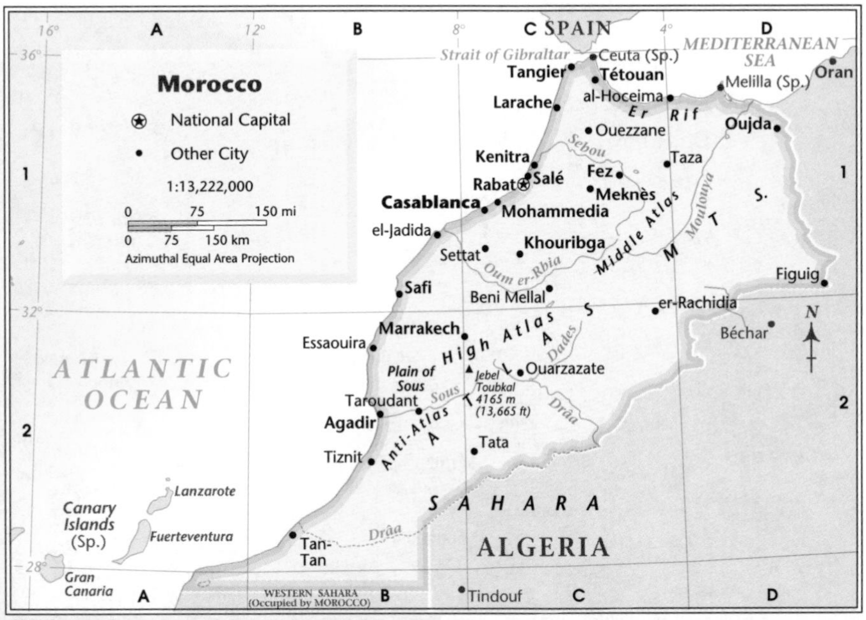

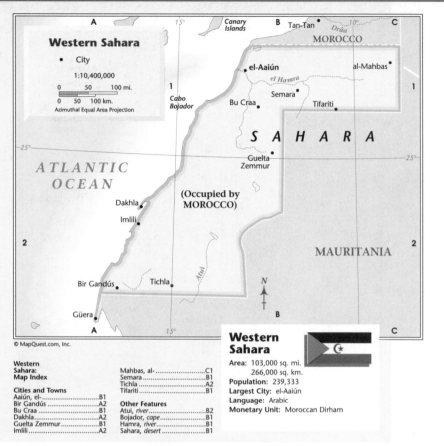

Western Sahara

- City

1:10,400,000

| 0 | 50 | 100 mi. |
| 0 | 50 | 100 km. |

Azimuthal Equal Area Projection

© MapQuest.com, Inc.

Western Sahara

Area: 103,000 sq. mi.
266,000 sq. km.
Population: 239,333
Largest City: el-Aaiún
Language: Arabic
Monetary Unit: Moroccan Dirham

Western Sahara:
Map Index

Cities and Towns
Aaiún, el- B1
Bir Gandús A2
Bu Craa B1
Dakhla A2
Guelta Zemmur B1
Imlili A2

Mahbas, al- C1
Semara B1
Tichla A2
Tifariti B1

Other Features
Atui, river B2
Bojador, cape B1
Hamra, river B1
Sahara, desert B1

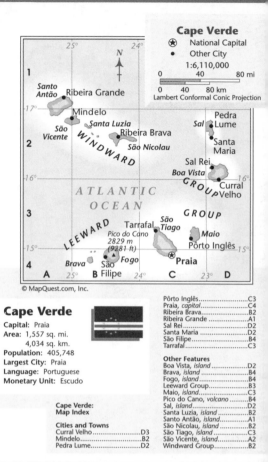

Cape Verde

- ⊛ National Capital
- • Other City

1:6,110,000

| 0 | 40 | 80 mi. |
| 0 | 40 | 80 km. |

Lambert Conformal Conic Projection

© MapQuest.com, Inc.

Cape Verde

Capital: Praia
Area: 1,557 sq. mi.
4,034 sq. km.
Population: 405,748
Largest City: Praia
Language: Portuguese
Monetary Unit: Escudo

Cape Verde:
Map Index

Cities and Towns
Curral Velho D3
Mindelo B2
Pedra Lume D2

Pôrto Inglês C3
Praia, capital C4
Ribeira Brava B2
Ribeira Grande A1
Sal Rei D2
Santa Maria D2
São Filipe B4
Tarrafal C3

Other Features
Boa Vista, island D2
Brava, island B4
Fogo, island B4
Leeward Group............B3
Maio, island C3
Pico do Cano, volcano ..B4
Sal, island D2
Santa Luzia, island A2
Santo Antão, island A1
São Nicolau, island B2
São Tiago, island C3
São Vicente, island A2
Windward Group..........B2

Mali:
Map Index

Cities and Towns
Ansongo D2
Bafoulabé A3
Bamako, capital B3
Bougouni B3
Bourem C2
Djenné C3
Gao D2
Goundam C2
Kayes A3
Kidal D2
Kita B3
Koulikoro B3
Koutiala B3
Ménaka D2
Mopti C3
Niono B3
Nioro du Sahel B2

San C3
Ségou B3
Sikasso B3
Taoudenni C1
Tessalit D1
Timbuktu C2

Other Features
Adrar des Iforas, massif ..D2
Azaouâd, region..........C2
Bani, river B3
Baoulé, river B3
Djouf, el-, desert B1
Erg Chech, desert C1
Hombori, mts. C2
Hombori Tondo, mt. C2
Niger, river B3
Sahara, desert C1
Sahel, region C2
Senegal, river A3

Mali

Capital: Bamako
Area: 482,077 sq. mi.
1,248,904 sq. km.
Population: 10,429,124
Largest City: Bamako
Language: French
Monetary Unit: Franc

Mauritania

Capital: Nouakchott
Area: 398,000 sq. mi.
1,031,088 sq. km.
Population: 2,581,738
Largest City: Nouakchott
Languages: Arabic, Wolof
Monetary Unit: Ouguiya

Mauritania

- ⊛ National Capital
- • Other City

1:2,350,000

| 0 | 150 | 300 mi |
| 0 | 150 | 300 km |

Lambert Conformal Conic Projection

© MapQuest.com, Inc.

Mali

- ⊛ National Capital
- • Other City

1:21,265,000

| 0 | 200 | 400 mi |
| 0 | 200 | 400 km |

Lambert Conformal Conic Projection

© MapQuest.com, Inc.

Mauritania:
Map Index

Cities and Towns
Akjoujt B3
Aleg B3
Atâr B2
Ayoûn el-Atroûs..........C3
Bîr Mogreïn C1
Fdérik B2
Kaédi B3
Kiffa C3
Néma D3
Nouadhibou A2
Nouakchott, capital A3

Ouadane....................B2
Rosso........................B3
Sélibaby B4
Tichit C3
Tidjikdja C3
Zouîrât B2

Other Features
Adrar, region B2
Djouf, el-, desert C3
Erg Iguidi, desert D1
Sahara, desert B3
Senegal, river B3
Tagânt, region C3

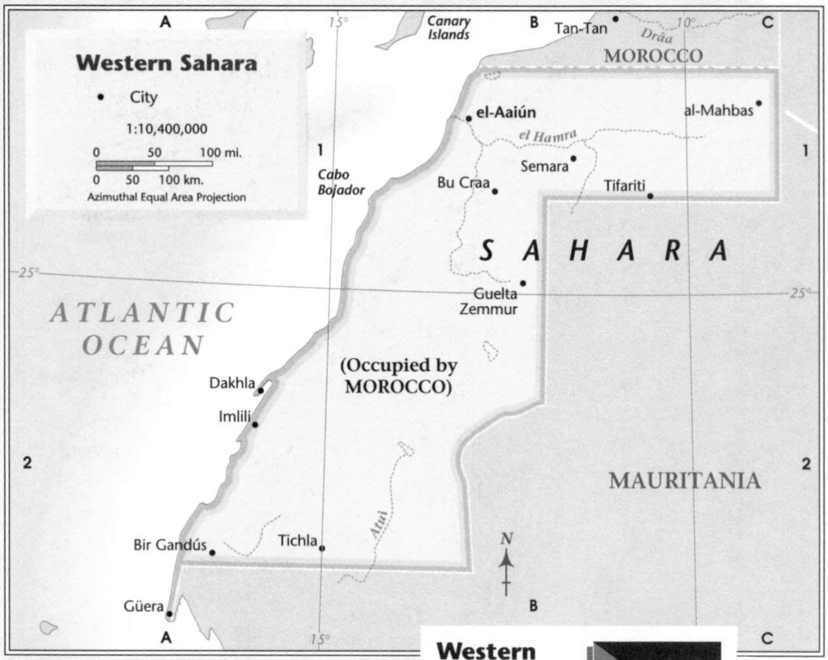

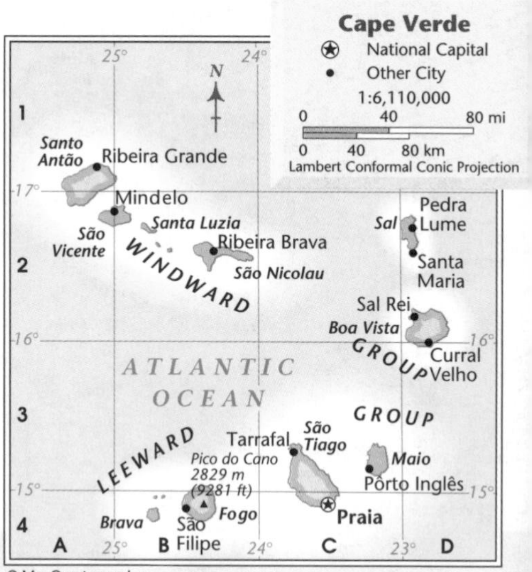

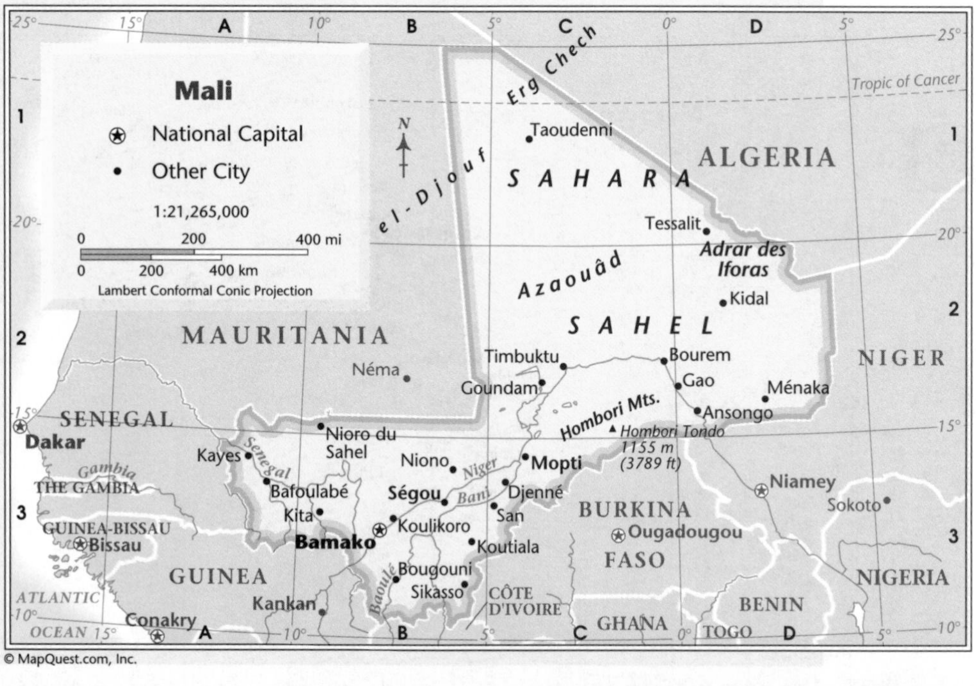

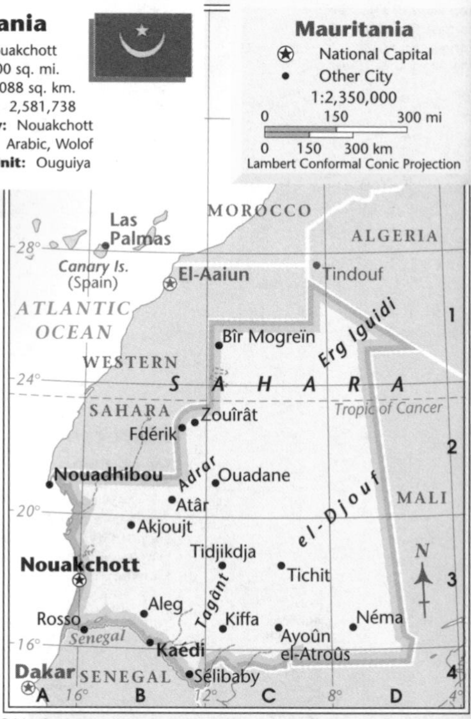

Niger

Capital: Niamey
Area: 497,000 sq. mi.
1,287,565 sq. km.
Population: 9,962,242
Largest City: Niamey
Language: French
Monetary Unit: CFA franc

Niger:
Map Index

Cities and Towns
Agadès B2
Arlit B2
Bilma C2
Birni Nkonni B3
Diffa C3
Djado C1
Dogondoutchi A3
Dosso A3
Gaya A3
Gouré C3
Maradi B3
Nguigmi C3
Niamey, *capital* A3
Tahoua B3
Téra A3
Tessaoua B3
Tillabéry A3
Zinder B3

Other Features
Aïr, *mts.* B2
Bagzane, *mt.* B2
Chad, *lake* C3
Dallol Bosso, *river* A3
Dillia, *river* C2
Djado, *plateau* C1
Erg du Ténéré, *desert* B2
Grand Erg de Bilma,
desert C2
Gréboun, *mt.* B1
Komadugu Yobe, *river* C3
Manga, *region* C2
Niger, *river* A3
Sahara, *desert* A1
Sahel, *region* A3
Talak, *region* B2
Ténéré, *desert* C1

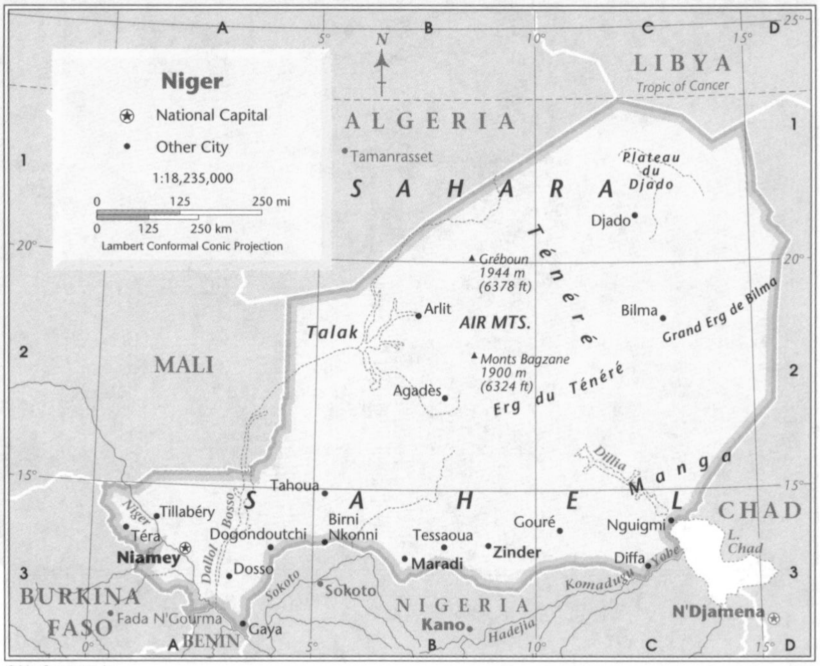

© MapQuest.com, Inc.

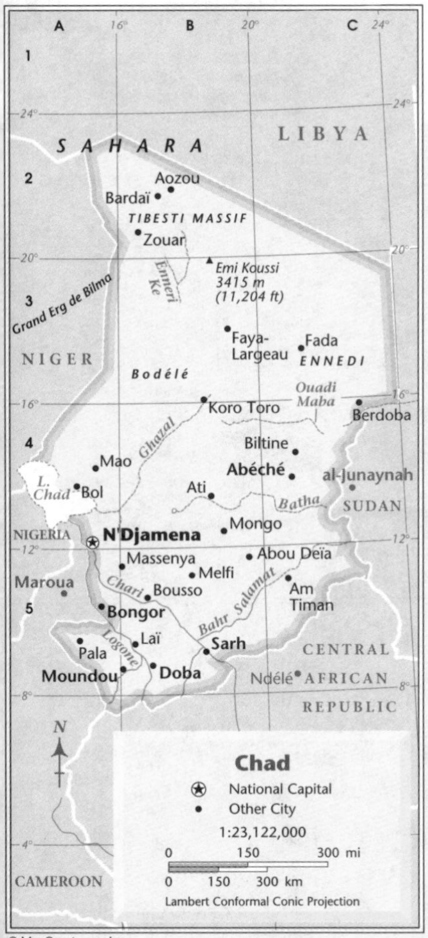

© MapQuest.com, Inc.

Chad

Capital: N'Djamena
Area: 495,755 sq. mi.
1,248,339 sq. km.
Population: 7,557,436
Largest City: N'Djamena
Languages: French, Arabic
Monetary Unit: CFA franc

Chad:
Map Index

Cities and Towns
Abéché C4
Abou Deïa B5
Am Timan C5
Aozou B2
Ati B4
Bardaï B2
Berdoba C4
Biltine C4
Bol A4
Bongor B5
Bousso B5
Doba B5
Fada C3
Faya-Largeau B3
Koro Toro B4
Laï B5
Mao A4
Massenya B5
Melfi B5
Mongo B4
Moundou B5
N'Djamena, *capital* A4
Pala A5
Sarh B5
Zouar B2

Other Features
Bahr Salamat, *river* B5
Batha, *river* C4
Bodélé, *depression* B3
Chad, *lake* A4
Chari, *river* A5
Emi Koussi, *mt.* B3
Ennedi, *plateau* C3
Enneri Ke, *river* B3
Ghazal, *river* B4
Grand Erg de Bilma,
desert A3
Logone, *river* A5
Ouadi Maba, *river* C4
Sahara, *desert* A2
Tibesti, *massif* B2

Sudan:
Map Index

Cities and Towns
Atbarah C2
Babanusah B3
Damazin, ad- C3
Dunqulah C1
Fashir, al- B2
Halaib D1
Juba C4
Junaynah, al- A2
Kaduqli B3
Kassala D2
Khartoum, *capital* C2
Khartoum North C2
Khashm al-Qirbah C2
Kuraymah C1
Kusti C2
Malakal C3
Nuhud, an- B2
Nyala B2
Omdurman C2
Pibor Post C3
Port Sudan D1
Qadarif, al- C2
Rumbek B3
Sannar C2
Ubayyid, al- C2
Wadi Halfa C1
Wad Madani C2
Waw B3
Yambio B4

Other Features
Akobo, *river* C3
Atbarah, *river* C2
Bahr al-Arab, *river* B3
Bahr al-Ghazal, *river* C3
Bahr al-Jabal, *river* C3
Blue Nile, *river* C2
Kangen, *river* C3
Kinyeti, *mt.* C4
Libyan, *desert* B1
Lol, *river* B3
Nasser, *lake* C1
Nile, *river* C1, C2
Nuba, *mts.* C3
Nubian, *desert* C1
Red, *sea* D1
Red Sea, *hills* D1
Sobat, *river* C3
Sudd, *region* B3
Sue, *river* B3
Wadi al-Malik, *river* B2
Wadi Howar, *river* B2
White Nile, *river* C3

Sudan

Capital: Khartoum
Area: 966,757 sq. mi.
2,530,459 sq. km.
Population: 34,475,690
Largest City: Khartoum
Language: Arabic
Monetary Unit: Pound

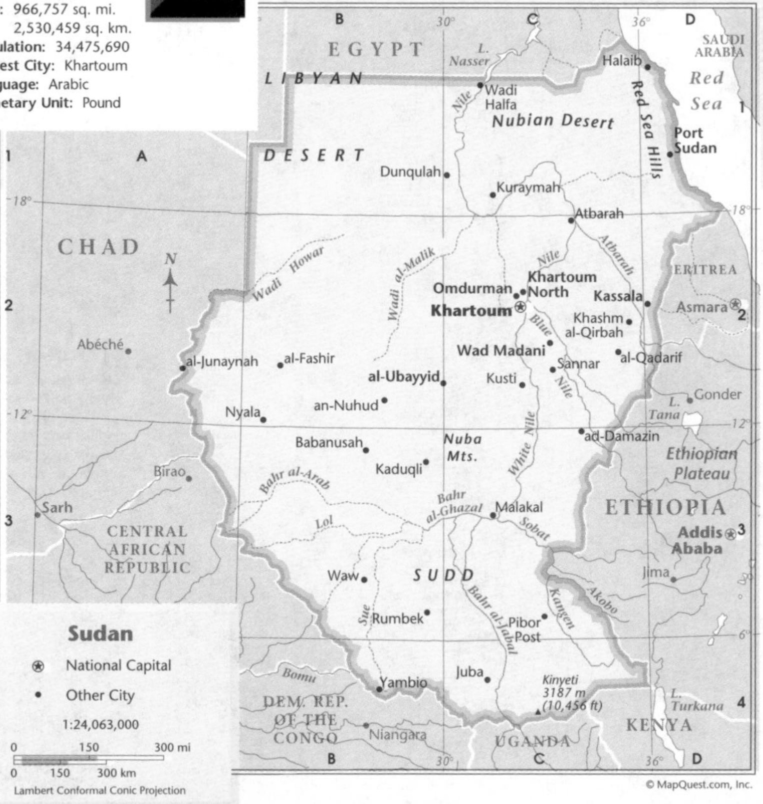

© MapQuest.com, Inc.

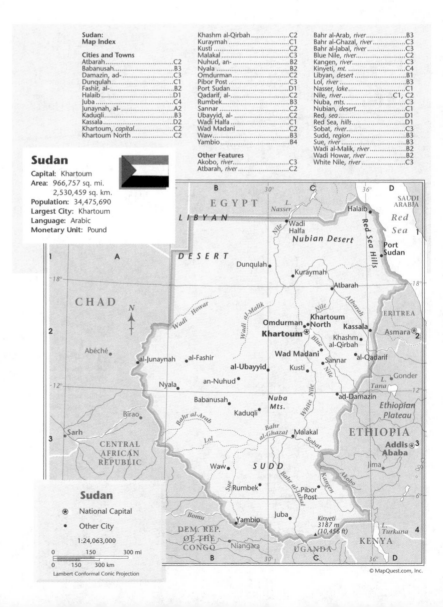

Eritrea

Capital: Asmara
Area: 45,300 sq. mi.
117,358 sq. km.
Population: 3,984,723
Largest City: Asmara
Language: Tigrinya
Monetary Unit: Ethiopian birr

Eritrea

⊛ National Capital
• Other City
1:13,000,000

| 0 | 90 | 180 mi |
| 0 | 90 | 180 km |

Mercator Projection

Eritrea:
Map Index

Cities and Towns
Adi Keyih B2
Adi Ugri B2
Akordat A2
Asmara, *capital* B2
Assab D3
Ed C3
Keren B2
Massawa B2
Nakfa B1
Teseney A2
Tio C2

Other Features
Bab al-Mandab, *strait* D3
Dahlak, *archipelago* C2
Danakil, *desert* C2
Gash, *river* B2
Red, *sea* C1

© MapQuest.com, Inc.

Djibouti

⊛ National Capital
• Other City
1:5,500,000

| 0 | 25 | 50 mi |
| 0 | 25 | 50 km |

Transverse Mercator Proj.

Djibouti:
Map Index

Cities and Towns
Alayli Dadda B2
Ali Adde B2
Ali-Sabieh B2
Arta B2
As Ela B2
Balho B1
Dikhil B2
Djibouti, *capital* B2
Dorra B2
Holhol B2
Khor Angar C1
Loyada C2
Obock B2
Randa B2
Tadjoura B2
Yoboki B2

Other Features
Abhé, *lake* A2
Aden, *gulf* C1
Assal, *lake* B2
Bab al-Mandab, *strait* C1
Gaggade, *plain* C2
Mabla, *mts.* B1
Moussa Ali, *mt.* B1
Red, *sea* C1
Tadjoura, *gulf* B2

© MapQuest.com, Inc.

Djibouti

Capital: Djibouti
Area: 8,950 sq. mi.
23,187 sq. km.
Population: 447,439
Largest City: Djibouti
Languages: Cushitic languages
Monetary Unit: Franc

Ethiopia

⊛ National Capital
• Other City

1:15,053,000

| 0 | 100 | 200 mi |
| 0 | 100 | 200 km |

Mercator Projection

Ethiopia

Capital: Addis Ababa
Area: 437,794 sq. mi.
1,134,181 sq. km.
Population: 59,680,383
Largest City: Addis Ababa
Language: Amharic
Monetary Unit: Birr

Ethiopia:
Map Index

Cities and Towns
Addis Ababa, *capital* C2
Adwa C1
Arba Minch B3
Asela C3
Asosa B2
Awasa C3
Bahir Dar B2
Debre Birhan C2
Debre Markos B2
Degeh Bur D2
Dese C2
Dire Dawa D2
Goba C3
Gonder B1
Gore B2

Harer D2
Imi D3
Jima B3
Mekele C1
Nazret C2
Negele C3
Nekemte B2
Shewa Gimira B3
Weldiya C2
Werder D3

Other Features
Abaya, *lake* B3
Abhe, *lake* C2
Akobo, *river* A3
Atbara, *river* B1
Awash, *river* C2
Baro, *river* B2
Blue Nile, *river* B2
Choke, *mts.* B2
Dawa, *river* C3
Denakil, *desert* C1
Dinder, *river* B1
Ethiopian, *plateau* C2
Genale, *river* C3
Great Rift, *valley* C3
Ogaden, *region* D3
Omo, *river* B3
Provisional
Administrative Line D3
Ras Dashen, *mt.* C1
Tana, *lake* B1
Tekeze, *river* B1
Turkana, *lake* B3
Wabe Gestro, *river* C3
Wabe Shebele, *river* D3
Ziway, *lake* C3

© MapQuest.com, Inc.

Somalia:
Map Index

Cities and Towns
Baraawe A3
Baydhabo A3
Beledweyne B3
Benderbeyla C2
Berbera B1
Boosaaso B1

Burco B2
Ceerigaabo B1
Dhuusamareeb B2
Eyl C2
Gaalkacyo B2
Garoowe B2
Hargeysa A2
Hobyo B2
Jamaame A3
Jawhar B3
Jilib A3
Kismayu A4
Luuq A3
Marka A3
Mogadishu, *capital* B3
Qardho B2
Xuddur A3

Other Features
Aden, *gulf* B1
Gees Gwardafuy, *cape* C1
Juba, *river* A3
Nugaal, *valley* B2
Raas Xaafuun, *cape* C1
Surud Ad, *mt.* B1
Webi Shabeelle, *river* B3

Somalia

Capital: Mogadishu
Area: 246,300 sq. mi.
638,083 sq. km.
Population: 7,140,643
Largest City: Mogadishu
Language: Somali, Arabic
Monetary Unit: Shilling

Somalia

⊛ National Capital
• Other City

1:22,100,000

| 0 | 150 | 300 mi |
| 0 | 150 | 300 km |

Miller Cylindrical Projection

© MapQuest.com, Inc.

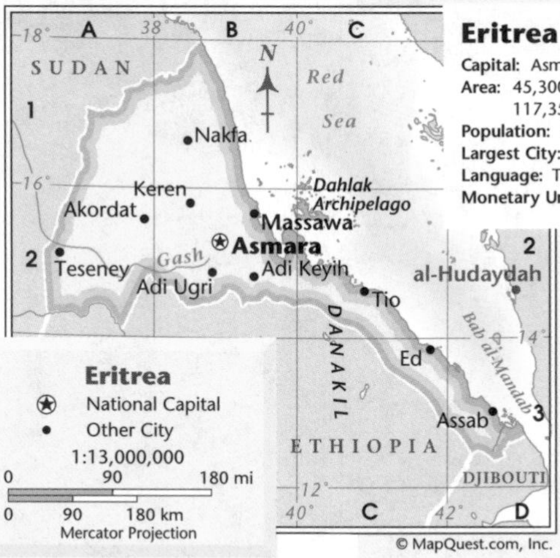

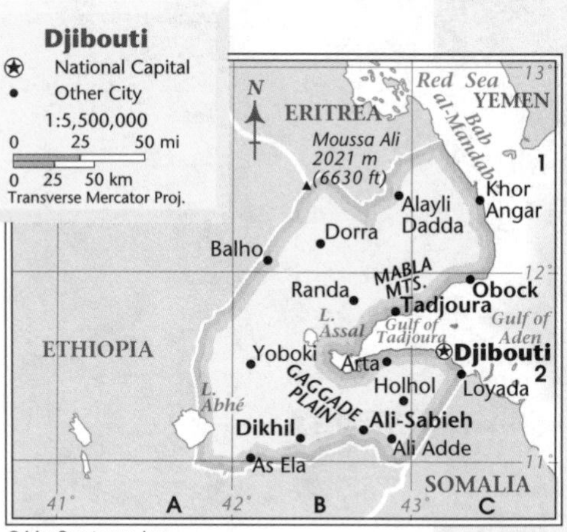

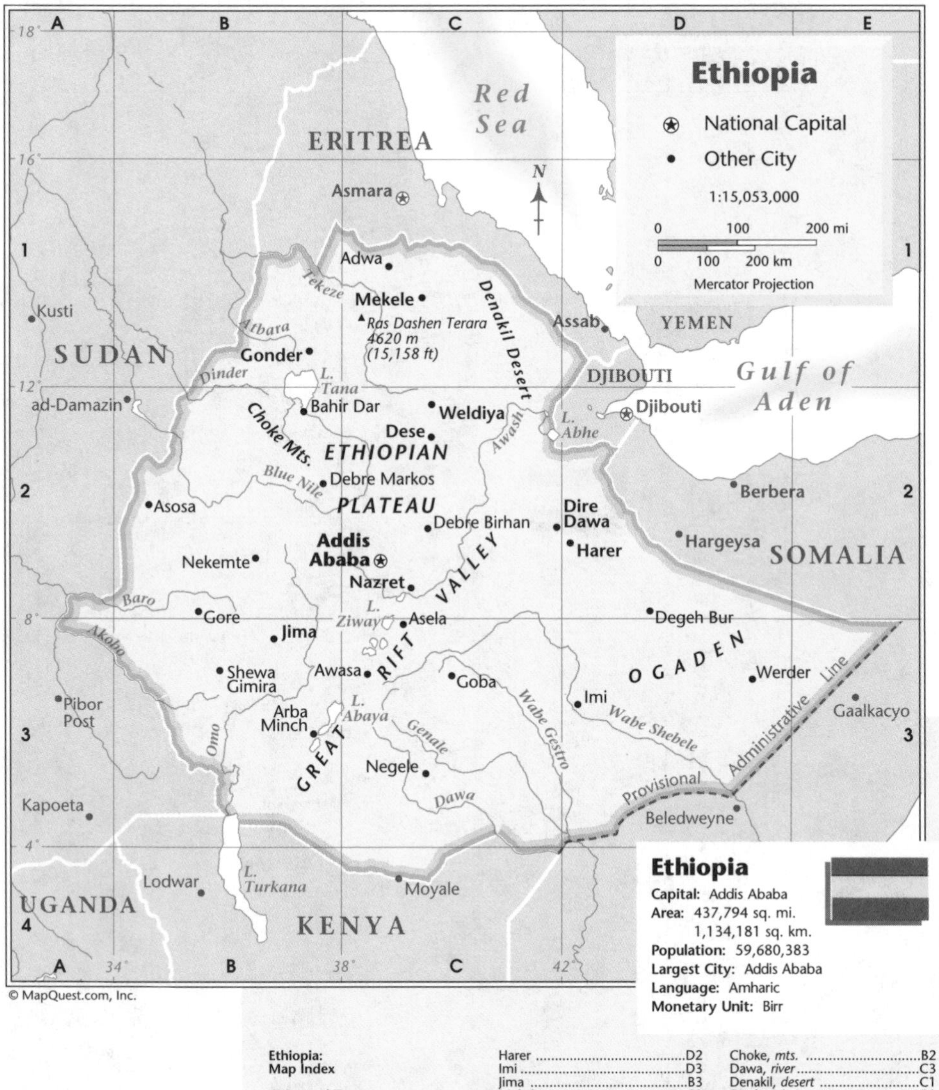

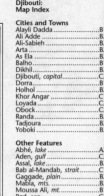

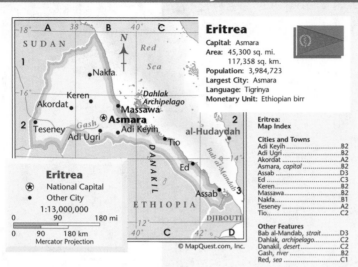

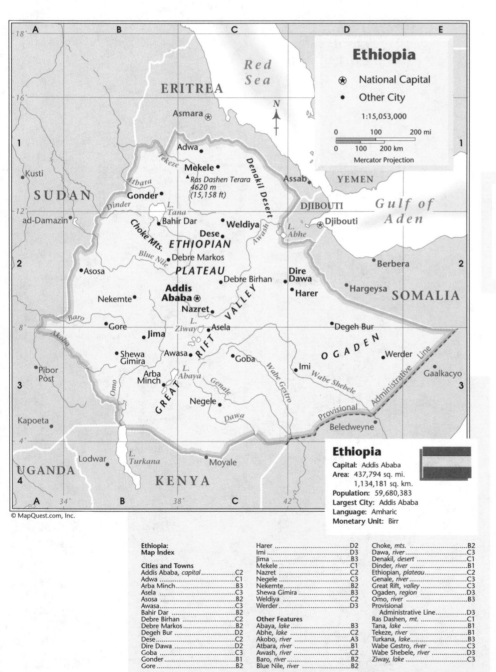

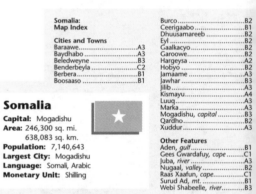

Kenya

Capital: Nairobi
Area: 224,961 sq. mi.
     582,801 sq. km.
Population: 28,808,658
Largest City: Nairobi
Language: Swahili, English
Monetary Unit: Shilling

Kenya

⊛ National Capital
• Other City

1:12,105,000

0   100   200 mi
0   100   200 km
Mercator Projection

Kenya:
Map Index

Provinces
Central D4
Coast E5
Eastern E3
Nairobi Area D4
North-Eastern F3
Nyanza C4
Rift Valley D3
Western C3

Cities and Towns
Eldoret C3
Embu D4
Garissa E4
Kakamega C3
Kericho C4
Kisumu C4
Kitale C3
Lamu F5
Lodwar C2
Machakos D4
Malindi F5
Marsabit E2
Meru D3
Mombasa E5
Moyale E2

Nairobi, capital D4
Nakuru D4
Nyeri D4
Ramu F2
Thika D4
Tsavo E5
Wajir F3

Other Features
Aberdare, range D4
Athi, river E5
Baringo, lake D3
Chalbi, desert D2
Daua, river F1
Galana, river E5
Great Rift, valley C3
Kenya, mt. D4
Laga Bor, river E2
Lorian, swamp E3
Lotikipi, plain C1
Magadi, lake D4
Mara, river C4
Ngiro, river D3
Nzoia, river C3
Tana, river F4
Turkana (Rudolf), lake D2
Turkwel, river C2
Victoria, lake B4
Yatta, plateau E5

Uganda

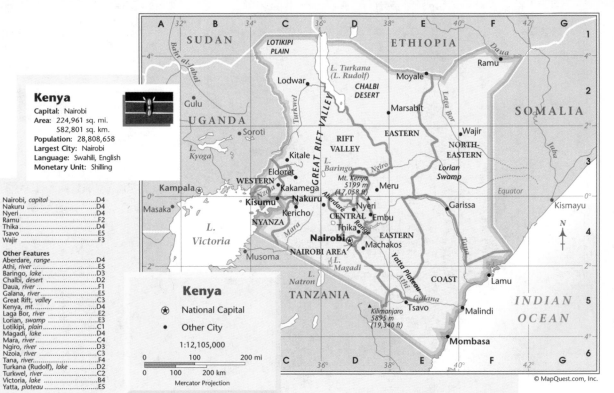

Capital: Kampala
Area: 93,070 sq. mi.
     241,114 sq. km.
Population: 22,804,973
Largest City: Kampala
Language: English
Monetary Unit: Shilling

Uganda

⊛ National Capital
• Other City

1:11,600,000

0   75   150 mi
0   75   150 km
Mercator Projection

Uganda:
Map Index

Cities and Towns
Arua B2
Atiak C2
Entebbe C3
Fort Portal B3
Gulu C2
Jinja C3
Kabale A4
Kampala, capital C3
Kitgum C2
Lira C2
Loyoro D2
Masaka B4
Masindi B3
Mbale D3
Mbarara B4
Moroto D2

Mubende B3
Soroti C3
Tororo D3

Other Features
Achwa, river C2
Albert, lake A3
Albert Nile, river B2
Bahr al-Jabal, river B2
Edward, lake A4
Elgon, mt. D3
George, lake A4
Kafu, river B3
Kagera, river B4
Kyoga, lake C3
Margherita, peak A3
Ruwenzori, range B3
Sese, islands C4
Victoria, lake C4
Victoria Nile, river B2,C3

Burundi

Capital: Bujumbura
Area: 10,740 sq. mi.
     27,824 sq. km.
Population: 5,735,937
Largest City: Bujumbura
Languages: French, Kirundi
Monetary Unit: Franc

Burundi:
Map Index

Cities and Towns
Bubanza B2
Bujumbura, capital B2
Bururi B2
Cankuzo C2
Gitega B2
Karuzi B2
Makamba B3
Muramvya B2
Muyinga C1
Ngozi B1

Rutana B2
Ruyigi C2

Other Features
Heha, mt. B2
Kagera, river C1
Malagarasi, river B2
Ruvubu, river B2
Ruzizi, river A1
Tanganyika, lake B2

Burundi

⊛ National Capital
• Other City

1:6,548,000

0   50   100 mi
0   50   100 km
Conic Equidistant Projection

Rwanda

⊛ National Capital
• Other City

1:4,624,000

0   25   50 mi
0   25   50 km
Gauss-Krüger Projection

© MapQuest.com, Inc.

Rwanda

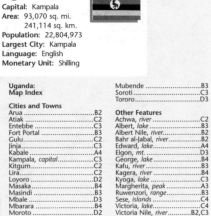

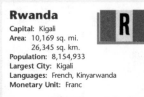

Capital: Kigali
Area: 10,169 sq. mi.
     26,345 sq. km.
Population: 8,154,933
Largest City: Kigali
Languages: French, Kinyarwanda
Monetary Unit: Franc

Rwanda:
Map Index

Cities and Towns
Butare B2
Byumba C1
Cyangugu A2
Gikongoro B2
Gisenyi B2
Gitarama B2
Kagitumba C1
Kibungo C2
Kibuye B2
Kigali, capital B1
Nyanza B2
Ruhengeri B1

Other Features
Akanyaru, river B2

Bulera, lake B1
Cyohoha Sud, lake C2
Ihema, lake C1
Kagera National Park C1
Kagera, river C1, C2
Karisimbi, mt. A1
Kivu, lake A2
Muhazi, lake B2
Nyabarongo, river C2
Ruhondo, lake B2
Ruhwa, river B2
Ruzizi, river A2
Rwayakizinga, lake C1
Rweru, lake C2
Virunga, mts. B1

© MapQuest.com, Inc.

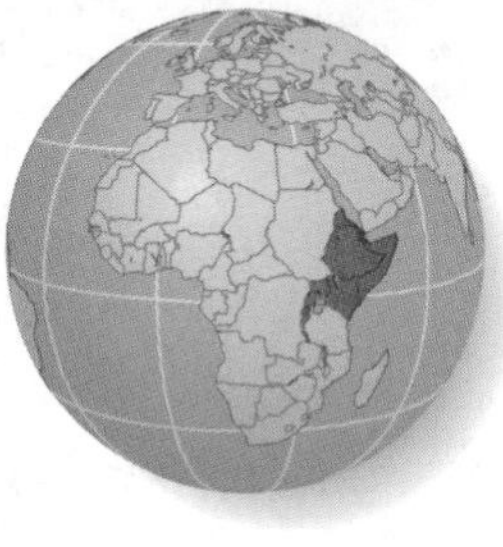

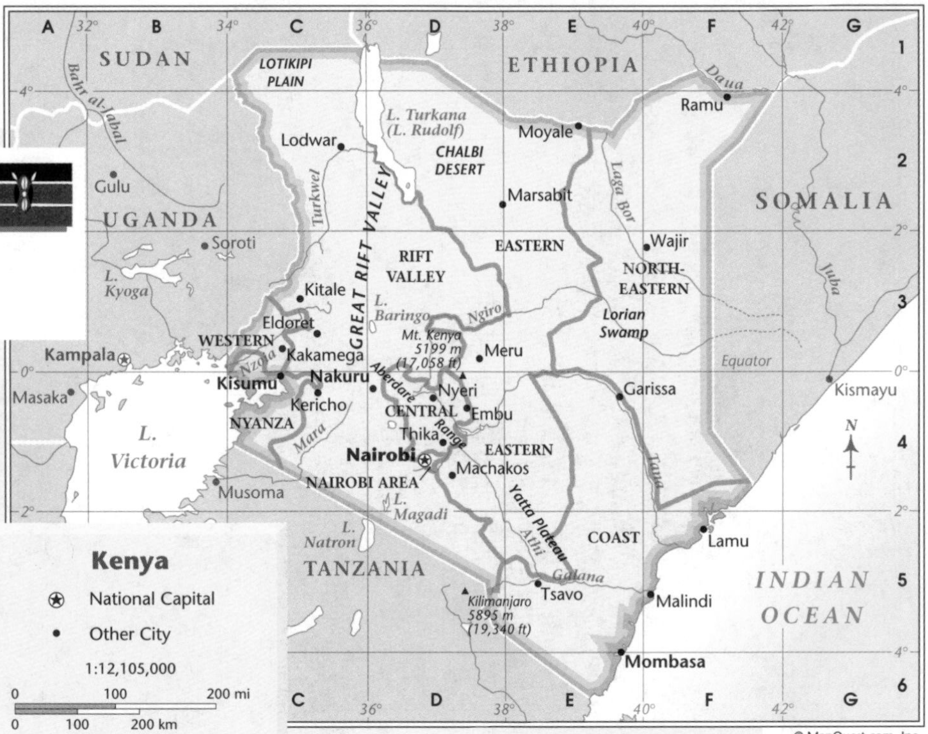

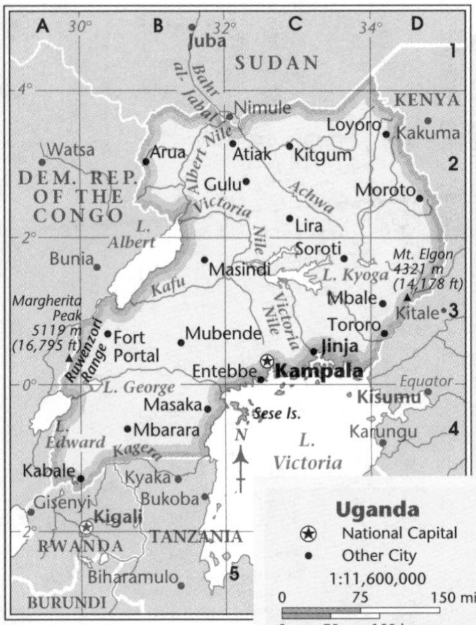

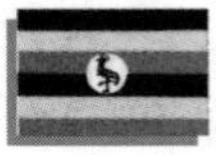

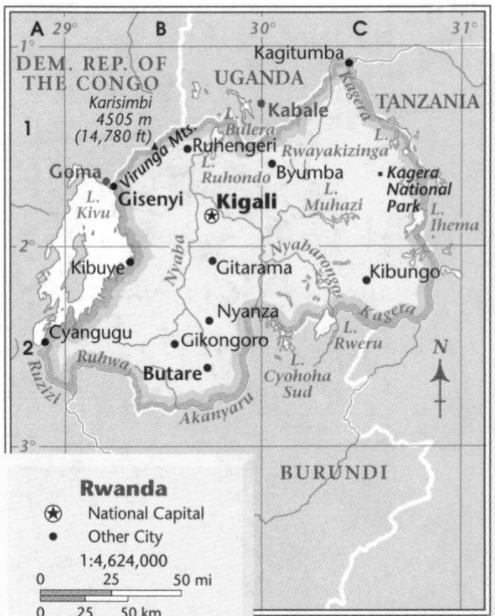

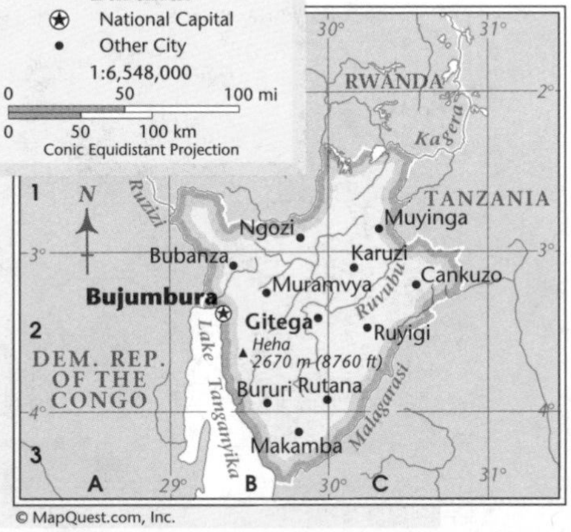

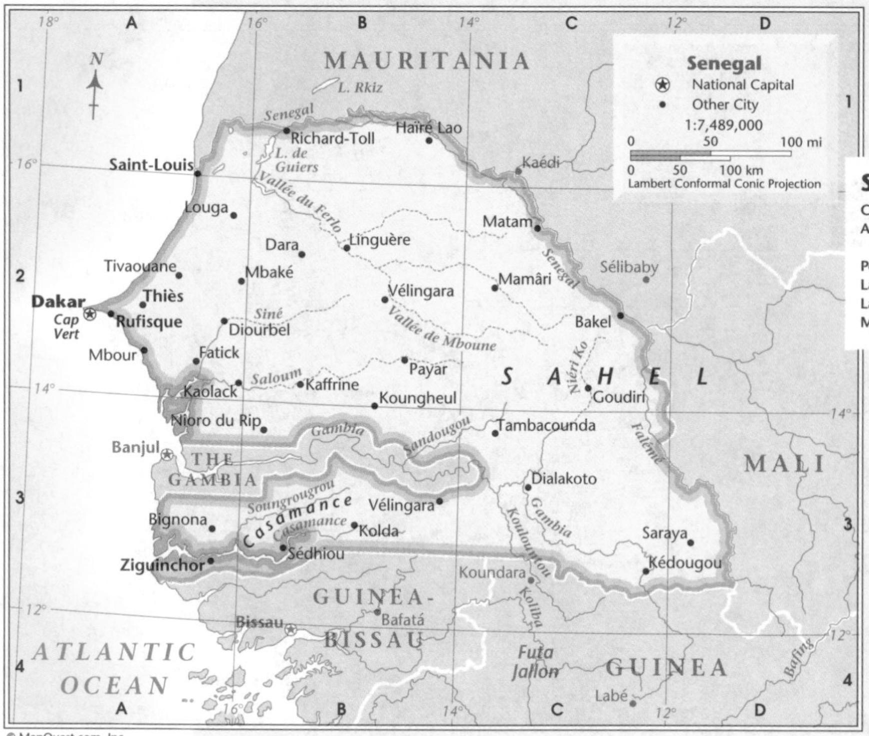

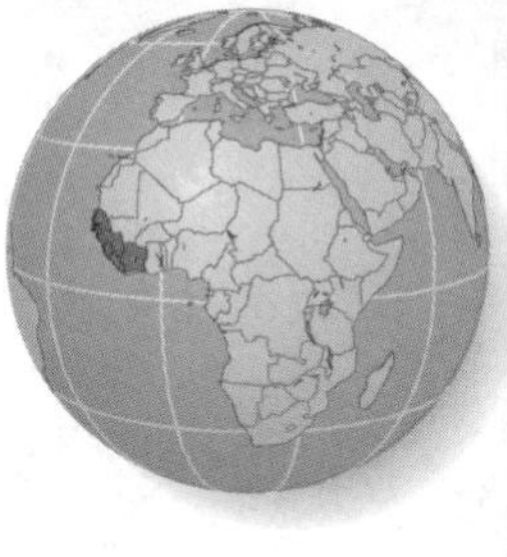

Senegal

Capital: Dakar
Area: 75,951 sq. mi.
196,764 sq. km.
Population: 10,051,930
Largest City: Dakar
Language: French
Monetary Unit: CFA franc

Senegal: Map Index

Cities and Towns

Bakel....C2
Bignona....A3
Dakar, *capital*....A2
Dara....B2
Dialakoto....C3
Diourbel....A2
Fatick....A2
Goudiri....C2
Hairé Lao....B1
Kaffrine....B2
Kaolack....A2
Kédougou....C3
Kolda....B3
Koungheul....B2
Linguère....B2
Louga....A2
Mamâri....C2
Matam....C2
Mbaké....A2
Mbour....A2
Nioro du Rip....B3
Payar....B2
Richard-Toll....B1
Rufisque....A2
Saint-Louis....A1
Saraya....D3
Sédhiou....B3
Tambacounda....C3
Thiès....A2
Tivaouane....A2
Vélingara....B2
Vélingara....B3
Ziguinchor....A3

Other Features

Casamance, *region*....B3
Casamance, *river*....B3
Falémé, *river*....C3
Ferlo, *river*....B2
Gambia, *river*....C3
Guiers, *lake*....B1
Koulountou, *river*....C3
Mboune, *river*....B2
Niéri Ko, *river*....C2
Sahel, *region*....C2
Saloum, *river*....B2
Sandougou, *river*....B3
Senegal, *river*....B1, C2
Siné, *river*....B2
Soungrougrou, *river*....B3
Vert, *cape*....A2

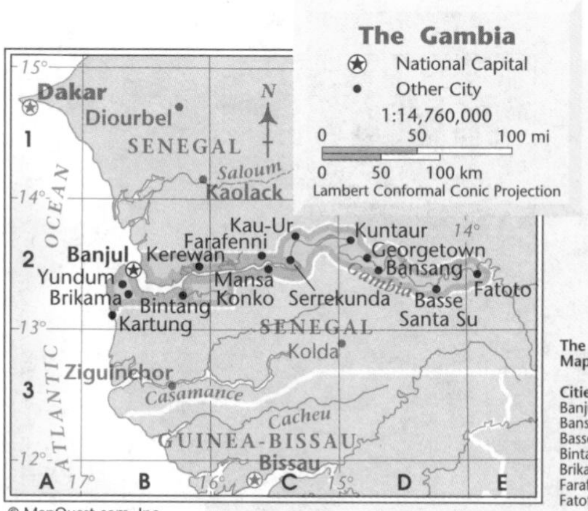

The Gambia

Capital: Banjul
Area: 4,127 sq. mi.
10,692 sq. km.
Population: 1,336,320
Largest City: Banjul
Language: English
Monetary Unit: Dalasi

The Gambia: Map Index

Cities and Towns

Banjul, *capital*....B2
Bansang....D2
Basse Santa Su....D2
Bintang....B2
Brikama....B2
Farafenni....C2
Fatoto....E2
Georgetown....D2
Kartung....B2
Kau-Ur....C2
Kerewan....B2
Kuntaur....D2
Mansa Konko....C2
Serrekunda....C2
Yundum....B2

Other Feature

Gambia, *river*....D2

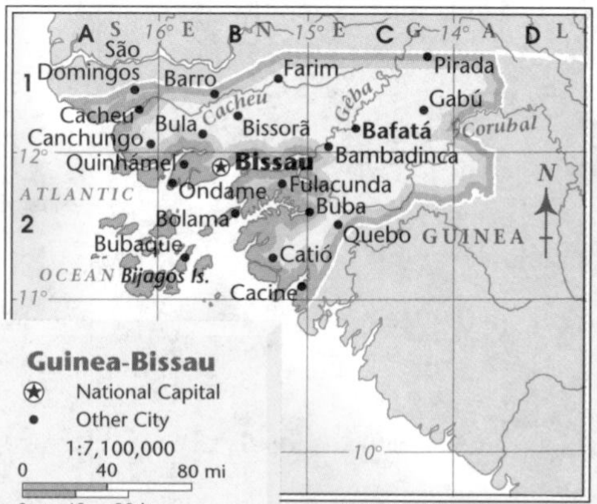

Guinea-Bissau

Capital: Bissau
Area: 13,948 sq. mi.
36,135 sq. km.
Population: 1,234,555
Largest City: Bissau
Language: Portuguese
Monetary Unit: CFA franc

Guinea-Bissau: Map Index

Cities and Towns

Bafatá....C1
Bambadinca....C1
Barro....B1
Bissau, *capital*....B2
Bissorã....B1
Bolama....B2
Buba....C2
Bubaque....B2
Bula....B1
Cacheu....A1
Cacine....C2
Canchungo....A1
Catió....B2
Farim....B1
Fulacunda....B2
Gabú....C1
Ondame....B2
Pirada....C1
Quebo....C2
Quinhámel....B2
São Domingos....A1

Other Features

Bijagós, *islands*....A2
Cacheu, *river*....B1
Corubal, *river*....D1
Gêba, *river*....C1

Guinea: Map Index

Cities and Towns

Beyla....D3
Conakry, *capital*....B3
Coyah....B3
Dabola....C2
Fria....B2
Guéckédou....C3
Kailahun....C3
Kali....C1
Kamsar....A2
Kankan....D2
Kérouané....D3
Kindia....B2
Kissidougou....C3
Kouroussa....D2
Labé....B2
Lélouma....B2
Macenta....D3
Mamou....B2
Niagassola....D1
Nzérékoré....D4
Siguiri....D2
Tougué....C2
Yomou....D4

Other Features

Bafing, *river*....C2
Futa Jallon, *plateau*....B1
Gambia, *river*....B2
Los, *islands*....A3
Milo, *river*....D3
Niger, *river*....C2
Nimba, *mts.*....D4
Tinkissa, *river*....C2

Guinea

Capital: Conakry
Area: 94,926 sq. mi.
245,922 sq. km.
Population: 7,538,953
Largest City: Conakry
Language: French
Monetary Unit: Guinea franc

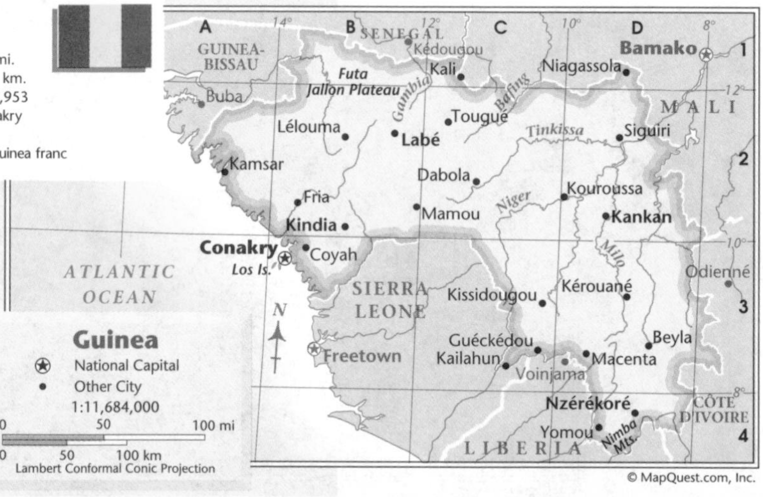

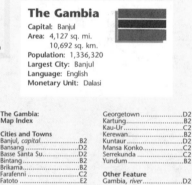

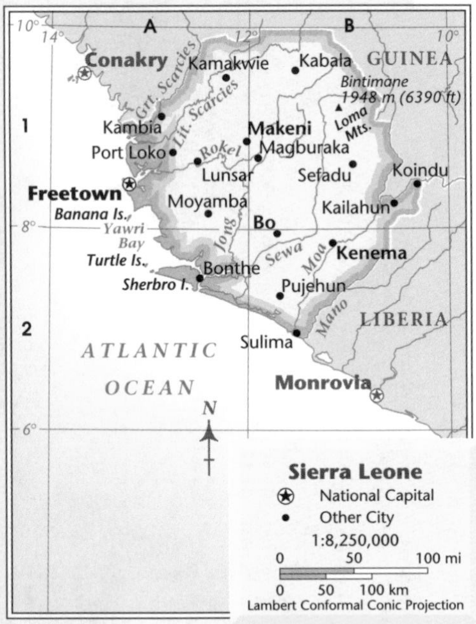

Sierra Leone

National Capital

Other City

1:8,250,000

0 50 100 mi

0 50 100 km

Lambert Conformal Conic Projection

Côte d'Ivoire (Ivory Coast)

National Capital

Other City

1:9,789,000

0 75 150 mi

0 75 150 km

Lambert Conformal Conic Projection

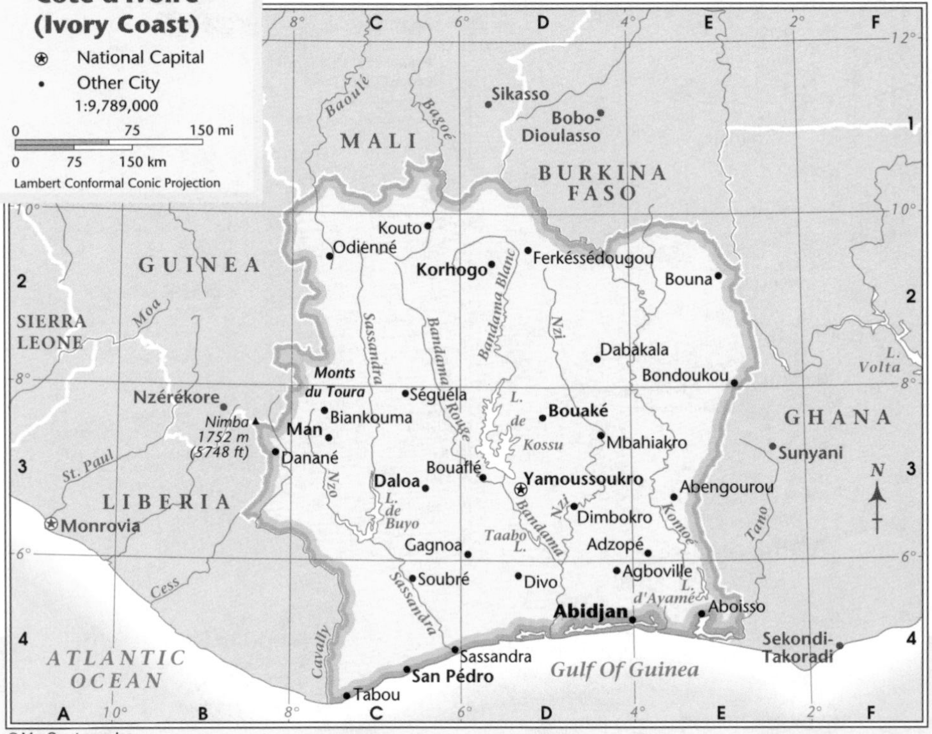

Sierra Leone

Capital: Freetown
Area: 27,699 sq. mi.
71,759 sq. km.
Population: 5,296,651
Largest City: Freetown
Language: English
Monetary Unit: Leone

Sierra Leone: Map Index

Cities and Towns
Bo B2
Bonthe A2
Freetown, *capital* A1
Kabala B1
Kailahun B1
Kamakwie A1
Kambia A1
Kenema B2
Koindu B1
Lunsar A1
Magburaka B1
Makeni B1
Moyamba A1
Port Loko A1
Pujehun B2
Sefadu B1
Sulima B2

Other Features
Banana, *islands* A1
Bintimane, *mt.* B1
Great Scarcies, *river* A1
Jong, *river* A2
Little Scarcies, *river* A1
Loma, *mts.* B1
Mano, *river* B2
Moa, *river* B2
Rokel, *river* A1
Sewa, *river* B2
Sherbro, *island* A2
Turtle, *islands* A2
Yawri, *bay* A2

Côte d'Ivoire

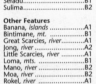

Capital: Yamoussoukro
Area: 124,504 sq. mi.
322,549 sq. km.
Population: 15,818,068
Largest City: Abidjan
Language: French
Monetary Unit: CFA franc

Côte d'Ivoire: Map Index

Cities and Towns
Abengourou E3
Abidjan D4
Aboisso E4
Adzopé E3
Agboville D4
Biankouma C3
Bondoukou E2
Bouaflé D3
Bouaké D3
Bouna E2
Dabakala D2
Daloa C3
Danané B3
Dimbokro D3
Divo D4
Ferkéssédougou D2
Gagnoa D3
Korhogo D2
Kouto C2
Man C3
Mbahiakro D3
Odienné C2
San Pédro C4
Sassandra C4
Séguéla C3
Soubré C4
Tabou C4
Yamoussoukro, *capital* D3

Other Features
Ayamé, *lake* E4
Bagoé, *river* C1
Bandama, *river* D3
Bandama Blanc, *river* D2
Bandama Rouge, *river* C2
Baoulé, *river* C1
Buyo, *lake* C3
Cavally, *river* C4
Guinea, *gulf* D4
Komoé, *river* E3
Kossu, *lake* D3
Nimba, *mt.* B3
Nzi, *river* D3
Nzo, *river* C3
Sassandra, *river* C2, C4
Taabo, *lake* D3
Tano, *river* E3
Toura, *mts.* C2

Liberia

Capital: Monrovia
Area: 38,250 sq. mi.
99,093 sq. km.
Population: 2,923,725
Largest City: Monrovia
Language: English
Monetary Unit: Dollar

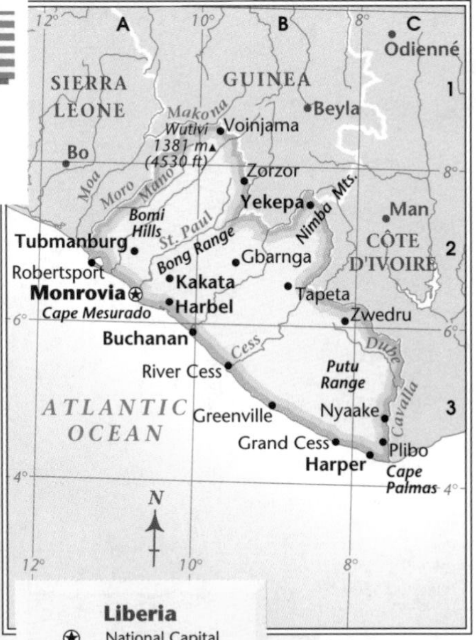

Liberia: Map Index

Cities and Towns
Buchanan A3
Gbarnga B2
Grand Cess B3
Greenville B3
Harbel A2
Harper C3
Kakata A2
Monrovia, *capital* A2
Nyaake C3
Plibo C3
River Cess B3
Robertsport A2
Tapeta B2
Tubmanburg A2
Voinjama B1
Yekepa B2
Zorzor B2
Zwedru B2

Other Features
Bomi, *hills* A2
Bong, *range* A2
Cavalla, *river* C3
Cess, *river* B3
Dube, *river* C3
Makona, *river* A1
Mano, *river* A2
Mesurado, *cape* A2
Moro, *river* A2
Nimba, *mts.* B2
Palmas, *cape* C3
Putu, *range* B3
St. Paul, *river* A2
Wutivi, *mt.* B1

Liberia

National Capital

Other City

1:11,221,000

0 60 120 mi

0 60 120 km

Lambert Conformal Conic Projection

São Tomé & Príncipe

Capital: São Tomé
Area: 386 sq. mi.
1,000 sq. km.
Population: 154,878
Largest City: São Tomé
Language: Portuguese
Monetary Unit: Dobra

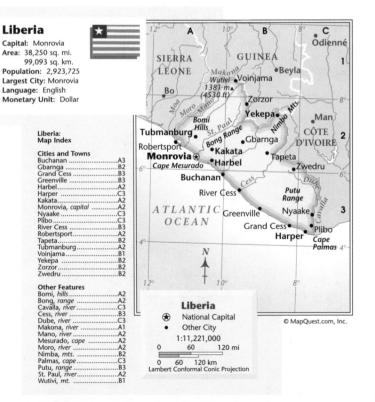

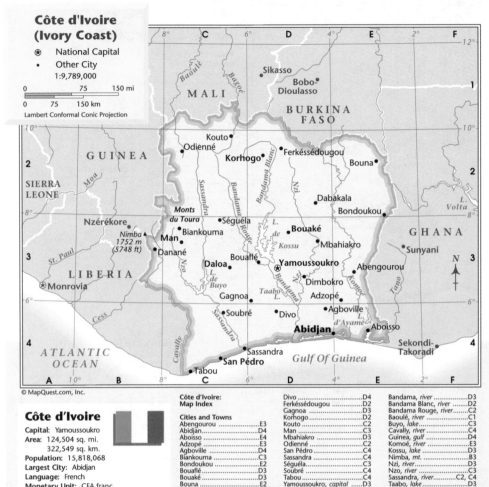

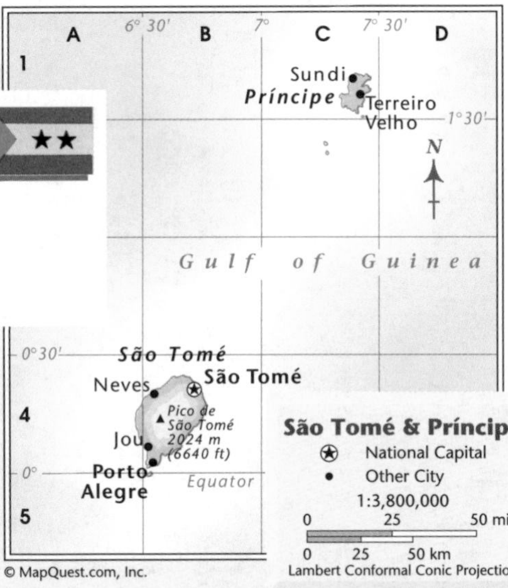

São Tomé & Príncipe: Map Index

Cities and Towns
Jou B4
Neves B4
Porto Alegre B4
São Tomé, *capital* B4
Sundi C1
Terreiro Velho C1

Other Features
Príncipe, *island* C1
São Tomé, *island* B4
São Tomé, *mt.* B4

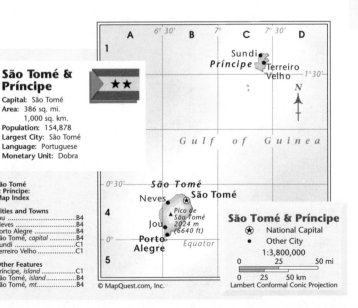

São Tomé & Príncipe

National Capital

Other City

1:3,800,000

0 25 50 mi

0 25 50 km

Lambert Conformal Conic Projection

Ghana

Capital: Accra
Area: 92,098 sq. mi.
238,596 sq. km.
Population: 18,887,626
Largest City: Accra
Language: English
Monetary Unit: Cedi

Ghana:
Map Index

Cities and Towns
Accra, capital B4
Awaso...............................A3
Axim.................................A4
Bawku..............................B1
Bimbila.............................C2
Bole..................................A2
Bolgatanga B1
Cape Coast B4
Dunkwa.............................B4
Ejura.................................B3
Elmina..............................B4
Ho....................................C3
Keta..................................C4
Koforidua..........................B3
Kpandu.............................C3
Kumasi..............................B3
Nkawkaw...........................B3
Nsawam............................B4
Obuasi..............................B3
Oda..................................B4
Prestea.............................A4
Salaga...............................B2
Sekondi-Takoradi...............B4

Sunyani.............................A3
Tamale..............................B2
Tema.................................C4
Wa....................................A1
Wenchi..............................A3
Winneba............................B4
Yendi................................B2

Other Features
Afadjoto, mt. C3
Afram, river B3
Akosombo, dam C3
Ankobra, river A4
Black Volta, river A2
Daka, river B2
Guinea, gulf C4
Kulpawn, river B1
Kwahu, plateau B3
Oti, river C2
Pra, river B4
Pru, river B3
Red Volta, river B1
Tano, river A3
Volta, lake C3
Volta, river C3
White Volta, river B1

Ghana

⊛ National Capital
• Other City

1:9,560,000

0   50   100 mi
0   50   100 km
Lambert Conformal Conic Projection

© MapQuest.com, Inc.

Burkina Faso

Burkina Faso

⊛ National Capital
• Other City

1:14,785,000

0   100   200 mi
0   100   200 km
Lambert Conformal Conic Projection

© MapQuest.com, Inc.

Capital: Ouagadougou
Area: 105,946 sq. mi.
274,472 sq. km.
Population: 11,575,898
Largest City: Ouagadougou
Language: French
Monetary Unit: CFA franc

Burkina Faso:
Map Index

Cities and Towns
Bobo-Dioulasso....................B3
Dédougou...........................C2
Dori...................................D1
Gaoua................................C3
Koudougou.........................C2
Léo....................................C3
Ouagadougou, capital D2
Ouahigouya........................C2
Tenkodogo.........................D3

Other Features
Black Volta, river B3
Red Volta, river D3
Sirba, river D2
Téna Kourou, mt. B3
White Volta, river D2

Benin

Benin

⊛ National Capital
• Other City

1:14,800,000

0   100   200 mi
0   100   200 km
Lambert Conformal Conic Projection

© MapQuest.com, Inc.

Benin

Capital: Porto-Novo
Area: 43,500 sq. mi.
112,694 sq. km.
Population: 6,305,567
Largest City: Cotonou
Language: French
Monetary Unit: CFA franc

Benin:
Map Index

Cities and Towns
Abomey A4
Bassila A3
Cotonou B4
Djougou A3
Kandi B2
Lokossa A4
Malanville B1
Natitingou A2
Nikki B3
Ouidah B4
Parakou B3
Pobé B4

Porto-Novo, capital..............B4
Savalou A3
Savé B3
Segbana B2
Tchaourou B3

Other Features
Alibori, river B2
Chaîne de l'Atacora, mts. A2
Couffo, river A4
Guinea, gulf A4
Mékrou, river A2
Mono, river A4
Niger, river B1
Ouémé, river B3
Sota, river B2

Togo

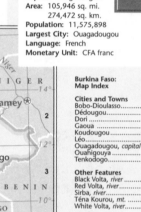

Capital: Lomé
Area: 21,925 sq. mi.
56,801 sq. km.
Population: 5,081,413
Largest City: Lomé
Language: French
Monetary Unit: CFA franc

Togo:
Map Index

Cities and Towns
Amlamé B3
Aného B3
Anié B3
Atakpamé B3
Badou B3
Bafilo B2
Bassar B2
Blitta B2
Dapaong B1
Kanté B2
Kara B2
Kpalimé B3
Kpémé B3
Lomé, capital B3
Mango B1
Niamtougou B2
Sokodé B2
Sotouboua B2
Tabligbo B3
Tchamba B2
Tsévié B3

Other Features
Agou, mt. B3
Benin, bight B4
Mono, river B3
Oti, river B1

Togo

⊛ National Capital
• Other City

1:8,600,000

0   50   100 mi
0   50   100 km
Lambert Conformal Conic Projection

© MapQuest.com, Inc

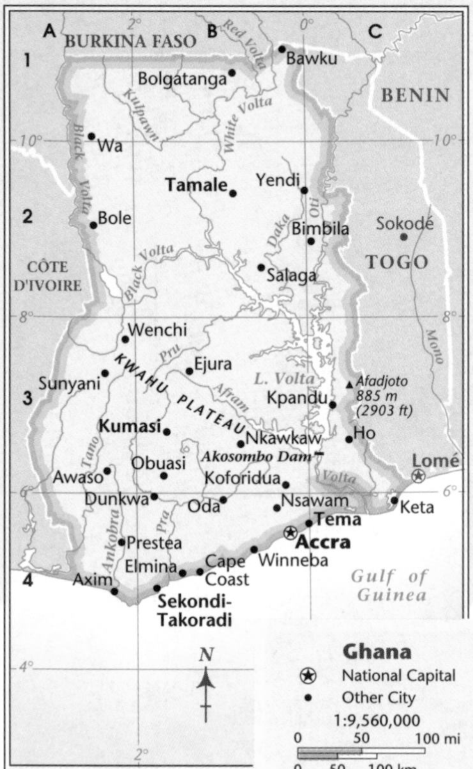

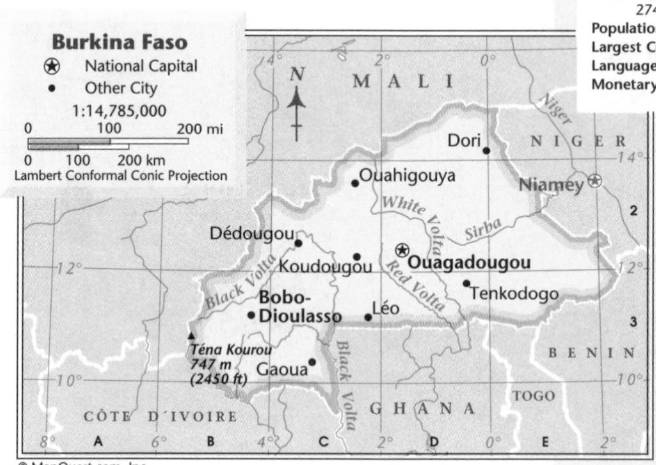

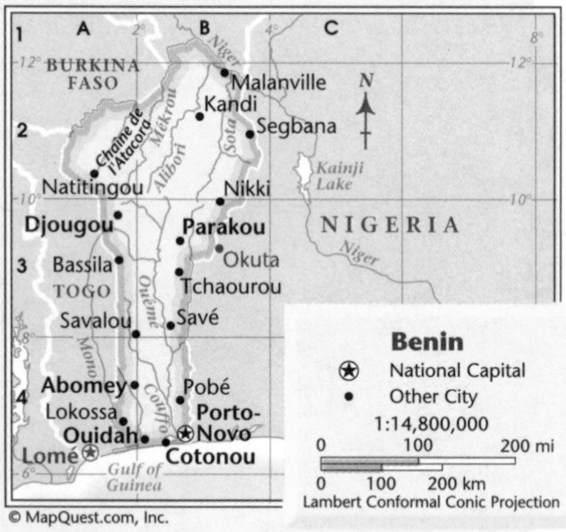

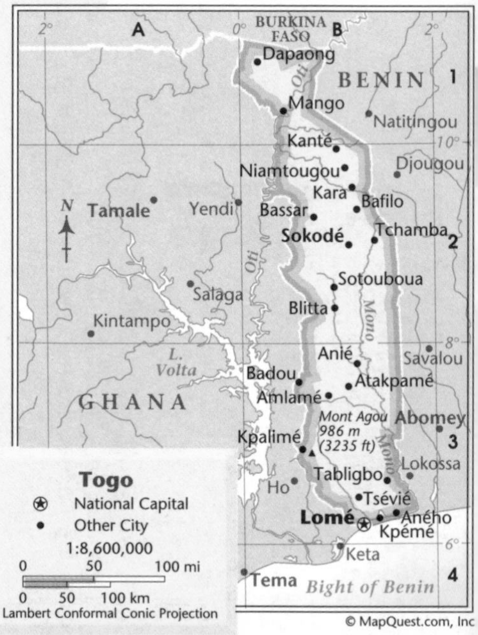

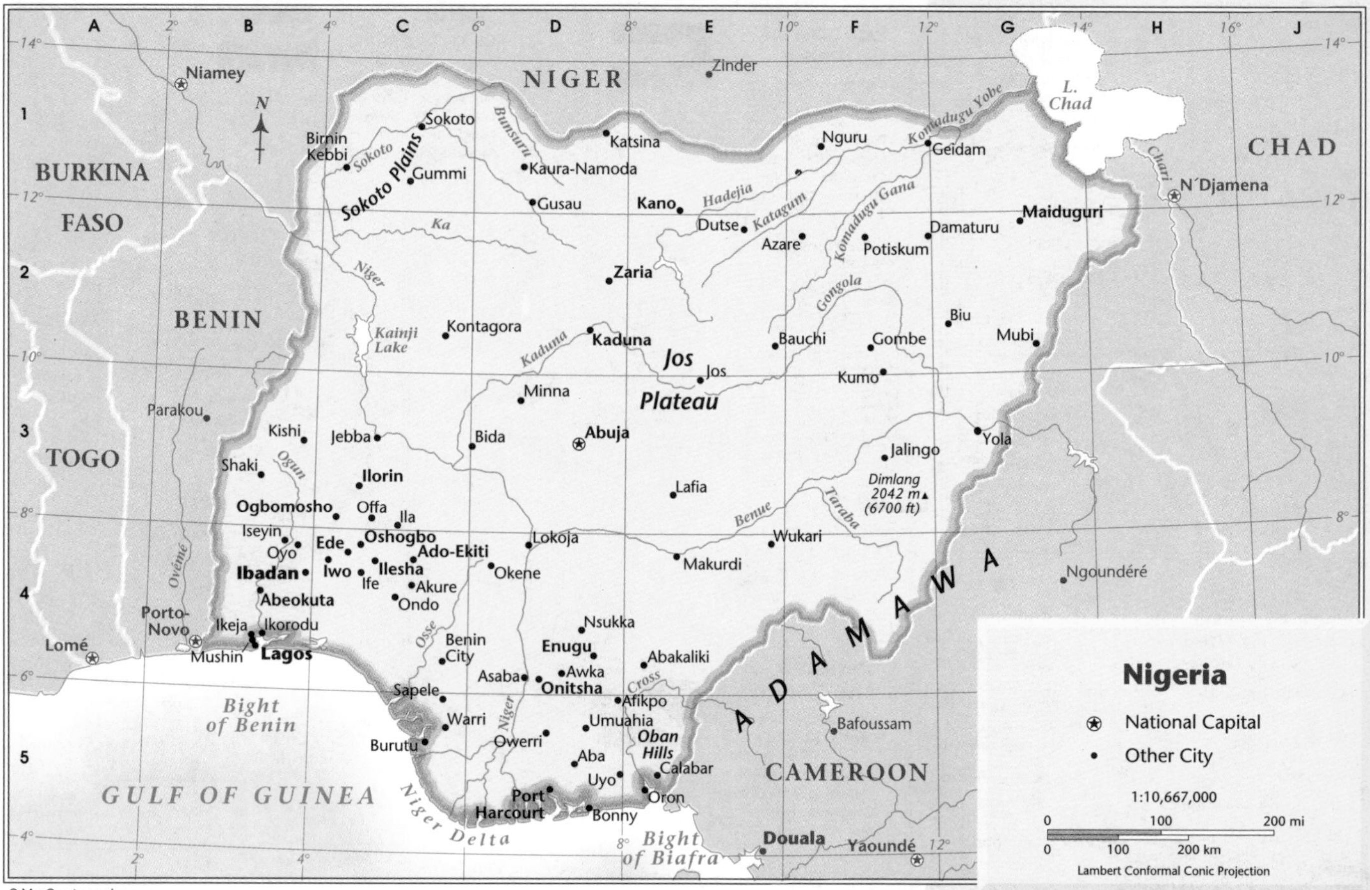

Nigeria

Capital: Abuja
Area: 356,669 sq. mi.
924,013 sq. km.
Population: 113,828,587
Largest City: Lagos
Language: English
Monetary Unit: Naira

Nigeria:
Map Index

Cities and Towns
Aba D5
Abakaliki....E4
Abeokuta B4
Abuja, *capital*....D3
Ado-Ekiti C4
Afikpo D5
Akure....C4
Asaba D4
Awka D4
Azare F2
Bauchi E2
Benin City C4
Bida....D3
Birnin Kebbi....C1
Biu G2
Bonny D5
Burutu C5
Calabar E5
Damaturu....F2
Dutse E2
Ede C4
Enugu D4
Geidam F1
Gombe....F2
Gummi C1
Gusau D1
Ibadan B4
Ife C4
Ikeja....B4
Ikorodu B4
Ila C3
Ilesha....C4
Ilorin C3
Iseyin B4
Iwo C4
Jalingo F3
Jebba....C3
Jos E3
Kaduna D2
Kano E1
Katsina D1
Kaura-Namoda D1
Kishi....B3
Kontagora C2
Kumo....F2
Lafia....E3
Lagos....B4
Lokoja D4
Maiduguri G2
Makurdi E4
Minna D3
Mubi....G2
Mushin B4
Nguru F1
Nsukka D4
Offa....C3
Ogbomosho C3
Okene....D4
Ondo....C4
Onitsha D4
Oron E5
Oshogbo....C4
Owerri....D5
Oyo B4
Port Harcourt D5
Potiskum F2
Sapele C5
Shaki B3
Sokoto....C1
Umuahia D5
Uyo....D5
Warri C5
Wukari E4
Yola....G3
Zaria D2

Other Features
Adamawa, *massif* E5
Benin, *bight* B5
Benue, *river* E3
Bunsuru, *river* D1
Chad, *lake*....G1
Cross, *river*....E4
Dimlang, *mt.* F3
Gongola, *river* F2
Guinea, *gulf*....B5
Hadejia, *river* E1
Jos, *plateau*....E2
Ka, *river*....C2
Kaduna, *river*....D2
Kainji, *lake*....C2
Katagum, *river* E2
Komadugu Gana, *river* F2
Komadugu Yobe, *river* F1
Niger, *delta* C5
Niger, *river* C2, D5
Oban, *hills* E5
Ogun, *river*....B3
Osse, *river* C4
Sokoto, *plains* C1
Sokoto, *river* C1
Taraba, *river* F3

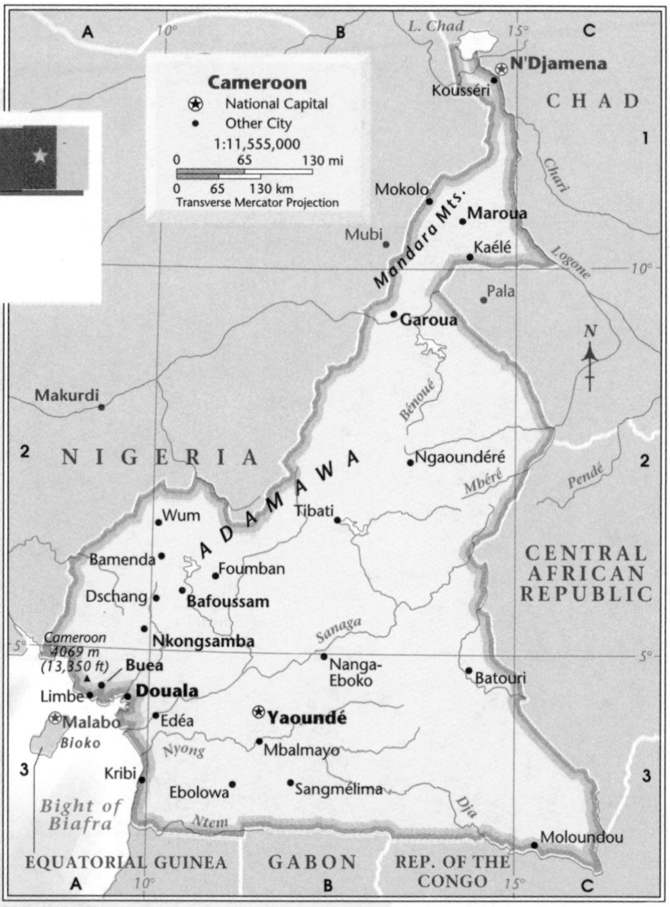

Cameroon

Capital: Yaoundé
Area: 183,569 sq. mi.
475,567 sq. km.
Population: 15,456,092
Largest City: Douala
Languages: English, French
Monetary Unit: CFA franc

Cameroon:
Map Index

Cities and Towns
Bafoussam B2
Bamenda....B2
Batouri B3
Buea....A3
Douala A3
Dschang....B2
Ebolowa B3
Edéa B3
Foumban....B2
Garoua B2
Kaélé B1
Kousséri....B1
Kribi A3
Limbe....A3
Maroua....B1
Mbalmayo....B3
Mokolo....B1
Moloundou....C3
Nanga-Eboko B3
Ngaoundéré....B2
Nkongsamba....A2
Sangmélima B3
Tibati....B2
Wum B2
Yaoundé, *capital*....B3

Other Features
Adamawa, *massif*....B2
Bénoué, *river* B2
Biafra, *bight*....A3
Cameroon, *mt.* A3
Chad, *lake* B1
Chari, *river* C1
Dja, *river*....B3
Logone, *river*....C1
Mandara, *mts.* B1
Mbéré, *river*....B2
Ntem, *river*....B3
Nyong, *river* B3
Sanaga, *river*....B2

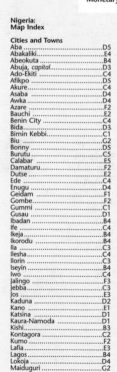

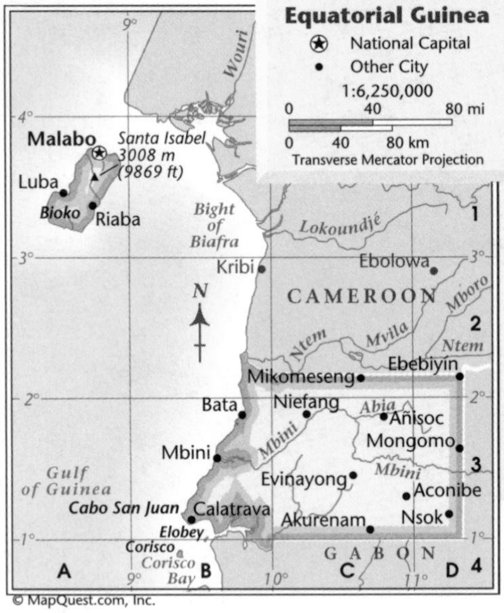

Equatorial Guinea

★ National Capital
● Other City

1:6,250,000

0   40   80 mi
0   40   80 km
Transverse Mercator Projection

© MapQuest.com, Inc.

Equatorial Guinea

Capital: Malabo
Area: 10,831 sq. mi.
28,060 sq. km.
Population: 465,746
Largest City: Malabo
Language: Spanish
Monetary Unit: CFA franc

Equatorial Guinea:
Map Index

Cities and Towns
Aconibe C3
Akurenam C3
Añisoc C3
Bata B3
Calatrava B3
Ebebiyín D2
Evinayong C3
Luba A1
Malabo, *capital* A1
Mbini B3
Mikomeseng C2
Mongomo D3

Niefang C3
Nsok D3
Riaba A1

Other Features
Abia, *river* C3
Biafra, *bight* B1
Bioko, *island* A1
Corisco, *bay* B4
Corisco, *island* B4
Elobey, *islands* B3
Guinea, *gulf* A3
Mbini, *river* C3
Mboro, *river* D4
San Juan, *cape* B3
Santa Isabel, *peak* A1

Gabon

Capital: Libreville
Area: 103,347 sq. mi.
267,738 sq. km.
Population: 1,225,853
Largest City: Libreville
Language: French
Monetary Unit: CFA franc

Gabon

★ National Capital
● Other City

1:11,850,000

0   75   150 mi
0   75   150 km
Azimuthal Equal Area Projection

© MapQuest.com, Inc.

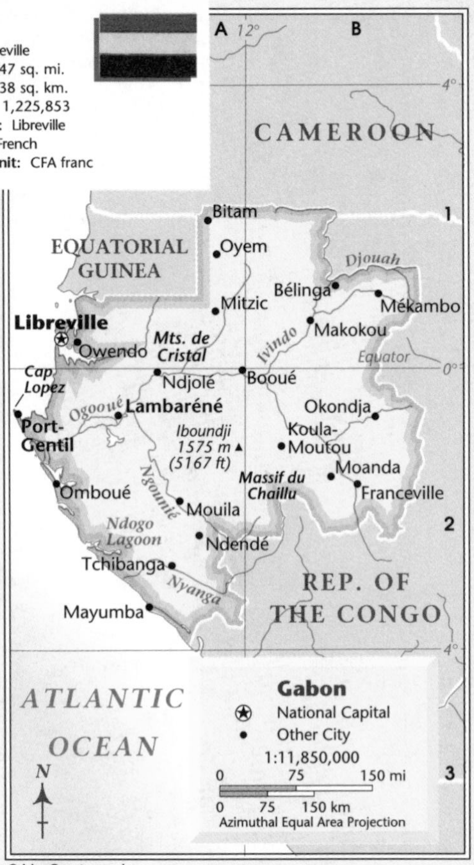

Gabon:
Map Index

Cities and Towns
Bélinga B1
Bitam A1
Booué A2
Franceville B2
Koula-Moutou B2
Lambaréné A2
Libreville, *capital* A1
Makokou B1
Mayumba A2
Mékambo B1
Mitzic A1
Moanda B2
Mouila A2
Ndendé A2
Ndjolé A2

Okondja B2
Omboué A2
Owendo A1
Oyem A1
Port-Gentil A2
Tchibanga A2

Other Features
Chaillu, *mts.* B2
Cristal, *mts.* A1
Djouah, *river* B1
Iboundji, *mt.* A2
Ivindo, *river* B1
Lopez, *cape* A2
Ndogo, *lagoon* A2
Ngounié, *river* A2
Nyanga, *river* A2
Ogooué, *river* A2

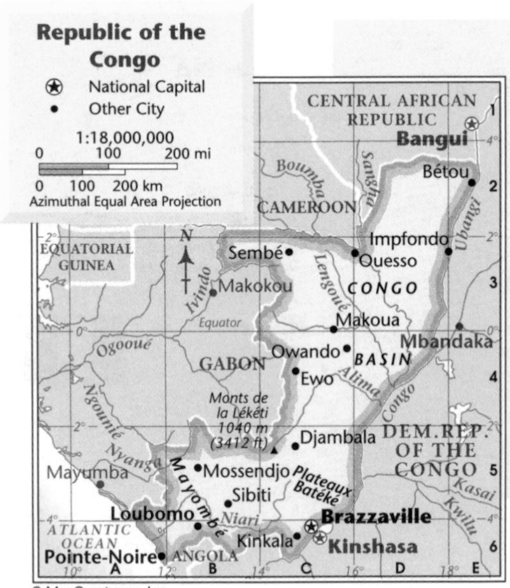

Republic of the Congo

★ National Capital
● Other City

1:18,000,000

0   100   200 mi
0   100   200 km
Azimuthal Equal Area Projection

© MapQuest.com, Inc.

Republic of the Congo

Capital: Brazzaville
Area: 132,047 sq. mi.
342,091 sq. km.
Population: 2,716,814
Largest City: Brazzaville
Language: French
Monetary Unit: CFA franc

Republic of the Congo:
Map Index

Cities and Towns
Bétou E2
Brazzaville, *capital* C6
Djambala C5
Ewo C4
Impfondo D3
Kinkala C6
Loubomo B6
Makoua C4
Mossendjo B5
Ouesso D3
Owando C4
Pointe-Noire A6

Sembé C3
Sibiti B5

Other Features
Alima, *river* D4
Batéké, *plateau* C5
Congo, *basin* D3
Congo, *river* D4
Ivindo, *river* B3
Léketi, *mts.* C5
Lengoué, *river* C3
Mayombé, *massif* B5
Niari, *river* B5
Nyanga, *river* A5
Sangha, *river* D2
Ubangi, *river* E2

Central African Republic (C.A.R.)

Capital: Bangui
Area: 240,324 sq. mi.
622,601 sq. km.
Population: 3,444,951
Largest City: Bangui
Language: French
Monetary Unit: CFA franc

Central African Republic:
Map Index

Cities and Towns
Bambari B2
Bangassou B3
Bangui, *capital* A3
Batangafo A2
Berbérati A3
Birao B1
Bossangoa A2
Bouar A2
Bria B2
Kaga Bandoro A2
Mobaye B2
Ndélé B2
Nola A3
Obo C2
Yalinga B2

Other Features
Chari, *river* A2
Chinko, *river* B2
Gribingui, *river* A2
Kadei, *river* A3
Kotto, *river* B2
Lobaye, *river* A2
Mambéré, *river* A2
Massif des Bongos, *range* ..B2
Mpoko, *river* A2
Ouaka, *river* B2
Ouarra, *river* C2
Ouham, *river* A2
Pendé, *river* A2
Toussoro, *mt.* B2
Ubangi, *river* A3

© MapQuest.com, Inc.

Central African Republic

★ National Capital
● Other City

1:12,895,000

0   75   150 mi
0   75   150 km
Lambert Conformal Conic Projection

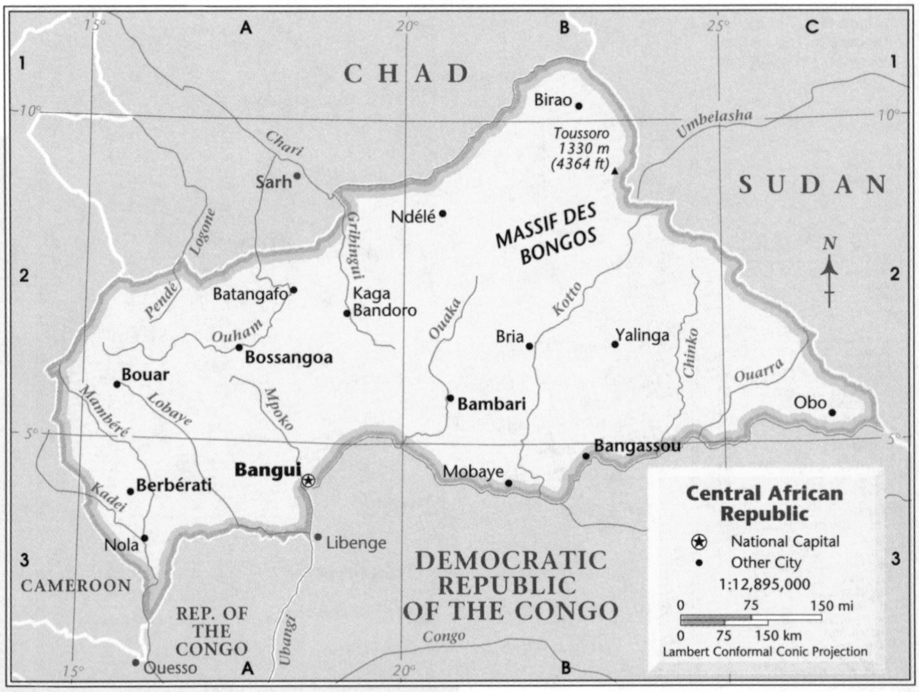

Democratic Republic of the Congo

Capital: Kinshasa
Area: 905,446 sq. mi.
2,345,715 sq. km.
Population: 50,481,305
Largest City: Kinshasa
Language: French
Monetary Unit: Congolese franc

Democratic Republic of the Congo: Map Index

Regions
Bandundu B2
Bas-Congo A2
Équateur B1
Kasai-Occidental B2
Kasai-Oriental B2
Katanga C3
Kinshasa B2
Maniema C2
Nord-Kivu C2
Orientale C1
Sud-Kivu C2

Cities and Towns
Banana A2
Bandundu B2
Boende B2
Bolobo B2
Boma A2
Bondo B1
Bukavu C2
Bumba B1
Bunia C1
Buta C1
Dilolo B3
Gemena B1
Goma C2
Ikela B2
Ilebo B2
Inga A2
Isiro C1
Kabalo C2
Kahemba B2
Kalemie C2
Kamina C3
Kananga B2
Kikwit B2
Kindu C2
Kinshasa, *capital* A2
Kisangani C1
Kolwezi C3
Likasi C3
Lisala B1
Lodja B2
Lubumbashi C3
Lusambo B2
Manono C2
Matadi A2
Mbandaka B2
Mbanza-Ngungu A2
Mbuji-Mayi B2
Moba C2
Mwene-Ditu B2
Tshikapa B2
Uvira C2
Watsa C1
Yangambi C1

Other Features
Albert, *lake* C1
Aruwimi, *river* C1
Bomu, *river* C1
Congo, *river* B1
Congo Basin, *region* B1
Edward, *lake* C2
Kasai, *river* B2
Katanga, *plateau* B3
Kivu, *lake* C2
Kwa, *river* B2
Kwango, *river* B2
Lomami, *river* C2
Lualaba, *river* C2
Luapula, *river* C3
Lukuga, *river* C2
Luvua, *river* C2
Mai-Ndombe, *lake* B2
Margherita, *peak* C1
Mitumba, *mts.* C2
Mweru, *lake* C3
Sankuru, *river* B2
Tanganyika, *lake* C2
Tshuapa, *river* B2
Tumba, *lake* B2
Ubangi, *river* B1
Uele, *river* C1
Upemba, *lake* C3

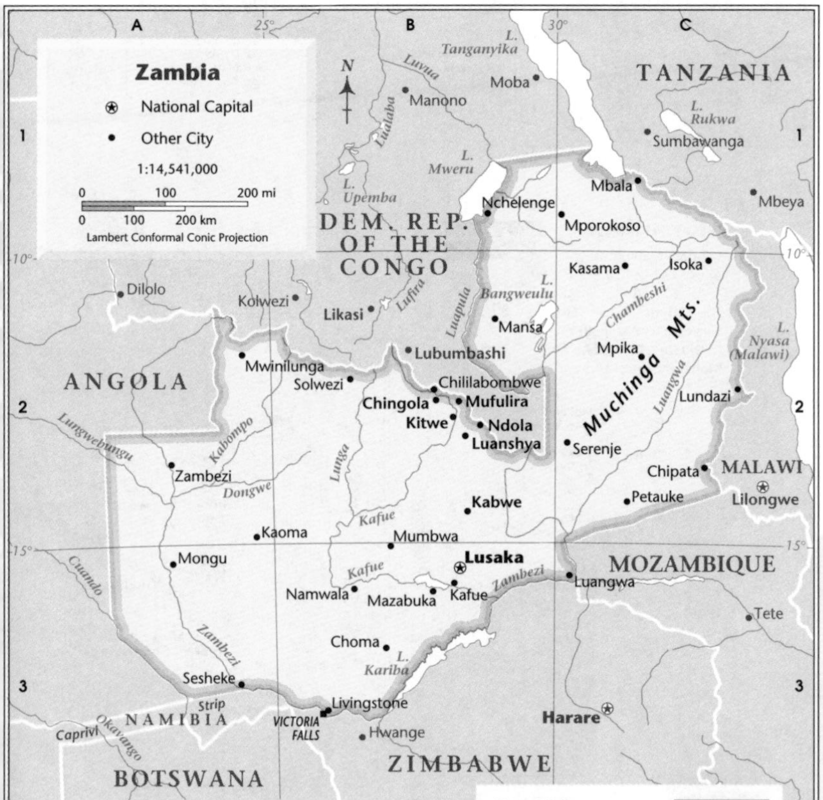

Zambia

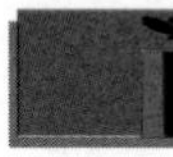

Capital: Lusaka
Area: 290,586 sq. mi.
752,813 sq. km.
Population: 9,663,535
Largest City: Lusaka
Language: English
Monetary Unit: Kwacha

Zambia: Map Index

Cities and Towns
Chililabombwe B2
Chingola B2
Chipata C2
Choma B3
Isoka C2
Kabwe B2
Kafue B3
Kaoma A2
Kasama C2
Kitwe B2
Livingstone B3
Luangwa C3
Luanshya B2
Lundazi C2
Lusaka, *capital* B3
Mansa B2
Mazabuka B3
Mbala C1
Mongu A3
Mpika C2
Mporokoso C1
Mufulira B2
Mumbwa B3
Mwinilunga A2
Namwala B3
Nchelenge B1
Ndola B2
Petauke C2
Serenje C2
Sesheke A3
Solwezi B2
Zambezi A2

Other Features
Bangweulu, *lake* B2
Chambeshi, *river* C2
Cuando, *river* A3
Dongwe, *river* A2
Kabompo, *river* A2
Kafue, *river* B2
Kariba, *lake* B3
Luangwa, *river* C2
Luapula, *river* B2
Lunga, *river* B2
Lungwebungu, *river* A2
Luvua, *river* B1
Muchinga, *mts.* C2
Mweru, *lake* B1
Tanganyika, *lake* C1
Victoria, *falls* B3
Zambezi, *river* A3, B3

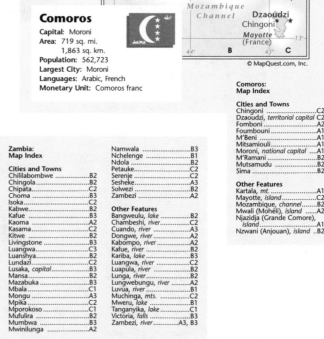

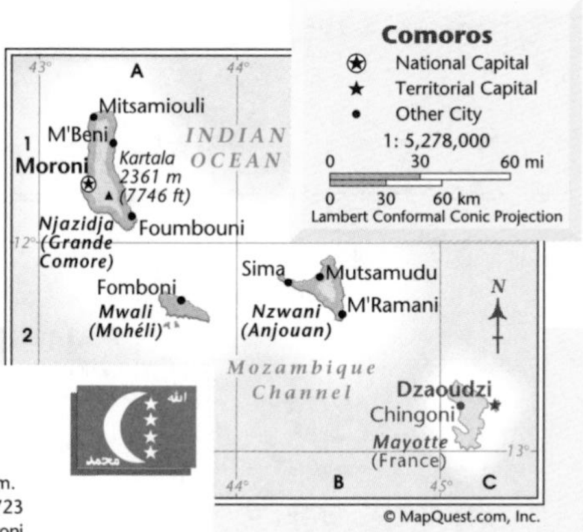

Comoros

Capital: Moroni
Area: 719 sq. mi.
1,863 sq. km.
Population: 562,723
Largest City: Moroni
Languages: Arabic, French
Monetary Unit: Comoros franc

Comoros: Map Index

Cities and Towns
Chingoni C2
Dzaoudzi, *territorial capital* C2
Fomboni A2
Foumbouni A1
M'Beni A1
Mitsamiouli A1
Moroni, *national capital* A1
M'Ramani B2
Mutsamudu B2
Sima B2

Other Features
Kartala, *mt.* A1
Mayotte, *island* C2
Mozambique, *channel* B2
Mwali (Mohéli), *island* A2
Njazidja (Grande Comore), *island* A1
Nzwani (Anjouan), *island* B2

Tanzania
⊛ National Capital
• Other City
1:11,000,000

0   100   200 mi
0   100   200 km
Lambert Conformal Conic Projection

Tanzania
Capital: Dar es-Salaam
Area: 364,017 sq. mi.
  943,049 sq. km.
Population: 31,270,820
Largest City: Dar es-Salaam
Languages: Swahili, English
Monetary Unit: Shilling

Tanzania:
Map Index

Cities and Towns
Arusha	C1
Bukoba	B1
Dar es-Salaam, *capital*	C2
Dodoma	C2
Iringa	C2
Kigoma	A1
Kilwa Kivinje	C2
Lindi	C2
Mbeya	B2
Morogoro	C2
Moshi	C1
Mpanda	B2
Mtwara	D3
Musoma	B1
Mwanza	B1
Ngara	B1
Shinyanga	B1
Singida	B1
Songea	C3
Sumbawanga	B2
Tabora	B2
Tanga	C2
Wete	C1
Zanzibar	C2

Other Features
Eyasi, *lake*	B1
Great Rift, *valley*	B2, C1
Great Ruaha, *river*	C2

Igombe, *river*	B1
Kagera, *river*	B1
Kilimanjaro, *mt.*	C1
Kilombero, *river*	C2
Kipengere, *range*	B2
Luwegu, *river*	C2
Mafia, *island*	C2
Malagarasi, *river*	B2
Manyara, *lake*	C1
Mara, *river*	B1
Masai, *steppe*	C1
Mbemkuru, *river*	C3
Moyowosi, *river*	B1
Natron, *lake*	C1
Ngorongoro, *crater*	C1
Njombe, *river*	B2
Nyasa (Malawi), *lake*	B3
Pangani, *river*	C1
Pemba, *island*	C1
Ruaha Natl. Park	B2
Rufiji, *river*	C2
Rukwa, *lake*	B2
Rungwa, *river*	B2
Ruvuma, *river*	C3
Serengeti Natl. Park	B1
Tanganyika, *lake*	A2
Tarangire Natl. Park	C1
Ugalla, *river*	B2
Victoria, *lake*	B1
Wami, *river*	C2
Wembere, *river*	B1
Zanzibar, *island*	C2

© MapQuest.com, Inc.

Malawi
Capital: Lilongwe
Area: 45,747 sq. mi.
  118,516 sq. km.
Population: 10,000,416
Largest City: Blantyre
Languages: English, Chichewa
Monetary Unit: Kwacha

Mozambique
Capital: Maputo
Area: 313,661 sq. mi.
  812,593 sq. km.
Population: 19,124,335.
Largest City: Maputo
Language: Portuguese
Monetary Unit: Metical

Mozambique
⊛ National Capital
• Other City
1:25,181,000

0   150   300 mi
0   150   300 km
Modified Lambert Conformal Conic Projection

Malawi:
Map Index

Cities and Towns
Blantyre	B3
Chitipa	B1
Dedza	B2
Karonga	B1
Kasungu	B2
Lilongwe, *capital*	B2
Mchinji	A2
Monkey Bay	B2
Mzimba	B2
Mzuzu	B2
Nkhata Bay	B2
Nkhotakota	B2
Nsanje	B3
Salima	B2
Zomba	B3

Other Features
Bua, *river*	B2
Chilwa, *lake*	C3
Great Rift, *valley*	B1
Malawi (Nyasa), *lake*	B1
Malombe, *lake*	B2
Nyika, *plateau*	B2
Sapitwa, *mt.*	B3
Shire, *river*	B3
Songwe, *river*	B1

Malawi
⊛ National Capital
• Other City
1:10,756,000

0   70   140 mi
0   70   140 km
Lambert Conformal Conic Projection

© MapQuest.com, Inc.

Mozambique:
Map Index

Cities and Towns
Angoche	C3
Beira	B3
Chimoio	B3
Chinde	C3
Cuamba	C2
Inhambane	B5
Lichinga	B2
Maputo, *capital*	B5
Moçambique	D2
Mocímboa da Praia	D1
Nacala	D2
Nampula	C2
Pebane	C3
Pemba	D2
Quelimane	C3
Tete	B3
Vilanculos	B4
Xai-Xai	B5

Other Features
Binga, *mt.*	B3
Búzi, *river*	B4
Cabora Bassa, *dam*	B2
Cabora Bassa, *lake*	A2
Changane, *river*	B4
Chilwa, *lake*	B2
Chire, *river*	B3
Lebombo, *mts.*	A4
Limpopo, *river*	B4
Lugenda, *river*	C1
Lúrio, *river*	C2
Mozambique, *channel*	C3
Namuli, *highlands*	C2
Nyasa (Malawi), *lake*	B2
Rovuma, *river*	C1
Save, *river*	B4
Zambezi, *river*	B3

© MapQuest.com, Inc.

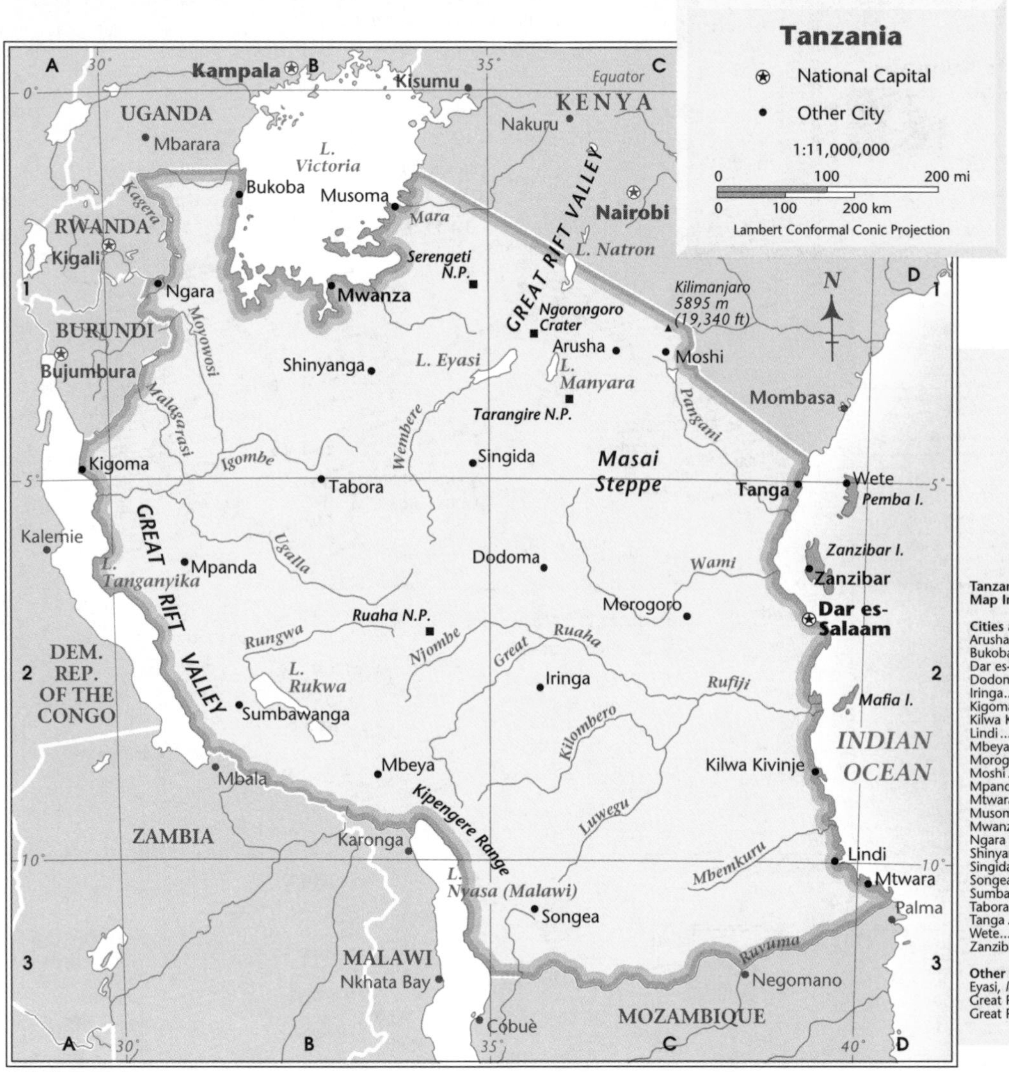

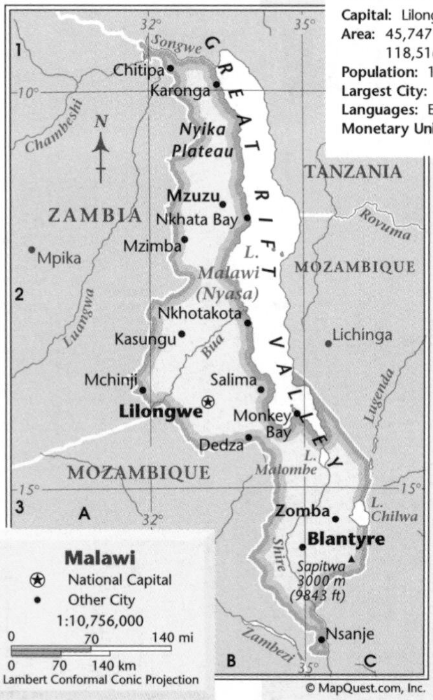

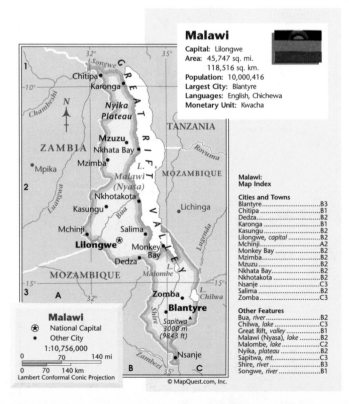

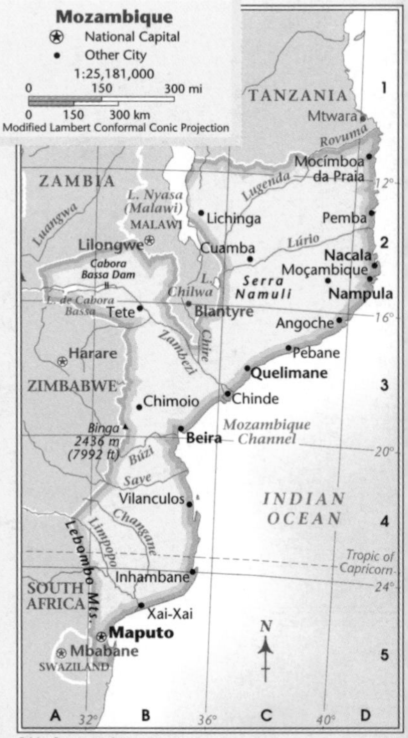

Mauritius
National Capital
Other City
1:1,635,000
0 10 20 mi
0 10 20 km
Transverse Mercator Projection

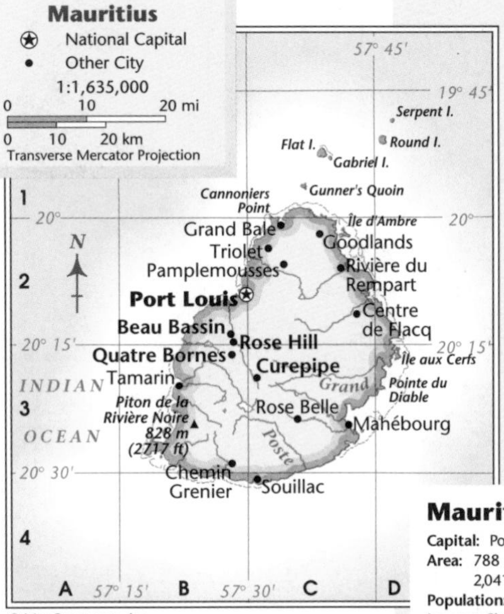

Mauritius:
Map Index

Cities and Towns

Beau Bassin	B2
Centre de Flacq	C2
Chemin Grenier	B3
Curepipe	C3
Goodlands	C2
Grand Baie	C2
Mahébourg	C3
Pamplemousses	C2
Port Louis, *capital*	B2
Quatre Bornes	B3
Rivière du Rempart	C2
Rose Belle	C3
Rose Hill	B2
Souillac	C4
Tamarin	B3
Triolet	C2

Other Features

Ambre, *island*	C2
Cannoniers, *point*	C1
Cerfs, *island*	D3
Diable, *point*	D3
Flat, *island*	C1
Gabriel, *island*	C1
Grand, *river*	C3
Gunner's Quoin, *island*	C1
Poste, *river*	C3
Rivière Noire, *mt.*	B3
Round, *island*	D1
Serpent, *island*	D1

Mauritius

Capital: Port Louis
Area: 788 sq. mi.
2,041 sq. km.
Population: 1,182,212
Largest City: Port Louis
Language: English
Monetary Unit: Rupee

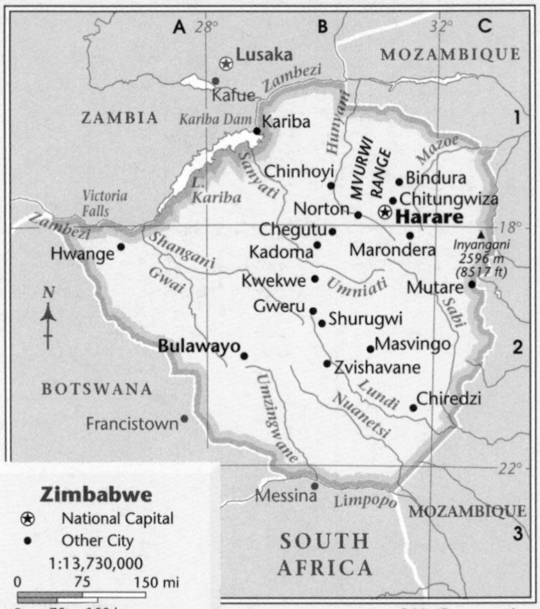

Zimbabwe
National Capital
Other City
1:13,730,000
0 75 150 mi
0 75 150 km
Lambert Conformal Conic Projection

Zimbabwe

Capital: Harare
Area: 150,872 sq. mi.
390,860 sq. km.
Population: 11,163,160
Largest City: Harare
Language: English
Monetary Unit: Dollar

Zimbabwe:
Map Index

Cities and Towns

Bindura	B1
Bulawayo	B2
Chegutu	B2
Chinhoyi	B1
Chiredzi	B2
Chitungwiza	B1
Gweru	B2
Harare, *capital*	B1
Hwange	A2
Kadoma	B2
Kariba	B1
Kwekwe	B2
Marondera	B2
Masvingo	B2
Mutare	C2
Norton	B1
Shurugwi	B2
Zvishavane	B2

Other Features

Gwai, *river*	A2
Hunyani, *river*	B1
Inyangani, *mt.*	C2
Kariba, *lake*	A1
Limpopo, *river*	B3
Lundi, *river*	B2
Mazoe, *river*	B1
Mvurwi, *range*	B1
Nuanetsi, *river*	B2
Sabi, *river*	C2
Sanyati, *river*	B1
Shangani, *river*	A2
Umniati, *river*	B2
Umzingwani, *river*	B2
Victoria, *falls*	A1
Zambezi, *river*	A1, B1

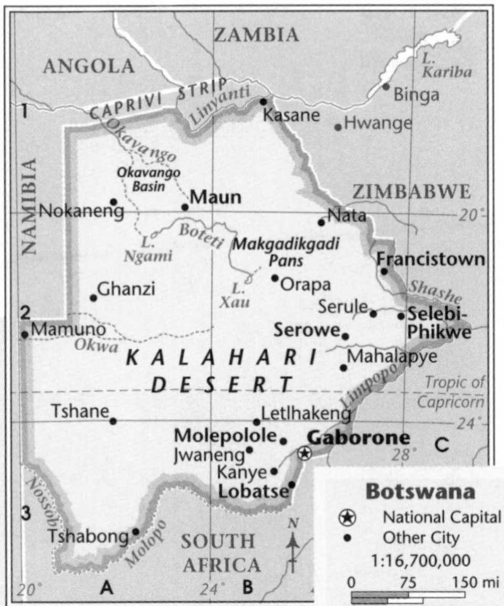

Botswana
National Capital
Other City
1:16,700,000
0 75 150 mi
0 75 150 km
Lambert Conformal Conic Proj.

Botswana

Capital: Gaborone
Area: 224,607 sq. mi.
581,883 sq. km.
Population: 1,464,167
Largest City: Gaborone
Language: English
Monetary Unit: Pula

Botswana:
Map Index

Cities and Towns

Francistown	B2
Gaborone, *capital*	B3
Ghanzi	A2
Jwaneng	B3
Kanye	B3
Kasane	B1
Letlhakeng	B3
Lobatse	B3
Mahalapye	B2
Mamuno	A2
Maun	A1
Molepolole	B3
Nata	B2
Nokaneng	A1
Orapa	B2
Selebi-Phikwe	C2
Serowe	B2
Serule	B2
Tshabong	A3
Tshane	A3

Other Features

Boteti, *river*	A2
Kalahari, *desert*	A2
Limpopo, *river*	B2
Linyanti, *river*	A1
Makgadikgadi, *salt pans*	B2
Molopo, *river*	A3
Ngami, *lake*	A2
Nossob, *river*	A3
Okavango, *basin*	A1
Okavango, *river*	A1
Okwa, *river*	A2
Shashe, *river*	C2
Xau, *lake*	B2

Madagascar
National Capital
Other City
1:17,474,000
0 100 200 mi
0 100 200 km
Lambert Conformal Conic Projection

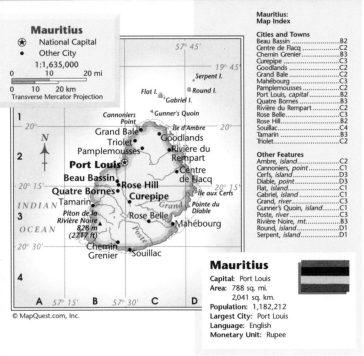

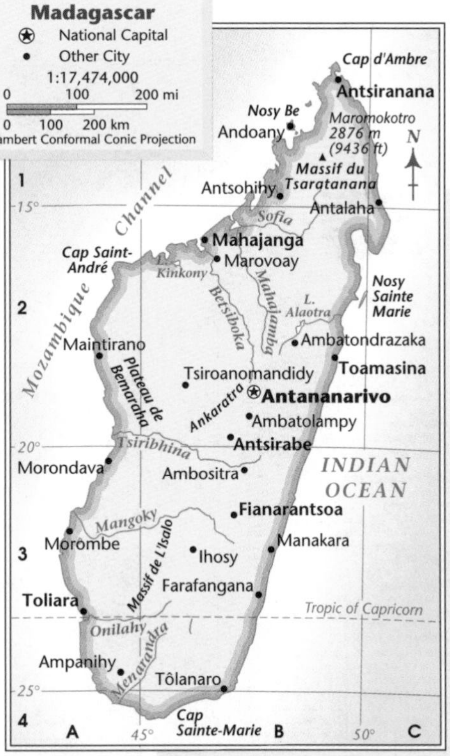

Madagascar

Capital: Antananarivo
Area: 226,658 sq. mi.
587,197 sq. km.
Population: 14,873,387
Largest City: Antananarivo
Languages: Malagasy, French
Monetary Unit: Malagasy franc

Madagascar:
Map Index

Cities and Towns

Ambatolampy	B2
Ambatondrazaka	B2
Ambositra	B3
Ampanihy	A3
Andoany	B1
Antalaha	C1
Antananarivo, *capital*	B2
Antsirabe	B2
Antsiranana	B1
Antsohihy	B1
Farafangana	B3
Fianarantsoa	B3
Ihosy	B3
Mahajanga	B2
Maintirano	A2
Manakara	B3
Marovoay	B2
Morombe	A3
Morondava	A3
Toamasina	B2
Tôlanaro	B3
Toliara	A3
Tsiroanomandidy	B2

Other Features

Alaotra, *lake*	B2
Ambre, *cape*	B1
Ankaratra, *mts.*	B2
Bemaraha, *plateau*	A2
Betsiboka, *river*	B2
Kinkony, *lake*	B2
L'Isalo, *mts.*	B3
Mahajamba, *river*	B2
Mangoky, *river*	A3
Maromokotro, *mt.*	B1
Menarandra, *river*	A3
Mozambique, *channel*	A2
Nosy Be, *island*	B1
Nosy Sainte Marie, *island*	B2
Onilahy, *river*	A3
Saint-André, *cape*	A2
Sainte-Marie, *cape*	B4
Sofia, *river*	B2
Tsaratanana, *mts.*	B1
Tsiribihina, *river*	B2

Angola

National Capital
Other City
1:17,333,000
0   100   200 mi
0   100   200 km
Lambert Conformal Conic Projection

© MapQuest.com, Inc.

Seychelles

National Capital
Other City
1:18,500,000
0   100   200 mi
0   100   200 km
Lambert Conformal
Conic Projection

© MapQuest.com, Inc.

Angola:
Map Index

Provinces
Bengo B3
Benguela B4
Bié C4
Cabinda B1
Cuando Cubango D5
Cuanza Norte B2
Cuanza Sul B3
Cunene C5
Huambo C4
Huíla B4
Luanda B3
Lunda Norte D2
Lunda Sul D3
Malanje C2
Moxico D4
Namibe B5
Uíge C2
Zaire B2

Cities and Towns
Benguela B4
Bentiaba B4
Cabinda B1
Cangamba D4
Catumbela B4
Caungula D2

Caxito B2
Cazombo E3
Cuíto Cuanavale D5
Dondo B3
Huambo C4
Kuito C4
Lobito B4
Luanda, capital B2
Luau E3
Lubango B5
Lucapa D2
Luena D3
Luremo C2
Malanje C2
Maquela do Zombo C2
Mavinga D5
M'banza Congo B2
Menongue C4
Namibe B5
N'dalatando B3
N'zeto B2
Ondjiva C5
Quibala C3
Quibemba C3
Quimbele C2
Saurimo D3
Soyo B3
Sumbe B3
Tombua B5
Uíge C2
Xangongo C5

Other Features
Bié, plateau C4
Chicapa, river D3
Cuando, river D4
Cuango, river D2
Cuanza, river C3
Cubal, river B4
Cubango, river D5
Cuito, river C4
Cunene, river B5, C4
Dande, river B2
Kasai, river D3
Môco, mt. C4
Zambezi, river E3

Angola

Capital: Luanda
Area: 481,354 sq. mi.
    1,247,031 sq. km.
Population: 11,177,537
Largest City: Luanda
Language: Portuguese
Monetary Unit: Kwanza

Seychelles

Capital: Victoria
Area: 176 sq. mi.
    456 sq. km.
Population: 79,164
Largest City: Victoria
Languages: English, French
Monetary Unit: Rupee

Seychelles:
Map Index

Cities and Towns
Anse Boileau ....Inset
Anse Royale ....Inset
Cascade ....Inset
De Quincy Village ....Inset
Misere ....Inset

Port Glaud ....Inset
Takamaka ....Inset
Victoria, capital ....Inset

Other Features
Aldabra, islands A2
Amirante, islands B2
Cerf, island ....Inset
Cosmoledo, island group A2

Farquhar, island group B2
La Digue, island C1
Mahé, island ....C1, Inset
Mahé, island group B1
Praslin, island C1
St. Anne, island ....Inset
Silhouette, island C1

Namibia

Capital: Windhoek
Area: 318,146 sq. mi.
    824,212 sq. km.
Population: 1,648,270
Largest City: Windhoek
Language: English, Afrikaans
Monetary Unit: Rand

Namibia:
Map Index

Cities and Towns
Bethanien C4
Gobabis C2
Grootfontein C1
Karasburg C4
Karibib B2
Katima Mulilo E1
Keetmanshoop C4
Khorixas B2
Lüderitz B4
Maltahöhe B3
Mariental C3
Okahandja C2
Okakarara C2
Omaruru B2
Ondangwa B1
Opuwo A1
Oranjemund B4
Oshakati B1
Otavi C1
Otjiwarongo B2
Outjo B2
Rehoboth C3
Rundu C1

Swakopmund B2
Tsumeb C1
Tsumkwe D1
Walvis Bay B2
Windhoek, capital C2

Other Features
Auob, river C3
Brandberg, mt. B2
Caprivi, strip D1
Eiseb, river D2
Etosha, pan B1
Fish, river C4
Kalahari, desert C3
Kaoko Veld, mts. A1
Kaukau Veld, region C2
Kunene, river A1
Linyanti, river E1
Namib, desert A1, B3
Nossob, river C3
Okavango, river C1
Omatako, river C1
Orange, river C4
Ruacana, falls A1
Skeleton, coast A1
Ugab, river B2
Zambezi, river E1

Namibia

National Capital
Other City
1:16,153,000
0   100   200 mi
0   100   200 km
Lambert Conformal Conic Projection

© MapQuest.com, Inc.

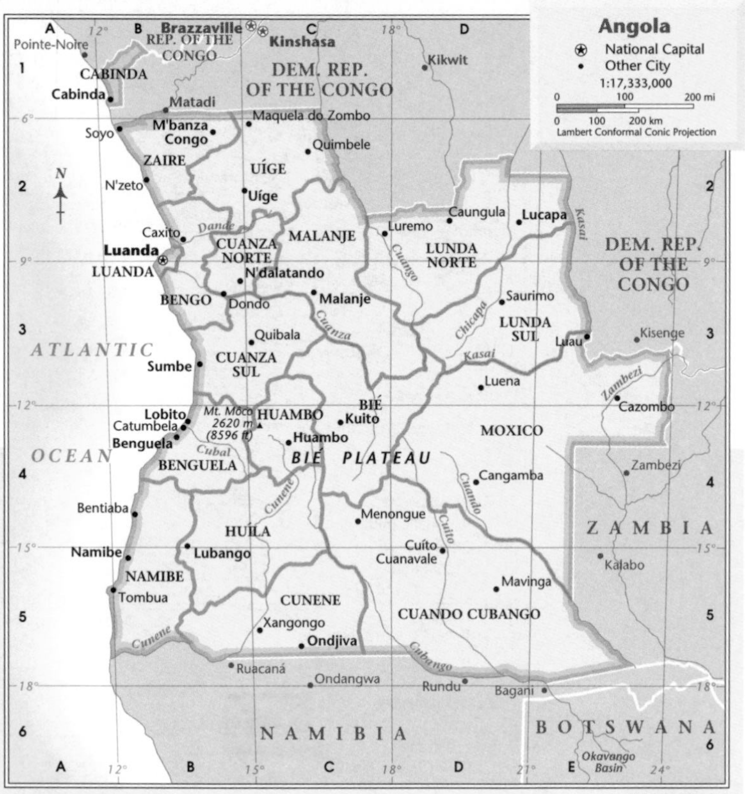

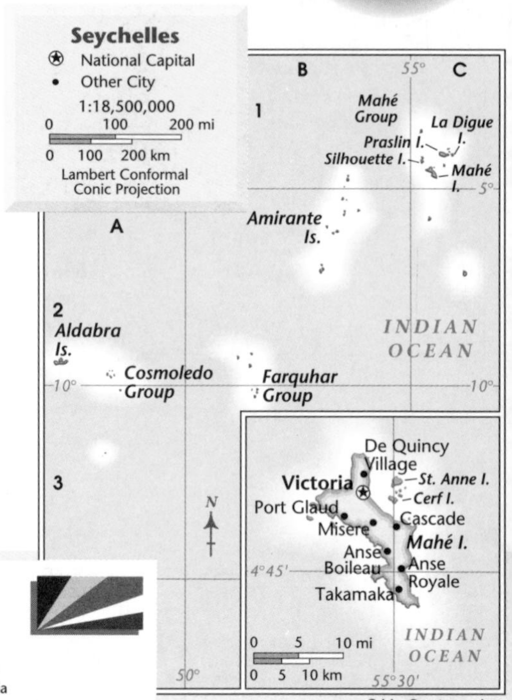

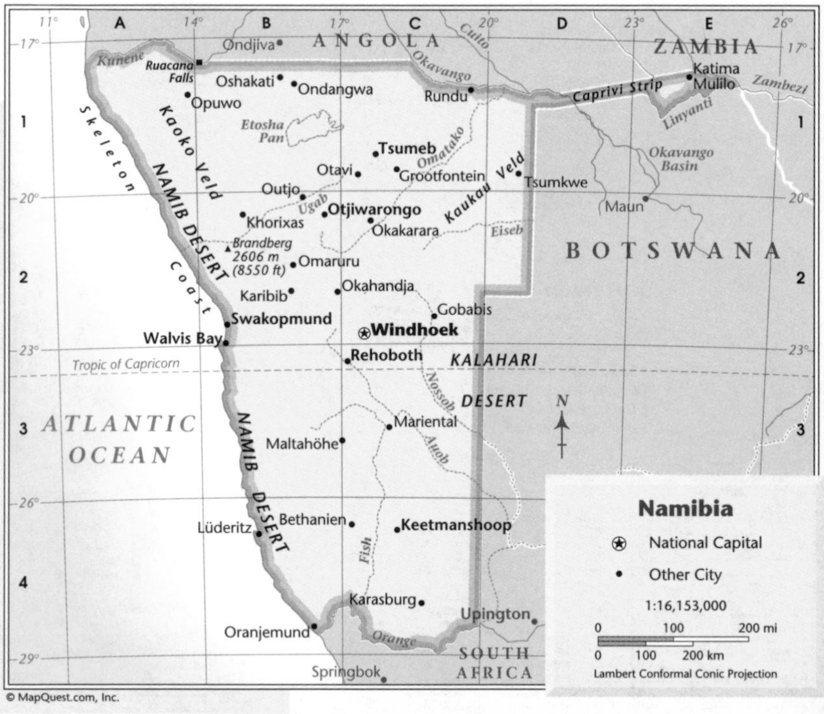

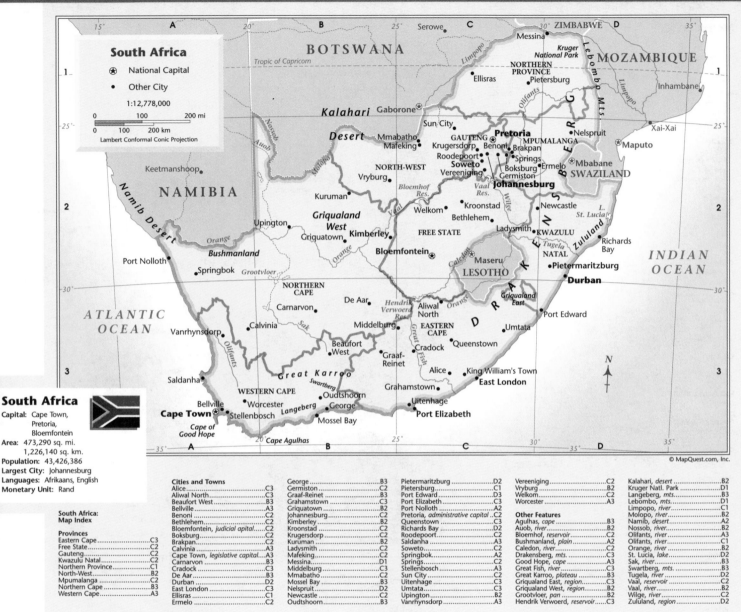

South Africa

* ⊛ National Capital
* • Other City

1:12,778,000

0   100   200 mi
0   100   200 km

Lambert Conformal Conic Projection

© MapQuest.com, Inc.

South Africa

Capital: Cape Town, Pretoria, Bloemfontein
Area: 473,290 sq. mi.
1,226,140 sq. km.
Population: 43,426,386
Largest City: Johannesburg
Languages: Afrikaans, English
Monetary Unit: Rand

South Africa:
Map Index

Provinces
Eastern Cape............C3
Free State................C2
Gauteng...................C2
Kwazulu Natal...........C1
Northern Province.....C1
North-West...............B2
Mpumalanga.............C2
Northern Cape..........B3
Western Cape...........A3

Cities and Towns
Alice..........................C3
Aliwal North...............C3
Beaufort West............B3
Bellville.....................A3
Benoni......................C2
Bethlehem.................C2
Bloemfontein, judicial apital.....C2
Boksburg...................C2
Brakpan....................C2
Calvinia.....................A3
Cape Town, legislative capital...A3
Carnarvon..................B3
Cradock.....................C3
De Aar......................B3
Durban......................D2
East London...............C3
Ellisras.....................C1
Ermelo......................C2

George.......................B3
Germiston...................C2
Graaf-Reinet...............C3
Grahamstown..............C3
Griquatown..................B2
Johannesburg.............C2
Kimberley...................B2
Kroonstad...................C2
Krugersdorp................C2
Kuruman....................B2
Ladysmith..................C2
Mafeking....................C2
Messina.....................D1
Middelburg.................B3
Mmabatho..................C2
Mossel Bay.................B3
Nelspruit...................D2
Newcastle..................C2
Oudtshoorn................B3

Pietermaritzburg.........D2
Pietersburg................C1
Port Edward...............D3
Port Elizabeth............C3
Port Nolloth...............A3
Pretoria, administrative capital ..C2
Queenstown...............C3
Richards Bay..............D2
Roodepoort................C2
Saldanha...................A3
Soweto......................C2
Springbok..................A2
Springs.....................C2
Stellenbosch..............A3
Sun City....................C2
Uitenhage..................C3
Umtata......................C3
Upington...................B2
Vanrhynsdorp.............A3

Vereeniging................C2
Vryburg.....................B2
Welkom.....................C2
Worcester..................A3

Other Features
Agulhas, cape.............B3
Auob, river................A2
Bloemhof, reservoir......C2
Bushmanland, plain.....A2
Caledon, river............C2
Drakensberg, mts.........C3
Good Hope, cape.........A3
Great Fish, river.........C3
Great Karroo, plateau...B3
Griqualand East, region..C2
Griqualand West, region..B2
Grootvloer, pan...........B2
Hendrik Verhoerd, reservoir....C3

Kalahari, desert...........B2
Kruger Natl. Park.........D1
Langeberg, mts...........B3
Lebombo, mts............D1
Limpopo, river............C1
Molopo, river.............B2
Namib, desert............A2
Nossob, river.............A3
Olifants, river............C1
Olifants, river............A3
Orange, river.............B2
St. Lucia, lake...........D2
Sak, river..................B3
Swartberg, mts...........B3
Tugela, river..............D2
Vaal, reservoir............C2
Vaal, river.................B2
Wilge, river................C2
Zululand, region..........D2

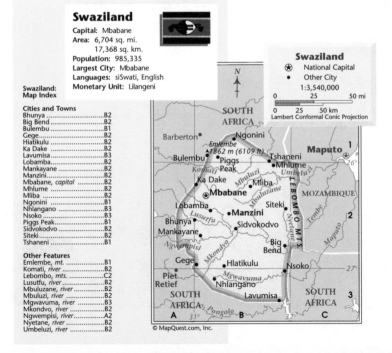

Swaziland

Capital: Mbabane
Area: 6,704 sq. mi.
17,368 sq. km.
Population: 985,335
Largest City: Mbabane
Languages: siSwati, English
Monetary Unit: Lilangeni

Swaziland:
Map Index

Cities and Towns
Bhunya B2
Big Bend B2
Bulembu B1
Gege B2
Hiatikulu B2
Ka Dake B2
Lavumisa B3
Lobamba B2
Mankayane B2
Manzini B2
Mbabane, capital B2
Mhlume B2
Mliba B2
Ngonini B1
Nhlangano B3
Nsoko B3
Piggs Peak B1
Sidvokodvo B2
Siteki B2
Tshaneni B1

Other Features
Emlembe, mt. B1
Komati, river B2
Lebombo, mts. C2
Lusutfu, river B2
Mbuluzane, river B2
Mbuluzi, river B2
Mgwavuma, river B2
Mkondvo, river B2
Ngwempisi, river A2
Nyetane, river B2
Umbeluzi, river B2

Swaziland

* ⊛ National Capital
* • Other City

1:3,540,000

0   25   50 mi
0   25   50 km

Lambert Conformal Conic Projection

© MapQuest.com, Inc.

Lesotho

Capital: Maseru
Area: 11,716 sq. mi.
30,352 sq. km.
Population: 2,128,950
Largest City: Maseru
Language: English
Monetary Unit: Loti

Lesotho:
Map Index

Cities and Towns
Butha-Buthe B1
Leribe B1
Libono B1
Mafeteng A2
Maseru, capital A2
Mohales Hoek A3
Mokhotlong C2
Morija A2
Pitseng B1
Qachas Nek B3
Quthing A3
Roma B2
Sekake B2
Teyateyaneng A2
Thaba-Tseka B2

Other Features
Caledon, river A1
Central, range B2
Drakensberg, mts. B3
Makhaleng, river A2
Maloti, mts. B2
Matsoku, river B2
Orange, river A3, B2
Sources, mt. B1
Thabana Ntlenyana, mt. ..C2
Tsedike, river B3

Lesotho

* ⊛ National Capital
* • Other City

1:5,811,000

0   30   60 mi
0   30   60 km

Lambert Conformal Conic Projection

© MapQuest.com, Inc.

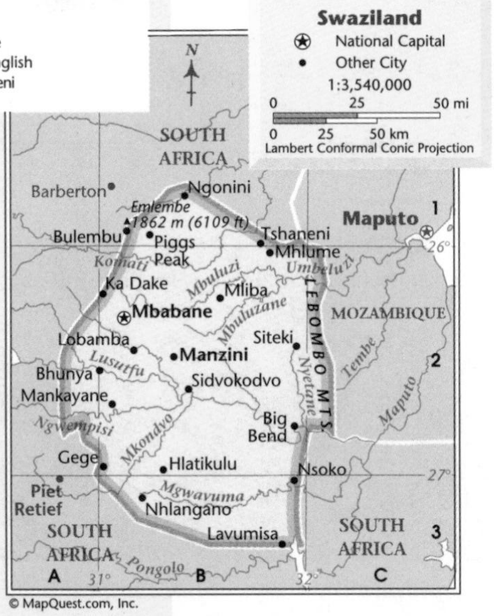

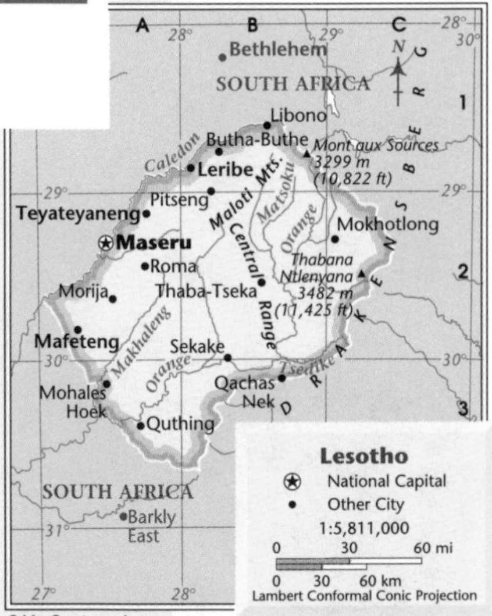

MAJOR CITIES

Argentina
Buenos Aires	2,961,000
Córdoba	1,148,000
Rosario	895,000

Bolivia
La Paz	739,000
Santa Cruz	833,000
El Alto	527,000

Brazil
São Paulo	10,018,000
Rio de Janeiro	5,606,000
Salvador	2,263,000
Belo Horizonte	2,097,000
Fortaleza	1,917,000
Brasília	1,738,000
Curitiba	1,409,000
Recife	1,330,000
Pôrto Alegre	1,296,000
Belém	1,168,000
Manaus	1,138,000

Chile
Santiago	4,641,000
Puente Alto	363,000

Colombia
Bogotá	4,945,000
Cali	1,666,000
Medellín	1,630,000
Barranquilla	994,000

Ecuador
Guayaquil	1,974,000
Quito	1,444,000

Falkland Islands
Stanley	1,200

French Guiana
Cayenne	41,000

Guyana
Georgetown	195,000

Paraguay
Asunción	547,000

Peru
Lima	5,682,000
Arequipa	619,000
Trujillo	509,000

Suriname
Paramaribo	216,000

Uruguay
Montevideo	1,303,000

Venezuela
Caracas	3,673,000
Maracaibo	1,221,000
Barquisimeto	954,000
Valencia	911,000

International comparability of city population data is limited by various data inconsistencies.

CITIES
⊛ National Capital
★ Territorial Capital
• Other City

ELEVATIONS
	Feet	Meters
	13,120	4000
	6560	2000
	1640	500
	656	200
	0	0
	Below sea level	

South America: Population, by nation (in millions)

BRAZIL	COLOM.	ARGEN.	PERU	VENEZ.	All other S. Am. countries
171.9	39.3	36.7	26.6	23.2	45.6

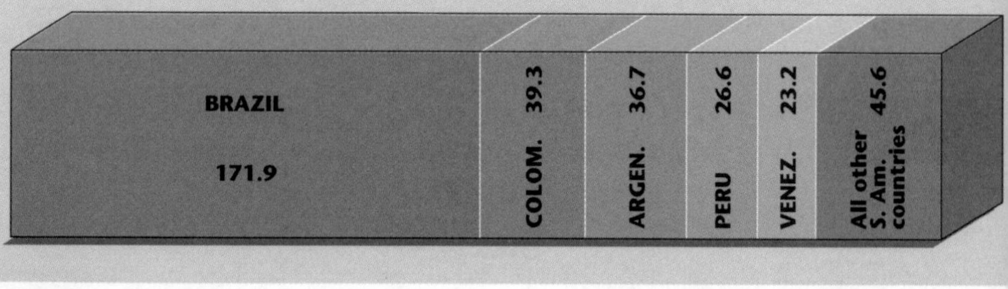

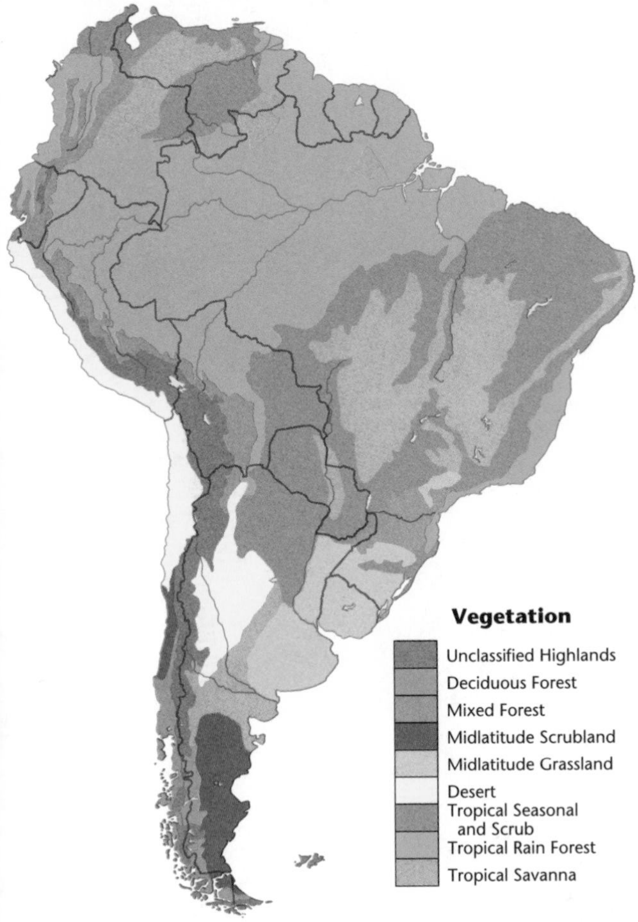
Vegetation
Unclassified Highlands
Deciduous Forest
Mixed Forest
Midlatitude Scrubland
Midlatitude Grassland
Desert
Tropical Seasonal and Scrub
Tropical Rain Forest
Tropical Savanna

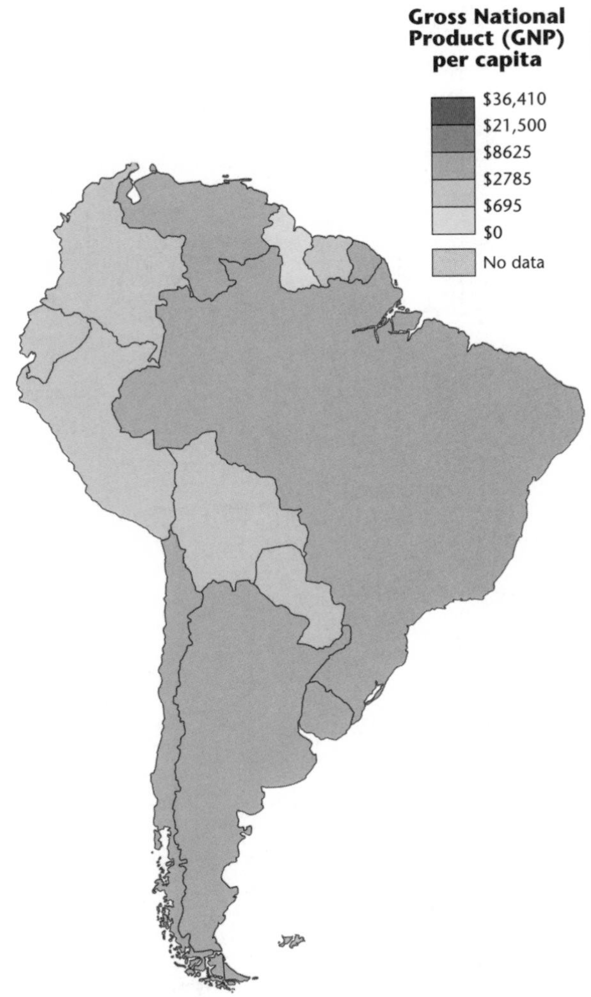
Gross National Product (GNP) per capita
$36,410
$21,500
$8625
$2785
$695
$0
No data

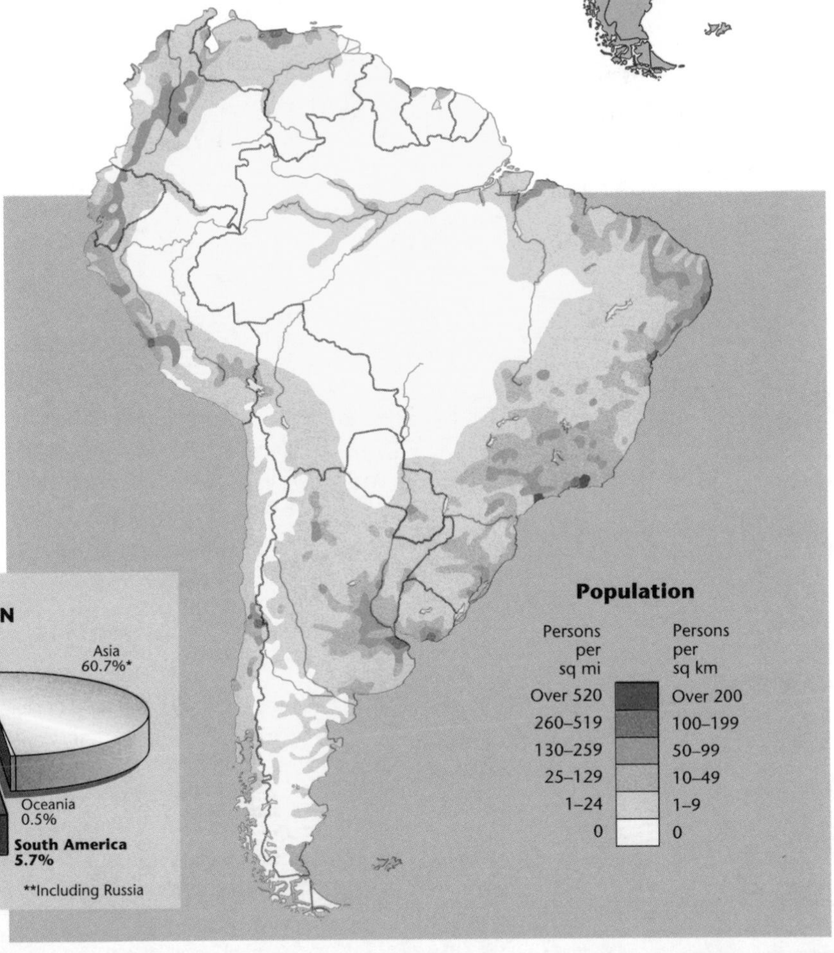
Population
Persons per sq mi
Persons per sq km
Over 520
Over 200
260–519
100–199
130–259
50–99
25–129
10–49
1–24
1–9
0
0

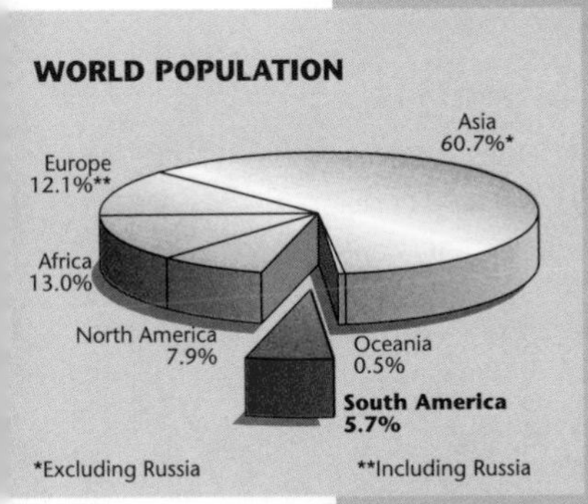
WORLD POPULATION
Asia 60.7%*
Europe 12.1%**
Africa 13.0%
North America 7.9%
Oceania 0.5%
South America 5.7%
*Excluding Russia
**Including Russia

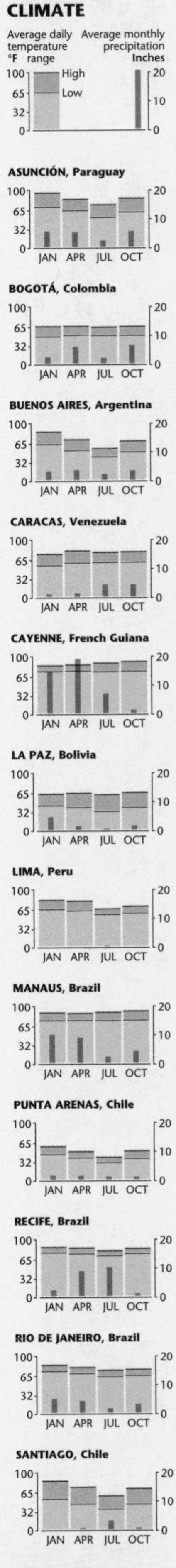
CLIMATE
Average daily temperature °F range
Average monthly precipitation Inches
High
Low
ASUNCIÓN, Paraguay
BOGOTÁ, Colombia
BUENOS AIRES, Argentina
CARACAS, Venezuela
CAYENNE, French Guiana
LA PAZ, Bolivia
LIMA, Peru
MANAUS, Brazil
PUNTA ARENAS, Chile
RECIFE, Brazil
RIO DE JANEIRO, Brazil
SANTIAGO, Chile
JAN APR JUL OCT

BOLIVIA
PARAGUAY
BRAZIL
URUGUAY
CHILE
PACIFIC OCEAN
ATLANTIC OCEAN
ATACAMA DESERT
ANDES
GRAN CHACO
PAMPAS
PATAGONIA
Tropic of Capricorn
Chuquicamata
Antofagasta
JUJUY
Embarcación
San Salvador de Jujuy
Llullaillaco 6723 m (22,057 ft)
Salta
SALTA
San Miguel de Tucumán
TUCUMÁN
Ojos del Salado 6880 m (22,572 ft)
CATAMARCA
SANTIAGO DEL ESTERO
Santiago del Estero
Catamarca
La Rioja
LA RIOJA
La Serena
CÓRDOBA
Córdoba
SAN JUAN
San Juan
Mercedario 6770 m (22,211 ft)
Champaquí 2850 m (9350 ft)
Sierras de Córdoba
Villa María
Aconcagua 6960 m (22,834 ft)
Mendoza
Godoy Cruz
Santiago
Tupungato 6800 m (22,310 ft)
San Luis
SAN LUIS
Río Cuarto
San Rafael
MENDOZA
Domuyo 4709 m (15,450 ft)
Concepción
LA PAMPA
Santa Rosa
NEUQUÉN
Neuquén
Bahía Blanca
Lanín 3776 m (12,389 ft)
RÍO NEGRO
San Antonio Oeste
Viedma
Punta Rasa
San Carlos de Bariloche
Puerto Montt
Golfo San Matías
Península Valdés
Chiloé
Esquel
CHUBUT
Rawson
Comodoro Rivadavia
Golfo San Jorge
Coihaique
Península Taitao
L. Buenos Aires
Cabo Tres Puntas
Puerto Deseado
SANTA CRUZ
L. San Martín
L. Cardiel
Fitzroy 3375 m (11,073 ft)
L. Viedma
Santa Cruz
Puerto Santa Cruz
Calafate
L. Argentino
Bahía Grande
Gallegos
Río Gallegos
Punta Dungeness
Strait of Magellan
Punta Arenas
TIERRA DEL FUEGO
Ushuaia
Isla de los Estados
Beagle Channel
Cape Horn
Pilcomayo
Bermejo
FORMOSA
Formosa
Concepción
Asunción
Paraguay
Paraná
Foz do Iguaçu
Iguaçu Falls
Iguaçu
Curitiba
CHACO
Presidencia Roque Sáenz Peña
Resistencia
Corrientes
MISIONES
Posadas
CORRIENTES
Reconquista
SANTA FE
Salado
L. Mar Chiquita
San Francisco
Santa Fe
Paraná
Curuzú Cuatiá
Santa Maria
ENTRE RÍOS
Uruguay
Concordia
Pôrto Alegre
L. dos Patos
Pelotas
Negro
Rosario
San Nicolás
DISTRITO FEDERAL
Buenos Aires
Avellaneda
Montevideo
Lanús
Lomas de Zamora
La Plata
Río de la Plata
BUENOS AIRES
Olavarría
Tandil
Cabo San Antonio
Mar del Plata
Necochea
Desaguadero
Atuel
Colorado
Chubut
Chico
Deseado
West Falkland I.
East Falkland I.
Stanley
Falkland Islands (Islas Malvinas) (Br.) (claimed by Argentina)
N
Argentina
National Capital
Territorial Capital
Other City
1:17,760,000
0 200 400 mi
0 200 400 km
Modified Chamberlain Trimetric Projection

Paraguay

National Capital
Other City

1:10,375,000

0   50   100 mi
0   50   100 km
Conic Equidistant Projection

© MapQuest.com, Inc.

Argentina

Capital: Buenos Aires
Area: 1,073,518 sq. mi.
2,781,134 sq. km.
Population: 36,737,664
Largest City: Buenos Aires
Language: Spanish
Monetary Unit: Peso

Argentina: Map Index

Provinces

Buenos Aires C4
Catamarca B2
Chaco C2
Chubut B5
Córdoba C3
Corrientes D2
Distrito Federal D3
Entre Ríos D3
Formosa D1
Jujuy B1
La Pampa B4
La Rioja B2
Mendoza B3
Misiones E2
Neuquén B4
Río Negro B5
Salta B3
San Juan B3
San Luis B3
Santa Cruz A6
Santa Fe C2
Santiago del Estero C2
Tierra del Fuego B7
Tucumán B2

Cities and Towns

Avellaneda D3
Bahía Blanca C4
Buenos Aires, *capital* ...D3
Calafate A7
Catamarca B2
Comodoro Rivadavia B6
Concordia D3
Córdoba C3
Corrientes D2
Curuzú Cuatiá D2
Embarcación C1
Esquel A5
Formosa D2
Godoy Cruz B3
Lanús D3

La Plata D4
La Rioja B2
Lomas de Zamora D4
Mar del Plata D4
Mendoza B3
Necochea D4
Neuquén B4
Olavarría C4
Paraná C3
Posadas D2
Presidencia Roque
  Sáenz Peña C2
Puerto Deseado B6
Puerto Santa Cruz B6
Rawson B5
Reconquista D2
Resistencia D2
Río Cuarto C3
Río Gallegos B7
Rosario C3
Salta B3
San Antonio Oeste B5
San Carlos de Bariloche ..A5
San Francisco C3
San Juan B3
San Luis B3
San Miguel de Tucumán ..B2
San Nicolás C3
San Rafael B4
San Salvador de Jujuy ...B1
Santa Fe C3
Santa Rosa C4
Santiago del Estero C2
Tandil D4
Ushuaia B7
Viedma C5
Villa María C3

Other Features

Aconcagua, *mt.* A3
Andes, *mts.* A6–B1
Argentino, *lake* A7
Atuel, *river* B4
Beagle, *channel* B7
Bermejo, *river* C2

Blanca, *bay* C4
Buenos Aires, *lake* A6
Cardiel, *lake* A6
Champaquí, *mt.* C3
Chico, *river* B6
Chubut, *river* A5
Colorado, *river* B4
Córdoba, *range* B3
Desaguadero, *river* B2
Deseado, *river* B6
Domuyo, *volcano* A4
Dungeness, *point* B7
Estados, *island* C7
Fitzroy, *mt.* A6
Gallegos, *river* A7
Gran Chaco, *region* C1
Grande, *bay* B7
Iguaçu, *falls* E2
Iguaçu, *river* E2
Lanín, *volcano* A4
Llullaillaco, *volcano* B1
Magellan, *strait* B7
Mar Chiquita, *lake* C3
Mercedario, *mt* B3
Negro, *river* B4
Ojos del Salado, *mt.* B2
Pampas, *plain* C4
Paraguay, *river* D2
Paraná, *river* D2
Patagonia, *region* A6
Pilcomayo, *river* C1
Plata, Río de la, *estuary* .D3
Rasa, *point* C5
Salado, *river* B3
Salado, *river* C2
San Antonio, *cape* D4
San Jorge, *gulf* B6
San Martín, *lake* A6
San Matías, *gulf* C5
Santa Cruz, *river* A7
Tres Puntas, *cape* B6
Tupungato, *mt.* B3
Uruguay, *river* D3
Valdés, *peninsula* C5
Viedma, *lake* A6

Paraguay

Capital: Asunción
Area: 157,048 sq. mi.
406,752 sq. km.
Population: 5,434,095
Largest City: Asunción
Language: Spanish
Monetary Unit: Guarani

Paraguay: Map Index

Departments

Alto Paraguay C2
Alto Paraná E4
Amambay E3
Asunción D4
Boquerón B3
Caaguazú D4
Caazapá D5
Canendiyú D5
Central D4
Concepción D3
Cordillera D4
Guairá D4
Itapúa E5
Misiones D5
Ñeembucú C5
Paraguarí D5
Presidente Hayes C4
San Pedro D4

Cities and Towns

Abaí E4
Asunción, *capital* D4
Caacupé D4
Caaguazú E4
Caazapá D5
Capitán Pablo Lagerenza ..B1
Ciudad del Este E4
Concepción D3
Coronel Oviedo D4
Doctor Pedro P. Peña A3
Encarnación E5

Filadelfia B3
Fuerte Olimpo D2
General
  Eugenio A. Garay A2
Mariscal Estigarribia B3
Paraguarí D4
Pedro Juan Caballero E3
Pilar C5
Pozo Colorado C3
Puerto Bahía C2
Puerto Pinasco D3
Salto del Guairá E4
San Juan Bautista D5
San Lorenzo D4
San Pedro D4
Villa Hayes D4
Villarrica D4

Other Features

Acaray, *river* E4
Amambay, *mts.* E3
Apa, *river* D3
Chaco Boreal, *region* B2
Gran Chaco, *region* B3
Iguazú, *falls* E4
Itaipú, *reservoir* E4
Jejuí-Guazú, *river* D4
Montelindo, *river* C3
Paraguay, *river* C2, C5
Paraná, *river* C5, E5
Pilcomayo, *river* B3, C4
Tebicuary, *river* D5
Verde, *river* C3
Ypané, *river* D3
Ypoá, *lake* D4

Uruguay

National Capital
Other City

1:6,625,000

0   40   80 mi
0   40   80 km
Lambert Conformal Conic Projection

Uruguay

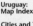

Capital: Montevideo
Area: 68,037 sq. mi.
176,215 sq. km.
Population: 3,308,523
Largest City: Montevideo
Language: Spanish
Monetary Unit: New peso

Uruguay: Map Index

Cities and Towns

Artigas B1
Bella Unión B1
Canelones B3
Carmelo A2
Colonia A2
Durazno B2
Florida B3
Fray Bentos A2
Las Piedras B3
Melo C2
Mercedes A2
Minas C3
Montevideo, *capital* B3
Nueva Palmira A2
Pando C3
Paso de los Toros B2
Paysandú A2
Piedra Sola B2
Punta del Este C3
Rivera C1
Rocha C3
Salto B1
San Carlos C3
San José B3
Tacuarembó C1
Treinta y Tres C2
Trinidad B2

Other Features

Arapey Grande, *river* B1
Baygorria, *lake* B2
Cebollati, *river* C2
Cuareim, *river* B1
Daymán, *river* B1
Grande, *range* C2
Haedo, *range* B2
Merín, *lagoon* D2
Mirador Nacional, *mt.* C3
Negra, *lagoon* D2
Negro, *river* B2
Paso de Palmar, *lake* B2
Plata, *river* B3
Queguay Grande, *river* B2
Rincón del Bonete, *lake* B2
Salto Grande, *reservoir* B1
San José, *river* B2
San Salvador, *river* A2
Santa Ana, *range* C1
Santa Lucía, *river* B3
Tacuarembó, *river* C1
Tacuarí, *river* D2
Uruguay, *river* A1
Yaguarí, *river* C1
Yaguarón, *river* D2
Yi, *river* C2

© MapQuest.com, Inc.

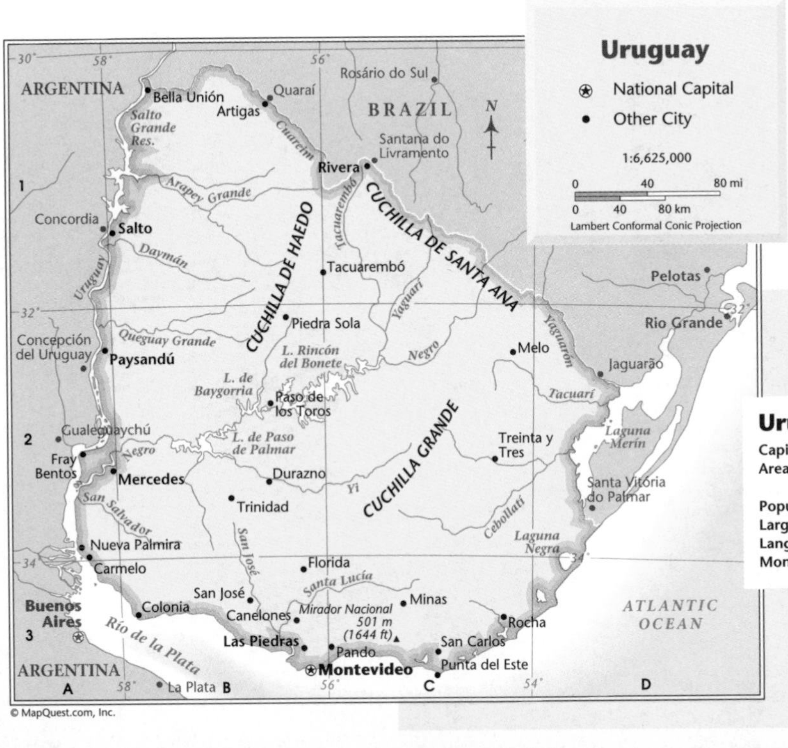

Chile

Capital: Santiago
Area: 292,135 sq. mi.
756,826 sq. km.
Population: 14,973,843
Largest City: Santiago
Language: Spanish
Monetary Unit: Peso

Chile: Map Index

Regions
Aisén del General Carlos Ibáñez del Campo B8
Antofagasta C2
Atacama B3
Bío-Bío B6
Coquimbo B4
El Libertador General Bernardo O'Higgins B4
La Araucanía B6
Los Lagos B7
Magallanes y Antártica Chilena B9
Maule B5, B6
Región Metropolitana ....B4, Inset
Tarapacá C1
Valparaíso ....B4, Inset

Cities and Towns
Aguada de Cachinal C2
Aguas Blancas C2
Algarrobo ....Inset
Altamira C3
Ancud B7
Angol B6
Antofagasta B2
Arica B1
Balmaceda B8
Calama C2
Casablanca ....Inset
Castro B7
Cerro Castillo B9
Chaitén B7
Chañaral B3
Chiapa C1
Chile Chico B8
Chillán B6
Chuquicamata C2
Cochrane B8
Coihaique B8
Colina ....Inset
Collaguasi C2
Concepción B6
Conchalí ....Inset
Constitución B5
Copiapó B3
Coquimbo B3
Curicó B4
El Tabo ....Inset
El Trebolar ....Inset
Freirina B3
Gatico B2
Illapel B4
Iquique B2
Lampa ....Inset
La Serena B3
La Unión B7
Lebu B6
Linares B5
Los Andes B4
Los Ángeles B6
Maipú ....Inset
Mamiña C2
Melipilla ....Inset
Ñuñoa ....Inset
Osorno B7
Ovalle B4
Parral B6
Pisagua B1
Porvenir B9
Potrerillos C3
Puente Alto ....Inset
Puerto Aisén B8
Puerto Cisnes B7
Puerto Montt B7
Puerto Natales B9
Puerto Varas B7
Puerto Williams C9
Punta Arenas B9
Punta Delgada B9
Putre C1
Quellón B7
Quillota B4
Quilpué ....Inset
Rancagua B4
Rungue ....Inset
San Antonio ....B4, Inset
San Bernardo ....Inset
San Félix B3
San Fernando B4
San Pedro de Atacama C2
Santa Inés ....Inset
Santiago, *capital* ....B4, Inset
Socompa C2
Talagante ....Inset
Talca B5
Talcahuano B6
Taltal B3
Temuco B6
Tilomonte C2
Tocopilla B2
Tomé B6
Unión C2
Valdivia B6
Vallenar B3
Valparaíso ....B4, Inset
Victoria B6
Viña del Mar ....B4, Inset

Other Features
Aconcagua, *river* B4
Ancud, *gulf* B7
Andes, *mts.* B8, C4
Atacama, *desert* C2
Bascuñán, *cape* B3
Bío-Bío, *river* B6
Brunswick, *peninsula* B9
Buenos Aires, *lake* B8
Campana, *island* A8
Chiloé, *island* B7
Chonos, *archipelago* B7
Cochrane, *lake* B8
Concepción, *bay* B6
Copiapó, *river* B3
Corcovado, *gulf* B7
Desolación, *island* B9
Domeyko, *mts.* C3
Dungeness, *point* C9
Duque de York, *island* A9
Elqui, *river* B3
Fitzroy, *mt.* B8
Galera, *point* B6
Horn, *cape* C9
Hoste, *island* C9
Imperial, *river* B6
Lanín, *volcano* B6
Lengua de Vaca, *point* B4
Llanquihue, *lake* B7
Llullaillaco, *volcano* C2
Loa, *river* B2
Madre de Dios, *island* A9
Magdalena, *island* B7
Magellan, *strait* B9
Maipo, *river* ....B4, Inset
Maule, *river* B5
Navarino, *island* C9
Occidental, *mts.* C1
Ojos del Salado, *mt.* C3
Ollagüe, *volcano* C2
Penas, *gulf* B8
Rapel, *river* B4
Reina Adelaida, *archipelago* B9
San Martín, *lake* B8
San Valentín, *mt.* B8
Santa Inés, *island* B9
Taitao, *peninsula* A8
Tierra del Fuego, *island* C9
Toltén, *river* B6
Wellington, *island* A8

Peru

Capital: Lima
Area: 496,225 sq. mi.
1,285,216 sq. km.
Population: 26,624,582
Largest City: Lima
Languages: Spanish, Quechua
Monetary Unit: Nuevo Sol

**Peru:
Map Index**

Cities and Towns
Abancay C3
Arequipa C4
Ayacucho C3
Cajamarca B2
Callao B3
Cerro de Pasco B3
Chachapoyas B2
Chiclayo B2
Chimbote B2
Chincha Alta B3
Cuzco C3
Huacho B3
Huancavelica B3
Huancayo B3
Huánuco B2
Huaraz B2
Ica B3
Ilo C4
Iquitos C1
Juliaca C4
La Oroya B3
Lima, *capital* B3
Mollendo C4
Moquegua C4
Moyobamba B2
Nazca C3
Pacasmayo B2
Paita A2
Patavilca B3
Pisco B3
Piura A2
Pucallpa C2
Puerto Maldonado D3
Puno C4
Salaverry B2
San Juan B4
Sicuani C3
Sullana A1
Tacna C4
Talara A1
Tarapoto B2
Tingo María B2
Trujillo B2
Tumbes A1
Yurimaguas B2

Other Features
Amazon, *river* C1
Andes, *mts.* B1, C3
Apurímac, *river* C3
Central, *mts.* B2
Colca, *river* C4
Coropuna, *mt.* C4
Guayaquil, *gulf* A1
Huallaga, *river* B2
Huascarán, *mt.* B2
La Montaña, *region* C2
Machupicchu, *ruins* C3
Madre de Dios, *river* C3
Mantaro, *river* B3
Marañón, *river* B1, B2
Napo, *river* C1
Negra, *point* A2
Occidental, *mts.* B2, C4
Oriental, *mts.* B2, C3
Pastaza, *river* B1
Purús, *river* C3
Putumayo, *river* C1
Santiago, *river* B1
Sechura, *desert* A2
Tambo, *river* C3
Tambo, *river* C4
Tigre, *river* B1
Titicaca, *lake* D4
Ucayali, *river* C2
Urubamba, *river* C3
Vilcabamba, *mts.* C3
Yavarí, *river* C1

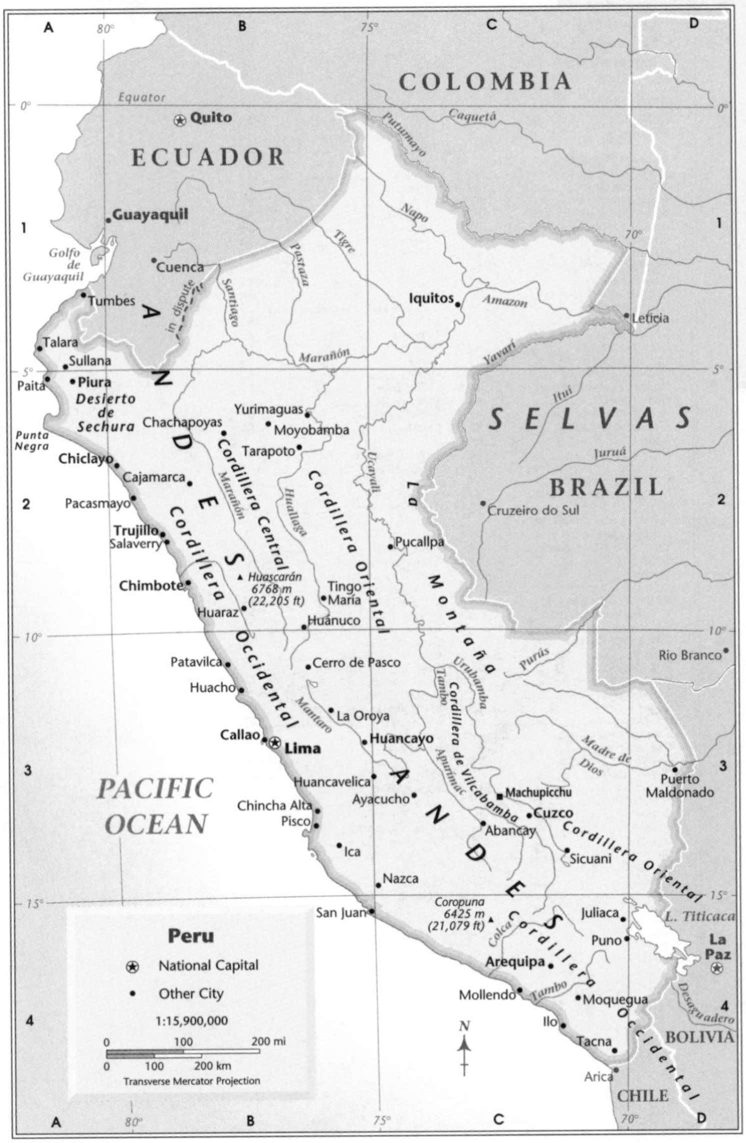

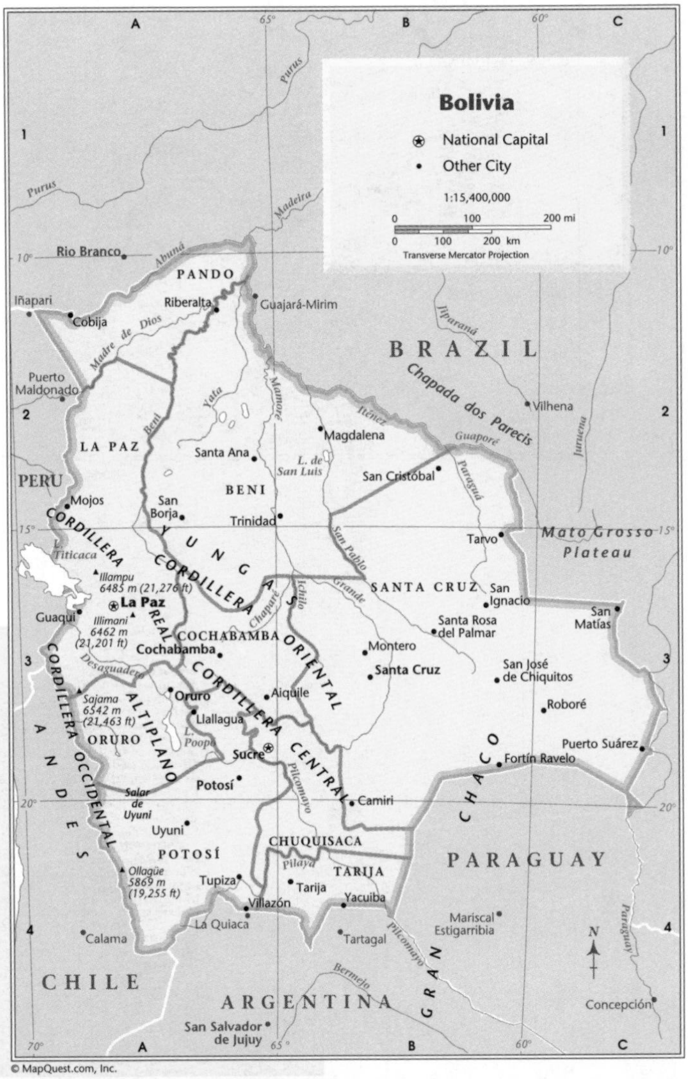

**Bolivia:
Map Index**

Departments
Beni A2
Chuquisaca B4
Cochabamba A3
La Paz A2
Oruro A3
Pando A2
Potosí A4
Santa Cruz B3
Tarija B4

Cities and Towns
Aiquile A3
Camiri B4
Cobija A2
Cochabamba A3
Fortín Ravelo B3
Guaqui A3
La Paz, *capital* A3
Llallagua A3
Magdalena B2
Mojos A2
Montero B3
Oruro A3
Potosí A3
Puerto Suárez C3
Riberalta A2
Roboré C3
San Borja A2
San Cristóbal B2
San Ignacio B3
San José de Chiquitos B3
San Matías C3
Santa Ana A2
Santa Cruz B3
Santa Rosa del Palmar B3
Sucre, *capital* A3
Tarija B4
Tarvo B3
Trinidad B2
Tupiza A4
Uyuni A4
Villazón A4
Yacuiba B4

Other Features
Abuná, *river* A2
Altiplano, *plateau* A3
Beni, *river* A2
Chaparé, *river* A3
Cordillera Central, *mts.* A3
Cordillera Occidental, *mts.* A3
Cordillera Oriental, *mts.* A3
Cordillera Real, *mts.* A3
Desaguadero, *river* A3
Gran Chaco, *region* B4
Grande, *river* B3
Guaporé, *river* B2
Ichilo, *river* B3
Illampu, *mt.* A3
Illimani, *mt.* A3
Iténez, *river* B2
Madre de Dios, *river* A2
Mamoré, *river* A2
Ollagüe, *volcano.* A4
Paraguá, *river* B2
Paraguay, *river* C4
Pilaya, *river* B4
Pilcomayo, *river* B3
Poopó, *lake* A3
Sajama, *mt.* A3
Salar de Uyuni, *salt flat* A4
San Luis, *lake* B2
San Pablo, *river* B3
Titicaca, *lake* A3
Yata, *river* A2
Yungas, *region* A3

Bolivia

Capital: La Paz, Sucre
Area: 424,164 sq. mi.
1,098,871 sq. km.
Population: 7,982,850
Largest City: La Paz
Languages: Spanish, Quechua, Aymara
Monetary Unit: Boliviano

Banco Serranilla
Cayo de Roncador
Isla de Providencia
SAN ANDRÉS Y PROVIDENCIA
Isla de San Andrés
Cayos de Albuquerque
0 25 50 mi
0 25 50 km

Caribbean Sea

PANAMA
Panamá
Gulf of Panama
Turbo

PACIFIC OCEAN

Punta Gallinas
Península de la Guajira
Ríohacha
Golfo de Venezuela
Coro
Santa Marta
Pico Cristóbal Colón 5775 m (18,947 ft)
LA GUAJIRA
Barranquilla
ATLÁNTICO
Maracaibo
Sierra Nevada de Santa Marta
Cartagena
Valledupar
MAGDALENA
CÉSAR
Sincelejo
SUCRE
Montería
CÓRDOBA
BOLÍVAR
NORTE DE SANTANDER
Cúcuta
San Cristóbal
L. de Maracaibo
Mérida
VENEZUELA
Barquisimeto
Cojedes
Bucaramanga
Barrancabermeja
SANTANDER
Arauca
ARAUCA
San Fernando de Apure
Apure
ANTIOQUIA
Medellín
Cravo Norte
RISARALDA
CALDAS
BOYACÁ
Manizales
Tunja
Quibdó
CHOCÓ
CUNDINAMARCA
Tolima 5215 m (17,110 ft)
Bogotá
Villavicencio
CASANARE
Yopal
Orocué
Meta
VICHADA
Puerto Carreño
Orinoco
LLANOS
CORDILLERA OCCIDENTAL
CORDILLERA CENTRAL
CORDILLERA ORIENTAL
Pereira
QUINDÍO
Ibagué
Armenia
TOLIMA
Buenaventura
VALLE DEL CAUCA
Palmira
Cali
Huila 5750 m (18,865 ft)
CAUCA
Neiva
HUILA
META
Vista Hermosa
San José del Guaviare
GUAVIARE
Puerto Inírida
GUAINÍA
Guainía
San Felipe
Popayán
Patía
NARIÑO
Tumaco
Pasto
Mocoa
PUTUMAYO
Florencia
CAQUETÁ
Miraflores
VAUPÉS
Mitú
Vaupés
Apaporis
Quito ECUADOR
Puerto Leguízamo
Putumayo
Caquetá
São Gabriel de Cachoeria
AMAZONAS
El Encanto
Napo
Japurá
BRAZIL
Içá
PERU
Iquitos
Amazon
Leticia
Yavari

N

Colombia
⊛ National Capital
• Other City
1:13,825,000
0 100 200 mi
0 100 200 km
Transverse Mercator Projection

© MapQuest.com, Inc.

Colombia
Capital: Bogotá
Area: 440,831 sq. mi.
1,142,049 sq. km.
Population: 39,309,422
Largest City: Bogotá
Language: Spanish
Monetary Unit: Peso

Colombia:
Map Index

Internal Divisions
Amazonas (commissary) B5
Antioquia (dept.) B3
Arauca (intendency) C3
Atlántico (dept.) B2
Bolívar (dept.) B2
Boyacá (dept.) B3
Caldas (dept.) B3
Capital District B4
Caquetá (dept.) B4
Casanare (intendency) B4
Cauca (dept.) A4
César (dept.) B2
Chocó (dept.) A3
Córdoba (dept.) B2
Cundinamarca (dept.) B3
Guainía (commissary) C4
Guaviare (commissary) B4
Huila (dept.) A4
La Guajira (dept.) B2
Magdalena (dept.) B2
Meta (dept.) B4
Nariño (dept.) A4
Norte de Santander (dept.) ..B2
Putumayo (intendency) A4
Quindío (dept.) B3
Risaralda (dept.) B3
San Andrés y Providencia
(intendency) ....Inset
Santander (dept.) B3
Sucre (dept.) B2
Tolima (dept.) B4
Valle del Cauca (dept.) A4
Vaupés (commissary) C4
Vichada (commissary) C3

Cities and Towns
Arauca C3
Armenia B3
Barrancabermeja B3
Barranquilla B2
Bogotá, capital B3
Bucaramanga B3
Buenaventura A4
Cali A4
Cartagena B2
Cravo Norte C3
Cúcuta B3
El Encanto B5
Florencia B4
Ibagué B3
Leticia C6
Manizales B3
Medellín B3
Miraflores B4
Mitú C4

Mocoa A4
Montería B2
Neiva B4
Orocué C3
Palmira A4
Pasto A4
Pereira B3
Popayán A4
Puerto Carreño D3
Puerto Inírida D4
Puerto Leguízamo B5
Quibdó A3
Ríohacha B2
San Felipe D4
San José del Guaviare B4
Santa Marta B2
Sincelejo B2
Tumaco A4
Tunja B3
Turbo A2
Valledupar B2
Villavicencio B3
Vista Hermosa B3
Yopal B3

Other Features
Albuquerque, cays ....Inset
Amazon, river C5
Andes, range A4
Apaporis, river C4
Atrato, river A3
Caquetá, river B5
Cauca, river B3
Cordillera Central, range A4
Cordillera Occidental,
range A4
Cordillera Oriental, range B4
Cristóbal Colón, peak B2
Gallinas, point C1
Guainía, river C4
Guajira, peninsula C1
Guaviare, river C3
Huila, mt. A4
Llanos, prairie C3
Magdalena, river B3
Meta, river C3
Orinoco, river D3
Patía, river A4
Providencia, island ....Inset
Putumayo, river B5
Roncador, cay ....Inset
San Andrés, island ....Inset
San Juan, river A3
Serranilla, bank ....Inset
Sierra Nevada de Santa
Marta, mts. B2
Tolima, mt. B3
Vaupés, river B4
Vichada, river C3

Venezuela:
Map Index

Internal Divisions
Amazonas (territory) C3
Anzoátegui (state) D2
Apure (state) C2
Aragua (state) C2
Barinas (state) C2
Bolívar (state) D2
Carabobo (state) C2
Cojedes (state) C2
Delta Amacuro (territory) D2
Dependencias Federales C1
Distrito Federal C1
Falcón (state) B1
Guárico (state) C2
Lara (state) B1
Mérida (state) B2
Miranda (state) C1
Monagas (state) D2
Nueva Esparta (state) D1
Portuguesa (state) C2
Sucre (state) D1
Táchira (state) B2
Trujillo (state) B2
Yaracuy (state) C1
Zulia (state) B2

Cities and Towns
Acarigua C2
Anaco D2
Barcelona D1
Barinas B2
Barquisimeto C1
Baruta C1
Cabimas B1
Calabozo C2
Canaima D2
Caracas, capital C1
Carora C1
Carúpano D1
Ciudad Bolívar D2
Ciudad Guayana D2
Coro C1
Cumaná D1
El Tigre D2
Guanare C2
Güiria D1
La Asunción D1
La Guaira Maiquetía C1
Los Teques C1
Maiquetía C1
Maracaibo B1
Maracay C1
Maturín D2
Mérida B2

Petare C1
Puerto Ayacucho C2
Puerto Cabello C1
Puerto La Cruz D1
Punto Fijo B1
San Cristóbal B2
San Felipe C1
San Fernando de Apure C2
San Juan de Los Morros C2
Santa Elena de Uairén D3
Trujillo B2
Tucupita D2
Valencia C1
Valera B2

Other Features
Angel, falls D2
Apure, river C2
Arauca, river C2
Bolívar, mt. B2
Caroní, river D2
Casiquiare, river C3
Caura, river D2
Cojedes, river C2
Guri, reservoir D2
Guiana, highlands D2
La Tortuga, island C1
Llanos, plain B2

Maracaibo, lake B2
Margarita, island D1
Mérida, mts. B2
Meta, river C2
Neblina, mt. C3
Negro, river B3
Orinoco, river C3, D2
Pacaraima, mts. D3
Paria, gulf D1
Parima, mts. D3
Roraima, mt. D2
Venezuela, gulf B1

Venezuela
Capital: Caracas
Area: 352,144 sq. mi.
912,050 sq. km.
Population: 23,203,466
Largest City: Caracas
Language: Spanish
Monetary Unit: Bolivar

Ecuador

Capital: Quito
Area: 105,037 sq. mi.
272,117 sq. km.
Population: 12,562,496
Largest City: Guayaquil
Language: Spanish
Monetary Unit: Sucre

Ecuador: Map Index

Provinces

Azuay ... B4
Bolívar ... B3
Cañar ... B4
Carchi ... C2
Chimborazo ... B3
Cotopaxi ... B3
El Oro ... B4
Esmeraldas ... B2
Galápagos ... Inset
Guayas ... A4
Imbabura ... B2
Loja ... B5
Los Ríos ... B3
Manabí ... A3
Morona-Santiago ... C4
Napo ... C3
Pastaza ... C3
Pichincha ... B2
Sucumbíos ... C3
Tungurahua ... B3
Zamora-Chinchipe ... B5

Cities and Towns

Ambato ... B3
Azogues ... B4
Babahoyo ... B3
Baquerizo Moreno ... Inset
Chone ... A3
Cuenca ... B4
Esmeraldas ... B2
Guaranda ... B3
Guayaquil ... B4
Ibarra ... B2
Jipijapa ... A3
La Libertad ... A4
Latacunga ... B3
Loja ... B4
Macas ... B4
Machala ... B4
Manta ... A3
Milagro ... B4
Nueva Loja ... C2
Nuevo Rocafuerte ... D3
Otavalo ... B2
Portoviejo ... A3
Puerto Bolívar ... B4
Puyo ... C3
Quevedo ... B3
Quito, *capital* ... B3
Riobamba ... B3
San Lorenzo ... B2
Santa Rosa ... B4
Santo Domingo de los Colorados ... B3
Tena ... C3
Tulcán ... C2
Zamora ... B5

Other Features

Aguarico, *river* ... C3
Andes, *mts.* ... B4
Cayambe, *mt.* ... C3
Chimborazo, *mt.* ... B3
Chira, *river* ... A5
Cordillera Occidental, *mts.* ... B4
Cordillera Oriental, *mts.* ... C4
Cotopaxi, *mt.* ... B3
Curaray, *river* ... C3
Daule, *river* ... B3
Española, *island* ... Inset
Fernandina, *island* ... Inset
Galera, *point* ... A2
Guaillabamba, *river* ... B2
Guayaquil, *gulf* ... A4
Guayas, *river* ... B4
Isabela, *island* ... Inset
Manta, *bay* ... A3
Marchena, *island* ... Inset
Napo, *river* ... C3
Pastaza, *river* ... C4
Pinta, *island* ... Inset
Plata, *island* ... A3
Puná, *island* ... A4
Putumayo, *river* ... D2
San Cristóbal, *island* ... Inset
San Lorenzo, *cape* ... A3
San Salvador, *island* ... Inset
Santa Cruz, *island* ... Inset
Santa Elena, *point* ... A4
Santa María, *island* ... Inset
Santiago, *river* ... B4
Tigre, *river* ... C3
Vinces, *river* ... B3
Wolf, *mt.* ... Inset
Zamora, *river* ... B4

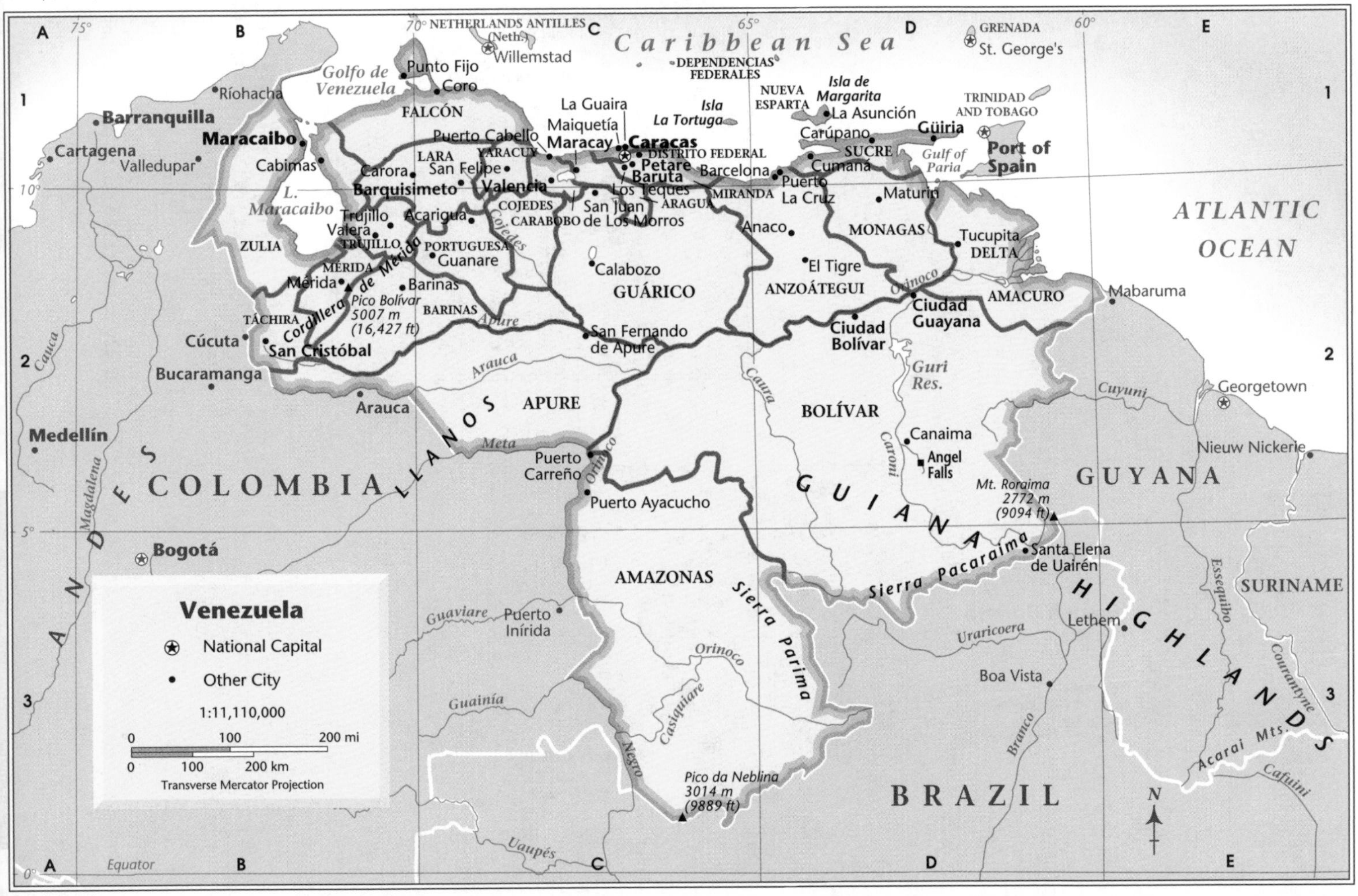

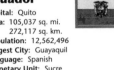

Guyana

★ National Capital
● Other City

1:10,660,000

0   75   150 mi
0   75   150 km
Transverse Mercator Projection

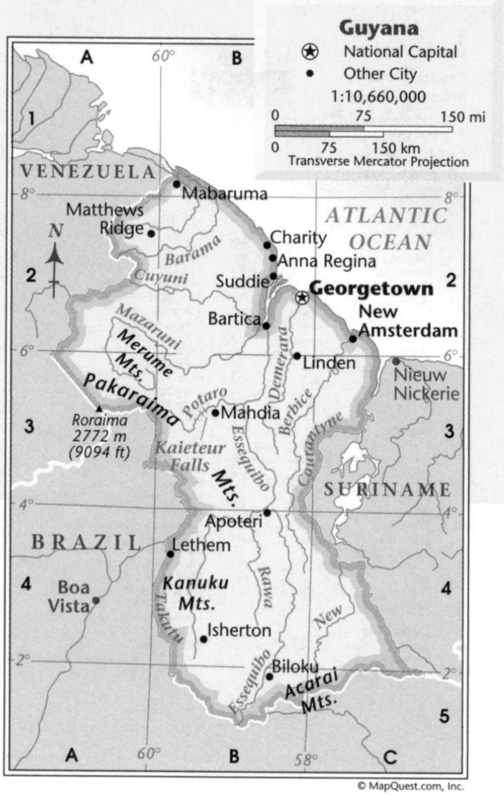

Guyana

Capital: Georgetown
Area: 83,000 sq. mi.
    214,969 sq. km.
Population: 705,156
Largest City: Georgetown
Language: English
Monetary Unit: Guyana dollar

Guyana: Map Index

Cities and Towns

Anna Regina	B2
Apoteri	B4
Bartica	B2
Biloku	B5
Charity	B2
Georgetown, *capital*	B2
Isherton	B4
Lethem	B4
Linden	B3
Mabaruma	B1
Mahdia	B3
Matthews Ridge	A2
New Amsterdam	C2
Suddie	B2

Other Features

Acarai, *mts.*	B5
Barama, *river*	B2
Berbice, *river*	B3
Courantyne, *river*	B3
Cuyuni, *river*	A2
Demerara, *river*	B3
Essequibo, *river*	B3, B5
Kaieteur, *falls*	B3
Kanuku, *mts.*	B4
Mazaruni, *river*	A2
Merume, *mts.*	A2
New, *river*	C4
Pakaraima, *mts.*	A3
Potaro, *river*	B3
Rawa, *river*	B4
Roraima, *mt.*	A3
Takutu, *river*	B4

Suriname

★ National Capital
● Other City

1:9,840,000

0   60   120 mi
0   60   120 km
Conic Equidistant Projection

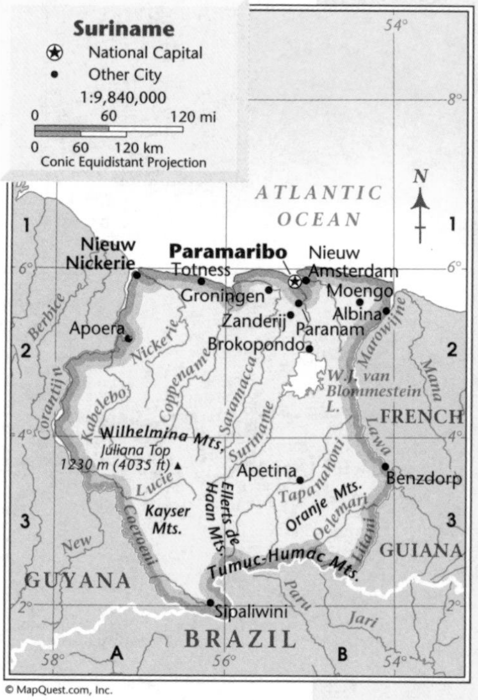

Suriname

Capital: Paramaribo
Area: 63,037 sq. mi.
    163,265 sq. km.
Population: 431,156
Largest City: Paramaribo
Language: Dutch
Monetary Unit: Suriname guilder

Suriname: Map Index

Cities and Towns

Albina	B2
Apetina	B3
Apoera	A2
Benzdorp	B3
Brokopondo	B2
Groningen	B2
Moengo	B2
Nieuw Amsterdam	B2
Nieuw Nickerie	A2
Paramaribo, *capital*	B2
Paranam	B2
Sipaliwini	A3
Totness	A2
Zanderij	B2

Other Features

Coeroeni, *river*	A3
Coppename, *river*	A2
Corantijn, *river*	A2
Ellerts de Haan, *mts.*	A3
Juliana Top, *mt.*	A3
Kabelebo, *river*	A2
Kayser, *mts.*	A3
Lawa, *river*	B2
Litani, *river*	B3
Lucie, *river*	A3
Marowijne, *river*	B2
Nickerie, *river*	A2
Oelemari, *river*	B3
Oranje, *mts.*	B3
Saramacca, *river*	B2
Suriname, *river*	B3
Tapanahoni, *river*	B3
Tumuc-Humac, *mts.*	B3
Wilhelmina, *mts.*	A2
W.J. van Blommestein, *lake*	B2

French Guiana: Map Index

Cities and Towns

Apatou	A1
Cacao	B1
Camopi	B2
Cayenne, *capital*	B1
Grand Santi	A1
Iracoubo	B1
Kaw	B1
Kourou	B1
Mana	B1
Maripasoula	A2
Ouanary	C1
Régina	B1
Rémire	B1
Saint-Élie	B1
Saint-Georges	C2
Saint-Laurent du Maroni	A1
Saül	B2

Other Features

Camopi, *river*	B2
Devil's, *island*	B1
Lawa, *river*	A2
Litani, *river*	A2
Mana, *river*	A1
Maroni, *river*	A1
Oyapock, *river*	B2
Salut, *islands*	B1
Tampok, *river*	A2
Tumuc-Humac, *mts.*	A2

French Guiana

Capital: Cayenne
Area: 35,135 sq. mi.
    91,000 sq. km.
Population: 167,982
Largest City: Cayenne
Language: French
Monetary Unit: French franc

French Guiana

★ Territorial Capital
● Other City

1:8,410,000

0   50   100 mi
0   50   100 km
Conic Equidistant Projection

Brazil: Map Index

States and Federal District

Acre A2
Alagoas E2
Amapá C1
Amazonas B2
Bahia D3
Ceará E2
Espírito Santo D3
Federal District D3
Goiás D3
Maranhão D2
Mato Grosso C3
Mato Grosso do Sul C4
Minas Gerais D3
Pará C2
Paraíba E2
Paraná C4
Pernambuco E2
Piauí D2
Rio de Janeiro .... D4, Inset I
Rio Grande do Norte E2
Rio Grande do Sul C4
Rondônia B3
Roraima B1
Santa Catarina C4
São Paulo .... C4, Inset II
Sergipe E3
Tocantins D3

Cities and Towns

Alagoinhas E3
Altamira C2
Anápolis D3
Aracaju E3
Bacabal D2
Bauru D4
Belém D2
Belford Roxo .... Inset I
Belo Horizonte D3
Boa Vista B1
Bom Jesus da Lapa D3
Brasília, *capital* D3
Cáceres C3
Cachimbo C2
Campina Grande E2
Campinas D4
Campo Grande C4
Campos D4
Campos Elísios .... Inset I
Carapicuíba .... Inset II
Corumbá C3
Cotia .... Inset II
Cruzeiro do Sul A2
Cubatão .... Inset II
Cuiabá C3
Curitiba D4
Diadema .... Inset II
Dourados C4
Duque de Caxias .... Inset I
Feira de Santana E3
Floriano D2
Florianópolis D4
Fortaleza E2
Foz do Iguaçu C4
Goiânia D3
Governador Valadares D3
Guajara Mirim B3
Guarujá .... Inset II
Guarulhos .... Inset II
Ilhéus E3
Imbariê .... Inset I
Imperatriz D2
Inhomirim .... Inset I
Ipiíba .... Inset I
Itabira D3
Itabuna E3
Itaipu .... Inset I
Itajaí D4
Itapecerica da Serra .... Inset II
Itapeva .... Inset II
Itaquaquecetuba .... Inset II
Jaboatão E2
Jacare-Acanga C2
Japeri .... Inset I
Jir Paraná B3
João Pessoa E2
Joinville D4
Juàzeiro D2
Juàzeiro do Norte E2
Juiz de Fora D4
Jundiai D4
Lajes C4
Londrina C4
Macapá C1
Maceió E2
Majé .... Inset I
Manaus C2
Maraba D2
Mariana D3
Mauá .... Inset II
Mogi das Cruzes .... Inset II
Monjolo .... Inset I
Montes Claros D3
Mozzoro E2
Natal E2
Neves .... Inset I
Nilópolis .... Inset I
Niterói .... D4, Inset I
Nova Iguaçu .... Inset I
Olinda E2
Osasco .... Inset II
Palmas D3
Paranaguá D4
Parnaiba D2
Passo Fundo C4
Paulo Afonso E2
Pelotas C5
Petrólina D2
Petrópolis .... D4, Inset I
Piracicaba D4
Poá .... Inset II
Pôrto Alegre C5
Pôrto Velho B2
Queimados .... Inset I
Randonopolis C3
Recife E2
Ribeirão Pires .... Inset II
Ribeirão Prêto D4
Rio Branco B2
Rio de Janeiro .... D4, Inset I
Rio Grande C5
Rio Verde C3
Salvador E3
Santa Maria C4
Santana do Livramento C5
Santarém C2
Santo André .... Inset II
Santos .... D4, Inset II
São Bernardo do Campo .... Inset II
São Caetano do Sul .... Inset II
São Gonçalo .... Inset I
São João de Meriti .... Inset I
São José do Rio Prêto D4
São Luís D2
São Paulo .... D4, Inset II
São Vincente .... Inset II
Sobral D2
Sorocaba D4
Suzano .... Inset II
Taboão da Serra .... Inset II
Tefé B2
Teresina D2
Tubarão D4
Uberaba D3
Uberlândia D3
Vincente de Carvalho .... Inset II
Vitória D4
Vitória da Conquista D3
Volta Redonda D4

Other Features

Acaraí, *range* C1
Açúcar, *mt.* .... Inset I
Amazon, *basin* B2
Amazon, *river* B2
Araguaia, *river* C3
Aripuanã, *river* C2
Baleia, *point* E3
Bandeira, *mt.* D4
Billings, *reservoir* .... Inset II
Branco, *river* B1
Brazilian, *highlands* D3
Caviana, *island* D1
Chapada dos Parecis, *range* C3
Corcovado, *mt.* .... Inset I
Corumbau, *point* E3
Furnas, *reservoir* D4
Geral, *range* C4
Grande, *river* D3
Guandu, *river* .... Inset I
Guaporé, *river* B3
Guiana, *highlands* B1
Içá, *river* B2
Iguaçu, *falls* C4
Itaipu, *reservoir* C4
Japurá, *river* B2
Jari, *river* C1
Javari, *river* A2
Juruá, *river* B2
Juruena, *river* C3
Madeira, *river* B2
Mantiqueira, *range* D4
Mar, *range* D4
Marajó, *island* D2
Mato Grosso, *plateau* C3
Mexiana, *island* D1
Neblina, *mt.* B1
Negro, *river* B2
Órgãos, *range* .... Inset I
Pantanal, *lowland* C4
Pará, *river* C2
Paraguai, *river* C3
Paraná, *river* C4
Parima, *range* B1
Parnaíba, *river* D2
Patos, *lagoon* C5
Paulo Afonso, *falls* E2
Pedra Açú, *mt.* .... Inset I
Purus, *river* B2
Roncador, *range* C3
São Francisco, *river* D3
Selvas, *region* B2
Sobradinho, *reservoir* D3
Tapajós, *river* C2
Taquari, *river* C3
Teles Pires, *river* C2
Tietê, *river* .... Inset II
Tocantins, *river* D2
Tucuruí, *reservoir* D2
Tumucumaque, *range* C1
Uruguai, *river* C4
Xingu, *river* C3

Brazil

Capital: Brasília
Area: 3,286,470 sq. mi.
8,514,171 sq. km.
Population: 171,853,126
Largest City: São Paulo
Language: Portuguese
Monetary Unit: Real

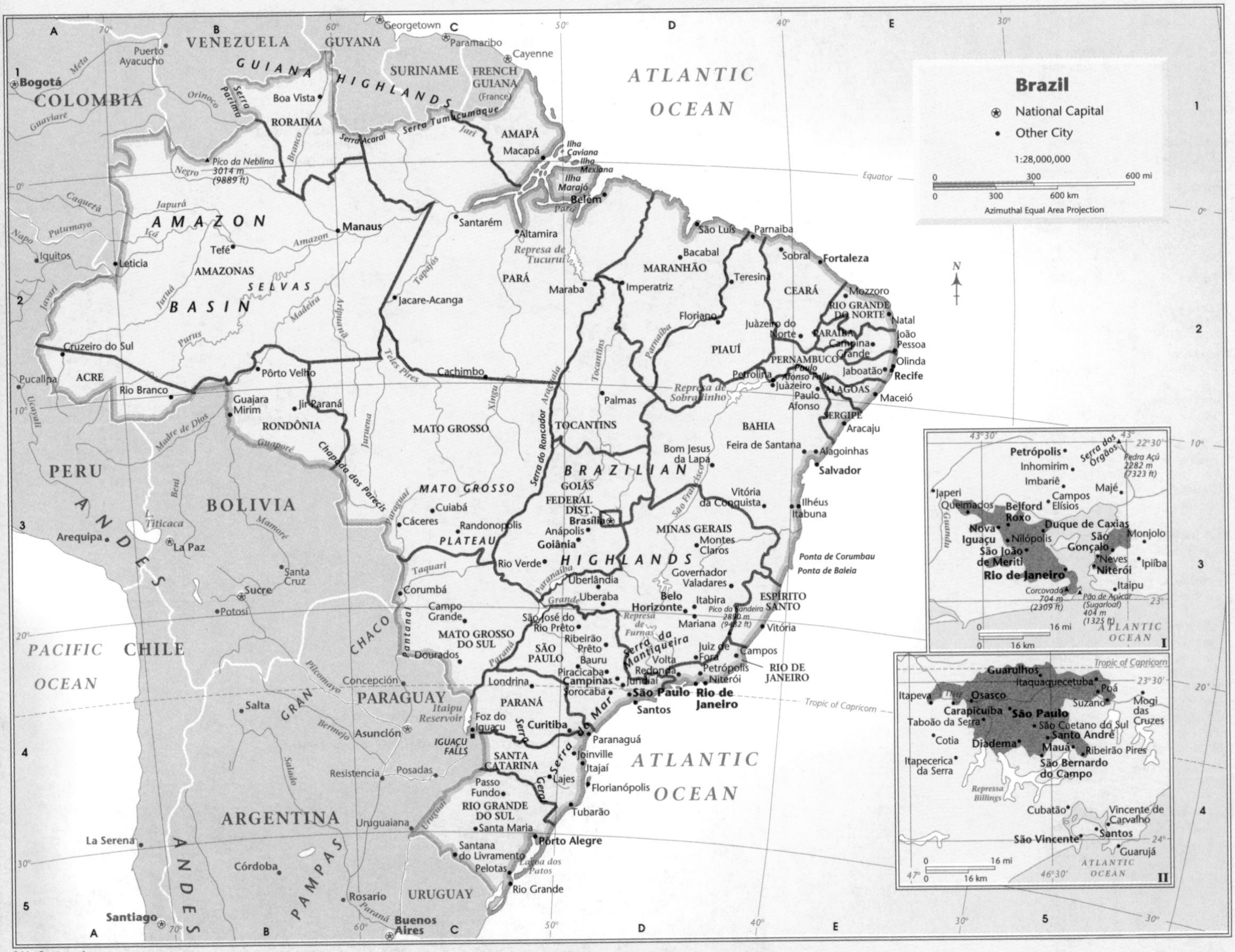

MAJOR CITIES

Antigua & Barbuda
St. Johns 27,000

Bahamas
Nassau 172,000

Barbados
Bridgetown 6,000

Belize
Belize City 45,000
Belmopan 4,000

Canada (metro)
Toronto 4,264,000
Montréal 3,327,000
Vancouver 1,832,000
Ottawa 1,010,000

Costa Rica
San José 324,000

Cuba
Havana 2,185,000

Dominica
Roseau 16,000

Dominican Republic
Santo Domingo 2,135,000

El Salvador (metro)
San Salvador 1,214,000

Grenada
St. George's 30,000

Guatemala (metro)
Guatemala 2,205,000

Haiti
Port-au-Prince 884,000

Honduras (metro)
Tegucigalpa 995,000

Jamaica (metro)
Kingston 587,000

Mexico
Mexico City 8,489,000
Guadalajara 1,633,000
Puebla 1,223,000

Nicaragua (metro)
Managua 1,124,000

Panama
Panamá 465,000

Puerto Rico
San Juan 428,000

St. Kitts & Nevis
Basseterre 15,000

St. Lucia
Castries 45,000

St. Vincent & Grenadines
Kingstown 15,000

Trinidad & Tobago
Port of Spain 43,000

United States
New York 7,381,000
Los Angeles 3,554,000
Chicago 2,722,000
Houston 1,744,000
Philadelphia 1,478,000
San Diego 1,171,000
Phoenix 1,159,000
Washington, D.C. 543,000

International comparability of city population data is limited by various data inconsistencies.

North America: Population, by nation (in millions)

UNITED STATES	MEXICO	CANADA	GUATEM.	CUBA	All other N. Am. countries
272.6	100.3	31.0	12.3	11.1	48.5

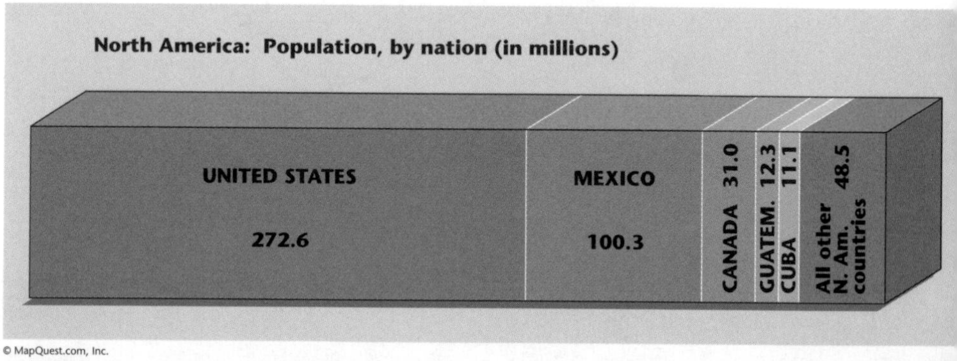

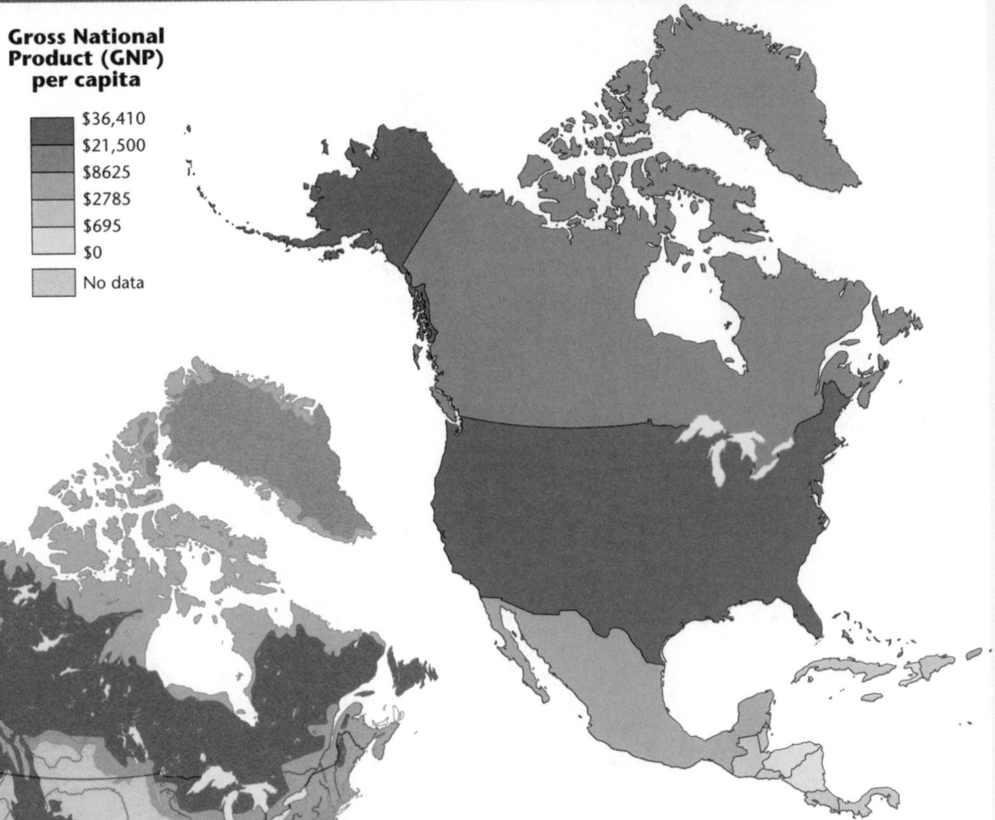
Gross National Product (GNP) per capita
$36,410
$21,500
$8625
$2785
$695
$0
No data

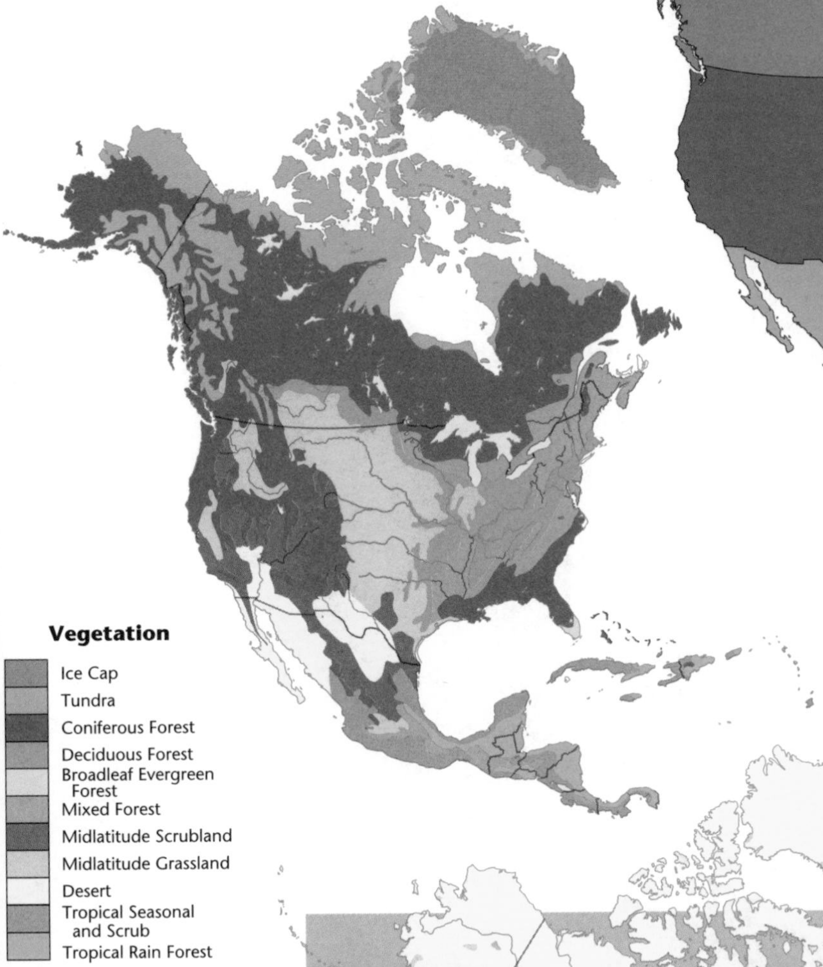
Vegetation
Ice Cap
Tundra
Coniferous Forest
Deciduous Forest
Broadleaf Evergreen Forest
Mixed Forest
Midlatitude Scrubland
Midlatitude Grassland
Desert
Tropical Seasonal and Scrub
Tropical Rain Forest

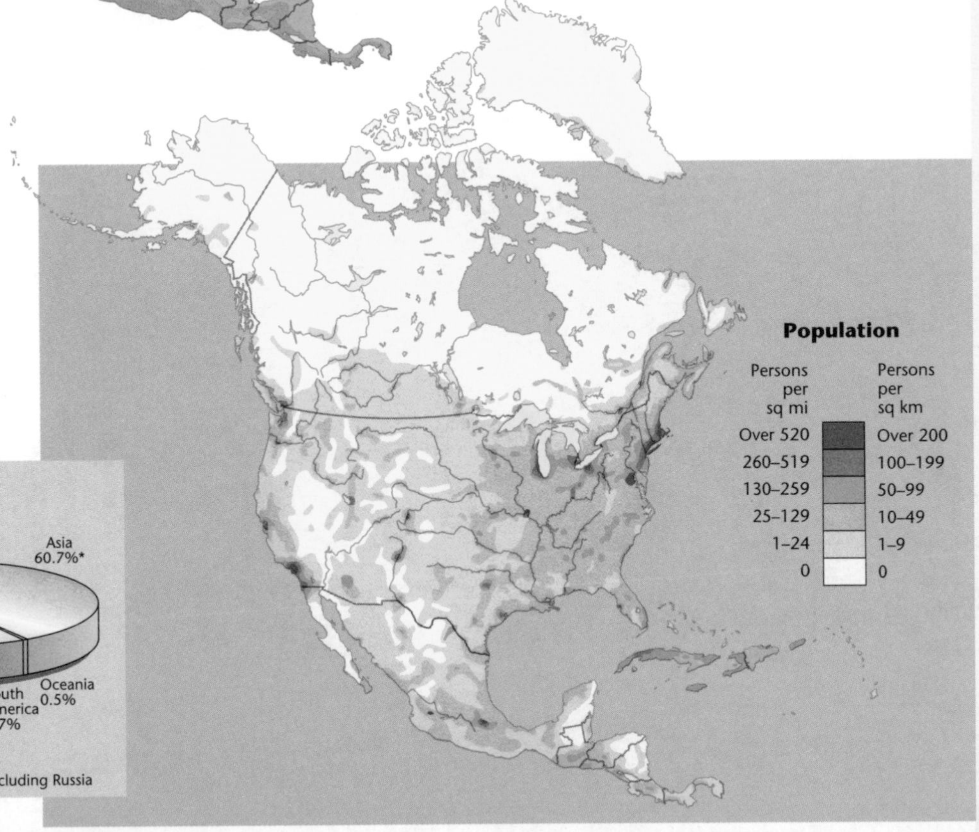
Population
Persons per sq mi
Persons per sq km
Over 520
Over 200
260–519
100–199
130–259
50–99
25–129
10–49
1–24
1–9
0
0

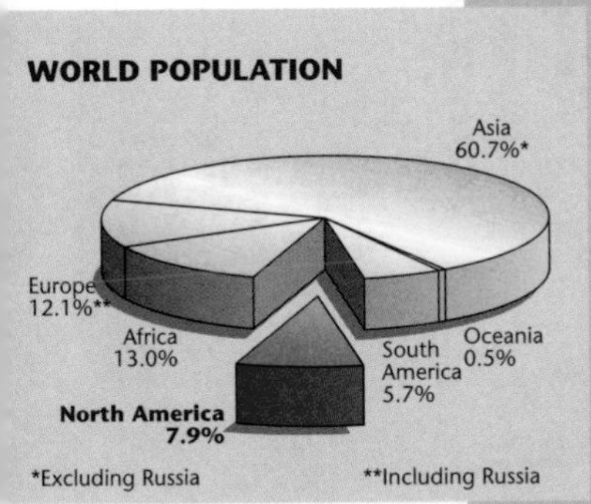
WORLD POPULATION
Asia 60.7%*
Europe 12.1%**
Africa 13.0%
North America 7.9%
South America 5.7%
Oceania 0.5%
*Excluding Russia
**Including Russia

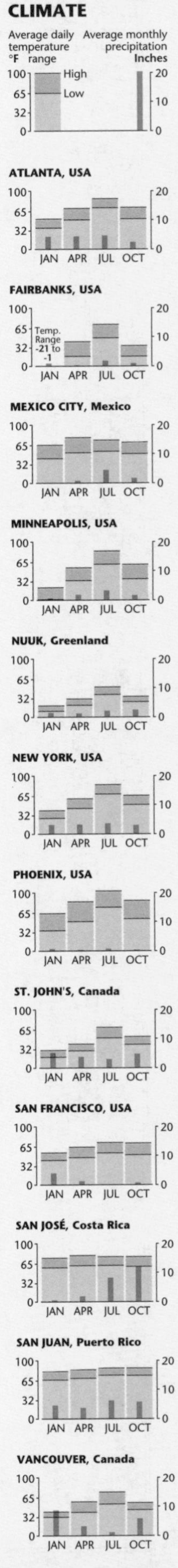
CLIMATE
Average daily temperature °F range
Average monthly precipitation Inches
High
Low
ATLANTA, USA
FAIRBANKS, USA
Temp. Range -21 to -1
MEXICO CITY, Mexico
MINNEAPOLIS, USA
NUUK, Greenland
NEW YORK, USA
PHOENIX, USA
ST. JOHN'S, Canada
SAN FRANCISCO, USA
SAN JOSÉ, Costa Rica
SAN JUAN, Puerto Rico
VANCOUVER, Canada
JAN APR JUL OCT

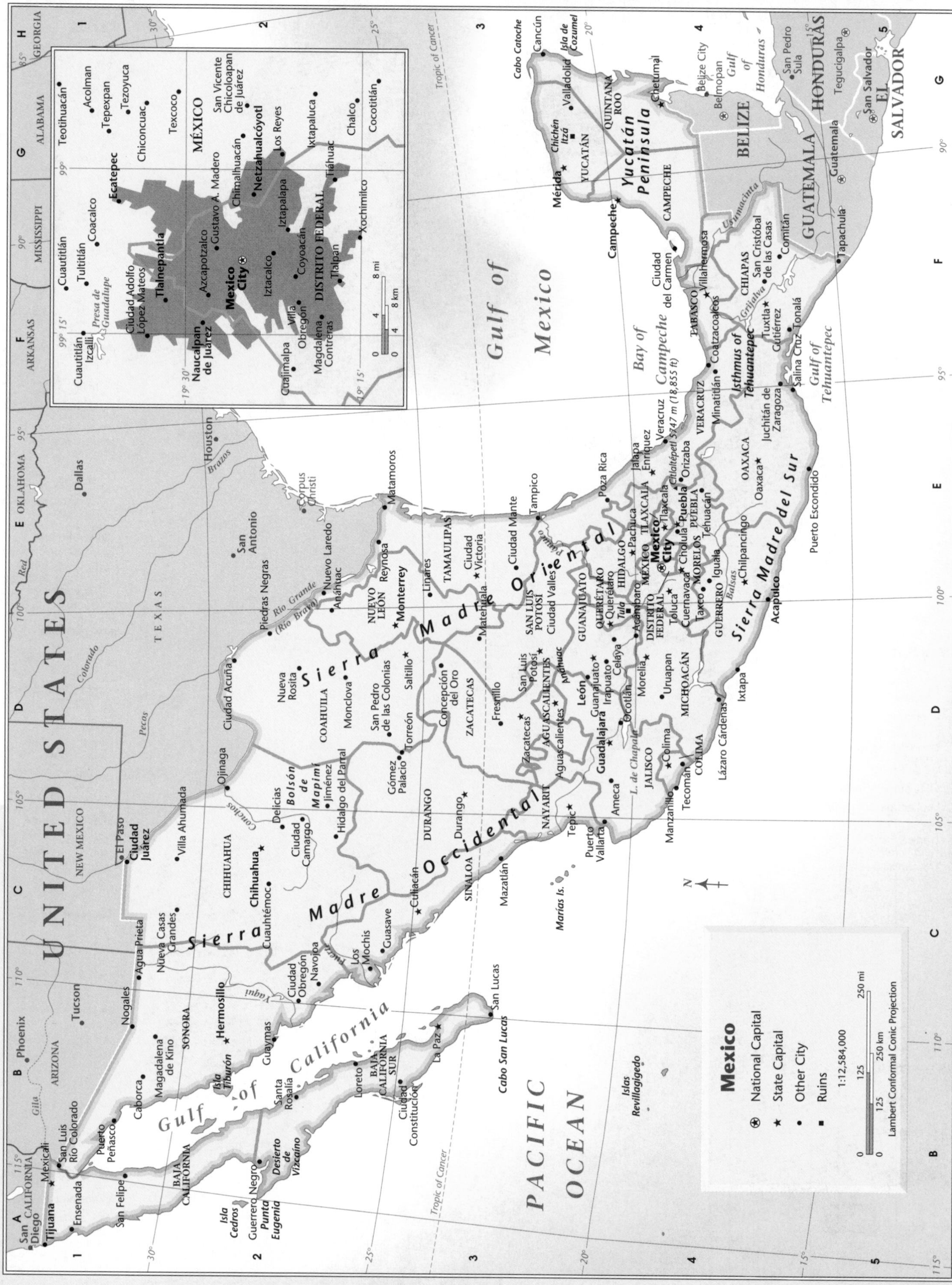
Mexico
National Capital
State Capital
Other City
Ruins
1:12,584,000
0 125 250 mi
0 125 250 km
Lambert Conformal Conic Projection
UNITED STATES
Gulf of Mexico
Bay of Campeche
PACIFIC OCEAN
Gulf of California
Gulf of Tehuantepec
Gulf of Honduras
Yucatán Peninsula
Isthmus of Tehuantepec
Sierra Madre Occidental
Sierra Madre Oriental
Sierra Madre del Sur
Bolsón de Mapimí
Desierto de Vizcaíno
Tropic of Cancer
Citlaltépetl 5747 m (18,855 ft)
BAJA CALIFORNIA
BAJA CALIFORNIA SUR
SONORA
CHIHUAHUA
COAHUILA
NUEVO LEÓN
TAMAULIPAS
SINALOA
DURANGO
ZACATECAS
NAYARIT
JALISCO
COLIMA
MICHOACÁN
AGUASCALIENTES
SAN LUIS POTOSÍ
GUANAJUATO
QUERÉTARO
HIDALGO
MÉXICO
DISTRITO FEDERAL
TLAXCALA
PUEBLA
MORELOS
GUERRERO
OAXACA
VERACRUZ
TABASCO
CHIAPAS
CAMPECHE
YUCATÁN
QUINTANA ROO
BELIZE
GUATEMALA
HONDURAS
EL SALVADOR
Mexico City
Tijuana
Mexicali
Hermosillo
Chihuahua
Ciudad Juárez
Monterrey
Saltillo
Guadalajara
Acapulco
Veracruz
Mérida
Cancún
Chichén Itzá
Campeche
Chetumal
Oaxaca
Puebla
Tampico
Mazatlán
Culiacán
La Paz
San Lucas
Cabo San Lucas
Islas Revillagigedo
Marías Is.
Tehuantepec
Cuautitlán
Tlalnepantla
Ecatepec
Netzahualcóyotl
Naucalpan de Juárez
Azcapotzalco
Gustavo A. Madero
Iztapalapa
Coyoacán
Xochimilco
Tlalpan
Magdalena Contreras
Cuajimalpa
Villa Obregón
Iztacalco
Tláhuac
Chalco
Texcoco
Teotihuacán
Presa de Guadalupe
DISTRITO FEDERAL
MÉXICO
0 4 8 mi
0 4 8 km
© MapQuest.com, Inc.

Mexico

Capital: Mexico City
Area: 756,066 sq. mi.
1,958,720 sq. km.
Population: 100,294,036
Largest City: Mexico City
Language: Spanish
Monetary Unit: New peso

Mexico: Map Index

States
Aguascalientes D3
Baja California A1
Baja California Sur B2
Campeche F4
Chiapas F4
Chihuahua C2
Coahuila D2
Colima D4
Distrito Federal ......E4, Inset
Durango C3
Guanajuato D3
Guerrero D4
Hidalgo E3
Jalisco D4
México ......E4, Inset
Michoacán D4
Morelos E4
Nayarit C3
Nuevo León D2
Oaxaca E4
Puebla E4
Querétaro D3
Quintana Roo G4
San Luis Potosí D3
Sinaloa C3
Sonora B1
Tabasco F4
Tamaulipas E3
Tlaxcala E4
Veracruz E4
Yucatán G3
Zacatecas D3

Cities and Towns
Acámbaro D4
Acapulco E4
Acolman ......Inset
Agua Prieta C1
Aguascalientes, *state capital* D3
Ameca D3
Anáhuac D2
Azcapotzalco ......Inset
Caborca B1
Campeche, *state capital* F4
Cancún G3
Celaya D3
Chalco ......Inset
Chetumal, *state capital* G4
Chiconcuac ......Inset
Chihuahua, *state capital* C2
Chilpancingo, *state capital* E4
Chimalhuacán ......Inset
Cholula E4
Ciudad Acuña D2
Ciudad Adolfo López Mateos ......Inset
Ciudad Camargo C2
Ciudad Constitución B3
Ciudad del Carmen F4
Ciudad Juárez C1
Ciudad Mante E3
Ciudad Obregón C2
Ciudad Valles E3
Ciudad Victoria, *state capital* E3
Coacalco ......Inset
Coatzacoalcos F4
Cocotitlán ......Inset
Colima, *state capital* D4
Comitán F4
Concepción del Oro D3
Coyoacán ......Inset
Cuajimalpa ......Inset
Cuauhtémoc C2
Cuautitlán ......Inset
Cuautitlán Izcalli ......Inset
Cuernavaca, *state capital* E4
Culiacán, *state capital* C3
Delicias C2
Durango, *state capital* D3
Ecatepec ......Inset
Ensenada A1
Fresnillo D3
Gómez Palacio D2
Guadalajara, *state capital* D3
Guanajuato, *state capital* D3
Guasave C2
Guaymas B2
Guerrero Negro B2
Gustavo A. Madero ......Inset
Hermosillo, *state capital* B2
Hidalgo del Parral C2
Iguala E4
Irapuato D3
Ixtapa D4
Ixtapaluca ......Inset
Iztacalco ......Inset
Iztapalapa ......Inset
Jalapa Enríquez, *state capital* E4
Jiménez D2
Juchitán de Zaragoza F4
La Paz, *state capital* B3
Lázaro Cárdenas D4
León D3
Linares E3
Loreto B2
Los Mochis C2
Los Reyes ......Inset
Magdalena de Kino B1
Magdalena Contreras ......Inset
Manzanillo D4
Matamoros E2
Matehuala D3
Mazatlán C3
Mérida, *state capital* G3
Mexicali, *state capital* A1
Mexico City, *national capital* ......E4, Inset
Minatitlán F4
Monclova D2
Monterrey, *state capital* D2
Morelia, *state capital* D4
Naucalpan de Juárez ......Inset
Navojoa C2
Netzahualcóyotl ......Inset
Nogales B1
Nueva Casas Grandes C1
Nueva Rosita D2
Nuevo Laredo E2
Oaxaca, *state capital* E4
Ocotlán D3
Ojinaga D2
Orizaba E4
Pachuca, *state capital* E3
Piedras Negras D2
Poza Rica E3
Puebla, *state capital* E4
Puerto Escondido E4
Puerto Peñasco B1
Puerto Vallarta C3
Querétaro, *statr capital* D3
Reynosa E2
Salina Cruz E4
Saltillo, *state capital* D2
San Cristóbal de las Casas F4
San Felipe B1
San Lucas C3
San Luis Potosí, *state capital* D3
San Luis Río Colorado B1
San Pedro de las Colonias D2
Santa Rosalía B2
San Vicente Chicoloapan de Juárez ......Inset
Tampico E3
Tapachula F5
Taxco E4
Tecomán D4
Tehuacán E4
Teotihuacán ......Inset
Tepexpan ......Inset
Tepic, *state capital* D3
Texcoco ......Inset
Tezoyuca ......Inset
Tiáhuac ......Inset
Tijuana A1
Tlaipan ......Inset
Tlalnepantla ......Inset
Tlaxcala, *state capital* E4
Toluca, *state capital* E4
Tonalá F4
Torreón D2
Tultitlán ......Inset
Tuxtla Gutiérrez, *state capital* F4
Uruapan D4
Valladolid G3
Veracruz E4
Villa Ahumada C1
Villahermosa, *state capital* F4
Villa Obregón ......Inset
Xochimilco ......Inset
Zacatecas, *state capital* D3

Other Features
Anáhuac, *depression* D3
Balsas, *river* E4
Bolsón de Mapimí, *depression* D2
California, *gulf* B1
Campeche, *bay* F4
Catoche, *cape* G3
Cedros, *island* A2
Chapala, *lake* D3
Chichén Itzá, *ruins* G3
Citlaltépetl, *mt.* E4
Conchos, *river* C2
Cozumel, *island* G3
Eugenia, *point* A2
Fuerte, *river* C2
Grijalva, *river* F4
Guadalupe, *reservoir* ......Inset
Marías, *islands* C3
Pánuco, *river* E3
Revillagigedo, *islands* B4
Rio Grande (Río Bravo), *river* D2
San Lucas, *cape* B3
Sierra Madre del Sur, *mts.* D4
Sierra Madre Occidental, *mts.* C2
Sierra Madre Oriental, *mts.* D2
Tehuantepec, *gulf* E4
Tehuantepec, *isthmus* F4
Tiburón, *island* B2
Tula, *ruins* D3
Usumacinta, *river* F4
Vizcaíno, *desert* B2
Yaqui, *river* C2
Yucatán, *peninsula* G4

MEXICO
Paxbán
Belize City
Belmopan
BELIZE
L. Petén-Itzá
Tikal
Flores
La Libertad
San Pedro
Usumacinta
Pasión
Comitán
Chixoy
Chinajá
San Luis
Gulf of Honduras
Puerto Barrios
Santo Tomás de Castilla
Sarstún
Cobán
L. de Izabal
San Pedro Sula
Tacaná 4093 m (13,428 ft)
Huehuetenango
Salamá
Motagua
Tajumulco 4220 m (13,845 ft)
Zacapa
HONDURAS
Suchiate
Sierra Madre
Quetzaltenango
Guatemala City
Santa Rosa de Copán
Mazatenango
L. de Atitlán
Antigua
Jutiapa
Champerico
Escuintla
Paz
Santa Ana
San Salvador
San José
EL SALVADOR
PACIFIC OCEAN
Guatemala
National Capital
Other City
1:8,150,000
0 50 100 mi
0 50 100 km
Lambert Conformal Conic Projection
N

© MapQuest.com, Inc.

Guatemala

Capital: Guatemala City
Area: 42,042 sq. mi.
108,917 sq. km.
Population: 12,335,580
Largest City: Guatemala City
Language: Spanish
Monetary Unit: Quetzal

Guatemala: Map Index

Cities and Towns
Antigua C5
Champerico B5
Chinajá C4
Cobán C4
Escuintla C5
Flores D3
Guatemala City, *capital* C5
Huehuetenango B4
Jutiapa D5
La Libertad C3
Mazatenango B5
Paxbán C2
Puerto Barrios E4
Quetzaltenango B5
Salamá C4
San José C6
San Luis D3
Santo Tomás de Castilla E4
Tikal D2
Zacapa D5

Other Features
Atitlán, *lake* B5
Chixoy, *river* C4
Honduras, *gulf* E3
Izabal, *lake* E4
Motagua, *river* D4
Pasión, *river* C3
Paz, *river* C6
Petén-Itzá, *lake* D3
San Pedro, *river* C2
Sarstún, *river* D4
Sierra Madre, *mts.* C5
Suchiate, *river* A5
Tacaná, *volcano* A4
Tajumulco, *volcano* B4
Usumacinta, *river* C3

MEXICO
Corozal
Hondo
New
Progresso
Orange Walk
Neustadt
Maskall
Ambergris Cay
Caribbean Sea
Hill Bank
Belize City
Belize
Turneffe Islands
Belmopan
San Ignacio
Dangriga
Glover Reef
Victoria 1122 m (3681 ft)
Maya Mts.
Placentia
San Antonio
Punta Gorda
Sarstoon
GUATEMALA
N
Belize
National Capital
Other City
1:5,590,000
0 25 50 mi
0 25 50 km
Lambert Conformal Conic Projection

© MapQuest.com, Inc.

Belize

Capital: Belmopan
Area: 8,867 sq. mi.
22,972 sq. km.
Population: 235,789
Largest City: Belize City
Language: English
Monetary Unit: Belize dollar

Belize: Map Index

Cities and Towns
Belize City B2
Belmopan, *capital* B2
Corozal B1
Dangriga B2
Hill Bank B2
Maskall B2
Neustadt A2
Orange Walk B1
Placentia B3
Progresso B1
Punta Gorda B3
San Antonio A3
San Ignacio A2

Other Features
Ambergris Cay, *island* C2
Belize, *river* B2
Glover, *reef* C3
Hondo, *river* B1
Maya, *mts.* A3
New, *river* B1
Sarstoon, *river* A4
Turneffe, *islands* C2
Victoria, *peak* B3

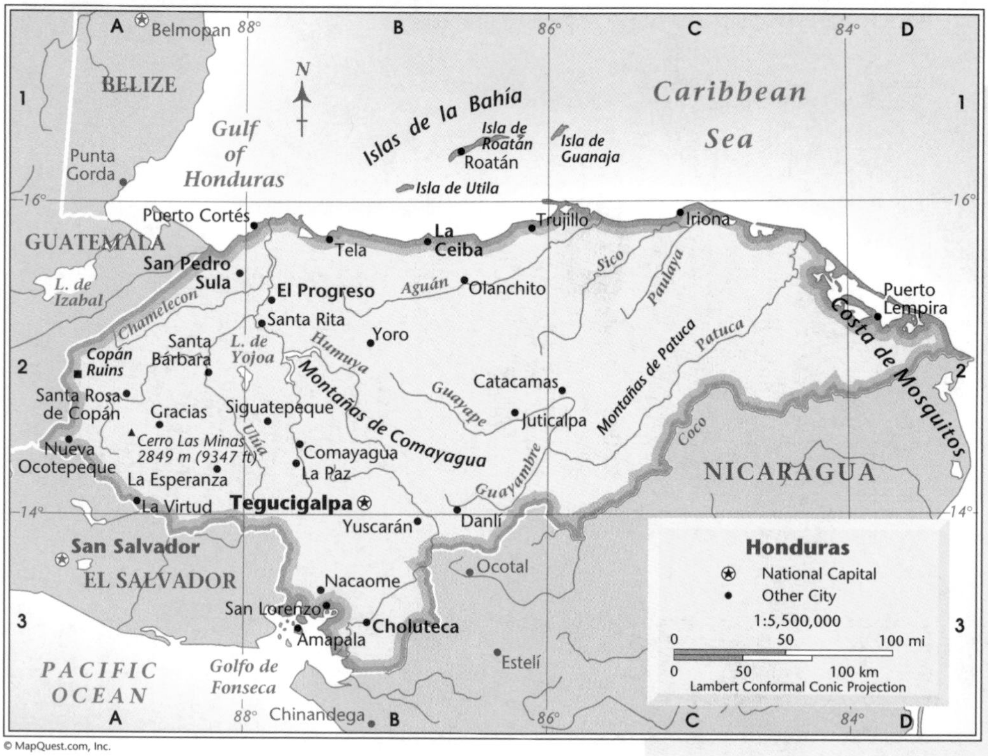

Honduras

Capital: Tegucigalpa
Area: 43,277 sq. mi.
112,117 sq. km.
Population: 5,997,327
Largest City: Tegucigalpa
Language: Spanish
Monetary Unit: Lempira

Honduras:
Map Index

Cities and Towns
Amapala B3
Catacamas C2
Choluteca B3
Comayagua....B2
Danlí B2
El Progreso B2
Gracias A2
Iriona C2
Juticalpa B2
La Ceiba B2
La Esperanza A2
La Paz B2
La Virtud A2
Nacaome....B3
Nueva Ocotepeque....A2
Olanchito B2
Puerto Cortés B2
Puerto Lempira....D2
Roatán....B1
San Lorenzo B3
San Pedro Sula A2
Santa Bárbara A2
Santa Rita B2
Santa Rosa de Copán A2
Siguatepeque B2
Tegucigalpa, *capital*....B2
Tela B2
Trujillo B2
Yoro B2
Yuscarán B3

Other Features
Aguán, *river*....B2
Bahía, *islands*....B1
Caribbean, *sea* C1
Chamelecon, *river* A2
Coco, *river* C2
Comayagua, *mts.* B2
Copán, *ruins* A2
Fonseca, *gulf* B3
Guanaja, *island* C1
Guayambre, *river*....B2
Guayape, *river* B2
Honduras, *gulf*....A1
Humuya, *river* B2
Las Minas, *mt.* A2
Mosquitos, *coast*....D2
Patuca, *mts.* C2
Patuca, *river* C2
Paulaya, *river*....C2
Roatán, *island* B1
Sico, *river* C2
Ulúa, *river* B2
Utila, *island* B1
Yojoa, *lake*....B2

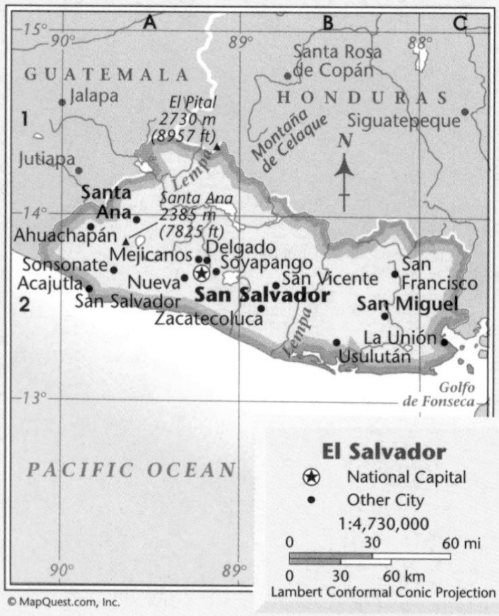

El Salvador

Capital: San Salvador
Area: 8,124 sq. mi.
21,047 sq. km.
Population: 5,839,079
Largest City: San Salvador
Language: Spanish
Monetary Unit: Colón

El Salvador:
Map Index

Cities and Towns
Acajutla....A2
Ahuachapán....A2
Delgado....A2
La Unión C2
Mejicanos A2
Nueva San Salvador A2
San Francisco B2
San Miguel....B2
San Salvador, *capital* A2
Santa Ana A2
San Vicente B2
Sonsonate A2
Soyapango....A2
Usulután B2
Zacatecoluca B2

Other Features
El Pital, *mt.* A1
Fonseca, *gulf* C2
Lempa, *river*....A1, B2
Santa Ana, *volcano* A2

Costa Rica:
Map Index

Cities and Towns
Alajuela B2
Cartago....C3
Colorado....C2
Golfito C4
Heredia B2
La Cruz A1
Liberia A2
Limón C3
Los Chiles B1
Puerto Jiménez C4
Puerto Quepos B3
Puntarenas B3
San José, *capital*....B3
Santa Cruz A2

Other Features
Arenal, *lake* B2
Central, *range* B2
Chirripó, *mt.* C3
Chirripó, *river* C2
Coronado, *bay* B3
Dulce, *gulf*....C4
Frio, *river*....B2
General, *river*....C3
Grande, *river* B3
Guanacaste, *range*....A2
Irazú, *volcano* C3
Nicoya, *gulf*....B3
Papagayo, *gulf*....A2
Pirris, *river* B3
Reventazón, *river*....C3
San Carlos, *river*....B2
San Juan, *river* B2
Sarapiquí *river* B2
Sixaola, *river* C3
Talamanca, *range* C3
Tempisque, *river* A2

Costa Rica

Capital: San José
Area: 19,730 sq. mi.
51,114 sq. km.
Population: 3,674,490
Largest City: San José
Language: Spanish
Monetary Unit: Colón

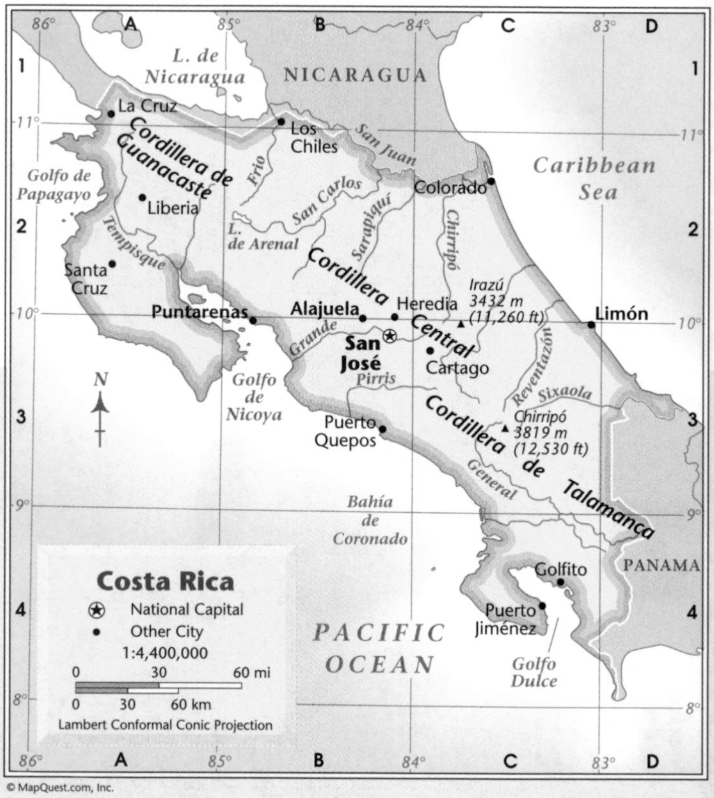

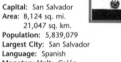

Nicaragua

Capital: Managua
Area: 50,880 sq. mi.
  131,813 sq. km.
Population: 4,717,132
Largest City: Managua
Language: Spanish
Monetary Unit: Córdoba

Nicaragua Map Legend
Nicaragua
★ National Capital
• Other City
1:4,400,000
0   25   50 mi
0   25   50 km
Lambert Conformal Conic Projection

Nicaragua: Map Index

Cities and Towns
Bluefields C3
Boaco B2
Bocay B1
Chinandega A2
Colonia Nueva Guinea B3
Corinto A2
Diriamba A3
Estelí A2
Granada B3
Jinotega B2
Jinotepe A3
Juigalpa B2
La Rosita B2
León A2
Managua, capital A2
Masaya A3
Matagalpa B2
Nagarote A2
Ocotal A2
Prinzapolka C2
Puerto Cabezas C1
Puerto Sandino A2
Rama B2
Río Blanco B2
Río Grande A2
Rivas B3
San Carlos B3
San Juan del Norte C3
San Juan del Sur B3
Siuna B2
Somoto A2
Waspam C1
Wiwili B2

Other Features
Bambana, river B2
Bismuna, lagoon C1
Bluefields, bay C3
Bocay, river B2
Chontaleña, mts. B3
Coco, river A2, C1
Cosiguina, mt. A2
Cosiguina, point A2
Dariense, mts. B2
Escondido, river B2
Fonseca, gulf A2
Gracias a Dios, cape C1
Grande de Matagalpa, river ..B2
Huapí, mts. B2
Isabelia, mts. B2
Kurinwás, river B2
Maíz, islands C2
Managua, lake A2
Mico, river B2
Miskitos, cays C1
Mogotón, mt. A2
Mosquitos, coast C2
Nicaragua, lake B3
Ometepe, island B3
Perlas, lagoon C2
Perlas, point C2
Prinzapolka, river B2
San Juan, river B3
San Juan del Norte, bay C3
Siquia, river B3
Solentiname, island B3
Tipitapa, river A2
Tuma, river B2
Wawa, river B1
Zapatera, island B3

© MapQuest.com, Inc.

Panama Map Legend
Panama
★ National Capital
• Other City
1:6,400,000
0   40   80 mi
0   40   80 km
Lambert Conformal Conic Projection

Panama

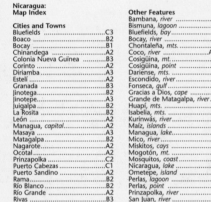

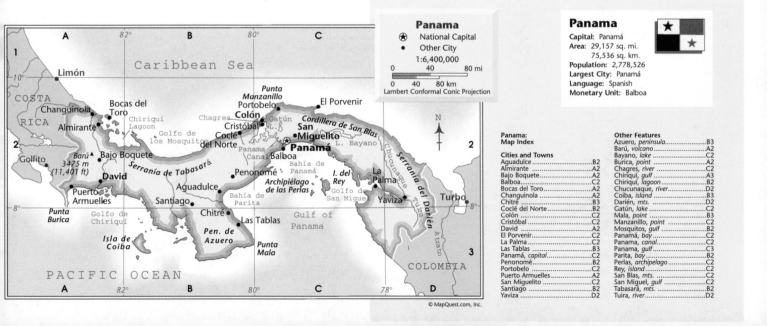

Capital: Panamá
Area: 29,157 sq. mi.
  75,536 sq. km.
Population: 2,778,526
Largest City: Panamá
Language: Spanish
Monetary Unit: Balboa

Panama: Map Index

Cities and Towns
Aguadulce B2
Almirante A2
Bajo Boquete A2
Balboa C2
Bocas del Toro A2
Changuinola A2
Chitré B3
Coclé del Norte B2
Colón C2
Cristóbal C2
David A2
El Porvenir C2
La Palma C2
Las Tablas B3
Panamá, capital C2
Penonomé B2
Portobelo C2
Puerto Armuelles A2
San Miguelito C2
Santiago B2
Yaviza D2

Other Features
Azuero, peninsula B3
Barú, volcano A2
Bayano, lake C2
Burica, point A2
Chagres, river C2
Chiriquí, gulf A3
Chiriquí, lagoon B2
Chucunaque, river D2
Coiba, island B3
Darién, mts. D2
Gatún, lake C2
Mala, point B3
Manzanillo, point C2
Mosquitos, gulf C2
Panamá, bay C2
Panama, canal C2
Panama, gulf C3
Parita, bay B2
Perlas, archipelago C2
Rey, island C2
San Blas, mts. C2
San Miguel, gulf C2
Tabasará, mts. B2
Tuira, river D2

© MapQuest.com, Inc.

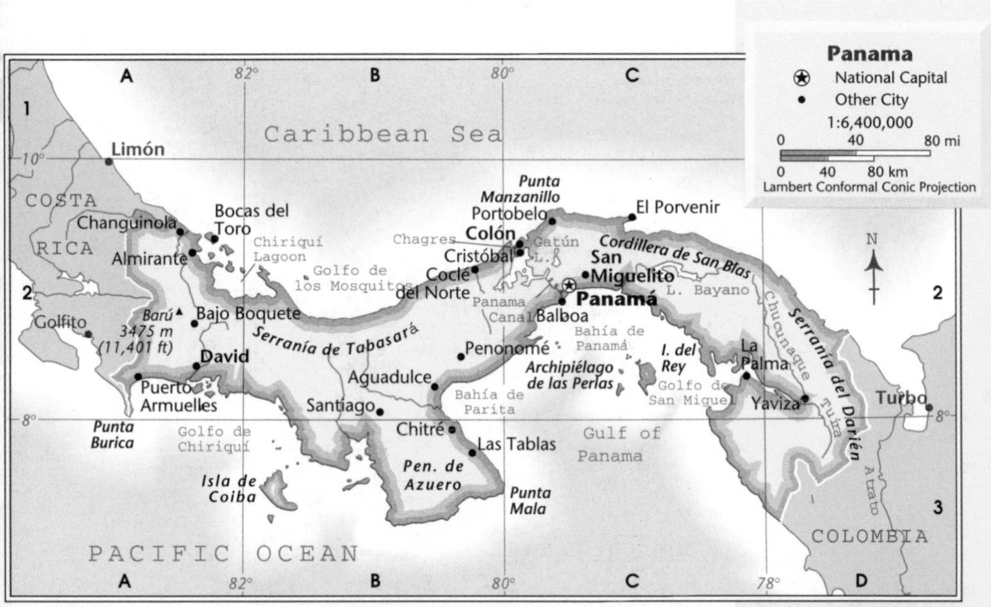

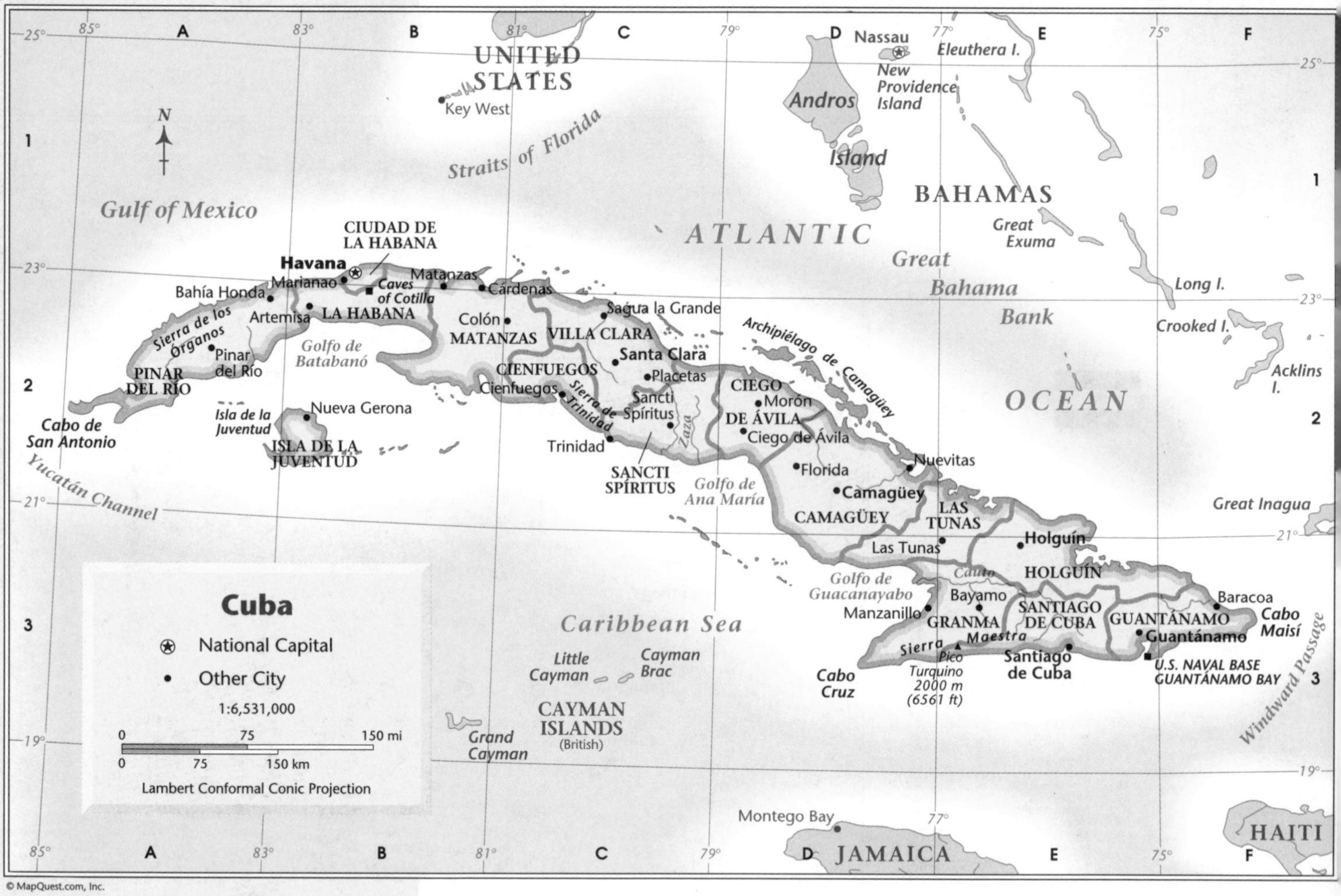

Cuba

Capital: Havana
Area: 42,804 sq. mi.
110,890 sq. km.
Population: 11,096,395
Largest City: Havana
Language: Spanish
Monetary Unit: Peso

Cuba:
Map Index

Provinces
Camagüey D2
Ciego de Ávila D2
Cienfuegos C2
Ciudad de La Habana B1
Granma E3
Guantánamo E3
Holguín E3
Isla de la Juventud (special municipality) B2
La Habana B2
Las Tunas E2
Matanzas B2
Pinar del Río A2
Sancti Spíritus C2
Santiago de Cuba E3
Villa Clara C2

Cities and Towns
Artemisa B2
Bahía Honda A2
Baracoa F3
Bayamo E3
Camagüey D2
Cárdenas B1
Ciego de Ávila D2
Cienfuegos C2
Colón C2
Florida D2
Guantánamo E3
Havana, *capital* B1
Holguín E3
Las Tunas E3
Manzanillo D3
Marianao B1
Matanzas B1
Morón D2
Nueva Gerona B2
Nuevitas D2
Pinar del Río A2
Placetas C2
Sagua la Grande C2
Sancti Spíritus C2
Santa Clara C2
Santiago de Cuba E3
Trinidad C2

Other Features
Ana María, *gulf* D2
Batabanó, *gulf* B2
Camagüey, *archipelago* D2
Cauto, *river* E3
Cotilla, *caves* B2
Cruz, *cape* D3
Florida, *straits* B1
Guacanayabo, *gulf* D3
Juventud, *island* B2
Maestra, *mts.* D3
Maisí, *cape* F3
Mexico, *gulf* A1
Órganos, *mts.* A2
San Antonio, *cape* A2
Trinidad, *mts.* C2
Turquino, *mt.* E3
U.S. Naval Base Guantánamo Bay E3
Windward, *passage* F3
Yucatán, *channel* A2
Zaza, *river* C2

Jamaica

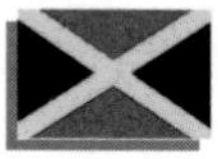

Capital: Kingston
Area: 4,244 sq. mi.
10,995 sq. km.
Population: 2,652,443
Largest City: Kingston
Language: English
Monetary Unit: Dollar

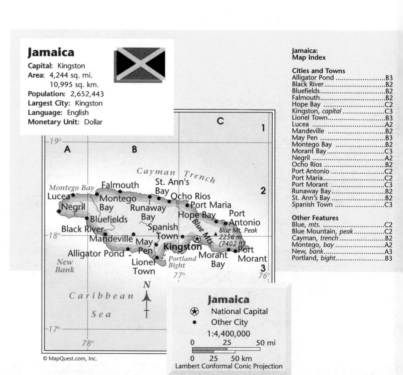

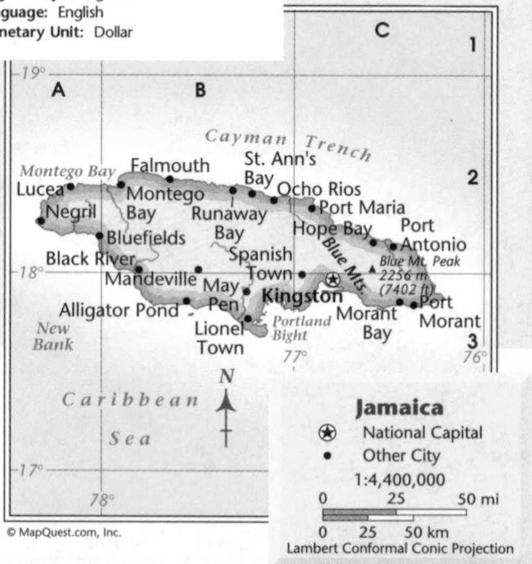

Jamaica:
Map Index

Cities and Towns
Alligator Pond B3
Black River B2
Bluefields B2
Falmouth B2
Hope Bay C2
Kingston, *capital* C3
Lionel Town B3
Lucea A2
Mandeville B2
May Pen B3
Montego Bay B2
Morant Bay C3
Negril A2
Ocho Rios B2
Port Antonio C2
Port Maria C2
Port Morant C3
Runaway Bay B2
St. Ann's Bay B2
Spanish Town C3

Other Features
Blue, *mts.* C2
Blue Mountain, *peak* C2
Cayman, *trench* B2
Montego, *bay* A2
New, *bank* A3
Portland, *bight* B3

Dominican Republic: Map Index

Provinces

Azua ... B2
Bahoruco ... A2
Barahona ... A2
Dajabón ... A1
Distrito Nacional ... B2
Duarte ... C1
El Seibo ... C2
Espaillat ... B1
Hato Mayor ... C2
Independencia ... A2
La Altagracia ... D2
La Estrelleta ... A1
La Romana ... D2
La Vega ... B2
María Trinidad Sánchez ... B1
Monseñor Nouel ... B2
Monte Cristi ... A1
Monte Plata ... C2
Pedernales ... A3
Peravia ... B2
Puerto Plata ... B1
Salcedo ... B1
Samaná ... C1
Sánchez Ramírez ... B1
San Cristóbal ... B2
San Juan ... A2
San Pedro de Macorís ... C2
Santiago ... B1
Santiago Rodríguez ... A1
Valverde ... B1

Cities and Towns

Azua ... B2
Baní ... B2
Barahona ... A2
Bonao ... B2
Cabrera ... C1
Comendador ... A2
Cotuí ... B1
Dajabón ... A1
El Macao ... D2
El Seibo ... C2
Hato Mayor ... C2
Higüey ... D2
Jimaní ... A2
La Romana ... D2
La Vega ... B1
Luperón ... B1
Mao ... A1
Miches ... C2
Moca ... B1
Monte Cristi ... A1
Monte Plata ... C2
Nagua ... C1
Neiba ... A2
Oviedo ... A3
Pedernales ... A2
Pedro Santana ... A1
Puerto Plata ... B1
Sabana de la Mar ... C1
Sabaneta ... A1
Salcedo ... B1
Samaná ... C1
San Cristóbal ... B2
San Francisco de Macorís ... B1
San José de las Matas ... A1
San Juan ... A2
San Pedro de Macorís ... C2
Santiago ... B1
Santo Domingo, *capital* ... C2
Sousúa ... B1

Other Features

Bahoruco, *mts.* ... A2
Beata, *cape* ... A3
Beata, *island* ... A3
Calderas, *bay* ... B2
Camú, *river* ... B1
Central, *range* ... B2
Cibao, *valley* ... A1
Duarte, *mt.* ... B1
Engaño, *cape* ... D2
Enriquillo, *lake* ... A2
Mona, *passage* ... D2
Neiba, *mts.* ... A2
Ocoa, *bay* ... B2
Oriental, *range* ... C2
Ozama, *river* ... B2
Samaná, *bay* ... C1
Samaná, *cape* ... C1
Saona, *island* ... D2
Septentrional, *range* ... A1
Soco, *river* ... C2
Yaque del Norte, *river* ... A1
Yaque del Sur, *river* ... A2
Yuna, *river* ... B2

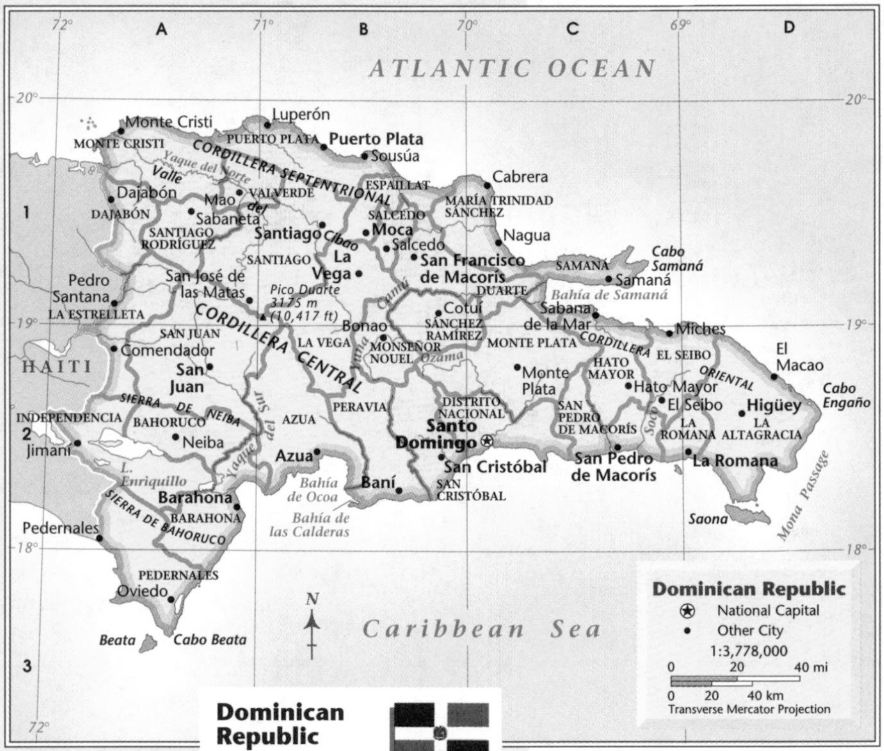

Dominican Republic

Capital: Santo Domingo
Area: 18,704 sq. mi.
48,456 sq. km.
Population: 8,129,734
Largest City: Santo Domingo
Language: Spanish
Monetary Unit: Peso

Haiti

National Capital
Other City
1:5,593,000
0 30 60 mi
0 30 60 km
Lambert Conformal Conic Projection

Haiti: Map Index

Departments

Artibonite ... C1
Centre ... D1
Grand Ande ... B2
Nord ... C1
Nord-Est ... D1
Nord-Ouest ... B1
Ouest ... C2
Sud ... B2
Sud-Est ... C2

Cities and Towns

Anse-à-Galets ... C2
Belle-Anse ... C2
Cap-Haïtien ... C1
Dame-Marie ... A2
Ennery ... C1
Gonaïves ... C1
Hinche ... C1
Jacmel ... C2
Jérémie ... A2
Léogâne ... C2
Les Cayes ... B2
Miragoâne ... B2
Mirebalais ... C2
Port-au-Prince, *capital* ... C2
Port-de-Paix ... C1
Port-Salut ... B2
Saint-Marc ... C1

Other Features

Artibonite, *river* ... C1
Gonâve, *gulf* ... B1
Gonâve, *island* ... B2
Gravois, *point* ... B3
Pic de la Selle, *mt.* ... D2
Port-au-Prince, *bay* ... C2
Tortuga, *island* ... C1
Vache, *island* ... B2
Windward, *passage* ... B1

Haiti

Capital: Port-au-Prince
Area: 10,695 sq. mi.
27,614 sq. km.
Population: 6,884,264
Largest City: Port-au-Prince
Languages: French, Creole
Monetary Unit: Gourde

The Bahamas

Capital: Nassau
Area: 5,382 sq. mi.
13,943 sq. km.
Population: 283,705
Largest City: Nassau
Languages: English, Creole
Monetary Unit: Dollar

Turks and Caicos Is.

Capital: Grand Turk
Area: 193 sq. mi.
500 sq. km.
Population: 16,863
Largest City: Grand Turk
Language: English
Monetary Unit: U.S. Dollar

Bahamas and Turks & Caicos Islands: Map Index

Bahamas

Cities and Towns

Alice Town ... B2
Arthur's Town ... B3
Freeport ... A2
Kemps Bay ... B3
Marsh Harbour ... B2
Matthew Town ... C4
Nassau, *capital* ... B2
Nicholls' Town ... A2
Sandy Point ... B2

Other Features

Acklins, *island* ... C4
Andros, *island* ... A3
Cat, *island* ... B3
Crooked, *island* ... C4
Crooked Island, *passage* ... C4
Eleuthera, *island* ... B2
Exuma, *sound* ... B3
Grand Bahama, *island* ... A2
Great Abaco, *island* ... B2
Great Bahama, *bank* ... A3
Great Exuma, *island* ... B3
Great Inagua, *island* ... C4
Harbour, *island* ... B2
Little Inagua, *island* ... C4
Long, *island* ... C3
Mayaguana, *island* ... C4
Mayaguana, *passage* ... C4
New Providence, *island* ... B3
Northeast Providence, *channel* ... B2
Rum, *cay* ... C3
Samana, *cay* ... C3
San Salvador, *island* ... C3
Water, *cays* ... A3

Turks & Caicos Islands

Cities and Towns

Cockburn Harbour ... D4
Grand Turk, *capital* ... D4

Other Features

Ambergris, *cay* ... D4
Caicos, *islands* ... D4
Grand Turk, *island* ... D4
Providenciales, *island* ... C4
Salt, *cay* ... D4
Turks, *islands* ... D4

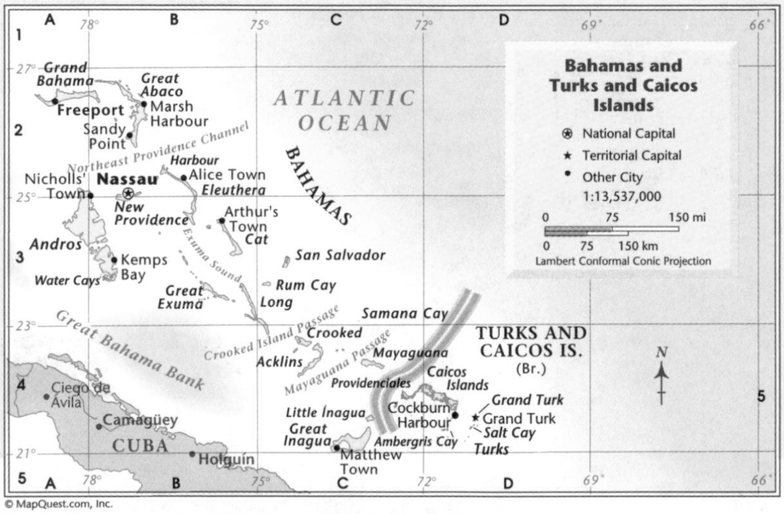

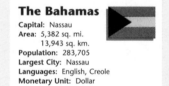

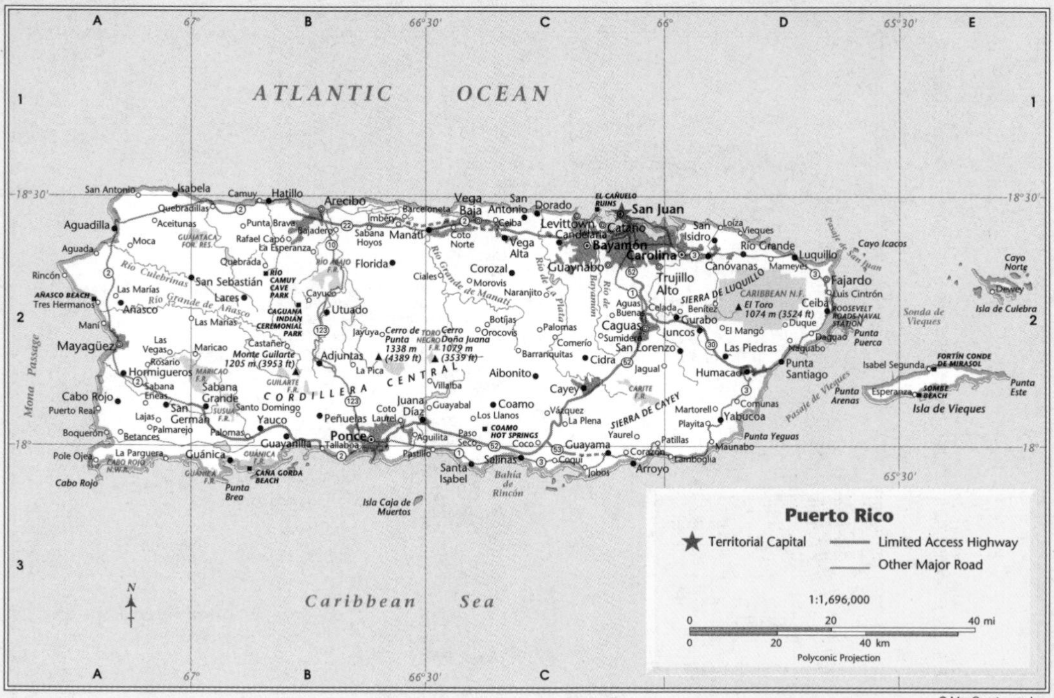

Puerto Rico

Capital: San Juan
Area: 3,492 sq. mi.
9,047 sq. km.
Population: 3,887,652
Largest City: San Juan
Languages: Spanish, English
Monetary Unit: U.S. dollar

Puerto Rico: Map Index

Cities and Towns
Adjuntas B2
Aguada A2
Aguadilla A2
Aguas Buenas C2
Aguilita B2
Aibonito C2
Añasco A2
Arecibo B2
Arroyo C3
Bajadero B2
Barceloneta B2
Barranquitas C2
Bayamón C2
Cabo Rojo A2
Caguas C2
Camuy B2
Candelaria C2
Canóvanas D2
Carolina D2
Cataño C2
Cayey C2
Ceiba C2
Ceiba D2
Celada D2
Ciales C2
Cidra C2
Coamo C2
Coco C2
Comerío C2
Coquí C3
Corazón C3
Corozal C2
Coto Laurel B2
Dorado C2
Fajardo D2
Florida B2
Guánica B3
Guayama C3
Guayanilla B2
Guaynabo C2
Gurabo D2
Hatillo B2
Hormigueros A2
Humacao D2
Imbéry B2
Isabela A1
Jayuya B2
Jobos C3
Juana Díaz B2
Juncos D2
Lajas A2
Lares B2
Las Piedras D2
Levittown C2
Loíza D2
Luquillo D2
Manatí B2
Martorell D2
Maunabo D2
Mayagüez A2
Moca A2
Naguabo D2
Pastillo C3
Patillas C2
Peñuelas B2
Ponce B2
Puerto Real A2
Punta Santiago D2
Quebradillas B2
Río Grande D2
Sabana Grande B2
Salinas C3
San Antonio C2
San Germán A2
San Isidro D2
San Juan, *capital* C2
San Lorenzo D2
San Sebastián B2
Santa Isabel C3
Santo Domingo B2
Trujillo Alto C2
Utuado B2
Vega Alta C2
Vega Baja C2
Vieques D2
Villalba C2
Yabucoa D2
Yauco B2

Other Features
Añasco, *beach* A2
Arenas, *point* D2
Bayamón, *river* C2
Brea, *point* B3
Cabo Rojo Natl. Wildlife Refuge A3
Caguana Indian Ceremonial Park B2
Caja de Muertos, *island* B3
Caña Gorda, *beach* B3
Caribbean, *sea* B3
Caribbean Natl. Forest D2
Carite Forest Reserve C2
Coamo Hot Springs C2
Cordillera Central, *mts.* B2
Culebra, *island* E2
Culebrinas, *river* A2
Doña Juana, *mt.* C2
El Cañuelo, *ruins* C2
El Toro, *mt.* D2
Este, *point* E2
Fortín Conde de Mirasol, *fort* E2
Grande de Añasco, *river* A2
Grande de Manatí, *river* C2
Guajataca Forest Reserve B2
Guánica Forest Reserve B3
Guilarte, *mt.* B2
Guilarte Forest Reserve B2
Icacos, *key* D2
La Plata, *river* C2
Maricao Forest Reserve B2
Mona, *passage* A2
Norte, *key* E2
Puerca, *point* D2
Punta, *mt.* B2
Rincón, *bay* C3
Río Abajo Forest Reserve B2
Río Camuy Cave Park B2
Rojo, *cape* A3
Roosevelt Roads Naval Station D2
San Juan, *passage* D2
Sierra de Cayey, *mts.* C2
Sierra de Luquillo, *mts.* D2
Sombe, *beach* E2
Susua Forest Reserve B2
Toro Negro Forest Reserve C2
Vieques, *island* E2
Vieques, *passage* D2
Vieques, *sound* E2
Yeguas, *point* D2

Antigua and Barbuda

Capital: St. John's
Area: 171 sq. mi.
443 sq. km.
Population: 64,246
Largest City: St. John's
Language: English
Monetary Unit: East Caribbean dollar

Antigua and Barbuda: Map Index

Cities and Towns
Bolands D5
Cedar Grove E5
Codrington E2
Falmouth E5
Freetown E5
Old Road D5
St. John's, *capital* D5

Other Features
Antigua, *island* D4
Barbuda, *island* E3
Boggy, *peak* D5
Cobb, *cove* E1
Codrington, *lagoon* D1
Goat, *point* D1
Gravenor, *bay* E2
Palmetto, *point* D2
Redonda, *island* A6
Shirley, *cape* E6
Spanish, *point* E2
Willoughby, *bay* E5

Dominica: Map Index

Cities and Towns
Berekua B4
Castle Bruce B2
Colihaut A2
Glanvillia A2
La Plaine B3
Laudat B3
Marigot B2
Massacre B3
Pointe Michel B3
Pont Cassé B3
Portsmouth A2
Rosalie B3
Roseau, *capital* B3
Saint Joseph A3
Salibia B2
Salisbury A2
Soufrière B4
Vieille Case B1
Wesley B2

Other Features
Boiling, *lake* B3
Dominica, *passage* A1
Grand, *bay* B4
Layou, *river* B3
Morne Diablotin, *mt.* B2
Roseau, *river* B3
Toulaman, *river* B2

Dominica

Capital: Roseau
Area: 290 sq. mi.
751 sq. km.
Population: 64,881
Largest City: Roseau
Language: English
Monetary Unit: East Caribbean dollar

St. Kitts & Nevis: Map Index

Cities and Towns
Basseterre, *capital* B2
Bath C3
Cayon B1
Charlestown C3
Cotton Ground C2
Dieppe Bay Town B1
Fig Tree C3
Newcastle C2
Old Road Town B2
St. Paul's A1
Sandy Point Town A1
Zion C3

Other Features
Great Salt, *pond* C2
Nag's Head, *cape* C2
Narrows, *strait* C2
Nevis, *island* C3
St. Kitts (St. Christopher), *island* B2

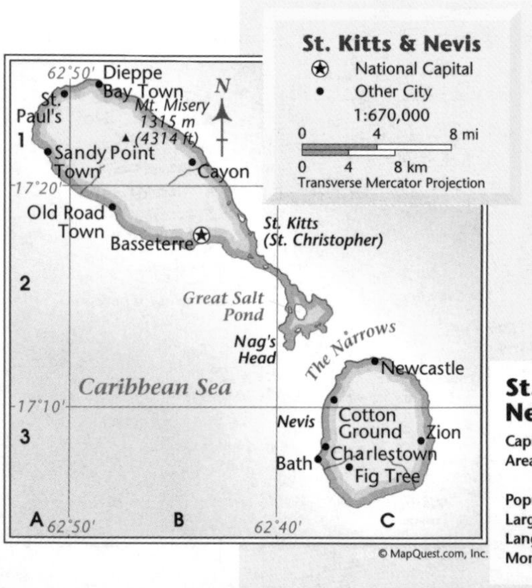

St. Kitts & Nevis

Capital: Basseterre
Area: 104 sq. mi.
269 sq. km.
Population: 42,838
Largest City: Basseterre
Language: English
Monetary Unit: East Caribbean dollar

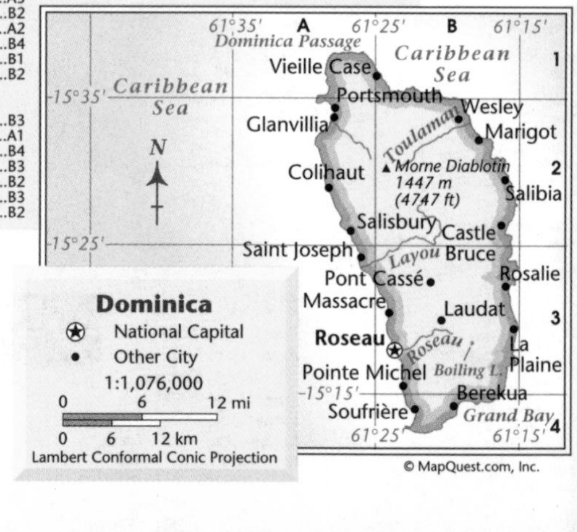

St. Lucia

Capital: Castries
Area: 238 sq. mi.
617 sq. km.
Population: 154,020
Largest City: Castries
Language: English
Monetary Unit: East Caribbean dollar

St. Lucia:
Map Index

Cities and Towns
Canaries.............................A2
Castries, *capital*..............B1
Choiseul............................A3
Dauphin.............................B1
Dennery.............................B2
Desruisseau.......................B3
Grand Anse........................B1
Gros Islet..........................B1
Laborie..............................B3
La Croix Maingot.................A2
Micoud...............................B3
Mon Repos.........................B2

Other Features
Canelles, *river*.................B3
Cul de Sac, *river*..............B2
Fond d'Or, *river*................B2
Gimie, *mt.*......................A2
Maria, *islands*.................B3
Moule à Chique, *cape*......B3
Point, *cape*......................B1
Saint Lucia, *channel*........B1
Saint Vincent, *passage*.....B4
Soufrière, *volcano*............A2

St. Lucia

⊛ National Capital
• Other City
1:1,000,000
0   5   10 mi
0   5   10 km
Miller Cylindrical Projection

© MapQuest.com, Inc.

Barbados

Capital: Bridgetown
Area: 166 sq. mi.
430 sq. km.
Population: 259,191
Largest City: Bridgetown
Language: English
Monetary Unit: Dollar

Barbados
⊛ National Capital
• Other City
1:809,000
0   5   10 mi
0   5   10 km
Azimuthal Equal Area Projection

© MapQuest.com, Inc.

Barbados:
Map Index

Cities and Towns
Bathsheba...........................B3
Belair.................................B4
Blackmans..........................B3
Bridgetown, *capital*..........A4
Holetown............................A3
Oistins...............................B5
Portland.............................A2
Seawell..............................C4
Speightstown......................A2
Spring Hall.........................A2
The Crane..........................C4
Thicket..............................C4

Other Features
Bruce Vale, *river*..............B3
Carlisle, *bay*....................A4
Constitution, *river*............B4
Hillaby, *mt.*.....................A3
North, *point*.....................A1
Ragged, *point*..................C3
South, *point*....................B5

St. Vincent and the Grenadines:
Map Index

Cities and Towns
Ashton...............................A4
Barrouallie.........................B2
Biabou...............................B2
Charlestown.......................A3
Derrick..............................B3
Georgetown........................B2
Kingstown, *capital*...........B2
Lovell Village......................B3
New Sandy Bay...................B1
Port Elizabeth....................B2
Stubbs...............................B2

Other Features
Baleine, *bay*....................B1
Baliceaux, *island*.............B3
Bequia, *island*.................B2
Canouan, *island*..............B3
Grenadines, *islands*.........A3
Mayreau, *island*..............A4
Mt. Wynn, *bay*.................B2
Mustique, *island*.............B3
North Mayreau, *channel*....A3
Palm, *island*....................A4
Petit Canouan, *island*.......B3
Petit Mustique, *island*......B3
Petit St. Vincent, *island*....A4
St. Vincent, *island*...........B2
Savan, *island*..................B3
Soufrière, *mt.*..................B1
Tobago, *cays*...................A4
Union, *island*...................A4
Windward, *islands*............B4

St. Vincent and the Grenadines

⊛ National Capital
• Other City
1:1,900,000
0   10   20 mi
0   10   20 km
Miller Cylindrical Projection

© MapQuest.com, Inc.

St. Vincent and The Grenadines

Capital: Kingstown
Area: 150 sq. mi.
389 sq. km.
Population: 120,519
Largest City: Kingstown
Languages: English, French patois
Monetary Unit: East Caribbean dollar

Trinidad & Tobago

Capital: Port of Spain
Area: 1,980 sq. mi.
5,130 sq. km.
Population: 1,102,096
Largest City: Port of Spain
Language: English
Monetary Unit: Dollar

Trinidad & Tobago:
Map Index

Cities and Towns
Arima.................................A2
Canaan..............................B1
Chaguanas.........................A2

Charlotteville.......................B1
Couva.................................A2
Fullarton.............................A2
Guayaguayare......................A2
Matelot...............................A2
Moruga...............................A2
Pierreville...........................A2
Plymouth............................B1
Point Fortin........................A2
Port of Spain, *capital*.......A2
Princes Town......................A2
Rio Claro............................A2
St. Augustine......................A2
San Fernando......................A2
San Francique.....................A2
Sangre Grande....................A2
Scarborough.......................B1
Siparia...............................A2
Toco..................................B2

Other Features
El Cerro del Aripo, *mt.*......A2
Paria, *gulf*........................A2
Pitch, *lake*.......................A2
Tobago, *island*.................B1
Trinidad, *island*................A2

Trinidad & Tobago

⊛ National Capital
• Other City
1:2,700,000
0   15   30 mi
0   15   30 km
Azimuthal Equal Area Projection

© MapQuest.com, Inc.

Grenada:
Map Index

Cities and Towns
Grand Bay...........................C1
Grand Roy...........................B2
Hillsborough........................C1
Marquis...............................B2
St. David's...........................B2
St. George's, *capital*..........A2
Sauteurs.............................B2
Tivoli..................................B2

Other Features
Bird, *island*......................B2

Caille, *island*....................B1
Carriacou, *island*..............C1
Diamond, *island*...............B1
Frigate, *island*..................C1
Grenada, *island*................B2
Grenadines, *island*
group..........................B1, C1
Large, *island*....................C1
Les Tantes, *island*............C1
Petit Martinique, *island*.....C1
Ronde, *island*...................B1
St. Catherine, *mt.*............B2
Salines, *point*...................A2
Sandy, *island*...................B2

Grenada

⊛ National Capital
• Other City
1:1,260,000
0   8   16 mi
0   8   16 km
Transverse Mercator Projection

Grenada

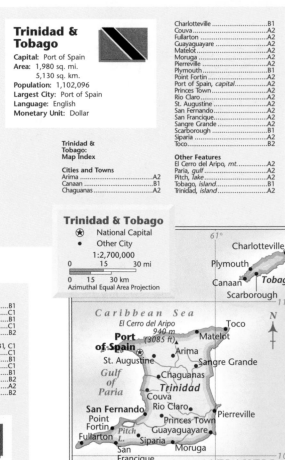

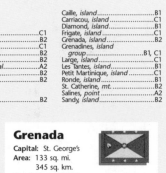

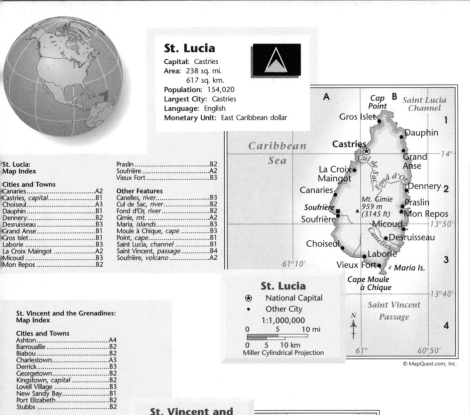

Capital: St. George's
Area: 133 sq. mi.
345 sq. km.
Population: 97,008
Largest City: St. George's
Language: English
Monetary Unit: East Caribbean dollar

© MapQuest.com, Inc.

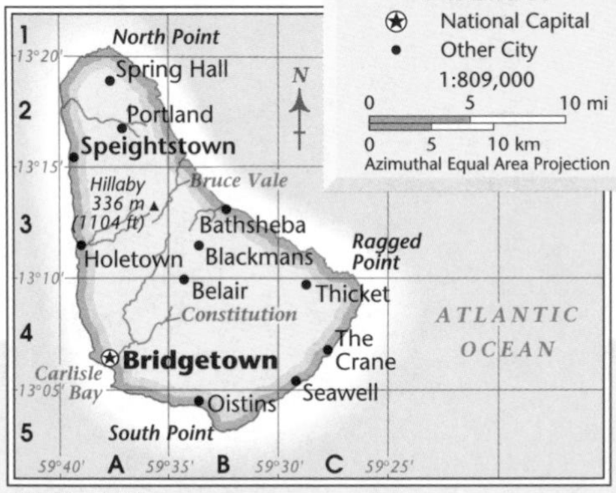

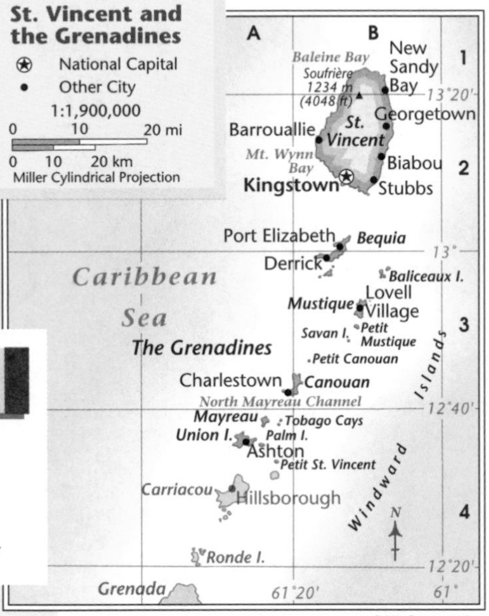

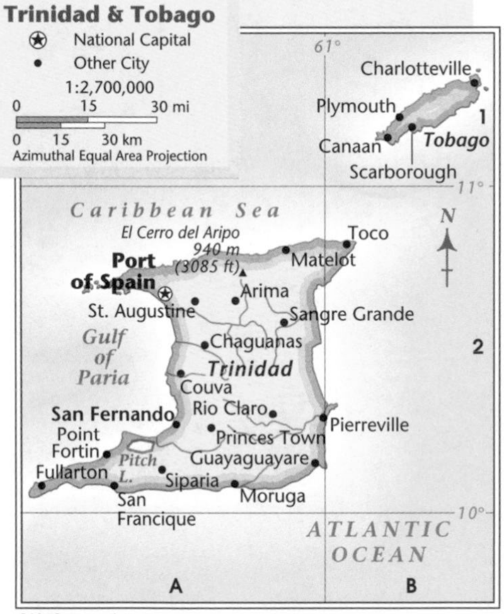

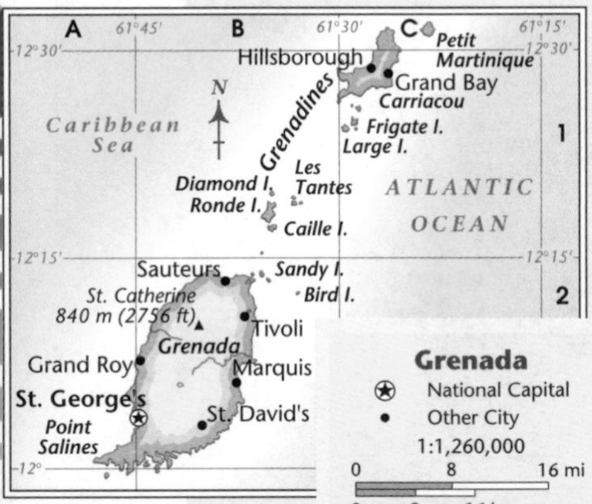

© MapQuest.com, Inc.

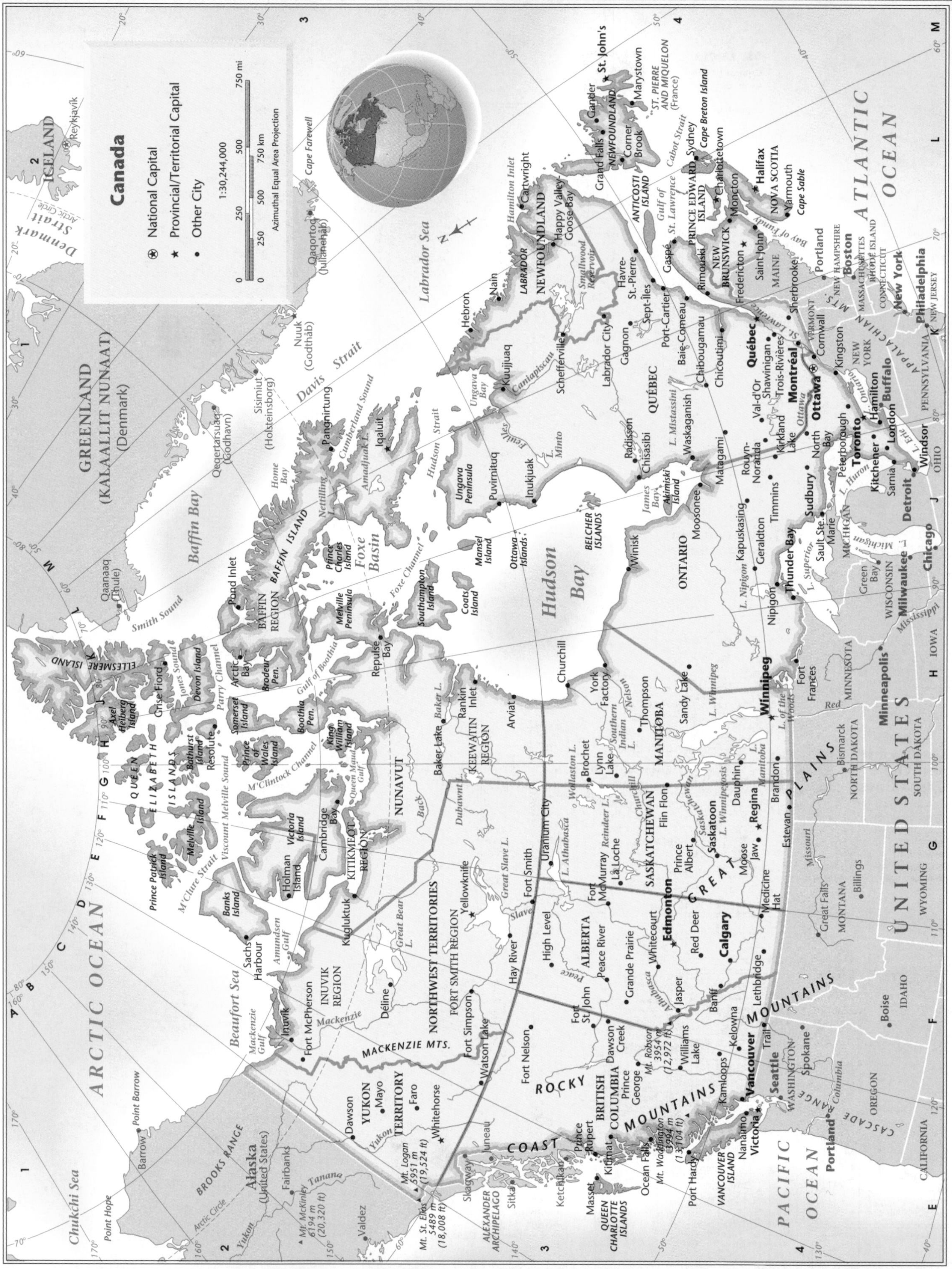

Canada

⊛ National Capital
★ Provincial/Territorial Capital
• Other City

1:30,244,000

Azimuthal Equal Area Projection

ICELAND

Reykjavik

GREENLAND
(KALAALLIT NUNAAT)
(Denmark)

Denmark Strait

Qaanaaq
(Thule)

Qaqortoq
(Julianehåb)

Nuuk
(Godthåb)

Sisimiut
(Holsteinsborg)

Qeqertarsuaq
(Godhavn)

Cape Farewell

Baffin Bay

Davis Strait

Labrador Sea

Smith Sound

ELLESMERE ISLAND

QUEEN ELIZABETH ISLANDS

Axel Heiberg Island

Prince Patrick Island

Crise Fiord

Devon Island

Jones Sound

Bathurst Island

Cornwallis Island

Resolute

Melville Island

Parry Channel

Somerset Island

Prince of Wales Island

Brodeur Pen.

Arctic Bay

BAFFIN REGION

BAFFIN ISLAND

Pangnirtung

Cumberland Sound

Home Bay

Nettilling L.

Prince Charles Island

Melville Peninsula

Foxe Basin

Foxe Channel

Iqaluit

Amadjuak L.

Hudson Strait

Pond Inlet

Nain

Hebron

LABRADOR

NEWFOUNDLAND

Cartwright

Hamilton Inlet

Happy Valley-Goose Bay

Smallwood Reservoir

Havre-St-Pierre

Sept-Îles

Gander

St. John's

Corner Brook

NEWFOUNDLAND

Grand Falls

Marystown

ST-PIERRE AND MIQUELON (France)

Cabot Strait

Cape Breton Island

Sydney

PRINCE EDWARD ISLAND

Charlottetown

NOVA SCOTIA

Halifax

Cape Sable

Yarmouth

Bay of Fundy

Moncton

NEW BRUNSWICK

Fredericton

Saint John

Gaspé

Rimouski

Baie-Comeau

Port-Cartier

Gagnon

Labrador City

Schefferville

QUÉBEC

L. Mistassini

Chibougamau

Chicoutimi

Waskaganish

Radisson

Chisasibi

Matagami

L. Minto

Kuujjuaq

Ungava Bay

Ungava Peninsula

Feuilles

Puvirnituq

Inukjuak

Akimiski Island

James Bay

Ottawa Islands

BELCHER ISLANDS

Mansel Island

Coats Island

Southampton Island

Repulse Bay

Gulf of Boothia

Boothia Pen.

King William Island

Committee Bay

Back

Baker Lake

Baker L.

Chesterfield Inlet

Rankin Inlet

Arviat

KEEWATIN REGION

NUNAVUT

Wollaston L.

Dubawnt L.

Brochet

Lynn Lake

Reindeer L.

Southern Indian L.

Thompson

Churchill

York Factory

HUDSON BAY

Winisk

Moosonee

ONTARIO

L. Nipigon

Kapuskasing

Geraldton

Timmins

Kirkland Lake

Rouyn-Noranda

Val-d'Or

Shawinigan

Trois-Rivières

Québec ★

Montréal

Ottawa ⊛

Cornwall

Kingston

VERMONT

NEW HAMPSHIRE

MAINE

Sherbrooke

Portland

St. Lawrence

Gulf of St. Lawrence

ANTICOSTI ISLAND

ATLANTIC OCEAN

Boston

MASSACHUSETTS

RHODE ISLAND

CONNECTICUT

New York

NEW JERSEY

Philadelphia

PENNSYLVANIA

APPALACHIAN MTS.

Buffalo

NEW YORK

Hamilton

London

Toronto

Peterborough

Kitchener

Windsor

Sarnia

OHIO

Detroit

North Bay

Sudbury

Sault Ste. Marie

Thunder Bay

Nipigon

L. Superior

L. Huron

L. Michigan

MICHIGAN

Green Bay

Milwaukee

Chicago

WISCONSIN

Mississippi

IOWA

MINNESOTA

Minneapolis

Fort Frances

L. of the Woods

Winnipeg

MANITOBA

L. Winnipeg

Sandy Lake

Flin Flon

Saskatchewan

SASKATCHEWAN

Prince Albert

Saskatoon

L. Winnipegosis

L. Manitoba

Dauphin

Brandon

Regina ★

Moose Jaw

Estevan

GREAT PLAINS

Bismarck

NORTH DAKOTA

SOUTH DAKOTA

UNITED STATES

Medicine Hat

Lethbridge

Swift Current

Missouri

Great Falls

MONTANA

WYOMING

Billings

ALBERTA

Calgary

Red Deer

Edmonton

Whitecourt

La Loche

Fort McMurray

Uranium City

L. Athabasca

Fort Smith

FORT SMITH REGION

Great Slave L.

Yellowknife ★

Slave

Hay River

Fort Simpson

NORTHWEST TERRITORIES

Fort Resolution

Great Bear L.

Déline

Fort McPherson

Inuvik

INUVIK REGION

Mackenzie

MACKENZIE MTS.

Watson Lake

Fort Nelson

Fort St. John

Dawson Creek

Peace River

Grande Prairie

High Level

Peace

Athabasca

ROCKY MOUNTAINS

BRITISH COLUMBIA

Prince George

Jasper

Banff

Mt. Robson 3954 m (12,972 ft) ▲

Kelowna

Kamloops

Williams Lake

Quesnel

Prince Rupert

Kitimat

Ocean Falls

Port Hardy

Nanaimo

VANCOUVER ISLAND

Victoria ★

Vancouver

Trail

COAST MOUNTAINS

Mt. Waddington 3994 m (13,104 ft) ▲

QUEEN CHARLOTTE ISLANDS

Masset

Skagway

Juneau

Ketchikan

Sitka

ALEXANDER ARCHIPELAGO

Seattle

WASHINGTON

Spokane

Portland

OREGON

IDAHO

Boise

CASCADE RANGE

Columbia

Mt. Logan 5951 m (19,524 ft) ▲

Mt. St. Elias 5489 m (18,008 ft) ▲

YUKON TERRITORY

Whitehorse ★

Faro

Mayo

Dawson

Yukon

Alaska (United States)

Fairbanks

Mt. McKinley 6194 m (20,320 ft) ▲

BROOKS RANGE

Arctic Circle

Point Barrow

Barrow

Point Hope

Chukchi Sea

Tanana

Valdez

PACIFIC OCEAN

ARCTIC OCEAN

Beaufort Sea

Mackenzie Gulf

Amundsen Gulf

Banks Island

Sachs Harbour

Kugluktuk

Holman Island

Victoria Island

Cambridge Bay

KITIKMEOT REGION

Queen Maud Gulf

Coronation Gulf

M'Clintock Channel

Viscount Melville Sound

M'Clure Strait

Melville Island

Prince of Wales Strait

**Canada:
Map Index**

ALBERTA

Cities and Towns
Banff F3
Calgary F3
Edmonton, *capital* F3
Fort McMurray F3
Grande Prairie F3
High Level F3
Jasper F3
Lethbridge F4
Medicine Hat F4
Peace River F3
Red Deer F3
Whitecourt F3

Other Features
Athabasca, *river* F3
Peace, *river* F3

BRITISH COLUMBIA

Cities and Towns
Dawson Creek E3
Fort Nelson E3
Fort St. John E3
Kamloops E3
Kelowna F4
Kitimat E3
Masset D3
Nanaimo E4
Ocean Falls E3
Port Hardy E3
Prince George E3
Prince Rupert D3
Trail F4
Vancouver E4
Victoria, *capital* E4
Williams Lake E3

Other Features
Coast, *mts.* D3
Fraser, *river* E3
Queen Charlotte, *islands* D3
Robson, *mt.* F3
Rocky, *mts.* E3
Vancouver, *island* E4
Waddington, *mt.* E3

MANITOBA

Cities and Towns
Brandon H4
Brochet G3
Churchill H3
Dauphin G3
Flin Flon G3
Lynn Lake G3
Thompson H3
Winnipeg, *capital* H4
York Factory H3

Other Features
Churchill, *river* G3
Hudson, *bay* J3
Manitoba, *lake* H3
Nelson, *river* H3
Saskatchewan, *river* G3
Southern Indian, *lake* H3
Winnipeg, *lake* H3
Winnipegosis, *lake* G3

NEW BRUNSWICK

Cities and Towns
Fredericton, *capital* L4
Moncton L4
Saint John L4

Other Feature
Fundy, *bay* L4

NEWFOUNDLAND

Cities and Towns
Cartwright M3
Corner Brook M4
Gander M4
Grand Falls M4
Happy Valley-Goose Bay L3
Hebron L3
Labrador City L3
Marystown M4
Nain L3
St. John's, *capital* M4

Other Features
Cabot, *strait* M4
Hamilton, *inlet* M3
Labrador, *region* L3
Labrador, *sea* M3
St. Lawrence, *gulf* L4
Smallwood, *reservoir* L3

NORTHWEST TERRITORIES

Cities and Towns
Arviat H2
Déline E2
Fort McPherson D2
Fort Simpson E2
Fort Smith F2
Hay River F2
Holman Island F1
Inuvik D2
Sachs Harbour E1
Yellowknife, *capital* F2

Other Features
Amundsen, *gulf* E1
Banks, *island* E1
Beaufort, *sea* D1
Fort Smith, *region* E2
Great Bear, *lake* F2
Great Slave, *lake* F2
Inuvik, *region* E2
Mackenzie, *gulf* D2
Mackenzie, *mts.* D2
Mackenzie, *river* D2
M'Clure, *strait* E1
Melville, *island* F1
Prince Patrick, *island* E1
Slave, *river* F2
Victoria, *island* F1
Viscount Melville, *sound* F1

NUNAVUT

Cities and Towns
Arctic Bay J1
Baker Lake H2
Cambridge Bay G2
Grise Fiord J1
Iqaluit, *capital* L2
Kugluktuk F2
Pangnirtung L2
Pond Inlet K1
Rankin Inlet H2
Repulse Bay J2
Resolute H1

Other Features
Amadjuak, *lake* K2
Axel Heiberg, *island* H1
Back, *river* G2
Baffin, *bay* L1
Baffin, *island* K1
Baffin, *region* J1
Baker, *lake* H2
Bathurst, *island* H1
Belcher, *islands* K3
Boothia, *gulf* J2
Boothia, *peninsula* H1
Brodeur, *peninsula* J1
Coats, *island* J2
Cumberland, *sound* L2
Davis, *strait* M2
Devon, *island* J1
Dubawnt, *lake* G2
Ellesmere, *island* K1
Foxe, *basin* K2
Foxe, *channel* J2
Home, *bay* L2
Hudson, *bay* J3
Hudson, *strait* K2
James, *bay* J3
Jones, *sound* J1
Keewatin, *region* H2
King William, *island* H2
Kitikmeot, *region* F2
Mansel, *island* J2
M'Clintock, *channel* G1
Melville, *island* G1
Melville, *peninsula* J2
Nettilling, *lake* K2
Ottawa, *islands* J3
Parry, *channel* J1
Prince Charles, *island* K2
Prince of Wales, *island* H1
Queen Elizabeth, *islands* F1
Queen Maud, *gulf* G2
Smith, *sound* K1
Somerset, *island* H1
Southampton, *island* J2
Victoria, *island* G1

NOVA SCOTIA

Cities and Towns
Halifax, *capital* L4
Sydney M4
Yarmouth L4

Other Features
Cabot, *strait* M4
Cape Breton, *island* M4
Fundy, *bay* L4
Sable, *cape* L4

ONTARIO

Cities and Towns
Cornwall K4
Fort Frances H4
Geraldton J4
Hamilton K4
Kapuskasing J4
Kingston K4
Kirkland Lake K4
Kitchener J4
London J4
Moosonee J3
Nipigon J4
North Bay K4
Ottawa, *national capital* K4
Peterborough K4
Sandy Lake H3
Sarnia J4
Sault Ste. Marie J4
Sudbury J4
Thunder Bay J4
Timmins J4
Toronto, *capital* K4
Windsor J4
Winisk J3

Other Features
Akimiski, *island* J3
Albany, *river* H3
Erie, *lake* J4
Hudson, bay J3
Huron, *lake* J4
James, *bay* J3
Nipigon, *lake* J3
Ontario, *lake* K4
Ottawa, *river* K4
Superior, *lake* J4
Woods, *lake* H4

PRINCE EDWARD ISLAND

Cities and Towns
Charlottetown, *capital* L4

QUÉBEC

Cities and Towns
Baie-Comeau L4
Chibougamau K4
Chicoutimi K4
Chisasibi K3
Gagnon L3
Gaspé L4
Havre-St.-Pierre L3
Inukjuak K3
Kuujjuaq L3
Matagami K4
Montréal K4
Port-Cartier L3
Puvirnituq K2
Québec, *capital* K4
Radisson K3
Rimouski L4
Rouyn-Noranda K4
Schefferville L3
Sept-Îles L3
Shawinigan K4
Sherbrooke K4
Trois-Rivières K4
Val-d'Or K4
Waskaganish K3

Other Features
Anticosti, *island* L4
Caniapiscau, *river* L3
Feuilles, *river* K3
Hudson, *bay* J3
Hudson, *strait* K2
James, *bay* J3
Minto, *lake* K3
Mistassini, *lake* K3
Ottawa, *river* K4
St. Lawrence, *gulf* L4
St. Lawrence, *river* K4
Ungava, *bay* L3
Ungava, *peninsula* K2

SASKATCHEWAN

Cities and Towns
Estevan G4
La Loche G3
Moose Jaw G3
Prince Albert G3
Regina, *capital* G3
Saskatoon G3
Uranium City G3

Other Features
Athabasca, *lake* G3
Churchill, *river* G3
Great Plains, *plain* G3
Reindeer, *lake* G3
Saskatchewan, *river* G3
Wollaston, *lake* G3

YUKON TERRITORY

Cities and Towns
Dawson D2
Faro D2
Mayo D2
Watson Lake E2
Whitehorse, *capital* D2

Other Features
Beaufort, *sea* D1
Logan, *mt.* C2
St. Elias, *mt.* C2
Yukon, *river* D2

Canada

Capital: Ottawa
Area: 3,849,674 sq. mi.
9,973,249 sq. km.
Population: 31,006,347
Largest City: Toronto
Languages: English, French
Monetary Unit: Canadian dollar

Alberta
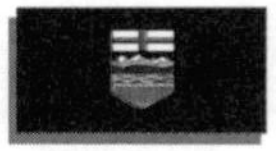

Capital: Edmonton
Area: 255,287 sq. mi.
661,265 sq. km.
Population: 2,696,826
Largest City: Edmonton

British Columbia
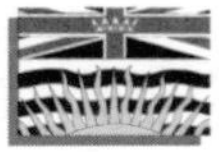

Capital: Victoria
Area: 365,947 sq. mi.
948,049 sq. km.
Population: 3,724,500
Largest City: Vancouver

Manitoba

Capital: Winnipeg
Area: 250,947 sq. mi.
650,122 sq. km.
Population: 1,113,898
Largest City: Winnipeg

New Brunswick

Capital: Fredericton
Area: 28,355 sq. mi.
73,459 sq. km.
Population: 738,133
Largest City: Saint John

Newfoundland
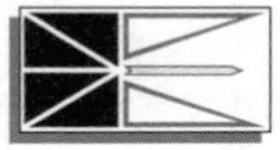

Capital: St. John's
Area: 156,949 sq. mi.
406,604 sq. km.
Population: 551,792
Largest City: St. John's

Northwest Territories

Capital: Yellowknife
Area: 520,850 sq. mi.
1,349,000 sq. km.
Population: 39,672
Largest City: Yellowknife

Nova Scotia

Capital: Halifax
Area: 21,425 sq. mi.
55,505 sq. km.
Population: 909,282
Largest City: Halifax

Nunavut

Capital: Iqaluit
Area: 800,775 sq. mi.
2,074,000 sq. km.
Population: 24,730
Largest City: Iqaluit

Ontario

Capital: Toronto
Area: 412,581 sq. mi.
1,068,863 sq. km.
Population: 10,753,573
Largest City: Toronto

Prince Edward Island

Capital: Charlottetown
Area: 2,185 sq. mi.
5,661 sq. km.
Population: 134,557
Largest City: Charlottetown

Québec

Capital: Québec
Area: 594,860 sq. mi.
1,541,088 sq. km.
Population: 7,138,795
Largest City: Montréal

Saskatchewan

Capital: Regina
Area: 251,866 sq. mi.
652,503 sq. km.
Population: 990,237
Largest City: Saskatoon

Yukon Territory

Capital: Whitehorse
Area: 186,661 sq. mi.
483,578 sq. km.
Population: 30,766
Largest City: Whitehorse

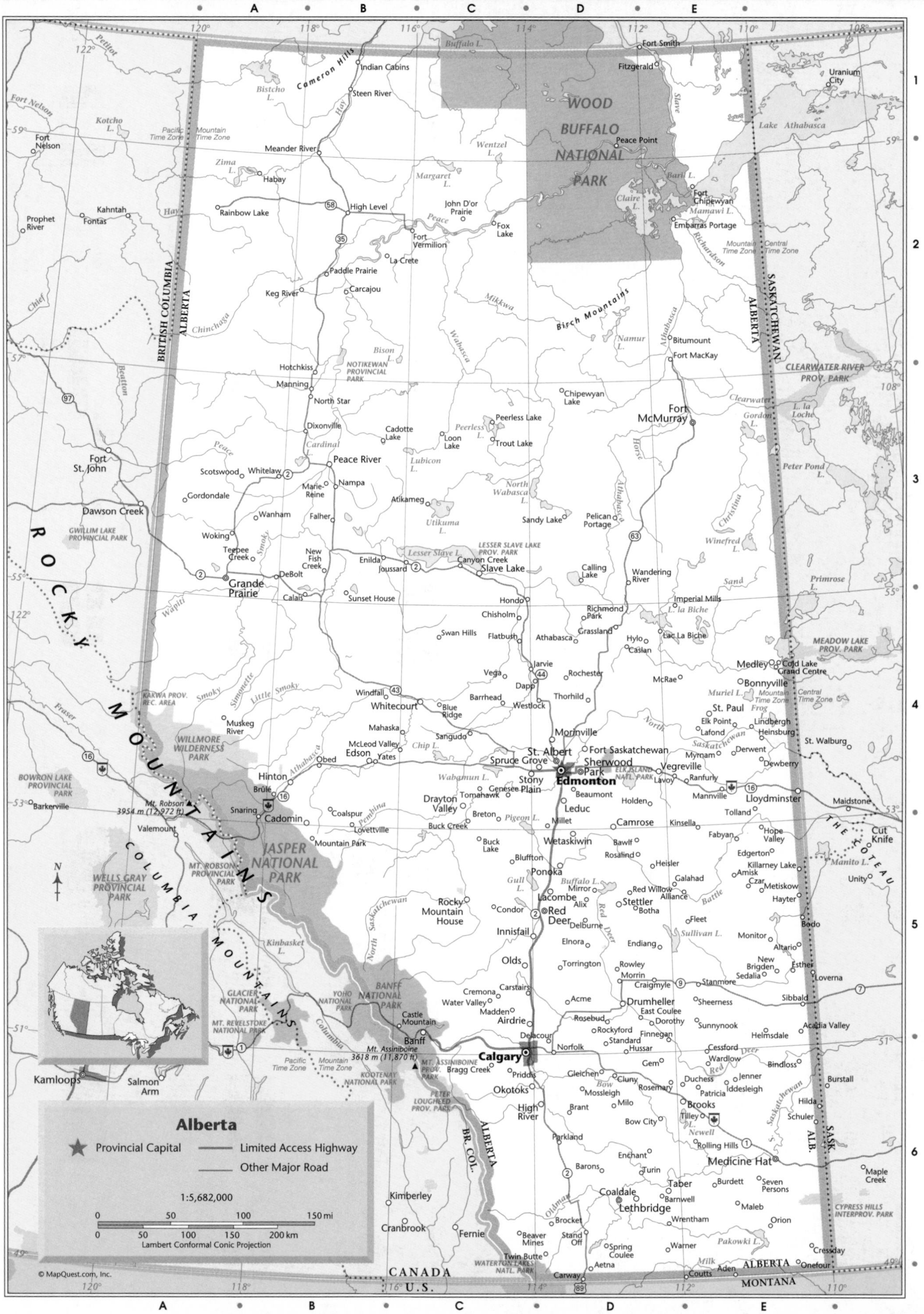

A
B
C
D
E
1
2
3
4
5
6
Alberta
Provincial Capital
Limited Access Highway
Other Major Road
1:5,682,000
0 50 100 150 mi
0 50 100 150 200 km
Lambert Conformal Conic Projection
© MapQuest.com, Inc.
WOOD BUFFALO NATIONAL PARK
ROCKY MOUNTAINS
COLUMBIA MOUNTAINS
JASPER NATIONAL PARK
BANFF NATIONAL PARK
YOHO NATIONAL PARK
GLACIER NATIONAL PARK
MT. REVELSTOKE NATIONAL PARK
KOOTENAY NATIONAL PARK
MT. ASSINIBOINE PROV. PARK
PETER LOUGHEED PROV. PARK
WATERTON LAKES NATL. PARK
WELLS GRAY PROVINCIAL PARK
BOWRON LAKE PROVINCIAL PARK
MT. ROBSON PROVINCIAL PARK
WILLMORE WILDERNESS PARK
KAKWA PROV. REC. AREA
GWILLIM LAKE PROVINCIAL PARK
NOTIKEWAN PROVINCIAL PARK
LESSER SLAVE LAKE PROV. PARK
ELK ISLAND NATL. PARK
CLEARWATER RIVER PROV. PARK
MEADOW LAKE PROV. PARK
CYPRESS HILLS INTERPROV. PARK
BRITISH COLUMBIA
ALBERTA
SASKATCHEWAN
BR. COL.
ALB.
SASK.
CANADA
U.S.
MONTANA
THE COTEAU
Cameron Hills
Birch Mountains
Pacific Time Zone
Mountain Time Zone
Central Time Zone
Mt. Robson 3954 m (12,972 ft)
Mt. Assiniboine 3618 m (11,870 ft)
Edmonton
Calgary
Red Deer
Lethbridge
Medicine Hat
Grande Prairie
Fort McMurray
Peace River
Fort Chipewyan
Fort Smith
Fitzgerald
Peace Point
Indian Cabins
Steen River
Meander River
High Level
Rainbow Lake
Habay
Fort Vermilion
La Crete
John D'or Prairie
Fox Lake
Embarras Portage
Paddle Prairie
Keg River
Carcajou
Bitumount
Fort MacKay
Hotchkiss
Manning
North Star
Dixonville
Cadotte Lake
Loon Lake
Peerless Lake
Trout Lake
Chipewyan Lake
Whitelaw
Scotswood
Gordondale
Nampa
Marie-Reine
Falher
Wanham
Woking
Teepee Creek
DeBolt
Calais
Sunset House
New Fish Creek
Enilda
Joussard
Canyon Creek
Slave Lake
Atikameg
Sandy Lake
Pelican Portage
Calling Lake
Wandering River
Hondo
Chisholm
Flatbush
Swan Hills
Athabasca
Grassland
Richmond Park
Imperial Mills
Lac La Biche
Hylo
Caslan
Vega
Jarvie
Rochester
Dapp
Westlock
Barrhead
Thorhild
McRae
Medley
Cold Lake
Grand Centre
Bonnyville
St. Paul
Elk Point
Lafond
Lindbergh
Heinsburg
St. Walburg
Windfall
Whitecourt
Blue Ridge
Mahaska
Sangudo
Muskeg River
McLeod Valley
Edson
Yates
Obed
Hinton
Brûlé
Snaring
Cadomin
Valemount
Barkerville
Coalspur
Lovettville
Mountain Park
Morinville
St. Albert
Fort Saskatchewan
Spruce Grove
Sherwood Park
Stony Plain
Genesee
Tomahawk
Drayton Valley
Breton
Buck Creek
Beaumont
Leduc
Millet
Vegreville
Lavoy
Ranfurly
Mannville
Myrnam
Derwent
Dewberry
Lloydminster
Maidstone
Tolland
Holden
Camrose
Kinsella
Fabyan
Hope Valley
Cut Knife
Wetaskiwin
Bawlf
Rosalind
Buck Lake
Bluffton
Ponoka
Heisler
Galahad
Edgerton
Killarney Lake
Amisk
Czar
Metiskow
Hayter
Unity
Rocky Mountain House
Condor
Lacombe
Mirror
Alix
Red Willow
Alliance
Stettler
Botha
Delburne
Fleet
Innisfail
Elnora
Endiang
Monitor
Altario
Bodo
Olds
Torrington
Rowley
Morrin
Craigmyle
Stanmore
New Brigden
Sedalia
Esther
Loverna
Cremona
Carstairs
Water Valley
Madden
Acme
Drumheller
East Coulee
Sheerness
Sibbald
Castle Mountain
Banff
Airdrie
Rosebud
Rockyford
Dorothy
Sunnynook
Helmsdale
Acadia Valley
Delacour
Norfolk
Standard
Finnegan
Hussar
Cessford
Wardlow
Bindloss
Bragg Creek
Priddis
Gleichen
Cluny
Gem
Duchess
Jenner
Burstall
Okotoks
Mossleigh
Rosemary
Patricia
Iddesleigh
Hilda
High River
Brant
Milo
Brooks
Bow City
Tilley
Schuler
Parkland
Rolling Hills
Barons
Enchant
Turin
Maple Creek
Taber
Burdett
Seven Persons
Coaldale
Barnwell
Maleb
Wrentham
Orion
Brocket
Stand Off
Beaver Mines
Spring Coulee
Warner
Twin Butte
Aetna
Carway
Coutts
Aden
Cressday
Onefour
Kimberley
Cranbrook
Fernie
Kamloops
Salmon Arm
Dawson Creek
Fort St. John
Fort Nelson
Prophet River
Kahntah
Fontas
Uranium City
Lake Athabasca
Bistcho L.
Zima L.
Kotcho L.
Margaret L.
Wentzel L.
Claire L.
Baril L.
Mamawi L.
Bison L.
Cardinal L.
Lubicon L.
Peerless L.
North Wabasca L.
Utikuma L.
Lesser Slave L.
Namur L.
Gordon L.
L. la Loche
Peter Pond L.
Winefred L.
Primrose L.
L. la Biche
Muriel L.
Frog L.
Chip L.
Wabamun L.
Pigeon L.
Gull L.
Buffalo L.
Sullivan L.
Manito L.
Kinbasket L.
Newell L.
Pakowki L.
Buffalo L.
Peace
Hay
Slave
Athabasca
Clearwater
Christina
Wabasca
Mikkwa
Chinchaga
Chief
Petitot
Fort Nelson
Beatton
Smoky
Wapiti
Simonette
Little Smoky
Fraser
Pembina
North Saskatchewan
Saskatchewan
Red Deer
Bow
Oldman
Milk
Columbia
Battle
Horse
Sand
Richardson
Red
Sask.
58
35
97
2
43
44
63
16
1
9
7
2
89
120°
118°
116°
114°
112°
110°
108°
122°
59°
57°
55°
53°
51°
49°

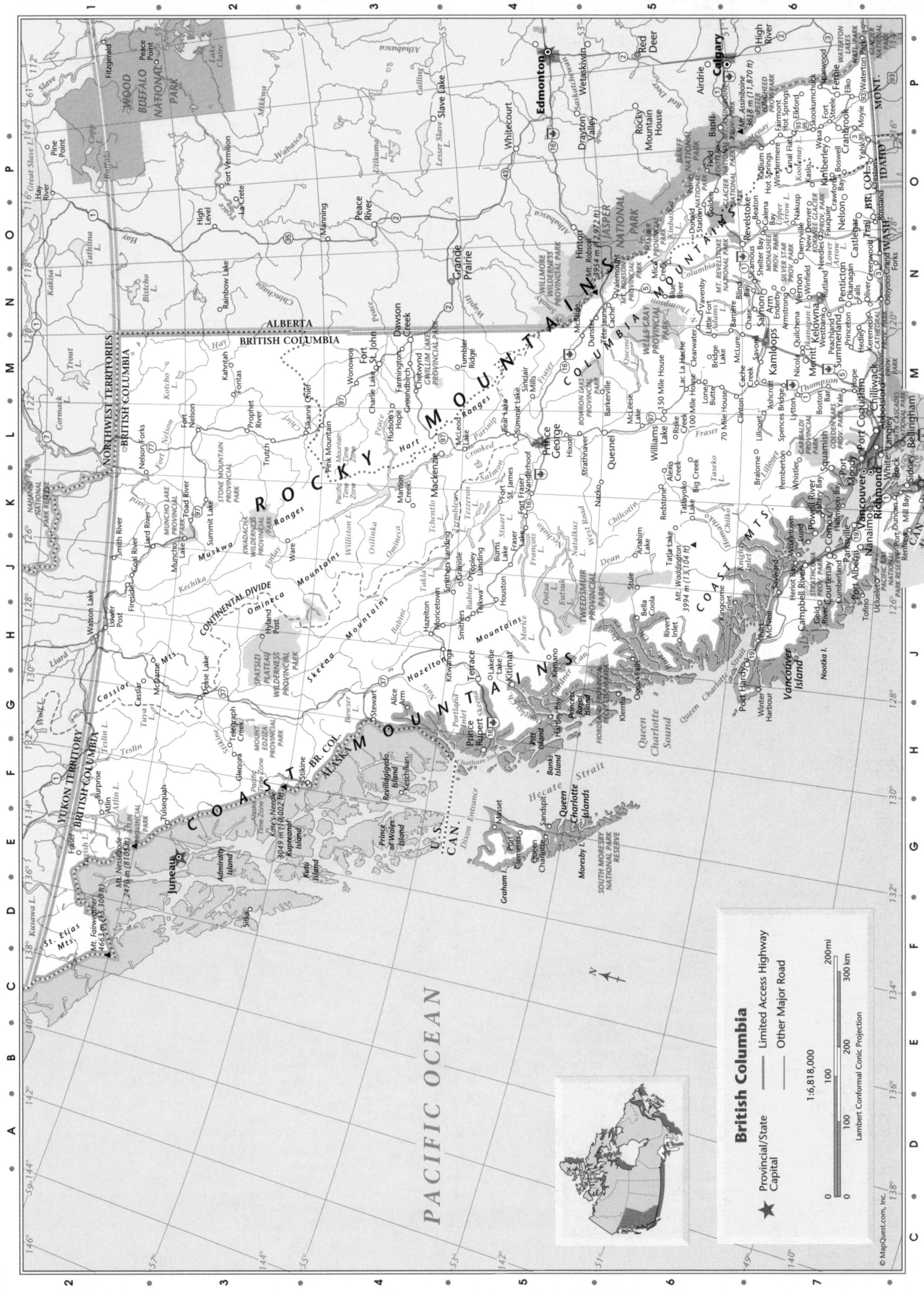
British Columbia
Provincial/State Capital
Limited Access Highway
Other Major Road
1:6,818,000
0 100 200mi
0 100 200 300 km
Lambert Conformal Conic Projection
PACIFIC OCEAN
ROCKY MOUNTAINS
COAST MOUNTAINS
COLUMBIA MOUNTAINS
COAST MTS.
ALBERTA
BRITISH COLUMBIA
YUKON TERRITORY
NORTHWEST TERRITORIES
Edmonton
Calgary
Victoria
Vancouver
Prince George
Prince Rupert
Kamloops
Kelowna
Juneau
Queen Charlotte Islands
Vancouver Island
Queen Charlotte Sound
Hecate Strait
WOOD BUFFALO NATIONAL PARK
JASPER NATIONAL PARK
BANFF NATIONAL PARK
© MapQuest.com, Inc.

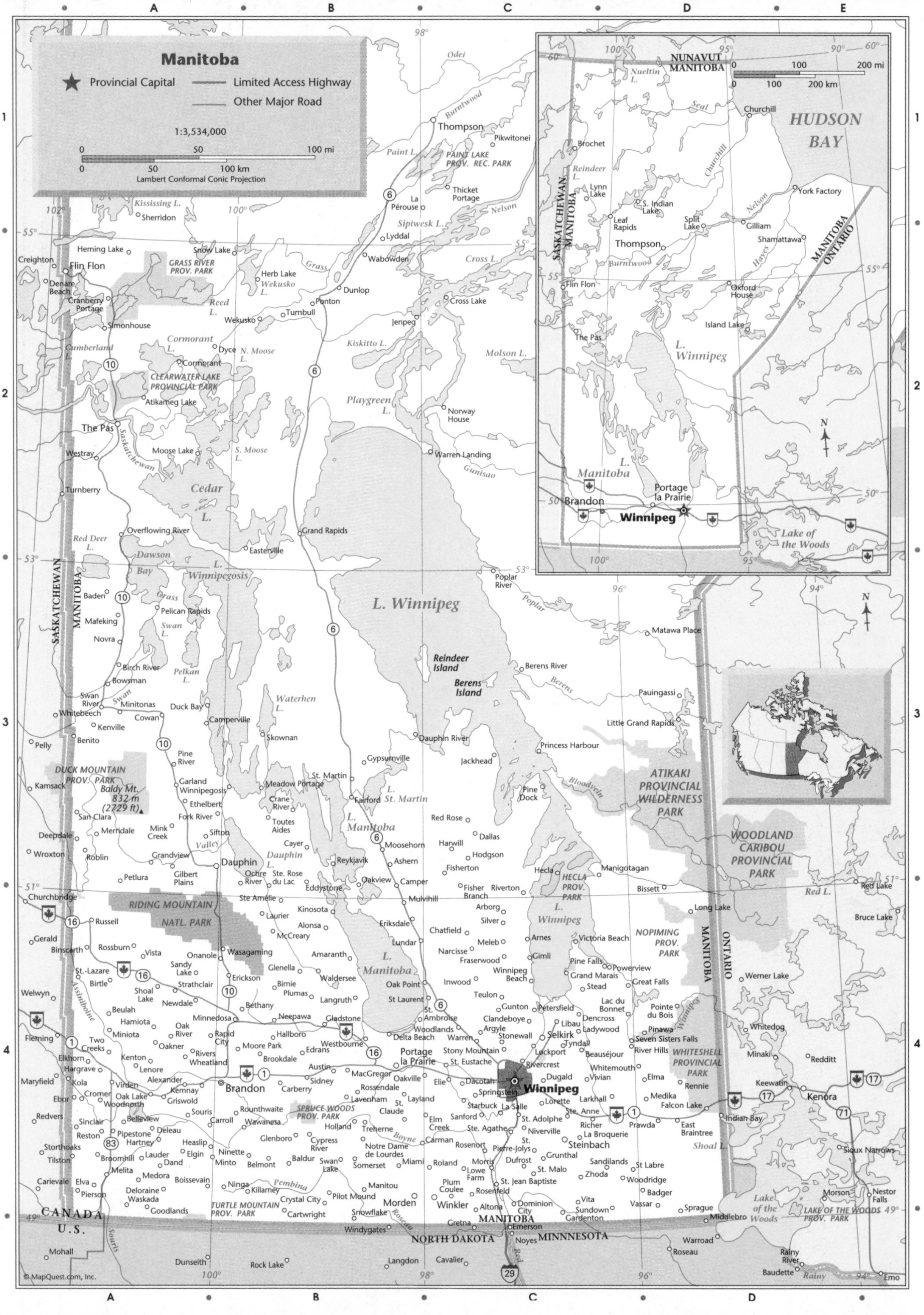
Manitoba
Provincial Capital
Limited Access Highway
Other Major Road
1:3,534,000
0
50
100 mi
0
50
100 km
Lambert Conformal Conic Projection
A
B
C
D
E
1
2
3
4
NUNAVUT
MANITOBA
HUDSON BAY
Nueltin L.
Churchill
Brochet
Reindeer L.
Lynn Lake
S. Indian Lake
Leaf Rapids
Split Lake
York Factory
Gilliam
Shamattawa
Thompson
Flin Flon
Oxford House
Island Lake
The Pas
L. Winnipeg
L. Manitoba
Brandon
Portage la Prairie
Winnipeg
Lake of the Woods
SASKATCHEWAN
MANITOBA
ONTARIO
Thompson
Pikwitonei
Paint L.
PAINT LAKE PROV. REC. PARK
La Pérouse
Thicket Portage
Nelson
Sipiwesk L.
Lyddal
Kississing L.
Sherridon
Heming Lake
Snow Lake
GRASS RIVER PROV. PARK
Wabowden
Cross L.
Creighton
Flin Flon
Denare Beach
Cranberry Portage
Herb Lake
Wekusko L.
Dunlop
Ponton
Cross Lake
Reed L.
Wekusko
Turnbull
Jenpeg
Simonhouse
Cormorant L.
Cormorant
Dyce
N. Moose L.
Kiskitto L.
Molson L.
Cumberland L.
CLEARWATER LAKE PROVINCIAL PARK
Atikameg Lake
Playgreen L.
Norway House
The Pas
Moose Lake
S. Moose L.
Warren Landing
Westray
Saskatchewan
Gunisao
Cedar L.
Turnberry
Overflowing River
Grand Rapids
Red Deer L.
Easterville
Dawson Bay
L. Winnipegosis
L. Winnipeg
Poplar River
Baden
Pelican Rapids
Mafeking
Swan L.
Novra
Matawa Place
Birch River
Pelkan L.
Reindeer Island
Berens Island
Berens River
Bowsman
Waterhen L.
Swan River
Minitonas
Duck Bay
Pauingassi
Whitebeech
Cowan
Camperville
Kenville
Skownan
Dauphin River
Little Grand Rapids
Pelly
Benito
Princess Harbour
Pine River
Gypsumville
Jackhead
DUCK MOUNTAIN PROV. PARK
Baldy Mt. 832 m (2729 ft)
Garland
Winnipegosis
Meadow Portage
St. Martin
L. St. Martin
Kamsack
Ethelbert
Crane River
Fairford
Pine Dock
ATIKAKI PROVINCIAL WILDERNESS PARK
Bloodvein
San Clara
Fork River
Toutes Aides
Red Rose
Merridale
Mink Creek
Sifton
Valley
Moosehorn
Harwill
Dallas
WOODLAND CARIBOU PROVINCIAL PARK
Deepdale
Cayer
Dauphin L.
Reykjavik
Ashern
Hodgson
Wroxton
Roblin
Grandview
Dauphin
Ochre River
Ste. Rose du Lac
Fisherton
Hecla
Manigotagan
Petlura
Gilbert Plains
Eddystone
Oakview
Camper
Fisher Branch
Riverton
HECLA PROV. PARK
Bissett
Red Lake
Red L.
Churchbridge
RIDING MOUNTAIN NATL. PARK
Ste Amélie
Mulvihill
Arborg
Long Lake
Russell
Kinosota
Laurier
Silver
Alonsa
Eriksdale
Bruce Lake
Gerald
McCreary
Chatfield
Arnes
Victoria Beach
NOPIMING PROV. PARK
Binscarth
Rossburn
Vista
Onanole
Wasagaming
Amaranth
Lundar
Meleb
Gimli
Narcisse
Fraserwood
Sandy Lake
Glenella
Winnipeg Beach
Pine Falls
Powerview
St.-Lazare
Birtle
Strathclair
Erickson
Waldersee
Oak Point
Inwood
Grand Marais
Stead
Great Falls
Werner Lake
Welwyn
Shoal Lake
Birnie
Plumas
Langruth
St Laurent
Teulon
Lac du Bonnet
Beulah
Newdale
Bethany
Gunton
Petersfield
Pointe du Bois
Minnedosa
Neepawa
Gladstone
St. Ambroise
Clandeboye
Dencross
Hamiota
Oak River
Rapid City
Hallboro
Woodlands
Argyle
Libau
Ladywood
Pinawa
Whitedog
Fleming
Miniota
Delta Beach
Stonewall
Selkirk
Seven Sisters Falls
Elkhorn
Two Creeks
Oakner
Moore Park
Westbourne
Warren
Tyndall
River Hills
Minaki
Rivers
Edrans
Portage la Prairie
Stony Mountain
Lockport
Beauséjour
WHITESHELL PROVINCIAL PARK
Reddit
Kenton
Wheatland
Brookdale
St. Eustache
Rivercrest
Whitemouth
Hargrave
Lenore
Austin
MacGregor
Oakville
Elie
Dacotah
Dugald
Vivian
Elma
Rennie
Keewatin
Kenora
Maryfield
Kola
Virden
Alexander
Brandon
Sidney
Rossendale
Winnipeg
Ebor
Cromer
Oak Lake
Woodnorth
Griswold
Carberry
Lavenham
Layland
Starbuck
Springstein
Lorette
Larkhall
Medika
Falcon Lake
Souris
Rounthwaite
SPRUCE WOODS PROV. PARK
St. Claude
La Salle
Ste. Anne
Redvers
Sinclair
Belleview
Carroll
Wawanesa
Elm Creek
Sanford
St. Adolphe
Prawda
Indian Bay
Reston
Pipestone
Deleau
Holland
Treherne
Ste. Agathe
Niverville
Richer
La Broquerie
East Braintree
Storthoaks
Hartney
Heaslip
Glenboro
Cypress River
Boyne
Carman
St.
Shoal L.
Tilston
Broomhill
Lauder
Elgin
Ninette
Baldur
Notre Dame de Lourdes
Rosenort
Pierre-Jolys
Steinbach
Grunthal
Sioux Narrows
Melita
Dand
Minto
Belmont
Swan Lake
Somerset
Miami
Roland
Morris
Dufrost
Sandilands
St Labre
Medora
Boissevain
Lowe Farm
St. Malo
Zhoda
Carievale
Elva
Pierson
Deloraine
Ninga
Killarney
Pembina
Manitou
Plum Coulee
St. Jean Baptiste
Woodridge
Badger
Morson
Nestor Falls
Waskada
Goodlands
TURTLE MOUNTAIN PROV. PARK
Crystal City
Cartwright
Pilot Mound
Snowflake
Morden
Winkler
Rosenfeld
Altona
Dominion City
Vita
Sundown
Vassar
Sprague
Gardenton
Lake of the Woods
LAKE OF THE WOODS PROV. PARK
CANADA
U.S.
Windygates
Gretna
MANITOBA
Emerson
Middlebro
NORTH DAKOTA
Noyes
MINNESOTA
Warroad
Roseau
Mohall
Souris
Dunseith
Rock Lake
Langdon
Cavalier
Red
Rainy River
Baudette
Rainy
Emo
© MapQuest.com, Inc.

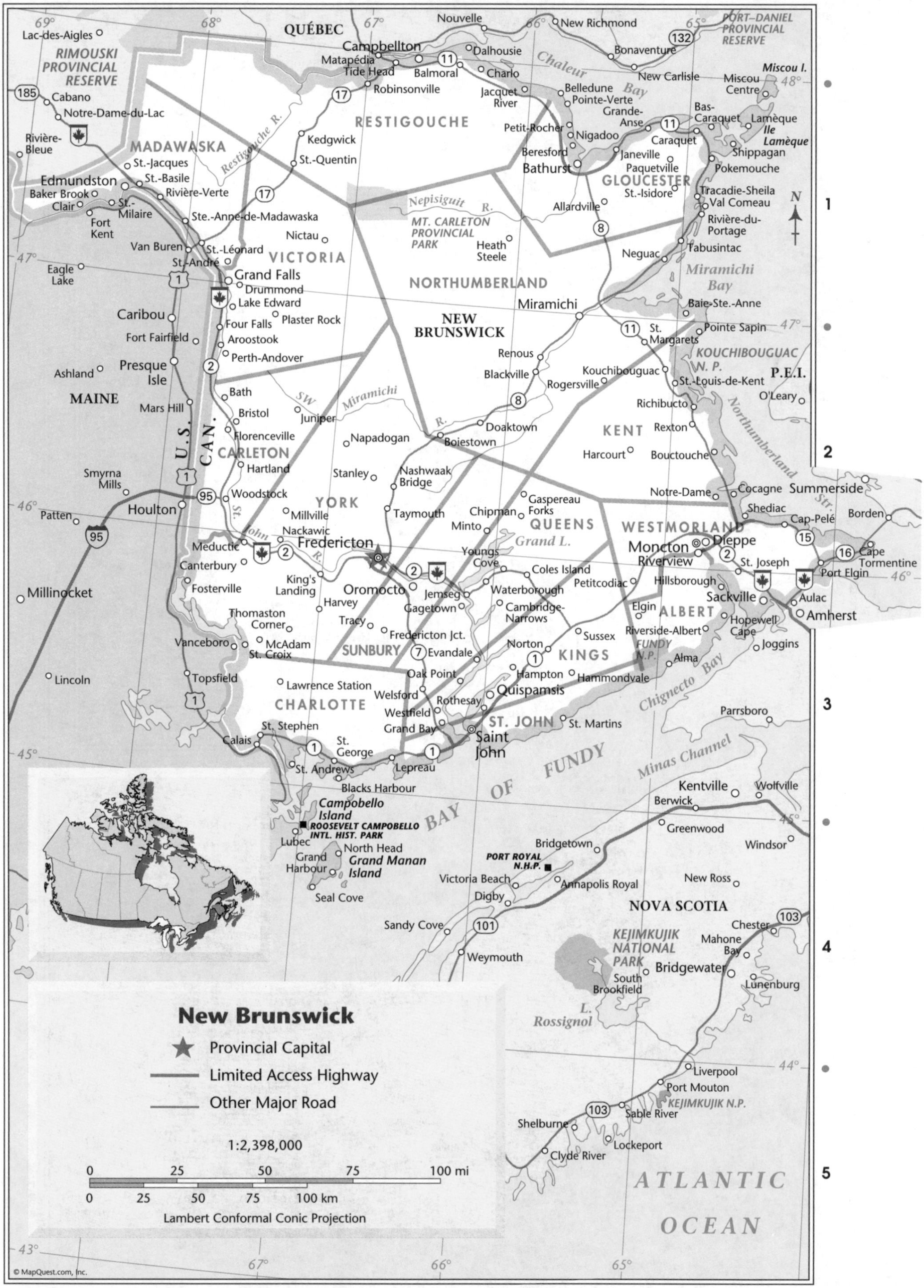
QUÉBEC
RIMOUSKI PROVINCIAL RESERVE
PORT-DANIEL PROVINCIAL RESERVE
Chaleur Bay
RESTIGOUCHE
MADAWASKA
VICTORIA
GLOUCESTER
NORTHUMBERLAND
NEW BRUNSWICK
MT. CARLETON PROVINCIAL PARK
Miramichi Bay
KOUCHIBOUGUAC N. P.
P.E.I.
MAINE
U.S.
CAN.
CARLETON
YORK
KENT
QUEENS
WESTMORLAND
ALBERT
SUNBURY
KINGS
CHARLOTTE
ST. JOHN
FUNDY N.P.
Chignecto Bay
BAY OF FUNDY
Minas Channel
Campobello Island
ROOSEVELT CAMPOBELLO INTL. HIST. PARK
Grand Manan Island
PORT ROYAL N.H.P.
NOVA SCOTIA
KEJIMKUJIK NATIONAL PARK
KEJIMKUJIK N.P.
L. Rossignol
ATLANTIC OCEAN
Northumberland Str.
Fredericton
Saint John
Moncton
Miramichi
Bathurst
Campbellton
Edmundston
Grand Falls
Houlton
Caribou
Presque Isle
Summerside
Amherst
Kentville
Bridgewater
New Brunswick
Provincial Capital
Limited Access Highway
Other Major Road
1:2,398,000
0 25 50 75 100 mi
0 25 50 75 100 km
Lambert Conformal Conic Projection
© MapQuest.com, Inc.

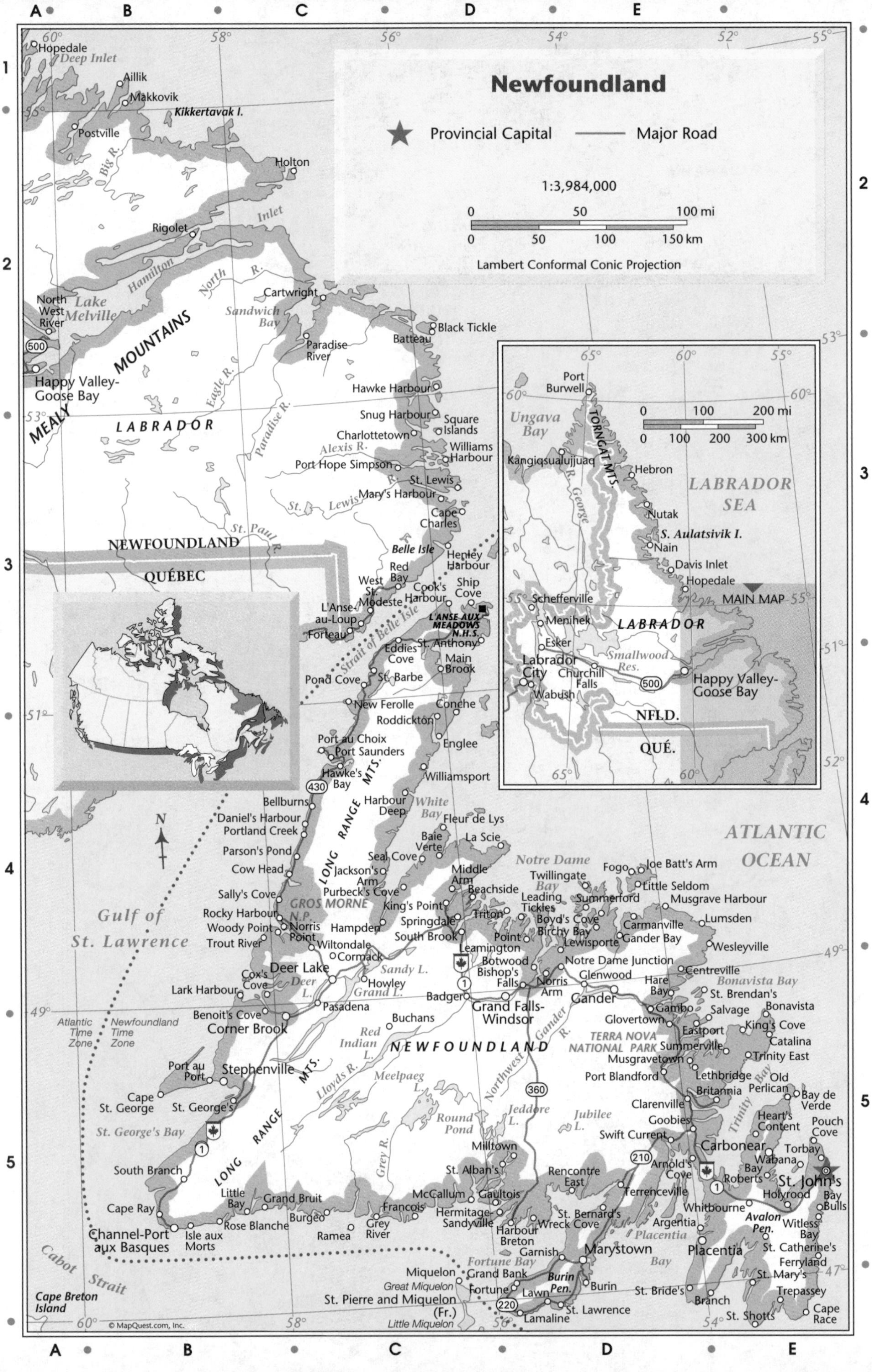
Newfoundland
Provincial Capital
Major Road
1:3,984,000
0 50 100 mi
0 50 100 150 km
Lambert Conformal Conic Projection
Hopedale
Deep Inlet
Aillik
Makkovik
Kikkertavak I.
Postville
Big R.
Holton
Rigolet
Inlet
Hamilton
North R.
Lake Melville
North West River
Cartwright
Sandwich Bay
MEALY MOUNTAINS
Happy Valley-Goose Bay
Paradise River
Black Tickle
Batteau
Eagle R.
Paradise R.
Hawke Harbour
Snug Harbour
Square Islands
LABRADOR
Charlottetown
Alexis R.
Williams Harbour
Port Hope Simpson
St. Lewis
St. Lewis R.
Mary's Harbour
Cape Charles
St. Paul R.
NEWFOUNDLAND
QUÉBEC
Belle Isle
Henley Harbour
Red Bay
West St. Modeste
Cook's Harbour
Ship Cove
L'Anse-au-Loup
L'ANSE AUX MEADOWS N.H.S.
Forteau
Strait of Belle Isle
Eddies Cove
St. Anthony
Main Brook
Pond Cove
St. Barbe
New Ferolle
Conche
Roddickton
Port au Choix
Port Saunders
Englee
Hawke's Bay
Williamsport
Bellburns
Harbour Deep
White Bay
Daniel's Harbour
Fleur de Lys
Portland Creek
Baie Verte
La Scie
Parson's Pond
Seal Cove
Cow Head
Jackson's Arm
Middle Arm
Notre Dame Bay
Fogo
Joe Batt's Arm
Twillingate
Little Seldom
Sally's Cove
Purbeck's Cove
Beachside
Musgrave Harbour
GROS MORNE N.P.
Rocky Harbour
King's Point
Leading Tickles
Summerford
Lumsden
Woody Point
Norris Point
Hampden
Springdale
Triton
Boyd's Cove
Carmanville
Trout River
South Brook
Point Leamington
Birchy Bay
Lewisporte
Gander Bay
Wesleyville
Wiltondale
Cormack
Botwood
Notre Dame Junction
Centreville
Deer Lake
Sandy L.
Bishop's Falls
Glenwood
Hare Bay
Bonavista Bay
Cox's Cove
Deer L.
Howley
Norris Arm
Lark Harbour
Grand L.
Badger
Gander
St. Brendan's
Pasadena
Grand Falls-Windsor
Gambo
Bonavista
Benoit's Cove
Buchans
Glovertown
Salvage
King's Cove
Corner Brook
Gander R.
Eastport
Catalina
Atlantic Time Zone
Newfoundland Time Zone
Red Indian L.
NEWFOUNDLAND
TERRA NOVA NATIONAL PARK
Summerville
Trinity East
Musgravetown
Port au Port
Stephenville
Lloyds R.
Meelpaeg L.
Northwest
Port Blandford
Lethbridge
Old Perlican
Britannia
Trinity Bay
Cape St. George
St. George's
Jeddore L.
Jubilee L.
Clarenville
Bay de Verde
Round Pond
Goobies
Heart's Content
Pouch Cove
St. George's Bay
LONG RANGE MTS.
Swift Current
Carbonear
Torbay
Milltown
Wabana
Grey R.
Arnold's Cove
Bay Roberts
St. John's
South Branch
St. Alban's
Rencontre East
Holyrood
Bay Bulls
Little Bay
Grand Bruit
McCallum
Gaultois
Terrenceville
Whitbourne
Cape Ray
Francois
Hermitage-Sandyville
St. Bernard's
Argentia
Avalon Pen.
Witless Bay
Rose Blanche
Burgeo
Grey River
Wreck Cove
Placentia
Channel-Port aux Basques
Isle aux Morts
Ramea
Harbour Breton
Garnish
Marystown
Placentia Bay
St. Catherine's
Ferryland
Fortune Bay
Cabot Strait
Miquelon
Grand Bank
Burin Pen.
St. Mary's
Great Miquelon
Fortune
Burin
St. Bride's
Trepassey
Cape Breton Island
St. Pierre and Miquelon (Fr.)
Lawn
St. Lawrence
Branch
Lamaline
Cape Race
St. Shotts
Little Miquelon
© MapQuest.com, Inc.
Gulf of St. Lawrence
ATLANTIC OCEAN
Port Burwell
Ungava Bay
TORNGAT MTS.
0 100 200 mi
0 100 200 300 km
Kangiqsualujjuaq
Hebron
George R.
LABRADOR SEA
Nutak
S. Aulatsivik I.
Nain
Davis Inlet
Hopedale
MAIN MAP
Schefferville
Menihek
LABRADOR
Esker
Smallwood Res.
Labrador City
Churchill Falls
Wabush
Happy Valley-Goose Bay
NFLD.
QUÉ.
N
A B C D E
1 2 3 4 5
60° 58° 56° 54° 52° 55° 53° 51° 49° 47° 65°

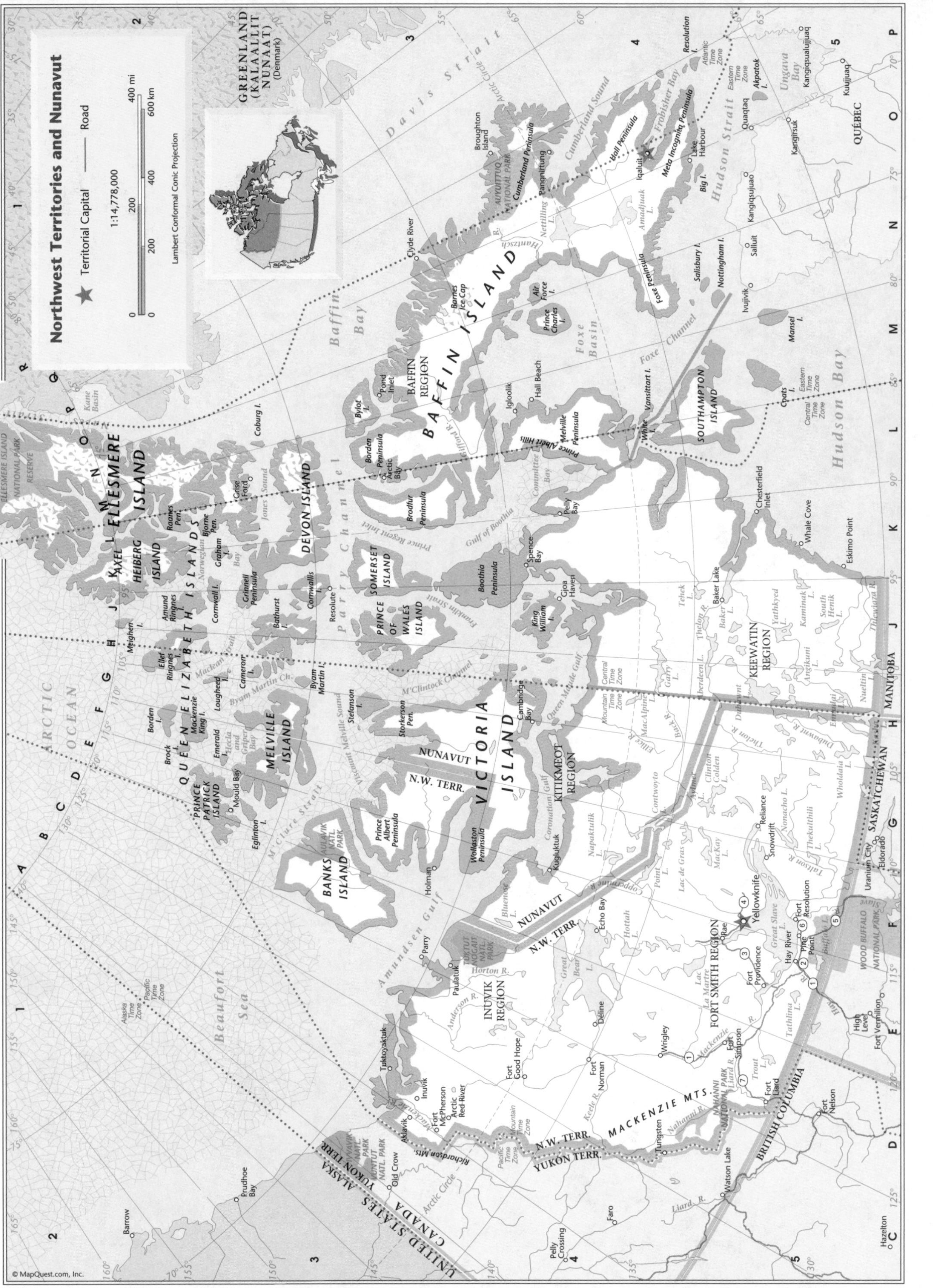
Northwest Territories and Nunavut
Territorial Capital
Road
1:14,778,000
Lambert Conformal Conic Projection
GREENLAND (KALAALLIT NUNAAT) (Denmark)
ARCTIC OCEAN
Beaufort Sea
Baffin Bay
Davis Strait
Hudson Bay
Hudson Strait
Foxe Basin
Foxe Channel
Ungava Bay
Amundsen Gulf
Parry Channel
ELLESMERE ISLAND
AXEL HEIBERG ISLAND
QUEEN ELIZABETH ISLANDS
DEVON ISLAND
MELVILLE ISLAND
PRINCE PATRICK ISLAND
BANKS ISLAND
VICTORIA ISLAND
PRINCE OF WALES ISLAND
SOMERSET ISLAND
BAFFIN ISLAND
SOUTHAMPTON ISLAND
BAFFIN REGION
KITIKMEOT REGION
KEEWATIN REGION
INUVIK REGION
FORT SMITH REGION
NUNAVUT
N.W. TERR.
YUKON TERR.
MACKENZIE MTS.
BRITISH COLUMBIA
ALBERTA
SASKATCHEWAN
MANITOBA
QUÉBEC
UNITED STATES
CANADA
ALASKA
Iqaluit
Yellowknife
Alert
Resolute
Inuvik
Tuktoyaktuk
Aklavik
Fort McPherson
Fort Good Hope
Fort Norman
Wrigley
Fort Simpson
Fort Liard
Fort Providence
Hay River
Pine Point
Fort Resolution
Rae
Holman
Paulatuk
Kugluktuk
Cambridge Bay
Gjoa Haven
Spence Bay
Pelly Bay
Igloolik
Hall Beach
Pond Inlet
Arctic Bay
Clyde River
Broughton Island
Pangnirtung
Lake Harbour
Baker Lake
Chesterfield Inlet
Whale Cove
Eskimo Point
Coral Harbour
Great Bear L.
Great Slave L.
WOOD BUFFALO NATIONAL PARK
NAHANNI NATIONAL PARK
AUYUITTUQ NATIONAL PARK
AULAVIK NATL. PARK
TUKTUT NOGAIT NATL. PARK
ELLESMERE ISLAND NATIONAL PARK RESERVE
Arctic Circle
Central Time Zone
Mountain Time Zone
Eastern Time Zone
Atlantic Time Zone
Pacific Time Zone
© MapQuest.com, Inc.

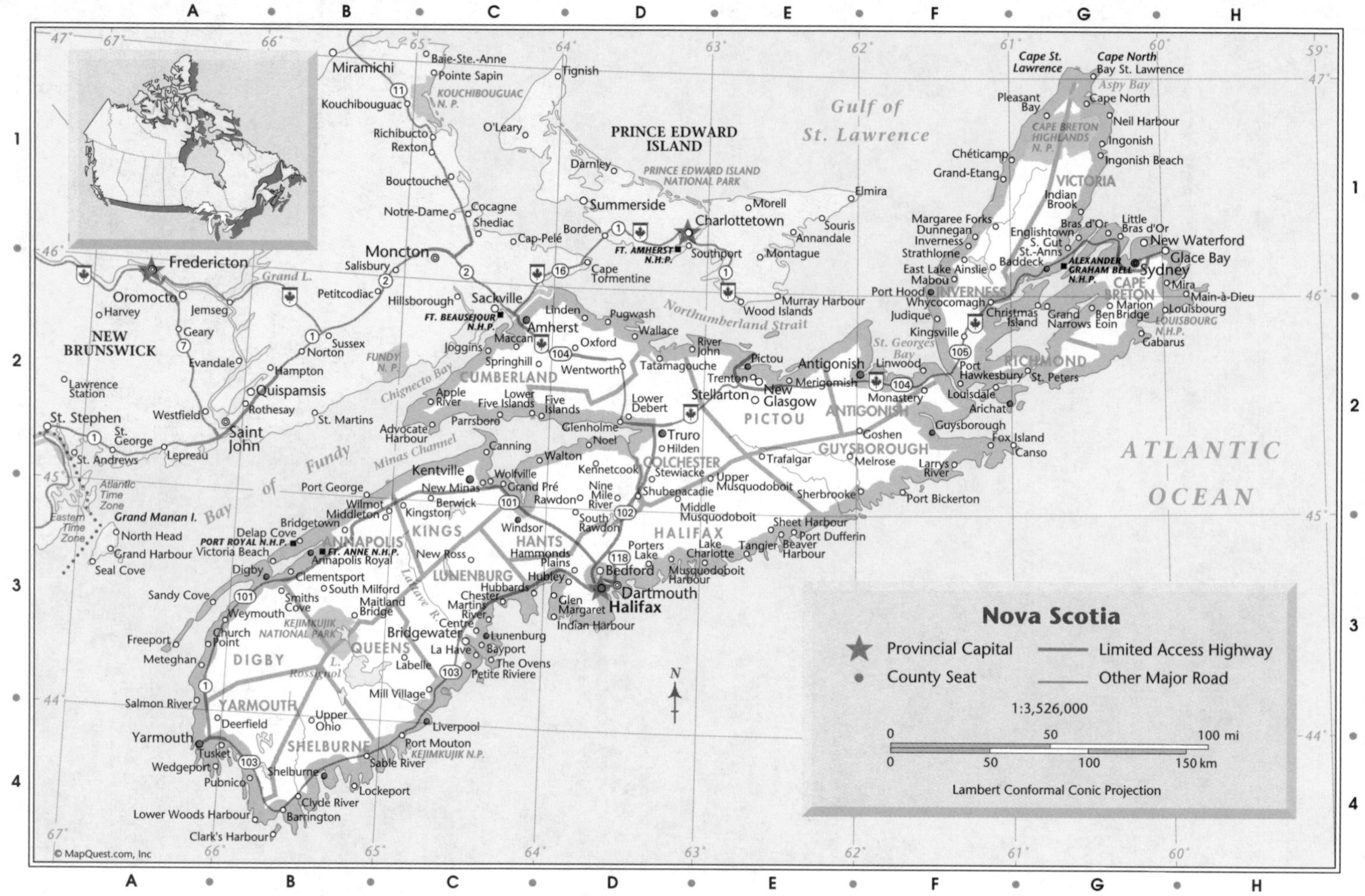
Nova Scotia
Provincial Capital
County Seat
Limited Access Highway
Other Major Road
1:3,526,000
0 50 100 mi
0 50 100 150 km
Lambert Conformal Conic Projection
© MapQuest.com, Inc
Gulf of St. Lawrence
ATLANTIC OCEAN
PRINCE EDWARD ISLAND
NEW BRUNSWICK
Bay of Fundy
Minas Channel
Chignecto Bay
Northumberland Strait
Atlantic Time Zone
Eastern Time Zone
CUMBERLAND
COLCHESTER
PICTOU
ANTIGONISH
GUYSBOROUGH
HALIFAX
HANTS
KINGS
ANNAPOLIS
LUNENBURG
QUEENS
DIGBY
YARMOUTH
SHELBURNE
INVERNESS
VICTORIA
CAPE BRETON
RICHMOND
CAPE BRETON HIGHLANDS N. P.
KEJIMKUJIK NATIONAL PARK
KEJIMKUJIK N.P.
FUNDY N. P.
KOUCHIBOUGUAC N. P.
PRINCE EDWARD ISLAND NATIONAL PARK
FT. BEAUSEJOUR N.H.P.
FT. AMHERST N.H.P.
PORT ROYAL N.H.P.
FT. ANNE N.H.P.
ALEXANDER GRAHAM BELL N.H.P.
LOUISBOURG N.H.P.
Fredericton
Charlottetown
Halifax
Dartmouth
Bedford
Moncton
Saint John
Sydney
Truro
Amherst
Kentville
Yarmouth
Summerside
Antigonish
New Glasgow
Pictou
Stellarton
Bridgewater
Liverpool
Digby
Windsor
Wolfville
Lunenburg
Shelburne
Glace Bay
New Waterford
Louisbourg
Port Hawkesbury
Guysborough
Canso
Cheticamp
Baddeck
Ingonish
Cape North
Cape St. Lawrence
Bay St. Lawrence
Miramichi
Tignish
Grand Manan I.
Grand L.
L. Rossignol
La Have R.

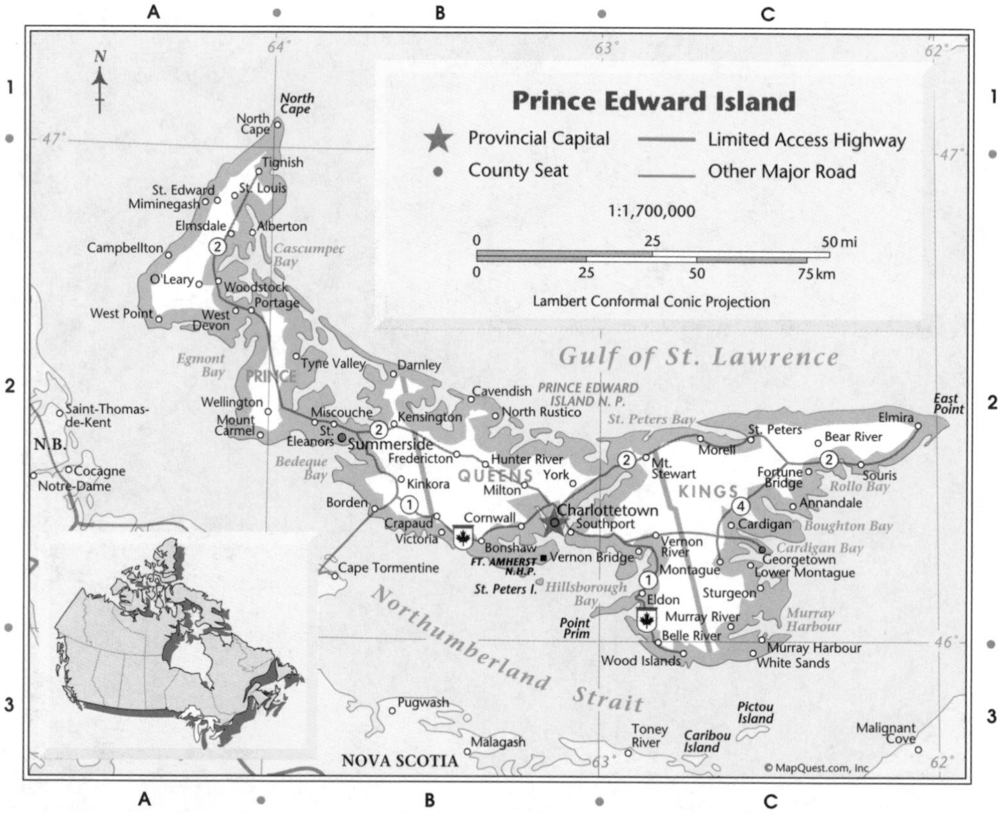
Prince Edward Island
Provincial Capital
County Seat
Limited Access Highway
Other Major Road
1:1,700,000
0 25 50 mi
0 25 50 75 km
Lambert Conformal Conic Projection
© MapQuest.com, Inc
Gulf of St. Lawrence
Northumberland Strait
PRINCE
QUEENS
KINGS
PRINCE EDWARD ISLAND N. P.
FT. AMHERST N.H.P.
N.B.
NOVA SCOTIA
North Cape
Tignish
St. Louis
St. Edward
Miminegash
Elmsdale
Alberton
Campbellton
Cascumpec Bay
O'Leary
Woodstock
West Point
West Devon
Portage
Egmont Bay
Tyne Valley
Darnley
Wellington
Mount Carmel
Miscouche
St. Eleanors
Summerside
Kensington
Cavendish
North Rustico
Bedeque Bay
Fredericton
Kinkora
Hunter River
York
Milton
Borden
Crapaud
Victoria
Cornwall
Bonshaw
Charlottetown
Southport
Vernon Bridge
Vernon River
Montague
Mt. Stewart
Morell
St. Peters
St. Peters Bay
Bear River
Elmira
East Point
Souris
Fortune Bridge
Rollo Bay
Annandale
Cardigan
Boughton Bay
Cardigan Bay
Georgetown
Lower Montague
Sturgeon
Murray River
Murray Harbour
White Sands
Belle River
Wood Islands
Eldon
Point Prim
Hillsborough Bay
St. Peters I.
Cape Tormentine
Saint-Thomas-de-Kent
Cocagne
Notre-Dame
Pugwash
Malagash
Toney River
Caribou Island
Pictou Island
Malignant Cove

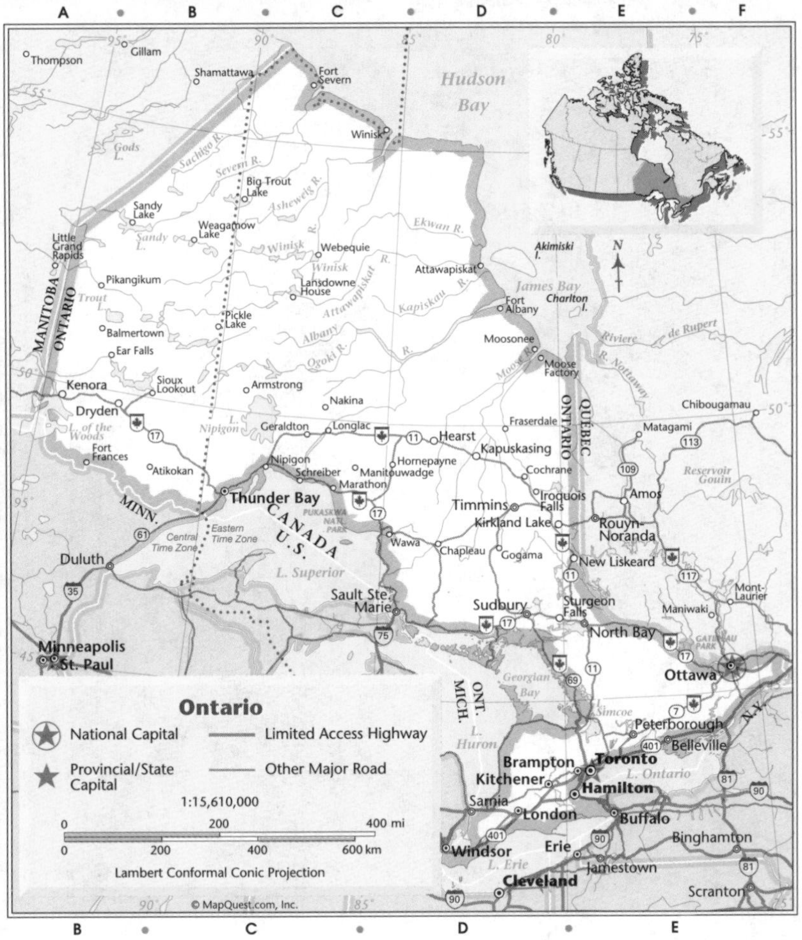
Ontario
National Capital
Provincial/State Capital
Limited Access Highway
Other Major Road
1:15,610,000
0 200 400 mi
0 200 400 600 km
Lambert Conformal Conic Projection
© MapQuest.com, Inc.
Hudson Bay
James Bay
Akimiski I.
Charlton I.
L. Superior
L. Huron
L. Ontario
L. Erie
Georgian Bay
L. Simcoe
L. Nipigon
L. of the Woods
MANITOBA
ONTARIO
QUÉBEC
MINN.
MICH.
ONT.
N.Y.
CANADA
U.S.
Central Time Zone
Eastern Time Zone
Thompson
Gillam
Shamattawa
Fort Severn
Winisk
Big Trout Lake
Sandy Lake
Weagamow Lake
Webequie
Little Grand Rapids
Pikangikum
Lansdowne House
Attawapiskat
Fort Albany
Pickle Lake
Balmertown
Ear Falls
Moosonee
Moose Factory
Sioux Lookout
Armstrong
Kenora
Dryden
Nakina
Fraserdale
Chibougamau
Geraldton
Longlac
Hearst
Matagami
Fort Frances
Atikokan
Nipigon
Schreiber
Manitouwadge
Hornepayne
Kapuskasing
Cochrane
Marathon
Thunder Bay
Iroquois Falls
Amos
Timmins
Kirkland Lake
Rouyn-Noranda
Wawa
Chapleau
Gogama
New Liskeard
Duluth
Sault Ste. Marie
Sudbury
Sturgeon Falls
Maniwaki
Mont-Laurier
North Bay
Minneapolis
St. Paul
Ottawa
Peterborough
Belleville
Brampton
Toronto
Kitchener
Hamilton
Sarnia
London
Buffalo
Binghamton
Windsor
Erie
Jamestown
Cleveland
Scranton

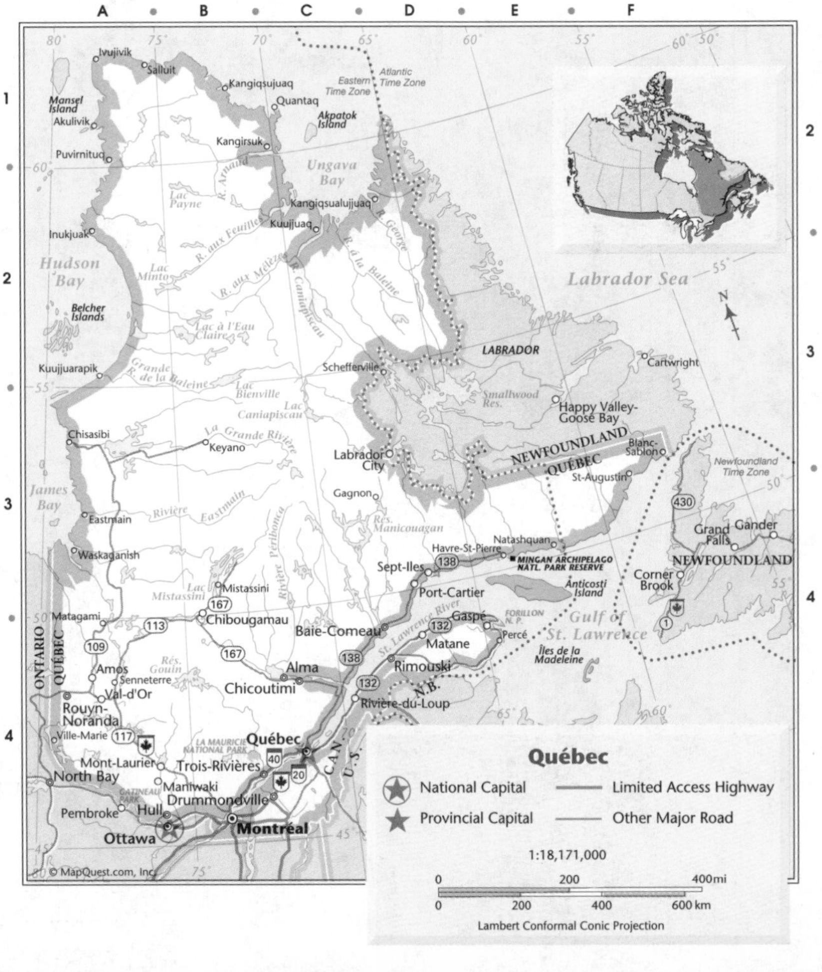
Québec
National Capital
Provincial Capital
Limited Access Highway
Other Major Road
1:18,171,000
0 200 400 mi
0 200 400 600 km
Lambert Conformal Conic Projection
© MapQuest.com, Inc.
Hudson Bay
James Bay
Ungava Bay
Labrador Sea
Gulf of St. Lawrence
Mansel Island
Akpatok Island
Belcher Islands
Anticosti Island
Îles de la Madeleine
LABRADOR
NEWFOUNDLAND
QUÉBEC
ONTARIO
N.B.
Atlantic Time Zone
Eastern Time Zone
Newfoundland Time Zone
Ivujivik
Salluit
Kangiqsujuaq
Quantaq
Akulivik
Kangirsuk
Puvirnituq
Kangiqsualujjuaq
Kuujjuaq
Inukjuak
Lac Payne
Lac Minto
Lac à l'Eau Claire
Kuujjuarapik
Schefferville
Cartwright
Lac Bienville
Lac Caniapiscau
Smallwood Res.
Happy Valley-Goose Bay
Chisasibi
Keyano
Labrador City
Blanc-Sablon
St-Augustin
Gagnon
Eastmain
Waskaganish
Natashquan
Havre-St-Pierre
MINGAN ARCHIPELAGO NATL. PARK RESERVE
Sept-Îles
Port-Cartier
Grand Falls
Gander
Corner Brook
Mistassini
Matagami
Chibougamau
Baie-Comeau
Gaspé
Percé
Matane
Rimouski
Amos
Senneterre
Val-d'Or
Alma
Chicoutimi
Rouyn-Noranda
Rivière-du-Loup
Ville-Marie
Québec
Mont-Laurier
Trois-Rivières
North Bay
Maniwaki
Drummondville
Pembroke
Hull
Ottawa
Montréal

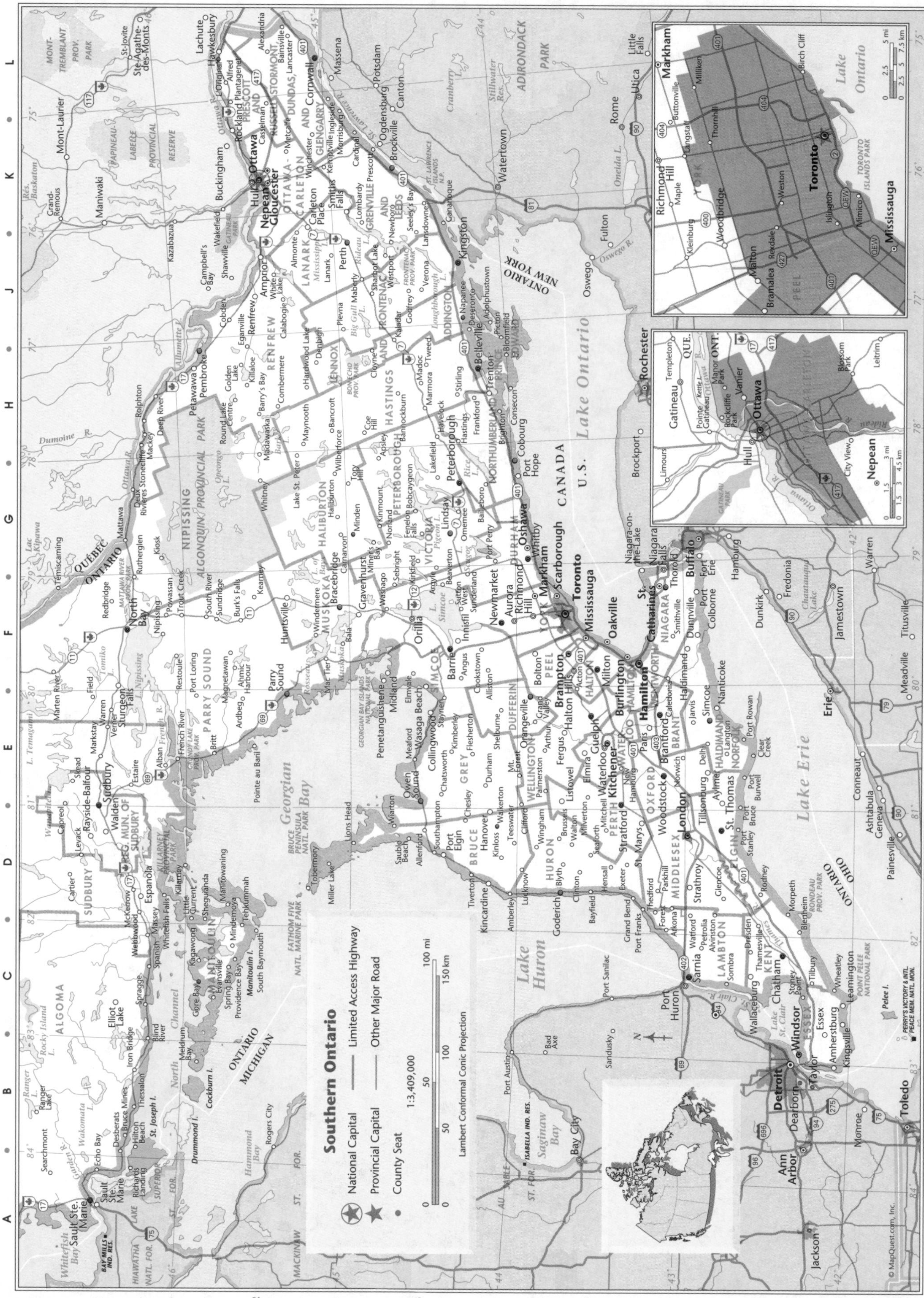
Southern Ontario
National Capital
Provincial Capital
County Seat
Limited Access Highway
Other Major Road
1:3,409,000
0 50 100 mi
0 50 100 150 km
Lambert Conformal Conic Projection
Lake Huron
Georgian Bay
Lake Ontario
Lake Erie
ONTARIO
MICHIGAN
QUÉBEC
NEW YORK
OHIO
CANADA
U.S.
ALGONQUIN PROVINCIAL PARK
Toronto
Ottawa
Nepean
Markham
Mississauga
Richmond Hill
Hull
© MapQuest.com, Inc.

Southern Québec

★ National Capital
★ Provincial Capital

— Limited Access Highway
— Other Major Road

1:3,580,000

Lambert Conformal Conic Projection

0   50   100   150 km
0   50   100 mi

Montréal (inset)
Repentigny, Terrebonne, Bois-des-Filion, Ste-Thérèse, Lorraine, Blainville, Deux-Montagnes, St-Eustache, Pierrefonds, Île Bizard, Pointe-Claire, Dollard, Ste-Anne, Laval, Île Jésus, St-Laurent, St-Léonard, Montréal-Nord, Anjou, Boucherville, Longueuil, St-Lambert, Brossard, La Prairie, Candiac, Delson, St-Constant, Kahnawake, Châteauguay, Lachine, La Salle, Verdun, Mont-Royal, Hampstead, Westmount, Île Perrot

Québec (inset)
Beauport, Île d'Orléans, Charlesbourg, Vanier, Québec, Ste-Foy, L'Ancienne-Lorette, Loretteville, St-Émile, Cap-Rouge, Sillery, Lévis, St-Romuald, Charny, Bernières, St-Rédempteur, St-Jean-Chrysostome

Gaspé Peninsula, Forillon Nat'l Park, Cloridorme, Grande-Vallée, L'Anse-à-Valleau, Rivière-au-Renard, Cap-aux-Os, Gaspé, Douglastown, Barachois, Grande-Rivière, Chandler, Percé, Murdochville, Mont-St-Pierre, La Martre, Marsoui, Ste-Anne-des-Monts, Cap-Chat, Les Méchins, Matane, Baie-des-Sables, Sayabec, Amqui, Causapscal, Carleton, New Carlisle, New Richmond, Nouvelle, Pointe-à-la-Croix, Campbellton, Matapédia, Escuminac, Dalhousie

St-Lawrence River, Gros-Morne, Les Islets-Caribou, Pointe-des-Monts, Godbout, Franquelin, Baie-Comeau, Pointe-Lebel, Ragueneau, Betsiamites, Colombier, Forestville, Labrieville, Sault-au-Mouton, Les Escoumins

Chibougamau, Mistassini, Dolbeau, Normandin, La Doré, St-Félicien, Roberval, Chambord, Lac-Bouchette, St-Henri-de-Taillon, Ste-Monique, Alma, St-Bruno, Métabetchouan, Péribonka, Ste-Rose-du-Nord, St-Félix-d'Otis, La Baie, Chicoutimi, Jonquière, St-Ambroise, St-Ludger-de-Milot, St-David-de-Falardeau, St-Fulgence

Laurentides Provincial Reserve, Réserve Faunique des Laurentides, La Malbaie, Clermont, Baie-St-Paul, Les Éboulements, St-Siméon, Baie-Ste-Catherine, Tadoussac, Rivière-du-Loup, Cacouna, L'Isle-Verte, Trois-Pistoles, Le Bic, Rimouski, St-Fabien, St-Cyprien, St-Hubert

Montréal, Laval, Ottawa, Hull, Gatineau, Aylmer, Buckingham, Maniwaki, Mont-Laurier, Val-des-Bois, Notre-Dame-du-Laus, Ste-Anne-du-Lac, Ferme-Neuve, Lac-Saguay, Ste-Véronique, L'Annonciation, Mont-Tremblant, Mont-Laurier, St-Donat, St-Côme, Joliette, St-Jérôme, Ste-Agathe-des-Monts, St-Sauveur, Lachute, Ste-Scholastique, Mirabel, Vaudreuil, Salaberry-de-Valleyfield, Châteauguay, Cornwall, Massena, Malone

Trois-Rivières, Cap-de-la-Madeleine, Shawinigan, Grand-Mère, La Tuque, Rivière-aux-Rats, Rivière-Matawin, Parent, St-Maurice Provincial Reserve, Mastigouche Provincial Reserve, Louiseville, Sorel, Tracy, Nicolet, Bécancour, Drummondville, St-Hyacinthe, Granby, Waterloo, Cowansville, Bedford, St-Jean-sur-Richelieu, Contrecœur, Beloeil, Sherbrooke, Magog, Coaticook, Lac-Mégantic, Thetford Mines, Victoriaville, Plessisville, Princeville, Asbestos, Windsor, Richmond, East Angus, Black Lake, Scotstown, Woburn

Lévis, Montmagny, St-Jean-Port-Joli, La Pocatière, St-Pascal, Kamouraska, Rivière-Bleue, Cabano, Notre-Dame-du-Lac, Dégelis, Edmundston

St-Georges, Beauceville, St-Joseph-de-Beauce, Ste-Marie, St-Philémon, St-Raphaël, Lac-Etchemin, St-Camille-de-Lellis, St-Fabien-de-Panet, St-Martin, St-Prosper, Jackman, Lac Mégantic

Maine, N.H., Vt., N.Y., Ont., Qué., N.B., U.S., Canada, Atlantic Time Zone, Eastern Time Zone

Skowhegan, Bangor, Old Town, Belfast, Waterville, Rumford, Bethel

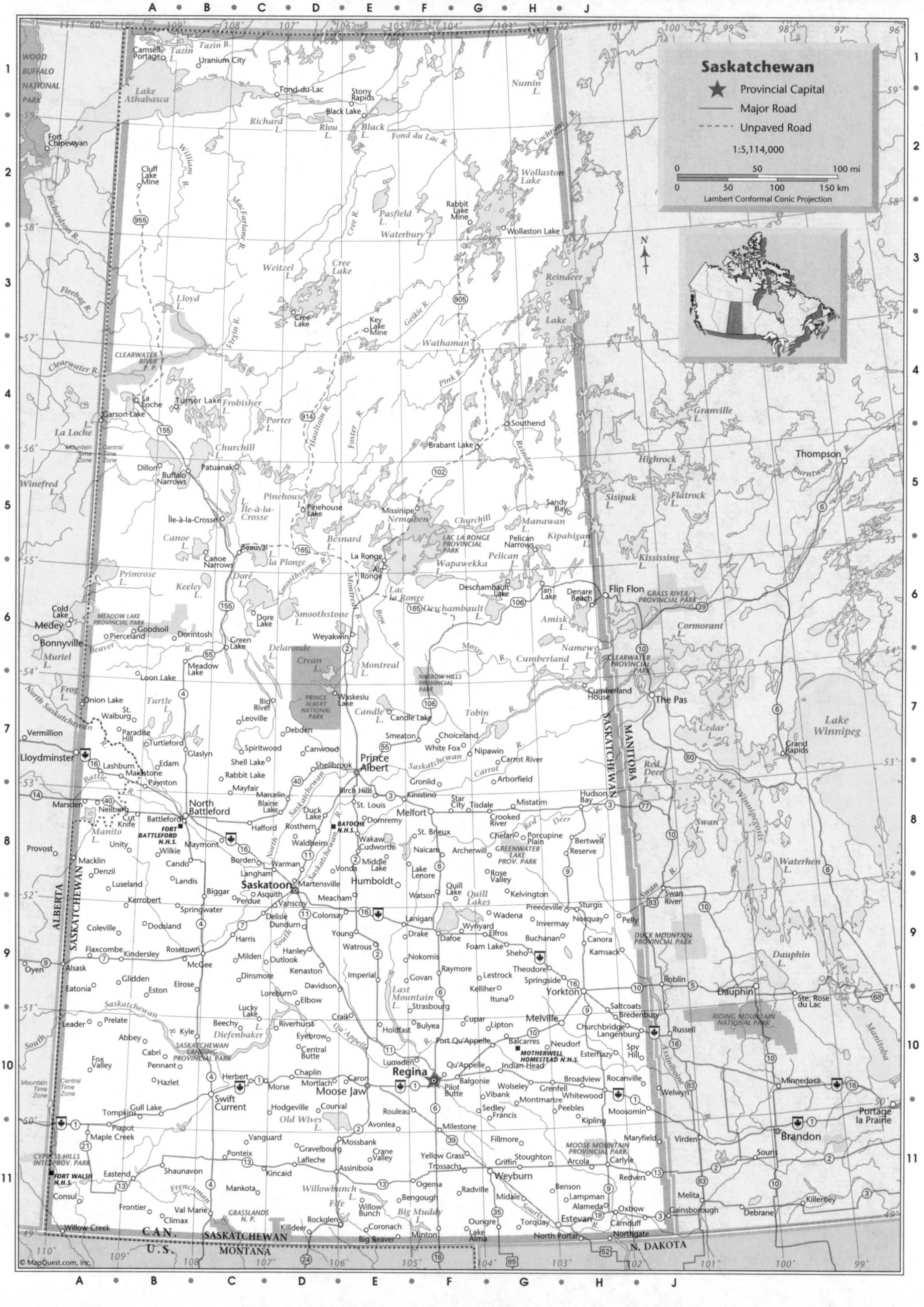
Saskatchewan
Provincial Capital
Major Road
Unpaved Road
1:5,114,000
0 50 100 mi
0 50 100 150 km
Lambert Conformal Conic Projection
N
A B C D E F G H J
1 2 3 4 5 6 7 8 9 10 11
WOOD BUFFALO NATIONAL PARK
Camsell Portage
Tazin L.
Tazin R.
Uranium City
Lake Athabasca
Fond-du-Lac
Stony Rapids
Black Lake
Richard L.
Riou L.
Black L.
Fond du Lac R.
Fort Chipewyan
Cochrane R.
Numin L.
Cluff Lake Mine
William R.
Richardson R.
MacFarlane R.
Cree R.
Wollaston Lake
Rabbit Lake Mine
Pasfield L.
Waterbury L.
Weitzel L.
Cree Lake
Reindeer Lake
Firebag R.
Lloyd L.
Virgin R.
Key Lake Mine
Geikie R.
Wathaman L.
CLEARWATER RIVER P. P.
Clearwater R.
Pink R.
La Loche
Turnor Lake
Frobisher L.
Garson Lake
Porter L.
Haultain R.
Foster R.
Southend
La Loche L.
Churchill L.
Brabant Lake
Granville L.
Thompson
Burntwood R.
Highrock L.
Dillon
Buffalo Narrows
Patuanak
Winefred L.
Pinehouse L.
Pinehouse Lake
Missinipe
Nemeiben L.
Churchill R.
Sandy Bay
Sisipuk L.
Flatrock L.
Île-à-la-Crosse
Canoe L.
Canoe Narrows
Beauval
la Plonge
Besnard L.
LAC LA RONGE PROVINCIAL PARK
Manawan L.
Pelican Narrows
Kipahigan L.
La Ronge
Air Ronge
Wapawekka L.
Pelican L.
Kississing L.
Primrose L.
Keeley L.
Doré L.
Smoothstone R.
Montreal R.
Lac la Ronge
Deschambault Lake
Jan Lake
Denare Beach
Flin Flon
GRASS RIVER PROVINCIAL PARK
Cold Lake
MEADOW LAKE PROVINCIAL PARK
Dore Lake
Smoothstone L.
Deschambault L.
Amisk L.
Cormorant L.
Medley
Goodsoil
Pierceland
Dorintosh
Green Lake
Weyakwin
Bonnyville
Muriel L.
Beaver R.
Meadow Lake
Delaronde L.
Crean L.
Montreal L.
NARROW HILLS PROVINCIAL PARK
Cumberland L.
Namew L.
CLEARWATER PROVINCIAL PARK
Frog L.
Loon Lake
North Saskatchewan R.
Onion Lake
Turtle L.
St. Walburg
Big River
PRINCE ALBERT NATIONAL PARK
Waskesiu Lake
Candle L.
Candle Lake
Tobin L.
Cumberland House
The Pas
Lake Winnipeg
Vermillion
Paradise Hill
Leoville
Debden
Smeaton
Choiceland
Cedar L.
Turtleford
Spiritwood
Canwood
White Fox
Nipawin
Grand Rapids
Lloydminster
Lashburn
Maidstone
Edam
Glaslyn
Shell Lake
Shellbrook
Prince Albert
Carrot River
Red Deer L.
Paynton
Rabbit Lake
Saskatchewan R.
Gronlid
Arborfield
Lake Winnipegosis
Mayfair
Marcelin
Birch Hills
Kinistino
Star City
Tisdale
Mistatim
Hudson Bay
Marsden
Neilburg
Cut Knife
Battleford
North Battleford
Blaine Lake
Duck Lake
St. Louis
Melfort
Crooked River
Manito L.
FORT BATTLEFORD N.H.S.
Hafford
Rosthern
BATOCHE N.H.S.
Domremy
St. Brieux
Chelan
Porcupine Plain
Bertwell
Swan L.
Provost
Unity
Maymont
Waldheim
Wakaw
Cudworth
Naicam
Archerwill
GREENWATER LAKE PROV. PARK
Reserve
Wilkie
Macklin
Denzil
Borden
Warman
Vonda
Middle Lake
Waterhen L.
Cando
Luseland
Landis
Saskatoon
Martensville
Humboldt
Lake Lenore
Rose Valley
Quill Lake
Quill Lakes
Kelvington
Swan River
Kerrobert
Biggar
Asquith
Perdue
Meacham
Watson
Sturgis
Preeceville
Vanscoy
Springwater
Delisle
Colonsay
Lanigan
Wadena
Invermay
Norquay
Pelly
Coleville
Dodsland
Dundurn
Harris
Young
Drake
Dafoe
Wynyard
Elfros
Buchanan
Canora
DUCK MOUNTAIN PROVINCIAL PARK
Flaxcombe
Kindersley
Rosetown
Hanley
Watrous
Foam Lake
Sheho
Kamsack
Dauphin L.
Oyen
Alsask
McGee
Milden
Outlook
Nokomis
Theodore
Kenaston
Raymore
Lestrock
Springside
Roblin
Eatonia
Glidden
Dinsmore
Imperial
Govan
Yorkton
Dauphin
Eston
Elrose
Davidson
Kelliher
Ituna
Loreburn
Elbow
Last Mountain L.
Saltcoats
Ste. Rose du Lac
Lucky Lake
Strasbourg
Bredenbury
Leader
Prelate
Beechy
Riverhurst
Craik
Holdfast
Bulyea
Cupar
Lipton
Melville
Churchbridge
Langenburg
Russell
RIDING MOUNTAIN NATIONAL PARK
Abbey
Kyle
Diefenbaker L.
Eyebrow
Qu'Appelle
Fort Qu'Appelle
Balcarres
Neudorf
SASKATCHEWAN LANDING PROVINCIAL PARK
Cabri
Central Butte
MOTHERWELL HOMESTEAD N.H.S.
Esterhazy
Spy Hill
Fox Valley
Pennant
Lumsden
Indian Head
Hazlet
Herbert
Chaplin
Regina
Balgonie
Broadview
Rocanville
Minnedosa
Morse
Mortlach
Caron
Moose Jaw
Pilot Butte
Vibank
Wolseley
Grenfell
Whitewood
Welwyn
Gull Lake
Swift Current
Tompkins
Hodgeville
Courval
Rouleau
Sedley
Francis
Montmartre
Peebles
Moosomin
Portage la Prairie
Piapot
Maple Creek
Old Wives L.
Avonlea
Milestone
Kipling
Brandon
Vanguard
Mossbank
Fillmore
Maryfield
Virden
CYPRESS HILLS INTERPROV. PARK
Ponteix
Gravelbourg
Crane Valley
Yellow Grass
Stoughton
MOOSE MOUNTAIN PROVINCIAL PARK
Carlyle
Souris
Lafleche
Assiniboia
Trossachs
Griffin
Arcola
Shaunavon
Eastend
Kincaid
FORT WALSH N.H.S.
Redvers
Weyburn
Mankota
Willowbunch
Ogema
Radville
Benson
Consul
Frenchman R.
Fife L.
Bengough
Midale
Lampman
Alameda
Melita
Killarney
Frontier
Val Marie
Climax
GRASSLANDS N. P.
Willow Bunch
Big Muddy L.
Oxbow
Carnduff
Gainsborough
Debrane
Willow Creek
Killdeer
Rockglen
Coronach
Oungre
Torquay
Estevan
Lake Alma
Big Beaver
Minton
North Portal
Northgate
CAN.
U.S.
SASKATCHEWAN
MONTANA
N. DAKOTA
ALBERTA
MANITOBA
Mountain Time Zone
Central Time Zone
© MapQuest.com, Inc.

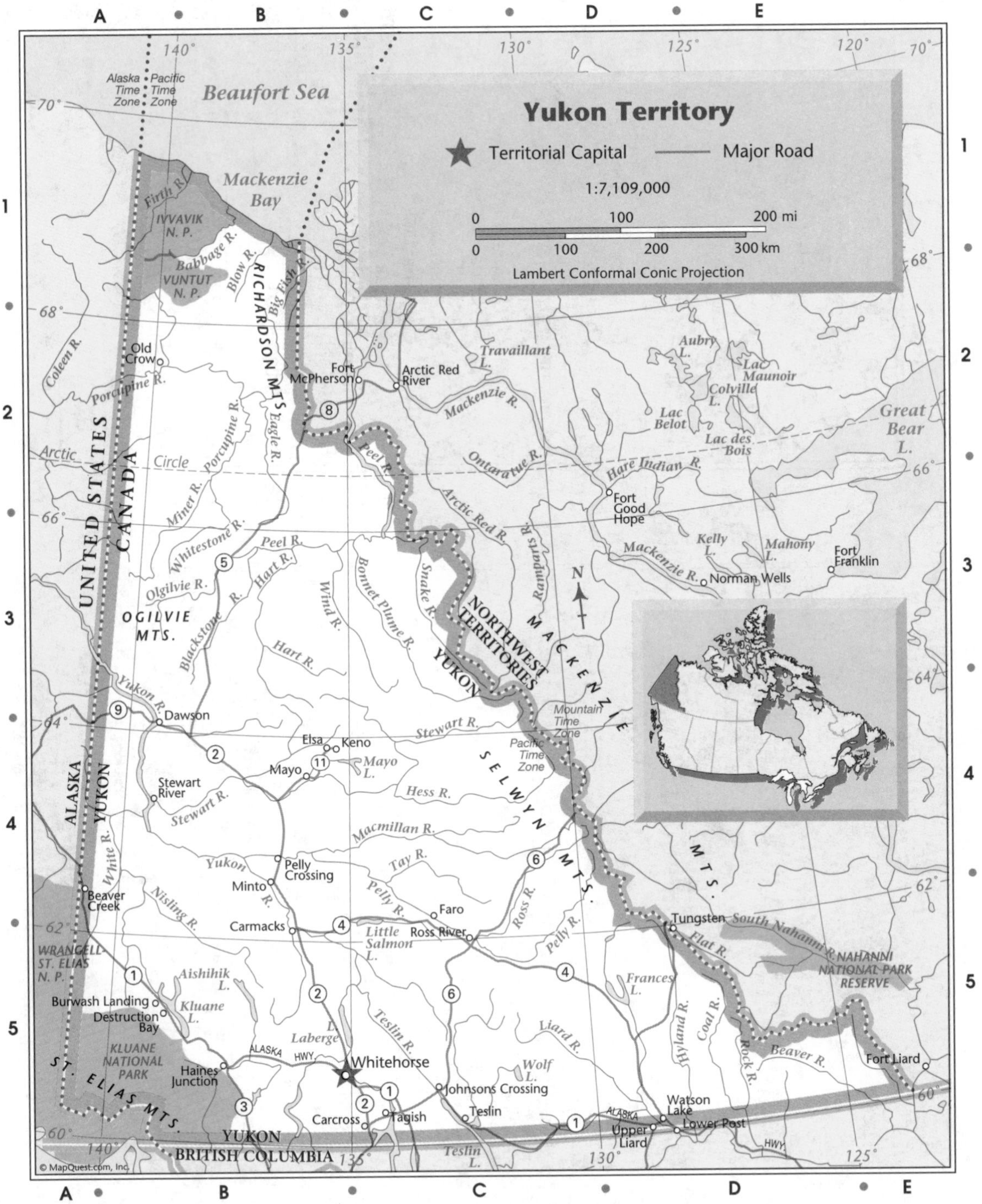
Yukon Territory
Territorial Capital
Major Road
1:7,109,000
0 100 200 mi
0 100 200 300 km
Lambert Conformal Conic Projection
Beaufort Sea
Mackenzie Bay
Alaska Time Zone
Pacific Time Zone
Mountain Time Zone
IVVAVIK N. P.
VUNTUT N. P.
RICHARDSON MTS.
OGILVIE MTS.
SELWYN MTS.
MACKENZIE MTS.
ST. ELIAS MTS.
UNITED STATES
CANADA
ALASKA
YUKON
NORTHWEST TERRITORIES
BRITISH COLUMBIA
KLUANE NATIONAL PARK
WRANGELL-ST. ELIAS N. P.
NAHANNI NATIONAL PARK RESERVE
Old Crow
Fort McPherson
Arctic Red River
Fort Good Hope
Norman Wells
Fort Franklin
Dawson
Elsa
Keno
Mayo
Stewart River
Pelly Crossing
Minto
Beaver Creek
Carmacks
Faro
Ross River
Burwash Landing
Destruction Bay
Haines Junction
Whitehorse
Carcross
Tagish
Johnsons Crossing
Teslin
Watson Lake
Upper Liard
Lower Post
Tungsten
Fort Liard
Great Bear L.
Aubry L.
Lac Maunoir
Colville L.
Lac Belot
Lac des Bois
Travaillant L.
Kelly L.
Mahony L.
Mayo L.
Little Salmon L.
Aishihik L.
Kluane L.
L. Laberge
Wolf L.
Frances L.
Teslin L.
Firth R.
Babbage R.
Blow R.
Big Fish R.
Coleen R.
Porcupine R.
Eagle R.
Peel R.
Miner R.
Whitestone R.
Ogilvie R.
Blackstone R.
Hart R.
Wind R.
Bonnet Plume R.
Snake R.
Yukon R.
Stewart R.
White R.
Nisling R.
Hess R.
Macmillan R.
Tay R.
Pelly R.
Ross R.
Teslin R.
Liard R.
Hyland R.
Coal R.
Rock R.
Beaver R.
Flat R.
South Nahanni R.
Mackenzie R.
Arctic Red R.
Ontaratue R.
Hare Indian R.
Ramparts R.
Arctic Circle
ALASKA HWY.
© MapQuest.com, Inc.

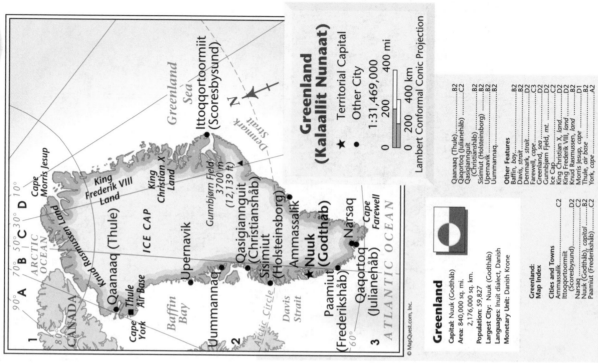

Greenland (Kalaallit Nunaat)

★ Territorial Capital
● Other City

1:31,469,000

0   200   400 km
0   200   400 mi

Lambert Conformal Conic Projection

Greenland
Sea

Denmark Strait

N

Cape Morris Jesup

King Frederik VIII Land

King Christian X Land

Gunnbjørn Field 3700 m (12,139 ft) ▲

ICE CAP

Ittoqqortoormiit (Scoresbysund)

Knud Rasmussen Land

Qaanaaq (Thule)

Upernavik

Uummannaq

Qasigiannguit (Christianshåb)

Sisimiut (Holsteinsborg)

Ammassalik

Nuuk (Godthåb) ★

Narsaq

Cape Farewell

Paamiut (Frederikshåb)

Qaqortoq (Julianehåb)

ARCTIC OCEAN

Thule Air Base ■

Cape York

Baffin Bay

Davis Strait

Arctic Circle

ATLANTIC OCEAN

CANADA

90° 80° 70° 60° 50° 40° 30° 20° 10° 0°

A   B   C   D

1   2   3

© MapQuest.com, Inc.

Greenland

Capital: Nuuk (Godthåb)
Area: 840,000 sq. mi.
2,176,000 sq. km.
Population: 59,827
Largest City: Nuuk (Godthåb)
Languages: Inuit dialect, Danish
Monetary Unit: Danish Krone

Greenland: Map Index

7   6   5   4   3

180°   160°   140°   120°   100°   80°   60°   40°   20°

Sea of Okhotsk

Sakhalin

Petropavlovsk

KAMCHATKA PEN.

Kamchatskiy

Klyuchevskaya Sopka 4750 m (15,584 ft) ▲

Yakutsk

VERKHOYANSK RANGE

S I B E R I A

RUSSIA

A S I A

Lena

Nordvik

Tiksi

Laptev Sea

New Siberian Is.

Severnaya Zemlya

TAYMYR PEN.

Norilsk

Yenisey

Dikson

Kara Sea

Novaya Zemlya

Ob

URAL MTS.

Pechora

Naryan-Mar

Northern Dvina

Arkhangelsk

Onega

Lake Onega

Lake Ladoga

Volga

Dnieper

Moscow ⊛

E U R O P E

UKRAINE

BELARUS

POLAND

LITH.

LATVIA

ESTONIA

Baltic Sea

FINLAND

St. Petersburg ⊛

Helsinki ⊛

Stockholm ⊛

SWEDEN

NORWAY

Oslo ⊛

Copenhagen ⊛

DEN.

North Sea

LAPLAND

KOLA PEN.

Murmansk

Barents Sea

Franz Josef Land

Svalbard (Nor.)

North Cape

Hammerfest

Tromsø

Norwegian Sea

KOLYMA RANGE

Kolyma

Arctic Circle

East Siberian Sea

International Date Line

Bering Sea

St. Lawrence I.

Nunivak I.

KODIAK I.

Bering Strait

Wrangel I.

Chukchi Sea

CHUKCHI RANGE

Nome

Pt. Barrow

Barrow

Beaufort Sea

ALASKA (U.S.)

Mt. McKinley 6194 m (20,320 ft) ▲

Anchorage

Juneau

Fairbanks

Yukon

BROOKS RANGE

COAST MTS.

MACKENZIE MTS.

Mackenzie

Great Bear Lake

Inuvik

Banks I.

Victoria Island

Resolute

Queen Elizabeth Islands

Ellesmere Island

CANADA

N O R T H   A M E R I C A

Baffin Island

Baffin Bay

Cape Farewell

ATLANTIC OCEAN

North Magnetic Pole

North Pole

SEA ICE

A R C T I C   O C E A N

Cape Morris Jesup

Alert

Qaanaaq (Thule)

GREENLAND (KALAALLIT-NUNAAT) (Denmark)

Nuuk (Godthåb)

Denmark Strait

Greenland Sea

Arctic Circle

ICELAND

Reykjavik ⊛

GREAT BRITAIN

Edinburgh

IRE.

Prime Meridian

8   9   10   11   12   13   14   15   16   17   18

Arctic Regions

⊛ National Capital
● Other City

1:43,520,000

0   400   800 km
0   400   800 mi

Polar Equal Area Projection

© MapQuest.com, Inc.

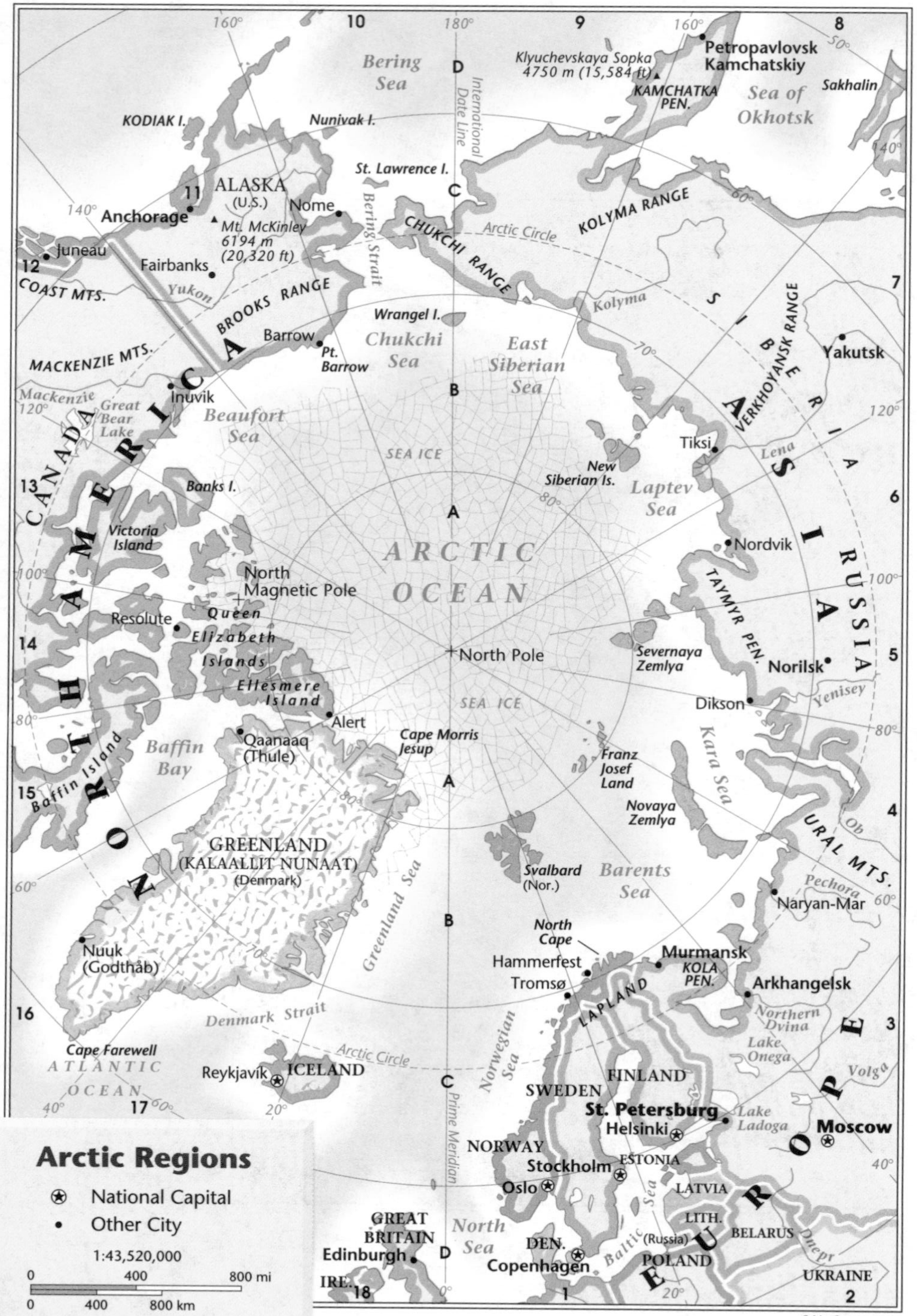

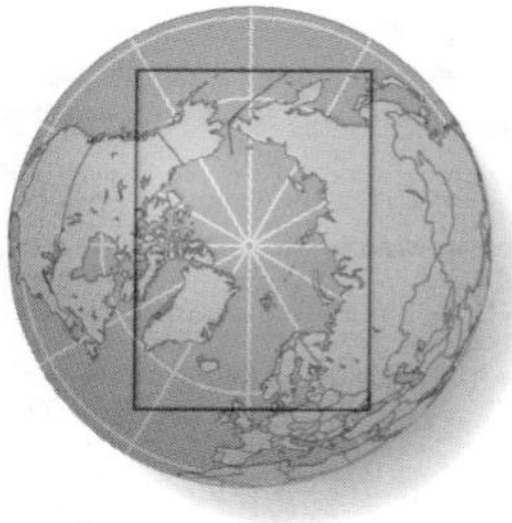

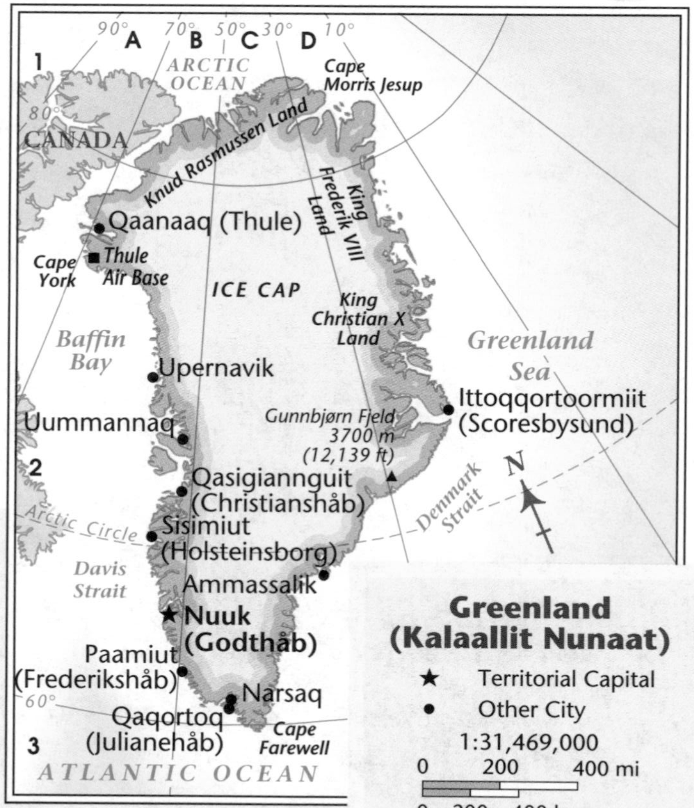

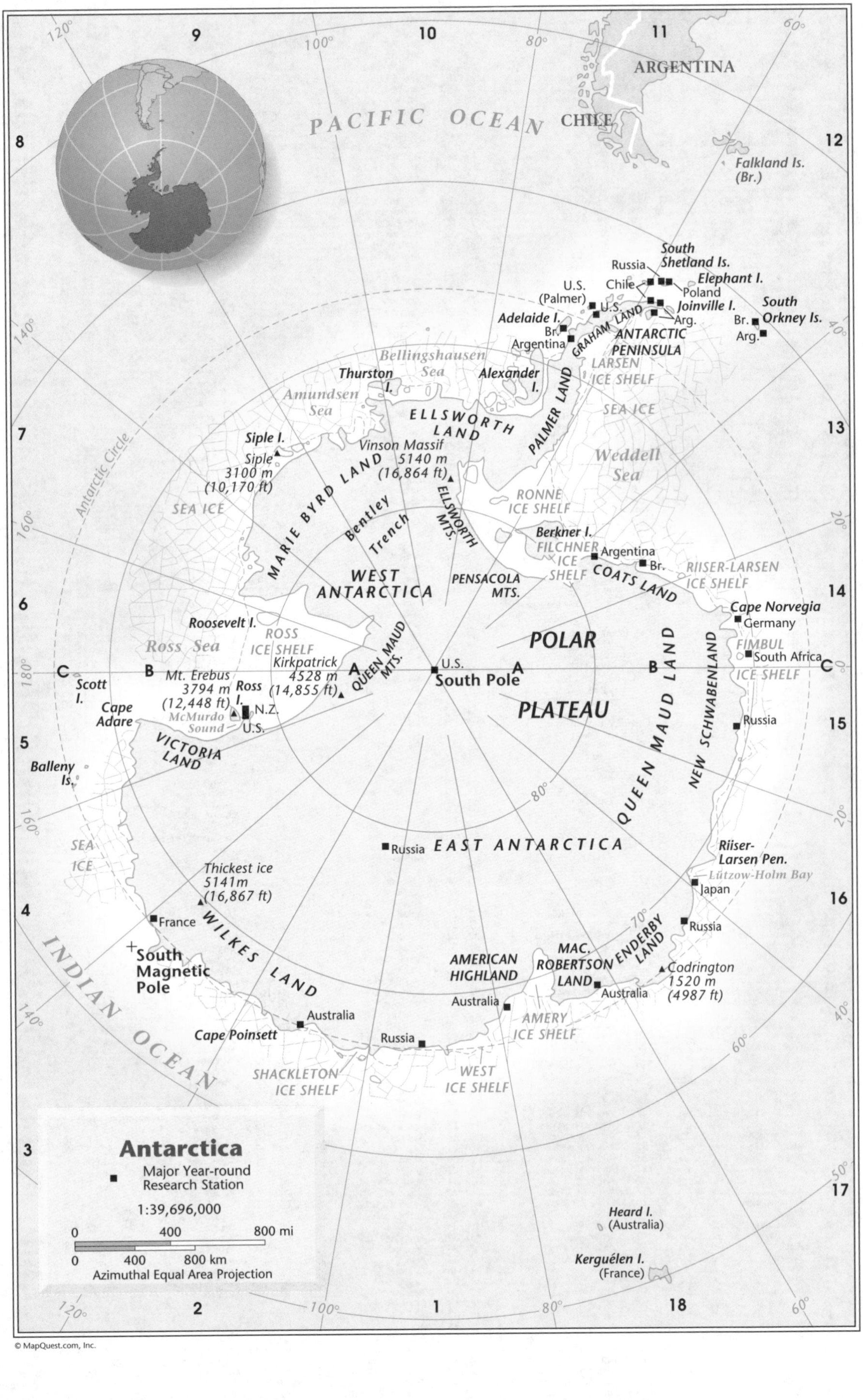
9
10
11
ARGENTINA
PACIFIC OCEAN
CHILE
8
12
Falkland Is. (Br.)
South Shetland Is.
Russia
Chile
Elephant I.
Poland
U.S. (Palmer)
U.S.
Joinville I.
Arg.
South Orkney Is.
Br.
Arg.
Adelaide I.
Br.
Argentina
GRAHAM LAND
ANTARCTIC PENINSULA
Bellingshausen Sea
Thurston I.
Alexander I.
LARSEN ICE SHELF
Amundsen Sea
ELLSWORTH LAND
PALMER LAND
SEA ICE
7
13
Siple I.
Siple 3100 m (10,170 ft)
Vinson Massif 5140 m (16,864 ft)
Weddell Sea
Antarctic Circle
MARIE BYRD LAND
ELLSWORTH MTS.
RONNE ICE SHELF
SEA ICE
Bentley Trench
Berkner I.
FILCHNER ICE SHELF
Argentina
Br.
RIISER-LARSEN ICE SHELF
WEST ANTARCTICA
PENSACOLA MTS.
COATS LAND
14
6
Cape Norvegia
Germany
Roosevelt I.
POLAR
ROSS ICE SHELF
Ross Sea
QUEEN MAUD MTS.
FIMBUL ICE SHELF
South Africa
Kirkpatrick 4528 m (14,855 ft)
U.S.
South Pole
C
B
A
A
B
C
Scott I.
Mt. Erebus 3794 m (12,448 ft)
Ross I.
N.Z.
McMurdo Sound
U.S.
Cape Adare
PLATEAU
QUEEN MAUD LAND
NEW SCHWABENLAND
Russia
15
5
VICTORIA LAND
Balleny Is.
SEA ICE
Russia
EAST ANTARCTICA
Riiser-Larsen Pen.
Lützow-Holm Bay
Japan
Thickest ice 5141m (16,867 ft)
16
4
France
WILKES LAND
Russia
South Magnetic Pole
AMERICAN HIGHLAND
MAC. ROBERTSON LAND
ENDERBY LAND
Codrington 1520 m (4987 ft)
Australia
Australia
INDIAN OCEAN
Australia
Cape Poinsett
Russia
AMERY ICE SHELF
SHACKLETON ICE SHELF
WEST ICE SHELF
3
Antarctica
Major Year-round Research Station
1:39,696,000
0 400 800 mi
0 400 800 km
Azimuthal Equal Area Projection
17
Heard I. (Australia)
Kerguélen I. (France)
2
1
18

A

Key Page
Aachen A3 40
Aaiún, el- B1 58
Aalst C2 33
Aarau C1 35
Aare, *river* B1, B2 35
Aba D5 65
Abadan B3 22
Abaí E4 75
Abakaliki E4 65
Abakan D6 44
Abancay C3 77
Abaya, *lake* B3 60
Abbeville C1 34
Abbey B10 104
Abbotsford L6 95
Abdali B1 24
Abéché C4 59
Abemama, *island* A1 17
Abengourou E3 63
Åbenrå B3 32
Abeokuta B4 65
Aberdeen Inset 10
Aberdeen C1 30
Aberdeen, Md. H4 99
Aberdeen, S. Dak. D1 126
Aberystwyth B3 30
Abha B2 24
Abhe, *lake* C2 60
Abia, *river* C3 66
Abidjan D4 63
Abilene, Tex. D2 126
Abkhazia, autonomous republic A3 45
Aboisso E4 63
Abomey A4 64
Abou Deïa B5 59
Abrantes A3 36
Abruzzi C2 38
Abşeron, *peninsula* C2 45
Abu Dhabi, *capital* C2 25
Abu Kamal B2 27
Abuja, *capital* D3 65
Abuná, *river* A2 77
Acadia Valley E5 94
Acajutla A2 86
Acámbaro D4 84
Acapulco E4 84
Acarai, *mts.* B5 80
Acaray, *river* E4 75
Acarigua C2 79
Accra, *capital* B4 64
Achill, *island* A2 31
Achinsk D6 44
Achwa, *river* C2 61
Acklins, *island* C4 89
Acme D5 94
Acolman Inset 84
Aconcagua, *mt.* A3 74
Aconcagua, *river* B4 76
Aconibe C3 66
Acquaviva A1 39
Acre A2 81
Acre (Akko) B1 26
Acton E4 102
Acton Vale D6 103
Açúcar, *mt.* Inset I 81
Adamawa, *massif* B2, E5 65
Adams, *lake* N5 95
Adana C3 27
Adapazarı B2 27
Adare, *cape* B5 107
Addis Ababa, *capital* C2 60
Addu, *atoll* A5 19
Adelaide, *island* C11 107
Adelaide, S.A., *capital* C3, Inset II 14
Aden B2 25
Aden E6 94
Aden, *gulf* B1, C2 60
Adi Keyih B2 60
Adi Ugri B2 60
Adige, *river* B1 38
Adirondack, *mts.*, N.Y. F1 126
Adjuntus B2 90
Admiralty, *islands* A2 15
Ado-Ekiti C4 65
Adolphustown H3 102
Adour, *river* B5 34
Adrar B2 57
Adrar des Iforas, *massif* D2 58
Adriatic, *sea* C2 38
Advocate Harbour C2 100
Adwa C1 60
Adygeya, republic E4 44
Adzopé E3 63
Aegean, *sea* C2 51
Ærø, *island* C4 32
Aetna D6 94
Afadjoto, *mt.* C3 64
Afghanistan 22
Afikpo D5 65
Afram, *river* B3 64
Afyon B2 27
Agadès B2 59
Agadir B2 57
Agartala F4 20
Agboville D4 63
Ağcabädi B2 45
Ağdam B3 45
Agen C4 34
Aginskiy Buryat, autonomous okrug D7 44
Aginskoye D7 44
Agou, *mt.* B3 64
Agra C3 20
Ağri E2 27
Agrigento C3 38
Agrínion B2 51
Ağstafa A2 45
Agua Prieta C1 84
Aguada A2 90
Aguadilla A2 90
Aguadulce B2 87
Aguán, *river* B2 86
Aguarico, *river* C3 79
Aguas Blancas C2 76
Aguas Buenas C2 90
Aguascalientes, *state capital* D3 84
Águilas F4 37
Aguilita B2 90
Agung, *mt.* C2 13
Agusan, *river* C4 12
Ahmadabad B4 20
Ahmadi, al- C2 24
Ahmic Harbour F2 102
Ahuachapán A2 86
Ahvaz B3 22
Ahwar B2 25
Aibonito C2 90
Aigáleo, *mts.* Inset 51
Ailinglapalap, *island* B2 16
Aillik B1 98
Ailuk, *island* B1 16
Aiquile A3 77
Air Force, *island* O3 99
Air Ronge E5 104
Air, *mts.* B2 59
Airdrie C5 94
Aishihik, *lake* B5 105
Aisne, *river* D2 34
Aiwo A2 16
Aix-en-Provence D5 34
Aix-les-Bains D4 34
Aíyina, *island* B3 51
Aizawl F4 20
Aizuwakamatsu C2 8
Ajaccio Inset I 34
Ajaria, autonomous republic A4 45
Ajdabiya D1 56
Ajka A2 43
Ajman C2 25
Ajmer B3 20
Akanyaru, *river* B2 61
Akashi B3 8
Akhalkalaki B4 45
Akhaltsikhe B4 45
Akharnaí Inset 51
Akhelóös, *river* B2 51
Akhmeta C3 45
Akhuryan, *river* C4 45
Akita D2 8
Akjoujt B3 58
Aklavik A3 99
Akobo, *river* A3 60
Akola C4 20
Akordat A2 60
Akosombo, *dam* C3 64
Akpatok, *island* P4 99
Akranes A2 52
Akron, Ohio E1 126
Aksaray C2 27
Aksu B1 10
Akulivik A1 101
Akure C4 65
Akurenam C3 66
Akureyri B2 52
Akuseki, *island* A4 8
Alabama E2 126
Alagoas E2 81
Alagoinhas E3 81
Alajuela B2 86
Alakol, *lake* E2 23
Alamayn, al- A1 56
Alameda H11 104
Alampur Inset II 20
Åland, *islands* B2 53
Alanya C3 27
Alarcón, *reservoir* E3 37
Alaska Inset I 126
Alaska, *gulf*, Alaska Inset I 126
Alaska, *range*, Alaska Inset I 126
Älät C3 45
Alaverdi B1 45
Alay, *mts.* B1, C3 23
Alayli Dadda B1 60
Alazani, *river* C4 45
Alba Iulia B2 43
Albacete F3 37
Alban E1 102
Albania 49
Albany, *capital*, N.Y. F1 126
Albany, Ga. E2 126
Albany, *river* C2 101
Albany, W.A. A3 14
Albert Nile, *river* B2 61
Albert, *canal* C1 33
Albert, *lake* B3 61
Alberton A2 100
Albi C5 34
Albina B2 80
Alboran, *sea* E4 37
Ålborg B1 32
Ålborg, *bay* C2 32
Albuquerque, *cays* Inset 78
Albuquerque, N. Mex. C2 126
Albury, N.S.W. D3 14
Alcalá de Henares Inset II 37
Alcañiz F2 37
Alcántara, *reservoir* C3 37
Alcázar de San Juan E3 37
Alcira F3 37
Alcobendas Inset II 37
Alcorcón E2, Inset II 37
Alcoy F3 37
Aldabra, *islands* A2 70
Aldan D8 44
Aldan, *river* D8 44
Alderney, *island* Inset II 30
Aleg B3 58
Alençon C2 34
Alert Q1 99
Alès D4 34
Alessandria B1 38
Ålesund B3 52
Aleutian *islands*, Alaska Inset I 126
Alexander A4 96
Alexander, *island* B11 107
Alexandra A4 15
Alexandria C4 43
Alexandria A1 56
Alexandria L2 102
Alexandria, La. D2 126
Alexandroúpolis C1 51
Alexis Creek L5 95
Alexis, *river* C3 98
Alfios, *river* B3 51
Alfred L2 102
Algarrobo Inset 76
Algarve, *region* A4 36
Algeciras D4 37
Algeria 57
Alghero B2 38
Algiers, *capital* B1 57
Ali Adde B2 60
Äli Bayramli C3 45
Ali-Sabieh B2 60
Aliákmon, *river* B1 51
Alibori, *river* B2 64
Alicante F3 37
Alice C3 71
Alice Arm H3 95
Alice Springs, N.T. C2 14
Alice Town B2 89
Aligarh C3 20
Alima, *river* D4 66
Aliwal North C3 71
Alix D5 94
Alkmaar B2 32
Allahabad D3 20
Allardville D1 97
Allen, *lake* B1 31
Allenford D3 102
Allentown, Pa. F1 126
Alleppey (Alappuzah) C7 20
Alliance E5 94
Allier, *river* C3 34
Alligator Pond B3 88
Alliston F3 102
Allumette, *lake* H2 102
Alma E3 97
Alma E3 103
Almada A3 36
Almadén D3 37
Almansa F3 37
Almaty (Alma-Ata) D2 23
Almehdralejo C3 37
Almelo D2 32
Almendra, *reservoir* C2 37
Almería E4 37
Almirante A2 87
Almonte J2 102
Alonsa B4 96
Alor Setar A1 13
Alor, *island* D2 13
Alotau B3 15
Alpena, Mich. E1 126
Alps, *mts.* 29
Alsace D2 34
Alsask A9 104
Alta E1 52
Altai, *mts.* B1 10
Altamira C2 81
Altamira C3 76
Altario E5 94
Altay B1 10
Altay B2 11
Altay, republic F4 44
Altdorf C2 35
Altiplano, *plateau* A3 77
Altona C4 96
Altun, *range* B2 10
Aluksne D2 46
Alvinston D5 102
Alytus C2 46
Alzette, *river* B2 33
Am Timan C5 59
Amadjuak, *lake* O4 99
Amadora A3 36
Amagasaki B3 8
Amahai D2 13
Amakusa, *islands* A3 8
Amambay, *mts.* E3 75
Amami, *island* Inset II 8
Amapá C1 81
Amapala B3 86
Amarah, al- C2 24
Amaranth B4 96
Amarillo, Tex. C2 126
Amasya C2 27
Amazon, *basin* B2 81
Amazon, *river* B2 81
Amazonas B2 81
Ambato B3 79
Ambatolampy B2 69
Ambatondrazaka B2 69
Amberg B4 40
Ambergris Cay, *island* C2 85
Ambergris, *cay* D4 89
Amberley D3 102
Ambon D2 13
Ambositra B3 69
Ambre, *cape* B1 69
Ambrym, *island* C3 18
Amdanga Inset II 20
Ameca D3 84
Ameland, *island* C1 32
American Samoa 18
Amersfoort C2 32
Amery Ice Shelf, *glacier* C18 107
Amherst C2 100
Amherstburg B5 102
Amiens C2 34
Amindivi, *islands* B6 20
Amirante, *islands* B2 70
Amisk E5 94
Amisk, *lake* H6 104
Amlamé B3 64
Amman, *capital* A2 26
Ammassalik C2 106
Ammersee, *lake* B4 40
Amos A4 101
Ampanihy A3 69
Amparai C4 19
Amqui J3 103
Amran A1 25
Amravati C4 20
Amritsar B2 20
Amsterdam, *capital* B2 32
Amstetten D2 39
Amu Darya, *river* B1, D2 22
Amund Ringnes, *island* J1 99
Amundsen, *gulf* C2 99
Amundsen, *sea* B9 107
Amur, *river* D8 44
Amyun A1 26
Ana María, *gulf* D2 88
Anabar C1 16
Anaco D2 79
Anadyr C10 44
Anadyr, *gulf* C11 44
Anahim Lake K5 95
Anáhuac D2 84
Anápolis D3 81
Añasco A2 90
Añasco, *beach* A2 90
Anatolia, *region* B2 27
Anatom, *island* C5 18
Anchorage, Alaska Inset I 126
Ancona C2 38
Ancud B7 76
Ancud, *gulf* B7 76
Andalusia D4 37
Andaman, *islands* F6 20
Andaman, *sea* B3 12
Anderlecht C2 33
Anderson, *river* C3 99
Andes, *mts.* 73
Andheri Inset I 20
Andizhan D2 23
Andoany B1 69
Andong C4 9
Andorra 36
Andorra la Vella, *capital* B2 36
Andreas, *cape* C1 27
Andros, *island* A3 89
Ándros, *island* C3 51
Androth, *island* B6 20
Aného B3 64
Anelghowhat C5 18
Anetan B1 16
Aneto, *mt.* G1 37
Angara, *river* D6 44
Angarsk D7 44
Angaur B4 17
Angel, *falls* D2 79
Angeles B3 12
Ångermanälven, *river* C2 53
Angers B3 34
Angikuni, *lake* H4 99
Angkor Thom, *ruins* B2 11
Angkor Wat, *ruins* B2 11
Anglesey, *island* B3 30
Angoche C3 68
Angol B6 76
Angola 70
Angoulême C4 34
Angus F3 102
Anholt, *island* C2 32
Anhui E2 10
Anibare B2 16
Anié B3 64
Añisoc C3 66
Anjou J5 103
Anju A3 9
Ankang D2 10
Ankara, *capital* C2 27
Ankaratra, *mts.* B2 69
Ankobra, *river* A4 64
Ann Arbor, Mich. E1 126
Anna Regina B2 80
Annaba B1 57
Annam, *mts.* A2 11
Annandale C2 100
Annapolis Royal B3 100
Annapolis, *capital*, Md. F2 126
Annapurna, *mt.* B2 19
Annecy D4 34
Anqing E2 10
Ansbach B4 40
Anse Boileau Inset 70
Anse Royale Inset 70
Anse-à-Galets C2 89
Anshan F1 10
Ansongo D2 58
Antalaha C1 69
Antalya B3 27
Antalya, *gulf* B3 27
Antananarivo, *capital* B2 69
Antarctic, *peninsula* C12 107
Antarctica 107
Antequera D4 37
Anti-Atlas, *ranges* B2 57
Anti-Lebanon, *mts.* B1 26
Anticosti, *island* D4 101
Antigonish F2 100
Antigua C5 85
Antigua, *island* D4 90
Antigua and Barbuda 90
Antioch (Antakya) D3 27
Antofagasta B2 76
Antrim, *mts.* A2 30
Antsirabe B2 69
Antsiranana B1 69
Antsohihy B1 69
Antwerp C1 33
Anuradhapura B3 19
Anyang E2 10
Anyang B4 9
Anyos B2 36
Aoa C1 18
Aoba, *island* B2 18
Aomori D1 8
Aoral, *mt.* C3 11
Aosta A1 38
Aozou B2 59
Apa, *river* D3 75
Apaporis, *river* C4 78
Apatity C3 44
Apatou A1 80
Apeldoorn C2 32
Apennines, *range* B1 38
Apetina B3 80
Api, *mt.* A2 19
Apia, *capital* C2 18
Apo, *volcano* C5 12
Apoera A2 80
Apolima, *island* B2 18
Apolima, *strait* B2 18
Apoteri B4 80
Appalachian, *mts.* E2 126
Apple River C2 100
Apsley G3 102
Apulia C2 38
Apure, *river* C2 79
Apurímac, *river* C3 77
Apuseni, *mts.* B2 43
Aqaba, *gulf* A3, B3 26
Aqabah, al- A3 26
Aqtau B2 23
Aqtobe B1 23
Aquileia C1 38
Aquitaine B4 34
Ara D3 20
Arabah, al-, *river* A2, B2 26
Arabian, *desert* B2 56
Arabian, *sea* A5, Inset I 20
Aracaju E3 81
Arachon B4 34
Arad A2 43
Aradah B3 25
Arafura, *sea* E2 13
Aragats, *mt.* B2 45
Aragón F2 37
Araguaia, *river* C3 81
Arak B3 22
Arakabesan, *island* B3 17
Arakan Yoma, *mts.* B2 12
Aral C2 23
Aral, *sea* A2, B2 23
Aran, *islands* B2 31
Aranda de Duero E2 37
Aranjuez E2 37
Aranyaprathet C3 12
Arapey Grande, *river* B1 75
Ararat B3 45
Ararat (Ağri Daği), *mt.* F2 27
Aras, *river* E2 27
Arauca C3 78
Arauca, *river* C2 79
Aravalli, *range* B3 20
Arawa B2 15
Arba Minch B3 60
Arborfield G7 104
Arborg C4 96
Archerwill G8 104
Arcola H11 104
Arctic Bay L2 99
Arctic Red River B3 99
Arda, *river* C4 50
Ardabil B2 22
Ardara B1 31
Ardbeg E2 102
Ardennes, *plateau* D2 33
Ardennes, *region* D1 34
Arecibo B2 90
Arekalong, *peninsula* C2 17
Arenal, *lake* B2 86
Arenas, *point* D2 90
Arendal B4 52
Arequipa C4 77
Arezzo B2 38
Argenteuil Inset II 34
Argentia D5 98
Argentina 74
Argentino, *lake* A7 74
Argeş, *river* C3 43
Arghandab, *river* B2 22
Argonne, *forest* D2 34
Árgos B3 51
Argyle C4 96
Argyle F3 102
Århus C2 32
Ari, *atoll* A3 19
Ariana C1 57
Arica B1 76
Arichat F2 100
Arima A2 91
Arinsal A2 36
Aripuanã, *river* C2 81
Arish, al- B1 56
Arizona B2 126
Arkansas D2 126
Arkansas, *river* D2 126
Arkhangelsk C4 44
Arklow C2 31
Arkona D4 102
Arles D5 34
Arlit B2 59
Arlon D3 33
Armagh A2 30
Armenia 45
Armenia B3 78
Armidale, N.S.W. E3 14
Armstrong N6 95
Armstrong C2 101
Arnaud, *river* B2 101
Arnes C4 96
Arnhem C3 32
Arnhem Land, *region* C1 14
Arnhem, *cape* C1 14
Arno, *island* C2 16
Arno, *river* B2 38
Arnold's Cove D5 98
Arnprior J2 102
Arnsberg B3 40
Aroostook B2 97
Arorae, *island* A2 17
Arpa, *river* C3 45
Arpajon Inset II 34
Arqalyq C1 23
Arran, *island* B2 30
Arras C1 34
Arroyo C3 90
Arta B2 60
Artashat B3 45
Artemisa B2 88
Arthur E4 102
Arthur's Town B3 89
Artibonite, *river* C1 89
Artigas B1 75
Artik A2 45
Artsvashen C2 45
Artvin E2 27
Aru, *islands* E2 13
Arua B2 61
Aruba, *island* 82
Arun, *river* D2 19
Arusha C1 68
Aruvi, *river* B3 19
Aruwimi, *river* C1 67
Arvayheer C2 11
As Ela B2 6
Asaba D4 6
Asadabad C2 2
Asahi Dake, *mt.* Inset I
Asahikawa Inset I
Asama, *mt.* C2
Asansol E4 2
Asau A2 1
Asbestos E6 10
Ascoli Piceno C2 3
Asela C3 6
Asenovgrad C3 5
Ashburton B3 1
Ashburton, *river* A2 1
Ashcroft M6 9
Ashdod B2 2
Ashern B3 9
Asheville, N.C. E2 12
Asheweig, *river* C2 10
Ashgabat, *capital* C3 2
Ashikaga C2
Ashizuri, *cape* B3
Ashmore and Cartier, *islands* B1 1
Ashqelon B2 2
Ashton A4 9
Ashuapmushuan, *river* C2 10
Asinara, *island* B2 3
Asipovichy D3 4
Asir, *region* B2 2
Askar B1 2
Asmara, *capital* B2 6
Asnam, el- B1 5
Aso, *mt.* A3
Asosa B2 6
Aspiring, *mt.* A3 1
Asprópirgos Inset 5
Asquith C8 10
Assab D3 6
Assal, *lake* B2 6
Assen D2 3
Assiniboia D11 10
Assiniboine, *mt.* P6 9
Assiniboine, *river* A4 9
Astana (Akmola), *capital* D1 2
Astara C3 4
Asti B1 3
Astipálaia, *island* C3 5
Astorga C1 3
Astrakhan E4 4
Astrolabe, *reefs* C2 1
Asturias C1 3
Asunción, *capital* D4 7
Aswan B3 5
Aswan High, *dam* B3 5
Asyut B2 5
At-Bashy D2 2
Atacama, *desert* C2 7
Atakpamé B3 6
Ataq B2 2
Atâr B2 5
Atatürk, *reservoir* D3 2
Atbara, *river* B1 6
Atbarah C2 5
Atbarah, *river* C2 5
Atbasar C1 2
Ath B2 3
Athabasca D4 9
Athabasca, *lake* A1 104
Athabasca, *river* B4, D3, E2 94
Athens, *capital* B3, Inset 51
Athens, Ga. E2 126
Athi, *river* E5 61
Athlone C2 31
Áthos, *mt.* C1 51
Ati B4 59
Atiak C2 61
Atikameg C3 94
Atikameg Lake A2 96
Atikokan B3 101
Atitlán, *lake* B5 85
Atlanta, *capital*, Ga. E2 126
Atlantic City, N.J. F2 126
Atlas, *mts.* A1, B2 57
Atlin F1 95
Atlin, *lake* F1 95
Atrai, *river* B4 21
Atrak, *river* D2 22
Atrato, *river* A3 78
Attapu D4 11
Attawapiskat D2 101
Attawapiskat, *river* C2 101
Atuel, *river* B4 74
Atyrau B2 23
Aua C1 18
Aube, *river* D3 34
Auch C5 34
Auckland B2 15
Augsburg B4 40
Augusta, *capital*, Maine G1 126
Augusta, Ga. E2 126
Auki B1 16
Aulac E3 97
Aunuu, *island* C1 18
Auob, *river* C3 70
Aur, *island* C2 16
Aurangabad C5 20
Aurillac C4 34
Aurora F3 102
Ausa, *river* C1 39
Austin B4 96
Austin, *capital*, Tex. D2 126
Australia 14
Australian Alps, *mts.* D3 14
Australian Capital Territory D3 14
Austria 39
Auvergne C4 34
Auxerre C3 34
Avalon, *peninsula* E5 98
Aveiro A2 36
Avellaneda D3 74
Avellino C2 38
Aviemore B1 30
Avignon D5 34
Ávila D2 37
Avilés D1 37
Avon, *islands* A2 18
Avon, *river* C3 30
Avonlea E10 104
Awaji B3 8

Key Page
Awaji, *island* B3 8
Awasa C3 60
Awash, *river* C2 60
Awaso A3 64
Awbari B2 56
Awka D4 65
Awwali, *river* A2 26
Axel Heiberg, *island* K1 99
Axim A4 64
Ayacucho C3 77
Ayagöz E2 23
Aydin A3 27
Ayer Chawan, *island* A1 13
Ayer's Cliff D6 103
Áyios Dhimítrios Inset 51
Aylesbury Inset III 30
Aylmer E5 102
Aylmer A6 103
Aylmer, *lake* G4 99
Aylmer, *lake* E6 103
Ayn, al- C2 25
Ayoûn el-Atroûs C3 58
Ayr B2 30
Aytos F3 50
Azaouâd, *region* C2 58
Azare F2 65
Azaz A1 27
Azcapotzalco Inset 84
Azerbaijan 45
Azerbaijan, *region* B2 22
Azogues B4 79
Azores, *islands* 5
Azov, *sea* D3 47
Azraq ash-Shishan B2 26
Azua B2 89
Azuero, *peninsula* B3 87

B

Ba, *river* B3 11
Baalbek B1 26
Bab al-Mandab, *strait* C1 60
Babahoyo B3 79
Babanusah B3 59
Babar, *island* D2 13
Babbage, *river* B1 105
Babda A2 26
Babelthuap, *island* C3 17
Babine, *lake* J4 95
Babine, *river* J3 95
Babruysk D3 47
Babu Bheri Inset II 20
Babuyan, *channel* B2 12
Babuyan, *islands* B2 12
Babylon, *ruins* B2 24
Bac Lieu A5 11
Bacabal D2 81
Bacău D2 43
Back, *river* H3 99
Bačka Palanka A2 49
Bacolod B4 12
Bad Ems A3 40
Bad Ischl C3 39
Bad Kreuznach A4 40
Bad Reichenhall C5 40
Badajoz C3 37
Badalona H2 37
Badanah B1 24
Badas A2 13
Baddeck G1 100
Baden C1 35
Baden E2 39
Baden A3 96
Baden-Baden B4 40
Baden-Württemberg B4 40
Badger D4 96
Badger C5 98
Badou B3 64
Bafatá C1 62
Baffin, *bay* L1 92
Baffin, *island* M2 99
Baffin, *region* N2 99
Bafilo B2 64
Bafing, *river* C2 62
Bafoulabé A3 58
Bafoussam B2 65
Baghdad, *capital* B2 24
Baghlan B1 22
Baglung B2 19
Bagmati, *river* C2 19
Bagoé, *river* C1 63
Baguio B2 12
Bagzane, *mt.* B2 59
Bahamas 89
Bahawalpur D4 21
Bahia D3 81
Bahía Blanca C4 74
Bahía Honda A2 88
Bahía, *islands* B1 86
Bahir Dar B2 60
Bahoruco, *mts.* A2 89
Bahr al-Arab, *river* B3 59
Bahr al-Ghazal, *river* C3 59
Bahr al-Jabal, *river* C3 59
Bahr Salamat, *river* B5 59
Bahrain 25
Bahrain, *gulf* A2 25
Baia Mare B2 43
Baicheng F1 10
Baidyabati Inset II 20
Baie Verte C4 98
Baie-Comeau H2 103
Baie-des-Sables J3 103
Baie-St-Paul F4 103
Baie-Ste.-Anne E1 97
Baie-Ste-Catherine G3 103
Bailieboro G3 102
Bainsville L2 102
Bair B2 26
Baiti B1 16
Baja B2 43
Baja California A1 84
Baja California Sur B2 84
Bajadero B2 90
Bajo Boquete A2 87
Bakel C2 62
Baker Brook A1 97
Baker Lake J4 99
Bakersfield, Calif. B2 126
Bakhardok C2 22
Bakhtaran B3 22
Bakhtiari, *region* B3 22
Bakony, *mts.* A2 43
Baku, *capital* C2 45
Bala F2 102
Bala, *lake* B3 30
Balabac, *island* A5 12
Balabac, *strait* A5 12
Balakän B2 45
Balaklava C4 47
Balaton, *lake* A2 43
Balboa C2 87
Balcarres G10 104
Baldur B4 96
Baldy, *mt.* A3 96
Balearic, *islands* G3 37
Balearic, *sea* G2 37
Baleia, *point* E3 81
Baleine, *river* C2 101
Balgonie F10 104
Balhaf B2 25
Balho B1 60
Bali, *island* C2 13
Baliceaux, *island* B3 91
Balıkesir A2 27
Balikpapan C2 13
Balkan, *mts.* B2 50
Balkh B1 22
Balkhash D2 23
Balkhash, *lake* D2 23
Ballancourt-sur-Essonne Inset II 34
Ballarat, Vic. D3 14
Balleny, *islands* C5 107
Ballerup D3 32
Ballina B1 31
Bally Inset II 20
Ballymena A2 30
Balmaceda B8 76
Balmertown B2 101
Balmoral C1 97
Balsas, *river* E4 84
Bălţi A2 50
Baltic, *sea* 29
Baltimore, Md. F2 126
Baluchistan, *region* E4 22
Balykchy E1 23
Balzers B2 33
Bam D4 22
Bamako, *capital* B3 58
Bamangachi Inset II 20
Bambadinca C1 62
Bambana, *river* B2 87
Bambari B2 66
Bamberg B4 40
Bamenda B2 65
Bamian B2 22
Ban Houayxay A1 11
Ban Phai C2 12
Banaba, *island* A2 17
Banana A2 67
Banana, *islands* A1 63
Bananga F7 20
Banat, *region* A3 43
Banbury C3 30
Bancroft H2 102
Banda Aceh A1 13
Banda, *sea* D2 13
Bandama Blanc, *river* D2 63
Bandama Rouge, *river* C2 63
Bandama, *river* D3 63
Bandar Beheshti E4 22
Bandar Lampung B2 13
Bandar Seri Begawan,
capital B2 13
Bandar-e Abbas D4 22
Bandar-e Anzali B2 22
Bandar-e Bushehr C4 22
Bandar-e Khomeyni B3 22
Bandar-e Torkeman C2 22
Bandeira, *mt.* D4 81
Bandra Inset I 20
Bandundu B2 67
Bandung B2 13
Banff C5 94
Bangalore C6 20
Bangar C2 13
Bangassou B3 66
Banggi, *island* D1 13
Banghiang, *river* C3 11
Bangka, *island* B2 13
Bangkok, *capital* B3 12
Bangladesh 21
Bangor B2 30
Bangor B3 30
Bangor, Maine G1 126
Bangui, *capital* A3 66
Bangweulu, *lake* B2 67
Baní B2 89
Bani Suwayf B2 56
Bani Walid B1 56
Bani, *river* B3 58
Baniyas A2 27
Banja Luka B1 48
Banjarmasin C2 13
Banjul, *capital* B2 62
Banks, *island* G4 95
Banks, *island* D2 99
Banks, *islands* B1 18
Banks, *peninsula* B3 15
Bann, *river* A2 30
Bannockburn H3 102
Bansang D2 62
Bansbaria Inset II 20
Banská Bystrica B2 42
Bantry B3 31
Bantry, *bay* B3 31
Baoding E2 10
Baoshan C3 10
Baotou E1 10
Baoulé, *river* B3 58
Baqubah B2 24
Baquerizo Moreno Inset 79
Bar A3 49
Bar-le-Duc D2 34
Baraawe A3 60
Barabinsk D5 44
Baracaldo E1 37
Barachois M3 103
Baracoa F3 88
Barahona A2 89
Baraki Barak B2 22
Barakpur Inset II 20
Baram, *river* D2 13
Barama, *river* B2 80
Baranagar Inset II 20
Baranavichy C3 47
Barasat Inset II 20
Barbados 91
Barbuda, *island* E3 90
Barcelona D1 79
Barcelona H2 37
Barceloneta B2 90
Bärdä B2 45
Bardaï B2 59
Bardejov C2 42
Bareilly C3 20
Barents, *sea* B3 44
Bargachia Inset II 20
Bari D2 38
Baril, *lake* E2 94
Barinas B2 79
Barind, *region* B4 21
Baris B3 56
Barisal D6 21
Bark, *lake* H2 102
Barkerville M4 95
Barkly, *tableland* C1 14
Barletta D2 38
Barnaul D6 44
Barnes, *ice cap* O3 99
Barnsley C3 30
Barnstaple B3 30
Barnwell D6 94
Baro, *river* B2 60
Barons D6 94
Barquisimeto C1 79
Barra, *island* A2 30
Barrancabermeja B3 78
Barranquilla B2 78
Barranquitas C2 90
Barreiro A3 36
Barrhead C4 94
Barrie F3 102
Barrière M5 95
Barrington B4 100
Barro B1 62
Barrouallie B2 91
Barrow, Alaska Inset I 126
Barrow, *river* C2 31
Barrow-in-Furness B2 30
Barry's Bay H2 102
Bartang, *river* B1 23
Bartica B2 80
Barú, *volcano* A2 87
Baruta C1 79
Baruun-Urt D2 11
Bas-Caraquet E1 97
Basarabeasca B2 50
Basel B1 35
Bashi, *channel* B1 12
Basilan B5 12
Basilan, *island* B5 12
Basildon Inset III 30
Basilicata C2 38
Baskatong, *reservoir* A5 103
Basque Country E1 37
Basra C2 24
Bass Rock, *islet* C2 30
Bass, *strait* D3 14
Bassar B2 64
Basse Santa Su D2 62
Basse-Normandie B2 34
Bassein B3 12
Basseterre, *capital* B2 90
Bassila A3 64
Bastia Inset I 34
Bastogne D2 33
Bata B3 66
Bataan, *peninsula* B3 12
Batabanó, *gulf* B2 88
Batan, *islands* B1 12
Batang C3 10
Batang Duri C2 13
Batangafo A2 66
Batangas B3 12
Batdambang B2 11
Bate, *bay* Inset IV 14
Batéké, *plateau* C5 66
Bath C3 90
Bath C3 30
Bath B2 97
Batha, *river* C4 59
Bathsheba B3 91
Bathurst D1 97
Bathurst, *island* J1 99
Batin, Wadi al-, *river* A2 24
Batinah, al-, *region* C1 25
Batman E3 27
Batna B1 57
Baton Rouge, *capital*, La. D2 126
Batouri B3 65
Batrun, al- A1 26
Batteau D2 98
Batticaloa C4 19
Battle, *river* A7 104
Battleford B8 104
Batu Pahat B2 13
Batumi A4 45
Baubau D2 13
Bauchi E2 65
Bauria Inset II 20
Bauru D4 81
Bauska C2 46
Bautzen C3 40
Bavaria B4 40
Bavarian Alps, *mts.* B5 40
Bawiti, al- A2 56
Bawku B1 64
Bawlf D5 94
Bay Bulls E5 98
Bay de Verde E5 98
Bay Roberts E5 98
Bay St. Lawrence G1 100
Bayamo E3 88
Bayamón C2 90
Bayamón, *river* C2 90
Bayan Har, *range* C2 10
Bayanhongor C2 11
Bayda, al- B2 25
Bayda, al- D1 56
Baydhabo A3 60
Bayerischer Wald, *mts.* C4 40
Bayeux B2 34
Bayfield D4 102
Baygorria, *lake* B2 75
Baykal, *lake* D7 44
Bayonne B5 34
Bayport C3 100
Bayramaly D3 22
Bayreuth B4 40
Bays, *lake* F2 102
Baza E4 37
Bazardüzü Daği, *mt.* B2 45
Bazin, *river* A4 103
Beachside D4 98
Beagle, *channel* B7 74
Bear Lake L4 95
Bear River C2 100
Beata, *cape* A3 89
Beata, *island* A3 89
Beaton O6 95
Beau Bassin B2 69
Beauceville F5 103
Beaufort West B3 71
Beaufort, *sea* B1 105
Beaulac E6 103
Beaumont D4 94
Beaumont, Tex. D2 126
Beauport L5 103
Beaupré F4 103
Beauséjour C4 96
Beauvais C2 34
Beauval C5 104
Beaver Creek A4 105
Beaver Harbour E3 100
Beaver Hill, *lake* D2 96
Beaver Mines C6 94
Beaver, *river* A6 104
Beaver, *river* D5 105
Beaverton F3 102
Bécancour D5 103
Bečej B2 49
Béchar A1 57
Bedeque, *bay* B2 100
Bedford C3 30
Bedford D3 100
Bedford D6 103
Bedok B1 13
Beechy C10 104
Beersheba B2 26
Behala Inset II 20
Bei'an F1 10
Beihai D3 10
Beijing, *capital* E2 10
Beira B3 68
Beirut, *capital* A2 26
Beja B3 36
Béja B1 57
Bejaïa B1 57
Bejaïa, *gulf* B1 57
Béjar D2 37
Bekaa, *valley* A2 26
Békéscsaba C2 43
Bela C4 21
Belair B4 91
Belapurpada Inset I 20
Belarus 47
Belasica, *mts.* C2 48
Belaya Tserkov C2 47
Beledweyne B3 60
Belém D2 81
Bélep, *islands* C2 18
Belfast B2 30
Belford Roxo Inset I 81
Belfort D3 34
Belfort, *gap* D3 34
Belgaum B5 20
Belgium 33
Belgrade, *capital* B2 49
Beli Drim, *river* B3 49
Bélinga B1 66
Belitung, *island* B2 13
Belize 85
Belize City B2 85
Belize, *river* B2 85
Bella Coola J5 95
Bella Unión B1 75
Bellary C5 20
Bellburns C4 98
Belle Isle, *strait* C3 98
Belle River C3 100
Belle, *island* B3 34
Belle, *island* C3 98
Belle-Anse C2 89
Belledune D1 97
Belleview A4 96
Belleville H3 102
Bellingham L7 95
Bellingham, Wash. A1 126
Bellingshausen, *sea* B10 107
Bellinzona D2 35
Bellona, *island* A2 16
Belluno C1 38
Bellville A3 71
Belmont B4 96
Belmopan, *capital* B2 85
Belo Horizonte D3 81
Beloeil C6 103
Belomorsk C3 44
Bemaraha, *plateau* A2 69
Bemidji, Minn. D1 126
Ben Eoin G2 100
Ben Nevis, *mt.* B2 30
Benavente D1 37
Bend, Oreg. A1 126
Bender (Tighina) B2 50
Benderbeyla C2 60
Bendigo, Vic. D3 14
Benevento C2 38
Bengal, *bay* E5 20
Bengbu E2 10
Benghazi D1 56
Bengkulu B2 13
Bengough E11 104
Benguela B4 70
Beni Mellal C1 57
Beni, *river* A2 77
Benidorm F3 37
Benin 64
Benin City C4 65
Benin, *bight* B5 65
Benito A3 96
Benoit's Cove B5 98
Benoni C2 71
Bénoué, *river* B2 65
Benson G11 104
Bentiaba B4 70
Benue, *river* E3 65
Benxi F1 10
Benzdorp B3 80
Beqa, *island* B3 17
Bequia, *island* B2 91
Berat A3 49
Berbera B1 60
Berbérati A3 66
Berbice, *river* B3 80
Berdoba C4 59
Berdyansk D3 47
Berekua B4 90
Berens River C3 96
Berens, *island* C3 96
Berens, *river* C3 96
Beresford D1 97
Berezniki D4 44
Bergamo B1 38
Bergen B3 52
Bergen op Zoom B3 32
Bergerac C4 34
Bergisch Gladbach A3 40
Bering, *sea* Inset I 126
Bering, *strait* C11 44
Berkner, *island* B12 107
Berlin, *capital* C2 40
Bermejo, *river* C2 74
Bermuda, *island* 82
Bern, *capital* B2 35
Bernburg B3 40
Bernese Alps, *mts.* B2 35
Bernières K6 103
Berounka, *river* A3 42
Bertwell H8 104
Berwick C2 100
Berwick-upon-Tweed C2 30
Besançon D3 34
Beskid, *mts.* D4 41
Besnard, *lake* D5 104
Besor, *river* B2 26
Bethanien C4 70
Bethany B4 96
Bethel, Alaska Inset I 126
Bethierville C5 103
Bethlehem C2 71
Béticos, *mts.* E4 37
Bétou E2 66
Betsiamites H3 103
Betsiamites, *river* G2 103
Betsiboka, *river* B2 69
Bette, *mt.* C3 56
Beulah A4 96
Beyla D3 62
Beyneu B2 23
Beyşehir, *lake* B3 27
Béziers C5 34
Bhadrakh E4 20
Bhadreswar Inset II 20
Bhagalpur E3 20
Bhairahawa B2 19
Bhaktapur C2 19
Bhamapur D5 20
Bhamo C1 12
Bhandup Inset I 20
Bharatpur C3 20
Bhatapara D4 20
Bhatpara Inset II 20
Bhavnagar B4 20
Bhayandar Inset I 20
Bheri, *river* B2 19
Bhima, *river* C5 20
Bhimpur Inset II 20
Bhiwandi Inset I 20
Bhopal C4 20
Bhubaneswar E4 20
Bhuj A4 20
Bhunya B2 71
Bhutan 19
Biabou B2 91
Biafra, *bight* A3 65
Biak, *island* E2 13
Biała Podlaska F2 41
Białystok F2 41
Biankouma C3 63
Biarritz B5 34
Bicaz, *reservoir* D2 43
Biche, *lake* E4 94
Bida D3 65
Bié, *plateau* C4 70
Biel B1 35
Biel, *lake* B1 35
Biele Karpaty, *mts.* A2 42
Bielefeld B2 40
Bielsko-Biała D4 41
Bien Hoa B4 11
Bienville, *lake* B2 101
Big Beaver E11 104
Big Bend B2 71
Big Creek L5 95
Big Fish, *river* B1 105
Big Gull, *lake* J3 102
Big Muddy, *lake* F11 104
Big River C7 104
Big Trout Lake C2 101
Big, *island* O4 99
Big, *river* B2 98
Biggar C8 104
Bignona A3 62
Bigstone, *river* D1 96
Bihać A1 48
Bihar E3 20
Bihor, *mts.* B2 43
Bijagós, *islands* A2 62
Bijapur C5 20
Bijeljina C1 48
Bikaner B3 20
Bikar, *island* C1 16
Bikini, *island* B1 16
Bilaspur D4 20
Biläsuvar C3 45
Bilauktaung, *range* B3, C3 12
Bilbao E1 37
Billings, Mont. C1 126
Billings, *reservoir* Inset II 81
Bilma C2 59
Biloku B5 80
Biloxi, Miss. E2 126
Biltine C4 59
Bimbila C2 64
Binche C2 33
Bindloss E6 94
Bindura B1 69
Binga, *mt.* B3 68
Bingen A4 40
Binscarth A4 96
Bint Jubayl A2 26
Bintang B2 62
Bintimane, *mt.* B1 63
Bío-Bío, *river* B6 76
Bioko, *island* A1 66
Bir Gandús A2 58
Bir Morgrein C1 58
Birak B2 56
Birao B1 66
Biratnagar D3 19
Birch Cliff K5 102
Birch Hills E7 104
Birch River A3 96
Birch, *mts.* D2 94
Birchy Bay D4 98
Bird, *island* B2 91
Birendranagar B2 19
Birganj C2 19
Birjand D3 22
Birkat Qarun, *lake* B2 56
Birkenhead B3 30
Birkirkara B2 36
Birlad D2 43
Birmingham C3 30
Birmingham, Ala. E2 126
Birni Nkonni B3 59
Birnie B4 96
Birnin Kebbi C1 65
Birobizhan E8 44
Birtle A4 96
Biržai C1 46
Birzebbuga C3 36
Biscay, *bay* B4 34
Bishkek, *capital* D1 23
Bishnupur Inset II 20
Bishop's Falls D4 98
Biskra B1 57
Bislig C4 12
Bismarck, *archipelago* A2 15
Bismarck, *capital*, N. Dak. C1 126
Bismarck, *range* A2 15
Bismarck, *sea* A2 15
Bismuna, *lagoon* C1 87
Bison, *lake* B2 94
Bissau, *capital* A2 62
Bissett D3 96
Bissorã B1 62
Bistcho, *lake* A1 94
Bistriţa C2 43
Bistriţa, *river* C2 43
Bitam A1 66
Bitola B2 48
Bitumount E2 94
Biu G2 65
Biwa, *lake* B3 8
Biysk D6 44
Bizard, *island* H5 103
Bizerte B1 57
Bjorne, *peninsula* L1 99
Black (Da), *river* A2 11
Black Country, *region* C3 30
Black Lake E1 104
Black River B2 88
Black Tickle D2 98
Black Volta, *river* A2, B3 64
Black, *forest* A4 40
Black, *hills*, S. Dak. C1 126
Black, *lake* E1 104
Black, *sea* 29
Blackburn C3 30
Blackmans B3 91
Blackpool C3 30
Blacks Harbour C3 97
Blackstone, *river* B3 105
Blackville D2 97
Blackwater, *river* B2, C1 31
Blagoevgrad B4 50
Blagoveshchensk D4 44
Blagoveshchensk D8 44
Blaine Lake D8 104
Blainville H5 103
Blanc, *mt.* D4 34
Blanc, *reservoir* C4 103
Blanc-Sablon E3 101
Blanca, *bay* C4 74
Blanda, *river* B2 52
Blantyre B3 68
Blarney B3 31
Blatec C2 48
Blenheim B3 15
Blenheim D5 102
Blida B1 57
Bligh Water, *sound* B2 17
Blind Bay N6 95
Blind River C1 102
Blitta B2 64
Bloemfontein,
judicial capital C2 71
Blois C3 34
Bloodvein, *river* C3 96
Bloomfield H4 102
Bloomington, Ind. E2 126
Blossom Park H6 102
Blow, *river* B1 105
Blue Mountain, *peak* C2 88
Blue Nile, *river* C2 59
Blue Ridge C4 94
Blue River N5 95
Blue, *mts.* E3 14
Blue, *mts.* C2 88
Bluefields B2 88
Bluefields C3 87

Key Page
Bluenose, *lake* E3 99
Bluffton C5 94
Blyth D4 102
Bo B2 63
Bo Hai, *gulf* E2 10
Boa Vista B1 81
Boa Vista, *island* D2 58
Boaco B2 87
Bobcaygeon G3 102
Bobo-Dioulasso B3 64
Bocas del Toro A2 87
Bocay B1 87
Bocay, *river* B2 87
Bocholt A3 40
Bochum A3 40
Bodaybo D7 44
Bodo E5 94
Bodø C2 52
Boende B2 67
Boggeragh, *mts.* B2 31
Boggy, *peak* D5 90
Bogor B2 13
Bogotá, *capital* B3 78
Bogra C4 21
Bohemia, *region* A3 42
Bohemian, *forest* A3 42
Bohemian-Moravian, *heights* B3 42
Bohol, *island* C4 12
Bohol, *sea* C4 12
Boiestown C2 97
Boilleau F3 103
Bois-des-Filion H5 103
Boise, *capital*, Idaho B1 126
Boissevain A4 96
Boknafjord, *fjord* B4 52
Boksburg C2 71
Bol A4 59
Bolama B2 62
Bolands D5 90
Bole A2 64
Bolgatanga B1 64
Bolívar, *mt.* B2 79
Bolivia 77
Bolligen B2 35
Bolnisi C4 45
Bolobo B2 67
Bologna B1 38
Bolovens, *plateau* D4 11
Bolsena, *lake* B2 38
Bolsón de Mapimí, *depression* D2 84
Bolton C3 30
Bolton F4 102
Bolu B2 27
Bolzano B1 38
Bom Jesus da Lapa D3 81
Boma A2 67
Bombay B5, Inset I 20
Bombay, *harbor* Inset I 20
Bomu, *river* C1 67
Bon Pays, *region* B2 33
Bon, *cape* C1 57
Bonaire, *island* 82
Bonao B2 89
Bonaventure L3 103
Bonaventure, *river* L3 103
Bonavista E5 98
Bonavista, *bay* E5 98
Bondo B1 67
Bondoukou E2 63
Bondy Inset II 34
Bongor A5 59
Bonin, *islands* Inset III 8
Bonn A3 40
Bonnet Plume, *river* C3 105
Bonny D5 65
Bonnyville E4 94
Bonshaw B2 100
Bonthe A2 63
Bööntsagaan, *lake* B2 11
Boosaaso B1 60
Boothia, *gulf* K2 99
Boothia, *peninsula* K2 99
Booué A2 66
Bor C2 49
Borås B3 53
Bordeaux B4 34
Borden B2 100
Borden C8 104
Borden, *island* F1 99
Borden, *peninsula* M2 99
Bordoy, *island* Inset 32
Borgo Maggiore B1 39
Borivli Inset I 20
Borjomi B4 45
Borneo, *island* C1 13
Bornholm, *island* E3 32
Bosanska Gradiška B1 48
Bosanska Krupa A1 48
Bosna, *river* B1 48
Bosnia & Hercegovina 48
Boso, *peninsula* D3 8
Bosporus, *strait* B2 27
Bossangoa A2 66
Bosten, *lake* B1 10
Boston C3 30
Boston Bar M6 95
Boston, *capital*, Mass. F1 126
Boswell O6 95
Botany, *bay* Inset IV 14
Boteti, *river* A2 69
Botha D5 94
Bothnia, *gulf* B2, D2 53
Botna, *river* B2 50
Botoșani D2 43
Botrange, *mt.* E2 33
Botswana 69
Botte Donato, *mt.* D3 38
Bottrop A3 40
Botwood D4 98
Bouaflé D3 63
Bouaké D3 63
Bouar A2 66
Boucherville J5 103
Bouctouche E2 97
Bougainville, *island* B2 15
Boughton, *bay* C2 100
Bougouni B3 58
Boulder, Colo. C2 126
Boulogne-Billancourt Inset II 34
Boulogne-sur-Mer C1 34
Bouna E2 63
Bourail C2 18
Bourem C2 58
Bourg-en-Bresse D3 34
Bourges C3 34
Bourgogne C3 34
Bourke, N.S.W. D3 14
Bournemouth C4 30
Bousso B5 59
Bow City D6 94
Bow, *river* D6 94
Bow, *river* E6 104
Bowen, Qld. D2 14
Bowling Green, Ky. E2 126
Bowser, *lake* H3 95
Bowsman A3 96
Boyd's Cove D4 98
Boyne, *river* C2 31
Boyne, *river* B4 96
Bozeman, Mont. B1 126
Brabant Lake G4 104
Brač, *island* C3 48
Bracciano, *lake* C2 38
Bracebridge F2 102
Bradford C3 30
Braga A2 36
Bragança B2 36
Bragg Creek C6 94
Brahmanbaria E5 21
Brahmaputra, *river* F3 20
Brăila D3 43
Braintree Inset III 30
Brakpan C2 71
Bralorne L6 95
Bramalea H5 102
Brampton F4 102
Branch E5 98
Branco, *river* B1 81
Brandberg, *mt.* B2 70
Brandenburg C2 40
Brandon B4, C2 96
Brant D6 94
Brantford E4 102
Bras d'Or G1 100
Brasília, *capital* D3 81
Brașov C3 43
Bratislava, *capital* A2 42
Bratsk D7 44
Braunau C2 39
Brava, *coast* H2 37
Brava, *island* B4 58
Brazil 81
Brazilian, *highlands* D3 81
Brazzaville, *capital* C6 66
Brčko B1 48
Brea, *point* B3 90
Břeclav C4 42
Brecon Beacons, *mts.* B3 30
Breda B3 32
Bredenbury H10 104
Bregalnica, *river* C2 48
Breidhafjördhur, *fjord* A2 52
Bremen B2 40
Bremerhaven B2 40
Brenner, *pass* B3 39
Brentwood Inset III 30
Brescia B1 38
Brest A3 47
Brest A2 34
Bretagne B2 34
Breton C4 94
Bria B2 66
Briançon D4 34
Briceni A1 50
Bridge Lake M5 95
Bridgeport, Conn. F1 126
Bridgetown B3 100
Bridgetown, *capital* A4 91
Bridgewater C3 100
Brienzersee, *lake* B2 35
Brighton C4 30
Brighton H3 102
Brikama B2 62
Brindisi D2 38
Brisbane, Qld., *capital* E2, Inset III 14
Brisbane, *river* Inset III 14
Bristol C3 30
Bristol B2 97
Bristol, *channel* B3 30
Britannia E5 98
Britt E2 102
Brive-la-Gaillarde C4 34
Brno C3 42
Broadview H10 104
Brochet C1 96
Brock, *island* F1 99
Brocket D6 94
Brockville K3 102
Brodfur, *peninsula* L2 99
Broken Hill, N.S.W. D3 14
Brokopondo B2 80
Brolin C3 30
Bromptonville E6 103
Brookdale B4 96
Brooks E6 94
Brooks *range*, Alaska Inset I 126
Broome, W.A. B1 14
Broomhill A4 96
Brossard J6 103
Brownsville, Tex. D3 126
Bruce Mines B1 102
Bruce Peninsula N.P. D2 102
Brugge B1 33
Brugge-Ghent, *canal* B1 33
Brûlé B4 94
Brunei 13
Brunei, *bay* C1 13
Brunei, *river* B2 13
Brunswick B2 40
Brunswick, Ga. E2 126
Brunswick, *peninsula* B9 76
Brussels D4 102
Brussels, *capital* C2 33
Bryan, Tex. D2 126
Bryansk D3 44
Bsharri B1 26
Bu Craa B1 58
Bua, *river* B2 68
Buada B2 16
Buala A1 16
Buba C2 62
Bubanza B2 61
Bubaque B2 62
Bubiyan, *island* C2 24
Bucaramanga B3 78
Buchanan A3 63
Buchanan H9 104
Buchans C5 98
Bucharest, *capital* D3 43
Buck Creek C4 94
Buck Lake C5 94
Buckingham A6 103
Budapest, *capital* B2 43
Buea A3 65
Buenaventura A4 78
Buendía, *reservoir* E2 37
Buene, *river* A2 49
Buenos Aires, *capital* D3 74
Buenos Aires, *lake* A6 74
Buffalo Narrows B5 104
Buffalo, *lake* D5 94
Buffalo, *lake* E4 99
Buffalo, N.Y. F1 126
Bug, *river* E2, F3 41
Bugeac, *region* B3 50
Bugojno B1 48
Buhayrat al-Asad, *lake* B1 27
Buj-Buj Inset II 20
Bujumbura, *capital* B2 61
Buka, *island* B2 15
Bukavu C2 67
Bukhara B3 23
Bukit Pagon, *mt.* C3 13
Bukit Panjang B1 13
Bukit Timah B1 13
Bükk, *mts.* C1 43
Bukoba B1 68
Bula B1 62
Bulawayo B2 69
Bulembu B1 71
Bulgan C2 11
Bulgaria 50
Bulle B2 35
Bulyea F10 104
Bumba B1 67
Bunbury, W.A. A3 14
Bundaberg, Qld. E2 14
Bungo, *channel* B3 8
Bunia C1 67
Bunsuru, *river* D1 65
Buon Me Thuot B4 11
Buqayq C1 24
Buraydah B1 24
Burco B2 60
Burdekin, *river* D1 14
Burdett E6 94
Burdur, *lake* B3 27
Burdwan E4 20
Büren B3 40
Burgas F3 50
Burgeo C5 98
Burgos E1 37
Burhanpur C4 20
Burica, *point* A2 87
Burin D5 98
Burin, *peninsula* D5 98
Buriram C3 12
Burk's Falls F2 102
Burke, *channel* J5 95
Burkina Faso 64
Burlington F4 102
Burlington, Vt. F1 126
Burma (Myanmar) 12
Burnley C3 30
Burns Lake K4 95
Burntwood, *lake* A1 96
Burntwood, *river* B1, C1, D2 96
Bursa B2 27
Burtnieku, *lake* C2 46
Buru, *island* D2 13
Burundi 61
Bururi B2 61
Burutu C5 65
Burwash Landing B5 105
Bury C3 30
Bury St. Edmunds D3 30
Buryatiya, republic D7 44
Bushmanland, *plain* A2 71
Buta C1 67
Butare B2 61
Bute, *island* B2 30
Butha-Buthe B1 71
Butte, Mont. B1 126
Buttonville K5 102
Butuan C4 12
Butwal B2 19
Buurgplaatz, *mt.* B1 33
Buxton C3 30
Buyant-Uhaa D3 11
Buyo, *lake* C3 63
Büyük Menderes, *lake* A3 27
Buzău D3 43
Búzi, *river* B4 68
Büzmeyin C2 22
Byam Martin, *channel* G1 99
Byam Martin, *island* H1 99
Byarezina, *river* D3 47
Byblos, *ruins* A1 26
Bydgoszcz C2 41
Byelaruskaya Hrada, *range* C3 47
Bylot, *island* N2 99
Bytom D3 41
Byumba C1 61

C

Ca Mau A5 11
Ca, *river* A2 11
Caacupé D4 75
Caaguazú E4 75
Caazapá D5 75
Cabanatuan B3 12
Cabano H4 103
Cabimas B1 79
Cabinda B1 70
Cabo Rojo A2 90
Cabora Bassa, *dam* B2 68
Cabora Bassa, *lake* A2 68
Caborca B1 84
Cabrera C1 89
Cabrera, *island* H3 37
Çabri B10 104
Čačak B3 49
Cacao B1 80
Cáceres C3 81
Cáceres C3 37
Cache Creek M6 95
Cacheu A1 62
Cacheu, *river* B1 62
Cachimbo C2 81
Cacine B2 62
Cacouna G4 103
Cadiz B4 12
Cádiz C4 37
Cádiz, *gulf* C4 37
Cadomin B4 94
Cadotte Lake B3 94
Caen B2 34
Caerleon C3 30
Caernarfon B3 30
Cagayan de Oro C4 12
Cagayan Sulu, *island* A5 12
Cagayan, *islands* B4 12
Cagayan, *river* B2 12
Cagliari B3 38
Cagliari, *gulf* B3 38
Caguas C2 90
Caha, *mts.* B3 31
Cahors C4 34
Cahul B3 50
Caicos, *islands* D4 89
Caidasm da Rainha A3 36
Caille, *island* B1 91
Cairns, Qld. D1 14
Cairo, *capital* B1 56
Cairo, Ill. E2 126
Caja de Muertos, *island* B3 90
Cajamarca B2 77
Calabar E5 65
Calabogie J2 102
Calabozo C2 79
Calabria D3 38
Calafate A7 74
Calais C1 34
Calais B3 94
Calais B3 97
Calama C2 76
Calamian, *islands* A3 12
Calapan B3 12
Călărași D3 43
Calatayud F2 37
Calatrava B3 66
Calbayog C3 12
Calcutta E4, Inset II 20
Caledon, *river* A1, C2 71
Caledonia F4 102
Calgary C5 94
Cali A4 78
California B2 126
California, *gulf* B1 84
Callao B3 77
Calling Lake D3 94
Caltanissetta C3 38
Calvi Inset I 34
Calvinia A3 71
Cam Ranh B4 11
Camagüey D2 88
Camagüey, *archipelago* D2 88
Camberley Inset III 30
Cambodia 11
Cambrai C1 34
Cambrian, *mts.* B3 30
Cambridge D3 30
Cambridge Bay G3 99
Cambridge-Narrows D3 97
Cameron, *hills* B1 94
Cameron, *island* H1 99
Cameroon 65
Cameroon, *mt.* A3 65
Camiri B4 77
Camopi B2 80
Camopi, *river* B2 80
Campana, *island* A8 76
Campania C2 38
Campbell River K6 95
Campbellton C1 97
Campbellton A2 100
Campbellton K4 103
Campbelltown, N.S.W. Inset IV 14
Campbelltown, S.A. Inset II 14
Campbeltown B2 30
Campeche, *bay* F4 84
Campeche, *state capital* F4 84
Camper B3 96
Camperville A3 96
Campina Grande E2 81
Campinas D4 81
Campo Grande C4 81
Campobasso C2 38
Campobello, *island* C4 97
Campos D4 81
Campos Elísios Inset I 81
Camrose D4 94
Camsell Portage A1 104
Camú, *river* B1 89
Camuy B2 90
Can Tho A4 11
Caña Gorda, *beach* B3 90
Canaan B1 91
Canada 92
Canaima D2 79
Çanakkale A2 27
Canal Flats P6 95
Canaray, *islands* Inset I 37
Canaries A2 91
Canary, *islands* 55
Canaveral, *cape*, Fla. E3 126
Canberra, A.C.T., *natl. capital* D3 14
Canchungo A1 62
Cancún G3 84
Candelaria C2 90
Candiac J6 103
Candle Lake E7 104
Cando B8 104
Canelles, *river* B3 91
Canelones B3 75
Cangamba D4 70
Cangzhou E2 10
Caniapiscau, *lake* C3 101
Caniapiscau, *river* C2 101
Çankırı C2 27
Cankuzo C2 61
Cannes D5 34
Canning C2 100
Canning, *river* Inset I 14
Canoe Narrows B5 104
Canoe, *lake* B5 104
Canora H9 104
Canossa B1 38
Canouan, *island* B3 91
Canóvanas D2 90
Canso G2 100
Cantabria D1 37
Cantábrica, *mts.* C1 37
Canterbury D3 30
Canterbury B3 97
Canterbury, *bight* B3 15
Canterbury, *plains* B3 15
Canton, *island* B2 17
Canwood D7 104
Canyon Creek C3 94
Cao Bang B1 11
Cap-aux-Os M3 103
Cap-Chat K2 103
Cap-de-la-Madeleine D5 103
Cap-Haïtien C1 89
Cap-Pelé E2 97
Cap-Rouge K6 103
Cap-St-Ignace F4 103
Cape Charles D3 98
Cape Coast B4 64
Cape Girardeau, Mo. E2 126
Cape North G1 100
Cape Race E5 98
Cape Ray B5 98
Cape St. George B5 98
Cape Tormentine E2 97
Cape Town, *legislative capital* A3 71
Cape Verde 58
Cape York, *peninsula* D1 14
Capitán Pablo Lagerenza B1 75
Caplan L3 103
Caprara, *point* B2 38
Capreol D1 102
Capri, *island* C2 38
Capua C2 38
Caquetá, *river* B5 78
Car Nicobar, *island* F7 20
Caracas, *capital* C1 79
Caramoan, *peninsula* B3 12
Carapicuíba Inset II 81
Caraquet E1 97
Carberry B4 96
Carbonara, *cape* B3 38
Carbonear E5 98
Carbonia B3 38
Carcajou B2 94
Carcassonne C5 34
Carcross C5 105
Cardamom, *mts.* A3 11
Cárdenas B1 88
Cardiel, *lake* A6 74
Cardiff B3 30
Cardigan C2 100
Cardigan, *bay* B3 30
Cardigan, *bay* C2 100
Cardinal K3 102
Cardinal, *lake* B3 94
Caribbean, *sea* 82
Carievale A4 96
Carleton K3 103
Carleton Place J2 102
Carlingford C1 31
Carlingford, *lake* C1 31
Carlisle C2 30
Carlisle, *bay* A4 91
Carlow C2 31
Carlsbad, N. Mex. C2 126
Carlyle H11 104
Carmacks B4 105
Carman B4 96
Carmanville D4 98
Carmarthen B3 30
Carmelo A2 75
Carnac B3 34
Carnarvon B3 71
Carnarvon G2 102
Carnarvon, W.A. A2 14
Carnduff J11 104
Carnic Alps, *range* C4 39
Carnsore, *point* C2 31
Carolina D2 90
Caroline, *island* D2 17
Caroline, *islands* B2 15
Caron E10 104
Caroní, *river* D2 79
Carora C1 79
Carpathian, *mts.* 43
Carpentaria, *gulf* C1 14
Carrantuohill, *mt.* B3 31
Carriacou, *island* C1 91
Carrick-on-Shannon B2 31
Carroll A4 96
Carrot River G7 104
Carson City, *capital*, Nev. B2 126
Carstairs C5 94
Cartagena B2 78
Cartagena F4 37
Cartago C3 86
Carthage, ruin C1 57
Cartier D1 102
Cartwright B4 96
Cartwright C2 98
Carúpano D1 79
Carvoeiro, *cape* A3 36
Carway D6 94
Casa Grande, Ariz. B2 126
Casablanca Inset 76
Casablanca C1 57
Casamance, *region* B3 62
Casamance, *river* B3 62
Cascade Inset 70
Cascade, *range* A1 126
Cascapedia, *river* K3 103
Cascumpec, *bay* B2 100
Caserta C2 38
Cashel C2 31
Casiquiare, *river* C3 79
Caslan D4 94
Casper, Wyo. C1 126
Caspian, *depression* B2 23
Caspian, *sea* 7
Casselman K2 102
Cassiar H1 95
Cassiar, *mts.* G1 95
Castel Gandolfo C2 38
Castellón de la Plana F3 37
Castelo Branco B3 36
Castile and León D1, E1 37
Castile-la Mancha E3 37
Castle Bruce B2 90
Castle Mountain C5 94
Castlebar B2 31
Castlegar O6 95
Castries, *capital* B1 91
Castro B7 76
Cat, *island* B3 89
Catacamas C2 86
Catalina E5 98
Catalonia G2 37
Catamarca B2 74
Catanduanes, *island* C3 12
Catania C3 38
Cataño C2 90
Catanzaro D3 38
Catió B2 62
Catoche, *cape* G3 84
Catumbela B4 70
Cauca, *river* B3 78
Caucasus, *mts.* A1, A2 45
Caungula D2 70
Caura, *river* D2 79
Causapscal J3 103
Căușeni B2 50
Cauto, *river* E3 88
Cauvery, *river* C6 20
Cavalla, *river* C3 63
Cavally, *river* C4 63
Cavan C2 31
Cavendish B2 100
Caviana, *island* D1 81
Caxito B2 70
Cayambe, *mt.* C3 79
Cayenne, *capital* B1 80
Cayer B3 96
Cayey C2 90
Cayman, *trench* B2 88
Cayman, *islands* 88
Cayon B1 90
Cazombo E3 70
Ceará E2 81
Cebollatí, *river* C2 75
Cebu B4 12
Cebu, *island* B4 12
Cedar City, Utah B2 126
Cedar Grove E5 90
Cedar Rapids, Iowa D1 126
Cedar, *lake* A2 96
Cedros, *island* A2 84
Ceduna, S.A. C3 14
Ceerigaabo B1 60
Cefalù C3 38
Cegléd B2 43
Ceiba C2 90
Ceiba D2 90
Celada D2 90
Celaya D3 84
Celebes (Sulawesi), *island* D2 13
Celebes, *sea* D1 13
Celje C2 48
Celtic, *sea* B3 31
Central African Republic 66
Central Butte D10 104
Central Makran, *range* B4 21
Central Siberian, *plateau* C7 44
Centre C3 34
Centre C3 100
Centre de Flacq C2 69
Centreville E4 98
Ceram, *island* D2 13
Ceram, *sea* D2 13
Cerf, *island* Inset 70
Cernavodă E3 43
Cerro Castillo B9 76
Cerro de Pasco B3 77
Cervati, *mt.* C2 38
Cesis C2 46
České Budějovice B4 42
Cess, *river* B3 63
Cessford E6 94
Cetinje A3 49
Ceuta D5 37
Cévennes, *mts.* C4 34
Ceyhan, *river* D3 27
Chachapoyas B2 77
Chaco Boreal, *region* B2 75
Chad 59
Chad, *lake* A4, C3 59
Chaeryŏng, *river* A3 9
Chagai, *hills* B4 21
Chaghcharan B2 22
Chagres, *river* C2 87
Chaguanas A2 91
Chaitén B7 76
Chaiyaphum C3 12
Chalco Inset 84
Chaleur, *bay* D1 97
Chalna C6 21
Châlons-sur-Marne D2 34
Chambal, *river* C3 20
Chambéry D4 34
Chambeshi, *river* C2 67
Chambord D3 103
Chamelecon, *river* A2 86
Chamonix-Mont-Blanc D4 34
Champagne Castle, *mt.* C2 71
Champagne-Ardenne D2 34
Champaquí, *mt.* C3 74
Champasak C4 11

Key Page
Champerico B5 85
Champlain D5 103
Chañaral B3 76
Chança, *river* B4 36
Chandannagar Inset II 20
Chandigarh C2 20
Chandler M3 103
Chandpur D5 21
Chandrapur C5 20
Chang (Yangtze), *river* D2, E2 10
Changane, *river* B4 68
Changchun F1 10
Changde E3 10
Changhua B1 9
Changi B1 13
Changjin B2 9
Changjin, *river* B2 9
Changsha E3 10
Changuinola A2 87
Changyŏn A3 9
Changzhi E2 10
Changzhou F2 10
Channel *islands*, Calif. A2 126
Channel-Port aux Basques B5 98
Chantilly C2 34
Chao Phraya, *river* B3 12
Chapada dos Parecis, *range* C3 81
Chapala, *lake* D3 84
Chaparé, *river* A3 77
Chapleau D3 101
Chaplin D10 104
Chardzhou D2 22
Charente, *river* B4 34
Chari, *river* A5 59
Charikar B1 22
Charity B2 80
Charleroi C2 33
Charles A1 96
Charlesbourg E5, Inset 103
Charleston, *capital*, W. Va. E2 126
Charleston, S.C. F2 126
Charlestown C3 90
Charlestown A3 91
Charleville Mézières D2 34
Charleville, Qld. D2 14
Charlie Lake M3 95
Charlo C1 97
Charlotte, N.C. E2 126
Charlottetown C3 98
Charlottetown B2 100
Charlotteville B1 91
Charny E5, K6 103
Charters Towers, Qld. D2 14
Chartres C2 34
Chase N6 95
Châteauguay C6, H6 103
Châteauroux C3 34
Châtellerault C3 34
Chatfield C4 96
Chatham Inset III 30
Chatham C5 102
Chatham, *sound* G4 95
Chatkal, *river* B2 23
Chatsworth E3 102
Chattanooga, Tenn. E2 126
Chau Doc A4 11
Chaumont D2 34
Chaves B2 36
Cheb A2 42
Cheboksary D4 44
Chech'ŏn C4 9
Chechnya, republic E4 44
Cheduba, *island* B2 12
Chegutu B2 69
Cheju Inset 9
Cheju, *island* Inset 9
Cheju, *strait* Inset 9
Chek Keng Inset 10
Chelan G8 104
Cheleken A2 22
Chelif, *river* B1 57
Chelles Inset II 34
Chełm F3 41
Chelmsford D3, Inset III 30
Cheltenham C3 30
Chelyabinsk D5 44
Chelyuskin, *cape* B7 44
Chembur Inset I 20
Chemin Grenier B3 69
Chemnitz C3 40
Chenab, *river* D3 21
Chenachane A2 57
Chene Inset I 20
Chénéville A6 103
Chengde E1 10
Chengdu D2 10
Chennai (Madras) D6 20
Cherbourg B2 34
Cherepovets D3 44
Cherkassy C2 47
Chernigov C1 47
Chernivtsi B2 47
Cherrapunji F3 20
Cherryville N6 95
Cherskiy C10 44
Cherskiy, *range* C8 44
Chesapeake, *bay* F2 126
Chesley D3 102
Chester C3 30
Chester C3 100
Chesterfield C3 30
Chesterfield Inlet K4 99
Chesterfield, *islands* A2 18
Cheticamp G1 100
Chetumal, *state capital* G4 84
Chetwynd M3 95
Cheviot, *hills* C2 30
Chevreuse Inset II 34
Cheyenne, *capital*, Wyo. C1 126
Chhukha A2 19
Chi, *river* C2 12
Chiai B2 9
Chiang Mai B2 12
Chiang Rai B2 12
Chiapa C1 76
Chiapas F4 84
Chiatura B3 45
Chiba D3 8
Chibougamau B2 103
Chibougamau, *lake* B2 103
Chicago, Ill. E1 126
Chicapa, *river* D3 70
Chichén Itzá, *ruins* G3 84
Chichester C4 30
Chichi, *island* Inset III 8
Chiclayo B2 77
Chico, *river* B6 74
Chiconcuac Inset 84
Chicoutimi E3 103
Chief, *river* L2 95
Chiem, *lake* C5 40
Chiesanuova B2 39
Chieti C2 38
Chifeng E1 10
Chignecto, *bay* C2 100
Chihuahua, *state capital* C2 84
Chilcotin, *river* K5 95
Chile 76
Chile Chico B8 76
Chililabombwe B2 67
Chilko, *lake* K5 95
Chillán B6 76
Chilliwack M6 95
Chiloé, *island* B7 76
Chilpancingo, *state capital* E4 84
Chilung B1 9
Chilwa, *lake* B2, C3 68
Chimalhuacán Inset 84
Chimay C2 33
Chimborazo, *mt.* B3 79
Chimbote B2 77
Chimoio B3 68
Chin, *hills* B2 12
China 10
Chinajá C4 85
Chinandega A2 87
Chincha Alta B3 77
Chinchaga, *river* A2 94
Chinde C3 68
Chindwin, *river* B1 12
Chingola B2 67
Chingoni C2 67
Chinhae C5 9
Chinhoyi B1 69
Chiniot D3 21
Chinju C5 9
Chinko, *river* B2 66
Chioggia C1 38
Chip, *lake* C4 94
Chipata C2 67
Chipewyan Lake D3 94
Chipman D2 97
Chira, *river* A5 79
Chirchiq, *river* C2 23
Chire, *river* B3 68
Chiredzi B2 69
Chiriquí, *gulf* A3 87
Chiriquí, *lagoon* B2 87
Chirner Inset I 20
Chirripó, *mt.* C3 86
Chirripó, *river* C2 86
Chisasibi A3 101
Chisholm C4 94
Chişinău, *capital* B2 50
Chita D7 44
Chitipa B1 68
Chitose Inset I 8
Chitral D2 21
Chitré B3 87
Chittagong E6 21
Chitungwiza B1 69
Chixoy, *river* C4 85
Choa Chu Kang A1 13
Choiceland F7 104
Choiseul A3 91
Choiseul, *island* A1 16
Choisy-le Roi Inset II 34
Chojnice C2 41
Choke, *mts.* B2 60
Cholet B3 34
Cholpon-Ata E1 23
Cholula E4 84
Choluteca B3 86
Choma B3 67
Chon Lhari, *mt.* A1 19
Chon Buri B3 12
Chone A3 79
Ch'ŏngch'ŏn, *river* A3 9
Ch'ŏngjin C2 9
Ch'ŏngju B4 9
Ch'ŏngju A3 9
Chongqing D3 10
Chonju B5 9
Chonos, *archipelago* B7 76
Chontaleña, *mts.* B2 87
Chornobyl' C1 47
Chorzów D3 41
Choshui, *river* B2 9
Choybalsan D2 11
Christchurch B3 15
Christina, *river* E3 94
Christmas Island G2 100
Chu, *river* D1 23
Chubut, *river* A5 74
Chucunaque, *river* D2 87
Chugoku, *mts.* B3 8
Chukchi, *peninsula* C11 44
Chukchi, *range* C10 44
Chukchi, *sea* B11 44
Chukotka, autonomous okrug C10 44
Chumphon B4 12
Chunan B1 9
Ch'unch'ŏn B4 9
Chung Hau Inset 10
Chungho B1 9
Ch'ungju B4 9
Chungli B1 9
Chungqing, Ind. Mun. D3 10
Chungyang, *range* B2 9
Chuquicamata C2 76
Chur D2 35
Church Point A3 100
Churchbridge A4 96
Churchbridge J10 104
Churchill D1 96
Churchill Falls D3 98
Churchill, *lake* B4 104
Churchill, *river* D1 96
Churia, *mts.* B2 19
Chute-aux-Outardes H2 103
Chuuk, *islands* C2 15
Chuvashiya, republic D4 44
Ciales C2 90
Cibao, *valley* A1 89
Cicia, *island* C2 17
Cidra C2 90
Ciechánow E2 41
Ciego de Ávila D2 88
Cienfuegos C2 88
Cieza F3 37
Cijara, *reservoir* D3 37
Cikobia, *island* C1 17
Cilacap B2 13
Cilician Gates, *pass* C3 27
Cimone, *mt.* B1 38
Cincinnati, Ohio E2 126
Cirebon B2 13
Citlaltépetl, *mt.* E4 84
City View G6 102
Ciudad Acuña D2 84
Ciudad Bolívar D2 79
Ciudad Camargo C2 84
Ciudad Constitución B3 84
Ciudad del Carmen F4 84
Ciudad del Este E4 75
Ciudad Guayana D2 79
Ciudad Juárez C1 84
Ciudad Mante E3 84
Ciudad Obregón C2 84
Ciudad Real E3 37
Ciudad Rodrigo C2 37
Ciudad Valles E3 84
Ciudad Victoria, *state capital* E3 84
Ciudadela H2 37
Civitavecchia B2 38
Clair A1 97
Claire, *lake* D2 94
Clandeboye C4 96
Clara C2 31
Clarenville D5 98
Clark's Harbour B4 100
Clarksville, Tenn. E2 126
Clear Creek E5 102
Clear, *cape* B3 31
Clearwater M5 95
Clearwater, *river* E3 94
Clementsport B3 100
Clermont F4 103
Clermont-Ferrand C4 34
Clervaux B1 33
Clerve, *river* B1 33
Cleveland, Ohio E1 126
Clichy Inset II 34
Clifden A2 31
Clifford E4 102
Climax B11 104
Clinton M5 95
Clinton D4 102
Clinton Colden, *lake* G4 99
Cloncurry, Qld. D2 14
Clonmel C2 31
Cloridorme M2 103
Clovis, N. Mex. C2 126
Cloyne H3 102
Cluff Lake Mine A2 104
Cluj-Napoca B2 43
Cluny D3 34
Cluny D6 94
Clutha, *river* A4 15
Clyde River B4 100
Clyde River P2 99
Clyde, *estuary* B2 30
Clyde, *river* B2 30
Clydebank B2 30
Coacalco Inset 84
Coahuila D2 84
Coal River J1 95
Coal, *river* D5 105
Coaldale D6 94
Coalspur B4 94
Coamo C2 90
Coast, *mts.* F2, J5 95
Coast, *ranges* A1, A2 126
Coaticook E6 103
Coats Land, *region* B13 107
Coats, *island* M4 99
Coatzacoalcos F4 84
Cobán C4 85
Cobden J2 102
Cóbh B3 31
Cobham, *river* D2 96
Cobija A2 77
Cobourg G4 102
Coburg B3 40
Coburg, *island* N1 99
Cocagne E2 97
Cochabamba A3 77
Cochin (Kochi) C7 20
Cochrane B8 76
Cochrane D3 101
Cochrane, *lake* B8 76
Cochrane, *river* H2 104
Cockburn Harbour D4 89
Cockburn, *island* B2 102
Coclé del Norte B2 87
Coco C2 90
Coco, *islands* B3 12
Coco, *river* A2, C1 87
Cocos, *islands* 5
Cocotitlán Inset 84
Cod, *cape*, Mass. G1 126
Codri, *region* A3 50
Codrington E2 90
Codrington, *mt.* C17 107
Cody, Wyo. C1 126
Coe Hill H3 102
Coeroeni, *river* A3 80
Coeur d'Alene, Idaho B1 126
Cogalnic, *river* B2 50
Cognac B4 34
Coiba, *island* B3 87
Coihaique B8 76
Coimbatore C6 20
Coimbra A2 36
Cojedes, *river* C2 79
Colca, *river* C4 77
Colchester D3 30
Cold Lake E4 94
Coleraine A2 30
Coles Island D3 97
Coleville A9 104
Colihaut A2 90
Colima, *state capital* D4 84
Colina Inset 76
Coll, *island* A2 30
Collaguasi C2 76
Collingwood B3 15
Collingwood E3 102
Colmar D2 34
Cologne A3 40
Colombia 78
Colombier H3 103
Colombo, *capital* A5 19
Colón C2 87
Colón C2 88
Colonia A2 15
Colonia B3 75
Colonia Nueva Gúinea B3 87
Colonsay E9 104
Colonsay, *island* A2 30
Colorado C2 86
Colorado C2 126
Colorado Springs, Colo. C2 126
Colorado, *plateau* B2 126
Colorado, *river* B4 74
Colorado, *river* B2 126
Columbia, *capital*, S.C. E2 126
Columbia, *mts.* M4 95
Columbia, *plateau* B1 126
Columbia, *river* B1 126
Columbus, *capital*, Ohio E2 126
Columbus, Ga. E2 126
Coma Pedrosa, *mt.* A1 36
Comayagua B2 86
Comayagua, *mts.* B2 86
Combermere H2 102
Comendador A2 89
Comerío C2 90
Comilla E5 21
Comino, *island* B1 36
Cominotto, *island* B1 36
Comitán F4 84
Committee, *bay* L3 99
Communisim, *peak.* B1 23
Como B1 38
Como, *lake* B1 38
Comodoro Rivadavia B6 74
Comorin, *cape* C7 20
Comoros 67
Comox K6 95
Compiègne C2 34
Compton E6 103
Comrat B2 50
Con Son, *islands* B5 11
Conakry, *capital* B3 62
Concepción B6 76
Concepción D3 75
Concepción del Oro D3 84
Conchalí Inset 76
Conche D4 98
Conchos, *river* C2 84
Concord, *capital*, N.H. F1 126
Concordia D3 74
Condor C5 94
Congo, Dem Rep of 67
Congo, Rep of 66
Congo, *basin* D3 66
Congo, *river* D4 66
Congo, *river* B1 67
Conn, *lake* B1 31
Connecticut F1 126
Connemara, *region* B2 31
Consecon H4 102
Constance B5 40
Constance (Bodensee), *lake* D1 35
Constanţa E3 43
Constantine B1 57
Constitución B5 76
Consul A11 104
Contrecoeur C6 103
Contwoyto, *lake* G3 99
Conwy B3 30
Coober Pedy, S.A. C2 14
Cook's Harbour D3 98
Cook, *mt.* B3 15
Cook, *strait* B3 15
Cookshire E6 103
Cookstown F3 102
Coos Bay, Oreg. A1 126
Copán, *ruins* A2 86
Copenhagen, *capital* D3 32
Copiapó B3 76
Copiapó, *river* B3 76
Coppename, *river* A2 80
Coppermine, *river* F3 99
Coquí C3 90
Coquimbo B3 76
Coral, *sea* E1 14
Corantijn, *river* A2 80
Corazón C3 90
Corbeil-Essonnes Inset II 34
Corcovado, *gulf* B7 76
Corcovado, *mt.* Inset I 81
Córdoba C3 74
Córdoba D4 37
Córdoba, *range* B3 74
Corinth B3 51
Corinth, *gulf* B2 51
Corinth, *isthmus* B3 51
Corinto A2 87
Corisco, *bay* B4 66
Corisco, *island* B4 66
Cork B3 31
Cormack C4 98
Cormoran, *reef* B2 17
Cormorant A2 96
Cormorant, *lake* A2 96
Cornellá de Llogregat G2 37
Corner Brook C5 98
Corno, *mt.* C2 38
Cornwall B2 100
Cornwall L2 102
Cornwall, *island* K1 99
Cornwallis, *island* J1 99
Coro C1 79
Coromandel, *peninsula* C2 15
Coronach E11 104
Coronado, *bay* B3 86
Coronation, *gulf* F3 99
Coronel Oviedo D4 75
Coropuna, *mt.* C4 77
Corozal B1 85
Corozal C2 90
Corpus Christi, Tex. D3 126
Corregidor, *island* B3 12
Corrib, *lake* B2 31
Corrientes D2 74
Corse Inset I 34
Corsica, *island* Inset I 34
Cortina d'Ampezzo C1 38
Cortona B2 38
Corubal, *river* D1 62
Çoruh, *river* E2 27
Çorum C2 27
Corumbá C3 81
Corumbau, *point* E3 81
Corvallis, Oreg. A1 126
Cosenza D3 38
Coslada Inset II 37
Cosmoledo, *island group* A2 70
Costa Rica 86
Cotabato C5 12
Côte d'Ivoire 63
Cotentin, *peninsula* B2 34
Cotia Inset II 81
Coto Laurel B2 90
Cotonou B4 64
Cotopaxi, *mt.* B3 79
Cotswold, *hills* C3 30
Cottbus C3 40
Cotton Ground C2 90
Cotuí B1 89
Coubert Inset II 34
Couffo, *river* B4 64
Courantyne, *river* B3 80
Courland, *lagoon* A2 46
Courtenay K6 95
Courval D10 104
Coutts E6 94
Couva A2 91
Coventry C3 30
Covilhã B2 36
Cow Head C4 98
Cowan A3 96
Cowansville D6 103
Cowes C4 30
Cox's Bazar E7 21
Cox's Cove B4 98
Coyah B3 62
Coyoacán Inset 84
Cozumel, *island* G3 84
Cradock C3 71
Craigmyle D5 94
Craik E9 104
Craiova B3 43
Cranberry Portage A2 96
Cranbrook P6 95
Crane River B3 96
Crane Valley E11 104
Crapaud B2 100
Cravo Norte C3 78
Crawford Bay O6 95
Crawley Inset III 30
Crean, *lake* D6 104
Cree Lake D3 104
Cree, *river* E2 104
Cremona B1 38
Cremona C5 94
Cres, *island* B3 48
Cressday E6 94
Creston O6 95
Crete, *island* C4 51
Crete, *sea* C4 51
Créteil Inset II 34
Crewe C3 30
Crimean, *mts.* C4 47
Crimean, *peninsula* C3 47
Cristal, *mts.* A1 66
Cristóbal C2 87
Cristóbal Colón, *peak* B2 78
Crna Gora, *mts.* B3 49
Crna, *river* B2 48
Croatia 48
Crocker, *range* D2 13
Cromer A4 96
Crooked River G8 104
Crooked, *island* C4 89
Crooked, *river* L4 95
Cross Lake C2 96
Cross, *river* E4 65
Crotone D3 38
Cruz, *cape* D3 88
Cruzeiro do Sul A2 81
Crystal City B4 96
Cu Lao Thu, *island* B4 11
Cuajimalpa Inset 84
Cuamba C2 68
Cuando, *river* D4 70
Cuango, *river* D2 70
Cuanza, *river* C3 70
Cuareim, *river* B1 75
Cuauhtémoc C2 84
Cuautitlán Inset 84
Cuautitlán Izcalli Inset 84
Cuba 88
Cubal, *river* B4 70
Cubango, *river* D5 70
Cubatão Inset II 81
Cúcuta B3 78
Cuddalore C6 20
Cudworth E8 104
Cuenca B4 79
Cuenca E2 37
Cuernavaca, *state capital* E4 84
Cuiabá C3 81
Cuíto Cuanavale D5 70
Cuito, *river* D4 70
Cukorova, *region* C3 27
Culebra, *island* E2 90
Culebrinas, *river* A2 90
Culiacán, *state capital* C3 84
Cumaná D1 79
Cumberland K6 95
Cumberland House H7 104
Cumberland, *lake* H6 104
Cumberland, *peninsula* P3 99
Cumberland, *sound* P3 99
Cumbrian, *mts.* B2 30
Cunene, *river* B5, C4 70
Cuneo A1 38
Cupar B2 30
Cupar F10 104
Curaçao, *island* 82
Curaray, *river* C3 79
Curepipe C3 69
Curicó B4 76
Curitiba D4 81
Curral Velho D3 58
Curuzú Cuatiá D2 74
Cut Knife A8 104
Cuttack E4 20
Cuxhaven B2 40
Cuyo, *islands* B4 12
Cuyuni, *river* A2 80
Cuzco C3 77
Cyangugu A2 61
Cyclades, *islands* C3 51
Cypress River B4 96
Cyprus 27
Czar E5 94
Czech Republic 42
Częstochowa D3 41

D

Da Lat B4 11
Da Nang B3 11
Dabakala D2 63
Dabola C2 62
Dachang D3 10
Dachau B4 40
Dacotah C4 96
Dades, *river* C2 57
Dadu C4 21
Dafoe F9 104
Dagestan, republic E4 44
Dagupan B2 12
Dahlak, *archipelago* C2 60
Dahna, ad-, *desert* B1 24
Dahuk B1 24
Dajabón A1 89
Daka, *river* B2 64
Dakar, *capital* A2 62
Dakhla A2 58
Đakovica B3 49
Dalälven, *river* C2 53
Dalandzadgad C3 11
Dalhousie C1 97
Dalhousie K3 103
Dali D2 10
Dalian F2 10
Dallas C3 96
Dallas, Tex. D2 126
Dallol Bosso, *river* A3 59
Dalmatia, *region* B3 48
Daloa C3 63
Dalvík B2 52
Daly, *river* C1 14
Daman B4 20
Damanhur B1 56
Damascus, *capital* A3 27
Damaturu F2 65
Damavand, *mt.* C2 22
Damazin, ad- C3 59
Dame-Marie A2 89
Damietta B1 56
Damietta, *river* B1 56
Dammam, ad- C1 24
Dammartin-en-Goële Inset II 34
Dampier, W.A. A2 14
Damur, ad- A2 26
Danakil, *desert* C2 60
Danané B3 63
Dand A4 96
Dande, *river* B2 70
Dandeldhura A2 19
Dandong F1 10
Dangara A1 23
Dangme, *river* C2 19
Dangrek, *mts.* C3 12
Dangriga B2 85
Daniel's Harbour C4 98
Danjiangkou E2 10
Danlí B2 86
Danube, *river* 29
Danville D6 103
Danville, Va. F2 126
Dao Phu Quoc, *island* A4 11
Dapaong B1 64
Dapp D4 94
Daqing F1 10
Dar es-Salaam, *capital* C2 68
Dara A3 27
Dara B2 62
Đaravica, *mt.* B3 49
Darbhanga E3 20
Darhan C2 11
Darién, *mts.* D2 87
Dariense, *mts.* B2 87
Darjiling E3 20
Darling, *range* A3 14
Darling, *river* D3 14
Darlington C2 30
Darłowo C1 41
Darmstadt B4 40
Darnah D1 56
Darnley B2 100
Dartmoor, *plateau* B4 30
Dartmouth D3 100
Daru A2 15
Darwin, N.T., *capital* C1 14
Dashhowuz C2 22
Dasht-e Kavir, *desert* D3 22
Dasht-e Lut, *desert* D3 22
Datong E1 10
Daua, *river* F1 61
Daugavpils D3 46
Daule, *river* B3 79
Dauphin B1 91
Dauphin A3 96
Dauphin River B3 96
Dauphin, *lake* B3 96

	Key	Page
Davao	C5	12
Davao, *gulf*	C5	12
Davenport, Iowa	D1	126
David	A2	87
Davidson	D9	104
Davis Inlet	E3	98
Davis, *strait*	M2	92
Davos	D2	35
Dawa, *river*	C3	60
Dawhat as-Salwa, *bay*	B3	25
Dawkah	B2	25
Dawna, *range*	B2	12
Dawson	B3	105
Dawson Creek	M3	95
Dawson, *bay*	A2	96
Daymán, *river*	B1	75
Dayr az-Zawr	B2	27
Dayton, Ohio	E2	126
Daytona Beach, Fla.	E3	126
De Aar	B3	71
De Quincy Village	Inset	70
Dead Sea, *lake*	A2	26
Dead, *sea*	B2	26
Dean, *channel*	J5	95
Dean, *river*	K5	95
Dease Lake	G2	95
Death, *valley*, Calif.	B2	126
Deauville	C2	34
Debar	A2	48
Debden	D7	104
Debed, *river*	B2	45
DeBolt	A3	94
Debre Birhan	C2	60
Debre Markos	B2	60
Debrecen	C2	43
Decatur, Ill.	E2	126
Deccan, *plateau*	C5	20
Děčín	B2	42
Dédougou	C2	64
Dedza	B2	68
Dee, *river*	B3, C1	30
Deep River	H1	102
Deep, *inlet*	B1	98
Deepdale	A3	96
Deer Lake	C4	98
Deerfield	A4	100
Degeh Bur	D2	60
Dégelis	H4	103
Dehiwala-Mt. Lavinia	A5	19
Dehra Dun	C2	20
Dej	B2	43
Del Rio, Tex.	C3	126
Delacour	D5	94
Delap Cove	B3	100
Delaronde, *lake*	C6	104
Delaware	F2	126
Delburne	D5	94
Deleau	A4	96
Delft	B2	32
Delft, *island*	A2	19
Delfzijl	D1	32
Delgado	A2	86
Delhi	C3	20
Delhi	E5	102
Delicias	C2	84
Déline	D3	99
Delisle	C9	104
Deloraine	A4	96
Delos, *island*	C3	51
Delson	J6	103
Delta Beach	B4	96
Demerara, *river*	B3	80
Den Helder	B2	32
Denakil, *desert*	C1	60
Denare Beach	H6	104
Denbigh	H2	102
Dencross	C4	96
Dender, *river*	B2	33
Denigomodu	A2	16
Denmark		**32**
Denmark, *strait*	D2	106
Dennery	B2	91
Denpasar	C2	13
D'Entrecasteaux, *islands*	B2	15
D'Entrecasteaux, *reefs*	C1	18
Denver, *capital*, Colo.	C2	126
Denzil	A8	104
Dera Ghazi Khan	D3	21
Dera Ismail Khan	D3	21
Derby	C3	30
Derg, *lake*	B2	31
Derrick	B3	91
Derventa	B1	48
Derwent	E4	94
Des Moines, *capital*, Iowa	D1	126
Desaguadero, *river*	B2	74
Desaguadero, *river*	A3	77
Desberats	B1	102
Deschaillons	D5	103
Deschambault Lake	G6	104
Dese	C2	60
Deseado, *river*	B6	74
Deseronto	H3	102
Desna, *river*	C1	47
Desolación, *island*	B9	76
Desruisseau	B3	91
Dessau	C3	40
Destruction Bay	B5	105
Detmold	B3	40
Detroit, Mich.	E1	126
Deux Rivieres	G1	102
Deux-Montagnes	H5	103
Deva	B3	43
Deventer	D2	32
Devil's, *island*	B1	80
Devoll, *river*	B3	49
Devon, *island*	L1	99
Devonport, Tas.	D4	14
Dewberry	E4	94
Dezful	B3	22
Dháfni	Inset	51
Dhahran	C1	24
Dhaka, *capital*	D5	21
Dhamar	A2	25
Dhangarhi	A2	19
Dhankuta	D2	19
Dharan	D3	19
Dhaulagiri, *mt.*	B2	19
Dhofar, *region*	B3	25
Dhulagarh	Inset II	20
Dhuusamareeb	B2	60
Diadema	Inset II	81
Dialakoto	C3	62
Diamond, *island*	B1	91
Dibrugarh	F3	20
Diefenbaker, *lake*	C10	104
Diekirch	B2	33
Dien Bien Phu	A2	11
Dieppe	C2	34
Dieppe	E2	97
Dieppe Bay Town	B1	90
Diffa	C3	59
Differdange	A2	33
Digby	B3	100
Digne	D4	34
Digul, *river*	E2	13
Dijon	D3	34
Dikhil	B2	60
Dikson	B6	44
Dili	D2	13
Dilijan	B2	45
Dillon	B5	104
Dilolo	B3	67
Dimbokro	D3	63
Dimitrovgrad	D3	50
Dimlang, *mt.*	F3	65
Dimona	B2	26
Dinagat, *island*	C4	12
Dinajpur	B3	21
Dinant	C2	33
Dinara, *mt.*	A2, C3	48
Dinaric Alps, *mts.*	A1, B3	48
Dinder, *river*	B1	60
Dingle	A2	31
Dingle, *bay*	A2	31
Dingli	B2	36
Dinsmore	C9	104
Diourbel	A2	62
Dipolog	B4	12
Dire Dawa	D2	60
Diriamba	A3	87
Dispur	F3	20
Diu	B4	20
Diuata, *mts.*	C4	12
Divo	D4	63
Divriği	D2	27
Diwaniyah, ad-	C2	24
Dixon Entrance, *channel*	F4	95
Dixonville	B3	94
Diyala, *river*	C2	24
Diyarbakır	E3	27
Dja, *river*	B3	65
Djado	C1	59
Djambala	C5	66
Djanet	B2	57
Djelfa	B1	57
Djenné	C3	58
Djerba, *island*	C3	57
Djibouti		**60**
Djibouti, *capital*	C2	60
Djouah, *river*	B1	66
Djouf, el-, *desert*	B1, C3	58
Djougou	A3	64
Dnepr-Bug, *canal*	B3	47
Dneprodzerzhinsk	C2	47
Dnieper, *river*	C1, E3	47
Dniester, *river*	B2	47
Dnipropetrovsk	D2	47
Doaktown	C2	97
Doba	B5	59
Doboj	B1	48
Dobrich	F2	50
Dobruja, *region*	E3	43
Doctor Pedro P. Peña	A3	75
Dodecanese, *islands*	C3	51
Dodge City, Kans.	C2	126
Dodoma	C2	68
Dodsland	B9	104
Doetinchem	D3	32
Dogo, *island*	B2	8
Dogondoutchi	A3	59
Doha, *capital*	D3	25
Doiran, *lake*	C2	48
Dolbeau	D3	103
Dôle	D3	34
Dolomites, *range*	B1	38
Domagnano	B1	39
Domeyko, *mts.*	C3	76
Dominica		**90**
Dominica, *passage*	A1	90
Dominican Republic		**89**
Dominion City	C4	96
Domont	Inset II	34
Domremy	E8	104
Domuyo, *volcano*	A4	74
Don Benito	D3	37
Doña Juana, *mt.*	C2	90
Donald Station	O5	95
Doncaster	C3	30
Dondo	B3	70
Donegal	B1	31
Donegal, *bay*	B1	31
Donets, *basin*	D2	47
Donetsk	D2	47
Dong Hoi	B3	11
Dong Nai, *river*	B4	11
Dongting, *lake*	E3	10
Dongwe, *river*	A2	67
Donnacona	E5	103
Dor, *lake*	C6	104
Dorado	C2	90
Dorchester	C4	30
Dordogne, *river*	C4	34
Dordrecht	B3	32
Dore Lake	C6	104
Dörgön, *lake*	B2	11
Dori	D1	64
Dorintosh	B6	104
Dorking	Inset III	30
Dornoch	B1	30
Dorohoi	D2	43
Dorothy	D5	94
Dorra	B1	60
Dortmund	A3	40
Dorval	H6	103
Dos Hermanas	D4	37
Dosquet	E5	103
Dosso	A3	59
Dothan, Ala.	E2	126
Douai	C1	34
Douala	A3	65
Doubs, *river*	A1	35
Douglas	B2	30
Douglas, *channel*	H4	95
Douglastown	M3	103
Dourados	C4	81
Douro, *river*	B2	36
Dover	D3	30
Dover, *capital*, Del.	F2	126
Dover, *strait*	D4	30
Dovrefjell, *mts.*	B3	52
Dozen, *island*	B2	8
Drâa, *river*	A1, B2, C2	57
Draguignan	D5	34
Drake	E9	104
Drakensberg, *mts.*	B3, C3	71
Drammen	C4	52
Drava, *river*	A2	43
Drayton Valley	C4	94
Dresden	C3	40
Dresden	C5	102
Dreux	C2	34
Drin, *river*	A1	49
Drina, *river*	A2	49
Drobeta-Turnu Severin	B3	43
Drogheda	C2	31
Drumheller	D5	94
Drummond	B2	97
Drummondville	D6	103
Druskininkai	B2	46
Dryden	B3	101
Dschang	B2	65
Duars, *plain*	A3	19
Duarte, *mt.*	B1	89
Dubăsari	B2	50
Dubawnt, *lake*	H4	99
Dubawnt, *river*	H4	99
Dubayy	C2	25
Dubbo, N.S.W.	D3	14
Dube, *river*	C3	63
Dublin, *capital*	C2	31
Dubrovnik	D4	48
Dubuque, Iowa	D1	126
Dubysa, *river*	B2	46
Duchess	E6	94
Duck Bay	A3	96
Duck Lake	D8	104
Dudelange	B2	33
Dudinka	C6	44
Dudley	C3	30
Duero, *river*	D2	37
Dufourspitze, *mt.*	B3	35
Dufrost	C4	96
Dugald	C4	96
Duisburg	A3	40
Dukhan	B3	25
Dulce, *gulf*	C4	86
Duluth, Minn.	D1	126
Dum-Dum	Inset II	20
Duma	A1	26
Dumaguete	B4	12
Dumbås	B3	52
Dumfries	B2	30
Dumjor	Inset II	20
Dún Laoghaire	C2	31
Dunaújváros	B2	43
Duncan	L7	95
Duncansby, *cape*	B1	30
Dund-Us	B2	11
Dundalk	C2	31
Dundee	C2	30
Dundurn	D9	104
Dunedin	B4	15
Dunfermline	B2	30
Dungarvan	C2	31
Dunkirk (Dunkerque)	C1	34
Dunkwa	B4	64
Dunlop	B2	96
Dunnegan	F1	100
Dunnville	F5	102
Dunqulah	C1	59
Dunsinane, *mt.*	B2	30
Dunstable	Inset III	30
Dunster	N4	95
Duqm	C2	25
Duque de Caxias	Inset I	81
Duque de York, *island*	A9	76
Durance, *river*	D5	34
Durango, Colo.	C2	126
Durango, *state capital*	D3	84
Durazno	B2	75
Durban	D2	71
Durham	C2	30
Durham	E3	102
Durham, N.C.	F2	126
Durmitor, *mts.*	A3	49
Durrës	A2	49
Dushanbe, *capital*	A1	23
Düsseldorf	A3	40
Dutse	E2	65
Dyce	A2	96
Dyje, *river*	B4	42
Dzaoudzi, *territorial capital*	C2	67
Dzavhan, *river*	B2	11
Dzhugdzhur, *range*	D8	44
Dzungaria, *desert basin*	B1	10
Dzyarzhynskaya Hara, *mt.*	C3	47

E

	Key	Page
Eagle, *river*	B2	98
Eagle, *river*	B2	105
Ear Falls	B2	101
East Angus	E6	103
East Antarctica	B1	107
East Braintree	D4	96
East China, *sea*		7
East Coast Bays	B2	15
East Coulee	D5	94
East Frisian, *islands*	A2	40
East Lake Ainslie	F1	100
East London	C3	71
East Point	C2	100
East Siberian, *sea*	B10	44
East York	K5	102
East, *cape*	C2	15
Eastbourne	D4	30
Eastend	B11	104
Eastern Ghats, *mts.*	C6	20
Easterville	B2	96
Eastmain	A3	101
Eastmain, *river*	B3	101
Eastport	E5	98
Eatonia	A9	104
Eau Claire, Wis.	D1	126
Eauripik, *atoll*	B2	15
Ebebiyín	D2	66
Eberswalde	C2	40
Ebolowa	B3	65
Ebon, *island*	B3	16
Ebor	A4	96
Ebro, *river*	F1	37
Ecatepec	Inset	84
Echo Bay	E3	99
Echo Bay	A1	102
Echternach	B2	33
Écija	D4	37
Ecuador		**79**
Ed	C3	60
Edam	C2	32
Edam	B7	104
Eddies Cove	C3	98
Eddystone	B3	96
Ede	C4	65
Ede	C2	32
Edéa	B3	65
Edgerton	E5	94
Edinburgh	B2	30
Edirne	A2	27
Edmonton, *capital*	D4	94
Edmundston	A1	97
Edmundston	H4	103
Édouard, *lake*	D4	103
Edrans	B4	96
Edson	B4	94
Edward, *lake*	A4	61
Edwards *plateau*, Tex.	C2	126
Eems, *river*	D1	32
Éfaté, *island*	C3	18
Egadi, *islands*	C3	38
Eganville	H2	102
Eger	C2	43
Egersund	B4	52
Eglinton, *island*	E1	99
Egmont, *bay*	A2	100
Egmont, *cape*	B2	15
Egmont, *mt.*	B2	15
Eğridir, *lake*	B2	27
Egypt		**56**
Eifel, *plateau*	A3	40
Eigg, *island*	A2	30
Eindhoven	C3	32
Einsiedeln	C1	35
Eiseb, *river*	D2	70
Eisenach	B3	40
Eisenhüttenstadt	C2	40
Eisleben	B3	40
Ejmiatsin	B2	45
Ejura	B3	64
Ekibastuz	D1	23
Ekwan, *river*	D2	101
El Cañuelo, *ruins*	C2	90
El Cerro del Aripo, *mt.*	A2	91
El Encanto	B5	78
El Ferrol	B1	37
El Macao	D2	89
El Paso, Tex.	C2	126
El Pital, *mt.*	A1	86
El Porvenir	C2	87
El Progreso	B2	86
El Salvador		**86**
El Seibo	C2	89
El Serrat	B1	36
El Tabo	Inset	76
El Tigre	D2	79
El Toro, *mt.*	D2	90
El Trebolar	Inset	76
Elat	B3	26
Elâzığ	D2	27
Elba, *island*	B2	38
Elbasan	B2	49
Elbe, *river*	B2, C3	40
Elbert *mt.*, Colo.	C2	126
Elbląg	D1	41
Elbow	D9	104
Elburz, *mts.*	C2	22
Elche	F3	37
Eldon	C2	100
Eldoret	C3	61
Elephant, *island*	C12	107
Elephanta, *island*	Inset I	20
Eleuthera, *island*	B2	89
Elevsís	Inset	51
Elfros	G9	104
Elgin	B1	30
Elgin	A4	96
Elgin	D3	97
Elgon, *mt.*	D3	61
Eli Malk, *island*	B3	17
Elie	C4	96
Elista	E4	44
Ełk	F4	41
Elk Point	E4	94
Elkford	P6	95
Elkhorn	A4	96
Elkhovo	E3	50
Elko	P6	95
Elko, Nev.	B1	126
Ellef Ringnes, *island*	H1	99
Ellerts de Haan, *mts.*	A3	80
Ellesmere, *island*	M1	99
Ellice, *river*	G3	99
Ellinikón	Inset	51
Elliot Lake	C1	102
Ellisras	C1	71
Ellsworth Land, *region*	B10	107
Ellsworth, *mts.*	B10	107
Elm Creek	C4	96
Elma	D4	96
Elmina	B4	64
Elmira	C2	100
Elmira	E4	102
Elmsdale	A2	100
Elmvale	F3	102
Elnora	D5	94
Elqui, *river*	B3	76
Elrose	B9	104
Elsa	B4	105
Elva	A4	96
Elvas	B3	36
Ely	D3	30
Ely, Nev.	B2	126
Embarcación	C1	74
Embarras Portage	E2	94
Embi	B2	23
Embu	D4	61
Emden	A2	40
Emerald, *island*	F1	99
Emerald, Qld.	D2	14
Emerson	C4	96
Emi Koussi, *mt.*	B3	59
Emilia-Romagna	B1	38
Emlembe, *mt.*	B1	71
Emmeloord	C2	32
Emmen	D2	32
Emporia, Kans.	D2	126
Ems, *river*	A2	40
Encarnación	E5	75
Enchant	D6	94
Ende	D2	13
Enderbury, *island*	B2	17
Enderby	N6	95
Enderby Land, *region*	C17	107
Endiang	D5	94
Enewetak, *island*	A1	16
Engadine, *valley*	D2	35
Engaño, *cape*	D2	89
Enggano, *island*	B2	13
Englee	C4	98
English, *channel*	C4	30
Englishtown	G1	100
Enguri, *river*	A3	45
Enid, Okla.	D2	126
Enilda	B3	94
Enna	C3	38
Ennadai, *lake*	H4	99
Ennery	C1	89
Ennis	B2	31
Ennistymon	B2	31
Enns, *river*	D3	39
Enriquillo, *lake*	A2	89
Enschede	D2	32
Ensenada	A1	84
Ensenguly	A3	22
Entebbe	C3	61
Enugu	D4	65
Épi, *island*	C3	18
Epinal	D2	34
Episkopi	A2	27
Epsom	Inset III	30
Equatorial, *channel*	A5	19
Equatorial Guinea		**66**
Er Rif, *range*	C1	57
Erciyes Daği, *mt.*	C2	27
Érd	B2	43
Erdenet	C2	11
Erebus, *mt.*	B5	107
Erenhot	E1	10
Erfurt	B3	40
Erg Chech, *desert*	C1	58
Erg Iguidi, *desert*	D1	58
Erickson	B4	96
Erie, *lake*	E5	102
Erie, Pa.	E1	126
Eriksdale	B4	96
Erimo, *cape*	Inset I	8
Eritrea		**60**
Erlangen	B4	40
Ermelo	C2	71
Erne, *river*	A2	30
Errigal, *mt.*	B1	31
Erromango, *island*	C4	18
Ersekë	B3	49
Erzen, *river*	A2	49
Erzgebirge, *mts.*	C3	40
Erzincan	D2	27
Erzurum	E2	27
Esbjerg	B3	32
Esch-sur-Alzette	A2	33
Eschen	B1	33
Escondido, *river*	B2	87
Escuintla	C5	85
Escuminac	K3	103
Esfahan	C3	22
Esil	C1	23
Esker	D3	98
Eskifjördhur	C2	52
Eskilstuna	C3	53
Eskimo Point	K4	99
Eskişehir	B2	27
Esla, *river*	D2	37
Esmeraldas	B2	79
Espanola	D1	102
Española, *island*	Inset	79
Esperance, W.A.	B3	14
Espichel, *cape*	A3	36
Espírito Santo	D3	81
Espiritu Santo, *island*	B2	18
Espoo	B2	53
Esquel	A5	74
Essaouira	B2	57
Essen	A3	40
Essequibo, *river*	B3, B5	80
Essex	C5	102
Esslingen	B4	40
Estados, *island*	C7	74
Estaire	E1	102
Estany d'Engolasters, *lake*	B2	36
Este, *point*	E2	90
Estelí	A2	87
Esterhazy	H10	104
Estevan	G11	104
Esther	E5	94
Eston	B9	104
Estonia		**46**
Estoril	A3	36
Estrela, *mts.*	B2	36
Esztergom	B2	43
Etchemin, *river*	L6	103
Ethelbert	A3	96
Ethiopia		**60**
Ethiopia, *plateau*	C2	60
Etna, *mt.*	C3	38
Etobicoke	J5	102
Etosha, *pan*	B1	70
Etrechy	Inset II	34
Etrek, *river*	B3	22
Ettelbruck	B2	33
'Eua, *island*	C4	17
Euboea, *island*	B2	51
Eugene, Oreg.	A1	126
Eugenia, *point*	A2	84
Euphrates, *river*	C2	24
Eureka, Calif.	A1	126
Eutsuk, *lake*	J4	95
Evandale	C3	97
Evansville	C2	102
Evansville, Ind.	E2	126
Evenkiya, autonomous okrug	C6	44
Everest, *mt.*	C2	19
Everett, Wash.	A1	126
Evinayong	C3	66
Évora	B3	36
Évreux	C2	34
Évry	Inset II	34
Ewa	B1	16
Ewell	Inset III	30
Ewo	C4	66
Exeter	B4	30
Exeter	D4	102
Exmoor, *plateau*	B3	30
Extremadura	C3	37
Exuma, *sound*	B3	89
Eyasi, *lake*	B1	68
Eyebrow	D10	104
Eyl	B2	60
Eyre, *lake*	C2	14
Eyre, *peninsula*	C3	14
Eysturoy, *island*	Inset	32

F

	Key	Page
Fabyan	E5	94
Fada	C3	59
Fadiffolu, *atoll*	A2	19
Faenza	B1	38
Faeroe, *islands*	Inset	32
Fagamalo	B1	18
Făgăras	C3	43
Fagasa	B1	18
Fagatogo	B1	18
Fair, *island*	Inset I	30
Fairbanks, Alaska	Inset I	126
Fairford	B3	96
Fairmont Hot Springs	P6	95
Fairweather, *mt.*	D1	95
Faisalabad	D3	21
Faizabad	D3	20
Fajardo	D2	90
Fakfak	E2	13
Falciano	C1	39
Falcon Lake	D4	96
Falelatai	B2	18
Falelima	A2	18
Falémé, *river*	C2	62
Faleniu	B1	18
Fălești	A2	50
Falher	B3	94
Falkland, *islands*	C7	74
Fallujah, al-	B2	24
Falmouth	B2	88
Falmouth	E5	90
False Divi, *point*	D5	20
Falster, *island*	D4	32
Falun	C2	53
Famagusta	B1	27
Fan Si Pan, *mt.*	A1	11
Fangliao	B2	9
Fanø, *island*	B3	32
Farafangana	B3	69
Farafenni	C2	62
Farah	A2	22
Farah, *river*	A2	22
Faraulep, *atoll*	B2	15
Farewell, *cape*	B3	15
Farewell, *cape*	C3	106
Farghona	D2	23
Fargo, N. Dak.	D1	126
Faridpur	C5	21
Farim	B1	62
Farmington	M3	95
Farmington, N. Mex.	C2	126
Farnham	Inset III	30
Faro	B4	36
Faro	C4	105
Farquhar, *island group*	B2	70
Farrellton	A6	103
Fashir, al-	B2	59
Fatick	A2	62
Fatoto	E2	62
Fauquier	N6	95
Faxaflói, *bay*	A2	52
Faxälven, *river*	C2	53
Faya-Largeau	B3	59
Faylakah, *island*	C2	24
Fayyum, al-	B2	56
Fdérik	B2	58
Fehmarn, *island*	B1	40
Fehmarn, *strait*	C4	32
Feira de Santana	E3	81
Feldkirch	A3	39
Felidu, *atoll*	A3	19
Felixstowe	D3	30
Fen, *river*	E2	10
Fenelon Falls	G3	102
Fengshan	B2	9
Fengyüan	B1	9
Feni, *islands*	B2	15
Fens, *region*	D3	30
Feodosiya	D3	47
Fergana, *valley*	D2	23
Fergus	E4	102
Ferkéssédougou	D2	63
Ferlo, *river*	B2	62
Ferme-Neuve	A5	103
Fernandina, *island*	Inset	79
Fernie	P6	95
Ferrara	B1	38
Ferryland	E5	98
Fethiye	B3	27
Feuilles, *river*	B2	101
Feyzabad	C1	22
Fez	C1	57

	Key	Page
narantsoa	B3	69
chtelberg, *mt.*	C3	40
chtelgebirge, *mts.*	B4	40
eld	O5	95
eld	E1	102
er	A3	49
e, *lake*	E11	104
g Tree	C3	90
gueira da Foz	A2	36
gueres	H1	37
guig	D1	57
i		17
adelfia	B3	75
chner Ice Shelf, *glacier*	B12	107
fla, *island*	B3	36
lmore	G11	104
mbul Ice Shelf, *glacier*	B14	107
nisterre, *cape*	B1	37
nland		**53**
nland, *gulf*	C3	53
nlay, *river*	J2	95
nn, *river*	C1	31
nnegan	D5	94
nnmark, *plateau*	E2	52
reside	J1	95
rth, *river*	A1	105
sh, *river*	C4	70
sher Branch	C3	96
sherton	C3	96
shguard	B3	30
tzgerald	E1	94
tzroy, *mt.*	B8	76
tzroy, *river*	B1	14
ve Islands	C2	100
agstaff, Ariz.	B2	126
at, *island*	C1	69
atbush	C4	94
axcombe	A9	104
eet	E5	94
eetwood	C3	30
eming	A4	96
ensburg	B1	40
esherton	E3	102
eur de Lys	C4	98
evoland, *polder*	C2	32
in Flon	A2, C2	96
inders, *range*	C3	14
inders, *river*	D1	14
int, *island*	D3	17
int, Mich.	E1	126
odden Field, *plain*	C2	30
orence	B2	38
orence, S.C.	F2	126
orenceville	B2	97
orencia	B4	78
ores	D3	85
ores, *island*	D2	13
ores, *sea*	C2	13
oreşti	B2	50
oriano	D2	81
orianópolis	D4	81
orida	B3	75
orida	D2	88
orida	B2	90
orida	E3	126
orida Keys, Fla.	E3	126
orida, *straits*	B1	88
orø	A3	52
ly, *river*	A2	15
oam Lake	G9	104
oča	B2	48
ocşani	D3	43
oggia	C2	38
ogo	D4	98
ogo, *island*	B4	58
oix	C5	34
olkestone	D3	30
omboni	A2	67
ond du Lac, *river*	F2	104
ond-du-Lac	C1	104
onseca, *gulf*	B3, C2	86
ontainebleau	C2	34
ontas	M2	95
ontvieille	A2	35
onuafobu (Falcon), *island*	B3	17
onualei, *island*	C2	17
Forest	D4	102
Forestville	G3	103
Fork River	A3	96
Forli	C1	38
Formentera, *island*	G3	37
Formosa	D2	74
Fort Albany	D2	101
Fort Chipewyan	E2	94
Fort Collins, Colo.	C1	126
Fort Erie	G5	102
Fort Frances	B3	101
Fort Fraser	K4	95
Fort Good Hope	C3	99
Fort Lauderdale, Fla.	E3	126
Fort Liard	D4	99
Fort MacKay	E2	94
Fort McMurray	E3	94
Fort McPherson	B3	99
Fort Myers, Fla.	E3	126
Fort Nelson	L2	95
Fort Nelson, *river*	L1	95
Fort Norman	C4	99
Fort Portal	B3	61
Fort Providence	E4	99
Fort Qu'Appelle	G10	104
Fort Resolution	F4	99
Fort Saskatchewan	D4	94
Fort Severn	C1	101
Fort Simpson	D4	99
Fort Smith, Ark.	D2	126
Fort Smith, *region*	E4	99
Fort St. James	K4	95
Fort St. John	M3	95
Fort Steele	P6	95
Fort Stockton, Tex.	C2	126
Fort Vermilion	C2	94
Fort Wayne, Ind.	E1	126
Fort William	B2	30
Fort Worth, Tex.	D2	126
Fortaleza	E2	81
Forteau	C3	98
Forth, *estuary*	C2	30
Forth, *river*	B2	30
Fortín Conde de Mirasol, *fort*	E2	90
Fortín Ravelo	B3	77
Fortune	D5	98
Fortune Bridge	C2	100
Fortune, *bay*	D5	98
Foster, *river*	E4	104
Fosterville	B3	97
Foumban	B2	65
Foumbouni	A1	67
Four Falls	B2	97
Foveaux, *strait*	A4	15
Fox Island	F2	100
Fox Lake	C2	94
Fox Valley	A10	104
Foxe, *basin*	N3	99
Foxe, *channel*	M3	99
Foxe, *peninsula*	N4	99
Foyle, *inlet*	C1	31
Foyle, *lake*	A2	30
Foyle, *river*	A2	30
Foz do Iguaçu	C4	81
France		**34**
Frances, *lake*	D5	105
Franceville	B2	66
Franche-Comté	D3	34
Francis	G10	104
Francistown	B2	69
Francois	C5	98
François, *lake*	K4	95
Franconian Jura, *mts.*	B4	40
Frankenwald, *mts.*	B3	40
Frankford	H3	102
Frankfort, *capital*, Ky.	E2	126
Frankfurt am Main	B3	40
Frankfurt an der Oder	C2	40
Franklin, *strait*	J2	99
Franquelin	J2	103
Franz Josef Land, *islands*	A4	44
Fraser	E1	95
Fraser Lake	K4	95
Fraser, *river*	L5, M4	95
Fraserburgh	C1	30
Fraserdale	D2	101
Fraserwood	C4	96
Fray Bentos	A2	75
Fredericia	B3	32
Fredericton	C3	97
Fredericton	B2	100
Fredericton Jct.	C3	97
Frederiksberg	D3	32
Frederikshavn	C1	32
Fredrikstad	C4	52
Freeport	A2	89
Freeport	A3	100
Freetown	E5	90
Freetown, *capital*	A1	63
Freiberg	C3	40
Freiburg	A5	40
Freirina	B3	76
Fréjus	D5	34
Fremantle, W.A.	A3, Inset I	14
French Guiana		**80**
French River	E1	102
Frenchman, *river*	B11	104
Fresnillo	D3	84
Fresno, Calif.	B2	126
Fria	B2	62
Fribourg	B2	35
Friedrichshafen	B5	40
Frigate, *island*	C1	91
Frisches Haff, *bay*	D1	41
Friuli-Venezia Giulia	C1	38
Frobisher, *lake*	C4	104
Frog, *lake*	E4	94
Frome, *lake*	D2	14
Frontier	B11	104
Frosinone	C2	38
Fruška Gora, *mts.*	A2	49
Frutigen	B2	35
Frýdek-Místek	D3	42
Fua'amotu	B4	17
Fuenlabrada	Inset II	37
Fuerte Olimpo	D2	75
Fuerte, *river*	C2	84
Fuerteventura, *island*	Inset I	37
Fuhayhil, al-	C2	24
Fujayrah, al-	D2	25
Fuji, *mt.*	C3	8
Fujian	E3	10
Fujisawa	C3	8
Fukue	A3	8
Fukue, *island*	A3	8
Fukui	C2	8
Fukuoka	A3	8
Fukushima	D2	8
Fukuyama	B3	8
Fulacunda	B2	62
Fuladi, *mt.*	B2	22
Fulda	B3	40
Fulda, *river*	B3	40
Fullarton	A2	91
Funabashi	D3	8
Funafuti, *capital*	C3	16
Funafuti, *island*	C3	16
Fundy, *bay*	A3	100
Furnas, *reservoir*	D4	81
Fürstenfeld	E3	39
Fürth	B4	40
Fushun	F1	10
Futa Jallon, *plateau*	B1	62
Futuna, *island*	C4	18
Fuxin	F1	10
Fuzhou	E3	10
Fyn, *island*	C3	32

G

	Key	Page
Gaalkacyo	B2	60
Gabarus	G2	100
Gabès	C3	57
Gabès, *gulf*	C2	57
Gaborone, *capital*	B3	69
Gabon		**66**
Gabriel, *island*	C1	69
Gabrovo	D3	50
Gabú	C1	62
Gacko	B2	48
Gaeta	C2	38
Gafsa	B2	57
Gagetown	C3	97
Gagnoa	D3	63
Gagnon	C3	101
Gagra	A2	45
Gainesville, Fla.	E3	126
Gainsborough	J11	104
Gairdner, *lake*	C3	14
Gaizina, *mt.*	C2	46
Galahad	E5	94
Galana, *river*	E5	61
Galápagos, *islands*	Inset	79
Galaţi	E3	43
Galena Bay	O6	95
Galicia	C1	37
Galilee, *region*	B1	26
Galle	B5	19
Gallegos, *river*	A7	74
Gallinas, *point*	C1	78
Gällivare	D1	53
Galoa	B3	17
Galveston, Tex.	D3	126
Galway	B2	31
Galway, *bay*	B2	31
Gam, *river*	A1	11
Gambia, The		**62**
Gambia, *river*	B2, C3, D2	62
Gambo	D5	98
Gamprin	B1	33
Gan, *river*	E3	10
Gananoque	J3	102
Gäncä	B2	45
Gander	D5	98
Gander Bay	D4	98
Gandhinagar	B4	20
Ganganagar	B3	20
Ganges, *river*	E3	20
Gangtok	E3	20
Gansu	C1, D2	10
Ganzhou	E3	10
Gao	D2	58
Gaoua	C3	64
Gap	D4	34
Garabil, *plateau*	D3	22
Garabogazköl, *lake*	A2	22
Garda, *lake*	B1	38
Garden Hill	D2	96
Garden Reach	Inset II	20
Garden, *island*	Inset I	14
Garden, *river*	A1	102
Gardenton	C4	96
Gardez	B2	22
Gardner, *canal*	H4	95
Gardner, *island*	B2	17
Garissa	E4	61
Garland	A3	96
Garmisch-Partenkirchen	B5	40
Garnish	D5	98
Garonne, *river*	C4	34
Garoowe	B2	60
Garoua	B2	65
Garry, *lake*	H3	99
Garson Lake	A4	104
Garulia	Inset II	20
Gary, Ind.	E1	126
Gascoyne, *river*	A2	14
Gash, *river*	B2	60
Gaspé	M3	103
Gaspé, *peninsula*	L3	103
Gaspereau Forks	D2	97
Gatal, *cape*	E4	37
Gateshead	C2	30
Gatico	B2	76
Gatineau	A6	103
Gatineau Park	A6	103
Gatineau, *river*	A4, A5	103
Gatún, *lake*	C2	87
Gau, *island*	B3	17
Gauhati	F3	20
Gaultois	D5	98
Gavarr	C2	45
Gävle	C2	53
Gaya	E4	20
Gaya	A3	59
Gazanjyk	B2	22
Gazelle, *peninsula*	B2	15
Gaziantep	D3	27
Gbarnga	B2	63
Gdańsk	D1	41
Gdańsk, *gulf*	D1	41
Gdynia	D1	41
Gêba, *river*	C1	62
Geelong, Vic.	D3	14
Gege	B2	71
Geidam	F1	65
Geikie, *river*	F3	104
Gejiu	D3	10
Gela	C3	38
Gelibolu (Gallipoli)	A2	27
Gelsenkirchen	A3	40
Gem	D6	94
Gembloux	C2	33
Gemena	B1	67
General Eugenio A. Garay	A2	75
General Santos	C5	12
General, *river*	C3	86
Genesee	C4	94
Geneva	A2	35
Geneva, *lake*	A2	35
Genk	D2	33
Gennargentu, *mts.*	B2	38
Genoa	B1	38
Genoa, *gulf*	B1	38
Gentilly	Inset II	34
Gentofte	D3	32
George	B3	71
George Town	A2	13
George, *river*	C2	101
Georgetown	B2	91
Georgetown	D2	62
Georgetown	C2	100
Georgetown, *capital*	B2	80
Georgia		**45**
Georgia	E2	126
Georgian, *bay*	E2	102
Gera	C3	40
Geral, *range*	C4	81
Gerald	A4	96
Geraldton	C3	101
Geraldton, W.A.	A2	14
Gerlachovka, *mt.*	C2	42
Germany		**40**
Germiston	C2	71
Gerona	H2	37
Getafe	E2, Inset II	37
Gevgelija	C2	48
Geylegphug	B3	19
Ghabah	C2	25
Ghadamis	A1	56
Ghaghara, *river*	D3	20
Ghana		**64**
Ghanzi	A2	69
Ghardaia	B1	57
Gharyan	B1	56
Ghat	B3	56
Ghatkopar	Inset I	20
Ghaydah, al-	C1	25
Ghazal, *river*	B4	59
Ghazni	B2	22
Ghent	B1	33
Ghurdaqah, al-	B2	56
Giant's Causeway, *headland*	A2	30
Gibraltar		**36**
Gibraltar, *strait*	D5	37
Gibson, *desert*	B2	14
Giessen	B3	40
Gifford, *river*	M2	99
Gifu	C3	8
Giglio, *island*	B2	38
Gijón	D1	37
Gikongoro	B2	61
Gilbert Plains	A3	96
Gilbert, *islands*	A1	17
Gilbert, *river*	D1	14
Gilgit	E2	21
Gilliam	D1	96
Gillingham	D3	30
Gimie, *mt.*	A2	91
Gimli	C4	96
Giresun	D2	27
Gironde, *river*	B4	34
Gisborne	C2	15
Gisenyi	B1	61
Gitarama	B2	61
Gitega	B2	61
Giurgiu	C4	43
Giza	B2	56
Gizo	A1	16
Gjirokastër	B3	49
Gjoa Haven	J3	99
Gjøvik	C3	52
Glace Bay	H1	100
Gladstone	B4	96
Gladstone, Qld.	E2	14
Glåma, *river*	C3	52
Glanvillia	A2	90
Glasgow	B2	30
Glasgow, Mont.	C1	126
Glaslyn	B7	104
Glastonbury	C3	30
Gleichen	D6	94
Glen Margaret	D3	100
Glenboro	B4	96
Glencoe	D5	102
Glenella	B4	96
Glenholme	D2	100
Glenora	G2	95
Glenwood	D5	98
Glidden	A9	104
Glifádha	Inset	51
Glittertinden, *mt.*	B3	52
Gliwice	D3	41
Głogów	C3	41
Gloucester	C3	30
Gloucester	K2	102
Glover, *reef*	C3	85
Glovertown	D5	98
Gmünd	D2	39
Goba	C3	60
Gobabis	C2	70
Gobi, *desert*	D1	10
Godavari, *river*	C5	20
Godbout	J2	103
Goderich	D4	102
Godfrey	J3	102
Godoy Cruz	B3	74
Gods, *lake*	D2	96
Gogama	D3	101
Goiânia	D3	81
Goiás	D3	81
Golan Heights, occupied terr.	A3	27
Gold Coast, Qld.	E2	14
Gold River	J6	95
Golden	O5	95
Golden Lake	H2	102
Golea, el-	B2	57
Golfito	C4	86
Golmud	C2	10
Golyama Kamchiya, *river*	E2	50
Goma	C2	67
Gombe	F2	65
Gomera, *island*	Inset I	37
Gómez Palacio	D2	84
Gonaïves	C1	89
Gonâve, *gulf*	B1	89
Gonâve, *island*	B2	89
Gonder	B1	60
Gongola, *river*	F2	65
Goobies	E5	98
Good Hope, *cape*	A3	71
Goodlands	C2	69
Goodlands	A4	96
Goodsoil	A6	104
Göppingen	B4	40
Gorakhpur	D3	20
Goražde	B2	48
Gordon, *lake*	E3	94
Gordondale	A3	94
Gore	B2	60
Gore Bay	C2	102
Gori	C4	45
Goris	D3	45
Gorizia	C1	38
Görlitz	C3	40
Gorlovka	D2	47
Gorno-Altay, *republic*	D6	44
Gorno-Altaysk	D6	44
Goroka	A2	15
Gorontalo	D1	13
Gorzów Wielkopolski	B2	41
Gosford, N.S.W.	E3	14
Goshen	F2	100
Goslar	B3	40
Gospić	B3	48
Gosport	C4	30
Göta, *canal*	B3	53
Göteborg och Bohus	B3	53
Gotha	B3	40
Gotland, *island*	C3	53
Gotsu	B3	8
Göttingen	B3	40
Gouda	B2	32
Goudiri	C2	62
Gouin, *reservoir*	B3	103
Goundam	C2	58
Gouré	C3	59
Govan	E9	104
Governador Valadares	D3	81
Gowd-e Zereh, *lake*	A3	22
Göyçay	B2	45
Gozo, *island*	A1	36
Graaf-Reinet	B3	71
Gračanica	B1	48
Gracias	A2	86
Grafton, N.S.W.	E2	14
Graham Land, *region*	C11	107
Graham, *island*	F4	95
Graham, *island*	K1	99
Grahamstown	C3	71
Grampian, *mts.*	B2	30
Gran Canaria, *island*	Inset I	37
Gran Chaco, *region*	B3	75
Granada	B3	87
Granada	E4	37
Granby	D6	103
Grand Anse	B1	91
Grand Bahama, *island*	A2	89
Grand Bale	C2	69
Grand Bank	D5	98
Grand Bay	C1	91
Grand Bay	C3	97
Grand Bend	D4	102
Grand Bruit	B5	98
Grand Canyon, Ariz.	B2	126
Grand Centre	E4	94
Grand Cess	B3	63
Grand Erg Occidental, *desert*	B1	57
Grand Erg Oriental, *desert*	B2	57
Grand Falls	B1	97
Grand Falls-Windsor	D5	98
Grand Forks	N6	95
Grand Forks, N. Dak.	D1	126
Grand Island, Nebr.	D1	126
Grand Junction, Colo.	C2	126
Grand Manan, *island*	C4	97
Grand Marais	C4	96
Grand Narrows	G2	100
Grand Pré	C2	100
Grand Rapids	B2	96
Grand Rapids, Mich.	E1	126
Grand Roy	B2	91
Grand Santi	A1	80
Grand Turk, *capital*	D4	89
Grand Turk, *island*	D4	89
Grand Valley	E4	102
Grand, *canal*	C2	31
Grand, *harbor*	C2	36
Grand, *lake*	D2	97
Grand, *lake*	C4	98
Grand, *river*	C3	69
Grand-Etang	F1	100
Grand-Mère	D5	103
Grand-Remous	A5	103
Grande Baleine, *river*	A2	101
Grande de Añasco, *river*	A2	90
Grande de Manatí, *river*	C2	90
Grande de Matagalpa, *river*	B2	87
Grande Prairie	A3	94
Grande, *bay*	B7	74
Grande, *range*	C2	75
Grande, *river*	B3	77
Grande, *river*	D3	81
Grande, *river*	B3	86
Grande-Anse	D1	97
Grande-Rivière	M3	103
Grande-Vallée	M2	103
Grândola	A3	36
Grandview	A3	96
Granisle	J4	95
Grantham	C3	30
Granville Lake	A1	96
Gras, *lake*	F4	99
Grass, *river*	A3, B2	96
Grassland	D4	94
Grauspitz, *mt.*	B2	33
Gravelbourg	D11	104
Gravenhurst	F3	102
Gravesend	Inset III	30
Gravois, *point*	B3	89
Graz	D3	39
Great Abaco, *island*	B2	89
Great Alföld, *plain*	B2	43
Great Artesian, *basin*	D2	14
Great Australian, *bight*	B3	14
Great Bahama, bank	B4	89
Great Barrier, *island*	C2	15
Great Barrier, *reef*	D1	14
Great *basin*, Nev.	B2	126
Great Bear, *lake*	D3	99
Great Britain		**30**
Great Dividing, *range*	D1, D3	14
Great Exuma, *island*	B3	89
Great Falls	C4	96
Great Falls, Mont.	B1	126
Great Fish, *river*	C3	71
Great Inagua, *island*	C4	89
Great Indian, *desert*	B3	20
Great Karroo, *plateau*	B3	71
Great Nicobar, *island*	F7	20
Great Rift, *valley*		55
Great Ruaha, *river*	C2	68
Great Salt, *lake*, Utah	B1	126
Great Sand Sea, *desert*	A2	56
Great Sandy, *desert*	B2	14
Great Scarcies, *river*	A1	63
Great Sea, *reef*	B1	17
Great Slave, *lake*	F4	99
Great Victoria, *desert*	B2	14
Great Wall of China	D2	10
Great Yarmouth	D3	30
Great Zab, *river*	B1	24
Great, *plains*	C1	126
Greater Hinggan, *range*	F1	10
Greater Sunda, *islands*	B2	13
Gréboun, *mt.*	B1	59
Gredos, *mts.*	D2	37
Greece		**51**
Greeley, Colo.	C1	126
Greely, *fjord*	L1	99
Green Bay, Wis.	E1	126
Green Lake	C6	104
Green, *islands*	B2	15
Greenland		**106**
Greenland, *sea*	D2	106
Greenock	B2	30
Greensboro, N.C.	F2	126
Greenville	B3	63
Greenville, S.C.	E2	126
Greenwood	N6	95
Greifswald	C1	40
Grenå	C2	32
Grenada		**91**
Grenada, *island*	B2	91
Grenadines, *islands*	A3, B1, C1	91
Grenfell	H10	104
Grenoble	D4	34
Gretna	C4	96
Greve	D3	32
Grevenmacher	B2	33
Grey River	C5	98
Grey, *range*	D2	14
Greymouth	B3	15
Gribingui, *river*	A2	66
Griffin	G11	104
Griffith, N.S.W.	D3	14
Grijalva, *river*	F4	84
Grimsby	C3	30
Grimsey, *island*	B1	52
Grinnell, *peninsula*	J1	99
Griqualand East, *region*	C3	71
Griqualand West, *region*	B2	71
Griquatown	B2	71
Grise Ford	M1	99
Griswold	A4	96
Groningen	B2	80
Groningen	D1	32
Gronlid	F7	104
Groote Eylandt, *island*	C1	14
Grootfontein	C1	70
Grootvloer, *pan*	B2	71
Gros Islet	B1	91
Gros Morne Natl. Park	C4	98
Gros-Morne	L2	103
Grosseto	B2	38
Grossglockner, *mt.*	C3	39
Groundbirch	M3	95
Groznyy	E4	44
Grudziądz	D2	41
Grunthal	C4	96
Guacanayabo, *gulf*	D3	88
Guadalajara	E2	37
Guadalajara, *state capital*	D3	84
Guadalcanal, *island*	A1	16
Guadalquivir, *river*	D4	37
Guadalupe, *reservoir*	Inset	84
Guadarrama, *mts.*	D2	37
Guadeloupe, *island*		82
Guadiana, *river*	C3	37
Guaillabamba, *river*	B2	79
Guainía, *river*	C4	78
Guajara Mirim	B3	81
Guajira, *peninsula*	C1	78
Guam, *island*		5
Guanacaste, *range*	A2	86
Guanaja, *island*	C1	86
Guanajuato, *state capital*	D3	84
Guanare	C2	79
Guandu, *river*	Inset I	81
Guangdong	E3	10
Guangxi Zhuang	D3	10
Guangzhou	E3	10
Guánica	B3	90
Guantánamo	E3	88
Guaporé, *river*	B3	81
Guaqui	A3	77
Guaranda	B3	79
Guarda	B2	36
Guarujá	Inset II	81
Guarulhos	Inset II	81
Guasave	C2	84
Guatemala		**85**
Guatemala City, *capital*	C5	85
Guaviare, *river*	C4	78
Guayaguayare	A2	91
Guayama	C3	90
Guayambre, *river*	B2	86
Guayanilla	B2	90
Guayape, *river*	B2	86
Guayaquil	B4	79
Guayaquil, *gulf*	A4	79
Guayas, *river*	B4	79
Guaymas	B2	84
Guaynabo	C2	90
Guben	C3	40
Gudauta	A2	45
Gudenå, *river*	B2	32
Guecho	E1	37
Guéckédou	C3	62
Guelph	E4	102
Guelta Zemmur	B1	58
Guéret	C3	34
Guernica Y Luno	E1	37
Guernsey, *island*	Inset II	30
Guerrero	D4	84
Guerrero Negro	B2	84
Guiana, *highlands*	D2	79
Guiers, *lake*	B1	62
Guilarte, *mt.*	B2	90

Key Page

Guildford C3 30
Guilin E3 10
Guimarães A2 36
Guinea **62**
Guinea, *gulf* 55
Guinea-Bissau **62**
Güiria D1 79
Guiyang D3 10
Guizhou D3 10
Gujranwala E3 21
Gujrat E3 21
Gulbarga C5 20
Gulbene D2 46
Gulf Coastal, *plain* D3 126
Gulistan C2 23
Gull Lake B10 104
Gull, *lake* C5 94
Gulu C2 61
Gumdag B2 22
Gummi C1 65
Gunisao, *river* C2 96
Gunnbjørn Fjeld, *mt.* D2 106
Gunton C4 96
Guntur D5 20
Gurabo D2 90
Guri, *reservoir* D2 79
Gusau D1 65
Gushgy D3 22
Gushgy, *river* D3 22
Gushikawa Inset II 8
Gustavo A. Madero Inset 84
Güstrow C2 40
Guyana **80**
Guysborough F2 100
Gwadar B5 21
Gwai, *river* A2 69
Gwalior C3 20
Gweru B2 69
Gyda, *peninsula* B5 44
Gympie, Qld. E2 14
Gyöngyös B2 43
Győr A2 43
Gypsumville B3 96
Gyumri A2 45
Gyzylarbat B2 22

H

Ha Giang A1 11
Ha'apai, *island group* B3 17
Haapsalu B2 46
Haarlem B2 32
Habarut C1 25
Habay A2 94
Haboro Inset I 8
Hachijo, *island* C3 8
Hachinohe D1 8
Hachioji C3 8
Haddummati, *atoll* A4 19
Hadejia, *river* E1 65
Hadera B1 26
Haderslev B3 32
Hadhramaut, *district* B1 25
Hadithah, al- B2 24
Haedo, *range* B2 75
Haeju A3 9
Hafford C8 104
Hafnarfjördhur A3 52
Hagen A3 40
Hague, *cape* B2 34
Haha, *island* Inset III 8
Haifa B1 26
Haifa, *bay* B1 26
Haikou E4 10
Hail B1 24
Hailar E1 10
Hainan D4 10
Haines Junction B5 105
Haiphong B2 11
Hairé Lao B1 62
Haiti **89**
Hajdúböszörmény C2 43
Haji Ibrahim, *mt.* B1 24
Hajjah A1 25
Haka B2 12
Hakodate D1, Inset I 8
Halab (Aleppo) A1 27
Halaib D1 59
Halba B1 26
Halberstadt B3 40
Haldimand F5 102
Halfmoon Bay L6 95
Haliburton G2 102
Halifax C3 30
Halifax, *capital* D3 100
Halil, *river* D4 22
Halisahar Inset II 20
Hall Beach M3 99
Hall, *peninsula* P4 99
Halla-san, *mt.* Inset 9
Hallboro B4 96
Halle C2 33
Halle B3 40
Hallingdal, *valley* B3 52
Halmahera, *island* D1 13
Halmstad B3 53
Haltiatunturi, mt B1 53
Halton Hills F4 102
Hamadan B3 22
Hamah A2 27
Hamamatsu C3 8
Hamar C3 52
Hambantota C5 19
Hamburg B2 40
Hämeenlinna B2 53
Hameln B2 40
Hamersley, *range* A2 14
Hamgyŏng, *mts.* C2 9
Hamhŭng B3 9
Hami C1 10
Hamilton C2 15
Hamilton B2 30
Hamilton F4 102
Hamilton, *inlet* B2 98
Hamiota A4 96
Hamm A3 40
Hammamat, al- C1 57
Hammamet, *gulf* C1 57
Hammerfest E1 52
Hammonds Plains D3 100
Hammondvale D3 97
Hampden C4 98
Hampstead J5 103
Hampton D3 97
Hamun-e Jaz Murian, *lake* D4 22
Hamun-e Saberi, *lake* A2 22
Han, *river* E2 10
Han, *river* B4 9
Hanau B3 40
Handan E2 10
Hangayn, *mts.* B2 11
Hangö B3 53
Hangzhou F2 10
Hanley D9 104
Hannibal, Mo. D2 126
Hannover B2 40
Hanoi, *capital* A2 11
Hanover D3 102
Hantzsch, *river* O3 99
Hanzhong D2 10
Haora E4, Inset II 20
Haparanda D1 53
Happy Valley-Goose Bay A2, E4 98
Har Us, *lake* B2 11
Harad C1 24
Harare, *capital* B1 69
Harbel A2 63
Harbin F1 10
Harbour Breton D5 98
Harbour Deep C4 98
Harbour, *island* B2 89
Harcourt D2 97
Hardangerfjord, *fjord* B4 52
Hardangervidda, *plateau* B3 52
Hardwood Lake H2 102
Hare Bay D5 98
Harer D2 60
Hargeysa A2 60
Hargrave A4 96
Harirud, *river* A2 22
Harlow Inset III 30
Härnösand C2 53
Harper C3 63
Harris C9 104
Harrisburg, *capital*, Pa. F1 126
Harrogate C2 30
Harstad D2 52
Hart, *ranges* L3 95
Hart, *river* B3 105
Hartford, *capital*, Conn. F1 126
Hartland B2 97
Hartley Bay H4 95
Hartney A4 96
Harvey C3 97
Harwill C3 96
Harz, *mts.* B3 40
Hasa, al-, *region* C1 24
Hasakah, al- B1 27
Hashtadan, *region* E3 22
Haslemere Inset III 30
Hasselt D2 33
Hastings C2 15
Hastings D4 30
Hastings H3 102
Hat Yai B5 12
Hatillo B2 90
Hato Mayor C2 89
Hatteras *cape*, N.C. F2 126
Hattiesburg, Miss. E2 126
Haugesund B4 52
Haultain, *river* D4 104
Haute-Normandie C2 34
Havana, *capital* B1 88
Havel, *river* C2 40
Havelock H3 102
Havířov D3 42
Havre, Mont. C1 126
Havre-St-Pierre D3 101
Hawaii Inset II 126
Hawaii *island*, Hawaii Inset II 126
Hawalli C2 24
Hawar, *islands* B2 25
Hawea, *lake* A3 15
Hawf C1 25
Hawick C2 30
Hawke Harbour D2 98
Hawke's Bay C4 98
Hawke, *bay* C2 15
Hawkesbury L2 102
Hay River E4 99
Hay, *river* A2, B1 94
Hayes, *river* D1, D2 96
Hayma C2 25
Hayter E5 94
Hazelton J3 95
Hazelton, *mts.* H3 95
Hazlet B10 104
Hazm, al- A1 25
Hearst D3 101
Heart's Content E5 98
Heaslip A4 96
Heath Steele C1 97
Hebei E2 10
Hebrides, *sea* A1 30
Hebron E3 98
Hecate, *strait* G4 95
Hecla C3 96
Hecla and Griper, *bay* F1 99
Hedley M6 95
Heerenveen C2 32
Heerlen C4 32
Hefei E2 10
Hegang G1 10
Heha, *mt.* B2 61
Heidelberg B4 40
Heidenheim B4 40
Heilbronn B4 40
Heilong (Amur), *river* F1 10
Heilongjiang F1 10
Heimaey, *island* A3 52
Heinsburg E4 94
Heisler D5 94
Hekla, *volcano* B3 52
Hel D1 41
Helen, *reef* Inset 17
Helena, *capital*, Mont. B1 126
Helgoland, *island* A1 40
Hellin F3 37
Helmand, *river* A2 22
Helmsdale E5 94
Helsingborg B3 53
Helsingør D2 32
Helsinki, *capital* B2 53
Heming Lake A2 96
Henan E2 10
Henashi, *cape* C1 8
Hengch'un B2 9
Hengelo D2 32
Hengyang E3 10
Henley Harbour D3 98
Hensall D4 102
Henzada B3 12
Herat A2 22
Herb Lake B2 96
Herbert C10 104
Heredia B2 86
Hereford C3 30
Heriot Bay K6 95
Hermitage-Sandyville D5 98
Hermon, *mt.* A3 27
Hermosillo, *state capital* B2 84
Hernád, *river* C1 43
Herne A3 40
Herning B2 32
Hertford Inset III 30
Herzliyya B1 26
Hess, *river* C4 105
Hesse B3 40
Hetauda C2 19
Hiatikulu B2 71
Hibbing, Minn. D1 126
Hicks Bay C2 15
Hidaka, *mts.* Inset I 8
Hidalgo E3 84
Hidalgo del Parral C2 84
Hieflau D3 39
Hierro, *island* Inset I 37
Higashiosaka B3 8
High Atlas, ranges B2 57
High Level B2 94
High River D6 94
High Tatra, *mts.* D4 41
High Wycombe Inset III 30
Highrock A1 96
Highrock, *lake* A1 96
Higüey D2 89
Hiiumaa, *island* B2 46
Hijaz, al-, *region* A1 24
Hilda E6 94
Hilden D2 100
Hildesheim B2 40
Hill Bank B2 85
Hillaby, *mt.* A3 91
Hillah, al- B2 24
Hillerød D3 32
Hillsborough C1 91
Hillsborough E3 97
Hillsborough, *bay* B2 100
Hilo, Hawaii Inset II 126
Hilton Beach B1 102
Hilversum C2 32
Himalayas, *mts.* 7
Himeji B3 8
Hinche C1 89
Hindelang B5 40
Hindu Kush, *range* B1 22
Hino, *cape* B3 8
Hinton B4 94
Hirakata B3 8
Hirakud, *reservoir* D4 20
Hirara Inset II 8
Hirmil, al- B1 26
Hirosake D1 8
Hiroshima B3 8
Hirtshals B1 32
Hisabpur Inset II 20
Hitachi D2 8
Hixon L4 95
Hjørring B1 32
Hkakabo Razi, *mt.* C1 12
Ho C3 64
Ho Chi Minh City B4 11
Hoa Binh A2 11
Hobart, Tas., *capital* D4 14
Hobsons, *bay* Inset V 14
Hobyo B2 60
Hoceima, al- D1 57
Hodgeville D10 104
Hodgson C3 96
Hódmezővásárhely C2 43
Hoeryŏng C1 9
Hof B3 40
Höfn C2 52
Hohe Tauern, *mts.* C3 39
Hohhot E1 10
Hokkaido, *island* D1, Inset I 8
Hoktemberyan B2 45
Holbæk C3 32
Holden D4 94
Holdfast E10 104
Holetown A3 91
Holguín E3 88
Holhol B2 60
Holland B4 96
Holman E2 99
Holon B1 26
Holstebro B2 32
Holton C2 98
Holyhead B3 30
Holyrood E5 98
Holywood B2 30
Homathko, *river* K5 95
Hombori Tondo, *mt.* C2 58
Hombori, *mts.* C2 58
Homer, Alaska Inset I 126
Homo, *bay* B2 18
Homs A2 27
Homyel E3 47
Hon Gai B2 11
Hondo C3 94
Hondo, *river* B1 85
Honduras **86**
Honduras, *gulf* A1 86
Hong Kong, S.A.R. E3 10
Hong Kong, *island* Inset 10
Hongze, *lake* E2 10
Honiara, *capital* A1 16
Honolulu, *capital*, Hawaii Inset II 126
Honshu, *island* C2 8
Hoogeveen D2 32
Hoorn C2 32
Hope M6 95
Hope Bay C2 88
Hope Valley E5 94
Hopedale A1 98
Hopedale E3 98
Hopewell Cape E3 97
Horgèn C1 35
Hormigueros A2 90
Hormuz, *strait* D4 22
Horn, *cape* C9 76
Horn, *cape* A1 52
Hornád, *river* C2 42
Hornavan, *lake* C1 53
Hornepayne D3 101
Horsburgh, *atoll* A2 19
Horse, *river* D3 94
Horsens B3 32
Horton, *river* D3 99
Hospitalet H2 37
Hoste, *island* C9 76
Hot Springs, Ark. D2 126
Hotan A2 10
Hotchkiss B2 94
Hottah, *lake* E3 99
Houghton, Mich. E1 126
Houmt Souk C3 57
Houston J4 95
Houston, Tex. D3 126
Hovd, *river* B2 11
Hove C4 30
Hoverla, *mt.* A2 47
Hövsgöl, *lake* C1 11
Howley C4 98
Hoy, *island* Inset I 30
Hradec Králové B2 42
Hrazdan B2 45
Hrazdan, *river* B2 45
Hrodna A3 47
Hron, *river* B2 42
Hsinchu B1 9
Hsinchuang B1 9
Hsintien B1 9
Hsinying B2 9
Hua Hin B3 12
Huacho B3 77
Huai, *river* E2 10
Huainan E2 10
Hualien B2 9
Huallaga, *river* B2 77
Huambo C4 70
Huancavelica B3 77
Huancayo B3 77
Huang (Yellow), *river* D2, E2 10
Huánuco B2 77
Huapí, *mts.* B2 87
Huaraz B2 77
Huascarán, *mt.* B2 77
Hubbards C3 100
Hubei E2 10
Hubley D3 100
Hubli-Dharwar C5 20
Hudaydah, al- A2 25
Huddersfield C3 30
Hudiksvall C2 53
Hudson Bay H8 104
Hudson's Hope M3 95
Hudson, *bay* J3 92
Hudson, *strait* O4 99
Hue B3 11
Huehuetenango B4 85
Huelva C4 37
Huesca F1 37
Hufuf, al- C1 24
Hugli, *river* Inset II 20
Hugli-Chunchura Inset II 20
Hŭich'ŏn B2 9
Huila, *mt.* A4 78
Hŭksan Chedo, *islands* A5 9
Hull A6 103
Hulun, *lake* E1 10
Hulwan B2 56
Humacao D2 90
Humber, *river* D3 30
Humboldt E8 104
Humenné C2 42
Humuya, *river* B2 86
Húnaflói, *bay* A2 52
Hunan E3 10
Hunedoara B3 43
Hungary **43**
Hŭngnam B3 9
Hünsruck, *mts.* A4 40
Hunter River B2 100
Huntington, W. Va. E2 126
Huntsville F2 102
Huntsville, Ala. E2 126
Hunyani, *river* B1 69
Huon, *islands* B1 18
Huon, *peninsula* A2 15
Huron, *lake* E1 126
Hussar D5 94
Hutchinson, Kans. D2 126
Hvannadalshnúkur, *mt.* B3 52
Hvar, *island* C3 48
Hvítá, *river* A2 52
Hwange A2 69
Hyargas, *lake* B2 11
Hyderabad C5 20
Hyderabad C5 21
Hyesan C2 9
Hyland Post H2 95
Hyland, *river* D5 105
Hylo D4 94
Hyvinkää B2 53

I

Ialomiţa, *river* D3 43
Ialpug, *river* B2 50
Iaşi D2 43
Ibadan B4 65
Ibagué B3 78
Ibar, *river* B3 49
Ibaraki B3 8
Ibarra B2 79
Ibb A2 25
Ibérico, *mts.* F2 37
Ibiza G4 37
Ibiza, *island* G3 37
Iboundji, *mt.* A2 66
Ibrahim, *river* A1 26
Ibri C1 25
Ica B3 77
Içá, *river* B2 81
Icacos, *key* D2 90
Ice Cap C2 106
Iceland **52**
Ich'ŏn B3 9
Ichihara D3 8
Ichikawa D3 8
Ichilo, *river* B3 77
Ichinomiya C3 8
Idaho B1 126
Idaho Falls, Idaho B1 126
Iddesleigh E6 94
Idfu B3 56
Ídhra, *island* B3 51
Idlib A2 27
Idrija B2 48
Ife C4 65
Igarka C6 44
Igloolik M3 99
Igombe, *river* B1 68
Iguaçu, *falls* C4 81
Iguaçu, *river* E2 74
Iguala E4 84
Iguazú, *falls* E4 75
Ih Bogd Uul, *mt.* C3 11
Ihavandiffulu, *atoll* A1 19
Ihosy B3 69
Ilan B1 9
Iijoki, *river* C1 53
Iisalmi C2 53
Ijevan C2 45
IJssel, *river* D2 32
IJsselmeer, *sea* C2 32
Ijuw C2 16
Ikaría, *island* C3 51
Ikeja B4 65
Ikela B2 67
Iki, *island* A3 8
Ikorodu B4 65
Ila C3 65
Ilam D3 19
Ilam B3 22
Île-à-la-Crosse C5 104
Île-de-France C2 34
Ilebo B2 67
Ilesha C4 65
Ilford D1 96
Ilhéus E3 81
Ili, *river* D2 23
Iligan C4 12
Illampu, *mt.* A3 77
Illapel B4 76
Illimani, *mt.* A3 77
Illinois E1 126
Illo C4 77
Iloilo B4 12
Ilorin C3 65
Imatra C2 53
Imbariè Inset I 81
Imbéry B2 90
Imi D3 60
Imjin, *river* B3 9
Imlili A2 58
Imperatriz D2 81
Imperial E9 104
Imperial Mills E4 94
Imperial, *river* B6 76
Impfondo D3 66
Imphal F4 20
Inari, *lake* C1 53
Inch'ŏn B4 9
Incles, *river* C1 36
Indalsälven, *river* B2 53
India **20**
Indian Bay D4 96
Indian Brook G1 100
Indian Cabins B1 94
Indian Harbour D3 100
Indian Head G10 104
Indiana E1 126
Indianapolis, *capital*, Ind. E2 126
Indigirka, *river* C9 44
Indispensable, *reefs* B2 16
Indonesia **13**
Indore C4 20
Indus, *river* C4, E2 21
Ingleside K3 102
Ingolstadt B4 40
Ingonish G1 100
Ingonish Beach G1 100
Ingushetiya, republic E4 44
Inhambane B5 68
Inhomirim Inset I 81
Inland, *sea* B3 8
Inn, *river* B3, C2 39
Inner Hebrides, *islands* A2 30
Inner Mongolia E1 10
Innisfail D5 94
Innisfil F3 102
Innsbruck B3 39
Inta C5 44
Interlaken B2 35
International Falls, Minn. D1 126
Inthanon, *mt.* B2 12
Inukjuak A2 101
Inuvik B3 99
Inuvik, *region* C3 99
Invercargill A4 15
Invermay G9 104
Inverness B1 30
Inverness F1 100
Inwood C4 96
Inyangani, *mt.* C2 69
Ioánnina B2 51
Ionian, *islands* B2 51
Ionian, *sea* A2 51
Iori, *river* C4 45
Iowa D1 126
Ipel', *river* B2 42
Ipiíba Inset I 81
Ipoh A2 1
Ipoly, *river* B1 4
Ipswich D3 3
Iqaluit, *capital*, Nunivut P4 9
Iquique B2 7
Iquitos C1 7
Iracoubo B1 8
Iráklion C4 51
Iran **22**
Iranshahr E4 2
Irapuato D3 8
Iraq **24**
Irazú, *volcano* C3 8
Irbe, *strait* A3 4
Irbid A1 2
Irbil B1 2
Ireland **31**
Iri B5 9
Irian Jaya, *region* E2 13
Iringa C2 68
Iriomote, *island* Inset II 8
Iriona C2 86
Irish, *sea* B3 30
Irkutsk D7 44
Iron Bridge B1 102
Iron Gate Reservoir B3 43
Iroquois Falls D3 101
Irrawaddy, *river* B2 12
Irtysh, *river* D1 23
Irtysh, *river* D5 44
Isabela A1 90
Isabela, *island* Inset 79
Isabelia, *mts.* B2 87
Ísafjördhur A1 52
Isangel C4 18
Isar, *river* C4 40
Ischia, *island* C2 38
Ise C3 8
Ise, *bay* C3 8
Isère, *river* D4 34
Isernia C2 38
Iseyin B4 65
Isherton B4 80
Ishigaki, *island* Inset II 8
Ishikari, *river* Inset I 8
Ishim D5 44
Ishim, *river* C1 23
Ishinomaki D2 8
Ishinomaki, *bay* D2 8
Ishizuchi, *mt.* B3 8
Isiro C1 67
İskenderun D3 27
Iskŭr, *river* C2 50
Islamabad, *capital* D3 21
Island Lake D2 96
Island, *lake* D2 96
Islay, *island* A2 30
Isle aux Morts B5 98
Islington J6 102
Ismailiyah, al- B1 56
Isoka C2 67
Isparta B3 27
Israel **26**
İstanbul B2 27
Istria, *peninsula* A2 48
Italy **38**
İzmir A2 27
İzmit B2 27
Itabira D3 81
Itabuna E3 81
Itaipu Inset I 81
Itaipú, *reservoir* E4 75
Itajaí D4 81
Itanagar F3 20
Itapecerica da Serra Inset II 81
Itapeva Inset II 81
Itaquaquecetuba Inset II 81
Iténez, *river* B2 77
Itháki, *island* B2 51
Ittoqqortoormiit (Scoresbysund) D2 106
Ituna G9 104
Ivalo C1 53
Ivano-Frankivsk A2 47
Ivanovo D3 44
Ivindo, *river* B1 66
Ivujivik A1 101
Iwaki D2 8
Iwakuni B3 8
Iwo C4 65
Iwo Jima, *island* Inset III 8
Ixelles C2 33
Ixtapa D4 84
Ixtapaluca Inset 84
Izabal, *lake* E4 85
Izhevsk D4 44
Izki C1 25
Izmail B3 47
Iztacalco Inset 84
Iztapalapa Inset 84
Izu, *islands* C3 8
Izu, *peninsula* C3 8
Izuhara A3 8

J

Jabal al-Akhdar, al-, *mts.* C1 25
Jabal al-Uwaynat, *mt.* D3 56
Jabal an-Nabi Shuayb, *mt.* A1 25
Jabal an-Nusayriyah, *mts.* A2 27
Jabal Katrinah, *mt.* B2 56
Jabal Ramm, *mt.* A3 26
Jabal Tuwayq, *mts.* B2 24
Jabal Zuqar, *island* A2 25
Jabalpur C4 20
Jaboatão E2 81
Jacare-Acanga C2 81
Jackhead C3 96
Jackson's Arm C4 98
Jackson, *capital*, Miss. D2 126
Jackson, port Inset IV 14
Jackson, Wyo. B1 126
Jacksonville, Fla. E2 126
Jacmel C2 89
Jacques-Cartier, *river* E4 103
Jacquet River C1 97
Jadabpur Inset II 20
Jadida, el- B1 57
Jaén E4 37

Key Page
affna B2 19
afr, al- B2 26
agdalpur D5 20
aghbub, al- D2 56
ahrah, al- B2 24
amaica 88
aipur C3 20
aipurhat B3 21
ajce B1 48
akarta, *capital* B2 13
akobstad B2 53
akupica, *mts.* B2 48
alal-Abad C2 23
alalabad C2 22
alapa Enríquez, *state capital* E4 84
alingo F3 65
alisco D4 84
alu D2 56
aluit, *island* B2 16
amaame A3 60
amalpur C4 21
ambi B2 13
ames, *bay* J3 92
ammu B2 20
amnagar B4 20
ampur Inset II 20
ämsä C2 53
amshedpur E4 20
amuna, *river* C4 21
an Lake H6 104
an Mayen, *island* 5
anai Inset II 20
anakpur C3 19
aneville D1 97
angy-Bazar B2 23
apan 8
apan, *sea* B2 8
apanese Alps, *mts.* C3 8
aperi Inset I 81
apurá, *river* B2 81
arama, *river* Inset II 37
arash A1 26
ari, *river* C1 81
arvie D4 94
arvis E5 102
ask D4 22
astrebac, *mts.* B3 49
ászberény B2 43
ava, *island* C2 13
ava, *sea* C2 13
avari, *river* A2 81
awf, al- A1 24
awf, al- D3 56
awhar B3 60
aya, *mt.* E2 13
ayapura F2 13
ayuya B2 90
azirah, al-, *region* B1 27
azzin A2 26
ebba C3 65
ebel Toubkal, *mt.* C2 57
eddore, *lake* D5 98
efferson City, *capital*, Mo. D2 126
ejuí-Guazú, *river* D4 75
ejur Inset II 20
ekabpils C2 46
elenia Góra B3 41
elgava B2 46
emseg C3 97
ena B3 40
engish Chokusu, *mt.* G1 23
enner E6 94
enpeg B2 96
érémie A2 89
Jerez de la Frontera C4 37
Jersey, *island* Inset II 30
Jerudong B2 13
Jerusalem, *capital* B2 26
Jesenice B2 48
Jessore C5 21
Jésus, *island* J5 103
Jetait A1 96
Jhang Sadar D3 21
Jhansi C3 20
Jhelum D3 21
Jhelum, *river* D3 21
Ji'an E3 10
Jiamusi G1 10
Jiangsu E2 10
Jiangxi E3 10
Jiddah A2 24
Jiddah, *island* A1 25
Jihlava B3 42
Jilib A3 60
Jilin F1 10
Jilin F1 10
Jima B3 60
Jimaní A2 89
Jiménez D2 84
Jinan E2 10
Jingdezhen E3 10
Jining E2 10
Jinja C3 61
Jinotega B2 87
Jinotepe A3 87
Jinsha (Yangtze), *river* C2 10
Jinzhou F1 10
Jipijapa A3 79
Jir Paraná B3 81
Jirgatol B1 23
Jiu, *river* B3 43
Jiujiang E3 10
Jixi G1 10
Jizan B2 24
Jizzakh C2 23
João Pessoa E2 81
Jobos C3 90
Jodhpur B3 20
Joe Batt's Arm D4 98
Joensuu C2 53
Joetsu C2 8
Joggins C2 100
Johannesburg C2 71
John D'or Prairie C2 94
Johnsons Crossing C5 105
Johor Baharu B2 13
Johor, *strait* B1 13
Joinville D4 81

Key Page
Joinville, *island* C12 107
Joka Inset II 20
Joliet, Ill. E1 126
Joliette C5 103
Jolo B5 12
Jolo, *island* B5 12
Jonava C2 46
Jones, *sound* L1 99
Jonesboro, Ark. D2 126
Jong, *river* A2 63
Jönköping B3 53
Jonquière E3 103
Joplin, Mo. D2 126
Jordan 26
Jordan, *river* A2 26
Jos E3 65
Jos, *plateau* E2 65
Jotunheimen, *mts.* B3 52
Jou B4 63
Joussard C3 94
Juan de Fuca, *strait* L7 95
Juana Díaz B2 90
Juàzeiro D2 81
Juàzeiro do Norte E2 81
Juba C4 59
Juba, *river* A3 60
Jubayl A1 26
Jubayl, al- C1 24
Jubilee, *lake* D5 98
Júcar, *river* F3 37
Juchitán de Zaragoza F4 84
Judique F2 100
Juigalpa B2 87
Juiz de Fora D4 81
Juliaca C4 77
Julian Alps, *mts.* A2 48
Juliana Top, *mt.* A3 80
Jullundur C2 20
Jumayliyah, al- C2 25
Jumla B2 19
Junagadh B4 20
Junaynah, al- A2 59
Juncos D2 90
Jundiai D4 81
Juneau, *capital*, Alaska Inset I 126
Jungfrau, *mt.* B2 35
Juniper B2 97
Juniyah A2 26
Juozapines, *mt.* C2 46
Jura, *island* B2 30
Jura, *mts.* A2 35
Jura, *river* A2 46
Jurbarkas B2 46
Jurmala B2 46
Jurong A1 13
Juruá, *river* B2 81
Juruena, *river* C3 81
Jutiapa D5 85
Juticalpa B2 86
Jutland, *peninsula* B3 32
Juventud, *island* B2 88
Južna, *river* B3 49
Jvari B3 45
Jwaneng B3 69
Jyväskylä C2 53

K

K2 (Godwin Austen), *mt.* A2 10
Ka Dake B2 71
Ka, *river* C2 65
Kabala B1 63
Kabale A4 61
Kabalo C2 67
Kabardino-Balkariya, republic E4 44
Kabelebo, *river* A2 80
Kabompo, *river* A2 67
Kabul, *capital* B2 22
Kabul, *river* B2 22
Kabwe B2 67
Kachovka C3 47
Kadavu, *island* B3 17
Kadei, *river* A3 66
Kadoma B2 69
Kaduna D2 65
Kaduna, *river* D2 65
Kaduqli B3 59
Kaédi B3 58
Kaélé B1 65
Kaeo B2 15
Kaesŏng B4 9
Kafan D3 45
Kaffrine B2 62
Kafr ad-Dawwar B1 56
Kafu, *river* B3 61
Kafue B3 67
Kafue, *river* B2 67
Kaga Bandoro A2 66
Kagawong C2 102
Kagera, *river* B4, C1, C2 61
Kagitumba C1 61
Kagoshima A4 8
Kahayan, *river* C2 13
Kahemba B2 67
Kahnawake H6 103
Kahntah M2 95
Kahoolawe *island*, Hawaii Inset II 126
Kai, *islands* E2 13
Kaieteur, *falls* B3 80
Kaifeng E2 10
Kaikoura B3 15
Kailahun C3 62
Kailahun B1 63
Kainji, *lake* C2 65
Kaiserslautern A4 40
Kaitaia B2 15
Kajaani C2 53
Kakamega C3 61
Kakata A2 63
Kakeroma, *island* Inset II 8
Kakhovka, *reservoir* C3 47
Kakinada D5 20
Kaladar H3 102
Kalahari, *desert* A2 69
Kalámai B3 51
Kalamáki Inset 51
Kälbäcär B2 45

Key Page
Kalemie C2 67
Kalgoorlie, W.A. B3 14
Kali C1 62
Kali, *river* B2 19
Kalimantan, *region* C2 13
Kaliningrad D3 44
Kalixälven, *river* D1 53
Kallithéa Inset 51
Kalmar C3 53
Kalmykiya, republic E4 44
Kalpeni, *island* B7 20
Kalu, *river* B5 19
Kalundborg C3 32
Kalutara A5 19
Kalwa Inset I 20
Kamakwie A1 63
Kaman Inset I 20
Kamaran, *island* A1 25
Kamarhati Inset II 20
Kambia A1 63
Kamchatka, *peninsula* D10 44
Kamchiya, *river* F2 50
Kamensk-Uralsky D5 44
Kamet, *mt.* C2 20
Kamina C3 67
Kaminak, *lake* J4 99
Kamloops M6 95
Kampala, *capital* C3 61
Kampong Cham D4 11
Kampong Chhnang C3 11
Kampong Saom B5 11
Kampong Thum C3 11
Kampot C5 11
Kamsack J9 104
Kamsar A2 62
Kamui, *cape* Inset I 8
Kananga B2 67
Kanazawa C2 8
Kanchenjunga, *mt.* D2 19
Kanchipuram C6 20
Kanchrapara Inset II 20
Kandi B2 64
Kandy B4 19
Kane, *basin* P1 99
Kangaroo, *island* C3 14
Kangen, *river* C3 59
Kanggye B2 9
Kanghwa, *bay* A4 9
Kangiqsualujjuaq C2 101
Kangiqsujuaq B1 101
Kangirsuk B1 101
Kangnŭng C4 9
Kangshan B2 9
Kankan D2 62
Kano E1 65
Kanpur D3 20
Kansaripara Inset II 20
Kansas D2 126
Kansas City, Kans. D2 126
Kansas City, Mo. D2 126
Kansay A1 23
Kansk D6 44
Kanté B2 64
Kanuku, *mts.* B4 80
Kanye B3 69
Kaohsiung B2 9
Kaoko Veld, *mts.* A1 70
Kaolack A2 62
Kaoma A2 67
Kaop'ing, *river* B2 9
Kapfenberg D3 39
Kapingamarangi, *atoll* C2 15
Kapiskau, *river* D2 101
Kaposvár A2 43
Kapuskasing D3 101
Kara B2 64
Kara, *sea* B5 44
Kara-Kum, *canal* D3 22
Kara-Kum, *desert* C2 22
Kara-Say F2 23
Karabakh, *canal* B2 45
Karachayevo-Cherkesiya, republic E4 44
Karachi C5 21
Karaj C2 22
Karak, al- A2 26
Karakol F1 23
Karakoram, *range* C1 20
Karaman C3 27
Karasburg C4 70
Karawanken, *range* D4 39
Karbala B2 24
Karcag C2 43
Kardiva, *channel* A2 19
Kärdla B1 46
Kareliya, republic C3 44
Kariba B1 69
Kariba, *lake* A1 69
Karibib B2 70
Karisimbi, *mt.* B1 61
Karkar, *island* A2 15
Karkinit, *bay* C3 47
Karlovac B2 48
Karlovy Vary A2 42
Karlskrona C3 53
Karlsruhe B4 40
Karlstad B3 53
Karnali, *river* B2 19
Karnaphuli, *reservoir* F6 21
Karnaphuli, *river* E6 21
Karonga B1 68
Karpas, *peninsula* C1 27
Kárpathos, *island* C4 51
Kars E2 27
Kartala, *mt.* A1 67
Kartung B2 62
Karun, *river* B3 22
Karuzi C2 61
Karviná D3 42
Kasai, *river* B1 67
Kasama C2 67
Kasane B1 69
Kasba, *lake* H4 99
Kashan C3 22
Kashi A2 10
Kashiwa D3 8
Kasinathpur Inset II 20
Kaslo O6 95
Kassala D2 59

Key Page
Kassel B3 40
Kasserine B2 57
Kastamonu C2 27
Kastoría B1 51
Kastrup D3 32
Kasugai C3 8
Kasungu B2 68
Kasur E3 21
Katagum, *river* E2 65
Katanga, *plateau* B3 67
Kateríni B1 51
Kate's Needle, *mt.* F2 95
Katherine, N.T. C1 14
Kathgodam C3 20
Kathiawar, *peninsula* B4 20
Kathmandu, *capital* C2 19
Katowice D3 41
Katrine, *lake* B2 30
Katsina D1 65
Kattegat, *strait* C2 32
Kau-Ur C2 62
Kauai *island*, Hawaii Inset II 126
Kaufbeuren B5 40
Kaukau Veld, *region* C2 70
Kaunas B2 46
Kaura-Namoda D1 65
Kavadarci C2 48
Kavajë A2 49
Kavála C1 51
Kavaratti, *island* B6 20
Kavieng B2 15
Kavir-e Namak, *desert* D3 22
Kaw B1 80
Kawagoe C3 8
Kawaguchi C3 8
Kawasaki C3 8
Kawhia B2 15
Kawthaung C4 12
Kayangel, *islands* C1 17
Kayes A3 58
Kayser, *mts.* A3 80
Kayseri C2 27
Kazakh Upland, *region* C2 23
Kazakhstan 23
Kazan D4 44
Kazanlŭk D3 50
Kazincbarcika C1 43
Kearney F2 102
Kearney, Nebr. D1 126
Keban, *reservoir* D2 27
Kebili B3 57
Kebir, *river* B1 26
Kebnekaise, *mt.* C1 53
Kechika, *river* J2 95
Kecskemét B2 43
Kėdainiai B2 46
Kedgwick B1 97
Kediri C2 13
Kédougou C3 62
Keele, *river* C4 99
Keeley, *lake* B6 104
Keetmanshoop C4 70
Keewatin, *region* J4 99
Kef, el- B1 57
Kefallinía, *island* B2 51
Keflavík A3 52
Keg River B2 94
Keila C1 46
Kékes, *mt.* C2 43
Kelang A2 13
Kelani, *river* B4 19
Kelliher G9 104
Kelowna N6 95
Kelsey C1 96
Keluang B2 13
Kelvington G8 104
Kemano J4 95
Kemerovo D6 44
Kemi B1 53
Kemijärvi C1 53
Kemijoki, *river* C1 53
Kemnay A4 96
Kempenland, *region* D1 33
Kemps Bay B3 89
Kempt, *lake* B4 103
Kempten B5 40
Kemptville K2 102
Kenaston D9 104
Kendal C2 30
Kendari D2 13
Kenema B2 63
Keng Tung C2 12
Kenilworth C3 30
Kenitra C1 57
Kennetcook D2 100
Keno B4 105
Kenora B3 101
Kensington B2 100
Kenton A4 96
Kentucky E2 126
Kentville C2 100
Kenville A3 96
Kenya 61
Kenya, *mt.* D4 61
Keokradong, *mt.* F7 21
Kerangan Nyatan B3 13
Keratsinion Inset 51
Kerch D3 47
Kerch, *strait* D3 47
Kerema A2 15
Keremeos N6 95
Keren B2 60
Kerewan B2 62
Kerguelen, *islands* 5
Kericho C4 61
Kerinci, *mt.* B2 13
Kerkennah, *islands* C2 57
Kerki D3 22
Kérkira A2 51
Kérkira, *island* A2 51
Kerman D3 22
Kerman, *region* D4 22
Kérouané D3 62
Kerrobert A9 104
Kerulen, *river* D2 11
Keszthely A2 43
Keta C4 64
Ketchikan, Alaska Inset I 126
Key Lake Mine E3 104

Key Page
Key West, Fla. E3 126
Keyano B3 101
Khabarovsk E8 44
Khabur, *river* B1 27
Khakasiya, republic D6 44
Khalándrion Inset 51
Khalkidhikí, *peninsula* B1 51
Khalkís B2 51
Khaluf C2 25
Khambhât, *gulf* B4 20
Khamis Mushayt B2 24
Khan-Tengri, *mt.* E2 23
Khanaqin C2 24
Khaniá B4 51
Khanka, *lake* G1 10
Khanty-Mansiya, autonomous okrug C5 44
Khanty-Mansiysk C5 44
Kharagpur E4 20
Kharg, *island* C4 22
Kharijah, al- B2 56
Kharijah, *oasis* B2 56
Kharj, al- B1 24
Kharkiv D1 47
Khartoum North C2 59
Khartoum, *capital* C2 59
Khashm al-Qirbah C2 59
Khashuri B4 45
Khasi, *hills* F3 20
Khaskovo D4 50
Khatanga B7 44
Khawr, al- D2 25
Kherson C3 47
Khíos, *island* C2 51
Khiran, al- C3 24
Khmelnytskyy B2 47
Khojak, *pass* C3 21
Khon Kaen C2 12
Khor Angar C1 60
Khorasan, *region* D2 22
Khorat, *plateau* C3 12
Khorixas B2 70
Khorramabad B3 22
Khorramshahr B3 22
Khorugh B2 23
Khouribga C1 57
Khowst B2 22
Khudzhand A1 23
Khujayli A2 23
Khulna C6 21
Khums, al- B1 56
Khuriya Muriya, *islands* C3 25
Khust A2 47
Khuzdar C4 21
Khuzestan, *region* B3 22
Khvoy A2 22
Khyber, *pass* D2 21
Kibungo C2 61
Kibuye B2 61
Kičevo A2 48
Kidal D2 58
Kidderminster C3 30
Kiel B1 40
Kiel, *bay* B1 40
Kielce E3 41
Kiev, *capital* C1 47
Kiev, *reservoir* C1 47
Kiffa C3 58
Kifisiá Inset 51
Kifissós, *river* B2 51
Kigali, *capital* B1 61
Kigoma A1 68
Kii, *channel* B3 8
Kii, *peninsula* B3 8
Kikinda B2 49
Kikkertavak, *island* B2 98
Kikwit B2 67
Kilchu C2 9
Kildare C2 31
Kilimanjaro, *mt.* C1 68
Kilinochchi B2 19
Kilkee B2 31
Kilkenny C2 31
Killala, *bay* B1 31
Killaloe H2 102
Killarney B2 31
Killarney B4 96
Killarney D1 102
Killarney Lake E5 94
Killdeer D11 104
Killeen, Tex. D2 126
Kilmarnock B2 30
Kilombero, *river* C2 68
Kilwa Kivinje C2 68
Kimbe B2 15
Kimberley B2 71
Kimberley O6 95
Kimberley E3 102
Kimberley, *plateau* B1 14
Kimch'aek C2 9
Kimch'ŏn C4 9
Kinabalu, *mt.* D1 13
Kinabatangan, *river* D2 13
Kinbasket, *lake* B5 94
Kinbasket, *lake* O5 95
Kincaid C11 104
Kincardine D3 102
Kindersley A9 104
Kindia B2 62
Kindu C2 67
King Leopold, *range* B1 14
King William, *island* J3 99
King's Cove E5 98
King's Landing B3 97
King's Lynn D3 30
King's Point C4 98
Kingcome Inlet J6 95
Kingman, Ariz. B2 126
Kingston C3 100
Kingston J3 102
Kingston upon Hull C3 30
Kingston upon Thames Inset III 30
Kingston, *capital* C3 88
Kingstown, *capital* B2 91
Kingsville F2 100
Kingsville C5 102
Kinistino E8 104
Kinkala C6 66
Kinkora B2 100

Key Page
Kinloss D3 102
Kinmount G3 102
Kinnairds, *cape* C1 30
Kinosota B4 96
Kinsarvik B3 52
Kinsella E5 94
Kinshasa, *capital* A2 67
Kinyeti, *mt.* C4 59
Kioa, *island* C2 17
Kiosk G1 102
Kipengere, *range* B2 68
Kipling H10 104
Kirakira B2 16
Kirensk D7 44
Kiribati 17
Kırıkkale C2 27
Kiritimati (Christmas), *island* D1 17
Kirkcaldy B2 30
Kirkenes F2 52
Kirkfield G3 102
Kirkland Lake D3 101
Kirkpatrick, *mt.* A5 107
Kirkuk B1 24
Kirkwall Inset I 30
Kirov D4 44
Kirovakan B2 45
Kirovograd C2 47
Kirşehir C2 27
Kirthar, *range* C4 21
Kiruna D1 53
Kisangani C1 67
Kishi B3 65
Kiskitto, *lake* B2 96
Kiskörei-víztároló, *lake* C2 43
Kiskunhalas B2 43
Kismayo A4 60
Kissidougou C3 62
Kississing, *lake* A1 96
Kisumu C4 61
Kita B3 58
Kita, *island* Inset III 8
Kitakami, *river* D2 8
Kitakyushu A3 8
Kitale C3 61
Kitami Inset I 8
Kitami, *mts.* Inset I 8
Kitchener E4 102
Kitgum C2 61
Kíthira, *island* B3 51
Kitikmeot, *region* G3 99
Kitimat H4 95
Kitwanga H3 95
Kitwe B2 67
Kivi, *lake* C2 53
Kivu, *lake* B1 61
Kızıl Irmak, *river* C2 27
Kjølen, *mts.* C1 53
Kladno B2 42
Klagenfurt D4 39
Klaipėda A2 46
Klamath Falls, Oreg. A1 126
Klarälven, *river* B2 53
Klatovy A3 42
Kleinburg J5 102
Klemtu H5 95
Kleve A3 40
Kloulklubed B3 17
Kluane, *lake* B5 105
Knee, *lake* D1 96
Knight, *inlet* K6 95
Knockboy, *mt.* B3 31
Knokke B1 33
Knoxville, Tenn. E2 126
Ko Chang, *island* C3 12
Ko Kut, *island* C4 12
Ko Phangan, *island* B4 12
Ko Samui, *island* B4 12
Ko Tarutao, *island* B5 12
Kobe B3 8
Koblenz A3 40
Kobuleti A4 45
Kočani C2 48
Kočevje B3 48
Kochi B3 8
Kodiak, Alaska Inset I 126
Kofarnihon, *river* A2 23
Köflach D3 39
Koforidua B3 64
Kofu C3 8
Køge D3 32
Kohima F3 20
Kohtla-Järve D1 46
Koindu B1 63
Koje-do, *island* C5 9
Kokkina A1 27
Kokkola B2 53
Kokshetau C1 23
Kola A4 96
Kola, *peninsula* C3 44
Kolari B1 53
Kolda B3 62
Kolding B3 32
Kolhapur B5 20
Kolín B2 42
Kołobrzeg B1 41
Kolpashevo D6 44
Kolshet Inset I 20
Kolumadulu, *atoll* A3 19
Kolwezi C3 67
Kolyma, *range* C10 44
Kolyma, *river* C9 44
Komadugu Gana, *river* F2 65
Komadugu Yobe, *river* F1 65
Komárno B3 42
Komárom B2 43
Komati, *river* B2 71
Komatsu C2 8
Komi, republic C4 44
Komi-Permyat, autonomous okrug D4 44
Komoé, *river* E3 63
Komotiní C1 51
Komsomolsk-na-Amure D8 44
Konar, *river* D2 21
Konduz B1 22
Konduz, *river* B1 22
Koné C2 18
Kong, *river* D4 11

	Key	Page
Konibodom	B1	23
Konin	D2	41
Konnagar	Inset II	20
Konotop	C1	47
Kontagora	C2	65
Kontum	B3	11
Konya	C3	27
Kootenay, *lake*	O6	95
Kootenay, *river*	P6	95
Kopaonik, *mts.*	B3	49
Kópavogur	A2	52
Koper	A3	48
Kopet, *mts.*	B2, D2	22
Koprivnica	C2	48
Korab, *mt.*	B2	49
Korab, *mt.*	A2	48
Korçë	B3	49
Korčula, *island*	C4	48
Korea, *bay*	A3	9
Korea, *strait*	C5	9
Korhogo	D2	63
Koriyama	D2	8
Korla	B1	10
Koro Toro	B4	59
Koro, *island*	B2	17
Koro, *sea*	B2	17
Koror, *capital*	B3	17
Koror, *island*	C3	17
Körös, *river*	C2	43
Korosten	B1	47
Kortrijk	B2	33
Koryak, *range*	C10	44
Koryakiya, autonomous okrug	C10	44
Kosŏng	C3	9
Kos, *island*	C3	51
Kosciusko, *mt.*	D3	14
Koshigaya	C3	8
Koshiki, *islands*	A4	8
Košice	C2	42
Kosovo, province	B3	49
Kosrae	D2	15
Kosrae, *island*	D2	15
Kossol, *passage*	C2	17
Kossol, *reef*	C2	17
Kossu, *lake*	D3	63
Koszalin	C1	41
Kota	C3	20
Kota Baharu	B1	13
Kota Kinabalu	D2	13
Kotcho, *lake*	M1	95
Kotka	C2	53
Kotlas	C4	44
Kotor, *gulf*	A3	49
Kotovsk	B2	47
Kotto, *river*	B2	66
Kouchibouguac	D2	97
Koudougou	C2	64
Koula-Moutou	B2	66
Koulikoro	B3	58
Koulountou, *river*	C3	62
Koumac	C2	18
Koungheul	B2	62
Kourou	B1	80
Kouroussa	D2	62
Kousséri	B1	65
Koutiala	B3	58
Kouto	C2	63
Kouvola	C2	53
Kovel	A1	47
Kowŏn	B3	9
Kowloon	Inset	10
Kowt-e Ashrow	B2	22
Kozáni	B1	51
Kozhikode	C6	20
Kozloduy	B2	50
Kozu, *island*	C3	8
Kožuf, *mts.*	C2	48
Kpalimé	B3	64
Kpandu	C3	64
Kpémé	B3	64
Kra, *isthmus*	B4	12
Kracheh	E3	11
Kragujevac	B2	49
Krakatau, *island*	B2	13
Kraków	D3	41
Kraljevo	B3	49
Kramatorsk	D2	47
Kranj	B2	48
Kranji	B1	13
Krasnodar	E3	44
Krasnoyarsk	D6	44
Krefeld	A3	40
Kremenchug	C2	47
Kretinga	A2	46
Kribi	A3	65
Krishna, *river*	C5	20
Kristiansand	B4	52
Kristianstad	B3	53
Kristiansund	B3	52
Kristinehamn	B3	53
Krk, *island*	B2	48
Krka, *river*	B3	48
Krong Kaoh Kong	A4	11
Kroonstad	C2	71
Krosnow	E4	41
Krško	C3	48
Krugersdorp	C2	71
Krujë	A2	49
Kruševac	B3	49
Kruševo	B2	48
Krychaw	E3	47
Kryvyi Rih	C2	47
Kuala Abang	B2	13
Kuala Belait	A2	13
Kuala Lumpur, *capital*	A2	13
Kuala Terengganu	B2	13
Kuantan	B2	13
Kuching	C2	13
Kuchino, *island*	A4	8
Kudymkar	D4	44
Kufstein	E3	99
Kugluktuk	C3	39
Kuito	C4	70
Kukës	B1	49
Kul, *river*	D4	22
Kula Kangri, *mt.*	B1	19
Kuldiga	A2	46
Kulmbach	B3	40
Kulob	A2	23
Kulpawn, *river*	B1	64
Kum, *river*	B4	9
Kumamoto	A3	8
Kumanovo	B1	48
Kumasi	B3	64
Kume, *island*	Inset II	8
Kumo	F2	65
Kunda	D1	46
Kunene, *river*	A1	70
Kunlun, *mts.*	B2	10
Kunming	D3	10
Kunsan	B5	9
Kuntaur	D2	62
Kuopio	C2	53
Kupa, *river*	B3	48
Kupang	D3	13
Kür, *river*	A2, C2	45
Kür-Aras, *lowland*	B2	45
Kura, *river*	E2	27
Kurashiki	B3	8
Kuraymah	C1	59
Kŭrdzhali	D4	50
Kure	B3	8
Kuressaare	B2	46
Kurgan	D5	44
Kuril, *islands*	E9	44
Kurinwás, *river*	B2	87
Kurla	Inset I	20
Kurnool	C5	20
Kuršėnai	B1	46
Kursk	D3	44
Kuru, *river*	C2	19
Kuruman	B2	71
Kurume	A3	8
Kurunegala	B4	19
Kushiro	Inset I	8
Kushtia	C5	21
Kusŏng	A3	9
Kusti	C2	59
Kut, al-	C2	24
Kütahya	B2	27
Kutaisi	B3	45
Kutch, *gulf*	A4	20
Kutno	D2	41
Kuujjuaq	C2	101
Kuujjuarapik	A2	101
Kuwait		**24**
Kuwait, *bay*	B2	24
Kuwait, *capital*	B2	24
Kwa, *river*	B2	67
Kwahu, *plateau*	B3	64
Kwajalein, *island*	B2	16
Kwangju	B5	9
Kwango, *river*	B2	67
Kwekwe	B2	69
Kyaukpyu	B2	12
Kyle	B10	104
Kyle of Lochalsh	B1	30
Kyoga, *lake*	C3	61
Kyŏngju	C5	9
Kyoto	B3	8
Kyrenia	B1	27
Kyrgyzstan		**23**
Kyrenia, *range*	B1	27
Kyushu, *island*	A3	8
Kyustendil	A3	50
Kyzyl	D6	44
Kyzyl-Kyya	C2	23
Kyzyl-Suu, *river*	C3	23
Kyzylkum, *desert*	B2	23

L

	Key	Page
La Asunción	D1	79
La Baie	F3	103
La Broquerie	C4	96
La Ceiba	B2	86
La Chaux-de-Fonds	A1	35
La Coma, *river*	B1	36
La Conception	B5	103
La Condamine	B1	35
La Coruña	B1	37
La Crete	B2	94
La Croix Maingot	A2	91
La Crosse, Wis.	D1	126
La Cruz	A1	86
La Digue, *island*	C1	70
La Doré	D3	103
La Esperanza	A2	86
La Goulette	C1	57
La Grande, *river*	B3	101
La Guadeloupe	F6	103
La Guaira Maiquetía	C1	79
La Have	C3	100
La Laguna	Inset I	37
La Libertad	A4	79
La Libertad	C3	85
La Loche	A4	104
La Louvière	C2	33
La Malbaie	F4	103
La Martre	K2	103
La Martre, *lake*	E4	99
La Montaña, *region*	C2	77
La Oroya	B3	77
La Palma	C2	87
La Palma, *island*	Inset I	37
La Paz	B2	86
La Paz, *capital*	A3	77
La Paz, *state capital*	B3	84
La Pérouse	B1	96
La Pérouse, *strait*	Inset I	8
La Plaine	B3	90
La Plata	D4	74
La Plata, *river*	C2	90
La Plonge, *lake*	C5	104
La Pocatière	F4	103
La Prairie	J6	103
La Rioja	B2	74
La Rioja	E1	37
La Rochelle	B3	34
La Roda	E3	37
La Romana	D2	89
La Ronge	E5	104
La Ronge, *lake*	E6	104
La Rosita	B2	87
La Salle	C4	96
La Salle	J6	103
La Scie	D4	98
La Serena	B3	76
La Spezia	B1	38
La Tortuga, *island*	C1	79
La Tuque	D4	103
La Unión	B7	76
La Unión	C2	86
La Vega	B1	89
La Virtud	A2	86
La-Roche-sur-Yon	B3	34
Labasa	B2	17
Labé	B2	62
Labe (Elbe), *river*	B2	42
Labelle	C3	100
Laberge, *lake*	B5	105
Labi	A3	13
Laborec, *river*	C2	42
Laborie	B3	91
Labrador City	D3	98
Labrieville	G2	103
Labu	C2	13
Labuan, *island*	D2	13
Laç	A2	49
Lac du Bonnet	C4	96
Lac La Biche	E4	94
Lac La Hache	M5	95
Lac Mégantic	F6	103
Lac-aux-Sables	D5	103
Lac-Bouchette	D3	103
Lac-des-Aigles	H4	103
Lac-des-îles	A5	103
Lac-Édouard	D4	103
Lac-Etchemin	F5	103
Lac-Nominingue	A5	103
Lac-Saguay	A5	103
Laccadive, *islands*	B6	20
Lachenaie	J5	103
Lachine	H6	103
Lachute	B6	103
Lacombe	D5	94
Ladhiqiyah, al- (Latakia)	A2	27
Ladoga, *lake*	C3	44
Ladysmith	C2	71
Ladywood	C4	96
Lae	A2	15
Lae, *island*	B2	16
Laem, *mt.*	B3	12
Læsø, *island*	C1	32
Lafayette, La.	D2	126
Lafia	E3	65
Lafleche	D11	104
Lafond	E4	94
Laghouat	B1	57
Lagodekhi	D4	45
Lagos	B4	65
Lagos	A4	36
Laguna de Bay, *lake*	B3	12
Lahave, *river*	C3	100
Lahij	A2	25
Lahn, *river*	B3	40
Lahore	E3	21
Lahti	C2	53
Laï	B5	59
Lairg	B1	30
Lajas	A2	90
Lajes	C4	81
Lakatoro	B3	18
Lake Alma	F11	104
Lake Charlotte	E3	100
Lake Edward	B2	97
Lake Harbour	O4	99
Lake Lenore	F8	104
Lake St. Peter	G2	102
Lake, district	B2	30
Lakeba, *island*	C3	17
Lakeba, *passage*	C3	17
Lakefield	G3	102
Lakelse Lake	H4	95
Lakhpat	A4	20
Laki, *volcano*	B2	52
Lakselv	F1	52
Lalitpur	C2	19
Lamaline	D5	98
Lamap	B3	18
Lambaréné	A2	66
Lambton	E6	103
Lamèque	E1	97
Lamèque, *island*	E1	97
Lami	B3	17
Lamía	B2	51
Lammermuir, *hills*	C2	30
Lamon, *bay*	B3	12
Lampa	Inset	76
Lampang	B2	12
Lampeter	B3	30
Lampman	H11	104
Lamu	F5	61
Lan, *island*	B2	9
Lanai *island*, Hawaii	Inset II	126
Lanark	J2	102
Lancaster	C2	30
Lancaster	L2	102
L'Ancienne-Lorette	K5	103
Land's End, *promontory*	B4	30
Lander, Wyo.	C1	126
Landes, *region*	B5	34
Landis	B8	104
Landshut	C4	40
Lang Son	B2	11
Langeburg, *mts.*	B3	71
Langeland, *island*	C4	32
Langenburg	J10	104
Langham	D8	104
Langkawi, *island*	A1	13
Langley	L6	95
Langruth	B4	96
Langstaff	K5	102
Langton	E5	102
Languedoc-Roussillon	C5	34
Lanigan	E9	104
Lanín, *volcano*	A4	74
Länkäran	C3	45
L'Annonciation	B5	103
Lansdowne	J3	102
Lansdowne House	C2	101
L'Anse-à-Valleau	M2	103
L'Anse-au-Loup	C3	98
L'Anse-aux-Gascons	M3	103
L'Anse-St-Jean	F3	103
Lansing, *capital*, Mich.	E1	126
Lantau, *island*	Inset	10
Lanús	D3	74
Lanzarote, *island*	Inset I	37
Lanzhou	D2	10
Lao Cai	A1	11
Laoag	B2	12
Laoang	C3	12
Laon	C2	34
Laos		**11**
Lapithos	B1	27
Lapland, *region*	B1	53
Lappeenranta	C2	53
Laptev, *sea*	B8	44
L'Aquila	C2	38
Larache	C1	57
Laramie, Wyo.	C1	126
Laredo, Tex.	D3	126
Lares	B2	90
Larestan, *region*	C4	22
Large, *island*	C1	91
Lárisa	B2	51
Lark Harbour	B4	98
Larkana	C4	21
Larkhall	C4	96
Larnaca	B2	27
Larne	B2	30
Larochette	B2	33
Larrys River	F2	100
Larsen Ice Shelf, *glacier*	C12	107
Las Cruces, N. Mex.	C2	126
Las Minas, *mt.*	A2	86
Las Palmas	Inset I	37
Las Piedras	D2	90
Las Piedras	B3	75
Las Tablas	B3	87
Las Tunas	E3	88
Las Vegas, N. Mex.	C2	126
Las Vegas, Nev.	B2	126
L'Ascension	B5	103
Lashburn	A7	104
Lashio	C2	12
Lashkar Gah	A2	22
Last Mountain, *lake*	E9	104
Latacunga	B3	79
Late, *island*	C2	17
Latina	C2	38
Latium	C2	38
Latvia		**46**
Lau, *island group*	C2	17
Laucala, *island*	C2	17
Laudat	B3	90
Lauder	A4	96
Launceston	B4	30
Launceston, Tas.	D4	14
Laurie River	A1	96
Laurier	B4	96
Lausanne	A2	35
Lautoka	A2	17
Laval	B2	34
Laval	C6, J5	103
Lavenham	B4	96
Lavoy	E4	94
Lavumisa	B3	71
Lawa, *river*	A2, B2	80
Lawn	D5	98
Lawrence Station	B3	97
Lawton, Okla.	D2	126
Layland	B4	96
Layou, *river*	B3	90
Lázaro Cárdenas	D4	84
Le Bic	H3	103
Le Creusot	D3	34
Le Havre	C2	34
Le Mans	C2	34
Le Puy	C4	34
Leader	A10	104
Leading Tickles	D4	98
Leaf Rapids	D1	96
Leamington	C5	102
l'Eau Claire, *lake*	B2	101
Lebanon		**26**
Lebanon, *mts.*	B1	26
Lebombo, *mts.*	C2, D1	71
Lebu	B6	76
Lecce	D2	38
Lech	B3	39
Lech, *river*	B4	40
Leduc	D4	94
Lee, *river*	B3	31
Leeds	C3	30
Leeuwarden	C1	32
Leeuwin, *cape*	A3	14
Leeward Group	B3	58
Lefka	A1	27
Lefkoniko	B1	27
Leganés	Inset II	37
Legazpi	B3	12
Legnica	C3	41
Leicester	C3	30
Leichhardt, *river*	D1	14
Leiden	B2	32
Leie, *river*	B2	33
Leikanger	B3	52
Leipzig	C3	40
Leiria	A3	36
Leitrim	H6	102
Leixões	A2	36
Lékéti, *mts.*	C5	66
Lélouma	B2	62
Lelystad	C2	32
Lempa, *river*	A1, B2	86
Lena, *river*	C8	44
Leneinsk	C2	23
Lenghu	C2	10
Lengoué, *river*	C3	66
Lenore	A4	96
Lens	C1	34
Lensk	C7	44
Léo	C3	64
Leoben	D3	39
Léogâne	C2	89
León	D3	84
León	A2	87
León	D1	37
Leone	B2	18
Leova	B2	50
Leoville	C7	104
Lepontine Alps, *mts.*	C2	35
Lepreau	C3	97
Lepsi	D2	23
Leribe	B1	71
Lérida	G2	37
Lerwick	Inset I	30
Les Çayes	B2	89
Les Éboulements	F4	103
Les Escaldes	B2	36
Les Escoumins	G3	103
Les Islets-Caribou	J2	103
Les Méchins	K3	103
Les Tantes, *island*	B1	91
Les Ulis	Inset II	34
Leskovac	B3	49
Lesosibirsk	D6	44
Lesotho		**71**
Lesser Caucasus, *mts.*	A2, B4	45
Lesser Hinggan, *range*	F1	10
Lesser Slave, *lake*	C3	94
Lesser Sunda, *islands*	C2	13
Lestrock	G9	104
Lésvos, *island*	C2	51
Leszno	C3	41
Lethbridge	D6	94
Lethbridge	E5	98
Lethem	B4	80
Leticia	C6	78
Letlhakeng	B3	69
Letterkenny	C1	31
Leuven	C2	33
Levack	D1	102
Levallois-Perret	Inset II	34
Leveque, *cape*	B1	14
Leverkusen	A3	40
Levice	B2	42
Lévis	E5, L6	103
Levittown	C2	90
Lewes	D4	30
Lewis, *island*	A1	30
Lewisporte	D4	98
Lewiston, Idaho	B1	126
Lewiston, Maine	F1	126
Lexington, Ky.	E2	126
Leyte, *island*	C4	12
Lhasa	C3	10
Lhobrak, *river*	C2	19
Lhuntshi	C2	19
Lianyungang	E2	10
Liao, *river*	F1	10
Liaoning	F1	10
Liaoyang	F1	10
Liaoyuan	F1	10
Liard River	J1	95
Liard, *river*	K1	95
Libau	C4	96
Liberec	B2	42
Liberia		**63**
Liberia	A2	86
Libono	B1	71
Libreville, *capital*	A1	66
Libya		**56**
Libyan, *desert*	A2, D2	56
Lichfield	C3	30
Lichinga	B2	68
Lida	B3	47
Liechtenstein		**33**
Liège	D2	33
Lieksa	D2	53
Lienz	C4	39
Liepāja	A2	46
Lièvre, *river*	A5	103
Lifford	C1	31
Lifou, *island*	D2	18
Lifuka, *island*	C3	17
Liguria	B1	38
Ligurian, *sea*	B2	38
Lihir, *group*	B2	15
Likasi	C3	67
Likiep, *island*	B1	16
Lille	C1	34
Lille, *strait*	B3	32
Lillehammer	C3	52
Lillooet	M6	95
Lillooet, *river*	L6	95
Lilongwe, *capital*	B2	68
Lima, *capital*	B3	77
Lima, *river*	A2	36
Limassol	B2	27
Limbazi	C2	46
Limbe	A3	65
Limbourg	D2	33
Limerick	B2	31
Limfjorden, *channel*	B2	32
Límnos, *island*	C2	51
Limoges	C4	34
Limón	C3	86
Limours	Inset II	34
Limousin	C4	34
Limpopo, *river*	C1	71
Linares	B5	76
Linares	E3	84
Linares	E3	37
Lincoln	C3	30
Lincoln, *capital*, Nebr.	D1	126
Lindau	B5	40
Lindbergh	E4	94
Linden	B3	80
Linden	D2	100
Lindi	C2	68
Lindsay	G3	102
Line, *islands*	D1	17
Lingayen, *gulf*	B2	12
Lingga, *island*	B2	13
Lingshi	A2	19
Linguère	B2	62
Linköping	C3	53
Linnhe, *lake*	B2	30
Linvanti, *river*	A1	69
Linwood	F2	100
Linz	D2	39
Lion, *gulf*	D5	34
Lionel Town	B3	88
Lions Head	D3	102
Lipa	B3	12
Lipari, *islands*	C3	38
Lipetsk	D3	44
Lippstadt	B3	40
Lipton	G10	104
Liptovský Mikuláš	B2	42
Lira	C2	61
Lisala	B1	67
L'Isalo, *mts.*	B3	69
Lisbon, *capital*	A3	36
Lisichansk	D2	47
L'Isle-Adam	Inset II	34
L'Isle-Verte	G3	103
Lismore, N.S.W.	E2	14
Listowel	E4	102
Litani, *river*	A2	26
Litani, *river*	A2, B3	80
Lithuania		**46**
Little Alföld, *plain*	A2	43
Little Andaman, *island*	F6	20
Little Bay	B5	98
Little Bras d'Or	G1	100
Little Current	D2	102
Little Fort	M5	95
Little Grand Rapids	D3	96
Little Inagua, *island*	C4	89
Little Rock, *capital*, Ark.	D2	126
Little Salmon, *lake*	C4	105
Little Scarcies, *river*	A1	63
Little Seldom	D4	98
Little Smoky, *river*	A4	94
Little St. Bernard, *pass*	D4	34
Little Zab, *river*	B1	24
Liuzhou	D3	10
Liverpool	C3	30
Liverpool	C3	100
Liverpool, *bay*	B3	30
Livingstone	B3	67
Livno	B2	48
Livorno	B2	38
Ljubljana, *capital*	B2	48
Ljusnanälven, *river*	B2	53
Llallagua	A3	77
Llandrindod Wells	B3	30
Llanos, *plain*	C2	79
Llanos, prairie	C3	78
Llanquihue, *lake*	B7	76
Lleyn, *peninsula*	B3	30
Llorts	B1	36
Lloyd, *lake*	B3	104
Lloydminster	E4	94
Lloydminster	A7	104
Lloyds, *river*	C5	98
Llullaillaco, *volcano*	B1	74
Lo Wu	Inset	10
Lo, *river*	A1	11
Loa, *river*	B2	76
Lobamba	B2	71
Lobatse	B3	69
Lobaye, *river*	A2	66
Lobito	B4	70
Locarno	C2	35
Lockeport	B4	100
Lockport	C4	96
Lod (Lydda)	B2	26
Lodja	B2	67
Lodwar	C2	61
Łódź	D3	41
Loei	B2	12
Loess, *plateau*	D2	10
Lofoten, *islands*	C2	52
Logan, *river*	Inset III	14
Logan, Utah	B1	126
Logone, *river*	A5	59
Logroño	E1	37
Loi-kaw	C2	12
Loire, *river*	C3	34
Loíza	D2	90
Loja	B4	79
Loja	D4	37
Lokka, *reservoir*	C1	53
Lokoja	D4	65
Lokossa	A4	64
Lol, *river*	B3	59
Lolland, *island*	C4	32
Lom	B2	50
Lomami, *river*	C2	67
Lomas de Zamora	D4	74
Lomawai	A3	17
Lombardy	B1	38
Lombardy	J3	102
Lombok, *island*	C2	13
Lomé, *capital*	B3	64
Lomond, *lake*	B2	30
Łomża	F2	41
London	D5	102
London, *capital*	C3, Inset III	30
Londonderry	A2	30
Londrina	C4	81
Lone Butte	M5	95
Long Beach, Calif.	B2	126
Long *island*, N.Y.	F1	126
Long Lake	D4	96
Long Range, *mts.*	B5, C4	98
Long Xuyen	A4	11
Long, *island*	C3	89
Longford	C2	31
Longlac	C3	101
Longreach, Qld.	D2	14
Longueuil	J5	103
Longview, Tex.	D2	126
Loon Lake	C3	94
Loon Lake	A6	104
Loop Head, *cape*	B2	31
Lop Buri	B3	12
Lop, *lake*	C1	10
Lorca	F4	37
Loreburn	D9	104
Lorengau	A2	15
Loreto	B2	84
Lorette	C4	96
Loretteville	K5	103
Lorient	B3	34
L'Original	L2	102
Lorne, *estuary*	A2	30
Lorraine	D2	34
Lorraine	H5	103
Los Andes	B4	76
Los Ángeles	B6	76
Los Angeles, Calif.	B2	126
Los Chiles	B1	86
Los Mochis	C2	84
Los Reyes	Inset	84
Los Teques	C1	79
Lot, *river*	C4	34
Louang Namtha	A1	11

Key Page
Loubomo B6 66
Louga A2 62
Lough Erne, *lake* A2 30
Loughborough, *lake* J3 102
Lougheed, *island* G1 99
Louisbourg H2 100
Louisdale F2 100
Louiseville D5 103
Louisiade, *archipelago* B3 15
Louisiana D2 126
Louisville, Ky. E2 126
Lourdes B5 34
Louri C2 19
Louvres Inset II 34
Lovech C2 50
Lovell Village B3 91
Lovettville B4 94
Lowe Farm C4 96
Lower Arrow, *lake* N6 95
Lower Debert D2 100
Lower Five Islands C2 100
Lower Hutt B3 15
Lower Montague C2 100
Lower Post H1 95
Lower Saxony B2 40
Lower Tunguska, *river* C6 44
Lower Woods Harbour B4 100
Lowestoft D3 30
Loyada C2 60
Loyalty, *islands* C2 18
Loyoro D2 61
Lualaba, *river* C2 67
Luanda, *capital* B2 70
Luang Prabang B2 11
Luang Prabang, *range* A3 11
Luang, *mt.* B4 12
Luangwa C3 67
Luangwa, *river* C2 67
Luanshya B2 67
Luapula, *river* B2, C3 67
Luau E3 70
Luba A1 66
Lubango B5 70
Lubbock, Tex. C2 126
Lübeck B2 40
Lubicon, *lake* C3 94
Lublin F3 41
Lubumbashi C3 67
Lucapa D2 70
Lucca B2 38
Lucea A2 88
Lucena B3 12
Lucena D4 37
Lučenec B2 42
Lucern, *lake* C2 35
Lucerne C1 35
Lucie, *river* A3 80
Luckenwalde C2 40
Lucknow D3 20
Lucknow D4 102
Lucky Lake C9 104
Luda Kamchiya, *river* E3 50
Lüderitz B4 70
Ludhiana C2 20
Ludogorie, *region* E2 50
Ludwigsburg B4 40
Ludwigshafen am Rhein B4 40
Luena D3 70
Lugano C3 35
Lugano, *lake* C3 35
Luganville B2 18
Lugenda, *river* C2 68
Lugo C1 37
Lugoj A3 43
Luhansk D2 47
Lukuga, *river* C2 67
Luleå D1 53
Luleälven, *river* D1 53
Lumphat F2 11
Lumsden E4 98
Lumsden F10 104
Lumut A2 13
Lund B3 53
Lund K6 95
Lundar B4 96
Lundazi C2 67
Lundi, *river* B2 69
Lüneburg B2 40
Lünen A3 40
Lunenburg C3 100
Lunga, *river* B2 67
Lungwebungu, *river* A2 67
Lunsar A1 63
Luoyang E2 10
Lupeni B3 43
Luperón B1 89
Luquillo D2 90
Luremo C2 70
Lúrio, *river* C2 68
Lusaka, *capital* B3 67
Lusambo B2 67
Luseland A8 104
Lushnjë A3 49
Lusutfu, *river* B2 71
Luton C3 30
Lutsk B1 47
Lützow-Holm, *bay* C16 107
Luuq A3 60
Luvua, *river* B1, C2 67
Luwegu, *river* C2 68
Luxembourg 33
Luxembourg, *capital* B2 33
Luxor B2 56
Luzarches Inset II 34
Luzhou D3 10
Luzon, *island* B3 12
Luzon, *strait* B2 12
Lviv A2 47
Lyddal B1 96
Lyme, *bay* C4 30
Lynn Lake C1 96
Lyon D4 34
Lytton M6 95

M

Ma, *river* A2 11
Maan A2 26
Maas, *river* C3, D3 32
Maastricht C4 32
Mabaruma B1 80
Maberly J3 102
Mabou F1 100
Mac Tier F2 102
MacAlpine, *lake* H3 99
Macapá C1 81
Macas B4 79
Macau, S.A.R. E3 10
Maccan C2 100
Macdonnell, *ranges* C2 14
Macedonia, F.Y.R. 48
Maceió E2 81
Macenta D3 62
Macerata C2 38
Macfarlane, *river* C2 104
Macgregor B4 96
Machakos D4 61
Machala B4 79
Machida C3 8
Machupicchu, *ruins* C3 77
MacKay, *lake* F4 99
MacKay, Qld. D2 14
Mackenzie L3 95
Mackenzie King, *island* F1 99
Mackenzie, *bay* B1 105
Mackenzie, *mts.* C4 99
Mackenzie, *river* B3, D4 99
Mackey H1 102
Macklin A8 104
Maclean, *strait* G1 99
Macmillan, *river* C4 105
Mâcon D3 34
Macon, Ga. E2 126
Madaba A2 26
Madagascar 69
Madan C4 50
Madang A2 15
Madawaska G2 102
Madden C5 94
Madeira, *island* 55
Madeira, *river* B2 81
Madhumati, *river* C5 21
Madhupur Tract, *region* D4 21
Madinat ath-Thawrah B2 27
Madison, *capital*, Wis. E1 126
Madiun C2 13
Madoc H3 102
Madre de Dios, *island* A9 76
Madre de Dios, *river* A2, C3 77
Madrid, *capital* E2, Inset II 37
Madriu, *river* B3 36
Madura, *island* C2 13
Madurai C7 20
Maebashi C2 8
Maestra, *mts.* D3 88
Maéwo, *island* C2 18
Mafeking A3 96
Mafeteng A2 71
Mafia, *island* C2 68
Mafikeng C1 71
Mafra A3 36
Mafraq, al- B1 26
Magadalena de Kino B1 84
Magadan D9 44
Magburaka B1 63
Magdagachi D8 44
Magdalena D3 77
Magdalena Contreras Inset 84
Magdalena, *island* B7 76
Magdalena, *river* B3 78
Magdeburg B2 40
Magelang C2 13
Magellan, *strait* B9 76
Maggiore, *lake* B1 38
Magnetawan F2 102
Magnitogorsk D4 44
Magog D6 103
Mahabharat, *range* B2 19
Mahajamba, *river* B2 69
Mahajanga B2 69
Mahalapye B2 69
Mahallah al-Kubra, al- B1 56
Mahanadi, *river* D4 20
Mahaska C4 94
Mahbas, al- C1 58
Mahdia B3 80
Mahdia C2 57
Mahé, *island* C1, Inset 70
Mahébourg C3 69
Mahilyow E3 47
Mahim, *bay* Inset I 20
Mahón J3 37
Mai-Ndombe, *lake* B2 67
Maidstone D3 30
Maidstone A7 104
Maiduguri G2 65
Main Brook C3 98
Main, *river* B4 40
Main-à-Dieu H1 100
Main-Danube, *canal* B4 40
Maine G1 126
Mainland, *island* Inset I 30
Maintirano A2 69
Mainz B4 40
Maio, *island* C3 58
Maipo, *river* B4, Inset 76
Maipú Inset 76
Maisí, *cape* F3 88
Maisons-Laffitte Inset II 34
Maitland Bridge B3 100
Maíz, *islands* C2 87
Maizuru B3 8
Majardah, *river* B1 57
Majé Inset I 81
Majorca, *island* H3 37
Majuro, *capital* C2 16
Majuro, *island* C2 16
Makamba B3 61
Makassar, *strait* C2 13
Makeni B1 63
Makeyevka D2 47
Makhachkala E4 44
Makhaleng, *river* A2 71
Makin, *island* A1 17
Makkovik B1 98
Makokou B1 66
Makona, *river* A1 63
Makoua C4 66
Makran Coast, *range* B5 21
Makung A2 9
Makurdi E4 65
Malabar, *coast* C4 20
Malabo, *capital* A1 66
Malacca, *strait* A1, A2 13
Malad Inset I 20
Maladzyechna C2 47
Málaga D4 37
Malagarasi, *river* B1 68
Malaita, *island* B1 16
Malakal C3 59
Malakula, *island* B3 18
Malang C2 13
Malanje C3 70
Malanville B2 64
Mälaren, *lake* C3 53
Malatya D2 27
Malawi 68
Malay, *peninsula* A1 13
Malaysia 13
Malbaie, *river* F4 103
Malbun B2 33
Malcolm, *atoll* A1 19
Malden, *island* D2 17
Maldives 19
Male Karpaty, *mts.* A2 42
Male, *atoll* A2 19
Male, *capital* A2 19
Maleb E6 94
Malegaon B4 20
Mali 58
Mali Rajinac, *mt.* B3 48
Malindi F5 61
Mallaig B1 30
Mallow B2 31
Malmberget D1 53
Malmédy E2 33
Malmö B3 53
Maloelap, *island* C2 16
Malombe, *lake* C2 68
Maloti, *mts.* B2 71
Malta 36
Maltahöhe B3 70
Malton J5 102
Mamâri C2 62
Mamawi, *lake* E2 94
Mambéré, *river* A2 66
Mamburao B3 12
Mamiña C2 76
Mamoré, *river* A2 77
Mamou B2 62
Mamry, *lake* E1 41
Mamtalah, al- B2 25
Mamuno A2 69
Man C3 63
Mana B1 80
Mana, *river* B1 80
Manado D1 13
Managua, *capital* A2 87
Managua, *lake* A2 87
Manakara B3 69
Manama, *capital* B1 25
Manatí B2 90
Manaus C2 81
Manawan, *lake* G5 104
Manbij A1 27
Manchester C3 30
Manchester, N.H. F1 126
Manchurian, *plain* F1 10
Mand, *river* C4 22
Mandalay C2 12
Mandalgov C2 11
Mandara, *mts.* B1 65
Mandaue B4 12
Mandeville B2 88
Mándra Inset 51
Mandurah, W.A. A3 14
Manfredonia C2 38
Manga, *region* C2 59
Mangalore B6 20
Mango B1 64
Mangoky, *river* A3 69
Manicouagan, *reservoir* C3 101
Manicougan Deux,
reservoir H2 103
Manigotagan C3 96
Manila, *bay* B3 12
Manila, *capital* B3 12
Manisa A2 27
Manito, *lake* A8 104
Manitoba, *lake* B3, B4, D2 96
Manitou B4 96
Manitoulin, *island* C2 102
Manitouwadge C3 101
Manitowaning D2 102
Maniwaki A5 103
Manizales B3 78
Mankato, Minn. D1 126
Mankayane B2 71
Mankota C11 104
Mankulam B2 19
Mannar A3 19
Mannar, *gulf* C7 20
Mannar, *island* A2 19
Mannheim B4 40
Manning B3 94
Mannville E4 94
Mano, *river* A2, B2 63
Manokwari E2 13
Manono C2 67
Manono, *island* B2 18
Manor Park H5 102
Manori, *point* Inset I 20
Manouane B4 103
Manpo B2 9
Mansa B2 67
Mansa Konko C2 62
Mansel, *island* M4 99
Manson Creek K3 95
Mansurah, al- B1 56
Manta A3 79
Manta, *bay* A3 79
Mantaro, *river* B3 77
Mantiqueira, *range* D4 81
Mantova B1 38
Mantua (Mantova) B1 38
Manukau B2 15
Manus, *island* A2 15
Manyara, *lake* C1 68
Manzanillo D3 88
Manzanillo D4 84
Manzini B2 71
Mao A1 89
Mao A4 59
Maple J5 102
Maple Creek A11 104
Maputo, *capital* B5 68
Maquela do Zombo C2 70
Mar Chiquita, *lake* C3 74
Mar del Plata D4 74
Mar, *range* D4 81
Mara, *river* C4 61
Maraba D2 81
Maracaibo B1 79
Maracaibo, *lake* B2 79
Maracay C1 79
Maradi B3 59
Marajó, *island* D2 81
Marakei, *island* A1 17
Maramasike, *island* B1 16
Maranhão D2 81
Marano, *river* C1 39
Marañón, *river* B1, B2 77
Maras D3 27
Marathon C3 101
Marbella D4 37
Marburg B3 40
Marcelin D8 104
Marche C2 38
Marchena, *island* Inset 79
Mardan D2 21
Mardin E3 27
Maré, *island* D2 18
Maremma, *region* B2 38
Margaree Forks F1 100
Margaret, *lake* C2 94
Margarita, *island* D1 79
Margate D3 30
Margherita, *peak* A3 61
Maria L3 103
Maria, *islands* B3 91
Mariana D3 81
Marianao B1 88
Marías, *islands* C3 84
Marib B1 25
Maribor C2 48
Marie Byrd Land, *region* B8 107
Marie-Reine B3 94
Mariehamn
(Maarianhamina) A2 53
Mariental C3 70
Marigot B2 90
Marijampolė B2 46
Marinduque, *island* B3 12
Marino C2 18
Marion Bridge G2 100
Maripasoula A2 80
Mariscal Estigarribia B3 75
Maritime Alps, *range* D4 34
Maritsa, *river* D3 50
Mariupol D3 47
Mariy El, republic D4 44
Marj Uyun A2 26
Marj, al- D1 56
Marka A3 60
Markham F4, K5 102
Markham, *river* A2 15
Markstay E1 102
Marl A3 40
Marmara, *sea* B2 27
Marmora H3 102
Marne, *river* C2, Inset II 34
Marneuli C4 45
Maromokotro, *mt.* B1 69
Marondera B2 69
Maroni, *river* A1 80
Maros, *river* C2 43
Maroua B1 65
Marovoay B2 69
Marowijne, *river* B2 80
Marquette, Mich. E1 126
Marquis B2 91
Marrakech B2 57
Marsa al-Burayqah C1 56
Marsabit E2 61
Marsala C3 38
Marsaxlokk, *bay* C3 36
Marsden A8 104
Marseille D5 34
Marsh Harbour B2 89
Marshall Is. 16
Marsoui L2 103
Martaban, *gulf* C3 12
Marten River F1 102
Martensville D8 104
Martin B2 42
Martinique, *island* 82
Martins River C3 100
Martorell D2 90
Martuni C2 45
Mary C3 22
Mary's Harbour D3 98
Maryborough, Qld. E2 14
Maryfield A4 96
Maryfield J11 104
Maryland F2 126
Marystown D5 98
Masada, *ruins* B2 26
Masai, *steppe* C1 68
Masaka B4 61
Masan C5 9
Masaya A3 87
Masbate B3 12
Masbate, *island* B3 12
Mascouche C6 103
Maseru, *capital* A2 71
Masfut D2 25
Mashhad D2 22
Masindi B3 61
Masirah, *gulf* C2 25
Masirah, *island* C2 25
Mask, *lake* B2 31
Maskall B2 85
Masqat, *capital* C1 25
Massachusetts F1 126
Massacre B3 90
Massawa B2 60
Massenya B5 59
Masset F4 95
Massey C1 102
Massif Central, *plateau* C4 34
Massif des Bongos, *range* B2 66
Massy Inset II 34
Masuda A3 8
Masvingo B2 69
Mat, *river* B2 49
Matadi A2 67
Matagalpa B2 87
Matagami A4 101
Matale B4 19
Matam C2 62
Matamoros E2 84
Matane J3 103
Matanzas B1 88
Matapédia C1 97
Matapédia K4 103
Matara B6 19
Mataram C2 13
Mataró H2 37
Matautu C2 18
Matawa Place D3 96
Matehuala D3 84
Matelot A2 91
Matera D2 38
Mathura C3 20
Matlock C3 30
Mato Grosso C3 81
Mato Grosso do Sul C4 81
Mato Grosso, *plateau* C3 81
Mátra, *mts.* B2 43
Matrah C1 25
Matruh A1 56
Matsoku, *river* B2 71
Matsudo C3 8
Matsue B3 8
Matsumae D1, Inset I 8
Matsumoto C2 8
Matsuyama B3 8
Mattawa G1 102
Mattawin, *river* C5 103
Matterhorn, *mt.* B3 35
Matthew Town C4 89
Matthews Ridge A2 80
Mauá Inset II 81
Maui, *island*, Hawaii Inset II 126
Maule, *river* B5 76
Maumturk, *mts.* B2 31
Maun A1 69
Mauna Loa, *mt.*, Hawaii Inset II 126
Maunabo D2 90
Mauren B1 33
Maurepas Inset II 34
Mauritania 58
Mauritius 69
Mavinga D5 70
May Pen B3 88
Maya, *mts.* A3 85
Mayaguana, *island* C4 89
Mayaguana, *passage* C4 89
Mayagüez A2 90
Maydi A1 25
Mayfair C7 104
Maymont C8 104
Maymyo C2 12
Maynooth C2 31
Maynooth H2 102
Mayo B4 105
Mayo, *lake* C4 105
Mayombé, *massif* B5 66
Mayon, *volcano* B3 12
Mayotte, *island* C2 67
Mayreau, *island* A4 91
Mayumba A2 66
Mazabuka B3 67
Mazandaran, *region* C2 22
Mazar-e Sharif B1 22
Mazaruni, *river* A2 80
Mazatenango B5 85
Mazatlán C3 84
Mažeikiai B1 46
Mazoe, *river* B1 69
Mazyr D3 47
Mbabane, *capital* B2 71
Mbahiakro D3 63
Mbaké A2 62
Mbala C1 67
Mbale D3 61
Mbalmayo B3 65
Mbandaka B2 67
M'banza Congo B2 70
Mbanza-Ngungu A2 67
Mbarara B4 61
Mbemkuru, *river* C3 68
M'Beni A1 67
Mbéré, *river* B2 65
Mbeya B2 68
Mbini B3 66
Mbini, *river* C3 66
Mboro, *river* D4 66
Mboune, *river* B2 62
Mbour A2 62
Mbuji-Mayi B2 67
Mbuluzane, *river* B2 71
Mbuluzi, *river* B2 71
McAdam B3 97
McAllen, Tex. D3 126
McBride M4 95
McCallum C5 98
McCreary B4 96
McDame H1 95
McGee B9 104
Mchinji A2 68
McKerrow D1 102
McKinley, *mt.*, Alaska Inset I 126
McLeese Lake L5 95
McLeod Lake L4 95
McLeod Valley C4 94
M'Clintock, *channel* H2 99
M'Clure, *strait* D2 99
McLure M5 95
McMurdo, *sound* B5 107
McRae E4 94
Meacham E8 104
Meadow Lake B6 104
Meadow Portage B3 96
Meaford E3 102
Mealy, *mts.* A3 98
Meander River B1 94
Mecca A2 24
Mechelen C1 33
Mecklenburg, *bay* B1 40
Mecklenburg-
Western Pomerania C2 40
Mecsek, *mts.* B2 43
Medan A1 13
Medellín B3 78
Medford, Oreg. A1 126
Medgidia E3 43
Mediaș C2 43
Medicine Hat E6 94
Medika D4 96
Medina A1 24
Medina del Campo D2 37
Medit B2 13
Mediterranean, *sea* 29
Medley E4 94
Medora A4 96
Meductic B3 97
Meelpaeg, *lake* C5 98
Meerut C3 20
Meghna, *river* D5 21
Meghri D4 45
Meighen, *island* J1 99
Meiktila B2 12
Meissen C3 40
Mejicanos A2 86
Mékambo B1 66
Mekele C1 60
Mékinac, *lake* D4 103
Meknès C1 57
Mekong, *delta* B5 11
Mekong, *river* A1, A4, C4, D3 11
Mékrou, *river* B2 64
Melaka B2 13
Melbourne, Fla. E3 126
Melbourne, Vic., *capital* D3 14
Meldrum Bay B2 102
Meleb C4 96
Melekeok C3 17
Mélèzes, *river* B2 101
Melfi B5 59
Melfort F8 104
Melipilla Inset 76
Melita A4 96
Melitopol D3 47
Mellieha B2 36
Mellieha, *bay* B2 36
Melo C2 75
Melrose E2 100
Melun Inset II 34
Melville H10 104
Melville, *island* C1 14
Melville, *island* F1 99
Melville, *lake* B2 98
Melville, *peninsula* M3 99
Memmingen B5 40
Memphis, Tenn. D2 126
Memphrémagog, *lake* D6 103
Menai, *strait* B3 30
Ménaka D2 58
Mende C4 34
Mendoza B3 74
Meneng B3 16
Menihek D3 98
Mennecy Inset II 34
Menongue C4 70
Mentawai, *islands* A2 13
Menzel Bourguiba B1 57
Meppel D2 32
Mequinenza, *lake* F2 37
Merano B1 38
Merauke F2 13
Mercedario, mt B3 74
Mercedes A2 75
Mergui C3 12
Mergui, *archipelago* C4 12
Mérida B2 79
Mérida C3 37
Mérida, *mts.* B2 79
Mérida, *state capital* G3 84
Meridian, Miss. E2 126
Merigomish E2 100
Merín, *lagoon* D2 75
Merir, *island* Inset 17
Merkys, *river* C2 46
Meron, *mt.* B1 26
Merredin, W.A. A3 14
Merrick, *mt.* B2 30
Merridale A3 96
Merritt M6 95
Mersch B2 33
Mersey, *river* C3 30
Mersin C3 27
Merthyr Tydfil B3 30
Meru D3 61
Merume, *mts.* A2 80
Mesaoria, *plain* B1 27
Meseta, *plateau* D3 37
Mesolóngion B2 51
Mesopotamia, *region* B2 24
Messina D1 71
Messina C3 38
Messina, *strait* C3 38
Mesta, *river* B4 50
Meta Incognita, *peninsula* P4 99
Meta, *river* C3 78
Métabetchouan E3 103
Metcalfe K2 102
Meteghan A3 100
Métis-sur-Mer J3 103
Metiskow E5 94
Metz D2 34
Meulan Inset II 34
Meuse, *river* D2 33
Mexiana, *island* D1 81
Mexicali, *state capital* A1 84
Mexico 84
Mexico City,
national capital E4, Inset 84
Mexico, *gulf* 82
Meymaneh A1 22
Meyungs B3 17
Mgwavuma, *river* B3 71
Mhlume B2 71
Miami B4 96

Key Page

Miami, Fla. E3 126
Mianwali D3 21
Miaoli B1 9
Mica Creek N5 95
Michalovce C2 42
Miches C2 89
Michigan E1 126
Michigan, *lake* E1 126
Michoacán D4 84
Mico, *river* B2 87
Micoud B3 91
Micronesia 15
Midale G11 104
Middelburg C3 71
Middelburg A3 32
Middle Andaman, *island* F6 20
Middle Arm C4 98
Middle Atlas, *ranges* C1 57
Middle Lake E8 104
Middle Musquodoboit D2 100
Middlebro D4 96
Middlesbrough C2 30
Middleton B3 100
Midi-Pyrénées C5 34
Midland F3 102
Midland, Tex. C2 126
Midlands, *region* C3 30
Miercurea Ciuc C2 43
Mieres D1 37
Mikkeli C2 53
Mikkwa, *river* C2 94
Mikomeseng C2 66
Míkonos, *island* C3 51
Mikura, *island* C3 8
Miladummadulu, *atoll* A1 19
Milagro B4 79
Milan B1 38
Milden C9 104
Mildura, Vic. D3 14
Miles City, Mont. C1 126
Milestone F10 104
Milford Haven B3 30
Milford Sound A3 15
Milh, *lake* B2 24
Mili, *island* C2 16
Milk, *river* E6 94
Mill Bay L7 95
Mill Village C3 100
Miller Lake D2 102
Millet D4 94
Milliken K5 102
Milltown D5 98
Millville B2 97
Milne, *bay* B3 15
Milo D6 94
Milo, *river* D3 62
Mílos, *island* C3 51
Milton B2 100
Milton F4 102
Milverton E4 102
Milwaukee, Wis. E1 126
Mimico J6 102
Miminegash A2 100
Mina Baranis C3 56
Mina Salman B1 25
Minami, *island* Inset III 8
Minas C3 75
Minas Gerais D3 81
Minas, *channel* C2 100
Minatitlán F4 84
Minch, *strait* B1 30
Mindanao, *island* C5 12
Mindelo B2 58
Mindemoya C2 102
Minden G3 102
Mindoro, *island* B3 12
Mindoro, *strait* B3 12
Miner's Bay G3 102
Miner, *river* B3 105
Mingäçevir B2 45
Mingäçevir, *reservoir* B2 45
Minho, *river* A1 36
Minicoy, *island* B7 20
Minija, *river* A2 46
Miniota A4 96
Minitonas A3 96
Mink Creek A3 96
Minna D3 65
Minneapolis, Minn. D1 126
Minnedosa B4 96
Minnesota D1 126
Miño, *river* C1 37
Minorca, *island* H2 37
Minot, N. Dak. C1 126
Minsk, *capital* C3 47
Minto B4 96
Minto C2 97
Minto B4 105
Minto, *lake* B2 101
Minton F11 104
Minya, al- B2 56
Miquelon, *island* M4 92
Mira H1 100
Mirabel B6 103
Mirador Nacional, *mt.* C3 75
Miraflores B4 78
Miragoâne B2 89
Miramichi D1 97
Miramichi, *bay* E1 97
Miranda de Ebro E1 37
Mirbat B3 25
Mirebalais C2 89
Miri D2 13
Mirnyy C7 44
Mirpur Khas C5 21
Mirror D5 94
Miscou, *island* E1 97
Miscouche B2 100
Misere Inset 70
Misery, *mt.* B1 90
Miskolc C1 43
Misool, *island* E2 13
Missinipe F5 104
Mississauga F4, J6 102
Mississippi D2 126
Mississippi, *lake* J2 102
Mississippi, *river* D1 126
Missoula, Mont. B1 126
Missouri D2 126
Missouri, *river* D1 126
Mistassibi, *river* D1 103
Mistassini D3 103
Mistassini, *lake* B3 101
Mistassini, *river* D2 103
Mistatim G8 104
Mistelbach E2 39
Misurata C1 56
Mitchell D4 102
Mitchell, *mt.*, N.C. E2 126
Mitchell, *river* D1 14
Mitchinamécus, *lake* A4 103
Mitilíni C2 51
Mito D2 8
Mitsamiouli A1 67
Mittelland, *canal* B2 40
Mitú C4 78
Mitumba, *mts.* C2 67
Mitzic A1 66
Miyake, *island* C3 8
Miyako D2 8
Miyako, *island* Inset II 8
Miyakonojo A4 8
Miyazaki A4 8
Mizen Head, *cape* B3 31
Mizo, *hills* F4 20
Mizpe Ramon B2 26
Mjøsa, *lake* C3 52
Mkondvo, *river* B2 71
Mliba B2 71
Mmabatho C2 71
Mo C2 52
Moa, *island* D2 13
Moa, *river* B2 63
Moab, Utah C2 126
Moala, *island group* B3 17
Moanda B2 66
Moba C2 67
Mobaye B3 66
Mobile, Ala. E2 126
Moca B1 89
Moca A2 90
Moçambique D2 68
Mocha, (Mukha, al-) A2 25
Mocímboa da Praia D1 68
Môco, *mt.* C4 70
Mocoa A4 78
Modena B1 38
Moengo B2 80
Moers A3 40
Mogadishu, *capital* B3 60
Mogami, *river* D2 8
Mogi das Cruzes Inset II 81
Mogilev Podolskiy B2 47
Mogocha D7 44
Mogotón, *mt.* A2 87
Mohács B2 43
Mohales Hoek A3 71
Mohammedia C1 57
Moher, *cliffs* B2 31
Mojave, *desert*, Calif. B2 126
Mojos A2 77
Mokhotlong C2 71
Mokolo B1 65
Mokpŏ B5 9
Mold B3 30
Moldavia, *region* D2 43
Molde B3 52
Moldova 50
Moldoveanu, *mt.* C3 43
Molepolole B3 69
Molise C2 38
Mollendo C4 77
Molokai *island*, Hawaii Inset II 126
Molopo, *river* B2 71
Moloundou C3 65
Molson, *lake* C2 96
Molucca, *sea* D2 13
Moluccas, *islands* D2 13
Mombasa E5 61
Mombetsu Inset I 8
Mon Repos B2 91
Møn, *island* D4 32
Mona, *passage* D2 89
Monaco 35
Monaco, *capital* B1 35
Monaghan C1 31
Monastery F2 100
Monastir C2 57
Mönchengladbach A3 40
Monclova D2 84
Moncton E2 97
Mondego, *cape* A2 36
Mondego, *river* B2 36
Monforte C1 37
Mongo B4 59
Mongolia 11
Mongolian, *plateau* C2 11
Mongomo D3 66
Mongu A3 67
Monitor E5 94
Monjolo Inset I 81
Monkey Bay B2 68
Mono, *river* A4, B2 64
Monopoli D2 38
Monrovia, *capital* A2 63
Mons B2 33
Mont-Carmel G4 103
Mont-Joli H3 103
Mont-Laurier A5 103
Mont-Royal J5 103
Mont-Saint-Michel B2 34
Mont-St-Pierre L2 103
Mont-Tremblant-Village B5 103
Montague C2 100
Montalto, *mt.* C3 38
Montana B2 50
Montana B1 126
Montargis C2 34
Montauban C4 34
Monte Carlo B1 35
Monte Cristi A1 89
Monte Plata C2 89
Montebello B6 103
Montecristo, *island* B2 38
Montegiardino B2 39
Montego Bay B2 88
Montélimar D4 34
Montelindo, *river* C3 75
Montenegro, *republic* A3 49
Montepulciano B2 38
Monterey, Calif. A2 126
Montería B2 78
Montero B3 77
Monterrey, *state capital* D2 84
Montes Claros D3 81
Montevideo, *capital* B3 75
Montgomery, *capital*, Ala. E2 126
Montluçon C3 34
Montmagny F5 103
Montmartre G10 104
Montpelier, *capital*, Vt. F1 126
Montpellier C5 34
Montréal C6, J5 103
Montréal, *island* J5 103
Montreal, *lake* E6 104
Montreal, *river* E6 104
Montreuil Inset II 34
Montreux A2 35
Montrose C2 30
Monywa B2 12
Monza B1 38
Moore Park B4 96
Moose Factory D2 101
Moose Jaw E10 104
Moose Lake A2 96
Moose, *river* D2 101
Moosehorn B3 96
Moosomin J10 104
Moosonee D2 101
Mopti C3 58
Moquegua C4 77
Moradabad C3 20
Morant Bay C3 88
Moratuwa A5 19
Morava, *river* A2, C3 42
Morava, *river* B3 49
Moravia, *region* C3 42
Moray, *estuary* B1 30
Morden B4 96
Mordoviya, *republic* E4 44
Moree, N.S.W. D2 14
Morehead A2 15
Morelia, *state capital* D4 84
Morell C2 100
Morelos E4 84
Morena, *mts.* D3 37
Moresby, *island* F5 95
Moreton, *bay* Inset III 14
Morgan City, La. D3 126
Morges A2 35
Morghab, *river* A1 22
Morghob B1 23
Morghob, *river* B1 23
Morice, *lake* J4 95
Moricetown J3 95
Morija A2 71
Morinville D4 94
Morioka D2 8
Morlaix B2 34
Morne Diablotin, *mt.* B2 90
Moro, *gulf* B5 12
Moro, *river* A2 63
Morocco 57
Morogoro C2 68
Morombe A3 69
Morón D2 88
Mörön C2 11
Morón de la Frontera D4 37
Morondava A3 69
Moroni, *national capital* A1 67
Morotai, *island* D1 13
Moroto D2 61
Morpeth D5 102
Morphou A1 27
Morrin D5 94
Morris C4 96
Morrisburg K3 102
Mors, *island* B2 32
Morse C10 104
Mortlach D10 104
Mortlock, *islands* C2 15
Moruga A2 91
Moscow, *capital* D3 44
Mosel, *river* A4 40
Moselle, *river* D2 34
Moshi C1 68
Mosjøen C2 52
Mosquitos, *coast* C3 87
Moss C4 52
Mossbank E11 104
Mossel Bay B3 71
Mossendjo B5 66
Mossleigh D6 94
Mossy, *river* F6 104
Most A1 42
Mostaganem B1 57
Mostar B2 48
Móstoles Inset II 37
Mosul B1 24
Motagua, *river* D4 85
Motherwell B2 30
Mouila A2 66
Mould Bay E1 99
Moule à Chique, *cape* B3 91
Moulmein C3 12
Moulouya, *river* D1 57
Moundou B5 59
Mount Carmel A2 100
Mt. Forest E4 102
Mount Gambier, S.A. D3 14
Mount Hagen A2 15
Mount Isa, Qld. C2 14
Mt. Stewart C2 100
Mountain Park B5 94
Moura B3 36
Mourne, *mts.* A2 30
Mouscron B2 33
Moussa Ali, *mt.* B1 60
Mouths of the Danube, *delta* E3 43
Mouths of the Ganges, *delta* C7 21
Mouths of the Indus, *delta* C5 21
Moyale E2 61
Moyamba A1 63
Moyie P6 95
Moyobamba B2 77
Moyowosi, *river* B1 68
Mozambique 68
Mozambique, *channel* 55
Mozzoro E2 81
Mpanda B2 68
Mpika C2 67
Mpoko, *river* A2 66
Mporokoso C1 67
Mqinvartsveri, *mt.* C3 45
M'Ramani B2 67
Mtkvari, *river* C4 45
Mtskheta C4 45
Mtwara D3 68
Muang Khammouan C3 11
Muang Không C4 11
Muang Khôngxédôn C4 11
Muang Paklay A2 11
Muang Pakxan B2 11
Muang Vangviang B2 11
Muang Xaignabouri A2 11
Muang Xay A1 11
Muang Xépôn D3 11
Muang Xon B1 11
Muar B2 13
Muara C1 13
Mubende B3 61
Mubi G2 65
Muchinga, *mts.* C2 67
Mudanjiang F1 10
Mudawwarah, al- B3 26
Mufulira B2 67
Muğla B3 27
Muharraq, al-, *island* B1 25
Mühlhausen B3 40
Mui Bai Bung, *point* A5 11
Mukalla, al- B2 25
Muko, *island* Inset III 8
Mulaku, *atoll* A3 19
Mulde, *river* C3 40
Mulhacén, *mt.* E4 37
Mülheim an der Ruhr A3 40
Mulhouse D3 34
Mull, *island* A2 30
Mullaittivu B2 19
Mullingar C2 31
Multan D3 21
Mulund Inset I 20
Mulvihill B4 96
Mumbra Inset I 20
Mumbwa B3 67
Mun, *river* C3 12
Muna, *island* D2 13
Munamägi, *mt.* D3 46
Muncho Lake K2 95
Munich B4 40
Munsan B4 9
Münster A3 40
Munster, *province* B2 31
Muonio B1 53
Muonioälven, *river* D1 53
Muoniojoki, *river* B1 53
Mur, *river* D3 39
Mura, *river* C2 48
Muramvya B2 61
Murat, *river* E2 27
Murchison, *river* A2 14
Murcia F4 37
Murdochville L3 103
Mureş, *river* B2 43
Murgab, *river* D3 22
Muriel, *lake* E4 94
Murilo, *atoll* C2 15
Müritz, *lake* C2 40
Murmansk C3 44
Muroran D1, Inset I 8
Muroto, *cape* B3 8
Murray Harbour C3 100
Murray River C2 100
Murray, *harbour* C2 100
Murray, *lake* A2 15
Murray, *river* D3 14
Murrumbidgee, *river* D3 14
Murska Sobota D2 48
Mürz, *river* D3 39
Murzuq B2 56
Muş E2 27
Mūša, *river* B1 46
Musala, *mt.* B3 50
Musan C1 9
Musgrave Harbour E4 98
Musgrave, *ranges* C2 14
Musgravetown E5 98
Mushin B4 65
Muskeg River A4 94
Muskegon, Mich. E1 126
Muskogee, Okla. D2 126
Muskoka, *lake* F2 102
Muskwa, *ranges* J2 95
Musoma B1 68
Musquodoboit Harbour D3 100
Mussau, *island* A2 15
Mustang B2 19
Mustique, *island* B3 91
Mustvee D2 46
Musu-dan, *point* C2 9
Mut A2 56
Mutare C2 69
Mutsamudu B2 67
Mutsu D1 8
Muyinga C1 61
Muyun Kum, *desert* D2 23
Muzaffarabad D2 21
Muynoq A2 23
Mwali (Mohéli), *island* A2 67
Mwanza B1 68
Mwene-Ditu B2 67
Mweru, *lake* B1, C3 67
Mwinilunga A2 67
My Tho B4 11
Myingyan B2 12
Myitkyina C1 12
Mykolaiv C3 47
Mymensingh D4 21
Myrnam E4 94
Mysore C6 20
Mzimba B2 68
Mzuzu B2 68

N

N'dalatando B3 70
N'Djamena, *capital* A4 59
N'zeto B2 70
Naas C2 31
Nabatiyah at-Tahta, an- A2 26
Naberezhnyye Chelny D4 44
Nabeul C1 57
Nabk, an- A2 27
Nabouwalu B2 17
Nacala D2 68
Nacaome B3 86
Nackawic B3 97
Nadi A2 17
Nadi, *bay* A2 17
Nadur B1 36
Naduri B2 17
Næstved C3 32
Nafud, an-, *desert* B1 24
Nag Hammadi B2 56
Naga B3 12
Naga, *hills* F3 20
Nagano C2 8
Nagaoka C2 8
Nagarote A2 87
Nagasaki A3 8
Nagorno-Karabakh, *autonomous region* B2 45
Nagoya C3 8
Nagpur C4 20
Nagua C1 89
Naguabo D2 90
Nagykanizsa A2 43
Naha Inset II 8
Nahanni, *river* C4 99
Nahariyya B1 26
Naicam F8 104
Naihati Inset II 20
Nain E3 98
Nairobi, *capital* D4 61
Najaf, an- B2 24
Najd, *region* B1 24
Najin D1 9
Najran B2 24
Nakadori, *island* A3 8
Nakano, *island* A4 8
Nakfa B1 60
Nakhichevan A3 45
Nakhodka E8 44
Nakhon Phanom C2 12
Nakhon Ratchasima C3 12
Nakhon Sawan B3 12
Nakhon Si Thammarat B4 12
Nakina C2 101
Nakodu B2 17
Nakskov C4 32
Naktong, *river* C5 9
Nakuru D4 61
Nakusp O6 95
Nal, *river* B4 21
Nalikul Inset II 20
Nam Dinh B2 11
Nam Ngum, *reservoir* B2 11
Nam Tok B3 12
Namangan D2 23
Namew, *lake* H6 104
Namib, *desert* A1, B3 70
Namibe B5 70
Namibia 70
Namoluk, *atoll* C2 15
Namonuito, *atoll* C2 15
Nampŏ A3 9
Nampa B3 94
Nampula C2 68
Namsos C3 52
Namu, *island* B2 16
Namuli, *highlands* C2 68
Namur C2 33
Namur, *lake* D2 94
Namwala B3 67
Nan B2 12
Nan Ling, *mts.* E3 10
Nan, *river* B2 12
Nanaimo L6 95
Nanchang E3 10
Nanchong D2 10
Nancy D2 34
Nanda Devi, *mt.* C2 20
Nanded C5 20
Nanga Parbat, *mt.* E2 21
Nanga-Eboko B3 65
Nangi Inset II 20
Nangnim-sanmaek, *mts.* B3 9
Nanjing E2 10
Nanning D3 10
Nanole Inset I 20
Nantŏu B2 9
Nanterre Inset II 34
Nantes B3 34
Nanticoke E5 102
Nanumanga, *island* B2 16
Nanumea, *island* B1 16
Nanyang E2 10
Nao, *cape* G3 37
Napadogan C2 97
Napaktulik, *lake* F3 99
Napanee J3 102
Napier C2 15
Naples C2 38
Naples, *bay* C2 38
Napo, *river* C1 77
Nara B3 8
Nara, *canal* C4 21
Narathiwat B5 12
Narayanganj D5 21
Narayani, *river* B2 19
Narbonne C5 34
Narcisse C4 96
Nares, *strait* O1 99
Narew, *river* E2 41
Narmada, *river* C4 20
Narrogin, W.A. A3 14
Narrows, *strait* C2 90
Narsaq C2 106
Narva E1 46
Narva, *river* D1 46
Narvik D2 52
Naryan-Mar C4 44
Naryn E2 23
Naryn, *river* E2 23
Nashshash, an- C3 25
Nashville, *capital*, Tenn. E2 126
Nashwaak Bridge C2 97
Näsi, *lake* B2 53
Nasik B4 20
Nasiriyah, an- C2 24
Nass, *river* H3 95
Nassau, *capital* B2 89
Nasser, *lake* B3 56
Nata B2 69
Natal E2 81
Natalkuz, *lake* K4 95
Natashquan D3 101
Natitingou A2 64
Natron, *lake* C1 68
Natuna Besar, *island* B1 13
Naucalpan de Juárez Inset 84
Naujoji Akmenė B1 46
Naumburg B3 40
Nauru 16
Navabad A1 23
Navarino, *island* C9 76
Navarra F1 37
Navojoa C2 84
Navua B3 17
Navua, *river* A3 17
Nawabshah C4 21
Nawoiy C2 23
Náxos, *island* C3 51
Nayarit C3 84
Nazareth B1 26
Nazca C3 77
Naze Inset II 8
Nazko L5 95
Nazret C2 60
Nchelenge B1 67
Ndélé B2 66
Ndendé A2 66
Ndjolé A2 66
Ndola B2 67
Néa Liósia Inset 51
Neagh, *lake* A2 30
Neápolis B3 51
Nebitdag B2 22
Neblina, *mt.* B1 81
Nebraska D1 126
Nechako, *river* K4 95
Neckar, *river* B4 40
Necochea D4 74
Neder Rijn, *river* C3 32
Nee Soon B1 13
Needles N6 95
Neepawa B4 96
Nefta A3 57
Negele C3 60
Negev, *region* B2 26
Negombo A4 19
Negra, *lagoon* D2 75
Negra, *point* A2 77
Negril A2 88
Negro, *river* B4 74
Negro, *river* B2 81
Negro, *river* C2 75
Negros, *island* B4 12
Neguac D1 97
Neiafu C2 17
Neiba A2 89
Neiba, *mts.* A2 89
Neijiang D3 10
Neil Harbour G1 100
Neilburg A8 104
Neisse, *river* C3 40
Neiva B4 78
Nekemte B2 60
Nellore C6 20
Nelson B3 15
Nelson O6 95
Nelson Forks L1 95
Nelson House B1 96
Nelson, *river* C1, D1 96
Nelspruit D2 71
Néma D3 58
Nemeiben, *lake* E5 104
Nemunas, *river* A2, C2 46
Nemuro Inset I 8
Nemuro, *strait* Inset I 8
Nenagh B2 31
Nendo, *island* C2 16
Nenetsiya, *autonomous okrug* C4 44
Nepal 19
Nepalganj B2 19
Nepean G6, K2 102
Nepisiguit, *river* C1 97
Neretva, *river* B2 48
Neris, *river* C2 46
Ness, *lake* B1 30
Nesselrode, *mt.* E1 95
Nestaocano, *river* C2 103
Netanya B1 26
Netherlands 32
Nettilling, *lake* O3 99
Netzahualcóyotl Inset 84
Neubrandenburg C2 40
Neuchâtel A2 35
Neuchâtel, *lake* A2 35
Neudorf G10 104
Neufchâteau D3 33
Neumünster B1 40
Neunkirchen A4 40
Neuquén B4 74
Neusiedler, *lake* E3 39
Neuss A3 40
Neustadt A2 85
Neustrelitz C2 40
Nevada B2 126
Nevada, *mts.* E4 37
Nevers C3 34
Neves B4 63
Neves Inset I 81
Nevėžis, *river* B2 46
Nevis, *island* C3 90
New Amsterdam C2 80
New Brigden E5 94
New Britain, *island* B2 15
New Caledonia, *island* C2 18
New Carlisle L4 103

Key Page
New Delhi, *capital* C3 20
New Denver O6 95
New England, *range* E3 14
New Ferolle C4 98
New Fish Creek B3 94
New Georgia Group, *islands* A1 16
New Glasgow E2 100
New Guinea, *island* A2 15
New Hamburg E4 102
New Hampshire F1 126
New Hanover, *island* B2 15
New Haven, Conn. F1 126
New Ireland, *island* B2 15
New Jersey F1 126
New Kowloon Inset 10
New Liskeard E3 101
New Mexico C2 126
New Minas C2 100
New Orleans, La. D3 126
New Plymouth B2 15
New Providence, *island* B3 89
New Richmond L3 103
New Ross C3 100
New Sandy Bay B1 91
New Schwabenland, *region* B16 107
New Siberian, *islands* B9 44
New South Wales D3 14
New Territories, *island* Inset 10
New Waterford G1 100
New Waterway, *channel* B3 32
New York F1 126
New York, N.Y. F1 126
New Zealand 15
New, *river* C4 80
New, *river* B1 85
Newark, N.J. F1 126
Newboro J3 102
Newcastle C2 90
Newcastle C2 71
Newcastle upon Tyne C2 30
Newcastle, N.S.W. E3 14
Newcastle-under-Lyme C3 30
Newdale A4 96
Newell, *lake* E6 94
Newman, W.A. A2 14
Newmarket D3 30
Newmarket F3 102
Newport C3 30
Newport News, Va. F2 126
Newquay B4 30
Newry A2 30
Newtown St. Boswells C2 30
Neyagawa B3 8
Neyshabur D2 22
Ngami, *lake* A2 69
Ngaoundéré B2 65
Ngara B1 68
Ngaramasch B4 17
Ngauruhoe, *mt.* C2 15
Ngerkeel B3 17
Ngemelis, *islands* B3 17
Ngermechau C2 17
Ngetbong C2 17
Ngiro, *river* D3 61
Ngoc Linh, *mt.* B3 11
Ngonini B1 71
Ngorongoro, *crater* C1 68
Ngounié, *river* A2 66
Ngozi B1 61
Nguigmi C3 59
Ngulu, *atoll* A2 15
Nguru F1 65
Ngwempisi, *river* A2 71
Nha Trang B4 11
Nhlangano B3 71
Niagara Falls F4 102
Niagara-on-the-Lake F4 102
Niagassola D1 62
Niamey, *capital* A3 59
Niamtougou B2 64
Niari, *river* B5 66
Nias, *island* A1 13
Nibok B2 16
Nicaragua 87
Nicaragua, *lake* B3 87
Nice D5 34
Nicholls' Town A2 89
Nickerie, *river* A2 80
Nicobar, *islands* F7 20
Nicola M6 95
Nicolet D5 103
Nicosia, *capital* B1 27
Nicoya, *gulf* B3 86
Nictau B1 97
Nidže, *mts.* B3 48
Niedere Tauern, *range* D3 39
Niefang C3 66
Nienburg B2 40
Niéri Ko, *river* C2 62
Nieuw Amsterdam B2 80
Nieuw Nickerie A2 80
Nigadoo D1 97
Niğde C3 27
Niger 59
Niger, *delta* C5 65
Niger, *river* B3 58
Nigeria 65
Nii, *island* C3 8
Niigata C2 8
Niihama B3 8
Niihau, *island*, Hawaii Inset II 126
Nijmegen C3 32
Níkaia Inset 51
Nikki B3 64
Nikko C2 8
Nikolayevsk-na-Amure D9 44
Nikopol C2 47
Nikšić A3 49
Nikunau, *island* A2 17
Nilandu, *atoll* A3 19
Nile, *river* B2 56
Nilgiri, *hills* C6 20
Nilópolis Inset I 81
Nimba, *mt.* B3 63
Nimba, *mts.* B2 63
Nîmes D5 34
Nine Mile River D2 100
Ninette B4 96
Ninga B4 96
Ningbo F3 10
Ningxia Hui D2 10
Ninigo, *group* A2 15
Niono B3 58
Nioro du Rip B3 62
Nioro du Sahel B2 58
Niort B3 34
Nipawin F7 104
Nipigon C3 101
Nipigon, *lake* C3 101
Nipissing F1 102
Nipissing, *lake* F1 102
Niš B3 49
Nišava, *river* C3 49
Nishino, *island* Inset III 8
Nishinomiya B3 8
Nisling, *river* B4 105
Niterói D4, Inset I 81
Nitra B2 42
Niuafo'ou, *island* B1 17
Niuatoputapu, *island* C1 17
Niulakita, *island* C4 16
Niutao, *island* B2 16
Niverville C4 96
Nizamabad C5 20
Nizhnevartosk C5 44
Nizhny Novgorod D4 44
Nizhny Tagil D4 44
Njazidja (Grande Comore), *island* A1 67
Njombe, *river* B2 68
Nkawkaw B3 64
Nkhata Bay B2 68
Nkhotakota B2 68
Nkongsamba A2 65
Noakhali E6 21
Nobeoka A3 8
Noel D2 100
Nogales B1 84
Nogales, Ariz. B2 126
Nojima, *cape* D3 8
Nok Kundi B4 21
Nokaneng A1 69
Nokomis E9 104
Nola A3 66
Nome, Alaska Inset I 126
Nonacho, *lake* G4 99
Nong Khai C2 12
Nonsan B4 9
Nonthaburi B3 12
Nootka, *island* J6 95
Norak A1 23
Nord-Ostsee, *canal* B1 40
Nord-Pas-de-Calais C1 34
Nordenham B2 40
Nordhausen B3 40
Nordhorn A2 40
Nordvik B7 44
Norfolk D5 94
Norfolk, Va. F2 126
Norilsk C6 44
Norland G3 102
Normandin D3 103
Norquay H9 104
Norra Storfjället, *mt.* C1 53
Norris Arm D4 98
Norris Point C4 98
Norrköping C3 53
Norte, *key* E2 90
N. Albanian Alps, *mts.* A1, B3 49
North Andaman, *island* F6 20
North Battleford B8 104
North Bay F1 102
North Cape B1 100
North Carolina F2 126
North China, *plain* E2 10
North Comino, *channel* B1 36
North Dakota C1 126
North Downs, *hills* C3 30
North Frisian, *islands* B4 32
North Holland, *canal* B2 32
North Korea 9
North Magnetic Pole B13 106
North Malosmadulu, *atoll* A2 19
N. Moose, *lake* B2 96
North Ossetiya, republic E4 44
North Platte, Nebr. C1 126
North Portal H11 104
North Rhine-Westphalia A3 40
North Rustico B2 100
North Saskatchewan, *river* D8 104
North Sea, *canal* B2 32
North Shields C2 30
North Siberian, *lowland* B6 44
North Star B3 94
North Taranaki, *bight* B2 15
N. Thompson, *river* N5 95
North Uist, *island* A1 30
North Wabasca, *lake* D3 94
North West River A2 98
North West, *cape* A2 14
North York K5 102
North, *cape* F1 52
North, *channel* A2 30
North, *channel* B1 102
North, *island* B2 15
North, *river* B2 98
North, *sea* 29
Northallerton C2 30
Northampton C3 30
Northeast, *polder* C2 32
Northeim B3 40
Northern Divina, *river* C4 44
Northern European, *plain* B2 40
Northern Sporades, *islands* B2 51
Northern Territory C2 14
Northgate H11 104
Northumberland, *strait* B3, D2 100
Northwest Gander, *river* D5 98
Norton D3 97
Norvegia, *cape* B14 107
Norway 52
Norway House C2 96
Norwegian, *bay* K1 99
Norwegian, *sea* A2 52
Norwich D3 30
Norwich E4 102
Nossob, *river* C3 70
Nosy Be, *island* B1 69
Nosy Sainte Marie, *island* B2 69
Noteć, *river* C2, D2 41
Noto, *peninsula* C2 8
Notre Dame de Lourdes B4 96
Notre Dame Junction D4 98
Notre Dame, *bay* D4 98
Notre-Dame E2 97
Notre-Dame-de-la-Merci B5 103
Notre-Dame-de-la-Salette A6 103
Notre-Dame-de-Lorette D2 103
Notre-Dame-du-Bon-Conseil D5 103
Notre-Dame-du-Lac H4 103
Notre-Dame-du-Laus A5 103
Nottingham C3 30
Nottingham, *island* N4 99
Nouadhibou A2 58
Nouakchott, *capital* A3 58
Nouméa, *capital* C2 18
Nouvelle K3 103
Nova Gorica A3 48
Nova Iguaçu Inset I 81
Novara B1 38
Novaya Zemlya, *islands* B4 44
Nové Zamky B3 42
Novgorod D3 44
Novi Pazar B3 49
Novi Sad A2 49
Novo Mesto C3 48
Novokuznetsk D6 44
Novosibirsk D6 44
Novra A3 96
Nowshak, *mt.* D2 21
Nowy Sącz E4 41
Nsanje C3 68
Nsawam B4 64
Nsok D3 66
Nsoko B3 71
Nsukka D4 65
Ntem, *river* B3 65
Nu'ulua, *island* D3 18
Nu'utele, *island* D3 18
Nuba, *mts.* C3 59
Nubian, *desert* C1 59
Nueltin, *lake* J4 99
Nueva Casas Grandes C1 84
Nueva Gerona B2 88
Nueva Loja C2 79
Nueva Ocotepeque A2 86
Nueva Palmira A2 75
Nueva Rosita D2 84
Nueva San Salvador A2 86
Nuevitas D2 88
Nuevo Laredo E2 84
Nuevo León D2 84
Nuevo Rocafuerte D3 79
Nuguria, *islands* B2 15
Nuhud, an- B2 59
Nui, *island* B2 16
Nuku'alofa, *capital* B4 17
Nukufetau, *island* C2 16
Nukulaelae, *island* C3 16
Nukuoro, *atoll* C2 15
Nukus A2 23
Nullarbor, *plain* B3 14
Numazu C3 8
Ñuñoa Inset 76
Nuoro B2 38
Nuremberg B4 40
Nutak E3 98
Nuuk (Godthåb), *capital* B2 106
Nuuuli B1 18
Nuwara Eliya B5 19
Nyaake C3 63
Nyaba, *river* B2 61
Nyala B2 59
Nyanga, *river* A2 66
Nyanza B2 61
Nyasa (Malawi), *lake* B2, B3 68
Nyborg C3 32
Nyeri D4 61
Nyetane, *river* B2 71
Nyika, *plateau* B2 68
Nyíregyháza C2 43
Nykøbing C4 32
Nyoman, *river* B3 47
Nyong, *river* B3 65
Nysa C3 41
Nzérékoré D4 62
Nzi, *river* D3 63
Nzo, *river* C3 63
Nzoia, *river* C3 61
Nzwani (Anjouan), *island* B2 67

O

O'Leary A2 100
Oahu, *island*, Hawaii Inset II 126
Oak Lake A4 96
Oak Point C4 96
Oak Point C3 97
Oak River A4 96
Oakland, Calif. A2 126
Oakner A4 96
Oakview B3 96
Oakville C4 96
Oakville F4 102
Oamaru B4 15
Oaxaca, *state capital* E4 84
Ob, *river* C5 44
Oban B2 30
Obed B4 94
Oberammergau B5 40
Oberhausen A3 40
Oberpfälzer Wald, *mts.* C4 40
Obi, *island* D2 13
Obihiro Inset I 8
Obo C2 66
Obock C2 60
Obuasi B3 64
Occidental, *mts.* B2, C4 77
Ocean Falls J5 95
Ochamchire A3 45
Ochil, *hills* B2 30
Ocho Rios B2 88
Ochre River B3 96
Ocoa, *bay* B2 89
Ocotal A2 87
Ocotlán D3 84
Oda B4 64
Odei, *river* C1 96
Odemira A4 36
Odense C3 32
Odense, *fjord* C3 32
Odenwald, *forest* B4 40
Oder, *river* B2, C3 41
Oderhaff, *lake* C2 40
Odesa C3 47
Odessa, Tex. C2 126
Odienné C2 63
Oeiras A3 36
Oelemari, *river* B3 80
Offa C3 65
Offenbach B3 40
Ofu, *island* A1 18
Ogaden, *region* D3 60
Ogbomosho C3 65
Ogden, Utah B1 126
Ogema F11 104
Ogilvie, *mts.* B3 105
Oglio, *river* B1 38
Ogoki, *river* C2 101
Ogooué, *river* A2 66
Ogosta, *river* B2 50
Ogražden, *mts.* C2 48
Ogre C2 46
Ogun, *river* B3 65
Ohio E1 126
Ohio, *river* E2 126
Ohonua C4 17
Ohrid A2 48
Ohrid, *lake* B2 49
Øibenik B3 48
Oise, *river* C2, Inset II 34
Oistins B5 91
Oita A3 8
Ojinaga D2 84
Ojos del Salado, *mt.* B2 74
Oka, *river* D4 44
Okahandja B2 70
Okakarara C2 70
Okanagan Falls N6 95
Okanagan, *lake* N6 95
Okara D3 21
Okavango, *basin* A1 69
Okavango, *river* A1 69
Okayama B3 8
Okazaki C3 8
Okeechobee, *lake*, Fla. E3 126
Okene D4 65
Okha D9 44
Okhotsk D9 44
Okhotsk, *sea* D9 44
Oki, *islands* B2 8
Okinawa, *island* Inset II 8
Okino Erabu, *island* Inset II 8
Oklahoma D2 126
Oklahoma City, *capital*, Okla. D2 126
Okondja B2 66
Okotoks C6 94
Okushiri, *island* C1, Inset I 8
Okwa, *river* A2 69
Ólafsvík A2 52
Olanchito B2 86
Öland, *island* C3 53
Olavarría C4 74
Olbia B2 38
Old Brahmaputra, *river* C4 21
Old Crow B2 105
Old Perlican E5 98
Old Road D5 90
Old Road Town B2 90
Old Wives, *lake* D10 104
Oldenburg B2 40
Oldham C3 30
Oldman, *river* D6 94
Olds C5 94
Olenek, *river* C7 44
Oléron, *island* B4 34
Olgilvie, *river* B3 105
Olhão A4 36
Olifants, *river* A3, C1 71
Olinda E2 81
Oliver N6 95
Ollagüe, *volcano* C2 76
Ollei C2 17
Olmaliq C2 23
Olomouc C3 42
Olongapo B3 12
Olosega, *island* A1 18
Olsztyn E2 41
Olt, *river* C3 43
Oltenița D3 43
Olympia, *capital*, Wash. A1 126
Olympus *mt.*, Wash. A1 126
Olympus, *mt.* A2 27
Olympus, *mt.* B1 51
Omagh A2 30
Omaha, beach B2 34
Omaha, Nebr. D1 126
Oman 25
Oman, *gulf* C1, D2 25
Omaruru B2 70
Omatako, *river* C1 70
Omboué A2 66
Omdurman C2 59
Omemee G3 102
Ometepe, *island* B3 87
Omineca, *mts.* J2 95
Omineca, *river* K3 95
Omiya C3 8
Omo, *river* B3 60
Omsk D5 44
Omuta A3 8
Onanole B4 96
Ondame B2 62
Ondangwa B1 70
Ondava, *river* C2 42
Ondjiva C5 70
Ondo C4 65
Öndörhaan D2 11
Onefour E6 94
Onega, *lake* C3 44
Onești D2 43
Ongjin A4 9
Ongole C5 20
Onilahy, *river* A3 69
Onion Lake A7 104
Onitsha D4 65
Ono, *island* B3 17
Onon, *river* D2 11
Onota, *island* A2 17
Onsŏng C1 9
Ontario, *lake* K4 92
Ontong Java, *island* A1 16
Oostende A1 33
Oostende-Brugge, *canal* B1 33
Oosterschelde, *channel* A3 32
Ootsa, *lake* J4 95
Opava C3 42
Opeongo, *lake* G2 102
Opole C3 41
Oporto (Porto) A2 36
Opuwo A1 70
Oqsu, *river* C2 23
Oradea A2 43
Oral B1 23
Oran A1 57
Orange Walk B1 85
Orange, N.S.W. D3 14
Orange, *river* A3, B2 71
Orangeville E4 102
Oranje, *mts.* B3 80
Oranjemund B4 70
Orapa B2 69
Ordino B2 36
Ordu D2 27
Örebro C3 53
Oregon A1 126
Orellana, *lake* D3 37
Orenburg D4 44
Orense C1 37
Øresund, *sound* D3 32
Órganos, *mts.* A2 88
Órgãos, *range* Inset I 81
Orhei B2 50
Orhon, *river* C2 11
Oriental, *mts.* B2, C3 77
Oriental, *range* C2 89
Orillia F3 102
Orinoco, *river* C3, D2 79
Orion E6 94
Oristano B3 38
Orizaba E4 84
Orkney, *islands* Inset I 30
Orlando, Fla. E3 126
Orléans C3 34
Orléans, *island* F5, L5 103
Ormoc C4 12
Orne, *river* B2 34
Örnsköldsvik C2 53
Orocué C3 78
Oroluk, *atoll* C2 15
Oromocto C3 97
Oron E5 65
Orontes, *river* A2 27
Orosháza C2 43
Orrefors C3 53
Orsha E2 47
Orsk D4 44
Ortegal, *cape* C1 37
Orumiyeh (Urmia) A2 22
Oruro A3 77
Oryakhovo B2 50
Os, *river* A3 36
Osaka B3 8
Osasco Inset II 81
Osh C2 23
Oshakati B1 70
Oshawa G4 102
Oshima, *peninsula* D1, Inset I 8
Oshogbo C4 65
Osijek D2 48
Osilinka, *river* K3 95
Öskemen (Ust-Kamenogorsk) E1 23
Oslo, *capital* C3 52
Oslofjord, *fjord* C4 52
Osnabrück B2 40
Osorno B7 76
Osoyoos N6 95
Oss C3 32
Osse, *river* C4 65
Österdalälven, *river* B2 53
Östersund B2 53
Ostrava D3 42
Ostrołęka E2 41
Osum, *river* B3 49
Osumi, *islands* A4 8
Osumi, *peninsula* A4 8
Osumi, *strait* A4 8
Osŭm, *river* C3 50
Otaru Inset I 8
Otavalo B2 79
Otavi C1 70
Oti, *river* B1, C2 64
Otjiwarongo B2 70
Otranto D2 38
Otranto, *strait* A3 49
Otsu B3 8
Ottawa H5, K2 102
Ottawa, *river* G1, G5 H5, K2 102
Otterlo C2 32
Ötztal Alps, *range* B4 39
Ou, *mts.* D2 8
Ou, *river* B1 11
Ouadane C2 58
Ouagadougou, *capital* D2 64
Ouahigouya C2 64
Ouaka, *river* B2 66
Ouanary C1 80
Ouargla B1 57
Ouarra, *river* C2 66
Ouarzazate C2 57
Oudtshoorn B3 71
Ouémé, *river* B3 64
Ouesso D3 66
Ouezzane C1 57
Ouham, *river* A2 66
Ouidah B4 64
Oujda D1 57
Oulu C1 53
Oulu, *lake* C2 53
Oulujoki, *river* C2 53
Oum er-Rbia, *river* C1 57
Ounasjoki, *river* B1 53
Oungre G11 104
Our, *river* B1 33
Ourthe, *river* D2 33
Ouse, *river* C2, D3 30
Outarde, *river* H2 103
Outer Hebrides, *islands* A1 30
Outjo B2 70
Outlook C9 104
Ouvéa, *island* C2 18
Ovalau, *island* B2 17
Ovalle B4 76
Overflakkee, *island* B3 32
Overflowing River A2 96
Oviedo A3 89
Oviedo D1 37
Owando C4 66
Owen Sound E3 102
Owen Stanley, *range* A2 15
Owendo A1 66
Owensboro, Ky. E2 126
Owerri D5 65
Oxbow H11 104
Oxford C3 30
Oxford D2 100
Oxford House D1, D2 96
Oxford, *lake* D2 96
Oyapock, *river* B2 80
Oyem A1 66
Oyo B4 65
Ozama, *river* B2 89
Ozark, *plateau* D2 126
Ózd C1 43
Özgön C2 23
Ozoir-la-Ferrière Inset II 34
Ozurgeti A4 45

P

Pa-an C3 12
Paamiut (Frederikshåb) C2 106
Pabna C4 21
Pacaraima, *mts.* D3 79
Pacasmayo B2 77
Pachuca, *state capital* E3 84
Padang B2 13
Paddle Prairie B2 94
Paderborn B3 40
Padma, *river* D5 21
Padua (Padova) B1 38
Paektu-san, *mt.* C2 9
Pagadian B5 12
Pago Pago, *capital* B1 18
Pahang, *river* B2 13
Paianía Inset 51
Päijänne, *lake* C2 53
Paint, *lake* B1 96
Paisley B2 30
Paita A2 77
Pakaraima, *mts.* A3 80
Pakistan 21
Pakowki, *lake* E6 94
Paks B2 43
Pakse C4 11
Pala A5 59
Palaiseau Inset II 34
Palana D10 44
Palanga A2 46
Palangkaraya C2 13
Palau 17
Palawan, *island* A4 12
Paldiski C1 46
Pale B2 48
Palembang B2 13
Palencia D1 37
Palermo C3 38
Palikir, *capital* C2 15
Palk, *strait* C7 20
Palliser, *cape* C3 15
Palm, *island* A4 91
Palma H3 37
Palmas D3 81
Palmer Land, *region* B11 107
Palmerston E4 102
Palmerston North C3 15
Palmira A4 78
Palmyra, *ruins* B2 27
Palos, *cape* F4 37
Palu C2 13
Pamirs, *mts.* B2 23
Pamirs, *region* A2 10
Pampas, *plain* C4 74
Pamplemousses C2 69
Pamplona F1 37
Panagyurishte C3 50
Panaji B5 20
Panama 87
Panama, *canal* C2 87
Panamá, *capital* C2 87
Panama, *gulf* C3 87
Panay, *gulf* B4 12
Panay, *island* B4 12
Pančevo B2 49
Panch'iao B1 9
Pandan, *strait* A2 13
Pandaruan, *river* C2 13
Pando C3 75
Panevėžys C2 46
Pangani, *river* C1 68
Pangkalpinang B2 13
Pangnirtung P3 99
Panihati Inset II 20
Panj A2 23
Panj, *river* B2 23
Panjakent A1 23
Panjgur B4 21
P'anmunjŏm B4 9
Pantanal, *lowland* C4 81
Pantelleria, *island* C3 38
Pánuco, *river* E3 84
Pápa A2 43
Papagayo, *gulf* A2 86
Paphos A2 27
Papua, *gulf* A2 15
Papua New Guinea 15
Paquetville D1 97
Pará C2 81
Pará, *river* C2 81
Paradise Hill A7 104

Key Page
Paradise River C2 98
Paraguá, *river* B2 77
Paraguai, *river* C3 81
Paraguarí D4 75
Paraguay 75
Paraguay, *river* C2, C5 75
Paraíba E2 81
Parakou B3 64
Paramaribo, *capital* B2 80
Paraná C3 74
Paraná C4 81
Paraná, *river* D2 74
Paranaguá D4 81
Paranam B2 80
Pardubice B2 42
Parent B4 103
Parepare C2 13
Paria, *gulf* D1 79
Parima, *range* B1 81
Paris, *capital* C2, Inset II 34
Paris E4 102
Parkhill D4 102
Parkland D6 94
Parksville K6 95
Parma B1 38
Parnaíba D2 81
Parnaíba, *river* D2 81
Pärnu C2 46
Pärnu, *river* C2 46
Paro A2 19
Paropamisus, *range* A2 22
Páros, *island* C3 51
Parral B6 76
Parrsboro C2 100
Parry D2 99
Parry Sound E2 102
Parry, *channel* J2 99
Parsnip, *river* L4 95
Parson's Pond C4 98
Pas de la Casa C2 36
Pasadena C5 98
Pasfield, *lake* E2 104
Pasión, *river* C3 85
Paso de los Toros B2 75
Paso de Palmar, *lake* B2 75
Passau C4 40
Passero, *cape* C3 38
Passo Fundo C4 81
Pastavy C2 47
Pastaza, *river* B1 77
Pastillo C3 90
Pasto A4 78
Patagonia, *region* A6 74
Patavilca B3 77
Paterson, N.J. F1 126
Patía, *river* A4 78
Patiala C2 20
Patillas C2 90
Patna E3 20
Patos, *lagoon* C5 81
Pátrai B2 51
Patricia E6 94
Pattani B5 12
Patuakhali D6 21
Patuanak C5 104
Patuca, *mts.* C2 86
Patuca, *river* C2 86
Pau B5 34
Pauingassi D3 96
Paulatuk D3 99
Paulaya, *river* C2 86
Paulo Afonso E2 81
Pavaiai B2 18
Pavia B1 38
Pavilosta A2 46
Pavlodar D1 23
Paxbán C2 85
Payar B2 62
Paye Inset I 20
Payne, *lake* B2 101
Paynton B7 104
Pays De La Loire B3 34
Paysandú A2 75
Paz, *river* C6 85
Pazardzhik C3 50
Peace Point D1 94
Peace River B3 94
Peace, *river* A3, C2 94
Peachland N6 95
Pebane C3 68
Peć B3 49
Pechora C4 44
Pechora, *river* C4 44
Pécs B2 43
Pedernales A2 89
Pedja, *river* C2 46
Pedra Açú, *mt.* Inset I 81
Pedra Lume D2 58
Pedro Juan Caballero E3 75
Pedro Santana A1 89
Peebles H10 104
Peel, *river* B3, C2 105
Peerless Lake C3 94
Pegasus, *bay* B3 15
Pegu C3 12
Peipus, *lake* D2 46
Pekalongan B2 13
Pekanbaru B1 13
Pelee, *island* C6 102
Peleliu, *island* B4 17
Peleng, *island* D2 13
Pelican Narrows H5 104
Pelican Portage D3 94
Pelican Rapids A3 96
Pelican, *lake* G5 104
Pelkan, *lake* A3 96
Pelly J9 104
Pelly Bay L3 99
Pelly Crossing B4 105
Pelly, *river* C4, C5 105
Pelotas C5 81
Pematangsiantar A1 13
Pemba D2 68
Pemba, *island* C2 68
Pemberton L6 95
Pembina, *river* B4 94
Pembina, *river* B4 96
Pembroke B3 30
Pembroke H2 102
Penas, *gulf* B8 76
Pendé, *river* A2 66
Pendleton, Oreg. B1 126
Penetanguishene F3 102
P'enghu (Pescadores), *islands* A2 9
Peniche A3 36
Peninsular Malaysia, *region* B2 13
Pennant B10 104
Pennine Alps, *mts.* B2 35
Pennines, *mts.* C2 30
Pennsylvania F1 126
Penonomé B2 87
Penrith C2 30
Pensacola, Fla. E2 126
Pensacola, *mts.* A11 107
Pentecost, *island* C2 18
Penticton N6 95
Peñuelas B2 90
Penza D4 44
Penzance B4 30
Penzhihua D3 10
Peoria, Ill. E1 126
Perak, *river* A2 13
Percé M3 103
Perdue C8 104
Pereira B3 78
Péribonca, *river* B3 101
Péribonka D3 103
Périgueux C4 34
Perim, *island* A2 25
Peristéri Inset 51
Perlas, *archipelago* C2 87
Perlas, *lagoon* C2 87
Perm D4 44
Pernambuco E2 81
Pernik B3 50
Perpignan C5 34
Perrot, *island* G6 103
Persian, *gulf* C1, C2, C3 24
Perth B2 30
Perth J3 102
Perth, W.A., *capital* A3, Inset I 14
Perth-Andover B2 97
Peru 77
Perugia C2 38
Pervomaysk C2 47
Pesaro C2 38
Pescadores, *channel* A2 9
Pescara C2 38
Peshawar D3 21
Peshkopi B2 49
Petah Tiqwa B1 26
Petare C1 79
Petauke C2 67
Petawawa H2 102
Petén-Itzá, *lake* D3 85
Peterborough C3 30
Peterborough G3 102
Peterhead C1 30
Petersfield C4 96
Petit Canouan, *island* B3 91
Petit Martinique, *island* C1 91
Petit Mustique, *island* B3 91
Petit St. Vincent, *island* A4 91
Petit-Rocher D1 97
Petitcodiac D3 97
Petite Riviere C3 100
Petlura A3 96
Petra, *ruins* A2 26
Petrich B4 50
Petrila B3 43
Petrolia C5 102
Petrólina D2 81
Petropavl C1 23
Petropavlovsk-Kamchatskiy D9 44
Petrópolis D4, Inset I 81
Petroşani B3 43
Petrozavodsk C3 44
Pevek C10 44
Peyia A2 27
Pforzheim B4 40
Phan Rang B4 11
Phan Thiet B4 11
Phatthalung B5 12
Phayao B2 12
Phetchabun B2 12
Phetchabun, *range* B3 12
Phetchaburi B3 12
Phichit B2 12
Philadelphia, Pa. F2 126
Philippine, *sea* C3 12
Philippine, *sea* B2 17
Philippines 12
Phitsanulok B2 12
Phnom Penh, *capital* C4 11
Phnum Tbeng Meanchey C2 11
Phoenix, *capital*, Ariz. B2 126
Phoenix, *island* B2 17
Phoenix, *islands* B2 17
Phôngsali B1 11
Phou Bia, *mt.* B2 11
Phra Nakhon Si Ayutthaya B3 12
Phuket B5 12
Phumi Samraong B1 11
Phuntsholing A3 19
Pianosa, *island* B2 38
Piapot A10 104
Piatra Neamţ D2 43
Piauí D2 81
Piave, *river* C1 38
Pibor Post C3 59
Pic de la Selle, *mt.* D2 89
Picardie C2 34
Pickle Lake B2 101
Pico do Cano, *volcano* B4 58
Picton H3 102
Pictou E2 100
Pidurutalagala, *mt.* B4 19
Piedmont A1 38
Piedra Sola B2 75
Piedras Negras D2 84
Pielinen, *lake* C2 53
Pierceland A6 104
Pierre, *capital*, S. Dak. C1 126
Pierrefonds G5 103
Pierreville A2 91
Pierson A4 96
Piešťany A2 42
Pietermaritzburg D2 71
Pietersburg C1 71
Pigeon, *lake* C4 94
Pigeon, *lake* G3 102
Piggs Peak B1 71
Pikangikum B2 101
Pikes *peak*, Colo. C2 126
Pikwitonei C1 96
Piła C2 41
Pilar C5 75
Pilaya, *river* B4 77
Pilcomayo, *river* B3, C4 75
Pilica, *river* E3 41
Pílos B3 51
Pilot Butte F10 104
Pilot Mound B4 96
Pinang, *island* A2 13
Pinar del Río A2 88
Pinawa D4 96
Pindus, *mts.* B2 51
Pine Bluff, Ark. D2 126
Pine Dock C3 96
Pine Falls C4 96
Pine Point F4 99
Pine River A3 96
Pinehouse Lake D5 104
Pines, *island* D2 18
Ping, *river* B2 12
P'ingtung B2 9
Pingxiang E3 10
Piniós, *river* B2 51
Pink Mountain L2 95
Pink, *river* F4 104
Pinsk C3 47
Pinta, *island* Inset 79
Piotrków Trybunalski D3 41
Pipestone A4 96
Pipmuacan, *reservoir* F2 103
Piracicaba D4 81
Pirada C1 62
Piraiévs B3, Inset 51
Pirmasens A4 40
Pirot C3 49
Pirris, *river* B3 86
Pisa B2 38
Pisagua B1 76
Pisco B3 77
Pistoia B2 38
Piteşti C3 43
Pitlochry B2 30
Pitseng B2 71
Pitt, *island* H4 95
Pittsburgh, Pa. E1 126
Piura A2 77
Placentia B3 85
Placentia D5 98
Placentia, *bay* D5 98
Placenza B1 38
Placetas C2 88
Planken B1 33
Plantagenet K2 102
Plasencia C2 37
Plaster Rock B2 97
Plata, Río de la, *estuary* D3 74
Plata, *river* B3 75
Platte, *river*, Nebr. C1 126
Plauen C3 40
Playgreen, *lake* B2 96
Pleasant Bay G1 100
Pleiku B4 11
Plenty, *bay* C2 15
Plessisville E5 103
Pleven C2 50
Plevna J3 102
Plibo C3 63
Pljevlja A3 49
Ploče C3 48
Płock D2 41
Ploieşti D3 43
Plovdiv C3 50
Plum Coulee C4 96
Plumas B4 96
Plymouth B1 91
Plymouth B4 30
Plzeň A3 42
Po, *river* A1, B1 38
Poá Inset II 81
Pobé B4 64
Pocatello, Idaho B1 126
Podgorica A3 49
Pogradec B3 49
Pohang C4 9
Pohnpei, *island* D2 15
Poinsett, *cape* C2 107
Point Fortin A2 91
Point Leamington D4 98
Point Pedro B2 19
Point Prim B2 100
Point, *lake* F3 99
Pointe au Baril E2 102
Pointe du Bois D4 96
Pointe Michel B3 90
Pointe Sapin E2 97
Pointe-a-la-Croix K3 103
Pointe-Claire H6 103
Pointe-des-Monts J2 103
Pointe-Lebel H2 103
Pointe-Noire A6 66
Pointe-Verte D1 97
Poisson Blanc, *reservoir* A6 103
Poissy Inset II 34
Poitiers C3 34
Poitou-Charentes C3 34
Pokemouche E1 97
Pokhara B2 19
Poland 41
Polar, *plateau* A14 107
Polba Inset II 20
Polis A1 27
Polonnaruwa C4 19
Polotsk D2 47
Poltava C2 47
Poltimore A6 103
Pomeranian, *bay* C1 40
Ponce B2 90
Pond Cove C3 98
Pond Inlet N2 99
Pondicherry C6 20
Ponferrada C1 37
Ponoka D5 94
Pont Cassé B3 90
Pont-Rouge E5 103
Pontchartrain Inset II 34
Ponteix C11 104
Pontevedra B1 37
Pontianak B2 13
Pontic, *mts.* D2 27
Pontine, *islands* C2 38
Pontine, *marshes* C2 38
Pontoise Inset II 34
Ponton B2 96
Poole C4 30
Poopó, *lake* A3 77
Popayán A4 78
Poperinge A2 33
Poplar River C3 96
Popomanaseu, *mt.* B1 16
Popondetta A2 15
Poprad C2 42
Porcupine Plain G8 104
Porcupine, *river* B2 105
Pori B2 53
Port Alberni K6 95
Port Antonio C2 88
Port au Choix C4 98
Port au Port B5 98
Port Augusta, S.A. C3 14
Port Bickerton F2 100
Port Blair F6 20
Port Blandford D5 98
Port Bruce E5 102
Port Burwell D3 98
Port Burwell E5 102
Port Clements F4 95
Port Colborne F5 102
Port Coquitlam L6 95
Port Dufferin E3 100
Port Elgin E3 97
Port Elgin D3 102
Port Elizabeth B2 91
Port Elizabeth C3 71
Port Franks D4 102
Port George B2 100
Port Glaud Inset 70
Port Harcourt D5 65
Port Hardy J6 95
Port Hawkesbury F2 100
Port Hedland, W.A. A2 14
Port Hood F1 100
Port Hope G4 102
Port Hope Simpson C3 98
Port Laoise C2 31
Port Lincoln, S.A. C3 14
Port Loko A1 63
Port Loring E2 102
Port Louis, *capital* B2 69
Port Macquarie, N.S.W. E3 14
Port Maria C2 88
Port McNeill J6 95
Port Moody L6 95
Port Morant C3 88
Port Moresby, *capital* A2 15
Port Mouton C4 100
Port Nolloth A2 71
Port of Spain, *capital* A2 91
Port Perry G3 102
Port Phillip, *bay* Inset V 14
Port Pirie, S.A. C3 14
Port Renfrew K7 95
Port Rowan E5 102
Port Said B1 56
Port Saunders C4 98
Port Stanley D5 102
Port Sudan D1 59
Port Talbot B3 30
Port-au-Prince, *bay* C2 89
Port-au-Prince, *capital* C2 89
Port-Cartier C3 101
Port-de-Paix C1 89
Port-Gentil A2 66
Port-Salut B2 89
Portadown A2 30
Portage A2 100
Portage la Prairie B4, D2 96
Portalegre B3 36
Porter, *lake* C4 104
Porters Lake D3 100
Porth Edward D3 71
Portimão A4 36
Portland A2 91
Portland Creek C4 98
Portland, *bight* B3 88
Portland, *inlet* G4 95
Portland, Maine F1 126
Portland, Oreg. A1 126
Portneuf, *river* C3 103
Porto Alegre B4 63
Pôrto Alegre C5 81
Pôrto Inglês C3 58
Pôrto Velho B2 81
Porto-Novo, *capital* B4 64
Porto-Vecchio Inset I 34
Portobelo C2 87
Portoviejo A3 79
Portree A1 30
Portsmouth C4 30
Portsmouth A2 90
Portsmouth, Va. F2 126
Portugal 36
Porvenir B9 76
Posadas D2 74
Poste, *river* C3 69
Postojna B3 48
Postville B2 98
Potaro, *river* B3 80
Potenza C2 38
Poti A3 45
Potiskum F2 65
Potnarvin C4 18
Potosí A3 77
Potrerillos C3 76
Potsdam C2 40
Pottuvil C5 19
Pouch Cove E5 98
Poutasi C3 18
Pouthisat B3 11
Považská Bystrica B2 42
Powassan F1 102
Powell River K6 95
Powerview C4 96
Poyang, *lake* E3 10
Poza Rica E3 84
Požarevac B2 49
Poznań C2 41
Pozo Colorado C3 75
Pra, *river* B4 64
Prachuap Khiri Khan B4 12
Prague, *capital* B2 42
Praia, *capital* C4 58
Praslin B2 91
Praslin, *island* C1 70
Prato B2 38
Prawda D4 96
Preeceville H9 104
Prelate A10 104
Preparis, *island* B3 12
Přerov C3 42
Prescott K3 102
Prescott, Ariz. B2 126
Presidencia Roque Sáenz Peña C2 74
Prešov C2 42
Prespa, *lake* B3 48
Presque Isle, Maine G1 126
Prestea A4 64
Preston C3 30
Pretoria, *administrative capital* C2 71
Préveza B2 51
Prey Veng D4 11
Priboj A3 49
Priddis C6 94
Prievidza B2 42
Prijedor A1 48
Prilep B2 48
Priluki C1 47
Primorsko F3 50
Primrose, *lake* A6 104
Prince Albert E7 104
Prince Albert, *hills* L3 99
Prince Albert, *peninsula* E2 99
Prince Charles, *island* N3 99
Prince George L4 95
Prince of Wales, *island* J2 99
Prince Patrick, *island* E1 99
Prince Regent, *inlet* K2 99
Prince Rupert G4 95
Princes Town A2 91
Princess Harbour C3 96
Princess Margriet, *canal* C1 32
Princess Royal, *island* H4 95
Princeton M6 95
Princeville E5 103
Príncipe, *island* C1 63
Prinzapolka C2 87
Prinzapolka, *river* B2 87
Pripyats, *marshes* C4 47
Pripyats, *river* C3 47
Priština B3 49
Privas D4 34
Prizren B3 49
Progresso B1 85
Prokopyevsk D6 44
Prokuplje B3 49
Prome B2 12
Prophet River L2 95
Prostějov C3 42
Provence-Alpes-Côte-d'Azur D4 34
Providence Bay C2 102
Providence, *capital*, R.I. F1 126
Providencia, *island* Inset 78
Providenciales, *island* C4 89
Provideniya C11 44
Provo, Utah B1 126
Pru, *river* B3 64
Prut, *river* B2 47
Przemyśl F4 41
Psel, *river* C1 47
Pskov D3 44
Pskov, *lake* D3 46
Ptsich, *river* D3 47
Ptuj C2 48
Pu'apu'a B2 18
Pubnico B4 100
Pucallpa C2 77
Puck D1 41
Puebla, *state capital* E4 84
Pueblo, Colo. C2 126
Puente Alto Inset 76
Puerca, *point* D2 90
Puerto Aisén B8 76
Puerto Armuelles A2 87
Puerto Ayacucho C2 79
Puerto Bahía C2 75
Puerto Barrios E4 85
Puerto Bolívar B4 79
Puerto Cabello C1 79
Puerto Cabezas C1 87
Puerto Carreño D3 78
Puerto Cisnes B7 76
Puerto Cortés B2 86
Puerto Deseado B6 74
Puerto Escondido E4 84
Puerto Inírida D4 78
Puerto Jiménez C4 86
Puerto Leguízamo B5 78
Puerto Lempira D2 86
Puerto Maldonado D3 77
Puerto Montt B7 76
Puerto Natales B9 76
Puerto Peñasco B1 84
Puerto Pinasco D3 75
Puerto Plata B1 89
Puerto Princesa A4 12
Puerto Real A2 90
Puerto Rico 90
Puerto Quepos B3 86
Puerto Sandino A2 87
Puerto Santa Cruz B7 74
Puerto Suárez C3 77
Puerto Vallarta C3 84
Puerto Varas B7 76
Puerto Williams C9 76
Puertollano D3 37
Puglia C2 38
Pugwash D2 100
Pujehun B2 63
Pukatawagan A1 96
Pukch'ŏng C2 9
Pukë A1 49
Pula A3 48
Pulangi, *river* C5 12
Puławy E3 41
Pulo Anna, *island* Inset 17
Pulusuk, *island* B2 15
Puná, *island* A4 79
Punakha A2 19
Pune B5 20
Punggol B1 13
P'ungsan C2 9
Puno C4 77
Punta, *mt.* B2 90
Punta Arenas B9 76
Punta del Este C3 75
Punta Delgada B9 76
Punta Gorda B3 85
Punta Santiago D2 90
Puntarenas B3 86
Punto Fijo B1 79
Purari, *river* A2 15
Purbeck's Cove C4 98
Purus, *river* B2 81
Pusan C5 9
Putao C1 12
Putre C1 76
Puttalam A3 19
Puttgarden B1 40
Putumayo, *river* B5 78
Puvirnituq A1 101
Puyo C3 79
Puysegur, *point* A4 15
Pyandzh, *river* B1 23
P'yŏnggang B3 9
P'yŏngsŏng A3 9
P'yŏngsan B3 9
P'yŏngyang, *capital* A3 9
Pyrenees, *range* C5 34

Q

Qaanaaq (Thule) B2 106
Qachas Nek B3 71
Qadarif, al- C2 59
Qaidam, *basin* C2 10
Qalat B2 22
Qalat Bishah B2 24
Qaleh-ye Now A2 22
Qaleh-ye Panjeh C1 22
Qamea, *island* C2 17
Qamishli, al- B1 27
Qandahar B2 22
Qaqortoq (Julianehåb) C2 106
Qaraghandy (Karaganda) D2 23
Qardho B2 60
Qareh, *river* B3 22
Qarokul, *lake* B1 23
Qarshi C3 23
Qaryah ash-Sharqiyah, al- B1 56
Qasigiannguit (Christianshåb) B2 106
Qasr as-Sabiyah C2 24
Qatar 25
Qatranah, al- B2 26
Qatrun, al- B3 56
Qattarah, *depression* A2 56
Qayrawan, al- C2 57
Qayyarah, al- B1 24
Qazvin B2 22
Qelelevu, *island* C2 17
Qeshm, *island* D4 22
Qilian, *range* C2 10
Qin Ling, *mts.* D2 10
Qina B2 56
Qingdao F2 10
Qinghai C2 10
Qinghai, *lake* C2 10
Qinhuangdao E2 10
Qiqihar F1 10
Qiryat Gat B2 26
Qiryat Shemona B1 26
Qishn C1 25
Qom C3 22
Qormi B2 36
Qostanay C1 23
Qu'Appelle G10 104
Qu'Appelle, *river* D10 104
Quang Ngai B3 11
Quantaq C1 101
Quanzhou E3 10
Quatre Bornes B3 69
Quba C2 45
Qubayyat, al- B1 26
Québec, *capital* E5, L6 103
Quebo C2 62
Quebradillas B2 90
Queen Charlotte F4 95
Queen Charlotte, *islands* G4 95
Queen Charlotte, *sound* H5 95
Queen Charlotte, *strait* H5 95
Queen Elizabeth, *islands* H1 99
Queen Maud Land, *region* B16 107
Queen Maud, *mts.* A5 107
Queen Maude, *gulf* H3 99
Queensland D2 14
Queenstown B1 13
Queenstown A3 15
Queenstown C3 71
Queenstown, Tas. D4 14
Queguay Grande, *river* B2 75
Queimados Inset I 81
Quelimane C3 68
Quellón B7 76
Queluz A3 36
Querétaro, *state capital* D3 84
Quesnel L5 95
Quesnel, *lake* M5 95
Quetta C3 21
Quetzaltenango B5 85
Quevedo B3 79
Quezon City B3 12
Qui Nhon B4 11
Quibala C3 70
Quibdó A3 78
Quilchena M6 95
Quill Lake F8 104
Quill, lakes F8 104

Key Page
Quillota B4 76
Quilpué Inset 76
Quimbele C2 70
Quimper A2 34
Quinhámel B2 62
Quintana Roo G4 84
Quispamsis D3 97
Quito, *capital* B3 79
Qunaytirah, al- A3 27
Qunfudhah, al- B2 24
Qunghirot A2 23
Quqon D2 23
Qurghonteppa A2 23
Qurnat as-Sawda, *mt.* B1 26
Quthing A3 71
Qyzylorda C2 23

R

Raahe B2 53
Raanes, *peninsula* L1 99
Raba C2 13
Rába, *river* A2 43
Rabat B2 36
Rabat, *capital* C1 57
Rabaul B2 15
Rabbit Lake C7 104
Rabbit Lake Mine G2 104
Rabi, *island* C2 17
Rach Gia A4 11
Rachidia, er- C2 57
Racine, Wis. E1 126
Rădăuţi C2 43
Radium Hot Springs O6 95
Radom E3 41
Radviliškis B2 46
Radville F11 104
Rae E4 99
Rafha B1 24
Rafter A1 96
Ragged, *point* C3 91
Ragueneau H2 103
Ragusa C3 38
Rahimyar Khan D4 21
Rainbow Lake A2 94
Rainier *mt.*, Wash. A1 126
Raipur D4 20
Rajang, *river* C2 13
Rajbiraj C3 19
Rajkot B4 20
Rajpur Inset II 20
Rajshahi B4 21
Rakaposhi, *mt.* E2 21
Raleigh, *capital*, N.C. F2 126
Ralik, *island chain* A1 16
Rama B2 87
Ramadi, ar- B2 24
Ramanbati Inset II 20
Ramat Gan B1 26
Ramea C5 98
Ramla B2 26
Ramon, *mt.* B2 26
Ramree, *island* B2 12
Ramtha, ar- B1 26
Ramu F2 61
Ramu, *river* A2 15
Rancagua B4 76
Rance, *river* B2 34
Ranchi E4 20
Randa B2 60
Randers C2 32
Randonopolis C3 81
Ranfurly E4 94
Rangamati F6 21
Ranger Lake B1 102
Rangitikei, *river* C2 15
Rangoon, *capital* C3 12
Rangpur C3 21
Ranong B4 12
Rapel, *river* B4 76
Rapid City A4 96
Rapid City, S. Dak. C1 126
Rapla C1 46
Rapti, *river* B2 19
Raqqah, ar- B2 27
Ras al-Khafji C1 24
Ras al-Khaymah C2 25
Ras an-Naqb A2 26
Ras Dashen, *mt.* C1 60
Ras Musandam, *cape* C1 25
Ras Tanura C1 24
Rasa, *point* C5 74
Rashayya A2 26
Rasht B2 22
Ratak, *island chain* B1 16
Ratchaburi B3 12
Rathlin, *island* A2 30
Ratingen A3 40
Ratnapura B5 19
Raukumara, *range* C2 15
Rauma B2 53
Raurkela D4 20
Raut, *river* B2 50
Ravenna C1 38
Ravensburg B5 40
Ravi, *river* D3 21
Rawa, *river* B4 80
Rawalpindi D3 21
Rawdatayn, ar- B2 24
Rawdon D2 100
Rawson B5 74
Raymore F9 104
Rayong B3 12
Rayside-Balfour D1 102
Raz, *point* A3 34
Razelm, *lake* E3 43
Razgrad E2 50
Ré, *island* B3 34
Reading C3 30
Rebun, *island* Inset I 8
Rechytsa E3 47
Recife E2 81
Recklinghausen A3 40
Reconquista D2 74
Red (Hong), *river* A2 11
Red Bay C3 98
Red Deer D5 94
Red Deer, *lake* A2 96
Red Deer, *river* D5, E6 94
Red Indian, *lake* C5 98
Red Rose C3 96
Red Sucker, *lake* E2 96
Red Volta, *river* B1, D3 64
Red Willow D5 94
Red, *river* C4 96
Red, *river* D2 126
Red, *sea* A1 24
Redange A2 33
Redbridge F1 102
Redding, Calif. A1 126
Redonda, *island* A6 90
Redstone L5 95
Redvers A4 96
Redvers J11 104
Ree, *lake* B2 31
Reed, *lake* A2 96
Regensburg C4 40
Reggio di Calabria C3 38
Reggio nell'Emilia B1 38
Reghin B2 43
Regina F10 104
Régina B1 80
Registan, *region* A2 22
Rehoboth C3 70
Rehovot B2 26
Reigate Inset III 30
Reims D2 34
Reina Adelaida, *archipelago* B9 76
Reindeer, *island* C3 96
Reindeer, *lake* H3 104
Reindeer, *river* G4 104
Reinosa D1 37
Reliance G4 99
Remagen A3 40
Remich B2 33
Rémire B1 80
Remscheid A3 40
Rencontre East D5 98
Renfrew J2 102
Rennell, *island* B2 16
Rennes B2 34
Rennie D4 96
Reno, Nev. B2 126
Renous D2 97
Repentigny K5 103
Reserve H8 104
Resistencia D2 74
Reşiţa A3 43
Resolute J2 99
Resolution, *island* P4 99
Restigouche, *river* B1 97
Reston A4 96
Restoule F1 102
Réunion, *island* 55
Reus G2 37
Reuss, *river* C2 35
Reutlingen B4 40
Revelstoke N6 95
Reventazón, *river* C3 86
Revillagigedo, *islands* B4 84
Rexdale J5 102
Rexton E2 97
Rey, *island* C2 87
Reykjavik B3 96
Reykjavík, *capital* A2 52
Reynosa E2 84
Rezekne D2 46
Reznas, *lake* D2 46
Rhaetian Alps, *mts.* D2 35
Rharsa, *salt marsh* A2 57
Rhine, *canal* B1, B2 33
Rhine, *river* A3, A4 40
Rhineland-Palatinate A4 40
Rhode Island F1 126
Rhodes D3 51
Rhodes, *island* D3 51
Rhodope, *mts.* C4 50
Rhondda B3 30
Rhône, *river* D4 34
Rhône-Alpes D4 34
Rhum, *island* A1 30
Riaba A1 66
Ribe B3 32
Ribeira Brava B2 58
Ribeira Grande A1 58
Ribeirão Pires Inset II 81
Ribeirão Prêto D4 81
Riberalta A2 77
Rîbniţa B2 50
Rice, *lake* G3 102
Richard, *lake* C1 104
Richard-Toll B1 62
Richards Bay D2 71
Richards Landing A1 102
Richardson, *mts.* B1 105
Richardson, *river* E2 94
Richelieu, *river* C6 103
Richer C4 96
Richibucto E2 97
Richmond L6 95
Richmond D6 103
Richmond Hill F4, K5 102
Richmond Park D4 94
Richmond, *capital*, Va. F2 126
Ricobayo, *reservoir* D2 37
Rida A2 25
Rideau, *lake* J3 102
Rideau, *river* H6 102
Riesa C3 40
Rieti C2 38
Riga, *capital* C2 46
Riga, *gulf* B2, B3 46
Rigolet B2 98
Riiser-Larsen Ice Shelf,
glacier B14 107
Riiser-Larsen, *peninsula* C16 107
Rijeka B2 48
Rila, *mts.* B3 50
Rimini C1 38
Rîmnicu Vîlcea C3 43
Rimouski H3 103
Rincón, *bay* C3 90
Rincón del Bonete, *lake* B2 75
Ringkøbing B2 32
Río Blanco B2 87
Rio Branco B2 81
Rio Claro A2 91
Río Cuarto C3 74
Rio de Janeiro D4, Inset I 81
Río Gallegos B7 74
Río Grande C5 81
Río Grande D2 90
Río Grande A2 87
Rio Grande (Río Bravo),
river D2 84
Rio Grande do Norte E2 81
Rio Grande do Sul C4 81
Rio Verde C3 81
Riobamba B3 79
Ríohacha B2 78
Rioni, *river* B3 45
Riou, *lake* D1 104
Rîşcani A2 50
Rishiri, *island* Inset I 8
Rishra Inset II 20
Riske Creek L5 95
Ritchies, *archipelago* F6 20
Rivas B3 87
River Cess B3 63
River Hills C4 96
River John D2 100
Rivera C1 75
Rivercrest C4 96
Riverhurst D10 104
Rivers A4 96
Rivers Inlet J5 95
Riverside, Calif. B2 126
Riverside-Albert E3 97
Riverton C3 96
Riverview E2 97
Rivière Bleue G4 103
Rivière du Loup C4 101
Rivière du Rempart C2 69
Rivière Noire, *mt.* B3 69
Rivière-à-Pierre D4 103
Rivière-au-Renard M3 103
Rivière-aux-Rats D4 103
Rivière-du-Loup G4 103
Rivière-du-Portage E1 97
Rivière-Matawin D5 103
Rivière-Ste-Marguerite G3 103
Rivière-Verte A1 97
Riyadh, *capital* B1 24
Riyaq B2 26
Roanne D3 34
Roanoke, Va. F2 126
Roatán B1 86
Roatán, *island* B1 86
Robertsport A2 63
Roberval D3 103
Robinsonville C1 97
Roblin A3 96
Roboré C3 77
Robson, *mt.* N4 95
Roca, *cape* A3 36
Rocanville J10 104
Rocha C3 75
Rochdale C3 30
Rochefort B4 34
Rochester D4 94
Rochester, Minn. D1 126
Rochester, N.Y. F1 126
Rock Island D6 103
Rock, *river* D5 105
Rockcliffe Park H5 102
Rockford, Ill. E1 126
Rockglen E11 104
Rockhampton, Qld. E2 14
Rockland K2 102
Rocky Harbour C4 98
Rocky Island, *lake* B1 102
Rocky Mountain House C5 94
Rocky, *mts.* 82
Rockyford D5 94
Roddickton C4 98
Rodez C4 34
Rodney D5 102
Roermond D3 32
Roeselare B2 33
Rogersville D2 97
Roi, *island* B2 16
Roi Et C2 12
Rojo, *cape* A3 90
Rokel, *river* A1 63
Roland C4 96
Rolling Hills E6 94
Rollo, *bay* C2 100
Rolphton H1 102
Roma A2 71
Roma, Qld. D2 14
Roman D2 43
Romania 43
Rome, *capital* C2 38
Rømø, *island* B3 32
Roncador, *cay* Inset 78
Roncador, *range* C3 81
Ronde, *island* B3 91
Rondônia B3 81
Rongelap, *island* B1 16
Rongerik, *island* B1 16
Rønne E3 32
Ronne Ice Shelf, *glacier* B11 107
Roodepoort C2 71
Roosevelt, *island* B6 107
Roosevelt Campobello
Intl. Hist. Park C4 97
Roper, *river* C1 14
Roraima B1 81
Roraima, *mt.* A3 80
Rosa, *mt.* A1 38
Rosalie B3 90
Rosalind D5 94
Rosario C3 74
Roscommon B2 31
Roscrea C2 31
Rose Belle C3 69
Rose Blanche B5 98
Rose Hill B2 69
Rose Valley G8 104
Rose, *island* B1 18
Roseau, *capital* B3 90
Roseau, *river* B4 96
Rosebud D5 94
Rosemary D6 94
Rosenfeld C4 96
Rosenheim C5 40
Rosenort C4 96
Rosetown B9 104
Rosetta, *river* B1 56
Roskilde D3 32
Ross Ice Shelf, *glacier* A6 107
Ross River C4 105
Ross, *island* B5 107
Ross, *river* C4 105
Ross, *sea* B6 107
Rossburn A4 96
Rosseau, *lake* F2 102
Rossel, *island* B3 15
Rossendale B4 96
Rossignol, *lake* B3 100
Rossland O6 95
Rosslare C2 31
Rosso B3 58
Rosthern D8 104
Rostock C1 40
Rostov-na-Donu E3 44
Roswell, N. Mex. C2 126
Rotherham C3 30
Rothesay D3 97
Rotorua C2 15
Rotterdam B3 32
Roubaix C1 34
Rouen C2 34
Rouleau F10 104
Round Lake Centre H2 102
Round, *island* D1 69
Round, *pond* C5 98
Rounthwaite B4 96
Routhierville J3 103
Rouyn-Noranda A4 101
Rovaniemi C1 53
Rovigo B1 38
Rovno B1 47
Rovuma, *river* C1 68
Rowley D5 94
Roxas B4 12
Royal, *canal* C2 31
Ruacana, *falls* B1 70
Ruahine, *range* C2 15
Ruapehu, *mt.* C2 15
Rub al-Khali
(Empty Quarter), *desert* C2 24
Rubtsovsk D6 44
Ruda Śląka D3 41
Rudnyy C1 23
Rufiji, *river* C2 68
Rufisque A2 62
Rügen, *island* C1 40
Ruggell B1 33
Ruhengeri B1 61
Ruhr, *river* B3 40
Ruhwa, *river* B2 61
Rukwa, *lake* B2 68
Rum, *cay* C3 89
Rumbek B3 59
Runaway Bay B2 88
Rundu C1 70
Rungue Inset 76
Rungwa, *river* B2 68
Rupel, *river* C1 33
Ruse D2 50
Russell A4 96
Russia 44
Rustavi C4 45
Rutana B2 61
Rutbah, ar- B2 24
Rutherglen F1 102
Rutland N6 95
Ruvubu, *river* C2 61
Ruvuma, *river* C3 68
Ruways, ar- B2, C1 25
Ruwenzori, *range* B3 61
Ruyigi C2 61
Ruzizi, *river* A1, A2 61
Ružomberok B2 42
Rwanda 61
Rweru, *lake* C2 61
Ryazan D3 44
Rybnik D3 41
Ryotsu C2 8
Rysy, *mt.* E4 41
Ryukyu, *islands* A4, Inset II 8
Rzeszów F3 41

S

's Hertogenbosch C3 32
Saale, *river* B3 40
Saar, *river* A4 40
Saarbrücken A4 40
Saaremaa, *island* B2 46
Saarland A4 40
Sab Abar A3 27
Šabac A2 49
Sabadell H2 37
Sabana de la Mar C1 89
Sabana Grande B2 90
Sabaneta A1 89
Sabha B2 56
Sable *cape*, Fla. E3 126
Sable River B4 100
Sabzevar D2 22
Sachigo, *river* B2 101
Sackville E3 97
Sacramento, *capital*, Calif. A2 126
Sadah A1 25
Sado, *island* C2 8
Sado, *river* A3 36
Safata, *bay* C3 18
Safed Koh, *range* D3 21
Safi B1 57
Safotu B1 18
Saga A3 8
Sagaing B2 12
Sagami, *bay* C3 8
Sagamihara C3 8
Saginaw, Mich. E1 126
Sagua la Grande C2 88
Saguenay, *river* F3 103
Sagunto F3 37
Sahara, *desert* 55
Saharanpur Panipat C3 20
Şahbuz A3 45
Sahel, *region* 55
Sahiwal D3 21
Sai Kung Inset 10
Saidpur B3 21
Saimaa, *lake* C2 53
St. Adolphe C4 96
St. Alban's D5 98
St. Albans C3, Inset III 30
St. Albert D4 94
St-Alexis-des-Monts C5 103
St-Ambroise E3 103
St. Ambroise B4 96
St.-Andé B1 97
St-André G4 103
St. Andrews C2 30
St. Andrews B3 97
St-Angèle-de-Mérici J3 103
St. Ann's Bay B2 88
St. Anne, *island* Inset 70
St. Anthony D3 98
St-Antoine C6 103
St-Apollinaire E5 103
St-Augustin E3 101
St. Augustine A2 91
St. Augustine, Fla. E3 126
St. Austell B4 30
St. Barbe C3 98
St.-Basile A1 97
St. Bernard's D5 98
St. Brendan's E5 98
St. Bride's D5 98
Saint-Brieuc B2 34
St. Brieux F8 104
St-Bruno E3 103
St-Camille-de-Lellis F5 103
St. Catharines F4 102
St. Catherine's E5 98
St. Catherine, *mt.* B2 91
St-Charles, *lake* K5 103
St. Clair, *lake* C5 102
St. Clair, *river* C5 102
St. Claude B4 96
Saint-Cloud Inset II 34
St. Cloud, Minn. D1 126
St-Côme C5 103
St-Constant J6 103
St. Croix B3 97
St-Cyprien H4 103
St-David-de-Falardeau E3 103
St. David's B2 91
St. David's B3 30
Saint-Denis Inset II 34
Saint-Dizier D2 34
St-Donat B5 103
St. Edward A2 100
St. Eleanors B2 100
St. Elias, *mts.* A5 105
Saint-Élie B1 80
St-Émile K5 103
Saint-Étienne D4 34
St. Eustache C4 96
St-Eustache H5 103
St-Fabien H3 103
St-Fabien-de-Panet F5 103
St-Félicien D3 103
St-Félix-d'Otis F3 103
St-François, *lake* E6 103
St-François, *river* D5 103
St.-Gédéon F6 103
St. George C3 97
St. George's B5 98
St. George's, *bay* B5 98
St. George's, *capital* A2 91
St. George's, *channel* B2 15
Saint George's, *channel* C3 31
St. George, Utah B2 126
St. Georges, *bay* F2 100
St-Georges F5 103
Saint-Georges C2 80
St-Germain G4 103
Saint-Germain-en-Laye Inset II 34
St. Gotthard, *pass* C2 35
St. Gotthard, *tunnel* C2 35
St. Helens C3 30
St-Henri-de-Taillon E3 103
St-Hubert G4 103
St-Hyacinthe D6 103
St-Ignace-du-Lac C5 103
St.-Isidore D1 97
St.-Jacques A1 97
St-Jacques-de-Leeds E5 103
St.-Jean, *lake* D3 103
St. Jean Baptiste C4 96
St-Jean-Chrysostome L6 103
St-Jean-de-Matha C5 103
St-Jean-Port-Joli F4 103
St-Jean-sur-Richelieu C6 103
St-Jérôme B6 103
Saint John C3 97
St. John, *river* B2 97
St. John's E5 98
St. John's, *capital* D5 90
Saint Joseph A3 90
St. Joseph E2 97
St. Joseph, *island* B1 102
St. Joseph, Mo. D2 126
St-Joseph-de-Beauce F5 103
St. Kitts
(St. Christopher), *island* B2 90
St. Kitts and Nevis 90
St Labre C4 96
St-Lambert J5 103
St Laurent C4 96
St-Laurent J5 103
Saint-Laurent du Maroni A1 80
St. Lawrence D5 98
St. Lawrence, *cape* G1 100
St. Lawrence, *gulf* L4 92
St. Lawrence, *river* K4 92
St. Lawrence Islands N.P. J3 102
St.-Lazare A4 96
St.-Leonard J5 103
St.-Léonard B1 97
St. Lewis D3 98
St. Lewis, *river* C3 98
Saint-Lô B2 34
Saint-Louis A1 62
St. Louis A2 100
St. Louis E8 104
St. Louis, Mo. D2 126
St-Louis, *lake* H6 103
St.-Louis-de-Kent E2 97
St.-Louis-de-Kent E2 97
St. Lucia 91
Saint Lucia, *channel* B1 91
St-Ludger F6 103
St. Ludger-de-Milot E3 103
St. Malo C4 96
St.-Malo E6 103
Saint-Malo B2 34
Saint-Malo, *gulf* B2 34
Saint-Marc C1 89
St-Marc-du-Lac-Long H4 103
St-Marcel F5 103
St-Marcellin H3 103
St. Margarets D2 97
St. Martin B3 96
St. Martin, *lake* B3 96
St. Martins D3 97
St. Mary's E5 98
St. Marys D4 102
St-Maurice, *river* C4 103
St-Michel F5 103
St-Michel-des-Saints C5 103
St.-Milaire A1 97
St. Moritz D2 35
Saint-Nazaire B3 34
St-Nicolas E5 103
St-Pacôme G4 103
St-Pamphile G5 103
St-Pascal G4 103
St. Paul E4 94
St. Paul, *capital*, Minn. D1 126
St. Paul, *river* A2 63
St. Paul, *river* C3 98
St. Paul's A1 90
Saint Paul's, *bay* B2 36
St. Peters G2 100
St. Peters C2 100
St. Peters, *bay* C2 100
St. Peters, *island* B2 100
St. Petersburg D3 44
St. Petersburg, Fla. E3 126
St-Philémon F5 103
St. Pierre, *island* M4 92
St. Pierre-Jolys C4 96
St.-Quentin B1 97
St-Raphaël F5 103
St-Rédempteur K6 103
St-Rémi-d'Amherst B5 103
St-Romuald L6 103
St. Shotts E5 98
St-Siméon G4 103
St. Stephen B3 97
St. Thomas D5 102
St-Tite-des-Caps F4 103
Saint-Tropez D5 34
St-Vallier F5 103
Saint Vincent, *passage* B4 91
St. Vincent, *gulf* Inset II 14
St. Vincent, *island* B2 91
St. Vincent and the Grenadines 91
St. Walburg A7 104
St-Zacharie F5 103
Ste-Agathe-des-Monts B5 103
Ste-Amélie B4 96
Ste-Anne-des-Monts K2 103
Ste-Anne-du-Lac A5 103
Ste-Apolline F5 103
Ste-Claire F5 103
Ste-Croix E5 103
Ste-Eulalie D5 103
Ste-Foy E5, K6 103
Ste-Luce H3 103
Ste-Marie E5 103
Ste-Monique E3 103
Ste-Rose-du-Nord F3 103
Ste-Thérèse H5 103
Ste-Véronique A5 103
Ste. Agathe C4 96
Ste. Anne C4 96
Ste. Rose du Lac B3 96
Ste.-Anne-de-Madawaska A1 97
Saintes B4 34
Sajama, *mt.* A3 77
Sak, *river* B3 71
Sakai B3 8
Sakarya, *river* B2 27
Sakha (Yakutiya), republic C8 44
Sakhalin, *island* I4 44
Şaki B2 45
Sakishima, *islands* Inset II 8
Sakon Nakhon C2 12
Sal Rei D2 58
Sal, *island* D2 58
Sala'ilua A2 18
Salaberry-de-Valleyfield B6 103
Salacgriva C2 46
Salado, *river* B3, C2 74
Salaga B2 64
Salahiyah A2 27
Salalah B3 25
Salamá C4 85
Salamanca D2 37
Salamís, *island* Inset 51
Salar de Uyuni, *salt flat* A4 77
Salaverry B2 77
Salcedo B1 89
Saldanha A3 71
Saldus B2 46
Salé C1 57
Salekhard C5 44
Salelologa B2 18
Salem C6 20
Salem, *capital*, Oreg. A1 126
Salerno C2 38
Salerno, *gulf* C2 38
Salford C3 30
Salgótarján B1 43
Salibia B2 90
Salihorsk C3 47
Salima B2 68
Salina Cruz E4 84
Salina, Kans. D2 126
Salinas C3 90
Salines, *point* A2 91
Salisbury A2 90
Salisbury C3 30
Salisbury, *island* N4 99
Sallut A1 101
Sallum, as- A1 56

Key Page
Sally's Cove C4 98
Salmon Arm N6 95
Salmon River A3 100
Salmon, Idaho B1 126
Salmon, *river* L4 95
Salo B2 53
Salonta A2 43
Saloum, *river* B2 62
Salsette, *island* Inset I 20
Salt Lake City, *capital*, Utah B1 126
Salt Water, *lake* Inset II 20
Salt, as- A1 26
Salt, *cay* D4 89
Salta B1 74
Saltcoats H9 104
Saltery Bay K6 95
Saltillo, *state capital* D2 84
Salto B1 75
Salto del Guairá E4 75
Salut, *islands* B1 80
Salvador E3 81
Salvage E5 98
Salween, *river* C2 10
Salyan C3 45
Salzach, *river* C3 39
Salzburg C3 39
Salzburg Alps, *range* C3 39
Salzgitter B2 40
Samaná C1 89
Samaná, *bay* C1 89
Samaná, *cape* C1 89
Samana, *cay* C3 89
Samangan B1 22
Samar, *island* C4 12
Samar, *sea* C3 12
Samara D4 44
Samarian, *hills* B1 26
Samarinda C2 13
Samarqand C3 23
Samarra B2 24
Samawah, as- C2 24
Sambalpur D4 20
Sambre, *river* C2 33
Samch'ŏk C4 9
Samina, *river* B2 33
Samoa 18
Samokov B3 50
Sámos, *island* C3 51
Samothráki, *island* C1 51
Samsø, *island* C3 32
Samsø, *strait* C3 32
Samsonvale, *lake* Inset III 14
Samsun D2 27
Samtredia B3 45
Samur, *river* B2 45
San C3 58
San Andrés, *island* Inset 78
San Angelo, Tex. C2 126
San Antonio B4, Inset 76
San Antonio A3 85
San Antonio C2 90
San Antonio Oeste B5 74
San Antonio, *cape* D4 74
San Antonio, *cape* A2 88
San Antonio, Tex. D3 126
San Baudilio de Llobregat G2 37
San Bernardino, Calif. B2 126
San Bernardo Inset 76
San Blas, *mts.* C2 87
San Borja A2 77
San Carlos B4 12
San Carlos C3 75
San Carlos B3 87
San Carlos de Bariloche A5 74
San Carlos, *river* B2 86
San Clara A3 96
San Cristóbal B2 77
San Cristóbal B2 79
San Cristóbal B2 89
San Cristóbal de las Casas F4 84
San Cristobal, *island* B2 16
San Cristóbal, *island* Inset 79
San Diego, Calif. B2 126
San Felipe D4 78
San Felipe B1 84
San Félix B3 76
San Fernando B2 12
San Fernando C4 37
San Fernando B4 76
San Fernando A2 91
San Fernando de Apure C2 79
San Francique A2 91
San Francisco C3 74
San Francisco B2 86
San Francisco de Macorís B1 89
San Francisco, Calif. A2 126
San Germán A2 90
San Gimignano B2 38
San Ignacio B3 77
San Ignacio A2 85
San Isidro D2 90
San Jorge, *gulf* B6 74
San José B3 86
San José C6 85
San José de Chiquitos B3 77
San José de las Matas A1 89
San José del Guaviare B4 78
San Jose, Calif. A2 126
San José, *capital* B3 86
San José, *river* B2 75
San Juan B3 74
San Juan B4 77
San Juan A2 89
San Juan, *capital* C2 90
San Juan, *passage* D2 90
San Juan Bautista D5 75
San Juan de Los Morros C2 79
San Juan del Norte C3 87
San Juan del Norte, *bay* C3 87
San Juan del Sur B3 87
San Juan, *river* A3 78
San Juan, *river* B3 87
San Lorenzo D4 75
San Lorenzo B2 79
San Lorenzo B3 86
San Lorenzo D2 90
San Lorenzo, *cape* A3 79
San Lucas C3 84
San Lucas, *cape* B3 84

Key Page
San Luis B3 74
San Luis D3 85
San Luis Potosí, *state capital* D3 84
San Luis Río Colorado B1 84
San Luis, *lake* B2 77
San Marino 39
San Marino, *capital* B1 39
San Marino, *river* A1 39
San Martín, *lake* A6 74
San Matías C3 77
San Matías, *gulf* C5 74
San Miguel B2 86
San Miguel de Tucumán B2 74
San Miguelito C2 87
San Nicolás C3 74
San Pablo B3 12
San Pablo, *river* B3 77
San Pawl il-Bahar B2 36
San Pedro D4 75
San Pédro C4 63
San Pedro de Atacama C2 76
San Pedro de las Colonias D2 84
San Pedro de Macorís C2 89
San Pedro Sula A2 86
San Pedro, *river* C2 85
San Pietro, *island* B3 38
San Rafael B3 74
San Remo A2 38
San Salvador de Jujuy B1 74
San Salvador, *capital* A2 86
San Salvador, *island* Inset 79
San Salvador, *island* C3 89
San Salvador, *river* A2 75
San Sebastián F1 37
San Sebastián B2 90
San Severo C2 38
San Valentín, *mt.* B8 76
San Vicente B2 86
San Vito, *cape* C3 38
San, *river* E2 11
San, *river* F3 41
Sana, *capital* A1 25
Sanaga, *river* B2 65
Sanandaj B2 22
Sanaw C1 25
Sancti Spíritus C2 88
Sand, *river* E3 94
Sandakan D2 13
Sanday, *island* Inset I 30
Sandilands C4 96
Sandougou, *river* B3 62
Sandoy, *island* Inset 32
Sandspit G4 95
Sandur Inset 32
Sandwich, *bay* C2 98
Sandy Bay H5 104
Sandy Cove A3 100
Sandy Lake D3 94
Sandy Lake A4 96
Sandy Lake B2 101
Sandy Point B2 89
Sandy Point Town A1 90
Sandy, *island* B2 18
Sandy, *island* B2 91
Sandy, *lake* C4 98
Sanford C4 96
Sangha, *river* D2 66
Sangmélima B3 65
Sangre Grande A2 91
Sangro, *river* C2 38
Sangudo C4 94
Sankosh, *river* B2 19
Sankrail Inset II 20
Sankt Gallen D1 35
Sankt Pölten D2 39
Sankuru, *river* B2 67
Sannar C2 59
Sanski Most A1 48
Sant Julià de Lòria A3 36
Sant'Antioco, *island* B3 38
Santa Ana A2 77
Santa Ana A2 86
Santa Ana, *range* C1 75
Santa Ana, *volcano* A2 86
Santa Bárbara A2 86
Santa Barbara, Calif. B2 126
Santa Catarina C4 81
Santa Clara C2 88
Santa Coloma de Gramanet H2 37
Santa Cruz B3 77
Santa Cruz A2 86
Santa Cruz de Tenerife Inset I 37
Santa Cruz, *island* Inset 79
Santa Cruz, *islands* C2 16
Santa Cruz, *river* A7 74
Santa Elena de Uairen D3 79
Santa Elena, *point* A4 79
Santa Fe C3 74
Santa Fe, N. Mex. C2 126
Santa Inés Inset 76
Santa Inés, *island* B9 76
Santa Isabel C3 90
Santa Isabel, *island* A1 16
Santa Isabel, *peak* A1 66
Santa Lucía, *river* B3 75
Santa Luzia, *island* B2 58
Santa Maria D2 58
Santa Maria C4 81
Santa Maria di Leuca, *cape* D3 38
Santa María, *island* B2 18
Santa María, *island* Inset 79
Santa Marta B2 78
Santa Rita B2 86
Santa Rosa C4 74
Santa Rosa B4 79
Santa Rosa de Copán A2 86
Santa Rosa del Palmar B3 77
Santa Rosalía B2 84
Santana do Livramento C5 81
Santander E1 37
Santarém A3 36
Santarém C2 81
Santiago B2 87
Santiago B1 89
Santiago de Compostela B1 37
Santiago de Cuba E3 88
Santiago del Estero C2 74
Santiago, *capital* B4, Inset 76

Key Page
Santiago, *river* B1 77
Santo André Inset II 81
Santo Antão, *island* A1 58
Santo Domingo B2 90
Santo Domingo de los Colorados B3 79
Santo Domingo, *capital* C2 89
Santo Tomás de Castilla E4 85
Santos D4, Inset II 81
Sanyati, *river* B1 69
São Bernardo do Campo Inset II 81
São Caetano do Sul Inset II 81
São Domingos A1 62
São Filipe B4 58
São Francisco, *river* D3 81
São Gonçalo Inset I 81
São João de Meriti Inset I 81
São José do Rio Prêto D4 81
São Luís D2 81
São Nicolau, *island* B2 58
São Paulo D4, Inset II 81
São Tiago, *island* C3 58
São Tomé, *capital* B4 63
São Tomé, *island* B4 63
São Tomé, *mt.* B4 63
São Tomé and Príncipe 63
São Vicente, *cape* A4 36
São Vicente, *island* A2 58
São Vincente Inset II 81
Saona, *island* D2 89
Saône, *river* D3 34
Sapele C5 65
Sapitwa, *mt.* C3 68
Sapporo Inset I 8
Sar, *passage* B3 17
Sar-e Pol B1 22
Sara Buri B3 12
Sarajevo, *capital* B2 48
Saramacca, *river* B2 80
Sarandë A4 49
Saransk D4 44
Sarapiquí, *river* B2 86
Sarasota, Fla. E3 126
Saratov D4 44
Saravan D4 11
Sarawak, state C2 13
Saraya D3 62
Sarbhang B3 19
Sarcelles Inset II 34
Sarda, *river* A2 19
Sardinia, *island* B2 38
Sargodha D3 21
Sarh B5 59
Sari C2 22
Sariwŏn A3 9
Sarjektjakko C1 53
Sark, *island* Inset II 30
Sarnia C5 102
Saronic, *gulf* Inset 51
Šar Planina, *mts.* B3 49
Sarstoon, *river* A4 85
Sarstún, *river* D4 85
Sary Tash C3 23
Sarygamysh Koli, *lake* B2 22
Saryshaghan D2 23
Sasamungga A1 16
Sasaram D4 20
Sasebo A3 8
Saskatchewan, *river* G3 92
Saskatoon D8 104
Sassandra C4 63
Sassandra, *river* C2, C4 63
Sassari B2 38
Sassnitz C1 40
Sata, *cape* A4 8
Satpura, *range* C4 20
Satsuma, *peninsula* A4 8
Sattahip B3 12
Satu Mare B2 43
Sauble Beach D3 102
Saudhárkrókur B2 52
Saudi Arabia 24
Saül B2 80
Sault Ste. Marie A1 102
Sault Ste. Marie, Mich. E1 126
Sault-au-Mouton G3 103
Saumur B3 34
Saurimo D3 70
Sauteurs B2 91
Sava, *river* B1, B2, C2 48
Savai'i, *island* A2 18
Savalou A3 64
Savan, *island* B3 91
Savannah, Ga. E2 126
Savannakhet C3 11
Savé B3 64
Savigny-sur-Orge Inset II 34
Savinja, *river* B2 48
Savona B1 38
Savona M6 95
Savonlinna C2 53
Savu, *sea* D2 13
Sawda, *mt.* B2 24
Sawhaj B2 56
Sawqirah C2 25
Sawqirah, *bay* C2 25
Saxony C3 40
Saxony-Anhalt B3 40
Sayabec J3 103
Sayan, *mts.* D6 44
Sayhut C1 25
Sayward K6 95
Saywun B1 25
Sázava, *river* B3 42
Scafell Pike, *mt.* B2 30
Scarborough C2 30
Scarborough B1 91
Scarborough F4, L5 102
Schaan B2 33
Schaerbeek C2 33
Schaffhausen C1 35
Schefferville D3 98
Schefferville C3 101
Schelde, *river* B2 33
Schellenberg B1 33
Scheveningen B2 32
Schiedam B3 32
Schiermonnikoog, *island* D1 32
Schleswig B1 40

Key Page
Schleswig-Holstein B2 40
Schouwen, *island* A3 32
Schreiber C3 101
Schuler E6 94
Schwäbisch Gmünd B4 40
Schwedt C2 40
Schweinfurt B3 40
Schwerin B2 40
Schweriner, *lake* B2 40
Schwyz C1 35
Scilly, *islands* A4 30
Scone B2 30
Sconser A1 30
Scotstown E6 103
Scotswood A3 94
Scott, *island* C5 107
Scottsbluff, Nebr. C1 126
Scugog, *lake* G3 102
Scunthorpe C3 30
Scutari, *lake* A1, A3 49
Sczecinek C2 41
Seaforth D4 102
Seal Cove C4 98
Seal, *river* D1 96
Searchmont A1 102
Seattle, Wash. A1 126
Seawell C4 91
Sebou, *river* C1 57
Sebright F3 102
Sechura, *desert* A2 77
Seda, *river* B3 36
Sedalia E5 94
Sedan D2 34
Sédhiou B3 62
Sedley F10 104
Seeley's Bay J3 102
Sefadu B1 63
Segbana B2 64
Ségou B3 58
Segovia D2 37
Séguéla C3 63
Segura, *river* E3 37
Seinäjoki B2 53
Seine, *river* C2, Inset II 34
Sekake B2 71
Sekondi-Takoradi B4 64
Selebi-Phikwe C2 69
Selenge Mörön, *river* C2 11
Sélibaby B4 58
Selínia Inset 51
Selkirk C4 96
Selvas, *region* B2 81
Selwyn, *mts.* C4 105
Seman, *river* A3 49
Semara B1 58
Semarang C2 13
Sembawang B1 13
Sembé C3 66
Semeru, *mt.* C2 13
Semey (Semipalatinsk) E1 23
Semmering, *pass* D3 39
Semois, *river* D3 33
Sempach C1 35
Sen, *river* D2 11
Senaki B3 45
Sendai D2 8
Senegal 62
Senegal, *river* B1, C2 62
Senkaku, *islands* Inset II 8
Senmonorom F3 11
Senne, *river* C2 33
Senneterre A4 101
Senta B2 49
Seoul, *capital* B4 9
Sepik, *river* A2 15
Sept-Îles C3 101
Septentrional, *range* A1 89
Serangoon B1 13
Serbia, republic B2 49
Seremban A2 13
Serenje C2 67
Sergipe E3 81
Seria A2 13
Serov D5 44
Serowe B2 69
Serpent, *island* D1 69
Sérrai B1 51
Serranilla, bank Inset 78
Serravalle B1 39
Serrekunda C2 62
Serule B2 69
Sese, *islands* C4 61
Sesheke A3 67
Seti, *river* A2 19
Sétif B1 57
Settat C1 57
Setúbal A3 36
Setúbal, *bay* A3 36
Sevan, *lake* C2 45
Sevastopol C4 47
Seven Persons E6 94
Seven Sisters Falls C4 96
Severn, *river* C3 30
Severn, *river* B2 101
Severnaya Zemlya, *islands* A6 44
Seville D4 37
Sevran Inset II 34
Sèvres Inset II 34
Sewa, *river* B2 63
Seward, Alaska Inset I 126
Seychelles 70
Sfax C2 57
Sfîntu Gheorghe C3 43
Sha Tin Inset 10
Shaanxi D2 10
Shabwah B1 25
Shache A2 10
Shackleton Ice Shelf, *glacier* C2 107
Shahr-e Kord C3 22
Shaki B3 65
Shalqar B2 23
Sham, ash- D1 25
Shamattawa E2 96
Shamgong B2 19
Shan, *plateau* C2 12
Shanchung B1 9
Shandong E2 10
Shangani, *river* A2 69
Shanghai F2 10

Key Page
Shannon B2 31
Shannon, *river* B2 31
Shantou E3 10
Shanxi E2 10
Shanxi F3 10
Shaoguan E3 10
Shaoxing F3 10
Shaoyang E3 10
Sharbot Lake J3 102
Sharjah C2 25
Shashe, *river* C2 69
Shashi E2 10
Shatt al-Arab, *river* C2 24
Shaunavon B11 104
Shawinigan D5 103
Sheberghan B1 22
Shediac E2 97
Sheerness E5 94
Sheet Harbour E3 100
Sheffield C3 30
Sheguianda D2 102
Sheho G9 104
Shek Pik Inset 10
Shelburne B4 100
Shelburne E3 102
Shelikhov, *gulf* C9 44
Shell Lake C7 104
Shellbrook D7 104
Shelter Bay N6 95
Shëngjin A2 49
Shenyang F1 10
Sherbro, *island* A2 63
Sherbrooke E2 100
Sherbrooke E6 103
Sheridan, Wyo. C1 126
Sherridon A1 96
Sherwood Park D4 94
Shetland, *islands* Inset I 30
Sheva Inset I 20
Shewa Gimira B3 60
Shibar, *pass* B2 22
Shibin al-Kawm B1 56
Shijiazhuang E2 10
Shikarpur C4 21
Shikoku, *island* B3 8
Shillong F3 20
Shimizu C3 8
Shimonoseki A3 8
Shimonoseki, *strait* A3 8
Shinano, *river* C2 8
Shinas C1 25
Shindand A2 22
Shinyanga B1 68
Shiono, *cape* B3 8
Ship Cove D3 98
Shippagan E1 97
Shirane, *mt.* C2 8
Shiraz C4 22
Shire, *river* B3 68
Shiretoko, *cape* Inset I 8
Shizuoka C3 8
Shkhara, *mt.* B3 45
Shkodër A1 49
Shkumbin, *river* A2 49
Shoal Lake A4 96
Sholapur C5 20
Shostka C1 47
Shreveport, La. D2 126
Shrewsbury C3 30
Shrirampur Inset II 20
Shubenacadie D2 100
Shubra al-Khaymah B1 56
Shumen E2 50
Shurugwi B2 69
Shwebo B2 12
Shymkent (Chimkent) C2 23
Siahan, *range* B4 21
Sialkot E3 21
Siargao, *island* C4 12
Šiauliai B2 46
Sibbald E5 94
Siberia, *region* C7 44
Siberut, *island* A2 13
Sibiti B5 66
Sibiu C3 43
Sibu C2 13
Sibuyan, *island* B3 12
Sibuyan, *sea* B3 12
Sicamous N6 95
Sichuan C2 10
Sicily, *island* C3 38
Sicily, *strait* B3 38
Sico, *river* C2 86
Sicuani C3 77
Sidi bel Abbès A1 57
Sidi Bou Zid B2 57
Sidlaw, *hills* B2 30
Sidney L7 95
Sidney B4 96
Sidon (Sayda) A2 26
Sidra, *gulf* C1 56
Sidvokodvo B2 71
Siedlce F2 41
Siegen B3 40
Siempang E1 11
Siemreab B2 11
Siena B2 38
Sieradz D3 41
Sierra de Cayey, *mts.* C2 90
Sierra de Loquillo, *mts.* D2 90
Sierra Leone 63
Sierra Madre, *mts.* B2 12
Sierra Madre, *mts.* C5 85
Sierra Nevada de Santa Marta, *mts.* B2 78
Sierra Nevada, *mts.*, Calif. A2 126
Sifton A3 96
Siggiewi B2 36
Sighetul Marmației B2 43
Sighișoara C2 43
Siglufjördhur B1 52
Siguatepeque B2 86
Siguiri D2 62
Siirt E3 27
Sikanni Chief L2 95
Sikasso B3 58
Sikhote Alin, *range* E8 44
Sikkim (state) E3 20
Šilalė B2 46

Key Page
Silay B4 12
Silesia, *region* C3 41
Silet B2 57
Silgarhi B2 19
Silhouette, *island* C1 70
Siliana B1 57
Silifke C3 27
Silisili, *mt.* B2 18
Silistra F1 50
Silkeborg B2 32
Sillery K6 103
Šilutė A2 46
Silvassi B4 20
Silver C4 96
Silver City, N. Mex. C2 126
Sima B2 67
Simcoe, *lake* E4 101
Simeulue, *island* A1 13
Simferopol C4 47
Simikot B1 19
Simla C2 20
Simon, *lake* A6 103
Simonette, *river* A4 94
Simonhouse A2 96
Simpson, *desert* C2 14
Sinai, *peninsula* B2 56
Sinaloa C3 84
Sincelejo B2 78
Sinclair A4 96
Sinclair Mills M4 95
Sindhuli Garhi C2 19
Siné, *river* B2 62
Sines A4 36
Singapore 13
Singapore, *capital* B1 13
Singapore, *island* B1 13
Singapore, *strait* B2 13
Singen B5 40
Singida B1 68
Singur Inset II 20
Sinope C2 27
Sinpo C2 9
Sint-Niklaas C1 33
Sint-Truiden D2 33
Sinŭiju A2 9
Sió, *river* B2 43
Siófok B2 43
Sion B2 35
Sioux City, Iowa D1 126
Sioux Falls, S. Dak. D1 126
Sioux Lookout B2 101
Sipaliwini A3 80
Siparia A2 91
Siping F1 10
Sipiwesk, *lake* C1 96
Siple, *island* B8 107
Siple, *mt.* B8 107
Siquia, *river* B2 87
Sirajganj C4 21
Sirba, *river* D2 64
Siret D2 43
Siret, *river* D2 43
Sirjan D4 22
Sisaket C3 12
Sisian D3 45
Sisimiut (Holsteinsborg) B2 106
Sisophon B2 11
Siteki B2 71
Sitka, Alaska Inset I 126
Sittang, *river* C2 12
Sittard C4 32
Sittwe B2 12
Siuna B2 87
Sivas D2 27
Siwah A2 56
Sixaola, *river* C3 86
Sjælland, *island* C3 32
Skagen C1 32
Skagerrak, *strait* A3 53
Skåne, *region* B3 53
Skaw, *cape* C1 32
Skead E1 102
Skeena, *mts.* H3 95
Skeena, *river* H4 95
Skeleton, *coast* A1 70
Skellefteå D2 53
Skellefteälven, *river* C1 53
Skien B4 52
Skierniewice E3 41
Skikda B1 57
Skíros, *island* C2 51
Skive B2 32
Skjern, *river* B3 32
Skookumchuck P6 95
Skopje, *capital* B2 48
Skovorodino D8 44
Skownan B3 96
Skye, *island* A1 30
Slagelse C3 32
Slaná, *river* C2 42
Slatina C3 43
Slave Lake C3 94
Slave, *river* F2 92
Slavonia, *region* C2 48
Slavonska Požega C2 48
Slavonski Brod D2 48
Sliema C2 36
Slieve Donard, *mt.* B2 30
Sligo B1 31
Sliven E3 50
Slobozia D3 43
Slough Inset III 30
Slovakia 42
Slovenia 48
Slovenskérudohorie, *mts.* B2 42
Sluch', *river* B1 47
Słupsk C1 41
Småland, *region* B3 53
Smallwood, *reservoir* D3 98
Smeaton F7 104
Smederevo B2 49
Smilovichi D3 47
Smiltene C2 46
Smith River J1 95
Smithers J4 95
Smithers Landing J3 95
Smiths Cove B3 100
Smiths Falls J3 102
Smithville F4 102

Key Page

Smoky, *river* A3, A4 94
Smolensk D3 44
Smolevichi D2 47
Smolyan C4 50
Smoothstone, *lake* D6 104
Smoothstone, *river* D6 104
Snake, *river* C3 105
Snake, *river* B1 126
Snaring A4 94
Sneek C1 32
Sněžka, *mt.* B2 42
Śniardwy, *lake* E2 41
Snow Lake A2 96
Snowdon, *mt.* B3 30
Snowdrift F4 99
Snowflake B4 96
Snug Harbour D3 98
Snuol E3 11
Soan-kundo, *islands* B5 9
Sobaek, *mts.* B5 9
Sobat, *river* C3 59
Sobradinho, *reservoir* D3 81
Sobral D2 81
Soc Trang A5 11
Sochi E3 44
Socompa C2 76
Socorro, N. Mex. C2 126
Socotra, *island* C2 25
Söderhamn C2 53
Sofia, *capital* B3 50
Sofia, *river* B2 69
Sognafjord, *fjord* B3 52
Soissons C2 34
Sŏjosŏn, *bay* A3 9
Sokchŏ C3 9
Sokodé B2 64
Sokoto C1 65
Sokoto, *plains* C1 65
Sokoto, *river* C1 65
Sol, *coast* D4 37
Sola B1 18
Soldeu B2 36
Solihull C3 30
Solingen A3 40
Solomon Is. 16
Solomon, *sea* B2 15
Solosolo C2 18
Solway, *estuary* B2 30
Solwezi B2 67
Somalia 60
Sombe, *beach* E2 90
Sombor A2 49
Sombra C5 102
Somerset B4 96
Somerset, *island* K2 99
Someş, *river* B2 43
Somme, *river* C2 34
Somoto A2 87
Son La A2 11
Son, *river* D4 20
Sonarpur Inset II 20
Sønderborg B4 32
Sondrio B1 38
Songea C3 68
Songhua, *river* F1 10
Songkhla B5 12
Songköl D2 23
Sŏngnam B4 9
Songnim A3 9
Songwe, *river* B1 68
Sonora B1 84
Sonsonate A2 86
Sonsoral, *island* Inset 17
Sooke L7 95
Sopron A2 43
Sor, *river* B3 36
Sorel C5 103
Soria E2 37
Sorø C3 32
Soroca B1 50
Sorocaba D4 81
Sorong E2 13
Soroti C3 61
Sorraia, *river* A3 36
Sorrento C2 38
Sosnowiec D3 41
Soso, *bay* B3 17
Sota, *river* B2 64
Sotk C2 45
Sotouboua B2 64
Soubré C4 63
Soufrière B4 90
Soufrière A2 91
Soufrière, *mt.* B1 91
Soufrière, *volcano* A2 91
Souillac C4 69
Soungrougrou, *river* B3 62
Sources, *mt.* B1 71
Souris A4 96
Souris C2 100
Souris, *river* G11 104
Sous, *plain* B2 57
Sous, *river* B2 57
Sousa B1 89
South Africa 71
South Andaman, *island* F6 20
S. Aulatsivik, *island* E3 98
South Australia C2 14
South Baymouth C2 102
South Bend, Ind. E1 126
South Branch B5 98
South Brook C4 98
South Carolina E2 126
South China, *sea* E4, Inset 10
South Comino, *channel* B2 36
South Dakota C1 126
South Downs, *hills* C3 30
South Dum-Dum Inset II 20
South Georgia, *island* 4
S. Gut St.-Anns G1 100
South Henik, *lake* J4 99
S. Indian Lake D1 96
South Korea 9
South Magnetic Pole C3 107
South Male, *atoll* A3 19
South Malosmadulu, *atoll* A2 19
South Milford B3 100
S. Moose, *lake* B2 96
South Orkney, *islands* C12 107

Key Page

South Ossetia, *region* B3 45
South Pole A17 107
South Rawdon D3 100
South River F2 102
South Ronaldsay, *island* Inset I 30
South Saskatchewan, *river* D8 104
South Shetland, *islands* C12 107
South Shields C2 30
South Taranaki, *bight* B2 15
South Uist, *island* A1 30
South West, *cape* A4 15
South, *island* A3 15
Southampton C4 30
Southampton D3 102
Southampton, *island* L4 99
Southend G4 104
Southend-on-Sea D3 30
Southern Alps, *mts.* A3 15
Southern Bug, *river* B2 47
Southern Uplands, *mts.* B2 30
Southland, *plains* A4 15
Southport C3 30
Southport B2 100
Sovetskaya Gavan E9 44
Soweto C2 71
Soya, *point* Inset I 8
Soyapango A2 86
Soyo B2 70
Sozh, *river* E3 47
Spa D2 33
Spain 37
Sousse C2 57
Spandau C2 40
Spanish C1 102
Spanish Town C3 88
Sparta B3 51
Spartansburg, S.C. E2 126
Spartivento, *cape* D3 38
Sparwood P6 95
Speightstown A2 91
Spence Bay K3 99
Spencer, *gulf* C3 14
Spences Bridge M6 95
Sperrin, *mts.* A2 30
Spessart, *mts.* B4 40
Spey, *river* B1 30
Speyer B4 40
Spiritwood C7 104
Spišská Nová Ves C2 42
Spithead, *channel* C4 30
Split C3 48
Split Lake D1 96
Splügen, *pass* D2 35
Spokane, Wash. B1 126
Spoleto C2 38
Spragge C1 102
Sprague D4 96
Spree, *river* C3 40
Spring Bay C2 102
Spring Coulee D6 94
Spring Hall A2 91
Springbok A2 71
Springdale C4 98
Springfield, *capital*, Ill. E2 126
Springfield, Mass. F1 126
Springfield, Mo. D2 126
Springhill C2 100
Springs C2 71
Springside H9 104
Springstein C4 96
Springwater B9 104
Spruce Grove D4 94
Spy Hill J10 104
Squamish L6 95
Square Islands D3 98
Sre Ambel B4 11
Srebrenica C1 48
Sredna Gora, *mts.* C3 50
Sremska Mitrovica A2 49
Sreng, *river* B2 11
Sri Lanka 19
Srinagar B2 20
Stafford C3 30
Stand Off D6 94
Standard D5 94
Stanley C2 97
Stanmore E5 94
Stanovoy, *range* D8 44
Star City F8 104
Stara Zagora D3 50
Starbuck C4 96
Starbuck, *island* D2 17
Starnberg, *lake* B5 40
Start, *point* B4 30
Staubbach, *falls* B2 35
Stavanger B4 52
Stavropol E4 44
Stayner E3 102
Stead C4 96
Steen River B1 94
Stefanson, *island* G2 99
Steinbach C4 96
Steinkjer C3 52
Stellarton E2 100
Stellenbosch A3 71
Stendal B2 40
Stepanavan B2 45
Stephenville B5 98
Stettler D5 94
Stevenage Inset III 30
Stevenson, *lake* C2 96
Stewart H3 95
Stewart River B4 105
Stewart, *island* A4 15
Stewart, *river* B4, C3 105
Stewiacke D2 100
Steyr D2 39
Stikine G3 95
Stikine, *river* G2 95
Stirling B2 30
Stirling H3 102
Štip C2 48
Stockerau E2 39
Stockholm, *capital* C3 53
Stoeng Treng D2 11
Stoke-on-Trent C3 30
Stonecliffe H1 102
Stoneham E4 103
Stonewall C4 96

Key Page

Stoney Point C5 102
Stony Mountain C4 96
Stony Plain D4 94
Stony Rapids E1 104
Storå, *river* B2 32
Storavan, *lake* C1 53
Store, *strait* C3 32
Storkerson, *peninsula* G2 99
Stornoway A1 30
Stornoway E6 103
Storsjön, *lake* B2 53
Storthoaks A4 96
Stoughton G11 104
Strakonice A3 42
Stralsund C1 40
Strangford B2 30
Stranraer B2 30
Strasbourg D2 34
Strasbourg F9 104
Stratford D4 102
Stratford E6 103
Stratford-upon-Avon C3 30
Strathclair A4 96
Strathlorne F1 100
Strathnaver L4 95
Strathroy D5 102
Straubing C4 40
Streymoy, *island* Inset 32
Stromboli, *island* C3 38
Stronsay, *island* Inset I 30
Struga A2 48
Struma, *river* A3 50
Strumica C2 48
Stryama, *river* C3 50
Stuart, *lake* K4 95
Stubbs B2 91
Stuie J5 95
Sturgeon C2 100
Sturgeon Falls D3 101
Sturgis H9 104
Stuttgart B4 40
Subotica A1 49
Suceava D2 43
Suchiate, *river* A5 85
Sucre, *capital* A3 77
Sudan 59
Sudbury E1 102
Sudd, *region* B3 59
Suddie B2 80
Sudeten, *mts.* B3 41
Sudirman, *range* E2 13
Suduroy, *island* Inset 32
Sue, *river* B3 59
Suez B2 56
Suez, *canal* B1 56
Suez, *gulf* B2 56
Sugandha Inset II 20
Suhar C1 25
Sühbaatar C2 11
Suhl B3 40
Suir, *river* C2 31
Suita B3 8
Sukabumi B2 13
Sukang B3 13
Sukhnah, as- B2 27
Sukhothai B2 12
Sukhumi A3 45
Sukkur C4 21
Sula, *islands* D2 13
Sulaiman, *range* C4 21
Sulaybikhat, as- B2 24
Sulaymaniyah, as- C1 24
Sulayyil, as- B2 24
Sulima B2 63
Sullana A1 77
Sullivan, *lake* E5 94
Sulu, *archipelago* B5 12
Sulu, *sea* A4 12
Süläktü A3 23
Sumatra, *island* B2 13
Šumava, *mts.* A3 42
Sumba, *island* D2 13
Sumbar, *river* B2 22
Sumbawa, *island* C2 13
Sumbawanga B2 68
Sumbe B3 70
Summerford D4 98
Summerland N6 95
Summerside B2 100
Summerville E5 98
Summit Lake K2 95
Summit Lake L4 95
Šumperk C3 42
Sumqayit C2 45
Sumy C1 47
Sun City C2 71
Sun Kosi, *river* C2 19
Sunch'ŏn B5 9
Sundarbans, *region* C7 21
Sunderland C2 30
Sunderland F3 102
Sundi C1 63
Sundown C4 96
Sundridge F2 102
Sundsvall C2 53
Sunnynook E5 94
Sunset House B3 94
Sunyani A3 64
Sup'ung, *reservoir* A2 9
Superior, *lake* J4 92
Superior, Wis. D1 126
Sur C1 25
Sur (Tyre) A2 26
Surab C4 21
Surabaya C2 13
Surakarta C2 13
Surat B4 20
Surat Thani B4 12
Sûre, *river* A2, B2 33
Surgut C5 44
Surigao C4 12
Surin C3 12
Suriname 80
Suriname, *river* B3 80
Surkhob, *river* B1 23
Surma, *river* E3 21
Surprise F1 95
Surt C1 56
Surtsey, *island* A3 52

Key Page

Surud Ad, *mt.* B1 60
Sussex D3 97
Susuman C9 44
Sutlej, *river* D4 21
Sutton West F3 102
Suva, *capital* B3 17
Suvadiva, *atoll* A4 19
Suwałki F1 41
Suwanose, *island* A4 8
Suwar, as- B2 27
Suwayda, as- A3 27
Suwŏn B4 9
Suzano Inset II 81
Suzhou F2 10
Svalbard, *islands* 5
Svay Rieng D4 11
Svendborg C3 32
Šventoji, *river* C2 46
Svetozarevo B3 49
Svilengrad E4 50
Svishtov D2 50
Svitavy C3 42
Svobodnyy D8 44
Swabian Jura, *mts.* B4 40
Swains, *island* A1 18
Swakopmund B2 70
Swan Hills C4 94
Swan Lake B4 96
Swan River A3 96
Swan, *lake* B3 96
Swan, *river* A3 96
Swan, *river* Inset I 14
Swansea B3 30
Swaziland 71
Sweden 53
Swift Current D5 98
Swift Current C10 104
Swindon C3 30
Świnoujście B2 41
Switzerland 35
Swords C2 31
Sydney G1 100
Sydney, *island* B2 17
Sydney, N.S.W.,
capital E3, Inset IV 14
Syktyvkar C4 44
Sylhet E4 21
Syracuse (Siracusa) C3 38
Syracuse, N.Y. F1 126
Syrdarya, *river* A1, C2 23
Syria 27
Syrian, *desert* B1 26
Szczecin B2 41
Szeged C2 43
Székesfehérvár B2 43
Szekszárd B2 43
Szentes C2 43
Szolnok C2 43
Szombathely A2 43

T

Taabo, *lake* D3 63
Tabar, *islands* B2 15
Tabasará, *mts.* B2 87
Tabasco F4 84
Tabelbala A2 57
Taber D6 94
Tablas, *island* B3 12
Tabligbo B3 64
Taboão da Serra Inset II 81
Tábor B3 42
Tabora B2 68
Tabou C4 63
Tabriz B2 22
Tabuaeran, *island* D1 17
Tabuk A1 24
Tabusintac D1 97
Tabwemasana, *mt.* B2 18
Tacaná, *volcano* A4 85
Tacloban C4 12
Tacna C4 77
Tacoma, Wash. A1 126
Tacuarembó C1 75
Tacuarembó, *river* C1 75
Tacuarí, *river* D2 75
Tadjoura B2 60
Tadmur B2 27
Tadoussac G3 103
Taebaek-Sanmaek, *mts.* C3 9
Taedong, *river* B3 9
Taegu C5 9
Taejŏn B4 9
Tafahi, *island* C1 17
Tafilah, at- A2 26
Taga C2 18
Taganrog, *gulf* D3 47
Tagish C5 105
Tagish, *lake* E1 95
Tagula, *island* B3 15
Tagus, *river* D3 37
Tahan, *mt.* B2 13
Tahat, *mt.* B2 57
Tahoua B3 59
Tai, *lake* C2 10
Tai'an E2 10
T'aichung B1 9
Taif, at- B2 24
T'ainan B2 9
Taipei, *capital* B1 9
Taitao, *peninsula* A8 76
T'aitung B2 9
Taiwan 9
Taiwan, *strait* E3 10
Taiyuan E2 10
Taizz A2 25
Tajikistan 23
Tajumulco, *volcano* B4 85
Tak B2 12
Taka, *island* B1 16
Takamaka Inset 70
Takamatsu B3 8
Takara, *island* A4 8
Takatsuki B3 8
Takev C5 11
Takipy A1 96
Takla Makan, *desert* B2 10
Takla, *lake* K3 95
Takua Pa B4 12

Key Page

Takutu, *river* B4 80
Talagante Inset 76
Talak, *region* B2 59
Talamanca, *range* C3 86
Talara A1 77
Talas C1 23
Talaud, *islands* D1 13
Talavera de la Reina D3 37
Talca B5 76
Talcahuano B6 76
Taldyqorghan D2 23
Talish, *mts.* C3 45
Tall Afar B1 24
Tallahassee, *capital*, Fla. E2 126
Tallinn, *capital* C1 46
Taloqan B1 22
Talsi B2 46
Taltal B3 76
Taltson, *river* F4 99
Tamale B2 64
Tamanrasset B2 57
Tamarin B3 69
Tamaulipas E3 84
Tambacounda C3 62
Tambo, *river* C3, C4 77
Tâmega, *river* B2 36
Tampa, Fla. E3 126
Tampere B2 53
Tampico E3 84
Tampines B1 13
Tampok, *river* B2 80
Tamsagbulag D2 11
Tamu B1 12
Tamworth, N.S.W. E3 14
Tan-Tan B2 57
Tana, *lake* B1 60
Tana, *river* F4 61
Tana, *river* F1 52
Tanabe B3 8
Tanch'ŏn C2 9
Tandil D4 74
Tanega, *island* A4 8
Tanen, *range* B2 12
Tanezrouft, *mts.* A2 57
Tanga C2 68
Tanga, *islands* B2 15
Tangail C4 21
Tanganyika, *lake* A2 68
Tanggula, *range* C2 10
Tangier C1 57
Tangier E3 100
Tangshan E2 10
Tanimbar, *islands* E2 13
Tanjungpinang B1 13
Tanna, *island* C4 18
Tano, *river* A3 64
Tanshui B1 9
Tanta B1 56
Tanzania 68
Taongi, *island* B1 16
Taoudenni C1 58
T'aoyüan B1 9
Tapa C1 46
Tapachula F5 84
Tapajós, *river* C2 81
Tapanahoni, *river* B3 80
Tapeta B2 63
Taquari, *river* C3 81
Tara D5 44
Tara, *river* A3 49
Taraba, *river* F3 65
Tarakan C1 13
Taranto D2 38
Taranto, *gulf* D2 38
Tarapoto B2 77
Tararua, *range* C3 15
Tarat B2 57
Tarawa, *capital* A1 17
Tarbes C5 34
Taree, N.S.W. E3 14
Tarif B2 25
Tarija B4 77
Tarim, *river* B1 10
Tarin Kowt B2 22
Tarnobrzeg E3 41
Tarnów E3 41
Taroudant B2 57
Tarrafal C3 58
Tarragona G2 37
Tarrasa G2 37
Tarsus C3 27
Tartu D2 46
Tartus A2 27
Tarvo B3 77
Taseko, *lake* L5 95
Tash Kömür C2 23
Tashigang C2 19
Tashir B1 45
Tashkent, *capital* C2 23
Tasikmalaya B2 13
Tasman, *bay* B3 15
Tasman, *sea* E3 14
Tasmania D4 14
Tata C2 57
Tatabánya B2 43
Tatamagouche D2 100
Tataouine C3 57
Tatar, *strait* D9 44
Tatarstan, republic D4 44
Tathlina, *lake* E4 99
Tatla Lake K5 95
Tatlayoko Lake K5 95
Tatra, *range* B2 42
Tau, *island* A1 18
Taumaruni C2 15
Taunggyi C2 12
Taunton C3 30
Taunus, *mts.* B3 40
Taupo C2 15
Taupo, *lake* C2 15
Tauragė B2 46
Tauranga C2 15
Taureau, *reservoir* C5 103
Taurus, *mts.* B3 27
Tauu, *islands* B3 15
Tavan Bogd Uul, *mt.* A2 11
Taverny Inset II 34
Taveuni, *island* C2 17
Tavoy C3 12

Key Page

Tavoy, *point* C3 12
Tawau D2 13
Tawi Tawi, *island* A5 12
Taxco E4 84
Tay Ninh B4 11
Tay, *estuary* C2 30
Tay, *lake* B2 30
Tay, *river* B2 30
Tay, *river* C4 105
Taymouth C2 97
Taymyr, *peninsula* B6 44
Taymyriya,
autonomous okrug B6 44
Taza C1 57
Tazin, *lake* A1 104
Tazin, *river* B1 104
Tbilisi, *capital* C4 45
Tchamba B2 64
Tchaourou B3 64
Tchentlo, *lake* K3 95
Tchibanga A2 66
Te Anau, *lake* A4 15
Tebicuary, *river* D5 75
Tecomán D4 84
Tecuci D3 43
Tedzhen C3 22
Tedzhen, *river* C3 22
Teepee Creek A3 94
Tees, *river* C2 30
Teeswater D3 102
Tefé B2 81
Tegal B2 13
Tegucigalpa, *capital* B2 86
Tehek, *lake* J4 99
Tehkummah D2 102
Tehran, *capital* C2 22
Tehuacán E4 84
Tehuantepec, *gulf* E4 84
Tehuantepec, *isthmus* F4 84
Teifi, *river* B3 30
Tekapo, *lake* B3 15
Tekeze, *river* B1 60
Tekirdağ A2 27
Tekong, *island* C1 13
Tel Aviv-Jaffa B1 26
Tela B2 86
Telavi C4 45
Telde Inset I 37
Telegraph Creek G2 95
Teles Pires, *river* C2 81
Telford C3 30
Telkwa J4 95
Telok Anson A2 13
Telšiai B2 46
Tema C4 64
Temagami, *lake* E1 102
Temburong, *river* C2 13
Temirtau D1 23
Tempisque, *river* A2 86
Temuco B6 76
Tena C3 79
Téna Kourou, *mt.* B3 64
Ténéré, *desert* C1 59
Tenerife, *island* Inset I 37
Tengiz, *lake* C1 23
Tenkodogo D3 64
Tennant Creek, N.T. C1 14
Tennessee E2 126
Tennessee, *river* E2 126
Tenojoki, *river* C1 53
Tenryu, *river* C3 8
Teotihuacán Inset 84
Tepexpan Inset 84
Tepic, *state capital* D3 84
Téra A3 59
Terai, *region* A2, C3 19
Teraina, *island* D1 17
Teramo C2 38
Teresina D2 81
Tereul F2 37
Termiz C3 23
Termoli C2 38
Ternate D1 13
Terni C2 38
Ternopil B2 47
Terrace H4 95
Terre Haute, Ind. E2 126
Terrebonne J5 103
Terreiro Velho C1 63
Terrenceville D5 98
Terschelling, *island* C1 32
Teseney A2 60
Teshio, *river* Inset I 8
Tesiyn, *river* B2 11
Teslić B1 48
Teslin C5 105
Teslin, *lake* C5 105
Teslin, *river* C5 105
Tessalit D1 58
Tessaoua B3 59
Testa del Gargano, *point* D2 38
Tete B3 68
Tête Jaune Cache N5 95
Tétouan C1 57
Tetovo A1 48
Teulada, *cape* B3 38
Teulon C4 96
Tewkesbury C3 30
Texarkana, Tex. D2 126
Texas D2 126
Texcoco Inset 84
Texel, *island* B1 32
Teyateyaneng A2 71
Tezoyuca Inset 84
Tezzeron, *lake* K4 95
Thaba-Tseka B2 71
Thabana Ntlenyana, *mt.* C2 71
Thai Nguyen A2 11
Thailand 12
Thailand, *gulf* B4, C4 12
Thames, *river* C3, Inset III 30
Thames, *river* D5 102
Thamesville D5 102
Thane Inset I 20
Thanh Hoa A2 11
Thanjavur C6 20
Thar, *desert* C4 21
Thásos C1 51
Thásos, *island* C1 51

	Key	Page
The Crane	C4	91
The Hague	B2	32
The Ovens	C3	100
The Pas	A2, C2	96
Thedford	D4	102
Thekulthili, *lake*	G4	99
Thelon, *river*	H4, J4	99
Theodore	H9	104
Thessalon	B1	102
Thessaloníki	B1	51
Thetford	D3	30
Thetford Mines	E5	103
Thicket	C4	91
Thicket Portage	C1	96
Thiès	A2	62
Thika	D4	61
Thimphu, *capital*	A2	19
Thingvellir	A2	52
Thio	C2	18
Thíra, *island*	C3	51
Thisted	B2	32
Thlewiaza, *river*	J4	99
Tholen, *island*	B3	32
Thomaston Corner	B3	97
Thompson	C1, D2	96
Thompson, *river*	M6	95
Thong Hoe	A1	13
Thorhild	D4	94
Thornhill	K5	102
Thorold	F4	102
Thrace, *region*	D4	50
Thracian, *plain*	C3	50
Three Kings, *islands*	B1	15
Thule, air base	B2	106
Thun	B2	35
Thunder Bay	C3	101
Thunersee, *lake*	B2	35
Thuringia	B3	40
Thuringian, *forest*	B3	40
Thurso	B1	30
Thurston, *island*	B9	107
Ti'avea	D2	18
Ti-n-Zaouâtene	B2	57
Tiáhuac	Inset	84
Tianjin	E2	10
Tibati	B2	65
Tiber, *river*	C2	38
Tiberias	B1	26
Tiberias (Galilee), *lake*	A1, B1	26
Tibesti, *massif*	B2	59
Tibet (Xizang)	B2	10
Tibet, *plateau*	B2	10
Tiburón, *island*	B2	84
Tichit	C3	58
Tichla	A2	58
Ticino, *river*	C2	35
Tide Head	C1	97
Tidjikdja	C3	58
Tien Shan, *range*	A1	10
Tierra del Fuego, *island*	C9	76
Tietê, *river*	Inset II	81
Tignish	A2	100
Tigre, *river*	B2	77
Tigris, *river*	B1	24
Tijuana	A1	84
Tikal	D2	85
Tikrit	B2	24
Tiksi	B8	44
Tiladummati, *atoll*	A1	19
Tilburg	C3	32
Tilbury	C5	102
Tillabéry	A3	59
Tilley	E6	94
Tillsonburg	E5	102
Tilomonte	C2	76
Tilston	A4	96
Timaru	B3	15
Timbuktu	C2	58
Timgad, *ruins*	B1	57
Timişoara	A3	43
Timmins	D3	101
Timor, *island*	D2	13
Timor, *sea*	B1	14
Tindouf	A2	57
Tingo María	B2	77
Tinkissa, *river*	C2	62
Tio	C2	60
Tipitapa, *river*	A2	87
Tipperary	B2	31
Tiranë, *capital*	A2	49
Tiraspol	B2	50
Tiree, *island*	A2	30
Tîrgovişte	C3	43
Tîrgu Jiu	B3	43
Tîrgu-Mureş	C2	43
Tîrgu Neamţ	D2	43
Tîrgu Ocna	D2	43
Tirich Mir, *mt.*	D2	21
Tirso, *river*	B2	38
Tiruchchirappalli	C6	20
Tisa, *river*	B2	49
Tisdale	F8	104
Tista, *river*	C2	21
Tisza, *river*	C2	43
Titagarh	Inset II	20
Titano, *mt.*	B1	39
Titicaca, *lake*	A3, D4	77
Titov Veles	B2	48
Titova Mitrovica	B3	49
Tivaouane	A2	62
Tiverton	B4	30
Tiverton	D3	102
Tivoli	B2	91
Tiznit	B2	57
Tlaipan	Inset	84
Tlalnepantla	Inset	84
Tlaxcala, *state capital*	E4	84
Tlemcen	A1	57
Toa Payoh	B1	13
Toad River	K2	95
Toamasina	B2	69
Toba Kakar, *range*	C3	21
Tobago, *cays*	A4	91
Tobago, *island*	B1	91
Tobermory	D2	102
Tobi, *island*	Inset	17
Tobin, *lake*	G7	104
Tobol, *river*	C1	23
Tobolsk	D5	44
Tobruk	D1	56
Tocantins	D3	81
Tocantins, *river*	D2	81
Toco	B2	91
Tocopilla	B2	76
Tofino	K6	95
Tofua, *island*	B3	17
Togo		**64**
Tokachi, *river*	Inset I	8
Tokaj	C1	43
Tokara, *islands*	A4	8
Tokat	D2	27
Tŏkchŏk-kundo, *islands*	A4	9
Tokmok	D1	23
Tokorozawa	C3	8
Toktogul	C2	23
Toku, *island*	C2	17
Tokuno, *island*	Inset II	8
Tokushima	B3	8
Tokuyama	A3	8
Tokyo, *capital*	C3	8
Tôlanaro	B3	69
Toledo	D3	37
Toledo, *mts.*	D3	37
Toledo, Ohio	E1	126
Toliara	A3	69
Tolima, *mt.*	B3	78
Tolland	E4	94
Toltén, *river*	B6	76
Toluca, *state capital*	E4	84
Tolyatti	D4	44
Tom Price, W.A.	A2	14
Tomahawk	C4	94
Tomakomai	Inset I	8
Tomanivi, *mt.*	B2	17
Tombua	B5	70
Tomé	B6	76
Tomelloso	E3	37
Tomiko, *lake*	F1	102
Tompkins	B10	104
Tomsk	D6	44
Tonalá	F4	84
Tonbridge	Inset III	30
Tone, *river*	C2	8
Tonga		**17**
Tongariro, *mt.*	C2	15
Tongatapu, *island*	B4	17
Tonghua	F1	10
Tongjosŏn, *bay*	B3	9
Tongliao	F1	10
Tongsa	B2	19
Tongsa, *river*	B2	19
Tonkin, *gulf*	B2	11
Tonle Sap, *lake*	B2,C3	11
Tonle Sap, *river*	B2	11
Toowoomba, Qld.	E2	14
Topeka, Kans.	D2	126
Topley Landing	J4	95
Torbay	B4	30
Torbay	E5	98
Torghay, *plateau*	C1	23
Tormes, *river*	D2	37
Torneälven, *river*	D1	53
Torngat, *mts.*	D3	98
Tornio	B1	53
Torniojoki, *river*	B1	53
Toronto, *capital*	F4, K5	102
Tororo	D3	61
Torquay	G11	104
Torre del Greco	C2	38
Torrejón de Ardoz	Inset II	37
Torrelavega	D1	37
Torrens, *lake*	C2	14
Torrens, *river*	Inset II	14
Torrente	F3	37
Torreón	D2	84
Torres, *islands*	B1	18
Torres, *strait*	D1	14
Torrington	D5	94
Tórshavn	Inset	32
Tortosa	G2	37
Tortosa, *cape*	G2	37
Tortuga, *island*	C1	89
Toruń	D2	41
Tõrva	C2	46
Tory Hill	G3	102
Tosa, *bay*	B3	8
Totness	A2	80
Tottori	B3	8
Touggourt	B1	57
Tougué	C2	62
Toulaman, *river*	B2	90
Touliu	B2	9
Toulon	D5	34
Toulouse	C5	34
Toungoo	C2	12
Toura, *mts.*	C2	63
Tourcoing	C1	34
Tournai	B2	33
Tours	C3	34
Toussoro, *mt.*	B2	66
Toutes Aides	B3	96
Tovuz	A2	45
Towada, *lake*	D1	8
Townsville, Qld.	D1	14
Toxkan, *river*	E2	23
Toyama	C2	8
Toyama, *bay*	C2	8
Toyohashi	C3	8
Toyonaka	B3	8
Toyota	C3	8
Tozeur	B3	57
Tqvarcheli	A3	45
Trabzon	D2	27
Tracadie-Sheila	E1	97
Tracy	C3	97
Tracy	C5	103
Trafalgar	E2	100
Trail	O6	95
Tralee	B2	31
Trang	B5	12
Transantarctic, *mts.*	B4	107
Transylvanian Alps, *mts.*	C3	43
Trapani	C3	38
Trasimeno, *lake*	C2	38
Trat	C3	12
Traun, *river*	D2	39
Traverse City, Mich.	E1	126
Trebinje	B2	48
Treherne	B4	96
Treinta y Tres	C2	75
Trembleur, *lake*	K4	95
Trenche, *river*	C3	103
Trenčín	B2	42
Trent, *river*	C3	30
Trentino-Alto Adige	B1	38
Trento	B1	38
Trenton	E2	100
Trenton	H3	102
Trenton, *capital*, N.J.	F1	126
Trepassey	E5	98
Tres Puntas, *cape*	B6	74
Treska, *river*	B2	48
Treviso	C1	38
Trier	A4	40
Triesen	B2	33
Triesenberg	B2	33
Trieste	C1	38
Trieste, *gulf*	A3	48
Triglav, *mt.*	A2	48
Tríkala	B2	51
Trim	C2	31
Trincomalee	C3	19
Trinidad	B2	77
Trinidad	B2	75
Trinidad	C2	88
Trinidad, *island*	A2	91
Trinidad, *mts.*	C2	88
Trinidad and Tobago		**91**
Trinity East	E5	98
Trinity, *bay*	E5	98
Triolet	C2	69
Tripoli (Tarabulus)	A1	26
Tripoli, *capital*	B1	56
Tripolitania, *region*	B1	56
Triton	D4	98
Trivandrum (Thiruvananthapuram)	C7	20
Trnava	A2	42
Trobriand, *islands*	B2	15
Trois-Pistoles	G3	103
Trois-Rivières	D5	103
Troisvierges	B1	33
Trollhättan	B3	53
Trombay	Inset I	20
Tromsø	D2	52
Trondheim	C3	52
Trondheimsfjord, *fjord*	B3	52
Trongisvágur	Inset	32
Troödos, *mts.*	A2	27
Trossachs	F11	104
Trout Creek	F1	102
Trout Lake	C3	94
Trout River	B4	98
Trout, *lake*	D4	99
Trout, *lake*	B2	101
Trouville	C2	34
Trowbridge	C3	30
Troyes	D2	34
Trujillo	B2	77
Trujillo	B2	79
Trujillo	B2	86
Trujillo Alto	C2	90
Truro	B4	30
Truro	D2	100
Trutch	L2	95
Trutnov	B2	42
Tsaratanana, *mts.*	B1	69
Tsavo	E5	61
Tsedike, *river*	B3	71
Tsengwen, *river*	B2	9
Tsetserleg	C2	11
Tsévié	B3	64
Tshabong	A3	69
Tshane	A3	69
Tshaneni	B1	71
Tshikapa	B2	67
Tshuapa, *river*	B2	67
Tsiribihina, *river*	B2	69
Tsiroanomandidy	B2	69
Tsiteli-Tsqaro	D4	45
Tskhinvali	B3	45
Tsnori	C4	45
Tsu, *island*	A3	8
Tsuen Wan	Inset	10
Tsugaru, *strait*	D1, Inset I	8
Tsumeb	C1	70
Tsumkwe	D1	70
Tsuruga	C3	8
Tsuruoka	C2	8
Tuam	B2	31
Tuas	A1	13
Tuasivi	B1	18
Tubarão	D4	81
Tübingen	B4	40
Tubmanburg	A2	63
Tucson, Ariz.	B2	126
Tucumcari, N. Mex.	C2	126
Tucupita	D2	79
Tucuruí, *reservoir*	D2	81
Tuen Mun	Inset	10
Tugela, *river*	D2	71
Tuguegarao	B2	12
Tuira, *river*	D2	87
Tuktoyaktuk	B3	99
Tuktut Nogait N.P.	D3	99
Tukums	B2	46
Tula	D3	44
Tula, *ruins*	D3	84
Tulcán	C2	79
Tulcea	E3	43
Tullamore	C2	31
Tulsa, Okla.	D2	126
Tulsequah	F2	95
Tulsipur	B2	19
Tultitlán	Inset	84
Tulun	D7	44
Tuma, *river*	B2	87
Tumaco	A4	78
Tumba, *lake*	B2	67
Tumbes	A1	77
Tumbler Ridge	M3	95
Tumen, *river*	C1	9
Tumuc-Humac, *mts.*	A2, B3	80
Tumucumaque, *range*	C1	81
Tunbridge Wells	D3	30
Tundzha, *river*	E3	50
Tungsten	C4	99
Tunis, *capital*	C1	57
Tunis, *gulf*	C1	57
Tunisia		**57**
Tunja	B3	78
Tupelo, Miss.	E2	126
Tupiza	A4	77
Tupungato, *mt.*	B3	74
Tur, at-	B2	56
Tura	C7	44
Turan, *lowland*	A2	23
Turayf	A1	24
Turbo	A2	78
Turda	B2	43
Turfan, *depression*	C1	10
Tŭrgovishte	E2	50
Türi	C2	46
Turin	A1	38
Turin	D6	94
Turkana (Rudolf), *lake*	D2	61
Turkeston, *mts.*	A1	23
Turkey		**27**
Turkmenbashi	A2	22
Turkmenistan		**22**
Turks and Caicos Islands		**89**
Turks, *islands*	D4	89
Turku	B2	53
Turkwel, *river*	C2	61
Turnberry	A2	96
Turnbull	B2	96
Turneffe, *islands*	C2	85
Turnhout	C1	33
Turnor Lake	B4	104
Turnu Măgurele	C4	43
Turquino, *mt.*	E3	88
Tursunzoda	A1	23
Turtle, *lake*	B7	104
Turtleford	B7	104
Tuscaloosa, Ala.	E2	126
Tuscany	B2	38
Tusket	B4	100
Tuticorin	C7	20
Tutong	B2	13
Tutong, *river*	B2	13
Tutuila, *island*	A1, C2	18
Tuul, *river*	C2	11
Tuvalu		**16**
Tuxtla Gutiérrez, *state capital*	F4	84
Tuy Hoa	B4	11
Tuya, *lake*	G1	95
Tuz, *lake*	C2	27
Tuzla	B1	48
Tweed	H3	102
Tweed, *river*	C2	30
Twillingate	D4	98
Twin Butte	D6	94
Twin Falls, Idaho	B1	126
Two Creeks	A4	96
Tychy	D3	41
Tynda	D8	44
Tyndall	C4	96
Tyne Valley	B2	100
Tyne, *river*	C2	30
Tyrrhenian, *sea*	B2	38
Tyumen	D5	44
Tyva, republic	D6	44
Tywi, *river*	B3	30

U

	Key	Page
Uaboe	B1	16
Ubangi, *river*	B1	67
Ubayyid, al-	C2	59
Ube	A3	8
Úbeda	E3	37
Úbeda	E3	37
Uberaba	D3	81
Uberlândia	D3	81
Ubin, *island*	B1	13
Ubon Ratchathani	C3	12
Ucayali, *river*	C2	77
Uccle	C2	33
Uchiura, *bay*	Inset I	8
Uchquduq	B2	23
Ucluelet	K7	95
Udaipur	B4	20
Uddevalla	B3	53
Uddjaur, *lake*	C1	53
Udine	C1	38
Udmurtiya, republic	D4	44
Udon Thani	C2	12
Udu, *point*	C2	17
Uele, *river*	C1	67
Uelzen	B2	40
Ufa	D4	44
Uga, *river*	B2	70
Ugalla, *river*	B2	68
Uganda		**61**
Uíge	C2	70
Uitenhage	C3	71
Ujae, *island*	B2	16
Ujelang, *island*	A2	16
Ujjain	C4	20
Ujung Pandang	C2	13
Ukhta	C4	44
Ukmergė	C2	46
Ukraine		**47**
Ulaan-Uul	C2	11
Ulaangom	B2	11
Ulan Bator, *capital*	C2	11
Ulan-Ude	D7	44
Ulansuhai, *lake*	D1	10
Ulchin	C4	9
Ulhas, *river*	Inset I	20
Uliastay	B2	11
Ulithi, *atoll*	B2	15
Ullŭng-do, *island*	D4	9
Ullapool	B1	30
Ulm	B4	40
Ulsan	C5	9
Ulster, *province*	C1	31
Ulu Dağ (Mt. Olympus), *mt.*	B2	27
Ulúa, *river*	B2	86
Ulubaria	Inset II	20
Uluru (Ayers Rock)	C2	14
Uman	C2	47
Umbeluzi, *river*	B2	71
Umboi, *island*	A2	15
Umbria	C2	38
Umeå	D2	53
Umeälven, *river*	C2	53
Umm al-Qaywayn	C2	25
Umm Bab	B3	25
Umm Qasr	C2	24
Umm Said (Musayid)	D4	25
Umniati, *river*	B2	69
Umtata	C3	71
Umuahia	D5	65
Umzingwani, *river*	B2	69
Una, *river*	A1	48
Unayzah	B1	24
Ungava, *bay*	L3	92
Ungheni	A2	50
Unión	C2	76
Union, *island*	A4	91
United Arab Emirates		**25**
United States		**126**
Unity	A8	104
Unst, *island*	Inset I	30
Upemba, *lake*	C3	67
Upernavik	B2	106
Upington	B2	71
Upolu, *island*	C2	18
Upper Arrow, *lake*	O6	95
Upper Liard	D5	105
Upper Lough Erne, *lake*	A	30
Upper Musquodoboit	E2	100
Upper Ohio	B4	100
Uppsala	C3	53
Ural, *mts.*	D4	44
Ural, *river*	B2	23
Uran	Inset I	20
Uranium City	B1	104
Urawa	C3	8
Urganch	B2	23
Urmia, *lake*	B2	22
Uroševac	B3	49
Uruapan	D4	84
Urubamba, *river*	C3	77
Uruguai, *river*	C4	81
Uruguay		**75**
Uruguay, *river*	D3	74
Urukthapel, *island*	B3	17
Ürümqi	B1	10
Usak	B2	27
Ushuaia	B7	74
Usk, *river*	C3	30
Üsküdar	B2	27
Usmas, *lake*	B2	46
Ussuri, *river*	E8	44
Ussuriysk	E8	44
Ust-Ilimsk	D7	44
Ust-Kamchatsk	D10	44
Ust-Kut	D7	44
Ust-Ordynskiy B uryat, autonomous okrug	D7	44
Ust-Ordynskiy	D7	44
Uster	C1	35
Ústí nad Labem	B2	42
Ustica, *island*	C3	38
Ustka	C1	41
Ustyurt, *plateau*	A2, B2	23
Usulután	B2	86
Usumacinta, *river*	F4	84
Utah	B2	126
Utah, beach	B2	34
Utan	Inset I	20
Utena	C2	46
Utikuma, *lake*	C3	94
Utila, *island*	B1	86
Utrecht	C2	32
Utsunomiya	C2	8
Uttaradit	B2	12
Utuado	B2	90
Utupua, *island*	C2	16
Uummannaq	B2	106
Uvira	C2	67
Uvs, *lake*	B1	11
Uwajima	B3	8
Uwaynat, al-	B2	56
Uyo	D5	65
Uyuni	A4	77
Uzbekistan		**23**
Uzhhorod	A2	47
Užice	A3	49

V

	Key	Page
Vaal, *reservoir*	C2	71
Vaal, *river*	B2	71
Vaalserberg, *mt.*	D4	32
Vaasa	B2	53
Vác	B2	43
Vache, *island*	B2	89
Vadodara	B4	20
Vadsø	F1	52
Vaduz, *capital*	B2	33
Vágar, *island*	Inset	32
Váh, *river*	A2	42
Vahsh, *river*	A1	23
Vaitupu, *island*	C2	16
Vakhan, *region*	C1	22
Val Comeau	E1	97
Val Marie	C11	104
Val-d'Or	A4	101
Val-des-Bois	A6	103
Valcourt	D6	103
Valdecaño	D2	37
Valdepeñas	E3	37
Valdés, *peninsula*	C5	74
Valdivia	B6	76
Valemount	N5	95
Valença	A1	36
Valence	D4	34
Valencia	C1	79
Valencia	F3	37
Valencia, *gulf*	G3	37
Valenciennes	C1	34
Valera	B2	79
Valga	D3	46
Valira d'Orient, *river*	B2	36
Valira, *river*	B2	36
Valjevo	A2	49
Valka	C2	46
Valladolid	G3	84
Valladolid	D2	37
Valle d'Aosta	A1	38
Valledupar	B2	78
Vallenar	B3	76
Valletta, *capital*	C2	36
Valley, *river*	A3	96
Valmiera	C2	46
Valparaíso	B4, Inset	76
Van	E2	27
Van, *lake*	E2	27
Vancouver	L6	95
Vancouver, *island*	J6	95
Vanderhoof	K4	95
Vänern, *lake*	B3	53
Vanguard	C11	104
Vanier	H5	102
Vanier	L5	103
Vanikolo, *islands*	C2	16
Vanimo	A2	15
Vannes	B3	34
Vanrhynsdorp	A3	71
Vanscoy	D8	104
Vansittart, *island*	M3	99
Vantaa	B2	53
Vanua Balavu, *island*	C2	17
Vanua Lava, *island*	B1	18
Vanua Levu, *island*	B2	17
Vanuatu		**18**
Varanasi	D3	20
Varaždin	C2	48
Vardar, *river*	C2	48
Varde, *river*	B3	32
Vardenis	C2	45
Varkaus	C2	53
Varna	F2	50
Vasai	Inset I	20
Vasai, *creek*	Inset I	20
Vaslui	D2	43
Vassar	D4	96
Västerås	C3	53
Vatican City		**39**
Vatnajökull, *ice cap*	B2	52
Vättern, *lake*	B3	53
Vatu Lele, *island*	A3	17
Vaudreuil	C6	103
Vaupés, *river*	B4	78
Vava'u, *island*	C2	17
Vavenby	N5	95
Vavuniya	B3	19
Vawkavysk	B3	47
Växjö	B3	53
Vayk	C3	45
Vega	C4	94
Vega Alta	C2	90
Vega Baja	C2	90
Vegreville	D4	94
Veimandu, *channel*	A3	19
Vejle	B3	32
Velika Morava, *river*	B2	49
Veliki, *canal*	A2	49
Veliko Tŭrnovo	D2	50
Vélingara	B3	62
Vélingara	B2	62
Vella Lavella, *island*	A1	16
Vellore	C6	20
Veneto	B1	38
Venezuela		**79**
Venezuela, *gulf*	B1	79
Venice	C1	38
Venice, *gulf*	C1	38
Venlo	D3	32
Venta, *river*	B1	46
Ventimiglia	A2	38
Ventspils	A2	46
Veracruz	E4	84
Vercelli	B1	38
Verde, *river*	C3	75
Verdun	D2	34
Verdun	J6	103
Vereeniging	C2	71
Verkhoyansk	C8	44
Verkhoyansk, *range*	C8	44
Vermillion, *river*	C4	103
Vermont	F1	126
Vernal, Utah	C1	126
Verner	E1	102
Vernon	N6	95
Vernon Bridge	C2	100
Vernon River	C2	100
Véroia	B1	51
Verona	B1	38
Verona	J3	102
Versailles	C2, Inset II	34
Vert, *cape*	A2	62
Verviers	D2	33
Vesoul	D3	34
Vesterålen, *islands*	C2	52
Vestmanna	Inset	32
Vestmannaeyjar	A3	52
Vesuvius, *volcano*	C2	38
Veszprém	A2	43
Vetauua, *island*	C1	17
Viana do Castelo	A2	36
Vianden	B2	33
Vibank	G10	104
Viborg	B2	32
Vicenza	B1	38
Vich	H2	37
Vichada, *river*	C3	78
Vichy	C3	34
Victoria	D3	14
Victoria	B6	76
Victoria	A1	36
Victoria	B2	100
Victoria Beach	C4	96
Victoria Beach	B3	100
Victoria Land, *region*	B5	107
Victoria Nile, *river*	C3	61
Victoria, *capital*	Inset	70
Victoria, *capital*	L7	95
Victoria, *falls*	B3	67
Victoria, *island*	F2	99
Victoria, *lake*	B4, C4	61
Victoria, *peak*	B3	85
Victoria, *river*	C1	14
Victoria, Tex.	D3	126
Victoriaville	E5	103
Vidin	A2	50
Viedma	C5	74
Viedma, *lake*	A6	74
Vieille Case	A1	90

Key Page
ienna, *capital* E2 39
ienne, *river* C3 34
ientiane, *capital* B3 11
eques D2 90
eques, *island* E2 90
eques, *passage* D2 90
eques, *sound* E2 90
ierzon C3 34
iet Tri A2 11
ietnam 11
ieux Fort B3 91
igan B2 12
ignemale, *mt.* B5 34
igo B1 37
ijayawada D5 20
ijosë, *river* A3 49
ila do Conde A2 36
ila Nova de Gaia A2 36
ila Real B2 36
ila Real de Santo Antonio B4 36
ila, *capital* C3 18
ilaine, *river* B3 34
ilanculos B4 68
ilcabamba, *mts.* C3 77
iljandi C2 46
ilkaviškis B2 46
illa Ahumada C1 84
illa Hayes D4 75
illa María C3 74
illa Obregón Inset 84
illach C4 39
illahermosa, *state capital* F4 84
illalba C2 90
illarreal de los Infantes F3 37
illarrica D4 75
illavicencio B3 78
illazón A4 77
ille-Marie A4 101
illeneuve-Saint-Georges Inset II 34
illeroy E5 103
ilnius, *capital* C2 46
ilyuy, *river* C7 44
ilyuysk C8 44
iña del Mar B4, Inset 76
incennes Inset II 34
incente de Carvalho Inset II 81
inces, *river* B3 79
indelälven, *river* C2 53
indhya, *range* C4 20
inh A2 11
innitsa B2 47
inson Massif, *mt.* B10 107
irden A4 96
irgin, *river* C3 104
irgin, *islands* 82
irginia F2 126
irtsu B2 46
irunga, *mts.* B1 61
isakhapatnam D5 20
isayan, *islands* B4 12
isayan, *sea* B4 12
isby C3 53
iscount Melville, *sound* F2 99
iseu B2 36
ista A4 96
ista Hermosa B4 78
istula, *river* D2, E3 41
ita C4 96
iterbo C2 38
iti Levu, *island* A2 17
itoria E1 37
itória D4 81
itória da Conquista D3 81
itsyebsk E2 47
ivian C4 96
izcaíno, *desert* B2 84
laardingen B3 32
ladivostok E8 44
lieland, *island* B1 32
lissingen A3 32
lorë A3 49
ltava, *river* B3 42
öcklabruck C2 39
oinjama B1 63
ojvodina, *province* A2 49
olcano, *islands* Inset III 8
olga, *river* E4 44
olgograd E4 44
ologda D3 44
ólos B2 51
olta Redonda D4 81
olta, *lake* C3 64
olta, *river* C3 64
onda D8 104
orkuta C5 44
oronezh D3 44
orotan, *river* C3 45
orskla, *river* C1 47
örts Järv, *lake* D2 46
õru D3 46
osges, *mts.* D2 34
ostok, *island* D3 17
ranje B3 49
ratsa B2 50
rbas A2 49
rbas, *river* B1 48
ršac B2 49
ryburg B2 71
ukovar D2 48
unaniu, *bay* A3 17
ung Tau-Con Dao B4 11
unisea B3 17

W

Va A1 64
Vaal, *river* C3 32
Vabag A2 15
Vabamun, *lake* C4 94
Vabana E5 98
Vabasca, *river* C2 94
Vabe Gestro, *river* C3 60
Vabe Shebele, *river* D3 60
Vabowden B2 96
Vabush D4 98
Vaco, Tex. D2 126
Vad Madani C2 59
Vaddan C2 56
Vaddenzee, *sound* C1 32
Waddington, *mt.* K5 95
Wadena G9 104
Wadi al-Malik, *river* B2 59
Wadi as-Sirhan, *depression* B2 26
Wadi Halfa C1 59
Wafrah, al- B3 24
Wagga Wagga, N.S.W. D3 14
Waigeo, *island* E2 13
Waikato, *river* C2 15
Waimamaku B2 15
Waingapu D2 13
Wairau, *river* B3 15
Waitaki, *river* B3 15
Wajh, al- A1 24
Wajir F3 61
Wakasa, *bay* B3 8
Wakaw E8 104
Wakayama B3 8
Wakefield C3 30
Wakkanai Inset I 8
Wakomata, *lake* B1 102
Wakrah, al- D3 25
Walachia, *region* B3 43
Wałbrzych C3 41
Walcheren, *island* A3 32
Walden D1 102
Waldersee B4 96
Waldheim D8 104
Walensee, *lake* D1 35
Walkerton D3 102
Wallace D2 100
Wallaceburg C5 102
Walsall C3 30
Walton C2 100
Walton D4 102
Walvis Bay B2 70
Wami, *river* C2 68
Wanaka, *lake* A3 15
Wanapitei, *lake* E1 102
Wandering River D3 94
Wando B5 9
Wanganui C2 15
Wanham A3 94
Wapawekka, *lake* F5 104
Wapawsik B1 96
Wapiti, *river* A4 94
Warangal C5 20
Warbah, *island* C1 24
Wardlow E6 94
Ware K2 95
Warman D8 104
Warner D6 94
Warren C4 96
Warren E1 102
Warren Landing C2 96
Warri C5 65
Warrington C3 30
Warrnambool, Vic. D3 14
Warsaw, *capital* E2 41
Warta, *river* B2, C2 41
Warwick C3 30
Wasa P6 95
Wasaga Beach F3 102
Wasagaming B4 96
Wash, *bay* D3 30
Washago F3 102
Washington A1 126
Washington, *cape* A3 17
Washington, *capital*, D.C. F2 126
Waskada A4 96
Waskaganish A3 101
Waskesiu Lake D7 104
Waspam C1 87
Water Valley C5 94
Water, *cays* A3 89
Waterborough C3 97
Waterbury, *lake* F2 104
Waterford C2 31
Waterhen, *lake* B3 96
Waterloo E4 102
Waterloo D6 103
Watertown, N.Y. F1 126
Watford Inset III 30
Watford D5 102
Wathaman, *lake* G3 104
Watrous E9 104
Watsa C1 67
Watson F8 104
Watson Lake D5 105
Wau A2 15
Wavre C2 33
Waw B3 59
Wawa D3 101
Wawa, *river* B1 87
Wawanesa B4 96
Weagamow Lake B2 101
Webbwood D1 102
Webequie C2 101
Webi Shabeelle, *river* B3 60
Weddell, *sea* B12 107
Wedgeport A4 100
Weert C3 32
Wei, *river* D2 10
Weiden C4 40
Weifang E2 10
Weimar B3 40
Weipa, Qld. D1 14
Weitzel, *lake* D3 104
Wekusko B2 96
Wekusko, *lake* B2 96
Weldiya C2 60
Welkom C2 71
Wellington A2 100
Wellington, *capital* B3 15
Wellington, *island* A8 76
Wels C2 39
Welsford C3 97
Welshpool B3 30
Welwyn A4 96
Wembere, *river* B1 68
Wenchi A3 64
Weno C2 15
Weno, *island* C2 15
Wenshan D3 10
Wentworth D2 100
Wentzel, *lake* C1 94
Wenzhou F3 10
Werder D3 60
Werra, *river* B3 40
Weser, *river* B2 40
Wesley B2 90
Wesleyville E4 98
West Antarctica A8 107
West Devon A2 100
West Frisian, *islands* B1 32
West Ice Shelf, *glacier* C1 107
West Palm Beach, Fla. E3 126
West Point A2 100
West Road, *river* K4 95
West Siberian, *plain* C5 44
West St. Modeste C3 98
West Virginia E2 126
Westbank N6 95
Westbourne B4 96
Western Australia B2 14
Western Dvina, *river* C2 46
Western Ghats, *mts.* B5 20
Western Sahara **58**
Western, *channel* C5 9
Westerschelde, *channel* A3 32
Westfield C3 97
Westlock D4 94
Westminster Inset III 30
Weston J5 102
Westport B3 15
Westport B2 31
Westport J3 102
Westray A2 96
Westray, *island* Inset I 30
Wetar, *island* D2 13
Wetaskiwin D5 94
Wete C1 68
Wetzlar B3 40
Wewak A1 15
Wexford C2 31
Weyakwin E6 104
Weyburn G11 104
Weymouth A3 100
Whakatane C2 15
Whale Cove K4 99
Whaletown K6 95
Whangarei B2 15
Wheatland A4 96
Wheatley C5 102
Wheeling, W. Va. E1 126
Whistler L6 95
Whitbourne E5 98
Whitby G4 102
White Fox F7 104
White Lake J2 102
White Nile, *river* C3 59
White Rock L6 95
White Sands C3 100
White Volta, *river* B1, D2 64
White, *bay* C4 98
White, *island* L3 99
White, *river* A4 105
White, *sea* C3 44
Whitecourt C4 94
Whitefish Falls D1 102
Whitefish, *bay* A1 102
Whitehaven B2 30
Whitehorse C5 105
Whitelaw A3 94
Whiteman, *range* A2 15
Whitemouth D4 96
Whitestone, *river* B3 105
Whitewood H10 104
Whitney G2 102
Whitney *mt.*, Calif. B2 126
Wholdaia, *lake* H4 99
Whyalla, S.A. C3 14
Whycocomagh F2 100
Wiarton D3 102
Wichita Falls, Tex. D2 126
Wichita, Kans. D2 126
Wick B1 30
Wicklow C2 31
Wicklow Head, *cape* D2 31
Wicklow, *mts.* C2 31
Wiener Neustadt E3 39
Wieprz, *river* F3 41
Wiesbaden B3 40
Wigan C3 30
Wight, *island* C4 30
Wilberforce G2 102
Wilge, *river* C2 71
Wilhelm, *mt.* A2 15
Wilhelmina, *canal* B3 32
Wilhelmina, *mts.* A2 80
Wilhelmshaven B2 40
Wilkes Land, *region* C3 107
Wilkie B8 104
William, *river* B2 104
Williams Harbour D3 98
Williams Lake L5 95
Williamsport C4 98
Williston, *lake* K3 95
Willow Bunch E11 104
Willow Creek A11 104
Willowbunch, *lake* E11 104
Wilmington, Del. F2 126
Wilmington, N.C. F2 126
Wilmot B3 100
Wiltondale C4 98
Wiltz A2 33
Winchester C3 30
Winchester K2 102
Wind, *river* B3 105
Windermere O6 95
Windermere F2 102
Windfall B4 94
Windhoek, *capital* C2 70
Windsor Inset III 30
Windsor C3 100
Windsor C5 102
Windsor D6 103
Windward Group B2 58
Windward, *islands* B4 91
Windward, *passage* F3 88
Winefred, *lake* E3 94
Winfield N6 95
Wingham D4 102
Winisk C1 101
Winisk, *lake* C2 101
Winisk, *river* C2 101
Winkler C4 96
Winneba B4 64
Winnemucca, Nev. B1 126
Winnipeg C4, D2 96
Winnipeg Beach C4 96
Winnipeg, *lake* B3, C4, D2 96
Winnipeg, *river* D4 96
Winnipegosis B3 96
Winnipegosis, *lake* A3 96
Winslow, Ariz. B2 126
Winston-Salem, N.C. E2 126
Winter Harbour H6 95
Winterthur C1 35
Wisconsin D1 126
Wismar B2 40
Witless Bay E5 98
Witten A3 40
Wittenberg C3 40
Wittenberge B2 40
Witu, *island* A2 15
Wiwili B2 87
Władysławowo D1 41
Włocławek D2 41
Woburn F6 103
Wodzisław Śląski D3 41
Woking A3 94
Wolf, *lake* C5 105
Wolfsberg D4 39
Wolfsburg B2 40
Wolfville C2 100
Wollaston Lake G2 104
Wollaston, *lake* H2 104
Wollaston, *peninsula* E3 99
Wollongong, N.S.W. E3 14
Wolseley G10 104
Wolverhampton C3 30
Wong, *river* A2 19
Wŏnju B4 9
Wonowon M3 95
Wŏnsan B3 9
Wood Islands C3 100
Woodbridge J5 102
Woodlands B1 13
Woodlands C4 96
Woodlark (Muyua), *island* B2 15
Woodnorth A4 96
Woodridge C4 96
Woods, *lake* B3 101
Woodstock B2 97
Woodstock A2 100
Woodstock E4 102
Woody Point C4 98
Woomera, S.A. C3 14
Worcester C3 30
Worcester A3 71
Worcester, Mass. F1 126
Worms B4 40
Wotho, *island* B1 16
Wotje, *island* B2 16
Wrangel, *island* B10 44
Wrath, *cape* B1 30
Wreck Cove D5 98
Wrentham D6 94
Wrigley D4 99
Wrocław C3 41
Wuhan E2 10
Wuhu E2 10
Wukari E4 65
Wum B2 65
Wuppertal A3 40
Würzburg B4 40
Wutivi, *mt.* B1 63
Wuwei D2 10
Wuxi F2 10
Wuzhong D2 10
Wuzhou E3 10
Wye, *river* C3 30
Wyndham, W.A. B1 14
Wynyard F9 104
Wyoming C1 126

X

Xaçmaz C2 45
Xai-Xai B5 68
Xam Nua C1 11
Xangongo C5 70
Xankändi B3 45
Xánthi C1 51
Xau, *lake* B2 69
Xi'an D2 10
Xi, *river* E3 10
Xiamen E3 10
Xiangfan E2 10
Xiangkhoang B2 11
Xiangtan E3 10
Xigaze B3 10
Xingu, *river* C3 81
Xining D2 10
Xinjiang Uygur B1 10
Xinxiang E2 10
Xinyang E2 10
Xochimilco Inset 84
Xuddur A3 60
Xuzhou E2 10

Y

Ya'an D2 10
Yablonovyy, *range* D7 44
Yabucoa D2 90
Yacuiba B4 77
Yafran B1 56
Yaguarí, *river* C1 75
Yaguarón, *river* D2 75
Yahk O6 95
Yakima, Wash. A1 126
Yaku, *island* A4 8
Yakutsk C8 44
Yala B5 12
Yale M6 95
Yalinga B2 66
Yalta C4 47
Yalu, *river* B2 9
Yamagata D2 8
Yamaguchi A3 8
Yamal, *peninsula* C5 44
Yamalo-Nenesiya, *autonomous okrug* C5 44
Yambio B4 59
Yambol E3 50
Yamoussoukro, *capital* D3 63
Yampi, *sound* B1 14
Yamuna, *river* C3 20
Yan, *river* B3 19
Yanbu al-Bahr A1 24
Yangambi C1 67
Yangdŏk B3 9
Yangquan E2 10
Yangtze, *river* C2, D2 10
Yangzhou E2 10
Yanji F1 10
Yantai F2 10
Yantra, *river* D2 50
Yao B3 8
Yaoundé, *capital* B3 65
Yap, *islands* A2 15
Yapen, *island* E2 13
Yaque del Norte, *river* A1 89
Yaque del Sur, *river* A2 89
Yaqui, *river* C2 84
Yare, *river* D3 30
Yaren, *capital* B3 16
Yariga, *mt.* C2 8
Yarmouth A4 100
Yaroslavl D3 44
Yasawa, *island group* A2 17
Yasuj C3 22
Yata, *river* A2 77
Yates B4 94
Yatsushiro A3 8
Yauco B2 90
Yavarí, *river* C1 77
Yaviza D2 87
Yazd C3 22
Yazd, *region* C3 22
Ybbs, *river* D2 39
Ye C3 12
Yeboah C3 30
Yecla F3 37
Yeguas, *point* D2 90
Yekaterinburg D5 44
Yekepa B2 63
Yell, *island* Inset I 30
Yellow Grass F11 104
Yellow, *sea* F2 10
Yellowknife, *capital* F4 99
Yemen **25**
Yen Bai A2 11
Yendi B2 64
Yenisey, *river* C6 44
Yeovil C4 30
Yerevan, *capital* B2 45
Yesilhrmak, *river* D2 27
Yeu, *island* B3 34
Yevlax B2 45
Yevpatoriya C3 47
Yevrey, autonomous oblast E8 44
Yi, *river* C2 75
Yialousa C1 27
Yibin D3 10
Yichang E2 10
Yichun F1 10
Yin Shan, *mts.* E1 10
Yinchuan D2 10
Yingkou F1 10
Yining B1 10
Ylikitka, *lake* C1 53
Ylivieska B2 53
Yoboki B2 60
Yogyakarta C2 13
Yojoa, *lake* B2 86
Yokkaichi C3 8
Yokohama C3 8
Yokosuka C3 8
Yola G3 65
Yom, *river* B2 12
Yomou D4 62
Yonago B3 8
Yonaguni, *island* Inset II 8
Yŏngju C4 9
Yonne, *river* C2 34
Yopal B3 78
York C3 30
York B2 100
York K5 102
York Factory E1 96
York, *cape* D1 14
Yorkton H9 104
Yoro B2 86
Yoron, *island* Inset II 8
Yoshino, *river* B3 8
Yoshkar-Ola D4 44
Yŏsu B5 9
Yotvata B3 26
Youghal C3 31
Young E9 104
Youngs Cove D2 97
Ypané, *river* D3 75
Ypoá, *lake* D4 75
Ypres A2 33
Ysyk-Köl, *lake* E1 23
Yü Shan, *mt.* B2 9
Yuan, *river* D3 10
Yubari Inset I 8
Yucatán, *channel* A2 88
Yucatán, *peninsula* G4 84
Yuen Long Inset 10
Yueyang E3 10
Yugoslavia **49**
Yukon, *river* D2 92
Yuma, Ariz. B2 126
Yumen C2 10
Yuna, *river* B2 89
Yundum B2 62
Yungas, *region* A3 77
Yungho B1 9
Yunnan C3 10
Yurimaguas B2 77
Yuscarán B3 86
Yushu C2 10
Yuzhno-Sakhalinsk E9 44
Yverdon A2 35

Z

Zaanstad B2 32
Zabbar C2 36
Zabid A2 25
Zabol E3 22
Zabrze D3 41
Zacapa D5 85
Zacatecas, *state capital* D3 84
Zacatecoluca B2 86
Zadar B3 48
Zafra C3 37
Zagazig B1 56
Zaghouan C1 57
Zagreb, *capital* B2 48
Zagros, *mts.* B3 22
Zahedan E4 22
Zahlah A2 26
Zaječar C3 49
Zákinthos, *island* B3 51
Zakopane D4 41
Zala, *river* A2 43
Zalaegerszeg A2 43
Zalău B2 43
Zambales, *mts.* B3 12
Zambezi A2 67
Zambezi, *river* A3, B3 67
Zambia **67**
Zamboanga B5 12
Zamboanga, *peninsula* B5 12
Zamora D2 37
Zamora B5 79
Zamora, *river* B4 79
Zamość F3 41
Zanderij B2 80
Zanjan B2 22
Zanzibar C2 68
Zao, *mt.* D2 8
Zapandna Morava, *river* B3 49
Zapatera, *island* B3 87
Zaporizhzhia D2 47
Zaqatala B2 45
Zarafobod A1 23
Zarafshon B2 23
Zaragoza F2 37
Zaranj A2 22
Zareh Sharan B2 22
Zaria D2 65
Zarqa, az- B1 26
Zarzis C3 57
Zavidovići B1 48
Zaysan E2 23
Zaysan, *lake* E2 23
Zebbug A1 36
Zeebrugge B1 33
Zefat B1 26
Zenica B1 48
Zeravshan, *mts.* A1 23
Zeravshan, *river* A1, B2 23
Zermatt B2 35
Zestaponi B3 45
Zeta, *river* A3 49
Zevulun, *plain* B1 26
Zêzere, *river* A3 36
Zhambyl (Dzhambul) D2 23
Zhangjiakou E1 10
Zhangye D2 10
Zhanjiang E3 10
Zhejiang E3 10
Zhelaniya, *cape* B5 44
Zhengzhou E2 10
Zhenjiang E2 10
Zhezqazghan C2 23
Zhitomir B1 47
Zhlobin D3 47
Zhob, *river* C3 21
Zhoda C4 96
Zhu, *river* E3 10
Zhuzhou E3 10
Zibo E2 10
Zielona Góra B3 41
Zigong D3 10
Ziguinchor A3 62
Žilina B2 42
Zillah C2 56
Zillertal Alps, *range* B3 39
Zima, *lake* A2 94
Zimbabwe **69**
Zinder B3 59
Zion C3 90
Zittau C3 40
Ziway, *lake* C3 60
Zlatibor, *mts.* A3 49
Zlín C3 42
Znojmo C4 42
Zomba C3 68
Zonguldak B2 27
Zorzor B2 63
Zouar B2 59
Zouîrât B2 58
Zrenjanin B2 49
Zug C1 35
Zugdidi A3 45
Zugspitze, *mt.* B5 40
Zuid-Willemsvaart, *canal* C3 32
Zújar, *reservoir* D3 37
Zululand, *region* D2 71
Zunyi D3 10
Zürich C1 35
Zürichsee, *lake* C1 35
Zurrieq B2 36
Zuwarah B1 56
Zvishavane B2 69
Zvolen B2 42
Zvornik C1 48
Zwedru B2 63
Zwickau C3 40
Zwolle D2 32
Zyryanka C9 44

Capital: Washington, D.C. **Population:** 272,640,000
Area: 3,787,300 sq. mi. **Largest City:** New York
9,809,200 sq. km. **Monetary Unit:** U.S. dollar

United States

⊛ National Capital
★ State/Provincial Capital
• Other City

1:19,100,000

0   150   300 mi
0   150   300 km

Albers Equal Area Projection

Hawaii
1:20,850,000
0   75   150 mi
0   75   150 km

Alaska
1:43,100,000
0   150   300 mi
0   150   300 km

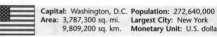

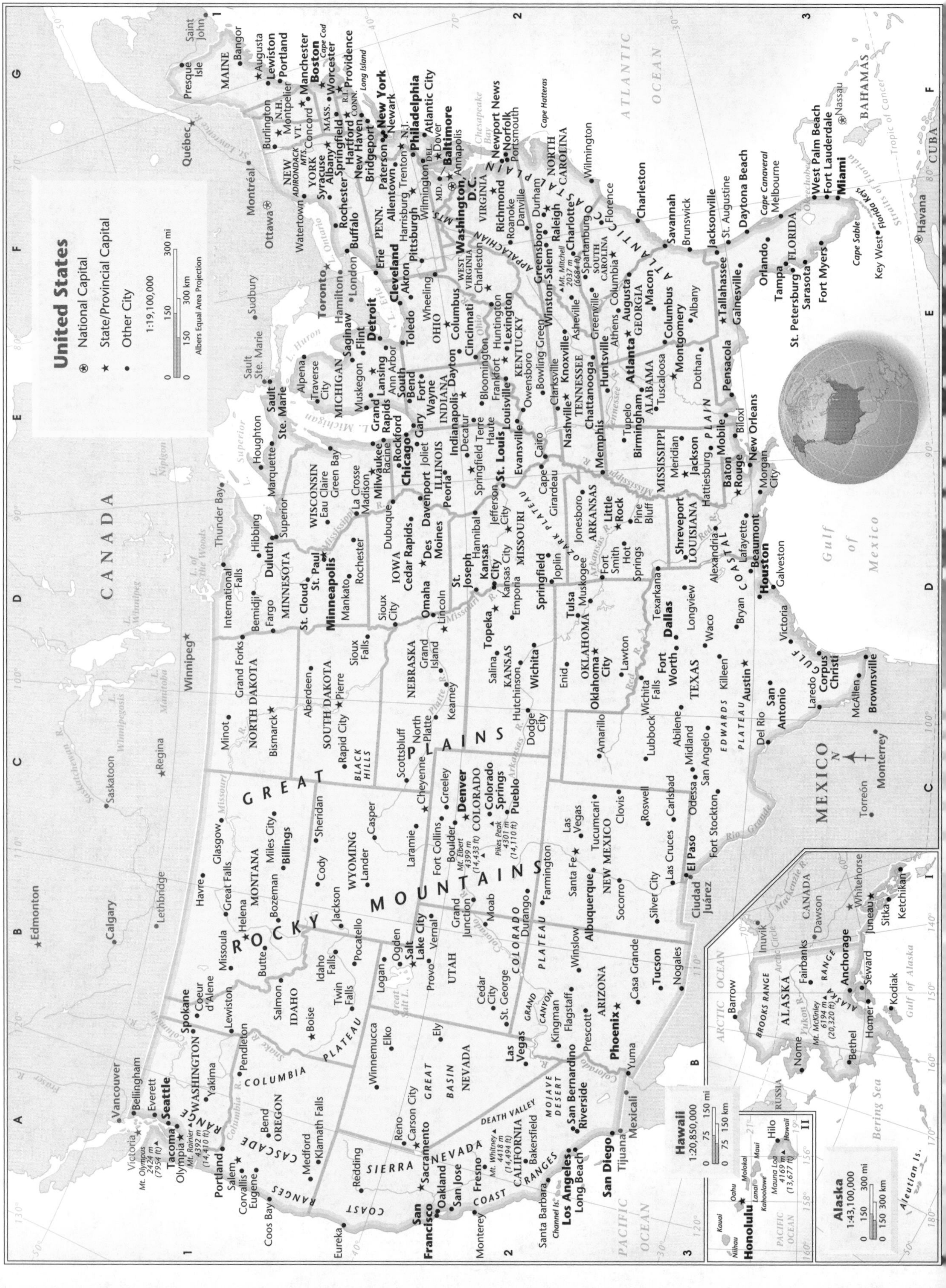

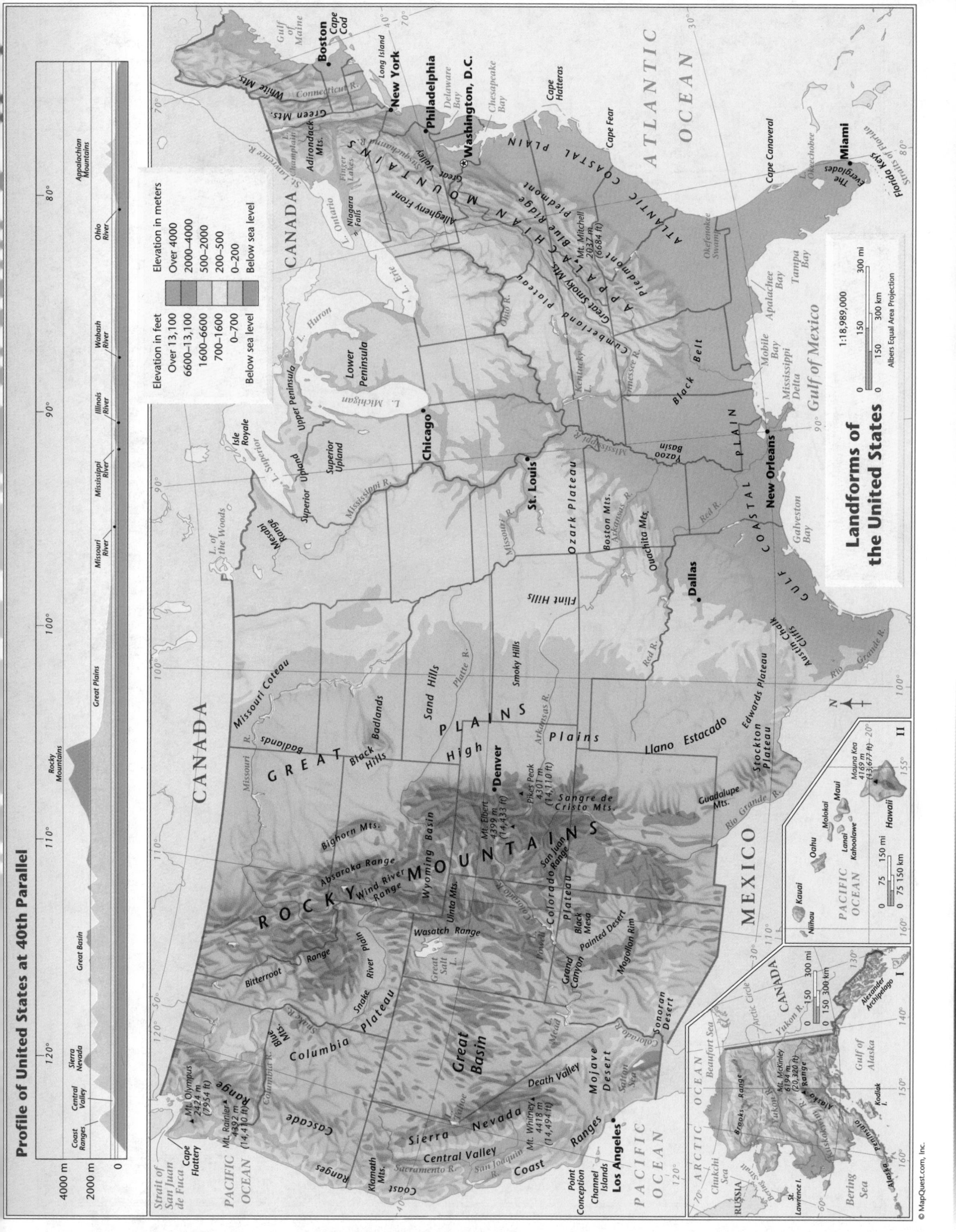

Profile of United States at 40th Parallel

4000 m
2000 m
0

Coast Ranges
Central Valley
Sierra Nevada
Great Basin
Rocky Mountains
Great Plains
Missouri River
Mississippi River
Illinois River
Wabash River
Ohio River
Appalachian Mountains

Elevation in meters
Over 4000
2000–4000
500–2000
0–200
Below sea level

Elevation in feet
Over 13,100
6600–13,100
1600–6600
700–1600
0–700
Below sea level

Landforms of the United States

1:18,989,000

0   150   300 mi
0   150   300 km
Albers Equal Area Projection

CANADA

PACIFIC OCEAN

Strait of San Juan de Fuca
Cape Flattery
Mt. Olympus 2424 m (7954 ft)
▲ Mt. Rainier 4392 m (14,410 ft)
Cascade Range
Klamath Mts.
Coast Ranges
Point Conception
Channel Islands
Los Angeles
Central Valley
Sacramento R.
San Joaquin R.
Sierra Nevada
▲ Mt. Whitney 4418 m (14,494 ft)
Mojave Desert
Salton Sea
Death Valley
Sonoran Desert
Columbia Plateau
Snake River Plain
Blue Mts.
Columbia R.
Snake R.
Range
Great Basin
Great Salt L.
Wasatch Range
L. Mead
Colorado R.
Colorado Plateau
Grand Canyon
Painted Desert
Black Mesa
Mogollon Rim
Powell
Uinta Mts.
Bighorn Mts.
Absaroka Range
Wind River Range
Wyoming Basin
San Juan Mts.
Sangre de Cristo Mts.
▲ Pikes Peak 4301 m (14,110 ft)
Denver
▲ Mt. Elbert 4399 m (14,433 ft)
R O C K Y   M O U N T A I N S
Guadalupe Mts.
Llano Estacado
Edwards Plateau
Stockton Plateau
Austin Chalk Cuesta
Rio Grande
MEXICO
Bitterroot Range
Missouri Coteau
Badlands
Missouri R.
Black Hills
Badlands
Sand Hills
Platte R.
High Plains
G R E A T   P L A I N S
Smoky Hills
Flint Hills
Arkansas R.
Red R.
Red R.
Dallas
Boston Mts.
Ouachita Mts.
Arkansas R.
Ozark Plateau
St. Louis
Missouri R.
Mississippi R.
Mississippi R.
Yazoo Basin
New Orleans
Galveston Bay
GULF COASTAL PLAIN
Black Belt
Mississippi Delta
Mobile Bay
Apalachee Bay
Tampa Bay
Gulf of Mexico
Okefenokee Swamp
The Everglades
L. Okeechobee
Miami
Florida Keys
Straits of Florida
Cape Canaveral
ATLANTIC COASTAL PLAIN
Cape Fear
Cape Hatteras
ATLANTIC OCEAN
Piedmont
Blue Ridge
Great Smoky Mts.
▲ Mt. Mitchell 2037 m (6684 ft)
A P P A L A C H I A N   M O U N T A I N S
Cumberland Plateau
Tennessee R.
Kentucky L.
Ohio R.
Allegheny Front
Susquehanna R.
Great Valley
Washington, D.C.
Philadelphia
Delaware Bay
Chesapeake Bay
New York
Long Island
Boston
Cape Cod
Gulf of Maine
White Mts.
Green Mts.
Connecticut R.
Adirondack Mts.
L. Champlain
St. Lawrence R.
Finger Lakes
Niagara Falls
L. Ontario
L. Erie
L. Huron
Chicago
L. Michigan
Lower Peninsula
Upper Peninsula
Superior Upland
Isle Royale
L. Superior
Mesabi Range
Superior Upland
L. of the Woods
CANADA
CANADA
N

Hawaii (inset II)
Kauai
Niihau
Oahu
Molokai
Lanai
Kahoolawe
Maui
Hawaii
▲ Mauna Kea 4169 m (13,677 ft)
PACIFIC OCEAN
0   75   150 mi
0   75   150 km

Alaska (inset I)
RUSSIA
Bering Sea
Chukchi Sea
ARCTIC OCEAN
Beaufort Sea
Arctic Circle
Brooks Range
Yukon R.
Alaska Range
▲ Mt. McKinley 6194 m (20,320 ft)
Gulf of Alaska
Kodiak I.
Alaska Peninsula
Aleutian Islands
St. Lawrence I.
Seward Peninsula
Norton Sound
Alexander Archipelago
CANADA
PACIFIC OCEAN
0   150   300 mi
0   150   300 km

© MapQuest.com, Inc.

Capital: Montgomery
Area: 52,400 sq. mi.
135,800 sq. km.
Population: 4,352,000
Largest City: Birmingham

Alabama

★ State Capital — Limited Access Highway
• County Seat — Other Major Road

1:2,443,000

0   25   50 mi
0 25 50 75 km

Albers Equal Area Projection

© MapQuest.com, Inc.

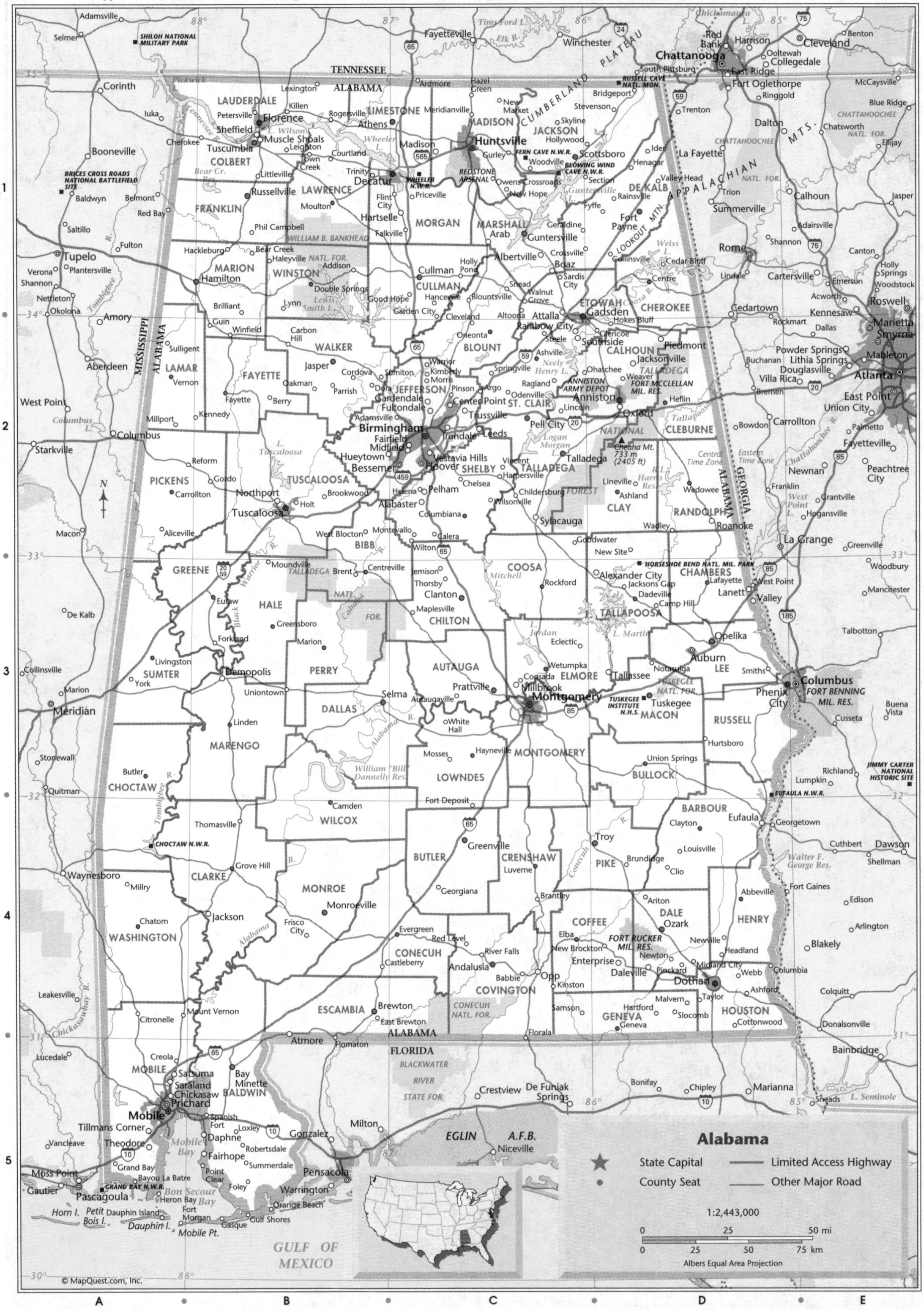

Capital: Juneau
Area: 656,400 sq. mi.
1,700,000 sq. km.
Population: 614,000
Largest City: Anchorage

Alaska

★ State/Territorial Capital
— Paved Road
--- Unpaved Road

1:11,795,000

Lambert Conformal Conic Projection

300 mi
450 km

RUSSIA

CANADA

MACKENZIE MOUNTAINS

SELWYN MTS.

N.W. TERR.

YUKON

BRITISH COLUMBIA

COAST MOUNTAINS

CONTINENTAL DIVIDE

DAWSON RANGE

RICHARDSON MTS.

Beaufort Sea

Chukchi Sea

ARCTIC OCEAN

NORTH SLOPE

BROOKS RANGE

ALASKA RANGE

KUSKOKWIM MOUNTAINS

SEWARD PENINSULA

LISBURNE PENINSULA

Norton Sound

Kotzebue Sound

YUKON DELTA N.W.R.

Bering Sea

Bristol Bay

ALASKA PENINSULA

ALEUTIAN ISLANDS

Gulf of Alaska

PACIFIC OCEAN

WRANGELL ST. ELIAS N.P. AND PRES.

KLUANE N.P.

CHUGACH NATL. FOR.

KENAI PEN.

Cook Inlet

Anchorage

Fairbanks

Juneau

Whitehorse

DENALI N.P. AND PRES.

Mt. McKinley 6194 m (20,320 ft)

Prudhoe Bay

Barrow

Nome

Bethel

Kodiak Island

St. Lawrence I.

Nunivak Island

St. Matthew I.

Pribilof Islands

ARCTIC NATL. WILDLIFE REF. (ARCTIC N.W.R.)

GATES OF THE ARCTIC N.P. AND PRES.

NOATAK NATL. PRES.

KOBUK VALLEY

SELAWIK N.W.R.

KANUTI N.W.R.

YUKON FLATS N.W.R.

STEESE N.R.A.

WHITE MTS. N.R.A.

YUKON-CHARLEY RIVERS NATL. PRES.

TETLIN N.W.R.

INNOKO N.W.R.

NOWITNA N.W.R.

KOYUKUK N.W.R.

TOGIAK N.W.R.

BECHAROF N.W.R.

ALASKA PENINSULA N.W.R.

ANIAKCHAK NATL. MON. AND PRES.

KATMAI N.P. & PRES.

KODIAK N.W.R.

KENAI N.W.R.

LAKE CLARK N.P. AND PRES.

KENAI FJORDS N.P.

TETLIN N.W.R.

GLACIER BAY N.P. AND PRES.

TONGASS NATL. FOR.

KLONDIKE GOLD RUSH N.H.P.

SITKA N.H.P.

ALEXANDER ARCHIPELAGO

Prince of Wales I.

Ketchikan

Sitka

Wrangell

Petersburg

Skagway

Haines

Yakutat

Valdez

Cordova

Seward

Homer

Kenai

Soldotna

Wasilla

Palmer

Healy

Cantwell

Talkeetna

McGrath

Galena

Tanana

Nenana

Delta Jct.

Tok

Northway Jct.

Eagle

Circle

Central

Fort Yukon

Arctic Village

Venetie

Bettles

Allakaket

Hughes

Huslia

Koyukuk

Ruby

Poorman

Ophir

Flat

Holy Cross

Russian Mission

Marshall

St. Mary's

Pilot Station

Emmonak

Alakanuk

Scammon Bay

Hooper Bay

Chevak

Kwethluk

Napaskiak

Eek

Quinhagak

Goodnews Bay

Togiak

Dillingham

Aleknagik

Naknek

King Salmon

Egegik

Pilot Point

Port Heiden

Chignik

Sand Point

Cold Bay

False Pass

Unalaska

Dutch Harbor

Akutan

CHUKCHI PENINSULA

St. Paul I.

St. George I.

Umnak Island

Unimak Island

Unalaska Island

Shumagin Islands

Sanak Island

Kodiak

Homer

Seldovia

Anchor Point

Ninilchik

Clam Gulch

Trinity Islands

Chirikof Island

Queen Charlotte Islands

MISTY FJORDS NATL. MON.

TWEEDSMUIR PROV. PARK

MUNCHO LAKE PROV. PARK

STONE MOUN. PROV. PARK

SPATSIZI PLATEAU WILDERNESS PROV. PARK

EDZIZA PROV. PARK

KWADACHA WILDERNESS PROV. PARK

ATLIN PROV. PARK

NAHANNI N.P.

CASSIAR MTS.

ALASKA HWY.

RICHARDSON HWY.

DALTON HWY.

STEESE HWY.

INTERNATIONAL DATE LINE

Arctic Circle

Alaska Time Zone

Pacific Time Zone

Mountain Time Zone

Hawaii-Aleutian Time Zone

Samoa Time Zone

Mt. McKinley 6194 m (20,320 ft)

Mt. St. Elias 5489 m (18,008 ft)

Mt. Logan 5951 m (19,524 ft)

Mt. Fairweather 4663 m (15,300 ft)

Mt. Blackburn 4996 m (16,390 ft)

Mt. Michelson 2700 m (8855 ft)

Mt. Joy 2236 m (7333 ft)

Mt. Veniaminof 2507 m (8225 ft)

Pavlof 2857 m (9372 ft)

Shishaldin 2857 m (9372 ft)

© MapQuest.com, Inc.

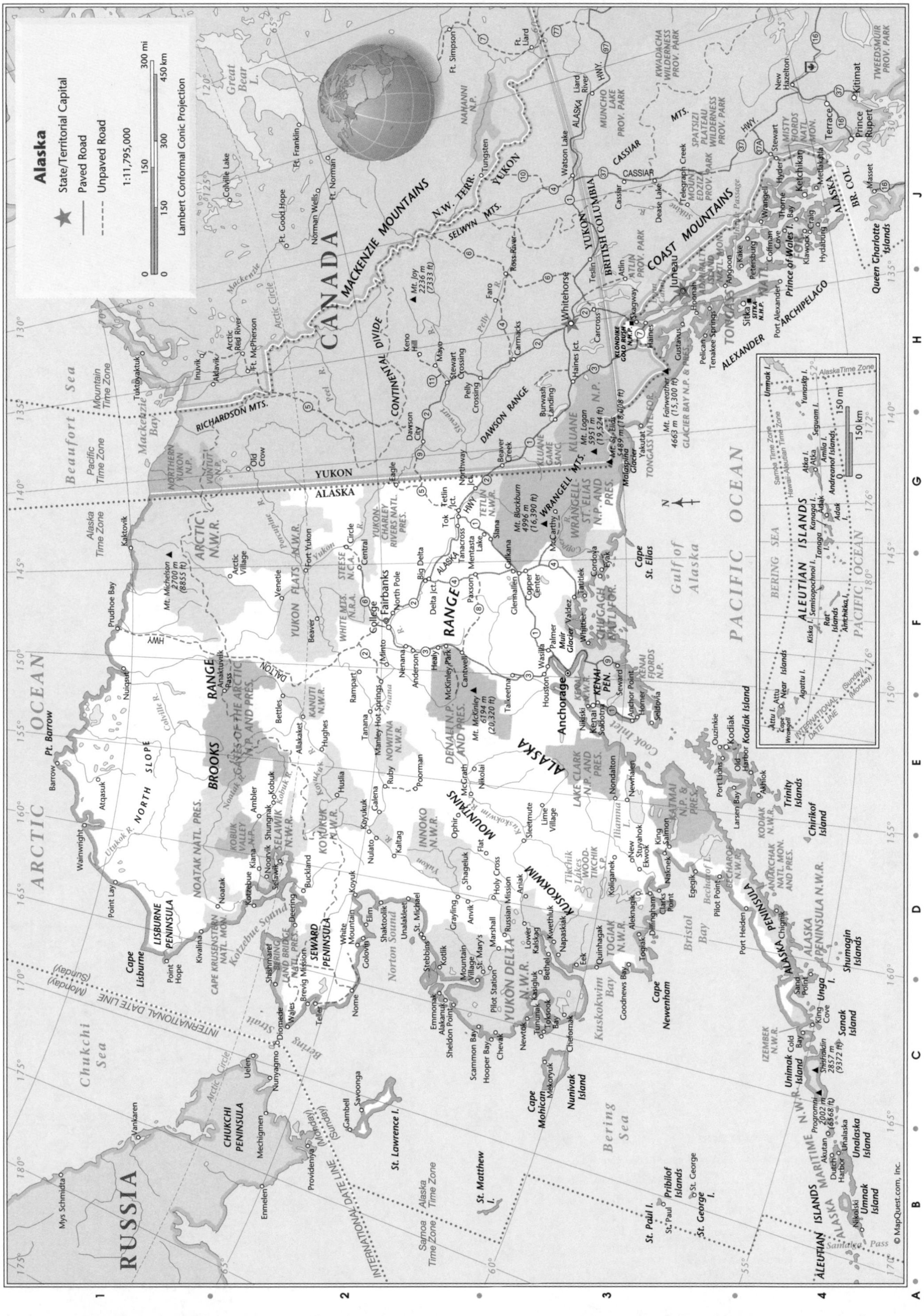

Capital: Phoenix
Area: 114,000 sq. mi.
295,300 sq. km.
Population: 4,669,000
Largest City: Phoenix

Arizona

★ State Capital
● County Seat

— Limited Access Highway
— Other Major Road

1:3,307,000

0 ___ 50 ___ 100mi
0 ___ 50 ___ 100 ___ 150 km
Albers Equal Area Projection

© MapQuest.com, Inc.

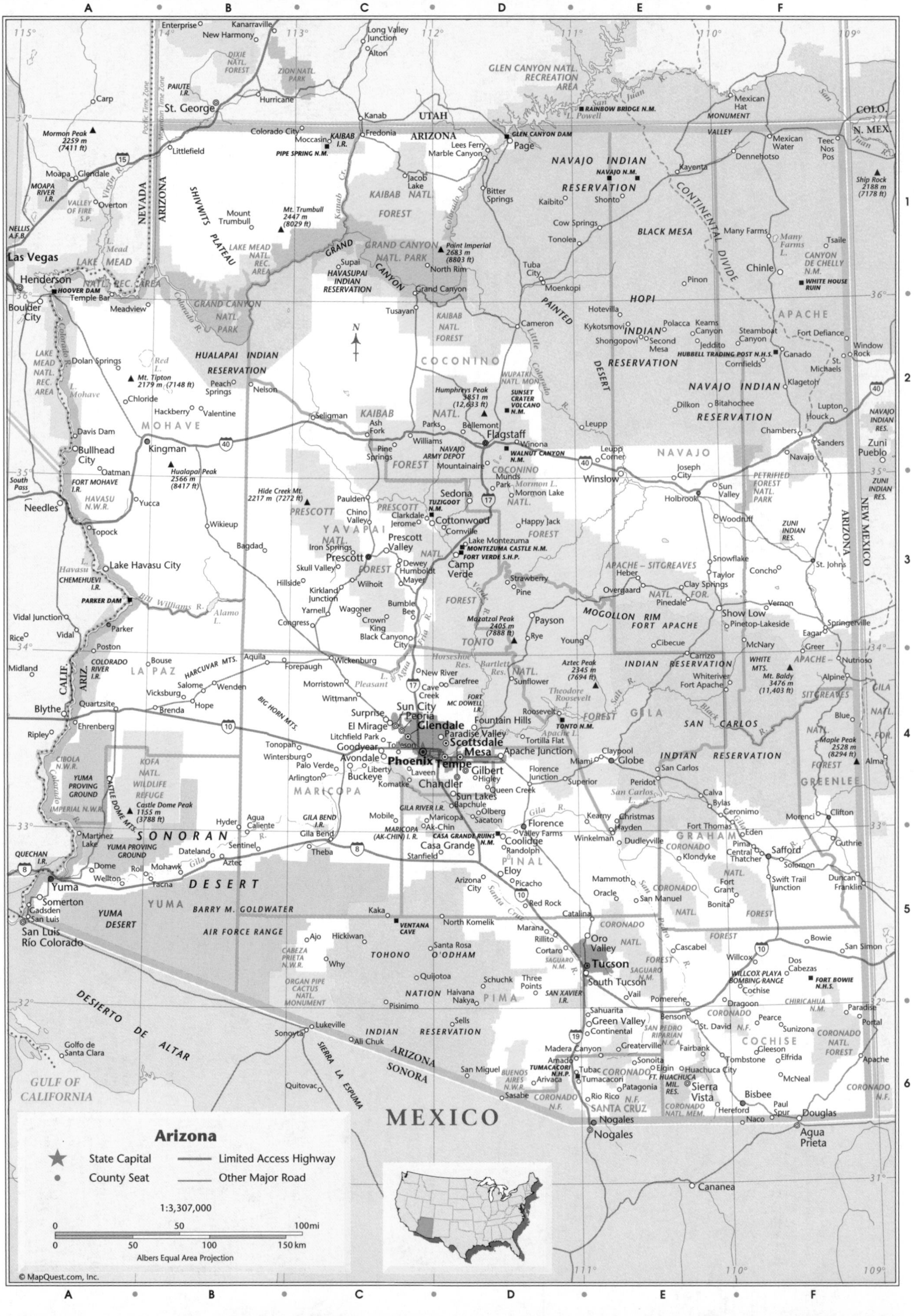

Capital: Little Rock
Area: 53,200 sq. mi.
137,700 sq. km.
Population: 2,538,000
Largest City: Little Rock

Arkansas

★ State Capital
• County Seat

Limited Access Highway
Other Major Road

1:2,507,000

Albers Equal Area Projection

© MapQuest.com, Inc.

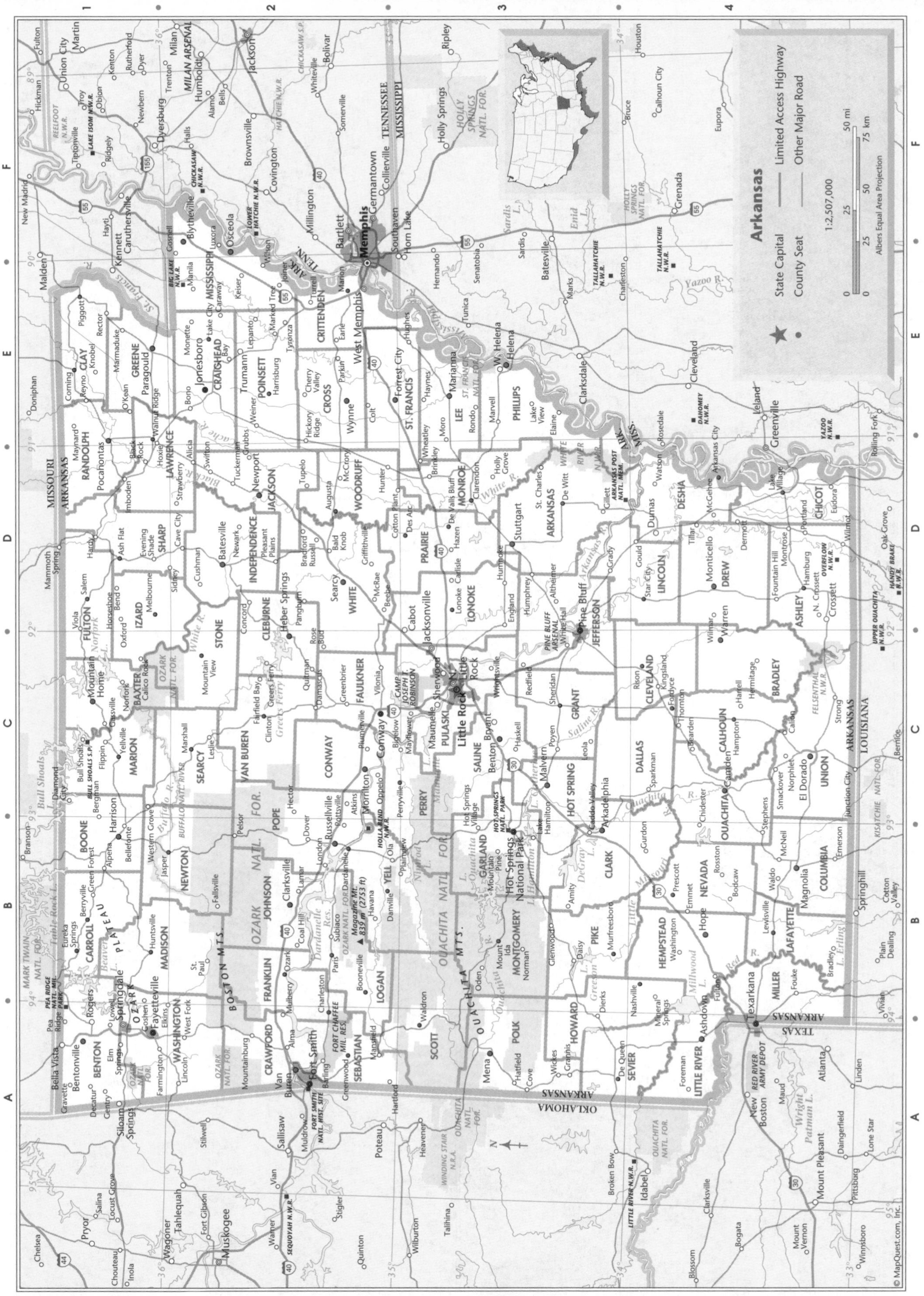

Capital: Sacramento
Area: 163,700 sq. mi.
424,000 sq. km.
Population: 32,667,000
Largest City: Los Angeles

California

★ State Capital
• County Seat

— Limited Access Highway
— Other Major Road

1:5,273,000

0   50   100 mi
0   50   100   150 km
Albers Equal Area Projection

© MapQuest.com, Inc.

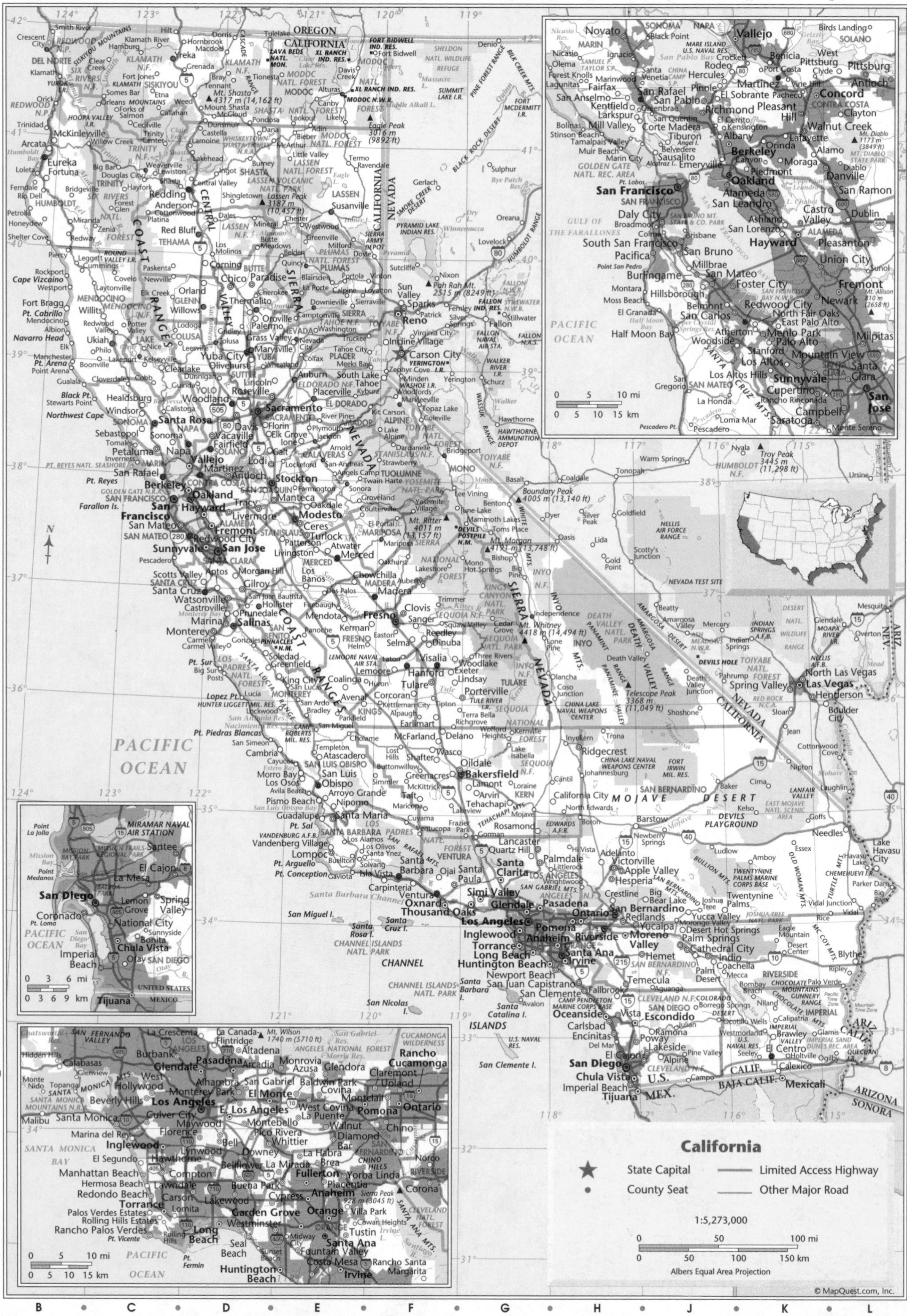

Capital: Denver
Area: 104,100 sq. mi.
269,600 sq. km.
Population: 3,971,000
Largest City: Denver

Colorado

★ State Capital
• County Seat
| Limited Access Highway
| Other Major Road

1:3,137,000
Albers Equal Area Projection

0   25   50 mi
0   25   50   75 km

© MapQuest.com, Inc.

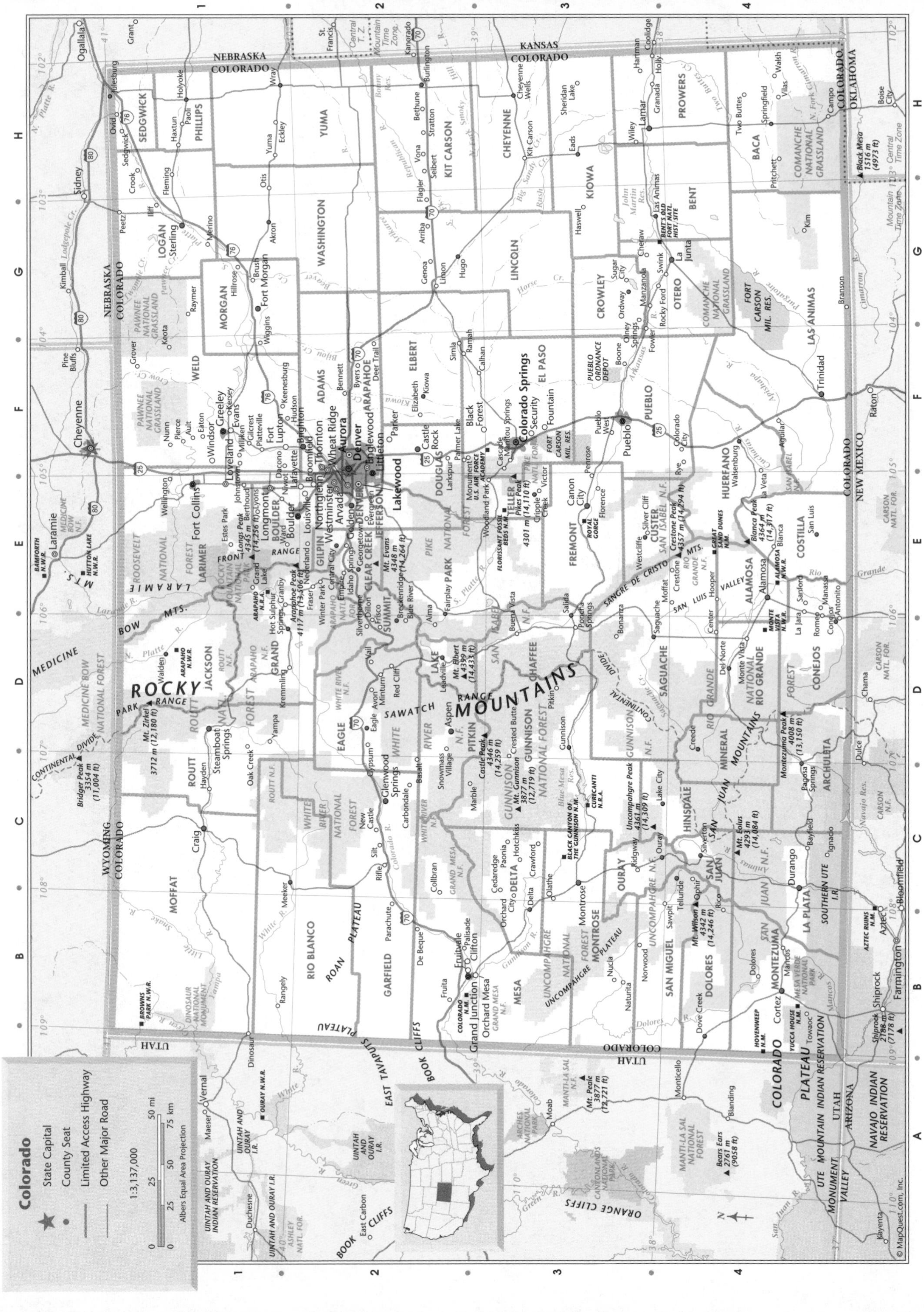

Capital: Hartford
Area: 5,500 sq. mi.
14,400 sq. km.
Population: 3,274,000
Largest City: Bridgeport

Connecticut

★ State Capital
— Limited Access Highway
— Other Major Road

1:750,000

Albers Equal Area Projection

© MapQuest.com, Inc.

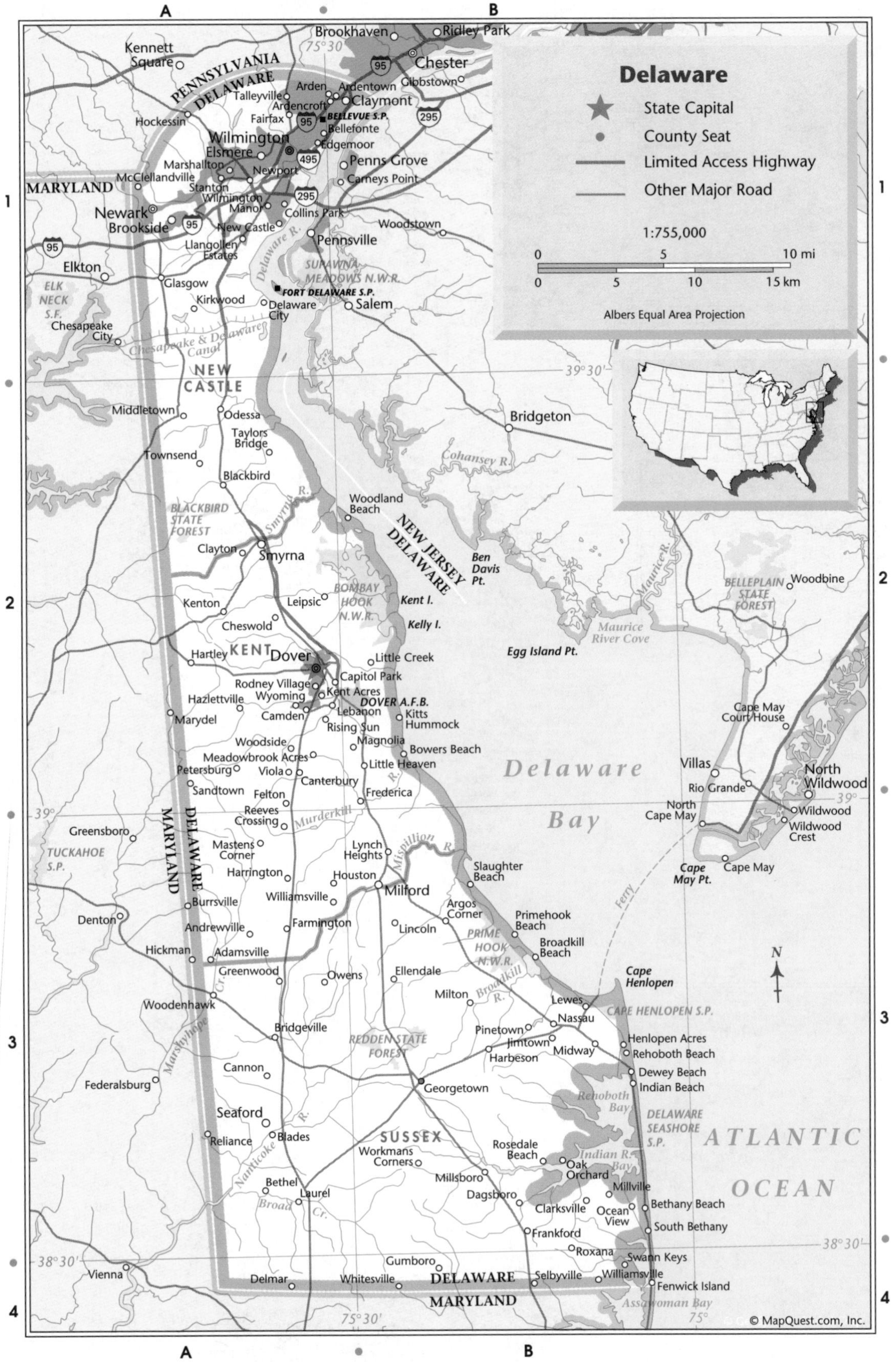
Delaware
State Capital
County Seat
Limited Access Highway
Other Major Road
1:755,000
0 5 10 mi
0 5 10 15 km
Albers Equal Area Projection
A
B
1
2
3
4
PENNSYLVANIA
DELAWARE
MARYLAND
NEW JERSEY
DELAWARE
NEW CASTLE
KENT
SUSSEX
Delaware Bay
ATLANTIC OCEAN
Brookhaven
Ridley Park
Chester
Kennett Square
Arden
Ardentown
Gibbstown
Talleyville
Ardencroft
Claymont
Hockessin
Fairfax
BELLEVUE S.P.
Bellefonte
Wilmington
Elsmere
Edgemoor
Marshallton
Newport
Penns Grove
McClellandville
Stanton
Carneys Point
Wilmington Manor
Collins Park
Newark
Brookside
New Castle
Woodstown
Llangollen Estates
Pennsville
Elkton
SUPAWNA MEADOWS N.W.R.
Glasgow
FORT DELAWARE S.P.
ELK NECK S.F.
Kirkwood
Delaware City
Salem
Chesapeake City
Chesapeake & Delaware Canal
39°30'
Middletown
Odessa
Taylors Bridge
Bridgeton
Townsend
Cohansey R.
Blackbird
BLACKBIRD STATE FOREST
Woodland Beach
Smyrna R.
Clayton
Smyrna
Ben Davis Pt.
Maurice R.
BELLEPLAIN STATE FOREST
Woodbine
BOMBAY HOOK N.W.R.
Kenton
Leipsic
Kent I.
Cheswold
Kelly I.
Maurice River Cove
Hartley
Dover
Little Creek
Egg Island Pt.
Capitol Park
Rodney Village
Kent Acres
Hazlettville
Wyoming
DOVER A.F.B.
Camden
Lebanon
Kitts Hummock
Marydel
Rising Sun
Cape May Court House
Woodside
Magnolia
Bowers Beach
Meadowbrook Acres
Petersburg
Viola
Little Heaven
Villas
North Wildwood
Canterbury
Sandtown
Rio Grande
Felton
Frederica
North Cape May
Wildwood
Reeves Crossing
Murderkill
39°
Wildwood Crest
Greensboro
Mastens Corner
Lynch Heights
Mispillion R.
Slaughter Beach
TUCKAHOE S.P.
Cape May Pt.
Cape May
Harrington
Houston
Milford
Burrsville
Williamsville
Argos Corner
Ferry
Denton
Primehook Beach
Farmington
Andrewville
Lincoln
PRIME HOOK N.W.R.
Broadkill Beach
Hickman
Adamsville
Greenwood
Owens
Ellendale
Cape Henlopen
N
Milton
Broadkill R.
Woodenhawk
Lewes
CAPE HENLOPEN S.P.
Nassau
Bridgeville
Pinetown
REDDEN STATE FOREST
Jimtown
Henlopen Acres
Midway
Harbeson
Rehoboth Beach
Cannon
Marshyhope Cr.
Dewey Beach
Federalsburg
Georgetown
Indian Beach
Rehoboth Bay
DELAWARE SEASHORE S.P.
Seaford
Blades
Reliance
Nanticoke R.
Rosedale Beach
Workmans Corners
Oak Orchard
Indian R. Bay
Bethel
Millsboro
Millville
Laurel
Dagsboro
Bethany Beach
Broad Cr.
Clarksville
Ocean View
South Bethany
Frankford
Roxana
38°30'
Swann Keys
Gumboro
Vienna
Williamsville
Selbyville
Delmar
Whitesville
Fenwick Island
Assawoman Bay
75°30'
75°
© MapQuest.com, Inc.

Capital: Tallahassee
Area: 65,800 sq. mi.
170,300 sq. km.
Population: 14,916,000
Largest City: Jacksonville

Capital: Atlanta
Area: 59,400 sq. mi.
153,900 sq. km.
Population: 7,642,000
Largest City: Atlanta

Georgia

★ State Capital
● County Seat
— Limited Access Highway
— Other Major Road

1:2,670,000

0   25   50   75 mi
0 25 50 75 100 km

Albers Equal Area Projection

© MapQuest.com, Inc.

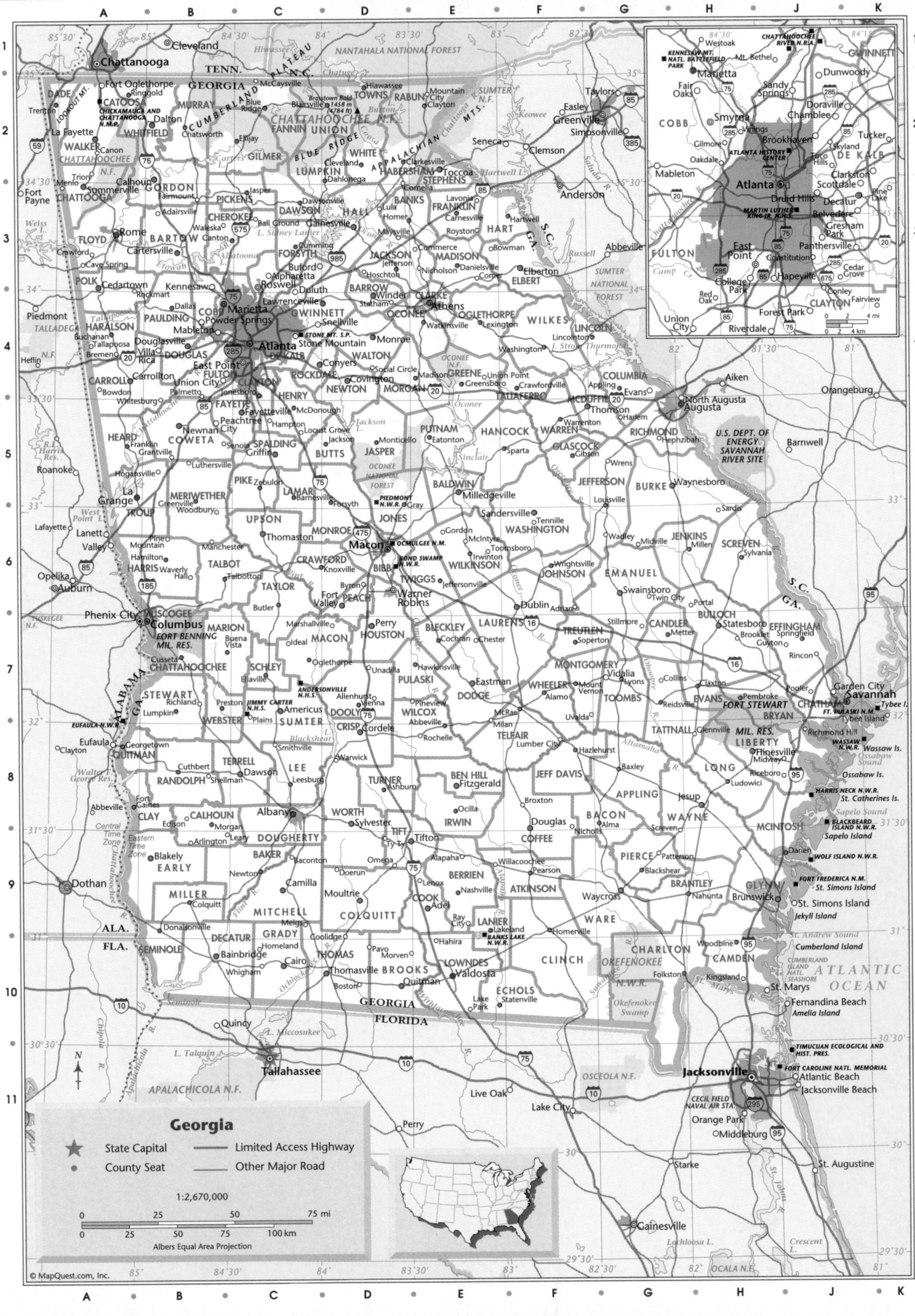

Capital: Honolulu
Area: 10,900 sq. mi.
28,300 sq. km.
Population: 1,193,000
Largest City: Honolulu

Hawaii
1:3,295,000
Mercator Projection

State Capital
County Seat
Limited Access Highway
Other Major Road

© MapQuest.com, Inc.

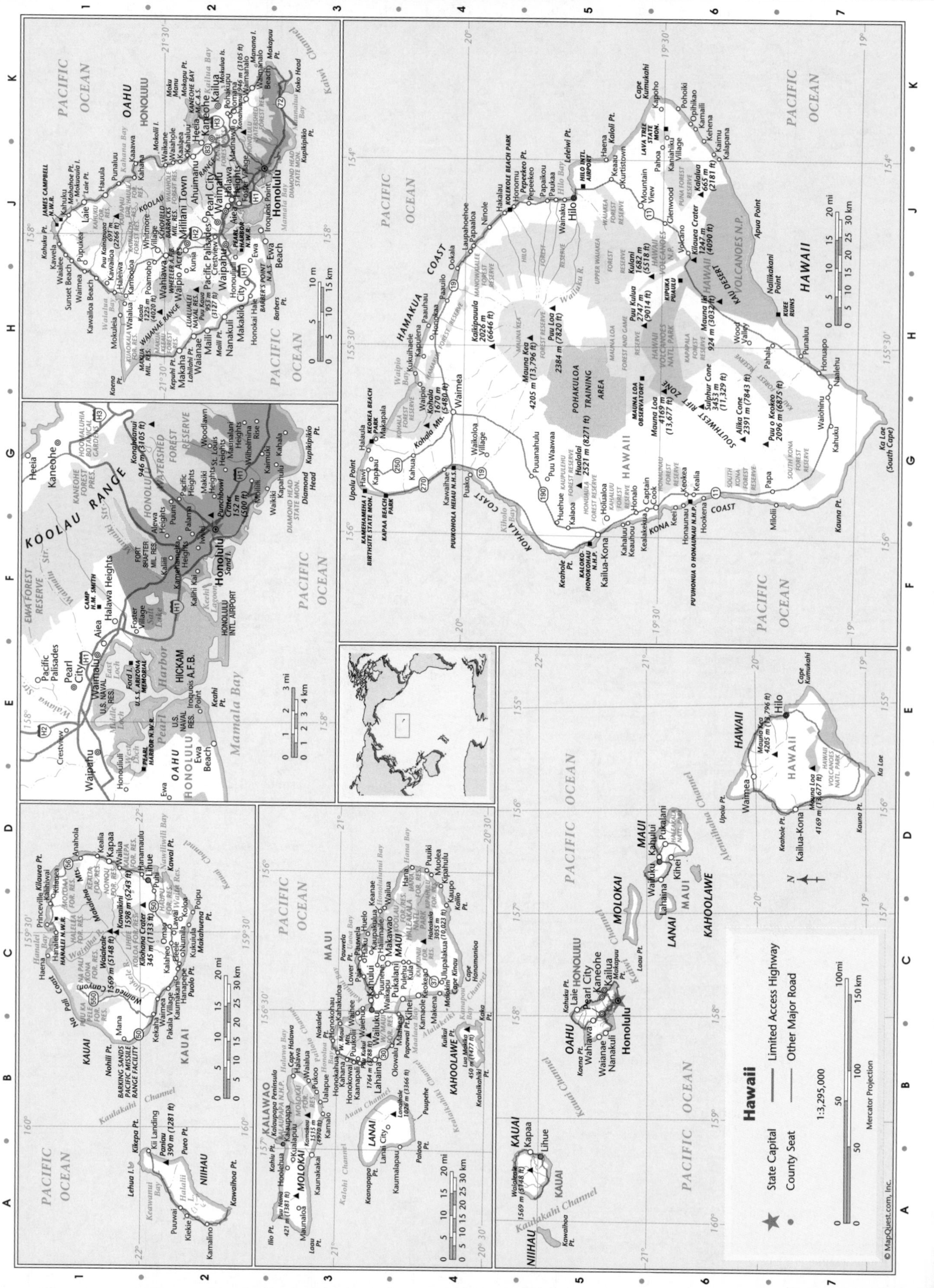

Capital: Boise
Area: 83,600 sq. mi.
216,500 sq. km.
Population: 1,229,000
Largest City: Boise

Idaho

★ State Capital
● County Seat

— Limited Access Highway
— Other Major Road

1:3,295,000

0   50   100mi
0   50   100   150 km

Albers Equal Area Projection

© MapQuest.com, Inc.

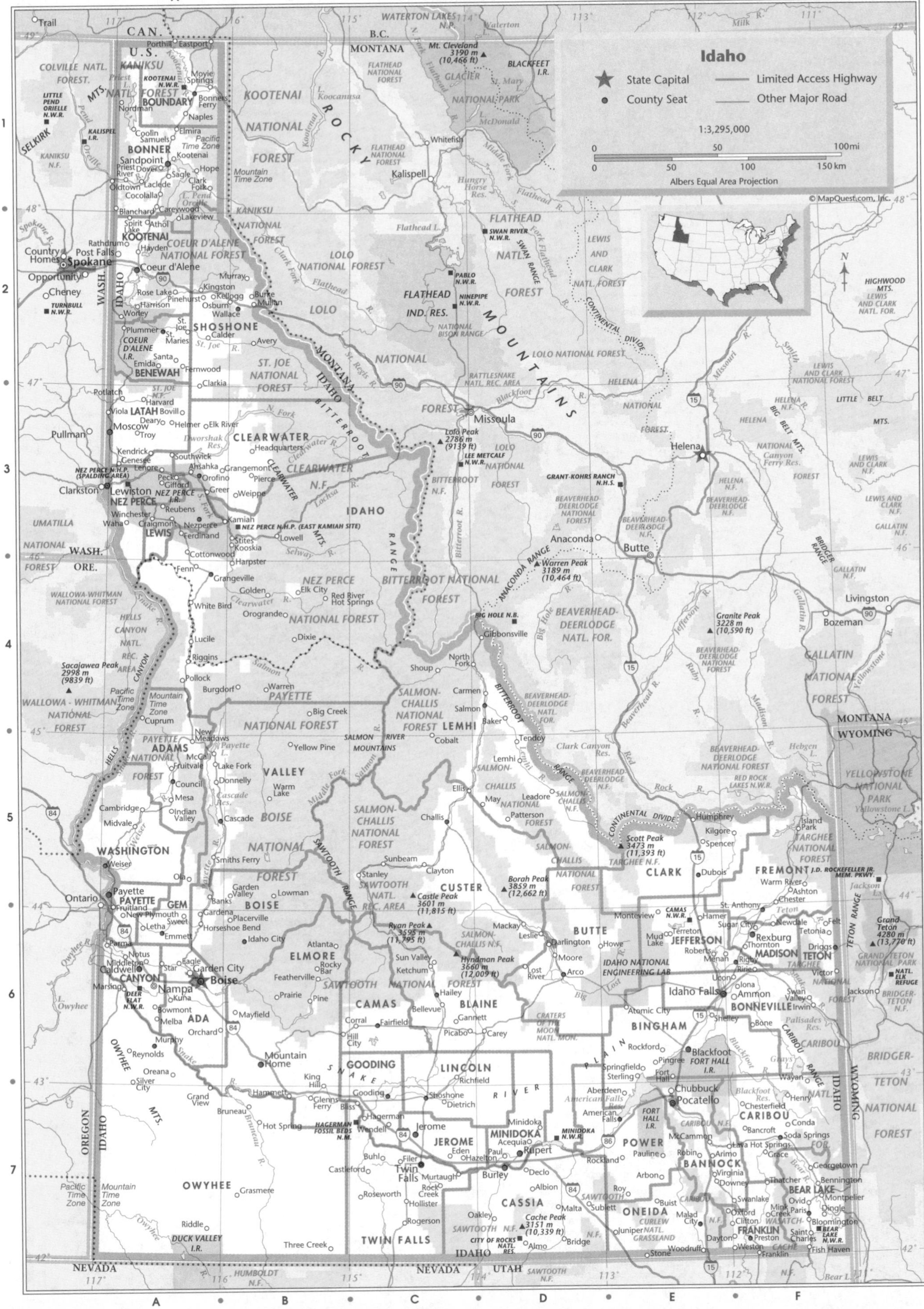

Capital: Springfield
Area: 57,900 sq. mi.
150,000 sq. km.
Population: 12,045,000
Largest City: Chicago

Illinois

★ State Capital
● County Seat

── Limited Access Highway
── Other Major Road

1:2,635,000

0   25   50 mi

0 25 50 75 km

Albers Equal Area Projection

© MapQuest.com, Inc.

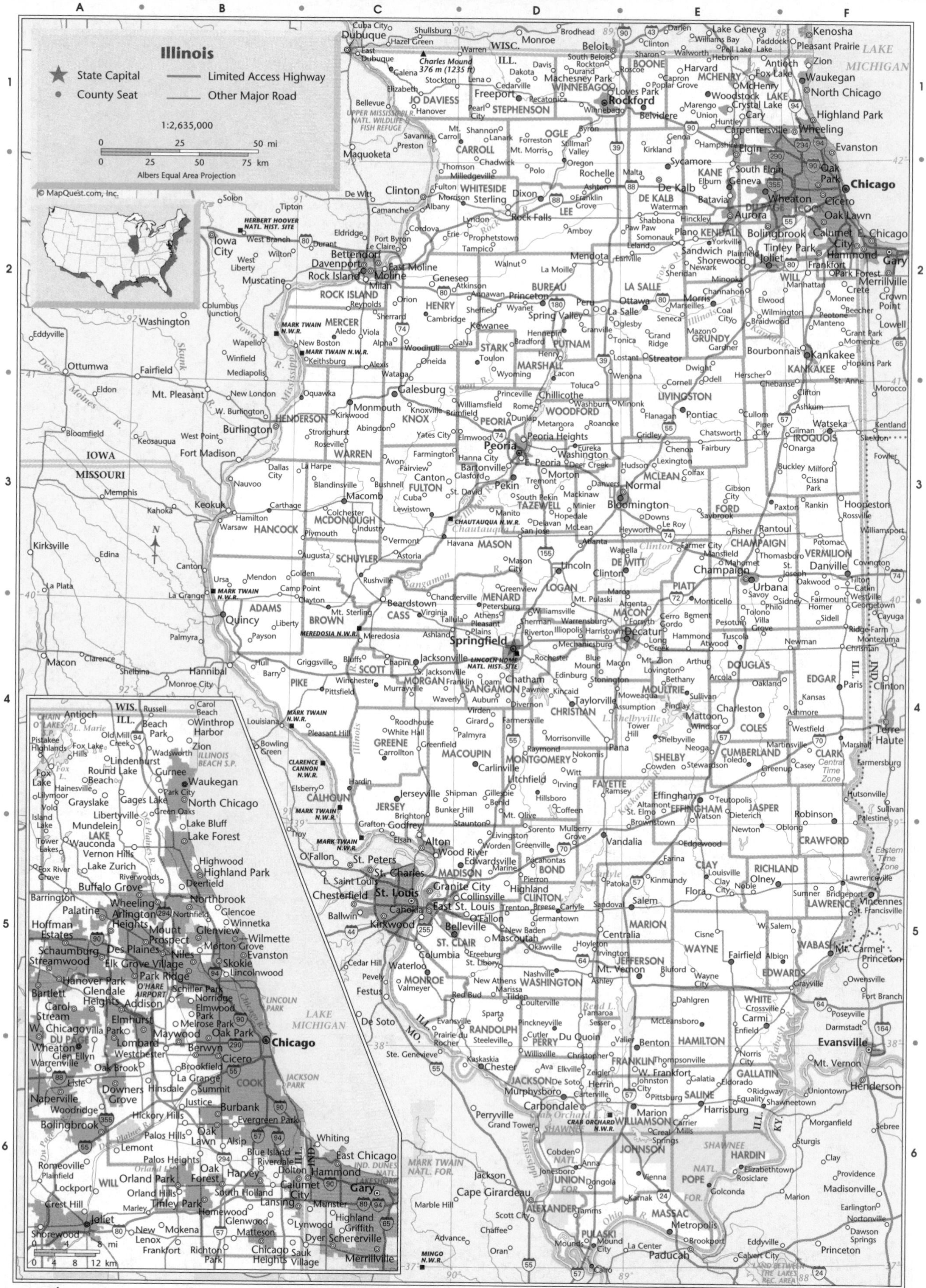

Capital: Indianapolis
Area: 36,400 sq. mi.
94,300 sq. km.
Population: 5,899,000
Largest City: Indianapolis

Lake Michigan
MICH.
IND.
ILLINOIS
INDIANA
OHIO
KY.
IND.

Central Time Zone
Eastern Time Zone

Indiana

★ State Capital
● County Seat

—— Limited Access Highway
—— Other Major Road

1:2,099,000

0   25   50 mi
0   25   50   75 km

Albers Equal Area Projection

© MapQuest.com, Inc.

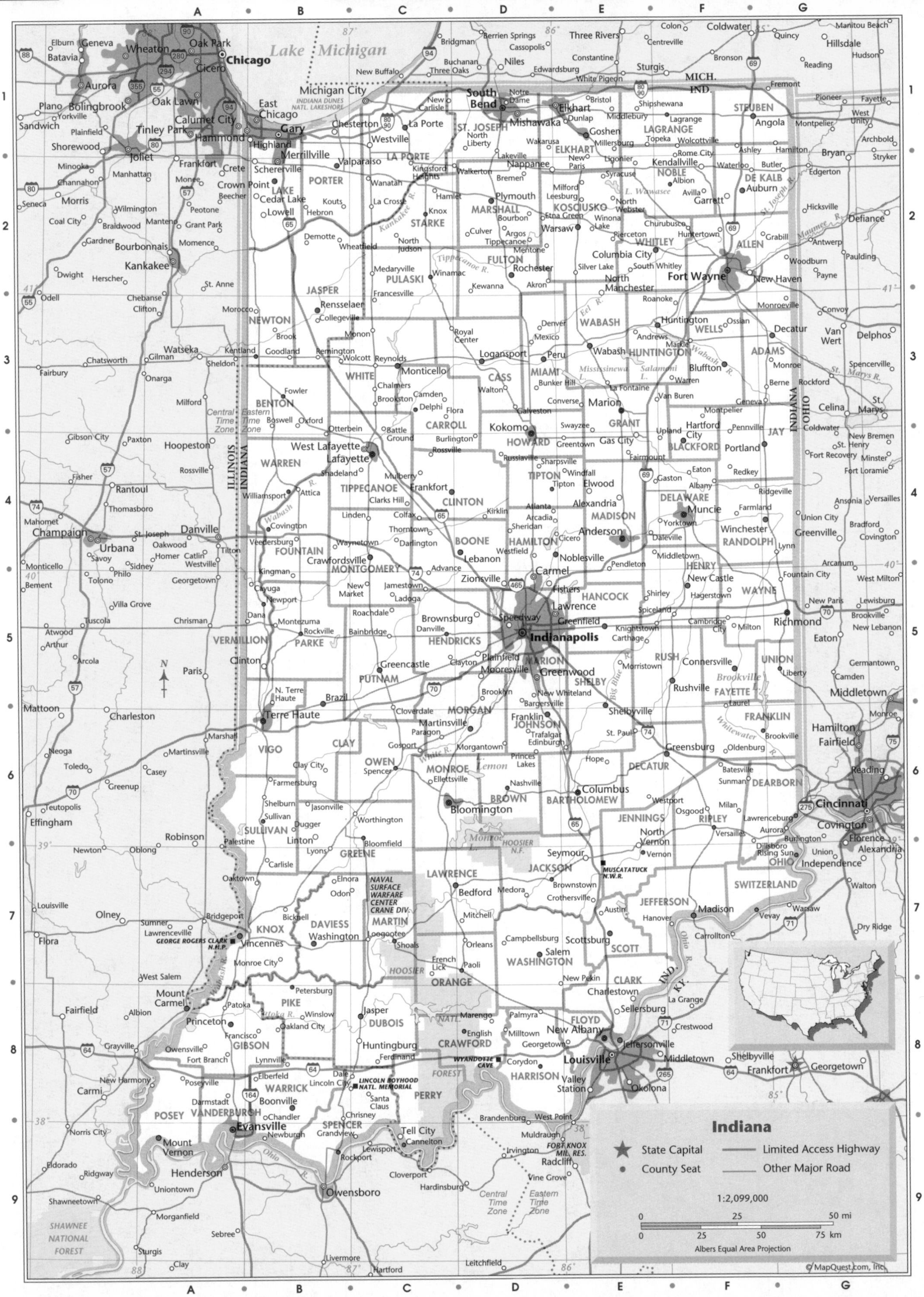

Capital: Des Moines
Area: 56,300 sq. mi.
145,800 sq. km.
Population: 2,862,000
Largest City: Des Moines

Iowa
1:2,500,000
Albers Equal Area Projection

★ State Capital
● County Seat

Limited Access Highway
Other Major Road

0   40   80   80 mi
0   40   80   120 km

© MapQuest.com, Inc.

KANSAS

Capital: Topeka
Area: 82,300 sq. mi.
213,100 sq. km.

Population: 2,629,000
Largest City: Wichita

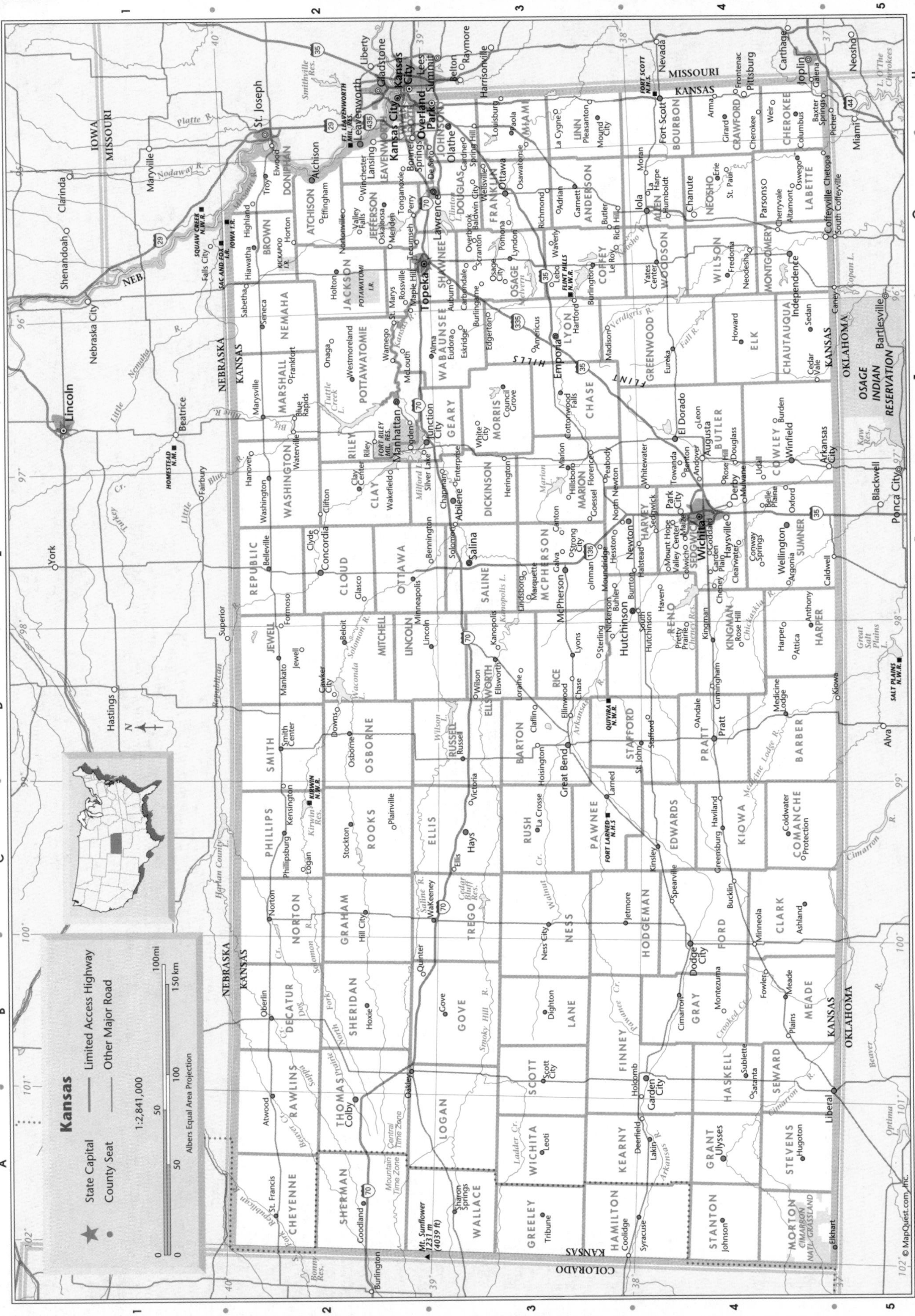

Capital: Frankfort
Area: 40,400 sq. mi.
104,700 sq. km.

Population: 3,936,000
Largest City: Louisville

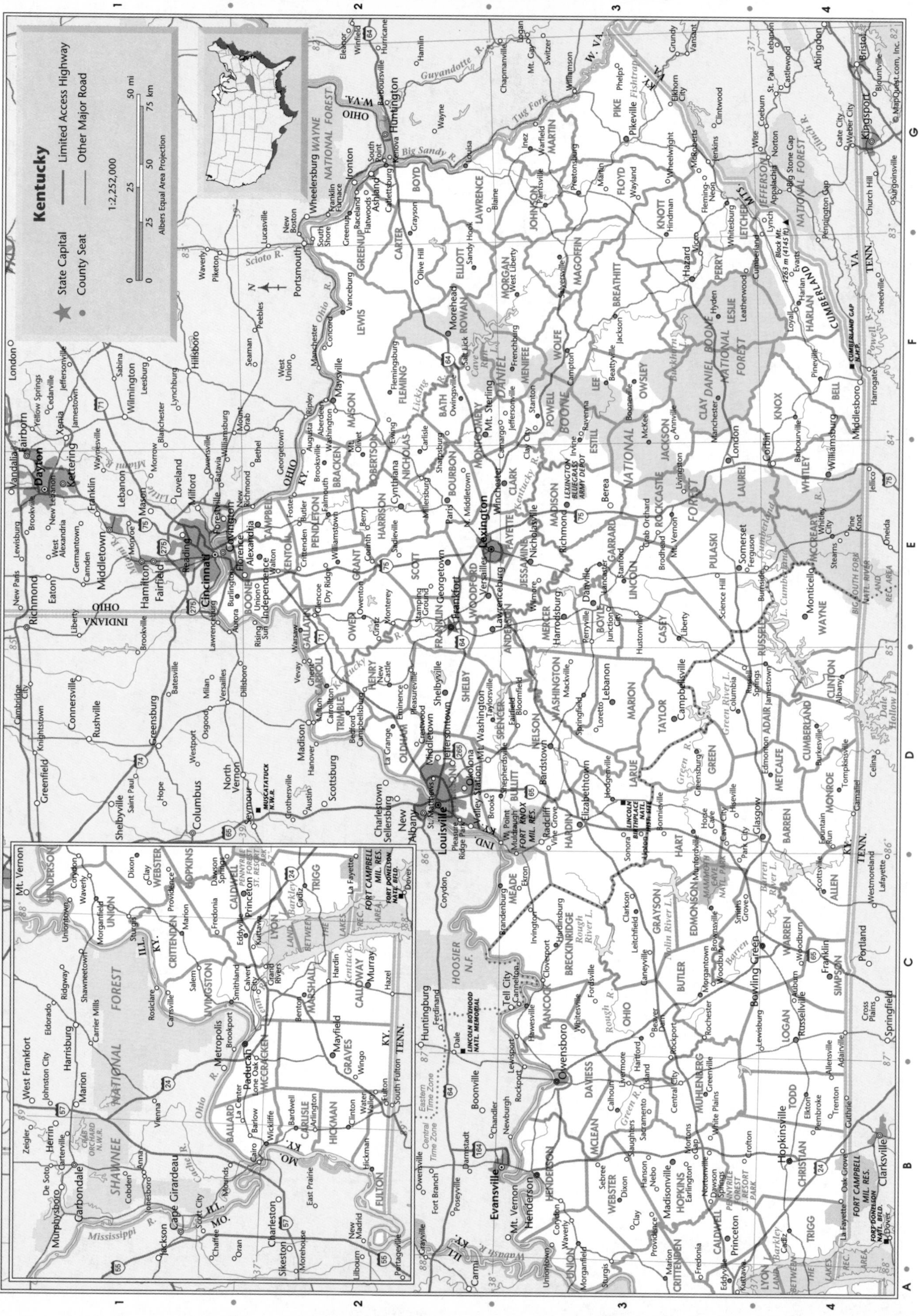

Capital: Baton Rouge
Area: 51,800 sq. mi.
134,300 sq. km.
Population: 4,369,000
Largest City: New Orleans

Louisiana

★ State Capital
● Parish Seat

━━━ Limited Access Highway
─── Other Major Road

1:2,750,000

Albers Equal Area Projection

© MapQuest.com, Inc.

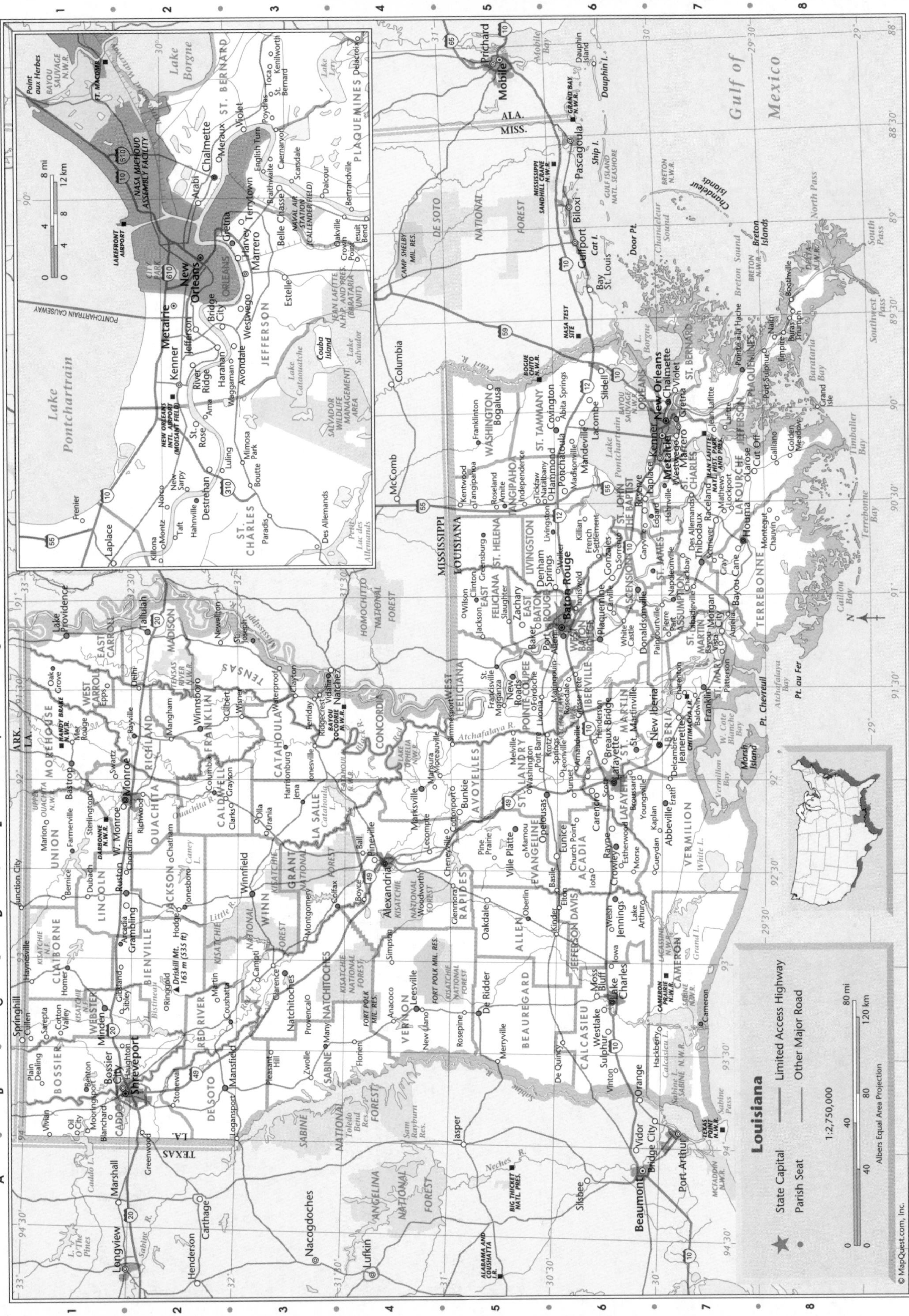

Capital: Augusta
Area: 35,400 sq. mi.
91,700 sq. km.
Population: 1,244,000
Largest City: Portland

Maine

★ State/Provincial Capital
● County Seat
— Limited Access Highway
— Other Major Road

1:2,074,000

0   25   50 mi
0   25   50   75 km

Albers Equal Area Projection

© MapQuest.com, Inc.

LAURENTIDES PROVINCIAL RESERVE

Baie-St-Paul
Mont-Carmel
Pohenegamook
Rivière-Bleue
St-Jacques
Edmundston
St-Basile
Madawaska
Grand Isle
Lille
Frenchville
Ste-Anne-de-Madawaska
Van Buren
St-Léonard
Grand Falls/Grand Sault
MT. CARLETON PROV. PARK
Plaster Rock

St-Pascal
La Pocatière
St-Roch-des-Aulnaies
St-Jean-Port-Joli
St-Aubert
Ste-Perpétue
Dickey
St. Francis
St. John
Soldier Pond
Fort Kent
Sinclair
Stockholm
Hamlin

St-Ferréal-les-Neiges
St-Tite-des-Caps
MT. STE-ANNE PROV. PARK
Beaupré
Ste-Anne-de-Beaupré
Château-Richer
Île d'Orléans
Cap-St-Ignace
Montmagny
St-Pamphile
Eagle Lake
Winterville
New Sweden
Limestone
Perham
Caribou
Washburn
Portage
Presque Isle
Mapleton
Fort Fairfield
Perth-Andover

Charlesbourg
Québec
Lévis-Lauzon
St-Romuald
St-Paul-de-Montminy
Clayton Lake
AROOSTOOK
Ashland
Masardis
Westfield
Squa Pan L.
Mars Hill
Bridgewater

Ste-Claire
St-Camille-de-Lellis
Munsungan L.
Oxbow
Monticello

Lac-Etchemin
Ste-Justine
Churchill L.
ALLAGASH WILDERNESS WATERWAY
Grand L. Seboeis
Littleton

St-Joseph-de-Beauce
Chamberlain L.
Grand L. Matagamon
Smyrna Mills
Houlton
Hodgdon
Linneus
Woodstock
Nackawic

East Broughton
Beauceville
St-Prosper
St-Zacharie
Chesuncook L.
Telos L.
BAXTER STATE PARK
Patten
Island Falls
North Amity
Orient

Thetford Mines
Ste-Georges
St-Méthode-de-Frontenac
La Guadeloupe
L. St-François
Lambton
St-Martin
St-Gédeon
Chesuncook
Sherman Station
Mt. Katahdin 1606 m (5268 ft)
Sherman Mills
Haynesville
Grand L.
Magaguadavic
Southwest Miramichi R.

FRONTENAC PROV. PARK
Lac Mégantic
L. Mégantic
Pittston Farm
Seboomook L.
Seboomook
North East Carry
Pemadumcook L.
Millinocket L.
Grindstone
Reed
Wytopitlock
Danforth
Eaton
Atlantic Time Zone
McAdam
Oromocto L.

Coburn Gore
Snow Mt. 1204 m (3948 ft)
SOMERSET
Moose River
Jackman
Rockwood
Moosehead
Kokadjo
Lily Bay
White Cap Mt. 1111 m (3644 ft)
West Seboeis
Millinocket
East Millinocket
Norcross
Kingman
Macwahoc
Mattawamkeag
Brookton
Vanceboro
Baskahegan L.

APPALACHIAN MOUNTAINS
QUÉBEC / MAINE
Aziscohos L.
Stratton
Eustis
Flagstaff L.
Long Pond
Lake Parlin
The Forks
Greenville
PISCATAQUIS
Brownville Junction
Seboeis
Seboeis L.
PENOBSCOT
Winn
Lincoln
Lee
Springfield
Topsfield
Waite
Big L.
PASSAMAQUODDY INDIAN TOWNSHIP I.R.
Princeton
St. Stephen
Calais
ST. CROIX ISLAND INTL. HIST. SITE

Shirley Mills
Monson
Brownville
Sebec
Milo
Howland
Burlington
Passadumkeag
Olamon
Grand Lake Stream
Woodland
Alexander
MOOSEHORN N.W.R.
Blacks Harbour

Sugarloaf Mt. 1291 m (4237 ft)
Carrabassett
Bingham
Dover-Foxcroft
Guilford
Piscataquis R.
Lagrange
Nicatous L.
Wesley
Northfield
PASSAMAQUODDY PLEASANT POINT I.R.
Eastport
Lubec

Wilsons Mills
Oquossoc
Rangeley
Saddleback Mt. 1255 m (4116 ft)
Mooselookmeguntic L.
Richardson Lakes
Upton
Umbagog L.
Kingfield
Salem
Phillips
New Vineyard
Madison
Norridgewock
Skowhegan
Caratunk
Solon
Wellington
Harmony
Corinna
Exeter Corners
East Corinth
Charleston
South Lagrange
Hudson
PENOBSCOT I.R.
Milford
Old Town
Orono
Great Pond
WASHINGTON
Dennysville
Whiting
West Quoddy Head

Berlin
Gorham
Gilead
Bethel
Newry
Mexico
Rumford
OXFORD
Byron
Weld
Dixfield
Chisholm
Farmington
FRANKLIN
Wilton
Mercer
New Portland
Athens
Hartland
Newport
Hermon
Pittsfield
Carmel
Bangor
Brewer
Hampden
East Holden
HANCOCK
Amherst
Waltham
Green Lake
Franklin
Deblois
Cherryfield
Harrington
Columbia Falls
Jonesboro
Machias
East Machias
Cutler

WHITE MTN. NATL. FOR.
WHITE MTS.
MAINE / N.H.
Andover
Bryant Pond
Canton
Livermore Falls
Belgrade
Oakland
Waterville
Winslow
Clinton
Burnham
Unity
China
Dixmont
Frankfort
Brooks
Swanville
Searsport
Stockton Springs
Bucksport
Orland
Ellsworth
Trenton
Blue Hill
Somesville
ACADIA NATL. PARK
Bar Harbor
Winter Harbor
Steuben
Milbridge
Jonesport
Great Wass I.
Cross I.

Buckfield
Livermore
Leeds
Turner
Greene
Winthrop
Augusta
Hallowell
Gardiner
KENNEBEC
South China
Searsmont
Liberty
Belfast
Castine
Islesboro Island
Sedgwick
Deer Isle
Stonington
Swans I.
Atlantic
Bass Harbor
Southwest Harbor
Mt. Desert I.
Frenchboro

North Waterford
Paris
South Paris
Norway
Oxford
Mechanic Falls
Auburn
Lewiston
ANDROSCOGGIN
Jefferson
Whitefield
Washington
Union
KNOX
Camden
Rockport
Rockland
Thomaston
North Haven
Isle au Haut
Long I.
ACADIA NATL. PARK
Penobscot Bay

Lovell
Bridgton
North Conway
Fryeburg
Conway
Naples
Casco
Gray
Lisbon
Lisbon Falls
SAGADAHOC
Wiscasset
Richmond
Dresden
Damariscotta
LINCOLN
Waldoboro
Owls Head
Vinalhaven I.
Vinalhaven

Hiram
Sebago L.
North Windham
Freeport
Yarmouth
Falmouth
Brunswick
Boothbay Harbor
Port Clyde
Monhegan I.
SEAL ISLAND N.W.R.
Matinicus I.

Limerick
Cornish
Hollis Center
Westbrook
Portland
CUMBERLAND
Casco Bay
Small Pt.
GULF OF MAINE

Wolfeboro
Kezar Falls
Shapleigh
Alfred
Springvale
Sanford
YORK
South Portland
Cape Elizabeth
Saco
Saco Bay
Old Orchard Beach
Biddeford

Rochester
Somersworth
Farmington
North Berwick
Berwick
Kennebunk
Kennebunkport
Ogunquit

Durham
Newmarket
Raymond
Epping
Exeter
Dover
Kittery
York
Portsmouth
ATLANTIC OCEAN

CANADA / U.S.
St. Lawrence River
St. John R.
Kennebec R.
Androscoggin
Penobscot R.
Moosehead L.
Allagash Wilderness Waterway
Eastern Time Zone
Atlantic Time Zone
NEW BRUNSWICK

Capital: Annapolis
Area: 12,400 sq. mi.
32,100 sq. km.
Population: 5,135,000
Largest City: Baltimore

Maryland

★ State Capital
• County Seat
— Limited Access Highway
— Other Major Road

1:1,261,000

©MapQuest.com, Inc.

Albers Equal Area Projection

30 mi
40 km

PENNSYLVANIA

W. VIRGINIA
VIRGINIA
W. VA.
VA.
MD.
PA.

DELAWARE
MARYLAND

DELAWARE BAY
ATLANTIC OCEAN
CHESAPEAKE BAY
Tangier Sound

ALLEGANY
GARRETT
WASHINGTON
FREDERICK
CARROLL
HARFORD
CECIL
BALTIMORE
HOWARD
MONTGOMERY
ANNE ARUNDEL
PRINCE GEORGES
CHARLES
CALVERT
ST. MARYS
KENT
QUEEN ANNES
CAROLINE
TALBOT
DORCHESTER
WICOMICO
SOMERSET
WORCESTER

Baltimore
Annapolis
Washington, D.C.
Cumberland
Hagerstown
Frederick
Westminster
Bel Air
Elkton
Towson
Dundalk
Columbia
Rockville
Gaithersburg
Bethesda
Silver Spring
Bowie
Laurel
Wheaton
Largo
Upper Marlboro
La Plata
Waldorf
Leonardtown
Chestertown
Centreville
Denton
Easton
Cambridge
Salisbury
Princess Anne
Snow Hill
Ocean City
Berlin

GETTYSBURG NATL. MIL. PARK
ANTIETAM N.B.
HARPERS FERRY N.H.P.
CATOCTIN MT. PARK
MONOCACY N.B.
CHESAPEAKE AND OHIO CANAL N.H.P.
GEORGE WASHINGTON BIRTHPLACE N.M.
BLACKWATER N.W.R.
MARTIN N.W.R.
EASTERN NECK N.W.R.
ASSATEAGUE ISLAND NATIONAL SEASHORE
CHINCOTEAGUE N.W.R.
ABERDEEN PROVING GROUND
ANDREWS A.F.B.
QUANTICO U.S.M.C. RES.
FORT BELVOIR MIL. RES.
FORT A.P. HILL MIL. RES.
PATUXENT N.A.T.C.
GREEN RIDGE S.F.
SAVAGE RIVER STATE FOREST
FORBES S.F.
BLUE RIDGE
ALLEGHENY FRONT

Susquehanna R.
Potomac R.
Patuxent R.
Choptank R.
Nanticoke R.
Pocomoke R.
Youghiogheny R.

Backbone Mt. (3360 ft) 1024 m
Mt. Storm L.

Cape Henlopen
Egg I. Pt.
Pt. Lookout
Smith I.

BOMBAY HOOK N.W.R.
PRIME HOOK N.W.R.

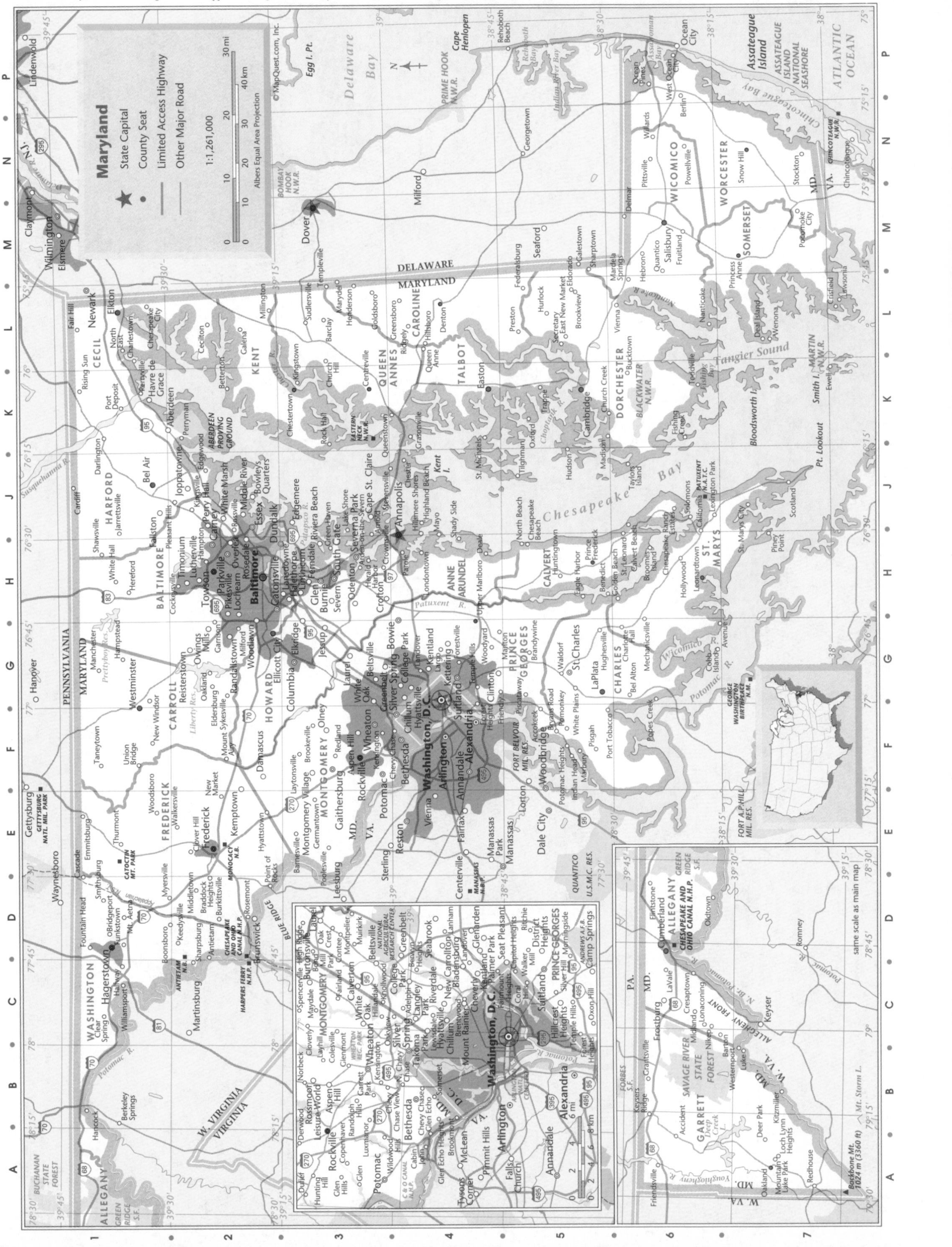

Capital: Boston
Area: 10,600 sq. mi. 27,300 sq. km.
Population: 6,147,000
Largest City: Boston

Massachusetts

Limited Access Highway
Other Major Road

1:1,241,000

★ State Capital
● County Seat

Lambert Conformal Conic Projection

© MapQuest.com, Inc.

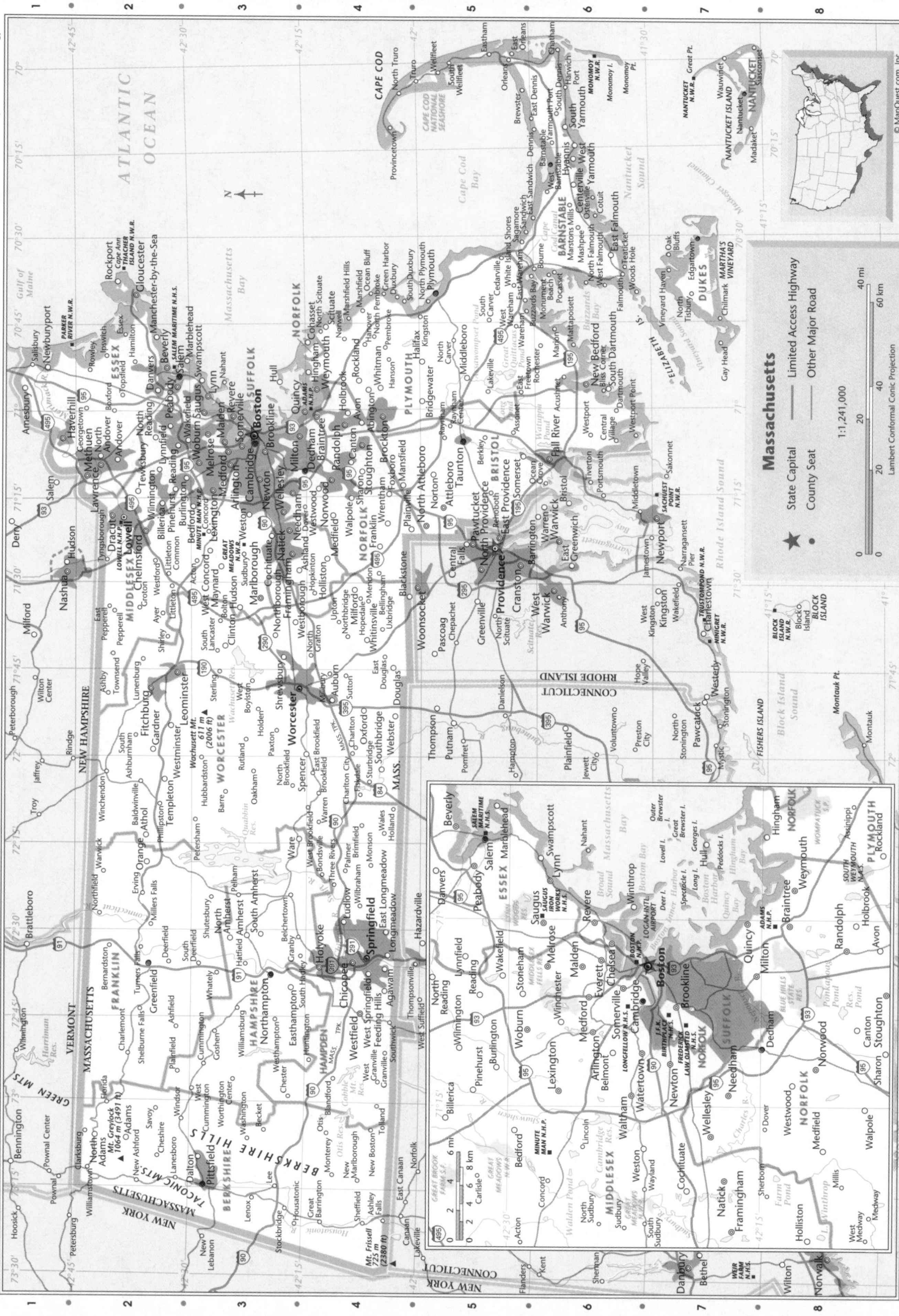

Capital: Lansing
Area: 96,700 sq. mi.
250,500 sq. km.
Population: 9,817,000
Largest City: Detroit

Michigan

★ State Capital — Limited Access Highway
• County Seat — Other Major Road

1:3,205,000

0   50   100 mi
0   50 100 150 km
Albers Equal Area Projection

© MapQuest.com, Inc.

Inset map (Apostle Islands / Gogebic area):

Central Time Zone | Eastern Time Zone — same scale as main map
LAKE SUPERIOR
APOSTLE ISLANDS NATL. LAKESHORE
APOSTLE ISLANDS
Outer I.
Madeline I.
Government Point 564 m (1850 ft)
Silver City
Ontonagon
White Pine
PORCUPINE MTS.
ONTONAGON
OTTAWA
Birch
Connorville
Merriweather
Bessemer
Wakefield
Ewen
Montreal
Hurley
Ironwood
Marenisco
Lake Gogebic
BAD RIVER I.R.
MICH.
GOGEBIC
Presque Isle
WIS.
Tuttle
Flambeau Flowage
Manitowish Waters
NORTHERN HIGHLAND AMERICAN LEGION S.F.
Manitowish
Butternut
Lac du Flambeau
LAC DU FLAMBEAU I.R.
Eagle River
Park Falls
CHEQUAMEGON N.F.
Minocqua

Main map labels:

Thunder Bay
Edward I.
Thunder Cape
Pie I.
ONT. MICH.
ISLE ROYALE
CANADA U.S.
ISLE ROYALE NATL. PARK
Sugar Mt. 415 m (1362 ft)
LAKE SUPERIOR
Fourteen Mile Pt.
Eagle River
Manitou I.
KEWEENAW
Keeweenaw Pt.
KEWEENAW PENINSULA
Traverse Pt.
Hancock
Houghton
Keweenaw Bay
HURON N.W.R.
HOUGHTON
L'Anse
L'ANSE I.R.
BARAGA
HURON MTS.
MT. Arvon 603 m (1979 ft)
OTTAWA N.F.
Ishpeming
Negaunee
Marquette
Laughing Fish Pt.
Grand I.
Au Sable Pt.
PICTURED ROCKS NATL. LAKESHORE
TAHQUAMENON FALLS S.P.
Whitefish Bay
Sault Ste. Marie
Eastern Time Zone
Central Time Zone
MARQUETTE
K.I. SAWYER A.F.B.
Munising
ALGER
Newberry
LUCE
HIAWATHA NATIONAL FOREST
BAY MILLS I.R.
Sault Ste. Marie
CHIPPEWA
ST. JOSEPH I.
Thessalon
Blind River
Elliot Lake
Massey
IRON
DICKINSON
Crystal Falls
DELTA
SCHOOLCRAFT
Manistique
Scott Pt.
Seul Choix Pt.
Gardens
MICHIGAN ISLANDS N.W.R.
MACKINAC
St. Ignace
Les Cheneaux Is.
North Channel
Clapperton I.
Barrie
DRUMMOND I.
COCKBURN I.
MANITOULIN ISLAND
NICOLET NATIONAL FOREST
Kingsford
Iron Mountain
Norway
Niagara
MENOMINEE
Gladstone
Escanaba
Big Bay De Noc
Summer I.
Pt. Detour
Hog I.
High I.
Beaver I.
Sturgeon Bay
BOIS BLANC I.
Cheboygan
Hammond Bay
Rogers City
Adams Pt.
ONTARIO
MICHIGAN
Great Duck I.
CANADA U.S.
SOKAOGON CHIPPEWA (POTAWATOMI) I.R.
Crandon
MENOMINEE INDIAN RES.
STOCKBRIDGE I.R.
Shawano
Peshtigo
Marinette
Menominee
St. Martin I.
GREEN BAY N.W.R.
Chambers I.
GRAVEL ISLAND N.W.R.
N. Manitou I.
S. Manitou I.
Leland
Charlevoix
Petoskey
EMMET
CHEBOYGAN
PRESQUE ISLE
Rogers City
Alpena
North Pt.
Howard
Oneida I.R.
Green Bay
De Pere
DOOR PENINSULA
Sturgeon Bay
SLEEPING BEAR DUNES NATL. LAKESHORE
Pt. Betsie
Crystal L.
Glen L.
Beulah
Traverse City
Bellaire
Boyne City
Gaylord
Atlanta
CHARLEVOIX
ANTRIM
OTSEGO
MONTMORENCY
ALPENA
CAMP GRAYLING MIL. RES.
Hubbard L.
Thunder Bay
MICHIGAN ISLANDS N.W.R.
South Pt.
LAKE HURON
New London
Appleton
Neenah
Kaukauna
Two Rivers
Manitowoc
Chilton
LAKE MICHIGAN
Manistee
Beulah
LEELANAU
GRAND TRAVERSE
BENZIE
KALKASKA
Grayling
CRAWFORD
OSCODA
Mio
ALCONA
Harrisville
Sturgeon Pt.
HURON N.F.
Au Sable Pt.
Omro
Oshkosh
Berlin
Ripon
L. Poygan
L. Winnebago
Central Time Zone
Eastern Time Zone
Big Sable Pt.
MANISTEE
MANISTEE NATIONAL
Ludington
WEXFORD
MISSAUKEE
Lake City
Cadillac
Houghton Lake
Roscommon
ROSCOMMON
Higgins L.
OGEMAW
West Branch
Skidway Lake
IOSCO
East Tawas
Tawas City
MASON
Baldwin
LAKE
Reed City
OSCEOLA
CLARE
Clare
Harrison
GLADWIN
Gladwin
ARENAC
Standish
Pt. Lookout
Pt. Au Gres
Sand Pt.
Pt. Aux Barques
WURTSMITH A.F.B.
Saginaw Bay
HURON
Bad Axe
Caro
Sandusky
Little Sable Pt.
Hart
OCEANA
NEWAYGO
White Cloud
Fremont
MECOSTA
Big Rapids
ISABELLA
Mt. Pleasant
St. Louis
Alma
Ithaca
MIDLAND
Midland
Carrollton
Shields
BAY
Bay City
Essexville
TUSCOLA
Vassar
Frankenmuth
SANILAC
Whitehall
Muskegon
North Muskegon
Muskegon Hts.
Norton Shores
MUSKEGON
Wolf Lake
MONTCALM
Stanton
Cedar Springs
Rockford
Greenville
Belding
GRATIOT
Chesaning
Owosso
Bridgeport
SAGINAW
Saginaw
Frankenmuth
Mt. Morris
Flushing
GENESEE
Flint
Burton
Grand Blanc
LAPEER
Lapeer
Imlay City
ST. CLAIR
Port Huron
Marysville
Sarnia
Ferrysburg
Spring Lake
Grand Haven
Coopersville
Sparta
Walker
Grand Rapids
KENT
Lowell
Ionia
IONIA
Portland
St. Johns
CLINTON
De Witt
SHIAWASSEE
Corunna
Durand
Holly
Fenton
Davison
Oxford
Lake Orion
Pontiac
OAKLAND
Romeo
Richmond
New Baltimore
Algonac
Marine City
St. Clair
OTTAWA
Holland
Zeeland
Jenison
Hudsonville
Wyoming
Kentwood
Cutlerville
Portland
Grand Ledge
Lansing
East Lansing
Okemos
Williamston
Fowlerville
LIVINGSTON
Howell
Brighton
Milford
Wixom
S. Lyon
MACOMB
Sterling Heights
Warren
Livonia
Detroit
Windsor
Tecumseh
Essex
ALLEGAN
Allegan
Wayland
Plainwell
BARRY
Hastings
Charlotte
EATON
Eaton Rapids
INGHAM
Holt
Mason
JACKSON
Chelsea
WASHTENAW
Ann Arbor
Ypsilanti
Saline
Milan
Flat Rock
Dearborn
Taylor
Romulus
South Haven
VAN BUREN
Paw Paw
Paw Paw Lake
KALAMAZOO
Kalamazoo
Portage
Battle Creek
Marshall
Albion
CALHOUN
Jackson
Michigan Center
Tecumseh
MONROE
Monroe
Rockwood
Benton Harbor
St. Joseph
BERRIEN
Dowagiac
CASS
Three Rivers
Centreville
ST. JOSEPH
Sturgis
Coldwater
BRANCH
Hillsdale
HILLSDALE
Hudson
Blissfield
LENAWEE
Adrian
Dundee
Temperance
Lambertville
Sylvania
Toledo
Maumee
Oregon
Perrysburg
OTTAWA N.W.R.
PERRYS VICTORY AND INT. PEACE MEM.
LAKE ERIE
Port Clinton
Kelleys I.
PELEE I.
PT. PELEE N.P.
Kingsville
Leamington
Amherstburg
Wallaceburg
MICHIGAN
INDIANA
Niles
Buchanan
Cassopolis
Elkhart
Goshen
Lagrange
Angola
Montpelier
Wauseon
Sylvania
CANADA U.S.
Michigan City
South Bend
Mishawaka
La Porte
Westville
Hammond
Gary
East Chicago
Calumet City
Chicago
Oak Park
Cicero
Bolingbrook
Joliet
Aurora
Batavia
Wheaton
De Kalb
Elgin
Carpentersville
Evanston
Highland Park
Lake Zurich
Wheeling
Waterman
Sandwich

Detroit area inset:

Rochester
Pontiac
Huron Heights
Union Lake
Keego Harbor
Sylvan Lake
Troy
Utica
Rochester Hills
Waldenburg
Chesterfield
Mount Clemens
Sterling Heights
MACOMB
Fraser
Warren
Clawson
OAKLAND
Birmingham
Beverly Hills
Royal Oak
Berkley
Madison Hts.
Center Line
Roseville
St. Clair Shores
Grosse Pte.
Woods
Franklin
Bingham Farms
Bloomfield Hills
Orchard Lake
West Acres
Keego
Farmington Hills
Farmington
Southfield
Oak Park
Ferndale
Hazel Park
Hamtramck
Eastpointe
Grosse Pointe Woods
Grosse Pointe Farms
Livonia
WAYNE
Highland Park
Detroit
Grosse Pointe Park
Grosse Pointe
Lake St. Clair
Westland
Garden City
Dearborn Hts.
Dearborn
U.S. CAN.
Windsor
MIDDLE ROUGE PARKWAY
LOWER ROUGE PARKWAY
Inkster
Melvindale
River Rouge
Ecorse
St. Clair Beach
Elmstead
Tecumseh
Wayne
Taylor
Allen Park
Lincoln Park
Southgate
Wyandotte
Romulus
La Salle
Oliver
0 3 6 mi
0 3 6 9 km

Capital: St. Paul
Area: 86,900 sq. mi.
225,200 sq. km.

Population: 4,725,000
Largest City: Minneapolis

Minnesota

★ State Capital   — Limited Access Highway
• County Seat   — Other Major Road

1:2,773,000

0   40   80 mi
0   40   80   120 km

Albers Equal Area Projection

© MapQuest.com, Inc.

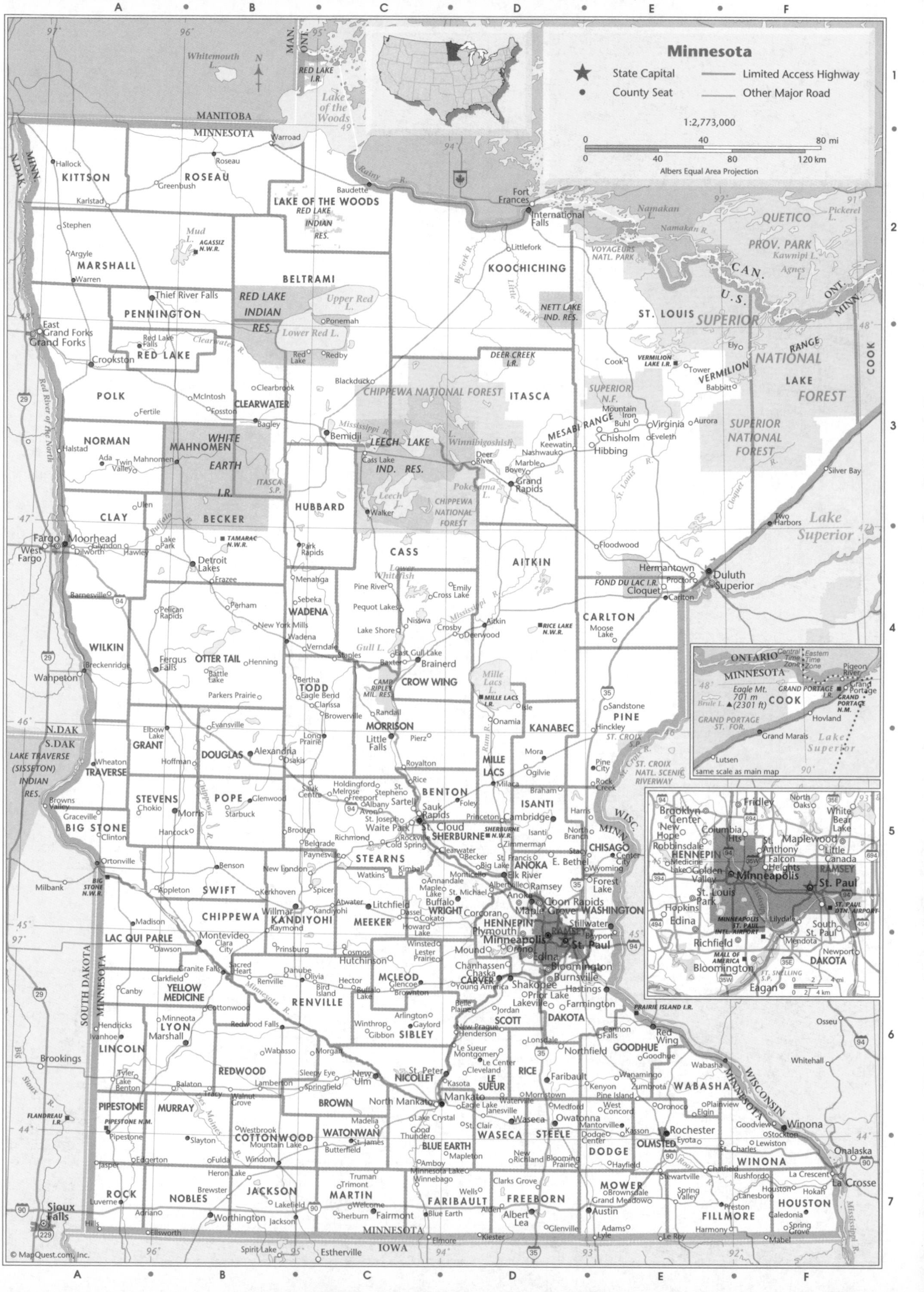

Capital: Jackson
Area: 48,400 sq. mi.
125,400 sq. km.
Population: 2,752,000
Largest City: Jackson

Mississippi

★ State Capital
• County Seat
— Limited Access Highway
— Other Major Road

1:2,386,000

0 40 80 mi
0 40 80 120 km

TENN.
MISS.
ALCORN
TIPPAH
BENTON
MARSHALL
DE SOTO
TUNICA
PANOLA
TATE
LAFAYETTE
UNION
PONTOTOC
PRENTISS
TISHOMINGO
LEE
ITAWAMBA
COAHOMA
QUITMAN
TALLAHATCHIE
YALOBUSHA
CALHOUN
CHICKASAW
MONROE
BOLIVAR
LEFLORE
GRENADA
CARROLL
MONTGOMERY
WEBSTER
CLAY
OKTIBBEHA
LOWNDES
SUNFLOWER
WASHINGTON
HUMPHREYS
HOLMES
ATTALA
CHOCTAW
WINSTON
NOXUBEE
SHARKEY
ISSAQUENA
YAZOO
LEAKE
NESHOBA
KEMPER
WARREN
MADISON
SCOTT
NEWTON
LAUDERDALE
HINDS
RANKIN
CLARKE
CLAIBORNE
COPIAH
SIMPSON
SMITH
JASPER
JEFFERSON
ADAMS
FRANKLIN
LINCOLN
LAWRENCE
JEFFERSON DAVIS
COVINGTON
JONES
WAYNE
WILKINSON
AMITE
PIKE
WALTHALL
MARION
LAMAR
FORREST
PERRY
GREENE
PEARL RIVER
STONE
GEORGE
HANCOCK
HARRISON
JACKSON
PINE HILLS

ARK.
LA.
ALABAMA
MISSISSIPPI
LOUISIANA
Gulf of Mexico
Gulf Island Natl. Seashore

Memphis, Germantown, Collierville, Southaven, Horn Lake, Olive Branch, Byhalia, Walnut, Corinth, Florence, Sheffield, Tuscumbia, Russellville, Iuka, Burnsville, Woodall Mtn. 246 m (806 ft), Holly Springs, Ripley, Booneville, Hernando, Ashland, Falkner, Kossuth, Rienzi, Jumpertown, Paden, Tishomingo, Coldwater, Senatobia, Potts Camp, Hickory Flat, Dumas, Blue Mountain, Myrtle, Baldwyn, Marietta, Golden, Red Bay, New Albany, Como, Crenshaw, Abbeville, Oxford, Blue Springs, Ecru, Guntown, Mantachie, Fulton, Tremont, Tunica, Sardis, Sledge, Falcon, Taylor, Toccopola, Pontotoc, Algoma, Sherman, Saltillo, Tupelo, Verona, Plantersville, Shannon, Smithville, Nettleton, Aberdeen, Hatley, Amory, Okolona, Houston, Calhoun City, Derma, Vardaman, Woodland, Mantee, Bruce, Coffeeville, Pittsboro, Slate Spring, Eupora, Maben, Mathiston, Walthall, West Point, Columbus, Starkville, Artesia, Crawford, Brooksville, Macon, Aliceville, Tuscaloosa, Demopolis

Greenville, Greenwood, Indianola, Leland, Metcalfe, Arcola, Moorhead, Itta Bena, Sidon, Carrollton, Winona, Kilmichael, Ackerman, Weir, Louisville, Noxapater, Shuqualak, Scooba, De Kalb, Philadelphia, Collinsville, Meridian, Marion, Conehatta, Decatur, Lake, Newton, Chunky, Hickory, Forest, Morton, Pelahatchie, Brandon, Pearl, Richland, Florence, Puckett, Raleigh, Sylvarena, Paulding, Pachuta, Quitman, Shubuta, Enterprise, Stonewall, Montrose, Louin, Bay Springs, Heidelberg, Sandersville, Laurel, Waynesboro, State Line, Shubuta

Jackson, Clinton, Ridgeland, Madison, Canton, Flora, Bentonia, Yazoo City, Satartia, Rolling Fork, Anguilla, Cary, Louise, Silver City, Belzoni, Isola, Inverness, Cruger, Tchula, Lexington, Durant, Goodman, Pickens, Sallis, Ethel, McCool, Kosciusko, Sebastopol, Lena, Walnut Grove, Union, Carthage

Vicksburg, Tallulah, Edwards, Raymond, Learned, Utica, Terry, Crystal Springs, Georgetown, Hazlehurst, Braxton, D'Lo, Mendenhall, Magee, Mize, Taylorsville, Soso, Bay Springs, Beauregard, Wesson, New Hebron, Mount Olive, Collins, Seminary, Ellisville, Richton, New Augusta, Beaumont, Leakesville, Natchez, Roxie, Meadville, Bude, Fayette, Monticello, Bassfield, Prentiss, Silver Creek, Sumrall, Petal, Hattiesburg, Camp Shelby Mil. Res., McLain, Lucedale

Woodville, Centreville, Liberty, Magnolia, McComb, Summit, Gloster, Crosby, Crosby, Tylertown, Columbia, Purvis, Lumberton, Poplarville, Picayune, Kiln, Wiggins, Lyman, Gulfport, Long Beach, Pass Christian, Bay St. Louis, Waveland, Pearlington, Slidell, Lacombe, D'Iberville, Biloxi, Ocean Springs, Gautier, Moss Point, Pascagoula, Vancleave, Saraland, Prichard, Mobile, Tillmans Corner, Theodore, Daphne, Fairhope, Diamondhead, Bogalusa, New Orleans, Kenner, Chalmette

Pine Bluff, Stuttgart, Marianna, Forrest City, West Helena, Helena, Friars Point, Clarksdale, Lula, Lyon, Marks, Lambert, Crowder, Pope, Duncan, Tutwiler, Alligator, Shelby, Winstonville, Mound Bayou, Merigold, Glendora, Gunnison, Rosedale, Pace, Drew, Renova, Cleveland, Boyle, Benoit, Shaw, Ruleville, Doddsville, Schlater, Sunflower, Moorhead, Hollandale, Beulah, Dumas, Monticello, Crossett, Overflow N.W.R., Bastrop, Mayersville, Lake Providence, Winnsboro, Port Gibson, Tensas River N.W.R., Poverty Point N.M.

NATIONAL WILDLIFE REFUGES: Arkabutla L., Sardis L., Enid L., Grenada L., Ross Barnett Res., Okatibbee L., Columbus L., Aberdeen L., Pickwick L., Bay Springs L.

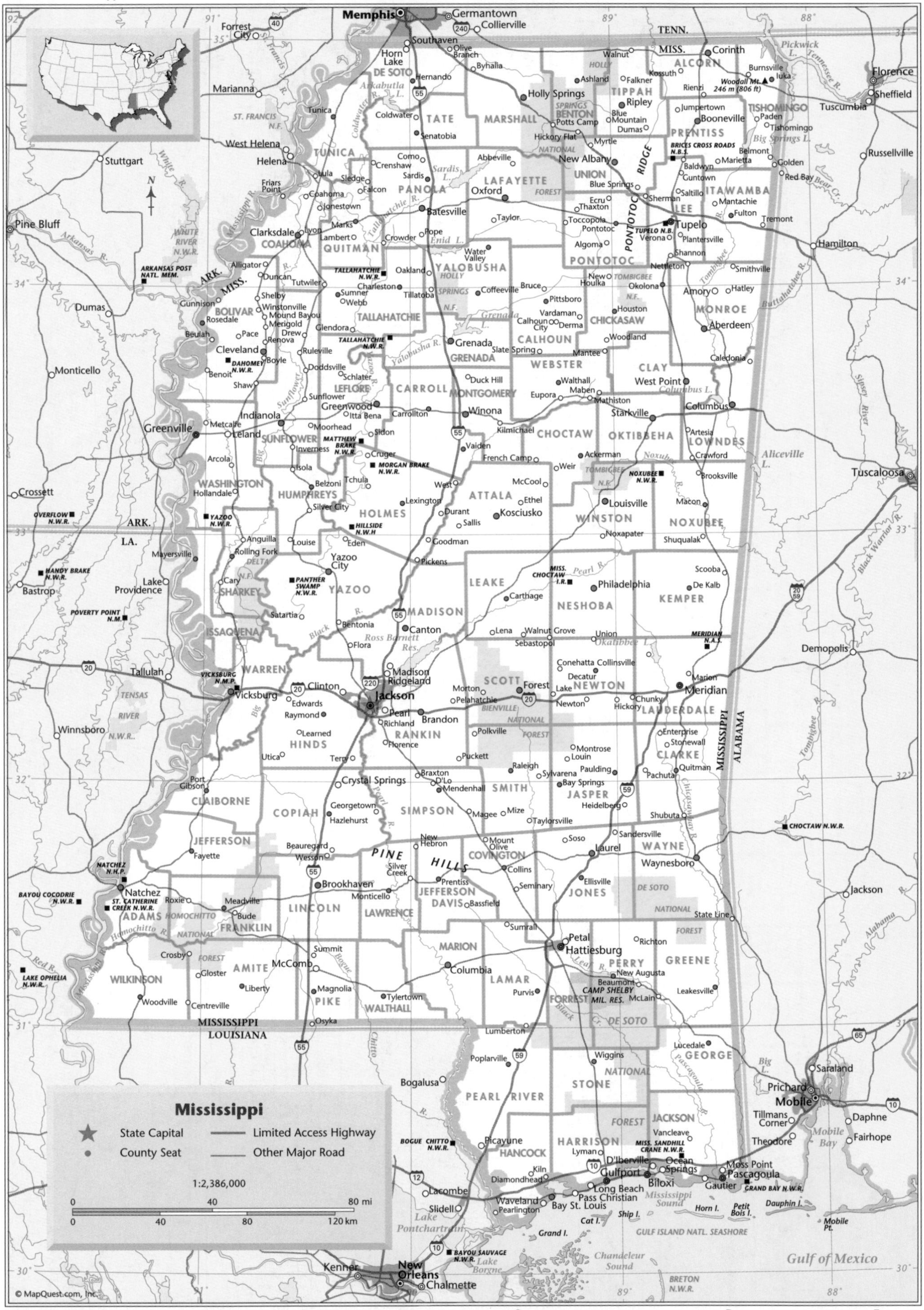

Capital: Jefferson City
Area: 69,700 sq. mi. 180,500 sq. km.
Population: 5,439,000
Largest City: Kansas City

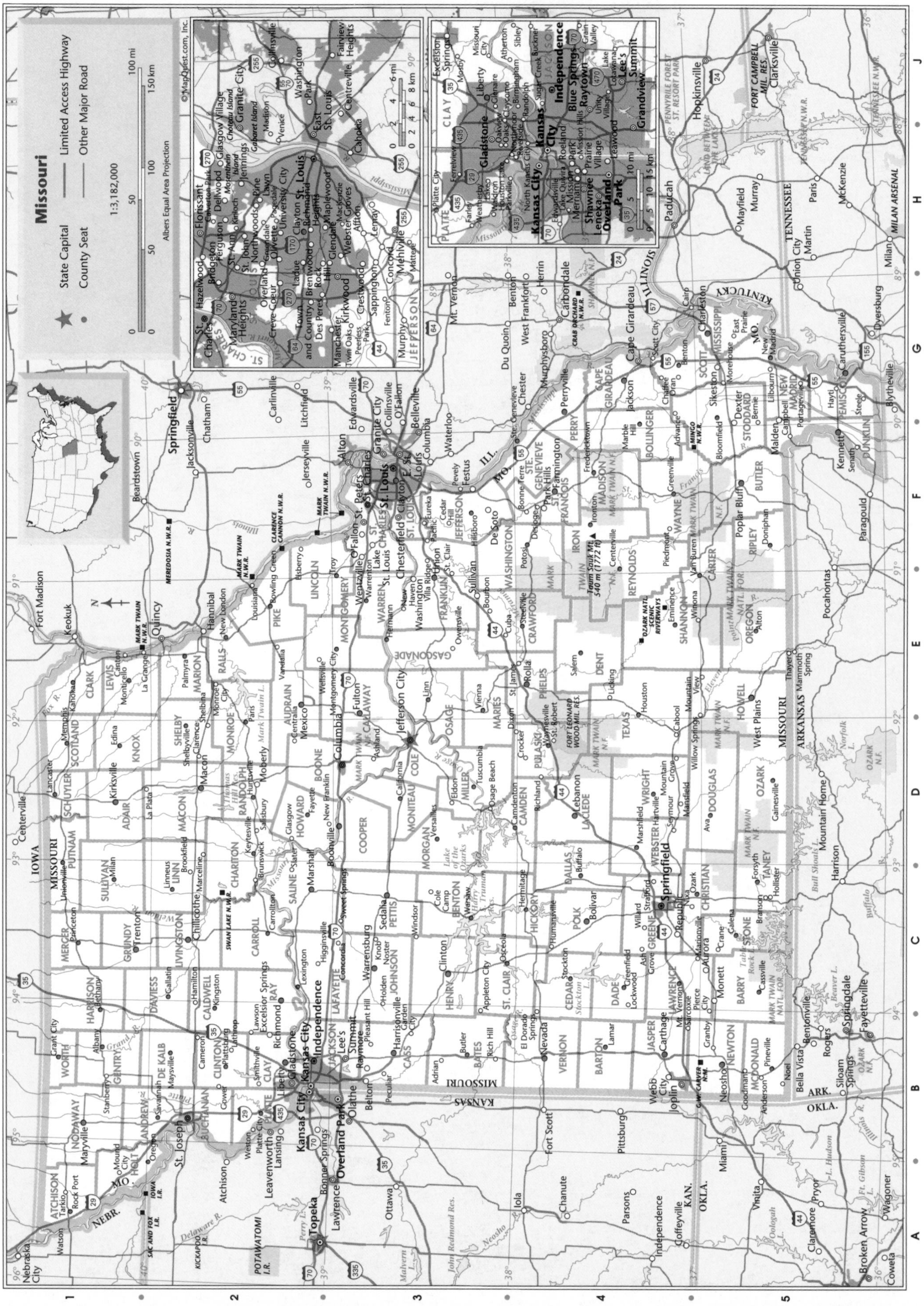

MONTANA

Capital: Helena
Area: 147,000 sq. mi.
380,800 sq. km.

Population: 880,000
Largest City: Billings

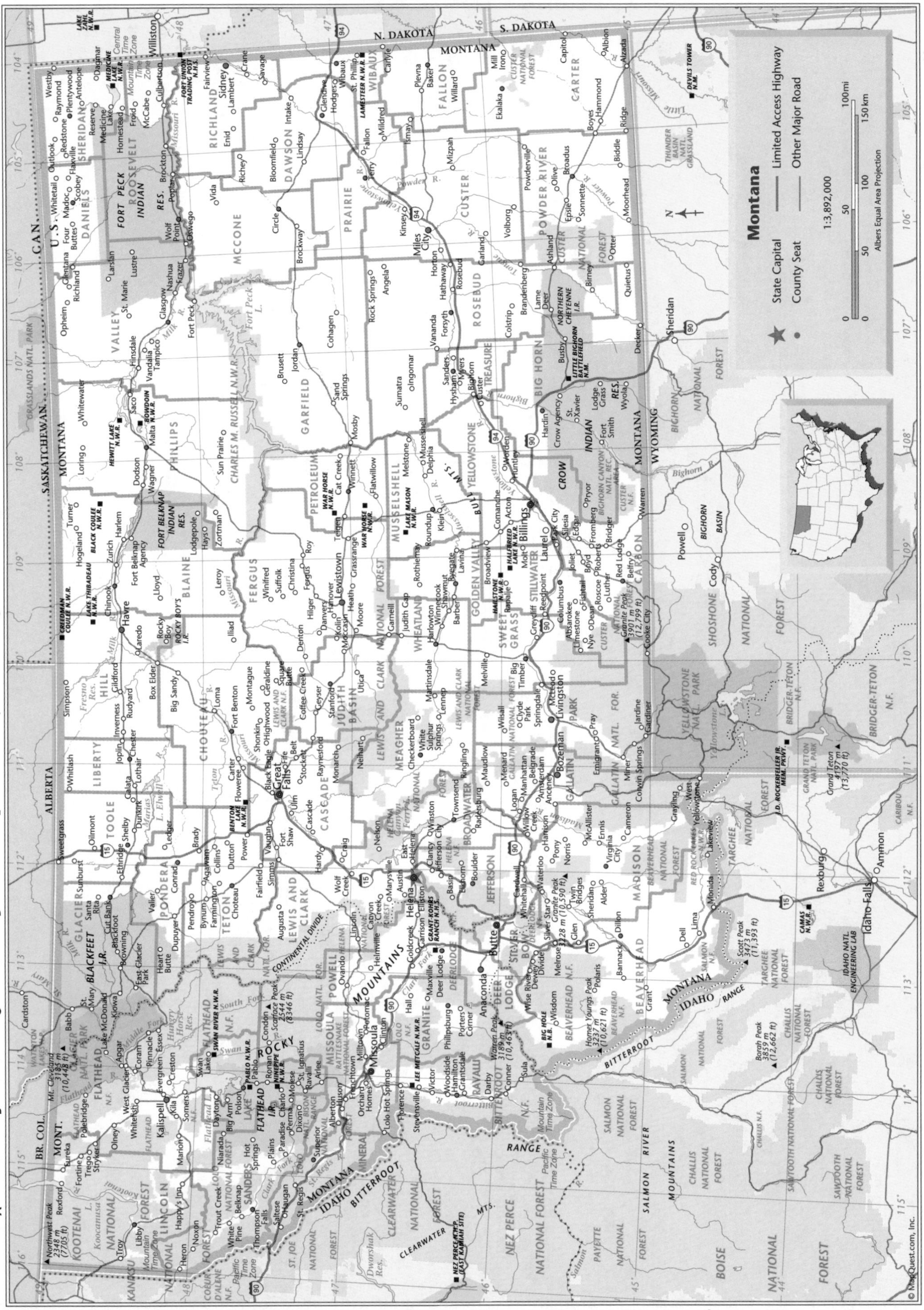

Capital: Lincoln
Area: 77,400 sq. mi.
200,300 sq. km.

Population: 1,663,000
Largest City: Omaha

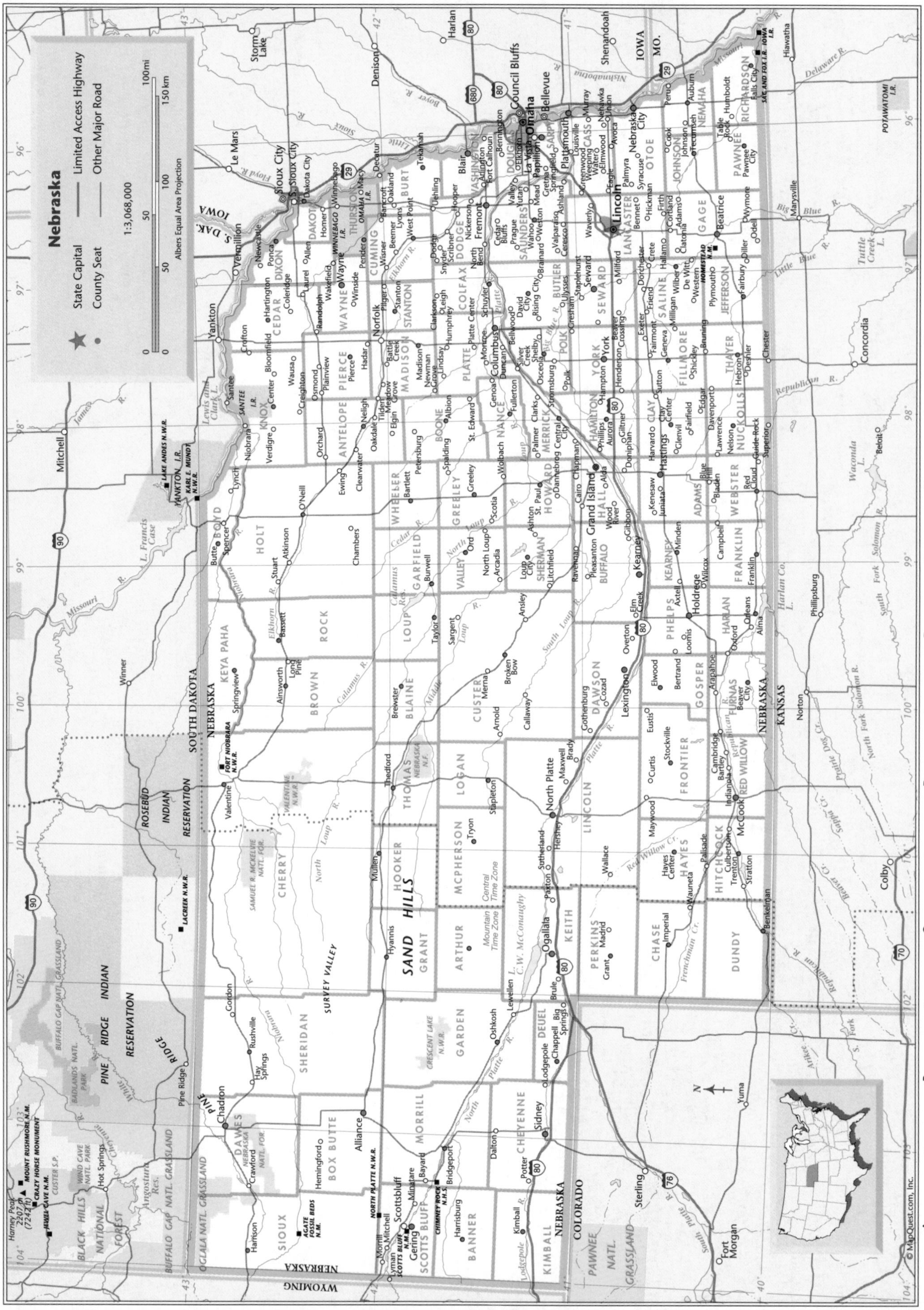

Capital: Carson City
Area: 110,600 sq. mi.
286,400 sq. km.
Population: 1,747,000
Largest City: Las Vegas

120° A 118° B 116° C 114°
42°

OREGON IDAHO
FORT McDERMITT IND. RES.
Owyhee
NEVADA
DUCK VALLEY IND. RES.

Denio
McDermitt
Owyhee
Jarbidge
Jackpot
Mountain City
Matterhorn 3304 m (10,839 ft)
Contact
Pacific Time Zone
Mountain Time Zone

FORT BIDWELL IND. RES.
Goose L.
Upper L.
Vya
Massacre L.
SHELDON NATL. WILDLIFE REFUGE
SUMMIT LAKE IND. RES.
FORT McDERMITT IND. RES.
Orovada
HUMBOLDT
Paradise Valley
HUMBOLDT NATL. FOR.
Charleston
ELKO
North Fork
Jack Creek
Tuscarora
Midas
Wilkins
Montello
GREAT SALT LAKE DESERT

MODOC NATL. FOR.
WASHOE
HUMBOLDT
DESERT VALLEY
OWYHEE DESERT
Mountain City
INDEPENDENCE MTS.
Marys R.

Golconda
Sulphur
Pronto
Winnemucca
Valmy
Dunphy
Carlin
Elko
Arthur
Wells
Deeth
Halleck
Cobre
Oasis
Pilot Peak 3263 m (10,704 ft)
WENDOVER RANGE
West Wendover
Shafter

Gerlach
Empire
Mill City
Imlay
Humboldt
Battle Mountain
Beowawe
Spring Creek
Ruby Dome 3471 m (11,387 ft)
Lamoille
Lee
TE-MOAK IND. RES.
Jiggs
Ruby Valley
Currie
DESERET TEST CENTER

PERSHING
Rye Patch Res.
Dry L.
Unionville
Mt. Tobin 2979 m (9775 ft)
SHOSHONE RANGE
Crescent Valley
HUMBOLDT NATL. FOR.
RUBY LAKE N.W.R.
Goshute L.
Lages
GOSHUTE IND. RES.
Ibapah Peak 3684 m (12,087 ft)

SIERRA ARMY DEPOT
PYRAMID LAKE IND. RES.
Flanigan
Oreana
Lovelock
Winnemucca L.
Pyramid L.
40°

PLUMAS NATL. FOR.
Sutcliffe
Nixon
GREAT BASIN
LANDER
EUREKA
Newark L.
Cherry Creek
Tippett
40°

TAHOE N.F.
Lemmon Valley
Sun Valley
Sparks
Reno
Verdi
Steamboat
Incline Village
Lake Tahoe
Zephyr Cove
Wadsworth
Fernley
Hazen
Fallon
Stillwater
CHURCHILL
Dixie Valley
FALLON N.W.R.
STILLWATER N.W.R.
FALLON IND. RES.
Cold Springs
Austin
North Toiyabe Peak 3290 m (10,793 ft)
Summit Mt. 3189 m (10,461 ft)
Eureka
WHITE PINE
McGill
Steptoe
Ruth
Ely
Lane
SCHELL CREEK RANGE
Mt. Moriah 3675 m (12,067 ft)

STOREY
Patrick
Silver Springs
Virginia City
LYON
Dayton
Carson City
Wabuska
WALKER RIVER IND. RES.
Middlegate
FALLON N.A.S.
SHOSHONE MOUNTAINS
TOIYABE RANGE
YOMBA IND. RES.
TOIYABE NATL. FOR.
Ione
Arc Dome 3588 m (11,773 ft)
Round Mountain
Mt. Jefferson 3642 m (11,949 ft)
TOIYABE NATL. FOR.
TOQUIMA RANGE
MONITOR RANGE
HOT CREEK RANGE
Duckwater
DUCKWATER IND. RES.
Currant
HUMBOLDT NATL. FOR.
EGAN RANGE
Preston
Lund
Minerva
Majors Place
Baker
Wheeler Peak 3982 m (13,063 ft)
GREAT BASIN N.P.
SNAKE RANGE
DESERT RANGE EXP. STA.

YERINGTON IND. RES.
Yerington
Mason
Schurz
WALKER RIVER IND. RES.
Gabbs
TOIYABE N.F.
Sunnyside
Atlanta
INDIAN PEAK RANGE

DOUGLAS
Minden
Gardnerville
WASHOE IND. RES.
Smith
Wellington
Topaz Lake
Mt. Grant 3426 m (11,239 ft)
Babbitt
Walker L.
MINERAL
Luning
Mina
SMOKY VALLEY
TOQUIMA RANGE
Warm Springs
Nyala
GRANT RANGE
HUMBOLDT NATL. FOR.
Adams-McGill Res.

South Lake Tahoe
ELDORADO N.F.
STANISLAUS NATL. FOR.
TOIYABE N.F.
Mono L.
Basalt
Coaldale
Tonopah
NYE
Pioche
Caselton
Ursine
38°

YOSEMITE NATL. PARK
Mt. Ritter 4010 m (13,157 ft)
Mt. Montgomery
Boundary Peak 4005 m (13,140 ft)
ESMERALDA
Silver Peak
Dyer
Goldfield
NELLIS AIR FORCE RANGE
Tempiute
Hiko
Panaca
Caliente
LINCOLN
Rachel
DIXIE NATL. FOR.

DEVILS POSTPILE NATL. MON.
Mt. Morgan 4190 m (13,748 ft)
SIERRA NATL. FOR.
INYO NATL. FOR.
White Mt. Peak 4342 m (14,246 ft)
Lida
Gold Point
Scotty's Junction
Ash Springs
Elgin
Alamo
Carp
PAHRANAGAT N.W.R.
Pacific Time Zone
Mountain Time Zone
PAIUTE IND. RES.

Madera
KINGS CANYON N.P.
Mt. Whitney 4418 m (14,494 ft)
INYO MTS.
DEATH VALLEY NATIONAL PARK
Beatty
NEVADA TEST SITE
NELLIS AIR FORCE RANGE
DESERT NATL.

SEQUOIA NATL. PARK
SIERRA NEVADA
SEQUOIA NATL. FOR.
CHINA LAKE NAVAL WEAPONS CENTER
Amargosa Valley
Mercury
ASH MEADOWS N.W.R.
DEVILS HOLE (DEATH VALLEY NATL. PARK)
Indian Springs
INDIAN SPRINGS A.F.B.
MOAPA RIVER IND. RES.
Glendale
Moapa
Overton
VALLEY OF FIRE S.P.
Mesquite
Bunkerville
ARIZONA

Lindsay
Corcoran
Porterville
KERN R.
DEATH VALLEY NATIONAL PARK
Amargosa R.
Pahrump
Charleston Park
NELLIS A.F.B.
N. Las Vegas
Las Vegas
Paradise
Henderson
Spring Valley
Blue Diamond
LAKE MEAD NATL. REC. AREA
Hoover Dam
Colorado R.
36°

FORT IRWIN MIL. RES.
RED ROCK N.C.A.
Sloan
Goodsprings
Sandy
Jean
CLARK
Boulder City
Nelson
BLACK MTS.
Red L.

Nevada
★ State Capital
● County Seat
─── Limited Access Highway
─── Other Major Road
1:3,364,000
0 50 100mi
0 50 100 150 km
Albers Equal Area Projection

MOJAVE NATL. PRESERVE
MOJAVE DESERT
Searchlight
Cottonwood Cove
Cal Nev Ari
Laughlin
Bullhead City
FORT MOJAVE IND. RES.
Kingman

© MapQuest.com, Inc.
120° A 118° B 116° C 114°

SIERRA
NEVADA
CALIFORNIA
WENDOVER
UTAH

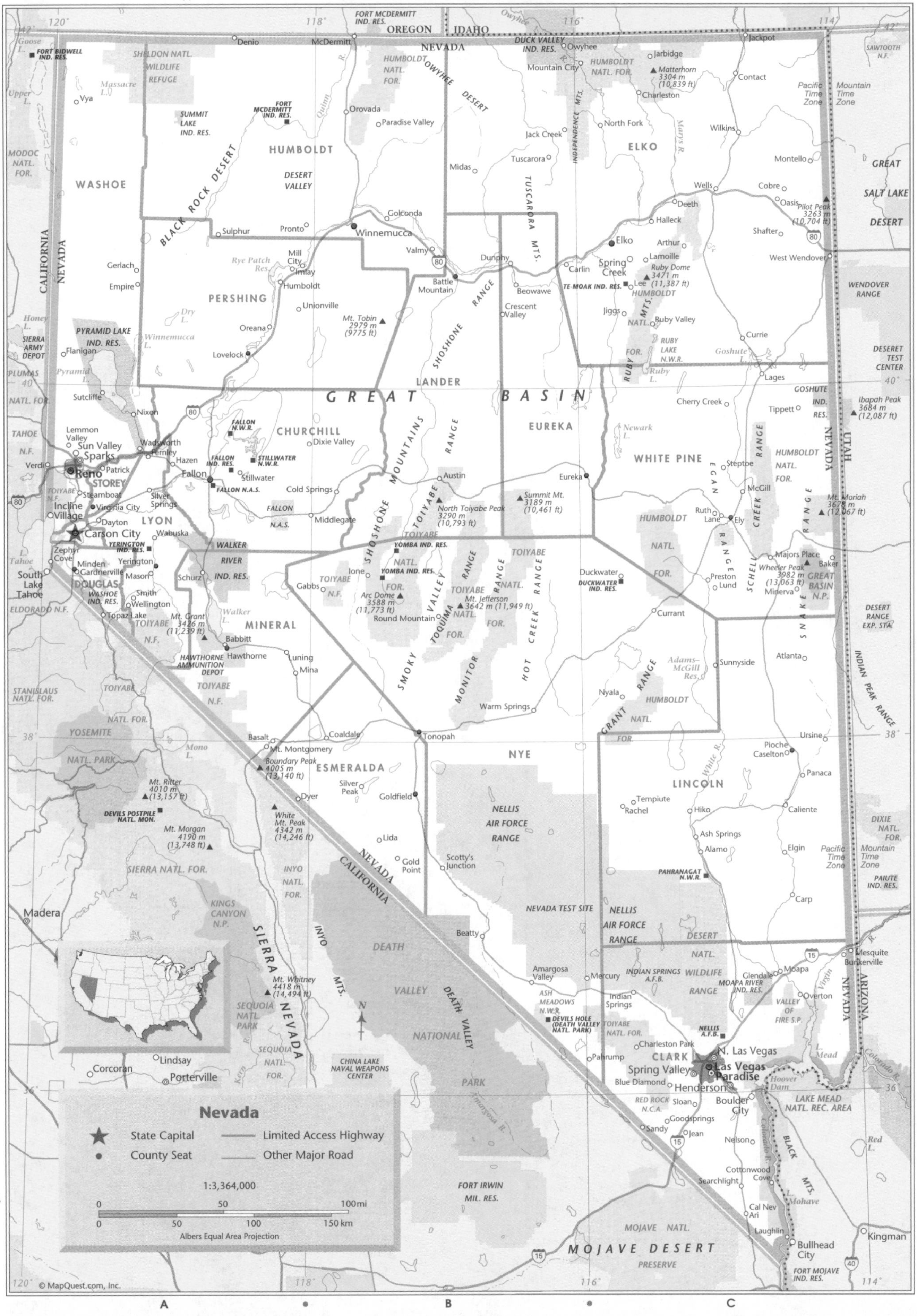

Capital: Concord
Area: 9,400 sq. mi.
24,200 sq. km.
Population: 1,185,000
Largest City: Manchester

New Hampshire

★ State Capital
• County Seat
— Limited Access Highway
— Other Major Road

1:1,395,000

0   25   50 mi
0   25   50   75 km

Albers Equal Area Projection

© MapQuest.com, Inc.

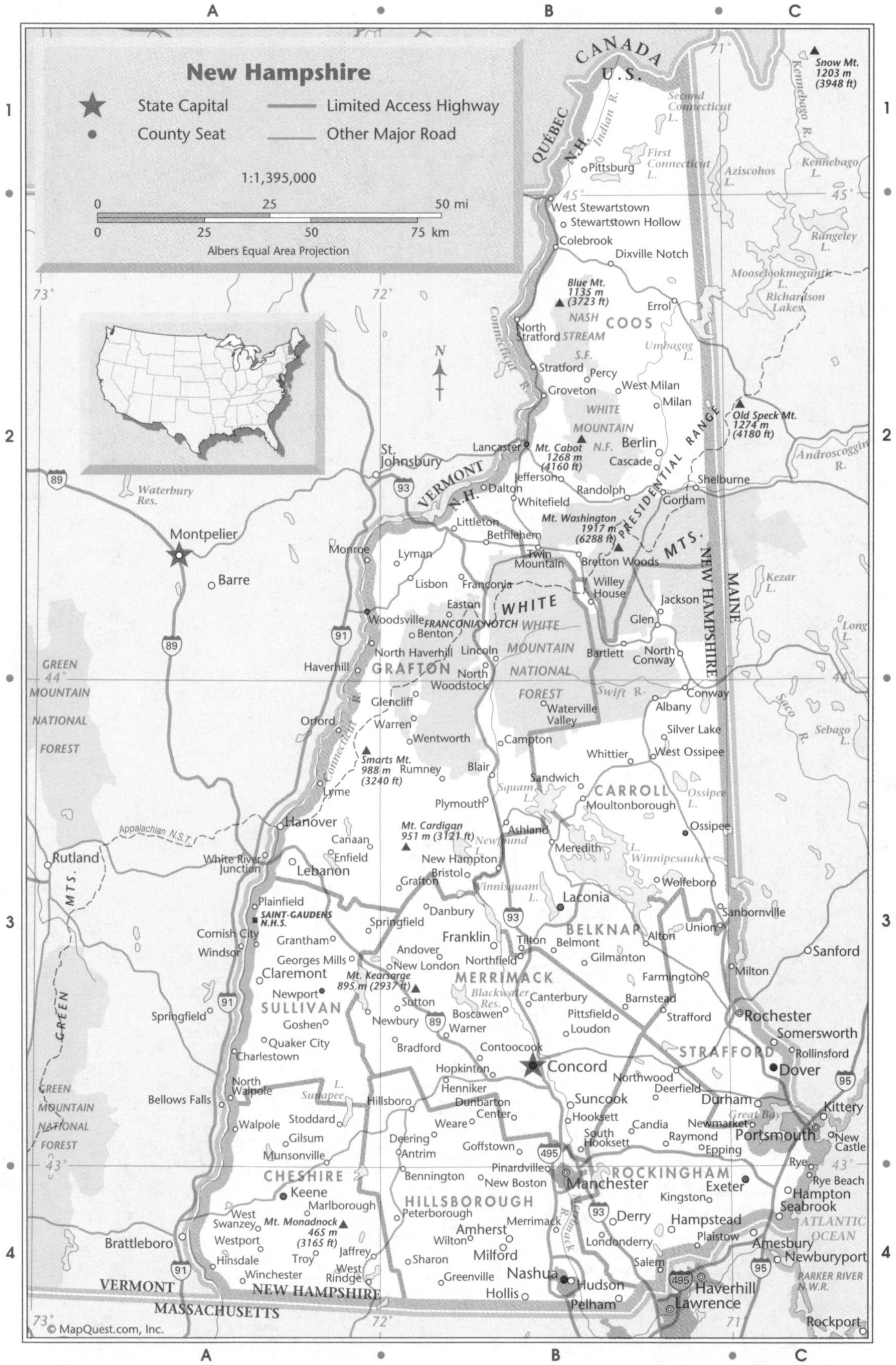

Capital: Trenton
Area: 8,700 sq. mi.
22,600 sq. km.
Population: 8,115,000
Largest City: Newark

New Jersey

★ State Capital
● County Seat

— Limited Access Highway
— Other Major Road

1:1,193,000

0   15   30 mi
0   15   30   45 km

Albers Equal Area Projection

© MapQuest.com, Inc.

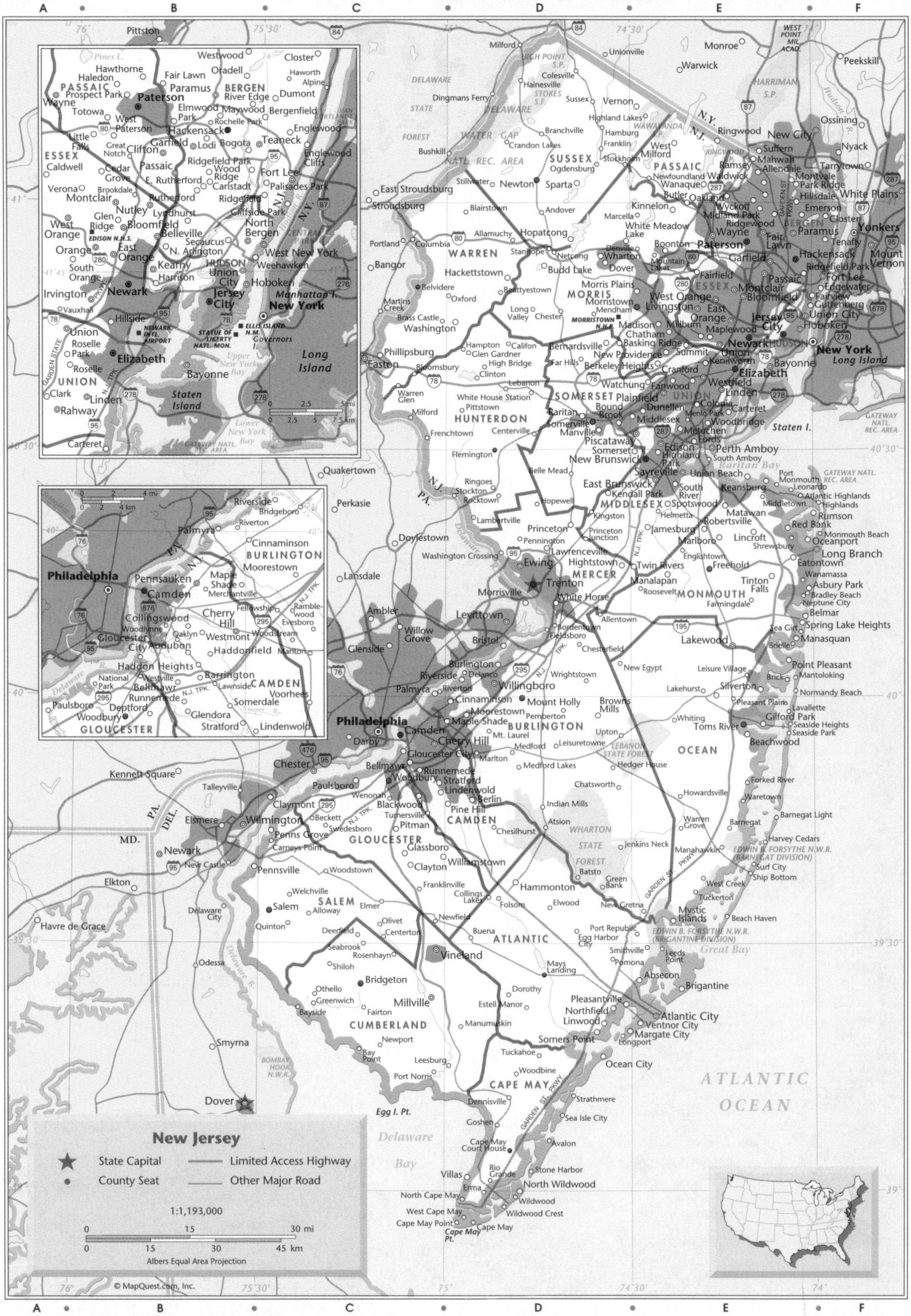

Capital: Santa Fe
Area: 121,600 sq. mi. 314,900 sq. km.
Population: 1,737,000
Largest City: Albuquerque

UTAH • ARIZ.
COLORADO
TEXAS
OKLA.
U.S. MEXICO
CHIHUAHUA

SAN JUAN NATIONAL FOREST
SOUTHERN UTE INDIAN RES.
UTE MOUNTAIN I.R.
NAVAJO INDIAN RES.
CANYON DE CHELLY NATL. MON.
MESA VERDE NATL. PARK
HOVENWEEP N.M.
YUCCA HOUSE N.M.
COMANCHE NATL. GRASSLAND
FORT CARSON MIL. RES.
SAN ISABEL N.F.
CARSON NATIONAL FOREST
APACHE
JICARILLA
RIO ARRIBA
SAN JUAN
MCKINLEY
NAVAJO I.R.
ZUNI INDIAN RES.
CIBOLA NATL. FOR.
EL MALPAIS NATL. CONS. AREA
EL MALPAIS NATL. MONUMENT
ACOMA INDIAN RES.
LAGUNA INDIAN RES.
ISLETA INDIAN RES.
SANDOVAL
JEMEZ IND. RES.
ZIA IND. RES.
COCHITI I.R.
BANDELIER NATL. MON.
LOS ALAMOS
SANTA FE
TAOS
SANGRE DE CRISTO MTS.
COLFAX
UNION
HARDING
MORA
SAN MIGUEL
TORRANCE
VALENCIA
CIBOLA
CATRON
APACHE - SITGREAVES NATL. FOR.
GILA NATIONAL FOREST
CIBOLA NATIONAL FOREST
SOCORRO
SEVILLETA N.W.R.
BOSQUE DEL APACHE N.W.R.
SALINAS PUEBLO MISSIONS N.M.
SALINAS PUEBLO MISSIONS N.M.
GUADALUPE
QUAY
CURRY
DE BACA
ROOSEVELT
LINCOLN
LINCOLN NATIONAL FOREST
CHAVES
BITTER LAKE N.W.R.
PECOS
LLANO ESTACADO
GRANT
GILA NATIONAL FOREST
CLIFF DWELLINGS N.M.
BLACK RANGE
SIERRA
WHITE SANDS MISSILE RANGE
WHITE SANDS NATL. MON.
MESCALERO APACHE INDIAN RES.
OTERO
DONA ANA
LUNA
HIDALGO
CORONADO NATIONAL FOREST
GUADALUPE MTS. NATL. PARK
CARLSBAD CAVERNS NATL. PARK
EDDY
LEA
GUADALUPE NATIONAL FOREST
FORT BLISS MIL. RES.
HOLLOMAN A.F.B.
CANNON A.F.B.
GRULLA N.W.R.

Major cities and towns:
Shiprock, Farmington, Aztec, Bloomfield, Kirtland, Durango, Cortez, Beklabito, Sanostee, Burnham, Newcomb, Toadlena, Sheep Springs, Crystal, Naschitti, Tohatchi, Mexican Springs, Window Rock, Gallup, Gamerco, Allisono, Church Rock, McGaffey, Thoreau, Prewitt, Milan, Grants, Bluewater, San Rafael, El Morro, Zuni, Black Rock, Ojo Caliente, Ramah, Fence Lake, Quemado, Omega, Pie Town, Datil, Magdalena, Aragon, Reserve, Luna, Apache Creek, Cruzville, Alma, Glenwood, Pleasanton, Buckhorn, Cliff, Gila, Mule Creek, Redrock, Virden, Lordsburg, Silver City, Pinos Altos, Santa Rita, Bayard, Hurley, Hanover, Mimbres, Monticello, Chloride, Cuchillo, Truth or Consequences, Hillsboro, Caballo, Las Palomas, Arrey, Derry, Garfield, Salem, Hatch, Rincon, Radium Springs, Deming, Columbus, Hachita, Animas, Rodeo, Cloverdale, Cotton City, Separ, Sunshine, San Miguel, Vado, Berino, Anthony, La Union, Chamberino, Canutillo, Sunland Park, El Paso, Cuidad Juarez, Fabens, Socorro, Guadalupe

Las Cruces, Mesilla, University Park, Fairacres, Dona Ana, Organ, Orogrande, Alamogordo, Tularosa, La Luz, High Rolls, Cloudcroft, Mayhill, Weed, Sacramento, Timberon, Pinon, Dunken, Hope, Artesia, Atoka, Lakewood, Carlsbad, Loving, Malaga, Black River Village, Whites City, Loco Hills, Maljamar, Lovington, Humble City, Nadine, Hobbs, Eunice, Jal, Tatum, Milnesand, Causey, Kenna, Elida, Portales, Clovis, Texico, Melrose, Grady, Ragland, Forrest, House, McAlister, Field, Jordan, Tucumcari, Montoya, San Jon, Logan, Nara Visa, Amistad, Bueyeros, Sedan, Clayton, Mt. Dora, Grenville, Des Moines, Capulin, Folsom, Raton, Trinidad, Texline

Santa Fe, Albuquerque, Rio Rancho, Bernalillo, Corrales, Alameda, Los Lunas, Belen, Bosque Farms, Isleta, Los Padillas, Peralta, Tome, Jarales, Casa Colorada, La Joya, Bernardo, Abeytas, Sabinal, Veguita, Polvadera, Lemitar, Escondida, Socorro, Luis Lopez, San Antonio, San Acacia, Bingham, White Oaks, Carrizozo, Nogal, Capitan, Fort Stanton, Lincoln, Hondo, Ruidoso, Alto, Ruidoso Downs, Bent, San Patricio, Picacho, Tinnie, Hondo, Riverside, Roswell, Dexter, Greenfield, Hagerman, Lake Arthur, Midway, Dora

Mountain peaks:
Shiprock 2188 m (7178 ft)
Montezuma Peak 4008 m (13,150 ft)
Wheeler Peak 4011 m (13,161 ft)
Baldy Mt. 3792 m (12,442 ft)
Cerro Vista 3639 m (11,939 ft)
Mt. Taylor 3445 m (11,301 ft)
Cebolleta Peak 2671 m (8762 ft)
Alegres Mt. 3122 m (10,244 ft)
Mt. Withington 3083 m (10,115 ft)
S. Baldy 3287 m (10,783 ft)
Whitewater Baldy 3319 m (10,890 ft)
Reeds Peak 3051 m (10,011 ft)
Sierra Blanca 3651 m (11,977 ft)
Gallinas Peak 2626 m (8615 ft)
Cooke's Peak 2563 m (8408 ft)
Burro Peak 2449 m (8035 ft)
Guadalupe Peak 2667 m (8751 ft)
Sierra Blanca 2100 m (6890 ft)
Mt. Livermore 2501 m (8206 ft)

RIO GRANDE
CONTINENTAL DIVIDE
PECOS R.
Conchas L.
Sumner L.
Elephant Butte Res.
Caballo Res.
JORNADA DEL MUERTO
SAN ANDRES MTS.
HUECO MTS.
Salt Basin
Playas L.
Mountain Time Zone / Central Time Zone

New Mexico

★ State Capital
● County Seat
── Limited Access Highway
── Other Major Road

1:3,409,000

0   50   100mi
0   50   100   150 km
Albers Equal Area Projection

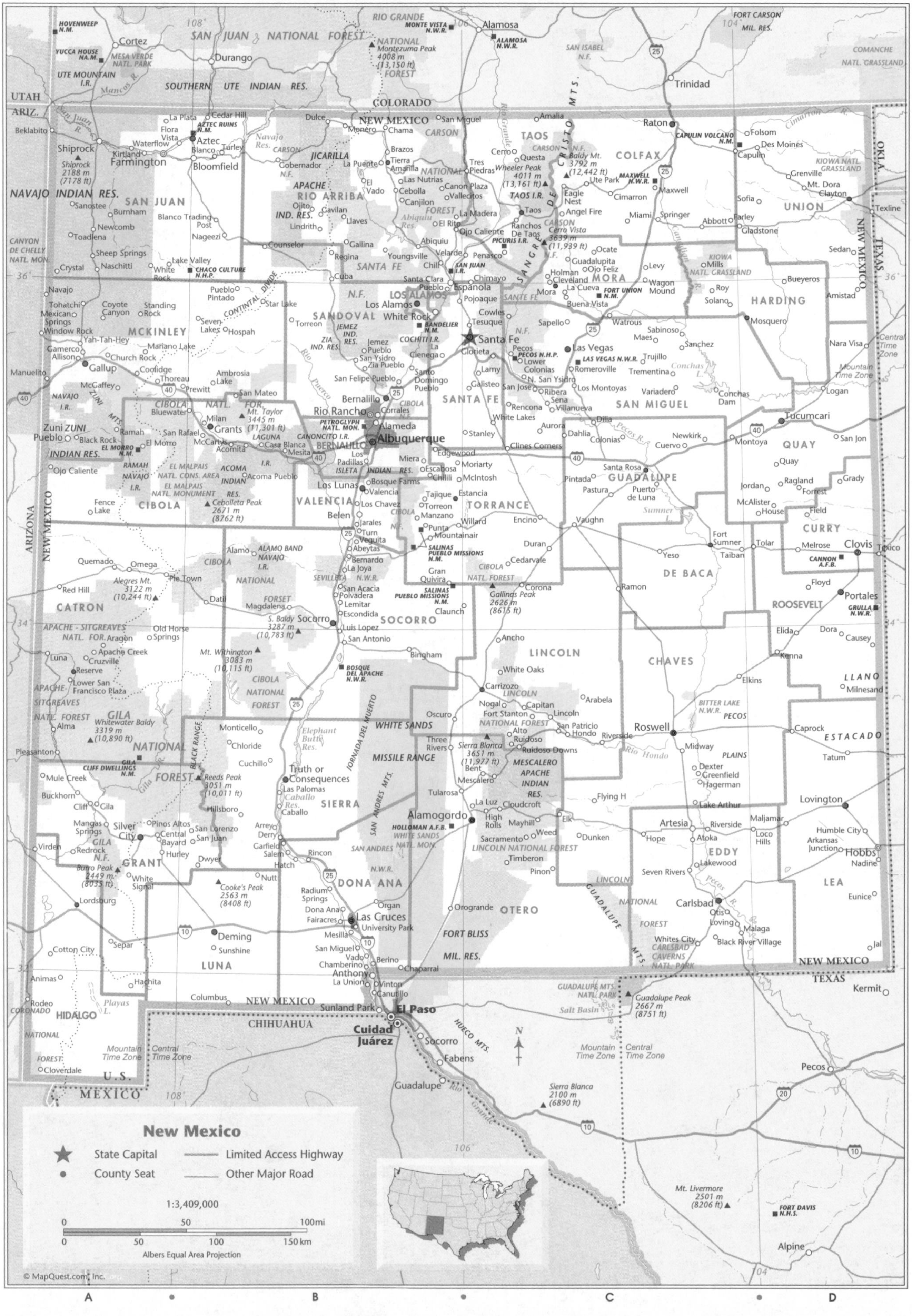

Capital: Albany
Area: 54,700 sq. mi. 141,100 sq. km.
Population: 18,175,000
Largest City: New York

New York

- ★ State Capital
- • County Seat

— Limited Access Highway
— Other Major Road

1:2,432,000

0 40 80 mi
0 40 80 120 km

Albers Equal Area Projection

same scale as main map

LAKE ONTARIO

LAKE ERIE

CANADA

UNITED STATES

ATLANTIC OCEAN

LONG ISLAND

ADIRONDACK MOUNTAINS

ADIRONDACK PARK

CATSKILL PARK

CATSKILL MTS.

Mt. Marcy 1629 m (5344 ft)

Slide Mountain 1281 m (4204 ft)

QUÉBEC

VT.

MASS.

CONN.

N.J.

PENNSYLVANIA

QUEBEC

ONTARIO

NEW YORK

MapQuest.com, Inc.

Capital: Raleigh
Area: 53,800 sq. mi.
139,400 sq. km.
Population: 7,546,000
Largest City: Charlotte

North Carolina

Limited Access Highway
Other Major Road

★ State Capital
• County Seat

1:2,600,000

Albers Equal Area Projection

0 40 80 80 mi
0 40 80 120 km

ATLANTIC OCEAN

VIRGINIA
NORTH CAROLINA
SOUTH CAROLINA

TENN.
N.C.
GA.

ONSLOW BAY
LONG BAY
THE GRAND STRAND

Mt. Mitchell 2037 m (6684 ft)
Mt. Rogers 1746 m (5729 ft)
Roan Mt. 1916 m (6285 ft)
Mt. Mitchell 2037 m (6684 ft)
Clingmans Dome 2025 m (6643 ft)
Standing Indian 1676 m (5499 ft)

Raleigh
Charlotte
Greensboro
Winston-Salem
Durham
Fayetteville
Wilmington
Asheville
Greenville
Rocky Mount
Goldsboro
Wilson
Kinston
Jacksonville
Gastonia
Concord
Salisbury
Hickory
Statesville
Monroe
Sanford
Lumberton
Greenville

© MapQuest.com, Inc.

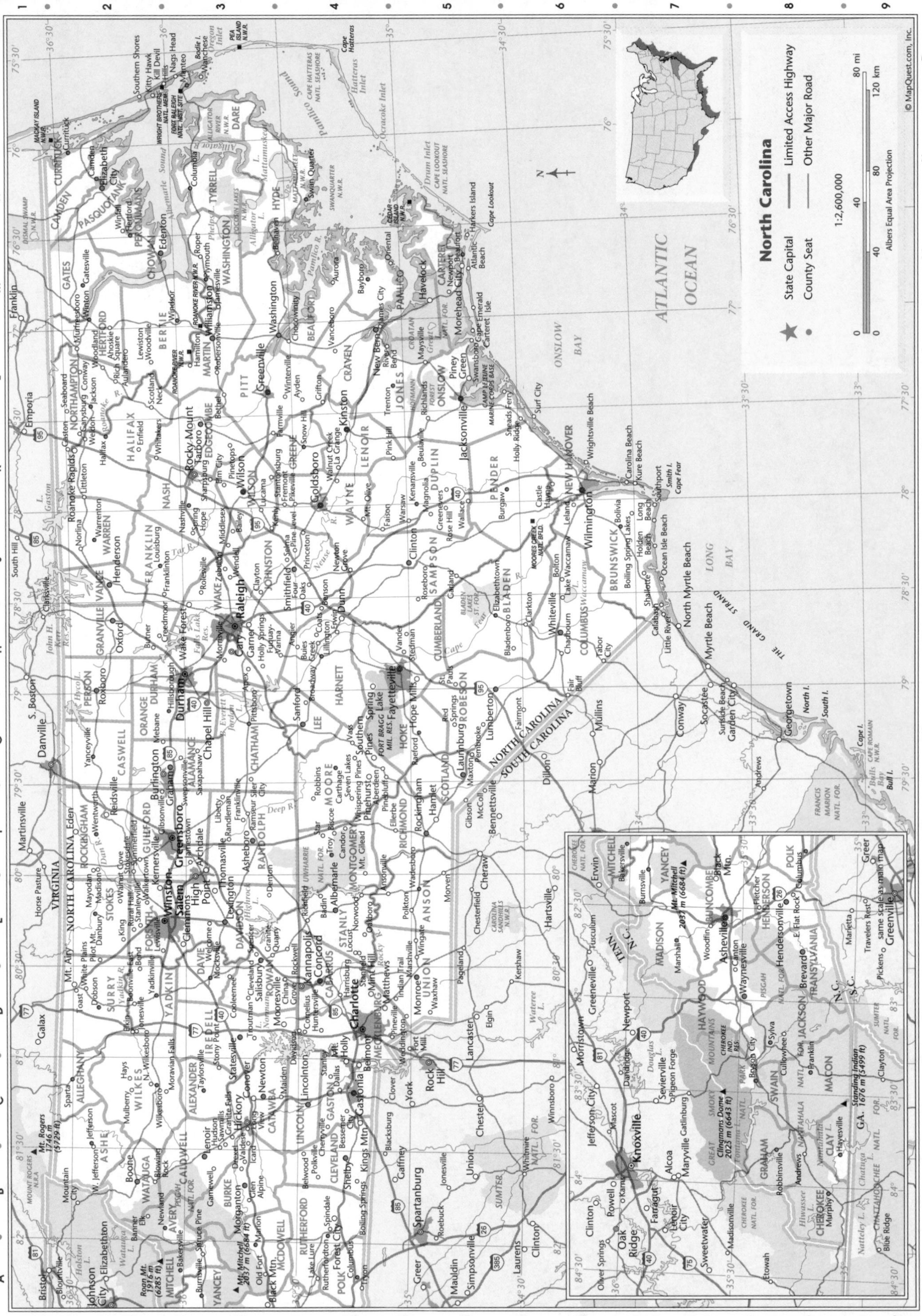

Capital: Bismarck
Area: 70,700 sq. mi.
183,100 sq. km.
Population: 638,000
Largest City: Fargo

North Dakota

1:2,617,000

Albers Equal Area Projection

State Capital ★
County Seat ●

—— Limited Access Highway
—— Other Major Road

0   40   80 mi
0   40   80   120 km

© MapQuest.com, Inc.

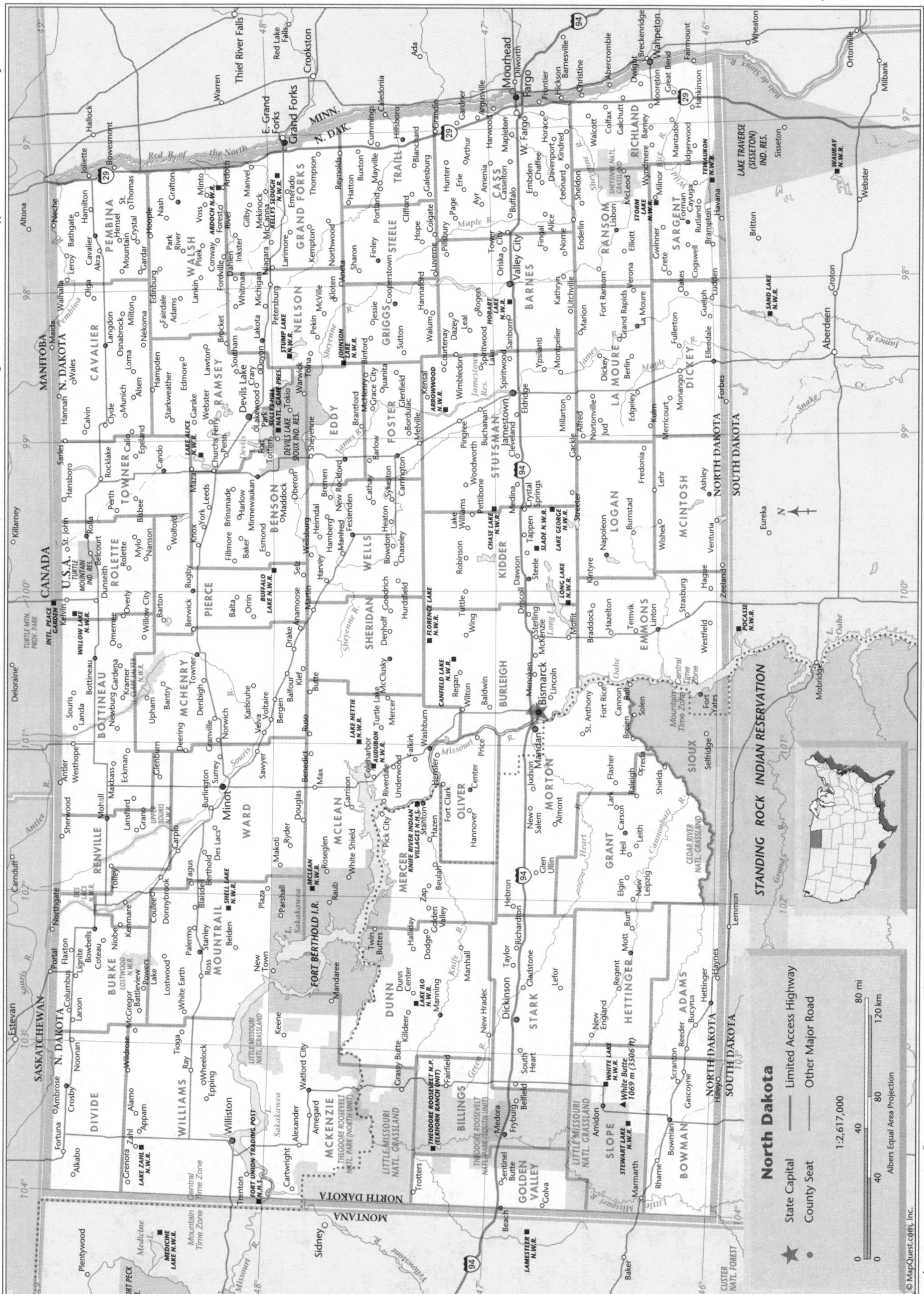

Capital: Columbus
Area: 44,800 sq. mi.
116,100 sq. km.
Population: 11,209,000
Largest City: Columbus

Ohio

★ State Capital — Limited Access Highway
• County Seat — Other Major Road

1:2,131,000

0 30 60 mi
0 30 60 90 km
Albers Equal Area Projection

© MapQuest.com, Inc.

Capital: Oklahoma City **Population:** 3,347,000
Area: 69,900 sq. mi. **Largest City:** Oklahoma City
181,000 sq. km.

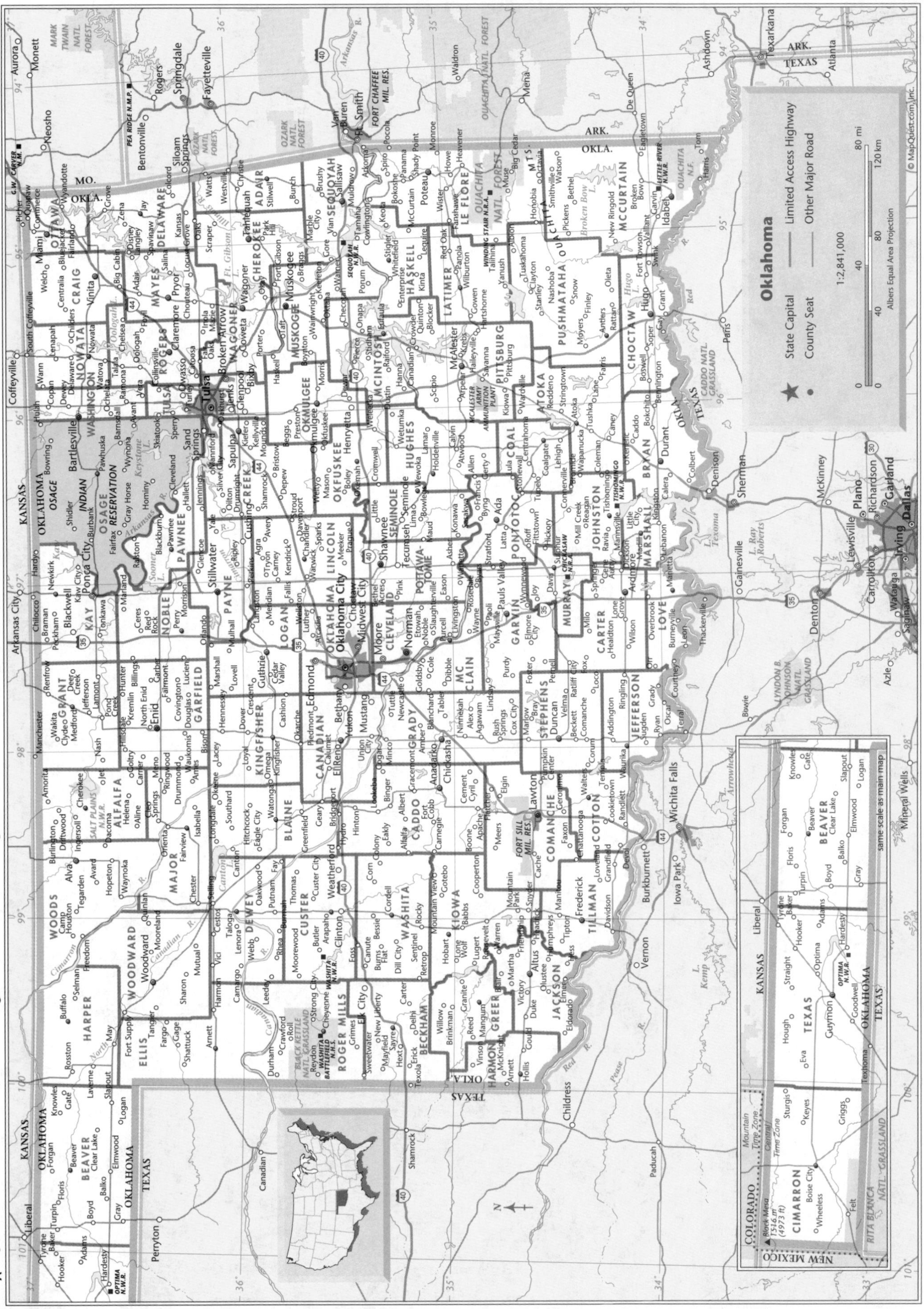

Capital: Salem
Area: 98,400 sq. mi.
254,800 sq. km.
Population: 3,282,000
Largest City: Portland

Oregon

Limited Access Highway
Other Major Road

1:3,545,000

★ State Capital
• County Seat

Albers Equal Area Projection

© MapQuest.com, Inc.

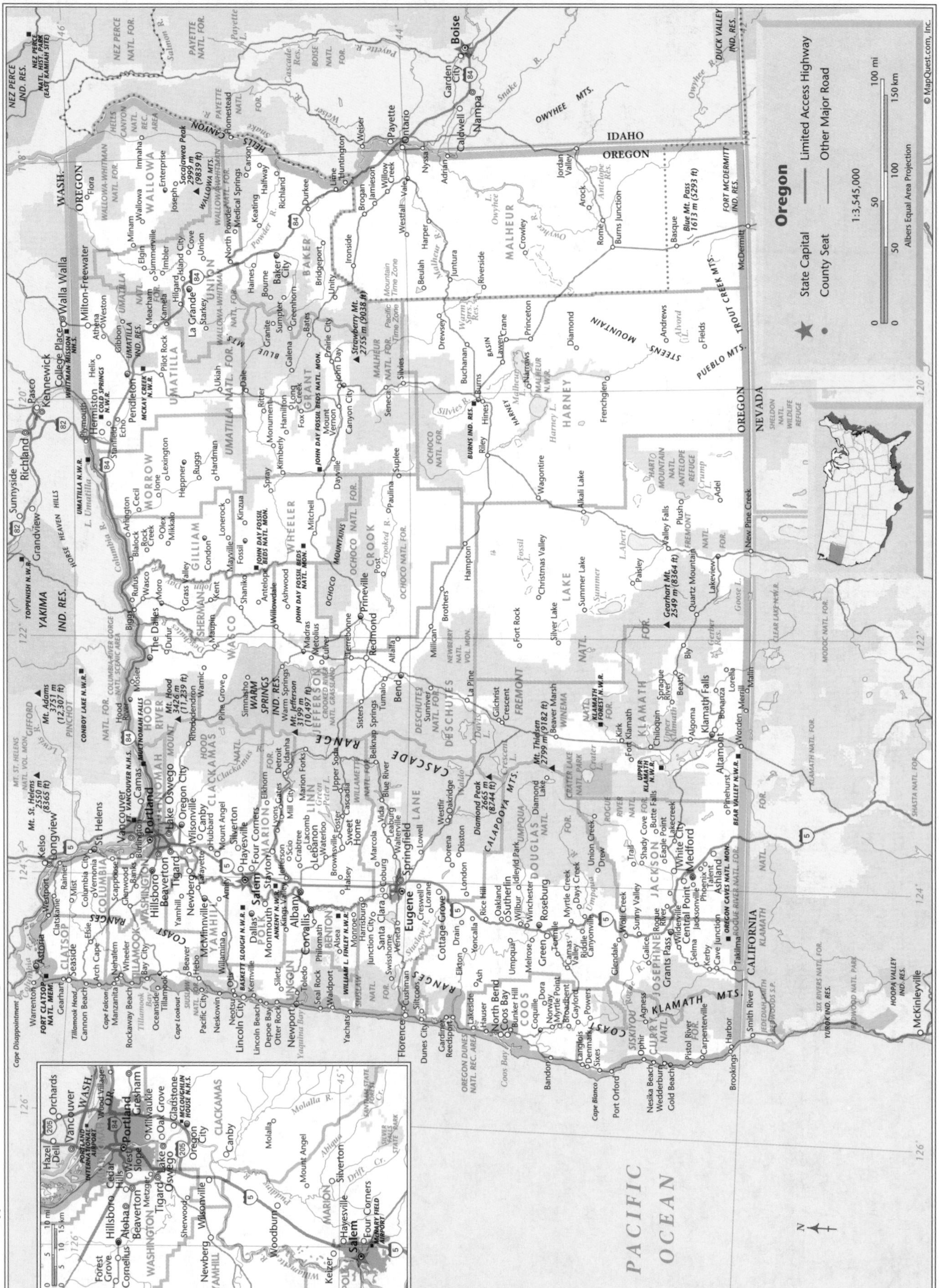

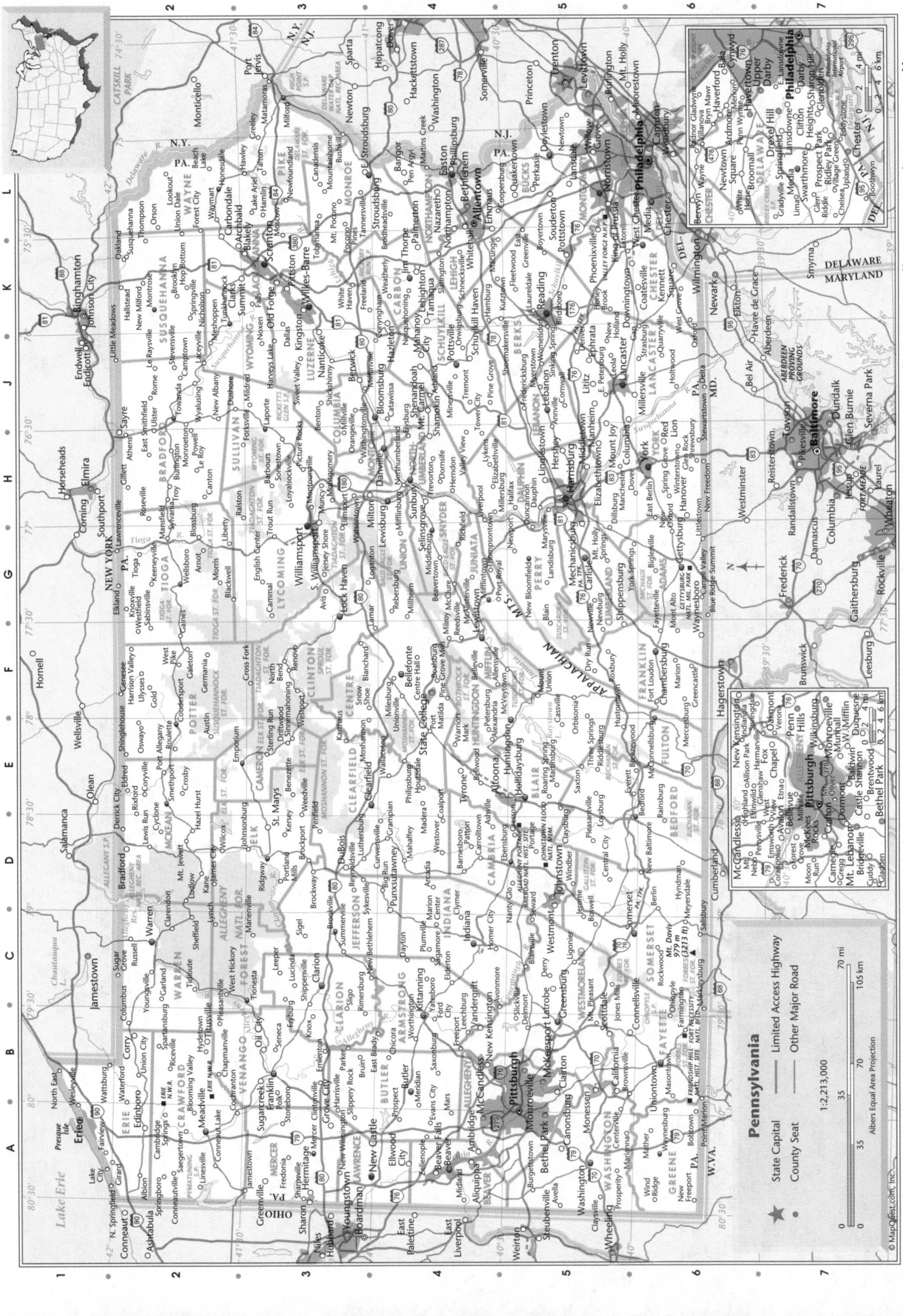
Pennsylvania
State Capital
County Seat
Limited Access Highway
Other Major Road
1:2,213,000
0 35 70 mi
0 35 70 105 km
Albers Equal Area Projection
© MapQuest.com, Inc.

Capital: Providence **Population:** 988,000
Area: 1,500 sq. mi. **Largest City:** Providence
4,000 sq. km.

Webster
DOUGLAS S.F.
MASSACHUSETTS
RHODE ISLAND
Slatersville
Woonsocket
Diamond Hill
Wallum Lake
Cumberland Hill
Manville
Glendale
Pascoag
Harrisville
Ashton
Tarkiln
Putnam
Berkeley
Valley Falls
Chepachet
Lonsdale
North Seekonk
West Glocester
Spragueville
Saylesville
Harmony
Central Falls
Pawtucket
Greenville
N. Providence
Rumford
PROVIDENCE
North Foster
Jerimoth Hill
247 m (812 ft)
North Scituate
Providence
ROGER WILLIAMS NATL. MEM.
East Providence
Seekonk
South Foster
Danielson
Foster Center
Scituate Res.
Clayville
Cranston
Pawtuxet
Moosup Valley
Hope
Fiskeville
West Barrington
Somerset
Ocean Grove
Rice City
Barrington
Warren
Moosup
Coventry Center
Anthony
Warwick
BRISTOL
Bristol
Plainfield
West Warwick
Quidnick
Washington
Fall River
KENT
Westport
East Greenwich
Nooseneck
Tiverton
PAUCHAUG S.F.
Narragansett Bay
Prudence
Portsmouth
Sakonnet
CONNECTICUT
RHODE ISLAND
Exeter
Wickford
Middletown
Adamsville
Arcadia
Hamilton
Little Compton
Rockville
Allenton
Slocum
NEWPORT
Wyoming
WASHINGTON
Saunderstown
Plum Point
TOURO SYNAGOGUE N.H.S.
Hope Valley
Usquepaug
Jamestown
Newport
SACHUEST POINT N.W.R.
Hopkinton
West Kingston
Kingston
Carolina
Shannock
Alton
Wakefield
Ashaway
Worden Pond
Narragansett Pier
Rhode Island Sound
Bradford
Perryville
Pawcatuck
Westerly
Charlestown
Jerusalem
Galilee
Dunn Corner
TRUSTOM POND N.W.R.
Green Hill
Matunuck
Point Judith
NINIGRET N.W.R.
Avondale
Weekapaug
Quonochontaug
Watch Hill

Block Island Sound

Sandy Pt.
BLOCK ISLAND N.W.R.

Block Island
Southeast Pt.
Block Island

Rhode Island

★ State Capital
— Limited Access Highway
— Other Major Road

1:505,000

0   5   10   15 mi
0 5 10 15 20 km

Albers Equal Area Projection

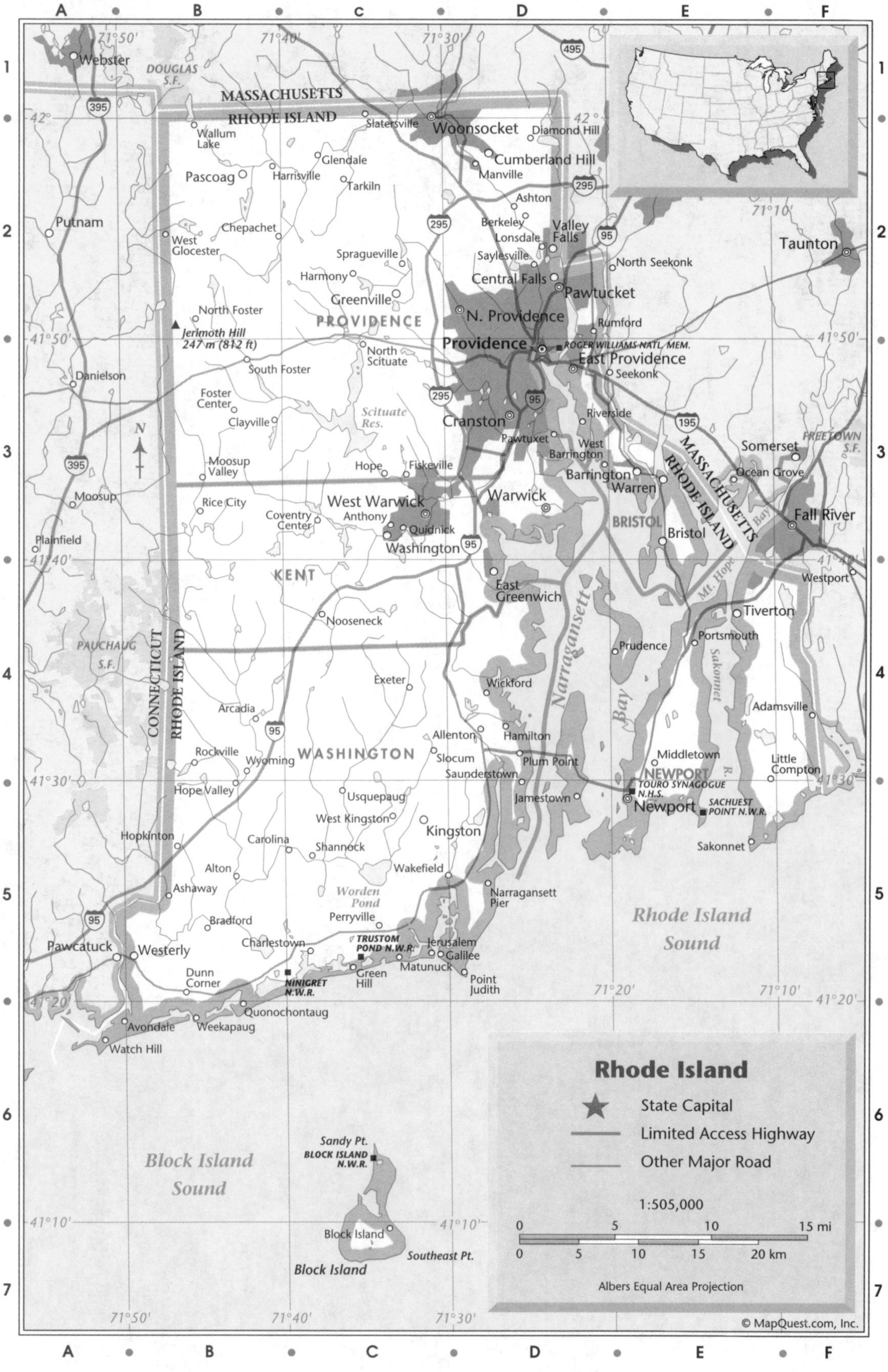

Capital: Columbia
Area: 32,000 sq. mi.
       82,900 sq. km.
Population: 3,836,000
Largest City: Columbia

South Carolina

| State Capital | ★ |
| County Seat | • |

Limited Access Highway
Other Major Road

1:2,148,000
Albers Equal Area Projection

0   30   60 mi
0   30   60   90 km

© MapQuest.com, Inc.

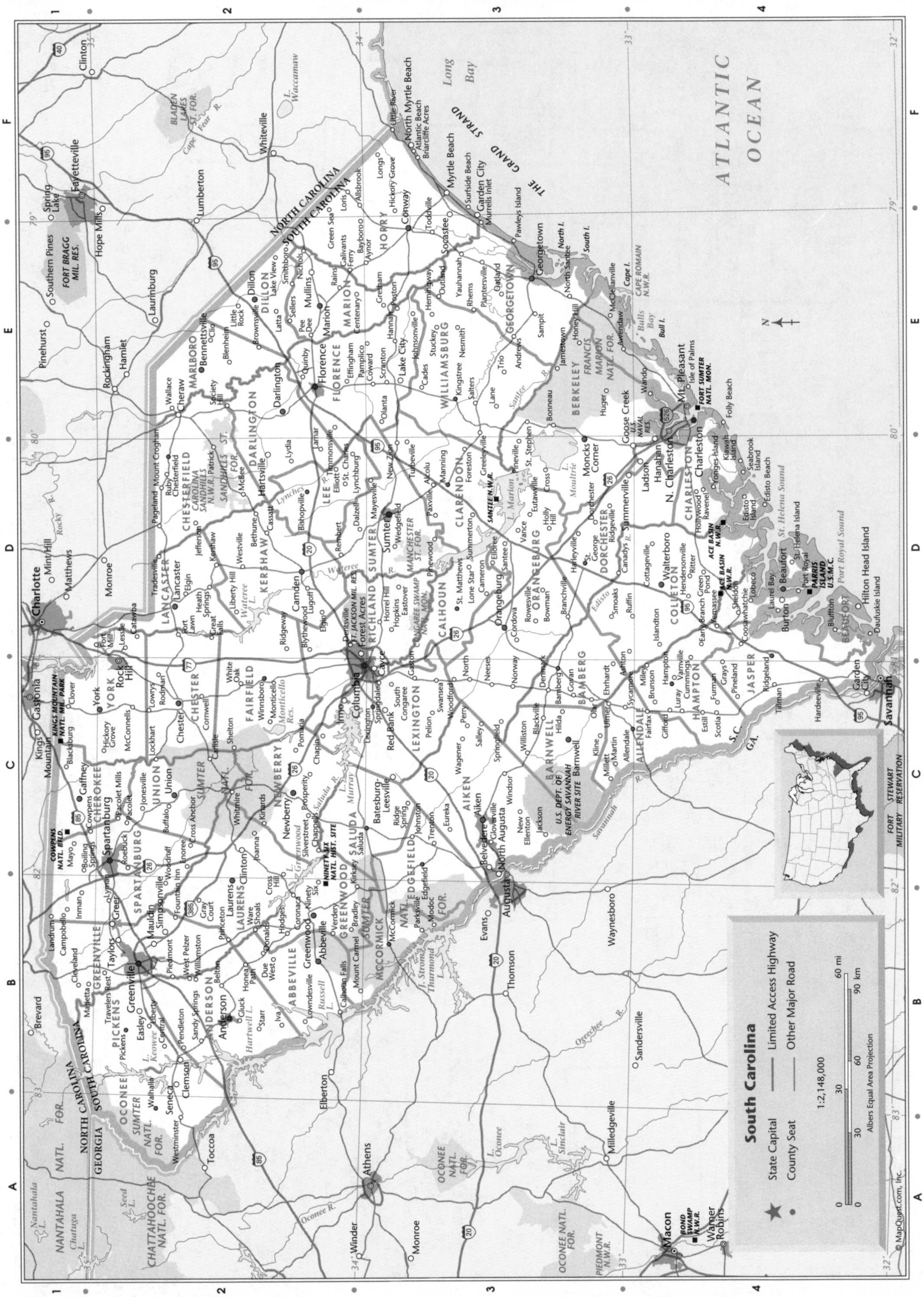

Capital: Pierre
Area: 77,100 sq. mi.
199,700 sq. km.
Population: 738,000
Largest City: Sioux Falls

South Dakota

State Capital ★
County Seat •

Limited Access Highway
Other Major Road

1:2,647,000

Albers Equal Area Projection

© MapQuest.com, Inc.

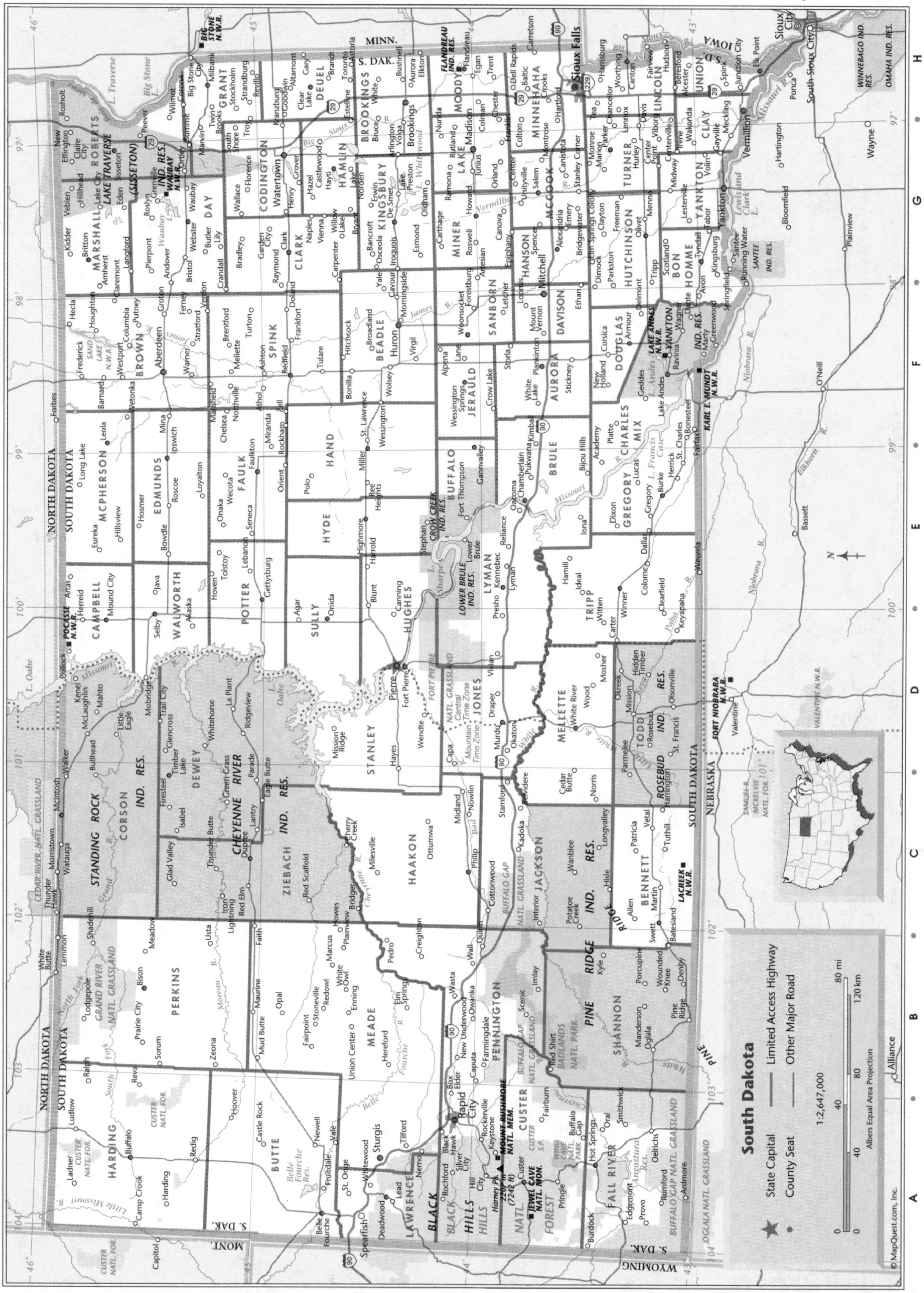

Capital: Nashville
Area: 42,100 sq. mi. 109,200 sq. km.
Population: 5,431,000
Largest City: Memphis

Tennessee

★ State Capital
● County Seat

── Limited Access Highway
── Other Major Road

1:2,352,000

0   40   80 mi

0   40   80   120 km

Albers Equal Area Projection

© MapQuest.com, Inc.

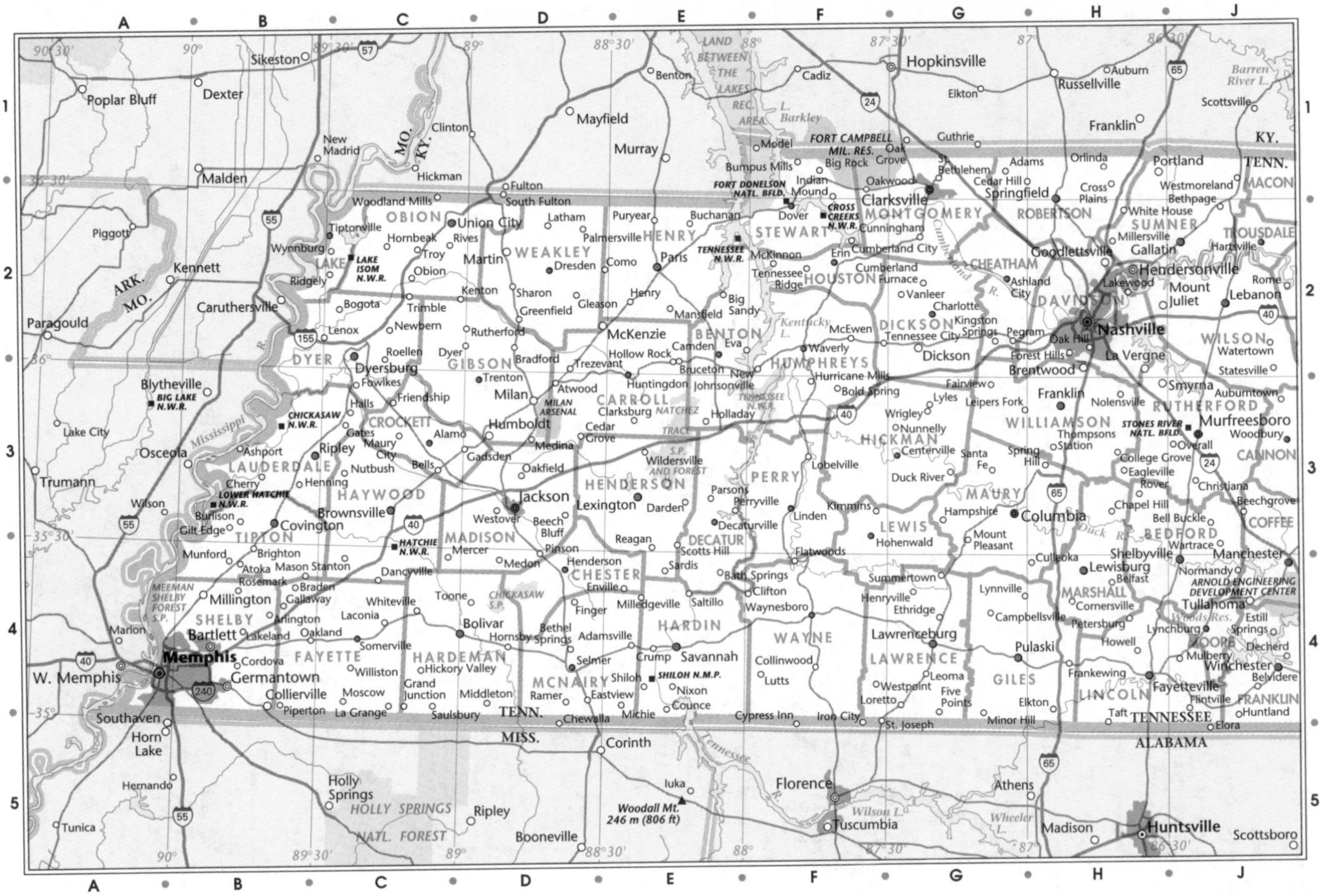

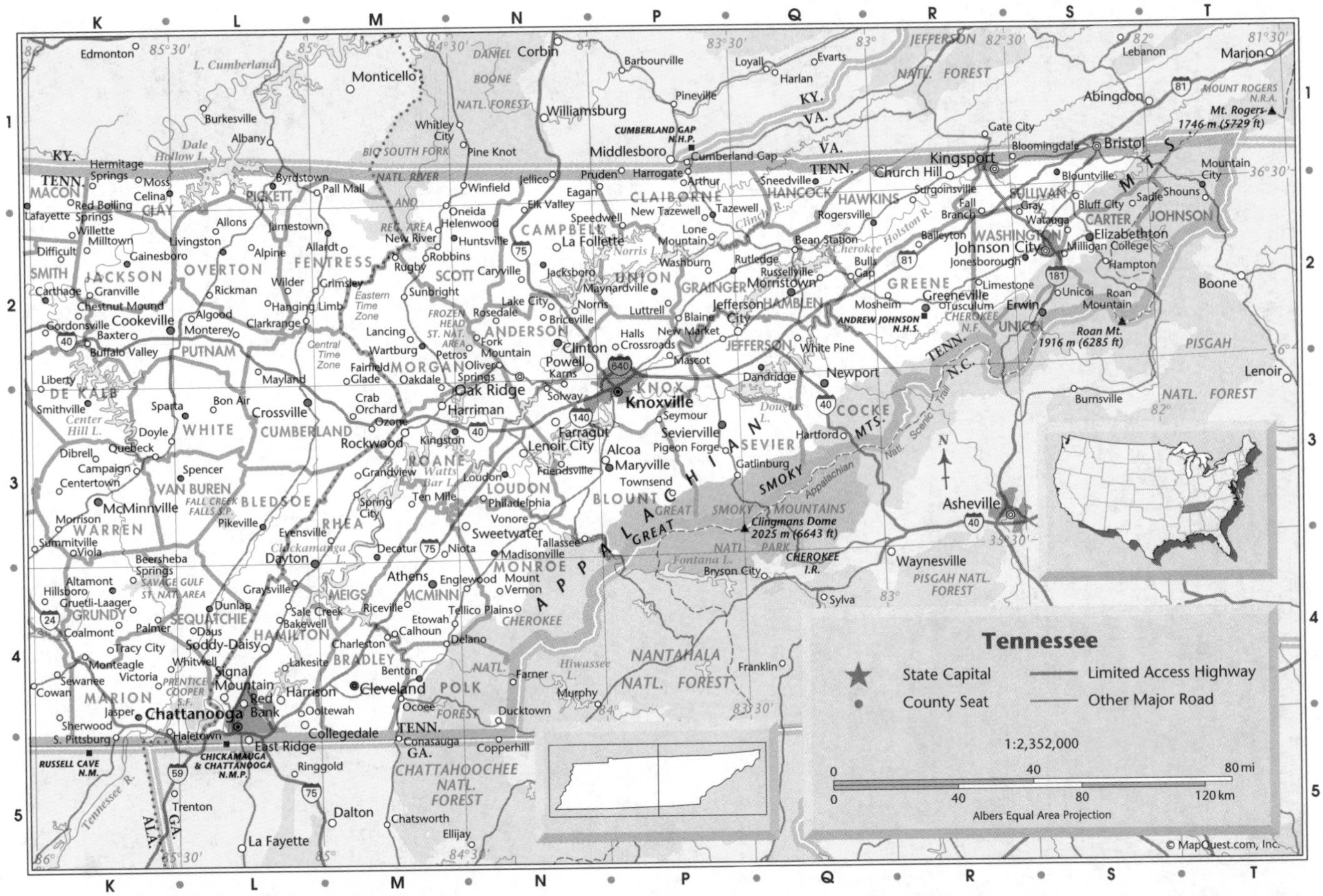

Capital: Austin
Area: 268,600 sq. mi.
695,700 sq. km.
Population: 19,760,000
Largest City: Houston

Texas

1:5,773,000

★ State Capital
• County Seat

— Limited Access Highway
— Other Major Road

Albers Equal Area Projection

© MapQuest.com, Inc.

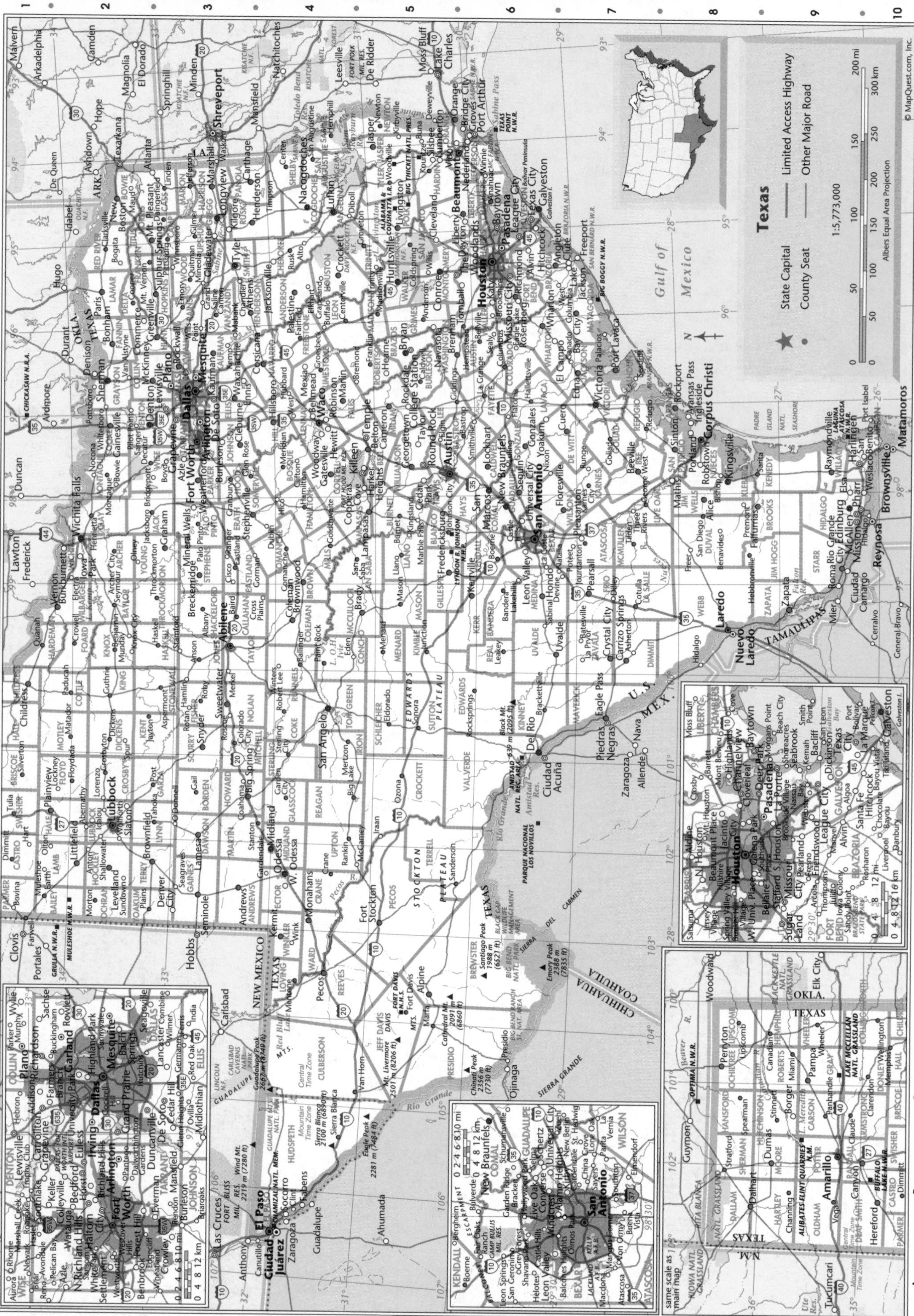

Capital: Salt Lake City
Area: 84,900 sq. mi.
219,900 sq. km.
Population: 2,100,000
Largest City: Salt Lake City

Utah

★ State Capital — Limited Access Highway
● County Seat — Other Major Road

1:2,830,000

0   40   80 mi
0   40   80   120 km
Albers Equal Area Projection

© MapQuest.com, Inc.

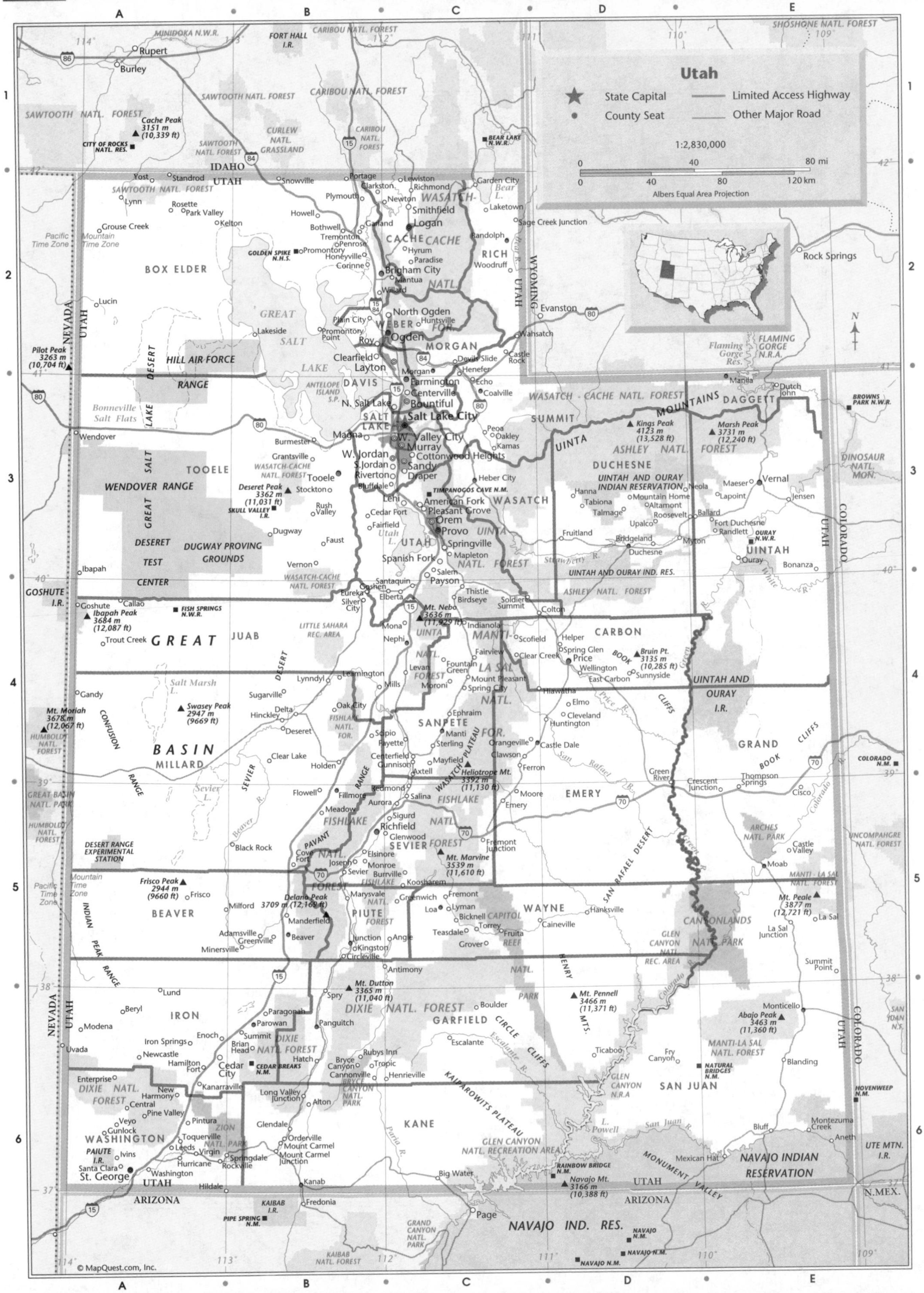

Capital: Montpelier
Area: 9,600 sq. mi.
24,900 sq. km.
Population: 591,000
Largest City: Burlington

Vermont

★ State Capital

• County Seat

━━ Limited Access Highway

━━ Other Major Road

1:1,291,000

0 — 20 — 40 mi

0 — 20 — 40 — 60 km

Albers Equal Area Projection

© MapQuest.com, Inc.

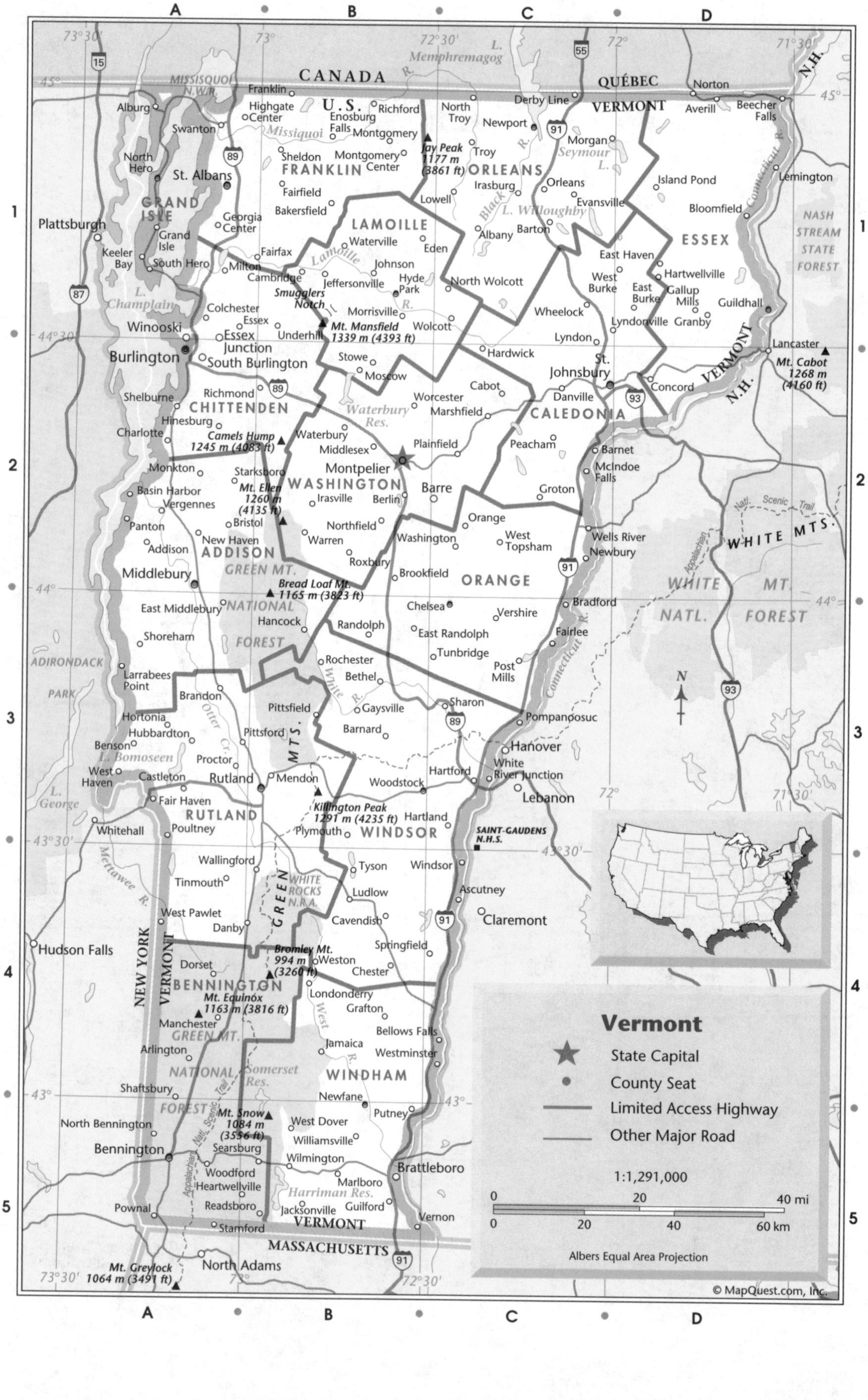

Capital: Richmond
Area: 42,800 sq. mi.
110,800 sq. km.

Population: 6,791,000
Largest City: Virginia Beach

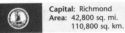

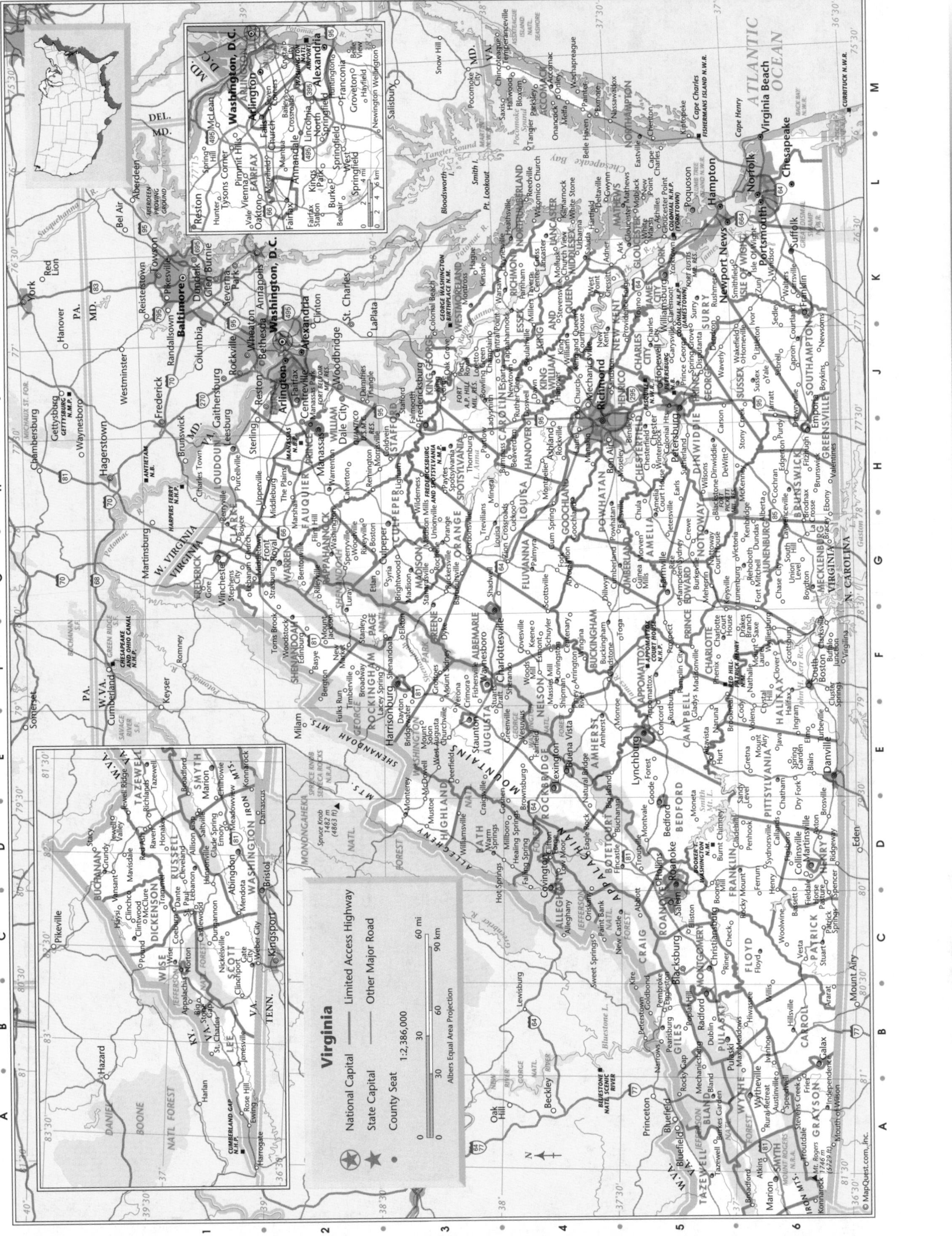

Capital: Olympia
Area: 71,300 sq. mi.
184,700 sq. km.

Population: 5,689,000
Largest City: Seattle

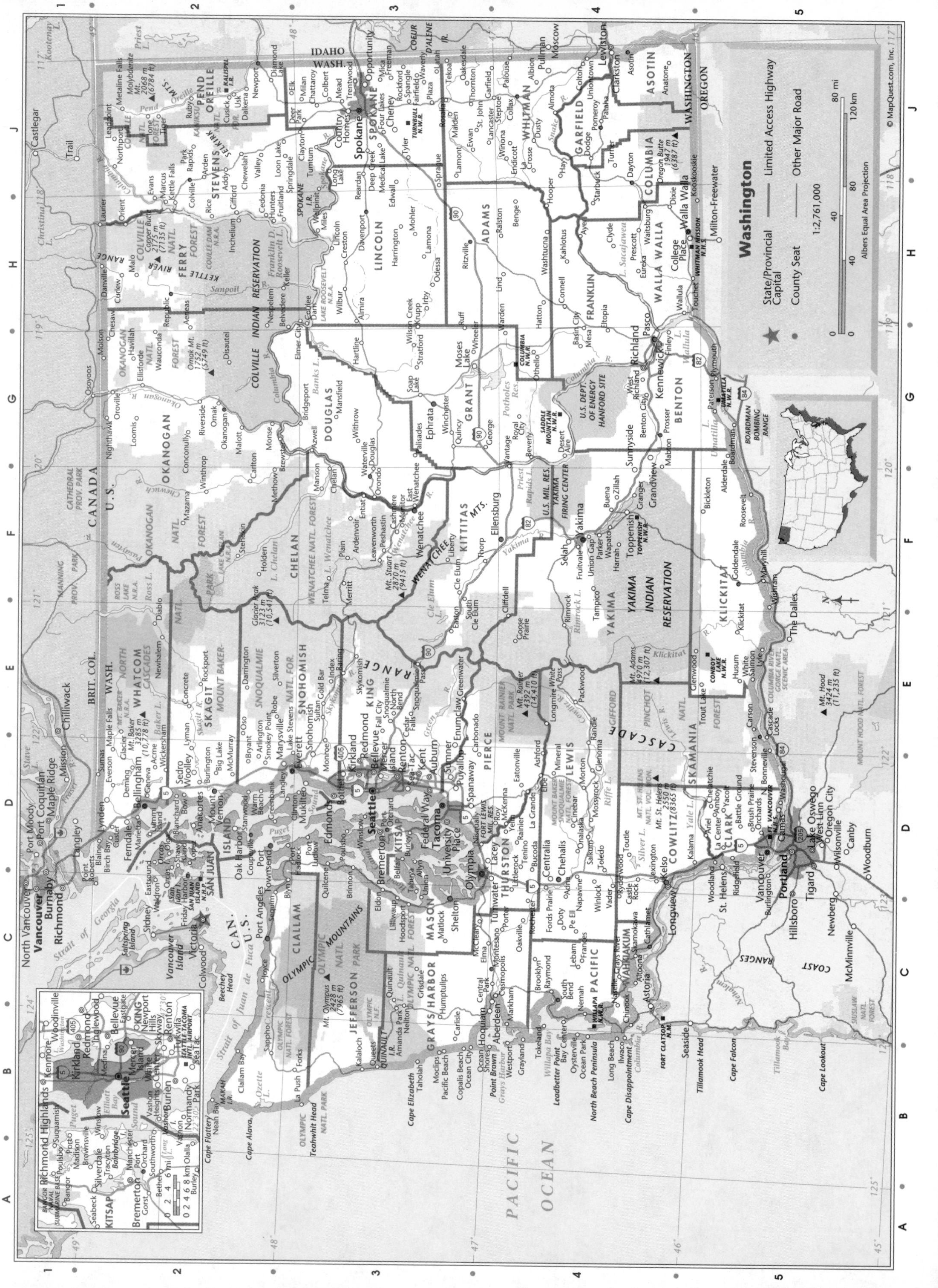

Capital: Charleston	Population: 1,811,000
Area: 24,200 sq. mi.	Largest City: Charleston
62,800 sq. km.	

West Virginia

State Capital ★
County Seat ●

Limited Access Highway
Other Major Road

1:1,830,000

0 30 60 mi
0 30 60 90 km

Albers Equal Area Projection

Inset (top right)

FREDERICKSBURG AND SPOTSYLVANIA N.M.P.

East Liverpool, Chester, New Cumberland, Weirton, Wellsburg, PA., W.VA., Steubenville, Martins Ferry, Wheeling, Bellaire, Moundsville, Cameron, Proctor, Littleton, HANCOCK, BROOKE, OHIO, MARSHALL, WETZEL

(same scale as main map)

Main map place labels

Hagerstown, Antietam N.B., Shepherdstown, Harpers Ferry N.H.P., Shanghai, Harpers Ferry, Charles Town, JEFFERSON, Hedgesville, Martinsburg, Berkeley Springs, BERKELEY, MORGAN, W.VA., VIRGINIA, Winchester, Front Royal, Culpeper

Cumberland, Frostburg, Carpendale, Keyser, New Creek, Fort Ashby, Springfield, Forks of Cacapon, Slanesville, Capon Bridge, Delray, Romney, Augusta, Wardensville, Old Fields, Moorefield, Lost City, Mathias, Baker, Rio, MINERAL, HAMPSHIRE, HARDY, Waynesboro

Mt. Davis (3213 ft), Frostburg, SAVAGE RIVER S.F., Elk Garden, Mount Storm, Scherr, Maysville, Henry, Bayard, Davis, Dorcas, Petersburg, Upper Tract, Riverton, Franklin, Brandywine, GRANT, PENDLETON, Harrisonburg, Staunton, WASHINGTON NATL. FOREST, Buena Vista, Lexington

Morgantown, Masontown, Reedsville, Kingwood, Terra Alta, Rowlesburg, Aurora, Bruceton Mills, Cuzzart, Newburg, PRESTON, TUCKER, Parsons, Montrose, Nestorville, Hambleton, Bowden, Harman, Bemis, MONONGAHELA NATL. FOREST, Gladwin, Circleville, Thornwood, SPRUCE KNOB SENECA ROCKS N.R.A., Spruce Knob (4863 ft)

FRIENDSHIP HILL NATL. HIST. SITE, FORBES S.F., Blacksville, PA., W.VA., Rivesville, Fairmont, Monongah, Shinnston, Wallace, Mannington, Bridgeport, Clarksburg, Salem, New Milton, West Union, Alma, Middlebourne, Smithfield, MARION, HARRISON, DODDRIDGE, TYLER, WETZEL, Lost Creek, Philippi, Belington, Elkins, Beverly, Mill Creek, Valley Head, Durbin, Green Bank, Cass, Dunmore, Frost, RANDOLPH, POCAHONTAS, Edray, Marlinton, Frankford, White Sulphur Springs, Covington

Cameron, Littleton, Hundred, New Martinsville, Proctor, Paden City, Sistersville, Friendly, St. Marys, Pine Grove, Pennsboro, Cairo, Harrisville, Pullman, Auburn, Ellenboro, Smithville, Tanner, Glenville, Burnsville, Stumptown, Flatwoods, Sutton, Birch River, Tioga, Craigsville, Summersville, Nallen, Mount Nebo, Lookout, Quinwood, Rupert, Rainelle, Meadow Bridge, Clintonville, Lewisburg, Ronceverte, Alderson, Union, Gap Mills, Waiteville, MARSHALL, PLEASANTS, RITCHIE, GILMER, WEBSTER, NICHOLAS, GREENBRIER, MONROE, Peterstown, Radford, Blacksburg

Parkersburg, Vienna, Marietta, Williamstown, Belleville, Mineralwells, Ravenswood, Sandyville, Ripley, Kenna, Cottageville, Walker, Evans, Leon, Reedy, Spencer, Elizabeth, Palestine, Petroleum, Macfarlan, Grantsville, Arnoldsburg, Looneyville, Newton, Clay, Wallback, Lizemores, Belva, Smithers, Gauley Bridge, Montgomery, Ansted, Mt. Hope, Oak Hill, Fayetteville, Beckley, Shady Spring, Hinton, Brooks, Talcott, WOOD, JACKSON, ROANE, CALHOUN, WIRT, CLAY, KANAWHA, FAYETTE, RALEIGH, SUMMERS, MERCER, WAYNE, LINCOLN, BOONE, LOGAN, MINGO, WYOMING, McDOWELL

South Charleston, Charleston, St. Albans, Nitro, Cross Lanes, Dunbar, Poca, Buffalo, Eleanor, Winfield, Hurricane, Milton, Barboursville, Huntington, Ceredo, Kenova, Hamlin, West Hamlin, Branchland, Harts, Griffithsville, Madison, Racine, Seth, Whitesville, Sylvester, Marmet, Rand, Cedar Grove, Pond Gap, Chelyan, Leewood, Kingston, Colcord, Pineville, Oceana, Man, Gilbert, Chapmanville, Logan, Stirrat, Amherstdale, Davy, Welch, War, Iaeger, Bradshaw, Matewan, Williamson, Delbarton, Kermit, Crum, Fort Gay, Wayne, East Lynn, Dunlow, Kiahsville, Lenore, Myrtle, Switzer, Mount Gay, Justice, Pineville, Baileysville, Mullens, Herndon, Glen Rogers, Lester, Sophia, Eccles, Mabscott, Sabine, Montcalm, Maybeurg, Bramwell, Bluefield, Princeton, Athens, Matoaka, Camp Creek, Lindside, Greenville, Peterstown, PUTNAM, CABELL, MASON, New Haven, Point Pleasant, Glenwood, Southside, Letart, Hartford

OHIO, OHIO R., Kanawha R., Big Sandy R., Guyandotte R., Tug Fork, Greenbrier R., Bluestone L., Summersville L., Sutton L., Gauley R., New River, KY., W.VA.

WAYNE NATL. FOREST, MONONGAHELA NATL. FOREST, GEORGE WASHINGTON NATL. FOREST, JEFFERSON NATL. FOREST, NEW RIVER GORGE NATL. RIVER, BLUESTONE NATL. SCENIC RIVER, GAULEY RIVER N.R.A., BOOKER T. WASHINGTON N.M., BUCHANAN S.F., FORBES S.F., CHESAPEAKE AND OHIO CANAL N.H.P., FORT NECESSITY NATL. BTFD.

APPALACHIAN MOUNTAINS, ALLEGHENY MOUNTAINS, SHENANDOAH MTN., GREEN RIDGE, SHENANDOAH, SHENANDOAH NATL. PARK

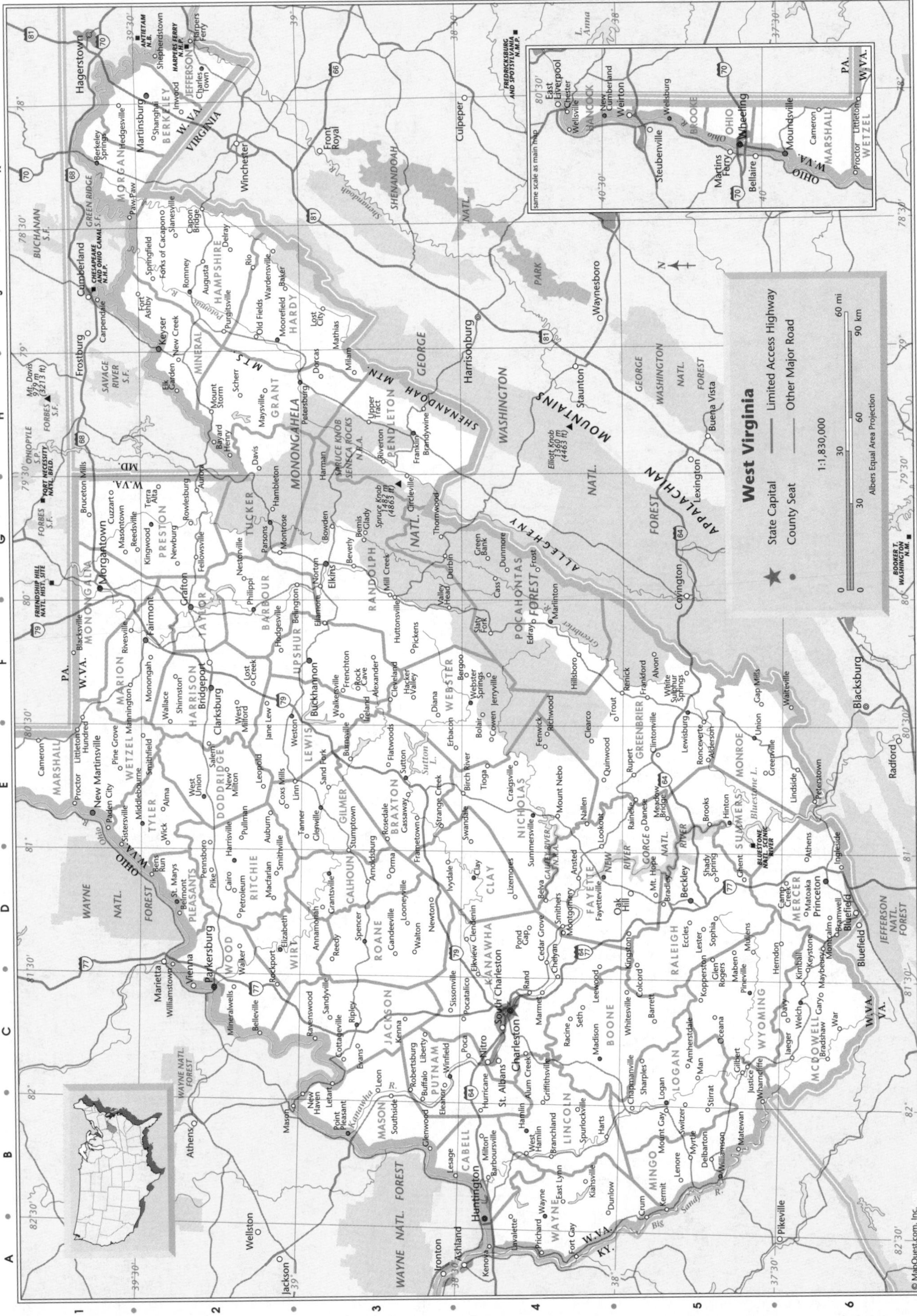

Capital: Madison
Area: 65,500 sq. mi. 169,600 sq. km.
Population: 5,224,000
Largest City: Milwaukee

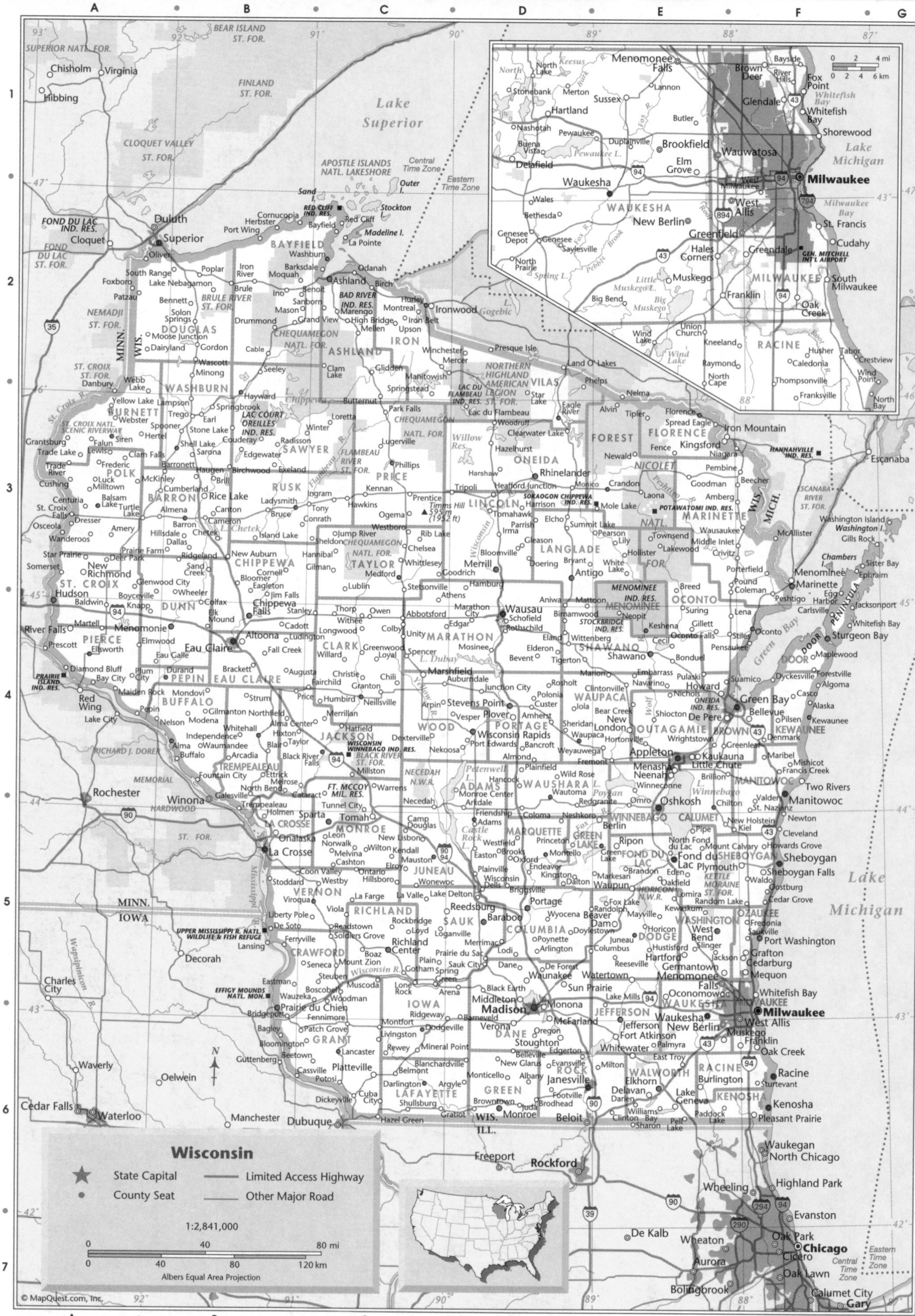

Capital: Cheyenne
Area: 97,800 sq. mi. 253,300 sq. km.
Population: 481,000
Largest City: Cheyenne

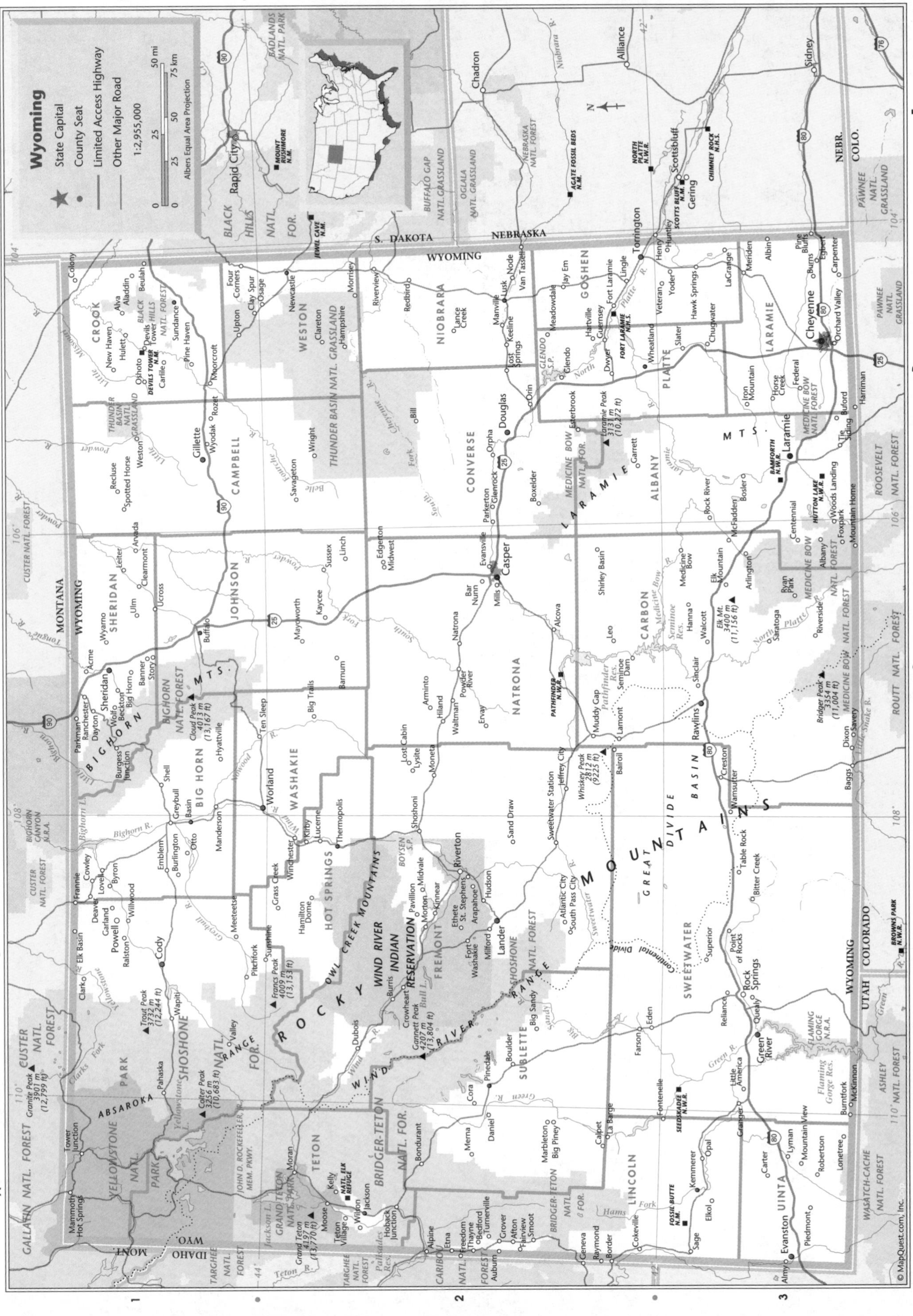

Abbreviations
N.H.P. National Historical Park
N.H.S. National Historic Site
N.M. National Monument
N.P. National Park
N.R.A. National Recreation Area

Key

Alabama ....page 128

Cities and Towns
Abbeville D4
Adamsville C2
Alabaster C2
Albertville C1
Alexander City D3
Aliceville A2
Andalusia C4
Anniston D2
Arab C1
Ashford D4
Ashland D2
Ashville C2
Athens C1
Atmore B4
Attalla C1
Auburn D3
Bay Minette B5
Bayou La Batre A5
Bessemer C2
Birmingham C2
Blountsville C1
Boaz C1
Brent B3
Brewton B4
Bridgeport D1
Brundidge D4
Butler A3
Calera C2
Camden B4
Camp Hill D3
Carbon Hill B2
Carrollton A2
Center Point C2
Centre D1
Centreville B3
Chatom A4
Chelsea C2
Cherokee B1
Chickasaw A5
Childersburg C2
Citronelle A4
Clanton C3
Clayton D4
Clio D4
Collinsville D1
Columbiana C2
Cordova B2
Cottonwood D4
Creola A5
Crossville D1
Cullman C1
Dadeville D3
Daleville D4
Daphne B5
Decatur C1
Demopolis B3
Dora B2
Dothan D4
Double Springs B1
East Brewton B4
Elba C4
Enterprise D4
Eufaula D4
Eutaw B3
Evergreen C4
Fairfield C2
Fairhope B5
Falkville C1
Fayette B2
Flomaton B4
Florala C4
Florence B1
Foley B5
Fort Morgan A5
Fort Payne D1
Frisco City B4
Fultondale C2
Gadsden D1
Gardendale C2
Gasque B5
Geneva D4
Georgiana C4
Glencoe D2
Good Hope C1
Goodwater C2
Gordo B2
Grand Bay A5
Greensboro B3
Greenville C4
Grove Hill B4
Guin B2
Gulf Shores B5
Guntersville C1
Haleyville B1
Hamilton B1
Hanceville C1
Hartford D4
Hartselle C1
Hayneville C3
Hazel Green C1
Headland D4
Heflin D2
Helena C2
Henagar D1
Heron Bay A5
Hokes Bluff D2
Holt B2
Hoover C2
Hueytown B2
Huntsville C1
Irondale C2
Jackson B4
Jacksonville D2
Jasper B2
Jemison C3
Lafayette D3
Lanett D3
Leeds C2
Lincoln C2
Linden B3
Lineville D2
Livingston A3
Luverne C4
Madison C1
Marion B3
Meridianville C1
Midfield C2
Midland City D4
Millbrook C3
Mobile A5
Monroeville B4
Montevallo C2
Montgomery, *capital* C3
Moulton B1
Moundville B3
Muscle Shoals B1
New Hope C1
Newton D4
Northport B2
Oneonta C2
Opelika D3
Opp C4
Orange Beach B5
Oxford D2
Ozark D4
Parrish B2
Pelham C2
Pell City C2
Petersville B1
Phenix City D3
Phil Campbell B1
Piedmont D2
Pinson C2
Point Clear B5
Prattville C3
Priceville C1
Prichard A5
Ragland C2
Rainbow City C2
Rainsville D1
Reform A2
Roanoke D2
Robertsdale B5
Rockford C3
Russellville B1
Samson C4
Saraland A5
Sardis City C1
Satsuma A5
Scottsboro C1
Selma B3
Sheffield B1
Slocomb D4
Smiths D3
Southside C2
Spanish Fort B5
Springville C2
Stevenson D1
Sulligent A2
Sumiton B2
Sylacauga C2
Talladega C2
Tallassee D3
Taylor D4
Theodore A5
Thomasville B4
Thorsby C3
Tillmans Corner A5
Town Creek B1
Trinity B1
Troy D4
Trussville C2
Tuscaloosa B2
Tuscumbia B1
Tuskegee D3
Union Springs D3
Uniontown B3
Valley D3
Vernon A2
Vestavia Hills C2
Vincent C2
Warrior C2
Weaver D2
Wedowee D2
West Blocton B2
Wetumpka C3
Winfield B2
York A3

Other Features
Alabama, *river* B4
Appalachian, *mts.* D1
Bear Creek, *reservoir* B1
Black Warrior, *river* B3
Bon Secour, *bay* B5
Cahaba, *river* B3
Cheaha, *mt.* D2
Conecuh, *river* C4
Coosa, *river* C3
Dauphin, *island* A5
Guntersville, *lake* C1
Jordan, *lake* C3
Lewis Smith, *lake* B1
Logan Morgan, *lake* C2
Lookout, *mt.* D1
Martin, *lake* D3
Mitchell, *lake* C3
Mobile, *bay* A5
Neely Henry, *lake* C2
Pickwick, *lake* A1
R.L. Harris, *reservoir* D2
Russell Cave Natl. Monument D1
Tallapoosa, *river* D2
Tennessee, *river* A1
Tombigbee, *river* A4
Tuscaloosa, *lake* B2
Tuskegee Institute Natl. Hist. Site D3
Weiss, *lake* D1
Wheeler, *lake* B1
William "Bill" Dannelly, *reservoir* B3
Wilson, *lake* B1

Alaska ....page 129

Cities and Towns
Adak Inset
Anchorage F2
Barrow D1
Bethel C2
Big Delta F2
College F2
Cordova F2
Craig J3
Delta Jct. F2
Dillingham D3
Fairbanks F2
Haines H3
Homer E3
Juneau, *capital* J3
Kenai E2
Ketchikan J3
Kodiak E3
Kotzebue C1
McKinley Park F2
Metlakatla J3
Nikiski E2
Nome B2
North Pole F2
Palmer F2
Petersburg J3
Prudhoe Bay F1
Seward F2
Sitka H3
Skagway H3
Soldotna E2
Talkeetna E2
Tok G2
Unalaska B4
Valdez F2
Wasilla F2
Whittier F2
Wrangell J3

Other Features
Adak, *island* Inset
Admiralty Island Natl. Monument J3
Agattu, *island* Inset
Alaska, *gulf* F3
Alaska, *peninsula* C3
Alaska, *range* E2
Aleutian, *islands* A4, Inset
Alexander, *archipelago* H3
Amchitka, *island* Inset
Amlia, *island* Inset
Andreanof, *islands* Inset
Aniakchak N.M. and Preserve D3
Atka, *island* Inset
Attu, *island* Inset
Barrow, *point* D1
Beaufort, *sea* H1
Becharof, *lake* D3
Bering, *sea* B3
Bering, *strait* B2
Blackburn, *mt.* G2
Bristol, *bay* C3
Brooks, *range* D1
Cape Krusenstern N.M. C1
Chirikof, *island* D3
Chukchi, *sea* A1
Colville, *river* E1
Cook, *inlet* E3
Copper, *river* G2
Denali Natl. Park and Preserve E2
Fairweather, *mt.* H3
Gates of the Arctic N.P. and Preserve E1
Glacier Bay N.P. and Preserve H3
Iliamna, *lake* D3
Inside Passage, *waterway* J3
Kanaga, *island* Inset
Katmai Natl. Park and Preserve D3
Kenai, *peninsula* E2
Kenai Fjords Natl. Park F3
Kiska, *island* Inset
Klondike Gold Rush N.H.P H3
Kobuk, *river* D1
Kobuk Valley Natl. Park D1
Kodiak, *island* E3
Kotzebue, *sound* C1
Koyukuk, *river* D1
Kuskokwim, *bay* C3
Kuskokwim, *mts.* D2
Kuskokwim, *river* D2
Lake Clark Natl. Park and Preserve E2
Lisburne, *cape* B1
Lisburne, *peninsula* C1
Logan, *mt.* G2
Lynn, *canal* J3
McKinley, *mt.* E2
Malaspina, *glacier* G3
Michelson, *mt.* G1
Mohican, *cape* B2
Muir, *glacier* F2
Near, *islands* Inset
Noatak, *river* D1
Norton, *sound* C2
Nunivak, *island* B3
Porcupine, *river* G1
Pribilof, *islands* B3
Prince of Wales, *island* J3
Progromni, *volcano* C4
Rat, *islands* Inset
St. Elias, *mt.* G2
St. George, *island* B3
St. Lawrence, *island* A2
St. Matthew, *island* A2
St. Paul, *island* A3
Samalga, *pass* B4
Sanak, *island* C4
Seguam, *island* Inset
Semisopochnoi, *island* Inset
Seward, *peninsula* C1
Shishaldin, *volcano* C4
Shumagin, *islands* D4
Sitka N.H.P. H3
Stikine, *river* J3
Tanaga, *island* F3
Tanana, *river* E2
Tikchik, *lakes* D2
Trinity, *islands* E3
Umnak, *island* Inset
Unalaska, *island* B4
Unga, *island* C3
Unimak, *island* C4
Utukok, *river* C1
White Mts. Natl. Rec. Area F1
Wrangell, *mts.* G2
Wrangell-St. Elias N.P. and Preserve G2
Yukon, *river* D2
Yukon-Charley Rivers Natl. Preserve G2
Yunaska, *island* Inset

Arizona ....page 130

Cities and Towns
Ajo C5
Apache Junction D4
Avondale C4
Bagdad B3
Benson E6
Bisbee F6
Bitahochee E2
Buckeye C4
Bullhead City A2
Camp Verde D3
Carefree D4
Casa Grande D5
Catalina E5
Cave Creek D4
Chandler D4
Chinle F1
Chino Valley C3
Cibecue E4
Clarkdale C3
Claypool E4
Clifton F4
Colorado City C1
Coolidge D5
Cornville D3
Cow Springs E1
Crown King C3
Douglas F6
Dudleyville E5
Eagar F3
El Mirage C4
Eloy D5
Flagstaff D2
Florence D4
Fort Defiance F2
Fountain Hills D4
Ganado F2
Geronimo E4
Gila Bend C5
Gilbert D4
Globe E4
Goodyear C4
Grand Canyon C1
Greaterville E6
Green Valley E6
Guthrie F5
Happy Jack D3
Holbrook E3
Huachuca City E6
Kayenta E1
Kearny E4
Kingman A2
Kirkland Junction C3
Lake Havasu City A3
Lake Montezuma D3
Litchfield Park C4
Mammoth E5
Many Farms F1
Marana D5
Mesa D4
Miami E4
Nogales E6
Oracle E5
Oro Valley E5
Page D1
Paradise Valley D4
Parker A3
Payson D3
Peoria C4
Phoenix, *capital* C4
Pima F5
Pinetop-Lakeside F3
Prescott C3
Prescott Valley C3
Quartzsite A4
Queen Creek D4
Randolph D5
Sacaton D4
Safford F5
Sahuarita E6
St. David E6
St. Johns F3
San Carlos E4
Sanders F2
San Manuel E5
Scottsdale D4
Sedona D3
Sells D6
Show Low E3
Sierra Vista E6
Snowflake E3
Somerton A5
South Tucson E5
Springerville F3
Sun City C4
Sun Lakes D4
Superior D4
Surprise C4
Taylor E3
Tempe D4
Thatcher F5
Three Points D5
Tolleson C4
Tombstone E6
Tuba City D1
Tucson E5
Whiteriver F4
Wickenburg C4
Willcox F5
Williams C2
Window Rock F2
Winslow E2
Yuma A5

Other Features
Agua Fria, *river* C4
Alamo, *lake* B3
Apache, *lake* D4
Aztec Peak, *mt.* E4
Baldy, *mt.* F4
Bartlett, *reservoir* D4
Big Horn, *mts.* B4
Bill Williams, *river* A3
Black, *mesa* E1
Black, *river* E4
Canyon De Chelly N.M. F1
Casa Grande Ruins N.M. D5
Castle Dome, *mts.* A4
Castle Dome Peak, *mt.* A4
Chiricahua Natl. Monument F6
Colorado, *river* B2, D1
Coronado Natl. Mem. E6
Gila, *river* B5, D4, F4
Glen Canyon, *dam* D1
Glen Canyon Natl. Rec. Area D1
Grand, *canyon* C1
Grand Canyon Natl. Park B2, C1
Harcuvar, *mts.* B4
Havasu, *lake* A3
Hide Creek, *mt.* C3
Hoover, *dam* A1
Hopi Indian Res. E2
Horseshoe, *reservoir* D4
Hualapai, *mt.* B3
Hubbell Trading Post N.H.S. F2
Humphreys Peak, *mt.* D2
Lake Mead Natl. Rec. Area B1
Little Colorado, *river* D2
Many Farms, *lake* F1
Maple Peak, *mt.* F4
Mazatzal Peak, *mt.* D3
Mohave, *lake* A2
Montezuma Castle N.M. D3
Monument, *valley* F1
Mormon, *lake* D3
Navajo Indian Res. E1, E2
Navajo Natl. Monument E1
Organ Pipe Cactus N.M. C5
Painted, *desert* D2
Parker, *dam* A3
Petrified Forest Natl. Park F3
Pipe Spring Natl. Monument C1
Pleasant, *lake* C4
Point Imperial, *mt.* D1
Powell, *lake* D1
Red, *lake* B2
Saguaro Natl. Monument E5
Salt, *river* E4
San Carlos, *lake* E4
San Pedro, *river* E5
Santa Cruz, *river* D5
Sonoran, *desert* B5
Sunset Crater Volcano N.M. D2
Theodore Roosevelt, *lake* D4
Tipton, *mt.* A2
Tonto Natl. Monument D4
Trumbull, *mt.* B1
Tumacacori Natl Hist. Park D6
Tuzigoot Natl. Monument C3
Ventana, *cave* C5
Verde, *river* D3
Virgin, *river* A1
Walnut Canyon Natl. Monument D2
White, *mts.* F4
White House, *ruin* F1
Wupatki Natl. Monument D2
Yuma, *desert* A5

Arkansas ....page 131

Cities and Towns
Alicia D2
Alma A2
Arkadelphia B3
Arkansas City D4
Ashdown A4
Ash Flat D1
Atkins C2
Augusta D2
Bald Knob D2
Barling A2
Batesville D2
Bay E2
Beebe D2
Bella Vista A1
Benton C3
Bentonville A1
Berryville B1
Blytheville F2
Bodcaw B4
Booneville B2
Brinkley D3
Bryant C3
Bull Shoals C1
Cabot D3
Camden C4
Caraway E2
Carlisle D3
Cave City D2
Charleston A2
Clarendon D3
Clarksville B2
Clinton C2
Conway C2
Corning E1
Crossett D4
Daisy B3
Damascus C2
Danville B2
Dardanelle B2
De Queen A3
Dermott D4
Des Arc D3
De Valls Bluff D3
De Witt D3
Dierks A3
Dumas D4
Earle E2
El Dorado C4
England D3
Eudora D4
Eureka Springs B1
Fairfield Bay C2
Fallsville B2
Farmington A1
Fayetteville A1
Fordyce C4
Foreman A4
Forrest City E2
Fort Smith A2
Fountain Hill D4
Gentry A1
Glenwood B3
Gosnell F2
Gould D4
Gravette A1
Greenbrier C2
Green Forest B1
Greenwood A2
Griffithville D2
Gurdon B4
Hamburg D4
Hampton C4
Harrisburg E2
Harrison B1
Haskell C3
Hatfield A3
Hazen D3
Heber Springs C2
Helena E3
Hope B4
Horseshoe Bend D1
Hot Springs National Park B3
Hot Springs Village B3
Hoxie E1
Hughes E3
Hunter D2
Huntsville B1
Jacksonville C3
Jasper B1
Jonesboro E2
Lake City E2
Lake Hamilton B3
Lake Village D4
Lepanto E2
Lewisville B4
Lincoln A2
Little Rock, *capital* C3
Lonoke D3
Luxora F2
McCrory D2
McGehee D4
McNeil B4
McRae D2
Magnolia B4
Malvern C3
Manila E2
Marianna E3
Marion E2
Marked Tree E2
Marshall C2
Marvell E3
Maumelle C3
Mayflower C3
Melbourne D1
Mena A3
Monticello D4
Morrilton C2
Mountain Home C1
Mountain View C2
Mount Ida B3
Mulberry A2
Murfreesboro B3
Nashville B4
Newport D2
North Crossett D4
North Little Rock C3
Oden B3
Osceola F2
Ozark B2
Paragould E1
Paris B2
Parkin E2
Pea Ridge A1
Pelsor B2
Perryville C2
Piggott E1
Pine Bluff D3
Pocahontas E1
Prescott B4
Rector E1
Rison C4
Rogers A1
Rose Bud C2
Russell D2
Russellville B2
St. Charles D3
St. Paul B2
Salem D1
Searcy D2
Sheridan C3
Sherwood C3
Siloam Springs A1
Smackover C4
Springdale A1
Springhill B4
Star City D4
Stuttgart D3
Texarkana A4
Tillar D4
Trumann E2
Tuckerman D2
Tupelo D2
Van Buren A2
Waldo B4
Waldron A3
Walnut Ridge E1
Warren C4
Washington B4
West Fork A2
West Helena E3
West Memphis E2
White Hall C3
Wynne E2
Yellville C1

Other Features
Arkansas, *river* D3
Arkansas Post Natl. Mem. D3
Beaver, *lake* B1
Black, *river* D2
Boston, *mts.* B2
Buffalo, *river* B1
Buffalo Natl. River C2
Bull Shoals, *lake* C1
Cache, *river* E2
Catherine, *lake* C3
Dardanelle, *reservoir* B2
DeGray, *lake* B3
Erling, *lake* B4
Fort Smith Natl. Hist Site A2
Greers Ferry, *lake* C2
Greeson, *lake* B3
Hamilton, *lake* B3
Hot Springs Natl. Park B3
Little Missouri, *river* B4
Magazine, *mt.* B2
Maumelle, *lake* C3
Millwood, *lake* B4
Mississippi, *river* E3
Nimrod, *lake* B3
Norfork, *lake* C1
Ouachita, *lake* B3
Ouachita, *mts.* A3
Ouachita, *river* B3, C4
Ozark, *plateau* B1
Pea Ridge Natl. Mil. Park A1
Red, *river* B4
St. Francis, *river* E1
Saline, *river* C3
Table Rock, *lake* B1
White, *river* C2, D3

California ....page 132

Cities and Towns
Adelanto H8
Alameda K2
Alamo L2
Albany K1
Alhambra D10
Alpine J10
Altadena D10
Alturas E1
Anaheim E11, H9
Anderson C2
Antioch D4, L1
Apple Valley H8
Aptos D5
Arcadia D10
Arcata A2
Arnold E4
Arroyo Grande E7
Arvin G7
Ashland K2
Atascadero E7
Atherton K3
Atwater E5
Auberry F5
Auburn E4
Avalon G9
Avenal E6
Azusa E10
Bakersfield G7
Baldwin Park E10
Barstow H8
Bell D10
Bellflower D11
Belmont K3
Belvedere J1
Benicia K1
Berkeley C5, K2
Beverly Hills C10
Big Bear Lake J8
Bishop G5
Black Point J1
Blythe L9
Bonita C9
Boron H8
Borrego Springs J9

	Key
Brawley	K10
Brea	E11
Bridgeport	F4
Brisbane	J2
Broadmoor	J2
Buellton	E8
Buena Park	E11
Burbank	C10
Burlingame	J3
Burney	D2
Buttonwillow	F7
Calabasas	B10
Calexico	K10
California City	H7
Calipatria	K9
Calistoga	C4
Cambria	D7
Campbell	L4
Canyon	K2
Carlsbad	H9
Carmel	D6
Carmel Valley	D6
Carpinteria	F8
Carson	D11
Castroville	D6
Cathedral City	J9
Cayucos	E7
Central Valley	C2
Ceres	E5
Chester	D2
Chico	D3
Chino	F10
Chowchilla	E5
Chula Vista	C9, H10
Claremont	F10
Clayton	L1
Clearlake	C4
Cloverdale	B4
Clovis	F6
Clyde	L1
Coachella	J9
Coalinga	E6
Cobb	C4
Colfax	E3
Colusa	D3
Compton	D11
Concord	L1
Corcoran	F6
Corning	C3
Corona	F11
Coronado	B8
Corte Madera	J1
Costa Mesa	E11
Cottonwood	C2
Covina	E10
Cowan Heights	E11
Crescent City	A1
Crestline	H8
Crockett	K1
Culver City	C10
Cupertino	L4
Cypress	D11
Daly City	J2
Danville	L2
Davis	D4
Delano	F7
Del Mar	H10
Desert Hot Springs	J9
Diablo	L2
Diamond Bar	E10
Dinuba	F6
Dos Palos	E6
Downey	D11
Downieville	E3
Dublin	L2
Dunsmuir	C1
Earlimart	F7
East Los Angeles	D10
Easton	F6
East Palo Alto	K3
El Cajon	C8, J10
El Centro	K10
El Cerrito	K1
El Granada	J3
Elk Grove	D4
El Monte	D10
El Segundo	C11
El Sobrante	K1
Emeryville	K2
Encinitas	H9
Escondido	H9
Eureka	A2
Exeter	F6
Fairfax	H1
Fairfield	D4
Fallbrook	H9
Ferndale	A2
Firebaugh	E6
Florence	D11
Florin	D4
Fort Bragg	B3
Fortuna	A2
Foster City	K3
Fountain Valley	E11
Frazier Park	G8
Fremont	D5, L3
Fresno	F6
Fullerton	E11
Galt	D4
Garden Grove	E11
Gilroy	D5
Glendale	D10, G8
Glendora	E10
Glenview	B10
Gonzales	D6
Grass Valley	D3
Greenacres	F7
Greenbrae	J1
Greenfield	D6
Greenville	E2
Gridley	D3
Groveland	E5
Guadalupe	E8
Half Moon Bay	J3
Hanford	F6
Hawthorne	C11
Hayfork	B2
Hayward	C5, L2
Healdsburg	C4
Hemet	J9
Hercules	K1
Hermosa Beach	C11
Hesperia	H8
Hidden Hills	B10
Hillsborough	J3
Hollister	D6
Holtville	K10
Huntington Beach	E11, G9
Huron	E6
Ignacio	J1
Imperial Beach	B9, H10
Independence	G6
Indio	J9
Inglewood	C11, G9
Ingot	C2
Inyokern	H7
Ione	E4
Irvine	E11, H9
Isla Vista	F8
Jackson	E4
Joshua Tree	J8
Julian	J9
Kelseyville	C4
Kensington	K1
Kentfield	J1
Kerman	E6
Kernville	G7
Kettleman City	F6
King City	D6
La Cañada-Flintridge	D10
La Crescenta	D10
Lafayette	K1
La Habra	E11
La Honda	K4
Lake Isabella	G7
Lakeport	C3
Lakeside	J10
Lakewood	D11
La Mesa	C8
La Mirada	D11
Lamont	G7
Lancaster	G8
La Puente	E10
Larkspur	J1
Laton	F6
Lawndale	C11
Lee Vining	F5
Lemon Grove	C8
Lemoore	F6
Lincoln	D4
Lindsay	F6
Littlerock	H8
Livermore	D5
Livingston	E5
Lockeford	D4
Lodi	D4
Loma Mar	K4
Lomita	C11
Lompoc	E8
Lone Pine	G6
Long Beach	D11, G9
Los Altos	K3
Los Altos Hills	K4
Los Angeles	D10, G8
Los Banos	E5
Los Molinos	C2
Los Osos	E7
Lynwood	D11
McCloud	C1
McFarland	F7
McKinleyville	A2
Madera	E6
Malibu	B10
Mammoth Lakes	G5
Manhattan Beach	C11
Manteca	D5
Marina	D6
Marina del Rey	C11
Marin City	J1
Marinwood	J1
Mariposa	F5
Markleeville	F4
Martinez	C4, K1
Marysville	D3
Maywood	D10
Mecca	J9
Mendota	E6
Menlo Park	K3
Merced	E5
Midway City	E11
Millbrae	J3
Mill Valley	J1
Milpitas	L3
Miranda	B2
Modesto	E5
Mojave	G7
Monrovia	E10
Montara	J3
Montclair	F10
Montebello	D10
Monte Nido	B10
Monterey	D6
Monterey Park	D10
Monte Sereno	L4
Moraga	K2
Moreno Valley	H9
Morgan Hill	D5
Morongo Valley	J8
Morro Bay	E7
Moss Beach	J3
Mountain View	K3
Mount Shasta	C1
Muir Beach	H1
Napa	C4
National City	C9
Needles	L8
Nevada City	D3
Newark	L3
Newberry Springs	J8
Newport Beach	H9
Nicasio	H1
Nice	C3
Nipomo	E7
Nipton	K7
Norco	F11
North Edwards	H7
North Fair Oaks	K3
Novato	H1
Oakdale	E5
Oakhurst	F5
Oakland	K2, C5
Oceanside	H9
Oildale	F7
Ojai	F8
Olema	H1
Olivehurst	D3
Ontario	F10, H8
Orange	E11
Orinda	K1
Orland	C3
Oroville	D3
Otay	C9
Oxnard	F8
Pacheco	L1
Pacifica	J2
Palermo	D3
Palmdale	G8
Palm Desert	J9
Palm Springs	J9
Palo Alto	K3
Palos Verdes Estates	C11
Paradise	D3
Pasadena	D10, G8
Patterson	D5
Petaluma	C4
Pico Rivera	D10
Piedmont	K2
Pine Valley	J10
Pinole	K1
Pismo Beach	E7
Pittsburg	L1
Placentia	E11
Placerville	E4
Pleasant Hill	L1
Pleasanton	L2
Pomona	E10, H8
Port Costa	K1
Porterville	G6
Portola	E3
Poway	H10
Prunedale	D6
Quartz Hill	G8
Quincy	E3
Ramona	J9
Rancho Cucamonga	F10
Rancho Palos Verdes	C11
Rancho Rinconada	L4
Rancho Santa Margarita	F11
Red Bluff	C2
Redding	C2
Redlands	H8
Redondo Beach	C11
Redwood City	C5, K3
Reedley	F6
Richgrove	F7
Richmond	J1
Ridgecrest	H7
Rio Dell	A2
Riverside	H9
Rodeo	K1
Rolling Hills	C11
Rolling Hills Estates	C11
Rosamond	G8
Roseville	D4
Sacramento, *capital*	D4
Salinas	D6
San Andreas	E4
San Anselmo	H1
San Bernardino	H8
San Bruno	J2
San Carlos	K3
San Clemente	H9
San Diego	B8, H10
San Francisco	C5, J2
San Gabriel	D10
Sanger	F6
San Gregorio	J4
San Jose	D5, L4
San Juan Bautista	D6
San Juan Capistrano	H9
San Leandro	K2
San Lorenzo	K2
San Luis Obispo	E7
San Mateo	C5, K3
San Pablo	J1
San Quentin	J1
San Rafael	C5, J1
San Ramon	L2
Santa Ana	E11, H9
Santa Barbara	F8
Santa Clara	L4
Santa Clarita	G8
Santa Cruz	C6
Santa Maria	E8
Santa Monica	C10
Santa Paula	F8
Santa Rosa	C4
Santa Venetia	J1
Santa Ynez	E8
Santee	C8
Saratoga	L4
Sausalito	J2
Scotts Valley	C5
Seal Beach	D11
Sebastopol	C4
Selma	F6
Shafter	F7
Shingletown	D2
Shoshone	J7
Simi Valley	G8
Soledad	D6
Solvang	E8
Sonoma	C4
Sonora	E5
South Lake Tahoe	F4
South San Francisco	J2
Spring Valley	C8
Squaw Valley	F6
Stanford	K3
Stinson Beach	H1
Stockton	D5
Sunnyvale	C5, L4
Sunol	L3
Sunset Beach	D11
Susanville	E2
Taft	F7
Tamalpais Valley	J1
Tehachapi	G7
Temecula	H9
Templeton	E7
Terra Bella	F7
Thermalito	D3
Thousand Oaks	G8
Tiburon	J1
Tipton	F6
Topanga	B10
Torrance	C11, G9
Tracy	D5
Truckee	E3
Tulare	F6
Turlock	E5
Tustin	E11
Twain Harte	E4
Twentynine Palms	J8
Ukiah	B3
Union City	L3
Upland	F10
Vacaville	D4
Vallejo	C4, K1
Vandenberg Village	E8
Ventucopa	F8
Ventura	F8
Victorville	H8
Villa Park	E11
Vine Hill	K1
Visalia	F6
Vista	H9
Walnut	E10
Walnut Creek	L1
Wasco	F7
Watsonville	D6
Weaverville	C2
Weed	C1
West Covina	E10
West Hollywood	C10
Westminster	E11
Westmorland	K9
West Pittsburg	L1
Westwood	E2
Wheatland	D3
Whittier	D10
Willits	B3
Willow Creek	B2
Willows	C3
Windsor	C4
Wofford Heights	G7
Woodlake	F6
Woodland	D4
Woodside	K3
Wrightwood	H8
Yorba Linda	E11
Yosemite Village	F5
Yreka	C1
Yuba City	D3
Yucaipa	H8
Yucca Valley	J8
Zenia	B2

Other Features

Alameda, *river*	L3
Alcatraz, *island*	J2
Allison, *mt.*	L3
Almanor, *lake*	D2
Amargosa, *range*	J6
Amargosa, *river*	J7
Angel, *island*	J1
Balboa, *park*	B8
Berryessa, *lake*	C4
Boundary, *peak*	G5
Bullion, *mts.*	J8
Cascade, *range*	D1
Central, *valley*	C2
Chabot, *lake*	K2
Channel, *islands*	F9
Channel Islands Natl. Park	E9, F9
Chatsworth, *reservoir*	B10
Chino, *river*	F10
Chocolate, *mts.*	K9
Clair Engle, *lake*	C1
Clear, *lake*	C3
Clear Lake, *reservoir*	D1
Coast, *ranges*	C2, D6
Colorado, *desert*	J9
Colorado, *river*	L9
Cucamonga, *river*	F11
Death, *valley*	H6
Death Valley Natl. Park	H6
Devils Postpile Natl. Monument	F5
Diablo, *mt.*	L1
Eagle, *lake*	E2
Eagle, *peak*	E1
Eel, *river*	B2
Estero, *bay*	E7
Farallon, *islands*	B5
Farallones, *gulf*	H2
Golden Gate Natl. Rec. Area	C5, J2
Goose, *lake*	E1
Grizzly, *bay*	L1
Half Moon, *bay*	J3
Honey, *lake*	E2
Humboldt, *bay*	A2
Imperial, *valley*	K9
Inyo, *mts.*	H6
Irvine, *lake*	F11
Joshua Tree Natl. Park	K8
Kern, *river*	G6
Kings, *river*	F6
Kings Canyon Natl. Park	G5
Klamath, *mts.*	B1
Klamath, *river*	B1
Lanfair, *valley*	K7
Lassen, *peak*	D2
Lassen Volcanic Natl. Park	D2
Lava Beds Natl. Monument	D1
McCoy, *mts.*	L9
Mad, *river*	B2
Merced, *river*	E5
Middle Alkali, *lake*	F1
Mission, *bay*	B8
Mission Bay, *park*	B8
Mojave, *desert*	H7
Mojave, *river*	J8
Mono, *lake*	G4
Monterey, *bay*	D6
Morgan, *mt.*	G5
Morris, *reservoir*	E10
Nacimiento, *reservoir*	D7
Napa, *river*	K1
Nicasio, *reservoir*	H1
Old Woman, *mts.*	K8
Oroville, *reservoir*	D3
Otay, *river*	C9
Panamint, *range*	H6
Panamint, *valley*	H6
Pescadero, *river*	J4
Pinnacles Natl. Monument	D6
Point Reyes Natl. Seashore	B4
Redwood Natl. Park	A1
Ritter, *mt.*	F5
Sacramento, *river*	C3
Salton, *sea*	K9
San Antonio, *reservoir*	D7
San Bernardino, *mts.*	J8
San Clemente, *island*	G10
San Diego, *bay*	B9
San Diego, *river*	B8
San Fernando, *valley*	B10
San Francisco, *bay*	J2
San Gabriel, *mts.*	G8
San Gabriel, *reservoir*	E10
San Joaquin, *river*	E5
San Luis Obispo, *bay*	E7
San Miguel, *island*	E8
San Nicolas, *island*	F9
San Pablo, *bay*	J1
San Rafael, *mts.*	F8
Santa Ana, *mts.*	F11
Santa Barbara, *channel*	E8
Santa Barbara, *island*	F9
Santa Catalina, *island*	G9
Santa Cruz, *island*	F8
Santa Cruz, *mts.*	J3
Santa Lucia, *range*	D6
Santa Monica, *bay*	B11
Santa Monica, *mts.*	B10
Santa Monica Mts. N.R.A.	B10
Santa Rosa, *island*	E9
Santiago, *river*	F11
Sequoia Natl. Park	G6
Shasta, *lake*	C2
Shasta, *mt.*	C1
Sierra, *peak*	F11
Sierra Nevada, *range*	D3, G5
Siskiyou, *mts.*	B1
Tahoe, *lake*	E3
Tehachapi, *mts.*	G8
Telescope, *peak*	H6
Trinity, *river*	B2
Tule, *river*	F6
Turtle, *mts.*	L8
Upper, *lake*	E1
Upper San Leandro, *reservoir*	L2
Vizcaino, *cape*	B3
Whiskeytown-Shasta-Trinity N.R.A.	D1
White, *mts.*	G5
Whitney, *mt.*	G6
Wilson, *mt.*	D10
Yosemite Natl. Park	F5

Colorado .... page 133

Cities and Towns

Akron	G1
Alamosa	E4
Arvada	E2
Aspen	D2
Aurora	F2
Avon	D2
Bennett	F2
Berthoud	E1
Black Forest	F2
Boulder	E1
Breckenridge	D2
Brighton	F2
Broomfield	E2
Brush	G1
Buena Vista	D3
Burlington	H2
Canon City	E3
Carbondale	C2
Castle Rock	F2
Cedaredge	C3
Center	D4
Central City	E2
Cheyenne Wells	H3
Clifton	B2
Colorado Springs	F3
Conejos	D4
Cortez	B4
Craig	C1
Crawford	C3
Creede	D4
Cripple Creek	E3
Dacono	F1
Del Norte	D4
Delta	B3
Denver, *capital*	F2
Dinosaur	A1
Dove Creek	B4
Durango	C4
Eads	H3
Eagle	D2
Eaton	F1
Englewood	F2
Estes Park	E1
Evans	F1
Evergreen	E2
Fairplay	E2
Florence	E3
Fort Collins	E1
Fort Lupton	F1
Fort Morgan	G1
Fountain	F3
Frisco	D2
Fruita	B2
Fruitvale	B2
Georgetown	E2
Glenwood Springs	C2
Golden	E2
Grand Junction	B2
Greeley	F1
Gunnison	D3
Gypsum	D2
Haswell	G3
Hayden	C1
Holyoke	H1
Hot Sulphur Springs	D1
Hugo	G2
Idaho Springs	E2
Johnstown	F1
Julesburg	H1
Keota	F1
Kiowa	F2
Kit Carson	H3
Lafayette	E2
La Junta	G4
Lake City	C3
Lakewood	E2
Lamar	H3
Las Animas	G3
Leadville	D2
Limon	G2
Littleton	F2
Longmont	E1
Louisville	E2
Loveland	E1
Manitou Springs	F3
Meeker	C1
Milliken	F1
Monte Vista	D4
Montrose	C3
Niwot	E1
Northglenn	F2
Olathe	C3
Orchard City	C3
Orchard Mesa	B2
Ordway	G3
Ouray	C3
Pagosa Springs	C4
Palisade	B2
Palmer Lake	F2
Paonia	C3
Parker	F2
Platteville	F1
Pritchett	H4
Pueblo	F3
Pueblo West	F3
Rangely	B1
Rifle	C2
Rocky Ford	G3
Saguache	D3
Salida	E3
San Luis	E4
Security	F3
Silverthorne	D2
Silverton	C4
Snowmass Village	D2
Springfield	H4
Steamboat Springs	D1
Sterling	G1
Telluride	C4
Thornton	F2
Trinidad	F4
Vail	D2
Vilas	H4
Walden	D1
Walsenburg	F4
Wellington	E1
Westcliffe	E3
Westminster	E2
Wheat Ridge	F2
Wiley	H3
Windsor	F1
Woodland Park	E3
Wray	H1
Yuma	H1

Other Features

Animas, *river*	C4
Apishapa, *river*	F4
Arapahoe, *peak*	E1
Arapaho Natl. Rec. Area	E1
Arikaree, *river*	G2
Arkansas, *river*	F3
Bent's Old Fort Natl. Hist. Site	G3
Black Canyon of the Gunnison Natl. Monument	C3
Blanca, *peak*	E4
Blue Mesa, *reservoir*	C3
Bonny, *reservoir*	H2
Castle, *peak*	D2
Colorado, *plateau*	A4
Colorado, *river*	C2
Colorado Natl. Monument	B2
Crestone, *peak*	E4
Cucharas, *river*	F4
Curecanti Natl. Rec. Area	C3
Dinosaur Natl. Monument	B1
Dolores, *river*	B3
Elbert, *mt.*	D2
Eolus, *mt.*	C4
Evans, *mt.*	E2
Florissant Fossil Beds N.M.	E3
Front, *range*	E1
Great Sand Dunes N.M.	E4
Green, *river*	B1
Gunnison, *mt.*	C3
Gunnison, *river*	B3
Hovenweep Natl. Monument	B4
John Martin, *reservoir*	G3
Laramie, *mts.*	E1
Laramie, *river*	E1
Little Snake, *river*	B1
Longs, *peak*	E1
Mancos, *river*	B4
Medicine Bow, *mts.*	D1
Mesa Verde Natl. Park	B4
Montezuma, *peak*	D4
North Fork Cimarron, *river*	H4
North Fork Smoky Hill, *river*	H2
North Platte, *river*	D1
Park, *range*	D1
Pikes, *peak*	E3
Purgatoire, *river*	G4
Rio Grande, *river*	E4
Roan, *plateau*	B2
Rocky, *mts.*	D1
Rocky Mt. Natl. Park	E1
Royal Gorge, *canyon*	E3
Sangre de Cristo, *mts.*	E3
San Juan, *mts.*	C4
San Luis, *valley*	E4
Sawatch, *range*	D2
South Fork Republican, *river*	G2
South Platte, *river*	E2, G1
Uncompahgre, *peak*	C3
U.S. Air Force Academy	F3
White, *river*	B1
Wilson, *mt.*	B4
Yampa, *river*	B1
Yucca House Natl. Monument	B4
Zirkel, *mt.*	D1

Connecticut .... page 134

Cities and Towns

Abington	G2
Andover	F3
Ansonia	C4
Attawaugan	H2
Avon	D2
Bakersville	C2
Ballouville	H2
Baltic	G3
Beacon Falls	C4
Berkshire	B4
Berlin	E3
Bethany	C4
Bethel	B4
Bethlehem	C3
Black Point	G4
Bloomfield	E2
Blue Hills	E2
Boardman Bridge	B3
Bolton	F2
Botsford	B4
Branford	D4
Bridgeport	C5
Bridgewater	B3
Bristol	D3
Broad Brook	E2
Brookfield	B4
Brookfield Center	B4
Brooklyn	H2
Burlington	D2
Burrville	C2
Cannondale	B5
Canterbury	H3
Canton	D2
Canton Center	D2
Centerbrook	F4
Central Village	H3
Chaplin	G2
Cheshire	D4
Chester	F4
Chesterfield	G4
Clarks Falls	H4
Clinton	E4
Colchester	F3
Colebrook	C2
Collinsville	D2
Columbia	F3
Cornwall	B2
Cornwall Bridge	B2
Coventry	F2
Cromwell	E3
Danbury	B4
Danielson	H2
Darien	B5
Dayville	H2
Deep River	F4
Derby	C4
Durham	E4
Eagleville	F2
East Brooklyn	H2
Eastford	G2
East Glastonbury	E3
East Granby	E2
East Haddam	F4
East Hampton	E3

	Key
East Hartford	E2
East Hartland	D2
East Haven	D4
East Killingly	H2
East Litchfield	C2
East Lyme	G4
Easton	B5
East Thompson	H1
East Village	C4
East Woodstock	H2
Ellington	F2
Enfield	E2
Essex	F4
Fairfield	B5
Falls Village	B2
Farmington	D3
Fitchman	G3
Flanders	B3
Franklin	G3
Gales Ferry	G4
Gaylordsville	B3
Georgetown	B5
Gilead	F3
Gilman	G3
Glasgo	H3
Glastonbury	E3
Goodrich Heights	E3
Goshen	C2
Granby	D2
Greenwich	A5
Grosvenor Dale	H2
Groton	G4
Groton Long Point	G4
Guilford	E4
Gurleyville	G2
Haddam	E4
Haddam Neck	E3
Hadlyme	F4
Hamburg	F4
Hamden	D4
Hampton	G2
Hanover	G3
Hartford, *capital*	E3
Harwinton	C2
Hawleyville	B4
Hazardville	E2
Hebron	F3
Higganum	E4
Hotchkissville	C3
Indian Neck	D5
Jewett City	H3
Kensington	D3
Killingworth	E4
Knollcrest	B4
Knollwood	F4
Lake Pocotopaug	E3
Lakeside	C3
Lakeside	C4
Laysville	F4
Lebanon	G3
Ledyard Center	G4
Liberty Hill	F3
Lime Rock	B2
Litchfield	C3
Lyons Plain	B5
Madison	E4
Manchester	E2
Mansfield Center	G3
Mansfield Four Corners	F2
Marble Dale	B3
Marion	D3
Meriden	D3
Merrow	F2
Middlebury	C3
Middlefield	E3
Middle Haddam	E3
Middletown	E3
Milford	C5
Mill Plain	A4
Milton	B2
Mohegan	G4
Monroe	C4
Montville	G4
Moosup	H3
Mystic	H4
Naugatuck	C4
New Britain	D3
New Canaan	B5
New Fairfield	B4
New Hartford	D2
New Haven	D4
Newington	E3
New London	G4
New Milford	B3
Newtown	B4
Niantic	G4
Noank	H4
Norfolk	C2
North Branford	D4
North Canton	D2
Northfield	C3
Northford	D4
North Franklin	G3
North Grosvenor Dale	H2
North Guilford	E4
North Haven	D4
North Stonington	H4
Northville	B3
North Westchester	F3
North Windham	G3
Norwalk	B5
Norwich	G3
Oakdale	G4
Oakville	C3
Old Lyme	F4
Old Mystic	H4
Old Saybrook	F4
Oneco	H3
Orange	C4
Oxford	C4
Park Lane	B3
Pawcatuck	H4
Perkins Corner	F3
Phoenixville	G2
Plainfield	H3
Plainville	D3
Plantsville	D3
Pleasant Valley	D2
Pleasure Beach	G4
Plymouth	C3
Pomfret	H2
Poquetanuck	G4
Poquonock	E2
Poquonock Bridge	G4
Portland	E3
Preston City	H3
Prospect	D4
Putnam	H2
Quaddick	H2
Quaker Hill	G4
Redding	B4
Redding Ridge	B4
Ridgebury	A4
Ridgefield	B4
Riverton	C2
Robertsville	C2
Rockfall	E3
Rockville	F2
Rocky Hill	E3
Roxbury	B3
Sachem Head	E5
Salem	F4
Salisbury	B2
Scantic	E2
Scitico	E2
Scotland	G3
Seymour	C4
Sharon	B2
Shelton	C4
Sherman	B3
Short Beach	D5
Simsbury	D2
Somers	F2
Sound View	F4
Southbury	C4
South Canaan	B2
South Chaplin	G2
South Glastonbury	E3
Southington	D3
South Kent	B3
South Killingly	H2
South Willington	F2
South Windham	G3
South Windsor	E2
Stafford	F2
Stafford Springs	F2
Staffordville	F2
Stamford	A5
Sterling	H3
Stevenson	C4
Stony Creek	E4
Storrs	F2
Straitsville	C4
Stratford	C5
Suffield	E2
Taconic	B1
Talcottville	F2
Tariffville	D2
Terryville	C3
Thompson	H2
Thompsonville	E2
Tolland	F2
Torrington	C2
Trumbull	C5
Uncasville	G4
Union	G2
Unionville	D2
Vernon	F2
Versailles	G3
Voluntown	H3
Wallingford	D4
Warren	B3
Warrenville	G2
Washington	B3
Washington Depot	B3
Waterbury	C3
Waterford	G4
Watertown	C3
Weatogue	D2
Westbrook	F4
West Cornwall	B2
Westford	G2
West Granby	D2
West Hartford	E2
West Hartland	D1
West Haven	D4
West Mystic	H4
West Norfolk	C1
Weston	B5
Westport	B5
West Redding	B4
West Simsbury	D2
West Stafford	F2
West Suffield	E2
West Willington	F2
Wethersfield	E3
Whigville	D3
Willimantic	G3
Wilton	B5
Winchester Center	C2
Windham	G3
Windsor	E2
Windsor Locks	E2
Winsted	C2
Winthrop	F4
Wolcott	D3
Woodbridge	C4
Woodmont	D5
Woodstock	H2
Woodstock Valley	G2
Woodville	B3
Yalesville	D4

Other Features

	Key
Appalachian Natl. Scenic Trail	B2
Bantam, *lake*	C3
Barkhamsted, *reservoir*	D2
Candlewood, *lake*	B4
Connecticut, *river*	E4
Easton, *reservoir*	B4
Farmington, *river*	D3
Frissell, *mt.*	B1
Gaillard, *lake*	D4
Hammonasset, *river*	E4
Hop, *river*	F3
Housatonic, *river*	B4
Long Island, *sound*	D5
Mt. Hope, *river*	G2
Natchaug, *river*	G2
Naugatuck, *river*	C4
Nepaug, *reservoir*	D2
Norwalk, *islands*	B5
Norwalk, *river*	B5
Quinebaug, *river*	H3
Saugatuck, *reservoir*	B4
Shenipsit, *lake*	F2
Shetucket, *river*	G3
Thames, *river*	G4
Waramaug, *lake*	B3
Weir Farm Natl. Hist. Site	B5
Willimantic, *river*	F2
Yantic, *river*	F3

Delaware ....page 135

Cities and Towns

	Key
Adamsville	A3
Andrewville	A3
Argos Corner	B3
Blackbird	A2
Broadkill Beach	B3
Brookside	A1
Burrsville	A3
Camden	A2
Cannon	A3
Canterbury	A2
Capitol Park	A2
Clarksville	B3
Claymont	B1
Collins Park	A1
Delaware City	A1
Dover, *capital*	A2
Edgemoor	A1
Elsmere	A1
Fairfax	A1
Georgetown	B3
Glasgow	A1
Gumboro	B4
Harbeson	B3
Harrington	A3
Hartley	A2
Hazlettville	A2
Hickman	A3
Hockessin	A1
Indian Beach	B3
Jimtown	B3
Kirkwood	A1
Kitts Hummock	B2
Laurel	A3
Lewes	B3
Lincoln	B3
Little Heaven	B2
Llangollen Estates	A1
Lynch Heights	B3
McClellandville	A1
Marshallton	A1
Marydel	A2
Mastens Corner	A3
Middletown	A2
Midway	B3
Milford	B3
Millsboro	B3
Milton	B3
Nassau	B3
Newark	A1
New Castle	A1
Oak Orchard	B3
Owens	A3
Petersburg	A2
Pinetown	B3
Primehook Beach	B3
Reeves Crossing	A3
Rehoboth Beach	B3
Reliance	A3
Rosedale Beach	B3
Roxana	B3
Sandtown	A2
Seaford	A3
Selbyville	B4
Smyrna	A2
Stanton	A1
Swann Keys	B4
Talleyville	A1
Taylors Bridge	A2
Whitesville	B4
Williamsville	A3
Williamsville	B4
Wilmington	A1
Wilmington Manor	A1
Woodenhawk	A3
Woodland Beach	B2
Workmans Corners	B3

Other Features

	Key
Broadkill, *river*	B3
Chesapeake & Delaware, *canal*	A1
Delaware, *bay*	B2
Delaware, *river*	A1
Henlopen, *cape*	B3
Indian River, *bay*	B3
Mispillion, *river*	B3
Murderkill, *river*	A3
Nanticoke, *river*	A3
Rehoboth, *bay*	B3
Smyrna, *river*	A2

Florida ....page 136

Cities and Towns

	Key
Alachua	C2
Altamonte Springs	D3
Anna Maria	C4
Apalachicola	A2
Apollo Beach	C4
Apopka	D3
Arcadia	D4
Archer	C2
Astor	D2
Atlantic Beach	D1
Auburndale	D3
Aventura	B3
Avon Park	D4
Baldwin	D1
Bal Harbour	B3
Bartow	D4
Bay Harbor Islands	B3
Bayonet Point	C3
Bee Ridge	C4
Belle Glade	E5
Belleview	C2
Beverly Hills	C3
Big Pine Key	D7
Biscayne Park	A3
Blountstown	A1
Boca Raton	E5
Bonifay	C6
Bonita Springs	D5
Boynton Beach	E5
Bradenton	C4
Brandon	C4
Bristol	A1
Bronson	C2
Brooksville	C3
Buckhead Ridge	E4
Bunnell	D2
Bushnell	C3
Callaway	C6
Cape Canaveral	E3
Cape Coral	D5
Carol City	A3, E6
Chattahoochee	A1
Chiefland	C2
Chipley	C6
Clearwater	C4
Clermont	D3
Clewiston	E5
Cocoa	E3
Cocoa Beach	E3
Coconut Grove	A3
Cooper City	A2
Coral Gables	A3, E6
Coral Springs	E5
Crawfordville	A1
Crescent City	D2
Crestview	B6
Cross City	B2
Crystal River	C3
Dade City	C3
Dania	B2
Davie	A2, E5
Daytona Beach	D2
De Bary	D3
Deerfield Beach	E5
De Funiak Springs	B6
De Land	D2
Delray Beach	E5
Deltona	D3
Destin	B6
Dunedin	C3
Dunnellon	C2
East Naples	D5
Eastpoint	A2
Edgewater	E3
El Portal	A3
Elfers	C3
Englewood	C5
Eustis	D3
Fellsmere	E4
Fernandina Beach	D1
Flagler Beach	D2
Florida City	E6
Fort Lauderdale	B2, E5
Fort Meade	D4
Fort Myers	D5
Fort Myers Beach	D5
Fort Myers Villas	D5
Fort Pierce	E4
Fort Walton Beach	B6
Frostproof	D4
Gainesville	C2
Gifford	E4
Golden Gate	D5
Gonzalez	A6
Goulds	E6
Greenacres City	E5
Green Cove Springs	D2
Gretna	A1
Gulf Breeze	A6
Haines City	D3
Hallandale	B3, E6
Havana	A1
Hawthorne	C2
Hialeah	A3, E6
Hialeah Gardens	A3
High Springs	C2
Hilliard	D1
Holiday	C3
Holly Hill	D2
Hollywood	A3, E5
Holmes Beach	C4
Homestead	E6
Homosassa Springs	C3
Hudson	C3
Immokalee	D5
Indian Harbour Beach	E3
Indian Rocks Beach	C4
Indiantown	E4
Inverness	C3
Jacksonville	D1
Jacksonville Beach	D1
Jasper	C1
Jensen Beach	E4
Jupiter	E5
Kendall	A4, E6
Key Biscayne	B4
Key Largo	E6
Keystone Heights	C2
Key West	D7
Kissimmee	D3
La Belle	D5
La Crosse	C2
Lady Lake	D3
Lake Buena Vista	D3
Lake Butler	C1
Lake City	C1
Lakeland	D3
Lake Mary	D3
Lake Panasoffkee	C3
Lake Wales	D4
Lake Worth	E5
Land O' Lakes	C3
Lantana	E5
Largo	C4
Lauderdale Lakes	A2
Lauderdale-by-the-Sea	B2
Lauderhill	A2
Lawtey	C1
Layton	E7
Leesburg	D3
Live Oak	C1
Longboat Key	C4
Lutz	C3
Lynn Haven	C6
Macclenny	C1
Madison	B1
Marathon	D7
Marco	D6
Margate	E5
Marianna	C6
Marineland	D2
Mayo	B1
Merritt Island	E3
Miami	A3, E6
Miami Beach	B3, E6
Miami Lakes	A3, A5
Miami Shores	A3, A5
Miami Springs	A3, A5
Middleburg	D1
Milton	A6
Mims	E3
Miramar	A3, E6
Monticello	B1
Moore Haven	D5
Mount Dora	D3
Naples	D5
Naples Manor	D5
Naples Park	D5
Naranja	E6
New Port Richey	C3
New Smyrna Beach	E2
Niceville	B6
Noma	C5
North Bay Village	A3
North Fort Myers	D5
North Miami	A3, E6
North Miami Beach	A3
North Naples	D5
North Port	C4
Oakland Park	B2, E5
Ocala	C2
Ocoee	D3
Okeechobee	E4
Oldsmar	C3
Olympia Hts.	A3
Opa-Locka	A3
Orange City	D3
Orange Park	D1
Orlando	D3
Ormond Beach	D2
Ormond-by-the-Sea	D2
Otter Creek	C2
Oviedo	D3
Pace	A6
Pahokee	E5
Palatka	D2
Palm Bay	E3
Palm Beach	E5
Palm Beach Gardens	E5
Palm Coast	D2
Palmetto	C4
Palm Harbor	C3
Panama City	C6
Pembroke Park	A3
Pembroke Pines	A3
Pennsuco	A3
Pensacola	A6
Perrine	E6
Perry	B1
Pierson	D2
Pine Castle	D3
Plantation	A2, E5
Plant City	C3
Polk City	D3
Pomona Park	D2
Port Charlotte	C5
Port Orange	E2
Port St. Joe	C7
Port St. Lucie	E4
Port Salerno	E4
Punta Gorda	C5
Quincy	A1
Raiford	C1
Ridge Manor	C3
Riverview	C4
Riviera Beach	E5
Rockledge	E3
Royal Palm Beach	E5
St. Augustine	D2
St. Augustine Shores	D2
St. Cloud	D3
St. Petersburg	C4
St. Petersburg Beach	C4
San Carlos Park	D5
Sanford	D3
Sanibel	C5
Sarasota	C4
Satellite Beach	E3
Sebastian	E4
Sebring	D4
Silver Springs	C2
Sneads	A1
South Miami	A3
South Venice	C4
Springfield	C6
Spring Hill	C3
Starke	C2
Stuart	E4
Sunrise	A2
Surfside	B3
Sweetwater	A3, E6
Tallahassee, *capital*	A1
Tamarac	A2, E5
Tampa	C4
Tarpon Springs	C3
Tavares	D3
Tavernier	E6
Temple Terrace	C3
Titusville	E3
Treasure Island	C4
Trenton	C2
Umatilla	D3
Venice	C4
Vero Beach	E4
Vilano Beach	D2
Virginia Gardens	A3
Warrington	A6
Wauchula	D4
Webster	C3
Weeki Wachee	C3
Welaka	D2
West Melbourne	E3
West Miami	A3
Weston	A2
West Palm Beach	E5
West Pensacola	A6
Westwood Lakes	A3
Wildwood	C3
Williston	C2
Wilton Manors	B2
Winter Garden	D3
Winter Haven	D3
Winter Park	D3
Woodville	A1
Yulee	D1
Zephyrhills	C3

Other Features

	Key
Amelia, *island*	D1
Apalachee, *bay*	A2
Apalachicola, *bay*	A2
Apalachicola, *river*	A1
Aucilla, *river*	B1
Big Cypress, *swamp*	D5
Biscayne, *bay*	B3, E6
Biscayne Natl. Park	E6
Boca Chica Key, *island*	D7
Caloosahatchee, *river*	D5
Canaveral, *cape*	E3
Canaveral Natl. Seashore	E3
Castillo de San Marcos N.M.	D2
Cedar Keys, *islands*	B2
Charlotte, *harbor*	C5
Chattahoochee, river	A1
Choctawhatchee, *bay*	B6
Crooked, *island*	C6
De Soto Natl. Memorial	C4
Deadman, *bay*	B2
Dog, *island*	A2
Dry Tortugas Natl. Park	C7
Elliott Key, *island*	E6
Escambia, *river*	A5
Everglades, *swamp*	A5, E6
Everglades Natl. Park	E6
Fisher, *island*	B3
Florida, *bay*	E6
Florida, *straits*	E7
Florida Keys, *islands*	D7
Fort Caroline Natl. Memorial	D1
Fort Matanzas Natl. Monument	D2
Gasparilla, *island*	C5
George, *lake*	D2
Gulf Islands Natl. Seashore	A6
Homosassa, *bay*	C3
Indian, *river*	B6
Iron, *mt.*	D4
Istokpoga, *lake*	D4
John F. Kennedy Space Center	E3
Key Biscayne, *island*	B3
Key Largo, *island*	E6
Kissimmee, *lake*	D4
Lochloosa, *lake*	D2
Marquesas Keys, *islands*	C7
Mexico, *gulf*	B5, B6
Ochlockonee, *river*	A1
Okeechobee, *lake*	E5
Okefenokee, *swamp*	C1
Peace, *river*	D4
Pensacola, *bay*	A6
Ponce de Leon, *bay*	D6
Romano, *cape*	D6
Sable, *cape*	D6
St. Andrews, *bay*	B6
St. George, *island*	A2
St. Johns, *river*	D2
St. Joseph, *bay*	C7
St. Marys, *river*	D1
St. Vincent, *island*	A2
San Blas, *cape*	C7
Sands Key, *island*	E6
Sanibel, *island*	C5
Santa Rosa, *island*	A6
Seminole, *lake*	A1
Sugarloaf Key, *island*	D7
Suwannee, *river*	C1, C2
Talquin, *lake*	A1
Tamiami, *canal*	A3
Tampa, *bay*	C4
Virginia Key, *island*	B3
Waccasassa, *bay*	C2
Withlacoochee, *river*	B1
Yellow, *river*	A6

Georgia ....page 137

Cities and Towns

	Key
Abbeville	E8
Adairsville	B3
Adel	E9
Alamo	F7
Albany	C8
Alma	G8
Alpharetta	C3
Americus	C7
Appling	G4
Arlington	B9
Ashburn	D8
Athens	E4
Atlanta, *capital*	C4, J3
Augusta	H5
Bainbridge	B10
Barnesville	C5
Baxley	G8
Belvedere	K3
Blackshear	G9
Blairsville	D2
Blakely	B9
Blue Ridge	C2
Boston	D10
Bremen	A4
Brookhaven	J2
Brunswick	H9
Buchanan	A4
Buena Vista	B7
Buford	C3
Butler	C6
Byron	D6
Cairo	C10
Calhoun	B2
Camilla	C9
Canton	B3
Carnesville	E3
Carrollton	A4
Cartersville	B3
Cedar Grove	J3
Cedartown	A3
Chamblee	J2
Chatsworth	B2
Clarkesville	D2
Clarkston	K2
Claxton	H7
Clayton	E2
Cleveland	D2
Cochran	E7
College Park	H3
Colquitt	B9
Columbus	B7
Commerce	E3
Conley	J4
Constitution	J3
Conyers	D4
Cordele	D8
Cornelia	D2
Covington	D4
Crawfordville	F4
Cumming	C3
Cusseta	B7
Cuthbert	B8
Dahlonega	D2
Dallas	B4
Dalton	B2
Danielsville	E3
Darien	J9
Dawson	C8
Dawsonville	C3
Decatur	K3
Donalsonville	B9
Doraville	K2
Douglas	F8
Douglasville	B4
Druid Hills	J3
Dublin	F6
Dunwoody	J2
Eastman	E7
East Point	C4, H3
Eatonton	E5
Elberton	F3
Ellaville	C7
Ellijay	C2
Evans	G4
Fair Oaks	H2
Fairview	K4
Fayetteville	C5
Fitzgerald	E8
Folkston	G10
Forest Park	J4
Forsyth	D5
Fort Gaines	A8
Fort Oglethorpe	A2
Fort Valley	D6
Franklin	A5
Gainesville	D3
Garden City	J7
Georgetown	A8
Gibson	F5
Gilmore	H2

Key
Glennville H8
Gordon E6
Gray D5
Greensboro E4
Greenville B5
Gresham Park J3
Griffin C5
Hahira E10
Hamilton B6
Hampton C5
Hapeville J3
Hartwell F3
Hawkinsville E7
Hazlehurst F8
Hephzibah G5
Hiawassee D2
Hinesville H8
Hogansville B5
Homer D3
Homerville F9
Irwinton E6
Jackson D5
Jasper C3
Jefferson E3
Jeffersonville E6
Jesup H8
Jonesboro C4
Kennesaw B3
Kingsland H10
Knoxville D6
La Fayette A2
La Grange A5
Lakeland E9
Lavonia E3
Lawrenceville D4
Leesburg C8
Lexington E4
Lincolnton G4
Locust Grove C5
Louisville G5
Ludowici H8
Lumber City F8
Lumpkin B7
Lyons G7
Mableton B4, G2
McDonough C5
McIntyre E6
Macon D6
McRae F7
Madison E4
Manchester B6
Marietta B4, H1
Marshallville D7
Metter G7
Milledgeville E5
Millen H6
Monroe D4
Monticello D5
Morgan B8
Moultrie D9
Mount Vernon F7
Mt. Bethel J1
Nashville E9
Newnan B5
Newton C9
Oakdale H2
Ocilla E8
Oglethorpe C7
Panthersville K3
Peachtree City B5
Pearson F9
Pembroke H7
Perry D7
Pooler J7
Powder Springs B4
Preston B7
Quitman E10
Red Oak H4
Reidsville G7
Richland B7
Richmond Hill J8
Rincon J7
Ringgold A2
Riverdale J4
Rochelle E8
Rockmart A3
Rome A3
Roswell C3
Royston E3
Sandersville F6
Sandy Springs J2
Savannah J7
Scottdale K3
Skyland J2
Smyrna H2
Snellville D4
Social Circle D4
Soperton F7
Sparta F5
Springfield J7
St. Marys H10
St. Simons Island J9
Statenville E10
Statesboro H7
Statham D4
Stone Mountain C4
Summerville A3
Swainsboro G6
Sylvania H6
Sylvester D8
Talbotton B6
Tennille F6
Thomaston C6
Thomasville D10
Thomson G5
Tifton E9
Toccoa E2
Toco Hills J2
Trenton A2
Trion A2
Tucker K2
Tybee Island K8
Unadilla D7
Union City B4, H4
Union Point E4
Valdosta E10
Vidalia G7
Vienna D7
Villa Rica B4
Wadley G6
Warner Robins D6
Warrenton F5
Washington F4
Watkinsville E4
Waycross G9
Waynesboro G5
Westoak H1
Winder D4
Woodbine H10
Wrens G5
Wrightsville F6

Key
Zebulon C5

Other Features
Alapaha, *river* E9
Allatoona, *lake* B3
Altamaha, *river* G8
Andersonville Natl. Hist. Site C7
Appalachian, *mts.* D2
Blackshear, *lake* D8
Blue, *ridge* C2
Brasstown Bald, *mt.* D2
Burton, *lake* D2
Carters, *lake* B2
Chattahoochee, *river* A5, A9, G3
Chattahoochee River N.R.A. J1
Chattooga, *river* E2
Chatuge, *lake* D1
Chickamauga and Chattanooga Natl. Military Park A2
Coosa, *river* D2
Cumberland, *island* J10
Cumberland Island Natl. Seashore J10
Etowah, *river* B3
Flint, *river* C9
Fort Frederica Natl. Monument J9
Fort Pulaski Natl. Monument K7
Hartwell, *lake* F2
Jackson, *lake* D5
Jekyll, *island* J9
Jimmy Carter Natl. Hist. Site C7
J. Strom Thurmond, *lake* G4
Lookout Mt., *ridge* A2
Martin Luther King Jr. N.H.S. J3
Ocmulgee Natl. Monument D6
Ochlockonee, *river* C10
Ocmulge, *river* E7
Oconee, *lake* E5
Oconee, *river* F6
Ogeechee, *river* F5
Ohoopee, *river* G7
Okefenokee, *swamp* G10
Ossabaw, *island* J8
Russell, *lake* F3
St. Catherines, *island* J8
St. Marys, *river* H10
St. Simons, *island* J9
Sapelo, *island* J9
Savannah, *river* H5
Seminole, *lake* B10
Sidney Lanier, *lake* C3
Sinclair, *lake* E5
Stone Mt. State Park C4
Suwannee, *river* F10
Tallapoosa, *river* A4
Tybee, *island* K7
Walter F. George, *reservoir* A8
Wassaw, *island* J8
Weiss, *lake* A3
West Point, *lake* A6
Withlacoochee, *river* E10

Hawaii page 138

Cities and Towns
Ahuimanu J2
Aiea F1, J2
Captain Cook G6
Crestview E1, J2
Eleele C2
Ewa D2, J2
Ewa Beach E2, J3
Foster Village F1, J2
Haena C1, J5
Halawa B3
Halawa Heights F1, J2
Haleiwa H1
Hana D4
Hanamaulu D1
Hanapepe C2
Hauula J1
Heeia G1, K2
Hilo E7, J5
Holualoa G5
Honalo G5
Honokaa H4
Honolulu, *capital* C5, F2, J2
Iroquois Point E2, J2
Kaanapali B3
Kahana B3, J1
Kahului C3, D6
Kailua C5, K2
Kailua-Kona D7, F5
Kalaheo C2
Kalaoa F5
Kalaupapa B3
Kaneohe C5, G1, K2
Kapaa A5, D1
Kaunakakai A3
Keaau J5
Kealakekua G5
Kealia D1, G6
Kekaha B2
Kihei C4, D6
Kilauea C1
Koloa C2
Kualapuu A3
Kula C4
Lahaina B3, D6
Laie C5, J1
Lanai City B3
Lawai C2
Lihue A5, D2
Maili H2
Makaha H2
Makakilo City H2
Makawao C3
Maunawili K2
Mililani Town J2
Mokuleia H1
Mountain View J5
Nanakuli B5, H2
Pacific Palisades E1, J2
Pahala H6
Papaikou J5
Pearl City C5, E1, J2
Pepeekeo J5
Pohakupu K2
Pukalani C3, D6
Pupukea J1
Volcano J6
Waialua B3, H1
Waianae B5, H2
Waihee C3
Waikiki G2
Waikoloa Village G4
Wailua C3, D1
Wailuku C3, D6
Waimalu E1, J2
Waimanalo K2
Waimanalo Beach K2

Key
Waimea C2, D6, H1
Waipahu E1, J2
Waipio H4
Waipio Acres J2
Whitmore Village J2

Other Features
Alenuihaha, *channel* D6
Alika Cone, *mt.* G6
Diamond Head, *point* G3
Ford, *island* E1
Haleakala, *mt.* C4
Haleakala Natl. Park C4, D6
Hamakua, *coast* H4
Hawaii, *island* E6, G5
Hawaii Volcanoes Natl. Park E7, H6
Hilo, *bay* J5
Hualalai, *mt.* G5
Kaala, *mt.* H1
Kaena, *point* B5, H1
Kahoolawe, *island* B4, D6
Kahului, *bay* C3
Kaikipauula, *mt.* H4
Kailua, *bay* K2
Kaiwi, *channel* C5, K3
Ka Lae (South Cape), *cape* D7, G7
Kalalua, *mt.* J6
Kalaupapa, *peninsula* B3
Kalaupapa Natl. Hist. Park B3
Kaloko-Honokohau Natl. Hist. Park F5
Kamakou, *mt.* B3
Kau, *desert* H6
Kauai, *channel* B5, D2
Kauai, *island* A5, B1
Kaulakahi, *channel* A5, B1
Kawaikini, *mt.* C1
Kiholo, *bay* G4
Kilauea, *crater* J6
Kilohana, *crater* C2
Kinau, *cape* C4
Kipuka Puaulu, *mt.* H6
Kohala, *coast* F5
Kohala, *mt.* G4
Kohala, *mts.* G4
Kona, *coast* F6
Konahuanui, *mt.* G2, K2
Koolau Range, *mts.* F1, J1
Kulani, *mt.* H5
Kumukahi, *cape* E7, K5
Lanai, *island* B3, C6
Lehua, *island* A1
Lua Makika, *mt.* B4
Maalaea, *bay* C4
Makaleha, *mts.* C1
Makapuu, *point* C5, K2
Mamala, *bay* E2, J3
Maui, *island* C3, D6
Mauna Iki, *mt.* H6
Mauna Kea, *mt.* E6, H5
Mauna Loa, *mt.* D7, H6
Maunalua, *bay* K3
Mokolii, *island* J2
Mokuauia, *island* J1
Mokulua, *islands* K2
Moku Manu, *island* K2
Molokai, *island* A3, C5
Molokini, *island* C4
Na Pali, *coast* B1
Niihau, *island* A2, A5
Oahu, *island* B5, D2, K1
Pearl, *harbor* E2
Punchbowl, *crater* G2
Pu'uhonua O Honaunau N.H.P. G6
Puu Kainapuaa, *mt.* J1
Puu Kaua, *mt.* H2
Puukohola Heiau Natl. Hist. Site G4
Puu Kukui, *mt.* B3
Puu Kulua, *mt.* H5
Puu Loa, *mt.* H5
Puu O Keokeo, *mt.* G6
Sand, *island* F2
Sulphur Cone, *mt.* G6
U.S.S. Arizona Memorial E1
Upolu, *point* D6, G3
Waialeale, *mt.* A5, C1
Waianae Range, *mts.* H1
Wailuku, *river* H5
Waimea, *canyon* C2
West Maui, *mts.* B3

Idaho page 139

Cities and Towns
Aberdeen E7
American Falls E7
Ammon F6
Arco D6
Banks A5
Bellevue C6
Bennington F7
Blackfoot E6
Boise, *capital* A6
Bonners Ferry A1
Buhl C7
Burley D7
Caldwell A6
Cascade A5
Challis C5
Chubbuck E7
Coeur d'Alene A2
Council A5
Driggs F6
Dubois E5
Eagle A6
Emmett A6
Fairfield C6
Filer C7
Fish Haven F7
Fruitland A6
Fruitvale A5
Garden City A6
Garden Valley A6
Glenns Ferry B7
Gooding C7
Grangeville A4
Hailey C6
Hayden A2
Idaho City B6
Idaho Falls E6
Jerome C7
Kamiah A3
Kellogg A2
Ketchum C6
Kuna A6
Laclede A1
Lewiston A3
McCall A5
Malad City E7
May D5
Middleton A6

Key
Montpelier F7
Moscow A3
Mountain Home B6
Murphy A6
Nampa A6
New Plymouth A6
Nezperce A3
Orofino A3
Osburn A2
Paris F7
Parma A6
Patterson D5
Pauline E7
Payette A5
Pinehurst A2
Pocatello E7
Post Falls A2
Preston F7
Priest River A1
Rathdrum A2
Rexburg F6
Rigby F6
Rupert D7
St. Anthony F6
St. Maries A2
Salmon D4
Sandpoint A1
Shelley E6
Shoshone C7
Soda Springs F7
Sugar City F6
Sun Valley C6
Thatcher F7
Twin Falls C7
Wallace B2
Weiser A5
Wendell C7

Other Features
American Falls, *reservoir* E7
Bear, *lake* F7
Bear, *river* F7
Big Lost, *river* D6
Bitterroot, *range* B3, D4
Blackfoot, *reservoir* F7
Blackfoot, *river* F6
Bruneau, *river* B7
Cache, *mt.* D7
Caribou, *range* F6
Cascade, *reservoir* A5
Castle, *mt.* C5
Clearwater, *mts.* B3
Clearwater, *river* B4
Craters of the Moon N.M. D6
Dworshak, *reservoir* A3
Grays, *lake* F6
Hagerman Fossil Beds N.M. C7
Hells, *canyon* A5
Hells Canyon Natl. Recreation Area A4
Kootenai, *river* A1
Lemhi, *river* D5
Lochsa, *river* B3
Middle Fork Salmon, *river* B5
Nez Perce N.H.P. A3, B3
North Fork Clearwater, *river* B3
Owyhee, *mts.* A6
Owyhee, *river* A6
Palisades, *reservoir* F6
Payette, *lake* A5
Payette, *river* A5
Pend Oreille, *lake* A1
Pend Oreille, *river* A1
Priest, *lake* A1
Ryan, *mt.* C6
St. Joe, *river* A2
Salmon, *river* B4
Salmon River, *mts.* C5
Sawtooth, *range* B5
Sawtooth Natl. Recreation Area C5
Scott, *mt.* E5
Snake, *river* A4
South Fork Selway, *river* B3
Teton, *river* F6
Weiser, *river* A5
Yellowstone Natl. Park F5

Illinois page 140

Cities and Towns
Abingdon C3
Addison B5
Albion E5
Aledo C2
Alsip B6
Altamont E4
Alton C5
Amboy D2
Anna D6
Antioch A4, E1
Arcola E4
Arlington Heights A5
Arthur E4
Ashland C4
Athens D4
Atlanta D3
Atwood E4
Auburn D4
Aurora E2
Barrington A5
Barry B4
Bartlett A5
Bartonville D3
Batavia E2
Beach Park B4
Beardstown C3
Beecher F2
Belleville D5
Belvidere E1
Bement E4
Benld D4
Benton E6
Berwyn B6
Bethany E4
Bloomington D3
Blue Island B6
Bolingbrook A6, E2
Bourbonnais F2
Braidwood E2
Breese D5
Bridgeport F5
Brighton C4
Brookfield B6
Buffalo Grove B5
Bunker Hill D4
Burbank B6
Bushnell C3
Byron D1
Cahokia C5
Cairo D6
Calumet City C6, F2

Key
Cambridge C2
Canton C3
Capron E1
Carbondale D6
Carlinville D4
Carlyle D5
Carmi E5
Carol Stream A5
Carpentersville E1
Carrier Mills E6
Carrollton C4
Carterville D6
Carthage B3
Cary E1
Casey F4
Catlin F3
Centralia D5
Cerro Gordo E4
Champaign E3
Channahon E2
Charleston E4
Chatham D4
Chenoa E3
Chester D6
Chicago B5, F2
Chicago Heights B6
Chillicothe D3
Christopher D6
Cicero B6, F2
Clifton F3
Clinton E3
Coal City E2
Colchester C3
Collinsville D5
Columbia C5
Crest Hill A6
Crete F2
Crystal Lake E1
Cuba C3
Danville F3
Decatur E4
Deerfield B5
De Kalb E2
Delavan D3
De Soto D6
Des Plaines B5
Dixon D2
Dolton B6
Downers Grove B6
Du Quoin D5
Dwight E2
Earlville E2
East Dubuque C1
East Moline C2
East Peoria D3
East St. Louis C5
Edwardsville D5
Effingham E4
Elburn E2
Eldorado E6
Elgin E1
Elizabethtown E6
Elk Grove Village B5
Elmhurst B5
Elmwood D3
Elmwood Park B5
Erie C2
Eureka D3
Evanston B5, F1
Evergreen Park B6
Fairbury E3
Fairfield E5
Farmer City E3
Farmington C3
Fisher E3
Flora E5
Forreston D1
Forsyth E4
Fox Lake A4, E1
Fox Lake Hills A4
Fox River Grove A5
Frankfort B6, F2
Freeburg D5
Freeport D1
Fulton C2
Gages Lake B4
Galena C1
Galesburg C3
Galva C2
Geneseo C2
Geneva E2
Genoa E1
Georgetown F4
Gibson City E3
Gillespie D4
Gilman F3
Girard D4
Glen Ellyn A5
Glencoe B5
Glendale Heights A5
Glenview B5
Glenwood B6
Godfrey C5
Golconda E6
Granite City C5
Granville D2
Grayslake A4
Grayville E5
Green Oaks B4
Greenup E4
Greenville D5
Gridley E3
Gurnee B4
Hainesville A4
Hamilton B3
Hampshire E1
Hanover Park A5
Hardin C4
Harrisburg E6
Harristown D4
Harvard E1
Harvey B6
Havana C3
Hennepin D2
Henry D2
Herrin D6
Herscher E2
Heyworth E3
Hickory Hills B6
Highland D5
Highland Park B5, F1
Highwood B5
Hillsboro D4
Hinckley E2
Hinsdale B6
Hoffman Estates A5
Homer F3
Homewood B6
Hoopeston F3
Huntley E1
Island Lake A5

Key
Jacksonville C4
Jerseyville C4
Johnston City E6
Joliet A6, E2
Jonesboro D6
Justice B6
Kankakee F2
Kaskaskia D6
Kewanee D2
Kincaid D4
Knoxville C3
Lacon D2
La Grange B6
La Harpe C3
Lake Bluff B5
Lake Forest B5
Lake Zurich A5
Lanark D1
La Salle D2
Lansing B6
Lawrenceville F5
Lemont B6
Lena D1
Le Roy E3
Lewistown C3
Lexington E3
Libertyville B5
Lilymoor A4
Lincoln D3
Lincolnwood B5
Lindenhurst A4
Lisle A6
Litchfield D4
Lockport A6
Lombard B6
Louisville E5
Loves Park D1
Lynwood C6
McHenry E1
Machesney Park D1
Mackinaw D3
McLeansboro E5
Macomb C3
Macon E4
Mahomet E3
Manhattan F2
Manito D3
Manteno F2
Marengo E1
Marion E6
Marissa D5
Marley B6
Maroa E3
Marseilles E2
Marshall F4
Mascoutah D5
Mason City D3
Matteson B6
Mattoon E4
Maywood B5
Melrose Park B5
Mendota D2
Metamora D3
Metropolis E6
Milan C2
Milford F3
Minonk D3
Minooka E2
Mokena B6
Moline C2
Momence F2
Monmouth C3
Monticello E3
Morris E2
Morrison D2
Morton D3
Morton Grove B5
Mound City D6
Mounds D6
Mount Carmel F5
Mount Carroll D1
Mount Morris D1
Mount Olive D4
Mount Prospect B5
Mount Pulaski D3
Mount Sterling C4
Mount Vernon E5
Mount Zion E4
Moweaqua D4
Mundelein A5
Murphysboro D6
Naperville A6
Nashville D5
Neoga E4
New Athens D5
New Baden D5
New Lenox B6
Newton E5
Niles B5
Nokomis D4
Normal E3
Norridge B5
Northbrook B5
North Chicago B4, F1
Northfield B5
Oak Brook B6
Oak Forest B6
Oak Lawn B6, F2
Oak Park B5, F2
Oakwood F3
Oblong F4
O'Fallon D5
Oglesby D2
Okawville D5
Old Mill Creek B4
Olney E5
Onarga F3
Oquawka C3
Oregon D1
Orion C2
Orland Hills B6
Orland Park B6
Ottawa E2
Palatine A5
Palestine F4
Palos Heights B6
Palos Hills B6
Pana D4
Paris F4
Park City B4
Park Forest F2
Park Ridge B5
Pawnee D4
Paxton E3
Pecatonica D1
Pekin D3
Peoria D3
Peoria Heights D3
Peotone F2
Peru D2
Petersburg D4

Key
Pinckneyville D5
Pittsfield C4
Plainfield A6, E2
Plano E2
Polo D2
Pontiac E3
Princeton D2
Princeville D3
Prophetstown D2
Quincy B4
Rantoul E3
Red Bud D5
Richton Park B6
Riverdale B6
Riverton D4
Riverwoods B5
Roanoke D3
Robinson F4
Rochelle D2
Rochester D4
Rock Falls D2
Rock Island C2
Rockford D1
Rockton D1
Rome D3
Romeoville A6
Roodhouse C4
Roscoe D1
Rosiclare E6
Rossville F3
Round Lake Beach A4
Rushville C3
Russell B4
St. David C3
St. Elmo E4
St. Joseph E3
St. Libory D5
Salem E5
Sandoval D5
Sandwich E2
Sauk Village C6
Savanna C1
Savoy E3
Schaumburg A5
Schiller Park B5
Seneca E2
Sesser D5
Shawneetown E6
Shelbyville E4
Sheridan E2
Sherman D4
Shorewood A6, E2
Skokie B5
Somonauk E2
South Beloit D1
South Elgin E2
South Holland B6
South Jacksonville C4
Sparta D5
Spring Valley D2
Springfield, *capital* D4
Staunton D4
Steeleville D5
Sterling D2
Stockland F3
Stockton C1
Streamwood A5
Streator E2
Sullivan E4
Summit B6
Sycamore E2
Taylorville D4
Teutopolis E4
Tilton F3
Tinley Park B6, F2
Toledo E4
Tolono E4
Toluca D3
Toulon D2
Tower Lakes A5
Tremont D3
Trenton D5
Tuscola E4
Urbana E3
Vandalia D5
Vernon Hills B5
Vienna E6
Villa Grove E4
Villa Park B5
Virden D4
Virginia C4
Volo A4
Wadsworth B4
Walnut D2
Wapella E3
Warren D1
Warrensburg D4
Warrenville A6
Warsaw B3
Washington D3
Waterloo C5
Watseka F3
Wauconda A5
Waukegan B4, F1
Waverly D4
Westchester B6
West Chicago A5
West Frankfort E6
Westville F3
Wheaton A6, E2
Wheeling B5, F1
White Hall C4
Wilmette B5
Wilmington E2
Winchester C4
Winnebago D1
Winnetka B5
Winthrop Harbor B4
Woodridge A6
Wood River C5
Woodstock E1
Wyoming D2
Yorkville E2
Zeigler D6
Zion B4, F1

Other Features
Carlyle, *lake* D5
Chautauqua, *lake* C3
Chicago, *river* B5
Clinton, *lake* E3
Crab Orchard, *lake* D6
Des Plaines, *river* A6, B4
Du Page, *river* A6
Fox, *lake* A4
Fox, *river* E2
Illinois, *river* D3
Ind. Dunes Natl. Lakeshore C6
Kankakee, *river* E2
Kaskaskia, *river* E4
Lincoln Home Natl. Hist. Site D4
Marie, *lake* A4
Michigan, *lake* F1
O'Hare, *airport* B5
Ohio, *river* D6
Orland, *lake* B6
Rend, *lake* D5
Rock, *river* D2
Sangamon, *river* C3
Shelbyville, *lake* E4
Spoon, *river* C3
Wabash, *river* E6

Indiana .... page 141

Cities and Towns

Albany F4
Albion F2
Alexandria E4
Anderson E4
Angola G1
Arcadia D4
Argos D2
Atlanta D4
Attica B4
Auburn F2
Aurora G6
Austin E7
Avilla F2
Bargersville D5
Batesville F6
Bedford D7
Berne G3
Bicknell B7
Bloomfield C6
Bloomington C6
Bluffton F3
Boonville B8
Bourbon D2
Brazil B5
Bremen D2
Brookston C3
Brookville F6
Brownsburg D5
Brownstown D7
Butler G2
Cambridge City F5
Cannelton C9
Carmel D5
Chandler B8
Charlestown E8
Chesterton B1
Churubusco F2
Cicero D4
Clayton C5
Clinton B5
Cloverdale C5
Columbia City E2
Columbus E6
Connersville F5
Corydon D8
Covington B4
Crawfordsville C4
Crothersville E7
Crown Point B2
Culver D2
Dale C8
Daleville E4
Danville C5
Darmstadt A8
Decatur G3
Delphi C3
Demotte B2
Dunlap E1
East Chicago B1
Eaton F4
Edinburgh E6
Elkhart E1
Ellettsville C6
Elwood E4
English D8
Evansville A9
Fairmount E4
Farmland F4
Ferdinand C8
Fishers D5
Flora C3
Fort Branch A8
Fort Wayne F2
Fowler B3
Frankfort C4
Franklin D6
Fremont G1
French Lick C7
Galveston D3
Garrett F2
Gary B1
Gas City E4
Geneva G3
Georgetown E8
Goshen E1
Greencastle C5
Greenfield E5
Greensburg F6
Greentown E4
Greenwood D5
Hagerstown F5
Hammond A1
Hanover F7
Hartford City F4
Hebron B2
Highland B1
Hope E6
Huntertown F2
Huntingburg C8
Huntington F3
Indianapolis, *capital* D5
Jasonville B6
Jasper C8
Jeffersonville E8
Kendallville F2
Kentland B3
Kingsford Heights C2
Knox C2
Kokomo D3
Kouts B2
Lafayette C4
Lagrange F1
Lakeville D1
La Porte C1
Lawrence D5
Lawrenceburg G6
Lebanon D4
Liberty G5
Ligonier E2
Lincoln City B8
Linton B6
Logansport D3
Loogootee C7
Lowell B2
Madison F7
Marion E3
Martinsville D6
Merrillville B2
Michigan City C1
Middlebury E1
Milan F6
Milford E2
Mishawaka D1
Mitchell D7
Monon C3
Monticello C3
Montpelier F3
Mooresville D5
Mount Vernon A9
Mulberry C4
Muncie F4
Nappanee D2
Nashville D6
New Albany E8
Newburgh B9
New Carlisle C1
New Castle F5
New Haven F2
Newport B5
New Whiteland D5
Noblesville D4
North Judson C2
North Liberty D1
North Manchester E2
North Terre Haute B5
North Vernon E6
Notre Dame D1
Oakland City B8
Odon C7
Orleans D7
Osgood F6
Ossian F3
Otterbein B3
Oxford B3
Paoli D7
Pendleton E4
Peru D3
Petersburg B8
Plainfield D5
Plymouth D2
Portland G4
Princeton A8
Redkey F4
Rensselaer B3
Richmond G5
Rising Sun G7
Rochester D2
Rockport B9
Rockville B5
Rushville F5
Salem D7
Schererville B2
Scottsburg E7
Sellersburg E8
Seymour E7
Shadeland C4
Shelbyville E5
Sheridan D4
Shoals C7
South Bend D1
South Whitley E2
Speedway D5
Spencer C6
Sullivan B6
Syracuse E2
Tell City C9
Terre Haute B6
Thorntown C4
Tippecanoe D2
Tipton D4
Union City G4
Upland F4
Valparaiso B2
Veedersburg B4
Vernon E7
Versailles F6
Vevay F7
Vincennes A7
Wabash E3
Wakarusa E1
Walkerton D2
Warsaw E2
Washington B7
Waterloo F2
Westfield D4
West Lafayette C4
Westport E6
Westville C1
Williamsport B4
Winamac C2
Winchester G4
Winona Lake E2
Woodburn G2
Worthington C6
Yorktown F4
Zionsville D5

Other Features
Big Blue, *river* E5
Brookville, *lake* F5
Eel, *river* E3
George Rogers Clark N.H.P. A7
Indiana Dunes Natl. Lakeshore B1
Kankakee, *river* C2
Lemon, *lake* D6
Lincoln Boyhood Natl. Memorial C8
Maumee, *river* G2
Michigan, *lake* B1
Mississinewa, *lake* E3
Monroe, *lake* D6
Ohio, *river* A9
Patoka, *river* B8
St. Joseph, *river* G2
Salamonie, *lake* E3
Tippecanoe, *river* C2
Wabash, *river* A8
Wawasee, *lake* E2
White, *river* C6
Whitewater, *river* F6

Iowa .... page 142

Cities and Towns

Ackley H2
Adel F4
Akron A2
Albia J5
Algona F1
Allison J2
Alta D2
Altoona H4
Ames G3
Anamosa M3
Ankeny G4
Asbury N3
Atlantic D5
Audubon E4
Avoca D5
Batavia K5
Bayard E4
Bedford E6
Belle Plaine K4
Bellevue P3
Belmond G2
Bettendorf P4
Bloomfield K6
Boone G3
Brighton L5
Britt G1
Brooklyn K4
Burlington M6
Camanche P4
Carlisle G5
Carroll E3
Carter Lake C5
Cascade N3
Cedar Falls K3
Cedar Rapids L4
Center Point L3
Centerville J6
Chariton H5
Charles City J1
Cherokee C2
Clarinda D6
Clarion G2
Clarksville J2
Clear Lake H1
Clinton P4
Colfax H4
Columbus Junction M5
Coon Rapids E4
Coralville L4
Corning E6
Corydon H6
Council Bluffs C5
Cresco K1
Creston F5
Dakota City F2
Dallas Center G4
Davenport N4
Decorah L1
Denison D4
Denver K2
Des Moines, *captial* G4
De Witt N4
Dubuque N2
Dunlap C4
Durant N4
Dyersville M3
Eagle Grove G2
Eldora H3
Eldridge N4
Elgin L2
Elkader M2
Emmetsburg E1
Epworth N3
Estherville E1
Evansdale K3
Fairfield L6
Farley M3
Fayette L2
Forest City G1
Fort Dodge F2
Fort Madison M6
Garner G1
Gilmore City F2
Glenwood C5
Greenfield F5
Grimes G4
Grinnell J4
Grundy Center J3
Guthrie Center E4
Guttenberg M2
Hampton H2
Harlan D4
Hartley D1
Hawarden B1
Hiawatha L3
Holstein C3
Hudson K3
Hull B1
Humboldt F2
Huxley G4
Ida Grove D3
Independence L3
Indianola G5
Iowa City L4
Iowa Falls H2
Jefferson F4
Jesup K3
Johnston G4
Kalona L5
Keokuk M7
Keosauqua L6
Knoxville H5
Lake City E3
Lake Mills G1
Lake View D3
Lamoni G6
La Porte City K3
Laurens E2
Le Claire P4
Le Mars B2
Lenox E6
Leon G6
Logan C4
Lovilia J5
Madrid G4
Manchester M3
Manly H1
Manning D4
Manson E2
Mapleton C3
Maquoketa N3
Marengo K4
Marion L4
Marshalltown J3
Mason City H1
Mediapolis M5
Melcher-Dallas H5
Milford D1
Missouri Valley C4
Monona M1
Monroe H4
Montezuma J4
Monticello M3
Mount Ayr F6
Mount Pleasant L6
Mount Vernon M4
Moville B3
Muscatine M5
Nashua J2
Nevada H3
New Hampton K1
New London M6
Newton H4
Nora Springs J1
North Liberty L4
Northwood H1
Norwalk G5
Oakland D5
Oelwein L2
Ogden F3
Onawa B3
Orange City B1
Osage J1
Osceola G5
Oskaloosa J5
Ottumwa K5
Park View N4
Parkersburg J2
Pella J5
Perry F4
Pleasantville H5
Pocahontas E2
Polk City G4
Postville L1
Prairie City H4
Primghar C1
Red Oak D5
Reinbeck J3
Remsen C2
Rock Rapids B1
Rock Valley B1
Rockwell City E3
Sac City E3
Sanborn C1
Sergeant Bluff B3
Sheldon C1
Shell Rock J2
Shenandoah D6
Sibley C1
Sidney C6
Sigourney K5
Sioux Center B1
Sioux City B2
Spencer D1
Spirit Lake D1
Storm Lake D2
Story City G3
Strawberry Point L2
Stuart F4
Sumner K2
Tama J4
Tipton M4
Toledo J4
Traer K3
Urbandale E4
Villisca E6
Vinton K3
Walcott N4
Wapello M5
Washington L5
Waterloo K3
Waukee G4
Waukon M1
Waverly K2
Webster City G2
West Branch M4
West Burlington M6
West Des Moines G4
West Liberty M4
West Union L2
Williamsburg L4
Wilton M4
Windsor Heights G4
Winterset F5
Woodbine C4

Other Features
Big Sioux, *river* A1
Boone, *river* G2
Cedar, *river* K3
Chariton, *river* H6
Clear, *lake* H1
Coralville, *lake* L4
Des Moines, *river* F3
Effigy Mounds Natl. Monument M1
Floyd, *river* B2
Fox, *river* K6
Iowa, *river* K4
Little Sioux, *river* D2
Maple, *river* D2
Mississippi, *river* M2
Missouri, *river* B4
Rathbun, *lake* J6
Red Rock, *lake* J5
Saylorville, *reservoir* G4
Skunk, *river* L5
Spirit, *lake* D1
Storm, *lake* D2
Turkey, *river* L2
Wapsipinicon, *river* K2
West Nishnabota, *river* K2

Kansas .... page 143

Cities and Towns

Abilene E3
Adrian G3
Alma F3
Andover E4
Anthony D4
Arkansas City E4
Arma H4
Ashland C4
Atchison G2
Atwood A2
Augusta F4
Baldwin City G3
Baxter Springs H4
Belle Plaine E4
Belleville E2
Beloit D2
Bonner Springs H2
Buhler E3
Burlington G3
Butler G3
Caldwell E4
Caney G4
Carbondale G3
Chanute G4
Chapman E3
Cheney E4
Cherryvale G4
Chetopa G4
Cimarron B4
Clay Center E2
Clearwater E4
Clifton E2
Coffeyville G4
Colby A2
Coldwater C4
Columbus H4
Concordia E2
Conway Springs E4
Coolidge A3
Cottonwood Falls F3
Council Grove F3
Derby E4
De Soto H3
Dighton B3
Dodge City B4
Douglass F4
El Dorado F4
Elkhart A4
Ellinwood D3
Ellis C3
Ellsworth D3
Emporia F3
Erie G4
Eudora F3
Eureka F4
Florence F3
Fort Scott H4
Fredonia G4
Frontenac H4
Galena H4
Garden City B4
Gardner H3
Garnett G3
Girard H4
Goddard E4
Goodland A2
Gove B3
Great Bend D3
Greensburg C4
Halstead E4
Harper D4
Hays C3
Haysville E4
Herington F3
Hesston E3
Hiawatha G2
Hill City C2
Hillsboro E3
Hoisington D3
Holcomb B4
Holton G2
Horton G2
Howard F4
Hoxie B2
Hugoton A4
Humboldt G4
Hutchinson E3
Independence G4
Iola G4
Iuka D4
Jetmore C3
Johnson A4
Junction City F2
Kansas City H2
Kansas City H2
Kingman D4
Kinsley C4
La Crosse C3
Lakin A4
Lansing H2
Larned C3
Lawrence G3
Leavenworth H2
Leoti A3
Liberal B4
Lincoln D2
Lindsborg E3
Lorraine D3
Louisburg H3
Lyndon G3
Lyons D3
McPherson E3
Maize E4
Manhattan F2
Mankato D2
Marion E3
Marysville F2
Meade B4
Medicine Lodge D4
Minneapolis E2
Mound City H3
Moundridge E3
Mulvane E4
Neodesha G4
Ness City C3
Newton E3
North Newton E3
Norton C2
Oakley B2
Oberlin B2
Ogden F2
Olathe H3
Osage City G3
Osawatomie H3
Osborne D2
Oskaloosa G2
Oswego G4
Ottawa G3
Overland Park H3
Paola H3
Park B2
Park City E4
Parsons G4
Peabody E3
Phillipsburg C2
Pittsburg H4
Plainville C2
Pratt D4
Rich Hill G3
Rose Hill D4
Rose Hill E4
Russell D3
Sabetha G2
St. Francis A2
St. John D3
St. Marys F2
Salina E3
Scott City B3
Sedan F4
Sedgwick E4
Seneca F2
Sharon Springs A3
Silver Lake F2
Smith Center D2
South Hutchinson E4
Spring Hill H3
Stafford D4
Sterling D3
Stockton C2
Sublette B4
Syracuse A4
Tecumseh G2
Tonganoxie G2
Topeka, *capital* G2
Towanda F4
Tribune A3
Troy G2
Ulysses A4
Valley Center E4

Key
Valley Falls G2
Wakeeney C2
Wamego E2
Washington E2
Waterville E2
Wellington E4
Wellsville G3
Westmoreland F2
Wichita E4
Winfield F4
Yates Center G4

Other Features
Arkansas, *river* A4, D3
Big Blue, *river* F2
Cedar Bluff, *reservoir* C3
Cheney, *reservoir* E4
Chikaskia, *river* D4
Cimarron, *river* A4
Clinton, *lake* G3
Fall, *river* F4
Flint Hills F4
Fort Larned Natl. Hist. Site C3
Fort Scott Natl. Hist. Site H4
Kanapolis, *lake* E3
Kansas, *river* F2
Kirwin, *reservoir* C2
Little Blue, *river* E1
Marion, *lake* E3
Medicine Lodge, *river* C4
Melvern, *lake* G3
Milford, *lake* F2
Missouri, *river* G2
Neosho, *river* G3
North Fork Solomon, *river* B2
Republican, *river* D1
Saline, *river* C2
Smoky Hill, *river* B3
Solomon, *river* D2
South Fork Republican, *river* A2
Sunflower, *mt.* A2
Tuttle Creek, *lake* F2
Verdigris, *river* F3
Waconda, *lake* D2
Wilson, *lake* D3

Kentucky ....page 144

Cities and Towns
Aberdeen F2
Albany D4
Alexandria E2
Allensville B4
Ashland G2
Auburn C4
Augusta E2
Barbourville F4
Bardstown D3
Bardwell B2
Beattyville F3
Beaver Dam C3
Bedford D2
Benton C2
Berea E3
Berry E2
Booneville F3
Bowling Green C4
Brandenburg C3
Brooks D2
Brooksville E2
Brownsville C3
Burkesville D4
Burlington E1
Butler E2
Cadiz B4, C2
Calhoun B3
Calvert City C2
Campbellsville D3
Campton F3
Carlisle E2
Carrollton D2
Carrsville C1
Catlettsburg G2
Cave City D3
Central City B3
Clay City F3
Clinton B2
Columbia D3
Concord F2
Corbin E4
Corinth E2
Covington E1
Crestwood D2
Cumberland G4
Cynthiana E2
Danville E3
Dawson Springs B3, C1
Dixon B3, C1
Dry Ridge E2
Earlington B3
Eddyville A3, C2
Edmonton D4
Ekron C3
Elizabethtown D3
Elkton B4
Eminence D2
Fairfield D3
Falmouth E2
Flatwoods G2
Flemingsburg F2
Florence E2
Foster E2
Frankfort, *capital* E2
Franklin C4
Frenchburg F3
Fulton B2
Georgetown E2
Glasgow D3
Gratz E2
Grayson G2
Greensburg D3
Greenup G2
Greenville B3
Guthrie B4
Hardinsburg C3
Harlan F4
Harrodsburg E3
Hartford C3
Hawesville C3
Hazard F3
Henderson B3
Hickman B2
Hindman G3
Hiseville D3
Hobson D3
Hodgenville D3
Hopkinsville B4
Horse Cave D3
Hyden F3
Independence E2
Inez G3
Irvine F3
Jackson F3
Jamestown D4
Jeffersontown D2
Jeffersonville F3
Jenkins G3
Junction City E3
La Fayette B4, C2
La Grange D2
Lancaster E3
Lawrenceburg E2
Leatherwood F3
Lebanon D3
Leitchfield C3
Lewisport C3
Lexington E2
Liberty E3
Livermore B3
Livingston E3
London E3
Louisa G2
Louisville D2
McKee F3
Mackville D3
Madisonville B3
Manchester F3
Marion A3, C1
Mayfield B2
Maysville F2
Middlesboro F4
Middletown D2
Monterey E2
Monticello E4
Morehead F2
Morganfield B3, C1
Morgantown C3
Mt. Olivet E2
Mt. Sterling F2
Mt. Vernon E3
Mt. Washington D2
Muldraugh C3
Munfordville D3
Murray C2
Nebo B3
New Castle D2
Nicholasville E3
Oak Grove B4
Okolona D2
Olive Hill F2
Owensboro B3
Owenton E2
Owingsville F2
Paducah C2
Paris E2
Patesville C3
Phelps G3
Pikeville G3
Pine Knot E4
Pineville F4
Pleasure Ridge Park D2
Prestonsburg G3
Princeton B3, C2
Providence B3, C1
Raceland G2
Radcliff D3
Richmond E3
Rochester C3
Russell Springs D3
Russellville C4
St. Matthews D2
Salyersville F3
Sandy Hook F3
Scottsville C4
Sebree B3
Shelbyville D2
Shepherdsville D3
Slaughters B3
Smithland C1
Somerset E3
South Shore G2
Springfield D3
Stanford E3
Stanton F3
Sturgis A3, C1
Taylorsville D2
Tompkinsville D4
Valley Station D2
Vanceburg F2
Versailles E2
Vicco F3
Vine Grove D3
Walton E2
Warsaw E2
West Liberty F3
Wheelwright G3
Whitesburg G3
Whitley City E4
Wickliffe B2
Williamsburg E4
Williamstown E2
Wilmore E3
Winchester E3
Woodbury C3
Zion B3

Other Features
Barkley, *lake* B4, C2
Barren, *river* C3
Barren River, *lake* C4
Big Sandy, *river* G2
Big South Fork Natl. River and Rec. Area E4
Buckhorn, *lake* F3
Cave Run, *lake* F2
Cumberland, *lake* E4
Cumberland, *river* E4
Cumberland Gap Natl. Hist. Park F4
Dale Hollow, *lake* D4
Fish Trap, *river* G3
Green, *river* B3, D3
Green River, *lake* D3
Kentucky, *lake* C2
Kentucky, *river* D2, E3
Licking, *river* F2
Lincoln Birthplace Natl. Hist. Site D3
Mammoth Cave Natl. Park C3
Nolin River, *lake* C3
Ohio, *river* F2
Rough, *river* C3
Rough River, *lake* C3
Tennessee, *river* C2
Tug Fork, *river* G3

Louisiana ....page 145

Cities and Towns
Abbeville E7
Abita Springs J6
Alexandria E4
Ama Inset
Amelia G7
Amite J5
Arabi Inset
Arcadia D1
Arnaudville F6
Avondale Inset
Baker G5
Baldwin F7
Ball E4
Basile D6
Bastrop F1
Baton Rouge, *captial* G6
Bayou Cane H7
Bayou Vista G7
Belle Chasse Inset
Bentley E3
Bernice E1
Bertrandville Inset
Bogalusa K5
Bossier City B1
Boyce D4
Braithwaite Inset
Breaux Bridge F6
Bridge City Inset
Broussard F6
Bunkie E5
Buras K8
Caernarvon Inset
Cameron C7
Carencro E6
Carville G6
Cecilia F6
Chalmette Inset, K7
Charenton F7
Chauvin H8
Church Point E6
Clinton G5
Colfax D3
Columbia E2
Cottonport E5
Coushatta C2
Covington J6
Crowley E6
Crown Point Inset
Cullen C1
Cut Off J7
Dalcour Inset
Delcambre F7
Delhi G2
Denham Springs H5
De Quincy C6
De Ridder C5
Des Allemands J7
Destrehan Inset
Donaldsonville H6
Edgard H6
Elton D6
English Turn Inset
Erath E7
Estelle Inset
Eunice E6
Farmerville E1
Ferriday F3
Franklin F7
Franklinton J5
Frenier Inset
Galliano J8
Garyville H6
Glenmora D5
Golden Meadow J8
Gonzales H6
Grambling D1
Grand Isle K8
Gray H7
Greensburg H5
Greenwood B2
Gretna Inset, J7
Gueydan E6
Hackberry C6
Hahnville Inset, J7
Hammond J5
Harahan Inset
Harrisonburg E2
Harvey Inset
Haughton C1
Haynesville C1
Henderson F6
Homer C1
Houma H7
Independence J5
Inniswold G6
Iota D6
Iowa C6
Jackson G5
Jeanerette F7
Jean Lafitte J7
Jefferson Inset
Jena E3
Jennings D6
Jesuit Bend Inset
Jonesboro D2
Jonesville F3
Kaplan E6
Kenilworth Inset
Kenner Inset, J7
Kentwood J5
Killona Inset
Kinder D6
Krotz Springs F5
Labadieville H7
Lacombe K6
Lafayette E6
Lafitte J7
Lake Arthur D6
Lake Charles C6
Lake Providence G1
Laplace Inset, J6
Larose J7
Lecompte E4
Leesville C4
Livingston H5
Lockport H7
Logansport B3
Luling Inset
Mamou E5
Mandeville J6
Mansfield B3
Mansura E4
Many C3
Marion E1
Marksville E4
Marrero Inset, J7
Melder D4
Melville F5
Meraux Inset
Metairie Inset, J7
Mimosa Park Inset
Minden C1
Monroe E1
Montegut H8
Montz Inset
Morgan City G7
Moss Bluff C6
Napoleonville G7
Natalbany J5
Natchitoches C3
Newellton G2
New Iberia F6
New Llano C4
New Orleans Inset, J7
New Roads G5
New Sarpy Inset
Norco Inset
Oakdale D5
Oak Grove G1
Oakville Inset
Oberlin D5
Oil City B1
Olla E3
Opelousas E5
Paincourtville G6
Paradis Inset
Patterson G7
Plaquemine G6
Point a la Hache K7
Ponchatoula J6
Port Allen G6
Port Barre F5
Port Sulphur K8
Poydras Inset
Raceland H7
Rayne E6
Rayville F2
Reserve H6
Richwood E2
Ringgold C2
River Ridge Inset
Ruston D1
St. Bernard Inset
St. Francisville G5
St. Joseph G3
St. Martinville F6
St. Rose Inset
Scarsdale Inset
Schriever H7
Scott E6
Shreveport B2
Simmesport F5
Slidell K6
Springhill C1
Stonewall B2
Sulphur C6
Sunset E6
Swartz F1
Taft Inset
Tallulah G2
Terrytown Inset
Thibodaux H7
Toca Inset
Vidalia G3
Ville Platte E5
Vinton B6
Violet Inset, K7
Vivian B1
Waggaman Inset
Walker H6
Washington E5
Welsh D6
Westlake C6
West Monroe E1
Westwego Inset, J7
White Castle G6
Winnfield D3
Winnsboro F2
Zachary G5
Zwolle B3

Other Features
Atchafalaya, *bay* G8
Atchafalaya, *river* F5
Barataria, *bay* K8
Bistineau, *lake* C2
Black, *river* F4
Borgne, *lake* Inset, K6
Breton, *islands* L8
Caddo, *lake* A1
Caillou, *bay* G8
Calcasieu, *lake* C7
Caney, *lake* E2
Catahoula, *lake* E3
Chandeleur, *islands* M7
Driskill, *mt.* C2
Grand, *lake* D7
Jean Lafitte N.H.P. and Preserve J7
Little, *river* D2
Marsh, *island* F7
Mississippi, *river* G3
Ouachita, *river* E2
Pearl, *river* K5
Pontchartrain, *lake* Inset, J6
Red, *river* C3
Sabine, *lake* B7
Sabine, *river* B5
Terrebonne, *bay* H8
Timbalier, *bay* J8
Toledo Bend, *reservoir* B4
Vermilion, *bay* F7
West Cote Blanche, *bay* F7
White, *lake* E7

Maine ....page 146

Cities and Towns
Alfred B5
Amherst D4
Athens C4
Auburn B4
Augusta, *capital* C4
Bangor D4
Bar Harbor D4
Bass Harbor D4
Bath C4
Belfast C4
Berwick B5
Biddeford B5
Boothbay Harbor C4
Brewer D4
Bridgton B4
Brunswick C4
Bucksport D4
Calais E3
Camden C4
Cape Elizabeth B5
Caribou D2
Chisholm B4
Clinton C4
Conway A4
Damariscotta C4
Dexter C3
Dixfield B4
Dover-Foxcroft C3
East Millinocket D3
Eastport F4
Ellsworth D4
Fairfield C4
Falmouth B5
Farmington B4
Fort Fairfield E2
Fort Kent D1
Frankfort D4
Franklin D4
Freeport B5
Frenchboro D4
Frenchville D1
Fryeburg B4
Gardiner C4
Greene B4
Hallowell C4
Hampden D4
Houlton E2
Howland D3
Kennebunk B5
Kittery B5
Lewiston B4
Lincoln D3
Lisbon Falls B4
Livermore Falls B4
Machias E4
Madawaska D1
Madison C4
Mars Hill E2
Mechanic Falls B4
Mexico B4
Milbridge E4
Milford D4
Millinocket D3
Milo D3
Norridgewock C4
North Amity E3
North Berwick B5
North Conway A4
North East Carry C3
North Windham B5
Norway B4
Oakland C4
Old Orchard Beach B5
Old Town D4
Orono D4
Oxford B4
Patten D3
Portland B5
Presque Isle D2
Richmond C4
Rockland C4
Rumford B4
Saco B5
Sanford B5
Skowhegan C4
South Paris B4
South Portland B5
Springvale B5
Thomaston C4
Van Buren E1
Waldoboro C4
Waterville C4
Westbrook B5
Westfield E2
Wilsons Mills A4
Wilton B4
Winslow C4
Winthrop C4
Wiscasset C4
Woodland E3
Yarmouth B5
York B5

Other Features
Acadia Natl. Park D4
Androscoggin, *river* B4
Appalachian, *mts.* A3
Aroostook, *river* D2
au Haut, *island* D4
Aziscohos, *lake* A3
Baskahegan, *lake* E3
Baxter State Park D2
Big, *lake* E3
Casco, *bay* C4
Chamberlain, *lake* C2
Chesuncook, *lake* C2
Churchill, *lake* C2
Cross, *island* E4
Deer, *island* D4
Elizabeth, *cape* B4
Flagstaff, *lake* B3
Grand, *lake* E3
Grand Matagamon, *lake* D2
Grand Seboeis, *lake* D2
Great Wass, *island* E4
Islesboro, *island* D4
Katahdin, *mt.* D3
Kennebec, *river* C3
Long, *island* D4
Maine, *gulf* C4
Matinicus, *island* D4
Mattawamkeag, *river* D2
Millinocket, *lake* D3
Monhegan, *island* C4
Moosehead, *lake* C3
Mooselookmeguntic, *lake* B4
Mt. Desert, *island* D4
Munsungan, *lake* D2
Nicatous, *lake* D3
Pemadumcook, *lake* C3
Penobscot, *bay* D4
Penobscot, *river* D3
Piscataquis, *river* C3
Richardson, *lakes* B4
Saco, *bay* B5
Saco, *river* B5
Saddleback, *mt.* B4
St. Croix, *river* E3
St. John, *river* C2
Sebago, *lake* B5
Sebec, *lake* C3
Seboeis, *lake* D3
Seboomook, *lake* C3
Snow, *mt.* B3
Sugarloaf, *mt.* B3
Swans, *island* D4
Telos, *lake* C2
Umbagog, *lake* A4
Vinalhaven, *island* D4
West Grand, *lake* E3
West Quoddy Head, *peninsula* F4
White Cap, *mt.* C3

Maryland ....page 147

Cities and Towns
Aberdeen K2
Accident A6
Accokeek F5
Adelphi C4
Annapolis, *capital* J4
Arden-on-the-Severn H3
Arnold J3
Aspen Hill B3, F3
Avenue G7
Baltimore H2
Bel Air J1
Beltsville C3, G3
Berlin P6
Berwyn Heights C4
Bethesda B4, F4
Bladensburg C4
Boonsboro D1
Bowie G4
Bowleys Quarters J2
Braddock Heights D2
Brandywine G5
Brentwood C4
Brunswick D2
Bucktown K6
Burtonsville C3
Cabin John A4
California J6
Calverton C3
Cambridge K5
Cape St. Claire J3
Camp Springs C5
Carney H2
Cascade D1
Catonsville H2
Centreville K3
Chesapeake Beach H5
Chesapeake Ranch Estates J6
Chestertown K3
Cheverly C4
Chillum C4, G4
Clinton G4
Clover Hill E2
Cloverly C3
Cockeysville H2
Colesville C3
College Park C4, G4
Columbia G3
Contee D3
Copenhaver A3
Coral Hills C5
Cresaptown C6
Crisfield L7
Crofton H3
Crownsville H3
Cumberland D6
Damascus F2
Deale H4
Delmar M6
Denton L4
Derwood A3
District Heights D5
Dufief A3
Dundalk H2
Easton K4
Edgemere J3
Edgewood J2
Eldersburg G2
Elkridge G3
Elkton L1
Ellicott City G2
Emmitsburg E1
Essex J2
Fair Hill L1
Fallston J1
Federalsburg L5
Ferndale H3
Forest Heights B5, G4
Forestville G4
Fountain Head D1
Frederick E2
Friendsville A6
Frostburg C6
Fruitland M6
Gaithersburg F3
Garrison G2
Germantown E3
Glen A3
Glenarden D4
Glen Burnie H3
Glen Echo Heights B4
Glen Hills A3
Glenmont B3
Golden Beach H6
Grantsville B6
Grasonville K4
Green Haven H3
Greenbelt D4, G3
Greensboro L4
Hagerstown D1
Halfway C1
Hampstead G1
Hampton H2
Hancock B1
Havre de Grace K1
Herald Harbor H3
High Ridge D3
Hillandale C3
Hillcrest Heights C5
Hillsmere Shores J4
Hughesville G5
Hunting Hill A3
Hurlock L5
Hyattstown E2
Hyattsville C4, G4
Indian Head F5
Jarrettsville J1
Jessup G3
Joppatowne J2
Kemptown E2
Kensington B3, F3
Kentland D4, G4
Kettering G4
Keysers Ridge B6
Kingstown K3
Kingsville J2
Knollwood C3
Lake Shore J3
Landover C4, G4
Langley Park C4
Lanham D4
Lansdowne H3
LaPlata G5
Largo G4
Laurel D3, G3
LaVale C6
Lawsonia L7
Layhill B3
Leonardtown H6
Lewisdale C4
Lexington Park J6
Linthicum H3
Lochearn H2
Londontown H4
Lutherville H2

Key
Luxmanor ... B3
Manchester ... G1
Marlton ... G4
Maydale ... C3
Middle River ... J2
Middletown ... D2
Milford ... G2
Montgomery Village ... F3
Montpelier ... D3
Mount Aetna ... D1
Mountain Lake Park ... A7
Mount Airy ... F2
Mount Rainier ... C4
Muirkirk ... D3
New Carrollton ... D4
Norbeck ... B3
North Chevy Chase ... B4
North East ... L1
Oak Crest ... D3
Oakland ... A7
Oakland ... G2
Oakview ... C3
Ocean City ... P6
Ocean Pines ... P6
Odenton ... H3
Olney ... F3
Overlea ... H2
Owings Mills ... G2
Oxon Hill ... C5
Palmer Park ... D4
Parkville ... H2
Parole ... H4
Perry Hall ... J2
Perryman ... K2
Perryville ... K1
Pikesville ... H2
Pleasant Hills ... J2
Pocomoke City ... M7
Poolesville ... E3
Potomac ... A3, F3
Potomac Heights ... F5
Preston ... L5
Prince Frederick ... H5
Princess Anne ... M7
Randallstown ... G2
Randolph Hills ... B3
Redhouse ... A7
Reisterstown ... G2
Rising Sun ... K1
Ritchie ... D5
Riverdale ... C4
Riviera Beach ... H3
Rock Hall ... K3
Rockville ... A3, F3
Rosedale ... H2
Rossmoor Leisure World ... B3
Rossville ... J2
St. Charles ... G5
St. Michaels ... K4
Salisbury ... M6
Seabrook ... D4
Seat Pleasant ... D5
Severn ... H3
Severna Park ... H3
Shady Side ... H4
Shawsville ... H1
Silver Hill ... C5
Silver Spring ... B4, F4
Snow Hill ... N7
South Gate ... H3
Spencerville ... C3
Stevensville ... J3
Suitland ... C5, G4
Sykesville ... G2
Takoma Park ... C4
Taneytown ... F1
Temple Hills ... C5, G4
Thurmont ... E1
Timonium ... H2
Towson ... H2
Upper Marlboro ... H4
Waldorf ... G5
Walker Mill ... D5
Walkersville ... E2
Westernport ... B7
Westminster ... F1
West Ocean City ... P6
Wheaton ... B3, F3
White Marsh ... J2
White Oak ... C3, G3
White Plains ... G5
Wildwood Hills ... A3
Williamsport ... C1
Woodlawn ... G2
Woodyard ... G4

Other Features
Allegheny Front, *mt. ridge* ... C7
Antietam Natl. Battlefield ... D2
Appalachian Natl. Scenic Trail ... D2
Assateague Island Natl. Seashore ... P7
Assawoman, *bay* ... P6
Backbone, *mt.* ... A7
Chesapeake, *bay* ... J5
Chesapeake and Ohio Canal N.H.P. ... A4, D2
Chester, *river* ... K3
Chincoteague, *bay* ... N7
Choptank, *river* ... K5
Deep Creek, *lake* ... A6
Liberty, *reservoir* ... G2
North Branch Potomac, *river* ... C7
Nanticoke, *river* ... L6
Patapsco, *river* ... H3
Patuxent, *river* ... H4
Potomac, *river* ... G6
Susquehanna, *river* ... J1
Wicomico, *river* ... G6
Youghiogheny, *river* ... A6

Massachusetts ... page 148

Cities and Towns
Abington ... L4
Acton ... A5, J3
Acushnet ... L6
Adams ... B2
Amesbury ... L1
Amherst ... D3
Andover ... K2
Arlington ... C6, K3
Ashby ... G2
Ashfield ... C2
Ashland ... J3
Assinippi ... F8
Assonet ... K5
Athol ... F2
Attleboro ... J5
Auburn ... G4
Avon ... D8, K4
Ayer ... H2
Baldwinville ... F2
Barnstable ... N6
Becket ... B3
Bedford ... B5, J3
Belchertown ... E3
Bellingham ... J4
Belmont ... C6
Berkley ... K5
Bernardston ... D2
Beverly ... F5, L2
Billerica ... B5, J2
Blackstone ... H4
Blandford ... C4
Bliss Corner ... L6
Bolton ... H3
Bondsville ... E4
Boston, *capital* ... D6, K3
Boxford ... L2
Braintree ... E8, K4
Brewster ... P5
Bridgewater ... L5
Brimfield ... F4
Brockton ... K4
Brookfield ... F4
Brookline ... C7, K3
Burlington ... C5, K2
Buzzards Bay ... M5
Cambridge ... D6, K3
Canton ... C8, K4
Carlisle ... B5
Cedarville ... M5
Centerville ... N6
Central Village ... K6
Charlton ... G4
Charlton City ... G4
Chatham ... Q6
Chelmsford ... J2
Chelsea ... D6
Cheshire ... B2
Chester ... C3
Chicopee ... D4
Chilmark ... M7
Clarksburg ... B2
Clinton ... H3
Cochituate ... B7, J3
Cohasset ... L4
Concord ... B6, J3
Cotuit ... N6
Dalton ... B3
Danvers ... E5, L2
Dartmouth ... K6
Dedham ... C7, K4
Dennis ... P6
Douglas ... H4
Dover ... B8, J4
Dracut ... J2
Duxbury ... M4
East Brookfield ... F4
East Dennis ... P6
East Douglas ... H4
East Falmouth ... M6
East Freetown ... L5
Eastham ... Q5
Easthampton ... D3
East Longmeadow ... D4
East Orleans ... Q5
East Pepperell ... H2
East Wareham ... M5
Edgartown ... M7
Erving ... E2
Essex ... L2
Everett ... D6
Fall River ... K6
Falmouth ... M6
Feeding Hills ... D4
Fiskdale ... F4
Fitchburg ... G2
Florida ... B2
Foxboro ... K4
Framingham ... A7, J3
Franklin ... J4
Gardner ... G2
Gay Head ... L7
Georgetown ... L2
Gloucester ... M2
Granby ... D3
Granville ... C4
Great Barrington ... A4
Greenfield ... D2
Green Harbor ... M4
Halifax ... L5
Hamilton ... L2
Hanover ... L4
Hanson ... L4
Haverhill ... K1
Hingham ... F8, L4
Holbrook ... E8, K4
Holland ... F4
Holliston ... A8, J4
Holyoke ... D4
Hopedale ... H4
Hopkinton ... H4
Hubbardston ... G3
Hudson ... H3
Hull ... F7, L3
Huntington ... C4
Hyannis ... N6
Ipswich ... L2
Kingston ... M5
Lakeville ... L5
Lawrence ... K2
Lee ... B3
Lenox ... A3
Leominster ... G2
Lexington ... C6, K3
Lincoln ... B6
Littleton ... H2
Littleton Common ... H2
Longmeadow ... D4
Lowell ... J2
Ludlow ... E4
Lunenburg ... H2
Lynn ... E6, L3
Lynnfield ... D5, K2
Madaket ... P7
Malden ... D6, K3
Manchester-by-the-Sea ... L2
Mansfield ... K4
Marblehead ... F5, L3
Marion ... L6
Marlborough ... H3
Marshfield ... M4
Marshfield Hills ... M4
Mashpee ... N6
Mattapoisett ... L6
Maynard ... J3
Medfield ... B8, J4
Medford ... D6, K3
Medway ... A8
Melrose ... D6, K3
Mendon ... H4
Methuen ... K2
Middleboro ... L5
Milford ... H4
Millis ... B8
Milton ... D7, K3
Monson ... E4
Monterey ... B4
Monument Beach ... M6
Nahant ... E6, L3
Nantucket ... P7
Natick ... B7, J3
Needham ... C7, K3
New Ashford ... B2
New Bedford ... L6
New Boston ... B4
Newburyport ... L1
New Marlborough ... B4
Newton ... C7, K3
North Adams ... B2
North Amherst ... D3
Northampton ... D3
North Andover ... K2
North Attleboro ... J5
Northborough ... H3
Northbridge ... H4
North Brookfield ... F3
North Carver ... L5
North Falmouth ... M6
Northfield ... E2
North Grafton ... H4
North Pembroke ... L4
North Plymouth ... M5
North Reading ... D5, K2
North Scituate ... L4
North Sudbury ... A6
North Tisbury ... M7
Norton ... K5
Norwell ... L4
Norwood ... C8, K4
Oakham ... F3
Ocean Bluff ... M4
Ocean Grove ... K6
Orange ... E2
Orleans ... Q5
Osterville ... N6
Otis ... B4
Oxford ... G4
Palmer ... E4
Paxton ... G3
Peabody ... E5, L2
Pelham ... E3
Pembroke ... L4
Pepperell ... H2
Petersham ... F3
Phillipston ... F2
Pinehurst ... C5, K2
Pittsfield ... B3
Plainfield ... C2
Plainville ... J4
Plymouth ... M5
Pocasset ... M6
Provincetown ... P4
Quincy ... E7, K3
Randolph ... D8, K4
Raynham ... K5
Raynham Center ... K5
Reading ... D5, K2
Rehoboth ... K5
Revere ... E6, K3
Rochester ... L6
Rockland ... E8, L4
Rockport ... M2
Rutland ... G3
Sagamore ... M5
Salem ... F5, L2
Salisbury ... L1
Sandwich ... N5
Saugus ... E6, K3
Savoy ... B2
Scituate ... L4
Sharon ... C8, K4
Sheffield ... A4
Shelburne Falls ... D2
Sherborn ... B8
Shirley ... H2
Shrewsbury ... H3
Shutesbury ... E3
Somerset ... K5
Somerville ... D6, K3
South Amherst ... D3
Southbridge ... F4
South Carver ... M5
South Deerfield ... D3
South Dennis ... P6
South Duxbury ... M4
South Lancaster ... H3
South Sudbury ... A7
South Wellfleet ... P5
South Yarmouth ... P6
Spencer ... G4
Springfield ... D4
Sterling ... G3
Stoneham ... D5
Stoughton ... D8, K4
Sturbridge ... F4
Sudbury ... A6, J3
Sutton ... G4
Swampscott ... E6, L3
Taunton ... K5
Teaticket ... M6
Templeton ... F2
Tewksbury ... K2
Three Rivers ... E4
Tolland ... B4
Topsfield ... L2
Truro ... P5
Turners Falls ... D2
Tyngsborough ... J2
Upton ... H4
Uxbridge ... H4
Vineyard Haven ... M7
Wakefield ... D5, K2
Wales ... F4
Walpole ... C8, J4
Waltham ... C6, B6
Ware ... F3
Wareham ... M5
Warren ... F4
Warwick ... E2
Washington ... B3
Watertown ... C6
Wauwinet ... P7
Wayland ... B7
Webster ... G4
Wellesley ... B7, J3
West Barnstable ... N6
Westborough ... H3
West Boylston ... G3
West Brookfield ... F4
West Concord ... J3
West Cummington ... C3
West Falmouth ... M6
Westfield ... D4
Westford ... J2
West Granville ... C4
Westhampton ... C3
West Medway ... A8
Westminster ... G2
Weston ... B6, J3
Westport ... K6
Westport Point ... K6
West Springfield ... D4
West Wareham ... L5
Westwood ... C8, K4
West Yarmouth ... P6
Weymouth ... E8, L4
Whately ... D3
White Island Shores ... M5
Whitinsville ... H4
Whitman ... L4
Wilbraham ... E4
Williamstown ... B2
Wilmington ... C5, K2
Winchendon ... F2
Winchester ... C6
Windsor ... B2
Winthrop ... E6
Woburn ... C5, K3
Worcester ... G3
Worthington Center ... C3
Wrentham ... J4
Yarmouth Port ... P6

Other Features
Adams Natl. Hist. Park ... E8, L4
Ann, *cape* ... M2
Berkshire, *hills* ... B4
Boston, *bay* ... E6
Boston, *harbor* ... E7
Boston Natl. Hist. Park ... D6
Buzzards, *bay* ... M6
Cape Cod, *bay* ... N5
Cape Cod, *canal* ... M5
Cape Cod Natl. Seashore ... P5
Charles, *river* ... B7
Chicopee, *river* ... D4
Cobble Mt., *reservoir* ... C4
Cod, *cape* ... P4
Connecticut, *river* ... E2
Deer, *island* ... E7
Elizabeth, *islands* ... L7
Frederick Law Olmsted N.H.S. ... C7
Georges, *island* ... E7
Greylock, *mt.* ... B2
Hingham, *bay* ... E7
Housatonic, *river* ... A4
J.F.K. Birthplace Natl. Hist. Site ... D7
Long, *island* ... E7
Longfellow Natl. Hist. Site ... D6
Lowell Natl. Hist. Park ... J2
Maine, *gulf* ... M1
Martha's Vineyard, *island* ... M7
Massachusetts, *bay* ... F6, M3
Merrimack, *river* ... K1
Minute Man Natl. Hist. Park ... B6, J3
Monomoy, *island* ... P6
Muskeget, *channel* ... N7
Nantucket, *island* ... P7
Neponset, *river* ... C7
Otis, *reservoir* ... B4
Peddocks, *island* ... E7
Quabbin, *reservoir* ... F3
Quincy, *bay* ... E7
Salem Maritime N.H.S. ... F5, L2
Saugus Iron Works N.H.S. ... E6
Shawsheen, *river* ... B6
Spectacle, *island* ... E7
Swift, *river* ... E4
Taconic, *mts.* ... A2
Wachusett, *reservoir* ... G3
Wachusett, *river* ... G3
Walden, *pond* ... B6

Michigan ... page 149

Cities and Towns
Adrian ... E8
Albion ... E7
Algonac ... G7
Allegan ... D7
Allendale ... C7
Allen Park ... A7
Alma ... E6
Alpena ... F4
Ann Arbor ... F7
Atlanta ... E5
Bad Axe ... G6
Baldwin ... D6
Battle Creek ... D7
Bay City ... F6
Belding ... D6
Bellaire ... D5
Belleville ... F7
Benton Harbor ... C7
Berkley ... A6
Bessemer ... C2
Beulah ... C5
Beverly Hills ... A6
Big Rapids ... D6
Birmingham ... A6
Blissfield ... F8
Bloomfield Hills ... A6
Boyne City ... D4
Bridgeport ... F6
Brighton ... F7
Buchanan ... C8
Burton ... F6
Cadillac ... D5
Carleton ... F7
Caro ... F6
Carrollton ... F6
Cassopolis ... C8
Cedar Springs ... D6
Center Line ... B6
Centreville ... D8
Charlevoix ... D4
Charlotte ... E7
Cheboygan ... E4
Chelsea ... E7
Chesaning ... E6
Chesterfield ... C6
Christmas ... C3
Clare ... E6
Clawson ... B6
Clio ... F6
Coldwater ... D8
Connorville ... C2
Coopersville ... D6
Crystal Falls ... A3
Cutlerville ... D7
Davison ... F6
Dearborn ... A7, F7
Dearborn Hts. ... A7
Detroit ... B7, F7
De Witt ... E7
Dowagiac ... C8
Dundee ... F8
Durand ... F7
Eagle River ... A2
East Lansing ... E7
Eastpointe ... B6
East Tawas ... F5
Eaton Rapids ... E7
Ecorse ... B7
Escanaba ... B4
Essexville ... F6
Farmington ... A6
Farmington Hills ... A6
Fenton ... F7
Ferndale ... B6
Ferrysburg ... C6
Flat Rock ... F7
Flint ... F6
Flushing ... F6
Fowlerville ... E7
Frankenmuth ... F6
Franklin ... A6
Fraser ... B6
Fremont ... D6
Garden City ... A7
Gaylord ... E4
Gladstone ... B4
Gladwin ... E6
Grand Blanc ... F7
Grand Haven ... C6
Grand Ledge ... E7
Grand Rapids ... D7
Grayling ... E5
Greenville ... D6
Grosse Pointe ... B7
Grosse Pointe Farms ... B6
Grosse Pointe Park ... B7
Grosse Pointe Shores ... B6
Grosse Pointe Woods ... B6
Hamtramck ... B7
Hancock ... A2
Harper Woods ... B6
Harrison ... E5
Harrisville ... F5
Hart ... C6
Hastings ... D7
Hazel Park ... B6
Highland Park ... B7
Hillsdale ... E8
Holland ... C7
Holly ... F7
Holt ... E7
Houghton ... A2
Houghton Lake ... E5
Howell ... F7
Hudson ... E8
Hudsonville ... D7
Huntington Woods ... A6
Huron Heights ... A6
Imlay City ... F6
Inkster ... A7
Ionia ... D6
Iron Mountain ... A4
Ironwood ... C2
Ishpeming ... B3
Ithaca ... E6
Jackson ... E7
Jenison ... D7
Kalamazoo ... D7
Kalkaska ... D5
Keego Harbor ... A6
Kentwood ... D7
Kingsford ... A4
Lake City ... D5
Lake Orion ... F7
Lambertville ... F8
L'Anse ... A3
Lansing, *capital* ... E7
Lapeer ... F6
Lincoln Park ... A7
Livonia ... A7, F7
Lowell ... D7
Ludington ... C6
Madison Hts. ... B6
Manistee ... C5
Manistique ... C4
Marenisco ... D2
Marine City ... G7
Marquette ... B3
Marshall ... E7
Marysville ... G7
Mason ... E7
Melvindale ... A7
Menominee ... B4
Merriweather ... D2
Michigan Center ... E7
Midland ... E6
Milan ... F7
Milford ... F7
Mio ... E5
Monroe ... F8
Mount Clemens ... B6
Mount Morris ... F6
Mount Pleasant ... E6
Munising ... C3
Muskegon ... C6
Muskegon Hts. ... C6
Negaunee ... B3
New Baltimore ... G7
Newberry ... D3
Niles ... C8
North Muskegon ... C6
Norton Shores ... C6
Norway ... B4
Oak Park ... A6
Okemos ... E7
Ontonagon ... D1
Orchard Lake ... A6
Otsego ... D7
Owosso ... E6
Oxford ... F7
Paw Paw ... D7
Paw Paw Lake ... C7
Petoskey ... E4
Plainwell ... D7
Pontiac ... A6, F7
Portage ... D7
Port Huron ... G7
Portland ... E7
Rapid River ... C4
Reed City ... D6
Richmond ... G7
River Rouge ... B7
Rochester Hills ... A6
Rockford ... D6
Rockwood ... F7
Rogers City ... F4
Romeo ... F7
Romulus ... F7
Roscommon ... E5
Roseville ... B6
Royal Oak ... B6
Saginaw ... F6
St. Clair ... G7
St. Clair Shores ... B6
St. Ignace ... E4
St. Johns ... E6
St. Joseph ... C7
St. Louis ... E6
Saline ... F7
Sandusky ... G6
Sault Ste. Marie ... E3
Shields ... E6
Silver City ... D1
Skidway Lake ... E5
Southfield ... A6
Southgate ... A7
South Haven ... C7
South Lyon ... F7
Sparta ... D6
Spring Lake ... C6
Standish ... F6
Stanton ... D6
Sterling Heights ... F7
Sturgis ... D8
Sylvan Lake ... A6
Tawas City ... F5
Taylor ... A7, F7
Tecumseh ... F7
Temperance ... F8
Three Rivers ... D7
Traverse City ... D5
Troy ... B6
Union Lake ... A6
Utica ... B6
Vassar ... F6
Wakefield ... C2
Waldenburg ... B6
Walker ... D7
Warren ... B6, F7
Wayland ... D7
Wayne ... A7
West Acres ... A6
West Branch ... E5
Westland ... A7
White Cloud ... D6
Whitehall ... C6
White Pine ... D2
Whitmore Lake ... F7
Williamston ... E7
Wixom ... F7
Wolf Lake ... C6
Wyandotte ... B7
Wyoming ... D7
Ypsilanti ... F7
Zeeland ... C7

Other Features
Arvon, *mt.* ... A3
Au Sable, *river* ... E5
Beaver, *island* ... D4
Big Bay De Noc, *bay* ... C4
Big Sable, *point* ... C5
Bois Blanc, *island* ... E4
Cass, *river* ... F6
Chambers, *island* ... B4
Detroit, *river* ... B7
Drummond, *island* ... F4
Erie, *lake* ... G8
Escanaba, *river* ... B3
Glen, *lake* ... D5
Gogebic, *lake* ... D2
Government Peak, *mt.* ... D1
Grand, *island* ... C3
Grand Traverse, *bay* ... D4
Green, *bay* ... B5
Hamlin, *lake* ... C5
Hammond, *bay* ... E4
Higgins, *lake* ... E5
High, *island* ... D4
Hog, *island* ... D4
Houghton, *lake* ... E5
Hubbard, *lake* ... F5
Huron, *bay* ... A3
Huron, *lake* ... G5
Huron, *mts.* ... A3
Indian, *lake* ... C3
Isle Royale, *island* ... A1
Isle Royale Natl. Park ... A2
Keweenaw, *bay* ... A3
Keweenaw, *peninsula* ... A2
Keweenaw, *point* ... B2
Lookout, *point* ... F5
Manistee, *river* ... D5
Manitou, *island* ... B2
Menominee, *river* ... B4
Michigamme, *reservoir* ... A3
Michigan, *lake* ... C5
North Manitou, *island* ... C4
Paint, *river* ... A3
Pictured Rocks Natl. Lakeshore ... C3
Porcupine, *mts.* ... D2
Saginaw, *bay* ... F6
St. Clair, *lake* ... G7
St. Martin, *island* ... C4
Sleeping Bear Dunes Natl. Lakeshore ... C5
South Fox, *island* ... D4
South Manitou, *island* ... C4
Straits of Mackinac ... E4
Sturgeon, *bay* ... D4
Superior, *lake* ... A2
Thunder, *bay* ... F5
Whitefish, *bay* ... E3
Wixom, *lake* ... E6

Minnesota ... page 150

Cities and Towns
Ada ... A3
Aitkin ... D4
Albany ... C5
Albert Lea ... D7
Albertville ... D5
Alexandria ... B5
Annandale ... C5
Anoka ... D5
Appleton ... A5
Arlington ... C6
Aurora ... E3
Austin ... E7
Babbitt ... F3
Bagley ... B3
Barnesville ... A4
Baudette ... C2
Baxter ... C4
Bayport ... E6

Key
Belle Plaine D6
Bemidji C3
Benson B5
Big Lake D5
Bird Island C6
Blooming Prairie D7
Bloomington D6
Blue Earth C7
Brainerd C4
Breckenridge A4
Brooklyn Center E5
Buffalo D5
Burnsville D6
Caledonia F7
Cambridge D5
Canby A6
Cannon Falls E6
Carlton E4
Center City E5
Chanhassen D6
Chaska D6
Chatfield E7
Chisholm E3
Clara City B6
Clarks Grove D7
Clearwater C5
Cloquet E4
Cokato C5
Cold Spring C5
Columbia Hts F5
Coon Rapids D5
Corcoran D5
Crookston A3
Crosby D4
Dawson A6
Detroit Lakes B4
Dilworth A4
Dodge Center E6
Duluth E4
Eagan F6
Eagle Lake D6
East Bethel D5
East Grand Forks A3
Edina D6
Elbow Lake B5
Elk River D5
Ely F3
Evansville B4
Eveleth E3
Eyota E7
Fairmont C7
Falcon Heights F5
Faribault D6
Farmington D6
Fergus Falls A4
Foley D5
Forest Lake E5
Fosston B3
Fridley F5
Gaylord C6
Glencoe C6
Glenwood B5
Golden Valley E5
Goodview F6
Grand Forks A3
Grand Marais F5
Grand Portage F4
Grand Rapids D3
Granite Falls B6
Hallock A2
Hastings E6
Hawley A4
Hayfield E7
Hermantown E4
Hibbing E3
Hokah F7
Hopkins E5
Hovland F4
Howard Lake C5
Hutchinson C6
International Falls D2
Ivanhoe A6
Jackson B7
Janesville D6
Jordan D6
Kasson E6
Kenyon E6
La Crescent F7
Lake Crystal C6
Lakefield B7
Lakeville D6
Le Center D6
Le Sueur D6
Lewiston F7
Litchfield C5
Little Canada F5
Little Falls C5
Long Prairie C5
Lonsdale D6
Lutsen E5
Luverne A7
McIntosh B3
Madelia C6
Madison A5
Mahnomen B3
Mankato D6
Mantorville E6
Maple Grove D5
Maple Lake C5
Mapleton D7
Maplewood F5
Marshall B6
Melrose C5
Mendota F6
Milaca D5
Minneapolis D6
Minneota B6
Montevideo B6
Montgomery D6
Monticello D5
Moorhead A4
Mora D5
Morris B5
Mound D6
Mountain Iron E3
Mountain Lake C7
New Hope E5
Newport F6
New Prague D6
New Ulm C6
Nisswa C4
North Branch E5
Northfield D6
North Mankato C6
North Oaks F5
Olivia C6
Orono D6
Oronoco E6
Ortonville A5
Osakis B5
Owatonna D6

Key
Park Rapids B4
Paynesville C5
Pelican Rapids A4
Perham B4
Pigeon River F4
Pine City E5
Pine Island E6
Pipestone A7
Plainview E6
Plymouth D5
Preston E7
Princeton D5
Prinsburg B6
Prior Lake D6
Proctor E4
Ramsey D5
Red Lake Falls A3
Red Wing E6
Redwood Falls B6
Renville B6
Richfield F6
Robbinsdale E5
Rochester E6
Roseau B2
Rushford F7
St. Anthony F5
St. Charles E7
St. Cloud C5
St. Francis D5
St. James C7
St. Joseph C5
St. Louis Park E5
St. Michael D5
St. Paul, *capital* D6
St. Peter D6
Sandstone E4
Sartell C5
Sauk Centre C5
Sauk Rapids C5
Shakopee D6
Silver Bay F3
Slayton B7
Sleepy Eye C6
South St. Paul F5
Spring Valley E7
Springfield C6
Staples C4
Stewartville E7
Stillwater E5
Thief River Falls A2
Tracy B6
Truman C7
Two Harbors F3
Tyler A6
Virginia E3
Wabasha E6
Wadena B4
Waite Park C5
Walker C3
Warren A2
Warroad B2
Waseca D6
Waterville D6
Wells D7
Wheaton A5
White Bear Lake F5
Willmar B5
Windom B7
Winnebago C7
Winona F6
Winsted C6
Winthrop C6
Worthington B7
Wyoming E5
Young America D6
Zimmerman D5
Zumbrota E6

Other Features
Big Fork, *river* D2
Brule, *lake* E4
Buffalo, *river* A4
Chippewa, *river* B5
Clearwater, *river* B3
Cloquet, *river* F3
Des Moines, *river* B6
Eagle, *mt.* F4
Grand Portage Natl. Monument F4
Gull, *lake* C4
Lake of the Woods, *lake* C1
Leech, *lake* C3
Little Fork, *river* D2
Lower Red, *lake* B3
Lower Whitefish, *lake* C4
Mall of America F6
Mesabi, *range* D3
Mille Lacs, *lake* D4
Minnesota, *river* B6
Mississippi, *river* C3
Mud, *lake* B2
Namakan, *lake* E2
Pipestone Natl. Monument A6
Pokegama, *lake* D3
Rainy, *river* C2
Red River of the North, *river* A3
Root, *river* E7
Rum, *river* D5
St. Croix, *river* E5
St. Louis, *river* E3
Superior, *lake* F3
Upper Red, *lake* C2
Vermilion, *range* F3
Voyageurs Natl. Park E2
Winnibigoshish, *lake* D3

Mississippi .... page 151

Cities and Towns
Aberdeen D2
Ackerman C2
Alligator B1
Amory D2
Ashland C1
Baldwyn D1
Bassfield C4
Batesville C1
Bay St. Louis C5
Bay Springs C4
Beauregard B4
Belmont D1
Belzoni B2
Biloxi D5
Blue Springs D1
Booneville D1
Brandon C3
Braxton C3
Brookhaven B4
Bruce C2
Calhoun City C2
Canton B3

Key
Carrollton C2
Carthage C3
Centreville A4
Charleston B1
Clarksdale B1
Cleveland B2
Clinton B3
Coahoma B1
Coffeeville C2
Coldwater C1
Collins C4
Collinsville D3
Columbia C4
Columbus D2
Como C1
Corinth D1
Crystal Springs B4
Decatur C3
De Kalb D3
Diamondhead C5
D'Iberville D5
Doddsville B2
Drew B2
Durant C2
Eden B3
Edwards B3
Ellisville C4
Eupora C2
Falcon B1
Falkner D1
Fayette A4
Flora B3
Florence B3
Forest C3
Friars Point B1
Fulton D1
Gautier D5
Glendora B2
Gloster A4
Golden D1
Goodman C3
Greenville A2
Greenwood B2
Grenada C2
Gulfport C5
Hattiesburg C4
Hazlehurst B4
Hernando C1
Hollandale B2
Holly Springs C1
Horn Lake B1
Houston D2
Indianola B2
Itta Bena B2
Iuka D1
Jackson, *capital* B3
Jonestown B1
Kiln C5
Kosciusko C2
Kossuth D1
Laurel C4
Leakesville D4
Learned B3
Leland B2
Lena C3
Lexington B2
Liberty B4
Long Beach C5
Louisville C2
Lucedale D5
Lula B1
Lumberton C4
Lyman C5
McComb B4
McCool C2
Macon D2
Madison B3
Magee C4
Magnolia B4
Mantee C2
Marion D3
Marks B1
Mayersville A3
Meadville B4
Mendenhall C4
Meridian D3
Monticello B4
Montrose C3
Moorhead B2
Morton C3
Moss Point D5
Mound Bayou B2
Natchez A4
Nettleton D1
New Albany D1
New Augusta C4
Newton C3
Ocean Springs D5
Okolona D1
Olive Branch C1
Oxford C1
Paden D1
Pascagoula D5
Pass Christian C5
Paulding C3
Pearl B3
Pearlington C5
Pelahatchie C3
Petal C4
Philadelphia C3
Picayune C5
Pickens C3
Pittsboro C2
Polkville C3
Pontotoc D1
Pope C1
Poplarville C5
Port Gibson B4
Prentiss C4
Purvis C4
Quitman D3
Raleigh C3
Raymond B3
Richland B3
Ridgeland B3
Ripley D1
Rolling Fork B3
Rosedale A2
Ruleville B2
Sallis C2
Saltillo D1
Sardis C1
Satartia B3
Seminary C4
Senatobia C1
Shannon D1
Shaw B2
Shelby B2
Shubuta D4
Silver Creek B4
Slate Spring C2

Key
Southaven B1
Starkville D2
Summit B4
Sumner B2
Sylvarena C3
Taylorsville C4
Tchula B2
Tillatoba C2
Toccopola C1
Tunica B1
Tupelo D1
Tutwiler B1
Tylertown B4
Union C3
Vaiden C2
Vancleave D5
Verona D1
Vicksburg B3
Walthall C2
Water Valley C1
Waveland C5
Waynesboro D4
Wesson B4
West C2
West Point D2
Wiggins C3
Winona C2
Woodland C2
Woodville A4
Yazoo City B3

Other Features
Arkabatula, *lake* B1
Big Black, *river* B3
Big Springs, *lake* D1
Big Sunflower, *river* B2
Bogue Chitto, *river* B4
Buttahatchee, *river* D2
Cat, *island* C5
Chickasawhay, *river* D4
Coldwater, *river* B1
Columbus, *lake* D2
Enid, *lake* C1
Grenada, *lake* C2
Gulf Island Natl. Seashore D5
Homochitto, *river* A4
Horn, *island* D5
Leaf, *river* C4
Mississippi, *river* B1
Mississppi, *sound* D5
Natchez Natl. Hist. Park A4
Noxubee, *river* D2
Okatibbee, *lake* D3
Pascagoula, *river* D5
Pearl, *river* C3
Petit Bois, *island* D5
Pickwick, *lake* D1
Pontotoc, *mt. ridge* D1
Ross Barnett, *reservoir* C3
Sardis, *lake* C1
Ship, *island* D5
Tallahatchie, *river* B1
Tombigbee, *river* D1
Tupelo Natl. Battlefield D1
Vicksburg Natl. Mil. Park B3
Woodall, *mt* D1
Yazoo, *river* B2

Missouri .... page 152

Cities and Towns
Adrian B3
Affton H3
Albany B1
Alton E5
Anderson B5
Appleton City B3
Ashland D3
Atherton J4
Aurora C5
Ava D5
Barnett D3
Belton B3
Benton G4
Bernie G5
Bethany B1
Birmingham J4
Bloomfield G5
Blue Springs J4
Bolivar C4
Bonne Terre F4
Boonville D3
Bowling Green E2
Branson C5
Brentwood H2
Bridgeton H2
Brookfield C2
Buckner J4
Buffalo C4
Butler B3
Cabool D4
California D3
Calverton Park H2
Camdenton D4
Cameron B2
Campbell F5
Canton E1
Cape Girardeau G4
Carrollton C2
Carthage B4
Caruthersville G5
Cassville C5
Cedar Hill F3
Centerville F4
Centralia D2
Chaffee G4
Charleston G5
Chesterfield F3
Chillicothe C2
Claycomo J4
Clayton F3, H2
Clinton C3
Columbia D3
Concord H3
Concordia C3
Crestwood H3
Creve Coeur H2
Cuba E3
Dellwood H2
Desloge F4
De Soto F3
Des Peres G2
Dexter G5
Dixon D3
Doniphan F5
East Prairie G5
Edina D1
Eldon D3
El Dorado Springs B4
Elsberry F2

Key
Eminence E4
Eureka F3
Excelsior Springs B2, J3
Farley H3
Farmington F4
Fayette D2
Fenton G3
Ferguson H2
Festus F3
Florissant H2
Forsyth C5
Fredericktown F4
Fulton E3
Gainesville D5
Galena C5
Gallatin C2
Gladstone B2, J3
Glasgow D2
Glasgow Village H2
Glendale H3
Grain Valley J4
Granby B5
Grandview J4
Grant City B1
Greenfield C4
Greenville F4
Hamilton C2
Hannibal E2
Harrisonville B3
Hartville D4
Hayti G5
Hazelwood H2
Hermann E3
Hermitage C4
Higginsville C2
Hillsboro F3
Holden C3
Hollister C5
Houston E4
Huntsville D2
Independence B2, J4
Ironton F4
Jackson G4
Jefferson City, *capital* D3
Jennings H2
Joplin B4
Kahoka E1
Kansas City B2, H4
Kennett F5
Keytesville D2
Kingston B2
Kinloch H2
Kirksville D1
Kirkwood H3
Knob Noster C3
Ladue H2
Lake Lotawana J4
Lake St. Louis F3
Lamar B4
Lancaster D1
La Plata D1
Lathrop B2
Lawson B2
Lebanon D4
Lee's Summit B3, J4
Lemay H3
Lexington C2
Liberty B2, J3
Licking E4
Lilbourn G5
Linn Creek D3
Linneus C2
Louisiana E2
Mackenzie H3
Macon D2
Malden G5
Manchester G3
Mansfield D4
Maplewood H3
Marble Hill G4
Marceline D2
Marionville C5
Marshall C2
Marshfield D4
Maryland Heights H2
Maryville B1
Mattese H3
Maysville B2
Mehlville H3
Memphis D1
Mexico E2
Milan C1
Millard D1
Moberly D2
Monett C5
Monroe City E2
Montgomery City E3
Monticello E1
Mosby J3
Mound City A1
Mountain Grove D4
Mountain View E4
Mt. Vernon C4
Murphy G3
Neosho B5
Nevada B4
New Haven E3
New London E2
New Madrid G5
Nixa C4
North Kansas City H4
Northwoods H2
Oaks J4
O'Fallon F3
Olivette H2
Oregon A2
Osage Beach D3
Osceola C3
Overland H2
Owensville E3
Ozark C4
Pacific F3
Pagedale H2
Palmyra E2
Paris D2
Park Hills F4
Parkville H4
Peculiar B3
Peerless Park G3
Perryville G4
Pevely F3
Piedmont F4
Pierce City C5
Pine Lawn H2
Pineville B5
Platte City B2, H3
Plattsburg B2
Pleasant Hill B3
Poplar Bluff F5
Portageville G5
Potosi F4

Key
Princeton C1
Randolph J4
Raymore B3
Raytown J4
Republic C4
Rich Hill B3
Richland D4
Richmond C2
Richmond Heights H2
Riverside H4
Rock Hill H2
Rock Port A1
Rolla E4
St. Ann H2
St. Charles F3, G2
St. Clair F3
Ste. Genevieve F4
St. James E3
St. John H2
St. Joseph B2
St. Louis F3, H2
St. Peters F3
St. Robert D4
Salem E4
Salisbury D2
Sappington H3
Sarcoxie B4
Savannah B2
Scott City G4
Sedalia C3
Senath F5
Seymour D4
Shelbina D2
Shelbyville D2
Shirley F4
Sikeston G5
Slater C2
Smithville B2
Springfield C4
Stanberry B1
Steele G5
Steelville E4
Stockton C4
Stoutsville E2
Sugar Creek J4
Sullivan E3
Sweet Springs C3
Tarkio A1
Thayer E5
Town and Country G2
Trenton C1
Troy F3
Tuscumbia D3
Union F3
Unionville C1
Unity Village J4
University City H2
Van Buren E5
Vandalia E2
Versailles D3
Vienna E3
Villa Ridge F3
Waldron H3
Warrensburg C3
Warrenton E3
Warsaw C3
Washington E3
Watson A1
Waynesville D4
Weatherby Lake H3
Webb City B4
Webster Groves H3
Wellsville E2
Wentzville F3
West Plains E5
Weston B2
Willard C4
Willow Springs E4
Windsor C3

Other Features
Bull Shoals, *lake* D5
Eleven Point, *river* E5
Fox, *river* E1
G.W. Carver Natl. Monument B5
Grand, *river* B1
Harry S. Truman, *reservoir* C3
Lake of the Ozarks, *lake* D3
Mark Twain, *lake* E2
Meramec, *river* E4
Mississippi, *river* G4
Missouri, *river* C2
Osage, *river* B4, D3
Ozark Natl. Scenic Riverways E4
Platte, *river* B2
St. Francis, *river* F4
Stockton, *lake* C4
Table Rock, *lake* C5
Taum Sauk, *mt.* F4
Thomas Hill, *reservoir* D2
Weldon, *river* C2

Montana.................. page 153

Cities and Towns
Anaconda D3
Baker M3
Belgrade E4
Big Timber F4
Billings H4
Boulder D3
Bozeman E4
Bridger H4
Broadus L4
Butte D3
Chester F1
Chinook G1
Choteau D2
Circle L2
Columbus G4
Conrad E1
Crow Agency J4
Cut Bank D1
Deer Lodge D3
Dell D5
Dillon D4
East Helena E3
Ekalaka M4
Evergreen B1
Forsyth K3
Fort Benton F2
Gardiner F4
Glasgow K1
Glendive M2
Great Falls E2
Hamilton B3
Hardin J4
Harlowton G3
Hathaway K3
Havre G1

Key
Helena, *capital* D3
Kalispell B1
Lame Deer K4
Laurel H4
Lewistown G2
Libby A1
Lincoln D3
Livingston F4
Lolo Hot Springs B3
Malta J1
Miles City L3
Missoula C3
Orchard Homes B3
Philipsburg C3
Plentywood M1
Polson B2
Pony E4
Red Lodge G4
Ronan B2
Roundup H3
Rudyard F1
St. Regis A2
Scobey L1
Shelby E1
Sidney M2
Somers B1
Stanford F2
Superior B2
Terry L3
Thompson Falls A2
Townsend E3
West Yellowstone E5
Whitefish B1
Wibaux M3
Wolf Point L1

Other Features
Bighorn, *river* J4
Bighorn Canyon Natl. Rec. Area H4
Bitterroot, *river* B3
Bull, *mts.* H3
Canyon Ferry *lake* E3
Clark Fork, *river* D3
Cleveland, *mt.* C1
Custer Battlefield Natl. Monument J4
Elwell, *lake* E1
Flathead, *lake* B2
Flathead *river* B1
Fort Peck, *lake* K2
Fresno, *reservoir* F1
Glacier Natl. Park C1
Granite Peak, *mt.* D4
Granite Peak, *mt.* G4
Grant-Kohrs Ranch N.H.S. D3
Homer Youngs Peak, *mt.* C4
Hungry Horse, *reservoir* C1
Koocanusa, *lake* A1
Kootenai, *river* A1
Little Missouri, *river* M5
Madison, *river* E4
Marias, *river* E1
Middle Fork, *river* C1
Milk, *river* D1
Missouri, *river* G2
Musselshell, *river* H3
Northwest Peak, *mt.* A1
Powder, *river* L3
Rocky, *mts.* C2
St. Mary, *river* C1
St. Regis, *river* B2
Scarface Peak, *mt.* C2
South Fork, *river* C2
Swan, *river* C2
Teton, *river* E2
Tongue, *river* K4
Warren Peak, *mt.* C4
Yellowstone, *river* L3
Yellowstone Natl. Park F5

Nebraska ....page 154

Cities and Towns
Ainsworth E2
Albion G3
Alliance B2
Alma F4
Ashland H3
Atkinson F2
Auburn J4
Aurora F4
Bartlett F3
Bassett E2
Beatrice H4
Beaver City E4
Bellevue J3
Benkelman C4
Blair H3
Brewster E3
Bridgeport A3
Broken Bow E3
Burwell E3
Butte F2
Center G2
Central City F3
Chadron B2
Chapman F3
Chappell B3
Clay Center F4
Columbus G3
Cozad E4
Crete H4
Dakota City H2
David City G3
Elkhorn H3
Elwood E4
Exeter G4
Fairbury G4
Falls City J4
Franklin F4
Fremont H3
Fullerton G3
Geneva G4
Gering A3
Gibbon F4
Gordon B2
Gothenburg D4
Grand Island F4
Grant C4
Greeley F3
Gretna H3
Guide Rock F4
Harrisburg A3
Harrison A2
Hartington G2
Hastings F4
Hayes Center C4
Hebron G4
Holdrege E4
Hyannis C3
Imperial C4
Kearney F4
Kimball A3
La Vista A3
Leigh G3
Lexington E4
Lincoln, *capital* H4
Loomis E4
Loup City F3
McCook D4
Madison G3
Milford G4
Minden F4
Mitchell A3
Mullen C2
Nebraska City J4
Neligh F2
Nelson F4
Norfolk G2
North Platte D3
Oakland H3
Ogallala C3
Omaha J3
O'Neill F2
Ord F3
Osceola G3
Oshkosh B3
Papillion H3
Pawnee City H4
Paxton C3
Pender H2
Pierce G2
Plainview G2
Plattsmouth J3
Plymouth H4
Ponca H2
Prague H3
Ravenna F3
Red Cloud F4
Rushville B2
St. Paul F3
Schuyler G3
Scottsbluff A3
Seward G4
Sidney B3
South Sioux City H2
Springfield H3
Springview E2
Stanton G3
Stapleton D3
Stockville D4
Superior F4
Sutton G4
Syracuse H4
Taylor E3
Tecumseh H4
Tekamah H3
Thedford D3
Trenton C4
Tryon D3
Valentine D2
Valley H3
Wahoo H3
Waverly H4
Wayne G2
West Point H3
Wilber H4
Wisner H3
Wymore H4
York G4

Other Features
Agate Fossil Beds N.M. A2
Arikee, *river* B5
Big Blue, *river* G3
C.W. McConaughy, *lake* C3
Calamus, *reservoir* E3
Calamus, *river* E2
Cedar, *river* F3
Chimney Rock Natl. Hist. Site A3
Elkhorn, *river* E2, G3
Harlan Co., *lake* E4
Homestead Natl. Monument H4
Lewis and Clark, *lake* G2
Little Blue, *river* G4
Loup, *river* F3
Middle Loup, *river* D3
Missouri, *river* J4
Niobrara, *river* B2, E2
North Loup, *river* C2, E3
North Platte, *river* B3
Pine, *mt. ridge* B2
Platte, *river* D4, G3
Republican, *river* D4
Sand, *hills* C3
Scotts Bluff Natl. Monument A3
South Fork Republican, *river* B5
South Loup, *river* E3

Nevada ....page 155

Cities and Towns
Alamo C3
Battle Mountain B1
Beatty B3
Boulder City C4
Carlin B1
Carson City, *capital* A2
Elko C1
Ely C2
Eureka C2
Fallon A2
Fernley A2
Gardnerville A2
Goldfield B3
Hawthorne A2
Henderson C3
Incline Village A2
Las Vegas C3
Laughlin C4
Lovelock A1
McGill C2
Mesquite C3
Minden A2
North Fork C1
North Las Vegas C3
Pahrump C3
Paradise C3
Pioche C3
Reno A2
Silver Peak B3
Sparks A2
Spring Creek C1
Spring Valley C3
Sun Valley A2
Tonopah B2
Virginia City A2
Wells C1
West Wendover C1
Winnemucca B1
Yerington A2
Zephyr Cove A2

Other Features
Arc Dome, *mt.* B2
Black Rock, *desert* A1
Boundary Peak, *mt.* A3
Colorado, *river* C4
Desert, *valley* A1
Egan, *range* C2
Goshute, *lake* C1
Grant, *mts.* C2
Grant, *mt.* A2
Great Basin C2
Great Basin Natl. Park C2
Hoover Dam C3
Hot Creek, *range* B2
Independence, *mts.* C1
Jefferson, *mt.* B2
Lake Mead Natl. Rec. Area C3
Marys, *river* C1
Matterhorn, *mt.* C1
Mead, *lake* C3
Mohave, *lake* C4
Monitor, *range* B2
Moriah, *mt.* C2
North Toiyabe Peak, *mt.* B2
Owyhee, *desert* B1
Owyhee, *river* B1
Pilot Peak, *mt.* C1
Pyramid, *lake* A1
Quinn, *river* B1
Ruby, *mts.* C1
Ruby Dome, *mt.* C1
Rye Patch, *reservoir* A1
Schell Creek, *range* C2
Shoshone, *mts.* B2
Shoshone, *range* B1
Smoky, *valley* B2
Snake, *range* C2
Summit, *mt.* B2
Tahoe, *lake* A2
Tobin, *mt.* B1
Toiyabe, *range* B2
Toquima, *range* B2
Tuscarora, *mts.* B1
Virgin, *river* C3
Walker, *lake* A2
Wheeler Peak, *mt.* C2
White, *river* C3

New Hampshire ....page 156

Cities and Towns
Albany B3
Amherst B4
Antrim B4
Barnstead B3
Bartlett B2
Benton B2
Berlin B2
Blair B3
Bradford B3
Bretton Woods B2
Bristol B3
Candia B3
Cascade B2
Claremont A3
Concord, *capital* B3
Contoocook B3
Conway B3
Cornish City A3
Dalton B2
Deerfield B3
Deering B3
Derry B4
Dixville Notch B2
Dover C3
Dunbarton Center B3
Durham C3
Easton B2
Enfield A3
Epping B3
Exeter C4
Farmington B3
Franklin B3
Gilmanton B3
Glencliff B3
Gorham B2
Groveton B2
Hampstead B4
Hampton C4
Hanover A3
Haverhill A2
Henniker B3
Hillsboro B3
Hinsdale A4
Hollis B4
Hooksett B3
Hudson B4
Jackson B2
Jaffrey A4
Jefferson B2
Keene A4
Laconia B3
Lancaster B2
Lebanon A3
Littleton B2
Loudon B3
Lyman B2
Manchester B3
Meredith B3
Merrimack B4
Milan B2
Milford B4
Monroe A2
Munsonville A3
Nashua B4
Newbury B3
New Castle C3
New London B3
Newmarket C3
Newport A3
North Conway B2
Northfield B3
North Haverhill A3
North Walpole A3
North Woodstock B2
Orford A3
Ossipee B3
Pelham B4
Percy B2
Peterborough B4
Pinardville B4
Pittsfield B3
Plymouth B3
Portsmouth C3
Quaker City A3
Randolph B2
Raymond B3
Rochester C3
Rumney B3
Rye C4
Sandwich B3
Sharon B4
Shelburne B2
Silver Lake B3
Somersworth C3
South Hooksett B3
Springfield A3
Stewartstown Hollow B2
Strafford B3
Stratford B2
Suncook B3
Sutton B3
Tilton B3
Warner B3
Waterville Valley B3
Westport A4
West Rindge A4
West Stewardstown B2
Whittier B3
Willey House B2
Winchester A4
Wolfeboro B3
Woodsville A2

Other Features
Appalachian Natl. Scenic Trail A3
Blackwater, *reservoir* B3
Blue, *mt.* B2
Cabot, *mt.* B2
Cardigan, *mt.* B3
Connecticut, *river* A3
First Connecticut, *lake* B1
Franconia, *notch* B2
Great, *bay* C3
Indian, *river* B1
Kearsarge, *mt.* B3
Merrimack, *river* B4
Monadnock, *mt.* A4
Newfound, *lake* B3
Ossipee, *lake* B3
Presidential, *mt. range* B2
Saint-Gaudens Natl. Hist. Site A3
Second Connecticut, *lake* B1
Smarts, *mt.* A3
Squam, *lake* B3
Sunapee, *lake* A3
Swift, *river* B3
Umbagog, *lake* B2
Washington, *mt.* B2
White, *mts.* B2
Winnipesaukee, *lake* B3
Winnisquam, *lake* B3

New Jersey ....page 157

Cities and Towns
Absecon E5
Allendale E1
Allentown D3
Alloway C4
Alpine C1
Asbury Park E3
Atlantic City E5
Atlantic Highlands E3
Atsion D4
Avalon D5
Barrington B3
Basking Ridge D2
Batsto D4
Bay Point C5
Bayonne E2
Bayside C5
Beachwood E4
Beattyestown D2
Beckett C4
Belle Mead D3
Belleville B2
Bellmawr B3, C4
Belmar E3
Belvidere C2
Bergenfield B1
Berkeley Heights E2
Berlin D4
Bernardsville D2
Blackwood C4
Blairstown D2
Bloomfield E2
Bogota B1
Boonton E2
Bordentown D3
Bound Brook D2
Bradley Beach E2
Brass Castle C2
Brick E3
Bridgeboro C3
Bridgeton C5
Brielle E3
Brigantine E5
Brookdale B1
Browns Mills D4
Budd Lake D2
Buena D4
Burlington D3
Butler E1
Caldwell A1
Camden B3, C4
Cape May D6
Cape May Court House D5
Carlstadt B1
Carneys Point C4
Carteret B2
Carteret E2
Cedar Grove B1
Centerton C4
Centerville D2
Chatham E2
Cherry Hill B3, C4
Chesilhurst D4
Chesterfield D3
Cinnaminson B3, D4
Clark A2
Clayton C4
Cliffside Park C2
Clifton B1
Clinton D2
Closter F2
Colesville D1
Collings Lakes D4
Collingswood B3
Colonia E2
Cranford E2
Deerfield C4
Delanco D3
Denville E2
Deptford B4
Dover D2
Dumont C1
Dunellen E2
East Brunswick E3
East Orange E2
East Rutherford B1
Eatontown E3
Edgewater F2
Edison E2
Egg Harbor City D4
Elizabeth E2
Elmer C4
Elmwood Park B1
Elwood D4
Emerson B2
Englewood C1
Englewood Cliffs C1
Englishtown E3
Erma D6
Estell Manor D5
Evesboro C3
Ewing D3
Fair Lawn B1, E2
Fairfield E2
Fairton C5
Fairview F2
Fanwood E2
Farmingdale E3
Fellowship C3
Fieldsboro D3
Flemington D3
Folsom D4
Fords E2
Forked River E4
Fort Lee F2
Franklin D1
Franklinville C4
Freehold E3
Frenchtown C2
Garfield E2
Gilford Park E4
Glassboro C4
Glen Gardner D2
Glen Ridge B2
Glendora A4
Gloucester City B3, C4
Goshen D5
Great Notch B1
Green Bank D4
Greenwich C5
Guttenberg F2
Hackensack B2
Hackettstown D2
Haddon Heights B3
Haddonfield B3
Hainesville D1
Haledon B1
Hamburg D1
Hammonton D4
Hampton D2
Harrison B2
Haworth C1
Hawthorne B1
Hedger House D4
High Bridge D2
Highland Lakes E1
Highland Park E3
Highlands F3
Hightstown D3
Hillsdale E1
Hillside B2
Hoboken B2
Hopatcong D2
Hopewell D3
Howardsville E4
Indian Mills D4
Irvington B2
Jamesburg E3
Jenkins Neck D4
Jersey City E2
Keansburg E3
Kearny B2
Kendall Park D3
Kenilworth E2
Kinnelon E2
Lakehurst E3
Lakewood E3
Lambertville D3
Lavallette E4
Lawnside B3
Lawrenceville D3
Leeds Point E5
Leisure Village E3
Leisuretowne D4
Leonardo E3
Lincroft E3
Linden E2
Lindenwold B4, C4
Linwood D5
Little Falls B1
Livingston E2
Lodi B1
Long Branch F3
Long Valley D2
Lyndhurst B2
Madison E2
Mahwah E1
Manahawkin E4
Manalapan E3
Manasquan E3
Manumuskin D5
Manville D2
Maple Shade B3, D4
Maplewood E2
Marcella E2
Margate City E5
Marlboro E3
Marlton C3, D4
Matawan E3
Mays Landing D5
Maywood B1
Medford Lakes D4
Mendham D2
Menlo Park E2
Merchantville B3
Metuchen E2
Middlesex E2
Middletown E3
Midland Park E2
Milford C2
Millburn E2
Millville C5
Monmouth Beach F3
Montclair E2
Montvale E1
Moorestown C3, D4
Morris Plains E2
Morristown E2
Mountain Lakes E2
Mount Holly D4
Mount Laurel D4
Mystic Islands E4
National Park B3
Neptune City E3
Netcong D2
Newark E2
New Brunswick E3
New Egypt D3
Newfield C4
New Gretna E4
Newfoundland E1
New Providence E2
Newton D1
Normandy Beach E3
North Arlington B2
North Bergen B2
North Cape May D6
Northfield D5
North Wildwood D5
Nutley B2
Oakland E2
Oaklyn B3
Ocean City D5
Oceanport E3
Ogdensburg D1
Olivet C4
Oradell B1
Orange B2
Othello C5
Oxford D2
Palisades Park B1
Palmyra B3, C3
Paramus B1, E2
Park Ridge E1
Passaic E2
Paterson E2
Paulsboro A4, C4
Pemberton D4
Pennington D3
Penns Grove C4
Pennsauken B3
Pennsville B4
Perth Amboy E2
Phillipsburg C2
Piscataway E2
Pine Hill D4
Pitman C4
Pittstown D2
Plainfield E2
Pleasant Plains E4
Pleasantville D5
Point Pleasant E3
Pomona D5
Port Monmouth E3
Port Norris C5
Princeton D3
Princeton Junction D3
Prospect Park B1
Quinton C4
Rahway A2
Ramblewood C3
Ramsey E1
Raritan D2
Red Bank E3
Ridgefield B2
Ridgefield Park B1, E2
Ridgewood E2
Ringoes D3
Ringwood E1
Rio Grande D5
River Edge B1
Riverside C3, D3
Riverton B3, C3
Robertsville E3
Rochelle Park B1
Rocktown D3
Roselle A2
Roselle Park A2
Rumson F3
Runnemede B4, C4
Rutherford B1
Salem C4
Sayreville E3
Seabrook C5
Sea Girt E3
Sea Isle City D5
Seaside Heights E4
Seaside Park E4
Secaucus B2
Ship Bottom E4
Shrewsbury E3
Silverton E3
Smithville E5
Somerdale B4
Somers Point D5
Somerset E3
Somerville D2
South Amboy E3
South Orange A2
South River E3
Sparta D1
Spotswood E3
Spring Lake Heights E3
Stanhope D2
Stillwater D1
Stockholm D1
Stratford B4, C4
Strathmere D5
Summit E2
Surf City E4
Sussex D1
Swedesboro C4
Teaneck B1
Tenafly F2
Tinton Falls E3
Toms River E4
Totowa B1
Trenton, *capital* D3
Tuckahoe D5
Tuckerton E4
Turnersville C4
Twin Rivers E3
Union E2
Union Beach E3
Union City E2
Upton D4
Vauxhall A2
Ventnor City E5
Vernon E1
Verona A1
Villas D5
Vineland C5
Voorhees C4
Waldwick E1
Wanamassa E3
Wanaque E1
Waretown E4
Warren Glen C2
Warren Grove E4
Washington D2
Washington Crossing D3
Watchung E2
Wayne A1, E2
Weehawken B2
Welchville C4
Wenonah C4
Westfield E2

Key
West Milford E1
Westmont B3
West New York C2
West Orange E2
West Paterson B1
Westville B3
Westwood B1
Wharton D2
White Horse D3
White House Station D2
White Meadow Lake D2
Whiting E4
Wildwood D6
Wildwood Crest D6
Williamstown D4
Willingboro D3
Woodbine D5
Woodbridge E2
Woodbury B4, C4
Woodlynne B3
Wood Ridge B1
Woodstown C4
Woodstream C3
Wrightstown D3
Wyckoff E1

Other Features
Cape May, *point* D6
Cooper, *river* B4
Delaware, *bay* C5
Delaware, *river* D3
Delaware Water Gap N.R.A. D1
Edison Natl. Hist. Site B2
Gateway Natl. Rec. Area F3
Great, *bay* E5
Hudson, *river* C2
Morristown Nat. Hist. Park D2
Pines, *lake* B1
Raritan, *bay* E3
Statue of Liberty N.M. B2

New Mexico ....page 158

Cities and Towns
Acoma Pueblo B2
Acomita B2
Alameda B2
Alamogordo C3
Albuquerque B2
Anthony B4
Artesia C3
Aztec B1
Bayard A3
Belen B2
Bernalillo B2
Bloomfield B1
Bosque Farms B2
Carlsbad C3
Carrizozo C3
Central A3
Chaparral B3
Chimayo C1
Clayton D1
Clovis D2
Corrales B2
Deming B3
Dulce B1
Elida D3
Elk C3
Elkins C3
Espanola B2
Estancia B2
Eunice D3
Fairacres B3
Farmington A1
Floyd D2
Fort Sumner C2
Gallup A2
Grants B2
Greenfield C3
Hobbs D3
Hurley A3
Jal D3
Jemez Pueblo B2
Kirtland A1
La Luz C3
Las Cruces B3
Las Vegas C2
Lordsburg A3
Los Alamos B2
Los Chavez B2
Los Lunas B2
Los Padillas B2
Lovington D3
Lower Colonias C2
Lower San Francisco Plaza A3
Maxwell C1
Mayhill C3
Mesilla B3
Milan B2
Mora C2
Moriarty B2
Mosquero D2
Navajo A2
Polvadera B2
Portales D2
Questa C1
Ranchos De Taos C1
Raton C1
Reserve A3
Rio Rancho B2
Roswell C3
Ruidoso C3
Sabinoso C2
San Felipe Pueblo B2
San Miguel B1
San Miguel B3
Santa Fe, *capital* C2
Santa Rosa C2
Santo Domingo Pueblo B2
Shiprock A1
Silver City A3
Socorro B2
Springer C1
Sunland Park B4
Taos C1
Tesuque C2
Tierra Amarilla B1
Truth or Consequences B3
Tucumcari D2
Tularosa B3
University Park B3
Ute Park C1
Valencia B2
Waterflow A1
Zuni Pueblo A2

Other Features
Abiquiu, *reservoir* B1
Alegres, *mt.* A2
Aztec Ruins Natl. Monument B1
Baldy, *mt.* C1
Bandelier Natl. Monument B2
Black, *mt. range* B3
Burro, *mt.* A3
Caballo, *reservoir* B3
Canadian, *river* C1
Capulin Volcano N.M. D1
Carlsbad Caverns Natl. Park C3
Cebolleta, *mt.* B2
Cerro Vista, *mt.* C1
Chaco Culture Natl. Hist. Park B1
Cimarron, *river* D1
Conchas, *lake* C2
Continental Divide, *mt. ridge* B2
Cooke's, *mt.* B3
Elephant Butte, *res.* B3
El Malpais Natl. Monument B2
El Morro Natl. Monument A2
Fort Union Natl. Monument C2
Gallinas, *mt.* C2
Gila, *river* A3
Gila Cliff Dwellings N.M. A3
Guadalupe, *mts.* C3
Jornada Del Muerto B3
Llano Estacado, *plateau* D3
Navajo, *reservoir* B1
Navajo Indian Res. A1
Pecos, *river* C2, C3
Pecos, *plains* C3
Pecos N.H.P. C2
Petroglyph Natl. Monument B2
Playas, *lake* A4
Reeds, *mt.* B3
Rio Grande, *river* C1
Rio Hondo, *river* C3
Rio Puerco, *river* B2
Salinas Pueblo Missions N.M. B2
San Andres, *mts.* B3
San Juan, *river* A1
Sangre De Cristo, *mts.* C1
Shiprock, *mt.* A1
Sierra Blanca, *mt.* C3
South Baldy, *mt.* B3
Sumner, *lake* C2
Taylor, *mt.* B2
Wheeler, *mt.* C1
White Sands Natl. Monument B3
Whitewater Baldy, *mt.* A3
Withington, *mt.* B3
Zuni, *mts.* A2

New York ....page 159

Cities and Towns
Adams H3
Adams Center H3
Akron C4
Albany, *capital* N5
Albion D4
Alden D5
Alfred E6
Allegany D6
Altamont M5
Amsterdam M5
Angola B5
Arcade D5
Astoria A3
Athens N6
Attica D5
Auburn G5
Avon E5
Bainbridge J6
Baldwinsville H4
Ballston Spa N4
Batavia D4
Bath F6
Beacon N7
Bedford-Stuyvesant A4
Belle Harbor A4
Belmont D6
Bensonhurst A4
Big Flats G6
Binghamton J6
Bloomfield F5
Bolivar D6
Boonville K4
Breezy Point A4
Brentwood C1
Brewerton H4
Bridgehampton E1
Brighton Beach A4
Broadalbin M4
Brockport E4
Brocton B6
Bronx A3, B1
Bronxville A2
Brooklyn A4, B2
Buffalo C5
Cairo M6
Calcium J2
Caledonia E5
Cambridge P4
Camden J4
Canajoharie L5
Canandaigua F5
Canarsie A4
Canastota J4
Canisteo E6
Canton K1
Carmel N7
Carthage J3
Castleton-on-Hudson N5
Catskill N6
Cayuga Heights H6
Cazenovia J5
Cedarhurst B4
Central Square H4
Chatham N6
Cheektowaga C5
Chittenango J4
Churchville E4
Clayton H2
Clinton K4
Clyde G4
Cobleskill L5
Cohoes N5
College Point A3
Colonie N5
Coney Island A4
Cooperstown L5
Corinth N4
Corning F6
Cortland H5
Coxsackie N6
Cuba D6
Dannemora N1
Dansville E5
Delhi L6
De Ruyter J5
Deposit K6
Dolgeville L4
Dover Plains N7
Dryden H6
Dundee G6
Dunkirk B6
East Atlantic Beach B4
Eastchester A2
East Hampton E1
East Islip C2
East New York A4
East Northport C1
East Patchogue D1
Eden C5
Elizabethtown N2
Ellenville M7
Elmira G6
Elmira Heights G6
Elmont B4
Endicott H6
Endwell H6
Fairmount H4
Far Rockaway B4
Fayette G5
Fine K2
Flatbush A4
Flushing A3
Fonda M5
Fort Edward N4
Fort Plain L5
Franklin Sq. B4
Franklinville D6
Fredonia B6
Freeport C2
Frewsburg B6
Friendship D6
Fulton H4
Geneseo E5
Geneva G5
Glen Cove B1
Glens Falls N4
Gloversville M4
Goshen M7
Gouverneur K2
Gowanda C6
Granville P4
Gravesend A4
Great Neck B1
Greece E4
Greene J6
Greenport E1
Greenwich P4
Groton H5
Hamburg C5
Hamilton J5
Hampton Bays E1
Hancock K7
Harlem A3
Hempstead B2
Herkimer L4
Hicksville C1
Highland N7
Hilton E4
Holbrook C1
Holland C5
Holley D4
Homer H5
Hoosick Falls P5
Hornell E6
Horseheads G6
Houghton D6
Howard Beach A4
Hudson N6
Hudson Falls N4
Huntington Station C1
Hurley M7
Ilion K4
Inwood B4
Irondequoit E4
Ithaca H6
Jamaica B2
Jamestown B6
Johnson City J6
Johnstown M4
Keeseville P1
Kew Gardens A4
Kinderhook N6
Kingston N7
Lake George N4
Lake Placid M2
Lake Pleasant M4
Lakewood B6
Lansing H5
Larchmont B2
Lawrence B4
Le Roy D5
Levittown C1
Liberty L7
Lima E5
Lindenhurst C2
Little Falls L4
Little Valley C6
Livingston Manor L7
Livonia E5
Lockport C4
Long Beach B2
Long Eddy K7
Long Island City A3
Long Lake M3
Loon Lake M1
Lowville K3
Lynbrook B4
Lyons G4
Malone M1
Mamaroneck B2
Manhasset Hills B3
Manhattan A3
Manlius J4
Manorhaven B3
Massapequa C2
Massena L1
Mastic D1
Mastic Beach D1
Mattituck E1
Mayville A6
Mechanicville N5
Medina D4
Mexico H4
Middleburgh M5
Middleport D4
Middletown M7
Millbrook N7
Mineola B1
Mohawk K5
Monroe A1
Montauk F1
Monticello L7
Montour Falls G6
Moravia H5
Mount Kisco B1
Mount Morris E5
Mount Vernon B1, C5
Munnsville J5
Nassau N5
Newark F4
Newburgh M7
New City B1
Newfane C4
New Hartford K4
New Hyde Park B3
New Paltz M7
New Rochelle B3
New York B2
Niagara Falls B4
Norfolk L1
North Collins C5
North Hills B3
North Syracuse H4
North Tonawanda C4
Norwich J5
Norwood L1
Nunda E5
Nyack B1
Oakfield D4
Ogdensburg K1
Olcott C4
Olean D6
Oneida J4
Oneonta K6
Ossining B1
Oswego H4
Owego H6
Oxford J6
Ozone Park A4
Painted Post F6
Palmyra F4
Pawling N7
Peekskill B1
Pelham A3
Pelham Manor A3
Penn Yan F5
Perry D5
Peru N1
Philadelphia J2
Philmont N6
Phoenix H4
Pine Bush M7
Plattsburgh P1
Port Henry P2
Port Jefferson D1
Port Morris A3
Port Washington B3
Potsdam L1
Poughkeepsie N7
Pulaski H3
Queens B4
Randolph C6
Ransomville C4
Ravena N6
Red Hook N7
Rensselaer N5
Rhinebeck N7
Richfield Springs L5
Riverhead D1
Rochester E4
Rockaway Point A4
Rocky Point D1
Rome K4
Rosendale M7
Rouses Point P1
Rye B2
Sackets Harbor H3
Sag Harbor E1
St. George A2
St. Johnsville L4
Salamanca C6
Sands Point B3
Saranac Lake M2
Saratoga Springs N4
Saugerties N6
Sayville D2
Schenectady N5
Schoharie M5
Scotia N5
Seneca Falls G5
Sherburne K5
Shortsville F5
Sidney K6
Silver Creek B5
Skaneateles H5
Sodus F4
Southampton E1
South Fallsburg L7
Southold E1
Southport G6
Spencerport E4
Springville C5
Stillwater N5
Stony Brook C1
Suffern A1
Syracuse H4
Throgs Neck A3
Ticonderoga P3
Troy N5
Trumansburg G5
Tupper Lake M2
Unadilla K6
Utica K4
Valley Stream B2
Victory Mills N4
Voorheesville N5
Walden M7
Walton K6
Wampsville J4
Wappingers Falls N7
Warrensburg N4
Warsaw D5
Warwick A1
Waterloo G5
Watertown J3
Waterville K5
Watkins Glen G6
Waverly G6
Wayland E5
Weedsport G4
Wellsville E6
West Carthage J3
Westfield A6
West Point N7
West Seneca C5
Whitehall P3
White Plains B1
Whitesboro K4
Whitestone A3
Williamsburg A4
Wilson C4
Wolcott G4
Woodmere B4
Woodstock M6
Yonkers B1
Yorktown Heights B1

Other Features
Adirondack, *mts.* L2
Adirondack Park M2
Appalachian Natl. Scenic Trail A1
Black, *lake* J2
Black, *river* K3
Cannonsville, *reservoir* K6
Catskill, *mts.* L7
Catskill Park L6
Cayuga, *lake* G5
Champlain, *lake* P1
Chenango, *river* J6
Cranberry, *lake* L2
Delaware, *river* K7
Erie, *canal* J4
Erie, *lake* A5
Fire Island Natl. Seashore D2
Fishers, *island* F1
Fort Stanwix Natl. Monument K4
Galloo, *island* H3
Gardiners, *island* F1
Gateway Natl. Rec. Area B2
Genesee, *river* D6
George, *lake* N3
Great Sacandaga, *lake* M4
Hinckley, *reservoir* K4
Home of F.D.R. Natl. Hist Site N7
Hudson, *river* M3
Indian, *lake* M3
J.F.K. Int'l Airport A4
Keuka, *lake* F5
Long, *island* E1
Long, *lake* M3
Long Island, *sound* C1
Marcy, *mt.* N2
Martin Van Buren Natl. Hist. Site N6
Mettawee, *river* P3
Mohawk, *river* L5
Oneida, *lake* J4
Ontario, *lake* E3
Pepacton, *reservoir* L6
Piseco, *lake* L4
St. Lawrence, *river* K1
Salmon River, *reservoir* J3
Saratoga, *lake* N4
Saratoga Natl. Hist. Park N4
Schoharie, *reservoir* M6
Schroon, *lake* N3
Slide, *mt.* M7
Staten, *island* A2
Stony, *island* H3
Susquehanna, *river* J6
Thousand, *islands* H2
Tupper, *lake* L2
Unadilla, *river* K5
Upper Saranac, *lake* M2
West Point Military Academy A1

North Carolina ....page 160

Cities and Towns
Aberdeen G4
Ahoskie L2
Albemarle E4
Andrews C8
Angier H3
Apex H3
Archdale F3
Asheboro F3
Asheville E7
Atlantic Beach M5
Ayden L4
Badin E4
Bakersville A2
Bayboro M4
Beaufort M5
Belhaven M3
Belmont C4
Benson H4
Bessemer City C4
Bethel L3
Biscoe F4
Black Mt. A3
Bladenboro H5
Blowing Rock B2
Boiling Spring Lakes J6
Boiling Springs B4
Bolivia J6
Boone B2
Brevard E8
Bryson City C8
Buies Creek H4
Burgaw K5
Burlington G2
Burnsville A3
Butner H2
Camden N2
Canton E7
Carolina Beach K6
Carthage G4
Cary H3
Chadbourn H6
Chapel Hill G3
Charlotte D4
Cherryville C4
China Grove D3
Clayton J3
Clemmons E3
Clinton J5
Coats H4
Columbia N3
Columbus A4
Concord D4
Conover C3
Cornelius D4
Creedmoor H2
Cullowhee D8
Currituck N2
Dallas C4
Danbury E2
Davidson D3
Denton E3
Dobson D2
Drexel B3
Dunn H4
Durham H2
E. Flat Rock E8
Eden F2
Edenton M2
Elizabeth City N2
Elizabethtown H5
Elkin D2
Elm City K3
Emerald Isle M5
Enfield K2
Erwin H4
Fairmont G5
Farmville K3
Fayetteville H4
Fletcher E8
Forest City B4
Four Oaks J4
Franklin C8
Franklinton J2
Fremont K3
Fuquay-Varina H3
Gamewell B3
Garner H3
Gastonia C4
Gatesville M2
Gibsonville F2
Goldsboro K4
Graham G2
Granite Falls C3
Granite Quarry E3
Greensboro F2
Greenville L3
Grifton L4
Halifax K2
Hamlet F5
Harkers Island M5
Harrisburg D4
Havelock M5
Hayesville C8
Hays C2
Henderson J2
Hendersonville E8
Hertford N2
Hickory C3
High Point E3
Hillsborough G2
Hope Mills H5
Hudson C3
Huntersville D4
Icard C3
Indian Trail D4
Jackson L2
Jacksonville L5
Jamestown F3
Jefferson C2
Jonesville D2
Kannapolis D4
Kenansville K5
Kenly J3
Kernersville E2
Kill Devil Hills P2
King E2
Kings Mt. C4
Kinston K4
Kitty Hawk P2
La Grange K4
Laurinburg G5
Leland J6
Lenoir B3
Lewisville E2
Lexington E3
Liberty F3
Lillington H4
Lincolnton C4
Locust E4
Long Beach J7
Long View C3
Louisburg J2
Lumberton G5
Madison F2
Maiden C3
Manteo P3
Marion A3
Marshall E7
Marshville E5
Matthews D4
Maxton G5
Mayodan F2
Mebane G2
Mint Hill D4
Mocksville D3
Monroe D5
Mooresville D3
Moravian Falls C2
Morehead City M5
Morganton B3
Mt. Airy D2
Mt. Gilead F4
Mt. Holly D4
Mt. Olive J4
Mulberry C2
Murfreesboro L2
Murphy B8
Nags Head P3
Nashville K3
New Bern L4
Newland B2
Newport M5
Newton C3
Norwood E4
North Wilkesboro C2
Oxford H2
Pembroke G5
Pinehurst G4
Pinetops K3
Pineville D4
Piney Green L5
Pittsboro G3
Plymouth M3
Polkville B4
Raeford G5
Raleigh, *capital* H3
Randleman F3
Red Springs G5
Reidsville F2
River Bend L4
Roanoke Rapids K2
Robbinsville C8
Robersonville L3
Rockingham F5
Rockwell E3
Rocky Mount K3
Rolesville J3
Rose Hill J5
Roseboro H5
Roxboro H2
Rural Hall E2
Rutherfordton B4
Salisbury E3
Sanford G4
Sawmills C3
Scotland Neck L2
Selma J3
Seven Lakes F4
Sharpsburg K3
Shelby B4
Siler City G3
Smithfield J3
Sneads Ferry L5
Snow Hill K4
Southern Pines G4
Southern Shores P2
Southport J7
Sparta C1
Spencer E3
Spindale B4

Key
Spring Lake H4
Spruce Pine A3
St. Pauls H5
Stanley C4
Stanleyville E2
Statesville D3
Stokesdale F2
Stony Point C3
Summerfield F2
Swan Quarter N4
Sylva D8
Tabor City H6
Tarboro K3
Taylorsville C3
Thomasville E3
Toast D2
Trenton L4
Troutman D3
Troy F4
Valdese B3
Wadesboro E5
Wake Forest H3
Wallace K5
Wanchese P3
Warrenton J2
Warsaw J5
Washington L3
Waxhaw D5
Waynesville D7
Weddington D4
Welcome E3
Weldon K2
Wendell J3
Wentworth F2
W. Jefferson C2
Whiteville H6
Wilkesboro C2
Williamston L3
Wilmington K6
Wilson K3
Windsor M2
Winfall N2
Wingate E5
Winston-Salem E2
Winterville L3
Winton M2
Woodfin E7
Wrightsville Beach K6
Yadkinville D2
Yanceyville G2
Zebulon J3

Other Features
Albemarle, *sound* N3
Alligator, *lake* N3
Alligator, *river* N3
B. Everett Jordan, *lake* G3
Bodie, *island* P3
Cape Fear, *river* H5
Cape Hatteras Natl. Seashore P4
Cape Lookout Natl. Seashore N5
Chatuga, *lake* C8
Clingmans Dome, *mt.* C7
Dan, *river* F2
Deep, *river* F3
Falls Lake, *reservoir* H3
Fear, *cape* K7
Fontana, *lake* C7
Fort Raleigh Natl. Hist. Site P3
Gaston, *lake* K1
Great, *lake* L5
Great Smoky Mts. Natl. Park C7
Hatteras, *cape* P4
Hatteras, *inlet* P4
Highrock, *lake* E3
Hiwassee, *lake* B8
Hyco, *lake* G2
John H. Kerr, *reservoir* H1
Lookout, *cape* M5
Mattamuskeet, *lake* N3
Mitchell, *mt.* A3
Nantahala, *lake* C8
Neuse, *river* J4
Norman, *lake* D3
Ocracoke, *inlet* N4
Oregon, *inlet* P3
Pamlico, *river* M4
Pamlico, *sound* P4
Phelps, *lake* N3
Roan, *mt.* A2
Roanoke, *river* K2
Rocky, *river* E4
Smith, *island* K7
Standing Indian, *mt.* C8
Tar, *river* J2
Waccamaw, *lake* J6
Wright Brothers Natl. Memorial P2
Yadkin, *river* D2

North Dakota .... page 161

Cities and Towns
Ashley F3
Beach A3
Belcourt F1
Beulah D2
Bismarck, *capital* E3
Bowman B3
Cando F1
Carrington F2
Casselton H3
Cavalier H1
Center D2
Cooperstown G2
Crosby B1
Devils Lake G1
Dickinson C3
Ellendale G3
Fargo J3
Fessenden F2
Finley H2
Forman H3
Fort Yates E3
Garrison D2
Grafton H1
Grand Forks H2
Harvey F2
Hazen D2
Hettinger C3
Hillsboro H2
Jamestown G3
Lakota G1
La Moure G3
Langdon G1
Larimore H2
Linton E3
Lisbon H3
McClusky E2
Mandan E3
Mayville H2
Mohall D1
Mott C3
Napoleon F3
New Rockford F2
New Town C1
Oakes G3
Park River H1
Rolla F1
Rugby F1
Stanley C1
Stanton D2
Steele F3
Tioga C1
Towner E1
Valley City H3
Wahpeton J3
Washburn D2
Watford City B2
West Fargo J3
Williston B1

Other Features
Cannonball, *river* D3
Devils, *lake* G1
Fort Union Trading Post N.H.S. A1
Green, *river* B2
Heart, *river* D3
Intl. Peace Garden E1
James, *river* F2
Jamestown, *reservoir* G2
Knife, *river* C2
Knife River Indian Villages N.H.S. D2
Little Missouri, *river* B3
Long, *lake* E3
Maple, *river* G3, H2
Missouri, *river* D2
Oahe, *lake* E3
Pembina, *river* G1
Sakakawea, *lake* C2
Sheyenne, *river* E2, G2, H3
Souris, *river* D1
Theodore Roosevelt N.P. B2, B3
White Butte, *mt.* B3
Wild Rice, *river* H3

Ohio .... page 162

Cities and Towns
Aberdeen C8
Ada C4
Akron G3
Alliance H4
Ansonia A5
Antrim H5
Antwerp A3
Arabia F8
Arcanum A6
Archbold B2
Arlington C4
Ashland F4
Ashtabula J2
Athens F7
Aurora H3
Avon Lake F2
Baltimore E6
Barberton G3
Barnesville H6
Batavia B7
Bay Village G9
Beachwood J9
Bedford J9
Bedford Heights J9
Bellaire J5
Bellefontaine C5
Bellevue E3
Bellville E4
Berea G9
Berlin Heights F3
Bethel B8
Beverly G6
Blanchester C7
Blissfield G5
Blue Ash C9
Bluffton C4
Boardman J3
Bowling Green C3
Bradford B5
Bremen F6
Brewster G4
Bridgetown B9
Broadview Heights H10
Brook Park G9
Brooklyn H9
Brookville B6
Brunswick G3
Bryan A3
Bucyrus E4
Burton H3
Cadiz J5
Caldwell G6
Cambridge G5
Camden A6
Canal Fulton G4
Canal Winchester E6
Canfield J3
Canton H4
Cardington E5
Carey D4
Carrollton H4
Cedarville C6
Celina A4
Centerburg E5
Chagrin Falls H3
Chardon H2
Chesterhill G7
Cheviot B9
Chillicothe E7
Cincinnati A7
Circleville E6
Cleveland G2
Cleveland Heights G2
Cleves A9
Clyde E3
Coldwater A5
Columbiana J4
Columbus, *capital* D6
Columbus Grove B4
Congress F4
Conneaut J2
Cortland J3
Coshocton G5
Covington B5
Crestline E4
Creston G4
Crooksville F6
Cuyahoga Falls H3
Dalton G4
Dayton B6
De Graff C5
Deer Park C9
Defiance B3
Delaware D5
Delhi Hills B9
Delphos B4
Delta C2
Deshler C3
Dover H4
Dresden F5
Dublin D5
Dunkinsville D8
E. Cleveland H8
East Liverpool J4
East Palestine J4
Eaton A6
Edgerton A3
Elida B4
Elyria F3
Euclid G2
Fairborn C6
Fairfield A7
Fairport Harbor H2
Fairview Park G9
Findlay C3
Fitchville F3
Forest C4
Forest Park B8
Forestville B7
Fort Recovery A5
Fort Shawnee B4
Fostoria D3
Franklin B6
Fredericktown E5
Fremont D3
Fresno G5
Gahanna E5
Galion E4
Gallipolis F8
Gambier F5
Garfield Hts. H9
Geneva J2
Genoa D2
Georgetown C8
Germantown B6
Gibsonburg D3
Grafton F3
Granville E5
Green G4
Green Springs D3
Greenfield D7
Greenville A5
Greenwich E3
Grove City D6
Hamilton A7
Hannibal J6
Harrisburg D6
Harrison A9
Heath F5
Hebron F6
Hicksville A3
Hillsboro C7
Hiram H3
Holgate B3
Hubbard J3
Huron E3
Independence H9
Jackson E7
Jackson Center B5
Jefferson J2
Jeffersonville C6
Johnstown E5
Keene G5
Kent H3
Kenton C4
Kettering B6
Kimbolton G5
Kirtland H2
Lakewood G9
Lancaster E6
Lebanon B7
Leipsic C3
Lewisburg A6
Lexington E4
Lima B4
Lisbon J4
Lodi G3
Logan F6
London D6
Lorain F3
Loudonville F4
Louisville H4
Loveland B7
Lucasville E8
Lyndhurst J8
McArthur F7
McConnelsville G6
Macedonia J10
Macksburg H6
Madeira C9
Manchester C8
Mansfield E4
Maple Hts. J9
Marietta H7
Marion D4
Martins Ferry J5
Marysville D5
Mason B7
Massillon G4
Maumee C2
Mayfield Hts. J9
Mechanicsburg C5
Medina G3
Mentor H2
Miamitown B9
Middleburg Heights G9
Middlefield H3
Middletown B6
Milan E3
Milford B7
Millersburg G4
Minerva H4
Minster B5
Monfort Heights B9
Monroe B7
Montgomery C9
Montpelier A2
Mount Gilead E4
Mount Healthy B9
Mount Orab C7
Mount Sterling D6
Mount Vernon E5
Napoleon B3
Nelsonville F7
Newark F5
New Baltimore B9
New Boston E8
New Bremen B5
New Carlisle B6
Newcomerstown G5
New Concord G6
New Lebanon B6
New Lexington F6
New London F3
New Paris A6
New Philadelphia H5
New Richmond B8
Newtown C9
Niles J3
North Baltimore C3
North Canton H4
North College Hill B9
North Kingsville J2
North Olmsted G3
North Royalton H10
Northfield J9
Northridge C6
Norwalk E3
Norwood C9
Oak Harbor D2
Oak Hill E8
Oberlin F3
Olmsted Falls G9
Oregon D2
Orrville G4
Orwell J2
Otsego G5
Ottawa B3
Painesville H2
Parma G3
Parma Heights H9
Pataskala E6
Paulding A3
Peebles D8
Pepper Pike J9
Perrysburg C2
Pickerington E6
Piketon E7
Pioneer A2
Piqua B5
Plain City D5
Plymouth E4
Pomeroy F7
Port Clinton E2
Portsmouth E8
Powhatan Point J6
Ravenna H3
Reading B7
Reynoldsburg E6
Richmond Heights J8
Richwood D5
Ripley C8
Rittman G4
Roseville F6
Russells Point C5
Sabina C7
Sagamore Hills J9
St. Bernard C9
St. Clairsville J5
St. Henry A5
St. Louisville F5
St. Marys B4
St. Paris C5
Salem J4
Salineville J4
Sandusky E3
Selma C6
Seven Hills H9
Shadyside J6
Shaker Hts. J9
Sharonville C9
Shelby E4
Shreve F4
Sidney B5
Silverton C9
Smithville G4
Solon J9
Somerset F6
South Charleston C6
South Euclid J8
South Point E9
Springdale C9
Springfield C6
Steubenville J5
Strasburg G4
Streetsboro H3
Strongsville G3
Stryker B3
Sugarcreek G5
Sunbury E5
Sylvania C2
The Village of Indian Hill C9
Tiffin D3
Tipp City B6
Toledo C2
Troy B5
Twinsburg J10
Uhrichsville H5
University Hts. J9
Upper Sandusky D4
Urbana C5
Utica F5
Van Wert A4
Vandalia B6
Venedocia B4
Vermilion F3
Versailles B5
Wapakoneta B4
Warren J3
Warrensville Heights J9
Warsaw G5
Washington Court House D6
Waterville C2
Wauseon B2
Waverly E7
Waynesville B6
Wellington F3
Wellston E7
Wellsville J4
West Alexandria A6
West Jefferson D6
West Lafayette G5
West Liberty C5
West Milton B6
West Salem F4
West Union C8
West Unity B2
Westerville E5
Westlake G9
Weston C3
Wheelersburg E8
Wickliffe J8
Wilkesville F7
Willard E3
Williamsburg B7
Williamsport D6
Williamsport E4
Wilmington C7
Woodsfield H6
Woodville D3
Wooster G4
Wyoming C9
Xenia C6
Yellow Springs C6
Youngstown J3

Other Features
Clendening, *lake* H5
Cuyahoga Valley N.R.A. H9
Erie, *lake* G1
Hocking, *river* F7
Hopewell Culture N.H.P. E7
James A. Garfield N.H.P. H2
Kelleys, *island* E2
Mohican, *river* F4
Muskingum, *river* G6
Ohio, *river* J6
Salt Fork, *lake* H5
Sandusky, *river* D3
Scioto, *river* D4
Senecaville, *lake* H6
William H. Taft Natl. Hist. Site C9

Oklahoma .... page 163

Cities and Towns
Ada F3
Agawam E3
Altus C3
Alva D1
Anadarko D2
Antlers G3
Apache D3
Arapaho D2
Ardmore E3
Arkoma H2
Atoka F3
Barnsdall F1
Bartlesville F1
Beaver B1
Bethel Acres E2
Bixby G2
Blackwell E1
Blanchard E2
Boise City B4
Bristow F2
Broken Arrow G1
Broken Bow H3
Buffalo C1
Cache D3
Calera F4
Carnegie D2
Catoosa G1
Chandler F2
Checotah G2
Chelsea G1
Cherokee D1
Cheyenne C2
Chickasha E2
Choctaw E2
Chouteau G1
Claremore G1
Cleveland F1
Clinton D2
Coalgate F3
Collinsville G1
Comanche E3
Commerce H1
Cordell D2
Corum D3
Coweta G2
Cushing F2
Davis E3
Dewey G1
Drumright F2
Durant F4
Eagletown H3
Edmond E2
Elk City C2
Enid E1
Eufaula G2
Fairfax F1
Fairview D1
Farris G3
Fittstown F3
Floris B1
Forgan B1
Fort Gibson G2
Frederick D3
Geary D2
Glenpool G2
Granite C3
Grove H1
Guthrie E2
Guymon C4
Harmon C1
Hartshorne G3
Haskell G2
Healdton E3
Heavener H3
Hennessey E1
Henryetta F2
Hobart C2
Holdenville F2
Hollis C3
Hominy F1
Hooker A1
Hugo G3
Idabel H4
Inola G1
Jay H1
Jenks G1
Joy E3
Kingfisher E2
Konawa F3
Krebs G3
Laverne C1
Lawton D3
Lenora C1
Lindsay E3
Locust Grove G1
Lone Grove E3
Loveland D3
Lovell E1
McAlester G3
McCurtain H2
McKnight C3
Madill F3
Mangum C3
Mannford F1
Marietta E4
Marlow E3
Medford E1
Midwest City E2
Minco E2
Moore E2
Muldrow H2
Muskogee G2
Mustang E2
Newcastle E2
Newkirk E1
Norman E2
Nowata G1
Oakhurst F1
Okeene D1
Okemah F2
Oklahoma City, *capital* E2
Okmulgee G2
Owasso G1
Panama H2
Pawhuska F1
Pawnee F1
Perkins E2
Perry E1
Picher H1
Piedmont E2
Ponca City E1
Poteau H2
Prague F2
Pryor Creek G1
Purcell E2
Roll C2
Sallisaw H2
Sand Springs F1
Sapulpa F1
Sayre C2
Seminole F2
Shattuck C1
Shawnee F2
Skiatook F1
Slaughterville E2
Snyder D3
Sparks F2
Spiro H2
Stanley G3
Stigler G2
Stillwater E1
Stilwell H2
Stratford F3
Stroud F2
Sulphur F3
Tahlequah H2
Talihina G3
Tecumseh F2
Tishomingo F3
Tonkawa E1
Tulsa G1
Turley G1
Tuttle E2
Vian H2
Vinita G1
Wagoner G2
Walters D3
Wanette E3
Warner G2
Warren C3
Watonga D2
Watova G1
Waukomis E1
Waurika D3
Weatherford D2
Westville H1
Wetumka F2
Wewoka F2
Wilburton G3
Wilson E3
Woodward C1
Wynnewood E3
Yale F1
Yukon E2

Other Features
Arkansas, *river* F1
Black Mesa, *mt.* B4
Broken Bow, *lake* H3
Canadian, *river* C2
Canton, *lake* D1
Chickasaw Natl. Rec. Area E3
Cimarron, *river* C1
Fort Gibson, *lake* G1
Hugo, *lake* G3
Illinois , *river* H2
Kaw, *lake* F1
Keystone, *lake* F1
North Canadian, *river* C1
Oologah, *lake* G1
Ouachita, *mts.* G3
Red, *river* C3
Sooner, *lake* F1
Texoma, *lake* F4
Washita Battlefield N.H.S. C2
Winding Stair Natl. Rec. Area H3

Oregon .... page 164

Cities and Towns
Albany B2
Aloha A2
Altamont C3
Ashland C3
Astoria B1
Baker City E2
Bandon B3
Beaverton A2, C2
Bend C2
Brookings B3
Brownsville C2
Burns D3
Canby A2, C2
Canyon City E2
Cedar Hills A2
Central Point C3
Clatskanie B1
Condon D2
Coos Bay B3
Coquille B3
Cornelius A2
Corvallis B2
Cottage Grove B3
Creswell B3
Crowley E3
Dallas B2
Eagle Point C3
Elgin E2
Enterprise E2
Eugene B2
Florence B3
Forest Grove A2
Fossil D2
Four Corners A2, C2
Glendale B3
Gold Beach B3
Grants Pass B3
Green B3
Gresham B2
Harbor B3
Harrisburg B2
Hayesville A2, C2
Heppner D2
Hermiston D2
Hillsboro A2, C2
Hines D3
Homestead F2
Hood River C2

Key
Hubbard C3
Jacksonville C3
Jefferson C2
John Day E2
Junction City B2
Juntura E3
Keizer A2
Klamath Falls C3
Lafayette B2
La Grande E2
Lakecreek C3
Lake Oswego A2, C2
Lakeside B3
Lakeview D3
Lebanon C2
Lexington D2
Lincoln Beach B2
Lincoln City B2
McMinnville B2
Madras C2
Meacham E2
Medford C3
Metzger A2
Mill City C2
Milton-Freewater E2
Milwaukie A2
Molalla A2
Monument D2
Moro D2
Mount Angel A2, C2
Mount Vernon D2
Myrtle Creek B3
Myrtle Point B3
Newberg A2, C2
Newport B2
North Bend B3
Nyssa E3
Oak Grove A2
Oakridge C3
Ontario F2
Oregon City A2, C2
Pendleton E2
Philomath B2
Phoenix C3
Pilot Rock E2
Portland A2, C2
Post D2
Prineville D2
Rainier C1
Redmond C2
Reedsport B3
Riley D3
Rogue River B3
Roseburg B3
Rufus D2
St. Helens C2
Stanfield D2
Salem, *capital* A2, B2
Santa Clara B2
Scappoose C2
Seaside B2
Seneca E2
Shady Cove C3
Sherwood A2
Silverton A2, C2
Springfield C2
Stayton C2
Sunriver C3
Sutherlin B3
Sweet Home C2
Talent C3
The Dalles C2
Tigard A2, C2
Tillamook B2
Toledo B2
Umpqua B3
Union E2
Vale E3
Veneta B2
Vernonia B2
Waldport B2
Warm Springs C2
Warrenton B1
Waterloo C2
West Slope A2
White City C3
Willamina B2
Wilsonville A2, C2
Woodburn A2
Wood Village B2

Other Features
Abert, *lake* D3
Blue, *mts.* E2
Calapooya, *mts.* C3
Cascade, *range* C3
Clackamas, *river* C2
Coast, *mt. ranges* B2
Columbia, *river* D2
Coos, *bay* B3
Crater, *lake* C3
Crater Lake Natl. Park C3
Crescent, *lake* C3
Crooked, *river* D2
Davis, *lake* C3
Deschutes, *river* C2
Diamond Peak, *mt.* C3
Gearhart Mtn., *mt.* D3
Green Peter, *lake* C2
Harney, *basin* D3
Harney, *lake* D3
Hells, *canyon* F2
Hells Canyon Natl. Rec. Area F2
Hood, *mt.* C2
Jefferson, *mt.* C2
John Day, *river* D2
John Day Fossil Beds N.M. D2
Klamath, *mts.* B3
Lookout, *cape* B2
McLoughlin house N.H.S. A2
Malheur, *lake* E3
Malheur, *river* E3
Molalla, *river* B2
Multnomah, *waterfalls* C2
Ochoco, *mts.* D2
Oregon Caves Natl. Monument B3
Oregon Dunes Natl. Rec. Area B3
Owyhee, *lake* E3
Owyhee, *river* E3
Powder, *river* E2
Pudding, *river* A2
Pueblo, *mts.* E3
Rogue, *river* B3
Sacajawea Peak, *mt.* E2
Silvies, *river* D3
Siuslaw, *river* B3
Snake, *river* F2
South Umpqua, *river* B3
Steens, *mts.* E3
Strawberry Mt., *mt.* E2
Summer, *lake* D3
Thielsen, *mt.* C3
Tillamook, *bay* B2
Trout Creek, *mts.* E3
Umatilla, *lake* D2
Upper Klamath, *lake* C3
Waldo, *lake* C3
Wallowa, *mts.* E2
Willamette, *river* A2

Pennsylvania ....page 165

Cities and Towns
Albion A2
Aliquippa A4
Allensville F4
Allentown L4
Allison Park E6
Altoona E4
Ambridge A4
Annville H5
Archbald K2
Ardmore M6
Arnot G2
Ashland J4
Athens H2
Austin E2
Avalon D7
Avis G3
Bala Cynwyd M6
Baldwin E7
Bangor L4
Barnesboro D4
Beaver A4
Beaver Falls A4
Beavertown G4
Bedford E5
Bellefonte F4
Belleville F4
Bellevue D7
Bellwood E4
Berlin D6
Berwick J3
Berwyn L6
Bethel Park A5, D7
Bethlehem L4
Birdsboro K5
Blairsville C5
Blakely K3
Bloomsburg J4
Blossburg G2
Boalsburg F4
Boothwyn L7
Boswell C5
Boyertown K5
Bradford D2
Brentwood E7
Bridgeville D7
Brockport D3
Brockway D3
Brodheadsville L4
Brooklyn K2
Brookville C3
Broomall L6
Brownsville B5
Bryn Mawr L6
Burgettstown A5
Butler B4
California B5
Cambridge Springs A2
Canonsburg A5
Canton H2
Carbondale K2
Carlisle G5
Carnegie D7
Carroll Valley G6
Carrolltown D4
Castle Shannon E7
Catawissa J4
Chambersburg F6
Chelsea L7
Chester L6, L7
Clairton B5
Clarion C3
Clarks Summit K2
Claysburg E5
Clearfield E3
Clifton Heights L7
Clymer C4
Coatesville K6
Columbia H5
Connellsville B6
Conyngham J4
Coopersburg L5
Coraopolis D7
Cornwall J5
Corry B2
Coudersport E2
Crafton D7
Cresson D5
Crosby E2
Cuddy D7
Curwensville D4
Dallas K3
Danville H4
Darby M7
Delmont B5
Denver J5
Derry C5
Dillsburg G5
Dormont D7
Dover H5
Downingtown K5
Doylestown L5
Drexel Hill M7
DuBois D3
Duncannon G5
Duquesne E7
Dushore J2
East Greenville K5
East Lansdowne M7
Easton L4
East Petersburg J5
East Stroudsburg L3
Ebensburg D4
Eddystone L7
Edinboro A2
Effinwild E6
Elizabethtown H5
Elizabethville H4
Elkland G2
Ellwood City A4
Elysburg H4
Emlenton B3
Emmaus L4
Emporium E2
Emsworth D7
Ephrata J5
Erie A1
Etna E7
Evans City A4
Everett E5
Exton K5
Fayetteville F6
Fleetwood K5
Ford City B4
Forest City L2
Forest Grove D7
Forksville H2
Fox Chapel E7
Freeland K3
Freeport B4
Galeton F2
Gettysburg G6
Girard A2
Gladden D7
Gladwyne M6
Glenolden M7
Glen Riddle L7
Glen Rock H6
Gradyville L7
Greencastle F6
Greensburg B5
Greenville A3
Gregg D7
Grove City A3
Hallstead K2
Hamburg K4
Hanover H6
Harmarville E6
Harrisburg, *capital* H5
Harrisville A3
Harveys Lake J3
Haverford M6
Havertown M6
Hazel Hurst D2
Hazleton K4
Hermitage A3
Herndon H4
Hershey H5
Highland D6
Hollidaysburg E5
Homer City C4
Honesdale L2
Huntingdon E5
Hyndman D6
Indiana C4
Indianola E6
Jersey Shore G3
Jim Thorpe K4
Johnsonburg D3
Johnstown D5
Kane D2
Kennett Square K6
King of Prussia L5
Kingston K3
Kittanning B4
Kutztown K5
Lake City A1
Lancaster J5
Lansdale L5
Lansdowne M7
Laporte J3
Latrobe C5
Lebanon J5
Leechburg B4
Lehighton K4
Levittown M5
Lewisburg H4
Lewistown F4
Ligonier C5
Lima L7
Linglestown H5
Lititz J5
Littlestown G6
Lock Haven G3
Lykens H4
McCandless A4, D6
McConnellsburg E6
McKees Rocks D7
McKeesport B5
Macungie K4
Mahanoy City J4
Manchester H5
Manheim J5
Mansfield G2
Mars A4
Martinsburg E5
Marysville H5
Masontown B6
Matamoras M3
Meadville A2
Mechanicsburg G5
Media L6, L7
Mercer A3
Mercersburg F6
Meridian B4
Merion M6
Meyersdale C6
Middleburg G4
Middletown H5
Midland A4
Mifflinburg G4
Mifflintown G4
Mifflinville J3
Milford M3
Millersburg H4
Millersville J6
Millheim G4
Millvale E7
Milroy F4
Milton H3
Minersville J4
Monessen B5
Monroeville B5, F7
Mont Alto F6
Montgomery H3
Montoursville H3
Montrose K2
Moon Run D7
Moscow K3
Mt. Carmel J4
Mt. Holly Springs G5
Mount Joy H5
Mt. Lebanon D7
Mt. Nebo D6
Mt. Oliver E7
Mt. Pleasant B5
Mt. Pocono L3
Mount Union F5
Muncy H3
Munhall E7
Myerstown J5
Nanticoke J3
Nanty Glo D5
Nazareth L4
Nesquehoning K4
New Bloomfield G5
New Castle A4
New Freedom H6
New Holland J5
New Kensington B4, F6
New Oxford G6
Newport G5
Newtown M5
Newtown Square L6
Newville G5
New Wilmington A3
Norristown L5
North East B1
Northampton L4
North Springfield A1
Northumberland H4
Oakmont E7
Oil City B3
Old Forge K3
Orwigsburg J4
Oxford J6
Palmerton K4
Patton D4
Pen Argyl L4
Penn Hills F7
Penn Wynne M6
Perkasie L5
Philadelphia L6, M7
Philipsburg E4
Phoenixville K5
Picture Rocks H3
Pine Grove J4
Pittsburgh B5, E7
Pittston K3
Pleasantville B2
Pleasantville D5
Point Marion B6
Polk B3
Port Allegany E2
Port Matilda E4
Portage D5
Portland Mills D3
Pottstown K5
Pottsville J4
Powell H2
Prospect Park L7
Punxsutawney D4
Quakertown L5
Quarryville J6
Radnor L6
Rainsburg D6
Reading K5
Red Lion H6
Renovo F3
Reynoldsville D3
Ridgway D3
Ridley Park L7
Roaring Spring E5
St. Marys D3
Saxonburg B4
Sayre H2
Schnecksville K4
Schuylkill Haven J4
Scottdale B5
Scranton K3
Selinsgrove H4
Shamokin H4
Sharon A3
Sharon Hill M7
Sharpsville A3
Sheffield C2
Shenandoah J4
Shippensburg F5
Shoemakersville K5
Shrewsbury H6
Sinking Spring J5
Slatington K4
Slippery Rock A3
Smethport E2
Somerset C5
Souderton L5
South Williamsport G3
Spring Grove H6
Springdale F6
Springfield L7
State College F4
Stewartstown H6
Strasburg J6
Stroudsburg L4
Sugarcreek B3
Sunbury H4
Susquehanna K2
Swarthmore L7
Sykesville D3
Tamaqua K4
Tionesta C3
Titusville B2
Tobyhanna L3
Towanda J2
Tower City H4
Tremont J4
Trevorton H4
Troy H2
Tunkhannock K2
Tyrone E4
Union City B2
Uniontown B6
Upland L7
Valley View H4
Vandergrift B4
Verona E7
Village Green L7
Villanova L6
Warren C2
Washington A5
Waterford A2
Watsontown H3
Waymart L2
Wayne L6
Waynesboro F6
Waynesburg A6
Weatherly K4
Wellsboro G2
Wesleyville A1
West Chester K6
West Grove K6
West Mifflin E7
Westmont D5
West Pike F2
West View E7
Whitehall K4
White Horse L6
Wilcox D2
Wilkes-Barre K3
Wilkinsburg E7
Williamsport G3
Willow Grove L5
Windber D5
Womelsdorf J5
York H6
York Springs G5
Youngsville C2
Zelienople A4

Other Features
Allegheny, *reservoir* D2
Allegheny, *river* B3
Allegheny Natl. Rec. Area D2
Allegheny Portage Railroad N.H.S. D5
Appalachian, *mts.* F5
Clarion, *river* C3
Conemaugh, *river* C4
Davis, *mt.* C6
Delaware, *river* L2
Delaware Water Gap N.R.A. M3
Erie, *lake* A1
Friendship Hill Natl. Hist. Site B6
Gettysburg Natl. Mil. Park G6
Johnstown Flood Natl. Memorial D5
Juniata, *river* F5
Lehigh, *river* K3
Ohio, *river* A4
Presque Isle, *island* A1
Raystown, *lake* E5
Schuylkill, *river* K5
Susquehanna, *river* J2
Tioga, *river* G2
Valley Forge Natl. Hist. Park L5

Rhode Island ....page 166

Cities and Towns
Adamsville F4
Allenton D4
Alton B5
Anthony C3
Arcadia B4
Ashaway B5
Ashton D2
Avondale A6
Barrington E3
Berkeley D2
Bradford B5
Bristol E3
Carolina C5
Central Falls D2
Charlestown C5
Chepachet B2
Clayville B3
Coventry Center C3
Cranston D3
Cumberland Hill D2
Diamond Hill D2
Dunn Corner B5
East Greenwich D4
East Providence D3
Exeter C4
Fiskeville C3
Foster Center B3
Galilee C5
Glendale C2
Green Hill C5
Greenville C2
Hamilton D4
Harmony C2
Harrisville B2
Hope C3
Hope Valley B5
Hopkinton B5
Jamestown D5
Jerusalem C5
Kingston C5
Little Compton E4
Lonsdale D2
Matunuck C5
Middletown E4
Moosup Valley B3
Narragansett Pier D5
Newport E5
Nooseneck C4
North Foster B2
North Providence D2
North Scituate C3
Pascoag B2
Pawtucket D2
Pawtuxet D3
Perryville C5
Plum Point D4
Point Judith D5
Portsmouth E4
Providence, *capital* D3
Prudence E4
Quidnick C3
Quonochontaug B6
Rice City B3
Riverside D3
Rockville B4
Rumford D2
Sakonnet E5
Saunderstown D5
Saylesville D2
Shannock C5
Slatersville C1
Slocum C4
South Foster B3
Spragueville C2
Tarkiln C2
Tiverton E4
Usquepaug C5
Valley Falls D2
Wakefield C5
Wallum Lake B2
Warren E3
Warwick D3
Washington C3
Watch Hill A6
Weekapaug B6
West Barrington D3
Westerly B5
West Glocester B2
West Kingston C5
West Warwick C3
Woonsocket C1
Wyoming B4

Other Features
Block, *island* C7
Block Island, *sound* B6
Mt. Hope, *bay* E4
Narragansett, *bay* D4
Rhode Island, *sound* E5
Roger Williams Natl. Mem. D3
Sakonnet, *river* E4
Scituate, *reservoir* C3
Touro Synagogue N.H.S. E5

South Carolina ....page 167

Cities and Towns
Abbeville B2
Aiken C3
Allendale C3
Anderson B2
Andrews E3
Bamberg C3
Barnwell C3
Batesburg-Leesville C3
Beaufort D4
Belton B2
Belvedere C3
Bennettsville E2
Bishopville D2
Blacksburg C1
Blackville C3
Boiling Springs C1
Brownsville E2
Buffalo C2
Burton D4
Calhoun Falls B2
Camden D2
Cayce C3
Central B2
Charleston E4
Cheraw E2
Chester C2
Chesterfield D2
Clemson B2
Clinton C2
Clover C1
Columbia, *capital* C2
Conway E3
Cowpens C1
Darlington E2
Denmark C3
Dentsville D2
Dillon E2
Easley B2
Edgefield C3
Elgin D2
Enoree C2
Estill C4
Fairfax C4
Florence E2
Folly Beach E4
Forest Acres D2
Foreston D3
Fort Mill D1
Fountain Inn B2
Furman C4
Gaffney C1
Garden City F3
Georgetown E3
Gifford C4
Gloverville C3
Goose Creek D3
Great Falls D2
Greeleyville E3
Greenville B2
Greenwood B2
Greer B2
Hampton C4
Hanahan D4
Hardeeville C4
Harleyville D3
Hartsville D2
Hickory Grove C2
Hickory Grove F3
Hilda C3
Hilton Head Island D4
Holly Hill D3
Hollywood D4
Honea Path B2
Horrel Hill D3
Inman B1
Irmo C2
Isle of Palms E4
Jackson C3
Jefferson D2
Joanna C2
Johnsonville E3
Johnston C3
Kershaw D2
Kiawah Island D4
Kingstree E3
Kline C3
Ladson D4
Lake City E3
Lancaster D2
Landrum B1
Lane E3
Latta E2
Laurel Bay D4
Laurens B2
Lexington C3
Liberty B2
Little River F3
Little Rock E2
Loris F2
Lugoff D2
Lyman B2
Lynchburg D2
McBee D2
McClellanville E3
McCormick B3
Manning D3
Marion E2
Mauldin B2
Mayesville D3
Mayo C1
Moncks Corner D3
Mt. Pleasant E4
Mullins E2
Murrells Inlet E3
Myrtle Beach F3
Neeses C3
New Ellenton C3
Newberry C2
Nichols E2
Ninety Six B2
North Augusta C3
North Charleston E4
North Myrtle Beach F3
Norway C3
Olanta E3
Olar C3
Orangeburg D3
Pacolet C2
Pacolet Mills C2
Pageland D2
Pamplico E3
Patrick D2
Pelion C3
Pendleton B2
Pickens B2
Piedmont B2
Pinewood D3
Pomaria C2
Port Royal D4
Ravenel D4
Red Bank C3
Ridgeland D4
Ridgeville D3
Ridgeway D2
Rock Hill C2
Roebuck C2
Rowesville D3

Key
Ruby D2
St. George D3
St. Matthews D3
St. Stephen E3
Salley C3
Salters E3
Saluda C3
Santee D3
Sellers E2
Seneca B2
Simpsonville B2
Socastee E3
Society Hill E2
South Congaree C3
Spartanburg C2
Springfield C3
Starr B2
Stuckey E3
Summerville D3
Sumter D3
Surfside Beach F3
Swansea C3
Sycamore C3
Taylors B2
Timmonsville E2
Travelers Rest B2
Trenton C3
Turbeville D3
Union C2
Varnville C4
Wagener C3
Walhalla A2
Walterboro D4
Ware Shoals B2
Westminster A2
Whitmire C2
Williamston B2
Williston C3
Winnsboro C2
Woodruff B2
Yemassee D4
York C2

Other Features
Bull, *island* E4
Bulls, *bay* E4
Cape, *island* E3
Congaree Swamp N.M. D3
Cowpens Natl. Bfld. C1
Edisto, *river* D3
Fort Sumter Natl. Monument E4
Greenwood, *lake* C2
Hartwell, *lake* B2
J. Strom Thurmond, *lake* B3
Keowee, *lake* B2
Kings Mt. Natl. Mil. Park C1
Long, *bay* F3
Lynches, *river* D2
Marion, *lake* D3
Monticello, *reservoir* C2
Moultrie, *lake* D3
Murray, *lake* C2
Ninety Six Natl. Hist. Site B2
North, *island* E3
Port Royal, *sound* D4
Russell, *lake* B2
St. Helena, *sound* D4
Saluda, *river* C2
Santee, *river* E3
Savannah, *river* C3
South, *island* E3
The Grand Strand F3
Wateree, *lake* D2
Wateree, *river* D2

South Dakota page 168

Cities and Towns
Aberdeen F1
Alexandria G3
Armour F3
Belle Fourche A2
Beresford H3
Black Hawk A2
Box Elder A2
Britton G1
Brookings H2
Burke E3
Canton H3
Chamberlain E3
Cherry Creek C2
Clark G2
Clear Lake H2
Custer A3
Deadwood A2
Dell Rapids H3
De Smet G2
Dupree C1
Elk Point H4
Faulkton E1
Flandreau H2
Fort Pierre D2
Freeman G3
Gettysburg E1
Hartford H3
Highmore E2
Hot Springs A3
Howard G2
Huron F2
Ipswich E1
Kadoka C3
Lake Andes F3
Lead A2
Lemmon B1
Lennox G3
Leola F1
Madison G2
Martin C3
Milbank H1
Miller E2
Mitchell G3
Mobridge D1
Murdo D3
Onida D2
Parker G3
Parkston G3
Philip C2
Pierre, *capital* D2
Pine Ridge B3
Plankinton F3
Platte F3
Rapid City A2
Redfield F2
Rosebud D3
Salem G3
Selby D1
Sioux Falls H3
Sisseton G1
Spearfish A2
Sturgis A2

Key
Timber Lake C1
Tyndall G4
Vermillion H4
Volga H2
Wagner F3
Watertown G2
Webster G1
Wessington Springs F2
White River D3
Winner E3
Woonsocket F2
Wounded Knee B3
Yankton G4

Other Features
Andes, *lake* F3
Angostura, *reservoir* A3
Bad, *river* C2
Badlands Natl. Park B3
Belle Fourche, *reservoir* A2
Belle Fourche, *river* A2
Big Sioux, *river* G2
Big Stone, *lake* H1
Black, *hills* A2
Bois de Sioux, *river* H1
Cheyenne, *river* C2
Francis Case, *lake* F3
Grand, *river* C1
Harney Peak, *mt.* A3
James, *river* F1
Jewel Cave Natl. Monument A3
Keya Paha, *river* D3
Lewis and Clark, *lake* G4
Little Missouri, *river* A1
Little White, *river* D3
Missouri, *river* E3
Moreau, *river* B1
Mount Rushmore Natl. Memorial A3
North Fork Grand, *river* B1
Oahe, *lake* D2
Pine, *ridge* B3
Sharpe, *lake* E2
South Fork Grand, *river* A1
Traverse, *lake* H1
Vermillion, *river* G3
Waubay, *lake* G1
White, *river* D3
Whitewood, *river* G2
Wind Cave Natl. Park A3

Tennessee page 169

Cities and Towns
Adamsville E4
Alamo C3
Alcoa P3
Algood L2
Altamont K4
Arlington B4
Ashland City G2
Athens M4
Bartlett B4
Baxter L2
Bells C3
Benton M4
Bethel Springs D4
Bethpage J2
Blaine P2
Blountville S1
Bluff City S2
Bolivar D4
Brentwood H2
Bristol S1
Brownsville C3
Bruceton E2
Buffalo Valley K2
Byrdstown L1
Camden E2
Campaign K3
Carthage K2
Caryville N2
Celina K1
Centerville G3
Charlotte G2
Chattanooga L4
Church Hill R1
Clarksville G1
Cleveland M4
Clinton N2
Collegedale L4
Collierville B4
Columbia G3
Conasauga M4
Cookeville L2
Covington B3
Cowan J4
Crossville L3
Dandridge Q2
Dayton L3
Decatur M3
Decaturville E3
Decherd J4
Dickson G2
Dover F2
Dresden D2
Dunlap L4
Dyer C2
Dyersburg C2
East Ridge L4
Elizabethton S2
Englewood N4
Erin F2
Erwin S2
Estill Springs J4
Etowah M4
Fairfield Glade M2
Farragut N3
Fayetteville H4
Forest Hills H2
Frankewing H4
Franklin H3
Gainesboro K2
Gallatin J2
Gatlinburg P3
Germantown B4
Gleason D2
Goodlettsville H2
Granville K2
Graysville L4
Greeneville R2
Greenfield D2
Grimsley M2
Gruetli-Laager K4
Halls C3
Halls Crossroads P2
Hampshire G3
Harriman M3
Hartsville J2
Henderson D4
Hendersonville H2

Key
Humboldt D3
Huntingdon E3
Huntsville N2
Jacksboro N2
Jackson D3
Jamestown M2
Jasper K4
Jefferson City Q2
Jellico N1
Johnson City S2
Jonesborough S2
Karns N3
Kenton C2
Kingsport R1
Kingston M3
Kingston Springs G2
Knoxville P3
Lafayette J1
La Follette N2
Lake City N2
Lakewood H2
La Vergne H2
Lawrenceburg G4
Lebanon J2
Lenoir City N3
Lewisburg H4
Lexington E3
Linden F3
Livingston L2
Loretto G4
Loudon N3
Lynchburg J4
McEwen F2
McKenzie D2
McKinnon F2
McMinnville K3
Madisonville N3
Manchester J4
Martin D2
Maryville P3
Mascot P2
Maynardville P2
Medon D4
Memphis A4
Middleton D4
Milan D3
Millersville H2
Milligan College S2
Millington B4
Monterey L2
Morristown Q2
Mosheim R2
Mountain City T1
Mount Juliet H2
Mount Pleasant G3
Munford B4
Murfreesboro J3
Nashville, *capital* H2
Newbern C2
New Johnsonville F2
New Tazewell P2
Nolensville H3
Norris N2
Oak Hill H2
Oak Ridge N2
Oliver Springs N2
Oneida M2
Overall J3
Paris E2
Parsons E3
Pegram G2
Pigeon Forge P3
Pikeville L3
Portland H1
Powell N2
Pulaski G4
Reagan E3
Red Bank L4
Ridgely C2
Ripley B3
Rockwood M3
Rogersville R2
Rutherford D2
Rutledge Q2
Savannah E4
Selmer D4
Sevierville P3
Sewanee K4
Shelbyville J4
Signal Mountain L4
Smithville K3
Smyrna H3
Sneedville Q1
Soddy-Daisy L4
Somerville C4
South Fulton D2
South Pittsburg K4
Sparta L3
Spencer L3
Spring City M3
Spring Hill H3
Springfield H1
Stanton C4
Surgoinsville R2
Sweetwater N3
Taft H4
Tazewell P2
Tellico Plains N4
Tennessee Ridge F2
Tiptonville C2
Tracy City K4
Trenton D3
Trimble C2
Tullahoma J4
Tusculum R2
Union City C2
Wartburg M2
Waverly F2
Waynesboro F4
Westmoreland J1
White House H2
White Pine Q2
Whitwell K4
Winchester J4
Woodbury J3

Other Features
Andrew Johnson Natl. Hist. Site R2
Appalachian, *mts.* N4
Appalachian Natl. Scenic Trail Q3
Barkley, *lake* F1
Big South Fork Natl. River and Rec. Area M1
Center Hill, *lake* K3
Cherokee, *lake* Q2
Chickamauga & Chattanooga Natl. Mil. Park L5
Chickamauga, *lake* M3
Clinch, *river* Q2
Clingmans Dome, *mt.* Q3
Cumberland, *river* G2

Key
Dale Hollow, *lake* L1
Douglas, *lake* Q3
Duck, *river* H3
Great Smoky, *mts.* P3
Great Smoky Mts. Natl. Park Q3
Holston, *river* R2
Kentucky, *lake* F2
Mississippi, *river* B3
Norris, *lake* P2
Roan, *mt.* S2
Shiloh Natl. Mil. Park E4
Tennessee, *river* E5, K5
Watts Bar, *lake* M3
Woods, *reservoir* J4

Texas page 170

Cities and Towns
Abernathy F2
Abilene H3
Addison C1
Alamo Heights B7
Albany H3
Algoa F9
Alice J8
Alpine D5
Alvin M6
Amarillo B9
Anahuac N6
Anderson M5
Andrews E3
Angleton M6
Anson H3
Anthony A3
Aransas Pass K8
Archer City J2
Arlington L3
Asherton H7
Aspermont G2
Atascosa A7
Athens M3
Atlanta N2
Austin, *capital* K5
Avondale A1
Azle K3
Bacliff G9
Baird H3
Balch Springs C2
Balcones Heights A7
Ballinger H4
Bandera H6
Barrett F8
Bastrop K5
Batesville H7
Bay City M7
Bayou Vista G10
Baytown N6
Beaumont N5
Beaumont Place F8
Beaver C8
Bedford B2
Beeville K7
Bellaire E8
Bellmead K4
Belton K4
Benavides J8
Benbrook A2
Benjamin H2
Bergheim A6
Big Lake F4
Big Spring F3
Bishop K8
Boerne J6
Bogata M2
Bonham L2
Borger C9
Bovina E1
Bowie K2
Bracken B6
Brackettville G6
Brady H4
Breckenridge J3
Brenham L5
Briar A1
Bridge City P5
Bridgeport K2
Brookshire M6
Brookside Village F9
Brownfield E2
Brownsville K10
Brownwood J4
Bryan L5
Buckingham C1
Buena Vista B7
Buffalo L4
Bulverde A6
Buna P5
Bunker Hill Village E8
Burkburnett J1
Burleson A3
Burleson K3
Burnet J5
Caldwell L5
Cameron L5
Canadian D9
Canton M3
Canutillo A4
Canyon B9
Carrizo Springs H7
Carrollton B1
Carthage N3
Castle Hills A6
Castle Hills J6
Cedar Hill B3
Cedar Park K5
Center N4
Centerville M4
Chandler M3
Channelview F8
Channing B9
Childress G1
Chocolate Bayou F10
Cisco J3
Clarendon C10
Clarksville M2
Claude C9
Cleburne K3
Cleveland M5
Clifton K4
Cloverleaf F8
Clute M6
Cockrell Hill B2
Coldspring M5
Coleman H4
College Station L5
Colleyville A2
Colorado City G3
Columbus L6
Comanche J4
Combine D2

Key
Commerce L2
Conroe M5
Converse B6
Cooper M2
Copperas Cove K4
Corpus Christi K8
Corsicana L3
Cotulla H7
Crane E4
Crockett M4
Crosby F8
Crosbyton F2
Crowell H2
Crowley A3
Crystal City H7
Cuero K6
Daingerfield N2
Dalhart B8
Dallas L3
Dalworthington Gardens B2
Danbury F10
Dayton N5
Decatur K2
Deer Park F8
Del Rio G6
Denison L2
Denton K2
Denver City E3
De Soto L3
Devine J6
Diboll N4
Dickens G2
Dickinson F9
Dilley H7
Dimmitt E1
Dublin J3
Dumas B9
Duncanville B2
Eagle Lake L6
Eagle Pass G7
Eastland J3
Eden H4
Edgecliff A3
Edinburg J9
Edna L7
El Campo L6
Eldorado G5
El Paso A4
Electra J1
Elgin K5
Elsa J9
Emory M3
Ennis L3
Euless B2
Everman A3
Fabens A4
Fair Oaks Ranch A6
Fairfield L4
Falfurrias J8
Farmers Branch B1
Farwell D1
Ferris C3
Flatonia K6
Floresville J6
Floydada F2
Forest Hill A2
Fort Davis D5
Fort Stockton E5
Fort Worth K3
Franklin L4
Fredericksburg J5
Freeport M7
Freer J8
Friendswood F9
Gail F3
Gainesville L2
Galena Park F8
Galveston N6
Ganado L6
Garden City F4
Garden Ridge B6
Gardendale B7
Garland C2
Gatesville K4
George West J7
Georgetown K5
Germann C3
Giddings L5
Gilmer N3
Gladewater N3
Glen Rose K3
Glenn Heights B3
Goldthwaite J4
Goliad K7
Gonzales K6
Gorman J3
Graham J2
Granbury K3
Grand Prairie B2
Grand Saline M3
Grapeland M4
Grapevine B1
Grapevine K3
Greenville L2
Groesbeck L4
Groves P6
Groveton M4
Guthrie G2
Hallettsville L6
Haltom City A2
Hamilton J4
Hamlin G3
Harker Heights K4
Harlingen K9
Haskell H2
Hearne L5
Hebbronville J8
Helotes A6
Hemphill P4
Hempstead L5
Henderson N3
Henrietta J2
Hereford B10
Hewitt K4
Hico J4
Hidalgo J9
Highland Park C2
Highlands F8
Hillsboro K3
Hitchcock F9
Hitchcock M6
Hollywood Park A6
Hondo H6
Houston M6
Hubbard L4
Huntsville M5
Hurst A2
Hutchins C2
Idalou F2
India C3
Ingleside K8

Key
Iowa Park J2
Irving B2
Jacinto City F8
Jacksboro J2
Jacksonville M4
Jasper P5
Jayton G2
Jefferson N3
Jersey Village E8
Johnson City J5
Jourdanton J7
Juliff E9
Junction H5
Karnes City K7
Katy M6
Kaufman L3
Keller A2
Kermit D4
Kerrick B8
Kerrville H5
Kilgore N3
Killeen K4
Kingsland J5
Kingsville K8
Kirby B7
Kirbyville P5
Knox City H2
Kountze N5
La Grange L6
Lake Jackson M7
Lakehills J6
La Marque G9
Lamesa F3
Lampasas J4
Lancaster C3
La Porte F9
La Pryor H7
Laredo H8
League City M6
Leakey H6
Leon Springs A6
Leon Valley J6
Levelland E2
Lewisville L2
Liberty N5
Linden N3
Lipscomb D8
Littlefield E2
Live Oak B6
Livingston N5
Llano J5
Lockhart K6
Lockney F1
Longview N3
Lubbock F2
Lufkin N4
Luling K6
Lumberton N5
Mabank L3
McAllen J9
McCamey E4
Macdona A7
McKinney L2
Madisonville M5
Mangus Corner A7
Mansfield A3
Manvel F9
Marble Falls J5
Marfa C5
Marlin L4
Marshall N3
Mason H5
Matador G1
Mathis K8
Memphis C10
Menard H5
Mentone D4
Meridian K4
Merkel G3
Mertzon G4
Mesquite F3
Mesquite L3
Mexia L4
Miami C9
Midland E4
Midlothian B3
Mineola M3
Mineral Wells J3
Mission J9
Missouri City M6
Monahans E4
Mont Belvieu G8
Montague K2
Morgans Point G8
Morton E2
Moss Bluff G8
Mt. Houston F8
Mt. Pleasant N2
Mt. Vernon M2
Muleshoe E1
Munday H2
Murphy C1
Nacogdoches N4
Nassau Bay F9
Navasota L5
Nederland N6
New Berlin C7
New Boston N2
New Braunfels J6
Newton P5
Nixon K6
Nocona K2
North Houston E8
North Richland Hills A2
Odessa E4
Olmos Park A7
Olney J2
Olton E1
Orange P5
Ovilla B3
Ozona F5
Paducah G1
Paint Rock H4
Palacios L7
Palestine M4
Palo Pinto J3
Pampa C9
Panhandle C9
Pantego B2
Paris M2
Parita B7
Parker C1
Pasadena M6
Pearland F9
Pearsall H7
Pecos D4
Pelican Bay A2
Perryton C8
Pharr J9
Pilot Point L2
Pittsburg N2

Key
Plains E2
Plainview F1
Plano L2
Pleasanton J7
Port Arthur P6
Port Bolivar G9
Port Isabel K9
Portland K8
Port Lavaca L7
Post F2
Poteet J6
Premont J8
Presidio C6
Quanah H1
Quitman M3
Ranger J3
Rankin F4
Raymondville K9
Red Oak C3
Refugio K7
Reno A2
Richardson C1
Richland Hills A2
Richmond M6
Rio Grande City J9
Roanoke A1
Robert Lee G4
Robinson K4
Robstown K8
Roby G3
Rockdale L5
Rockport K7
Rocksprings G5
Rockwall L3
Roma H9
Roscoe G3
Rosenberg M6
Rosharon E9
Rotan G3
Round Rock K5
Rowlett C2
Rusk M4
Sabinal H6
Sachse C1
St. Hedwig B7
San Angelo G4
San Antonio J6
San Augustine N4
San Benito K9
Sanderson E5
San Diego J8
Sandy Point E9
Sanger K2
San Geronimo A6
San Leon G9
San Marcos K6
San Saba J4
Sansom Park A2
Sarita K8
Satsuma E8
Sayers B7
Schertz B6
Schumansville C6
Seabrook F9
Seadrift L7
Seagoville C2
Seagraves E3
Sealy L6
Seguin K6
Selma B6
Seminole E3
Seymour H2
Shallowater E2
Shavano Park A6
Sherman L2
Shoreacres G9
Sierra Blanca B4
Silsbee N5
Silverton F1
Sinton K7
Slaton F2
Smith Point G9
Smithville K5
Snyder G3
Socorro A4
Sonora G5
South Houston F9
Southlake A1
Southside Place E8
Southton B7
Spearman C8
Spring Valley E8
Spur G2
Stafford E9
Stamford H3
Stanton F3
Stephenville J3
Sterling City G4
Stratford B8
Sugar Land E9
Sulphur Springs M2
Sundown E2
Sunnyvale C2
Sweetwater G3
Tahoka F2
Taylor K5
Temple K4
Texarkana N2
Texas City N6
The Woodlands M5
Thompsons E9
Three Rivers J7
Throckmorton H2
Tilden J7
Tomball M5
Trinity M5
Trophy Club A1
Tulia F1
Tyler M3
Universal City J6
University Park C2
Uvalde H6
Van Alstyne L2
Van Horn C4
Vega B9
Vernon H1
Victoria L7
Vidor N5
Von Ormy A7
Waco K4
Waskom N3
Watauga A2
Waxahachie L3
Weatherford K3
Webster F9
Wellington D10
Weslaco K9
West K4
West Columbia M6
West Odessa E4
Westover Hills A2

Key
West University Place E8
Westworth A2
Wharton L6
Wheatland A3
Wheeler D9
White Settlement A2
Whitesboro L2
Wichita Falls J2
Willis M5
Wills Point L3
Wilmer C3
Windcrest B6
Winnie N6
Winnsboro M3
Winters H4
Wolfforth F2
Woodville N5
Woodway K4
Wylie D1
Yoakum K6
Zapata H9
Zuehl B7

Other Features
Alibates Flint Quarries N.M. B9
Amistad, *reservoir* F6
Amistad Natl. Rec. Area G6
Balcones, *escarpment* A6
Big Bend Natl. Park D6
Big Thicket Natl. Preserve N5
Black, *mt.* G6
Canadian, *river* C9
Cathedral, *mt.* D5
Chamizal Natl. Mem. A4
Chinati Peak, *mt.* C6
Dallas-Fort Worth Intl. Airport B2
Davis, *mts.* C5
Eagle Peak, *mt.* B5
Edwards, *plateau* G5
Emory Peak, *mt.* D6
Falcon, *reservoir* H9
Fort Davis Natl. Hist. Site D5
Galveston, *bay* G9
Galveston, *island* N6
Guadalupe, *mts.* C3
Guadalupe Mts. Natl. Park C4
Guadalupe Peak, *mt.* C4
Kemp, *lake* H2
Livermore, *mt.* C5
Livingston, *lake* M5
Lyndon B. Johnson N.H.P. J5
Meredith, *lake* C9
Nueces, *river* J7
O.H. Ivie, *lake* H4
Padre Island Natl. Seashore K8
Pecos, *river* E4
Pelican, *island* G9
Red, *river* H1
Red Bluff, *lake* D4
Rio Grande, *river* F6
Sabine, *pass* P6
Sabine, *river* P5
Sam Rayburn, *reservoir* N4
Santiago Peak, *mt.* D6
Sierra Del Carmen, *mt.* D6
Stockton, *plateau* E5
Toledo Bend, *reservoir* P4

Utah .... page 171

Cities and Towns
American Fork C3
Beaver B5
Bicknell C5
Blanding E6
Bluffdale C3
Bountiful C3
Brigham City C2
Castle Dale C4
Cedar City A6
Centerville C3
Clearfield B2
Coalville C3
Cottonwood Heights C3
Delta B4
Draper C3
Duchesne D3
East Carbon D4
Enoch A6
Ephraim C4
Farmington C3
Ferron C4
Fillmore B5
Garland B2
Grantsville B3
Gunnison C4
Heber City C3
Helper D4
Hildale A6
Huntington D4
Hurricane A6
Hyrum C2
Ivins A6
Junction B5
Kanab B6
Lapoint E3
Layton C3
Lehi C3
Lewiston C2
Loa C5
Logan C2
Long Valley Junction B6
Maeser E3
Magna B3
Manila E3
Manti C4
Mapleton C3
Moab E5
Monroe B5
Monticello E6
Morgan C2
Mount Pleasant C4
Murray C3
Myton D3
N. Salt Lake C3
Nephi C4
North Ogden C2
Ogden C2
Orangeville C4
Orem C3
Panguitch B6
Parowan B6
Payson C3
Plain City B2
Pleasant Grove C3
Price D4
Provo C3
Randolph C2
Richfield B5
Richmond C2

Key
Riverton C3
Roosevelt D3
Roy B2
St. George A6
Salem C3
Salina C5
Salt Lake City, *capital* C3
Sandy C3
Santa Clara A6
Santaquin C4
Smithfield C2
South Jordan C3
Spanish Fork C3
Springville C3
Sugarville B4
Tooele B3
Tremonton B2
Vernal E3
Washington A6
Wellington D4
West Jordan C3
West Valley City C3
Willard B2

Other Features
Abajo Peak, *mt.* E6
Arches Natl. Park E5
Bear, *lake* C2
Bear, *river* C2
Beaver, *river* B5
Bonneville Salt Flats A3
Bruin Point, *mt.* D4
Bryce Canyon Natl. Park B6
Canyonlands Natl. Park E5
Capitol Reef Natl. Park C5
Cedar Breaks Natl. Monument B6
Colorado, *river* E5
Delano Peak, *mt.* B5
Deseret Peak, *mt.* B3
Dinosaur Natl. Monument E3
Dutton, *mt.* B5
Escalante, *river* C6
Flaming Gorge, *reservoir* E2
Flaming Gorge Natl. Rec. Area E2
Frisco Peak, *mt.* A5
Glen Canyon Natl. Rec. Area D6
Golden Spike Natl. Hist. Site B2
Great, *basin* A4
Great Salt, *lake* B2
Great Salt Lake, *desert* A3
Green, *river* D4
Heliotrope, *mt.* C4
Henry, *mts.* D6
Ibapah Peak, *mt.* A4
Kings Peak, *mt.* D3
Marsh Peak, *mt.* E3
Marvine, *mt.* C5
Monument, *valley* D6
Natural Bridges Natl. Monument E6
Navajo, *mt.* D6
Navajo Indian Res. E6
Nebo, *mt.* C4
Paria, *river* C6
Pavant, *range* B5
Peale, *mt.* E5
Pennell, *mt.* D6
Powell, *lake* D6
Price, *river* D4
Rainbow Bridge Natl. Monument D6
Salt Marsh, *lake* A4
San Juan, *river* D6
San Rafael, *river* D4
Sevier, *desert* B4
Sevier, *lake* A5
Strawberry, *river* D3
Swasey Peak, *mt.* A4
Timpanogos Cave N.M. C3
Uinta, *mts.* D3
Utah, *lake* C3
Wasatch, *plateau* C5
White, *river* E3
Zion Natl. Park A6

Vermont .... page 172

Cities and Towns
Addison A2
Albany C1
Ascutney C4
Averill D1
Bakersfield B1
Barnard B3
Barnet C2
Barre C2
Basin Harbor A2
Beecher Falls D1
Bellows Falls C4
Bennington A5
Benson A3
Berlin B2
Bethel B3
Bloomfield D1
Bradford C3
Brandon A3
Brattleboro B5
Bristol A2
Brookfield B2
Burlington A2
Cabot C2
Cambridge B1
Castleton A3
Cavendish B4
Charlotte A2
Chelsea C3
Colchester A1
Concord D2
Danby B4
Danville C2
Dorset A4
East Burke D1
East Haven D1
East Middlebury A3
East Randolph B3
Eden B1
Enosburg Falls B1
Essex A1
Essex Junction A1
Evansville C1
Fair Haven A3
Fairfax B1
Fairfield B1
Fairlee C3
Franklin B1
Gallup Mills D1
Gaysville B3
Georgia Center A1
Grafton B4
Granby D1
Grand Isle A1
Groton C2

Key
Guildhall D1
Guilford B5
Hancock B3
Hanover C3
Hardwick C2
Hartford C3
Hartland C3
Hartwellville A5
Heartwellville A5
Highgate Center A1
Hinesburg A2
Hortonia A3
Hubbardton A3
Hyde Park B1
Irasburg C1
Irasville B2
Jacksonville B5
Jamaica B4
Jeffersonville B1
Johnson B1
Keeler Bay A1
Larrabees Point A3
Lemington D1
Londonderry B4
Lowell C1
Lyndon C1
Lyndonville C1
McIndoe Falls C2
Marlboro B5
Mendon B3
Middlebury A2
Middlesex B2
Milton A1
Monkton A2
Montgomery B1
Montgomery Center B1
Montpelier, *capital* B2
Morgan C1
Morrisville B1
Moscow B2
Newbury C2
Newfane B4
New Haven A2
Newport C1
North Bennington A5
Northfield B2
North Hero A1
North Wolcott C1
Norton D1
Orange C2
Panton A2
Peacham C2
Pittsfield B3
Pittsford A3
Plainfield C2
Plymouth B3
Pompanoosuc C3
Post Mills C3
Poultney A3
Pownal A5
Proctor A3
Putney B5
Randolph B3
Readsboro B5
Richford B1
Richmond A2
Rochester B3
Roxbury B2
Rutland B3
St. Albans A1
St. Johnsbury C2
Searsburg B5
Shaftsbury A4
Sharon C3
Shelburne A2
Sheldon B1
Shoreham A3
South Burlington A2
South Hero A1
Springfield C4
Stamford A5
Starksboro A2
Swanton A1
Tinmouth A4
Troy C1
Tunbridge C3
Tyson B4
Underhill B1
Vergennes A2
Vernon B5
Vershire C3
Warren B2
Washington C2
Waterbury B2
Waterville B1
Wells River C2
West Burke D1
West Dover B5
West Haven A3
Westminster C4
Weston B4
West Pawlet A4
West Topsham C2
Wheelock C1
White River Junction C3
Williamsville B5
Wilmington B5
Windsor C4
Winooski A1
Wolcott C1
Woodford A5
Woodstock B3
Worcester B2

Other Features
Appalachian Natl. Scenic Trail A5
Black, *river* C1
Bomoseen, *lake* A3
Bread Loaf, *mt.* B2
Bromley, *mt.* B4
Camels Hump, *mt.* B2
Champlain, *lake* A1
Connecticut, *river* C3
Ellen, *mt.* B2
Equinox, *mt.* A4
Green, *mts.* B4
Harriman, *reservoir* B5
Jay Peak, *mt.* B1
Killington Peak, *mt.* B3
Lamoille, *river* B1
Mansfield, *mt.* B1
Mettawee, *river* A3
Missisquoi, *river* B1
Seymour, *lake* C1
Smugglers Notch, *pass* B1
Snow, *mt.* B5
Somerset, *reservoir* B4
Waterbury, *reservoir* B2
West, *river* B4
White, *river* B3
White Rocks N.R.A. B4

Key
Willoughby, *lake* C1

Virginia .... page 173

Cities and Towns
Abingdon D1
Accomac M4
Achilles L5
Alberta H6
Alexandria J2
Allison Gap D1
Altavista E5
Amelia Court House H5
Amherst E4
Annandale M2
Appalachia B1
Appomattox F5
Arlington J2
Ashland H4
Baileys Crossroads M2
Bassett C6
Basye F2
Bedford D5
Belleair L2
Belle Haven M4
Belle View M2
Bensley J5
Berryville H1
Big Stone Gap B1
Blacksburg B5
Blackstone H5
Bland A5
Bloxom M4
Bluefield A5
Bon Air H4
Bowling Green J3
Boyce G1
Boydton G6
Boykins J6
Bridgewater F3
Bristol D2
Brodnax G6
Brookneal F5
Brunswick H6
Buckingham F4
Buena Vista E4
Burke L2
Burkeville G5
Callands D6
Cape Charles L5
Castlewood C1
Centreville J2
Charles City J5
Charlotte Court House F5
Charlottesville F4
Chase City G6
Chatham E6
Cheriton M5
Chesapeake L6
Chester J5
Chesterfield H5
Chilhowie E1
Chincoteague M4
Christiansburg C5
Chula H5
Claremont K5
Clifton Forge D4
Clinchco C1
Clintwood C1
Coeburn C1
Collinsville D6
Colonial Beach K3
Colonial Hts. J5
Concord E5
Courtland J6
Covington C4
Crewe G5
Crimora F3
Crystal City M2
Crystal Hill F6
Culpeper G3
Cumberland G4
Dale City J2
Danville E6
Dendron K5
Dillwyn G4
Dinwiddie H5
Drakes Branch F6
Dublin B5
Dumfries J2
Dungannon C1
Eastville M5
Elkton F3
Emory D1
Emporia H6
Ewing A1
Fairfax J2
Fairfax Station L2
Falls Church M2
Falmouth J3
Farmville G5
Ferrum D6
Figsboro D6
Fincastle D5
Fishersville F3
Flint Hill G2
Floyd C6
Forest E5
Fort Mitchell G6
Franconia M2
Franklin K6
Fredericksburg J3
Fries B6
Front Royal G2
Galax B6
Gate City C1
Glade Spring D1
Gloucester K5
Gloucester Point K5
Goochland H4
Gordonsville G3
Goshen D4
Gretna E6
Grottoes F3
Groveton M2
Grundy D1
Halifax F6
Hampton L5
Hanover J4
Harrisonburg F3
Harrogate A1
Heathsville L4
Hollins D5
Hopewell J5
Horse Pasture D6
Huntington M2
Hurt E5
Independence A6
Isle of Wight K6
Jetersville G5

Key
Jonesville B1
Kenbridge G6
King and Queen Courthouse K4
King George J3
Kings Park L2
King William J4
Lancaster L4
Lawrenceville H6
Lebanon D1
Leesburg H1
Lexington E4
Lincolnia M2
Louisa G4
Lovingston F4
Lunenburg G6
Luray G2
Lynchburg E5
McLean M1
Madison G3
Manakin H4
Manassas J2
Manassas Park J2
Mantua L2
Marion A6
Martinsville D6
Mathews L5
Mechanicsburg A5
Mechanicsville J4
Meherrin G5
Millboro D4
Monterey D3
Montross K3
Mount Jackson F2
Narrows B5
New Castle C4
New Kent K4
New Market F2
Newport News L6
Newsoms J6
Norfolk L6
North Springfield M2
Norton C1
Nottoway Court House G5
Oakton L2
Onancock M4
Orange G3
Palmyra G4
Pearisburg B5
Petersburg J5
Peterstown B5
Pimmit Hills M1
Poquoson L5
Portsmouth L6
Powhatan H4
Prince George J5
Pulaski B5
Purcellville H1
Radford B5
Raven D1
Reston J2
Richlands D1
Richmond, *capital* J4
Ridgeway D6
Roanoke D5
Rocky Mount D6
Rustburg E5
Ruther Glen J4
Salem C5
Saltville D1
Saluda K4
Shenandoah F3
Smithfield K6
South Boston F6
South Hill G6
Spotsylvania H3
Springfield M2
Spring Hill M1
Stafford J3
Stanardsville G3
Staunton E3
Sterling J1
Stony Creek J6
Strasburg G2
Stuart C6
Stuarts Draft E3
Suffolk K6
Surry K5
Sussex J6
Tappahannock K4
Tazewell A5
Timberville F2
Triangle J2
Tysons Corner M1
Vale L1
Verona E3
Victoria G6
Vienna L1
Virginia Beach M6
Warm Springs D3
Warrenton H2
Warsaw K4
Washington G2
Waverly J5
Waynesboro F3
Weber City C1
Wellington M3
West Point K4
West Springfield M2
Williamsburg K5
Winchester G1
Wise C1
Woodbridge J2
Woodstock F2
Wytheville A6
Yorktown K5

Other Features
Allegheny, *mts.* D3
Anna, *lake* H3
Appalachian, *mts.* C5
Appomattox Court House N.H.P. F5
Arlington Natl. Cem. M2
Assateague Island Natl. Seashore M4
Booker T. Washington N.M. D5
Charles, *cape* M5
Chesapeake, *bay* L5
Colonial Natl. Hist. Park K5
Fredericksburg & Spotsylvania Natl. Mil. Park H3
Gaston, *lake* G6
George Washington Birthplace N.M. K3
Henry, *cape* M6
Iron, *mts.* A6
James, *river* K5
John H. Kerr, *reservoir* F6
Manassas Natl. Battlefield Park H2
Mount Rogers Natl. Rec. Area A6
Petersburg Natl. Battlefield J5
Potomac, *river* K3
Rappahannock, *river* J3
Rogers, *mt.* A6

Key

Shenandoah, *mts.* E3
Shenandoah, *river* F3
Shenandoah Natl. Park G2
Smith Mtn., *lake* D5
York, *river* K5

Washington ....page 174

Cities and Towns

Aberdeen C4
Amboy D5
Anacortes D2
Arlington D2
Asotin J4
Auburn D3
Bangor A1
Battle Ground D5
Bellingham D2
Belvedere H2
Benton City G4
Bethel A2
Birch Bay D2
Blaine D2
Boardman G5
Bothel D3
Bremerton D3
Brewster G2
Bridgeport G3
Bucoda D4
Burien B2
Burlington D2
Camas D5
Cashmere F3
Castle Rock D4
Cathlamet C4
Central Park C3
Centralia D4
Chehalis D4
Chelan F3
Cheney J3
Chewelah J2
Clarkston J4
Cle Elum F3
Clinton D3
Colfax J4
College Place H4
Colville J2
Connell H4
Cosmopolis C4
Country Homes J3
Coupeville D2
Davenport H3
Dayton J4
Deer Park J3
Dusty J4
Eastgate B2
Easton E3
Eastsound D2
East Wenatchee F3
Eatonville D4
Edmonds D3
Ellensburg F3
Elma C3
Elmer City H3
Enumclaw E3
Ephrata G3
Everett D2
Everson D2
Fall City E3
Federal Way D3
Ferndale D2
Fords Prairie C4
Forks B3
Four Lakes J3
Friday Harbor C2
Fruitvale F4
Goldendale F5
Gorst A2
Grandview G4
Granger F4
Hoquiam C3
Inglewood C2
Kelso D4
Kenmore B1
Kennewick G4
Kent D3
Kettle Falls H2
Kirkland D3
Lacey D3
La Grande D4
Lake Stevens D2
Leavenworth F3
Lexington D4
Longmire E4
Longview D4
Lynden D2
Mabton G4
McKenna D4
McMurray D2
Markham C4
Marysville D2
Medical Lake J3
Medina B2
Mercer Island D3
Merritt F3
Monroe D3
Montesano C4
Moses Lake G3
Mount Vernon D2
Mukilteo D3
Newhalem E2
Newport J2
Newport Hills B2
Normandy Park B2
North Bend E3
Oak Harbor D2
Ocean Park B4
Ocean Shores B3
Okanogan G2
Olalla B2
Olympia, *capital* D3
Omak G2
Opportunity J3
Orchards D5
Oroville G2
Othello G4
Oysterville B4
Pasco G4
Plymouth G5
Pomeroy J4
Port Angeles C2
Porter C4
Port Hadlock D2
Port Ludlow D3
Port Orchard D3
Port Townsend D2
Poulsbo D3
Prosser G4
Pullman J4
Puyallup D3
Quincy G3
Raymond C4
Redmond D3
Renton D3
Republic H2
Richland G4
Richmond Highlands B1
Ridgefield D5
Ritzville H3
St. John J3
Seabeck A2
Sea-Tac D3
Seattle D3
Sedro Woolley D2
Selah F4
Sequim C2
Shelton C3
Silverton E2
Skyway B2
Smokey Point D2
Snohomish D3
Snoqualmie E3
South Bend C4
Southworth B2
Spanaway D3
Spokane J3
Stanwood D2
Stevenson E5
Sultan E3
Sumas D2
Sumner D3
Sunnyside F4
Suquamish A1
Tacoma D3
Tekoa J3
Tenino D4
Tiger J2
Toppenish F4
Tracyton A2
Trentwood J3
Tukwila B2
Tumwater D3
Union Gap F4
University Place D3
Vancouver D5
Vashon B2
Walla Walla H4
Wapato F4
Warden G4
Washougal D5
Waterville F3
Wenatchee F3
Westport B4
West Richland G4
White Center B2
White Salmon E5
Winslow D3
Woodinville B1
Woodland D5
Yakima F4
Yelm D4
Zillah F4

Other Features

Adams, *mt.* E4
Bainbridge, *island* B2
Baker, *mt.* E2
Banks, *lake* G3
Cascade, *range* E4
Chelan, *lake* F2
Chewuch, *river* F2
Columbia, *river* G2
Copper Butte, *mt.* H2
Cowlitz, *river* E4
Disappointment, *cape* B4
Elliott, *bay* B2
Flattery, *cape* B2
Franklin D. Roosevelt, *lake* H2
Glacier Peak, *mt.* E2
Grays, *harbor* B4
Green, *river* E3
Hood, *canal* C3
Kettle River, *range* H2
Klickitat, *river* E4
Lake Chelan Natl. Rec. Area F2
Lake Roosevelt Natl. Rec. Area H2
Lewis, *river* E4
Mt. Baker Natl. Rec. Area E2
Mount Rainier Natl. Park E4
Mt. St. Helens Natl. Vol. Mon. D4
North Cascades Natl. Park E2
Okanogan, *river* G2
Olympic, *mts.* C3
Olympic Natl. Park C3
Olympus, *mt.* C3
Omak, *mt.* G2
Orcas, *island* D2
Oregon Butte, *mt.* J4
Ozette, *lake* B2
Pasayten, *river* F2
Pend Oreille, *river* J2
Potholes, *reservoir* G3
Priest Rapids, *lake* G4
Puget, *sound* B1, D2
Rainier, *mt.* E4
Riffe, *lake* D4
Rimrock, *lake* E4
Ross, *lake* F2
Ross Lake Natl. Rec. Area F2
Sacajawea, *lake* H4
St. Helens, *mt.* D4
San Juan, *island* C2
Sanpoil, *river* H2
Selkirk, *mts.* J2
Skagit, *river* E2
Skykomish, *river* E3
Snake, *river* J4
Spokane, *river* H3
Strait of Juan de Fuca B2
Stuart, *mt.* F3
Umatilla, *lake* G5
Vashon, *island* B2
Wallula, *lake* H4
Washington, *lake* B1
Wenatchee, *lake* F3
Wenatchee, *mts.* F3
Wenatchee, *river* F3
White, *pass* E4
Whitman Mission Natl. Hist. Site H4
Willapa, *bay* B4
Yakima, *river* F4
Yale, *lake* D4

West Virginia ....page 175

Cities and Towns

Ansted D4
Barboursville B4
Beckley D5
Belington G2
Berkeley Springs K1
Bluefield D6
Bradley D5
Bridgeport F2
Buckhannon F3
Charles Town L2
Charleston, *capital* C4
Chester K4
Circleville G3
Clarksburg F2
Clay D4
Clendenin D4
Craigsville E4
Davis H2
East Liverpool K4
Edray F4
Eleanor C3
Elizabeth D2
Elkins G3
Fairmont F2
Fayetteville D4
Fort Ashby J2
Franklin H3
Gary C6
Glenville E3
Grafton F2
Grantsville D3
Hamlin B4
Harpers Ferry L2
Harrisville D2
Hinton E5
Huntington B4
Hurricane B4
Inwood K2
Kenova A4
Keyser J2
Kingwood G2
Lewisburg F5
Logan C5
Madison C4
Mannington F1
Marlinton F4
Marmet C4
Martinsburg L2
Matewan B5
Middlebourne E2
Milton B4
Montgomery D4
Moorefield J2
Morgantown G1
Moundsville K6
Mt. Hope D5
Mullens D5
Newburg G2
New Cumberland K4
New Haven C3
New Martinsville E1
New Milton E2
Nitro C4
Oak Hill D5
Oceana C5
Orma D3
Paden City E1
Parkersburg C2
Parsons G2
Pennsboro E2
Petersburg H3
Peterstown E6
Philippi F2
Pineville C5
Point Pleasant B3
Princeton D6
Rainelle E5
Ravenswood C3
Reedy D3
Richwood E4
Ripley C3
Romney J2
Ronceverte F5
Rupert E5
St. Albans C4
St. Marys D2
Salem E2
Shady Spring D5
Shepherdstown L2
Shinnston F2
Sistersville E1
Slanesville J2
South Charleston C4
Spencer D3
Summersville E4
Sutton E3
Terra Alta G2
Union E5
Vienna C2
Wayne B4
Webster Springs F4
Weirton K5
Welch C6
Wellsburg K5
Wellsville K4
West Milford F2
Weston F2
West Union E2
Wheeling K5
White Sulphur Springs F5
Whitesville C5
Williamson B5
Williamstown D2
Winfield C3

Other Features

Allegheny, *mts.* G4
Big Sandy, *river* B5
Bluestone, *lake* E5
Bluestone Natl. Scenic River E5
Gauley River Natl. Rec. Area D4
Greenbrier, *river* F4
Harpers Ferry Natl. Hist. Park L2
Kanawha, *river* C4
New River Gorge Natl. River D5
Ohio, *river* E1
Potomac, *river* J2
Shenandoah, *mts.* H4
Spruce Knob, *mt.* G3
Spruce Knob Seneca Rocks N.R.A. H3
Sutton, *lake* E3

Wisconsin ....page 176

Cities and Towns

Abbotsford C4
Adams D5
Algoma F4
Alma B4
Altoona B4
Amery A3
Antigo D3
Appleton E4
Arcadia B4
Ashland C2
Augusta B4
Baldwin A4
Balsam Lake A3
Baraboo D5
Barronett A3
Bayside F1
Beaver Dam E5
Belleville D6
Bellevue F4
Beloit D6
Bennett B2
Berlin E5
Bethesda D2
Big Bend E2
Black River Falls C4
Bloomer B3
Bloomville D3
Boscobel C5
Breed E3
Brillion E4
Brodhead D6
Brookfield E1
Brown Deer F1
Bryant D3
Buena Vista D1
Burlington E6
Butler E1
Cadott B4
Cameron B3
Canton B3
Carlsville F4
Cedarburg F5
Cedar Grove F5
Chelsea C3
Chetek B3
Chili C4
Chilton E4
Chippewa Falls B4
Cleveland F5
Clinton E6
Clintonville E4
Colby C4
Coloma D4
Columbus D5
Conrath B3
Cornell B3
Cornucopia B2
Crandon E3
Crestview C6
Cuba City C6
Cudahy F2
Cumberland A3
Darlington C6
De Forest D5
De Pere E4
Delafield D1
Delavan E6
Denmark F4
Dodgeville C6
Duplainville E1
Durand B4
Eagle River D3
Easton D5
East Troy E6
Eau Claire B4
Edgar C4
Edgerton D6
Elkhorn E6
Ellsworth A4
Elm Grove E1
Elroy C5
Evansville D6
Fennimore C6
Florence E3
Fond du Lac E5
Forestville F4
Fort Atkinson E6
Fox Lake E5
Fox Point F1
Fredonia F5
Friendship D5
Galesville B4
Genesee D2
Genesee Depot D2
Germantown E5
Gillett E4
Glendale F1
Grafton F5
Green Bay F4
Greendale F2
Greenfield F2
Green Lake E5
Greenleaf E4
Hales Corners E2
Hamburg D3
Harrison D3
Hartford E5
Hartland D1
Hayward B2
Hillsboro C5
Hollister E3
Holmen B5
Horicon E5
Hortonville E4
Howard E4
Howards Grove F5
Hudson A4
Hurley C2
Husher F2
Jackson E5
Janesville D6
Jefferson E6
Juda D6
Jump River C3
Juneau E5
Kaukauna E4
Kenosha F6
Keshena E4
Kewaskum E5
Kewaunee F4
Kiel E5
Kneeland F2
Lac du Flambeau D3
La Crosse B5
Ladysmith B3
Lake Delton D5
Lake Geneva E6
Lake Mills E5
Lampson B3
Lancaster C6
La Pointe C2
Little Chute E4
Lodi D5
Lomira E5
McFarland D6
Madison, *capital* D5
Maiden Rock A4
Manitowish C2
Manitowoc F4
Marathon City D4
Marinette F3
Markesan E5
Marshfield C4
Mason B2
Mattoon D3
Mauston C5
Mayville E5
Medford C3
Menasha E4
Menomonee Falls E5
Menomonie B4
Mequon F5
Merrill D3
Middleton D5
Milton E6
Milwaukee F5
Mineral Point C6
Mishicot F4
Modena B4
Mole Lake E3
Mondovi B4
Monona D5
Monroe D6
Montello D5
Montfort C6
Mosinee D4
Muscoda C5
Muskego E6
Neenah E4
Neillsville C4
Nekoosa D4
New Berlin E6
New Glarus D6
New Holstein E5
New Lisbon C5
New London E4
New Richmond A3
Newton F5
Niagara F3
North Fond du Lac E5
North Lake D1
North Prairie D2
Oak Creek F6
Oconto F4
Oconto Falls E4
Odanah C2
Omro E4
Onalaska B5
Oostburg F5
Oregon D6
Osceola A3
Oshkosh E4
Paddock Lake E6
Palmyra E6
Park Falls C3
Pell Lake E6
Peshtigo F3
Pewaukee E1
Phillips C3
Platteville C6
Pleasant Prairie F6
Plover D4
Plymouth F5
Polonia D4
Portage D5
Port Edwards D4
Porterfield F3
Port Washington F5
Port Wing B2
Poynette D5
Prairie du Chien B5
Prairie du Sac D5
Prescott A4
Princeton D5
Pulaski E4
Racine F6
Randolph E5
Random Lake F5
Raymond F2
Reedsburg D5
Rhinelander D3
Rice Lake B3
Richland Center C5
Ridgeway D5
Ripon E5
River Falls A4
River Hills F1
Rothschild D4
St. Croix Falls A3
St. Francis F2
Sauk City D5
Saukville F5
Saylesville D2
Schofield D4
Shawano E4
Sheboygan F5
Sheboygan Falls F5
Shell Lake B3
Shorewood F1
Slinger E5
South Milwaukee F2
Sparta C5
Spencer C4
Spooner B3
Spread Eagle E3
Spring Green C5
Stanley C4
Stevens Point D4
Stonebank D1
Stoughton D6
Sturgeon Bay F4
Sturtevant F6
Summit Lake D3
Sun Prairie D5
Superior A2
Sussex E1
Tabor F2
Thompsonville F2
Thorp C4
Tomah C5
Tomahawk D3
Tony C3
Two Rivers F4
Verona D6
Viroqua C5
Wales D2
Wanderoos A3
Washburn C2
Watertown E5
Waukesha E6
Waunakee D5
Waupaca D4
Waupun E5
Wausau D4
Wautoma D4
Wauwatosa E1
Wauzeka C5
West Allis F6
West Bend E5
Westby C5
West Milwaukee F1
Weyauwega E4
Whitehall B4
Whitewater E6
Williams Bay E6
Wind Lake E2
Wind Point G2
Winneconne E4
Wisconsin Dells D5
Wisconsin Rapids D4
Wrightstown E4

Other Features

Apostle Islands Natl. Lakeshore C1
Big Muskego, *lake* E2
Castle Rock, *lake* D5
Chetek, *lake* B3
Chippewa, *lake* B3
Door, *peninsula* F4
Dubay, *lake* D4
Flambeau, *river* C3
Green, *bay* F4
Madeline, *island* C2
Michigan, *lake* G5
Mississippi, *river* B5
Outer, *island* C1
Peshtigo, *river* E3
Petenwell, *lake* D4
Pewaukee, *lake* D1
Poygan, *lake* E4
St. Croix Natl. Scenic Riverway A3
Sand, *island* C2
Spring, *lake* D2
Stockton, *island* C2
Superior, *lake* C1
Timms Hill, *mt.* C3
Winnebago, *lake* E4
Wisconsin, *river* D3
Wolf, *river* E4
Yellow, *river* C4

Wyoming ....page 177

Cities and Towns

Afton A2
Basin B1
Boxelder D2
Buffalo C1
Byron B1
Casper C2
Cheyenne, *capital* D3
Cody B1
Cokeville A2
Deaver B1
Douglas D2
Evanston A3
Evansville C2
Gillette D1
Glenrock D2
Green River B3
Greybull B1
Jackson A2
Kemmerer A3
Lander B2
Laramie D3
Lovell B1
Lusk D2
Lyman A3
Medicine Bow C3
Mills C2
Newcastle D2
Pinedale B2
Powell B1
Rawlins C3
Reliance B3
Riverton B2
Rock Springs B3
Saratoga C3
Sheridan C1
Sundance D1
Thermopolis B2
Torrington D2
Wamsutter C3
Wheatland D2
Worland C1

Other Features

Absaroka, *range* A1
Belle Fourche, *river* D2
Big Sandy, *river* B2
Bighorn, *lake* B1
Bighorn, *mts.* C1
Bighorn, *river* B1
Bighorn Canyon Natl. Rec. Area B1
Bridger Peak, *mt.* C3
Clarks Fork Yellowstone, *river* B1
Cloud Peak, *mt.* C1
Colter Peak, *mt.* A1
Continental Divide, *mt. ridge* B3
Devils Tower Natl. Monument D1
Elk, *mt.* C3
Flaming Gorge, *reservoir* B3
Flaming Gorge Natl. Rec. Area B3
Fort Laramie Natl. Hist. Site D2
Fossil Butte Natl. Monument A3
Francs Peak, *mt.* B2
Gannett Peak, *mt.* B2
Grand Teton, *mt.* A2
Grand Teton Natl. Park A2
Great Divide, *basin* B3
Green, *river* B3
Greybull, *river* B1
Jackson, *lake* A2
Laramie, *mts.* C2
Laramie, *river* D3
Laramie Peak, *mt.* D2
Little Bighorn, *river* C1
Little Missouri, *river* D1
Little Powder, *river* D1
Little Snake, *river* C3
Medicine Bow, *river* C2
North Platte, *river* D2
Nowood, *river* C1
Owl Creek, *mts.* B2
Pathfinder, *reservoir* C2
Powder, *river* D1
Rocky, *mts.* B2
Seminoe, *reservoir* C3
South Fork Cheyenne, *river* D2
South Fork Powder, *river* C2
Sweetwater, *river* B2
Teton, *river* A2
Tongue, *river* C1
Trout Peak, *mt.* B1
Whiskey Peak, *mt.* C2
Wind, *river* B2
Wind River, *range* B2
Yellowstone, *lake* A1
Yellowstone Natl. Park A1